The Phillimore
ATLAS and INDEX
of PARISH REGISTERS

BRITISH ISLES

British or German Ocean

Atlantic Ocean

North Channel

Irish Sea

St. George's Channel

Bristol Channel

British Channel

Meridian of Greenwich

Pentland Firth
MURRAY FIRTH
Cromarty
Sutherland
Caithness
Ross
Elgin
Banff
Aberdeen
Argyle
Forfar
Kinross
Stirling
Firth of Forth
Edinburgh
Berwick
Roxburgh
Selkirk
Dumfries
Kirkcudbright
Wigton

WESTERN ISLANDS
Lewis
St. Kilda

SCOTLAND

Donegal
Antrim
Tyrone
Down
Mayo
Sligo
Cavan
Galway
Roscommon
Clare
Limerick
Tipperary
Kilkenny
Wexford
Waterford
Cork
Kerry
Kildare
Wicklow
King's Co.
Queen's Co.

Isle of Man

Cumberland
Durham
York
Lancashire
Cheshire
Derby
Lincoln
Flint
Denbigh
Anglesey
Carnarvon
Montgomery
Shropshire
Stafford
Leicester
Cardigan Bay
Cardigan
Radnor
Worcester
Warwick
Northampton
Cambridge
Norfolk
Suffolk
Pembroke
Carmarthen
Hereford
Oxford
Bucks
Hertford
Essex
Glamorgan
Monmouth
Gloucester
Berks
London
Thames R.
Surrey
Kent
Wilts
Hampshire
Sussex
Somerset
Dorset
Devon
Cornwall
The Wash

BRISTOL CHANNEL
& Lundy I.
Eddystone Li. Ho.
Scilly Is.

Straits of Dover
Dieppe

British Miles.
10 20 30 40 50 60 70 80 90 100

The Phillimore
ATLAS and INDEX
of PARISH REGISTERS

3rd edition

edited by Cecil R. Humphery-Smith

Phillimore

First edition, 1984
Second edition, 1995
Reprinted 1999

Third edition, 2003

Published by
PHILLIMORE & CO. LTD
Shopwyke Manor Barn, Chichester, West Sussex, England
www.phillimore.co.uk

ISBN 1-86077-239-0
ISBN 13 978-1-86077-239-9

Printed and bound in Great Britain by
CAMBRIDGE PRINTING

Contents

THE ATLAS

For each region listed below, the Atlas contains (unless otherwise stated) a map of the pre-1832 parishes, and a topographical map from James Bell's *A New and Comprehensive Gazetteer of England and Wales* of 1834.

THE INDEX

Editor's Introduction

In this new edition we have introduced a map of the whole country showing the county boundaries before 1830 (see frontispiece). With each parish map in this Atlas is a reproduction of a topographical map from James Bell's *A New and Comprehensive Gazetteer of England and Wales* of 1834. A Scottish map is included from Henry Teesdale's Atlas of 1832. These maps should help a researcher to pinpoint the whereabouts and extent of a particular parish and the path someone might travel from one place to another in the light of local features.

There is a list of parishes for each county and a grid reference which will enable the user to find the place readily. Although a parish may be found in more than one square of a grid, the reference quoted should enable the reader to find the parish name with ease. Importantly, we have added to the Index the Registration District references corresponding to each parish for the period 1837-1851. This should assist researchers to move from General Registration of Births, Marriages and Deaths, to Census enumerators' records through to parochial records.

The indexes in this book provide outline information for ready reference consolidating into one source what can otherwise be discovered only by referring to many of these guides. They are nevertheless essential for the detail from original and copy sources that users of this book will require for further research.

A major change to the information in the Index has been the swapping of details regarding marriage indexes with that of census indexes. As many counties have now had the marriages in all parishes indexed for specific periods it was thought easier to summarise this in the end paragraph, and in its place provide a parish-by-parish breakdown of available census indexes. For example, indexes exist for that parish for the census years of 1851, 1871, 1881, 1891. These appear in the form 5,7,8,9. Mention needs to be made of the 1881 census index covering the whole country. We have not included 1901 as this was not available when we began our work on this edition and it has proved to be an unreliable source. We should also advise researchers in microfilm and CD-ROM indexes to use their findings with care.

For demographers, the 1841 Census on microfilm index held by Trevor Harris, P.O. Box 557, Morley, Pert 6062, Australia, for some counties may be useful, as are the several indexes to beneficiaries in Wills. Many counties' family history societies continue to make great strides in copying and indexing monumental inscriptions as well as registers.

Special mention must be made of the work of the Genealogical Society of Utah, the arm of the Church of Jesus Christ of Latter Day Saints, which has published the latest version of the International Genealogical Index on CD-ROM with magnificent access co-ordinates (*see* Note 1). It is making progress with the indexing of the 1881 Census, available on fiche for England and Wales. Genealogists, demographers and historians owe an immense debt to the organisers and volunteers who have made this great work possible, particularly to the G.S.U.

Sources for England and Wales

While the Institute has been maintaining its own listings of deposited parish records used in compiling this book, there is a useful series of publications by Local Population Studies. The *Original Parish Registers in Record Offices and Libraries* volumes outline the dates the registers extend to and where they can be found.

In both this publication and those of Local Population Studies only the earliest and latest years of the registers deposited in the appropriate record office are quoted. This is a combined figure encompassing the baptism, marriage and burial registers. Searchers must be aware that it is unlikely that all three types of register will extend in coverage to the stated dates and, of course, there might also be gaps within the series.

The *International Genealogical Index* is an index of millions of entries of baptisms and marriages (but no burials) arranged on a county basis for the period 1538-1881. It is an excellent finding aid, as are other indexes, but none must be regarded as a primary source. Searches can be made from microfiche copies at most county record offices and libraries. A complete set is also available at the Society of Genealogists and The Institute of Heraldic and Genealogical Studies from whom abstractions can be obtained.

A separate column has been included in this book to refer users to the large number of small marriage indexes available. It must be stressed that only information on those parishes indexed up to the end of 2001 has been included and by the time this book is in circulation more parishes may have been added. However, this will give an idea of the use and extent of the valuable work being done by individuals and family history societies. When requesting a search a stamped addressed envelope should be sent to the index holder together with the appropriate fee or a donation.

Boyd's Marriage Index is a typescript index of English marriages taken from copies of marriage registers, bishops' transcripts and marriage licences, and covering the period 1538-1837 for a large number of parishes. The only complete copies are in the possession of the Society of Genealogists (where they are free for inspection upon paying the appropriate membership fee or day fee), at the College of Arms and at the Genealogical Society of Salt Lake City, Utah. A partial copy of a large portion of the index is held at the Institute.

Pallot's Marriage Index is a handscript on thin paper slips of millions of marriages taken from original registers and bishops' transcripts for the period 1780-1837. It covers most of the 103 ancient parishes of the city of London and hundreds of other parishes up and down the country. This unique index is held at the Institute of Heraldic and Genealogical Studies. Details of searching facilities can be obtained on request. A copy of the Pallot Index of Marriages and that of Baptisms is available from the Institute on CD-ROM. Access to the original source may, however, be necessary because of the quality of the original slips.

With the passing of the Non Parochial Registers Act of 1840, all non-conformist registers were to be authenticated, and sent into the custody of the Registrar General. These registers are now held at the Public Record Office. However, many were not surrendered though some have now come to light and are in the hands of county record offices. Only those registers held at the Public Record Office have been noted in our Index. Record offices have published their own handlists and guides.

The Society of Genealogists has the largest collection of parish register copies to which they are continuing to add. Further information can be obtained from their publications listed below. They have also published a listing of parish register copies housed in other libraries and record offices throughout England and Wales. This list is now sadly out of date due to the enormous amount of transcription work which has been undertaken in the last decade. It is not within the scope of this publication to do more than refer users to the several useful publications which will provide fuller details and addresses of the many repositories where copies of registers can be found. Indeed, the abbreviated information in this index may mislead the searcher if reference is not made to the detail in the publications listed below which are essential aids to further research.

Mention must be made of the work of The Parish Register Transcription Society. Details of their publications on fiche may be obtained from 50 Silvester Road, Cowplain, Waterlooville, Hampshire PO8 8TL.

Sources for Scotland

Much of the work to put together an index for Scotland comparable with that for England and Wales has already been done by Kathleen B. Cory in *Tracing Your Scottish Ancestry* (Polygon 1990) and by Cecil Sinclair's *Tracing Your Scottish Ancestors in the*

Scottish Record Office (H.M.S.O. 1990). *Sources for Scottish Genealogy and Family History* by D.J. Steel (Phillimore for The Society of Genealogists) and *Key to the Parochial Registers of Scotland* by V. Ben Bloxham are also important research guides. All related records are centrally deposited at New Register House, Edinburgh. The dates of commencement of deposited original registers are given, in the second column, followed by the reference to the coordinates on the map. The end date can be taken as 1855 when General Registration begins in Scotland. There are no indexes prepared which are comparable with local marriage indexes, Boyd's or Pallot's, nor any significant number of transcripts of registers held in any one place. The IGI covers deposited registers, non-conformist records and all original parish registers have been separately filmed and indexed on microfiche. These are indexed by county and thereby form indexes of marriages, births and deaths, or baptisms and burials. They are widely available in libraries and societies' collections.

The maps are taken from those produced and sold separately for many years.

Scotland is particularly well covered for monumental inscriptions. The Scottish societies can provide further details:

The Scottish Genealogical Society, 15 Victoria Terrace, Edinburgh EH1 2JL
The Scottish Association for Family History Societies, 51/3 Mortonhall Road, Edinburgh EH9 2HN

Once the reader is used to the format of this book he will realise that it will enable him to answer such questions as: 'have the registers been deposited?' ... 'where are they to be found?'... 'what dates do they cover?'... 'have they been copied or indexed and by whom?'. The key is obviously to be used only as a guide in general terms. It indicates in what other publications further specific details can be found. These have been described in outline and can be purchased from the Institute. They are essential to effective and efficient use of this *Atlas and Index*. Discrepancies may well be found, since the publications referred to have been compiled independently and for much of the material in this edition we have relied upon information from county archivists. To them researchers must turn for details of those parishes which came into being after 1832. Some parishes were split in the 18th and 19th centuries, others absorbed older parish registers of decayed communities. These have been revealed since the practice of depositing registers began. The process of depositing registers with record offices has proceeded swiftly in the past decade while transcribing and indexing has slowed in pace.

It would be greatly appreciated if users of these maps and indexes would inform me of any errors that may be discovered so that justified amendments can be incorporated in new editions or in a leaflet. Ideas for improvement will also be considered.

Copyright

Copyright in the maps, index tables and text is ultimately vested in myself and The Trustees of The Institute of Heraldic and Genealogical Studies along with the compilers of the sources referred to from whom permission must be obtained for any reproduction in part or in whole. Many tracings, near copies and 'versions' of the Institute's maps have been made and some by those who should have better regard for our work. Because of the great deal of voluntary effort that has gone into this work as well as the enormous costs involved, photocopying is prohibited. We are well aware that several individuals, family history societies and other organisations have copied the maps for their own use in particular projects or for family history research. We particularly know of those who have followed precisely the outlines of the parish boundaries that we produced in the 1960s and later. We can well understand that no one wishes to reinvent the wheel. It is, however, appreciated when there is some acknowledgement for our pioneer work. Written permission is usually allowed for use of this material in conjunction with scholarly projects, but violations in 'professional' or commercial interest will be prosecuted in accordance with the Act.

Several significant alterations have been made to the format of this work. It becomes even more helpful to genealogists, local and family historians, and demographers than previous editions. It has been made possible by our efforts at the Institute; but none of the corrections and amendments would have been collected without collaboration and generous help from archivists, record officers and dedicated correspondents from around the country. I am well aware of their unfortunate financial constraints and pressure upon their time. I am immensely grateful to them all, especially those who were prompt and detailed in their responses.

We are much indebted to the Society of Genealogists for permission to take extracts from their publications in preparing the relevant columns in this Index.

The Maps

The unique production of a series of parish maps for each county of England and Wales was begun in 1959. Sources prior to 1832 were used to outline the parochial boundaries with the probate court jurisdictions affecting each shown in colour coding. In the process, of course, an index was made which formed the primary sources of the first Phillimore edition in 1984. This has now been entirely revised for two subsequent editions. In the beginning of this work there were few record offices in the counties, and none organised as they are today. My colleagues and I relied upon diocesan registrars and archdeacons, some of whom had their own parochial boundary maps, tithe maps, local antiquaries and clergy. The maps were made for the benefit of genealogists and local historians from whose viewpoint the juxtaposition of parishes is the most important, especially when (with the few indexes then available) 'blanket searching' of parish registers retained in the churches was a normal research process. Since the first appearance of the maps, several other 'experts' have come forward for each county and drawn our attention to amendments and corrections to be made. I cannot claim to be an expert on each county and have relied very much upon such people to whom I must express my heartfelt thanks for guidance and assistance. In consequence, however, the boundaries may well have altered beyond the original concepts of showing what they were before the boundary reforms of the 19th century. Indeed, corrections had been noticed which appear to have taken the latest versions of the maps into the second half of the 19th century. It would be foolish to argue with the archivists and those so much more familiar with the counties concerned than I. However, I personally take responsibility for the final decisions on amendments and corrections. Formerly I had used such spellings as pertained to parish names before 1832. Spellings (and dates) have now been amended so far as has seemed sensible as required by county archivists (*see* Note 2).

Each map now includes reference to neighbouring counties. This should prevent researchers continuing searches with an imaginary wall surrounding *their* particular county of interest. So very many times I have encountered the researcher who has exhausted every parish in *his* county when the marriage he seeks has been one mile across the county border.

The Index

The lists of deposited registers have been amended to include information provided by record offices. My own view has been that where a series of registers begins in (say) 1610 and there are no more than perhaps a dozen isolated entries in a late hand back to (say) 1550, it is misleading to give this early date for the beginning of the parish registers. However, so many dates have been 'corrected' by archivists and those expert in their own counties that I must take their word that my previous judgements have to be amended by the discovery of previously unknown material. Otherwise, I am faced with a further 20 years' checking original sources. I may have even less time left to me than when I last wrote this Introduction.

Most counties have produced their own guides to genealogical sources which are available in record offices and highly recommended. The excellent series of guides produced by Jeremy Gibson and his associates, published by The Federation of Family History Societies as well as The Society of Genealogists' pamphlets are also to be recommended to all users of this book. Brief guides to sources are noted in the editorial notes to each county to encourage users to turn to these more detailed resources.

Some indexers do not have any list of the parishes they have covered. Many indexes have gaps in them or are incomplete. Where there are two or more indexes in a county it is important to discover coverage from each source because they may or may not complement each other completely.

Names and addresses of holders of indexers are often changing. It is necessary to check these with the latest editions of Gibson Guides. As far as possible the annual FAMILY HISTORY DIARY (usually available in September from The Institute of Heraldic and Genealogical Studies, Northgate, Canterbury, CT1 1BA, or from local family history societies) contains updated names and addresses of importance, as well as much useful information.

Separate maps for each county are printed in a larger size (13 ins. by 17 ins.). The Institute also produces three maps showing Registration and Census Districts covering the periods 1837-51, 1852-1945, and 1946-1965, which are also available at modest prices from The Institute of Heraldic and Genealogical Studies, Northgate, Canterbury, CT1 1BA.

Acknowledgements

This new edition of *The Phillimore Atlas and Index of Parish Registers* derives from the work that I have done myself since 1959 and the contributions of many generations of students at the Institute of Heraldic and Genealogical Studies. Principally, the latest marathon effort that has updated the material for this edition has been supervised by Jeremy Palmer, with the help of Sarah Bulson, Debbie Foord and James Guy. The immense input of secretarial staff at the Institute also deserves acknowledgement. I take full responsibility for the result.

To the many members of staff and students of the Institute, to archivists, historians, parochial incumbents and local genealogists who have given so generously of their time, expertise and special knowledge to assist in the preparation of this work, as well as to the staff of Phillimore, our publishers, the Trustees of the Institute of Heraldic and Genealogical Studies join me once again in recording grateful thanks.

C.R. Humphery-Smith F.S.A.
Canterbury, 2002

Notes

1. The IGI column retains the 1988 listing because it is not possible to state what is or is not present on the 1992 version. There has, it appears, not been any update since 1992. The Institute has the latest version on CD-ROM.

2. Some dozen maps do not show one or two parishes which otherwise appear in the Index because registers have been deposited. Some are obviously chapelries or late formed parishes, the boundaries of which have not been determined. A few are ancient parishes, redundant in the 19th century, whose registers have since appeared and boundaries appear to have been absorbed:

Hampshire	Hinton Admiral (2A)	1810
Herefordshire	Ford	1742
Hertfordshire	London Colney (3E)	1826
Leicestershire	Stretton Parva (4G)	1592
Monmouth	Llandewi Rhydderch	1670
	Llanrihanyd Gobion (5H)	1751
Norfolk	Burgh Parva (M)	1594
	Frenze (2H)	1651
	Wilton (5G)	1634
Somerset	Bednall (6F)	1705
Staffordshire	Elkstone	1785
	Harford	1828
	Wilnecote	1763
North Wales	Isycoed	1749

Some parishes may have adjusted words prefixed, *Great, Long etc.*

List of Publications

Original Parish Registers in Record Offices and Libraries—Local Population Studies 1974 with four supplements; 1st, 1976; 2nd, 1978; 3rd, 1980; and 4th, 1982—Local Population Studies, Tawney House, Matlock, Derbyshire.

Mormon International Genealogical Index, 1988. *Parish and Vital Records Listing* published by The Genealogical Society of Utah.

Local Marriage Indexes (names and addresses are supplied at the end of each county index).

Parish Register Copies in the Library of the Society of Genealogists, 1992. Available on-line.

A List of Parishes in Boyd's Marriage Index, 1994—Society of Genealogists.

Parish Register Copies, Part Two, other than the Society of Genealogists' Collection—Society of Genealogists, 1974.

A Guide to Pallot Marriage and Baptismal Indexes—The Institute of Heraldic and Genealogical Studies.

Non Parochial Registers and Records in the Custody of the Registrar General—Public Record Office, 1859.

The National Index of Parish Registers (details from The Society). Published by The Society of Genealogists.

The following publications of Mr J.S.W. Gibson F.S.A., F.S.G. and collaborators are published by The Federation of Family History Societies, Units 15-16, Chesham Industrial Centre, Oram Street, Bury, BL9 6EN.

Bishops' Transcripts and Marriage Licences, 5th edition.

Census Returns 1841-1881 in Microfilm, 6th edition.

Coroners' Records in England and Wales, 2nd edition.

The Hearth Tax, Other Later Stuart Tax Lists and the Association Oath Rolls, 2nd edition.

Land Tax and Window Tax Assessments, 2nd edition.

List of Londoners, 3rd edition.

Local Census Listings, 1522-1930, 3rd edition.

Local Newspapers 1750-1920: A Select Location List, 2nd edition.

Marriage, Census and other Indexes for Family Historians, 8th edition.

Militia Lists and Musters, 1757-1876, 4th edition.

Poll Books, c.1696-1872, 3rd edition.

Poor Law Union Records in England and Wales:
>   Pt 1 - South East England and East Anglia
>   Pt 2 - Midlands and Northern England
>   Pt 3 - South West England, the Marches and Wales
>   Pt 4 - Gazetteer of England and Wales (lists parishes within each Poor Law Union).

Probate Jurisdictions: Where to Look for Wills, 5th edition.

Protestation Returns 1641-42 (1995).

Quarter Sessions Records for Family Historians, 4th edition.

Record Offices: How to Find Them, 9th edition.

Specialist Indexes for Family Historians, 2nd edition.

Tudor and Stuart Muster Rolls (1991).

Victuallers' Licences, 2nd edition.

Each record office publishes handlists, lists of deposited records, registers and copies or more comprehensive guides which are essential to users of this book. The addresses are given at the end of each county index.

Useful Addresses

Army Records Centre, Bourne Avenue, Hayes, Middlesex UB3 1RS

Borthwick Institute of Historical Research, St Anthony's Hall, Peaseholme Green, York YO1 7PW. 01904 642315

British Library, 96 Euston Road, London NW1 2DB. 0207 412 7513

Catholic Record Society, 114 Mount Street, London W1Y 6AH

Church of Jesus Christ of Latter Day Saints, Genealogical Society of Utah, 50 East North Temple, Salt Lake City, Utah 84150, U.S.A. English address: 751 Warwick Road, Solihull, West Midlands, B91 3DQ

College of Arms, Queen Victoria Street, London EC4V 4BT. 0207 248 2762

Council of Irish Genealogical Organisations, 186 Ashcroft, Raheny, Dublin 5, Ireland

Family Records Centre, Myddelton Street, Islington, London EC1R 1VW. 0208 392 5300

Federation of Family History Societies, Administrator, PO Box 2425, Coventry CV5 6YX

General Register Office (Ireland), Joyce House, 8-11 Lombard Street, East Dublin L2. 0035 31 6711000

General Register Office (Northern Ireland), Oxford House, 49-55 Chichester Street, Belfast BT1 4HL. 01232 252021

General Register Office for Scotland, HM New Register House, 2 Princes Street, Edinburgh EH1 3YY. 0131 334 0380

Guild of One-Name Studies, Box G, 14 Charterhouse Buildings, Goswell Road, London EC1M 7BA

Heraldry Society, P.O. Box 32, Maidenhead, Berkshire SL6 3FD. 0118 932 0210

Heraldry Society of Scotland, 25 Craigentinny Crescent, Edinburgh EH7 6QR

Home Office, Lunar House, 40 Wellesley Road, Croydon CR9 2BY

Huguenot Society and Library, University College, Gower Street, London WC1E 6BT. 0207 380 7094

Institute of Heraldic & Genealogical Studies, 79-82 Northgate, Canterbury, Kent CT1 1BA. 01227 768664; www.ihgs.ac.uk

Irish Genealogical Research Society, Irish Club, 82 Eaton Square, London SW1

Jewish Museum, Woburn House, Upper Woburn Place, London WC1H 0ED

Local Population Studies Society, Tawney House, Matlock, Derbyshire D24 3BT

Manorial Society of Great Britain, 104 Kennington Road, London SE11 6RE. 0207 735 6633

MOD, CS(R) 2b, Bourne Avenue, Hayes, Middlesex UB3 1RF

National Archives of Ireland, Bishop Street, Dublin 8. 0035 31 4072300

National Archives of Scotland, HM New Register House, 2 Princes Street, Edinburgh EH1 3YY

Naval Personnel Records, Room 2007 059(a), Ministry of Defence, Empress State Building, London SW6 1TR

Phillimore Bookshop, Shopwyke Manor Barn, Chichester, West Sussex PO20 2BG. 01243 787636; www.phillimore.co.uk

Principal Registry of the Family Division, First Avenue House, High Holborn, London. 0207 947 6000

Public Record Office, Ruskin Avenue, Kew, Richmond, Surrey TW9 4DU. 0208 876 3444

THE
ATLAS

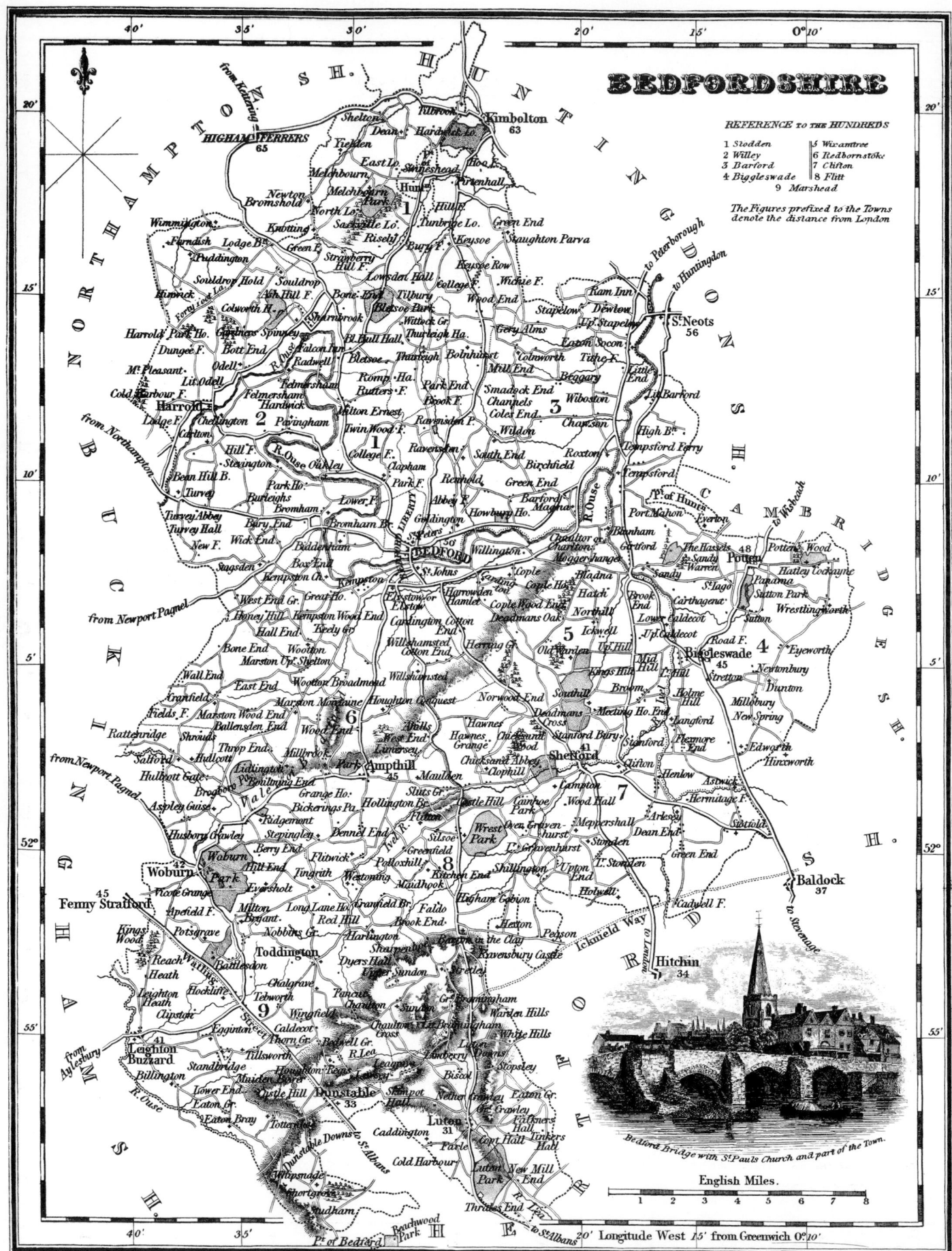

BEDFORDSHIRE

Engd. by Gray & Son

Publd. by Archd. Fullarton & Co. Glasgow.

REFERENCE to the HUNDREDS

1 Stodden
2 Willey
3 Barford
4 Biggleswade
9 Marshead
5 Wixamtree
6 Redbornstoke
7 Clifton
8 Flitt

The Figures prefixed to the Towns denote the distance from London

Bedford Bridge with St Pauls Church and part of the Town.

English Miles.

20' Longitude West 15' from Greenwich 0°10'

BEDFORDSHIRE

WITH DATES OF COMMENCEMENT OF REGISTERS FOR PARISHES FORMED BEFORE 1832

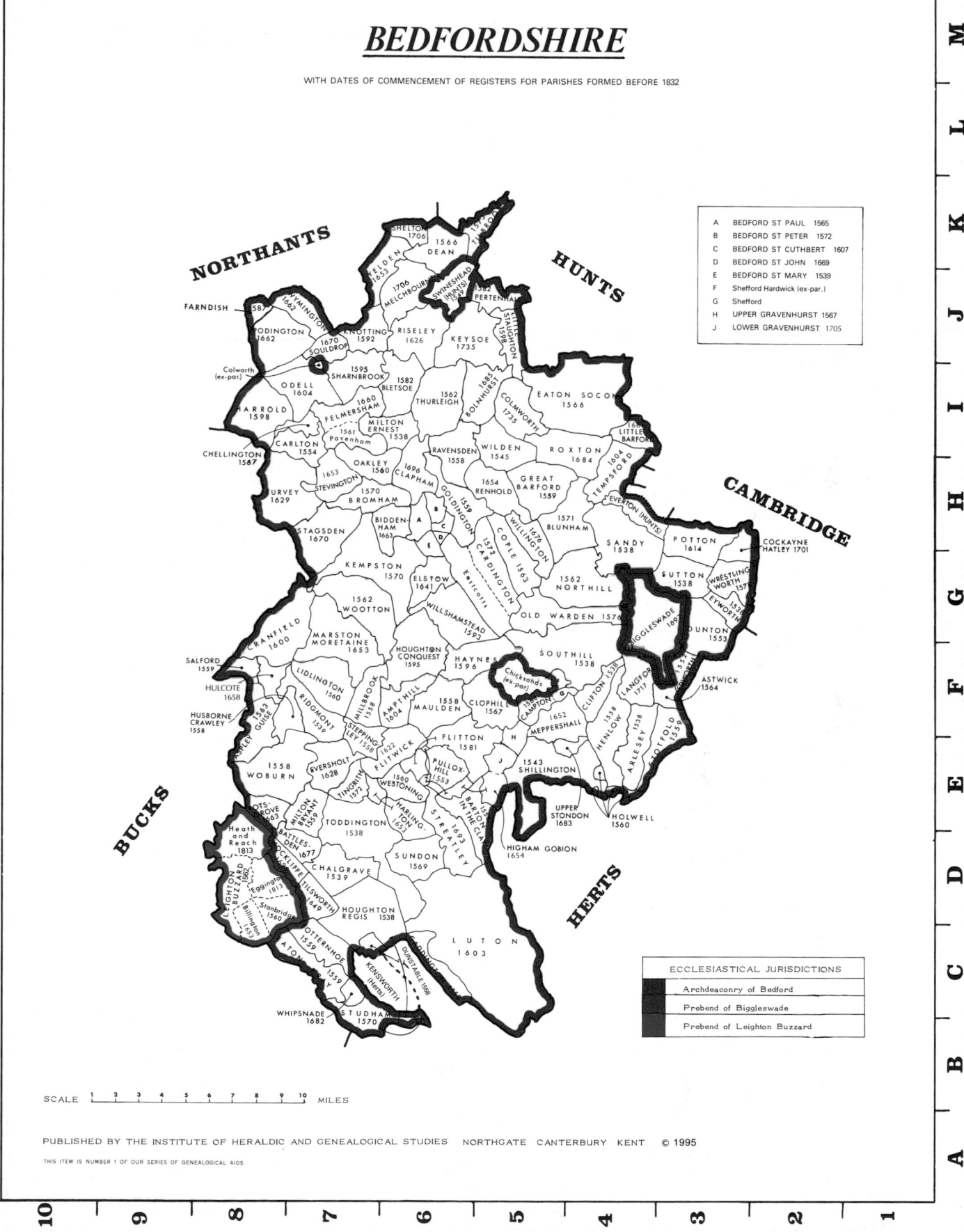

NORTHANTS

HUNTS

CAMBRIDGE

HERTS

BUCKS

A	BEDFORD ST PAUL	1565
B	BEDFORD ST PETER	1572
C	BEDFORD ST CUTHBERT	1607
D	BEDFORD ST JOHN	1669
E	BEDFORD ST MARY	1539
F	Shefford Hardwick (ex-par.)	
G	Shefford	
H	UPPER GRAVENHURST	1567
J	LOWER GRAVENHURST	1705

SHELTON 1706
DEAN 1566
TILBROOK
SWINESHEAD (HUNTS)
PERTENHALL 1582
FELDEN 1653
MELCHBOURN 1706
STAUGHTON 1598
FARNDISH
YMINGTON 1662
PODINGTON 1662
KNOTTING 1592
RISELEY 1626
KEYSOE 1735
SOULDROP 1670
Colworth (ex-par.)
SHARNBROOK 1595
BLETSOE 1582
BOLNHURST 1685
ODELL 1604
THURLEIGH 1562
COLMWORTH 1735
EATON SOCON 1566
HARROLD 1598
FELMERSHAM 1660
MILTON ERNEST 1538
LITTLE BARFORD 1666
CHELLINGTON 1567
CARLTON 1554
Pavenham 1561
RAVENSDEN 1558
WILDEN 1545
ROXTON 1684
TEMPSFORD 1604
URVEY 1629
OAKLEY 1560
CLAPHAM 1696
GOLDINGTON 1559
RENHOLD 1654
GREAT BARFORD 1559
BLUNHAM 1571
EVERTON (HUNTS)
STEVINGTON 1653
BROMHAM 1570
BIDDEN-HAM 1663
CARDINGTON 1572
COPLE 1563
WILLINGTON 1676
SANDY 1538
POTTON 1614
COCKAYNE HATLEY 1701
STAGSDEN 1670
KEMPSTON 1570
ELSTOW 1641
Eastcotts
OLD WARDEN 1576
NORTHILL 1562
SUTTON 1538
WRESTLING WORTH 1575
WOOTTON 1562
WILLSHAMSTEAD 1593
BIGGLESWADE 1538
EYWORTH 1538
SALFORD 1559
CRANFIELD 1600
MARSTON MORETAINE 1653
HOUGHTON CONQUEST 1595
HAYNES 1596
SOUTHILL 1538
DUNTON 1553
ASTWICK 1564
HULCOTE 1658
LIDLINGTON 1560
Chicksands (ex-par.)
CAMPTON
LANGFORD 1717
HUSBORNE CRAWLEY 1558
RIDGMONT 1558
MILLBROOK 1558
AMPTHILL 1604
MAULDEN 1558
CLOPHILL 1567
MEPPERSHALL 1652
CLIFTON 1538
HENLOW 1558
ARLESEY 1538
STOTFOLD 1559
STEPPING LEY 1556
FLITWICK 1622
FLITTON 1581
PULLOX-HILL 1553
SHILLINGTON 1543
HOLWELL 1560
WOBURN 1558
EVERSHOLT 1628
TINGRITH 1577
WESTONING 1560
STREATLEY 1693
UPPER STONDON 1683
HIGHAM GOBION 1654
POTS-GROVE 1663
HEATH and REACH 1813
BATTLES-DEN 1677
MILTON BRYANT 1559
HARLINGTON 1653
BARTON IN THE CLAY
TODDINGTON 1538
CHALGRAVE 1539
SUNDON 1569
LEIGHTON BUZZARD 1602
HOCKLIFFE 1662
Eggington 1813
TILSWORTH 1649
Stanbridge 1560
Billington 1653
HOUGHTON REGIS 1538
EATON 1559
TOTTERNHOE 1559
KENSWORTH (Herts)
DUNSTABLE 1558
CADDINGTON 1558
LUTON 1603
WHIPSNADE 1682
STUDHAM 1570

ECCLESIASTICAL JURISDICTIONS	
■	Archdeaconry of Bedford
	Prebend of Biggleswade
	Prebend of Leighton Buzzard

SCALE 1 2 3 4 5 6 7 8 9 10 MILES

PUBLISHED BY THE INSTITUTE OF HERALDIC AND GENEALOGICAL STUDIES NORTHGATE CANTERBURY KENT © 1995

THIS ITEM IS NUMBER 1 OF OUR SERIES OF GENEALOGICAL AIDS

WINDSOR CASTLE.
Engd by R. Scott

BERKSHIRE.

REFERENCE TO THE HUNDREDS.

1 Shrivenham	11 Lambourn
2 Faringdon	12 Faircross
3 Ganfield	13 Moreton
4 Ock	14 Theale
5 Hormer	15 Sonning
6 Moreton	16 Charlton
7 Reading	17 Ripplesmere
8 Compton	18 Wargrave
9 Wantage	19 Cookham
10 Kintbury Eagle	20 Beynhurst
	21 Bray

The Figures prefixed to the Towns denote the distance from London.

English Miles

Longitude West 30 from Greenwich

Published by Archd Fullarton & Co. Glasgow.

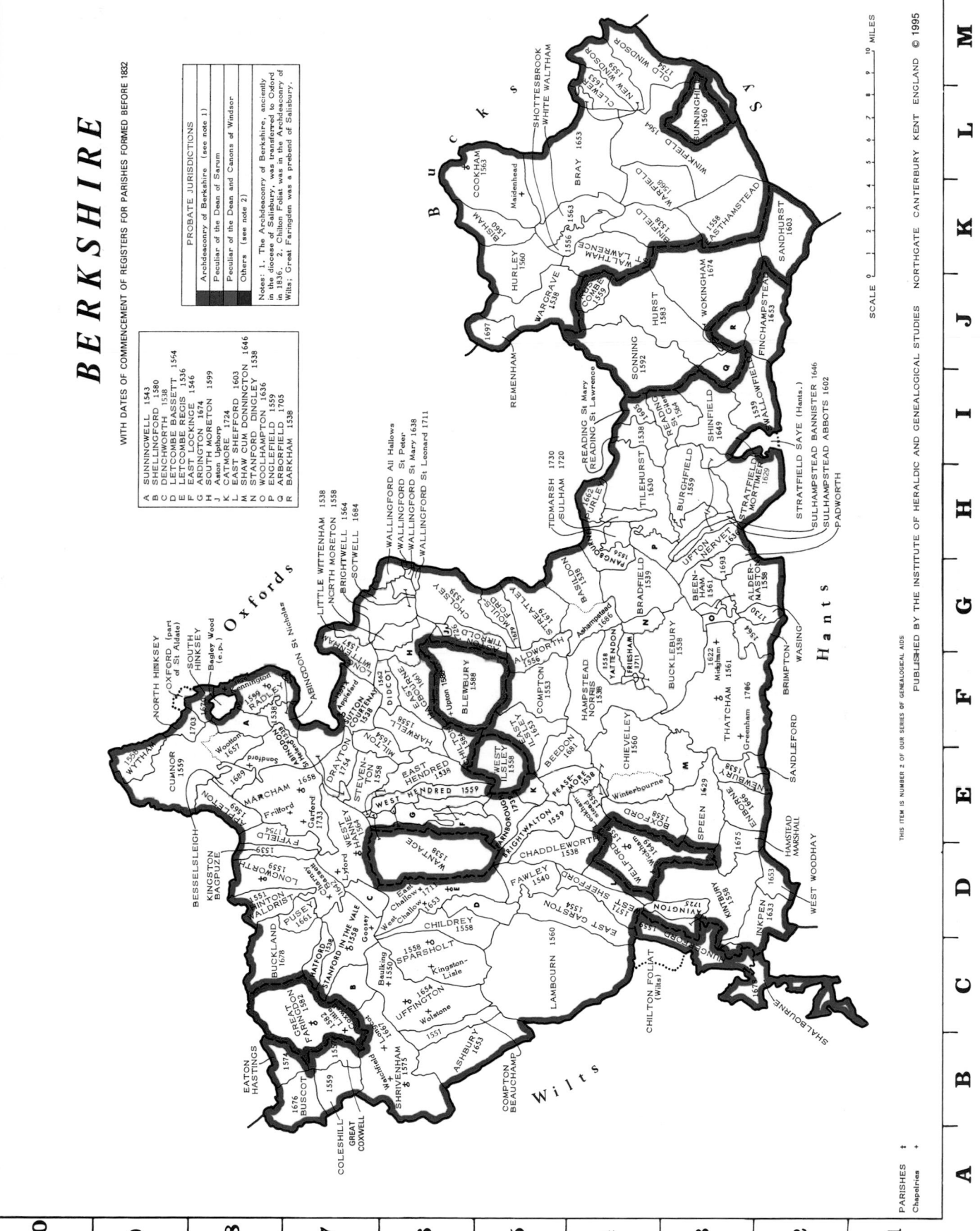

BERKSHIRE

WITH DATES OF COMMENCEMENT OF REGISTERS FOR PARISHES FORMED BEFORE 1832

PROBATE JURISDICTIONS

- Archdeaconry of Berkshire (see note 1)
- Peculiar of the Dean of Sarum
- Peculiar of the Dean and Canons of Windsor
- Others (see note 2)

Notes: 1. The Archdeaconry of Berkshire, anciently in the diocese of Salisbury, was transferred to Oxford in 1836. 2. Chilton Foliat was in the Archdeaconry of Wilts; Great Faringdon was a prebend of Salisbury.

A SUNNINGWELL 1543
B SHELLINGFORD 1580
C LETCHWORTH 1538
D LETCOMBE BASSETT 1554
E LETCOMBE REGIS 1536
F EAST LOCKINGE 1546
G ARDINGTON 1674
H SOUTH MORETON 1599
J Aston Upthorp
K CATMORE 1724
L EAST SHEFFORD 1603
M SHAW CUM DONNINGTON 1646
N STANFORD DINGLEY 1538
O WOOLHAMPTON 1636
P ENGLEFIELD 1559
Q ARBORFIELD 1705
R BARKHAM 1538

LITTLE WITTENHAM 1538
NORTH MORETON 1558
BRIGHTWELL 1564
SOTWELL 1684
WALLINGFORD All Hallows
WALLINGFORD St Peter
WALLINGFORD St Mary 1638
WALLINGFORD St Leonard 1711

SCALE 0 1 2 3 4 5 6 7 8 9 10 MILES

THIS ITEM IS NUMBER 2 OF OUR SERIES OF GENEALOGICAL AIDS

PUBLISHED BY THE INSTITUTE OF HERALDIC AND GENEALOGICAL STUDIES NORTHGATE CANTERBURY KENT ENGLAND © 1995

PARISHES †
Chapelries +

(Map of Berkshire showing parishes with dates, bordered by Oxfords, Bucks, Hants, and Wilts. Grid references A–M across and 1–10 down.)

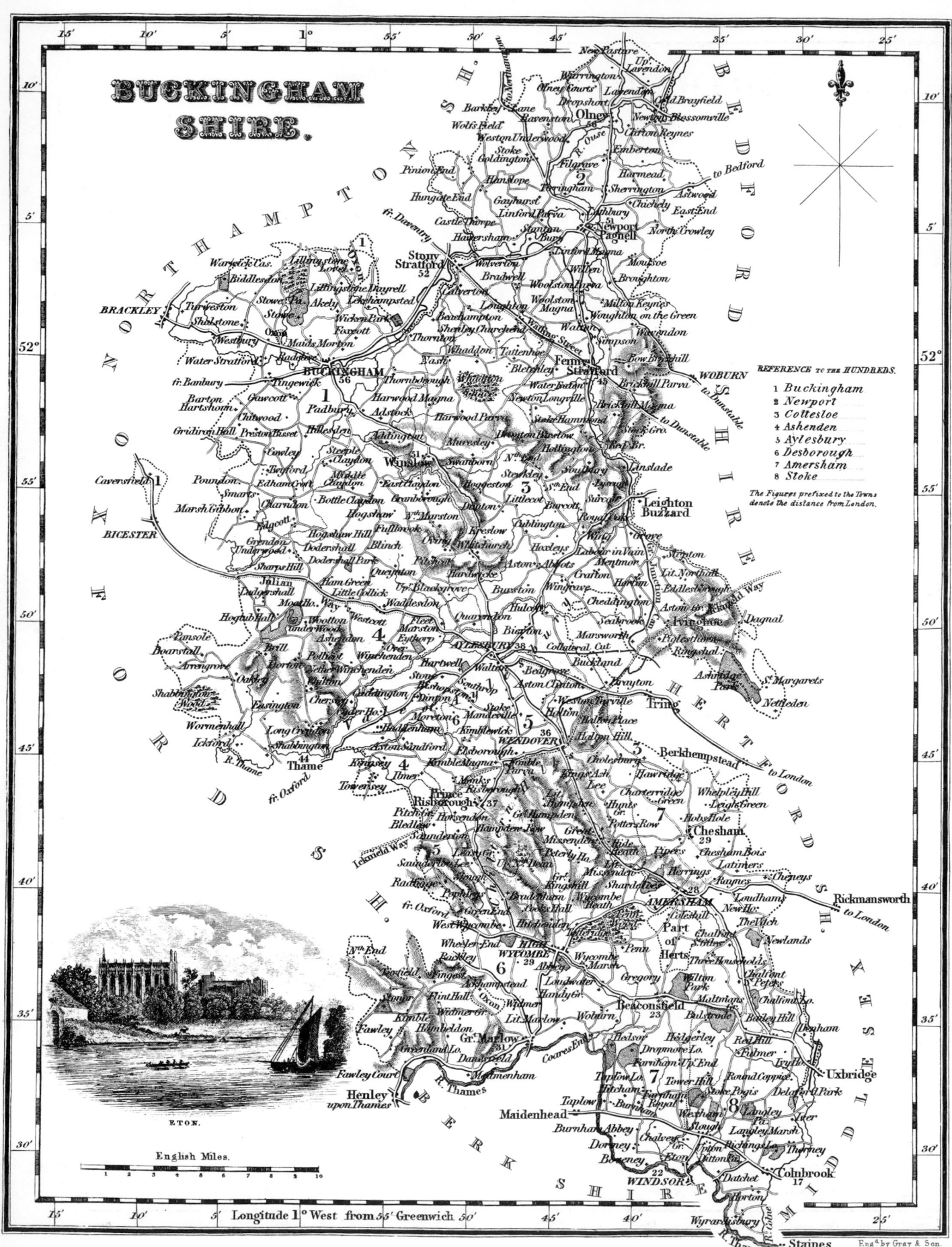

BUCKINGHAM SHIRE.

NORTHAMPTONSHIRE

BEDFORDSHIRE

HERTFORDSHIRE

MIDDLESEX

OXFORDSHIRE

BERKSHIRE

WINDSOR

REFERENCE to the HUNDREDS.

1 Buckingham
2 Newport
3 Cottesloe
4 Ashenden
5 Aylesbury
6 Desborough
7 Amersham
8 Stoke

The Figures prefixed to the Towns denote the distance from London.

ETON.

English Miles.

Longitude 1° West from Greenwich

Eng.d by Gray & Son.

Pub.d by Arch.d Fullarton & C.o Glasgow.

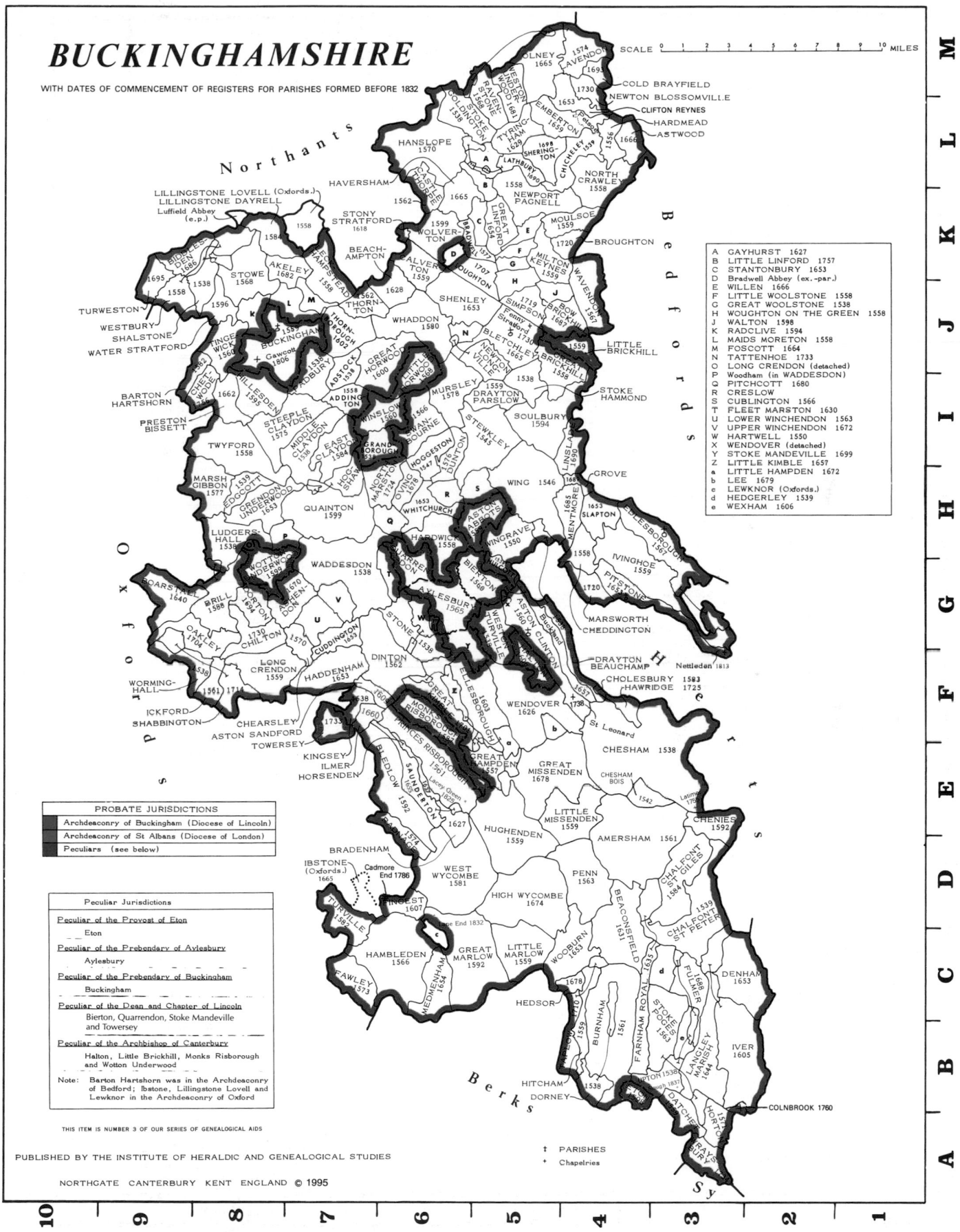

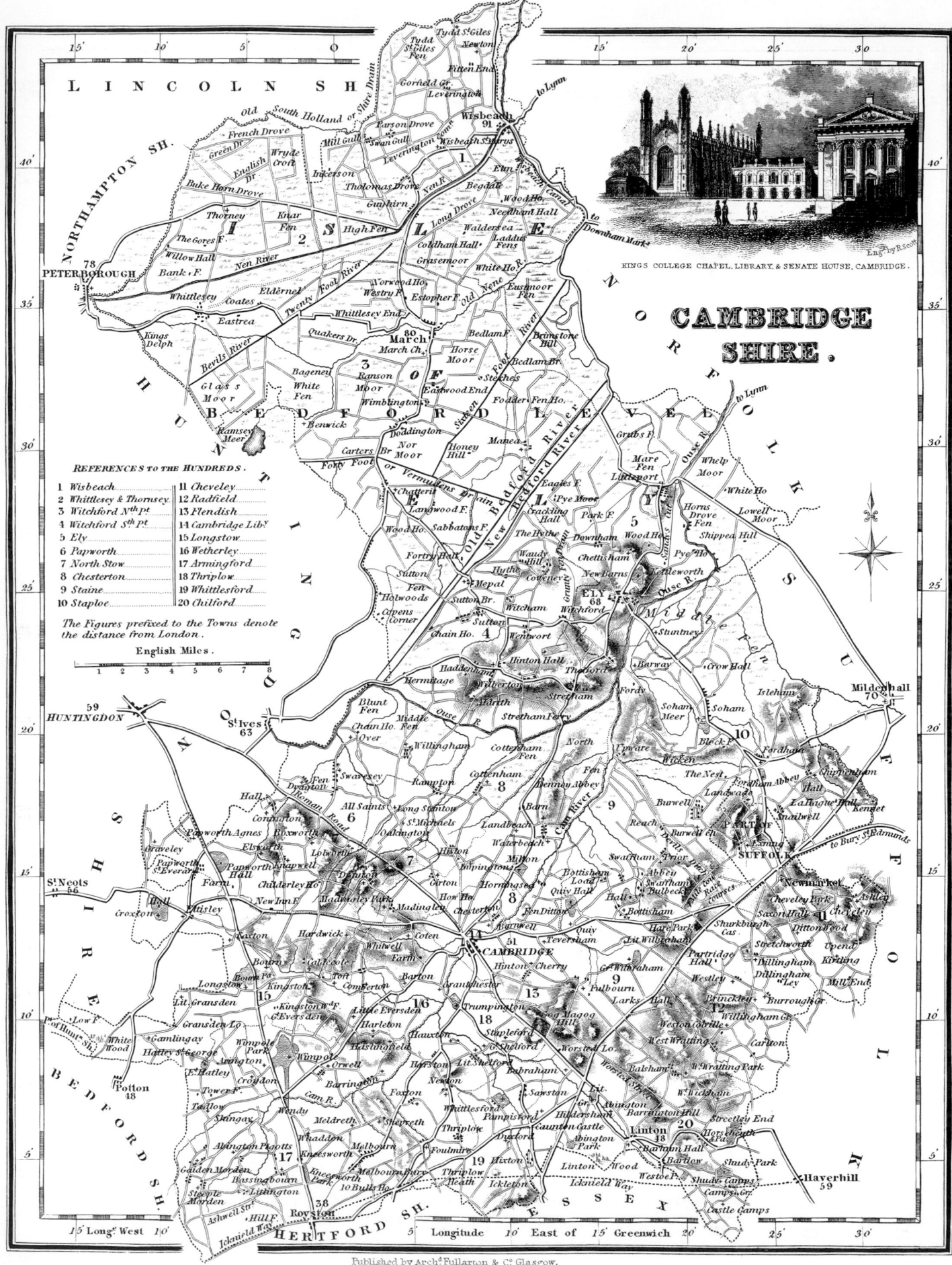

KINGS COLLEGE CHAPEL, LIBRARY, & SENATE HOUSE, CAMBRIDGE.

Eng.ᵈ by R.Scott

CAMBRIDGE SHIRE.

LINCOLN SH.

NORTHAMPTON SH.

NORFOLK

HUNTINGDON

BEDFORD

SUFFOLK

HERTFORD SH.

ESSEX

REFERENCES TO THE HUNDREDS.

1	Wisbeach	11	Cheveley
2	Whittlesey & Thornsey	12	Radfield
3	Witchford Nᵗʰ Pt.	13	Flendish
4	Witchford Sᵗʰ Pt.	14	Cambridge Libᵞ
5	Ely	15	Longstow
6	Papworth	16	Wetherley
7	North Stow	17	Armingford
8	Chesterton	18	Thriplow
9	Staine	19	Whittlesford
10	Staploe	20	Chilford

The Figures prefixed to the Towns denote
the distance from London.

English Miles.

Published by Archᵈ Fullarton & Cᵒ Glasgow.

Longitude   East of   Greenwich

Long.ᵉ West

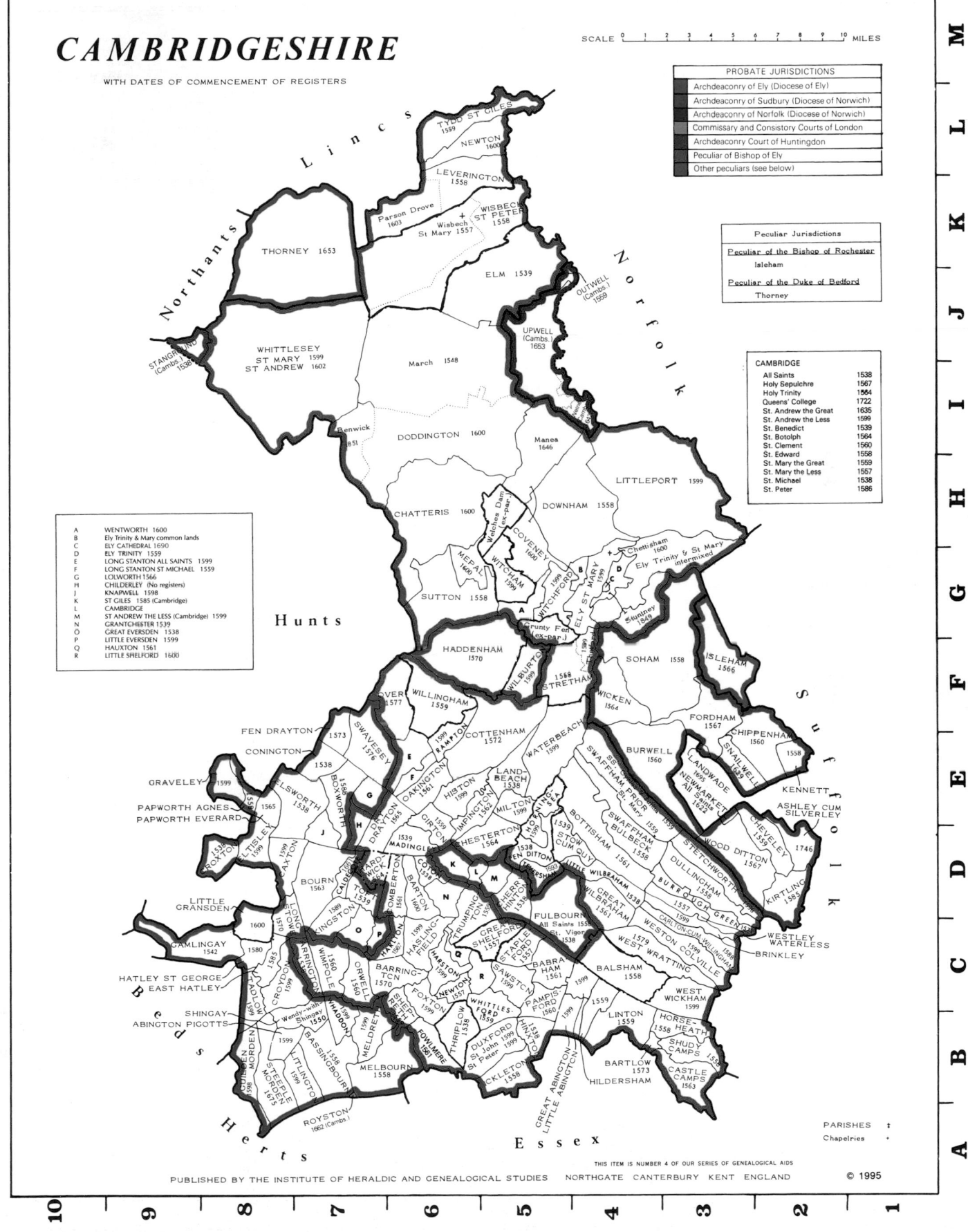

CAMBRIDGESHIRE

WITH DATES OF COMMENCEMENT OF REGISTERS

SCALE 0 1 2 3 4 5 6 7 8 9 10 MILES

PROBATE JURISDICTIONS

Archdeaconry of Ely (Diocese of Ely)
Archdeaconry of Sudbury (Diocese of Norwich)
Archdeaconry of Norfolk (Diocese of Norwich)
Commissary and Consistory Courts of London
Archdeaconry Court of Huntingdon
Peculiar of Bishop of Ely
Other peculiars (see below)

Peculiar Jurisdictions

Peculiar of the Bishop of Rochester
Isleham

Peculiar of the Duke of Bedford
Thorney

CAMBRIDGE

All Saints	1538
Holy Sepulchre	1567
Holy Trinity	1564
Queens' College	1722
St. Andrew the Great	1635
St. Andrew the Less	1599
St. Benedict	1539
St. Botolph	1564
St. Clement	1560
St. Edward	1558
St. Mary the Great	1559
St. Mary the Less	1557
St. Michael	1538
St. Peter	1586

A	WENTWORTH	1600
B	Ely Trinity & Mary common lands	
C	ELY CATHEDRAL	1690
D	ELY TRINITY	1559
E	LONG STANTON ALL SAINTS	1599
F	LONG STANTON ST MICHAEL	1559
G	LOLWORTH	1566
H	CHILDERLEY	(No registers)
J	KNAPWELL	1598
K	ST GILES	1585 (Cambridge)
L	CAMBRIDGE	
M	ST ANDREW THE LESS	(Cambridge) 1599
N	GRANTCHESTER	1539
O	GREAT EVERSDEN	1538
P	LITTLE EVERSDEN	1599
Q	HAUXTON	1561
R	LITTLE SHELFORD	1600

Lincs
Northants
Norfolk
Suffolk
Hunts
Beds
Herts
Essex

TYDD ST GILES 1599
NEWTON 1600
LEVERINGTON 1558
Parson Drove 1603
WISBECH ST PETER 1558
Wisbech St Mary 1557
THORNEY 1653
ELM 1539
OUTWELL (Cambs.) 1559
UPWELL (Cambs.) 1653
WHITTLESEY ST MARY 1599 ST ANDREW 1602
STANGROUND (Cambs.) 1538
March 1548
Benwick 1851
DODDINGTON 1600
Manea 1646
LITTLEPORT 1599
CHATTERIS 1600
Watches Dam (ex par.)
COVENEY 1600
DOWNHAM 1558
Chettisham 1600
Ely Trinity & St Mary intermixed
MEPAL 1600
WITCHAM 1599
WITCHFORD 1599
ELY ST MARY
Stuntney 1849
SUTTON 1558
Grunty Fen (ex-par.)
HADDENHAM 1570
WILBURTON 1599
STRETHAM 1568
SOHAM 1558
ISLEHAM 1566
OVER 1577
WILLINGHAM 1559
WICKEN 1564
FORDHAM 1567
CHIPPENHAM 1560
FEN DRAYTON 1573
SWAVESEY 1576
RAMPTON 1599
COTTENHAM 1572
WATERBEACH 1599
BURWELL 1560
SNAILWELL 1559
CONINGTON 1538
ELSWORTH 1538
BOXWORTH 1568
OAKINGTON 1561
HISTON 1599
LANDBEACH 1538
SWAFFHAM PRIOR SS St Mary
SWAFFHAM BULBECK 1558
LANDWADE 1695
KENNETT 1558
GRAVELEY 1599
DRAYTON 1565
IMPINGTON 1562
MILTON 1599
STOW CUM QUY 1599
SWAFFHAM BULBECK 1558
NEWMARKET All Saints 1622
ASHLEY CUM SILVERLEY
PAPWORTH AGNES
PAPWORTH EVERARD 1565
KNAPWELL 1539
MADINGLEY
CHESTERTON 1564
FEN DITTON 1538
BOTTISHAM 1539
STETCHWORTH 1567
WOOD DITTON 1567
CHEVELEY 1559
1746
CROXTON 1538
LT TISLEY 1599
CALDECOTE
HARDWICK 1599
COTON 1538
LITTLE WILBRAHAM 1599
DULLINGHAM 1558
KIRTLING 1585
BOURN 1563
LONG STOWTON 1570
KINGSTON 1599
TOFT 1599
BARTON 1601
TRUMPINGTON 1599
GREAT WILBRAHAM 1561
BURROUGH GREEN 1557
LITTLE GRANSDEN 1600
CAXTON 1585
BOURN
COMBERTON 1561
GRANTCHESTER
HASLINGFIELD 1599
GREAT SHELFORD 1557
FULBOURN All Saints 1558 St. Vigor 1538
WESTON COLVILLE
WESTLEY WATERLESS
BRINKLEY
GAMLINGAY 1542
CROYDON 1599
ARRINGTON 1560
WIMPOLE 1560
ORWELL 1561
LITTLE SHELFORD
HAUXTON
STAPLEFORD 1557
BABRAHAM 1561
WEST WRATTING 1579
BALSHAM 1558
HATLEY ST GEORGE EAST HATLEY
WENDY with SHINGAY 1550
WHADDON 1599
BARRINGTON 1570
HARSTON 1599
NEWTON 1557
SAWSTON 1599
PAMPISFORD 1560
LINTON 1559
WEST WICKHAM 1599
SHINGAY
ABINGTON PIGOTTS
TADLOW 1585
MELDRETH 1558
SHEPRETH 1599
FOXTON 1599
THRIPLOW 1538
WHITTLESFORD 1599
DUXFORD St John St Peter 1599
HINXTON 1538
HORSEHEATH 1558
SHUDY CAMPS 1558
MORDEN 1599
STEEPLE MORDEN 1615
LITLINGTON 1599
BASSINGBOURN 1558
FOWLMERE 1661
MELBOURN 1558
ICKLETON 1558
GREAT ABINGTON LITTLE ABINGTON
BARTLOW 1573
HILDERSHAM
CASTLE CAMPS 1563
ROYSTON 1662 (Cambs)

PARISHES ‡
Chapelries +

THIS ITEM IS NUMBER 4 OF OUR SERIES OF GENEALOGICAL AIDS

PUBLISHED BY THE INSTITUTE OF HERALDIC AND GENEALOGICAL STUDIES   NORTHGATE   CANTERBURY   KENT   ENGLAND   © 1995

M L K J I H G F E D C B A
10 9 8 7 6 5 4 3 2 1

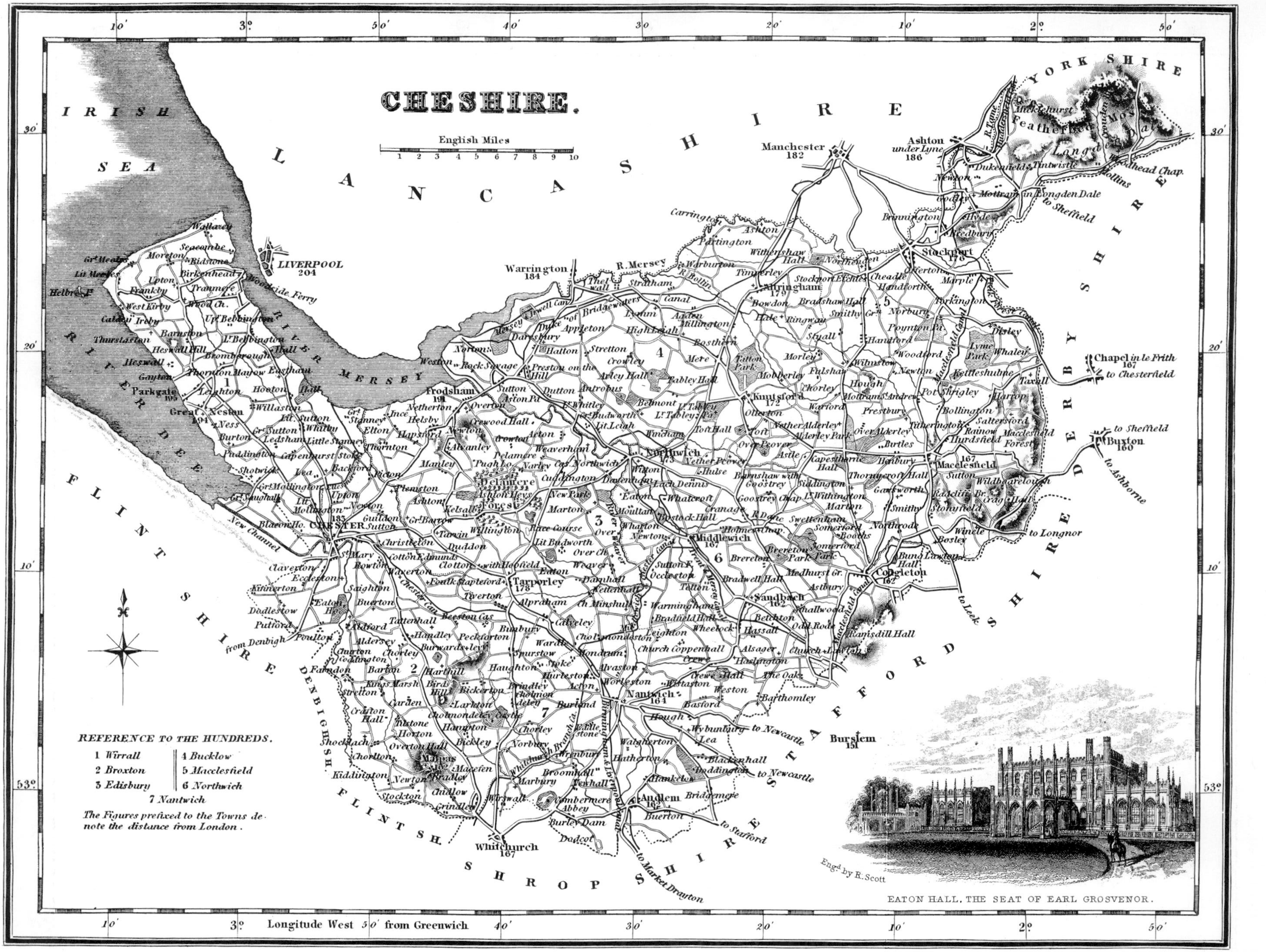

CHESHIRE.

English Miles
1 2 3 4 5 6 7 8 9 10

YORKSHIRE

DERBYSHIRE

LANCASHIRE

STAFFORDSHIRE

SHROPSHIRE

FLINTSHIRE

DENBIGHSHIRE

IRISH SEA

RIVER MERSEY

RIVER DEE

Liverpool 204
Manchester 182
Ashton under Lyne 186
Warrington 184
Whitchurch 161
Nantwich
Chapel in le Frith 167
Buxton 160

to Sheffield
to Chesterfield
to Ashborne
to Longnor
to Leek
to Newcastle
to Newcastle
to Stafford
to Market Drayton
from Denbigh

Birmingham & Liverpool Canal
Trent Mersey Canal
New Channel

EATON HALL, THE SEAT OF EARL GROSVENOR.

Engd. by R. Scott.

REFERENCE TO THE HUNDREDS.

1 Wirrall   4 Bucklow
2 Broxton   5 Macclesfield
3 Edisbury   6 Northwich
                 7 Nantwich

The Figures prefixed to the Towns denote the distance from London.

Longitude West 3° from Greenwich

Published by Archd. Fullarton & Co. Glasgow.

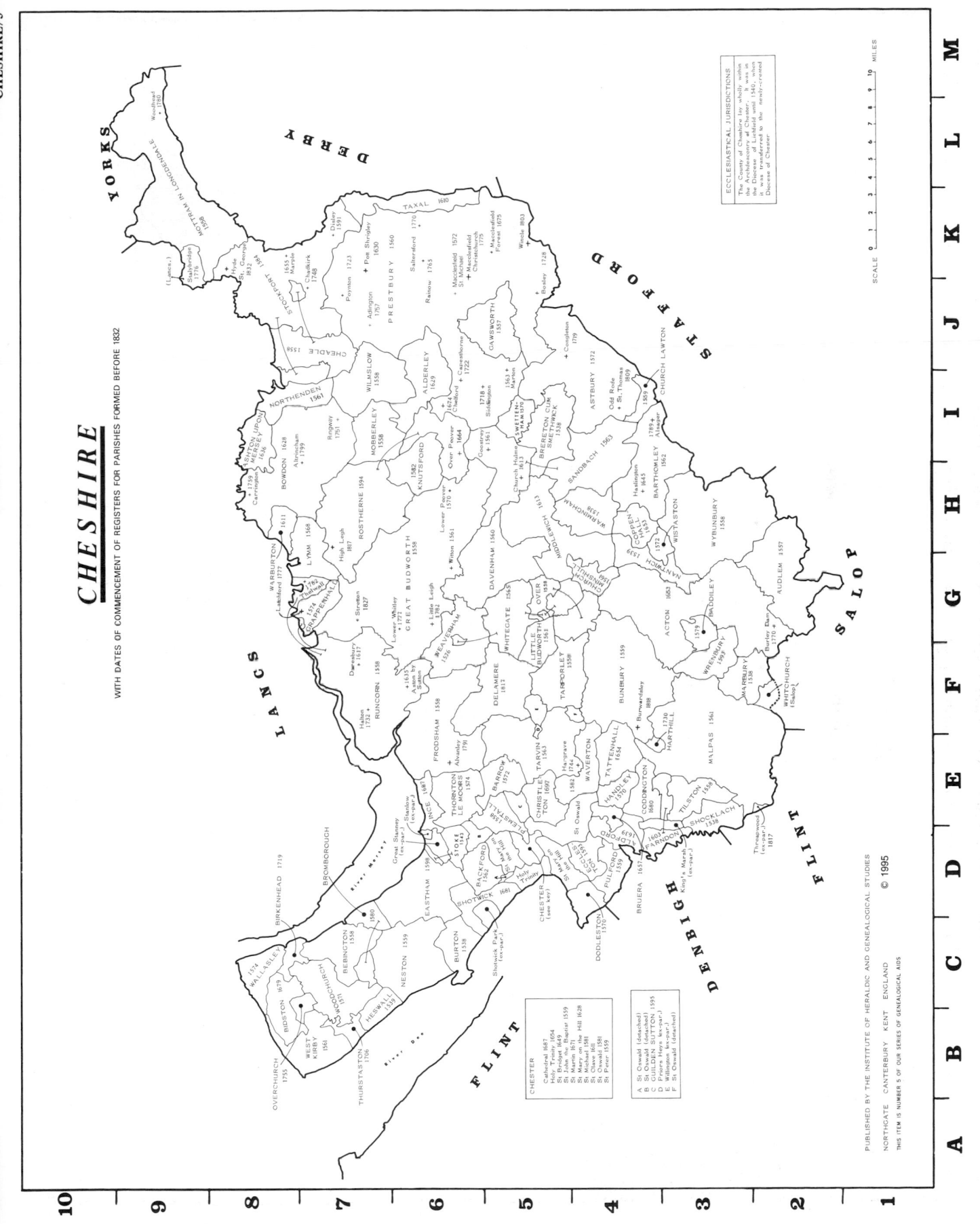

CHESHIRE

WITH DATES OF COMMENCEMENT OF REGISTERS FOR PARISHES FORMED BEFORE 1832

ECCLESIASTICAL JURISDICTIONS

The County of Cheshire lay wholly within the Archdeaconry of Chester but was in the Diocese of Lichfield until 1540, when it was transferred to the newly-created Diocese of Chester

SCALE 0 1 2 3 4 5 6 7 8 9 10 MILES

CHESTER
Cathedral 1687
Holy Trinity 1654
St Bridget 1649
St John the Baptist 1559
St Martin 1671
St Mary on the Hill 1628
St Michael 1581
St Olave 1611
St Oswald 1581
St Peter 1559

A St Oswald (detached)
B St Oswald (detached)
C GUILDEN SUTTON 1595
D Pixors Hays (ex-par.)
E Willington (ex-par.)
F St Oswald (detached)

PUBLISHED BY THE INSTITUTE OF HERALDIC AND GENEALOGICAL STUDIES

NORTHGATE CANTERBURY KENT ENGLAND

THIS ITEM IS NUMBER 5 OF OUR SERIES OF GENEALOGICAL AIDS

© 1995

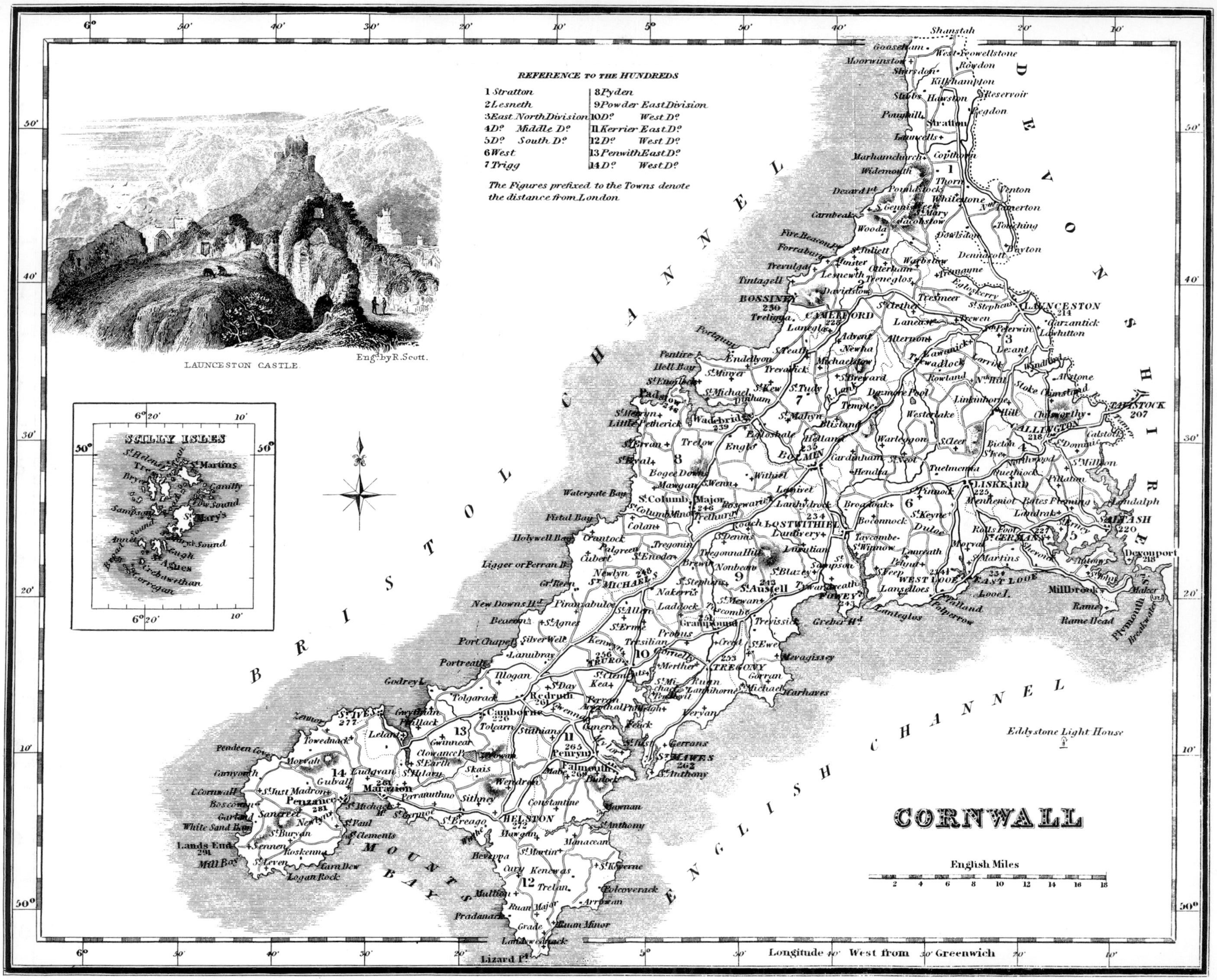

CORNWALL

English Miles

Published by Archd. Fullarton & Co. Glasgow.

DEVONSHIRE

D E V O N

E N G L I S H   C H A N N E L

B R I S T O L   C H A N N E L

B A Y S

MOUNTS

Eddystone Light House

Longitude 4° West from 30' Greenwich

REFERENCE TO THE HUNDREDS

1 Stratton
2 Lesneth
3 East North Division
4 D° Middle D°
5 D° South D°
6 West
7 Trigg

8 Pyder
9 Powder East Division
10 D° West D°
11 Kerrier East D°
12 D° West D°
13 Powith East D°
14 D° West D°

The Figures prefixed to the Towns denote
the distance from London.

LAUNCESTON CASTLE.

Eng.d by R. Scott.

SCILLY ISLES

CORNWALL PARISHES

WITH DATES OF COMMENCEMENT OF REGISTERS FOR PARISHES FORMED BEFORE 1832

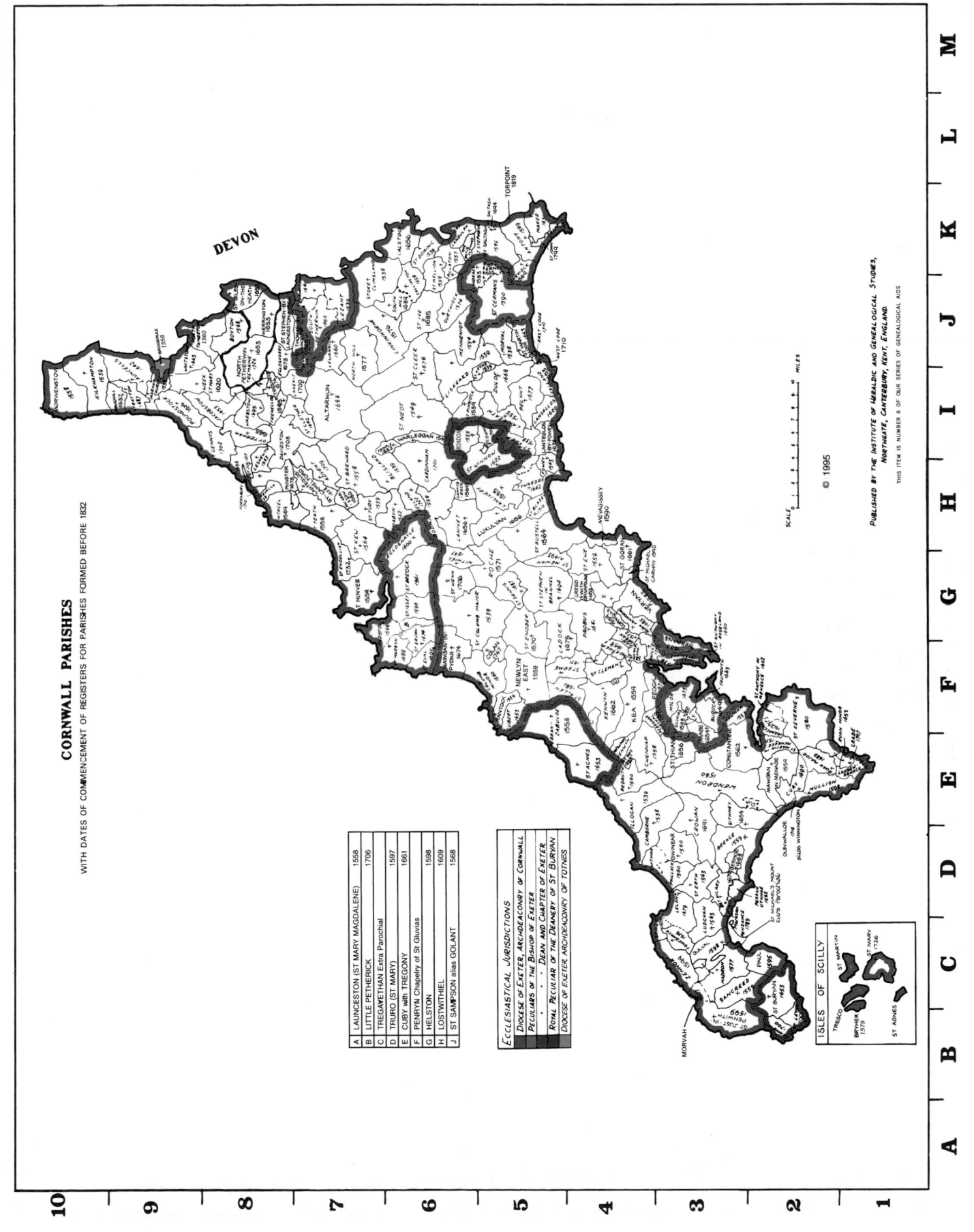

DEVON

A	LAUNCESTON (ST MARY MAGDALENE)	1558
B	LITTLE PETHERICK	1706
C	TREGAVETHAN Extra Parochial	
D	TRURO (ST MARY)	1597
E	CUBY with TREGONY	1661
F	PENRYN Chapelry of St Gluvias	
G	HELSTON	1598
H	LOSTWITHIEL	1609
J	ST SAMPSON alias GOLANT	1568

ECCLESIASTICAL JURISDICTIONS

DIOCESE OF EXETER, ARCHDEACONRY OF CORNWALL
PECULIARS OF THE BISHOP OF EXETER
DEAN AND CHAPTER OF EXETER
ROYAL PECULIAR OF THE DEANERY OF ST BURYAN
DIOCESE OF EXETER ARCHDEACONRY OF TOTNES

ISLES OF SCILLY

TRESCO
BRYHER 1579
ST MARTIN
ST MARY 1726
ST AGNES

SCALE

© 1995

PUBLISHED BY THE INSTITUTE OF HERALDIC AND GENEALOGICAL STUDIES,
NORTHGATE, CANTERBURY, KENT, ENGLAND

THIS ITEM IS NUMBER 6 OF OUR SERIES OF GENEALOGICAL AIDS

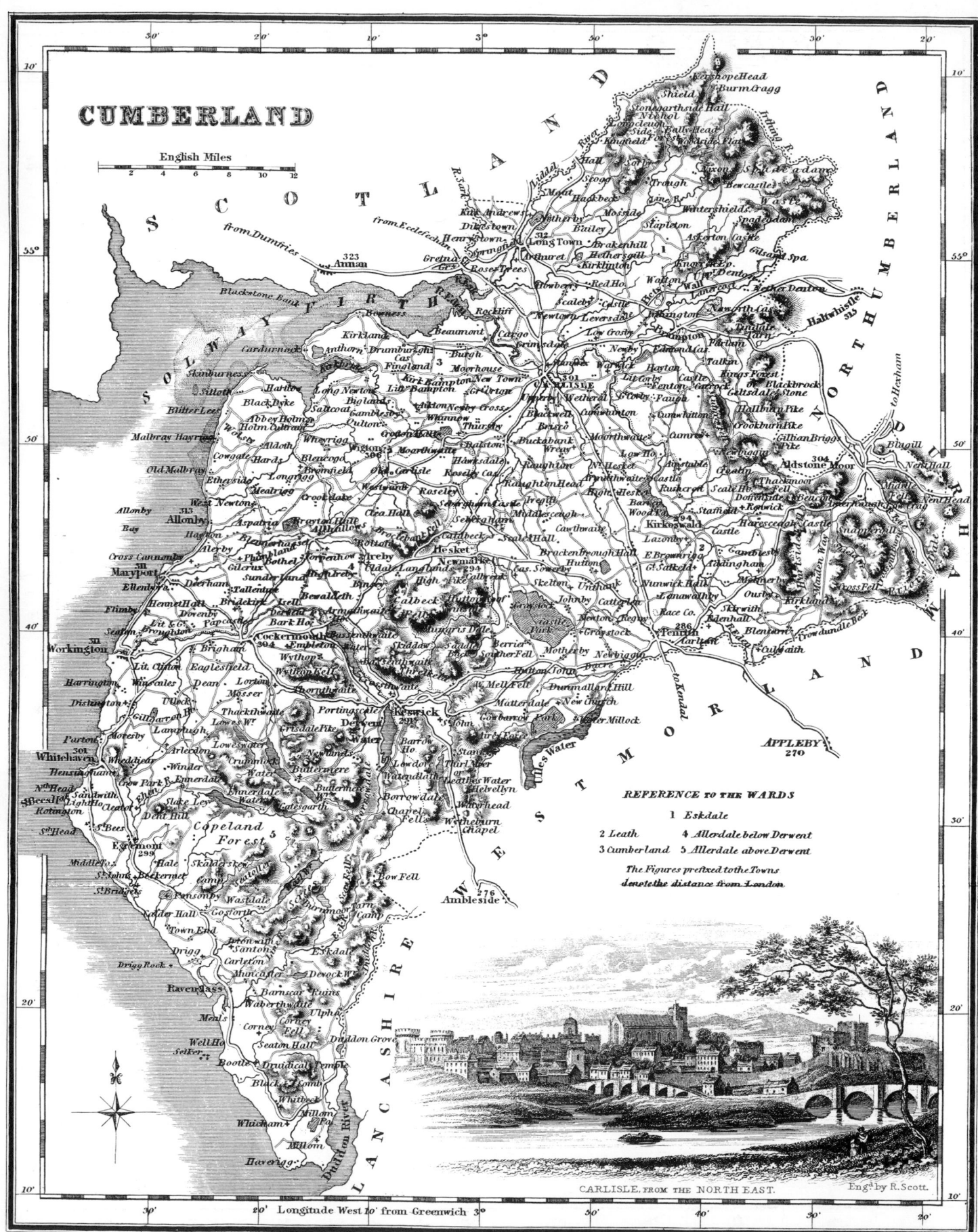

CUMBERLAND

English Miles

SCOTLAND

SOLWAY FIRTH

NORTHUMBERLAND

DURHAM

WESTMORLAND

LANCASHIRE

REFERENCE TO THE WARDS

1 Eskdale
2 Leath   4 Allerdale below Derwent
3 Cumberland   5 Allerdale above Derwent

*The Figures prefixed to the Towns
denote the distance from London*

CARLISLE, FROM THE NORTH EAST.

Engᵈ by R. Scott.

Published by Archᵈ Fullarton & Cᵒ Glasgow

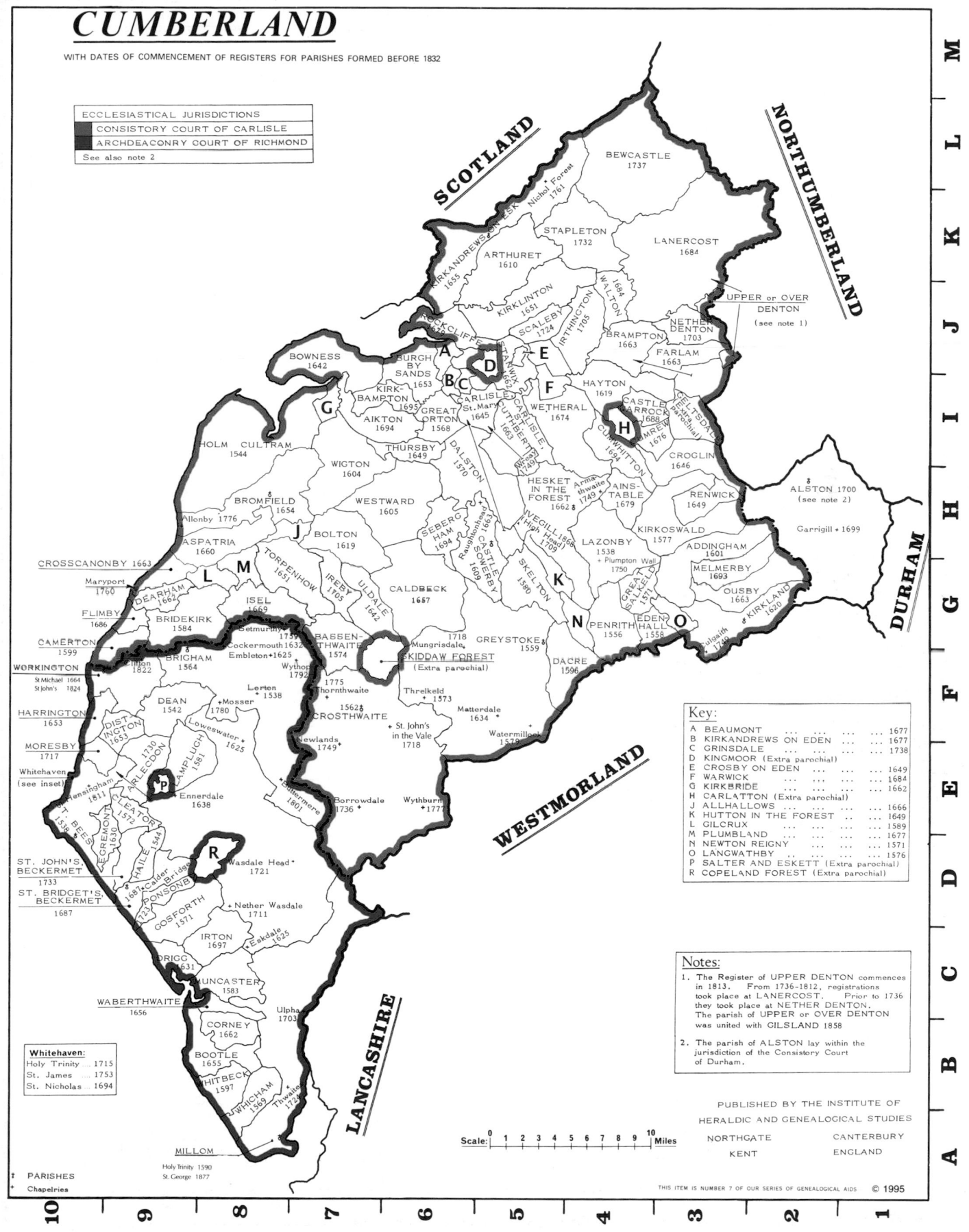

CUMBERLAND

WITH DATES OF COMMENCEMENT OF REGISTERS FOR PARISHES FORMED BEFORE 1832

ECCLESIASTICAL JURISDICTIONS
CONSISTORY COURT OF CARLISLE
ARCHDEACONRY COURT OF RICHMOND
See also note 2

SCOTLAND

NORTHUMBERLAND

WESTMORLAND

LANCASHIRE

DURHAM

Key:
A	BEAUMONT	1677
B	KIRKANDREWS ON EDEN	1677
C	GRINSDALE	1738
D	KINGMOOR (Extra parochial)	
E	CROSBY ON EDEN	1649
F	WARWICK	1684
G	KIRKBRIDE	1662
H	CARLATTON (Extra parochial)	
J	ALLHALLOWS	1666
K	HUTTON IN THE FOREST	1649
L	GILCRUX	1589
M	PLUMBLAND	1677
N	NEWTON REIGNY	1571
O	LANGWATHBY	1576
P	SALTER AND ESKETT (Extra parochial)	
R	COPELAND FOREST (Extra parochial)	

Notes:

1. The Register of UPPER DENTON commences in 1813. From 1736-1812, registrations took place at LANERCOST. Prior to 1736 they took place at NETHER DENTON. The parish of UPPER or OVER DENTON was united with GILSLAND 1858

2. The parish of ALSTON lay within the jurisdiction of the Consistory Court of Durham.

PUBLISHED BY THE INSTITUTE OF
HERALDIC AND GENEALOGICAL STUDIES
NORTHGATE   CANTERBURY
KENT   ENGLAND

THIS ITEM IS NUMBER 7 OF OUR SERIES OF GENEALOGICAL AIDS   © 1995

Whitehaven:
Holy Trinity ... 1715
St. James 1753
St. Nicholas .. 1694

Scale: 0 1 2 3 4 5 6 7 8 9 10 Miles

ṡ PARISHES
+ Chapelries

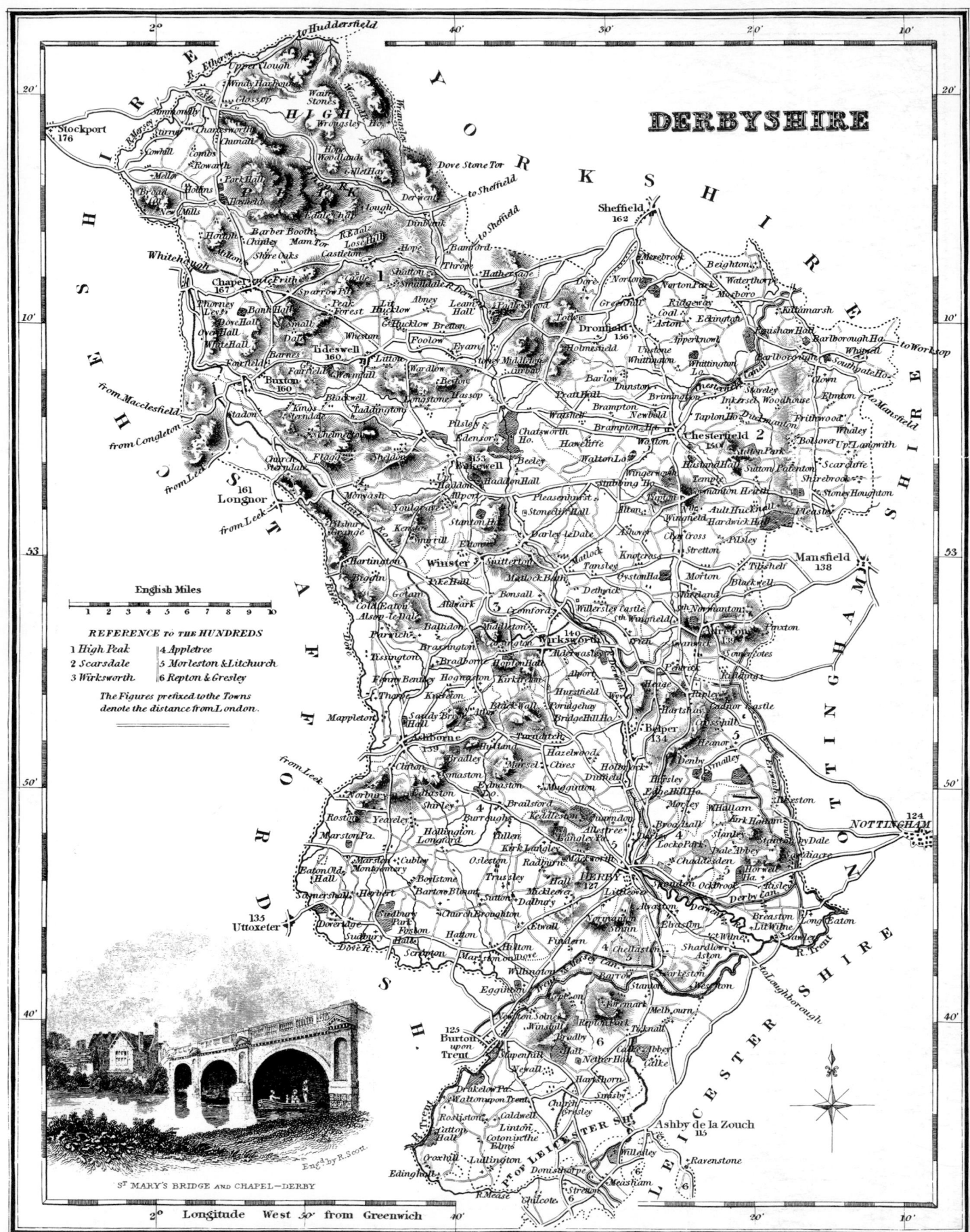

DERBYSHIRE

REFERENCE TO THE HUNDREDS

1 High Peak   4 Appletree
2 Scarsdale   5 Morleston & Litchurch
3 Wirksworth   6 Repton & Gresley

The Figures prefixed to the Towns
denote the distance from London.

English Miles

St MARY'S BRIDGE AND CHAPEL—DERBY

Longitude West from Greenwich

Published by Archd. Fullarton & Co. Glasgow.

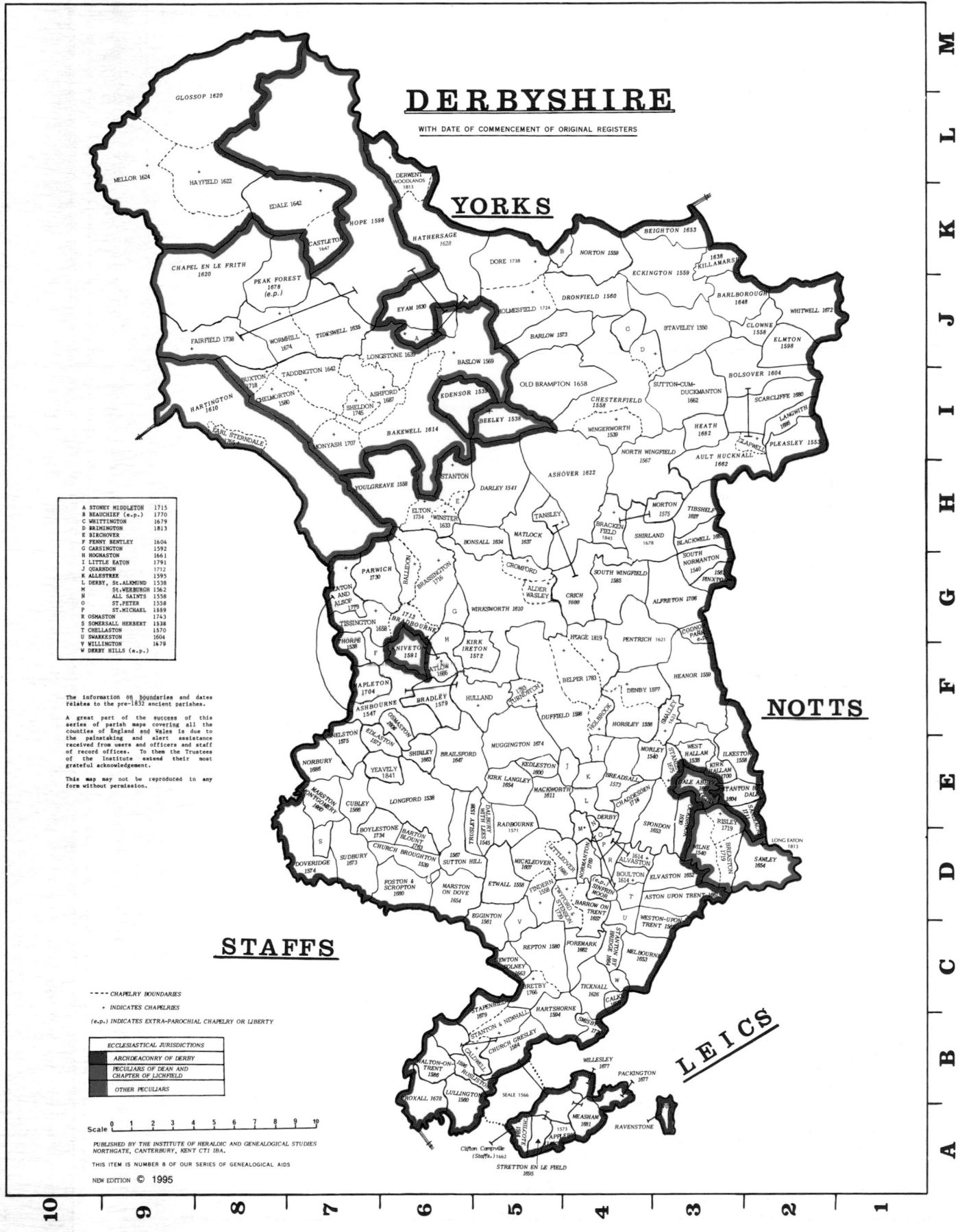

DERBYSHIRE
WITH DATE OF COMMENCEMENT OF ORIGINAL REGISTERS

YORKS

NOTTS

STAFFS

LEICS

GLOSSOP 1620

MELLOR 1624

HAYFIELD 1622

EDALE 1642

DERWENT WOODLANDS 1813

HOPE 1598

CASTLETON 1647

HATHERSAGE 1628

CHAPEL EN LE FRITH 1620

PEAK FOREST 1678 (e.p.)

FAIRFIELD 1738

WORMHILL 1674

TIDESWELL 1635

EYAM 1630

BEIGHTON 1653

NORTON 1559

DORE 1738

ECKINGTON 1559

1638 KILLAMARSH

BARLBOROUGH 1648

WHITWELL 1672

HOLMESFIELD 1724

DRONFIELD 1560

STAVELEY 1550

CLOWNE 1558

ELMTON 1598

BARLOW 1573

BUXTON 1718

TADDINGTON 1642

ASHFORD 1580

SHELDON 1745

LONGSTONE 1639

BASLOW 1569

EDENSOR 1539

OLD BRAMPTON 1658

CHESTERFIELD 1558

SUTTON-CUM-DUCKMANTON 1662

BOLSOVER 1604

SCARCLIFFE 1680

LANGWITH 1686

HARTINGTON 1610

CHELMORTON 1580

BAKEWELL 1614

BEELEY 1538

WINGERWORTH 1539

HEATH 1682

CLAPWELL

PLEASLEY 1553

EARL STERNDALE

MONYASH 1707

STANTON

NORTH WINGFIELD 1567

AULT HUCKNALL 1662

YOULGREAVE 1558

DARLEY 1541

ASHOVER 1622

ELTON 1734

WINSTER 1633

TANSLEY

MORTON 1575

TIBSHELF 1627

PARWICH 1730

BONSALL 1634

MATLOCK 1637

BRACKEN FIELD 1845

SHIRLAND 1678

BLACKWELL 1683

BALLIDON

BRASSINGTON 1706

CROMFORD

SOUTH WINGFIELD 1585

SOUTH NORMANTON 1540

PINXTON

EATON AND ALSOP 1779

TISSINGTON 1658

BRADBOURNE 1713

ALDER WASLEY

CRICH 1600

ALFRETON 1706

CODNOR PARK

THORPE 1538

KNIVETON 1591

KIRK IRETON 1572

WIRKSWORTH 1610

HEAGE 1819

PENTRICH 1621

MAPLETON 1704

BRADLEY 1579

CARSINGTON

MATLOW 1686

HULLAND

BELPER 1783

DENBY 1577

HEANOR 1559

ASHBOURNE 1547

OSMASTON 1577

SHIRLEY 1663

BRAILSFORD 1647

MUGGINGTON 1674

DUFFIELD 1598

TURNDITCH

IDRIDGEHAY

HORSLEY 1558

SMALLEY 1623

MORLEY 1540

WEST HALLAM 1538

ILKESTON 1558

KIRK HALLAM 1700

SNELSTON 1575

YEAVELY 1841

KEDLESTON 1800

KIRK LANGLEY 1654

MACKWORTH 1611

BREADSALL 1573

CHADDESDEN 1718

DALE ABBEY 1666

STANTON BY DALE 1604

RISLEY 1719

NORBURY 1696

CUBLEY 1566

LONGFORD 1538

TRUSLEY 1538

DALBURY WITH LEES 1545

RADBOURNE 1571

DERBY

SPONDON 1653

MILNE 1540

BREASTON 1719

SAWLEY 1654

LONG EATON 1813

MARSTON MONTGOMERY 1692

BOYLESTONE 1734

BARTON BLOUNT 1561

SUTTON HILL

MICKLEOVER 1607

LITTLEOVER

NORMANTON 1780

ALVASTON 1614

ELVASTON 1652

DOVERIDGE 1574

SUDBURY 1673

CHURCH BROUGHTON 1539

FOSTON & SCROPTON 1690

MARSTON ON DOVE 1654

ETWALL 1558

FINDERN 1558

TWYFORD 1558

STENSON

BARROW ON TRENT 1657

BOULTON 1614

SINFIN MOOR

ASTON UPON TRENT 1658

WESTON-UPON-TRENT 1560

EGGINTON 1561

REPTON 1580

FOREMARK 1662

NEWTON SOLNEY 1663

TICKNALL 1626

MELBOURNE 1653

STANTON BY BRIDGE 1664

CALK

BRETBY 1766

HARTSHORNE 1594

SMISBY

WALTON-ON-TRENT 1586

CALDWELL

STAPENHILL 1679

STANTON & NEWHALL 1651

CHURCH GRESLEY 1584

WILLESLEY 1677

PACKINGTON 1677

CROXALL 1670

LULLINGTON 1580

LINTON 1580

SEALE 1566

MEASHAM 1681

CHILCOTE 1573

APPLEBY

RAVENSTONE

Clifton Campville (Staffs.) 1662

STRETTON EN LE FIELD 1695

Key (boxed list):

A STONEY MIDDLETON 1715
B BEAUCHIEF (e.p.) 1770
C WHITTINGTON 1679
D BRIMINGTON 1813
E BIRCHOVER
F FENNY BENTLEY 1604
G CARSINGTON 1592
H HOGNASTON 1661
I LITTLE EATON 1791
J QUARNDON 1712
K ALLESTREE 1595
L DERBY, St.ALKMUND 1538
M St.WERBURGH 1562
N ALL SAINTS 1558
O ST.PETER 1558
P ST.MICHAEL 1559
R OSMASTON 1743
S SOMERSALL HERBERT 1538
T CHELLASTON 1570
U SWARKESTON 1604
V WILLINGTON 1679
W DERBY HILLS (e.p.)

The information on boundaries and dates relates to the pre-1832 ancient parishes.

A great part of the success of this series of parish maps covering all the counties of England and Wales is due to the painstaking and alert assistance received from users and officers and staff of record offices. To them the Trustees of the Institute extend their most grateful acknowledgement.

This map may not be reproduced in any form without permission.

- - - - CHAPELRY BOUNDARIES

+ INDICATES CHAPELRIES

(e.p.) INDICATES EXTRA-PAROCHIAL CHAPELRY OR LIBERTY

ECCLESIASTICAL JURISDICTIONS

ARCHDEACONRY OF DERBY

PECULIARS OF DEAN AND CHAPTER OF LICHFIELD

OTHER PECULIARS

Scale 0 1 2 3 4 5 6 7 8 9 10

PUBLISHED BY THE INSTITUTE OF HERALDIC AND GENEALOGICAL STUDIES NORTHGATE, CANTERBURY, KENT CT1 1BA.

THIS ITEM IS NUMBER 8 OF OUR SERIES OF GENEALOGICAL AIDS

NEW EDITION © 1995

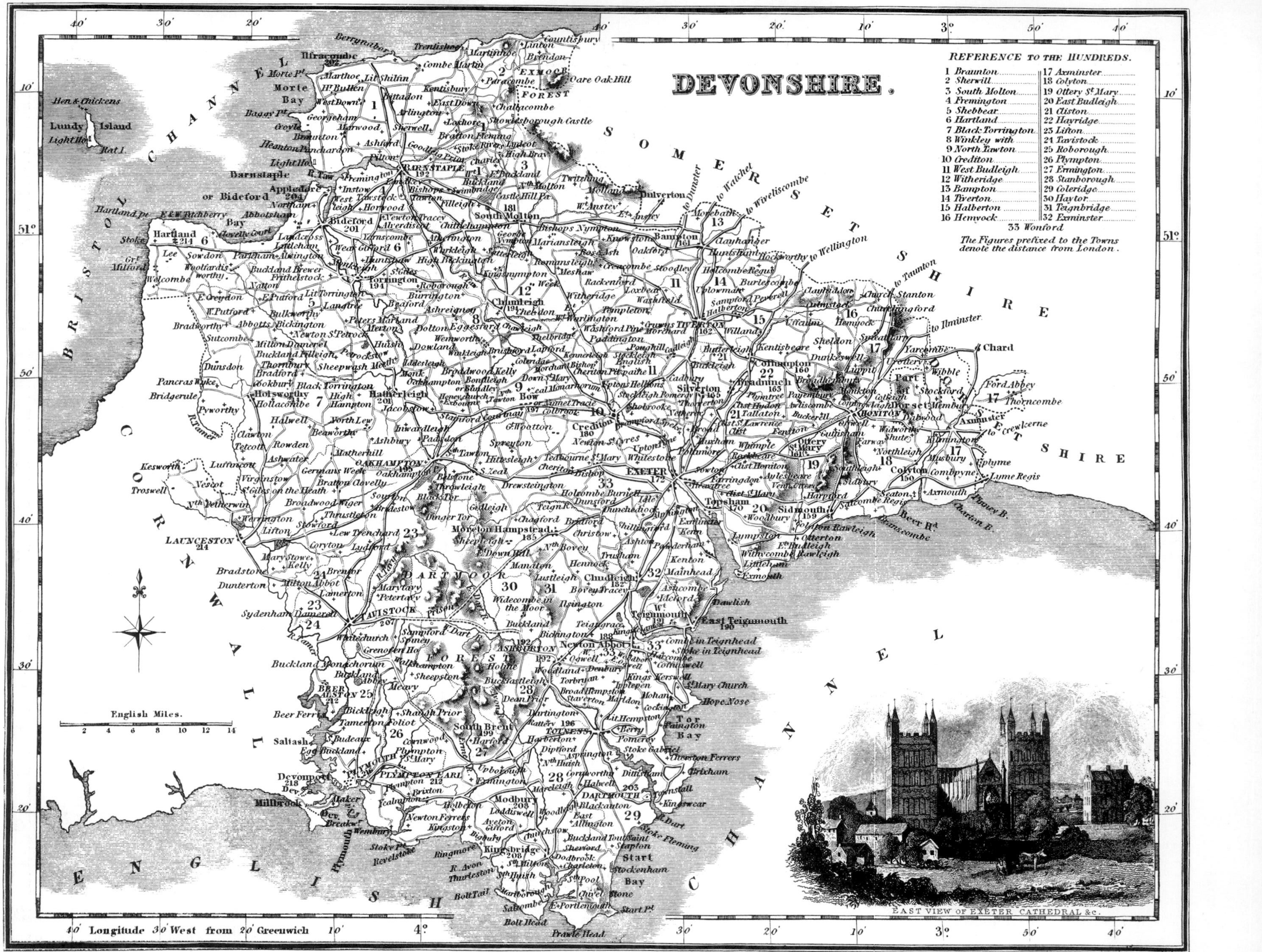

DEVONSHIRE.

REFERENCE TO THE HUNDREDS.

1 Braunton.	17 Axminster
2 Sherwill	18 Colyton.
3 South Molton	19 Ottery St Mary.
4 Fremington	20 East Budleigh.
5 Shebbear	21 Cliston.
6 Hartland	22 Haytridge.
7 Black Torrington.	23 Lifton.
8 Winkley with	24 Tavistock
9 North Newton	25 Roborough.
10 Crediton.	26 Plympton.
11 West Budleigh	27 Ermington.
12 Witheridge	28 Stanborough.
13 Bampton	29 Coleridge.
14 Tiverton.	30 Haytor.
15 Halberton.	31 Teignbridge.
16 Hemyock.	32 Exminster
	33 Wonford

The Figures prefixed to the Towns denote the distance from London.

SOMERSETSHIRE

DORSETSHIRE

CORNWALL

DEVONSHIRE

DARTMOOR FOREST

EXMOOR FOREST

BRISTOL CHANNEL

ENGLISH CHANNEL

Tor Bay

Start

Lundy Island

English Miles.

EAST VIEW OF EXETER CATHEDRAL &c.

Engd. by R. Scott

Published by Archd. Fullarton & Co. Glasgow.

Longitude 30' West from 20' Greenwich

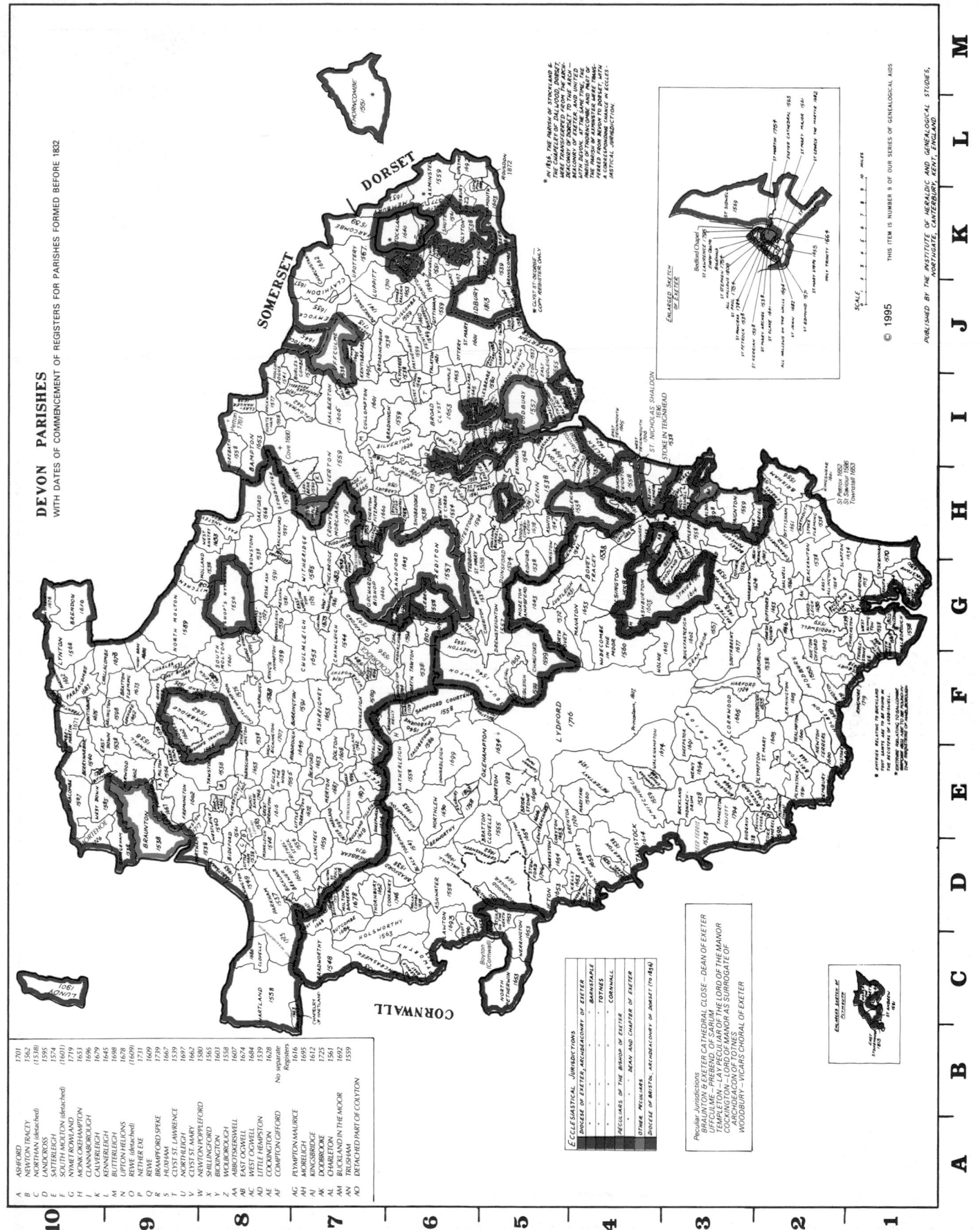

DEVON PARISHES

WITH DATES OF COMMENCEMENT OF REGISTERS FOR PARISHES FORMED BEFORE 1832

© 1995

THIS ITEM IS NUMBER 9 OF OUR SERIES OF GENEALOGICAL AIDS

PUBLISHED BY THE INSTITUTE OF HERALDIC AND GENEALOGICAL STUDIES, NORTHGATE, CANTERBURY, KENT, ENGLAND

DORSETSHIRE.

REFERENCE to the HUNDREDS and LIBERTIES.

Coombs Ditch	1	Loders & Bothramton*	20	Bradbury
Pimperne	2	Poorstock*	21	Cogdean
Rushmore	3	Buckland Newton*	22	Cranborne
Dewlish	4	Cerne Totcombe & Modbury	23	Knowlton
Corfe Castle	5	Whiteway	24	Loosebarrow
Bere Regis	6	Alten Pancras*	25	Monkton up Wimborne
Hundreds Barrow	7	Piddletrenthide*	26	Sixpeny Handley
Hasilor	8	Syding St Nicholas*	27	Wimborne St Giles
Culliford Tree	9	Culliford Tree	28	Alcester*
Win frith	10	St George	29	Gillingham*
Binden	11	Piddletown	30	Sherborne
Over Moigne*	12	Totterford	31	Yetmanster
Steborough	13	Uggescomb	32	Haldock*
Beaminster Forum & Redhone	14	Fordington	33	Ryme Intrinseca*
Eggerton	15	Isle of Portland*	34	Bromshall
Godderborne	16	Piddlehinton	35	Red Lane
Whitchurch Canonicorum	17	Sutton Peintz*	36	Sturminster-Newton Cas.
Broad Windsor*	18	Wayhouse*	37	Stower Provost*
Frampton	19	Wyke Regis & Elwall*	38	

The Names with a Star attached to them are Liberties.
The Figures prefixed to the Towns denote the distance from London §

English Miles.

Engᵈ by Gray & Son.

Longitude West 2° from Greenwich

Pubᵈ by A. & W.S Fullerton & Cᵒ Glasgow

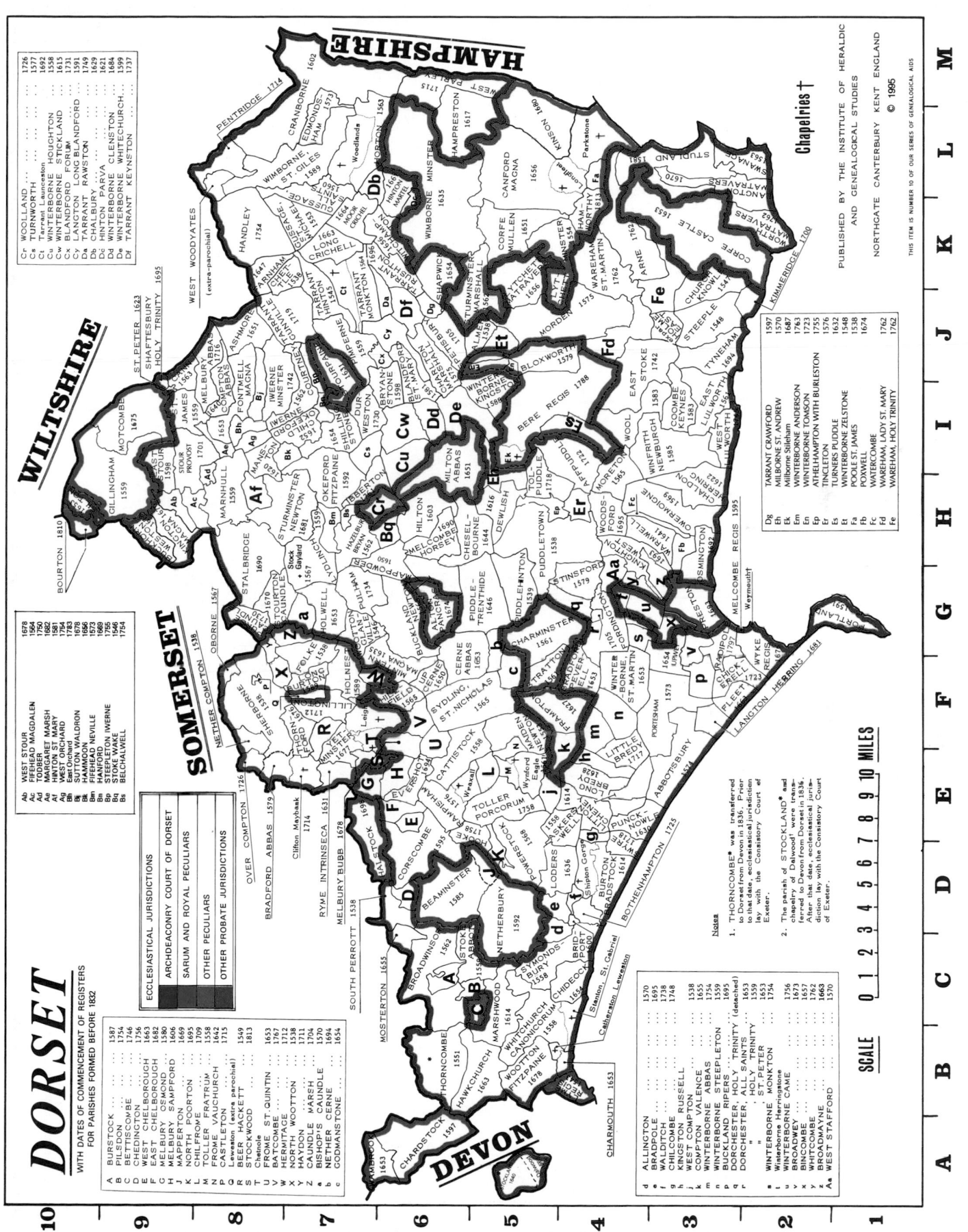

NORTH SEA

DURHAM

NORTHUMBERLAND

CUMBERLAND

WESTMORELD.

YORK

THE PREBENDS BRIDGE, THE CATHEDRAL &c. DURHAM.

Engd. by R. Scott

DURHAM

REFERENCE TO THE WARDS
1 Darlington   3 Easington
2 Chester   4 Stockton

The Figures prefixed to the Towns
denote the distance from London.

For the detached parts of Durham, see Northumberland.

English Miles.

Longitude West   from Greenwich

Published by Archd. Fullarton & Co. Glasgow.

DURHAM

WITH DATES OF COMMENCEMENT OF REGISTERS FOR PARISHES FORMED BEFORE 1832

PROBATE JURISDICTION

The Palatine and Episcopal Consistory of Durham had probate jurisdiction over the whole county.

DURHAM (A)	
St Margaret	1558
St Mary le Bow	1571
St Mary the Less	1558
St Mary Magdalen	1540
St Nicholas	1540
Cathedral	1609

HARTLE- POOL 1556
STRANTON 1580
GREATHAM 1564
HART 1577
ELWICK 1592
Wolviston 1759
BILLINGHAM 1569
MONK HESLEDON 1578
CASTLE EDEN 1694
EASINGTON 1570
NORTON 1574
Embleton 1651
SEDGEFIELD 1580
STOCKTON-ON-TEES 1616
ELTON 1573
EGGLESCLIFFE 1539
DINSDALE 1556
SOCKBURN 1580
HURWORTH 1559
LONG NEWTON 1564
MIDDLETON ST GEORGE 1616
Sadberge 1662
BISHOPTON 1649
GRINDON 1565
Carlton 1559
MARSHALL 1559
Stillington 1561
STAINTON-LE-STREET 1560
AYCLIFFE 1560
HAUGHTON-LE-SKERNE 1569
DARLINGTON 1590
CONISCLIFFE 1590
Denton 1576
GAINFORD 1560
KELLOE 1693
TRIMDON 1720
Garmondsway Moor 1641
Sherburn Hospital 1698
Whitwell House
BISHOP MIDDLEHAM 1559
MERRINGTON 1579
ST ANDREW AUCKLAND 1558
Croxdale 1696
WHITWORTH 1569
BISHOP AUCKLAND (ST ANNE) 1855
AUCKLAND 1543
ESCOMB 1543
ST HELEN AUCKLAND 1393
COCKFIELD 1578
STAINDROP 1635
WINSTON 1572
Whorlton 1626
Barnard Castle 1609
WHITBURN 1579
South Shields 1653
BOLDON 1571
MONKWEARMOUTH 1703
Sunderland 1719
BISHOP WEARMOUTH 1567
SEAHAM 1646
DALTON-LE-DALE 1653
Penshaw 1754
JARROW 1571
Heworth 1696
Gateshead Fell 1826
GATESHEAD 1559
WASHINGTON 1604
HOUGHTON-LE-SPRING 1563
Great Lumley
West Rainton 1825
PITTINGTON 1574
ST GILES DURHAM 1584
WHICKHAM 1576
Tanfield 1719
Lamesley 1603
CHESTER-LE-STREET 1582
WITTON GILBERT 1570
ST OSWALD DURHAM 1538
Esh 1567
RYTON 1581
Medomsley 1608
EBCHESTER 1619
LANCHESTER 1560
Satley 1797
BRANCEPETH 1599
WITTON-LE-WEAR 1558
Hamsterley 1580
WOLSINGHAM 1631
Wolsingham Park Moor 1697
MUGGLESWICK 1783
EDMONDBYERS 1700
Hunstonworth 1669
Heatherycleugh 1823
STANHOPE 1607
Weardale St John 1788
EGGLESTONE 1795
MIDDLETON-IN-TEESDALE 1578

SCALE 0 1 2 3 4 5 6 7 8 9 10 MILES

+ PARISHES
+ Chapelries

Northumberland

Yorks N. R.

Cumb

THIS ITEM IS NUMBER 11 OF OUR SERIES OF GENEALOGICAL AIDS

PUBLISHED BY THE INSTITUTE OF HERALDIC AND GENEALOGICAL STUDIES – NORTHGATE CANTERBURY KENT ENGLAND © 1995

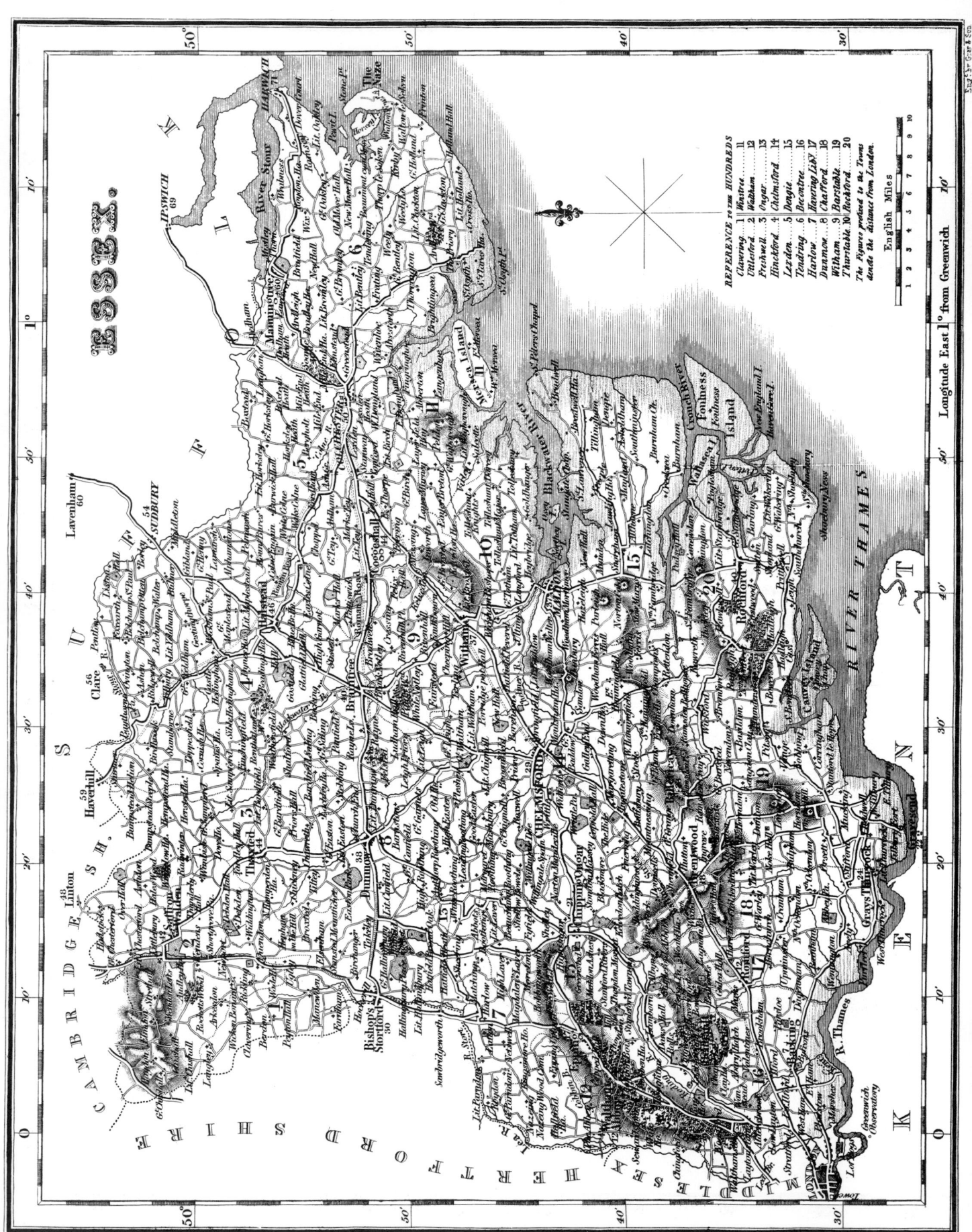

ESSEX.

REFERENCE to the HUNDREDS

Clavering	1	Waltham	11
Uttlesford	2	Witham	12
Freshwell	3	Ongar	13
Hinckford	4	Chelmsford	14
Lexden	5	Dengie	15
Tendring	6	Becontree	16
Harlow	7	Havering Lib.y	17
Dunmow	8	Chafford	18
Witham	9	Barstable	19
Thurstable	10	Rochford	20

The Figures prefixed to the Towns
denote the distance from London.

English Miles
1 2 3 4 5 6 7 8 9 10

Longitude East 1° from Greenwich

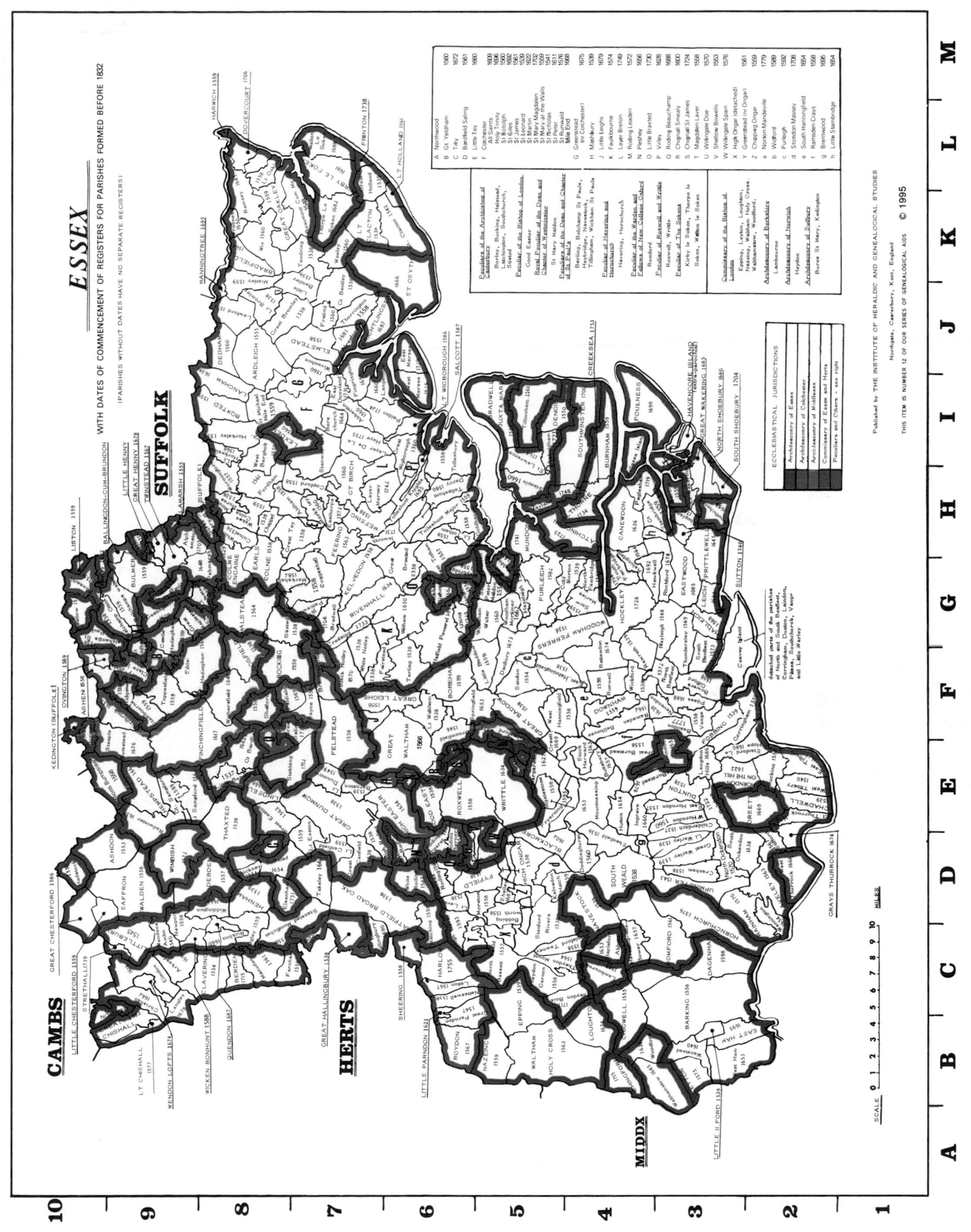

ESSEX

WITH DATES OF COMMENCEMENT OF REGISTERS FOR PARISHES FORMED BEFORE 1832

(PARISHES WITHOUT DATES HAVE NO SEPARATE REGISTERS)

Published by THE INSTITUTE OF HERALDIC AND GENEALOGICAL STUDIES

Northgate, Canterbury, Kent, England

THIS ITEM IS NUMBER 12 OF OUR SERIES OF GENEALOGICAL AIDS

© 1995

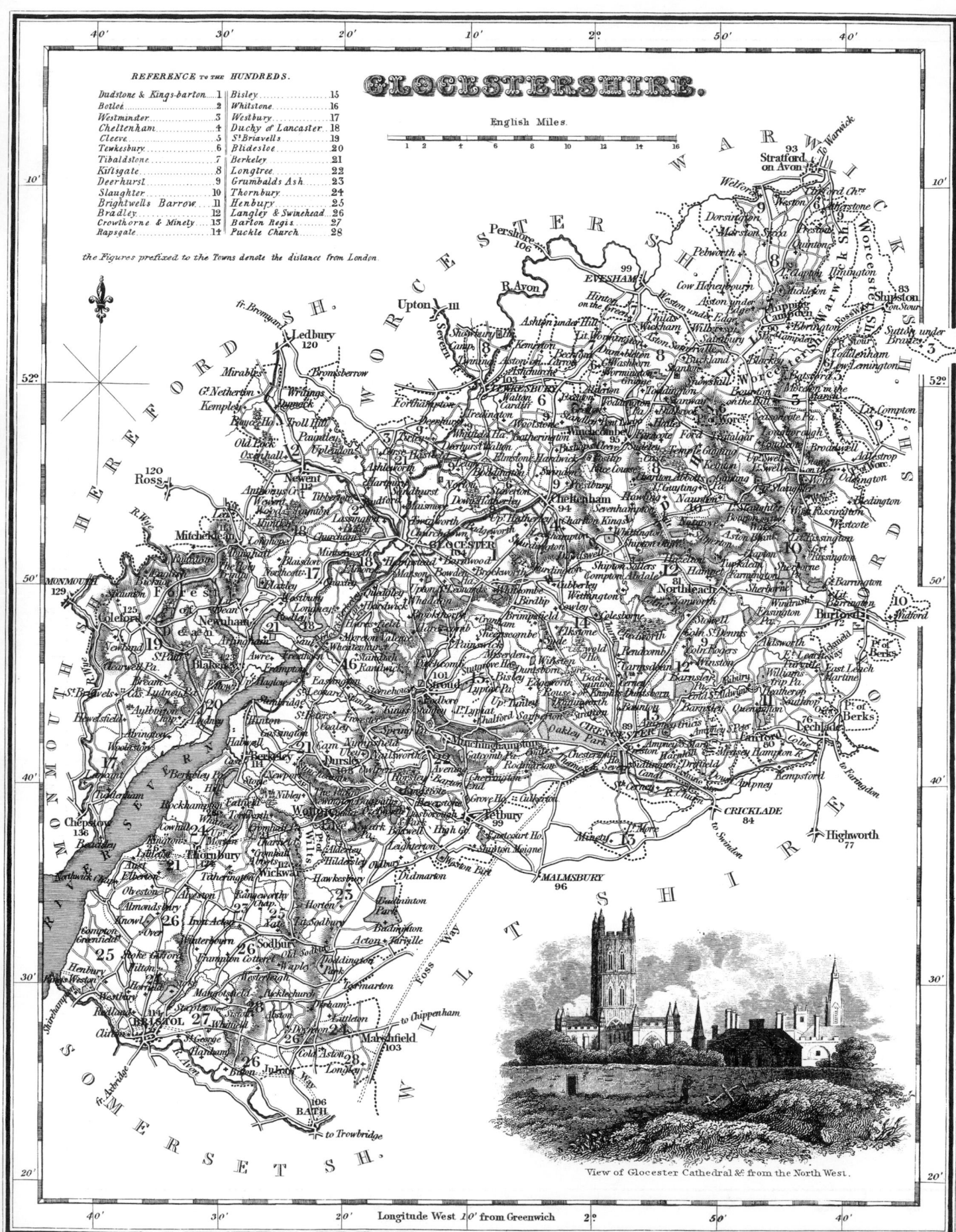

GLOCESTERSHIRE.

REFERENCE TO THE HUNDREDS.

Dudstone & Kings-barton	1	Bisley	15
Botloe	2	Whitstone	16
Westminster	3	Westbury	17
Cheltenham	4	Duchy of Lancaster	18
Cleeve	5	St Briavells	19
Tewkesbury	6	Blidesloe	20
Tibaldstone	7	Berkeley	21
Kiftsgate	8	Longtree	22
Deerhurst	9	Grumbalds Ash	23
Slaughter	10	Thornbury	24
Brightwells Barrow	11	Henbury	25
Bradley	12	Langley & Swinehead	26
Crowthorne & Minety	13	Barton Regis	27
Rapsgate	14	Puckle Church	28

the Figures prefixed to the Towns denote the distance from London.

English Miles.

View of Glocester Cathedral &c from the North West.

Engd. by Gray & Son.

Publd. by Archd. Fullarton & Co. Glasgow.

Longitude West 10' from Greenwich

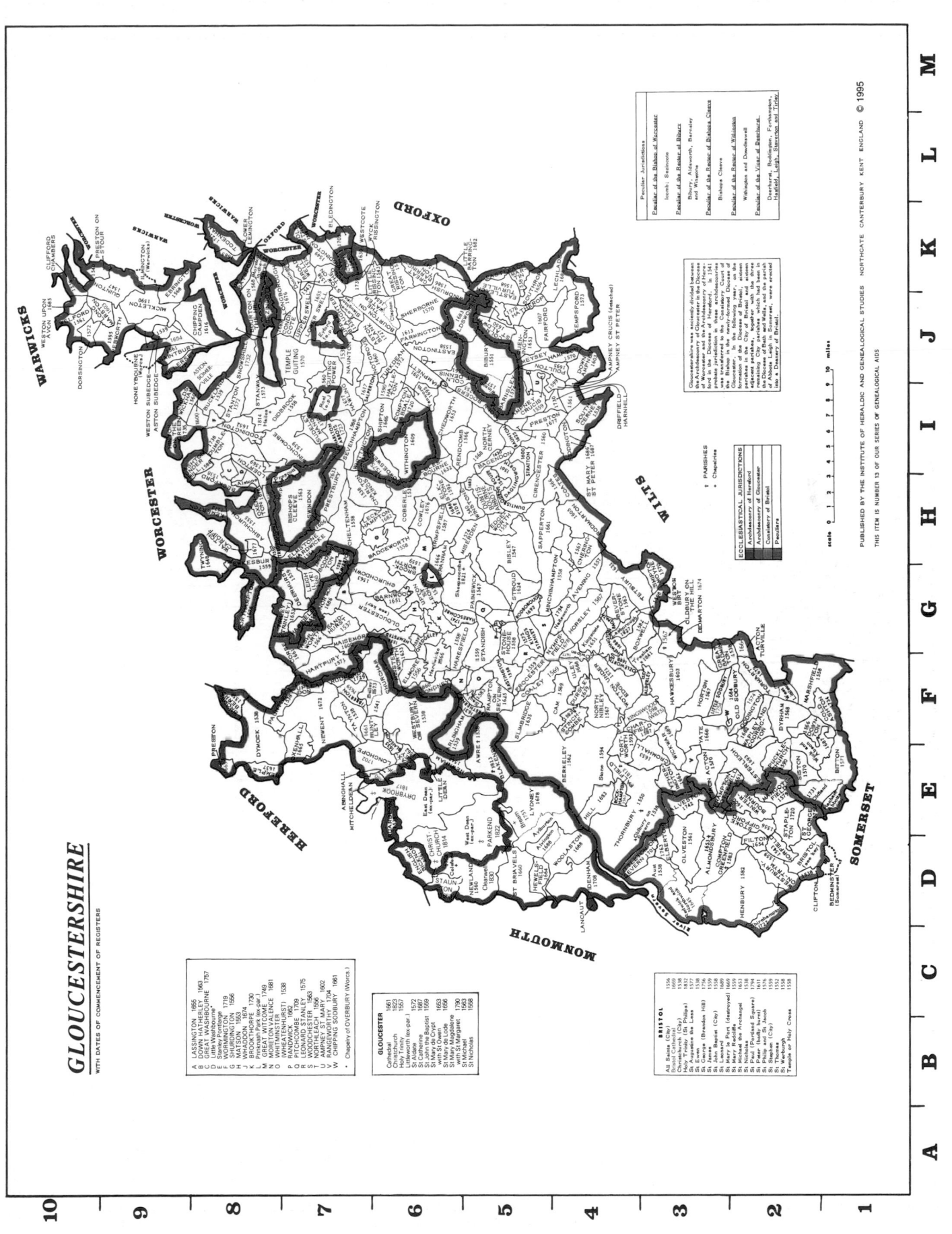

GLOUCESTERSHIRE
WITH DATES OF COMMENCEMENT OF REGISTERS

A LASSINGTON 1656
B DOWN HATHERLEY 1563
C GREAT WASHBOURNE 1757
D Little Washbourne†
E Stanley Pontlarge
F WORMINGTON 1719
G SHURDINGTON 1556
H MATSON 1563
J WHADDON 1674
K BROOKTHORPE 1730
L Prinknash Park (ex-par.)
M GREAT WITCOMBE 1749
N MORETON VALENCE 1681
O WHITMINSTER 1538
   (WHEATENHURST)
P RANDWICK 1662
Q LEONARD STANLEY 1575
R WOODCHESTER 1563
S NORTHLEACH 1566
T AMPNEY ST MARY 1602
U RANGEWORTHY 1704
W CHIPPING SODBURY 1661
* Chapelry of OVERBURY (Worcs.)

GLOUCESTER
Cathedral 1661
Christchurch 1823
Holy Trinity 1557
Littleworth (ex-par.) 1572
St Aldate 1887
St Catherine 1559
St John the Baptist 1663
St Mary de Crypt
   with St Owen 1656
St Mary Magdalene 1700
St Mary le Port (destroyed)
St Michael 1963
St Nicholas 1558

BRISTOL
All Saints (City) 1536
Bristol Cathedral 1669
Christchurch (City) 1538
Holy Trinity (St Philips) 1832
St Ewen 1577
St George (Brandon Hill) 1756
St James (City) 1559
St John Baptist (City) 1558
St Leonard 1689
St Mary le Port (destroyed) 1669
St Mary Radcliffe 1559
St Michael (City) 1653
St Nicholas 1538
St Paul (Portland Square) 1794
St Peter (badly burnt) 1611
St Philip and St Jacob 1576
St Stephen (City) 1559
St Thomas 1552
St Warburgh 1558
Temple or Holy Cross

ECCLESIASTICAL JURISDICTION
- Archdeaconry of Hereford
- Archdeaconry of Gloucester
- Deanery of Bristol
- Peculiars

† PARISHES
‡ Chapelries

scale 0 1 2 3 4 5 6 7 8 9 10 miles

Peculiar Jurisdictions
Peculiar of the Bishop of Worcester
   Icomb: Stanton

Peculiar of the Rector of Bibury
   Bibury, Aldsworth, Barnsley
   and Winson

Peculiar of the Rector of Bishops Cleeve
   Bishops Cleeve

Peculiar of the Rector of Withington
   Withington and Dowdeswell

Peculiar of the Vicar of Deerhurst
   Deerhurst, Boddington, Forthampton,
   Hasfield, Leigh, Staverton and Tirley

PUBLISHED BY THE INSTITUTE OF HERALDIC AND GENEALOGICAL STUDIES NORTHGATE CANTERBURY KENT ENGLAND © 1995

THIS ITEM IS NUMBER 13 OF OUR SERIES OF GENEALOGICAL AIDS

HAMPSHIRE, OR SOUTHAMPTON.

Eng.d by Gray & Son.

REFERENCE TO THE DIVISIONS HUNDREDS & LIBERTIES.

Andover Division	
Andover Hundred	1
Wherwell. D.o	2
Thorngate. D.o	3
Kings Somborn. D.e	4
Burton Stacey. D.o	5
Kingsclere Division	
Chuteley Hundred	6
Evingar. D.o	7
Kingsclere. D.o	8
Overton. D.o	9
Pastow. D.o	10
Basingstoke Divis.n	11
Basingstoke Hundred.	11
Bermondspit. D.o	12
Crondall. D.o	13
Holdshot. D.o	14
Odiham. D.o	15
Micheldever. D.o	16
Alton Division	
Alresford New Liberty	17
Alton Hundred. D.o	18
Bishops Sutton. D.o	19
Selborne. D.o	20
East Mean. D.o	21
Finch Dean. D.o	22
Fawley Division	
Bountisborough Hundred.	23
Buddlesgate. D.e	24
Fawley. D.e	25
Mansborough. D.o	26
Mainsbridge. D.o	27

Portsdown Division	
City of Winchester &c.	49
Alresford & Gosport Lib.s	28
B.rn Waltham H.d part of	29
Bosmere Hundred.	30
Fareham. D.o	31
Hambledon. D.o	32
Havant Liberty	33
Meon Stoke Hundred.	34
Portsdown. D.o	35
Titchfield. D.o	36
Beaulieu Liberty	37
B.rn Waltham H.d part of	38
Dibden Liberty	39
Lymington. D.o	40
New Forest Hundred	41
Redbridge. D.o	42
Ringwood. D.o	43
New Forest W.rn Divis.n	44
Bramore Liberty	45
Fordingbridge. D.o	46
Ringwood. D.o	47
Westover Liberty	48

City or Winchester &c.	49
Stoke Liberty	50
Borough of Portsmouth	50
Town & County of	51
Southampton	51
Isle of Wight Division	
East Medina Liberty	52
West Medina. D.o	53

The Figures prefixed to the Towns
Denote the distances from London.

English Miles

COUNTIES / PLACES:
BERKSHIRE — SURREY — SUSSEX — WILTS — DORSET

Newbury 56 · Guildford 30 · Godalming · Petworth 49 · Arundel · Haslemere 43 · Midhurst 50 · CHICHESTER 63 · Farnham 38 · WINCHESTER · Southampton · SALISBURY 81 · Downton 88 · Romsey · Stockbridge · Lymington · Christ Church 48 · Ringwood 92 · Fordingbridge · Cranbourne 93 · Wimborn Minster 100 · Poole 105 · Wareham 110 · Corfe Castle 113 · Blanford Forum 103 · Needles · Yarmouth · Newport 83 · SPITHEAD · ISLE OF WIGHT

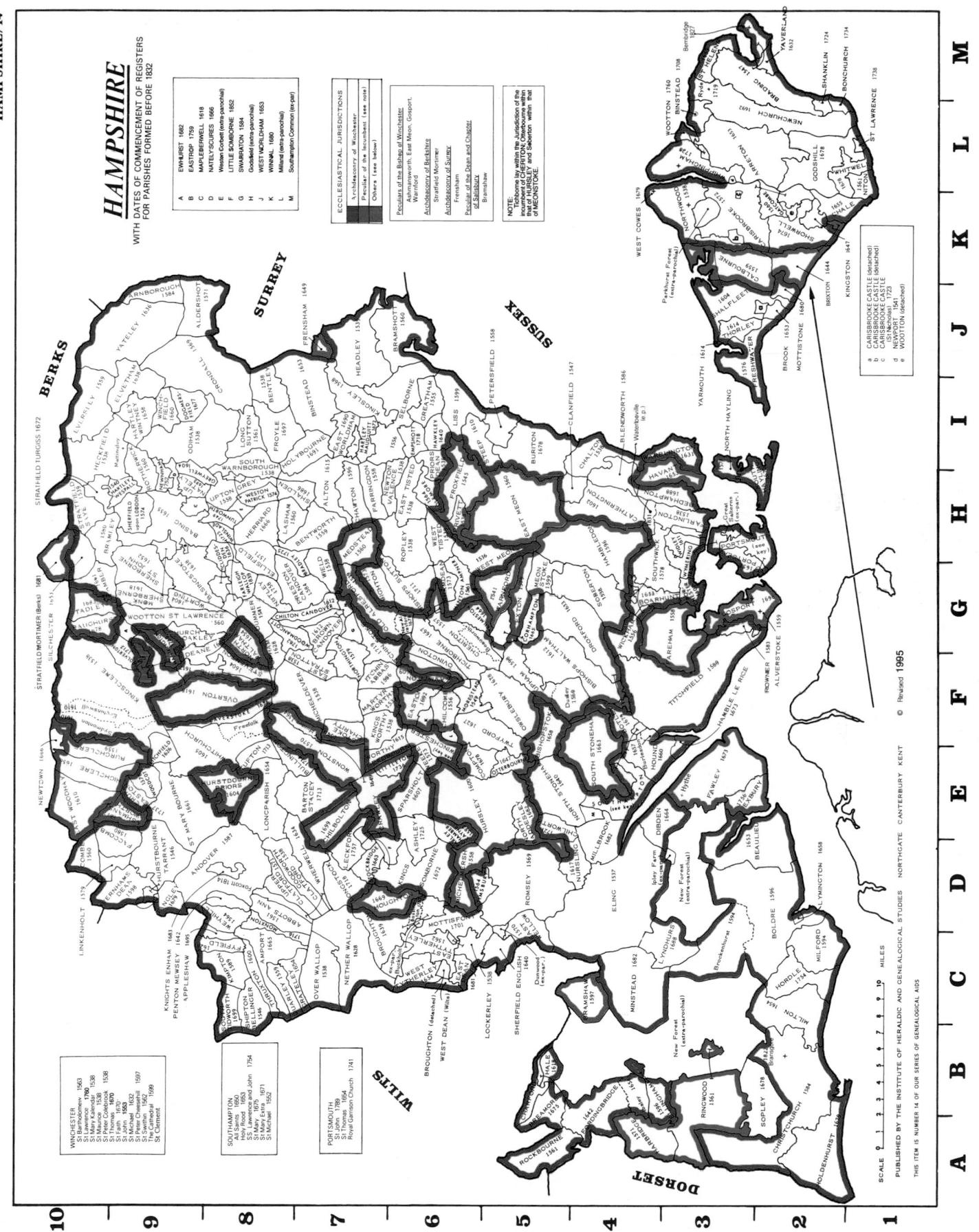

HAMPSHIRE

WITH DATES OF COMMENCEMENT OF REGISTERS
FOR PARISHES FORMED BEFORE 1832

A	EWHURST 1682
B	EASTROP 1759
C	MAPLEDERWELL 1618
D	NATELY SCURES 1666
E	Weston Corbett (extra-parochial)
F	LITTLE SOMBORNE 1852
G	SWARRATON 1584
H	Godsfield (extra-parochial)
J	WEST WORLDHAM 1653
K	WINNAL (extra-parochial)
L	Milland (extra-parochial)
M	Southampton Common (ex-par)

ECCLESIASTICAL JURISDICTIONS

Peculiars of the Bishop of Winchester

Peculiar of the Incumbent (see note)

Others (see below)

Peculiars of the Bishop of Winchester:
Ashmansworth, East Meon, Gosport,
Wanford

Archdeaconry of Berkshire:
Stratfield Mortimer

Archdeaconry of Surrey:
Frensham

Peculiar of the Dean and Chapter
of Salisbury:
Bramshaw

NOTE:
Titchborne lay within the Jurisdiction of the
incumbent of CHERITON, Otterbourne within
that of HURSLEY and Seberton within that
of MEONSTOKE.

a CARISBROOKE CASTLE (detached)
b CARISBROOKE CASTLE (detached)
c CARISBROOKE CASTLE (detached)
d NEWPORT 1541
e WOOTTON (detached)

WINCHESTER
St Bartholomew 1563
St Lawrence 1760
St Mary Kalendar 1538
St Maurice 1538
St Peter Colebrook 1538
St Thomas 1670
Faith 1670
St John 1563
St Michael 1632
St Peter Cheesehill 1597
St Swithin 1562
The Cathedral 1599
St Clement

SOUTHAMPTON
All Saints 1650
Holy Rood 1653
S.S. Lawrence and John 1665
St Mary Extra 1671
St Michael 1552

PORTSMOUTH
St John 1789
St Thomas 1654
Royal Garrison Church 1741

SCALE 0 1 2 3 4 5 6 7 8 9 10 MILES

PUBLISHED BY THE INSTITUTE OF HERALDIC AND GENEALOGICAL STUDIES NORTHGATE CANTERBURY KENT

THIS ITEM IS NUMBER 14 OF OUR SERIES OF GENEALOGICAL AIDS

© Revised 1995

BERKS

SURREY

SUSSEX

DORSET

WILTS

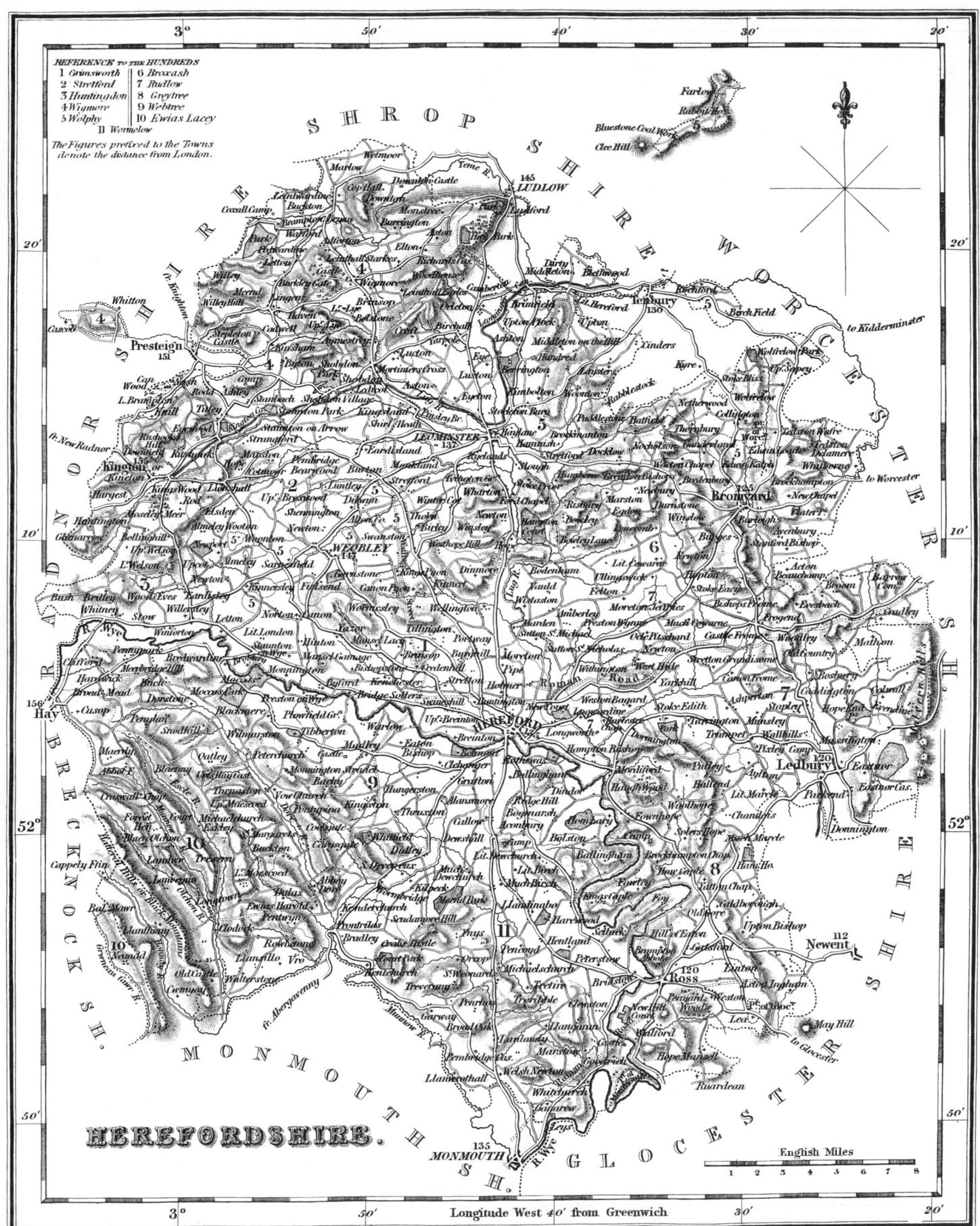

HEREFORDSHIRE.

REFERENCE TO THE HUNDREDS
1 Grimsworth   6 Broxash
2 Stretford   7 Radlow
3 Huntingdon   8 Greytree
4 Wigmore   9 Webtree
5 Wolphy   10 Ewias Lacey
          11 Wormelow

The Figures prefixed to the Towns
denote the distance from London.

English Miles

Longitude West 40' from Greenwich

Engᵈ on Steel by Gray & Son.

Pubᵈ by Archᵈ Fullarton & Cᵒ Glasgow

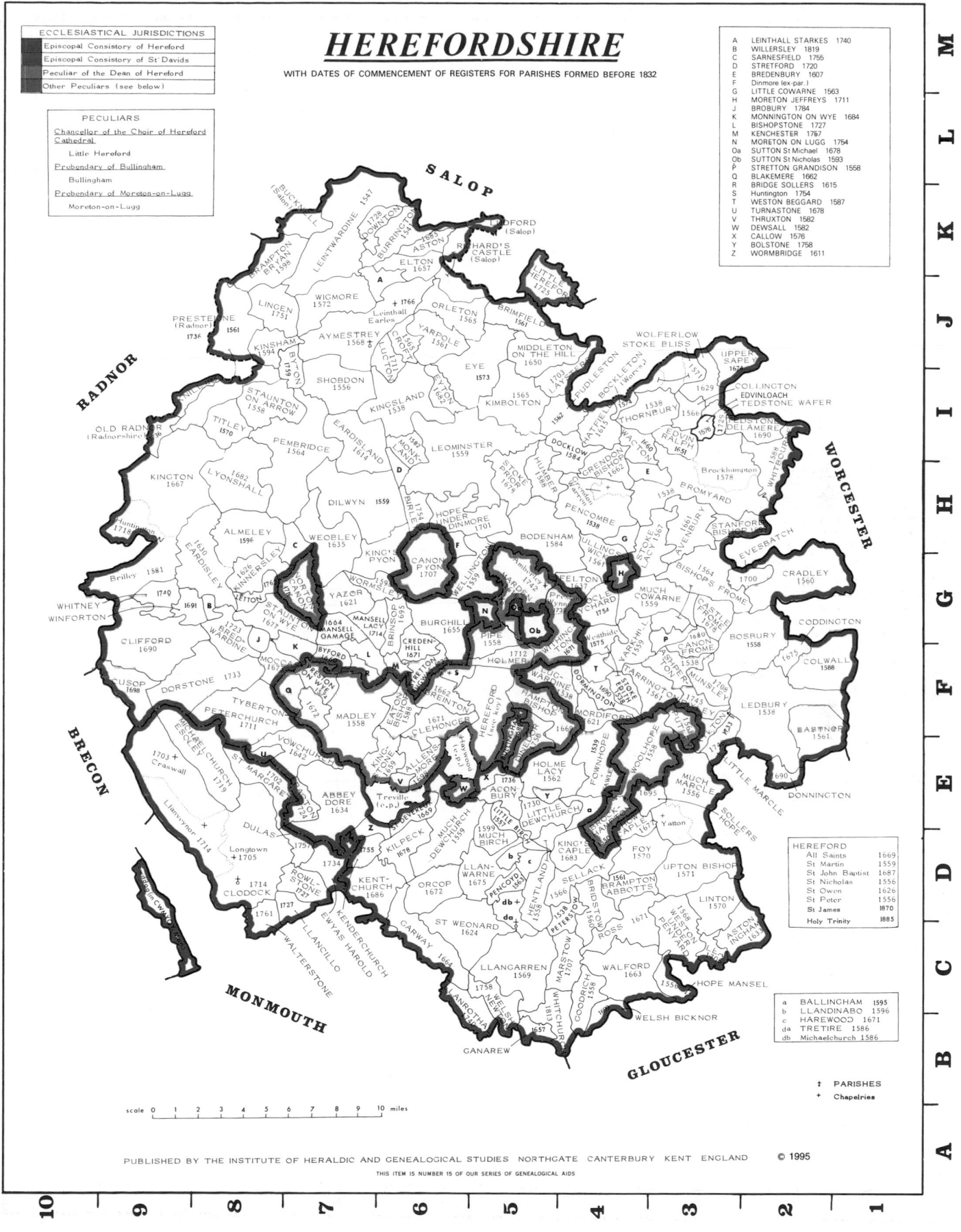

HEREFORDSHIRE

WITH DATES OF COMMENCEMENT OF REGISTERS FOR PARISHES FORMED BEFORE 1832

ECCLESIASTICAL JURISDICTIONS
- Episcopal Consistory of Hereford
- Episcopal Consistory of St Davids
- Peculiar of the Dean of Hereford
- Other Peculiars (see below)

PECULIARS
Chancellor of the Choir of Hereford Cathedral
   Little Hereford
Prebendary of Bullingham
   Bullingham
Prebendary of Moreton-on-Lugg
   Moreton-on-Lugg

A	LEINTHALL STARKES	1740
B	WILLERSLEY	1819
C	SARNESFIELD	1755
D	STRETFORD	1720
E	BREDENBURY	1607
F	Dinmore (ex-par.)	
G	LITTLE COWARNE	1563
H	MORETON JEFFREYS	1711
J	BROBURY	1784
K	MONNINGTON ON WYE	1684
L	BISHOPSTONE	1727
M	KENCHESTER	1767
N	MORETON ON LUGG	1754
Oa	SUTTON St Michael	1678
Ob	SUTTON St Nicholas	1593
P	STRETTON GRANDISON	1558
Q	BLAKEMERE	1662
R	BRIDGE SOLLERS	1615
S	Huntington	1754
T	WESTON BEGGARD	1587
U	TURNASTONE	1678
V	THRUXTON	1582
W	DEWSALL	1582
X	CALLOW	1576
Y	BOLSTONE	1758
Z	WORMBRIDGE	1611

HEREFORD

All Saints	1669
St Martin	1559
St John Baptist	1687
St Nicholas	1556
St Owen	1626
St Peter	1556
St James	1870
Holy Trinity	1885

a	BALLINGHAM	1595
b	LLANDINABO	1596
c	HAREWOOD	1671
da	TRETIRE	1586
db	Michaelchurch	1586

† PARISHES
+ Chapelries

scale 0 1 2 3 4 5 6 7 8 9 10 miles

PUBLISHED BY THE INSTITUTE OF HERALDIC AND GENEALOGICAL STUDIES NORTHGATE CANTERBURY KENT ENGLAND © 1995

THIS ITEM IS NUMBER 15 OF OUR SERIES OF GENEALOGICAL AIDS

HERTFORDSHIRE

Engᵈ on Steel by Gray & Son

Meridian of ⊙ Greenwich

REFERENCE TO THE HUNDREDS

1 Hertford	5 Hitchin
2 Broadwater	6 Odsey
3 Castle	7 Edwinstree
4 Dacorum	8 Braughing

Waltham Abbey 12

CAMBRIDGE SHIRE

BEDFORDSHIRE

BUCKINGHAMSHIRE

MIDDLESEX

ESSEX

English Miles

ST ALBAN'S ABBEY CHURCH

HERTFORDSHIRE

WITH DATES OF COMMENCEMENT OF REGISTERS FOR PARISHES FORMED BEFORE 1832

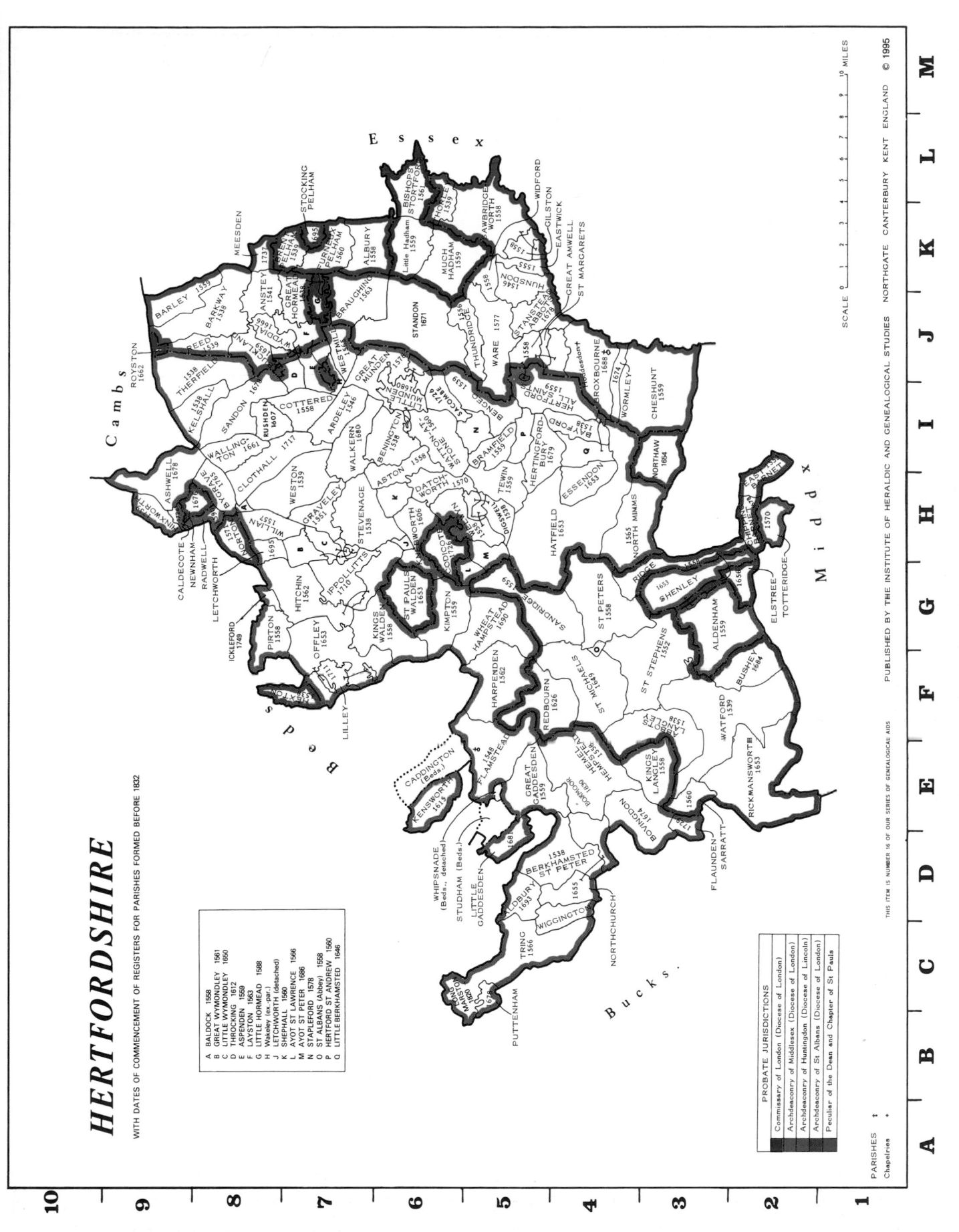

A BALDOCK 1558
B GREAT WYMONDLEY 1561
C LITTLE WYMONDLEY 1650
D THROCKING 1612
E ASPENDEN 1559
F LAYSTON 1563
G LITTLE HORMEAD 1588
H Wakeley (ex. par.)
J LETCHWORTH (detached)
K SHEPHALL 1560
L AYOT ST LAWRENCE 1566
M AYOT ST PETER 1686
N STAPLEFORD 1578
O ST ALBANS (Abbey) 1558
P HERTFORD ST ANDREW 1560
Q LITTLE BERKHAMSTED 1646

PROBATE JURISDICTIONS

Commissary of London (Diocese of London)
Archdeaconry of Middlesex (Diocese of London)
Archdeaconry of Huntingdon (Diocese of Lincoln)
Archdeaconry of St Albans (Diocese of London)
Peculiar of the Dean and Chapter of St Pauls

PARISHES †
Chapelries +

SCALE 0 1 2 3 4 5 6 7 8 9 10 MILES

PUBLISHED BY THE INSTITUTE OF HERALDIC AND GENEALOGICAL STUDIES   NORTHGATE   CANTERBURY   KENT   ENGLAND   © 1995

THIS ITEM IS NUMBER 16 OF OUR SERIES OF GENEALOGICAL AIDS

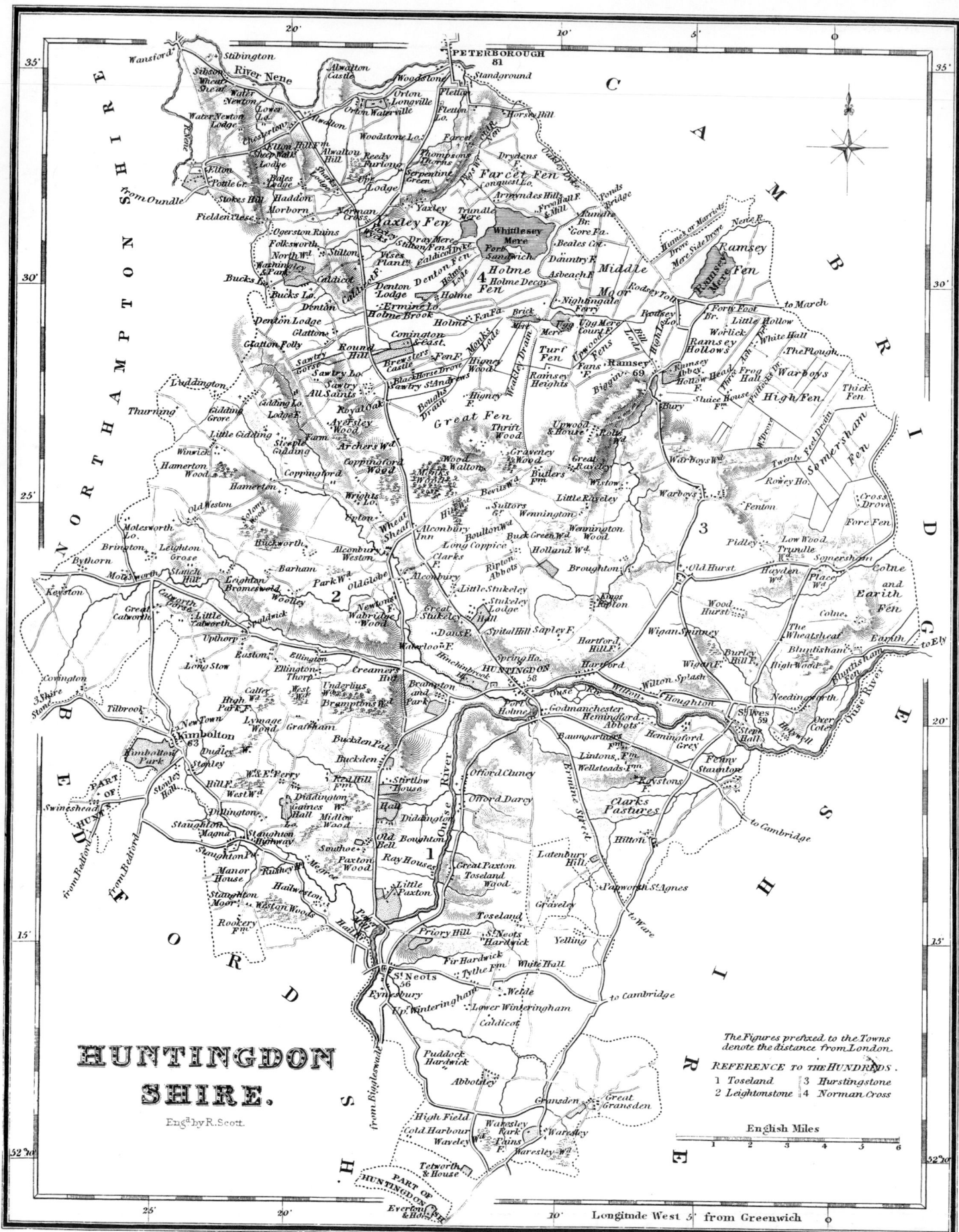

HUNTINGDON SHIRE.

Engd by R. Scott.

The Figures prefixed to the Towns
denote the distance from London.

REFERENCE TO THE HUNDREDS.
1 Toseland   3 Hurstingstone
2 Leightonstone   4 Norman Cross

English Miles

Published by Archd Fullarton & Co Glasgow.

Longitude West from Greenwich

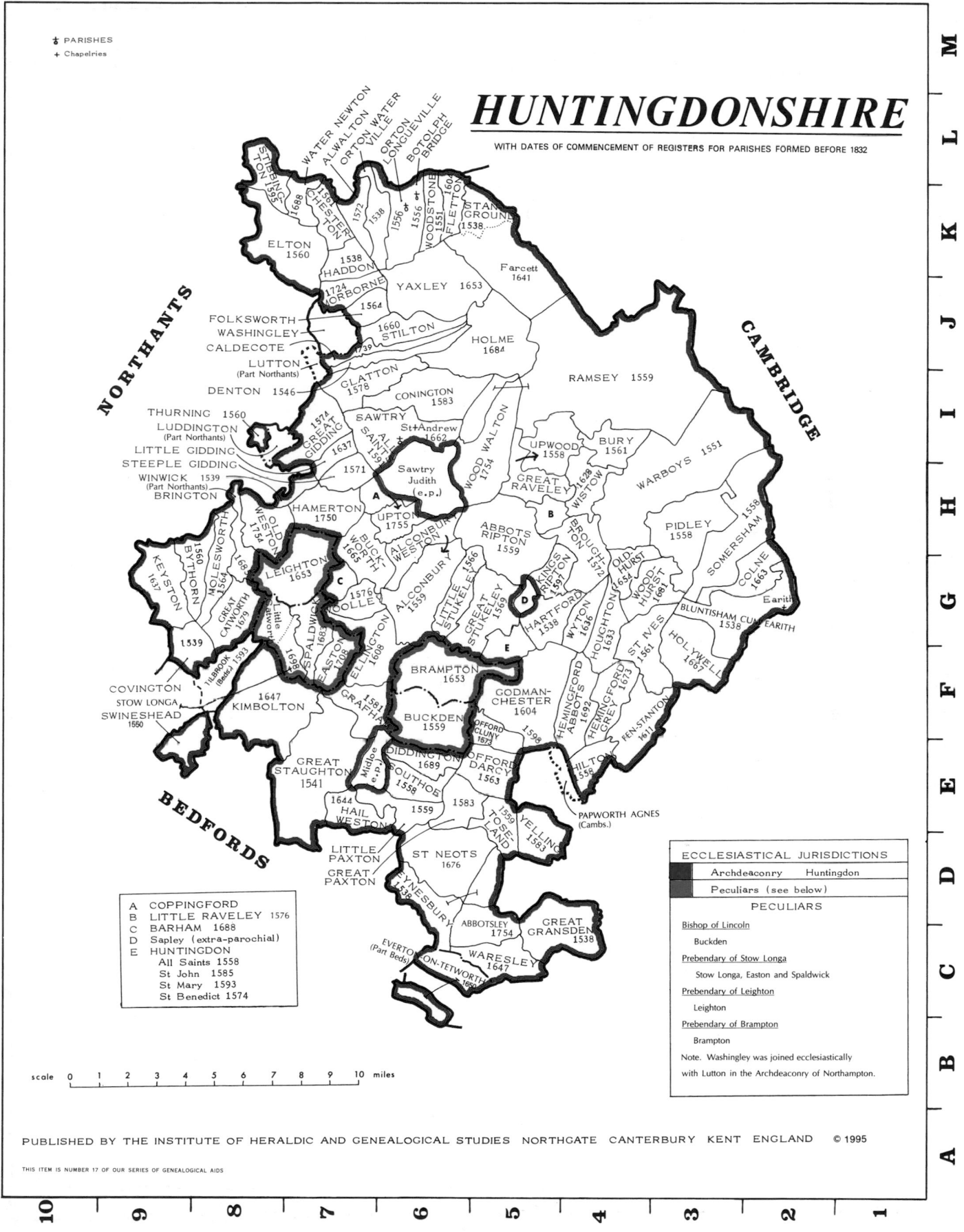

HUNTINGDONSHIRE

WITH DATES OF COMMENCEMENT OF REGISTERS FOR PARISHES FORMED BEFORE 1832

PARISHES
Chapelries

NORTHANTS

CAMBRIDGE

BEDFORDS

WATER NEWTON
ALWALTON
ORTON WATERVILLE
ORTON LONGUEVILLE
BOTOLPH BRIDGE
STEEPLE GIDDING 1595
CHESTERTON 1563
1688
1572
1538
1556
1556
1607
WOODSTONE 1551
FLETTON
STANGROUND 1538
ELTON 1560
HADDON 1538
MORBORNE 1724
1564
YAXLEY 1653
FARCETT 1641
FOLKSWORTH
WASHINGLEY
CALDECOTE
STILTON 1660
1739
HOLME 1684
LUTTON (Part Northants)
DENTON 1546
GLATTON 1578
CONINGTON 1583
RAMSEY 1559
THURNING 1560
LUDDINGTON (Part Northants)
LITTLE GIDDING
STEEPLE GIDDING
WINWICK 1539 (Part Northants)
BRINGTON
GREAT GIDDING 1637
SAWTRY ALL SAINTS 1591
St Andrew 1662
1574
1571
Sawtry Judith (e.p.)
WOOD WALTON 1754
UPWOOD 1558
BURY 1561
WARBOYS 1551
HAMERTON 1750
UPTON 1755
GREAT RAVELEY 1628
WISTOW
ABBOTS RIPTON 1559
BROUGHTON 1572
PIDLEY 1558
SOMERSHAM 1558
OLD WESTON 1754
BUCKWORTH 1665
ALCONBURY WESTON
COLNE 1663
KEYSTON 1637
BYTHORN 1560
MOLESWORTH 1681
1564
GREAT CATWORTH 1679
LEIGHTON 1653
WOOLLEY 1576
Little Catworth
ALCONBURY 1559
LITTLE STUKELEY 1566
GREAT STUKELEY 1569
KINGS RIPTON 1597
OLD HURST 1654
WOODHURST 1681
EARITH
BLUNTISHAM CUM EARITH 1538
1539
1591
SPALDWICK 1683
EASTON 1705
ELLINGTON 1608
HARTFORD 1538
WYTON 1636
HOUGHTON 1633
ST IVES 1561
HOLYWELL 1667
D
1698
COVINGTON
STOW LONGA
SWINESHEAD 1550
KIMBOLTON
GRAFHAM 1581
BRAMPTON 1653
GODMANCHESTER 1604
HEMINGFORD ABBOTS 1692
HEMINGFORD GREY 1673
FEN-STANTON 1611
1647
BUCKDEN 1559
OFFORD CLUNY 1673
1598
HILTON 1558
PAPWORTH AGNES (Cambs.)
GREAT STAUGHTON 1541
Midloe e.p.
DIDDINGTON 1689
SOUTHOE 1558
OFFORD DARCY 1563
1644
HAIL WESTON
1559
1583
TOSELAND 1559
YELLING 1583
LITTLE PAXTON
GREAT PAXTON
TYNESBURY 1538
ST NEOTS 1676
ABBOTSLEY 1754
GREAT GRANSDEN 1538
EVERTON (Part Beds)
SON-TETWORTH
WARESLEY 1647

A COPPINGFORD
B LITTLE RAVELEY 1576
C BARHAM 1688
D Sapley (extra-parochial)
E HUNTINGDON
   All Saints 1558
   St John 1585
   St Mary 1593
   St Benedict 1574

ECCLESIASTICAL JURISDICTIONS

Archdeaconry	Huntingdon
Peculiars	(see below)

PECULIARS

Bishop of Lincoln
   Buckden

Prebendary of Stow Longa
   Stow Longa, Easton and Spaldwick

Prebendary of Leighton
   Leighton

Prebendary of Brampton
   Brampton

Note. Washingley was joined ecclesiastically
with Lutton in the Archdeaconry of Northampton.

scale 0 1 2 3 4 5 6 7 8 9 10 miles

PUBLISHED BY THE INSTITUTE OF HERALDIC AND GENEALOGICAL STUDIES NORTHGATE CANTERBURY KENT ENGLAND © 1995

THIS ITEM IS NUMBER 17 OF OUR SERIES OF GENEALOGICAL AIDS

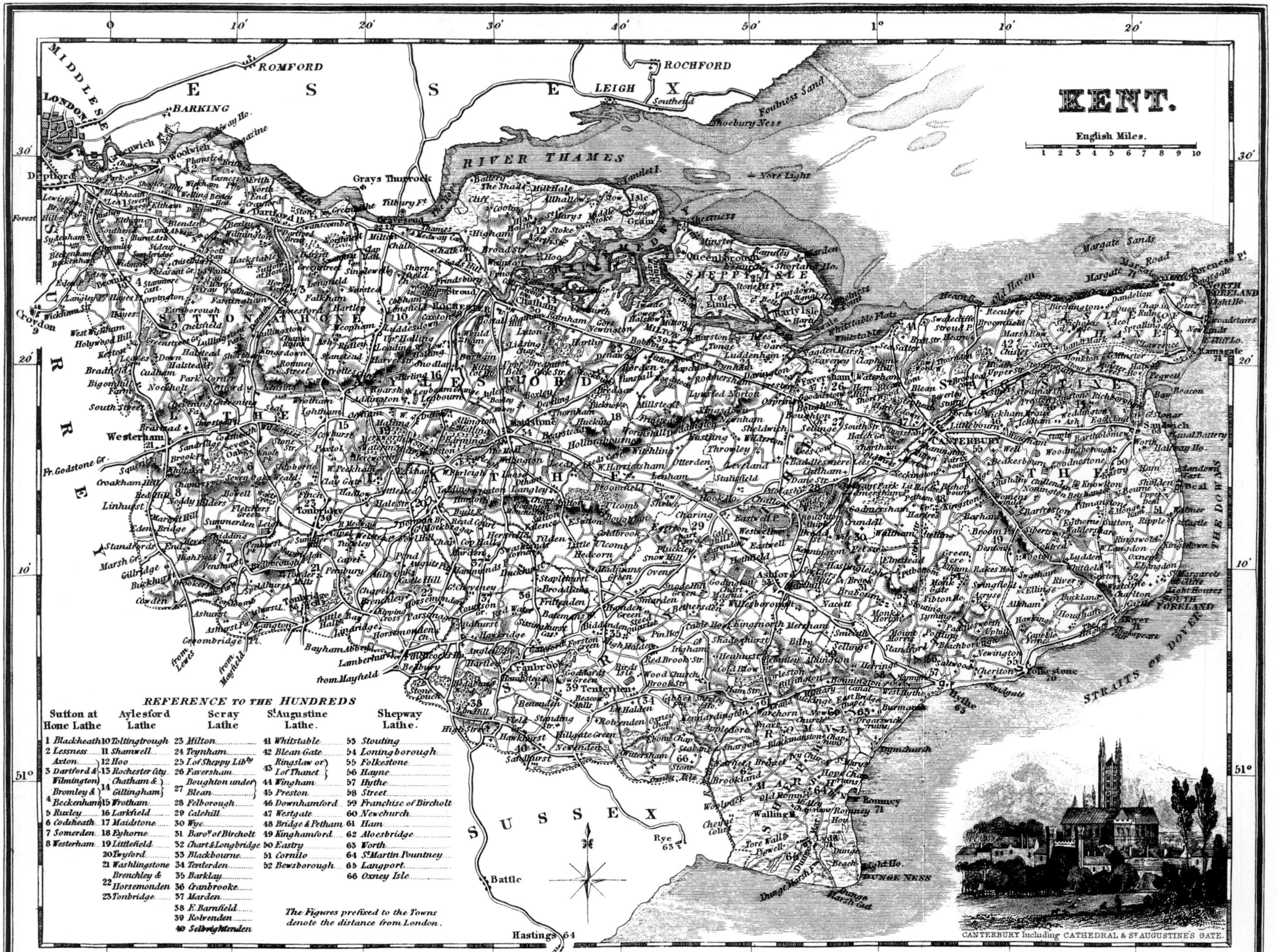

KENT.

English Miles.
1 2 3 4 5 6 7 8 9 10

Engd by R. Scott

CANTERBURY Including CATHEDRAL & St AUGUSTINES GATE.

RIVER THAMES

STRAIT of DOVER

THE DOWNS

MIDDLESEX

ESSEX

SURREY

SUSSEX

ROMFORD
BARKING Mo
LONDON
ROCHFORD
LEIGH
Southend
Grays Thurrock

Hastings 64
Rye 63½
Battle

REFERENCE TO THE HUNDREDS

Sutton at Home Lathe

1 Blackheath to Eltingborough
2 Lesnes
3 Dartford &
   Wilmington}
4 Beckenham
5 Bexley
6 Codsheath
7 Somerden
8 Westerham

Aylesford Lathe

9 Ruxley
10 Eltingborough
11 Shamwell
12 Hoo
13 Rochester City
14 Gillingham
15 Fotham
16 Larkfield
17 Maidstone
18 Eyhorne
19 Littlefield
20 Twyford
21 Washlingstone
22 Brenchley &
   Horsemonden
23 Toinbridge

Scray Lathe

24 Milton
25 Teynham
26 Ld. of Sharpy Libty
27 Faversham.
28 Boughton under
   Oldham &
29 Bean
30 Felborough
31 Calehill
32 Wye
33 Barony of Birchott
34 East Longbridge
35 Blackbourne
36 Tenterden
37 Barkley
38 Marden
39 Rolvenden
40 Selbrey Menden

St Augustine Lathe

41 Whitstable
42 Blean Gate
43 Ringslow or
   Ld of Thanet}
44 Wingham
45 Preston
46 Downhamford
47 Kinghamford
48 Bridge & Petham
49 Kinghamford
50 Eastry
51 Cornilo
52 Bewsborough

Shepway Lathe

53 Stouting
54 Loningborough
55 Folkestone
56 Hayne
57 Hythe
58 Street
59 Franchise of Bircholt
60 Newchurch
61 Ham
62 Blockbridge
63 Forth
64 St Martin Poulney
65 Langport
66 Oxney Isle

The Figures prefixed to the Towns denote the distance from London.

Longitude East 2° from Greenwich

Published by Archd. Fullarton & Co. Glasgow.

KENT PARISHES

WITH DATES OF COMMENCEMENT OF REGISTERS FOR PARISHES FORMED BEFORE 1832

M	SITTINGBOURNE	1561
N	BUCKLAND	(1562)
O	DAVINGTON	1549
P	GOODNESTONE	1569
R	LEAVELAND	1553
S	CANTERBURY	
	ALL SAINTS	1559
	CATHEDRAL	
	HOLY CROSS	1564
	ST. ANDREW	1560
	ST. GEORGE	1538
	ST. MARGARET	1653
	ST. MARY BREDMAN	1654
	ST. MARY MAGDALEN	1559
	ST. MILDRED	1560
	ST. PETER	1560
	ST. MARY, NORTHGATE	1559
T	ST. DUNSTAN	1559
U	ST. MARTIN	1640
W	ST. PAUL	1662
X		1604
Y	ST. MARY BREDIN	1688

Aa	ELMSTONE	1559
Ab	CHISLENDEN	1711
Ac	KNOWLTON	1552
Ad	HAM	
Ae	BETTESHANGER	1562

Af	BLACKMANSTONE	1715
Ag	ORGARSWICK	
Ah	PADDLESWORTH	1691
Ai	HAWKINGE	1691
Aj	CHARLTON	1690
Ak	ORKNEY	

A	DEPTFORD ST. NICHOLAS	1545
	ST. PAUL	1730
B	FOOTSCRAY Extra Parochial	1715
C	EAST WICKHAM	1715
D	IFIELD	1558
E	LONGFIELD	

F	ROCHESTER ST. MARGARET	1630
	ST. NICHOLAS	1624
	CATHEDRAL	1560
G	LEYBOURNE	1630
H	ALLINGTON Whetsted	1630
J	Tonbridge Wells, King Charles	1745
	Hely Trinity	1559
K		1558
L	BREDHURST	

ESSEX

MIDDLESEX

SURREY

SUSSEX

The Swale

River Medway

SCALE
0 2 4 6 8 10 MILES

N.B. PARISHES WITHOUT DATES HAVE NO SEPARATE REGISTERS

Ecclesiastical Jurisdictions
- ARCHDEACONRY OF CANTERBURY
- CONSISTORY COURT OF CANTERBURY
- ARCHDEACONRY OF ROCHESTER
- EXEMPT DEANERY OF SHOREHAM
- PECULIAR OF THE RECTOR OF CLIFFE

© 1995

THIS ITEM IS NUMBER 18 OF OUR SERIES OF GENEALOGICAL AIDS

PUBLISHED BY THE INSTITUTE OF HERALDIC AND GENEALOGICAL STUDIES, NORTHGATE, CANTERBURY, KENT, ENGLAND

A B C D E F G H I J K L M

1 2 3 4 5 6 7 8 9 10

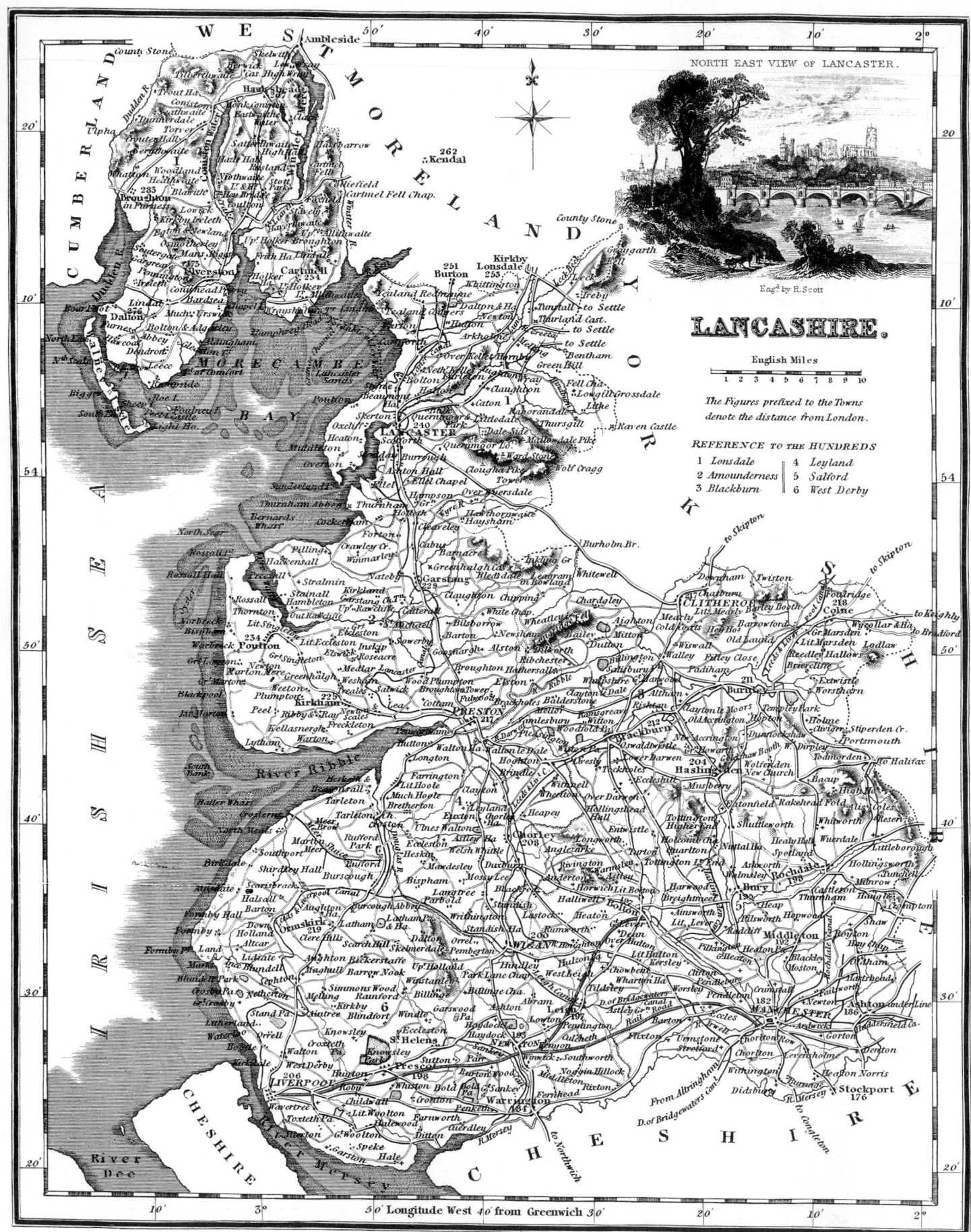

NORTH EAST VIEW OF LANCASTER.

Engd. by R. Scott

LANCASHIRE.

English Miles

1 2 3 4 5 6 7 8 9 10

The Figures prefixed to the Towns
denote the distance from London.

REFERENCE TO THE HUNDREDS

1 Lonsdale	4 Leyland
2 Amounderness	5 Salford
3 Blackburn	6 West Derby

Published by Archd. Fullarton & Co. Glasgow.

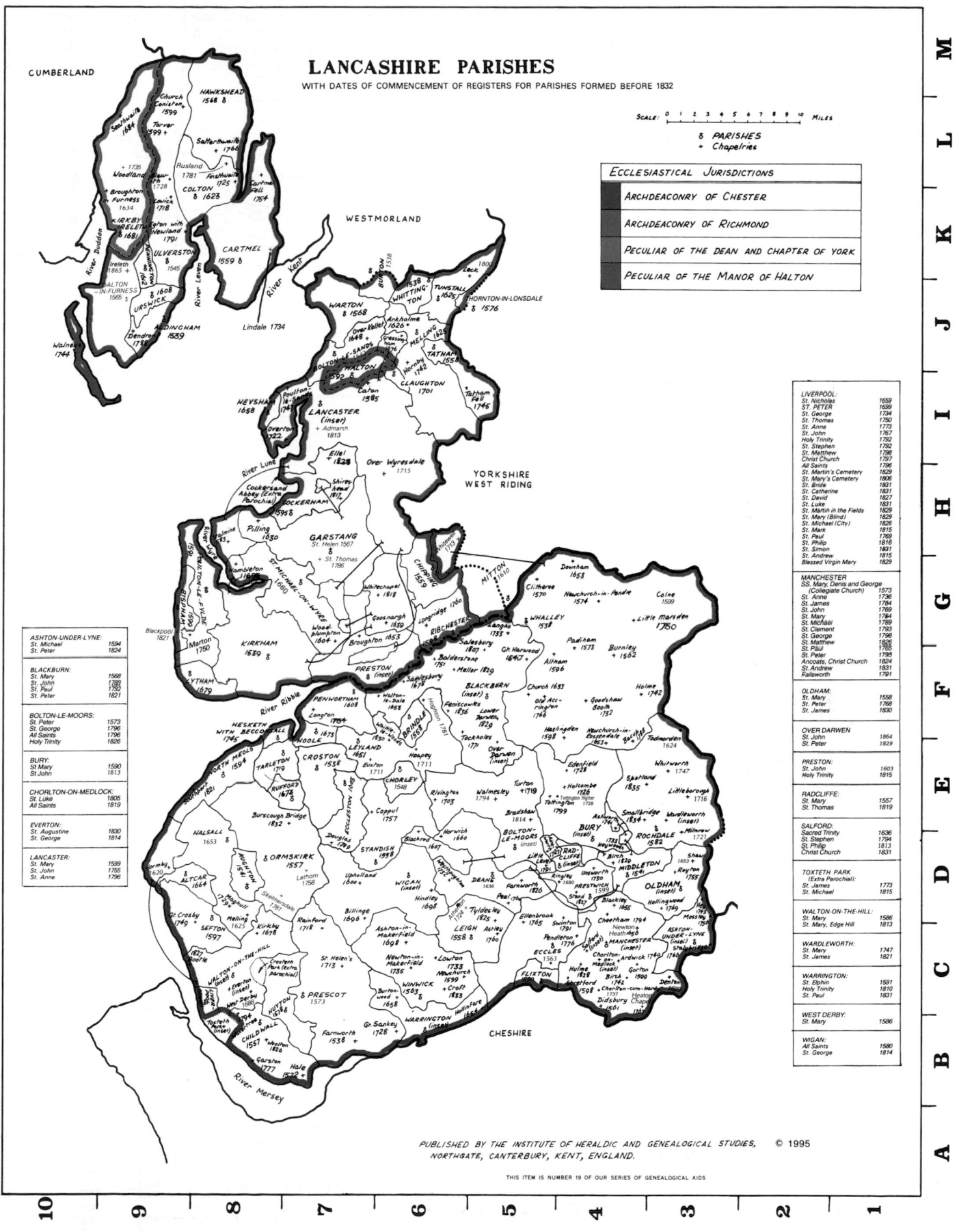

LANCASHIRE PARISHES

WITH DATES OF COMMENCEMENT OF REGISTERS FOR PARISHES FORMED BEFORE 1832

SCALE: 0 1 2 3 4 5 6 7 8 9 10 MILES

§ PARISHES
+ Chapelries

ECCLESIASTICAL JURISDICTIONS
ARCHDEACONRY OF CHESTER
ARCHDEACONRY OF RICHMOND
PECULIAR OF THE DEAN AND CHAPTER OF YORK
PECULIAR OF THE MANOR OF HALTON

CUMBERLAND

WESTMORLAND

YORKSHIRE WEST RIDING

CHESHIRE

LIVERPOOL:
St. Nicholas	1659
ST. PETER	1699
St. George	1734
St. Thomas	1750
St. Anne	1773
St. John	1767
Holy Trinity	1792
St. Stephen	1792
St. Matthew	1798
Christ Church	1797
All Saints	1796
St. Martin's Cemetery	1829
St. Mary's Cemetery	1806
St. Bride	1829
St. Catherine	1831
St. David	1827
St. Luke	1831
St. Martin in the Fields	1829
St. Mary (Blind)	1829
St. Mark (City)	1826
St. Mark	1815
St. Paul	1769
St. Philip	1816
St. Simon	1831
St. Andrew	1815
Blessed Virgin Mary	1829

MANCHESTER:
SS. Mary, Denis and George (Collegiate Church)	1573
St. Anne	1736
St. James	1784
St. John	1769
St. Mary	1764
St. Michael	1789
St. Clement	1793
St. George	1798
St. Matthew	1826
St. Paul	1765
St. Peter	1795
Ancoats, Christ Church	1824
St. Andrew	1831
Failsworth	1791

OLDHAM:
St. Mary	1558
St. Peter	1768
St. James	1830

OVER DARWEN:
St. John	1864
St. Peter	1829

PRESTON:
St. John	1603
Holy Trinity	1815

RADCLIFFE:
St. Mary	1557
St. Thomas	1819

SALFORD:
Sacred Trinity	1636
St. Stephen	1794
St. Philip	1813
Christ Church	1831

TOXTETH PARK (Extra Parochial):
St. James	1773
St. Michael	1815

WALTON-ON-THE-HILL:
St. Mary	1586
St. Mary, Edge Hill	1813

WARDLEWORTH:
St. Mary	1747
St. James	1821

WARRINGTON:
St. Elphin	1591
Holy Trinity	1810
St. Paul	1831

WEST DERBY:
St. Mary	1586

WIGAN:
All Saints	1580
St. George	1814

ASHTON-UNDER-LYNE:
St. Michael	1594
St. Peter	1824

BLACKBURN:
St. Mary	1568
St. John	1789
St. Paul	1792
St. Peter	1821

BOLTON-LE-MOORS:
St. Peter	1573
St. George	1796
All Saints	1796
Holy Trinity	1826

BURY:
St Mary	1590
St John	1813

CHORLTON-ON-MEDLOCK:
St. Luke	1805
All Saints	1819

EVERTON:
St. Augustine	1830
St. George	1814

LANCASTER:
St. Mary	1599
St. John	1755
St. Anne	1796

PUBLISHED BY THE INSTITUTE OF HERALDIC AND GENEALOGICAL STUDIES,
NORTHGATE, CANTERBURY, KENT, ENGLAND.

THIS ITEM IS NUMBER 19 OF OUR SERIES OF GENEALOGICAL AIDS

© 1995

M L K J I H G F E D C B A

10 9 8 7 6 5 4 3 2 1

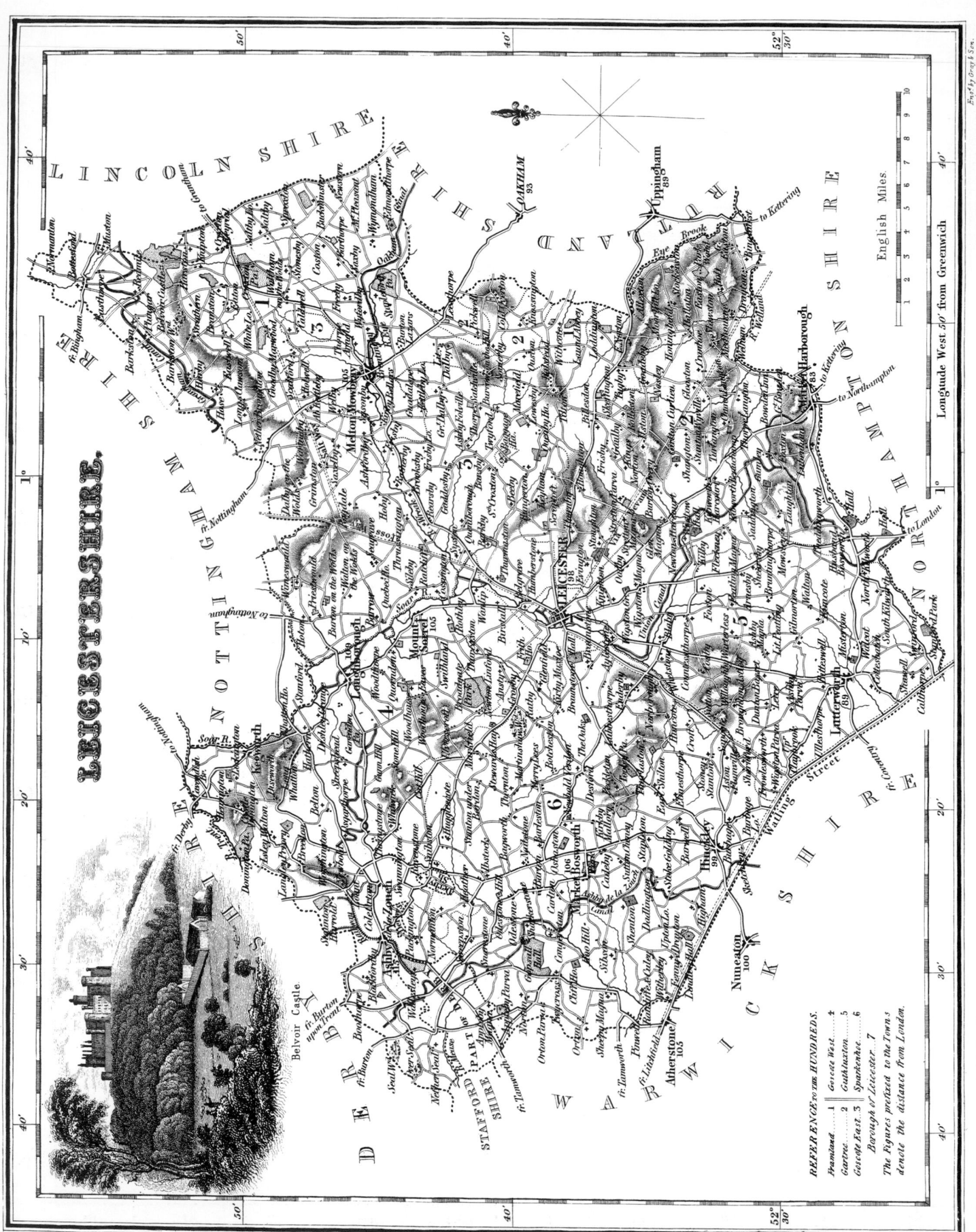

LEICESTERSHIRE.

LINCOLN SHIRE

RUTLAND SHIRE

NORTHAMPTON SHIRE

WARWICK SHIRE

NOTTINGHAM SHIRE

DERBY SHIRE

STAFFORD PART OF SHIRE

English Miles.

Longitude West 50' from Greenwich

Engd by Gray & Son.

Belvoir Castle.

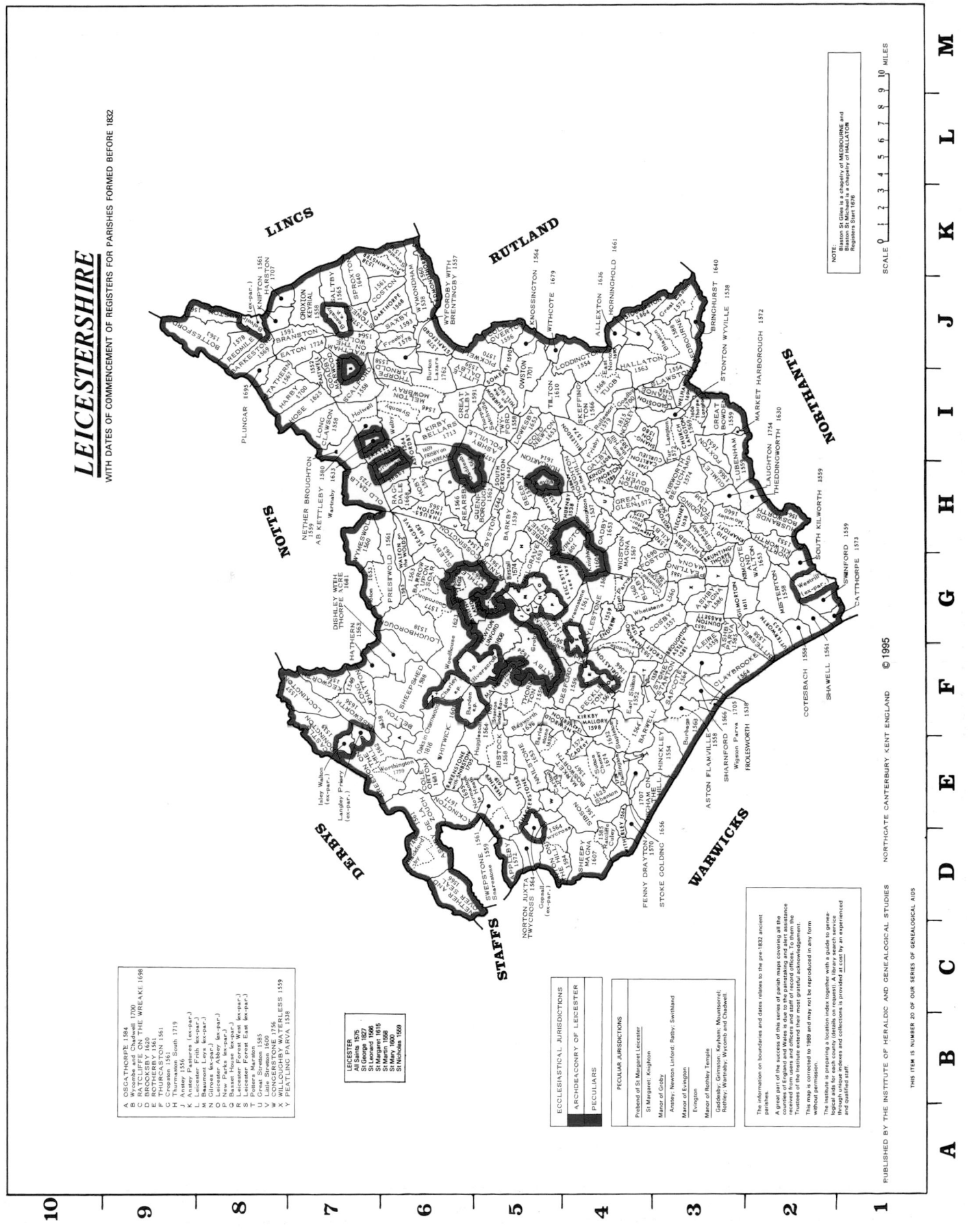

LEICESTERSHIRE

WITH DATES OF COMMENCEMENT OF REGISTERS FOR PARISHES FORMED BEFORE 1832

LINCS

RUTLAND

NOTTS

NORTHANTS

DERBYS

STAFFS

WARWICKS

NOTE:
Bliston St Giles is a chapelry of MEDBOURNE and
Bliston St Michael is a chapelry of HALLATON
Registers Start 1876

SCALE 0 1 2 3 4 5 6 7 8 9 10 MILES

A OSGATHORPE 1584
B Wycombe and Chadwell 1700
C RATCLIFFE ON THE WREAKE 1698
D BROOKSBY 1620
E ROTHERBY 1561
F THURCASTON 1561
G Cropston 1561
H Thurmaston South 1719
J Anstey 1556
K Leicester Frith (ex-par.)
L Anstey Pastures (ex-par.)
M Beaumont Leys (ex-par.)
N Gilroes (ex-par.)
O Leicester Abbey (ex-par.)
P New Parks (ex-par.)
R Basset House (ex-par.)
S Leicester Forest West (ex-par.)
T Leicester Forest East (ex-par.)
U Potters Marston
V Great Stretton 1565
W Little Stretton 1600
X CONGERSTONE 1756
Y WILLOUGHBY WATERLESS 1559
Z PEATLING PARVA 1538

LEICESTER
All Saints 1575
St George 1827
St Leonard 1566
St Margaret 1615
St Martin 1558
St Mary 1600
St Nicholas 1569

ECCLESIASTICAL JURISDICTIONS
ARCHDEACONRY OF LEICESTER
PECULIARS

PECULIAR JURISDICTIONS

Prebend of St Margaret Leicester

St Margaret: Knighton

Manor of Groby

Anstey, Newton Linford, Ratby, Swithland

Manor of Evington

Evington

Manor of Rothley Temple

Gaddesby, Grimston, Keyham, Mountsorrel;
Rothley, Wartnaby, Wycomb and Chadwell

The information on boundaries and dates relates to the pre-1832 ancient
parishes.

A great part of the success of this series of parish maps covering all the
counties of England and Wales is due to the painstaking and alert assistance
received from users and officers and staff of record offices. To them the
Trustees of the Institute extend their most grateful acknowledgement.

This map is corrected to 1989 and may not be reproduced in any form
without permission.

The Institute is preparing a location index together with a guide to genealogical aids for each county (details on request). A library search service
through unique indexes and collections is provided at cost by an experienced
and qualified staff.

PUBLISHED BY THE INSTITUTE OF HERALDIC AND GENEALOGICAL STUDIES   NORTHGATE CANTERBURY KENT ENGLAND   ©1995

THIS ITEM IS NUMBER 20 OF OUR SERIES OF GENEALOGICAL AIDS

A B C D E F G H I J K L M

10 9 8 7 6 5 4 3 2 1

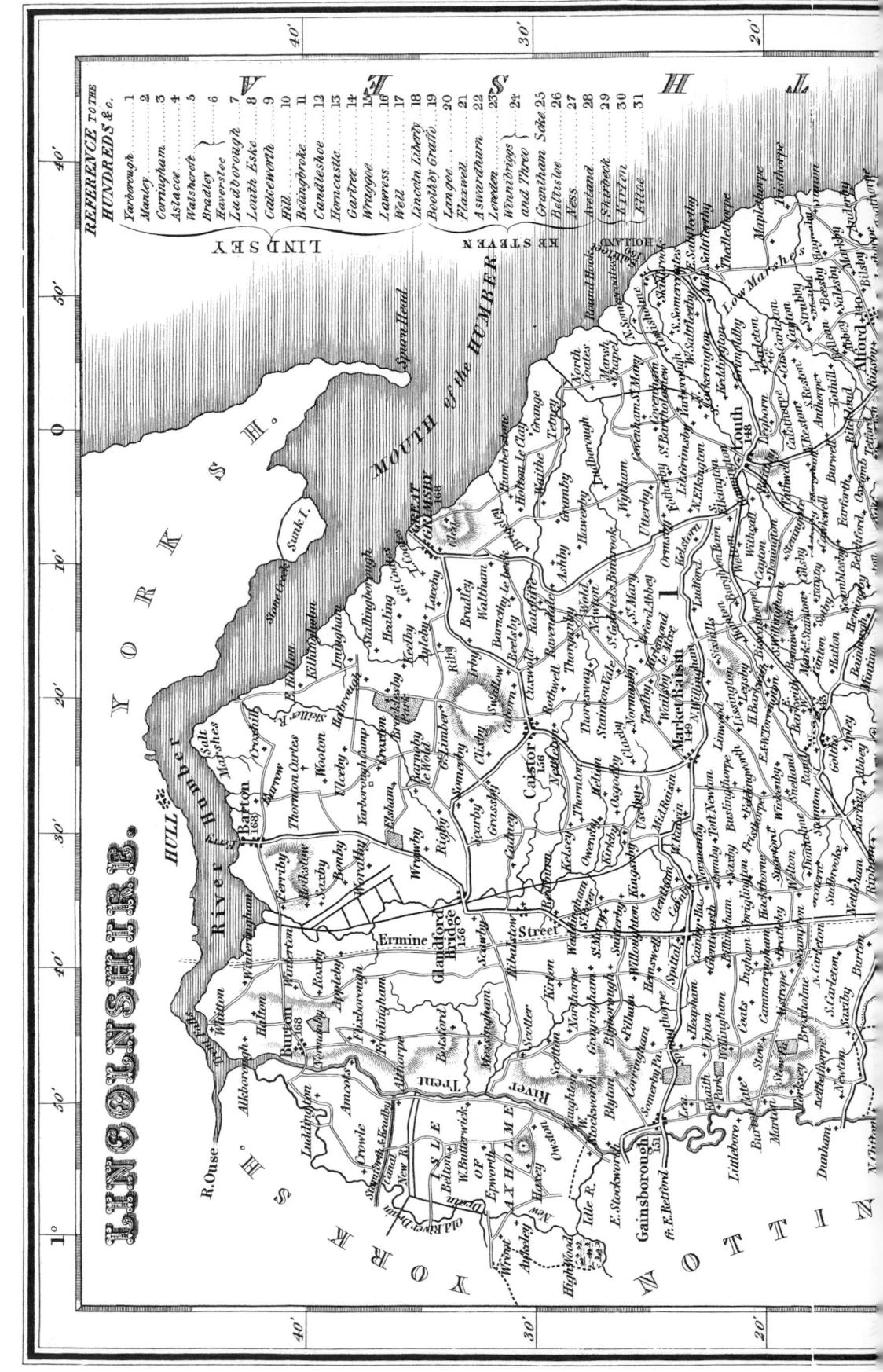

LINCOLNSHIRE.

LINDSEY

KESTEVEN

HOLLAND

YORKSHIRE

River Humber

HULL

R. Ouse

MOUTH of the HUMBER

YORK SH.

Sunk I.

Salt Marshes

Spurn Head

GREAT GRIMSBY 168

Barton 163

Ermine Street

Glanford Bridge 156

Burton 168

Trent

River Trent

ISLE OF AXHOLME

Castor 156

Market Raisen 149

LOUTH 148

Alford 150

Gainsborough 131

fr. E. Retford

NOTTIN

Caistor 156

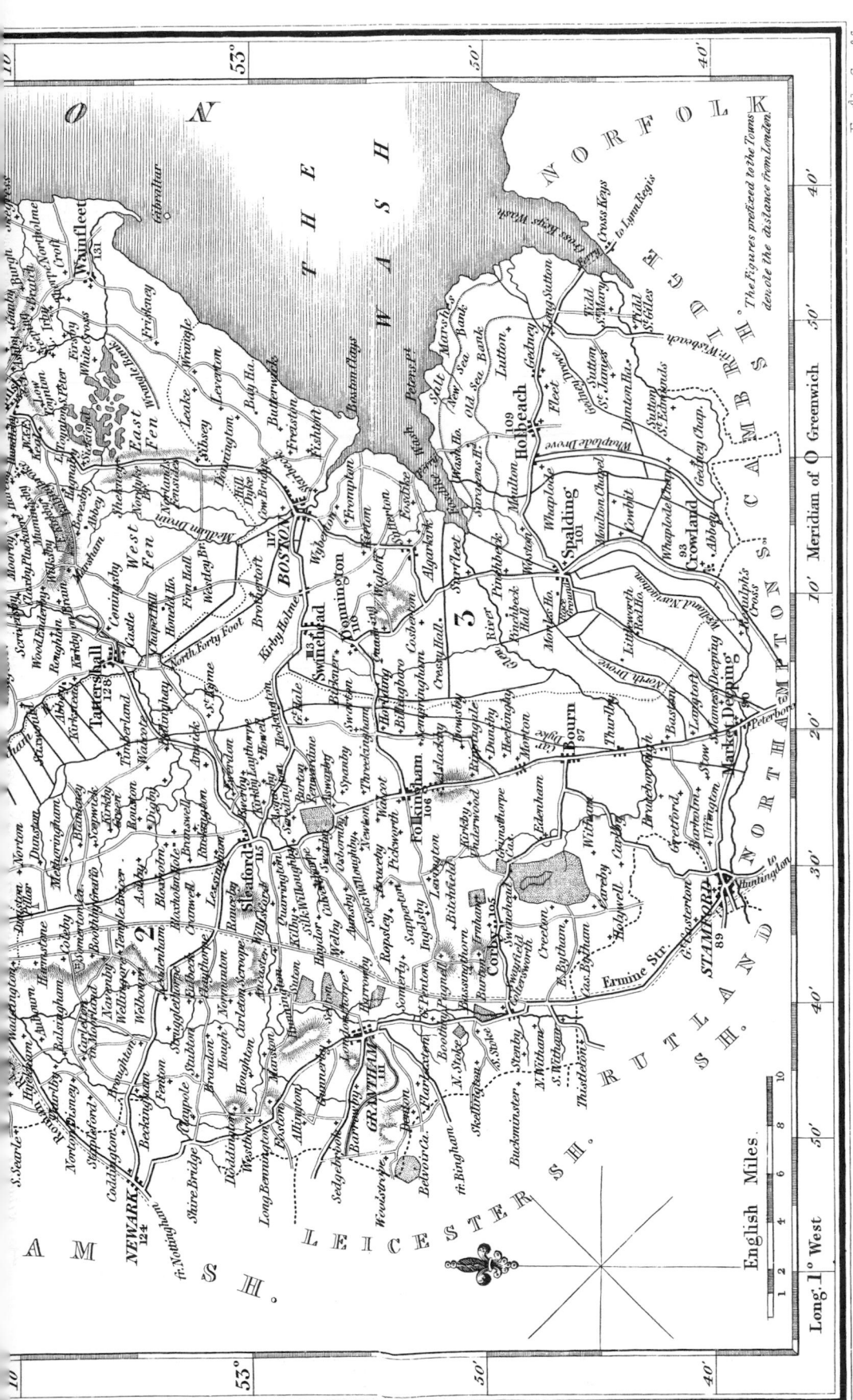

Pub. By Arch.^d Fullarton & Co Glasgow.

Eng.^d by Gray&Son.

English Miles.

Long.^{t.} 1° West

Meridian of ☉ Greenwich

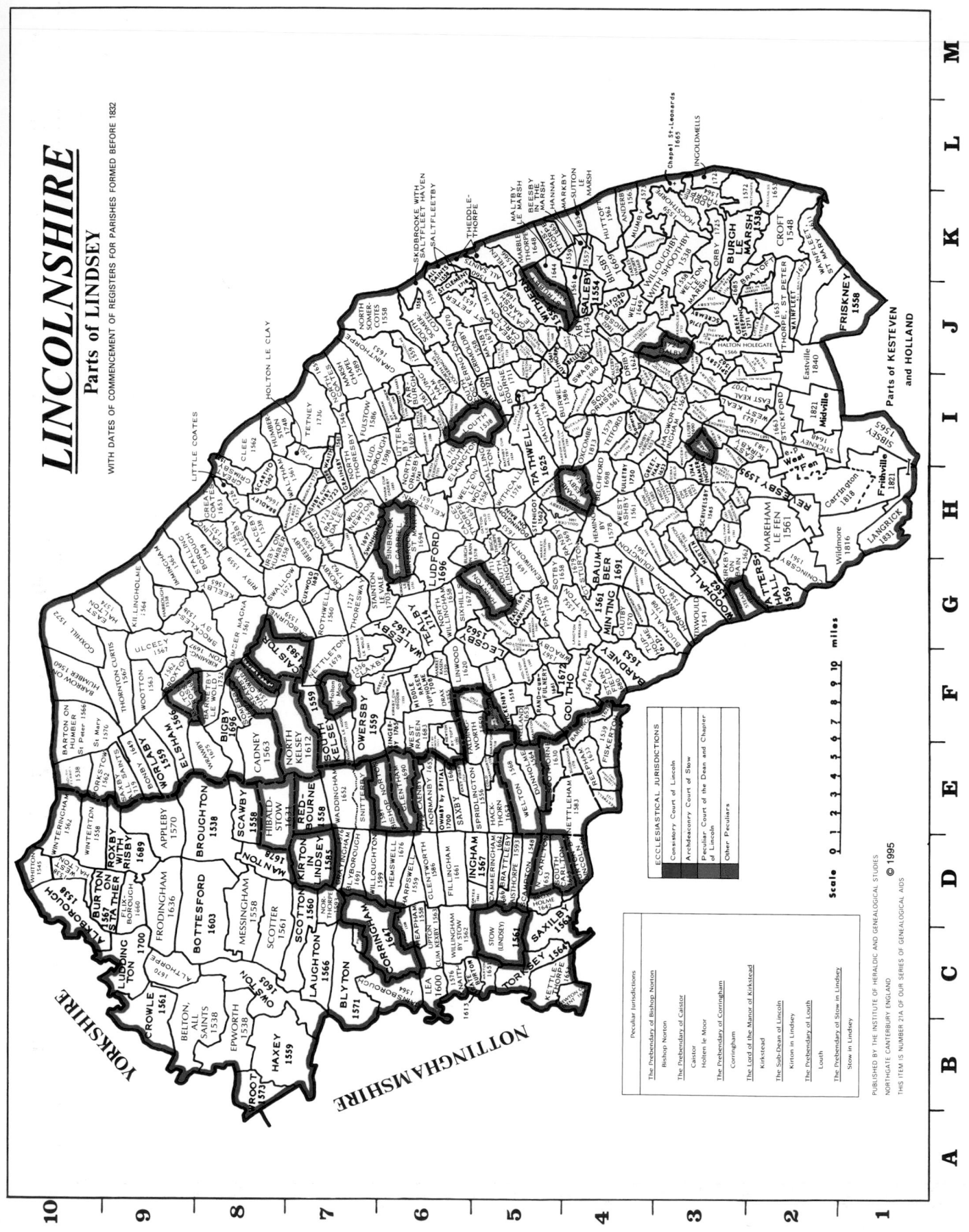

LINCOLNSHIRE
Parts of LINDSEY
WITH DATES OF COMMENCEMENT OF REGISTERS FOR PARISHES FORMED BEFORE 1832

ECCLESIASTICAL JURISDICTIONS

- Consistory Court of Lincoln
- Archdeaconry Court of Stow
- Peculiar Court of the Dean and Chapter of Lincoln
- Other Peculiars

Peculiar Jurisdictions

The Prebendary of Bishop Norton
Bishop Norton

The Prebendary of Caistor
Caistor
Holton le Moor

The Prebendary of Corringham
Corringham

The Lord of the Manor of Kirkstead
Kirkstead

The Sub-Dean of Lincoln
Kirton in Lindsey

The Prebendary of Louth
Louth

The Prebendary of Stow in Lindsey
Stow (Lindsey)

Scale 0 1 2 3 4 5 6 7 8 9 10 miles

PUBLISHED BY THE INSTITUTE OF HERALDIC AND GENEALOGICAL STUDIES
NORTHGATE CANTERBURY ENGLAND © 1995
THIS ITEM IS NUMBER 21A OF OUR SERIES OF GENEALOGICAL AIDS

YORKSHIRE

NOTTINGHAMSHIRE

Parts of KESTEVEN and HOLLAND

LINCOLNSHIRE

Parts of KESTEVEN and HOLLAND

WITH DATE OF COMMENCEMENT OF ORIGINAL REGISTERS

Ecclesiastical Jurisdictions

Consistory Court of Lincoln

Peculiar Court of Dean and Chapter of Lincoln

Peculiar Jurisdictions
The Prebendary of Heydour
Ashby, Culverthorpe, Heydour, Kelby and Oasby
The Prebendary of New Sleaford (Lafford)
Sleaford

Parts of LINDSEY

NORFOLK

CAMBRIDGE

NORTHANTS

RUTLAND

LEICESTERSHIRE

NOTTINGHAMSHIRE

Scale 0 1 2 3 4 5 6 7 8 9 10 Miles

STAMFORD:
ST. MICHAEL
ST. MARY
ST. GEORGE
ST. JOHN THE BAPTIST

GEDNEY 1558
Sutton St. Nicholas 1669
Long Sutton
Sutton St. Mary 1540
Sutton St. James
HOLBEACH 1560
FLEET 1652
WHAPLODE 1559
Whaplode Drove 1713
MOULTON 1558
WESTON 1678
SPALDING 1538
Cowbit 1704
Deeping Fen (e.p)
Crowland 1639
Deeping St. James
Market Deeping
West Deeping
Tallington
Barholm

WRANGLE 1653
LEAKE 1559
LEVERTON 1538
Benington 1638
FRIESTON 1660
FISHTOFT 1696
SKIRBECK 1661
Butterwick 1573
WYBERTON
FRAMPTON 1538
KIRTON 1562
Algarkirk 1678
SUTTERTON 1538
GOSBERTON 1659
SURFLEET
Holland Fen
Chapel Hill 1826
SWINESHEAD 1639
BICKER 1561
DONINGTON 1642
QUADRING 1583
PINCHBECK 1560
Dowsby 1670

BILLINGHAM
TIMBERLAND 1563
SOUTH KYME 1647
HECKINGTON 1559
GREAT HALE 1538
HELPRINGHAM 1583
SWATON 1681
HORBLING 1653
BILLINGBOROUGH
SEMPRINGHAM 1558
Aslackby
ASLACKBY
RIPPINGALE 1663
HACCONBY 1538
MORTON 1597
BOURNE 1562
WITHAM ON THE HILL 1670
THURLBY 1560

WASHINGBOROUGH 1564
BRANSTON 1681
NOCTON 1582
DUNSTON 1691
METHERINGHAM 1538
BLANKNEY 1558
SCOPWICK 1605
ASHBY DE LA LAUNDE
DIGBY 1679
DORRINGTON
ANWICK 1573
ROWSTON
RUSKINGTON 1564
EWERBY 1694
HOWELL
EVEDON
LEASINGHAM
QUARRINGTON
NEWTON
WALCOT 1546
KIRKBY LA THORPE
SILK WILLOUGHBY
OSBOURNBY
PICKWORTH 1583
INGHAM
THRECKINGHAM
FOLKINGHAM

LINCOLN
SKELLINGTHORPE 1563
DODDINGTON 1690
EAGLE 1568
THURLBY
BOULTHAM
WADDINGTON 1563
HARMSTON
COLEBY 1561
BOOTHBY GRAFFOE 1790
WELBOURN 1695
LEADENHAM
CAYTHORPE 1663
FULBECK
NORMANTON
CARLTON SCROOP 1561
HOUGH ON THE HILL 1646
SYSTON
BARKSTON
HONINGTON 1560
GREAT GONERBY 1560
LONDONTHORPE 1539
BELTON
SOMERBY
LITTLE PONTON
GREAT PONTON 1735
GRANTHAM 2951
BARROWBY 1538
HARLAXTON 1558
DENTON 1558
SOUTH STOKE 1660
STOKE ROCHFORD
LONG BENNINGTON 1560
FOSTON 1559
SEDGEBROOK

WELBY 1569
ROPSLEY
INGOLDSBY 1566
IRNHAM 1559
CORBY 1653
SWINSTEAD 1692
EDENHAM 1654
CASTLE BYTHAM 1537

WYVILLE
GUNBY St. Nicholas
STAINBY 1560
COLSTERWORTH 1653
NORTH WITHAM 1571
SOUTH WITHAM 989

BRACEBOROUGH
WILSTHORPE
UFFINGTON 1625

PUBLISHED BY THE INSTITUTE OF HERALDIC AND GENEALOGICAL STUDIES
NORTHGATE CANTERBURY ENGLAND

c 1995

THIS ITEM IS NUMBER 21B OF OUR SERIES OF GENEALOGICAL AIDS

A B C D E F G H I J K L M

1 2 3 4 5 6 7 8 9 10

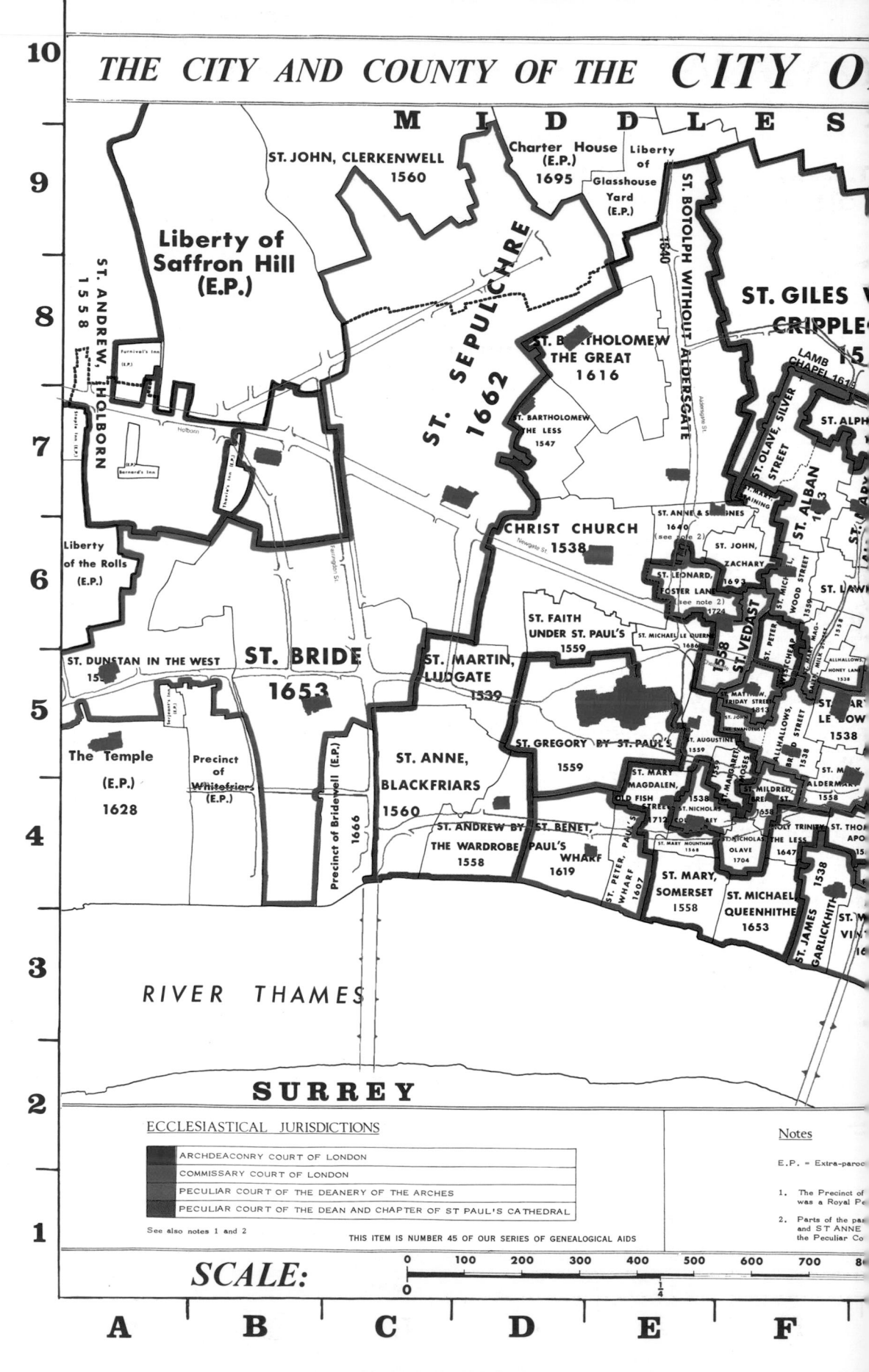

M I D D L E S

9

ST. JOHN, CLERKENWELL
1560

Charter House
(E.P.)
1695

Liberty
of
Glasshouse
Yard
(E.P.)

ST. BOTOLPH WITHOUT ALDERSGATE
1560

ST. GILES W
CRIPPLE
15

8

Liberty of
Saffron Hill
(E.P.)

ST. ANDREW, HOLBORN
1558

Furnival's Inn
(E.P.)

ST. BARTHOLOMEW
THE GREAT
1616

ST. SEPULCHRE
1662

LAMB
CHAPEL 161
ST. ALPH

ST. OLAVE, SILVER STREET

ST. BARTHOLOMEW
THE LESS
1547

7

Holborn

Staple Inn (E.P.)

Barnard's Inn

Thavie's Inn (E.P.)

ST. ALBAN
1 3

ST. MICH

WOOD STREET

ST. LAW

ST. ANNE & S JONES
1640
(see note 2)

ST. JOHN,
ZACHARY

ST. PETER

6

Liberty
of the Rolls
(E.P.)

CHRIST CHURCH
1538

Newgate St.

ST. FAITH
UNDER ST. PAUL'S
1559

ST. MICHAEL LE QUERN
1686

ST. LEONARD,
FOSTER LANE
1693
(see note 2)
1724

ST. VEDAST
1558

ALLHALLOWS
HONEY LANE
1538

5

ST. DUNSTAN IN THE WEST
15

ST. BRIDE
1653

ST. MARTIN,
LUDGATE
1339

ST. GREGORY BY ST. PAUL'S
1559

ST. MATTHEW,
FRIDAY STREET
1813

ST. JOHN
THE EVANGELIST

ST. AUGUSTINE
1559

ALLHALLOWS
BREAD STREET
1538

ST. MA
LE BOW
1538

The Temple
(E.P.)
1628

Precinct
of
Whitefriars
(E.P.)

Precinct of Bridewell (E.P.)
1666

ST. ANNE,
BLACKFRIARS
1560

ST. MARY
MAGDALEN,
OLD FISH
STREET
1712

ST. NICHOLAS
COLE ABBEY

ST. MARGARET
MOSES

ST. MILDRED
BREAD

ST. MARY
ALDERMARY
1558

4

ST. ANDREW BY ST. BENET,
THE WARDROBE PAUL'S
1558

ST. PAUL'S
WHARF
1619

ST. MARY MOUNTHAW

ST. NICHOLAS
OLAVE
1704

ST. NICHOLAS
OLAVE

HOLY TRINITY THE LESS
1647

ST. THO
APO

ST. PETER, PAUL'S
WHARF
1607

ST. MARY,
SOMERSET
1558

ST. MICHAEL
QUEENHITHE
1653

ST. JAMES
GARLICKHITH

ST. M
VIN

3

RIVER THAMES

2

SURREY

ECCLESIASTICAL JURISDICTIONS

ARCHDEACONRY COURT OF LONDON
COMMISSARY COURT OF LONDON
PECULIAR COURT OF THE DEANERY OF THE ARCHES
PECULIAR COURT OF THE DEAN AND CHAPTER OF ST PAUL'S CATHEDRAL

See also notes 1 and 2

THIS ITEM IS NUMBER 45 OF OUR SERIES OF GENEALOGICAL AIDS

Notes

E.P. = Extra-paroc

1. The Precinct of
was a Royal Pe

2. Parts of the par
and ST ANNE
the Peculiar Co

SCALE:

0   100   200   300   400   500   600   700   8

0

1/4

A   B   C   D   E   F

ONDON

WITH DATES OF COMMENCEMENT OF REGISTERS FOR PARISHES FORMED BEFORE 1832

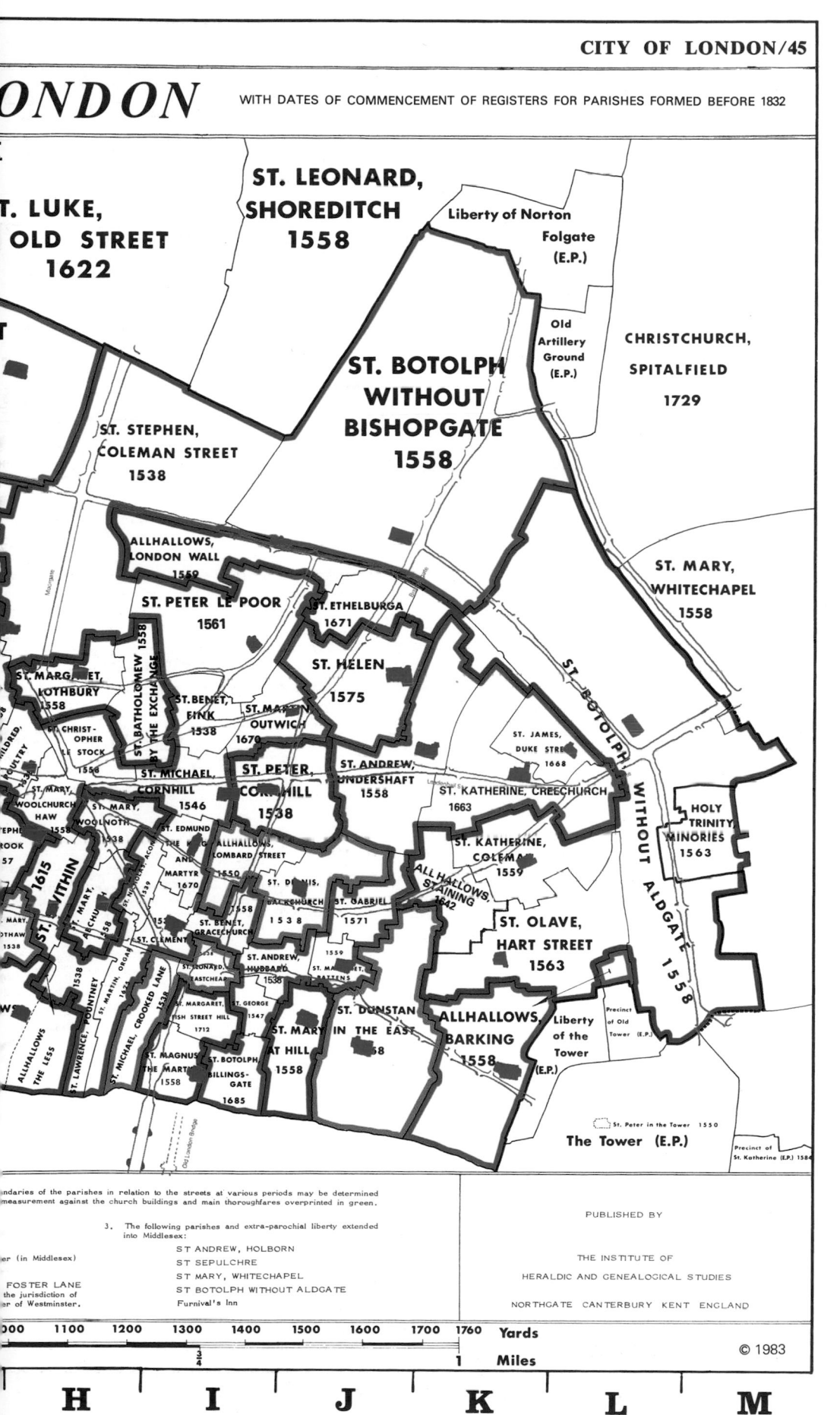

T. LUKE, OLD STREET 1622

ST. LEONARD, SHOREDITCH 1558

Liberty of Norton Folgate (E.P.)

Old Artillery Ground (E.P.)

CHRISTCHURCH, SPITALFIELD 1729

ST. BOTOLPH WITHOUT BISHOPGATE 1558

ST. STEPHEN, COLEMAN STREET 1538

ALLHALLOWS, LONDON WALL 1559

ST. PETER LE POOR 1561

ST. ETHELBURGA 1671

ST. MARY, WHITECHAPEL 1558

ST. HELEN 1575

ST. MARGARET, LOTHBURY 1558

ST. BATHOLOMEW 1558 BY THE EXCHANGE

ST. BENET, FINK 1538

ST. MARTIN OUTWICH 1670

ST. CHRIST-OPHER LE STOCK 1558

ST. JAMES, DUKE STRE 1668

ST. MICHAEL, CORNHILL 1546

ST. PETER, CORNHILL 1538

ST. ANDREW UNDERSHAFT 1558

ST. KATHERINE, CREECHURCH 1663

HOLY TRINITY MINORIES 1563

ST. MARY WOOLCHURCH HAW 1559

ST. MARY WOOLNOTH 1538

ST. EDMUND

THE KING AND MARTYR 1670

ALLHALLOWS, LOMBARD STREET 1550

ST. KATHERINE, COLEMA 1559

ALLHALLOWS STAINING 1642

ST. MARY WITHIN 1615

ST. MARY BOTHAW 1538

ST. DENNIS, BACKCHURCH 1558

ST. GABRIEL 1571

ST. BENET, GRACECHURCH

ST. OLAVE, HART STREET 1563

ST. CLEMENT

ST. LAWRENCE POUNTNEY

ST. MARTIN, ORGAR 1522

ST. MICHAEL, CROOKED LANE

ST. ANDREW, HUBBARD EASTCHEAP 1538

ST. MARGARET, PATTENS 1559

ALLHALLOWS THE LESS

ST. LEONARD, EASTCHEAP

ST. MARGARET, FISH STREET HILL 1712

ST. GEORGE 1547

ST. DUNSTAN IN THE EAST 1558

ALLHALLOWS, BARKING 1558

Precinct of Old Tower (E.P.)

ST. MAGNUS THE MARTYR 1558

ST. BOTOLPH, BILLINGS-GATE 1685

ST. MARY AT HILL 1558

Liberty of the Tower (E.P.)

St. Peter in the Tower 1550

The Tower (E.P.)

Precinct of St. Katherine (E.P.) 1584

ndaries of the parishes in relation to the streets at various periods may be determined
measurement against the church buildings and main thoroughfares overprinted in green.

3. The following parishes and extra-parochial liberty extended into Middlesex:

er (in Middlesex)

ST ANDREW, HOLBORN
ST SEPULCHRE
ST MARY, WHITECHAPEL

FOSTER LANE
the jurisdiction of
or of Westminster.

ST BOTOLPH WITHOUT ALDGATE
Furnival's Inn

PUBLISHED BY

THE INSTITUTE OF

HERALDIC AND GENEALOGICAL STUDIES

NORTHGATE CANTERBURY KENT ENGLAND

000   1100   1200   1300   1400   1500   1600   1700 1760   **Yards**

Miles

© 1983

H   I   J   K   L   M

MIDDLESEX.

The Figures prefixed to the Towns
denote the distance from London.

REFERENCE TO THE HUNDREDS

1 Spelthorne   4 Gore
2 Isleworth   5 Ossulton
3 Elthorne   6 Edmonton

English Miles.

ST PAULS CATHEDRAL. LONDON

Longitude 5′ East

Longitude West 5′ from Greenwich

Eng.d by R. Scott

Published by Arch.d Fullarton & C.o Glasgow

ESSEX

HERTFORDSHIRE

BUCKINGHAMSHIRE

BERKSHIRE

SURREY

KENT

LONDON

WESTMINSTER

SOUTHWARK

Waltham Abbey 12

Barking

Woodford

Woolwich

Greenwich

Watford 15

Rickmansworth 16

Chipping Barnet

Kingston 12

WINDSOR

R. Thames

MIDDLESEX

with date of commencement of registers

KEY

St. Marylebone

St.Marylebone 1668	All Souls, Langham Pl. 1825
Oxford Chapel 1736	Christ Church, Cosway St. 1825
Fitzroy Chapel 1786	St.Mary, Bryanstone Sq. 1825
	Holy Trinity, Marylebone Rd. 1828

St. Pancras

St.Pancras 1660	All Saints, Camden Town Chapel 1824
Percy Chapel 1776	St.Mary the Virgin, 1826
St.John the Baptist, 1804	Somerstown Chapel 1826
Kentish Town Chapel	St Peter, Regent Sq. Chapel 1829

Islington

St.Mary 1557	St.John, Upper Holloway 1829
Holy Trinity,	St.Paul, Canonbury 1830
Cloudsley Sq. 1829	

Clerkenwell

St.James 1561	Pentonville Chapel 1790
St.John the Baptist 1723	St.Mark, Myddleton Sq. 1828

Shoreditch

St.Leonard 1558	St.Leonard's Workhouse 1820
Aske's Hospital	St.John the Baptist, Hoxton 1826
Chapel 1696	St.Mary, Haggerston 1829
	Geffrey's Almshouses Chapel 1794

Hackney

St.John 1545	St.John of Jerusalem 1826
St.Barnabas with	St.Thomas 1827
St.Paul 1824	

ECCLESIASTICAL JURISDICTIONS

ARCHDEACONRY COURT OF MIDDLESEX
ARCHDEACONRY COURT OF LONDON
COMMISSARY COURT OF LONDON
PECULIAR COURT OF THE DEANERY OF CROYDON
PECULIAR COURT OF THE DEAN AND CHAPTER OF ST.PAUL'S CATHEDRAL
ROYAL PECULIAR OF THE DEAN AND CHAPTER OF WESTMINSTER

By the beginning of the eighteenth century, Paddington and much of Westminster had come under the jurisdiction of the Bishop of London or the Archdeacon of M'd'x. St. KATHERINE by the TOWER(Ad) was a single-parish Royal Peculiar

ESSEX

KENT

SURREY

BUCKINGHAMSHIRE

HERTFORDSHIRE

PUBLISHED BY THE INSTITUTE OF HERALDIC AND GENEALOGICAL STUDIES

NORTHGATE, CANTERBURY, KENT CT1 1BA. © 1995

THIS ITEM IS NUMBER 22 OF OUR SERIES OF GENEALOGICAL AIDS

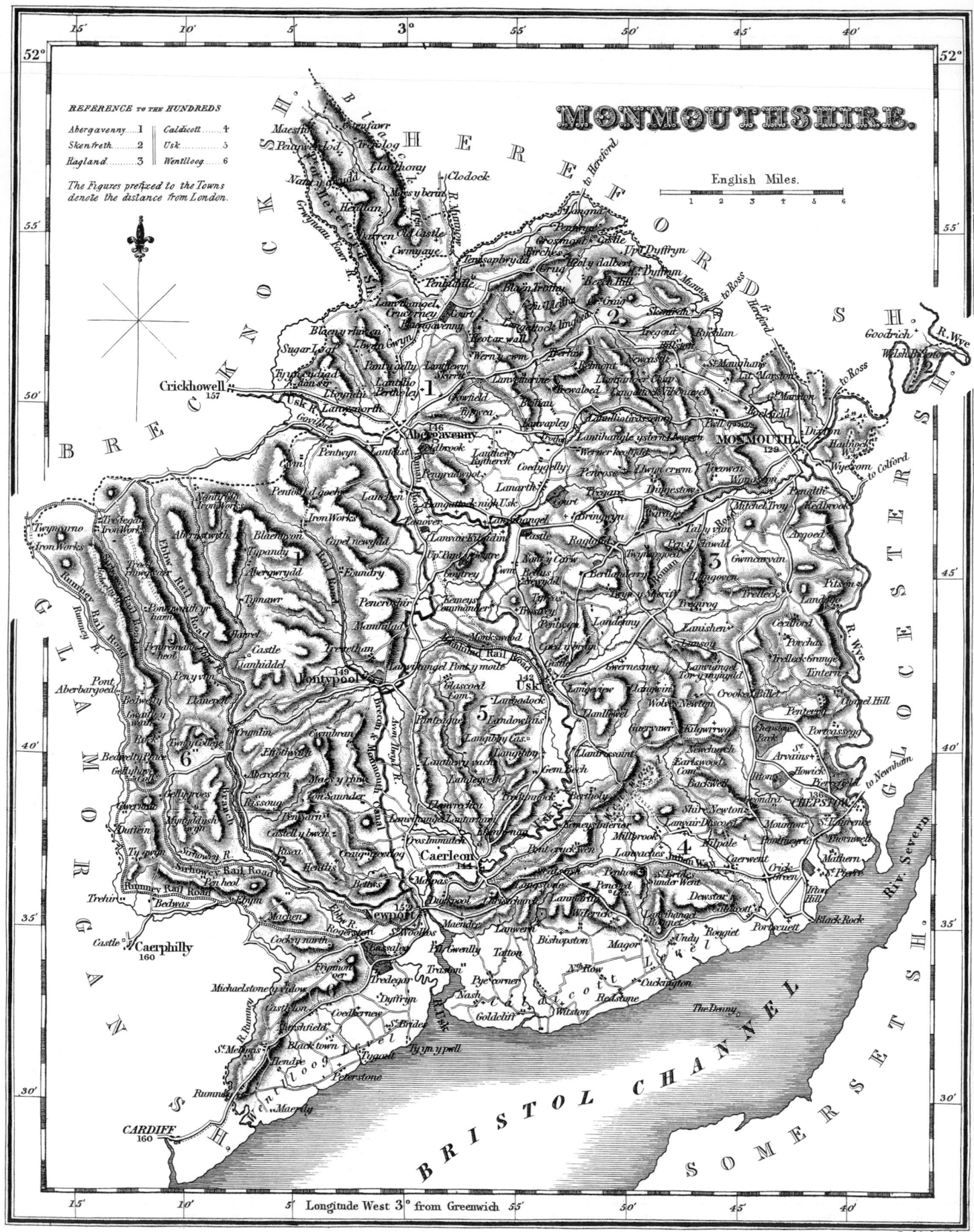

MONMOUTHSHIRE.

REFERENCE TO THE HUNDREDS

Abergavenny 1   Caldicott 4
Skenfreth 2   Usk 5
Ragland 3   Wentlloog 6

The Figures prefixed to the Towns
denote the distance from London.

English Miles.

Engd. by Gray & Son.

Pubd. by Archd. Fullarton & Co. Glasgow.

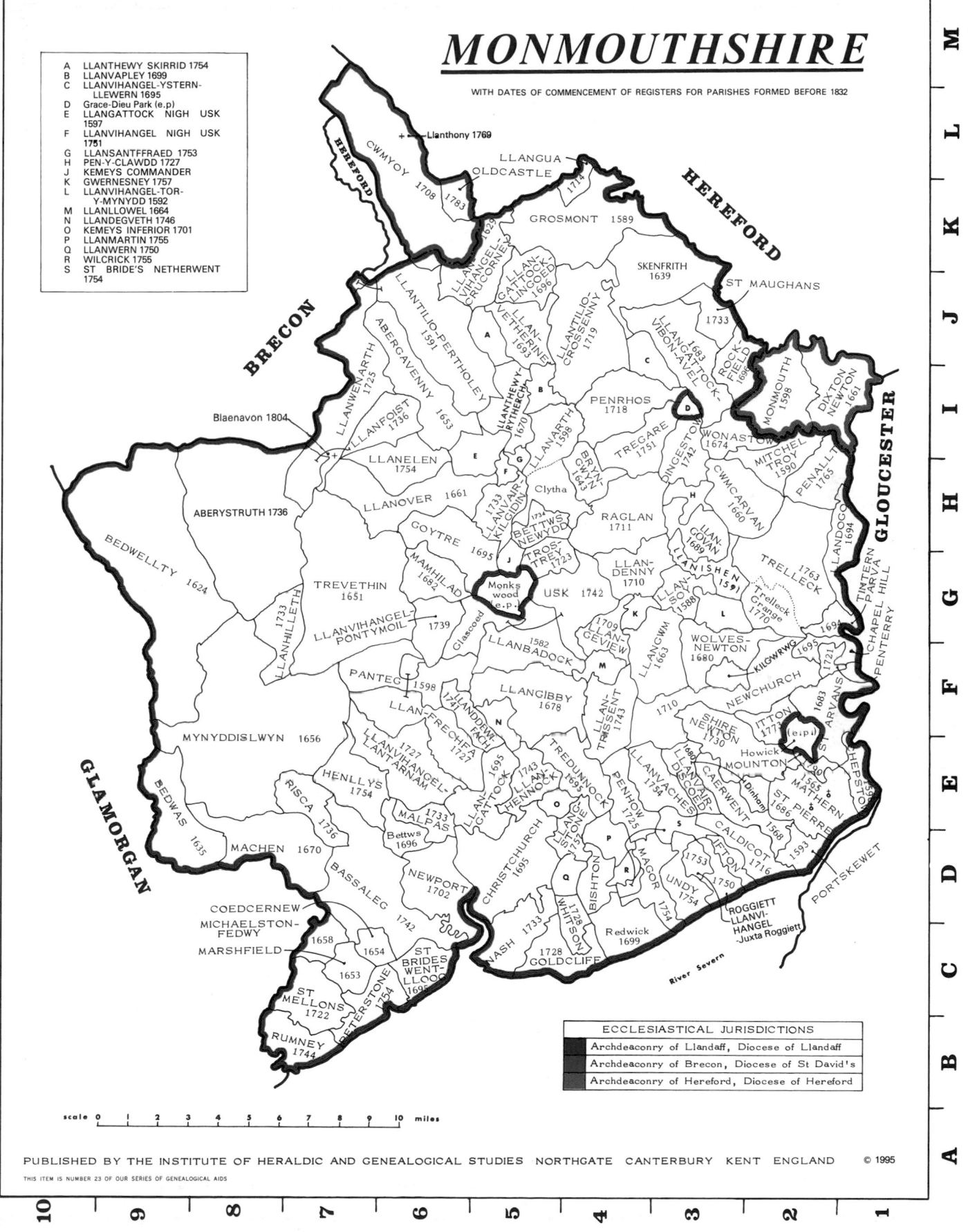

MONMOUTHSHIRE

WITH DATES OF COMMENCEMENT OF REGISTERS FOR PARISHES FORMED BEFORE 1832

A LLANTHEWY SKIRRID 1754
B LLANVAPLEY 1699
C LLANVIHANGEL-YSTERN-
     LLEWERN 1695
D Grace-Dieu Park (e.p)
E LLANGATTOCK NIGH USK
     1597
F LLANVIHANGEL NIGH USK
     1751
G LLANSANTFFRAED 1753
H PEN-Y-CLAWDD 1727
J KEMEYS COMMANDER
K GWERNESNEY 1757
L LLANVIHANGEL-TOR-
     Y-MYNYDD 1592
M LLANLLOWEL 1664
N LLANDEGVETH 1746
O KEMEYS INFERIOR 1701
P LLANMARTIN 1755
Q LLANWERN 1750
R WILCRICK 1755
S ST BRIDE'S NETHERWENT
     1754

HEREFORD
BRECON
GLOUCESTER
GLAMORGAN

Llanthony 1769
CWMYOY 1708 1783
LLANGUA
OLDCASTLE 1714
GROSMONT 1589
LLANGEL YSTERN 1629
LLAN-I-GATTOCK-LINGOED 1696
SKENFRITH 1639
ST MAUGHANS 1733
LLAN-VETHERINE 1693
LLANTILIO-PERTHOLEY 1591
LLANTILIO-CROSSENNY 1719
LLANGATTOCK-VIBON-AVEL 1683 1695
ABERGAVENNY 1653
LLANWENARTH 1725
LLANTHEWY-RYTHERCH 1670
LLANARTH 1598
PENRHOS 1718
C
MONMOUTH 1598
DIXTON NEWTON 1661
ROCK-FIELD 1695
Blaenavon 1804
LLANFOIST 1736
E
F
G
TREGARE 1751
DINGESTOW 1742
WONASTOW 1674
MITCHEL TROY 1590
PENALLT 1765
LANDOGO 1694
LLANELEN 1754
BRYN-GWYN 1643
Clytha
B
CWMCARVAN 1660
LLANOVER 1661
1733 LLANVAIR-KILGIDDIN
1734 BETTWS NEWYDD
RAGLAN 1711
LLAN-GOVEN 1689
TRELLECK 1763
TINTERN PARVA
ABERYSTRUTH 1736
GOYTRE 1695
J
TROS-TREY 1723
LLAN-DENNY 1710
LLAN-ISHEN 1591
Trelleck Grange 1770
CHAPEL HILL
PENTERRY HILL
BEDWELLTY 1624
MAMHILAD 1682
Monks wood e.p.
USK 1742
LLAN-SON 1588
1694
TREVETHIN 1651
Glascoed
LLANBADOCK 1582
1709 LLAN-GEVIEW
K
LLANGWM 1663
WOLVES-NEWTON 1680
KILGWRWG 1695 1721
NEWCHURCH
LLANVIHANGEL-PONTYMOIL
1739
PANTEG 1598
LLANDDEWI FACH 1741
M
LLANGIBBY 1678
LLAN-TRISSENT 1743
1710
SHIRE NEWTON 1730
ITTON 1771 (e.p)
CAERWENT
MYNYDDISLWYN 1656
LLAN-FRECHFA 1727
LLANVIHANGEL-LANTARNAM 1727
N
TREDUNNOCK 1695
Howick 1590
MOUNTON 1565
LLANVACHES 1754
Dinham
ST PIERRE 1686
MATHERN
CHEPSTOW
HENLLYS 1754
RISCA 1736
LLAN-HENNOCK 1695
O
PENHOW 1725
LLAN-GATTOCK 1695
MALPAS 1733
Bettws 1696
S
CALDICOT 1716
CLIFTON 1716
1568
1593
PORTSKEWET
MACHEN 1670
BASSALEG 1742
CHRISTCHURCH 1695
LLANMARTIN 1757
BISHTON
P
UNDY 1754
1753
ROGGIETT 1750
COEDCERNEW
NEWPORT 1702
Q
R
MAGOR
LLANVI-HANGEL -Juxta Roggiett
MICHAELSTON-FEDWY 1658
MARSHFIELD 1654
1653
NASH 1733
WHITSON 1728
Redwick 1699
River Severn
ST BRIDES WENT-LLOOG 1695
PETERSTONE 1754
GOLDCLIFE 1728
ST MELLONS 1722
RUMNEY 1744

ECCLESIASTICAL JURISDICTIONS
Archdeaconry of Llandaff, Diocese of Llandaff
Archdeaconry of Brecon, Diocese of St David's
Archdeaconry of Hereford, Diocese of Hereford

scale 0 1 2 3 4 5 6 7 8 9 10 miles

PUBLISHED BY THE INSTITUTE OF HERALDIC AND GENEALOGICAL STUDIES NORTHGATE CANTERBURY KENT ENGLAND   © 1995

THIS ITEM IS NUMBER 23 OF OUR SERIES OF GENEALOGICAL AIDS

10 9 8 7 6 5 4 3 2 1

M L K J I H G F E D C B A

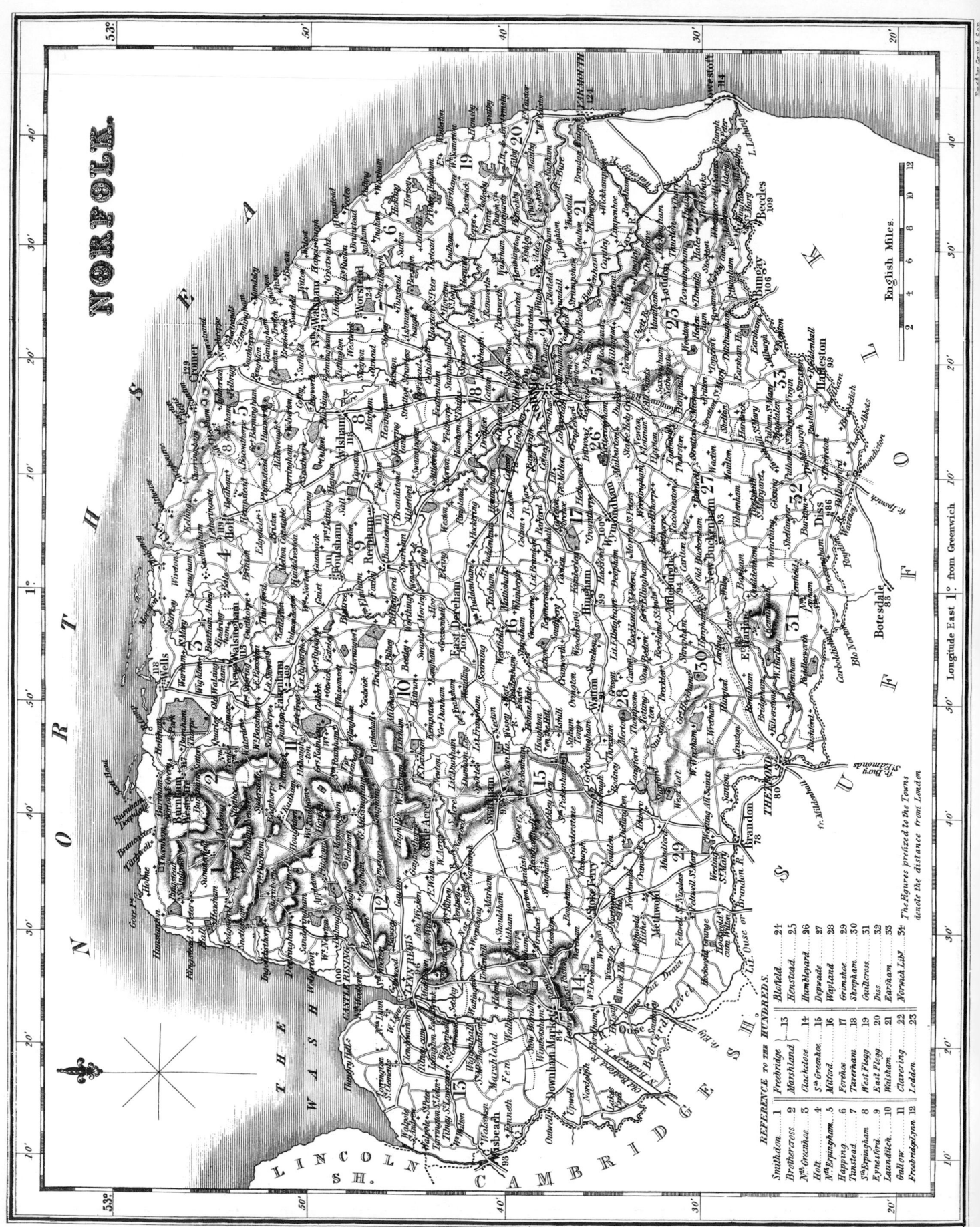

NORFOLK

NORTH SEA

THE WASH

LINCOLN SH.

CAMBRIDGESH.

SUFFOLK

English Miles.

Longitude East 1° from Greenwich

REFERENCE to the HUNDREDS.

Smithdon	1	Freebridge	13	Blofield	24
Brothercross	2	Marshland	14	Henstead	25
Nth. Greenhoe	3	Clackclose	14	Humbleyard	26
Holt	4	Sth. Greenhoe	16	Depwade	27
Nth. Erpingham	5	Mitford	16	Wayland	28
Happing	6	Forehoe	17	Grimshoe	29
Tunstead	7	Taverham	18	Shropham	30
Sth. Erpingham	8	East Flegg	19	Guiltcross	31
Eynesford	9	West Flegg	20	Diss	32
Launditch	10	Walsham	21	Earsham	33
Gallow	11	Clavering	22	Norwich Lib.	34
Freebridge-Lynn	12	Loddon	23		

The Figures prefixed to the Towns
denote the distance from London.

NORFOLK

WITH DATES OF COMMENCEMENT OF REGISTERS FOR PARISHES FORMED BEFORE 1832

ECCLESIASTICAL JURISDICTIONS

- Archdeaconry of Norwich
- Archdeaconry of Norfolk
- Peculiars of the Dean and Chapter of Norwich
- Other Peculiars

Peculiar Jurisdictions

- Peculiar of the Rector of Castle Rising — Castle Rising, North Wootton, Roydon All Saints and South Wootton
- Peculiar of the Bishop of Ely — Emneth
- Peculiar of the Rector of Great Cressingham — Thorpe next Norwich

NORWICH

St Andrew 1558
St Augustine 1558
St Benedict 1562
St Clement 1538
St Edmund 1550
St Etheldred 1666
St Giles 1538
St George at Colegate 1571
St George of Tombland 1538
St Gregory 1558
St James with Pockthorpe 1556
St John de Sepulchre 1632
St John of Timberhill 1558
St John of Timberhill 1559
St Julian 1559
St Lawrence 1558
St Margaret 1538
St Martin at Oak 1560
St Martin at Palace 1538
St Mary at Coslany 1558
St Mary in the Marsh 1663
St Michael at Coslany 1558
St Michael at Plea 1538
St Michael at Thorn 1785
St Paul 1997
St Peter of Mancroft 1538
St Peter per Mountergate 1538
St Peter Southgate 1558
St Saviour 1555
St Simon and Jude 1539
St Stephen 1538
St Swithin 1700
All Saints 1573

All the above parishes were in the jurisdiction of the Archdeacon of Norwich except St Clement, St Mary in the Marsh, St Paul, which were part of the Peculiar of the Dean and Chapter.

PUBLISHED BY THE INSTITUTE OF HERALDIC AND GENEALOGICAL STUDIES
NORTHGATE, CANTERBURY, KENT   © 1995

THIS ITEM IS NUMBER 24 OF OUR SERIES OF GENEALOGICAL AIDS

LINCOLN

CAMBRIDGE

SUFFOLK

scale 0 1 2 3 4 5 6 7 8 9 10 miles

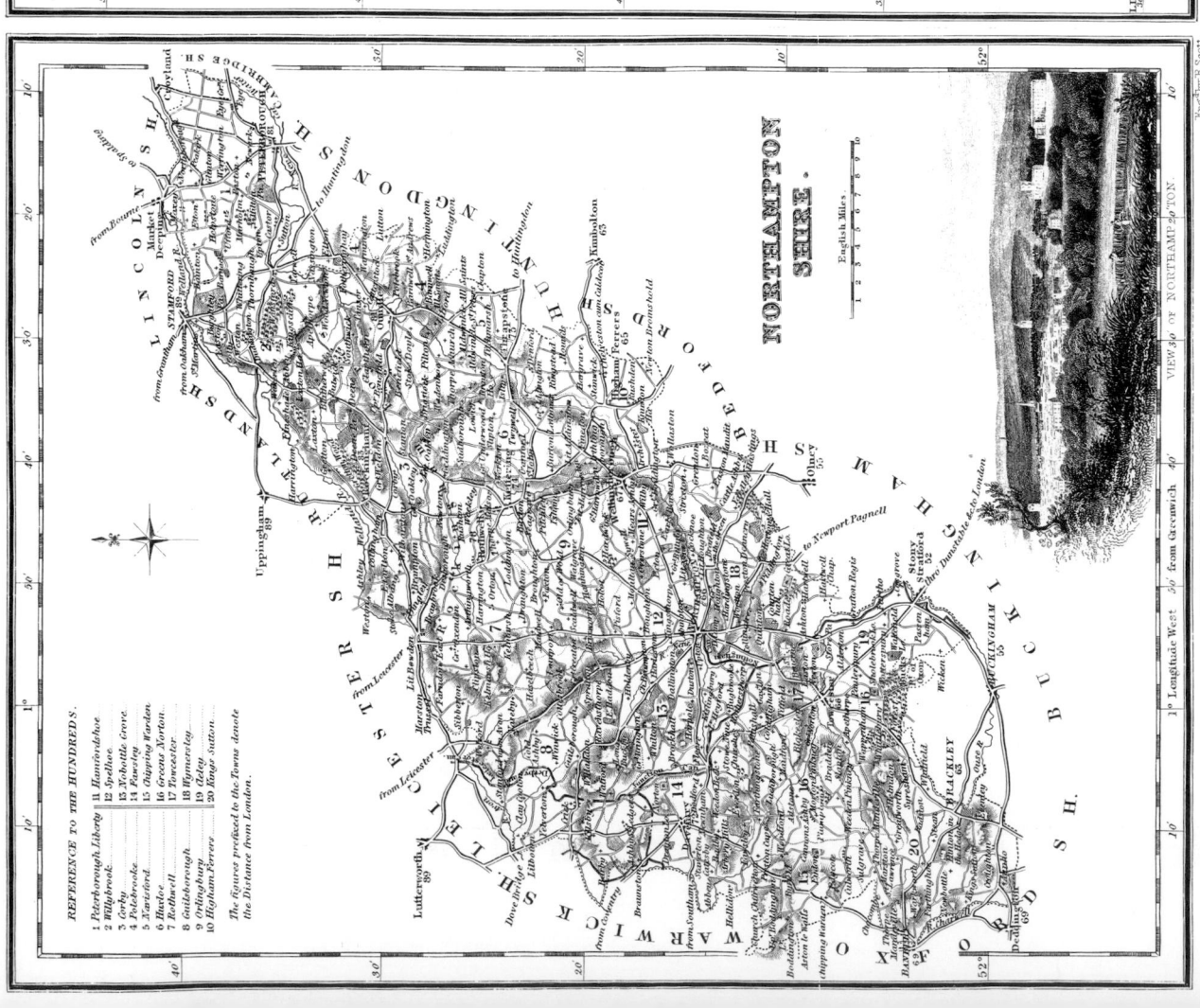

RUTLAND SHIRE

Eng.d by R. Scott

REFERENCE TO THE HUNDREDS.
1 Oakham Soke   3 East
2 Martinsley   4 Wrandike
                  5 Alstoe

The Figures prefixed to the Towns
denote the Distance from London.

English Miles.

Longitude West 30' from Greenwich

NORTHAMPTON SHIRE.

Eng.d by R. Scott

REFERENCE TO THE HUNDREDS.
1 Peterborough Liberty   11 Hamfordshoe
2 Willybrook   12 Spelhoe
3 Corby   13 Nobottle Grove
4 Polebrooke   14 Fawsley
5 Navisford   15 Chipping Warden
6 Huxloe   16 Greens Norton
7 Rothwell   17 Towcester
8 Guilsborough   18 Wymersley
9 Orlingbury   19 Cleley
10 Higham Ferrers   20 Kings Sutton

The figures prefixed to the Towns denote
the Distance from London.

English Miles.

VIEW OF NORTHAMPTON

Published by Archd. Fullarton & Co. Glasgow

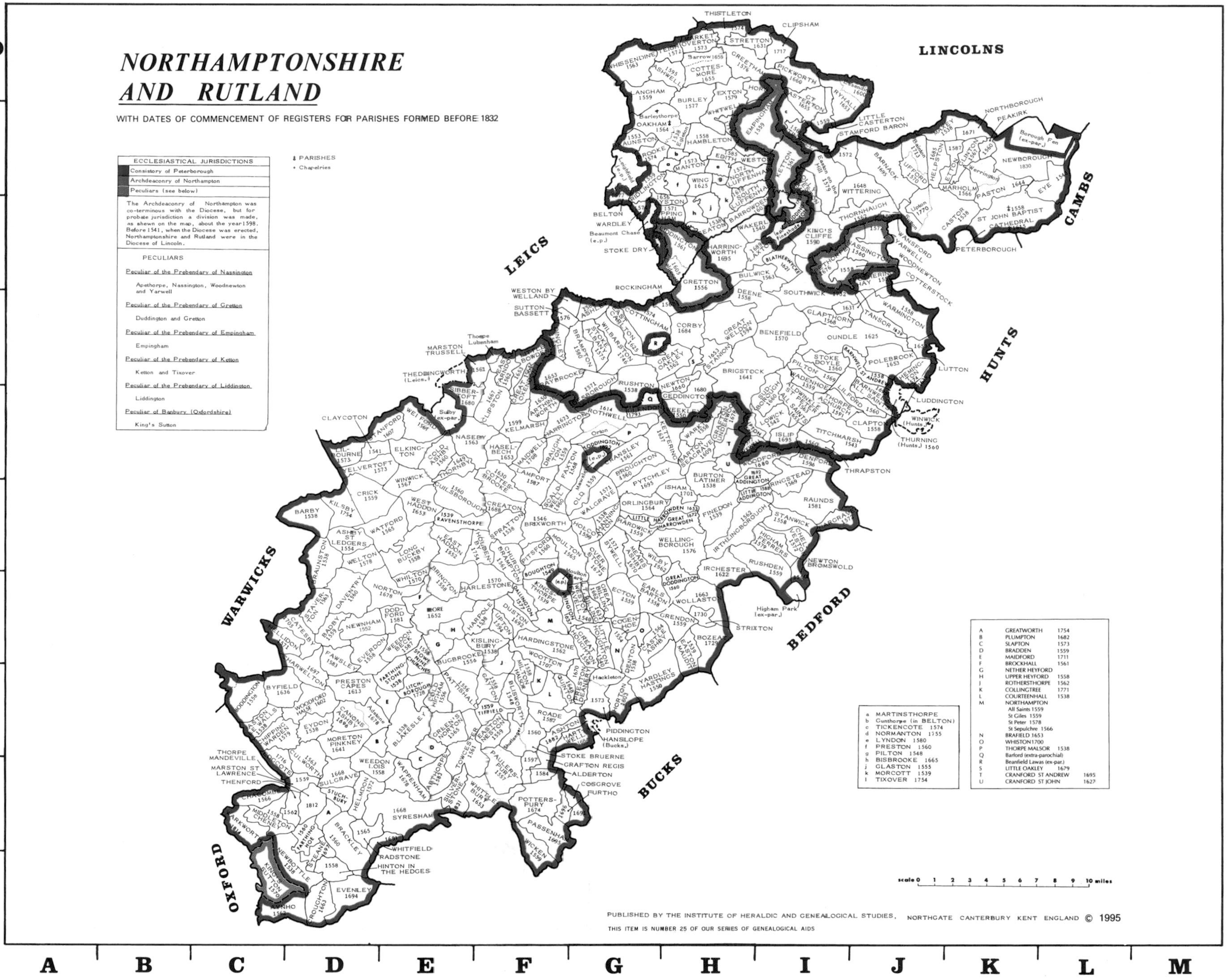

NORTHAMPTONSHIRE AND RUTLAND

WITH DATES OF COMMENCEMENT OF REGISTERS FOR PARISHES FORMED BEFORE 1832

§ PARISHES
• Chapelries

ECCLESIASTICAL JURISDICTIONS

Consistory of Peterborough.
Archdeaconry of Northampton.
Peculiars (see below)

The Archdeaconry of Northampton was co-terminous with the Diocese, but for probate jurisdiction a division was made, as shown on the map, about the year 1598. Before 1541, when the Diocese was erected, Northamptonshire and Rutland were in the Diocese of Lincoln.

PECULIARS

Peculiar of the Prebendary of Nassington.

Aenthorpe, Nassington, Woodnewton and Yarwell.

Peculiar of the Prebendary of Gretton.

Duddington and Gretton.

Peculiar of the Prebendary of Empingham.

Empingham.

Peculiar of the Prebendary of Ketton.

Ketton and Tixover.

Peculiar of the Prebendary of Liddington.

Liddington.

Peculiar of the Prebendary of Banbury (Oxfordshire).

King's Sutton.

A	GREATWORTH	1734
B	PLUMPTON	1662
C	SLAPTON	1573
D	BRADDEN	1559
E	MAIDFORD	1711
F	BROCKHALL	1561
G	NETHER HEYFORD	1558
H	UPPER HEYFORD	1562
I	ROTHERSTHORPE	1771
J	COLLINGTREE	1538
K	COURTEENHALL	
L	NORTHAMPTON	
	All Saints	1559
	St Giles	1559
M	St Peter	1578
N	St Sepulchre	1566
O	THORPE MALSOR	1538
P	WHISTON	1700
Q	Barford (extra-parochial)	1653
R	Beanfield Lawn (ex-par.)	1679
S	LITTLE OAKLEY	1695
T	CRANFORD ST ANDREW	1627
U	CRANFORD ST JOHN	

a	MARTINSTHORPE	
b	Gunthorpe (in BELTON)	1574
c	TICKENCOTE	1574
d	NORMANTON	1135
e	LYNDON	1580
f	PRESTON	1560
g	PILTON	1548
h	BISBROOKE	1665
i	GLASTON	1555
j	MORCOTT	1559
k	TIXOVER	1754

scale 0 1 2 3 4 5 6 7 8 9 10 miles

LINCOLNS

CAMBS

HUNTS

BEDFORD

BUCKS

OXFORD

WARWICKS

LEICS

PUBLISHED BY THE INSTITUTE OF HERALDIC AND GENEALOGICAL STUDIES, NORTHGATE CANTERBURY KENT ENGLAND © 1995

THIS ITEM IS NUMBER 25 OF OUR SERIES OF GENEALOGICAL AIDS

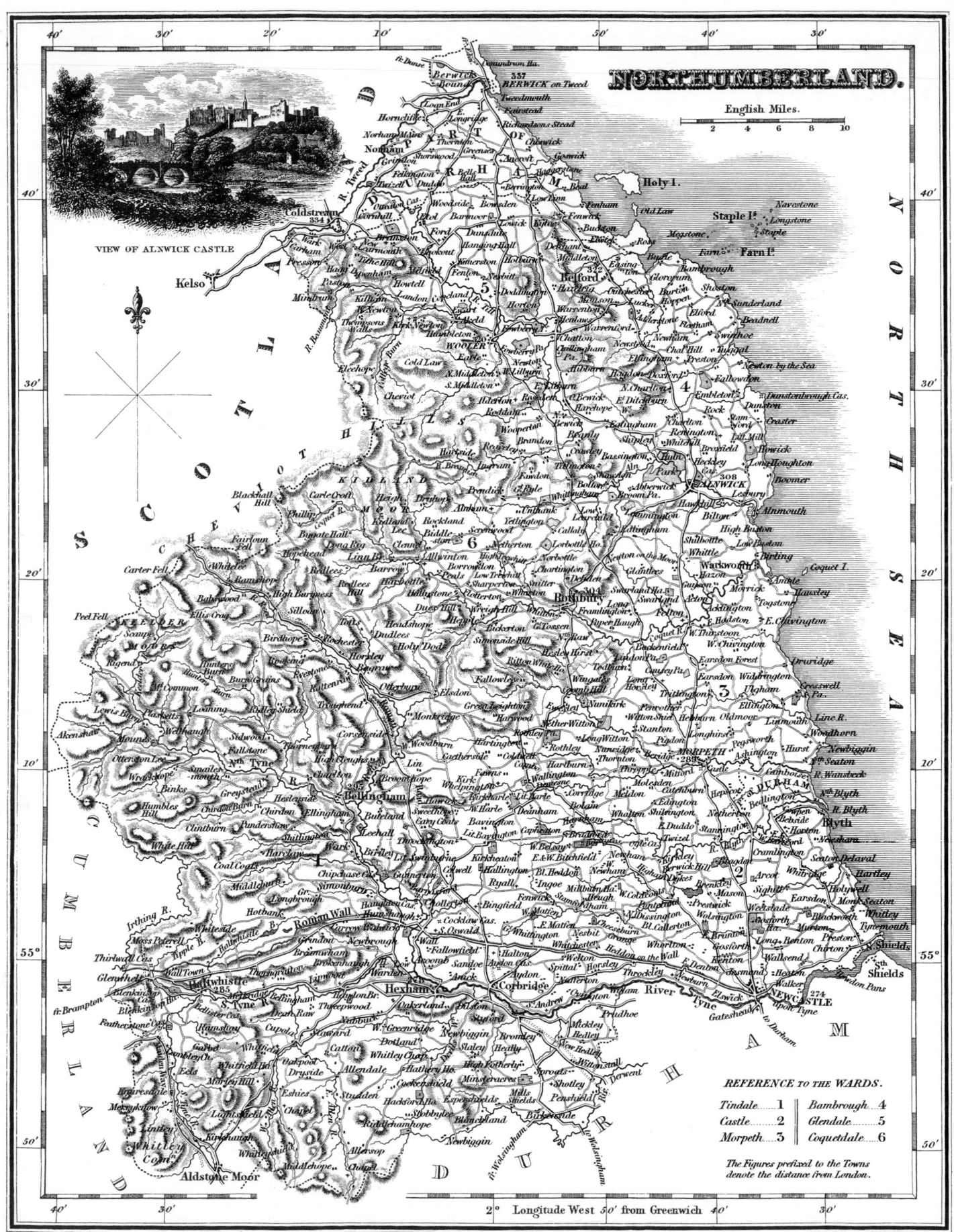

NORTHUMBERLAND.

VIEW OF ALNWICK CASTLE

REFERENCE TO THE WARDS.

Tindale	1	Bambrough	4
Castle	2	Glendale	5
Morpeth	3	Coquetdale	6

The Figures prefixed to the Towns denote the distance from London.

Longitude West from Greenwich

Pubᵈ by Archᵈ Fullarton & Cᵒ Glasgow.

Engᵈ on steel by Gray & Son.

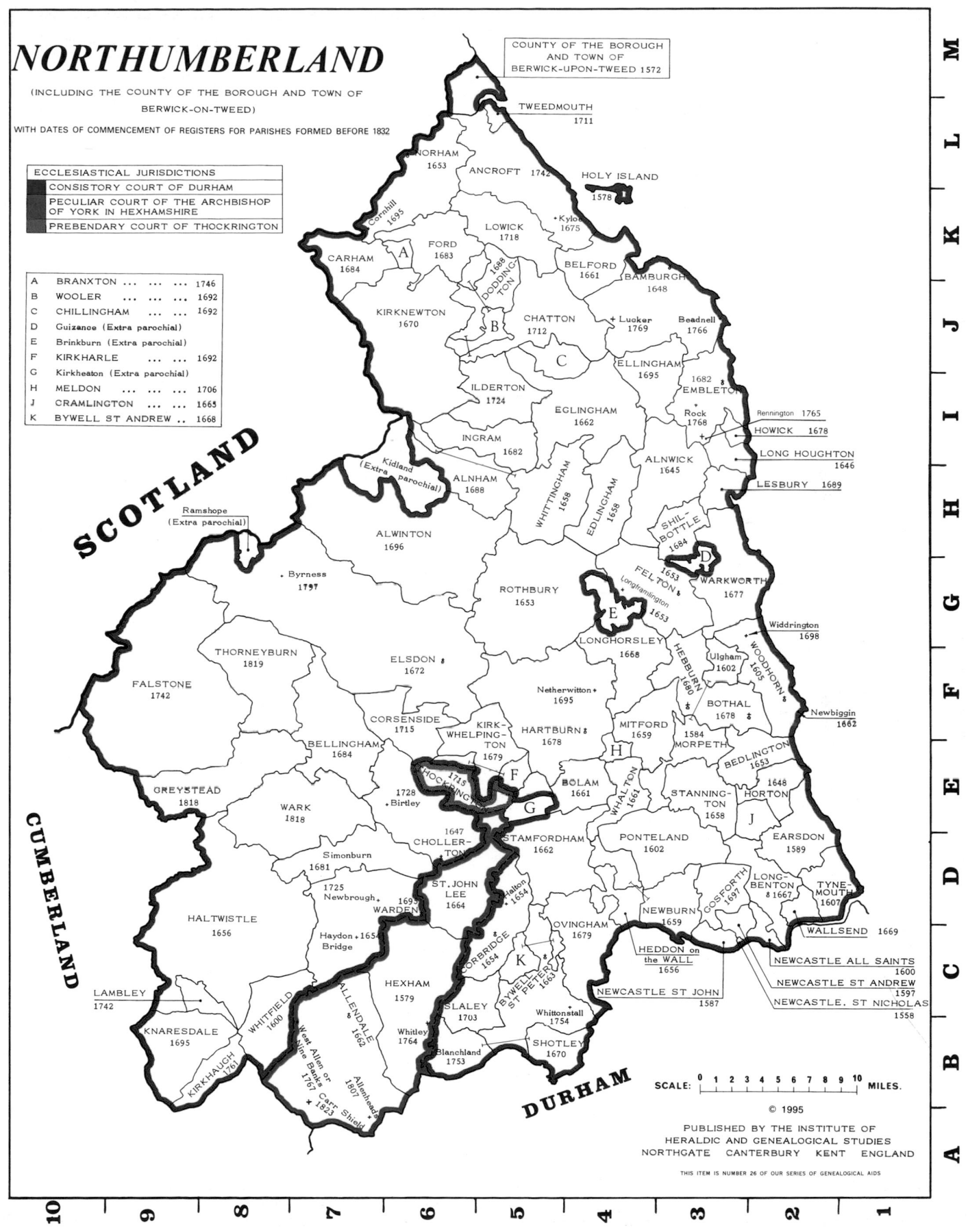

NORTHUMBERLAND

(INCLUDING THE COUNTY OF THE BOROUGH AND TOWN OF
BERWICK-ON-TWEED)

WITH DATES OF COMMENCEMENT OF REGISTERS FOR PARISHES FORMED BEFORE 1832

ECCLESIASTICAL JURISDICTIONS
CONSISTORY COURT OF DURHAM
PECULIAR COURT OF THE ARCHBISHOP
OF YORK IN HEXHAMSHIRE
PREBENDARY COURT OF THOCKRINGTON

A	BRANXTON	1746
B	WOOLER	1692
C	CHILLINGHAM	1692
D	Guizance (Extra parochial)	
E	Brinkburn (Extra parochial)	
F	KIRKHARLE	1692
G	Kirkheaton (Extra parochial)	
H	MELDON	1706
J	CRAMLINGTON	1665
K	BYWELL ST ANDREW ..	1668

COUNTY OF THE BOROUGH
AND TOWN OF
BERWICK-UPON-TWEED 1572

TWEEDMOUTH 1711

NORHAM 1653

ANCROFT 1742

HOLY ISLAND 1578

Cornhill 1695

+ Kyloe 1675

CARHAM 1684

FORD 1683

LOWICK 1718

BELFORD 1661

BAMBURGH 1648

DODDING-TON 1688

KIRKNEWTON 1670

CHATTON 1712

+ Lucker 1769

Beadnell 1766

ELLINGHAM 1695

EMBLETON 1682

ILDERTON 1724

EGLINGHAM 1662

Rock 1768

Rennington 1765

HOWICK 1678

LONG HOUGHTON 1646

INGRAM 1682

WHITTINGHAM 1658

ALNWICK 1645

LESBURY 1689

Kidland (Extra parochial)

ALNHAM 1688

EDLINGHAM 1658

SHIL-BOTTLE 1684

SCOTLAND

Ramshope (Extra parochial)

ALWINTON 1696

FEL-TON 1653

WARKWORTH 1677

+ Byrness 1797

ROTHBURY 1653

Longframlington 1653

WIDDRINGTON 1698

THORNEYBURN 1819

ELSDON 1672

LONGHORSLEY 1668

HEBBURN 1680

Ulgham 1602

WOODHORN 1605

FALSTONE 1742

Netherwitton 1695

MITFORD 1659

BOTHAL 1678

Newbiggin 1662

CORSENSIDE 1715

KIRK-WHELPING-TON 1679

HARTBURN 1678

MORPETH 1584

BELLINGHAM 1684

HOCKRINGTON 1713

BOLAM 1661

BEDLINGTON 1653

GREYSTEAD 1818

1728 + Birtley

STANNING-TON 1658

HORTON 1648

CUMBERLAND

WARK 1818

CHOLLER-TON 1647

STAMFORDHAM 1662

PONTELAND 1602

EARSDON 1589

Simonburn 1681

ST. JOHN LEE 1664

Halton 1654

GOSFORTH 1697

LONG-BENTON 1667

TYNE-MOUTH 1607

1725 Newbrough

1695 WARDEN

OVINGHAM 1679

NEWBURN 1659

WALLSEND 1669

HALTWISTLE 1656

Haydon 1654 Bridge

CORBRIDGE 1654

BYWELL ST PETER 1663

HEDDON on the WALL 1656

NEWCASTLE ALL SAINTS 1600

LAMBLEY 1742

WHITFIELD 1600

ALLENDALE 1662

HEXHAM 1579

SLALEY 1703

Whittonstall 1754

NEWCASTLE ST JOHN 1587

NEWCASTLE ST ANDREW 1597

NEWCASTLE. ST NICHOLAS 1558

KNARESDALE 1695

West Allen or Nine Banks 1761

Cerr Shield 1823

Whitley 1764

Blanchland 1753

SHOTLEY 1670

KIRKHAUGH 1761

Allenheads 1807

DURHAM

SCALE: 0 1 2 3 4 5 6 7 8 9 10 MILES.

© 1995

PUBLISHED BY THE INSTITUTE OF
HERALDIC AND GENEALOGICAL STUDIES
NORTHGATE CANTERBURY KENT ENGLAND

THIS ITEM IS NUMBER 26 OF OUR SERIES OF GENEALOGICAL AIDS

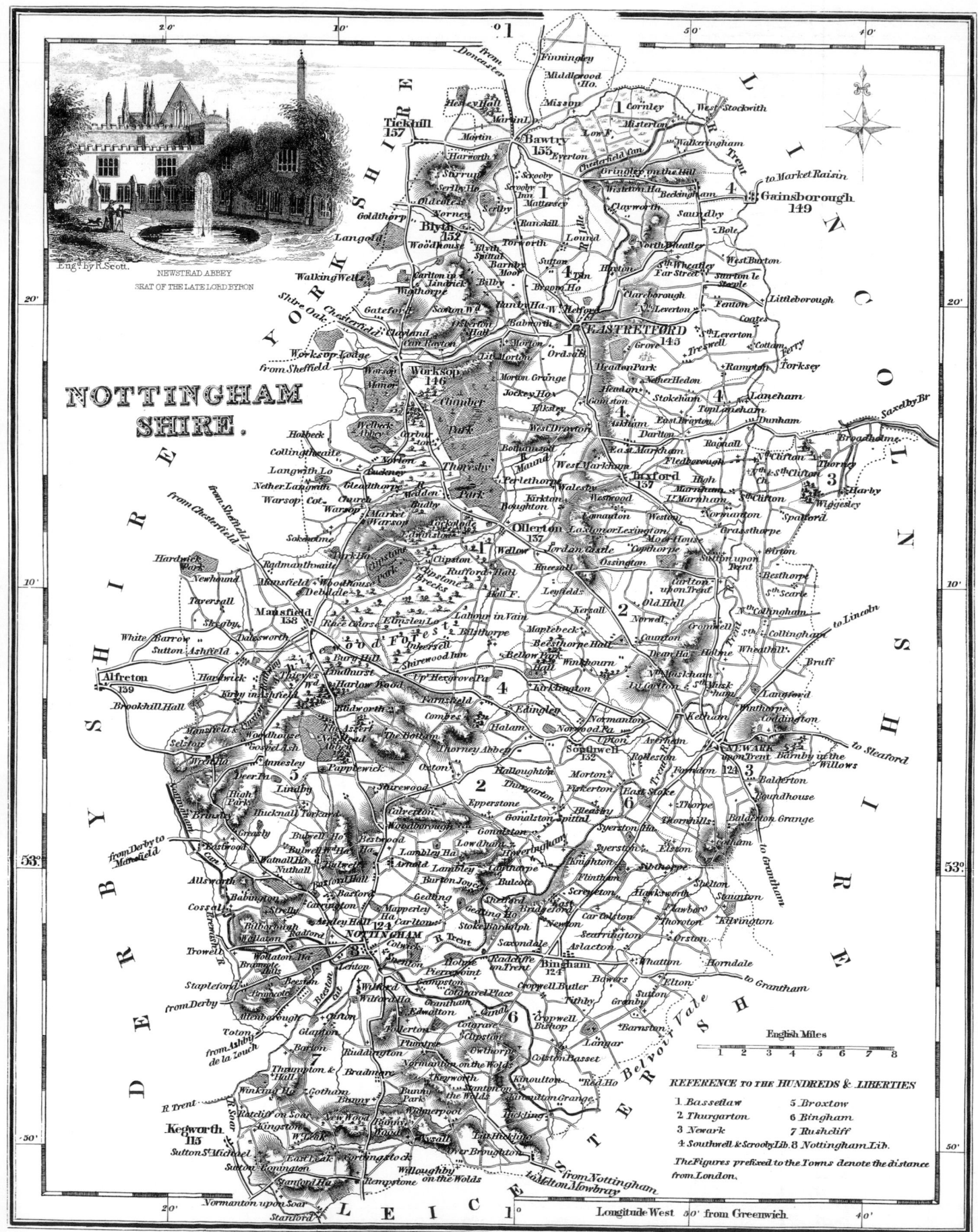

NOTTINGHAM SHIRE.

Eng.d by R.Scott.

NEWSTEAD ABBEY
SEAT OF THE LATE LORD BYRON

English Miles
1 2 3 4 5 6 7 8

REFERENCE TO THE HUNDREDS & LIBERTIES
1 Bassetlaw   5 Broxtow
2 Thurgarton   6 Bingham
3 Newark   7 Rushcliff
4 Southwell & Scrooby Lib. 8 Nottingham Lib.

The Figures prefixed to the Towns denote the distance
from London.

Longitude West 50' from Greenwich.

Published by Arch.d Fullarton & Co Glasgow

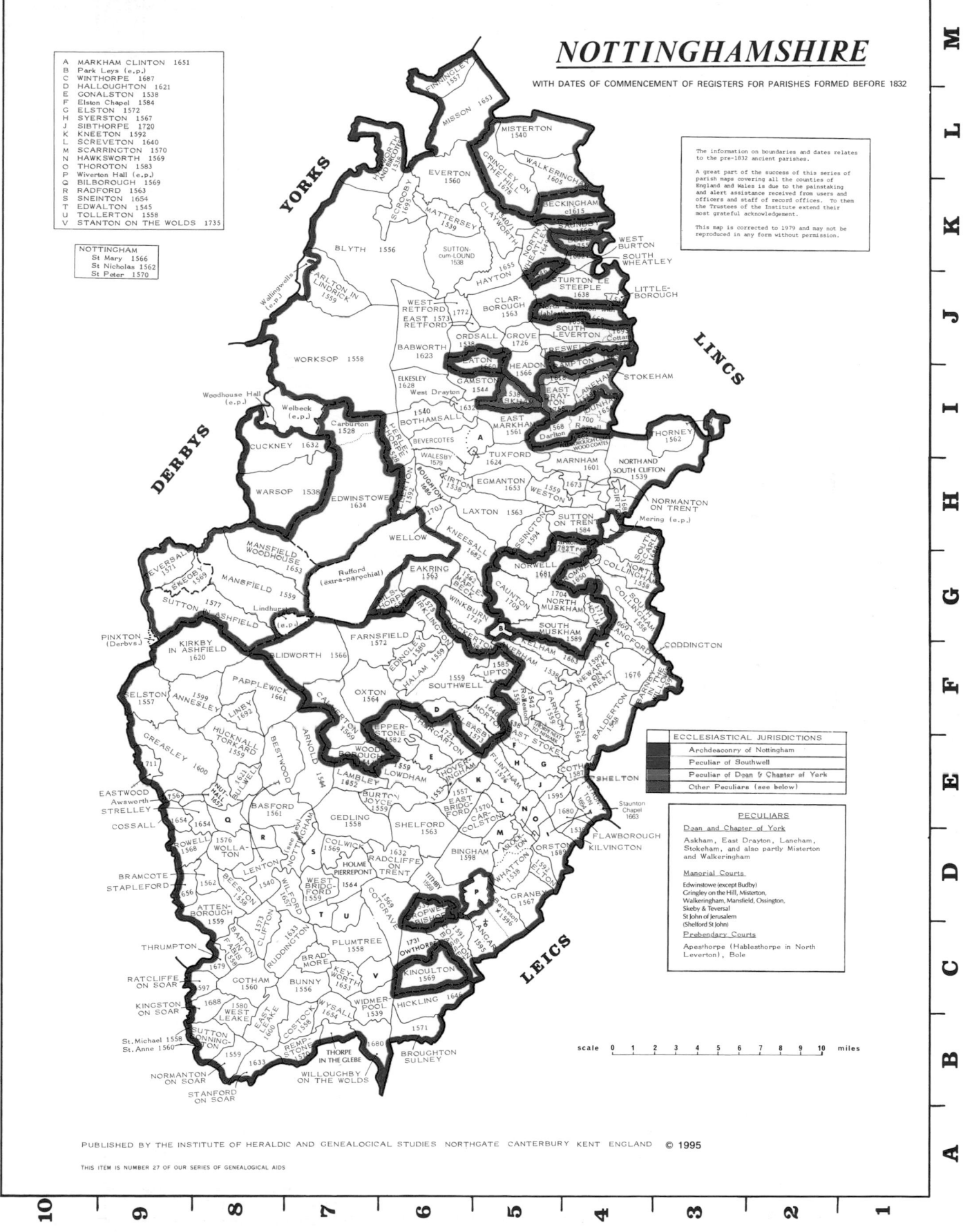

NOTTINGHAMSHIRE

WITH DATES OF COMMENCEMENT OF REGISTERS FOR PARISHES FORMED BEFORE 1832

A MARKHAM CLINTON 1651
B Park Leys (e.p.)
C WINTHORPE 1687
D HALLOUGHTON 1621
E GONALSTON 1538
F Elston Chapel 1584
G ELSTON 1572
H SYERSTON 1567
J SIBTHORPE 1720
K KNEETON 1592
L SCREVETON 1640
M SCARRINGTON 1570
N HAWKSWORTH 1569
O THOROTON 1583
P Wiverton Hall (e.p.)
Q BILBOROUGH 1569
R RADFORD 1563
S SNEINTON 1654
T EDWALTON 1545
U TOLLERTON 1558
V STANTON ON THE WOLDS 1735

NOTTINGHAM
St Mary 1566
St Nicholas 1562
St Peter 1570

The information on boundaries and dates relates
to the pre-1832 ancient parishes.

A great part of the success of this series of
parish maps covering all the counties of
England and Wales is due to the painstaking
and alert assistance received from users and
officers and staff of record offices. To them
the Trustees of the Institute extend their
most grateful acknowledgement.

This map is corrected to 1979 and may not be
reproduced in any form without permission.

ECCLESIASTICAL JURISDICTIONS

Archdeaconry of Nottingham

Peculiar of Southwell

Peculiar of Dean & Chapter of York

Other Peculiars (see below)

PECULIARS

Dean and Chapter of York

Askham, East Drayton, Laneham,
Stokeham, and also partly Misterton
and Walkeringham

Manorial Courts

Edwinstowe (except Budby)
Gringley on the Hill, Misterton,
Walkeringham, Mansfield, Ossington,
Skeby & Teversal
St John of Jerusalem
(Shelford St John)

Prebendary Courts

Apesthorpe (Hablesthorpe in North
Leverton), Bole

scale 0 1 2 3 4 5 6 7 8 9 10 miles

PUBLISHED BY THE INSTITUTE OF HERALDIC AND GENEALOGICAL STUDIES NORTHGATE CANTERBURY KENT ENGLAND © 1995

THIS ITEM IS NUMBER 27 OF OUR SERIES OF GENEALOGICAL AIDS

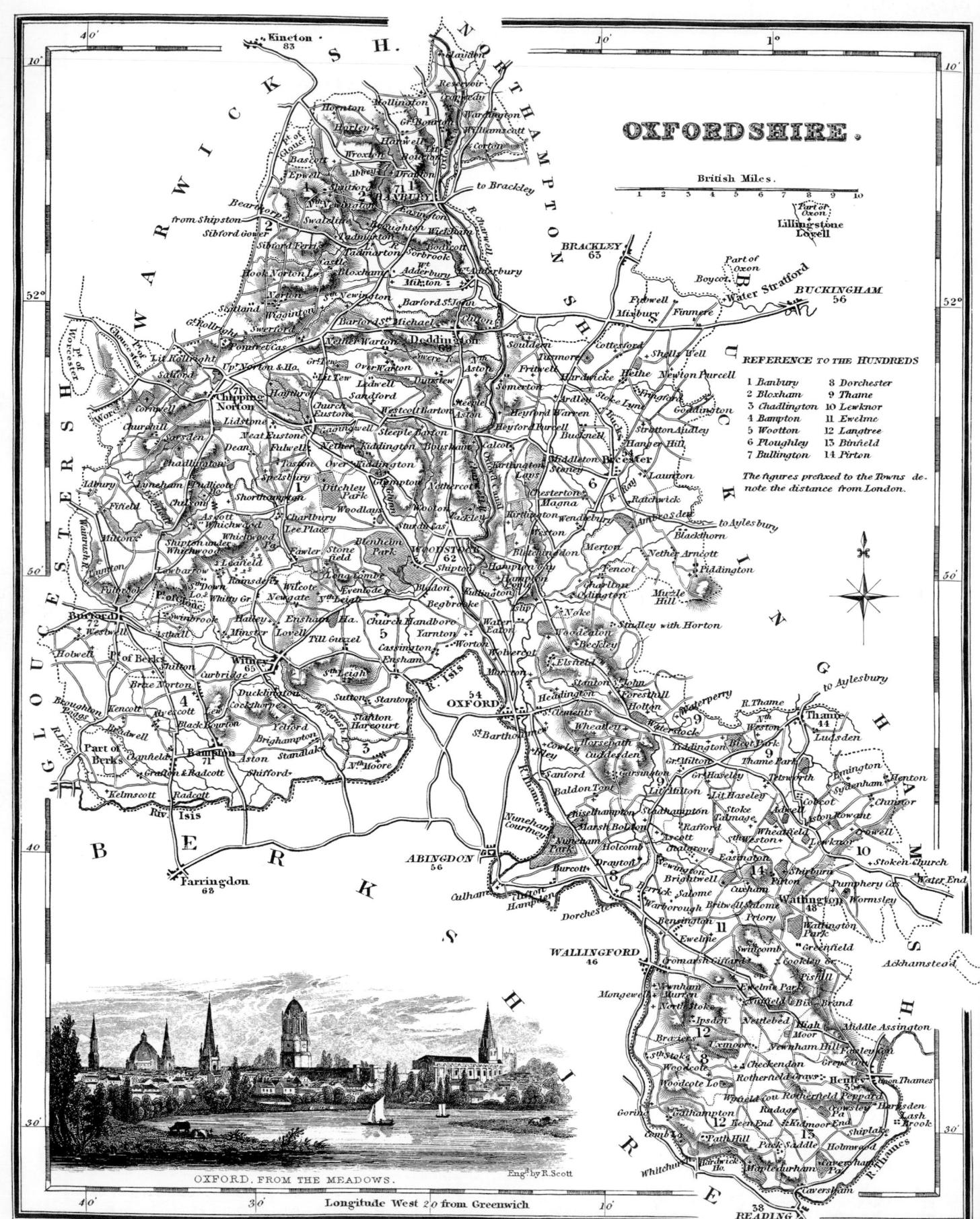

OXFORDSHIRE.

British Miles.
1 2 3 4 5 6 7 8 9 10

REFERENCE TO THE HUNDREDS

1 Banbury	8 Dorchester
2 Bloxham	9 Thame
3 Chadlington	10 Lewknor
4 Bampton	11 Ewelme
5 Wootton	12 Langtree
6 Ploughley	13 Binfield
7 Bullington	14 Pirton

The figures prefixed to the Towns denote the distance from London.

OXFORD, FROM THE MEADOWS.

Engd by R. Scott

Longitude West 2 0 from Greenwich

Published by Archd. Fullarton & Co Glasgow.

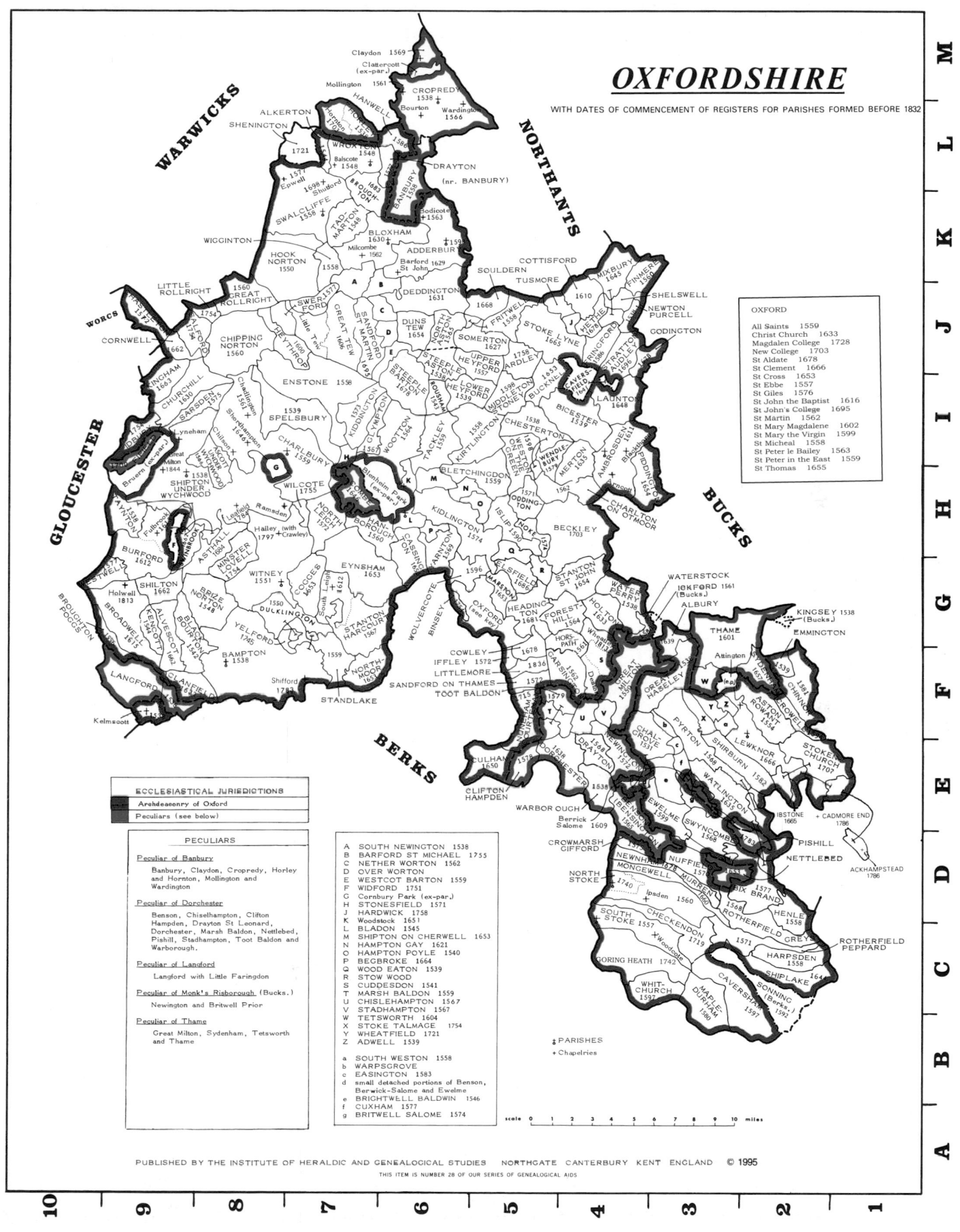

OXFORDSHIRE

WITH DATES OF COMMENCEMENT OF REGISTERS FOR PARISHES FORMED BEFORE 1832

WARWICKS

NORTHANTS

WORCS

GLOUCESTER

BUCKS

BERKS

OXFORD

All Saints	1559
Christ Church	1633
Magdalen College	1728
New College	1703
St Aldate	1678
St Clement	1666
St Cross	1653
St Ebbe	1557
St Giles	1576
St John the Baptist	1616
St John's College	1695
St Martin	1562
St Mary Magdalene	1602
St Mary the Virgin	1599
St Micheal	1558
St Peter le Bailey	1563
St Peter in the East	1559
St Thomas	1655

ECCLESIASTICAL JURISDICTIONS

Archdeaconry of Oxford

Peculiars (see below)

PECULIARS

Peculiar of Banbury
Banbury, Claydon, Cropredy, Horley and Hornton, Mollington and Wardington

Peculiar of Dorchester
Benson, Chiselhampton, Clifton Hampden, Drayton St Leonard, Dorchester, Marsh Baldon, Nettlebed, Pishill, Stadhampton, Toot Baldon and Warborough

Peculiar of Langford
Langford with Little Faringdon

Peculiar of Monk's Risborough (Bucks.)
Newington and Britwell Prior

Peculiar of Thame
Great Milton, Sydenham, Tetsworth and Thame

A	SOUTH NEWINGTON	1538
B	BARFORD ST MICHAEL	1755
C	NETHER WORTON	1562
D	OVER WORTON	1559
E	WESTCOT BARTON	1559
F	WIDFORD	1751
G	Cornbury Park (ex-par.)	
H	STONESFIELD	1571
J	HARDWICK	1758
K	Woodstock	1651
L	BLADON	1545
M	SHIPTON ON CHERWELL	1653
N	HAMPTON GAY	1621
O	HAMPTON POYLE	1540
P	BEGBROKE	1664
Q	WOOD EATON	1539
R	STOW WOOD	
S	CUDDESDON	1541
T	MARSH BALDON	1559
U	CHISLEHAMPTON	1567
V	STADHAMPTON	1567
W	TETSWORTH	1604
X	STOKE TALMAGE	1754
Y	WHEATFIELD	1721
Z	ADWELL	1539
a	SOUTH WESTON	1558
b	WARPSGROVE	
c	EASINGTON	1583
d	small detached portions of Benson, Berwick-Salome and Ewelme	
e	BRIGHTWELL BALDWIN	1546
f	CUXHAM	1577
g	BRITWELL SALOME	1574

‡ PARISHES
+ Chapelries

scale 0 1 2 3 4 5 6 7 8 9 10 miles

PUBLISHED BY THE INSTITUTE OF HERALDIC AND GENEALOGICAL STUDIES   NORTHGATE CANTERBURY KENT ENGLAND © 1995

THIS ITEM IS NUMBER 28 OF OUR SERIES OF GENEALOGICAL AIDS

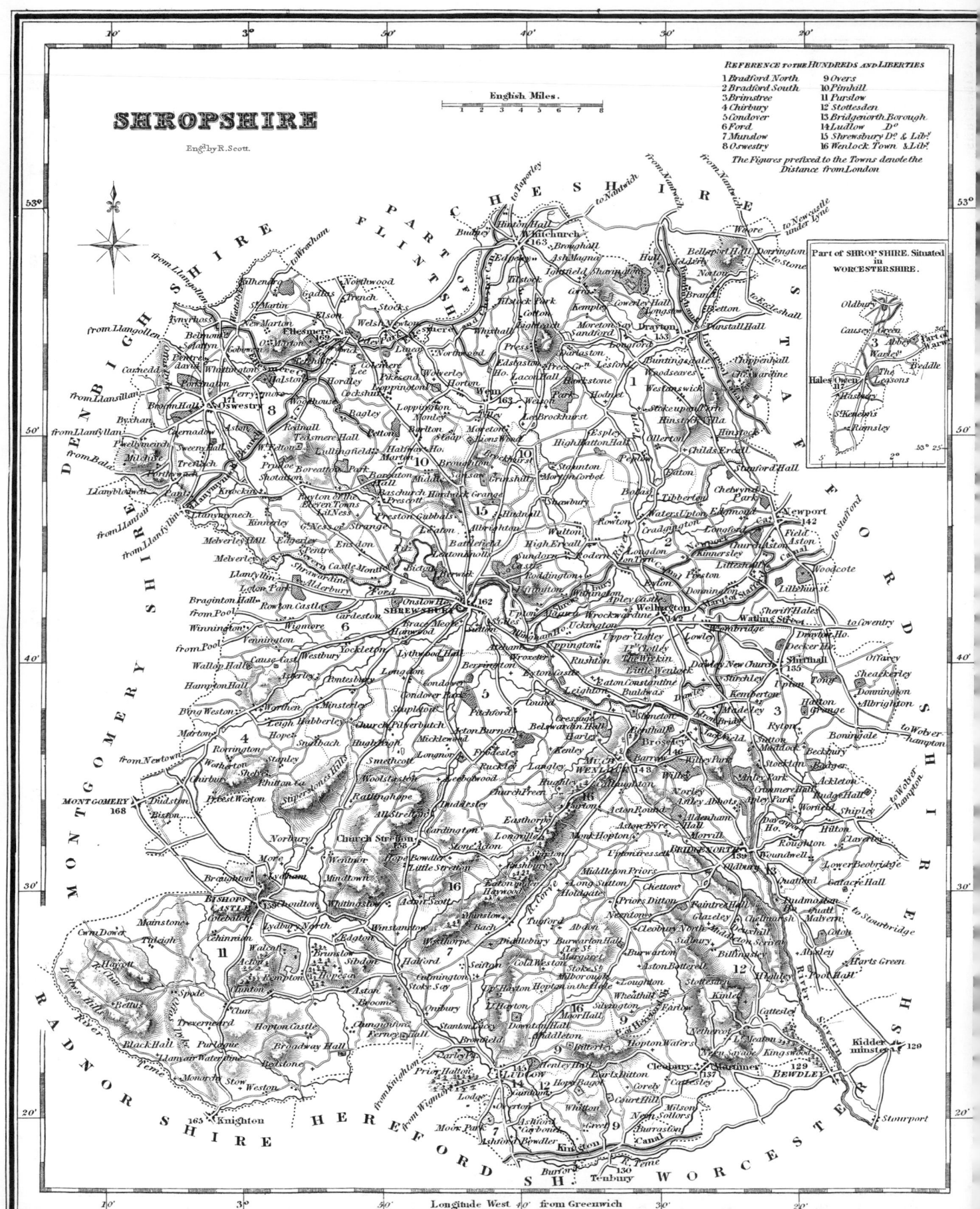

SHROPSHIRE

Engd by R. Scott.

English Miles.

Published by Archd Fullarton & Co. Glasgow.

REFERENCE TO THE HUNDREDS AND LIBERTIES

1 Bradford North	9 Overs
2 Bradford South	10 Pimhill
3 Brimstree	11 Purslow
4 Chirbury	12 Stottesden
5 Condover	13 Bridgenorth Borough
6 Ford	14 Ludlow Do
7 Munslow	15 Shrewsbury Do & Lib.
8 Oswestry	16 Wenlock Town & Lib.

The Figures prefixed to the Towns denote the Distance from London.

Part of SHROPSHIRE. Situated in WORCESTERSHIRE.

Longitude West from Greenwich

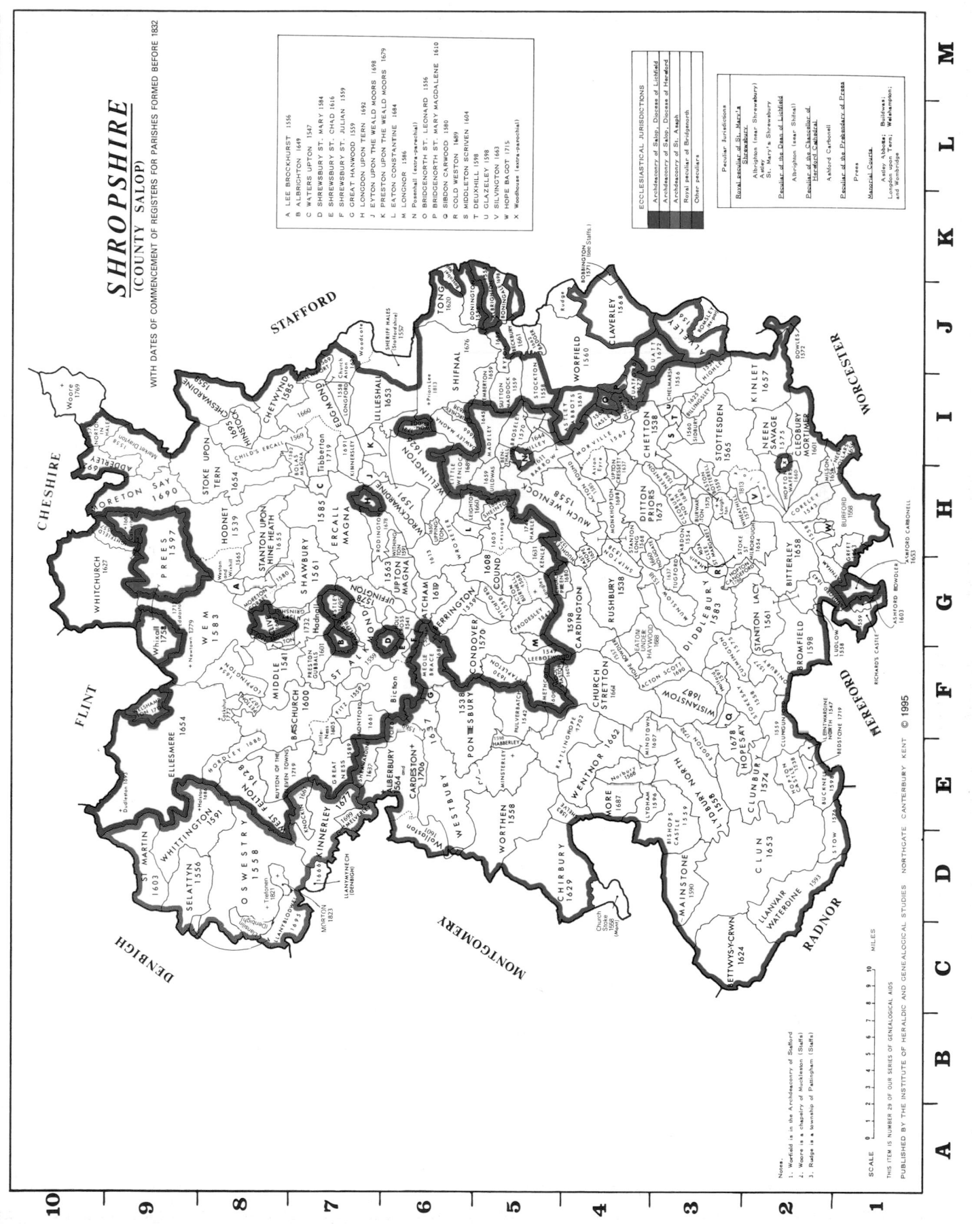

SHROPSHIRE
(COUNTY SALOP)

WITH DATES OF COMMENCEMENT OF REGISTERS FOR PARISHES FORMED BEFORE 1832

A LEE BROCKHURST 1556
B ALBRIGHTON 1649
C WATERS UPTON 1547
D SHREWSBURY ST. MARY 1584
E SHREWSBURY ST. CHAD 1616
F SHREWSBURY ST. JULIAN 1559
G GREAT HANWOOD 1559
H LONGDON UPON TERN 1692
J EYTON UPON THE WEALD MOORS 1698
K PRESTON UPON THE WEALD MOORS 1679
L EATON CONSTANTINE 1684
M LONGNOR 1586
N Posenhall (extra-parochial)
O BRIDGENORTH ST. LEONARD 1556
P BRIDGENORTH ST. MARY MAGDALENE 1610
Q SIBDON CARWOOD 1580
R COLD WESTON 1689
S MIDDLETON SCRIVEN 1604
T DEUXHILL 1598
U GLAZELEY 1598
V SILVINGTON 1663
W HOPE BAGOT (1715)
X Woodhouse (extra-parochial)

ECCLESIASTICAL JURISDICTIONS

Archdeaconry of Salop, Diocese of Lichfield
Archdeaconry of Salop, Diocese of Hereford
Archdeaconry of St. Asaph
Archdeaconry of Bridgenorth
Royal peculiar of Bridgenorth
Other peculiars

Peculiar Jurisdictions

Royal peculiar of St. Mary's
Shrewsbury
Albrighton (near Shrewsbury)
Astley
St. Mary's Shrewsbury

Peculiar of the Dean of Lichfield
Albrighton (near Shifnal)

Peculiar of the Chancellor of
Hereford Cathedral
Ashford Carbonell

Peculiar of the Prebendary of Prees
Prees

Manorial Courts
Astley Abbotts;   Buildwas;
Longden upon Tern;   Wenhampton;
and Wombridge

Notes
1. Worfield is in the Archdeaconry of Stafford.
2. Woore is a chapelry of Mucklestone (Staffs).
3. Rudge is a township of Pattingham (Staffs).

SCALE 0 1 2 3 4 5 6 7 8 9 10
MILES

THIS ITEM IS NUMBER 29 OF OUR SERIES OF GENEALOGICAL AIDS

PUBLISHED BY THE INSTITUTE OF HERALDIC AND GENEALOGICAL STUDIES NORTHGATE CANTERBURY KENT © 1995

STAFFORD
WORCESTER
HEREFORD
RADNOR
MONTGOMERY
DENBIGH
FLINT
CHESHIRE

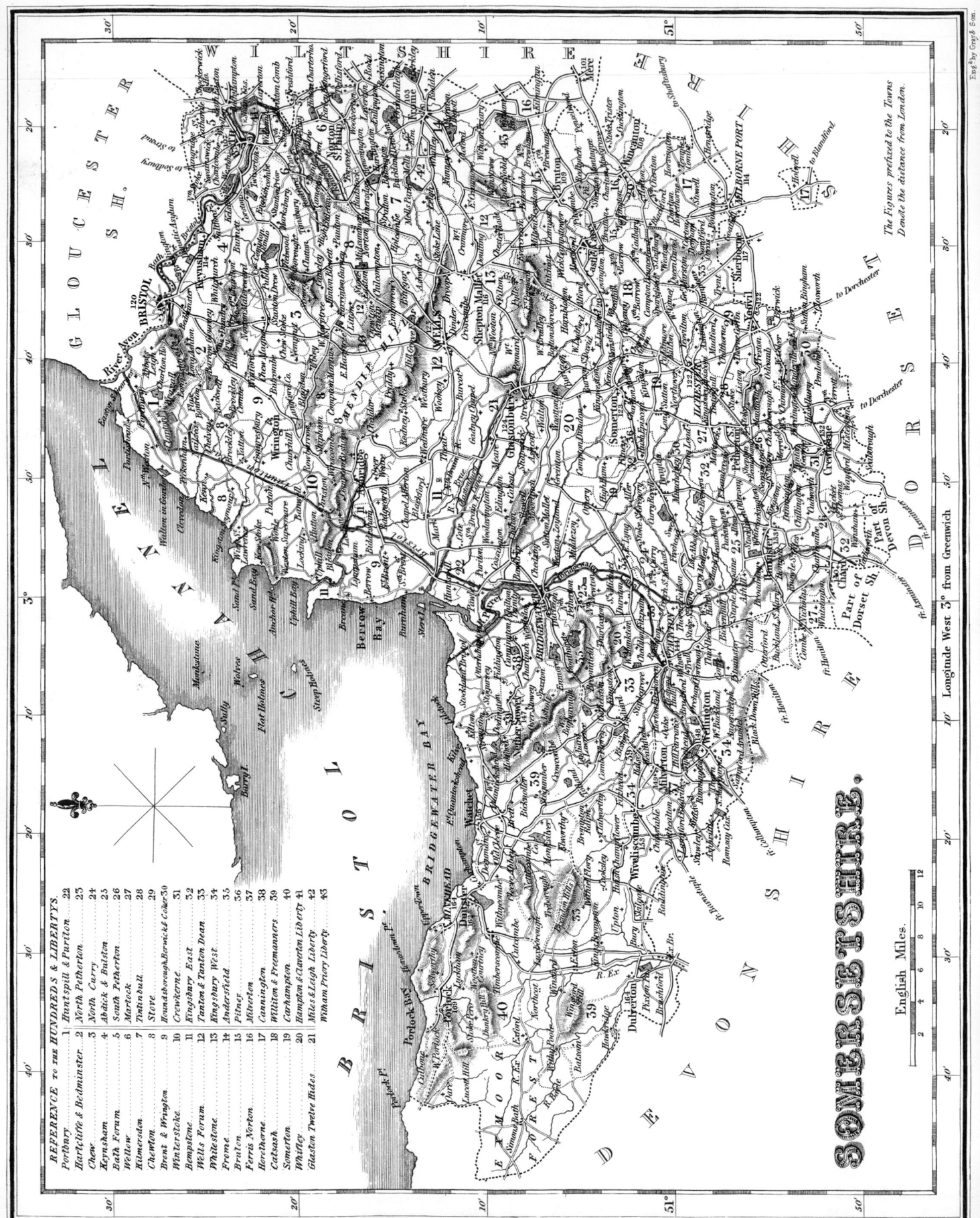

SOMERSETSHIRE.

REFERENCE to the HUNDREDS & LIBERTYS.

Portbury	1	Huntspill & Purton	22
Hartcliffe & Bedminster	2	North Petherton	23
Chew	3	North Curry	24
Keynsham	4	Abdick & Bulston	25
Bath Forum	5	South Petherton	26
Wellow	6	Martock	27
Kilmersdon	7	Tintinhull	28
Chewton	8	Stone	29
Brent & Wrington	9	Roundsborough Barwick Coker	30
Winterstoke	10	Crewkerne	31
Bempstone	11	Kingsbury East	32
Wells Forum	12	Tanton & Tanton Dean	33
Whitestone	13	Kingsbury West	34
Frome	14	Andersfield	35
Braton	15	Pitney	36
Ferris Norton	16	Milverton	37
Horethorne	17	Cannington	38
Catsash	18	Williton & Freemanners	39
Somerton	19	Carhampton	40
Whitley	20	Hampton & Claveton Liberty	41
Glaston Twelve Hides	21	Miles & Leigh Liberty	42
		Witham Priory Liberty	43

English Miles.

Eng.^d by Gray & Son.

The Figures prefixed to the Towns
Denote the distance from London.

Longitude West 3° from Greenwich

SOMERSET

WITH DATES OF COMMENCEMENT OF REGISTERS FOR PARISHES FORMED BEFORE 1832

Parish register date legend (selected readable entries):

Code	Parish	Date
Aa	THURLOXTON	1558
Ab	CHEDDON FITZPAINE	1558
Ac	HEATHFIELD	1703
Ad	OAKE	1630
Ae	EAST CHINNOCK	1647
Af	BROMPTON	1699
Ag	LUFTON	1746
Ah	THORNFALCON	1725
Ai	CURLAND	1634
Aj	BEER CROCOMBE	1542
Ak	ILCHESTER	1690
Al	NORTHOVER	1722
Am	HUISH EPISCOPI	1678
An	CHILTON CANTELO	1714
Ao	BARTON ST DAVID	1559
Ap	STOCKLINCH MAGDALEN	1712
Aq	SHEPTON BEAUCHAMP	1558
Ar	SEAVINGTON ST MARY	1716
As	SEAVINGTON ST MICHAEL	1558
At	LOPEN	1694
Au	KINGSTONE	1714
Av	WEST DOWLISH	1816
Aw	DOWLISH WAKE	1636
Ax	CRICKET MALHERBIE	1723
Ay	CHILLINGTON	1750
Az	DINNINGTON	1592
Ba	STOCKLINCH OTTERSEY	1558

Code	Parish	Date
A	Chelvey	1574
	BRICKSEA	1696
	FLAX BOURTON	1702
B	PUBLOW	1569
C	Pensford	1651
D	STANTON PRIOR	1572
E	BATH: St James	1569
	St Michael	1569
	SS Peter and Paul	1569
	DUNKERTON	1748
F	CHRISTON	1548
G	BIDDISHAM	1621
	ABBRIDGE	1562
	ROWBERROW	1723
H	HINTON BLEWETT	1563
I	HARRINGTON DOWN	1580
J	STONE EASTON	1572
K	STRATTON ON THE FOSSE	1641
L	HOLCOMBE	1698
M	WRITHINGTON	1675
N	BABINGTON	1725
O	HARDINGTON	
P	ELM	1697
Q	NETHER STOWEY	1640
R	DURLEIGH	1683
S	CHILTON TRINITY	1715
T	ST MICHAELCHURCH	1695

Code	Parish	Date
Ea	NORTON SUB HAMDON	1558
Eb	CHISELBOROUGH	1558
Ec	WEST CHINNOCK	1678
Ed	Middle Chinnock	1695
Ee	EAST CHINNOCK	1647
Ef	BROMPTON	1699
Eg	LUFTON	1746
Eh	THORNE COFFIN	1680
Ei	CHILTHORNE DOMER	1678
Ej	ILCHESTER	1690
Ek	NORTHOVER	1722
El	ASHINGTON	1567
Em	CHILTON CANTELO	1714
En	BARTON ST DAVID	1559
Eo	KEINTON MANDEVILLE	1281
Ep	EAST LYDFORD	1730
Eq	LOVINGTON	1777
Er	HORNBLOTTON	1763
Es	ALFORD	1554
Et	UPTON NOBLE	1657
Eu	MILTON CLEVEDON	1595
Ev	NORTH BARROW	1558
Ew	SOUTH BARROW	1678

§ PARISHES

	Parish	Date
§a	WESTON BAMPFYLDE	1632
§b	COMPTON PAUNCEFOOT	1559
§c	SOUTH CADBURY	1559
§d	BLACKFORD	1606
§e	MAPERTON	1558
§f	SUTTON MONTIS	1701

PECULIAR JURISDICTIONS

Peculiar of the Dean of Wells

Peculiar of the Dean and Chapter of Wells
Biddisham, Blinger, Broomfield, Corhampton, Chapel Allerton, Chilcompton, Dinder, Evercreech, Pucklechurch, Mark, Wedmore, Wookey, Wootton, Priddy, Wedmore, Wells St Cuthbert and Westbury

Peculiar of the Precentor of Wells
Bishops Lydeard, Cheddar, Combe St Nicholas, Long Sutton, Lovington, North Curry, South Barrow, Stoke St Gregory, Wells the Liberty of St Andrew, West Hatch, and Winsham

Peculiars of the Prebendaries of Wells
Ashill, Buckland Dinham, Compton Bishop, Combe Dunhen, Cudworth with Combe; Easton in Gordano; East Harptree; Headbury Plucknett; Henstridge; Ilton; Long Sutton; Timberscombe; Wan Lydford; White Lackington; Wivelscombe with Fitzhead; Yatton with Kenn

Peculiar of the Chancellor of Wells Cathedral
East Lambrook and Kingsbury Episcopi

Peculiar of the Provost of Wells Cathedral
Pilton

Peculiar of the Lord of the Manor of Ilminster
Ilminster

Peculiar of the Lord of the Manor of Witham Friary
Witham Friary

* Peculiar jurisdiction antiquated 1827 and the parish incorporated in the Archdeaconry of Wells

ECCLESIASTICAL JURISDICTIONS

	Archdeaconry of Bath
	Archdeaconry of Wells
	Archdeaconry of Taunton
	Peculiars

Abbots Leigh lay in the Diocese of Bristol

The Consistory Court of Bath and Wells had concurrent jurisdiction with the archidiaconal courts in the archdeaconries of Wells and Taunton, and sole jurisdiction in the archdeaconry of Bath.

GLOUCESTER · WILTS · DORSET · DEVON · EXMOOR (extra-parochial)

PUBLISHED BY THE INSTITUTE OF HERALDIC AND GENEALOGICAL STUDIES NORTHGATE CANTERBURY KENT ENGLAND © 1995

THIS ITEM IS NUMBER 30 OF OUR SERIES OF GENEALOGICAL AIDS

scale 0 1 2 3 4 5 6 7 8 9 10 miles

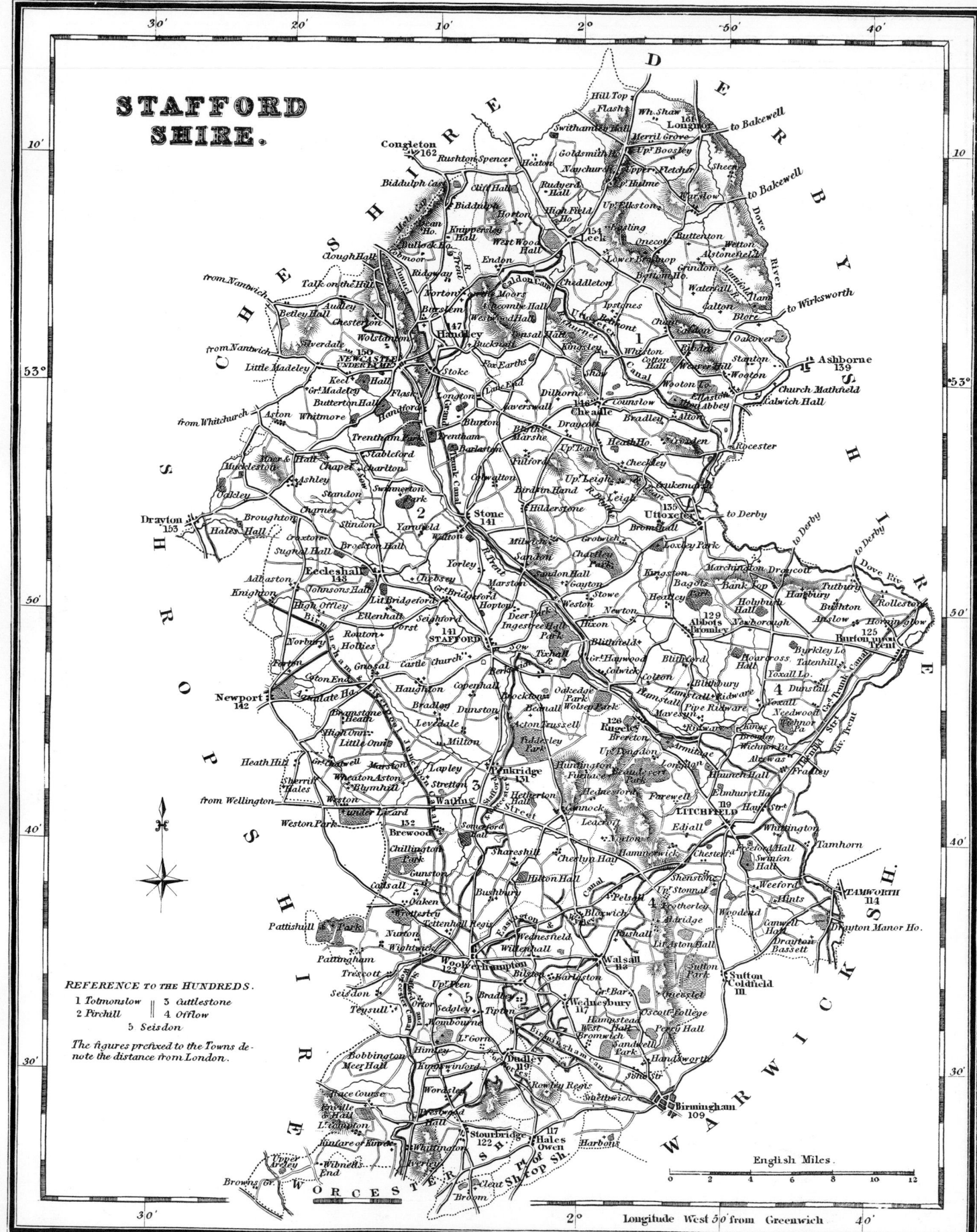

STAFFORD SHIRE.

REFERENCE TO THE HUNDREDS.
1 Totmonslow   3 Cuttlestone
2 Pirehill   4 Offlow
5 Seisdon

The figures prefixed to the Towns denote the distance from London.

English Miles.

Published by Archd. Fullarton & Co. Glasgow.

Engd. by R. Scott.

Longitude West from Greenwich

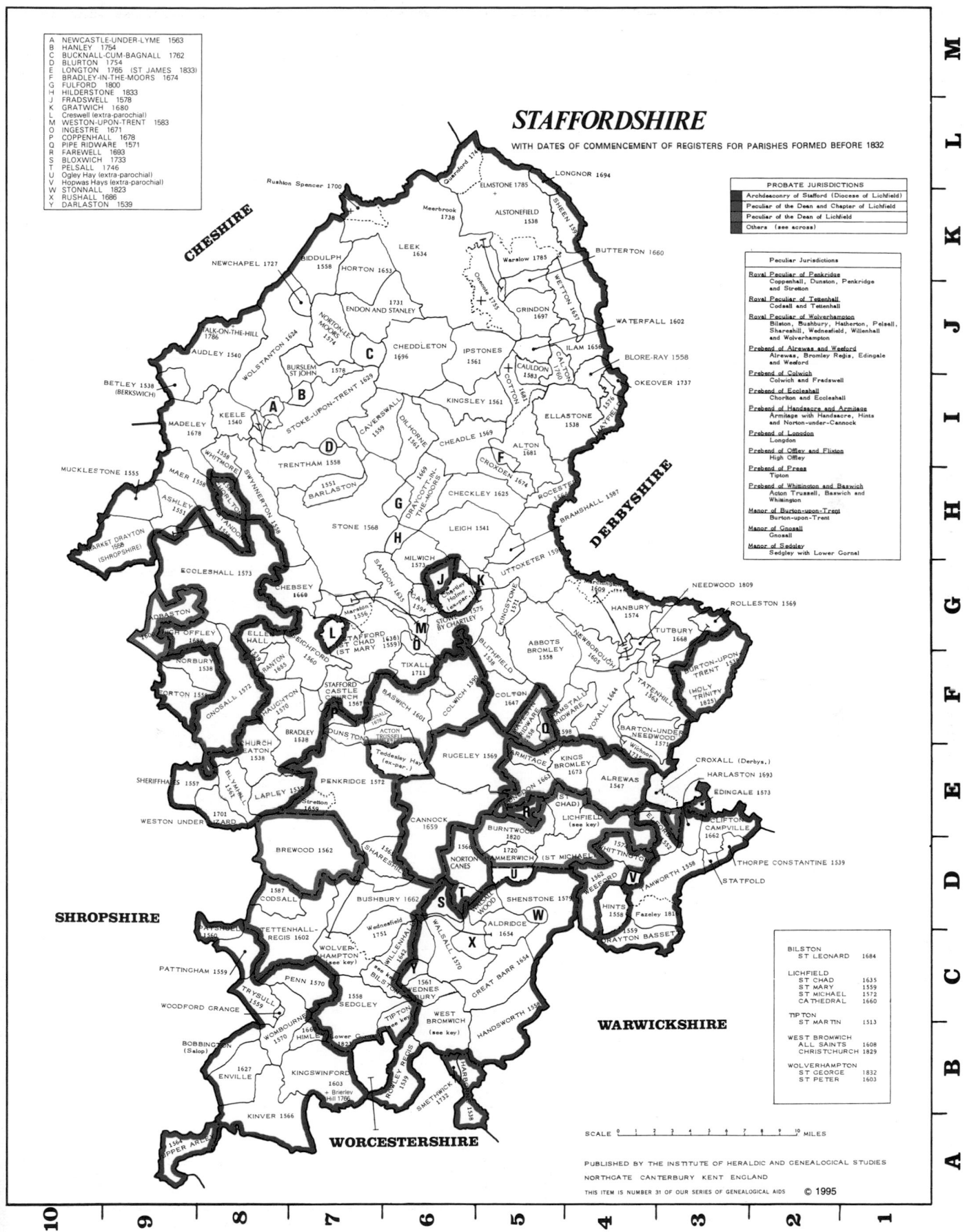

STAFFORDSHIRE
WITH DATES OF COMMENCEMENT OF REGISTERS FOR PARISHES FORMED BEFORE 1832

A NEWCASTLE-UNDER-LYME 1563
B HANLEY 1754
C BUCKNALL-CUM-BAGNALL 1762
D BLURTON 1754
E LONGTON 1765 (ST JAMES 1833)
F BRADLEY-IN-THE-MOORS 1674
G FULFORD 1800
H HILDERSTONE 1833
J FRADSWELL 1578
K GRATWICH 1680
L Creswell (extra-parochial)
M WESTON-UPON-TRENT 1583
O INGESTRE 1671
P COPPENHALL 1678
Q PIPE RIDWARE 1571
R FAREWELL 1693
S BLOXWICH 1733
T PELSALL 1746
U Ogley Hay (extra-parochial)
V Hopwas Hays (extra-parochial)
W STONNALL 1823
X RUSHALL 1686
Y DARLASTON 1539

PROBATE JURISDICTIONS
Archdeaconry of Stafford (Diocese of Lichfield)
Peculiar of the Dean and Chapter of Lichfield
Peculiar of the Dean of Lichfield
Others (see across)

Peculiar Jurisdictions
Royal Peculiar of Penkridge
Coppenhall, Dunston, Penkridge and Stretton
Royal Peculiar of Tettenhall
Codsall and Tettenhall
Royal Peculiar of Wolverhampton
Bilston, Bushbury, Hatherton, Pelsall, Shareshill, Wednesfield, Willenhall and Wolverhampton
Prebend of Alrewas and Weeford
Alrewas, Bromley Regis, Edingale and Weeford
Prebend of Colwich
Colwich and Fradswell
Prebend of Eccleshall
Chorlton and Eccleshall
Prebend of Handsacre and Armitage
Armitage with Handsacre, Hints and Norton-under-Cannock
Prebend of Longdon
Longdon
Prebend of Offley and Flixton
High Offley
Prebend of Prees
Tipton
Prebend of Whittington and Baswich
Acton Trussell, Baswich and Whittington
Manor of Burton-upon-Trent
Burton-upon-Trent
Manor of Gnosall
Gnosall
Manor of Sedgley
Sedgley with Lower Gornal

BILSTON
ST LEONARD 1684

LICHFIELD
ST CHAD 1635
ST MARY 1559
ST MICHAEL 1572
CATHEDRAL 1660

TIPTON
ST MARTIN 1513

WEST BROMWICH
ALL SAINTS 1608
CHRISTCHURCH 1829

WOLVERHAMPTON
ST GEORGE 1832
ST PETER 1603

SCALE 0 1 2 3 4 5 6 7 8 9 10 MILES

PUBLISHED BY THE INSTITUTE OF HERALDIC AND GENEALOGICAL STUDIES
NORTHGATE CANTERBURY KENT ENGLAND
THIS ITEM IS NUMBER 31 OF OUR SERIES OF GENEALOGICAL AIDS
© 1995

CHESHIRE
DERBYSHIRE
SHROPSHIRE
WARWICKSHIRE
WORCESTERSHIRE

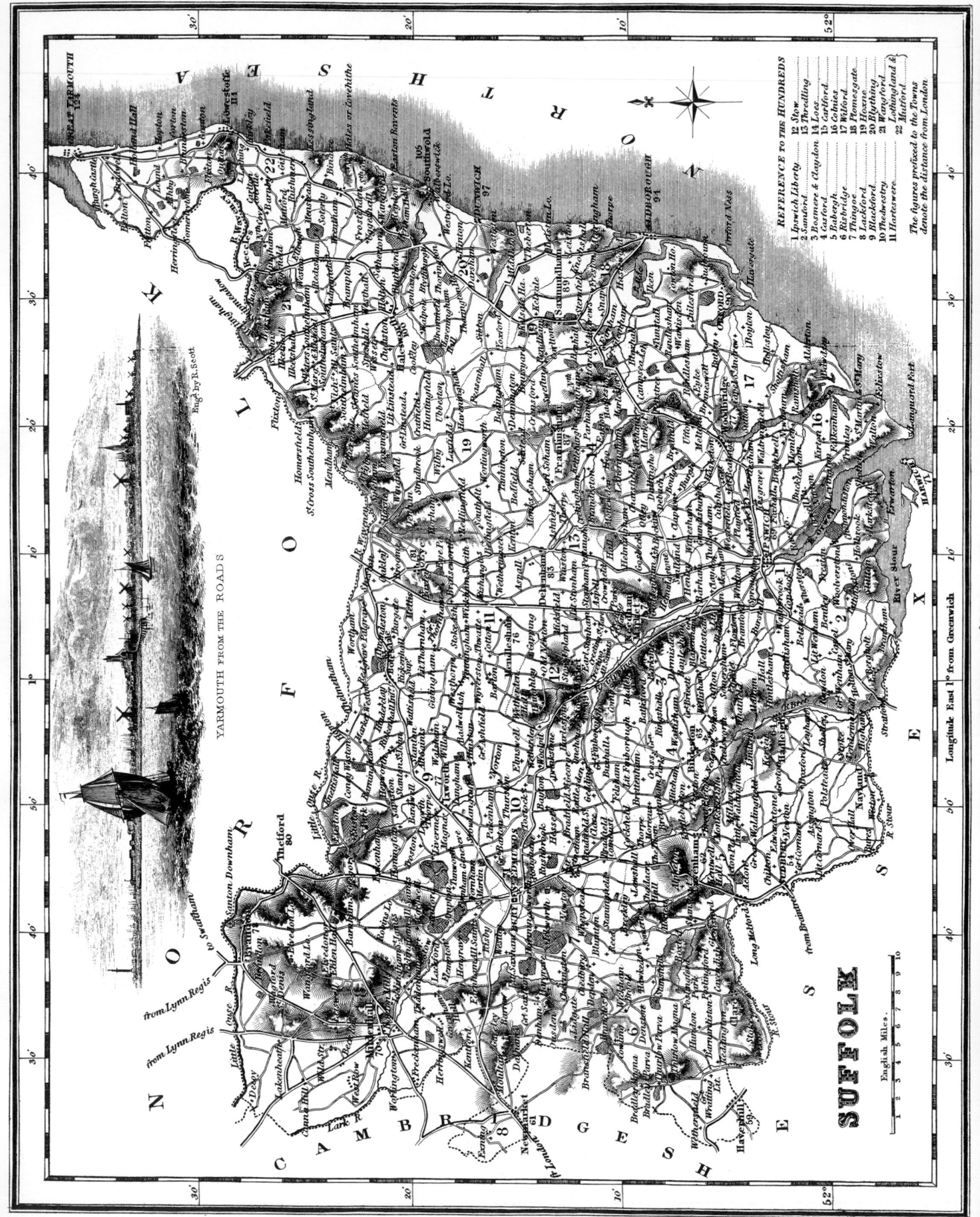

REFERENCE TO THE HUNDREDS

1 Ipswich Liberty	12 Stow
2 Samford	13 Thredling
3 Bosmere & Claydon	14 Loes
4 Carlford	15 Carlford
5 Babergh	16 Colnies
6 Risbridge	17 Wilford
7 Thingoe	18 Plomesgate
8 Lackford	19 Hoxne
9 Blackford	20 Blything
10 Thedwestry	21 Wangford
11 Hartesmere	22 Lothingland &
	Mutford

The figures prefixed to the Towns
denote the distance from London.

SUFFOLK

YARMOUTH FROM THE ROADS

Eng.d by R. Scott

English Miles.

Longitude East 1° from Greenwich

SUFFOLK

WITH DATES OF COMMENCEMENT OF REGISTERS FOR PARISHES FORMED BEFORE 1832

NORFOLK

ESSEX

CAMBRIDGE

River Stour

South Elmham
a. St. Cross
b. St. Margaret 1679
c. St. Peter
d. St. James 1705
e. All Saints & St. Nicholas 1708
f. St. Michael 1559

Ilketshall
a. St. Margaret 1538
b. St. Lawrence 1559
c. St. Andrew 1542
d. St. John 1538

Stanton
St. All Saints 1584
St. John Baptist 1579

Sudbury
All Saints 1564
St. Gregory 1653
St. Peter 1593

Fornham
a. St. Genevieve 1674
b. All Saints 1558
c. St. Martin 1539

Bury St. Edmunds
a. St. James 1558
b. St. Mary

Ipswich
St. Clement 1863
St. Helen 1677
St. Margaret 1538
St. Lawrence 1539
St. Mary at the Elms
St. Mary at the Quay 1559
St. Mary at the Tower 1538
St. Mary Stoke 1655
St. Matthew 1559
St. Nicholas 1539
St. Peter 1657
St. Stephen 1565

+ Chapelries

ECCLESIASTICAL JURISDICTIONS
Archdeaconry of Sudbury
Archdeaconry of Suffolk
Peculiars

Peculiars of the Abp. of Canterbury
Hadleigh
Monks Eleigh
Moulton

Peculiar of the Bishop of Rochester
Freckenham

SCALE 1 2 3 4 5 6 7 8 9 10 MILES

PUBLISHED BY THE INSTITUTE OF HERALDIC AND GENEALOGICAL STUDIES NORTHGATE CANTERBURY KENT © 1995

THIS ITEM IS NUMBER 32 OF OUR SERIES OF GENEALOGICAL AIDS

A	Flempton 1561	Ee	Shelland 1721
B	Ampton 1559	Ec	Harleston 1561
C	Little Livermere 1538	Ed	Stowupland 1559
D	Great Livermere 1559	Ee	Stowmarket 1538
E	Honington 1559	Ef	Gipping 1706
F	Ixworth Thorpe 1718	Eg	Stowmarket 1675
G	Stowlangtoft 1569	Eh	Great Finborough 1556
H	Hunston 1559	Ei	Onehouse 1561
I	Little Saxham 1569	Ek	Creeting St. Peter 1558
J	Rushbrooke 1566	El	Little Stonham 1542
K	Beyton 1539	Em	Creeting St. George 1709
L	Tostock 1675	En	Pettaugh 1663
M	Southwell Park 1710	Eo	Cretingham 1558
N	Chedburgh 1559	Ep	Kettleburgh 1561
O	Great Whelnetham 1557	Eq	Easton 1663
P	Little Whelnetham 1561	Er	Brandeston 1579
Q	Bradfield Combust 1538	Es	Swilland 1579
R	Bradfield St. Clare 1538	Et	Hemingston 1538
S	Bradfield St. George 1555	Eu	Ashbocking 1561
T	Gedding 1543	Ev	Henley 1559
U	Stanningfield 1561	Ew	Claydon 1559
V	Stradishall 1548	Ex	Flowton 1572
W	Somerton 1538	Ey	Burstall 1542
X	Barnardiston 1540	Ez	Debach 1539
Y	Stansted 1570		

Aa	Rickinghall Inferior 1652	Oa	Brettenham 1694
Ab	Rickinghall Superior 1557	Ob	Wetherden 1578
Ac	Botesdale 1538	Oc	Kettlebaston 1578
Ad	Thornham Magna 1766	Od	Chelsworth 1559
Ae	Thornham Parva 1710	Oe	Bildeston 1556
Af	Braiseworth 1709	Of	Naughton 1561
Ag	Stoke Ash 1538	Og	Great Finborough 1539
Ah	Thwaite St. George 1709	Oh	Wattisham 1538
Ai	Bedingfield 1563	Oi	Somersham 1675
Ak	Redingfields 1728	Ok	Great Bricett 1660
Al	Athelington 1694	Ol	Nettlestead 1618
Am	Southolt 1538	Om	Offton 1559
An	Linstead Magna 1655	Ow	Little Blakenham 1728
Ao	Linstead Parva 1539	Ox	Great Blakenham 1566
Ap	Redisham 1713	Ua	Whitton-cum-Thurston 1599
Aq	Shadingfield 1538	Ub	Westerfield 1538
Ar	Willingham 1696	Uc	Tuddenham St. Martin 1664
As	Rushmere 1718	Ud	Culpho 1700
At	Stoven 1653	Ue	Great Bealings 1539
Au	Wrangford 1678	Uf	Woodbridge 1546
Av	Aspall 1558	Ug	Kingrove 1558
Aw	Hevenningham 1539	Uh	Brightwell 1663
Ax	Ubbeston 1655	Ui	Waldringfield 1675
Ay	Thurlington 1561	Uk	Newbourn 1561
Az		Ul	Hemley 1698
		Um	Shottisham 1818
		Un	Alderton Priory (ex-par.)
		Uo	Ramsholt 1538
		Up	Levington 1662
		Uq	Stratton Hall
		Ur	Wolverstone 1559
		Us	Chelmondiston 1539
		Ut	Bourge 1538
		Uw	Carlton 1538

Gt. Yarmouth (Norfolk)

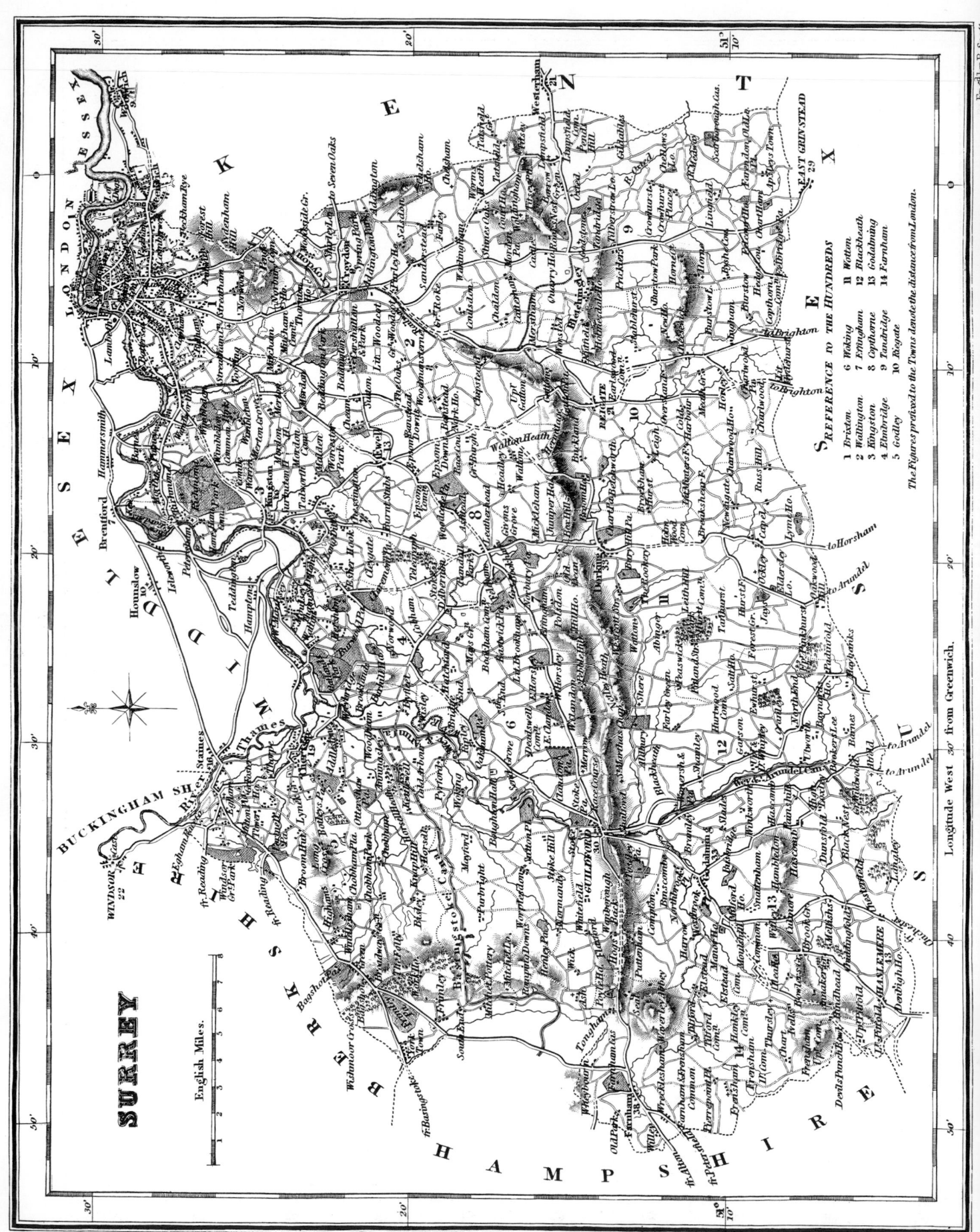

SURREY

English Miles.

Eng.d by R Scott

REFERENCE TO THE HUNDREDS

1 Brixton.
2 Wallington.
3 Kingston.
4 Elmbridge.
5 Godley.

6 Woking.
7 Effingham.
8 Copthorne.
9 Tandridge.
10 Reigate.

11 Wotton.
12 Blackheath.
13 Godalming.
14 Farnham.

The Figures prefixed to the Towns denote the distance from London.

Longitude West 30' from Greenwich.

SURREY

WITH DATES OF COMMENCEMENT OF REGISTERS FOR PARISHES FORMED BEFORE 1832

PROBATE JURISDICTIONS

Archdeaconry of Surrey (Diocese of Winchester)

Deanery of Croydon (Peculiar of the Abp of Canterbury)

Note: Addington and Lambeth were transferred to the Diocese of Canterbury in 1837. Battersea, Bermondsey, Camberwell, Clapham, Lambeth, Merton, Rotherhithe, Southwark, Streatham, Tooting and Wandsworth were transferred to the Diocese of London in 1846.

A	TOOTING GRAVENEY	1555
B	GUILDFORD ST MARY	1540
C	GUILDFORD HOLY TRINITY	1558
D	WEST CLANDON	1536
E	LITTLE BOOKHAM	1642
F	WOODMANSTERNE	1566
G	HASCOMBE	1646
H	CHILWORTH or ST MARTHA ON-THE-HILL	1779

BERMONDSEY
St James 1829
St Mary Magdalene 1548

CAMBERWELL
St George 1825
St Giles 1557

CLAPHAM
Holy Trinity 1551
St James, Clapham Park 1829

LAMBETH
Renfrew Road, Workhouse 1803
St John, Waterloo 1824
St Luke, W. Norwood 1825
St Mark, Kennington 1825
St Mary 1539
St Matthew, Brixton 1825

NEWINGTON
Holy Trinity 1825
St Mary 1561
St Peter, Walworth 1825

SOUTHWARK
Christ Church 1671
St George the Martyr 1602
St John Horsleydown 1733
St Olave 1582
St Saviour 1538
St Thomas 1614

PARISHES †
Chapelries +

SCALE 0 1 2 3 4 5 6 7 8 9 10 MILES

PUBLISHED BY THE INSTITUTE OF HERALDIC AND GENEALOGICAL STUDIES   NORTHGATE   CANTERBURY   KENT   ENGLAND © 1995

THIS ITEM IS NUMBER 33 OF OUR SERIES OF GENEALOGICAL AIDS

A   B   C   D   E   F   G   H   I   J   K   L   M

1   2   3   4   5   6   7   8   9   10

Kent

Sussex

Middlesex

Bucks

Berks

Hants

Parish names on map (selection): BERMONDSEY, ROTHERHITHE (St Mary), DEPTFORD (Kent), BATTERSEA (detached), LAMBETH, CLAPHAM, WANDSWORTH, STREATHAM, MITCHAM 1563, MERTON 1559, WIMBLEDON 1538, MORTLAKE 1599, BARNES 1714, KEW, RICHMOND, PETERSHAM, KINGSTON 1541, MALDEN 1564, CHESSINGTON 1627, THAMES DITTON 1663, LONG DITTON 1729, EAST MOLESEY, WEST MOLESEY 1639, WEYBRIDGE 1625, EGHAM 1560, THORP 1653, CHERTSEY 1606, CHOBHAM 1654, WINDLESHAM 1677, BISLEY 1561, HORSELL 1653, WOKING 1653, PIRBRIGHT 1574, WORPLESDON 1539, BYFLEET 1698, PYRFORD 1565, RIPLEY, SEND 1536, STOKE 1662, ASH 1548, SEALE 1538, PUTTENHAM 1562, COMPTON 1561, GUILDFORD ST NICHOLAS, SHALFORD 1594, WANBOROUGH, WONERSH 1563, ELSTEAD 1538, PEPERHAROW, GODALMING 1582, BRAMLEY, CRANLEIGH 1566, SHAMLEY, ALFOLD 1658, DUNSFOLD 1628, HAMBLEDON 1611, WITLEY 1653, THURSLEY 1613, CHIDDINGFOLD 1563, FRENSHAM 1649, FARNHAM 1539, WAVERLEY (e.p.), HASLEMERE, ALBURY 1559, SHERE 1546, ABINGER 1559, WOTTON 1596, EWHURST 1614, CRANLEIGH, EFFINGHAM 1565, EAST HORSLEY 1600, WEST HORSLEY 1600, OCKHAM, GREAT BOOKHAM 1632, FETCHAM 1559, LEATHERHEAD 1656, MICKLEHAM 1549, GREAT BOOKHAM, COBHAM 1562, STOKE D'ABERNON 1619, ESHER 1676, WALTON-ON-THAMES 1678, DORKING 1538, CAPEL 1653, OCKLEY 1539, NEWDIGATE 1559, CHARLWOOD 1595, HORLEY 1577, LEIGH 1579, REIGATE 1556, BETCHWORTH 1558, BUCKLAND 1560, WALTON-ON-THE-HILL 1581, HEADLEY 1661, ASHTEAD 1662, EPSOM 1695, EWELL 1604, CUDDINGTON 1538, CHEAM 1538, SUTTON 1636, BANSTEAD 1547, CARSHALTON, BEDDINGTON 1538, CROYDON 1538, WALLINGTON, WOODMANSTERNE, CHIPSTEAD 1656, GATTON 1599, MERSTHAM 1538, CHALDON 1564, COULSDON 1653, CATERHAM 1543, WARLINGHAM 1653, SANDERSTEAD 1563, FARLEY 1678, ADDINGTON 1559, CHELSHAM, WOLDINGHAM, TITSEY 1579, TATSFIELD 1574, OXTED 1603, LIMPSFIELD 1539, CROWHURST 1561, LINGFIELD 1559, GODSTONE 1662, TANDRIDGE 1672, BLETCHINGLEY 1538, NUTFIELD 1556, HORNE 1614, BURSTOW 1546, OAKWOOD, ALBURY (detached), WISLEY 1654.

Oakwood

Bramley +

Grimley 1590

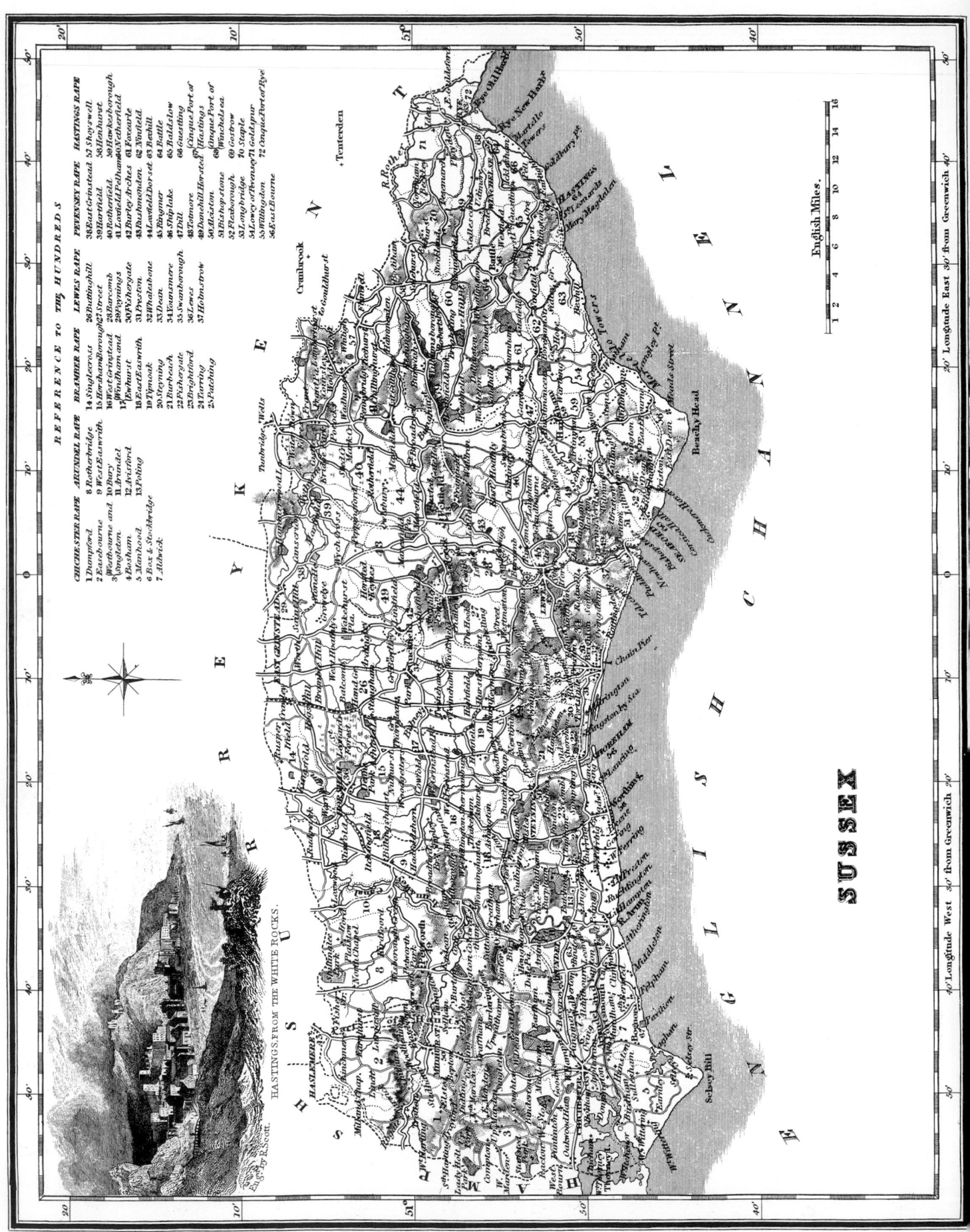

REFERENCE to THE HUNDREDS

CHICHESTER RAPE
1 Dumpford
2 Easebourne
3 Westbourne and Singleton
4 Bosham
5 Manhood
6 Box & Stockbridge
7 Aldwick

ARUNDEL RAPE
8 Rotherbridge
9 West Easwrith
10 Bury
11 Brandct
12 Avisford
13 Poling

BRAMBER RAPE
14 Singlecross
15 Horsham
16 West Grinstead
17 Windham and Ewhurst
18 East Easwrith
19 Tipnoak
20 Steyning
21 Burbeach
22 Fishergate
23 Brightford
24 Tarring
25 Patching

LEWES RAPE
26 Buttinghill
27 Street
28 Barcomb
29 Poynings
30 Fishergate
31 Preston
32 Whalesbone
33 Dean
34 Younsmere
35 Swanborough
36 Lewes
37 Holmstrow

PEVENSEY RAPE
38 East Grinstead
39 Hartfield
40 Rotherfield
41 Loxfield Pelham
42 Burley Arches
43 Rushmonden
44 Loxfield Dorset
45 Ringmer
46 Shiplake
47 Dill
48 Totnore
49 Danehill Horsted
50 Alciston
51 Bishopstone
52 Flexborough
53 Longbridge
54 Lowey of Pevensey
55 Willingdon
56 East Bourne

HASTINGS RAPE
57 Shoyswell
58 Henhurst
59 Hawksborough
60 Netherfield
61 Foxearle
62 Winfield
63 Bexhill
64 Battle
65 Baldslow
66 Guestling
67 Cinque Port of Hastings
68 Cinque Port or Winchelsea
69 Gostrow
70 Staple
71 Goldspur
72 Cinque Port of Rye

English Miles.
1 2 4 6 8 10 12 14 16

HASTINGS FROM THE WHITE ROCKS.

Engd by R. Scott.

SUSSEX

40' Longitude West 30' from Greenwich 20' 10' 0 10' 20' Longitude East 30' from Greenwich 40'

ENGLISH CHANNEL

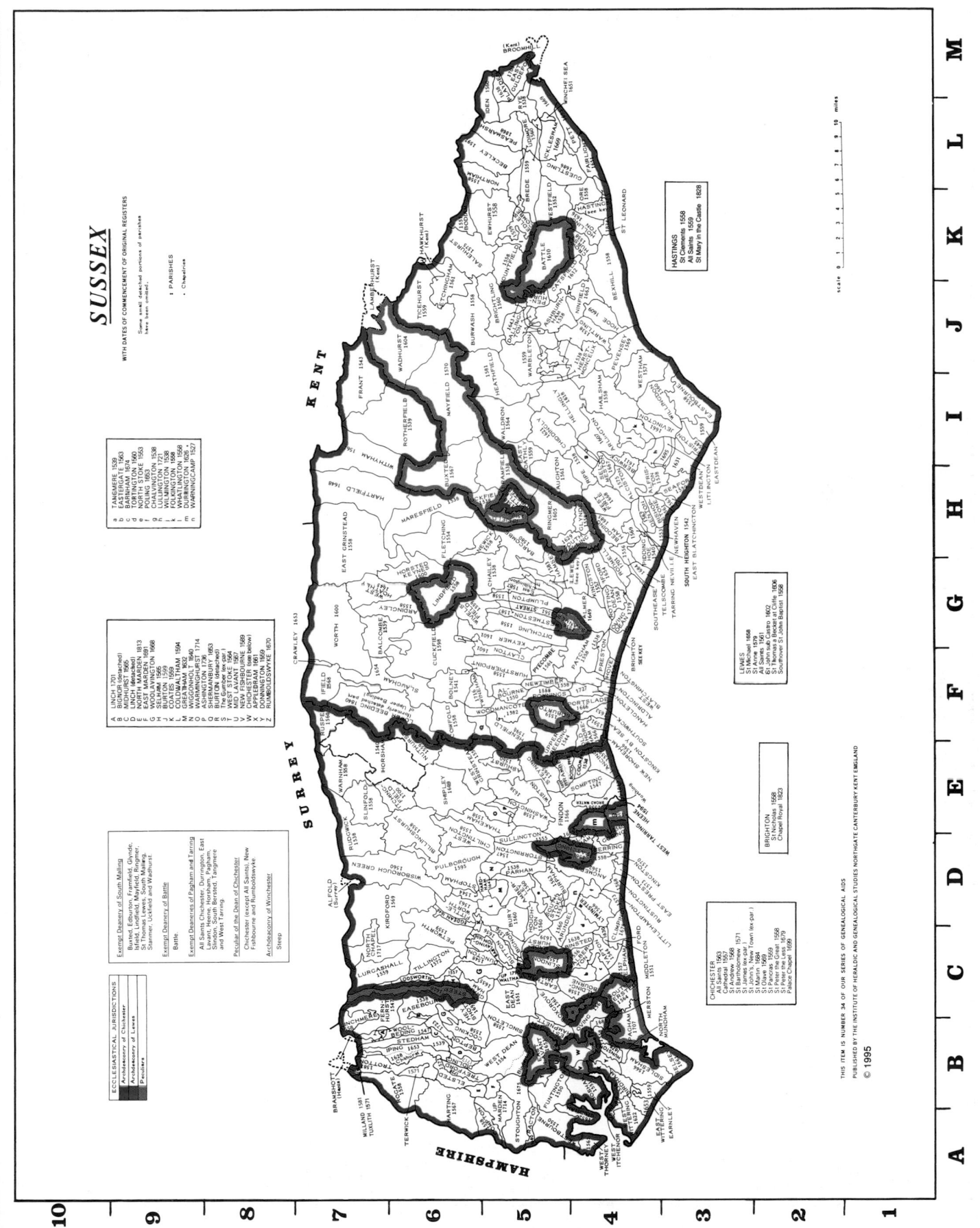

SUSSEX

WITH DATES OF COMMENCEMENT OF ORIGINAL REGISTERS

Some small detached portions of parishes
here have been omitted.

‡ PARISHES
• Chapelries

ECCLESIASTICAL JURISDICTIONS
- Archdeaconry of Chichester
- Archdeaconry of Lewes
- Peculiars

Exempt Deanery of South Malling
Buxted, Edburton, Framfield, Glynde,
Isfield, Lindfield, Mayfield, Ringmer,
St Thomas Lewes, South Malling,
Stanmer, Uckfield and Wadhurst.

Exempt Deanery of Battle
Battle

Exempt Deaneries of Pagham and Tarring
All Saints Chichester, Durrington, East
Lavant, Henne, Horsham, Pagham,
Sindon, South Bersted, Tangmere
and West Tarring.

Peculiar of the Dean of Chichester
Chichester (except All Saints), New
Fishbourne and Rumboldswyke.

Archdeaconry of Winchester

Steep

CHICHESTER
All Saints 1563
Cathedral 1567
St Andrew 1568
St Bartholomew 1571
St James (ex-par.)
St John's, New Town (ex-par.)
St Martin 1664
St Olave 1569
St Pancras 1559
St Peter the Great 1568
St Peter the Less 1679
Palace Chapel 1699

LEWES
St Michael 1668
St Anne 1579
All Saints 1561
St John sub Castro 1602
St Thomas à Becket at Cliffe 1606
Southover St John Baptist 1558

BRIGHTON
St Nicholas 1558
Chapel Royal 1823

HASTINGS
St Clements 1558
All Saints 1559
St Mary in the Castle 1828

a LINCH 1701
b BIGNOR (detached)
c MIDHURST 1565
d LYNCH (detached) 1674
e NORTH MARDEN 1813
f EAST MARDEN 1691
g POLING 1663
h WOOLAVINGTON 1668
i SELHAM 1565
j BURTON 1599
k FOLKINGTON 1538
l COATES 1559
m COLDWALTHAM 1594
n GREATHAM 1632
o WIGGONHOLT 1660
p WARMINGHURST 1714
q ASHINGTON 1736
r PARHAM 1663
s BURTON (detached)
t The Gumber (ex-par.)
u MID LAVANT 1567
v WEST STOKE 1564
w NEW FISHBOURNE 1589
x CHICHESTER (see below)
y APPLEDRAM 1661
z DONNINGTON 1559
Z RUMBOLDSWYKE 1670

TANGMERE 1539
EASTERGATE 1563
BARNHAM 1674
NORTH STOKE 1660
POLING 1663
WOOLAVINGTON 1668
SELHAM 1565
WILLINGTON 1721
WILMINGTON 1538
FOLKINGTON 1538
WHATLINGTON 1594
DURRINGTON 1626 •
WARNINGCAMP 1527

scale 0 1 2 3 4 5 6 7 8 9 10 miles

THIS ITEM IS NUMBER 34 OF OUR SERIES OF GENEALOGICAL AIDS

PUBLISHED BY THE INSTITUTE OF HERALDIC AND GENEALOGICAL STUDIES NORTHGATE CANTERBURY KENT ENGLAND

© 1995

KENT

SURREY

HAMPSHIRE

COVENTRY, WITH CHURCHES OF TRINITY & S.t MICHAELS.

Eng.d by R. Scott

WARWICKSHIRE.

English Miles.

1 2 3 4 5 6 7 8 9 10

REFERENCE to the HUNDREDS
1 Hemlingford   3 Barlichway
2 Knightlow   4 Kington
5 County of Coventry

The Figures prefixed to the Towns
denote the distance from London.

Longitude West 20′ from Greenwich

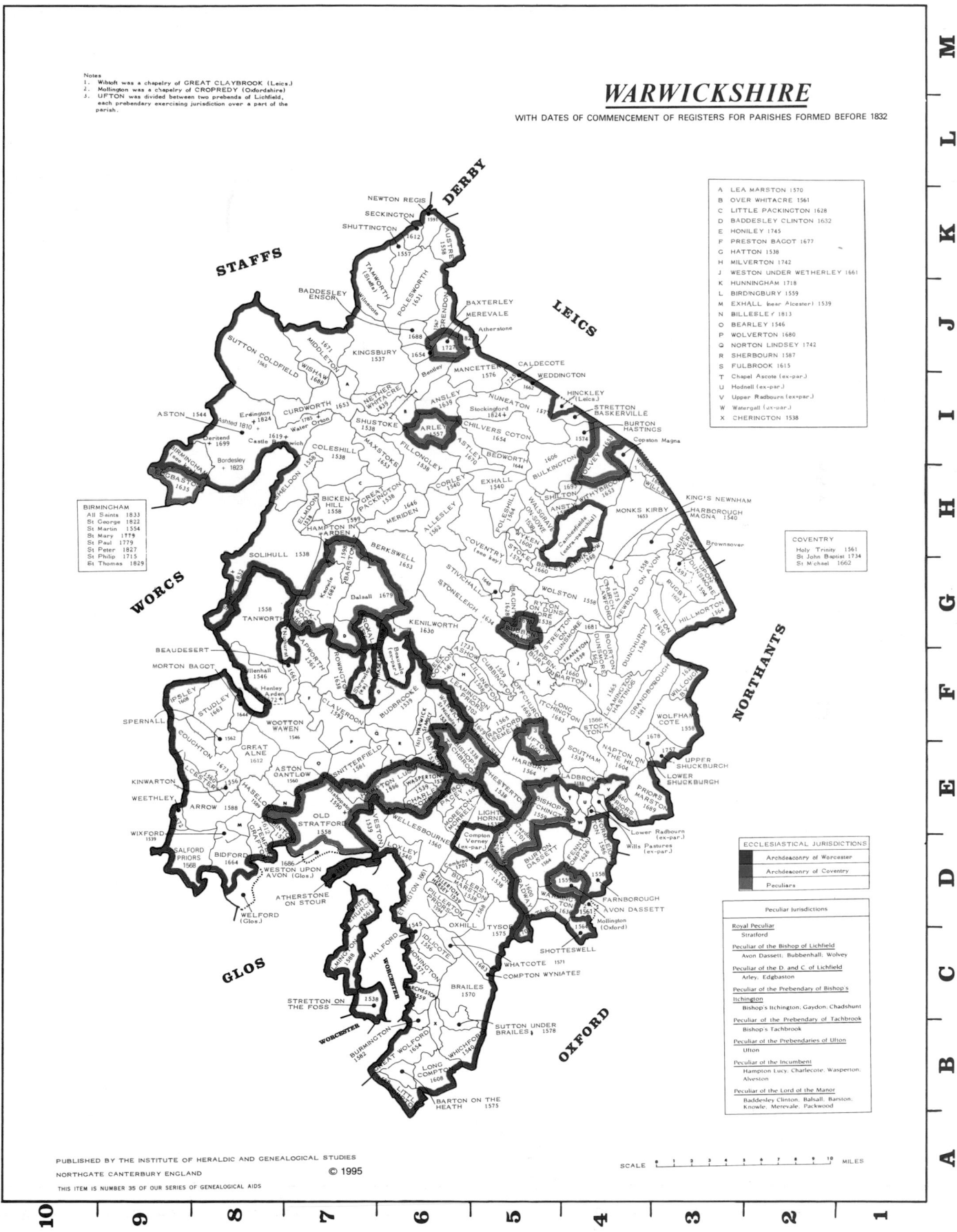

WARWICKSHIRE
WITH DATES OF COMMENCEMENT OF REGISTERS FOR PARISHES FORMED BEFORE 1832

Notes
1. Wibtoft was a chapelry of GREAT CLAYBROOK (Leics.)
2. Mollington was a chapelry of CROPREDY (Oxfordshire)
3. UFTON was divided between two prebends of Lichfield, each prebendary exercising jurisdiction over a part of the parish.

A LEA MARSTON 1570
B OVER WHITACRE 1561
C LITTLE PACKINGTON 1628
D BADDESLEY CLINTON 1632
E HONILEY 1745
F PRESTON BAGOT 1677
G HATTON 1538
H MILVERTON 1742
J WESTON UNDER WETHERLEY 1661
K HUNNINGHAM 1718
L BIRDINGBURY 1559
M EXHALL (near Alcester) 1539
N BILLESLEY 1813
O BEARLEY 1546
P WOLVERTON 1680
Q NORTON LINDSEY 1742
R SHERBOURN 1587
S FULBROOK 1615
T Chapel Ascote (ex-par.)
U Hodnell (ex-par.)
V Upper Radbourn (ex-par.)
W Watergall (ex-par.)
X CHERINGTON 1538

BIRMINGHAM
All Saints   1833
St George   1822
St Martin   1554
St Mary   1779
St Paul   1779
St Peter   1827
St Philip   1715
St Thomas   1829

COVENTRY
Holy Trinity   1561
St John Baptist 1734
St Michael   1662

ECCLESIASTICAL JURISDICTIONS
Archdeaconry of Worcester
Archdeaconry of Coventry
Peculiars

Peculiar Jurisdictions

Royal Peculiar
Stratford

Peculiar of the Bishop of Lichfield
Avon Dassett, Bubbenhall, Wolvey

Peculiar of the D. and C. of Lichfield
Arley, Edgbaston

Peculiar of the Prebendary of Bishop's Itchington
Bishop's Itchington, Gaydon, Chadshunt

Peculiar of the Prebendary of Tachbrook
Bishop's Tachbrook

Peculiar of the Prebendaries of Ufton
Ufton

Peculiar of the Incumbent
Hampton Lucy, Charlecote, Wasperton, Alveston

Peculiar of the Lord of the Manor
Baddesley Clinton, Balsall, Barston, Knowle, Merevale, Packwood

PUBLISHED BY THE INSTITUTE OF HERALDIC AND GENEALOGICAL STUDIES
NORTHGATE CANTERBURY ENGLAND
THIS ITEM IS NUMBER 35 OF OUR SERIES OF GENEALOGICAL AIDS

© 1995

SCALE   MILES

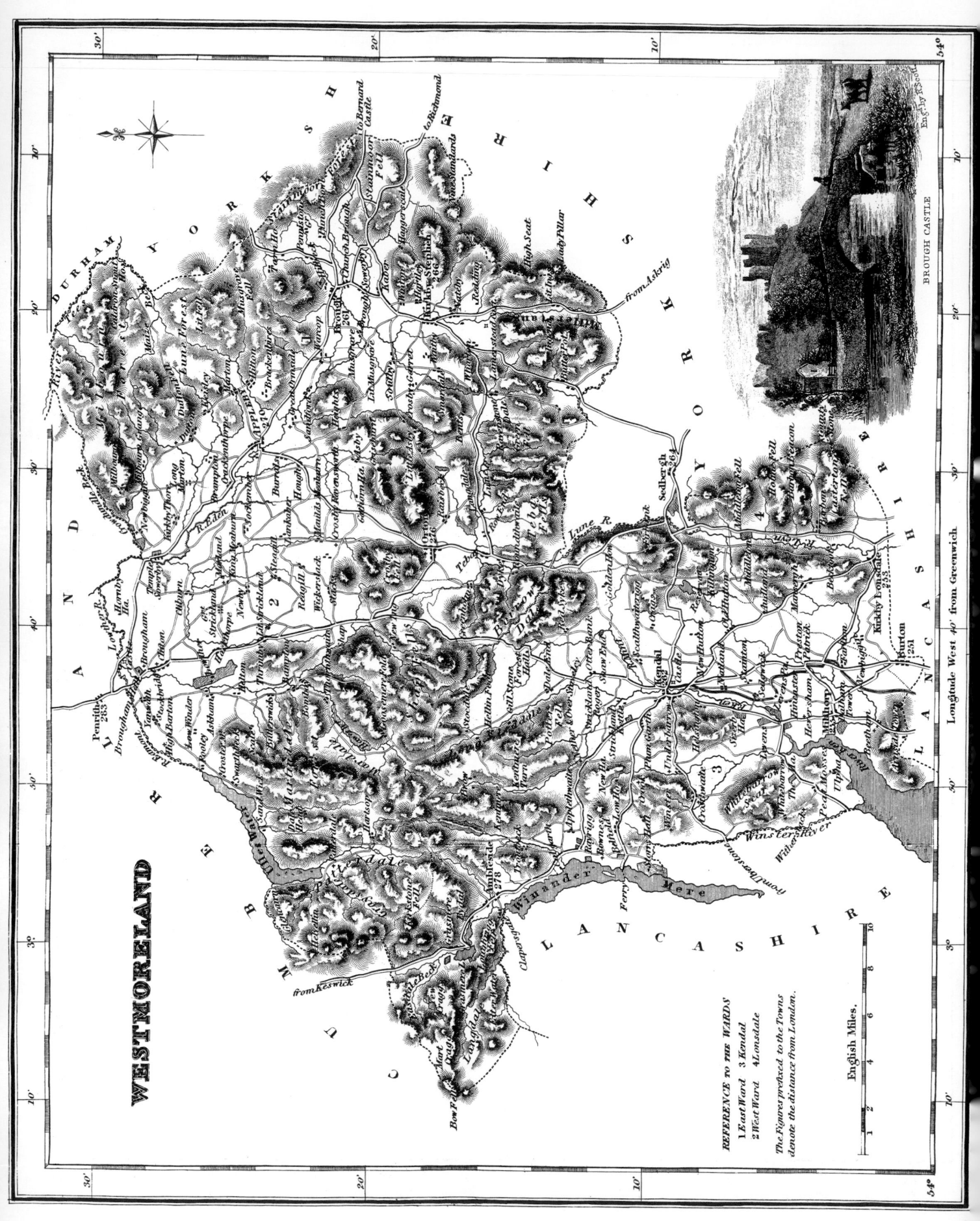

WESTMORELAND

BROUGH CASTLE

Eng.d by B. Scott

REFERENCE TO THE WARDS
1 East Ward   3 Kendal
2 West Ward   4 Lonsdale

The Figures prefixed to the Towns
denote the distance from London.

English Miles.

Longitude West 4° from Greenwich

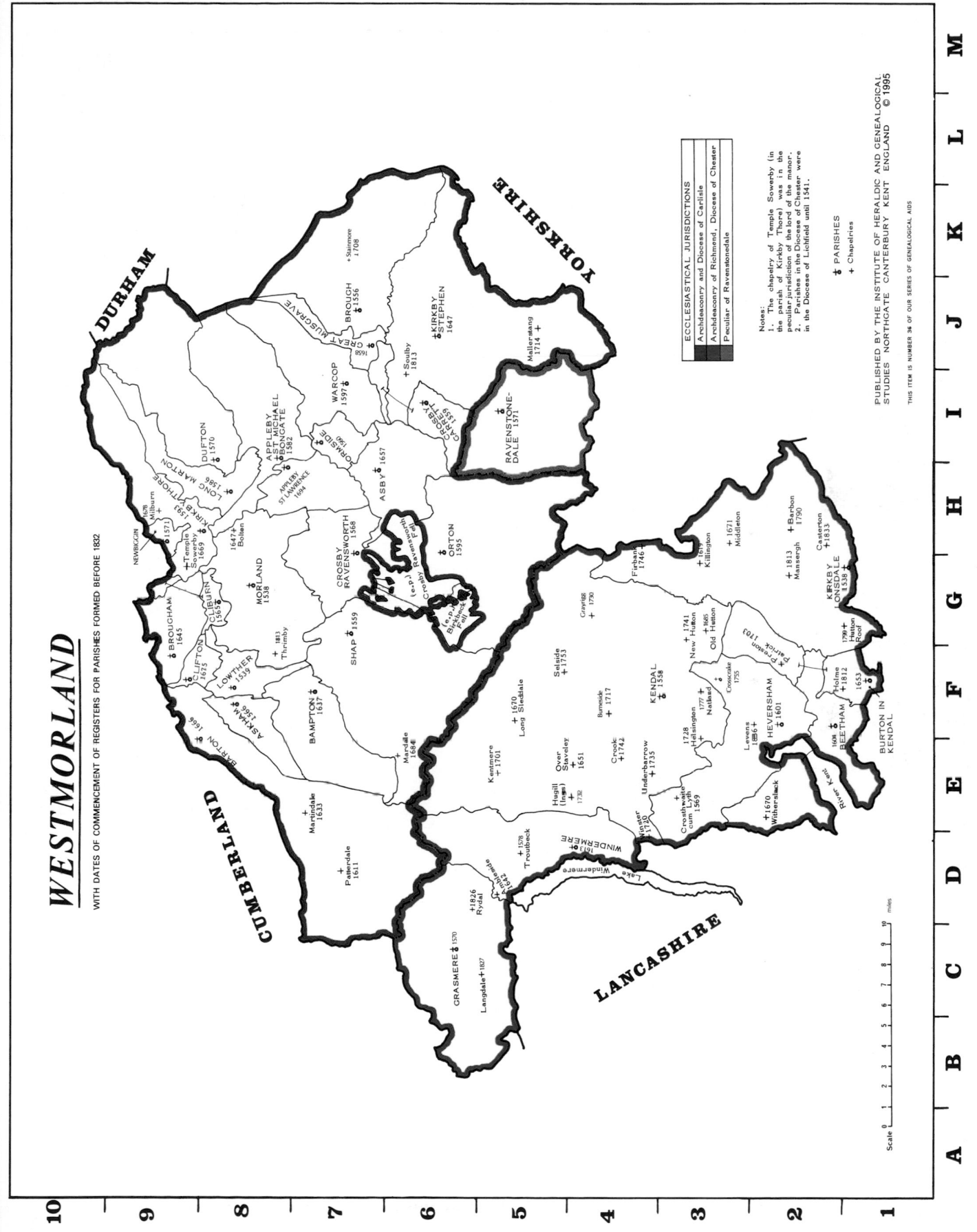

WESTMORLAND

WITH DATES OF COMMENCEMENT OF REGISTERS FOR PARISHES FORMED BEFORE 1832

DURHAM

CUMBERLAND

YORKSHIRE

LANCASHIRE

ECCLESIASTICAL JURISDICTIONS

Archdeaconry and Diocese of Carlisle
Archdeaconry of Richmond, Diocese of Chester
Peculiar of Ravenstonedale

Notes:
1. The chapelry of Temple Soverby (in the parish of Kirkby Thore) was in the peculiar jurisdiction of the lord of the manor.
2. Parishes in the Diocese of Chester were in the Diocese of Lichfield until 1541.

✝ PARISHES
✝ Chapelries

PUBLISHED BY THE INSTITUTE OF HERALDIC AND GENEALOGICAL
STUDIES NORTHGATE CANTERBURY KENT ENGLAND © 1995

THIS ITEM IS NUMBER 36 OF OUR SERIES OF GENEALOGICAL AIDS

Newbiggin 1678
Milburn 1571
+Temple Soverby 1669
Kirkby Thore 1592
DUFTON +1570
LONG MARTON +1586
APPLEBY ST MICHAEL BONGATE 1582
APPLEBY ST LAWRENCE 1694
ORMSIDE 1660
WARCOP 1597
ASBY ✝1657
Soulby 1813
+Stainmore 1708
BROUGH 1556
GREAT MUSGRAVE 8591
Crosby Garrett 1551
KIRKBY STEPHEN 1647
Mallerstang 1714 +
RAVENSTONE-DALE 1571
BROUGHAM 1645
CLIBURN 1565
+1813 Thrimby
MORLAND 1538
CROSBY RAVENSWORTH 1568
Crosby Ravensworth Fell (e.p.)
Birkbeck Fells (e.p.)
ORTON 1595
CLIFTON 1615
LOWTHER 1539
SHAP 1559
ASKHAM 1566
BAMPTON 1637
BARTON 1656
Mardale 1684
Martindale 1633
Patterdale 1611
Kentmere 1701
Long Sleddale +1670
Firbank 1746
+1671 Middleton
Killington +1619
Barbon 1790
+1813 Mansergh
Casterton 1833
KIRKBY LONSDALE 1538
Graythwaite +1730
Selside +1753
New Hutton 1741
Old Hutton +1685
Preston Patrick 1703
Crosscrake 1755
Hutton Roof 1790
Over Staveley 1651
Burneside +1717
Crook +1742
KENDAL 1558
Helsington 1777
Natland
Hugill (Ings) 1732
Underbarrow +1735
Helsington 1728
HEVERSHAM 1601
Levens 1856
Holme 1653
BEETHAM 1604
BURTON IN KENDAL
Winster 1630
+1613
Crosthwaite cum Lyth 1569
+1670 Witherslack
Troutbeck +1578
Ambleside 1642
GRASMERE ✝ 1570
Langdale +1827
+1826 Rydal
Lake Windermere
River Kent
WINDERMERE

Scale 0 1 2 3 4 5 6 7 8 9 10 miles

M L K J I H G F E D C B A

10 9 8 7 6 5 4 3 2 1

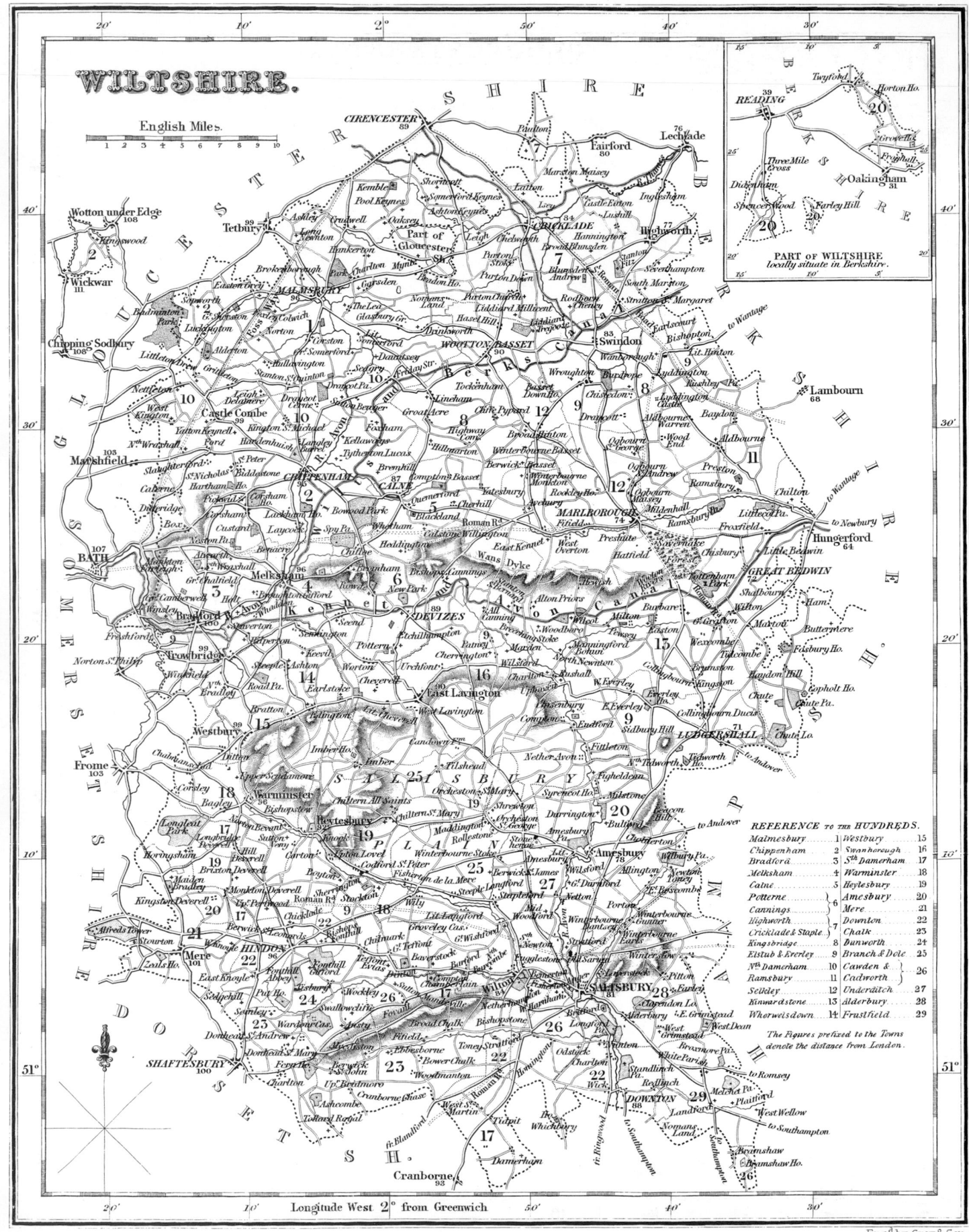

WILTSHIRE.

English Miles.

PART OF WILTSHIRE
locally situate in Berkshire.

REFERENCE TO THE HUNDREDS.

Malmesbury	1	Westbury	15
Chippenham	2	Swanborough	16
Bradford	3	Sth Damerham	17
Melksham	4	Warminster	18
Calne	5	Heytesbury	19
Potterne		Amesbury	20
Cannings	6	Mere	21
Highworth	7	Downton	22
Cricklade & Staple		Chalk	23
Kingsbridge	8	Dunworth	24
Elstub & Everley	9	Branch & Dole	25
Nth Damerham	10	Cawden &	
Ramsbury	11	Cadworth	26
Selkley	12	Underditch	27
Kinwardstone	13	Alderbury	28
Whorwelsdown	14	Frustfield	29

The Figures prefixed to the Towns
denote the distance from London.

Longitude West 2° from Greenwich

Engd by Gray & Son.

WILTSHIRE

WITH DATES OF COMMENCEMENT OF REGISTERS FOR PARISHES FORMED BEFORE 1832

ECCLESIASTICAL JURISDICTIONS
- ARCHDEACONRY OF SARUM
- ARCHDEACONRY OF WILTS
- PECULIAR OF THE DEAN OF SARUM
- OTHER PECULIARS
- DIOCESE OF GLOUCESTER
- ARCHDEACONRY OF WINCHESTER

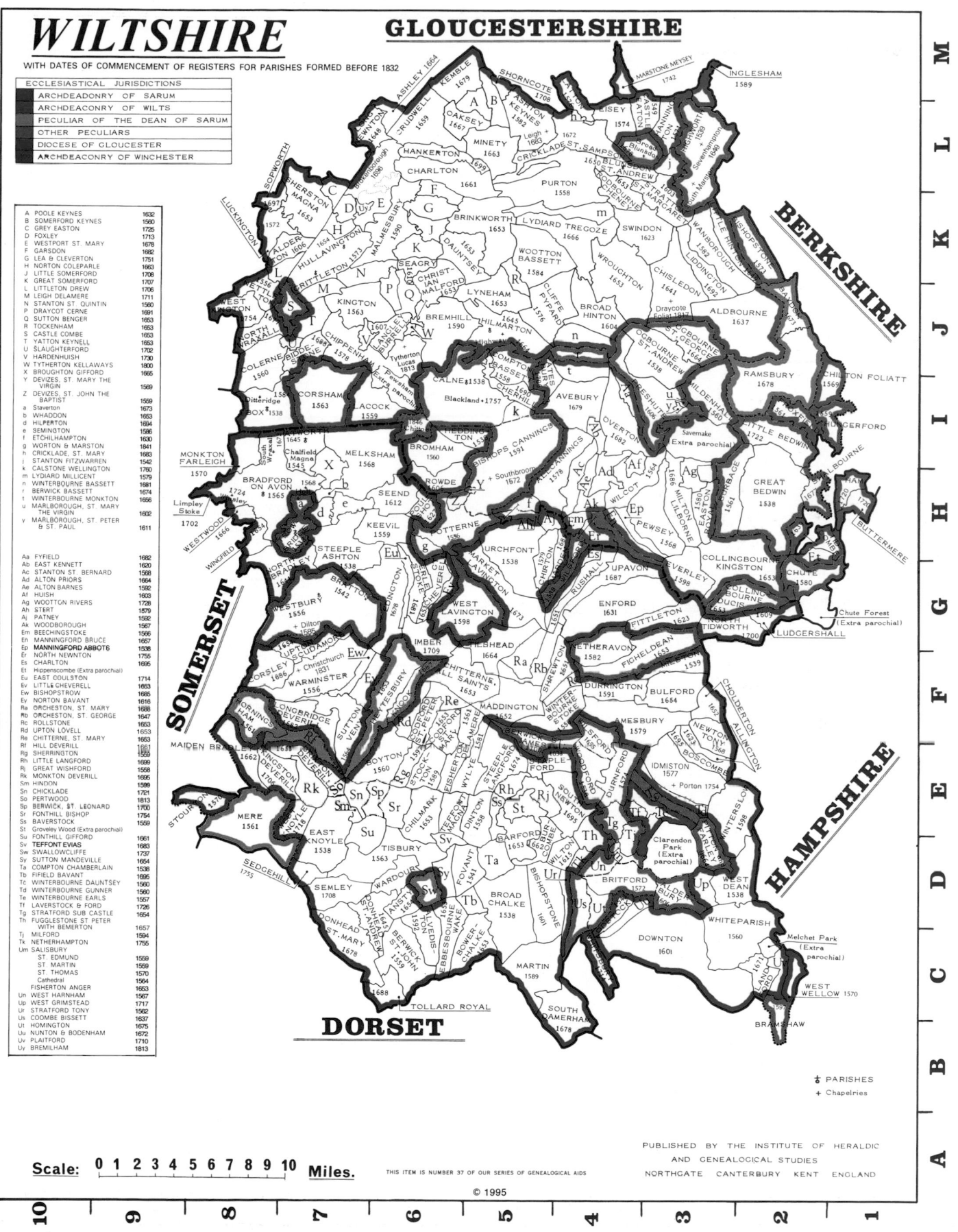

A	POOLE KEYNES	1632
B	SOMERFORD KEYNES	1560
C	GREY EASTON	1725
D	FOXLEY	1713
E	WESTPORT ST. MARY	1678
F	GARSDON	1682
G	LEA & CLEVERTON	1751
H	NORTON COLEPARLE	1663
J	LITTLE SOMERFORD	1708
K	GREAT SOMERFORD	1707
L	LITTLETON DREW	1706
M	LEIGH DELAMERE	1711
N	STANTON ST. QUINTIN	1560
P	DRAYCOT CERNE	1691
Q	SUTTON BENGER	1653
R	TOCKENHAM	1653
S	CASTLE COMBE	1653
T	YATTON KEYNELL	1653
U	SLAUGHTERFORD	1702
V	HARDENHUISH	1730
W	TYTHERTON KELLAWAYS	1800
X	BROUGHTON GIFFORD	1665
Y	DEVIZES, ST. MARY THE VIRGIN	1569
Z	DEVIZES, ST. JOHN THE BAPTIST	1559
a	Staverton	1673
b	WHADDON	1653
d	HILPERTON	1694
e	SEMINGTON	1586
f	ETCHILHAMPTON	1630
g	WORTON & MARSTON	1841
h	CRICKLADE, ST. MARY	1683
i	STANTON FITZWARREN	1542
k	CALSTONE WELLINGTON	1760
m	LYDIARD MILLICENT	1579
n	WINTERBOURNE BASSETT	1681
r	BERWICK BASSETT	1674
t	WINTERBOURNE MONKTON	1656
u	MARLBOROUGH, ST. MARY THE VIRGIN	1602
v	MARLBOROUGH, ST. PETER & ST. PAUL	1611

Aa	FYFIELD	1682
Ab	EAST KENNETT	1620
Ac	STANTON ST. BERNARD	1588
Ad	ALTON PRIORS	1664
Ae	ALTON BARNES	1592
Af	HUISH	1603
Ag	WOOTTON RIVERS	1728
Ah	STERT	1579
Aj	PATNEY	1592
Ak	WOODBOROUGH	1567
Am	BEECHINGSTOKE	1653
En	MANNINGFORD BRUCE	1657
Ep	**MANNINGFORD ABBOTS**	1538
Er	NORTH NEWNTON	1755
Es	CHARLTON	1695
Et	Hippenscombe (Extra parochial)	
Eu	EAST OULSTON	1714
Ev	LITTLE CHEVERELL	1653
Ew	BISHOPSTROW	1685
Ey	NORTON BAVANT	1616
Ra	ORCHESTON, ST. MARY	1688
Rb	ORCHESTON, ST. GEORGE	1647
Rc	ROLLSTONE	1653
Rd	UPTON LOVELL	1653
Re	CHITTERNE, ST. MARY	1653
Rf	HILL DEVERILL	1661
Rg	SHERRINGTON	1570
Rh	LITTLE LANGFORD	1699
Rj	GREAT WISHFORD	1558
Rk	MONKTON DEVERILL	1695
Sm	HINDON	1599
Sn	CHICKLADE	1721
Sc	PERTWOOD	1813
Sp	BERWICK, ST. LEONARD	1700
Sr	FONTHILL BISHOP	1653
Ss	BAVERSTOCK	1559
St	Groveley Wood (Extra parochial)	
Su	FONTHILL GIFFORD	1661
Sv	**TEFFONT EVIAS**	1683
Sx	SWALLOWCLIFFE	1737
Sy	SUTTON MANDEVILLE	1654
Ta	COMPTON CHAMBERLAIN	1538
Tb	FIFIELD BAVANT	1695
Tc	WINTERBOURNE DAUNTSEY	1560
Td	WINTERBOURNE GUNNER	1560
Te	WINTERBOURNE EARLS	1557
Tf	LAVERSTOCK & FORD	1726
Tg	STRATFORD SUB CASTLE	
Th	FUGGLESTONE ST PETER WITH BEMERTON	1657
Tj	MILFORD	1594
Tk	NETHERHAMPTON	1755
Um	SALISBURY	
	ST. EDMUND	1559
	ST. MARTIN	1559
	ST. THOMAS	1570
	Cathedral	1564
	FISHERTON ANGER	1653
Un	WEST HARNHAM	1567
Up	WEST GRIMSTEAD	1717
Ur	STRATFORD TONY	1562
Us	COOMBE BISSETT	1637
Ut	HOMINGTON	1675
Uu	NUNTON & BODENHAM	1672
Uv	PLAITFORD	1710
Uy	BREMILHAM	1813

GLOUCESTERSHIRE

BERKSHIRE

HAMPSHIRE

DORSET

SOMERSET

Scale: 0 1 2 3 4 5 6 7 8 9 10 Miles.

⚓ PARISHES
+ Chapelries

PUBLISHED BY THE INSTITUTE OF HERALDIC
AND GENEALOGICAL STUDIES
NORTHGATE CANTERBURY KENT ENGLAND

THIS ITEM IS NUMBER 37 OF OUR SERIES OF GENEALOGICAL AIDS

© 1995

WORCESTER SHIRE

REFERENCE TO THE HUNDREDS
1 Doddingtree   3 Oswaldslow
2 Halfshire   4 Pershore
                 5 Blackenhurst
The Figures prefixed to the Towns
denote the distance from London.

Birmingham 109
Solihull 108

Stratford on Avon 95
Shipston on Stour 85

Alcester 103

Chipping Campden 90
Broadway

Tewkesbury 103

Cleobury Mortimer 137
Bewdley 129
from Bridgenorth

Bromsgrove 125

WARWICK SHIRE
STAFFORD SHIRE
SHROP SHIRE
HEREFORD SHIRE
GLOUCESTER SHIRE

Worcester

R. Severn
River or Avon

English Miles
1 2 3 4 5 6 7 8 9 10

WORCESTER CATHEDRAL &C.

Longitude West 10' from Greenwich

Engraved by R. Scott

WORCESTERSHIRE

WITH DATES OF COMMENCEMENT OF REGISTERS FOR PARISHES FORMED BEFORE 1832

scale 0 1 2 3 4 5 6 7 8 9 10 miles

B	STOCKTON ON TEME 1567
C	SHELSLEY WALSH 1729
D	Kenswick (chapelry of Knightwick)
E	DOVERDALE 1704
F	Crutchfield (par.)
G	Westwood Park (ex-par.)
Hb	DROITWICH St Andrew 1571
Hc	DROITWICH St Peter 1544
J	MARTIN HUSSINGTREE 1538
K	WARNDON 1561
L	WHITTINGTON 1653
M	SPETCHLEY 1539
N	BREDICOT 1702
O	BROUGHTON HACKETT 1759
P	CHURCHILL 1564
Q	WHITE LADIES ASTON 1538
R	NORTH PIDDLE 1565
S	FLYFORD FLAVELL 1676
T	NAUNTON BEAUCHAMP 1559
U	EARLS CROOME 1644
V	Wyre Piddle 1670
W	LITTLE COMBERTON 1540
X	BRICKLEHAMPTON 1718
Ya	EVESHAM St Lawrence 1556
Yb	EVESHAM All saints 1539

† PARISHES

• Chapel in cries

ECCLESIASTICAL JURISDICTIONS

- Peculiar of the Dean and Chapter of Worcester
- Archdeaconry and Diocese of Worcester
- Archdeaconry of Salop, Diocese of Hereford
- Peculiars

PECULIAR JURISDICTIONS

Peculiar of the Dean and Chapter of Worcester
Berrow, Kempsey, Norton, Stoulton,
Tibberton. Wolverley, Worcester St Michael.

Peculiars of the Incumbents
Alvechurch, Bredon with Bredon's Norton
and Cutsdean, Hanbury, Hartlebury, Ripple
with Queenhill, Tredington, Fladbury with
Wyre Piddle. Throckmorton & Stock and
Bradley.

WORCESTER
Cathedral	1693
All Saints	1560
St Alban	1630
St Andrew	1656
St Clement	1694
St Helen	1538
St John Baptist	1558
St Martin	1538
St Michael	1546
St Nicholas	1563
St Oswald's Hospital	1695
St Peter the Great	1686
St Swithin	1538

STAFFS

SALOP

WARWICKS

GLOUCESTER

HEREFORD

PUBLISHED BY THE INSTITUTE OF HERALDIC AND GENEALOGICAL STUDIES   NORTHGATE CANTERBURY KENT ENGLAND   ©1995

THIS ITEM IS NUMBER 38 OF OUR SERIES OF GENEALOGICAL AIDS

EAST RIDING and AINSTY of YORKSHIRE

BEVERLEY MINSTER.

REFERENCE TO THE WAPENTAKES

1 Buckrose
2 Dickering
3 Ouse & Derwent
4 Harthill
5 Holderness

Drawn by Geo. Kemp Land Surveyor Leeds.

Engraved by James Neele & Co. Burleigh Street Strand.

Published by Archd. Fullarton & Co. Glasgow.

YORKSHIRE (EAST RIDING)

WITH DATES OF COMMENCEMENT OF REGISTERS FOR PARISHES FORMED BEFORE 1832

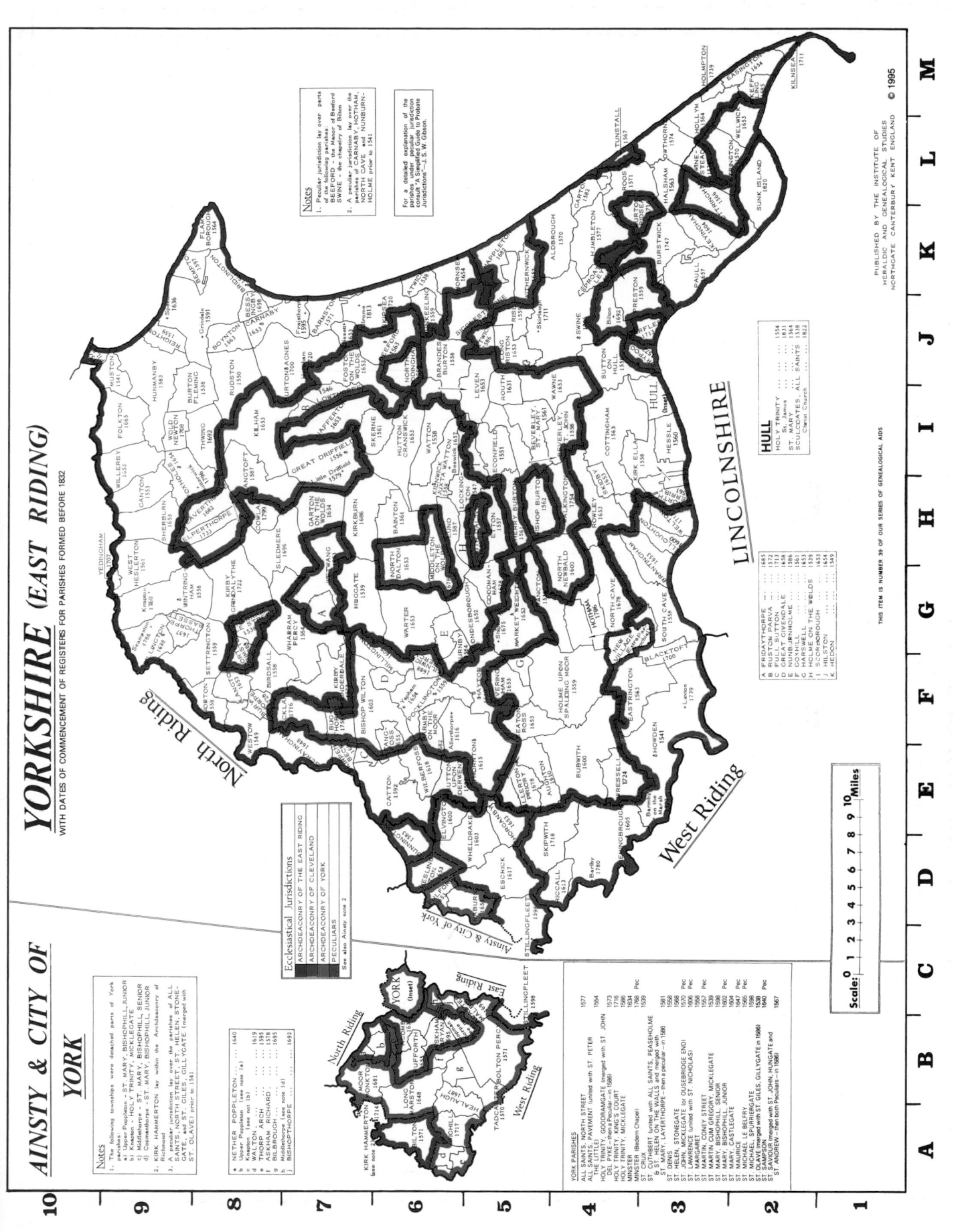

AINSTY & CITY OF YORK

Notes

1. The following townships were detached parts of York parishes:-
   a) Upper Poppleton - ST. MARY, BISHOPHILL JUNIOR
   b) Knapton - HOLY TRINITY, MICKLEGATE
   c) Middlethorpe - ST. MARY, BISHOPHILL SENIOR
   d) Copmanthorpe - ST. MARY, BISHOPHILL JUNIOR

2. KIRK HAMMERTON lay within the Archdeaconry of Richmond.

3. A peculiar jurisdiction lay over the parishes of ALL SAINTS, NORTH STREET, ST. HELEN, STONE-GATE, and ST. GILES, GILLYGATE (merged with ST. OLAVE) prior to 1341

a NETHER POPPLETON	1640
b Upper Population (see note 1a)	
c Knapton (see note 1b)	
d WALTON	1619
e THORP ARCH	1595
f ASKHAM RICHARD	1578
g BILBROUGH	1695
h Middlethorpe (see note 1c)	
i BISHOPTHORPE	1692

Notes

1. The jurisdiction lay over parts of the following parishes:
   BEEFORD - the Manor of Beeford
   SWINE - the chapelry of Bilton

2. A peculiar jurisdiction lay over the parishes of CARNABY, HOTHAM, NORTH CAVE and NUNBURN-HOLME prior to 1541

For a detailed explanation of the parishes under peculiar jurisdiction consult "A Simplified Guide to Probate Jurisdictions" - J. S. W. Gibson.

YORK PARISHES

ALL SAINTS, NORTH STREET	1577
ALL SAINTS, PAVEMENT (united with ST. PETER THE LITTLE)	1554
HOLY TRINITY, GOODRAMGATE (merged with ST. JOHN DEL PYKE - then a Peculiar)	1573
HOLY TRINITY, KING'S COURT	1716
HOLY TRINITY, MICKLEGATE	1586
MINSTER	1634
MINSTER (Bedern Chapel)	1539
ST. CRUX	1581
ST. CUTHBERT (united with ALL SAINTS, PEASHOLME & ST. HELEN ON THE WALLS and merged with ST. MARY, LAYERTHORPE - then a peculiar - in 1586	1558
ST. DENIS	1558
ST. HELEN, STONEGATE	1570 Pec
ST. JOHN, MICKLEGATE (or OUSEBRIDGE END)	1606 Pec
ST. LAWRENCE (united with ST. NICHOLAS)	1559
ST. MARTIN, CONEY STREET	1557
ST. MARTIN CUM GREGORY MICKLEGATE	1539
ST. MARY, BISHOPHILL SENIOR	1602
ST. MARY, BISHOPHILL JUNIOR	1604
ST. MAURICE	1647 Pec
ST. MICHAEL LE BELFRY	1565
ST. MICHAEL, SPURRIERGATE	1566
ST. OLAVE (merged with ST. GILES, GILLYGATE in 1586)	1538 Pec
ST. SAMPSON	1640
ST. SAVIOUR (merged with ST. JOHN, HUNGATE and ST. ANDREW - then both Peculiars - in 1586)	1567

HULL

HOLY TRINITY	1554
ST. James	1713
ST. MARY	1564
SCULCOATES, ALL SAINTS	1538
Christ Church	1822

A FRIDAYTHORPE	1665
B RUSTON PARVA	1572
C FULL SUTTON	1713
D GREAT GIVENDALE	1586
E NUNBURNHOLME	1561
F GOXHILL	1561
G HARSWELL	1653
H MELTON ON THE WOLDS	1639
J SCORBOROUGH	1653
K HEDON	1549

PUBLISHED BY THE INSTITUTE OF
HERALDIC AND GENEALOGICAL STUDIES
NORTHGATE CANTERBURY KENT ENGLAND

THIS ITEM IS NUMBER 39 OF OUR SERIES OF GENEALOGICAL AIDS

© 1995

Ecclesiastical Jurisdictions

- ARCHDEACONRY OF THE EAST RIDING
- ARCHDEACONRY OF CLEVELAND
- ARCHDEACONRY OF YORK
- PECULIARS

See also Ainsty note 2

Scale: 0 1 2 3 4 5 6 7 8 9 10 Miles

LINCOLNSHIRE

West Riding

North Riding

Ainsty & City of York

NORTH RIDING
OF
YORKSHIRE.

Engraved by Fullarton & C? Burleigh S? Strand

REFERENCE to the WAPENTAKES.

1. Gilling West.
2. Hang West.
3. Gilling East.
4. Hang East.
5. Hallikeld.
6. Allerton.
7. Birdforth.
8. Bulmer.
9. Rydale.
10. Langbargh.
11. Pickering.
12. Whitby Strand Lith.

NORTH SEA

DURHAM

WESTMORELAND

WEST RIDING

EAST RIDING

Scale of Miles

YORK MINSTER

Drawn by G. Kemp Land Surveyor Leeds.

Published by Fullartonn & C? Glasgow

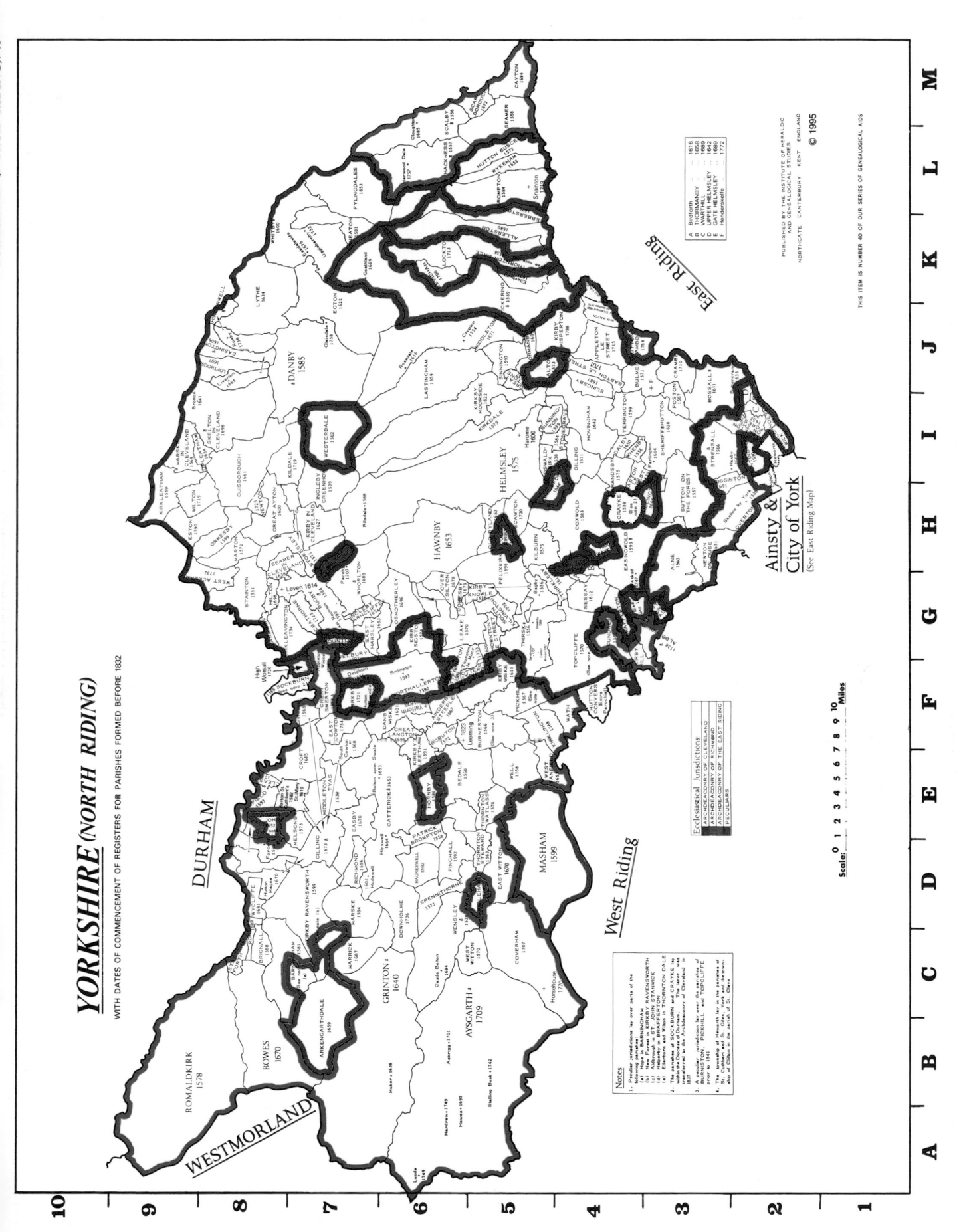

YORKSHIRE (NORTH RIDING)

WITH DATES OF COMMENCEMENT OF REGISTERS FOR PARISHES FORMED BEFORE 1832

DURHAM

WESTMORLAND

West Riding

East Riding

Ainsty & City of York
(See East Riding Map)

Ecclesiastical Jurisdictions

ARCHDEACONRY OF CLEVELAND
ARCHDEACONRY OF RICHMOND
ARCHDEACONRY OF THE EAST RIDING
PECULIARS

Scale: 0 1 2 3 4 5 6 7 8 9 10 Miles

Notes

1. Peculiar jurisdictions lay over parts of the following parishes
   (a) Hope in BARNINGHAM
   (b) New Forest in KIRKBY RAVENSWORTH
   (c) Aldbrough in ST JOHN STANWICK
   (d) Halperby in BRAFFERTON
   (e) Eskdaleto and Wiltonin THORNTON DALE

2. The parishes of SOCKBURN and CRAYKE lay within the Diocese of Durham. The latter was transferred to the Archdeaconry of Cleveland in 1837

3. A peculiar jurisdiction lay over the parishes of BURNESTON, PICKHILL, and TOPCLIFFE prior to 1541.

4. The township of Heworth lay in the parishes of St. Cuthbert and St. Giles, York and the township of Clifton in the parish of St. Olave.

ROMALDKIRK 1578

BOWES 1670

ARKENGARTHDALE 1639

GRINTON & 1640

AYSGARTH & 1709

MASHAM 1599

DANBY 1585

HELMSLEY 1575

HAWNBY 1653

WESTERDALE 1562

PUBLISHED BY THE INSTITUTE OF HERALDIC AND GENEALOGICAL STUDIES
NORTHGATE CANTERBURY KENT ENGLAND

© 1995

THIS ITEM IS NUMBER 40 OF OUR SERIES OF GENEALOGICAL AIDS

	1616
A Birdforth	1658
B THORMANBY	1689
C WARTHILL	1642
D UPPER HELMSLEY	1689
E GATE HELMSLEY	1772
F Hendarskelfe	

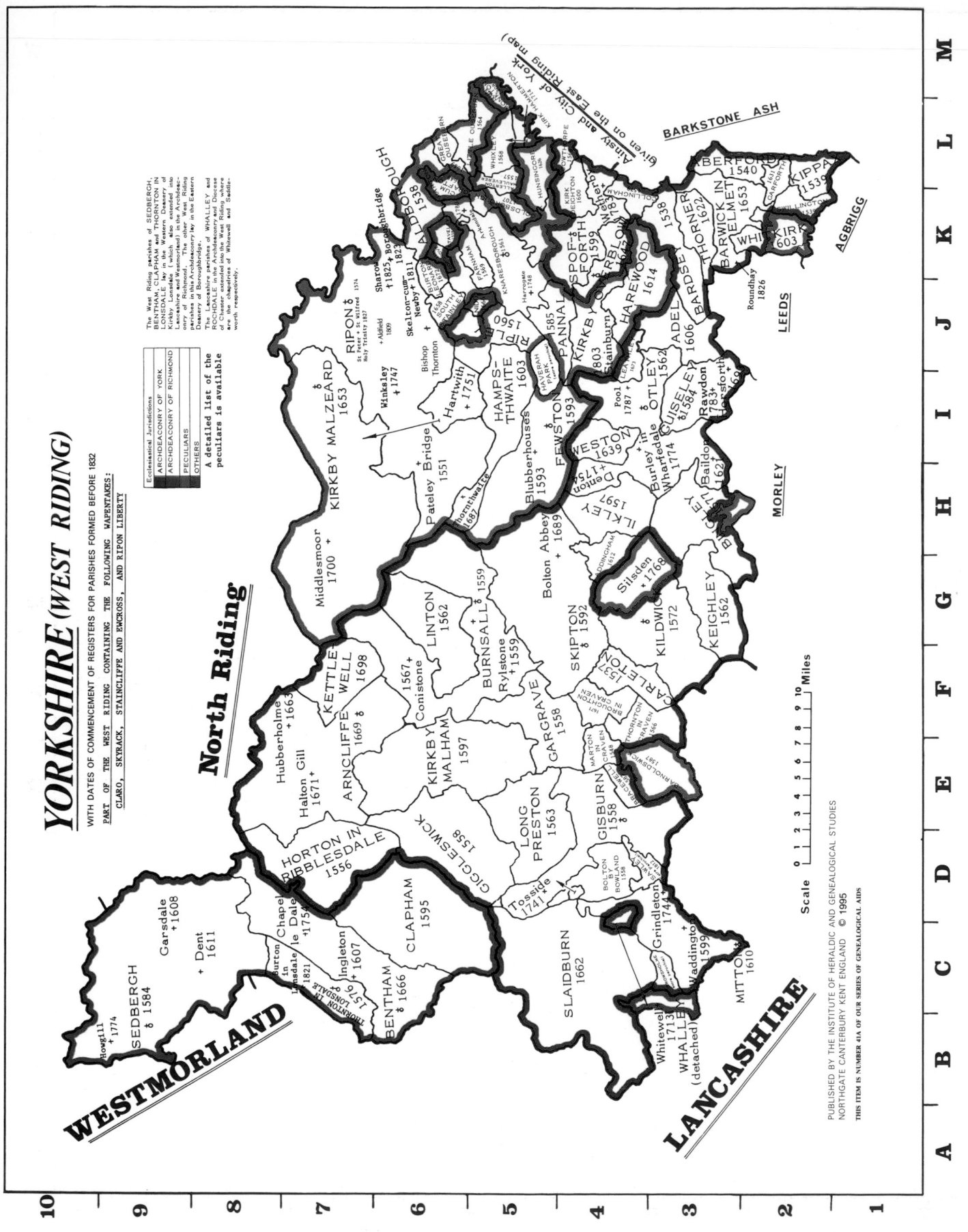

YORKSHIRE (WEST RIDING)

WITH DATES OF COMMENCEMENT OF REGISTERS FOR PARISHES FORMED BEFORE 1832

PART OF THE WEST RIDING CONTAINING THE FOLLOWING WAPENTAKES:
CLARO, SKYRACK, STAINCLIFFE AND EWCROSS, AND RIPON LIBERTY

Ecclesiastical Jurisdictions
- ARCHDEACONRY OF YORK
- ARCHDEACONRY OF RICHMOND
- PECULIARS
- OTHERS

A detailed list of the peculiars is available

The West Riding parishes of SEDBERGH, BENTHAM, CLAPHAM and THORNTON IN LONSDALE lay in the Western Deanery of Kirkby Lonsdale (which also extended into Lancashire and Westmorland) in the Archdeaconry of Richmond. The other West Riding parishes in this Archdeaconry lay in the Eastern Deanery of Boroughbridge.

The Lancashire parishes of WHALLEY and ROCHDALE in the Archdeaconry and Diocese of Chester extended into the West Riding where are the chapelries of Whitewell and Saddleworth respectively.

North Riding

WESTMORLAND

LANCASHIRE

BARKSTONE ASH

AGBRIGG

LEEDS

MORLEY

Howgill +1774
SEDBERGH ♂ 1584
Garsdale +1608
+ Dent 1611

Burton Chapel in Dale +1754
Ingleton + 1607
THORNTON IN LONSDALE 1576
Burton in Lonsdale 1821
BENTHAM ♂ 1666

HORTON IN RIBBLESDALE 1556

Halton Gill 1671+
Hubberholme +1663

Middlesmoor 1700 +

KIRKBY MALZEARD ♂ 1653

KETTLE WELL 1698 ♂
ARNCLIFFE 1669 ♂

1567+ Conistone
LINTON 1562

CLAPHAM 1595

KIRKBY MALHAM 1597

GIGGLESWICK 1558

BURNSALL ♂ 1559
+ Rylstone +1559

GARGRAVE 1558

LONG PRESTON 1563

SLAIDBURN 1662

Tossside 1741+

GISBURN 1558 ♂

Whitewell 1713
WHALLEY (detached)

Grindleton + 1744
Waddington 1599

MITTON + 1610

BOLTON BY BOWLAND 1558

MARTON IN CRAVEN
BRACEWELL
ARNOLDSWICK 1587

BROUGHTON IN CRAVEN
THORNTON IN CRAVEN
CARLETON 1537

SKIPTON ♂ 1592

KILDWICK ♂ 1592

KEIGHLEY 1562

Silsden + 1768

BINGLEY 1577

ADDINGHAM 1612

ILKLEY + 1597
Denton +1750
Burley in Wharfedale 1774

Baildon 1627+

Rawdon 1783+

Horsforth +1606

GUISELEY ♂ 1584

OTLEY 1562

ADEL 1606

BARDSEY

WESTON 1639

Pool 1787+
Leathley 1627+

KIRKBY OVERBLOW 1613
Stainburn +

HAREWOOD 1614

WEETON

PANNAL 803

HARROGATE +1748

Hampsthwaite HAVERAH PARK +1603

BLUBBERHOUSES 1593

FEWSTON 1593

Thruscross +1687

Thornthwaite

HAMPS- THWAITE 1603

Hartwith + 1751

Bishop Thornton

Pateley Bridge 1551

Winksley +1747

Sawley

RIPON ♂
St Peter + St Wilfred
Holy Trinity 1827

Sharow +1825
+ Adfield 1809

Skelton-cum-Newby + 1811

RIPL 1560

585

Markington 1811

SOUTH STAINLEY
NIDD 1607

KNARESBOROUGH
BURTON LEONARD

KIRKBY OF FORTH 1599

SPOFFORTH 1599

KIRK DEIGHTON 1600

Wetherby 1783+

SICKLINGHALL

Collingham

WHIXLEY 1566

GREAT OUSEBURN
LITTLE OUSEBURN
WHIXLEY

ALDBOROUGH 1538

+1574 Aldborough

Boroughbridge 1822+

MINSKIP

FARNHAM

ALLERTON MAULEVERER

Marton cum Grafton

HUNSINGORE 1600

COWTHORPE

ROUNDHAY 1826

BARWICK IN ELMET 1653

SHERBURN 1622

THORNER 1622

ABERFORD 1540

BARWICK IN ELMET 1653

GARFORTH 1631

KIPPAX 1539

WHITKIRK 1603

Roundhay 1826

Scale 0 1 2 3 4 5 6 7 8 9 10 Miles

PUBLISHED BY THE INSTITUTE OF HERALDIC AND GENEALOGICAL STUDIES
NORTHGATE CANTERBURY KENT ENGLAND © 1995

THIS ITEM IS NUMBER 41A OF OUR SERIES OF GENEALOGICAL AIDS

A B C D E F G H I J K L M

10 9 8 7 6 5 4 3 2 1

YORKSHIRE (WEST RIDING)

WITH DATES OF COMMENCEMENT OF REGISTERS FOR PARISHES FORMED BEFORE 1832

PART OF THE WEST RIDING CONTAINING THE FOLLOWING WAPENTAKES:
AGBRIGG, AINSTY, BARKSTONE ASH, MORLEY, OSGOLDCROSS, STAINCROSS,
STAFFORTH AND TICKHILL, DONCASTER SOKE AND LEEDS BOROUGH

The Lancashire parishes of WHALLEY and
ROCHDALE in the Archdeaconry and Diocese
of Chester extended into the West Riding as
are the chapelries of Whitewell and Saddleworth respectively.

The Nottinghamshire parishes of BLYTH and
FINNINGLEY in the Archdeaconry of Notting-
ham and Diocese of York extended into the
West Riding. The parish of ROSSINGTON,
wholly in the West Riding, also lay in this
Archdeaconry.

Ecclesiastical Jurisdictions
ARCHDEACONRY OF YORK
PECULIARS
OTHERS

A detailed list of the
peculiars is available

East Riding

(Ainsty and City of York
given on the East Riding map)

LINCOLNSHIRE

NOTTS.

DERBYSHIRE

CHESHIRE

LANCASHIRE

SKYRACK Wapentake

CALVERLEY 1574

LEEDS
St. Peter 1572
St. John 1725
Holy Trinity 1730
St. Paul 1796
St. Mary 1826
St. Mark 1827
Christ Church 1827

Oulton-cum-
Woodlesford 1827

ROTHWELL 1538

BRAMHAM 586

TADCASTER 1570

SHERBURN IN ELMET 1639

BRAYTON 1614

SELBY 1559

BIRKIN 1649

DRAX 1597

Carleton 1631

SNAITH 1587

Snaith Juxta 1617

KELLING TON 1597

WOMERS LEY 1564

CAMPSALL 1563

WISTOW 1590

Hook

Airmyn 1726

Rawcliffe 1689

THORNE 1565

FISH LAKE 1561

HATFIELD 1560

ARK SEY 1557

DONCASTER 1557

FINNINGLEY 1557

BLYTH 1556

Austerfield 1559

Bawtry 1653

TICKHILL 1538

MALTBY 1597

ASTON 1560

WHISTON

ROTHER HAM 1558

ECCLESFIELD 1558

SHEFFIELD
St. Peter 1560
St. Paul 1740
St. James 1789
St. George 1825
St. Philip 1828
St. Mary 1830

Attercliffe 1719

Tinsley 1711

Stannington 1830

Ecclesall 1784

Bradfield 1559

Bolsterstone 1658

Midhope 1772

PENISTONE 1644

Cumberworth 1653

SILKSTONE 1558

CAWTHORNE 1658

Wortley 1678

Wortley 1598

Worsborough 1750

DARFIELD 1559

Monk Bretton 1557

BARNSLEY

DARTON 1558

ROYSTON 1559

FELKIRK 1701

SOUTH KIRKBY 1559

HEMSWORTH 1654

FEATHER STONE 1558

NORMAN TON 1557

PONTEFRACT 1585

KIRK SMEATON 1604

WRAGBY 1538

WAKEFIELD 1613

HORBURY 1598

SANDAL MAGNA 1538

THORNHILL 1580

WOOLLEY 1651

EMLEY 1600

KIRKBURTON 1540

KIRK HEATON 1653

ALMONDBURY 1557

Honley 1829

HALIFAX 1538

Luddenden 1653

Heptonstall 1593

Haworth 1645

Wibsey 1640

Thornton 1678

Illingworth 1695

Wisden 1824

BRADFORD 1596

Horton 1808

Idle 1788

Lightcliffe 1538

Sowerby 1643

Sowerby Bridge 1709

RASTRICK 1614

Elland 1559

Stainland 1782

Ripponden 1684

Todmorden 1666

ROCHDALE 1768

SADDLEWORTH 1613

Dob Cross 1787

LEEDS

WISTOW

Scale 0 1 2 3 4 5 6 7 8 9 10 Miles

PUBLISHED BY THE INSTITUTE OF HERALDIC AND GENEALOGICAL STUDIES
NORTHGATE CANTERBURY KENT ENGLAND   © 1995

THIS ITEM IS NUMBER 4IB OF OUR SERIES OF GENEALOGICAL AIDS

A B C D E F G H I J K L M

1 2 3 4 5 6 7 8 9 10

WEST RIDING OF YORKSHIRE.

English Miles.

REFERENCE to the WAPENTAKES.
1 Staincliffe
2 Claro
3 Gyrack
4 Barkston Ash
5 Morley
6 Agbrigg
7 Staincross
8 Osgoldcross
9 Stratforth & Tickhill
10 Ainsty of York

NORTH RIDING

EAST RIDING

LINCOLNSHIRE

NOTTINGHAMSHIRE

DERBYSHIRE

CHESHIRE

LANCASHIRE

WESTMORELAND

PROPRIETORY SCHOOL WAKEFIELD

Drawn by G. Kemp Land Surveyor, Leeds.

Published by Archd. Fullarton &Co. Glasgow.

Engraved by Jas. Neele Burleigh Str. Strand.

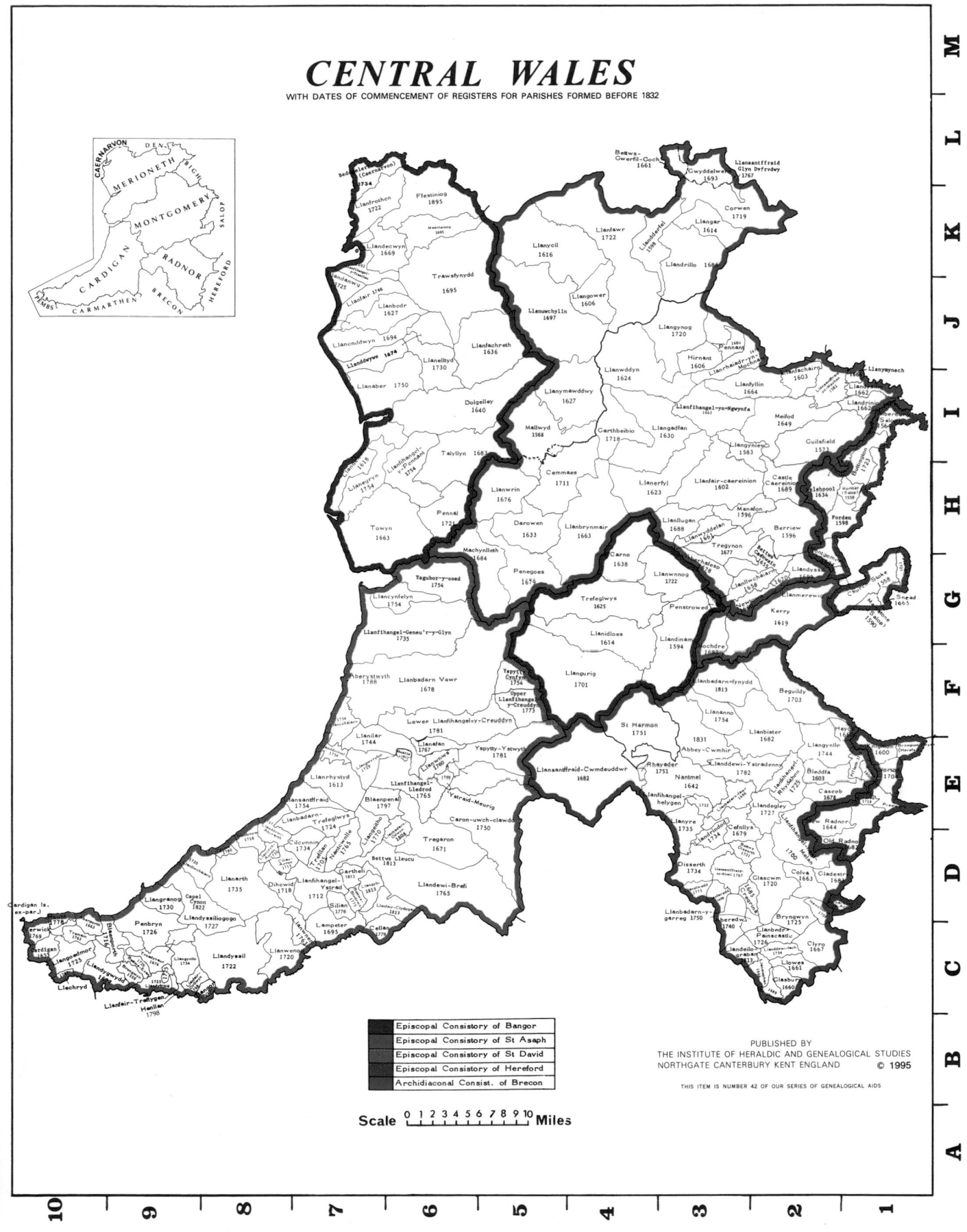

CENTRAL WALES
WITH DATES OF COMMENCEMENT OF REGISTERS FOR PARISHES FORMED BEFORE 1832

Episcopal Consistory of Bangor	
Episcopal Consistory of St Asaph	
Episcopal Consistory of St David	
Episcopal Consistory of Hereford	
Archidiaconal Consist. of Brecon	

Scale 0 1 2 3 4 5 6 7 8 9 10 Miles

PUBLISHED BY
THE INSTITUTE OF HERALDIC AND GENEALOGICAL STUDIES
NORTHGATE CANTERBURY KENT ENGLAND © 1995

THIS ITEM IS NUMBER 42 OF OUR SERIES OF GENEALOGICAL AIDS

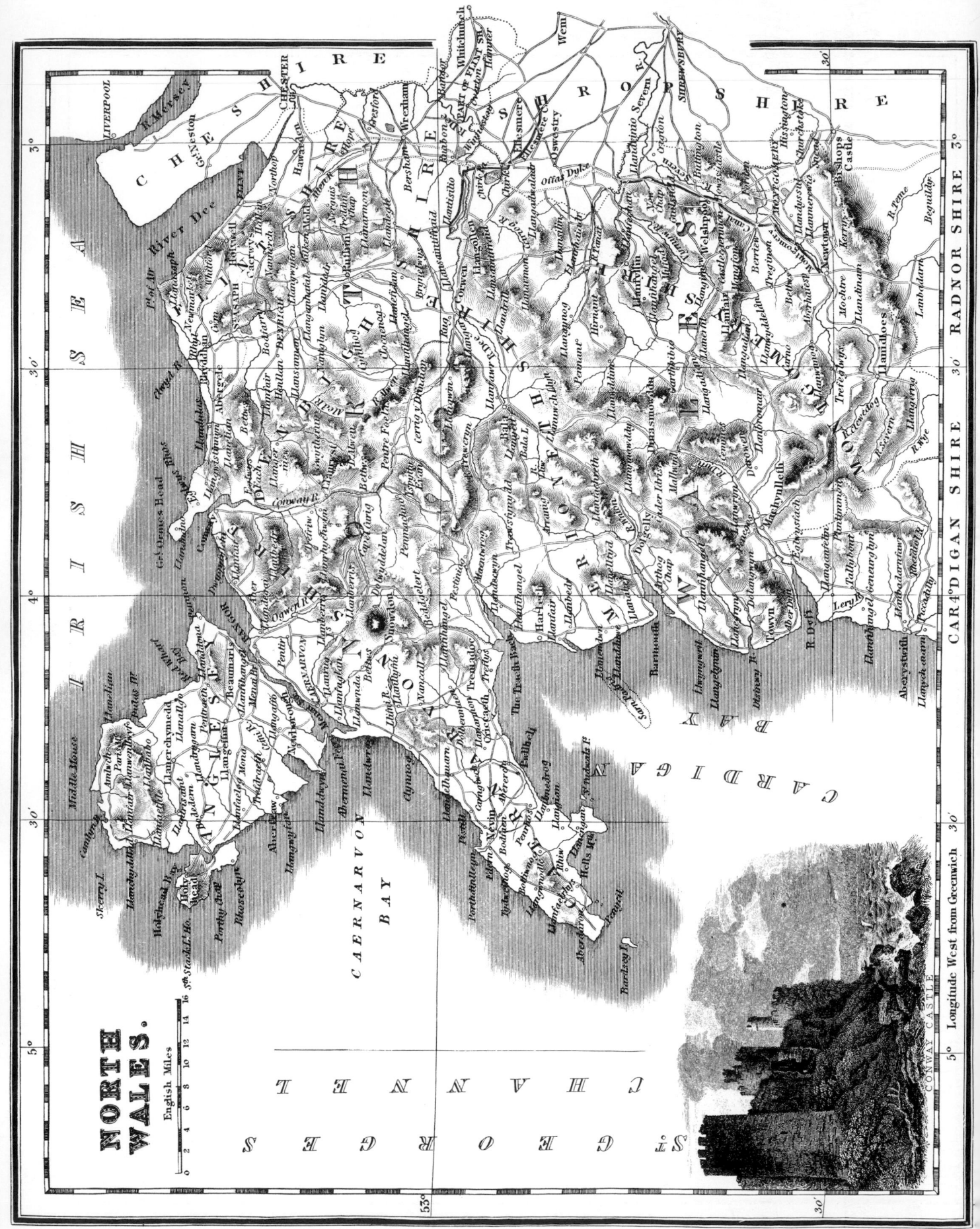

NORTH
WALES.

English Miles

0 2 4 6 8 10 12 14 16

IRISH SEA

CHESHIRE

LIVERPOOL

R. Mersey.

River Dee

FLINTSHIRE

DENBIGHSHIRE

MERIONETHSHIRE

MONTGOMERYSHIRE

SHROPSHIRE

RADNOR SHIRE

CAR⁴DIGAN SHIRE

ANGLESEY

CAERNARVONSHIRE

CAERNARVON BAY

CARDIGAN BAY

ST GEORGES CHANNEL

5° Longitude West from Greenwich 30'

CONWAY CASTLE

CHESTER

SHREWSBURY

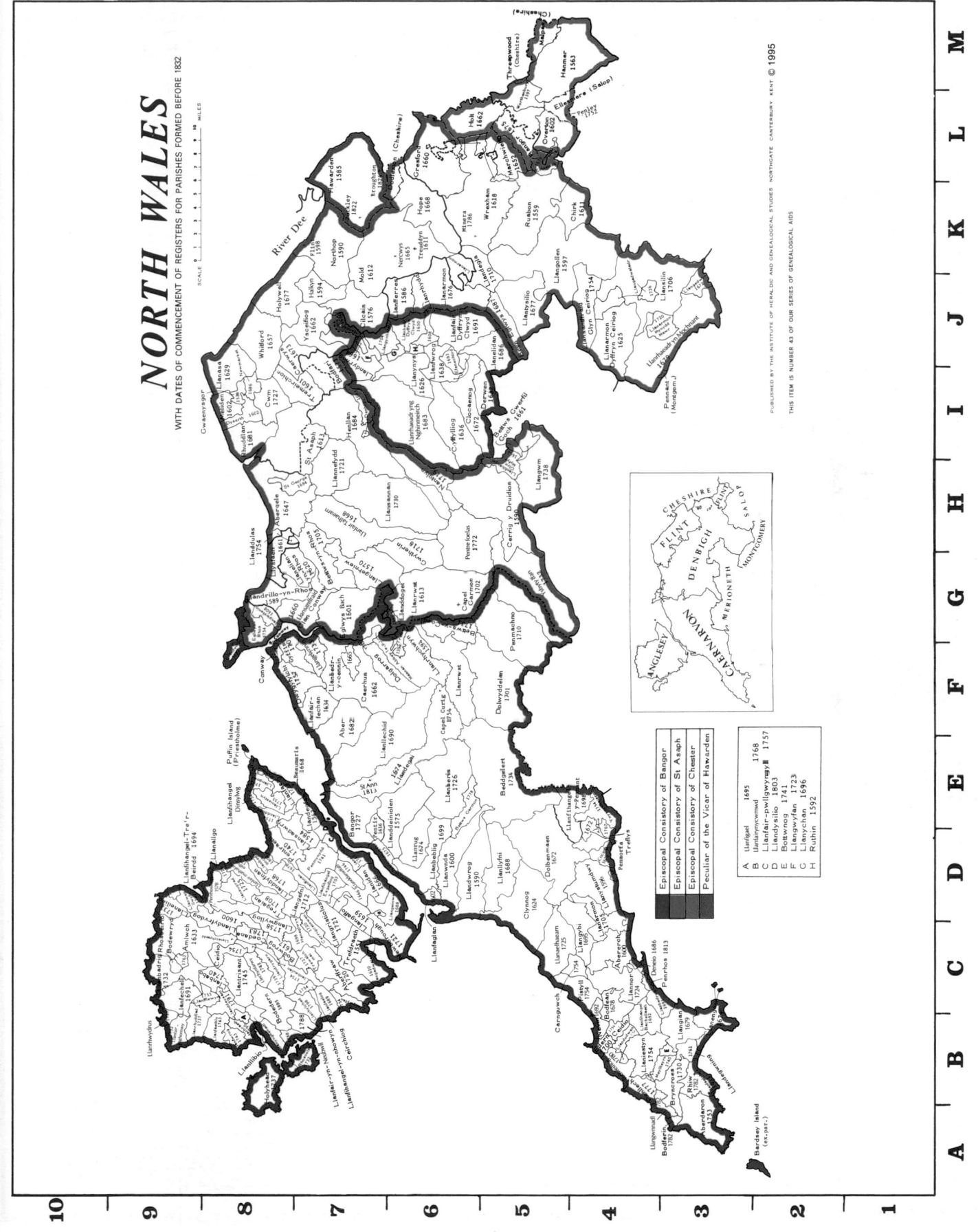

NORTH WALES

WITH DATES OF COMMENCEMENT OF REGISTERS FOR PARISHES FORMED BEFORE 1832

River Dee

SCALE

MILES

Episcopal Consistory of Bangor
Episcopal Consistory of St Asaph
Episcopal Consistory of Chester
Peculiar of the Vicar of Hawarden

A Llanfigael   1695
B Llanfairynmwwd   1768
C Llanfair-pwllgwyngyll 1757
D Llandysilio   1803
E Bottwnog   1741
F Llangwyfan   1723
G Llanychan   1696
H Ruthin   1592

PUBLISHED BY THE INSTITUTE OF HERALDIC AND GENEALOGICAL STUDIES NORTHGATE CANTERBURY KENT © 1995

THIS ITEM IS NUMBER 43 OF OUR SERIES OF GENEALOGICAL AIDS

CHESHIRE
FLINT
DENBIGH
CAERNARVON
ANGLESEY
MERIONETH
MONTGOMERY
SALOP

A B C D E F G H I J K L M

10 9 8 7 6 5 4 3 2 1

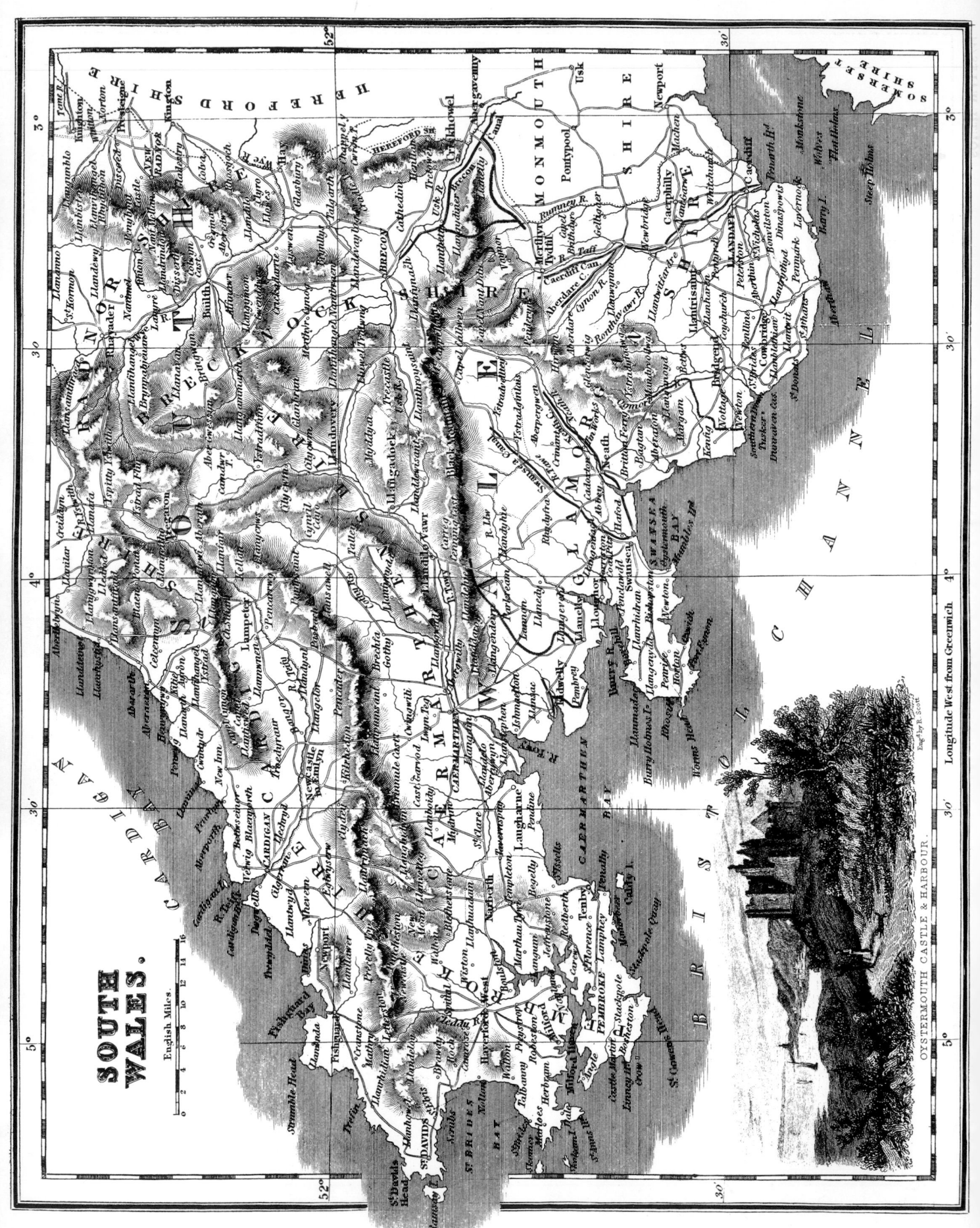

SOUTH WALES.

English Miles.
0 2 4 6 8 10 12 14 16

Longitude West from Greenwich.

OYSTERMOUTH CASTLE & HARBOUR.

Eng.d by R. Scott.

SOUTH WALES

WITH DATES OF COMMENCEMENT OF REGISTERS FOR PARISHES FORMED BEFORE 1832

PUBLISHED BY
THE INSTITUTE OF HERALDIC AND GENEALOGICAL STUDIES
NORTHGATE CANTERBURY KENT © 1995
THIS ITEM IS NUMBER 44 OF OUR SERIES OF GENEALOGICAL AIDS

Scale 0 1 2 3 4 5 6 7 8 9 10 Miles

A	Llanreithan 1786
Ba	St Martin Haverfordwest 1721
Bb	St Thomas Haverfordwest 1777
Bc	St Mary Haverfordwest 1678
C	Haroldston St Issels 1753
D	Coedcanlass
E	Upton
F	St Mary Brecon 1685
G	Llandefaelog-tref-graig 1755
H	Lanfihangel-Tal-y-llyn 1700
I	Llangsty-Tal-y-llyn 1718
J	St Andrew's Minor 1744
K	Llysworney 1754
L	Nash (ex-par.)
M	Llanmlhangel 1755
N	Llandough-juxta-Cowbridge 1583
O	Llanmaes 1583
P	St Mary Church 1577
Q	Flemingston 1726
R	Cowbridge 1718
S	Ystradowain 1757
T	Highlight (ex-par.)
U	Llanlltern 1725
U	St Brides super Ely 1747
W	St Georges 1693
X	Michaelston super Ely 1754
Y	Knelston
Z	Reynoldston 1713

Episcopal Consistory of St David

Episcopal Consistory of Llandaff

Archidiaconal Consist. of Brecon

RADNOR
BRECON
MON.
CARDIGAN
CARMARTHEN
GLAMORGAN
PEMBROKE

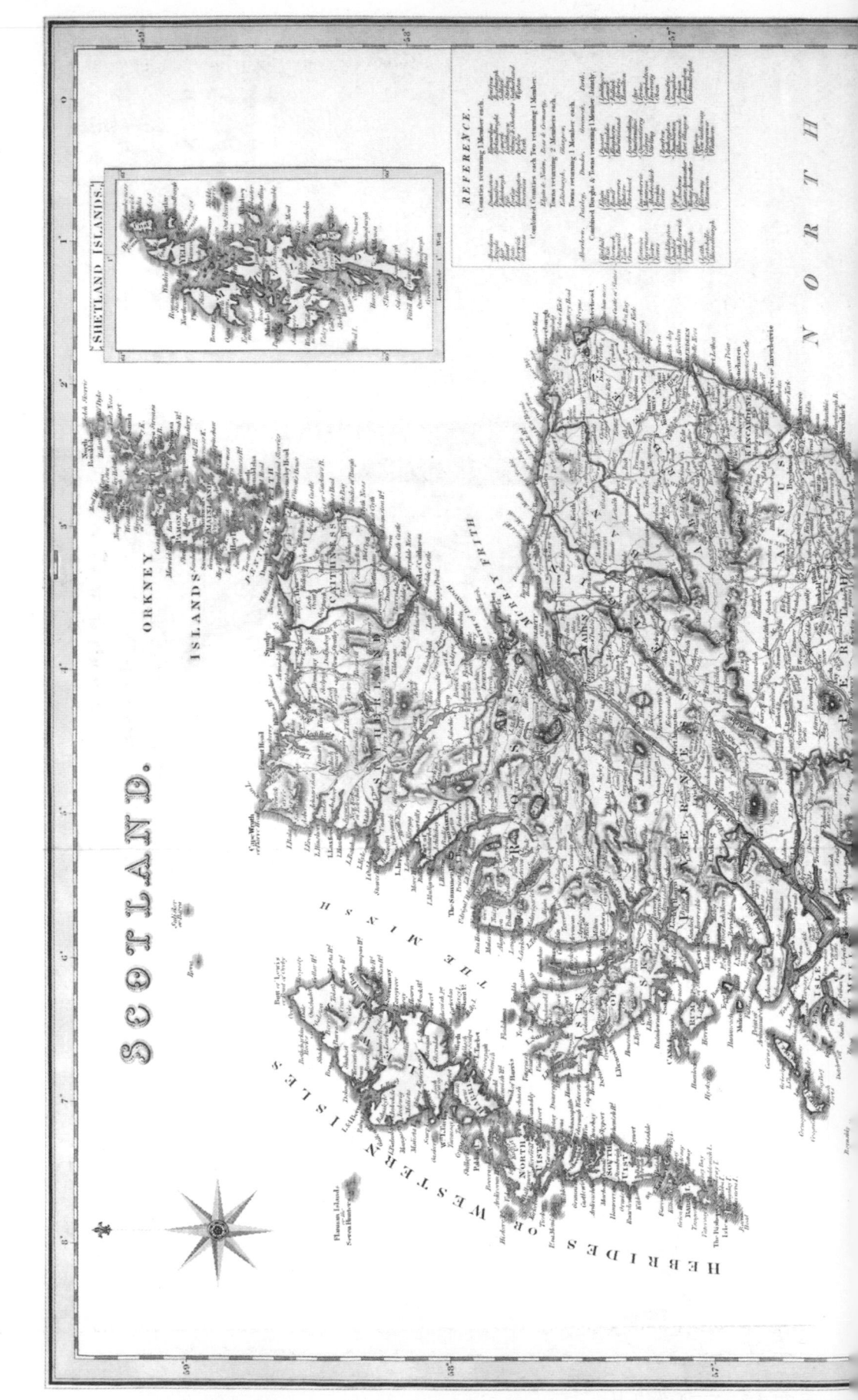

SCOTLAND.

SHETLAND ISLANDS.

ORKNEY ISLANDS.

HEBRIDES OR WESTERN ISLES.

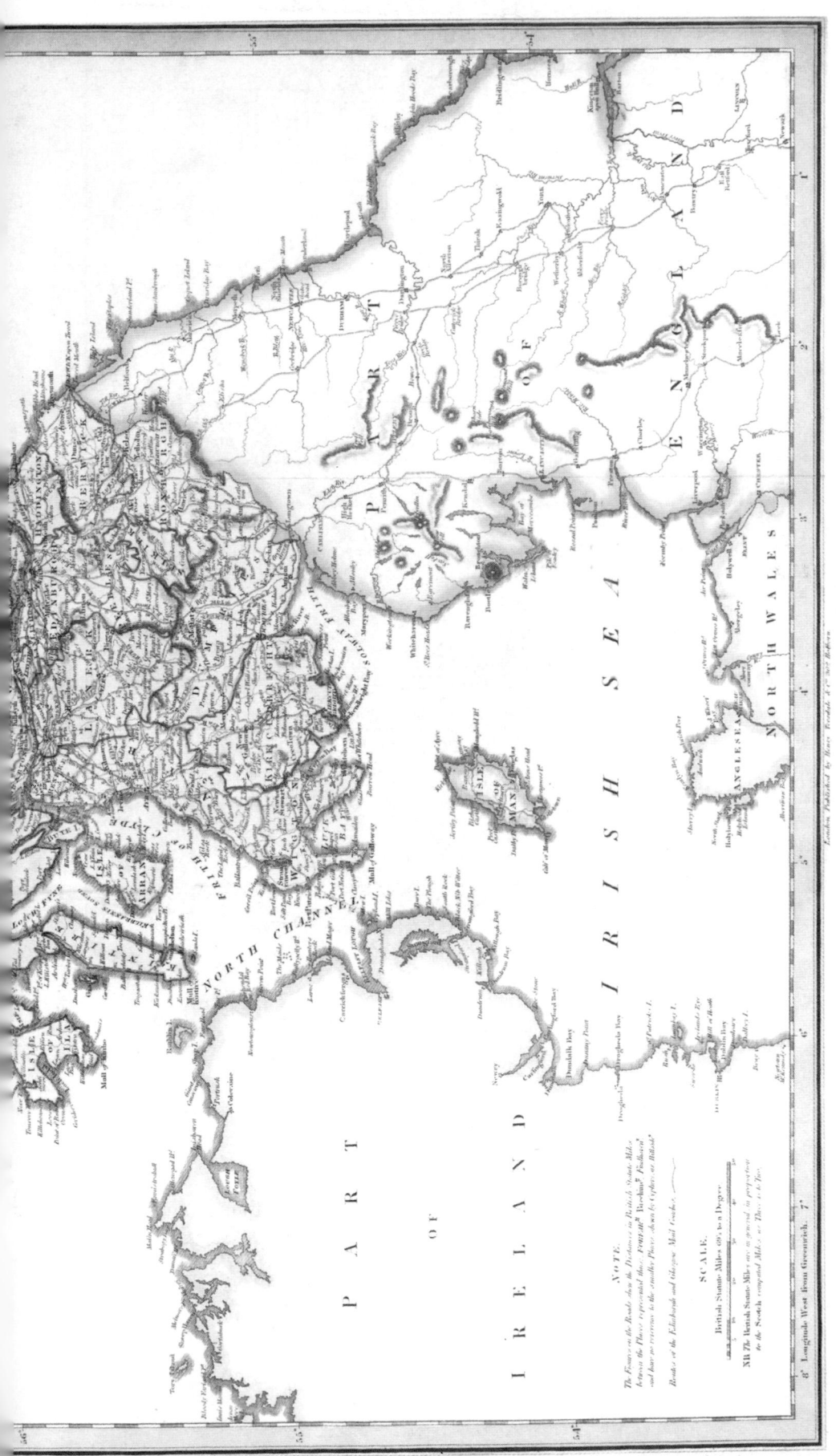

PART OF ENGLAND

IRISH SEA

NORTH WALES

ANGLESEY

ISLE OF MAN

NORTH CHANNEL

PART OF IRELAND

London Published by Henry Teesdale & Co. 302 Holborn.

NOTE.

The Figures on the Roads shew the Distances in British Statute Miles, between the Places represented thus. From the Nearest Figures, and have reference to the smaller Places shewn by Cyphers, as British.

Roads, or the Edinburgh and Glasgow Mail Coaches.

SCALE.

British Statute Miles 69½ to a Degree.

NB The British Statute Miles are in general in proportion to the Scotch computed Miles, as Three is to Ten.

8° Longitude West from Greenwich. 7°

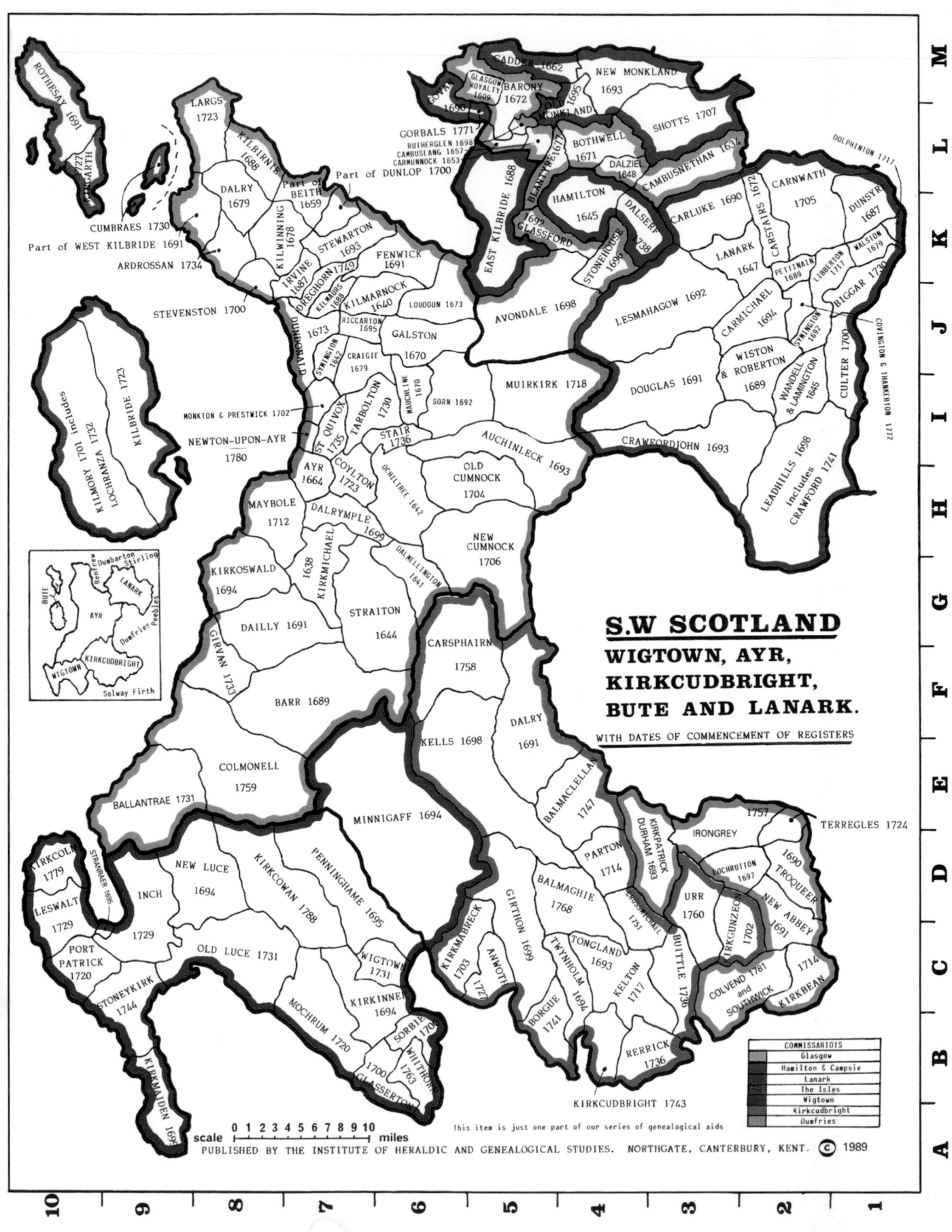

S.W SCOTLAND

WIGTOWN, AYR, KIRKCUDBRIGHT, BUTE AND LANARK.

WITH DATES OF COMMENCEMENT OF REGISTERS

ROTHESAY 1691
KINGARTH 1727
LARGS 1723
KILBIRNIE 1688
Part of BEITH 1659
Part of DUNLOP 1700
CUMBRAES 1730
DALRY 1679
Part of WEST KILBRIDE 1691
ARDROSSAN 1734
KILWINNING 1678
STEWARTON 1693
FENWICK 1691
STEVENSTON 1700
IRVINE 1687
DREGHORN 1749
KILMAURS 1688
KILMARNOCK 1640
LOUDOUN 1673
DUNDONALD
SYMINGTON 1642
RICCARTON 1695
GALSTON 1670
CRAIGIE 1679
MAUCHLINE 1670
SORN 1692
MUIRKIRK 1718
MONKTON & PRESTWICK 1702
ST QUIVOX 1735
TARBOLTON 1730
STAIR 1736
NEWTON-UPON-AYR 1780
AYR 1664
COYLTON 1723
OCHILTREE 1642
AUCHINLECK 1693
OLD CUMNOCK 1704
KILMORY 1701 includes LOCHRANZA 1732
KILBRIDE 1723
MAYBOLE 1712
DALRYMPLE 1699
DALMELLINGTON 1641
NEW CUMNOCK 1706
KIRKOSWALD 1694
KIRKMICHAEL 1638
STRAITON 1644
DAILLY 1691
GIRVAN 1733
CARSPHAIRN 1758
BARR 1689
KELLS 1698
DALRY 1691
COLMONELL 1759
MINNIGAFF 1694
BALLANTRAE 1731
BALMACLELLAN 1747
PARTON 1714
KIRKPATRICK DURHAM 1693
IRONGREY 1757
TERREGLES 1724
KIRKCOLM 1779
STRANRAER 1695
NEW LUCE 1694
KIRKCOWAN 1788
PENNINGHAME 1695
BALMAGHIE 1768
CROSSMICHAEL 1751
URR 1760
LOCHRUTTON 1697
KIRKGUNZEON 1702
TROQUEER 1690
NEW ABBEY 1691
LESWALT 1729
INCH 1729
GIRTHON 1699
KIRKMABRECK 1703
ANWOTH 1727
TWYNHOLM 1694
TONGLAND 1693
KELTON 1717
BUITTLE 1736
COLVEND 1781 and SOUTHWICK
KIRKBEAN 1714
PORT PATRICK 1720
OLD LUCE 1731
WIGTOWN 1731
BORGUE 1741
STONEYKIRK 1744
MOCHRUM 1720
KIRKINNER 1694
SORBIE 1700
RERRICK 1736
KIRKMAIDEN 1695
WHITHORN 1763
GLASSERTON
KIRKCUDBRIGHT 1743

CADDER 1662
GLASGOW ROYALTY 1609
BARONY 1672
GOVAN 1690
NEW MONKLAND 1693
OLD MONKLAND 1695
SHOTTS 1707
GORBALS 1771
RUTHERGLEN 1698
CAMBUSLANG 1657
CARMUNNOCK 1653
BLANTYRE 1677
BOTHWELL 1671
DALZIEL 1648
CAMBUSNETHAN 1624
DOLPHINTON 1717
EAST KILBRIDE 1688
HAMILTON 1645
GLASSFORD 1692
STONEHOUSE 1696
DALSERF 1738
CARLUKE 1690
CARSTAIRS 1672
CARNWATH 1705
DUNSYR 1687
LANARK 1647
PETTINAIN 1689
LIBBERTON 1717
WALSTON 1679
AVONDALE 1698
LESMAHAGOW 1692
CARMICHAEL 1694
SYMINGTON 1692
BIGGAR 1730
WISTON & ROBERTON 1689
WANDELL & LAMINGTON 1645
CULTER 1700
COVINGTON & THANKERTON 1772
DOUGLAS 1691
CRAWFORDJOHN 1693
LEADHILLS 1698 includes CRAWFORD 1741

scale 0 1 2 3 4 5 6 7 8 9 10 miles

This item is just one part of our series of genealogical aids

PUBLISHED BY THE INSTITUTE OF HERALDIC AND GENEALOGICAL STUDIES. NORTHGATE, CANTERBURY, KENT. © 1989

COMMISSARIOTS
Glasgow
Hamilton & Campsie
Lanark
The Isles
Wigtown
Kirkcudbright
Dumfries

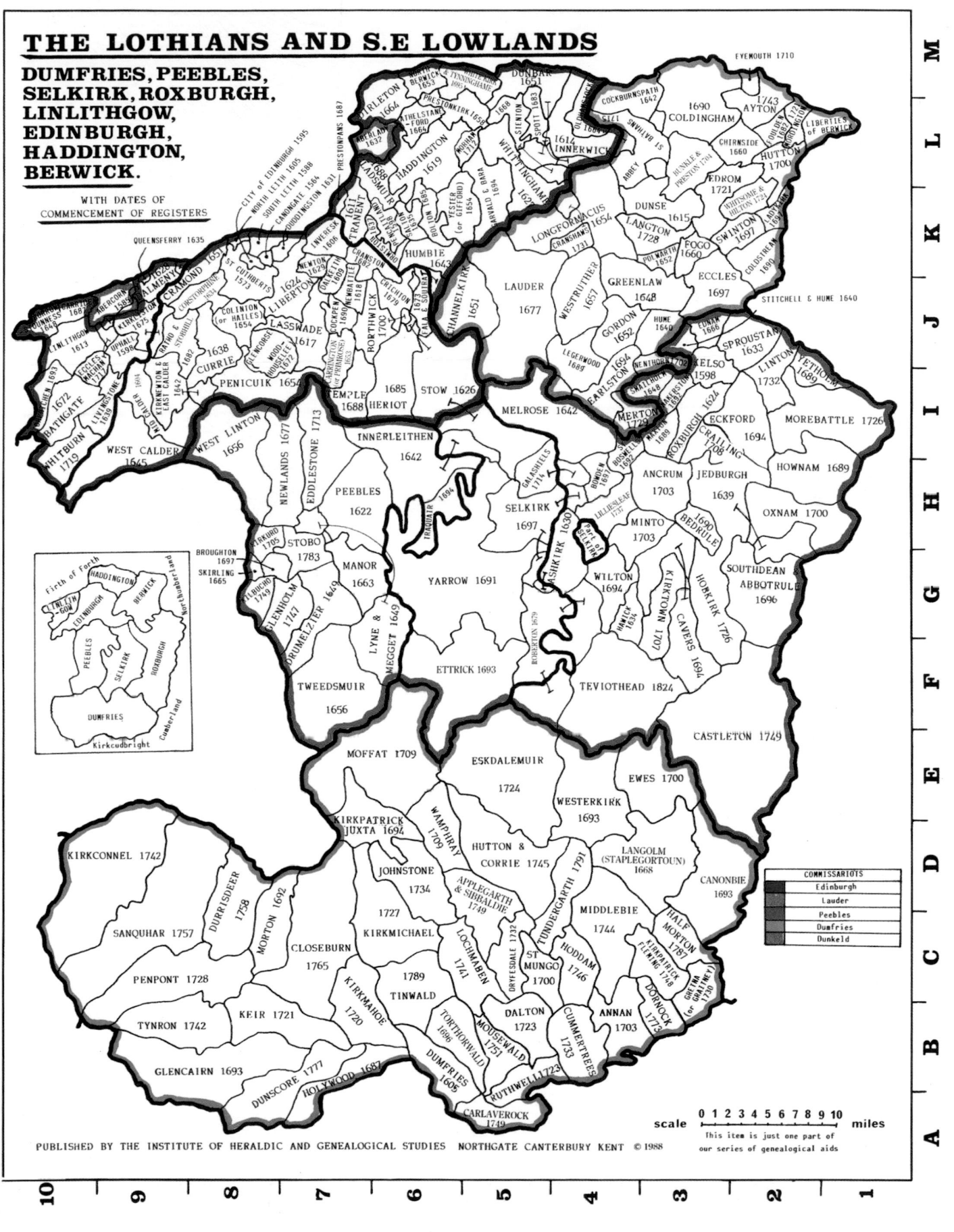

THE LOTHIANS AND S.E LOWLANDS

DUMFRIES, PEEBLES, SELKIRK, ROXBURGH, LINLITHGOW, EDINBURGH, HADDINGTON, BERWICK.

WITH DATES OF
COMMENCEMENT OF REGISTERS

EYEMOUTH 1710

COMMISSARIOTS
Edinburgh
Lauder
Peebles
Dumfries
Dunkeld

scale 0 1 2 3 4 5 6 7 8 9 10 miles

This item is just one part of
our series of genealogical aids

PUBLISHED BY THE INSTITUTE OF HERALDIC AND GENEALOGICAL STUDIES NORTHGATE CANTERBURY KENT © 1988

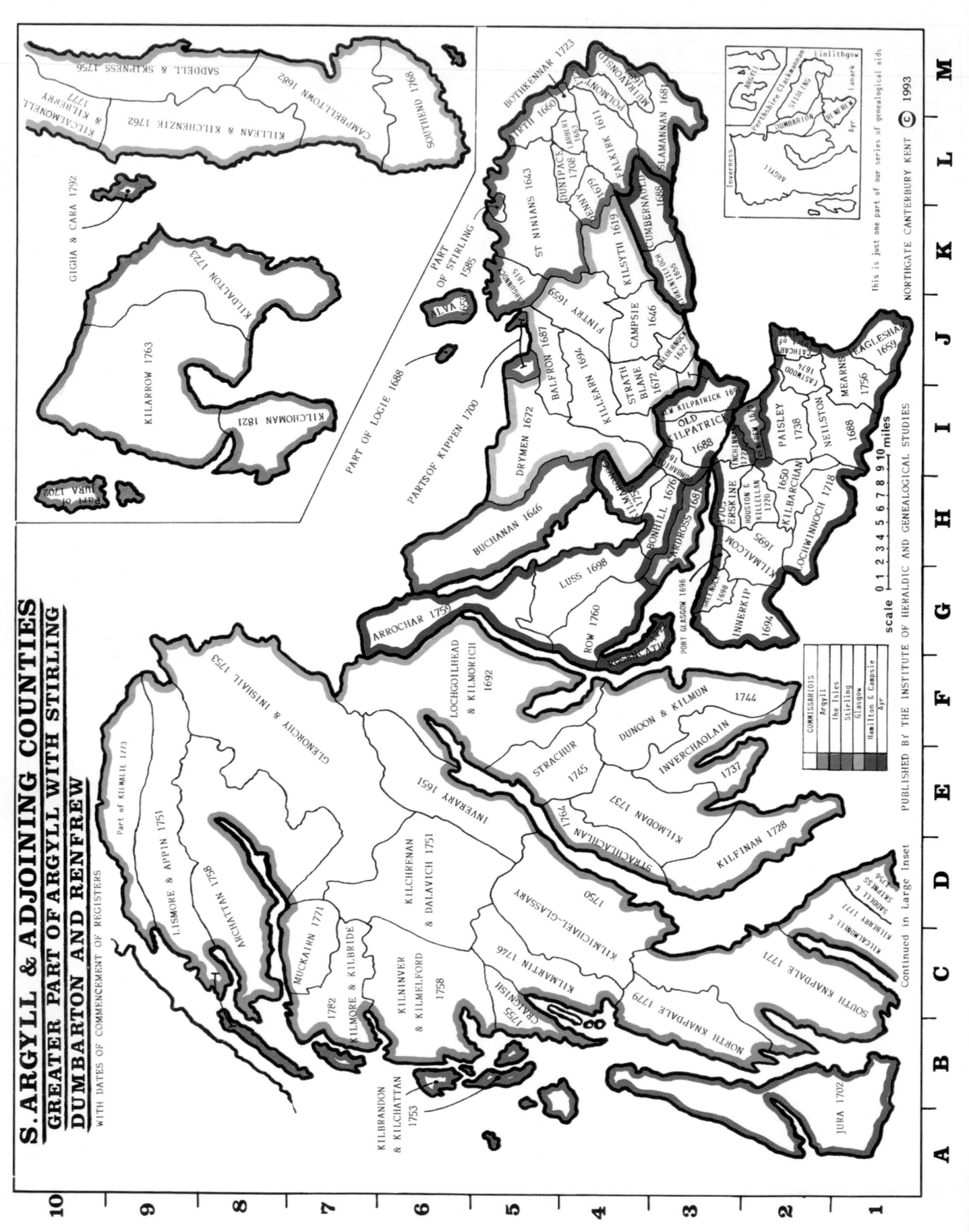

S. ARGYLL & ADJOINING COUNTIES
GREATER PART OF ARGYLL WITH STIRLING
DUMBARTON AND RENFREW
WITH DATES OF COMMENCEMENT OF REGISTERS

this is just one part of our series of genealogical aids

NORTHGATE CANTERBURY KENT © 1993

PUBLISHED BY THE INSTITUTE OF HERALDIC AND GENEALOGICAL STUDIES

scale 0 1 2 3 4 5 6 7 8 9 10 miles

Continued in Large Inset

COMMISSARIOTS	
Argyll	
The Isles	
Stirling	
Glasgow	
Hamilton & Campsie	
Ayr	

Left inset (Kintyre / islands):

SADDELL & SKIPNESS 1756
KILCALMONELL & KILBERRY 1777
KILLEAN & KILCHENZIE 1762
CAMPBELLTOWN 1682
SOUTHEND 1768
GIGHA & CARA 1792
KILDALTON 1723
KILARROW 1763
KILCHOMAN 1821
Part of JURA 1702

Main map labels:

BOTHKENNAR 1723
POLMONT 1723
MUIRAVONSIDE 1688
SLAMANNAN 1688
LARBERT 1663
DUNIPACE 1708
FALKIRK 1611
CUMBERNAULD 1688
DENNY 1679
HAMILTON 1699
ST NINIANS 1643
KILSYTH 1619
AIRTH 1585
GARGUNNOCK 1615
CAMPSIE 1646
FINTRY 1659
STRATH BLANE 1672
BALDERNOCK 1622
BALFRON 1687
KILLEARN 1694
NEW KILPATRICK 1692
OLD KILPATRICK 1688
DRYMEN 1672
PART OF STIRLING 1585
PART OF LOGIE 1688
ALVA 1652
PARTS OF KIPPEN 1700
BUCHANAN 1646
KILMARONOCK 1751
BONHILL 1676
CARDROSS 1681
DUMBARTON 1642
RENFREW 1673
INCHINNAN 1723
CATHCART 1690
GOVAN 1690
PORT GLASGOW 1696
OLD KILPATRICK
FAIFLEY
FASTWOOD 1674
PAISLEY 1738
MEARNS 1756
EAGLESHAM 1659
NEILSTON 1688
ERSKINE 1705
HOUSTON & KILLELLAN 1720
KILBARCHAN 1650
LOCHWINNOCH 1718
KILMALCOLM 1695
INNERKIP 1694
LUSS 1698
ROW 1760
ARROCHAR 1759
LOCHGOILHEAD & KILMORICH 1692
DUNOON & KILMUN 1744
STRACHUR 1745
INVERCHAOLAIN 1737
KILMODAN 1737
GLENORCHY & INISHAIL 1753
INVERARY 1651
STRACHLACHLAN 1764
KILFINAN 1728
Part of KILMALIE 1773
LISMORE & APPIN 1751
ARDCHATTAN 1758
KILBRANDON & KILCHATTAN 1753
MUCKAIRN 1771
KILMORE & KILBRIDE 1782
KILCHRENAN & DALAVICH 1751
KILNINVER & KILMELFORD 1758
KILMICHAEL-GLASSARY 1750
CRAIGNISH 1755
KILMARTIN 1766
NORTH KNAPDALE 1779
SOUTH KNAPDALE 1771
JURA 1702
KILCALMONELL & KILBERRY 1777
SADDELL & SKIPNESS 1756

Top right inset:
Inverness
Argyll
Perthshire
Clackmannan
Linlithgow
Stirling
Lanark
DUMBARTON
Renfrew
Ayr

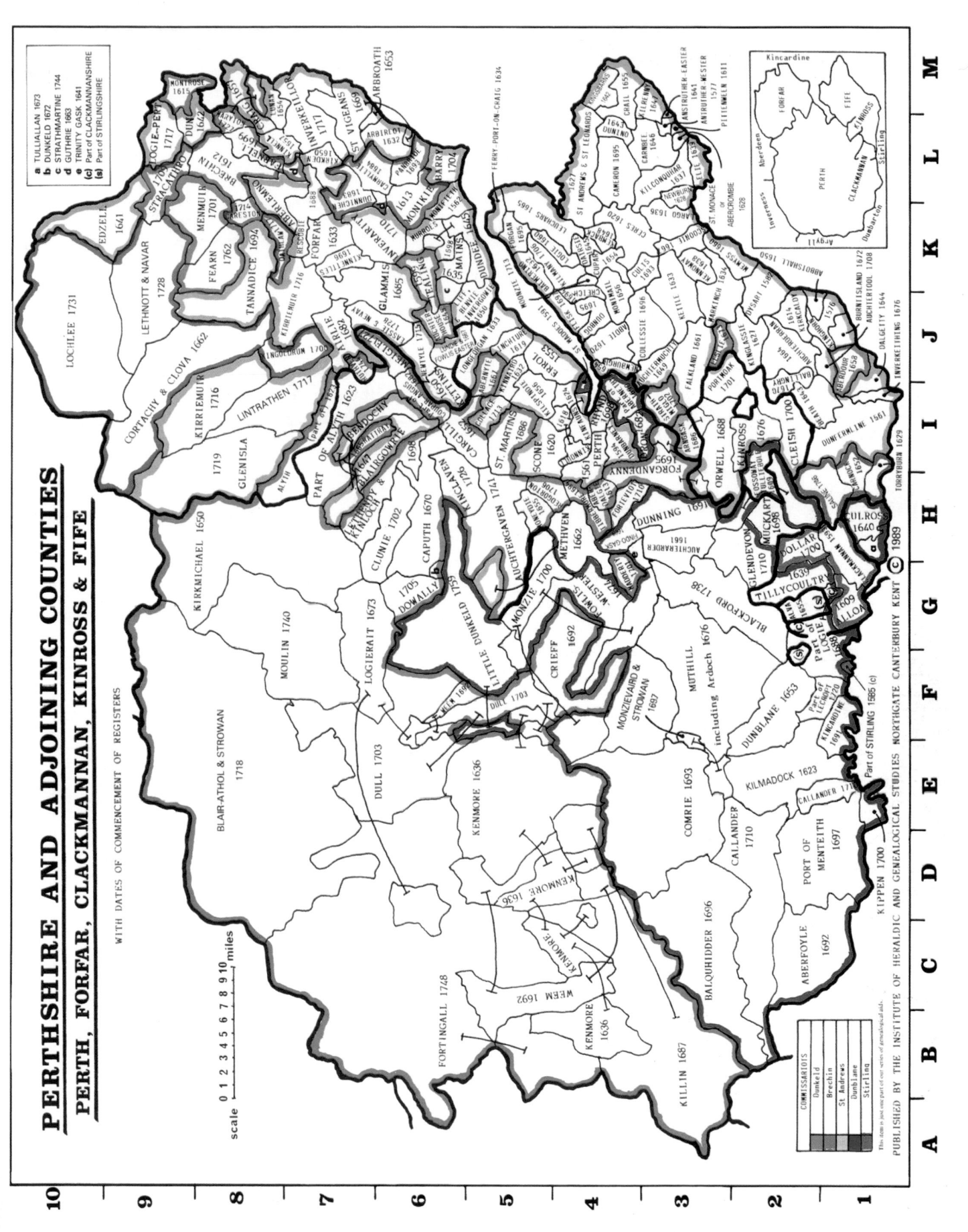

PERTHSHIRE AND ADJOINING COUNTIES
PERTH, FORFAR, CLACKMANNAN, KINROSS & FIFE

WITH DATES OF COMMENCEMENT OF REGISTERS

a TULLIALLAN 1673
b DUNKELD 1672
c STRATHMARTINE 1744
d TRINITY GASK 1641
(c) Part of CLACKMANNANSHIRE
(s) Part of STIRLINGSHIRE

scale 0 1 2 3 4 5 6 7 8 9 10 miles

COMMISSARIOTS
Dunkeld
Brechin
St Andrews
Dunblane
Stirling

This item is just one part of our series of genealogical aids.
PUBLISHED BY THE INSTITUTE OF HERALDIC AND GENEALOGICAL STUDIES NORTHGATE CANTERBURY KENT © 1989

KIPPEN 1700

Part of STIRLING 1585 (c)

N.E. SCOTLAND : NAIRN, ELGIN, BANFF, ABERDEEN, KINCARDINE

WITH DATES OF COMMENCEMENT OF REGISTERS

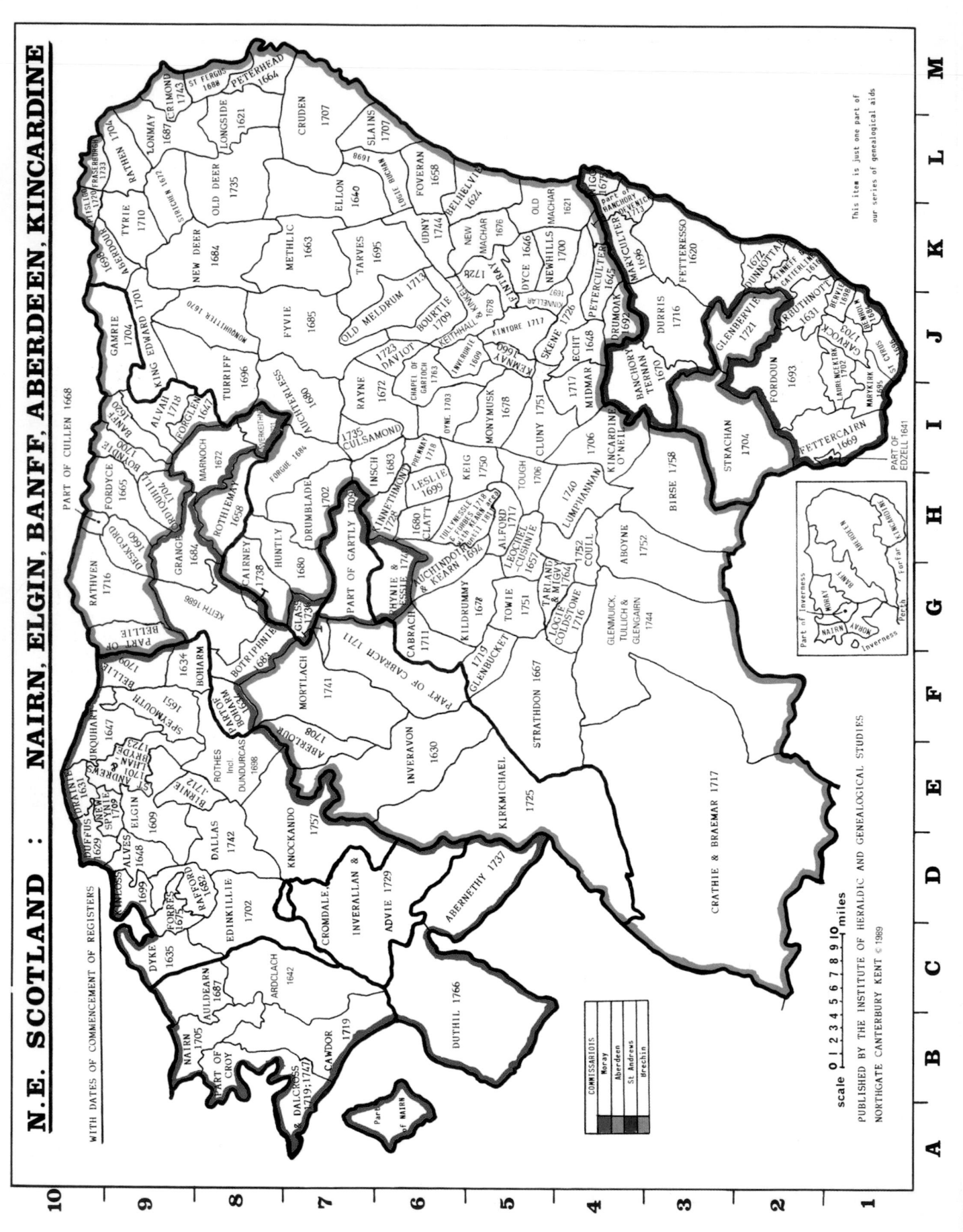

This item is just one part of our series of genealogical aids

PUBLISHED BY THE INSTITUTE OF HERALDIC AND GENEALOGICAL STUDIES

NORTHGATE CANTERBURY KENT © 1989

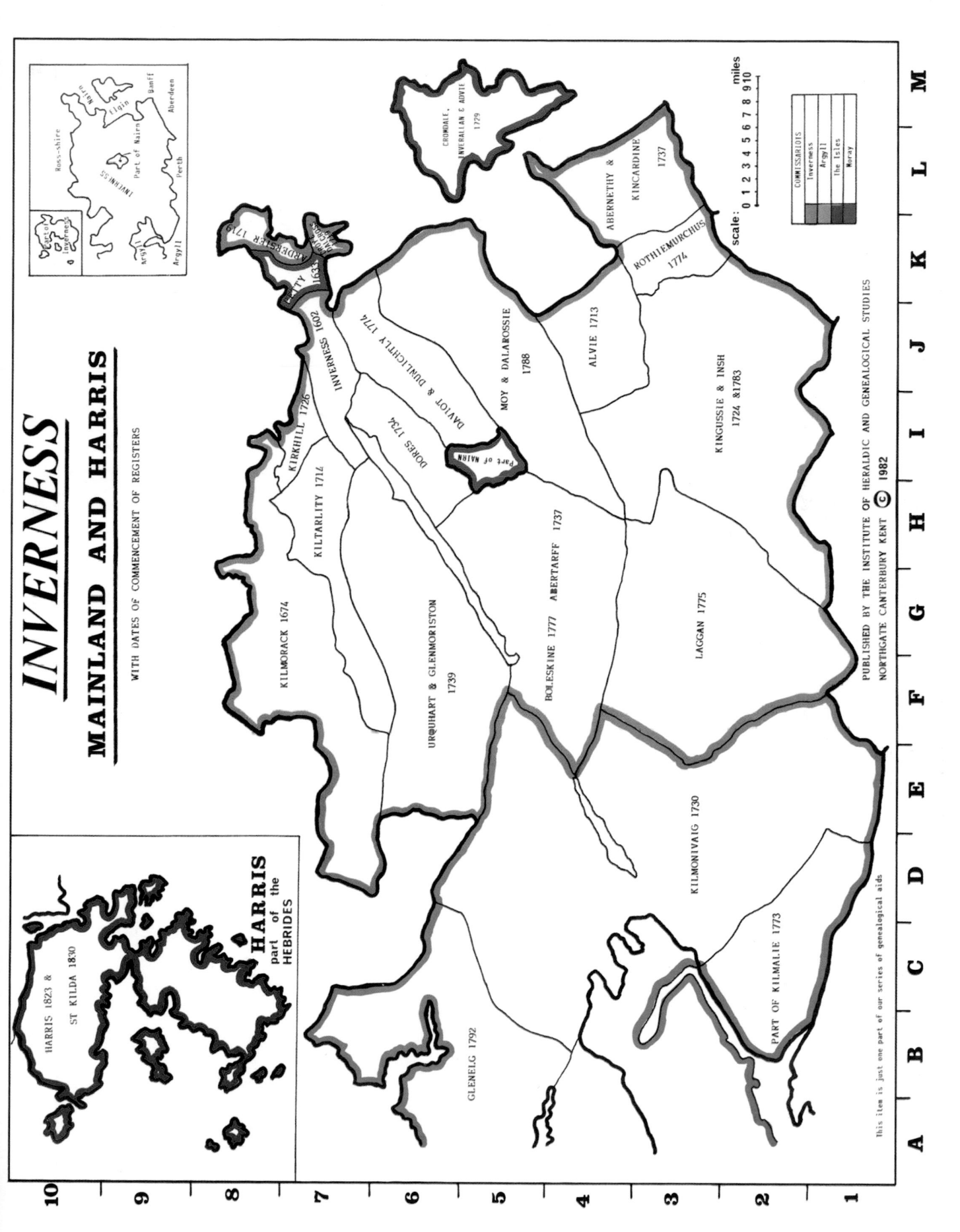

INVERNESS

MAINLAND AND HARRIS

WITH DATES OF COMMENCEMENT OF REGISTERS

HARRIS
part of the
HEBRIDES

HARRIS 1823 & ST KILDA 1830

KILMORACK 1674

KIRKHILL 1726

INVERNESS 1602

KILTARLITY 1714

URQUHART & GLENMORISTON 1739

DORRES 1734

DAVIOT & DUNLICHTY 1774

PETTY 1632

ARDERSIER 1710

CROY & DALCROSS 1635

MOY & DALAROSSIE 1788

Part of Nairn

ABERTARFF 1737

BOLESKINE 1777

GLENELG 1792

KILMONIVAIG 1730

LAGGAN 1775

PART OF KILMALIE 1773

ALVIE 1713

ROTHIEMURCHUS 1774

ABERNETHY & KINCARDINE 1737

CROMDALE, INVERALLAN & ADVIE 1729

KINGUSSIE & INSH 1724 &1783

scale: 0 1 2 3 4 5 6 7 8 9 10 miles

COMMISSARIOTS
Inverness
Argyll
The Isles
Moray

PUBLISHED BY THE INSTITUTE OF HERALDIC AND GENEALOGICAL STUDIES
NORTHGATE CANTERBURY KENT © 1982

This item is just one part of our series of genealogical aids

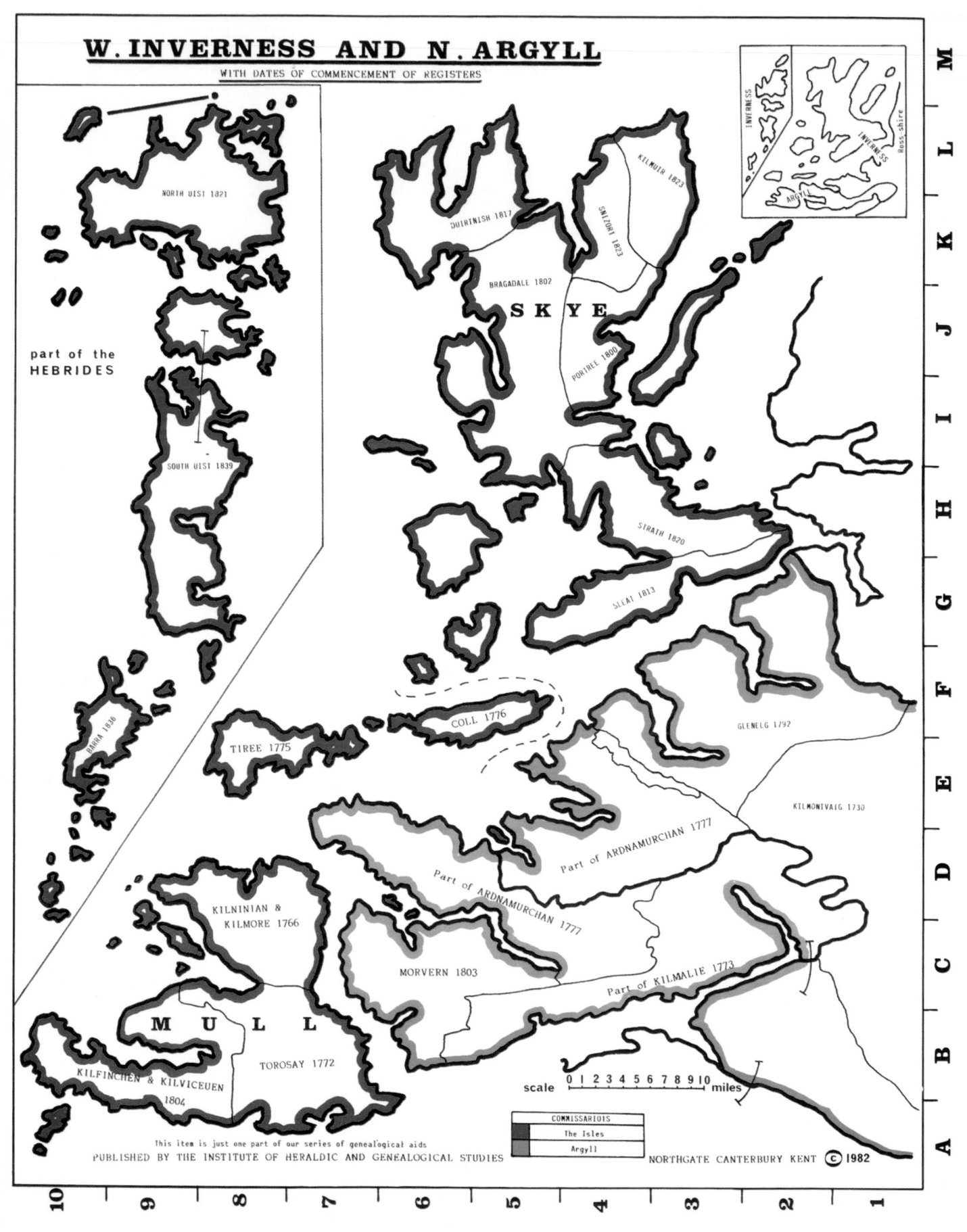

W. INVERNESS AND N. ARGYLL

WITH DATES OF COMMENCEMENT OF REGISTERS

part of the
HEBRIDES

NORTH UIST 1821

SOUTH UIST 1839

BARRA 1836

INVERNESS

INVERNESS

Ross-shire

ARGYLL

KILMUIR 1823

SNIZORT 1823

DUIRINISH 1817

BRACADALE 1802

S K Y E

PORTREE 1800

STRATH 1820

SLEAT 1813

GLENELG 1792

KILMONIVAIG 1730

COLL 1776

TIREE 1775

Part of ARDNAMURCHAN 1777

Part of ARDNAMURCHAN 1777

KILNINIAN &
KILMORE 1766

MORVERN 1803

Part of KILMALIE 1773

M U L L

TOROSAY 1772

KILFINCHEN & KILVICEUEN
1804

scale 0 1 2 3 4 5 6 7 8 9 10 miles

COMMISSARIOTS

The Isles

Argyll

This item is just one part of our series of genealogical aids

PUBLISHED BY THE INSTITUTE OF HERALDIC AND GENEALOGICAL STUDIES

NORTHGATE CANTERBURY KENT © 1982

M L K J I H G F E D C B A

10 9 8 7 6 5 4 3 2 1

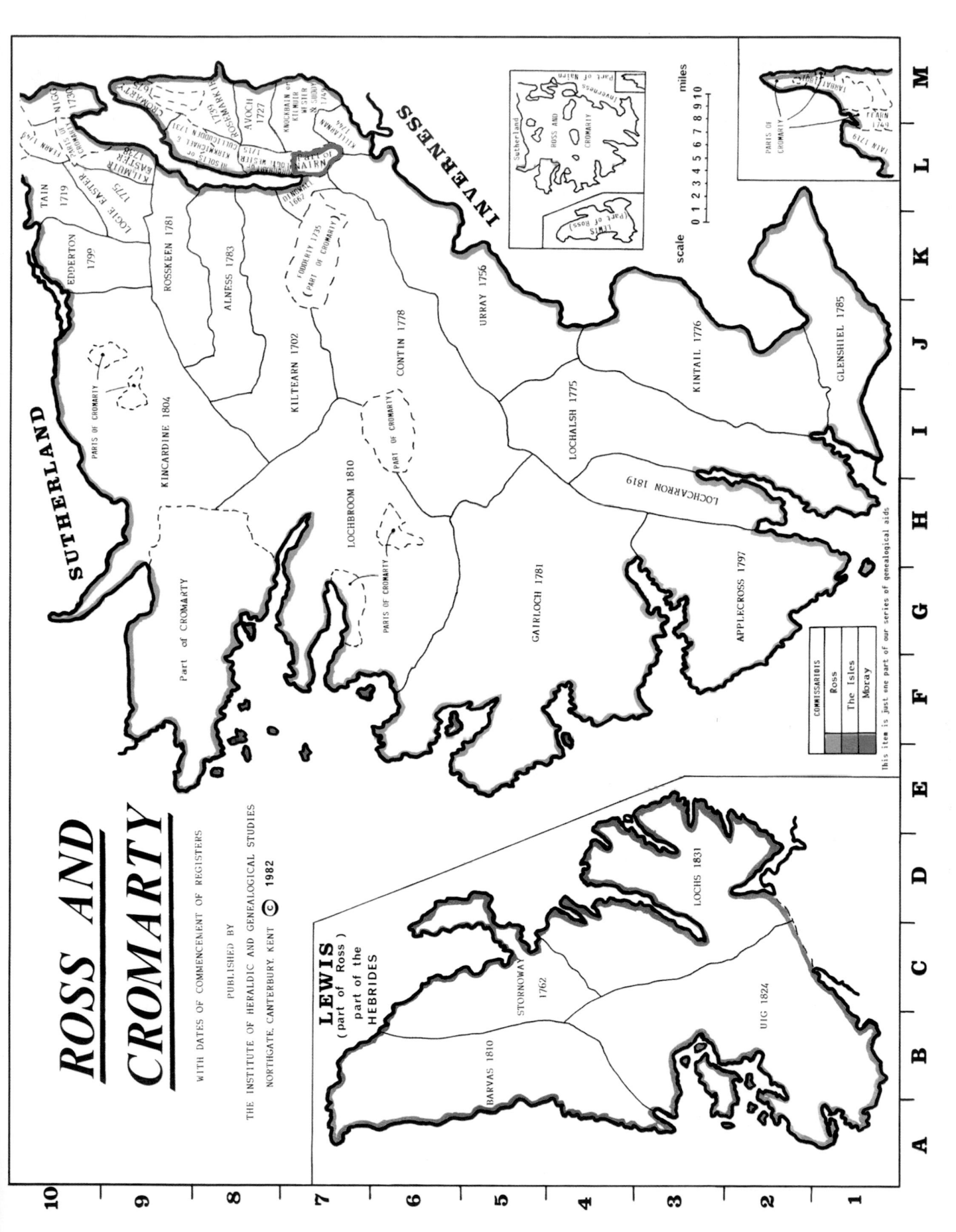

ROSS AND CROMARTY

WITH DATES OF COMMENCEMENT OF REGISTERS

PUBLISHED BY

THE INSTITUTE OF HERALDIC AND GENEALOGICAL STUDIES

NORTHGATE, CANTERBURY, KENT © 1982

LEWIS
(part of Ross)
part of the
HEBRIDES

SUTHERLAND

INVERNESS

Part of CROMARTY

PARTS OF CROMARTY

PARTS OF CROMARTY

NIGG 1730
TARBAT 1749
TAIN 1719
LOCHIE EASTER 1775
EDDERTON 1790
KILMUIR EASTER 1738
FEARN 1749
CROMARTY 1675
ROSSKEEN 1781
ALNESS 1783
KILTEARN 1702
KINCARDINE 1804
LOGIE WESTER 1750
ROSEMARKIE 1715
URQUHART 1707
FODDERTY 1735 (PART OF CROMARTY)
DINGWALL 1667
CONTIN 1778
URRAY 1756
PART of CROMARTY
LOCHBROOM 1810
GAIRLOCH 1781
APPLECROSS 1797
LOCHCARRON 1819
LOCHALSH 1775
KINTAIL 1776
GLENSHIEL 1785
AVOCH 1727
KNOCKBAIN or KILMUIR WESTER & SUDDIE 1744
KILLEARNAN 1744
NAIRN

BARVAS 1810
STORNOWAY 1762
UIG 1824
LOCHS 1831

TARBAT 1747
TAIN 1719
PARTS OF CROMARTY

PART of NAIRN
PART of INVERNESS
Sutherland
ROSS AND CROMARTY
LEWIS (part of Ross)

scale

miles
0 1 2 3 4 5 6 7 8 9 10

COMMISSARIOTS
Ross
The Isles
Moray

This item is just one part of our series of genealogical aids.

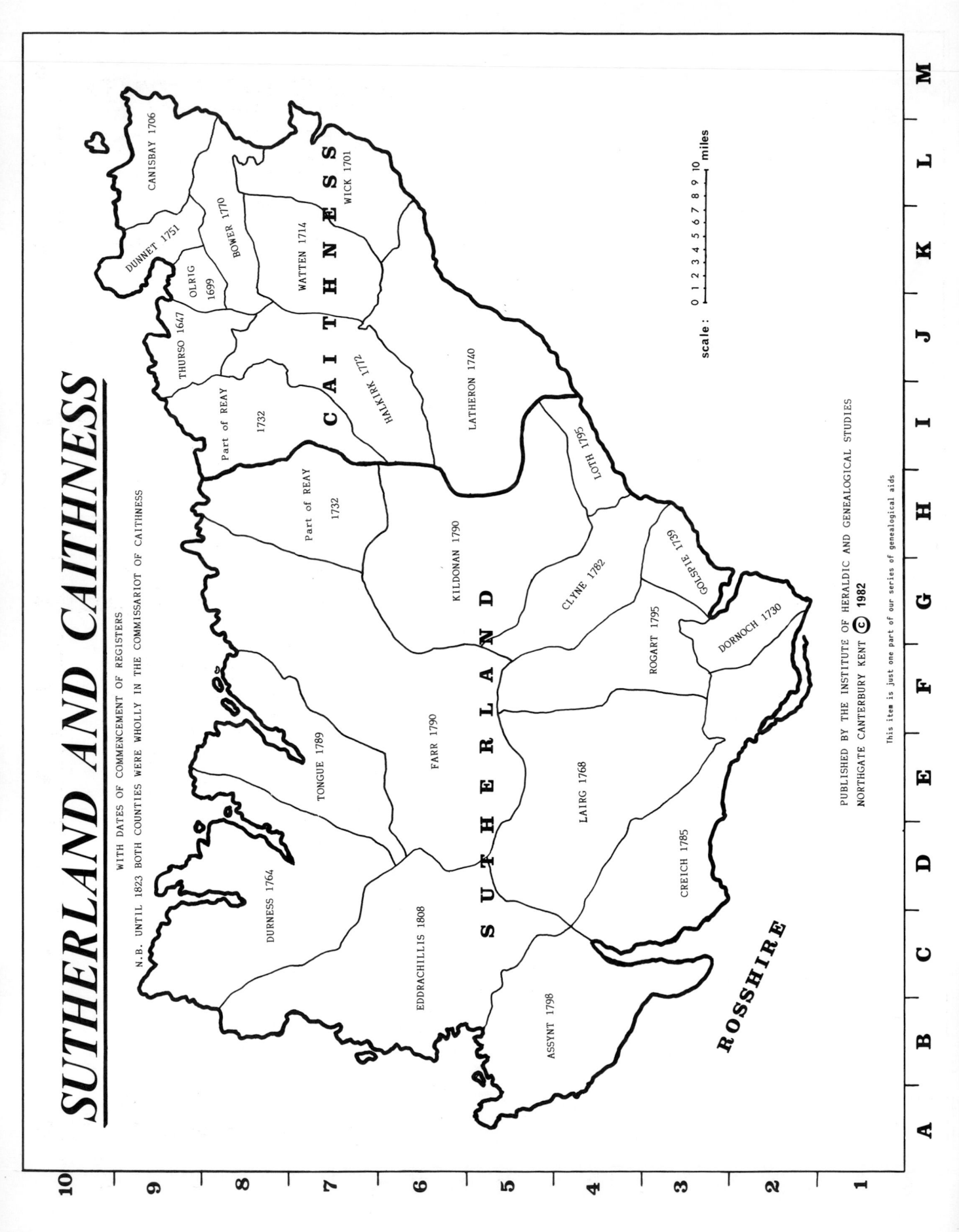

SUTHERLAND AND CAITHNESS

WITH DATES OF COMMENCEMENT OF REGISTERS

N.B. UNTIL 1823 BOTH COUNTIES WERE WHOLLY IN THE COMMISSARIOT OF CAITHNESS

CANISBAY 1706

DUNNET 1751

OLRIG 1699

BOWER 1770

WICK 1701

WATTEN 1714

THURSO 1647

Part of REAY 1732

HALKIRK 1772

CAITHNESS

LATHERON 1740

Part of REAY 1732

LOTH 1795

KILDONAN 1790

CLYNE 1782

GOLSPIE 1739

DURNESS 1764

TONGUE 1789

FARR 1790

ROGART 1795

DORNOCH 1730

SUTHERLAND

EDDRACHILLIS 1808

LAIRG 1768

CREICH 1785

ASSYNT 1798

ROSSHIRE

scale:
0 1 2 3 4 5 6 7 8 9 10 miles

PUBLISHED BY THE INSTITUTE OF HERALDIC AND GENEALOGICAL STUDIES
NORTHGATE CANTERBURY KENT © 1982

this item is just one part of our series of genealogical aids

A B C D E F G H I J K L M

10 9 8 7 6 5 4 3 2 1

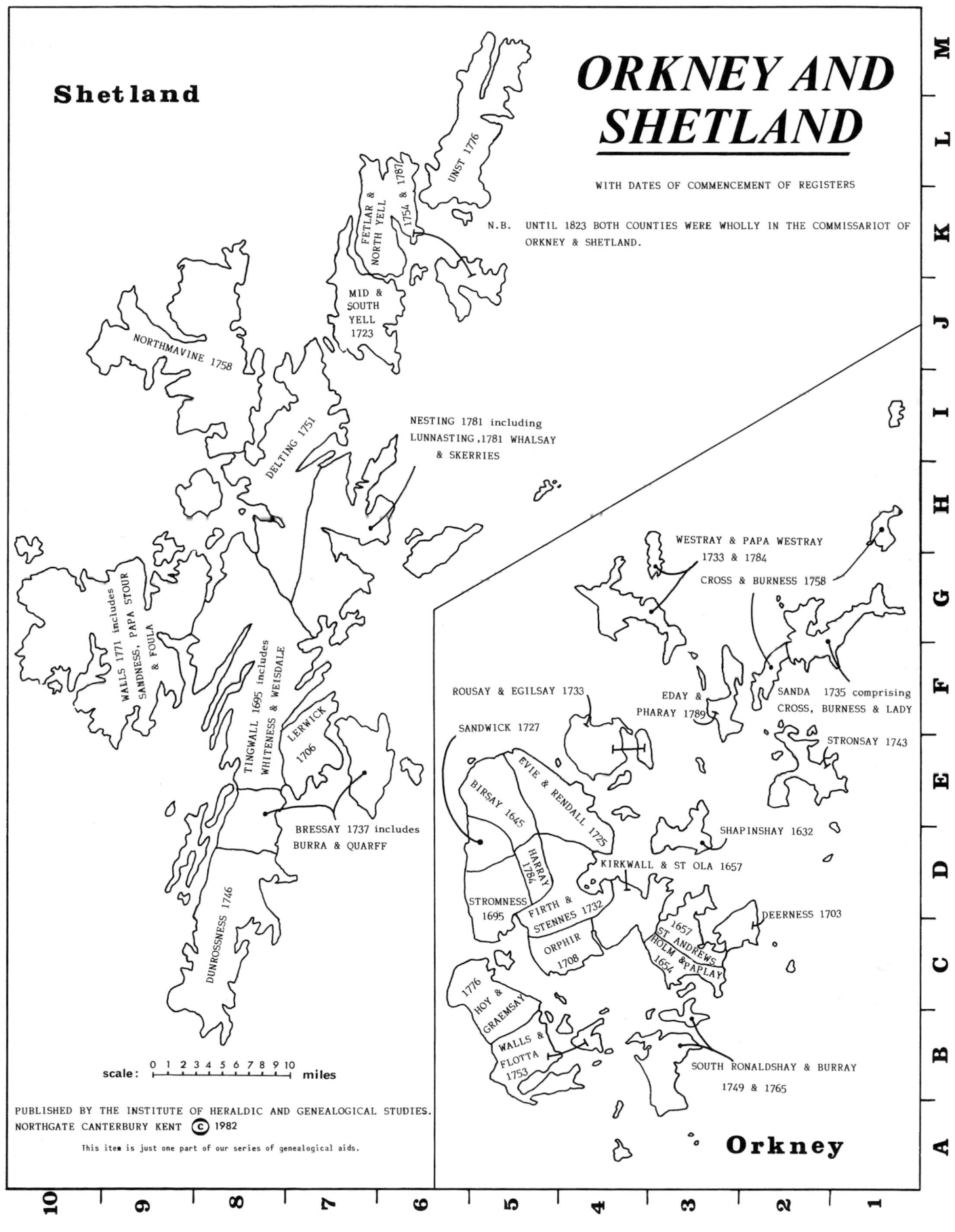

Shetland

ORKNEY AND
SHETLAND

WITH DATES OF COMMENCEMENT OF REGISTERS

N.B. UNTIL 1823 BOTH COUNTIES WERE WHOLLY IN THE COMMISSARIOT OF
ORKNEY & SHETLAND.

UNST 1776

FETLAR &
NORTH YELL
1754 & 1787

MID &
SOUTH
YELL
1723

NORTHMAVINE 1758

DELTING 1751

NESTING 1781 including
LUNNASTING, 1781 WHALSAY
& SKERRIES

WALLS 1771 includes PAPA STOUR
SANDNESS, & FOULA

TINGWALL 1695 includes
WHITENESS & WEISDALE

LERWICK
1706

BRESSAY 1737 includes
BURRA & QUARFF

DUNROSSNESS 1746

WESTRAY & PAPA WESTRAY
1733 & 1784

CROSS & BURNESS 1758

ROUSAY & EGILSAY 1733

EDAY &
PHARAY 1789

SANDA 1735 comprising
CROSS, BURNESS & LADY

STRONSAY 1743

SANDWICK 1727

EVIE & RENDALL 1725

BIRSAY 1645

HARRAY
1784

STROMNESS
1695

FIRTH &
STENNES 1732

ORPHIR
1708

SHAPINSHAY 1632

KIRKWALL & ST OLA 1657

DEERNESS 1703

1657
ST ANDREWS
HOLM & PAPLAY
1654

1776
HOY &
GRAEMSAY

WALLS &
FLOTTA
1753

SOUTH RONALDSHAY & BURRAY
1749 & 1765

Orkney

scale: 0 1 2 3 4 5 6 7 8 9 10 miles

PUBLISHED BY THE INSTITUTE OF HERALDIC AND GENEALOGICAL STUDIES.
NORTHGATE CANTERBURY KENT © 1982

This item is just one part of our series of genealogical aids.

M L K J I H G F E D C B A

10 9 8 7 6 5 4 3 2 1

THE
INDEX

BEDFORDSHIRE

parish name	deposited original registers	I.G.I.	local census indexes	copies of registers at Soc. Gen.	Boyd's marriage index	1837-1851 Registration District	Pallot's marriage index	non-conform. records at P.R.O.	map ref.
Ampthill	A 1604-1995	1602-1895	5,8	1602-1908		Ampthill	1790-1812		6F
Apsley Guise	A 1563-1996	1563-1880	5,8	1563-1920		Woburn		1815-1837	8E
Arlesey	A 1538-1992	1538-1885	5,8	1538-1909		Biggleswade			4E
Astwick	A 1564-1836	1602-1866	5,8	1563-1812		Biggleswade			3F
Barton in the Clay	A 1558-1968	1558-1885	5,8	1558-1922		Luton			6F
Battlesden	A 1677-1928	1602-1879	5,8	1602-1927		Woburn	1790-1811		8D
Bedford:								1743-1857	6H
St Cuthbert	A 1607-1974	1602-1885	5,8	1602-1904		Bedford	1790-1812		6H(C)
St John	A 1669-1937	1602-1885	5,8	1602-1940		Bedford	1791-1812		6H(D)
St Mary	A 1539-1972	1539-1885	5,8	1539-1908	1540-1837	Bedford	1780-1837		6H(E)
St Paul	A 1565-1944	1567-1892	5,8	1565-1901		Bedford			6H(A)
St Peter	A 1572-1981	1572-1884	5,8	1572-1905	1583-1837	Bedford	1780-1837		6H(B)
Biddenham	A 1663-1999	1602-1885	5,8	1602-1941		Bedford	1790-1812		7G
Biggleswade	A 1697-1974	1604-1885	5,8	1637-1907		Biggleswade	1790-1812	1790-1837	4G
Billington	A 1653-1990	1609-1885	5,8	1609-1931		Leighton Buzzard			8D
Bletsoe	A 1582-1974	1582-1885	5,8	1582-1925		Bedford			6I
Blunham	A 1571-1943	1571-1885	5,8	1571-1943		Biggleswade		1709-1837	5H
Cemetery				1902-1989		Biggleswade			5H
with Mogerhanger			5,8	1571-1812		Biggleswade			5H
Bolnhurst	A 1685-1995	1602-1875	5,8	1602-1938		Bedford	1790-1812		6I
Bromham	A 1570-1974	1570-1885	5,8	1570-1927		Bedford	1790-1812		7H
Caddington	A 1558-1970	1558-1880	5,8	1558-1911		Luton			6C
Campton	A 1568-1983	1568-1885	5,8	1568-1920		Biggleswade			5F
Cardington	A 1572-1955	1572-1885	5,8	1572-1919		Bedford	1790-1812	1796-1837	5G
Carlton	A 1554-1923	1554-1885	5,8	1554-1911		Bedford			8I
Chalgrave	A 1539-1987	1539-1885	5,8	1539-1908		Woburn			7D
Chellington	A 1567-1967	1567-1885	5,8	1567-1917		Bedford			7I
Chicksands (ex. par.)			5,8			Biggleswade			5F
Clapham	A 1696-1975	1603-1885	5,8	1603-1938		Bedford	1790-1812		6H
Clifton	A 1538-1990	1538-1885	5,8	1538-1929		Biggleswade			4F
Clophill	A 1567-1998	1567-1877	5,8	1567-1900		Ampthill			5F
Cockayne Hatley	A 1701-1839	1602-1885	5,8	1602-1812		Biggleswade	1790-1810		3G
Colmworth	A 1735-1979	1605-1885	5,8	1604-1925		Bedford			5I
Colworth (ex. par.)			5,8			Bedford			7I
Cople	A 1563-1993	1561-1885	5,8	1561-1933		Bedford	1790-1812		5H
Cranfield	A 1600-1981	1600-1885	5,8	1600-1916		Ampthill		1794-1837	8F
Dean	A 1566-1981	1566-1885	5,8	1566-1937		St Neots			6K
Dunstable	A 1558-1968	1558-1885	5,8	1558-1903	1558-1673	Luton		1772-1837	7C
Dunton	A 1553-1982	1553-1885	5,8	1553-1920		Biggleswade			3G
Eastcotts			5,8			Bedford			6G
Eaton Bray	A 1559-1968	1559-1885	5,8	1559-1925		Leighton Buzzard		1798-1837	7C
Eaton Socon	A 1566-1996	1566-1885	5,8	1566-1915		St Neots			5I
Edworth	A 1552-1972	1552-1885	5,8	1552-1940		Biggleswade	1793-1812		3F
Eggington	A 1813-1981	1611-1885	5,8	1813-1920		Leighton Buzzard			8D
Elstow	A 1641-1984	1602-1876	5,8	1602-1943		Bedford	1790-1812		6G
Eversholt	A 1628-1960	1582-1885	5,8	1602-1939		Woburn			7E
Everton (see Tetworth, Hunts)						Biggleswade			4H
Eyeworth	A 1538-1836	1538-1885	5,8	1538-1870		Biggleswade	1790-1812		3G
Farndish	A 1587-1966	1587-1885	5,8	1587-1882	1587-1734	Wellingborough			8J
Felmersham	A 1660-1985	1602-1885	5,8	1602-1937		Bedford	1790-1812		7I
Flitton	A 1581-1995	1581-1885	5,8	1581-1927		Ampthill			6E
Flitwick	A 1622-1999	1602-1885	5,8	1602-1812	1790-1796	Ampthill			6E
Goldington	A 1559-1980	1558-1880	5,8	1558-1927		Bedford			6H
Great Barford	A 1559-1977	1559-1877	5,8	1559-1911		Bedford			5H
Harlington	A 1653-1983	1602-1885	5,8	1602-1919		Woburn			6E
Harrold	A 1598-1994	1598-1885	5,8	1598-1923		Bedford		1812-1836	8I
Haynes	A 1596-1992	1596-1885	5,8	1596-1944		Ampthill	1790-1812		6F
Heath and Reach	A 1813-1995	1813-1885	5,8	1813-1929		Leighton Buzzard			8D
Henlow	A 1558-1976	1558-1885	5,8	1558-1919		Biggleswade			4E
Higham Gobion	A 1654-1996	1614-1885	5,8	1614-1886		Ampthill	1790-1812		5E
Hockliffe	A 1696-1985	1604-1885	5,8	1604-1944		Woburn		1808-1836	8D
Holwell	B 1560-1992	1560-1895	5,8	1838-1935		Hitchin	1790-1812		4E
Houghton Conquest	A 1595-1999	1539-1885	5,8	1539-1947		Ampthill			6F
Houghton Regis	A 1538-1962	1538-1885	5,8	1538-1914		Luton		1772-1836	7D
Hulcote	A 1658-1939	1605-1877	5,8	1605-1938		Woburn			8F
Husbourne Crawley	A 1558-1988	1558-1885	5,8	1557-1942		Woburn			8F
Kempston	A 1570-1984	1570-1875	5,8	1570-1812		Bedford			7G
Kensworth (Herts.)						Luton			7C
Keysoe	A 1735-1993	1602-1885	5,8	1602-1908		Bedford			6J
Knotting	A 1592-1941	1592-1885	5,8	1592-1938		Bedford	1790-1812		7J
Langford	A 1717-1979	1602-1885	5,8	1602-1922		Biggleswade			4F
Leighton Buzzard	A 1562-1985	1562-1885	5,8	1562-1963		Leighton Buzzard		1798-1837	8D
Lidlington	A 1560-1978	1560-1885	5,8	1560-1942		Ampthill			7F
Little Barford	A 1661-1970	1602-1885	5,8	1602-1882		St Neots	1790-1812		4I
Little Staughton	A 1598-1886	1598-1885	5,8	1598-1947		St Neots			5J
Lower Gravenshurst	A 1705-1970	1602-1885	5,8	1602-1912		Ampthill	1780-1837		5E(J)
Luton	A 1603-1904	1602-1888	5,8	1602-1901	1602-1700	Luton		1785-1854	6C
Marston Moretain	A 1653-1971	1602-1885	5,8	1602-1930		Ampthill			7G
Maulden	A 1558-1987	1558-1885	5,8	1558-1914		Ampthill		1730-1835	6F
Melchbourne	A 1706-1986	1602-1885	5,8	1602-1934		Bedford	1790-1812		6J
Meppershall	A 1652-1973	1602-1885	5,8	1602-1923		Biggleswade			5F
Millbrook	A 1558-1987	1558-1885	5,8	1558-1905		Ampthill			7F
Milton Bryan	A 1559-1894	1559-1885	5,8	1559-1943		Woburn			7E
Milton Ernest	A 1538-1984	1538-1885	5,8	1538-1937		Bedford			7I
Northill	A 1562-1971	1562-1885	5,8	1562-1918		Biggleswade	1790-1812		4G
Oakley	A 1560-1988	1560-1885	5,8	1560-1947		Bedford	1790-1812		7H
Odell	A 1604-1953	1602-1885	5,8	1602-1937		Bedford	1790-1812		7I
Old Warden	A 1576-1893	1576-1885	5,8	1576-1936		Biggleswade	1790-1812		5G
Pavenham	A 1561-1976	1561-1885	5,8	1561-1911		Bedford	1790-1812		7I

BEDFORDSHIRE

parish name	deposited original registers	I.G.I.	local census indexes	copies of registers at Soc. Gen.	Boyd's marriage index	1837-1851 Registration District	Pallot's marriage index	non-conform. records at P.R.O.	map ref.
Pertenhall	A 1582-1988	1582-1885	5,8	1582-1913		St Neots			5J
Podington	A 1662-1981	1602-1885	5,8	1602-1923	1663-1760	Wellingborough			8J
Potsgrove	A 1663-1965	1602-1885	5,8	1602-1922		Woburn			8E
Potton	A 1614-1980	1602-1885	5,8	1602-1917		Biggleswade			3H
Pulloxhill	A 1553-1987	1553-1885	5,8	1553-1914		Ampthill			6E
Ravensden	A 1558-1985	1565-1885	5,8	1558-1921		Bedford			6I
Renhold	A 1654-1897	1602-1885	5,8	1602-1912		Bedford			5H
Ridgmont	A 1539-1988	1539-1885	5,8	1539-1932		Woburn		1804-1836	7F
Riseley	A 1626-1967	1602-1885	5,8	1602-1913		Bedford			6J
Roxton	A 1684-1973	1602-1885	5,8	1602-1920		Bedford		1824-1836	5I
Salford	A 1559-1988	1558-1885	5,8	1558-1913		Woburn			8F
Sandy	A 1538-1964	1538-1885	5,8	1538-1906		Biggleswade	1790-1812		4H
Sharnbrook	A 1595-1974	1596-1885	5,8	1596-1929		Bedford			7I
Shefford Hardwick (ex.par.)			5,8			Biggleswade		1832-1936	5F(F)
Shelton	A 1706-1844	1603-1885	5,8	1602-1908		St Neots	1790-1812		6K
Shillington	A 1543-1946	1543-1885	5,8	1543-1913		Ampthill			5E
Souldrop	A 1670-1990	1602-1885	5,8	1602-1915		Bedford	1790-1812		7J
Southill	A 1538-1946	1538-1885	5,8	1538-1932		Biggleswade	1790-1812	1792-1837	5F
Stagsden	A 1670-1908	1602-1878	5,8	1602-1922		Bedford			7H
Stanbridge	A 1560-1974	1560-1885	5,8	1560-1923		Leighton Buzzard			8D
Steppingley	A 1558-1983	1559-1885	5,8	1558-1925		Ampthill			7E
Stevington	A 1653-1963	1603-1885	5,8	1603-1925		Bedford	1790-1812		7H
Stotfold	A 1559-1955	1559-1885	5,8	1559-1920		Biggleswade			4E
Streatley	A 1693-1837	1602-1895	5,8	1602-1945		Luton	1790-1812		6E
Studham	A 1570-1981	1569-1885	5,8	1570-1925	1570-1776	Luton			7C
Sundon	A 1569-1980	1569-1885	5,8	1569-1942		Luton	1790-1812		6D
Sutton	A 1538-1875	1538-1885	5,8	1538-1945		Biggleswade	1791-1812		3G
Swineshead (Hunts)						St Neots			6J
Tempsford	A 1604-1939	1571-1885	5,8	1602-1924		Biggleswade			4H
Thurleigh	A 1562-1966	1562-1885	5,8	1754-1911		Bedford			6I
Tilbrook	C 1573-1983	1602-1880	5,8	1573-1905		St Neots			5K
Tilsworth	A 1649-1979	1602-1885	5,8	1602-1938		Woburn			7D
Tingrith	A 1572-1978	1572-1885	5,8	1572-1931		Woburn			7E
Toddington	A 1558-1953	1540-1885	5,8	1558-1920		Woburn			7E
Totternhoe	A 1559-1984	1589-1885	5,8	1559-1944		Luton			7C
Turvey	A 1629-1975	1629-1885	5,8	1602-1946		Bedford		1829-1836	8H
Upper Gravenhurst	A 1567-1982	1567-1885	5,8	1567-1913		Ampthill	1780-1837		5E(H)
Upper Stondon	A 1683-1967	1602-1915	5,8	1602-1986		Biggleswade			5E
Westoning	A 1560-1980	1560-1812	5,8	1560-1943		Ampthill		1798-1836	6E
Whipsnade	A 1682-1985	1603-1885	5,8	1801-1923		Luton			7C
Wilden	A 1545-1982	1545-1885	5,8	1545-1945		Bedford			5I
Willington	A 1676-1929	1561-1885	5,8	1602-1940		Bedford	1790-1812		5H
Willshamstead	A 1593-1986	1593-1812	5,8	1593-1909		Bedford			6G
Woburn	A 1558-1967	1558-1885	5,8	1558-1926		Woburn	1790-1812	1791-1837	8E
Wootton	A 1562-1987	1561-1885	5,8	1561-1921		Bedford		1830-1837	7G
Wrestlingworth	A 1578-1883	1578-1885	5,8	1578-1931		Biggleswade	1790-1812		3G
Wymington	A 1662-1986	1662-1885	5,8	1602-1942		Wellingborough			7J
Yielden	A 1653-1978	1602-1885	5,8	1602-1914		Bedford	1790-1812		7J

Original registers deposited at:
A = Bedfordshire Record Office, County Hall, Cauldwell Street, Bedford MK42 9AP
B = Hertfordshire Record Office, County Hall, Hertford SG13 8DE
C = Huntingdonshire Record Office, Grammar School Walk, Huntingdon PE29 3LF

Study adjacent parishes in counties of Northamptonshire, Huntingdonshire, Cambridgeshire, Hertfordshire and Buckinghamshire

Bedfordshire Record Office – County Hall, Cauldwell Street, Bedford, MK42 9AP

The following useful indexes have been compiled – see Introduction
Census Index 1851 – Publications Officer, Beds. FHS, PO Box 214, Bedford, MK42 9RX
Bedford Prison 1851 – Society of Genealogists
Bedfordshire Marriage Index – County Archivist, Bedfordshire Record Office, County Hall, Cauldwell Street, Bedford, MK42 9AP covers the whole county to 1812.
Marriage Licences 1578-1618, 1747-1885 – County Archivist, Bedfordshire, Record Office, County Hall, Cauldwell Street, Bedford, MK42 9AP
Monumental Inscriptions – Mrs J Money, Beds. FHS, PO Box 214, Bedford, MK42 9RX

Bedfordshire is a very small county of irregular shape, its greatest length being 36 miles from north to south, and its greatest breadth 22 miles from east to west. It is watered by three principal rivers, the Ouse, Ivel and Lea. The population in 1841 was 107,936; in 1851, 124,936; in 1851, 124478; in 1861, 135,287; in 1871, 146,257; in 1881, 149,473.

The soils are chalk, chalk marl and green sand, with Oxford clay, cornbrash, limestone and oolite clay; the soil is generally good, fruitful and well tilled. The produce was coarse limestone, lime, fuller's earth from Woburn, coprolites, brick clay and bricks, coppice and brushwood, wheat, barley, oats, beans, hay, fruit, fat oxen, sheep, poultry, game, rabbits and eels. Market gardening was of considerable importance in this county and pickle farming was successfully pursued. Biggleswade, in particular, was the centre of industry. Thorough cultivation and generous treatment of the land are indispensable for the growth of the various crops needed in this industry. Many of the inhabitants were employed in the manufacture of lace, straw plait, straw bonnets and hats, bonnet blocks, bricks, tiles and pottery. Dunstable was the main seat of the straw trade.

The information in the Index is abbreviated, and may mislead the searcher if reference is not made to the details contained in the several publications listed in the Introduction. It is essential that users of this book check the appropriate works before making further enquiries.

BERKSHIRE

parish name	deposited original registers	I.G.I.	local census indexes	copies of registers at Soc. Gen.	Boyd's marriage index	1837-1851 Registration District	Pallot's marriage index	non-conform. records at P.R.O.	map ref.
Abingdon								1723-1837	7F
St Helen			5,6,7,8,9	1538-1837		Abingdon			7F
St Nicholas	A 1538-1978	1538-1877	5,6,7,8,9	1538-1880		Abingdon		1538-1835	7F
Aldermaston	A 1558-1992	1558-1869	5,8	1558-1840		Bradfield			2G
Aldworth	A 1556-1996	1556-1885	5,6,7,8,9			Wantage			5G
Appleford	A 1563-1989	1563-1837	5,6,7,8,9	1563-1837		Abingdon			7F
Appleton	A 1569-1990	1569-1812	5,6,7,8,9	1569-1839		Abingdon			8E
Arborfield	A 1705-1991	1705-1855	5,8	1580-1841		Wokingham		1765-1836	3J
Ardington	A 1674-1929	1674-1813	5,6,7,8,9	1607-1974		Wantage			6E
Ashampstead	A 1686-1980	1686-1813	5,8	1607-1837		Bradfield			4G
Ashbury	A 1653-1993	1704-1812	5,6,7,8,9	1612-1989		Faringdon			6B
Aston Tirrold	A 1726-1978	1727-1812	5,6,7,8,9	1607-1995		Wallingford		1738-1837	5G
Aston Upthorp (see Upton)									6G
Avington	A 1725-1994		5,8	1699-1835		Hungerford			3D
Bagley Wood (ex.par.)			5,6,7,8,9			Abingdon			8F
Barkham	A 1538-1998		5,8	1538-1732		Wokingham			3J
Basildon	A 1538-1982	1538-1813	5,8	1538-1753		Bradfield			4G
Baulking			5,6,7,8,9	1850-1989		Faringdon			6C
Beedon	A 1681-1985		5,6,7,8,9	1607-1840		Wantage			5F
Beenham	A 1561-1984	1561-1812	5,8	1561-1840		Bradfield			3G
Besselsleigh	A 1689-1994		5,6,7,8,9	1666-1994		Abingdon			8E
Binfield All Saints	A 1538-1987	1538-1812	5,8	1538-1841		Easthampstead			3K
Bisham	A 1560-1991	1560-1885	5,8	1560-1840		Cookham	1790-1812		5K
Blewbury	A 1588-1864	1588-1813	5,6,7,8,9	1588-1884		Wantage/Wallingford			6F
Boxford	A 1558-1982		5,8	1558-1981		Newbury			4E
Bradfield	A 1539-1989	1539-1833	5,8	1539-1838	1559-1812	Bradfield	1800-1812		4G
Bray	A 1652-1987	1653-1812	5,8	1653-1837		Cookham			4L
Brightwalton	A 1559-1979	1641-1825	5,6,7,8,9			Wantage			5E
Brightwell	A 1564-1974		5,6,7,8,9			Wallingford			7G
Brimpton	A 1678-1992		5,8	1607-1840		Newbury			2G
Buckland	A 1678-1930	1691-1859	5,6,7,8,9	1678-1974		Faringdon			8C
Bucklebury	A 1538-1910		5,8	1538-1840		Bradfield			3F
Burghfield	A 1559-1987	1559-1837	5,8	1607-1836		Bradfield			3H
Buscot	A 1676-1978	1676-1885	5,6,7,8,9	1607-1836	1676-1812	Faringdon	1800-1812		7B
Catmore	A 1724-1985		5,6,7,8,9	1736-1834		Wantage			5E
Chaddleworth	A 1538-1985	1538-1870	5,6,7,8,9	1607-1834		Wantage			5E
Charney Bassett	A 1642-1999	1641-1885	5,6,7,8,9	1607-1974		Faringdon			7D
Chieveley	A 1560-1974	1560-1885	5,8	1813-1874		Newbury			4F
Childrey	A 1558-1980	1558-1812	5,6,7,8,9			Wantage			6D
Chilton	A 1584-1974		5,6,7,8,9	1551-1995		Wantage			6F
Chilton Foliat (Wilts)									4C
Cholsey	A 1539-1929	1540-1838	5,6,7,8,9	1540-1917		Wallingford			6G
Clewer	A 1653-1990	1653-1812	5,8	1607-1837		Windsor			4M
Coleshill	A 1559-1990	1558-1875	5,6,7,8,9	1559-1980		Faringdon			7B
Compton	A 1553-1963	1553-1885	5,6,7,8,9			Wantage			5F
Compton Beauchamp	A 1551-1994	1551-1834	5,6,7,8,9	1551-1994		Faringdon			5C
Cookham	A 1563-1960	1563-1837	5,8	1563-1838		Cookham		1769-1837	5L
Cumnor	A 1559-1970	1607-1835	5,6,7,8,9	1559-1761		Abingdon			9E
Denchworth	A 1538-1969	1538-1835	5,6,7,8,9	1540-1912		Wantage	1790-1812		7D(C)
Didcot	A 1562-1960	1562-1678	5,6,7,8,9	1562-1840		Wallingford			6F
Drayton	A 1754-1979	1607-1836	5,6,7,8,9	1607-1837		Abingdon			7E
East Challow	A 1711-1974	1712-1812	5,6,7,8,9	1607-1991		Wantage			6D
East Garston	A 1554-1984	1554-1812	5,8	1554-1840		Hungerford			4D
East Hagbourne	A 1661-1908	1661-1837	5,6,7,8,9	1612-1993		Wallingford			6F
Easthampstead	A 1558-1966	1558-1867	5,8			Easthampstead			3K
East Hendred	A 1538-1988	1539-1837	5,6,7,8,9	1538-1974		Wantage			6E
East Ilsley	A 1653-1978		5,6,7,8,9	1654-1812		Wantage			5F
East Lockinge	A 1546-1897	1546-1897	5,6,7,8,9	1548-1872		Wantage			6E(F)
East Shefford	A 1603-1935	1603-1833	5,8	1603-1887		Hungerford			4D(L)
Eaton Hastings	A 1574-1961	1574-1885	5,6,7,8,9	1574-1981		Faringdon			7B
Enborne	A 1665-1974	1666-1885	5,8			Newbury			3E
Englefield	A 1559-1975	1561-1846	5,8			Bradfield			4H(P)
Farnborough	A 1739-1981	1739-1812	5,6,7,8,9			Wantage			5E
Fawley	A 1540-1987		5,6,7,8,9			Wantage			5D
Finchampstead	A 1653-1986	1653-1838	5,8	1607-1635		Wokingham			2J
Frilford (see Marcham)									7E
Frilsham	A 1711-1837	1711-1837	5,8	1607-1837		Bradfield			4G
Fyfield	A 1754-1979		5,6,7,8,9	1605-1913		Abingdon			7E
Garford	A 1733-1938	1733-1885	5,6,7,8,9			Abingdon			7E
Goosey			5,6,7,8,9	1850-1945		Wantage			7D
Great Coxwell	A 1557-1985	1557-1875	5,6,7,8,9	1557-1978		Faringdon			7B
Great Faringdon	A 1653-1974	1653-1812	5,6,7,8,9	1589-1974		Faringdon			7C
Greenham	A 1706-1979	1706-1812	5,8	1612-1840		Newbury			3F
Hamstead Marshall	A 1675-1970	1675-1812	5,8	1605-1837		Newbury			2E
Hamstead Norreys	A 1538-1973	1538-1875	5,6,7,8,9			Wantage			4F
Hanney	A 1564-1982	1565-1837	5,6,7,8,9	1564-1880	1564-1837	Wantage	1800-1837		7E
Harwell	A 1558-1962	1559-1837	5,6,7,8,9	1558-1962	1562-1837	Wantage			6F
Hatford	A 1538-1969		5,6,7,8,9	1535-1969		Faringdon			7C
Hinton Waldrist	A 1559-1979	1551-1875	5,6,7,8,9	1559-1974		Faringdon			8D
Hungerford	A 1559-1979	1559-1885	5,8	1559-1732		Hungerford		1806-1837	3C
Hurley	A 1560-1969	1560-1885	5,8	1560-1839		Cookham			5K
Hurst	A 1585-1950	1585-1844	5,8			Wokingham			3J
Inkpen	A 1633-1982	1633-1875	5,8	1541-1860		Hungerford			2D
Kennington			5,6,7,8,9	1829-1965		Abingdon			8F
Kingston Bagpuize	A 1539-1979	1539-1812	5,6,7,8,9	1539-1884		Abingdon			8E
Kingston Lisle	A 1559-1964	1559-1837	5,6,7,8,9	1559-1837	1559-1837	Faringdon	1800-1837		6C
Kintbury	A 1558-1981		5,8	1558-1842		Hungerford			3D
Lambourn	A 1560-1973	1560-1885	5,8	1560-1837		Hungerford			5C
Leckhampstead	A 1754-1985		5,8			Newbury			4E

111

parish name	deposited original registers	I.G.I.	local census indexes	copies of registers at Soc. Gen.	Boyd's marriage index	1837-1851 Registration District	Pallot's marriage index	non-conform. records at P.R.O.	map ref.
Letcombe Bassett	A 1564-1989		5,6,7,8,9	1564-1989		Wantage			5D(D)
Letcombe Regis	A 1536-1980	1536-1812	5,6,7,8,9			Wantage			6D(E)
Little Coxwell	A 1582-1949	1582-1836	5,6,7,8,9	1582-1984		Faringdon			7C
Little Wittenham	A 1538-1992	1538-1836	5,6,7,8,9	1539-1679	1539-1668	Wallingford			7G
Longcot and Fernham	A 1664-1994	1645-1899	5,6,7,8,9	1612-1989		Farringdon			6B
Long Wittenham	A 1561-1979	1561-1885	5,6,7,8,9	1561-1943		Wallingford			7G
Longworth	A 1559-1984	1559-1812	5,6,7,8,9	1559-1974		Faringdon/Abingdon			8D
Lyford	A 1843-1979		5,6,7,8,9			Abingdon			7D
Maidenhead		1796-1823	5,8			Cookham		1769-1837	5L
Marcham (with Garford)	A 1658-1977	1658-1812	5,6,7,8,9	1653-1804		Abingdon			7E
Midgham	A 1622-1983		5,8	1607-1840		Newbury			3G
Milton	A 1654-1987		5,6,7,8,9			Abingdon			6F
Moulsford	A 1754-1993	1705-1874	5,6,7,8,9	1607-1841		Wallingford			5G
Newbury St Nicolas	A1538-1988		5,8	1508-1844		Newbury		1695-1837	2E
New Windsor	A 1559-1967		5,8	1559-1837		Windsor		1782-1836	4M
Chapel Royal		1609-1877	5,8			Windsor		1647-1709	4M
St George's			5,8	1609-1956		Windsor			4M
North Hinksey	B 1703-1985	1703-1885	5,6,7,8,9	1607-1984		Abingdon			9F
North Moreton	A 1558-1991	1558-1812	5,6,7,8,9	1538-1996		Wallingford			6G
Old Windsor	A 1755-1940	1755-1812	5,8	1612-1772		Windsor		1782-1836	4M
Oxford (part of St Aldate)									9F
Padworth	A 1693-1991	1692-1885	5,8	1607-1838		Bradfield			3H
Pangbourne	A 1556-1935	1556-1823	5,8			Bradfield		1829-1836	4H
Peasemore	A 1538-1901	1538-1808	5,6,7,8,9	1538-1990		Wantage			4E
Purley	A 1662-1985	1662-1840	5,8	1662-1840	1662-1837	Bradfield	1830-1840		4H
Pusey			5,6,7,8,9	1607-1877		Faringdon			7D
Radley	A 1599-1998	1599-1885	5,6,7,8,9	1599-1961		Abingdon			8F
Reading								1705-1837	4I
St Giles	A 1564-1899	1564-1891	5,8			Reading			3I
St Laurence	A 1605-1963		5,8	1605-1837		Reading			4I
St Mary	A 1538-1954	1538-1876	5,8	1538-1812		Reading	1790-1812		4I
Remenham	A 1697-1963	1697-1789	5,7,8,9	1697-1963		Henley			5J
Ruscombe	A 1559-1906		5,8	1559-1812		Wokingham			4J
Sandford			5,6,7,8,9			Abingdon			8E
Sandhurst	A 1603-1977	1603-1810	5,8	1579-1837		Easthampstead			2K
Sandleford			5,8			Newbury			2E
Shalbourne (see Wilts)									2C
Shaw cum Donnington	A 1646-1985		5,8	1563-1960		Newbury			3E(M)
Shellingford	A 1580-1960	1582-1811	5,6,7,8,9	1578-1899	1582-1812	Faringdon			7C(B)
Shinfield	A 1649-1984	1649-1812	5,8			Wokingham			3I
Shottesbrooke	A 1566-1979		5,8	1566-1850		Cookham			4K
Shrivenham	A 1575-1972	1575-1875	5,6,7,8,9	1575-1941		Faringdon			6B
Sonning	A 1592-1947		5,7,8,9	1592-1846		Wokingham/Henley			4J
Sotwell	A 1684-1835		5,6,7,8,9	1607-1996		Wallingford			6G
South Hinksey	B 1670-1924	1670-1885	5,6,8,9	1607-1924		Abingdon			8F
South Moreton	A 1599-1944	1599-1834	5,6,7,8,9	1599-1996		Wallingford			6G(H)
Sparsholt	A 1558-1972	1558-1812	5,6,7,8,9	1559-1865	1558-1812	Wantage	1800-1812		6D
Speen	A 1629-2000		5,8	1614-1749		Newbury			3E
Stanford Dingley	A 1538-1979	1538-1894	5,8	1813-1837		Bradfield			4G(N)
Stanford-in-the-Vale	A 1558-1948	1555-1885	5,6,7,8,9	1555-1914		Faringdon			7C
Steventon	A 1558-1977	1558-1877	5,6,7,8,9	1558-1954		Abingdon			7E
Stratfield Mortimer	A 1629-1989		5,8	1615-1840		Bradfield		1805-1837	2H
Stratfield Saye (Hants)									2I
Streatley	A 1679-1987		5,8	1607-1840		Bradfield			5G
Sulham	A 1720-1983	1720-1875	5,8	1723-1837	1723-1836	Bradfield	1800-1837		4H
Sulhamstead Abbots	A 1602-1995	1602-1812	5,8	1602-1837		Bradfield			3H
Sulhamstead Bannister	A 1646-1994	1654-1804	5,8	1608-1837		Bradfield			3H
Sunninghill	A 1561-1962	1561-1837	5,8	1561-1841		Windsor			3L
Sunningwell	A 1543-1997	1543-1812	5,6,7,8,9	1741-1842		Abingdon			8F(A)
Sutton Courtenay	A 1538-1986	1538-1885	5,6,7,8,9	1538-1904		Abingdon			7F
Swallowfield	A 1539-1931	1636-1840	5,8			Wokingham			2I
Thatcham	A 1561-1992	1560-1812	5,8	1561-1840		Newbury		1807-1836	3F
Tidmarsh	A 1730-1998	1730-1812	5,8			Bradfield			4H
Tilehurst	A 1630-1986	1559-1885	5,8	1630-1754		Bradfield			4H
Uffington	A 1654-1988	1654-1838	5,6,7,8,9	1607-1990		Faringdon			6C
Ufton Nervet	A 1636-1991	1636-1812	5,8	1607-1837		Bradfield			3H
Upton	A 1588-1990	1588-1750	5,6,7,8,9	1558-1990		Wantage			6F
Wallingford								1788-1837	6H
All Hallows			5,6,7,8,9			Wallingford			6H
St Leonard	A 1711-1975		5,6,7,8,9	1605-1975		Wallingford			6H
St Mary	A 1638-1977		5,6,7,8,9	1813-1837		Wallingford			6H
St Peter	A 1711-1997		5,6,7,8,9	1605-1969		Wallingford			6H
Waltham St Lawrence	A 1558-1995	1559-1812	5,8	1559-1969		Cookham			4K
Wantage	A 1538-1944	1538-1837	5,6,7,8,9	1538-1837	1538-1837	Wantage		1829-1837	6D
Warfield	A 1568-1981	1594-1885	5,8	1568-1840		Easthampstead			3K
Wargrave	A 1538-1982	1538-1812	5,8	1538-1840		Wokingham			5J
Wasing	A 1730-1993	1730-1812	5,8	1607-1841		Newbury			2G
Watchfield	A 1858-1958		5,6,7,8,9	1858-1982		Faringdon			6B
Welford	A 1559-1982	1562-1812	5,8	1559-1812		Newbury	1800-1837		4E
West Challow	A 1653-1959	1653-1812	5,6,7,8,9	1607-1820		Wantage			6D
West Hendred	A 1558-1972	1559-1833	5,6,7,8,9	1558-1974	1559-1837	Wantage	1800-1837		6E
West Ilsley	A 1558-1967	1558-1812	5,6,7,8,9			Wantage			5E
West Shefford	A 1571-1982	1571-1860	5,8	1571-1840		Hungerford		1834-1837	4D
West Woodhay	A 1653-1986	1653-1812	5,8	1612-1851	1653-1812	Hungerford			2D
White Waltham	A 1563-1993	1565-1812	5,8	1563-1837		Cookham			4K
Wickham and Hoe Benham	A 1649-1812	1649-1812	5,8			Newbury		1800-1837	4D

BERKSHIRE

parish name	deposited original registers	I.G.I.	local census indexes	copies of registers at Soc. Gen.	Boyd's marriage index	1837-1851 Registration District	Pallot's marriage index	non-conform. records at P.R.O.	map ref.
Winkfield	A 1564-1988		5,8	1564-1841		Easthampstead			3L
Winterbourne	A 1564-1979	1565-1885	5,8	1567-1979		Newbury			4E
Wokingham All Saints	A 1674-1971	1674-1812	5,8			Wokingham		1813-1837	3J
Woolhampton	A 1636-1983		5,8	1607-1840		Newbury			3G(O)
Woolstone			5,6,7,8,9	1849-1988		Faringdon			6C
Wootton	A 1657-1979		5,6,7,8,9	1607-1952		Abingdon			8F
Wytham	B 1558-1938		5,6,7,8,9	1558-1984		Abingdon			9E
Yattendon	A 1558-1982	1558-1875	5,8			Bradfield			4F

Original registers deposited at:
A = Berkshire Record Office, 9 Coley Avenue, Reading, Berkshire, RG1 6AF
B = Oxfordshire Archives, St Luke's Church, Temple Road, Oxford, OX4 2EX

Study adjacent parishes in counties of Oxford, Buckinghamshire, Surrey, Hampshire and Wiltshire

Berkshire Record Office – 9 Coley Avenue, Reading, Berkshire, RG1 6AF

The following useful indexes have been compiled – see Introduction
Census Index 1851 – Berkshire FHS, C/O Geoff Mather, 18 Ravenswood Avenue, Crowthorne, Berkshire, RG45 6AY
Census Indexes 1841, 1861, 1871, 1891 – Oxfordshire FHS, Dr H Kearsey, Windmaill Place, Windmill Road, Minchinhampton, Stroud, Glos, GL6 9EE
Berkshire Marriage Index – Mrs P. Knight, Old Oak Cottage, The Pound, Cookham, Nr Maidenhead, Berks., SL6 9QE
Berkshire Marriages 1538-1837 (Indexed by Groom only) – Oxfordshire Archives, St Luke's Church, Temple Road, Oxford, OX4 2EX
North Berkshire Marriage Index 1538-1851 – Oxfordshire FHS, Dr H Kearsey, Windmaill Place, Windmill Road, Minchinhampton, Stroud, Glos, GL6 9EE
Berkshire Name Index – Berkshire FHS Research Centre, Yeomanry House, 131 Castle Hill, Reading, Berkshire, RG1 7TJ
General Berkshire Index – Mrs P. Knight, Old Oak Cottage, The Pound, Cookham, Nr Maidenhead, Berkshire, SL6 9QE

Berkshire is a county extremely irregular in shape; its greatest length being 42 miles from east to west and its greatest breadth about 28 miles from north to south. It is watered by six principal rivers: the Thames, Kennet, Lodden, Ock, Lambourn and Enborne. The population in 1841 was 161,759; in 1851, 170,065; in 1861, 176,256; in 1871, 196,475; in 1881, 218,363.

The soils are grey calcareous loam and clay. To the south of the county is the remarkably fertile Vale of Berkshire. Numerous herds of cattle were raised together with sheep, pigs and poultry. A considerable quantity of peat was dug around Newbury and other places. There were few industries but brewing was pursued in several towns especially Reading. Pins, ribbons and other silk goods were also made here. Newbury, once important for woollen cloths, became the great corn market of the county.

The information in the Index is abbreviated, and may mislead the searcher if reference is not made to the details contained in the several publications listed in the Introduction. It is essential that users of this book check the appropriate works before making further enquiries.

BUCKINGHAMSHIRE

parish name	deposited original registers	I.G.I.	local census indexes	copies of registers at Soc. Gen.	Boyd's marriage index	1837-1851 Registration District	Pallot's marriage index	non-conform. records at P.R.O.	map ref.
Addington	A 1558-1992	1558-1877	5,8,9	1558-1908		Buckingham	1790-1812		7I
Adstock	A 1538-1978	1538-1875	5,8,9			Buckingham			7I
Akeley	A 1682-1979	1600-1882	5,8,9	1600-1837		Buckingham			8K
Amersham	A 1561-1912	1561-1812	5,8,9	1561-1812	1561-1812	Amersham	1790-1812	1773-1837	4D
Ashendon	A 1732-1979	1732-1881	5,8,9	1732-1840		Aylesbury			7G
Aston Abbots	A 1559-1990	1559-1837	5,8,9	1559-1837		Aylesbury	1790-1812		5H
Aston Clinton	A 1560-1938	1560-1812	5,8,9	1560-1904	1560-1812	Aylesbury	1790-1812		5G
Aston Sandford	A 1609-1987		5,8,9			Aylesbury			7F
Astwood	A 1666-1914	1680-1875	5,8,9			Newport Pagnell			4L
Aylesbury	A 1565-1975	1564-1877	5,8,9	1564-1909		Aylesbury		1789-1837	6G
Barton Hartshorn	A 1752-1837	1752-1837	5,8,9	1575-1840		Buckingham			9I
Beachampton	A 1628-1998	1628-1836	5,8,9	1575-1833		Buckingham			6J
Beaconsfield	A 1631-1971	1575-1878	5,8,9	1540-1837	1631-1812	Amersham	1790-1812	1765-1837	4D
Biddlesden	A 1695-1993		5,8,9	1686-1987	1696-1837	Brackley			9K
Bierton	A 1560-1959		5,8,9	1560-1927		Aylesbury			5G
Bledlow	A 1592-1959	1868-1875	5,8,9	1590-1838		Wycombe			6E
Bletchley	A 1577-1986	1577-1881	5,8,9			Newport Pagnell			5J
Boarstall	A 1640-1888		5,8,9	1640-1888		Bicester			9G
Bow Brickhill	A 1653-1969	1653-1869	5,8,9	1600-1991		Newport Pagnell			4J
Bradenham	A 1627-1944	1627-1875	5,8,9	1627-1812	1627-1812	Wycombe	1790-1812		6E
Bradwell Abbey (ex.par.)			5,8,9			Newport Pagnell			6K(D)
Brill	A 1586-1953		5,8,9			Thame			8G
Broughton	A 1654-1837	1654-1837	5,8,9	1720-1837	1720-183	Newport Pagnell	1790-1837		4K
Buckingham	A 1558-1991		5,8,9	1559-1837		Buckingham		1785-1837	8J
Buckland	A 1653-1980		5,8,9	1609-1889		Aylesbury			5G
Burnham	A 1561-1967	1561-1812	5,8,9	1561-1812	1561-1812	Eton	1790-1812		4B
Cadmore End	A 1786-1972	1786-1878	5,8,9	1851-1853		Wycombe			6D
Calverton	A 1559-1942		5,8,9			Pottesbury			6K
Castle Thorpe			5,8,9			Newport Pagnell	1790-1837		6L
Chalfont St Giles	A 1584-1991	1584-1875	5,8,9	1584-1812	1584-1812	Amersham	1790-1812	1767-1836	3D
Chalfont St Peter	A 1538-1944	1538-1812	5,8,9	1538-1812	1538-1812	Amersham	1790-1812	1779-1836	3D
Chearsley	A 1570-1990	1570-1885	5,8,9	1570-1812		Aylesbury			7F
Cheddington	A 1539-1999	1539-1881	5,8,9	1552-1812	1552-1812	Leighton Buzzard	1790-1812		4G
Chenies	A 1592-1976	1592-1871	5,8,9	1592-1836	1593-1812	Amersham	1790-1836	1783-1812	3E
Chesham		1538-1837	5,8,9	1538-1837	1626-1837	Amersham	1790-1837	1778-1837	4E
Chesham Bois	A 1542-1974	1562-1884	5,8,9	1561-1812	1561-1812	Amersham			3E
Chetwode	A 1583-1948	1583-1877	5,8,9	1583-1840		Buckingham			8I
Chicheley	A 1539-1842	1539-1812	5,8,9	1539-1812	1539-1812	Newport Pagnell	1790-1812		4L
Chilton	A 1672-1930		5,8,9	1600-1824	1600-1812	Thame	1790-1824		8G
Cholesbury	A 1583-1887	1583-1875	5,8,9	1575-1840	1576-1812	Aylesbury	1790-1812		4F
Clifton Reynes	A 1653-1836	1653-1836	5,8,9			Newport Pagnell			4L
Cold Brayfield	A 1693-1836	1693-1836	5,8,9			Newport Pagnell			4M
Colnbrook	A 1760-1996	1760-1877	5,8,9			Eton			3B
Creslow			5,8,9			Aylesbury			6H(R)
Cublington	A 1566-1993	1566-1835	5,8,9	1566-1812		Aylesbury			5H(S)
Cuddington	A 1653-1986		5,8,9			Aylesbury			7G
Datchet	A 1559-1958	1559-1877	5,8,9	1559-1900		Eton			3B
Denham	A 1564-1980	1569-1812	5,8,9	1564-1911	1569-1812	Eton	1790-1812		3C
Dinton	A 1560-1996	1560-1881	5,8,9			Aylesbury			6F
Dorney	A 1538-1984	1538-1875	5,8,9	1538-1900	1540-1812	Eton	1790-1812		4B
Dorton	A 1694-1835	1694-1835	5,8,9	1590-1842	1703-1812	Thame			8G
Drayton Beauchamp	A 1538-1837		5,8,9	1538-1837		Aylesbury			4F
Drayton Parslow	A 1559-1991	1559-1837	5,8,9	1559-1837	1559-1837	Winslow	1790-1836		5I
Dunton	A 1577-1835	1577-1835	5,8,9	1577-1837		Winslow			6I
East Claydon	A 1583-1981		5,8,9	1584-1837		Winslow			7I
Edgcott	A 1538-1955	1538-1837	5,8,9	1538-1955		Buckingham	1790-1834		8H
Edlesborough	A 1567-1975	1567-1881	5,8,9	1568-1928	1562-1812	Leighton Buzzard	1790-1812		4H
Ellesborough	A 1603-1886	1603-1859	5,8,9	1603-1886		Wycombe			5F
Emberton	A 1658-1963		5,8,9			Newport Pagnell			5L
Eton	A 1598-1967	1594-1885	5,8,9	1594-1849		Eton			4B
Farnham Royal	A 1635-1975	1653-1881	5,8,9	1635-1786		Eton			4B
Fawley			5,8,9			Henley			7C
Fenny Stratford	A 1730-1987	1730-1860	5,8,9	1730-1901		Newport Pagnell	1790-1812		5J
Fingest	A 1607-1836	1607-1812	5,8,9	1607-1841	1601-1812	Wycombe	1790-1812		6D
Fleet Marston	A 1630-1964		5,8,9	1677-1691		Aylesbury			6G(T)
Foxcott	A 1664-1968	1664-1885	5,8,9	1752-1840		Buckingham			7J(M)
Fulmer	A 1658-1992	1658-1875	5,8,9	1688-1812	1688-1812	Eton	1790-1812		3C
Gawcott	A 1806-1967	1806-1875	5,8,9			Buckingham			8J
Gayhurst	A 1728-1834	1728-1836	5,8,9			Newport Pagnell			5L(A)
Granborough	A 1538-1964	1538-1875	5,8,9	1538-1754		Thame			7I
Great Brickhill	A 1559-1982		5,8,9	1558-1982		Newport Pagnell			5J
Great Hampden	A 1557-1835	1557-1812	5,8,9	1557-1812		Wycombe	1790-1812		5E
Great Horwood	A 1600-1974	1600-1875	5,8,9	1754-1837		Winslow		1822-1837	6J
Great Kimble	A 1701-1998	1701-1879	5,8,9			Wycombe			6F
Great Linford	A 1653-1965	1653-1881	5,8,9	1653-1882		Newport Pagnell			5K
Great Marlow	A 1592-1987	1592-1611	5,7,8,9	1592-1925		Wycombe		1774-1837	6C
Great Missenden	A 1678-1966	1575-1883	5,8,9	1575-1725		Amersham			5E
Great Woolstone	A 1813-1971	1538-1875	5,8,9	1538-1811		Newport Pagnell	1790-1812		5K(G)
Grendon Underwood	A 1560-1947	1813-1869	5,8,9	1560-1836		Aylesbury			8H
Grove	A 1689-1967	1690-1881	5,8,9	1711-1812	1711-1812	Leighton Buzzard	1790-1812		4H
Haddenham	A 1653-1979		5,7,8,9			Aylesbury		1823-1837	7F
Halton	A 1606-1988	1607-1879	5,8,9	1604-1849		Aylesbury			5F
Hambleden	A 1566-1981		5,8,9	1566-1837		Henley		1810-1836	6C
Hanslope			5,8,9	1575-1837		Newport Pagnell			6L
Hardmead	A 1556-1975	1555-1836	5,8,9	1575-1813	1576-1812	Newport Pagnell	1790-1813		4L
Hardwick with Weedon	A 1558-1865	1558-1849	5,8,9			Aylesbury			6H
Hartwell	A 1550-1935	1550-1884	5,8,9	1553-1812	1553-1812	Aylesbury	1790-1812		6G(W)
Haversham	A 1665-1975	1665-1877	5,8,9			Newport Pagnell			6K

BUCKINGHAMSHIRE

parish name	deposited original registers	I.G.I.	local census indexes	copies of registers at Soc. Gen.	Boyd's marriage index	1837-1851 Registration District	Pallot's marriage index	non-conform. records at P.R.O.	map ref.
Hawridge	A 1785-1848	1600-1848	5,8,9	1600-1840	1600-1812	Aylesbury	1790-1812		4F
Hedgerley	A 1539-1963	1539-1885	5,8,9	1539-1812	1539-1812	Eton	1790-1812		3C(d)
Hedsor	A 1678-1999	1678-1875	5,8,9	1600-1837	1676-1837	Wycombe	1790-1837		4C
High Wycombe	A 1610-1956	1600-1812	5,7,8,9	1600-1837	1600-1812	Wycombe	1790-1812	1762-1837	5D
Hillesden	A 1594-1951	1594-1875	5,8,9	1594-1812		Buckingham			8I
Hitcham	A 1559-1979	1754-1875	5,8,9	1559-1936	1580-1812	Eton	1790-1812		4B
Hoggeston	A 1547-1873	1547-1839	5,8,9	1547-1873		Winslow			6I
Hogshaw			5,8,9	1731-1801		Winslow			7H
Horsenden	A 1637-1849		5,8,9	1631-1842		Wycombe			6E
Horton	A 1571-1874		5,8,9	1571-1874		Eton			3A
Hughenden	A 1560-1963	1559-1876	5,8,9	1559-1812	1559-1812	Wycombe	1790-1812		5E
Hulcott	A 1539-1995		5,8,9	1539-1840		Aylesbury			5G
Ibstone (Oxon)						Wycombe			7D
Ickford	A 1561-1993		5,8,9			Thame			8F
Ilmer	A 1660-1837		5,8,9	1575-1899		Wycombe			7F
Iver	A 1605-1985	1605-1827	5,8,9	1605-1840	1605-1812	Eton	1790-1812		3B
Ivinghoe	A 1559-1982	1559-1881	5,8,9	1559-1986	1559-1812	Leighton Buzzard	1790-1812		4G
Kingsey	A 1538-1985		5,8,9	1538-1840		Thame			7F
Lacey Green	A 1825-1993		5,8,9			Wycombe			6E
Lane End	A 1832-1970		5,8,9			Wycombe			6D
Langley Marish	A 1645-1966	1644-1876	5,8,9	1644-1841		Eton			3B
Lathbury	A 1690-1839	1690-1839	5,8,9	1690-1837	1690-1837	Newport Pagnell	1790-1837		5L
Latimer	A 1756-1939	1756-1875	5,8,9	1756-1832	1756-1832	Amersham			3E
Lavendon	A 1574-1971	1574-1881	5,8,9			Newport Pagnell			4M
Leckhampstead	A 1558-1931	1558-1861	5,8,9	1558-1837		Buckingham	1790-1812		7K
Lee	A 1671-1959	1671-1872	5,8,9			Amersham			5F(b)
Lewknor (Oxon)						Wycome/Thame			6C(c)
Lillingstone Dayrell	A 1584-1980	1584-1875	5,8,9	1584-1870		Buckingham			8K
Lillingstone Lovell (Oxon)	A 1558-1836	1558-1840	5,8,9	1558-1840	1558-1840	Buckingham			7K
Linslade	A 1690-1976	1600-1812	5,8,9	1575-1812	1575-1812	Leighton Buzzard	1790-1812		4I
Little Brickhill	A 1559-1912		5,8,9	1559-1988		Newport Pagnell			4J
Little Hampden	A 1672-1844		5,8,9	1575-1840		Wycombe			5E(a)
Little Horwood	A 1568-1968	1568-1884	5,8,9	1754-1837		Winslow			6I
Little Kimble	A 1657-1992	1657-1877	5,8,9			Wycombe			6F(Z)
Little Linford	A 1757-1973		5,8,9			Newport Pagnell			5L(B)
Little Marlow	A 1559-1987		5,7,8,9	1559-1837		Wycombe			5C
Little Missenden	A 1559-1989	1559-1812	5,8,9	1559-1812	1559-1812	Wycombe	1790-1812		4E
Little Woolstone	A 1813-1962	1596-1876	5,8,9	1596-1813		Newport Pagnell	1790-1812		5K(F)
Long Crendon	A 1559-1969	1559-1875	5,8,9	1559-1684		Thame			8F
Long Crendon (det.)			5,8,9			Thame			8H(0)
Loughton	A 1720-1993	1707-1877	5,8,9	1707-1812		Newport Pagnell			6K
Lower Winchendon	A 1562-1979	1711-1883	5,8,9	1562-1752		Aylesbury			7G(U)
Ludgershall	A 1570-1979	1570-1882	5,8,9	1566-1837		Aylesbury			8H
Luffield Abbey (ex.par.)			5,8,9			Buckingham			8K
Maids Moreton	A 1558-1983	1558-1875	5,8,9	1558-1859		Buckingham			7J(L)
Marsh Gibbon	A 1576-1945	1558-1875	5,8,9			Buckingham			8H
Marsworth	A 1720-1992	1591-1812	5,8,9	1591-1812	1591-1812	Berkhamsted	1790-1837		4G
Medmenham	A 1654-1964	1575-1877	5,8,9	1575-1930		Henley			6C
Mentmore	A 1685-1990	1600-1880	5,8,9	1575-1837	1575-1812	Leighton Buzzard	1790-1829		4H
Middle Claydon	A 1538-1835		5,8,9			Buckingham			7I
Milton Keynes	A 1559-1893	1559-1943	5,8,9			Newport Pagnell			5K
Monks Risborough	A 1587-1986	1587-1876	5,8,9	1587-1841		Wycombe			6F
Moulsoe	A 1560-1993	1559-1836	5,8,9	1559-1837	1559-1837	Newport Pagnell	1790-1837		5K
Mursley	A 1578-1977	1578-1883	5,8,9	1575-1837		Winslow			6I
Nettleden	C 1813-1993		5,8,9	1600-1840		Berkhamsted			3F
Newport Pagnell	A 1558-1978	1558-1877	5,8,9	1558-1837	1558-1837	Newport Pagnell	1790-1837	1790-1837	5K
Newton Blossomville	A 1730-1930		5,8,9			Newport Pagnell			4L
Newton Longville	A 1560-1990	1560-1879	5,7,8,9	1560-1840		Newport Pagnell	1790-1837		5J
North Crawley	A 1558-1955		5,8,9	1700-1812		Newport Pagnell			4L
North Marston	A 1587-1938	1587-1875	5,8,9	1587-1911		Winsow			6H
Oakley	A 1726-1997	1727-1881	5,8,9			Thame			8G
Old Bradwell	A 1577-1979	1577-1881	5,8,9	1577-1914		Newport Pagnell			6K
Olney	A 1665-1973	1665-1877	5,8,9	1665-1837		Newport Pagnell	1790-1812	1819-1837	5M
Oving	A 1680-1931		5,8,9	1600-1837		Aylesbury			6H
Padbury	A 1538-1942	1538-1881	5,8,9	1538-1837		Buckingham			7I
Penn	A 1560-1943		5,8,9	1559-1837		Amersham			4D
Petsoe			5,8,9			Newprt Pagnell			4L
Pitchcott	A 1680-1979		5,8,9			Aylesbury			6H(Q)
Pitstone	A 1653-1972	1600-1882	5,8,9	1576-1812	1578-1812	Berkhamsted	1790-1812		4G
Preston Bissett	A 1630-1914	1630-1875	5,8,9	1576-1840		Buckingham			8I
Princes Risborough	A 1561-1936		5,8,9	1561-1870		Wycombe		1804-1837	6E
Quainton	A 1599-1959	1599-1881	5,8,9	1599-1883	1599-1837	Aylesbury			7H
Quarrendon			5,8,9			Aylesbury			6G
Radclive	A 1591-1992	1608-1836	5,8,9	1591-1890	1608-1812	Buckingham			8J(K)
Radnage	A 1574-1989	1754-1876	5,8,9	1574-1769		Wycombe	1790-1812		6E
Ravenstone	A 1568-1973	1568-1873	5,8,9	1568-1883		Newport Pagnell	1790-1812		5L
St Leonard	A 1738-1822	1738-1820	5,8,9	1738-1859		Aylesbury			4F
Saunderton	A 1655-1819		5,8,9	1813-1850		Wycombe	1790-1819		6E
Shabbington	A 1714-1982		5,8,9			Thame			8F
Shalstone	A 1538-1992		5,8,9	1538-1836		Buckingham			8J
Shenley	A 1703-1968	1653-1864	5,8,9	1703-1881		Winslow/Newport P			6J
Sherington	A 1698-1961	1698-1882	5,8,9	1698-1812	1698-1812	Newport Pagnell	1790-1812		5L
Simpson	A 1719-1995	1719-1877	5,8,9			Newport Pagnell			5J
Slapton	A 1653-1994	1575-1837	5,8,9	1575-1812	1651-1812	Leighton Buzzard	1790-1812		4H
Slough	A 1837-1965		5,8,9			Eton			3B
Soulbury	A 1594-1992	1575-1812	5,8,9	1575-1812	1575-1812	Leighton Buzzard	1790-1812	1816-1837	5I
Stantonbury	A 1657-1951	1666-1809	5,8,9			Newport Pagnell			5K(C)
Steeple Claydon	A 1575-1964			1754-1837	1754-1837	Buckingham			8I

parish name	deposited original registers	I.G.I.	local census indexes	copies of registers at Soc. Gen.	Boyd's marriage index	1837-1851 Registration District	Pallot's marriage index	non-conform. records at P.R.O.	map ref.
Stewkley	A 1545-1990	1545-1653	5,8,9	1545-1653		Winslow			5I
Stoke Goldington	A 1538-1950	1538-1877	5,8,9			Newport Pagnell			6L
Stoke Hammond	A 1534-1996	1534-1882	5,8,9			Leighton Buzzard			5I
Stoke Mandeville	A 1699-1997	1605-1700	5,8,9	1605-1840		Wycombe			6G(Y)
Stoke Poges	A 1563-1991	1563-1881	5,8,9	1563-1837	1563-1812	Eton	1790-1812		3B
Stone	A 1538-1996	1538-1881	5,8,9	1538-1812	1538-1812	Aylesbury			6G
Stony Stratford								1822-1837	6K
St Giles	A 1618-1968		5,8,9			Pottesbury			6K
St Mary Magdalen	A 1864-1968		5,8,9			Pottesbury			6K
Stowe	A 1568-1981		5,8,9	1569-1840		Buckingham			8K
Swanbourne	A 1565-1968	1565-1881	5,8,9	1565-1836		Winslow	1790-1836		6I
Taplow	A 1710-1897	1708-1875	5,8,9	1710-1893	1710-1812	Eton	1790-1812		4B
Tattenhoe	A 1733-1960	1733-1827	5,8,9	1813-1837		Winslow			6J(N)
Thornborough	A 1602-1999	1602-1846	5,8,9	1604-1837		Buckingham			7J
Thornton	A 1562-1990	1562-1812	5,8,9	1570-1812		Buckingham	1790-1812		7J
Tingewick	A 1560-1995	1560-1881	5,8,9	1569-1841	1569-1812	Buckingham			8J
Towersey	B 1589-1978		5,8,9	1581-1951		Thame			7F
Turville	A 1582-1989	1582-1812	5,8,9	1582-1852	1582-1812	Wycombe	1790-1812		7D
Turweston	A 1695-1996		5,8,9	1695-1851	1699-1837	Brackley			9J
Twyford	A 1558-1962	1558-1881	5,8,9	1635-1840		Buckingham			8I
Tyringham	A 1630-1950		5,8,9	1576-1836		Newport Pagnell			5L
Upper Winchendon	A 1606-1970		5,8,9	1606-1970		Aylesbury			7G(V)
Upton-cum-Chulvey	A 1539-1967	1539-1885	5,8,9	1539-1904		Eton			3B
Waddesdon	A 1538-1974	1538-1883	5,8,9			Aylesbury		1834-1836	7G
Walton	A 1598-1978	1598-1876	5,8,9	1598-1812		Newport Pagnell	1790-1812		5J(J)
Water Stratford	A 1596-1996	1596-1883	5,8,9	1597-1812	1597-1812	Buckingham			8J
Wavendon	A 1567-1964	1567-1881	5,8,9	1567-1783		Newport Pagnell			4J
Wendover	A 1626-1983	1600-1877	5,8,9	1576-1837	1576-1812	Wycombe	1790-1812	1819-1836	5F
Wendover (detached)			5,8,9			Wycombe			5G(X)
Westbury	A 1558-1995	1558-1837	5,8,9	1558-1837	1558-1837	Brackley	1790-1837		9J
Weston Turville	A 1538-1980		5,8,9			Aylesbury			5G
Weston Underwood	A 1681-1952	1681-1875	5,8,9			Newport Pagnell			5M
West Wycombe									6D
St Lawrence	A 1663-1983	1602-1877	5,8,9	1602-1641		Wycombe			6D
St Paul	A 1937-1966		5,8,9			Wycombe			6D
Wexham	A 1728-1985	1728-1876	5,8,9	1728-1981		Eton			3B(e)
Whaddon	A 1584-1995	1584-1842	5,7,8,9	1584-1837		Winslow			6J
Whitchurch	A 1653-1991		5,8,9			Aylesbury			6H
Willen	A 1665-1981	1575-1875	5,8,9	1600-1837	1600-1837	Newport Pagnell			5K(E)
Wing	A 1546-1998	1546-1881	5,8,9	1546-1837	1546-1812	Leighton Buzzard	1790-1812		5H
Wingrave	A 1550-1979		5,8,9	1550-1965		Aylesbury		1826-1836	5H
Winslow	A 1560-1994		5,8,9	1560-1837		Winslow		1819-1836	7I
Wolverton									6K
St George	A 1844-1965		5,8,9	1844-1903		Pottesbury			6K
Holy Trinity	A 1536-1979		5,8,9	1536-1850		Pottesbury			6K
St Mary	A 1864-1968		5,8,9			Pottesbury			6K
Wooburn	A 1653-1989	1653-1812	5,8,9	1653-1897	1653-1812	Wycombe	1790-1812	1773-1836	4C
Woodham (in Waddesdon)			5,8,9			Aylesbury			8H(P)
Worminghall	A 1538-1968		5,8,9			Thame			9F
Wotton Underwood	A 1599-1979	1599-1875	5,8,9	1599-1837		Aylesbury			8G
Woughton on the Green	A 1556-1997	1558-1876	5,8,9	1558-1812		Newport Pagnell	1790-1812		5J(H)
Wraysbury	A 1734-1962		5,8,9	1575-1766		Eton			3A

Original registers deposited at:
A = Buckinghamshire Record Office, County Hall, Aylesbury, HP20 1UU
B = Oxfordshire Record Office, St Luke's Church, Cowley, Oxford, OX4 2EX
C = Hertfordshire Archives & Local Studies, County Hall, Pegs Lane, Hertford, SG13 8DE

Study adjacent parishes in counties of Oxfordshire, Northamptonshire, Bedfordshire, Hertfordshire, Berkshire and Surrey

Buckinghamshire Record Office – County Hall, Aylesbury, HP20 1UU

The following useful indexes have been compiled – see Introduction
Census Index 1851 – Miss Shirley Nicholls, Faircross, Hare Lane, Little Kingshill, Great Missenden, Buckinghamshire, HP16 0EF
Census Index 1891 – Buckinghamshire FHS Sales, 3 Swallow Lane, Stoke Mandeville, Aylesbury, Bucks, HP22 5UW
Census Indexes 1851-1891 – Buckingham Genealogical Society – Mrs E McLaughlin, Varneys, Rudds Lane, Haddenham, Bucks, HP17 8JP
Buckingham FHS Marriage Index – C/O Mrs J Rees, 99 Aldrich Drive, Willen, Milton Keynes, MK15 9LJ complete to 1837
Buckinghamshire Genealogical Society Marriage Index – Mr A McLaughlin, Varneys, Rudds Lane, Haddenham, Bucks, HP17 8JP complete to 1837
Monumental Inscriptions – Mrs Ann Biggs, 18 Shelburne Road, High Wycombe, Buckinghamshire, HP12 3NJ
Buckinghamshire Wills & Administrations in the Prerogative Court of Canterbury 1700-1800 – Roy Clarke, 11 The Hyde, Weston Turville, Aylesbury, Buckinghamshire, HP22 5RP
Indexes of Marriage, Emigrants, Militia, Bastards, Settlement papers and Ancestors – Mrs Eve McLaughlin, Varneys, Rudds Lane, Haddenham, Aylesbury, Buckinghamshire, HP17 8JP
Buckinghamshire FHS Baptism Database – 1 Drove Cottages, Newhaven Road, Rodmell, Lewes, East Sussex BN7 3HD
Buckinghamshire FHS Burials Database – 1 Drove Cottages, Newhaven Road, Rodmell, Lewes, East Sussex BN7 3HD

Buckinghamshire's length from north to south is about 45 miles and its greatest breadth from east to west, crossing a slip of Hertfordshire, is nearly 23 miles. It is watered by three principal rivers: the Thames, Ouse and the Colne. The population in 1841 was 138,246; in 1851, 143,655; in 1861, 167,993; in 1871, 175,879; in 1881, 176,323.

The soils are chiefly chalk and flint. Great numbers of cattle were raised, dairy products being of considerable importance. Pigs and ducks were also reared and wheat, barley, oats, beans and saffron grown. The principal manufactures were lace and paper.

The information in the Index is abbreviated, and may mislead the searcher if reference is not made to the details contained in the several publications listed in the Introduction. It is essential that users of this book check the appropriate works before making further enquiries.

CAMBRIDGESHIRE

parish name	deposited original registers	I.G.I.	local census indexes	copies of registers at Soc. Gen.	Boyd's marriage index	1837-1851 Registration District	Pallot's marriage index	non-conform. records at P.R.O.	map ref.
Abington Pigotts	A 1729-1987	1599-1812	4,5,8	1559-1837	1599-1837	Royston	1790-1837		8B
Arrington	A 1538-1992	1546-1877	4,5,8	1538-1837	1538-1837	Caxton	1790-1837		7C
Ashley cum Silverley	A 1746-1939	1630-1876	4,5,6,8	1561-1837	1746-1837	Newmarket			2D
Babraham	A 1561-1925	1561-1876	4,5,8	1561-1925	1561-1837	Linton			5C
Balsham	A 1558-1994	1558-1876	4,5,8	1558-1851	1559-1837	Linton	1790-1812		4C
Barrington	A 1570-1994		4,5,8	1570-1890	1570-1837	Royston	1790-1837	1797-1837	6C
Bartlow	A 1573-2000	1573-1876	4,5,8	1573-1862	1600-1837	Linton			4B
Barton	A 1688-1989		4,5,8	1600-1851	1600-1837	Chesterton			6D
Bassingbourn with Kneesworth	A 1558-1989	1558-1876	4,5,8	1558-1851	1599-1837	Royston		1820-1837	7B
Benwick	A 1851-1982	1851-1876	4,5,8			North Witchford			7I
Bottisham	A 1561-1953	1562-1876	4,5,8	1563-1837	1563-1837	Newmarket			4E
Bourn		1564-1875	4,5,8	1563-1861	1599-1837	Caxton			7D
Boxworth	A 1588-1996	1588-1878	4,5,8	1588-1837	1588-1837	St Ives	1790-1812		7E
Brinkley	A 1684-1997	1599-1877	4,5,8	1599-1851	1599-1837	Newmarket			3C
Burrough Green	A 1571-1948	1571-1868	4,5,8	1571-1840	1599-1837	Newmarket			3D
Burwell	A 1560-1998	1562-1861	4,5,8	1561-1891	1561-1837	Newmarket		1747-1836	4E
Caldecote	A 1661-1837	1604-1880	4,5,8	1599-1918	1604-1812	Caxton	1790-1837		7D
Cambridge								1688-1840	6D(L)
All Saints	A 1538-1973	1539-1876	4,5,7,8	1538-1837	1639-1837	Cambridge	1790-1837		6D(L)
Holy Sepulchre	A 1567-1979	1569-1868	4,5,7,8	1569-1837	1569-1837	Cambridge	1790-1812		6D(L)
Holy Trinity	A 1564-1993	1566-1876	4,5,7,8	1564-1837	1564-1837	Cambridge			6D(L)
Queens' College			4,5,7,8	1722-1753		Cambridge			6D(L)
St Andrew the Great	A 1635-1984	1600-1837	4,5,7,8	1600-1860	1600-1837	Cambridge	1790-1837		6D(L)
St Andrew the Less	A 1753-1957	1599-1837	4,5,7,8	1599-1851	1599-1837	Cambridge	1790-1837		5D(M)
St Benedict	A 1539-1984	1539-1837	4,5,7,8	1539-1851	1539-1837	Cambridge	1790-1837		6D(L)
St Botolph	A 1564-1898	1564-1837	4,5,7,8	1564-1863	1564-1837	Cambridge	1790-1812		6D(L)
St Clement	A 1560-1882	1560-1876	4,5,7,8	1560-1992	1560-1837	Cambridge	1790-1837		6D(L)
St Edward	A 1558-1981	1559-1837	4,5,7,8	1558-1862	1558-1837	Cambridge	1790-1837		6D(L)
St Giles	A 1585-1974	1599-1837	4,5,7,8	1585-1860	1599-1837	Cambridge	1790-1837		6D(K)
St Mary the Great	A 1559-1974	1559-1837	4,5,7,8	1559-1851	1599-1837	Cambridge	1790-1837		6D(L)
St Mary the Less	A 1557-1944	1558-1837	4,5,7,8	1557-1890	1558-1837	Cambridge	1790-1837		6D(L)
St Michael	A 1538-1950	1538-1837	4,5,7,8	1538-1837	1539-1837	Cambridge	1790-1836		6D(L)
St Peter	A 1586-1971	1586-1758	4,5,7,8	1586-1758	1586-1758	Cambridge			6D(L)
Carlton-cum-Willingham	A 1588-1876	1588-1875	4,5,7,8	1588-1851	1599-1837	Linton			3C
Castle Camps	A 1563-1960	1563-1876	4,5,8	1563-1845	1567-1837	Linton			3B
Caxton	A 1741-1977	1599-1874	4,5,8	1599-1851	1600-1837	Caxton			8D
Chatteris	A 1614-1954	1600-1876	4,5,8	1600-1902	1600-1837	North Witchford		1778-1837	6H
Cherry Hinton	A 1538-1980	1538-1876	4,5,8	1538-1912	1538-1837	Chesterton			5D
Chesterton	A 1564-1969	1564-1876	4,5,8	1564-1923	1564-1837	Chesterton	1790-1837		6D
Chettisham, Ely	A 1700-1911		4,5,8	1600-1837	1600-1837	Ely			4G
Cheveley	A 1559-1965	1559-1876	4,5,8	1559-1902	1559-1837	Newmarket			2D
Childerley			4,5,8			Chesterton			7E(H)
Chippenham	A 1560-1992		4,5,8	1559-1880	1569-1837	Newmarket			2E
Comberton	A 1561-1967	1560-1876	4,5,8	1560-1924	1560-1837	Chesterton			6D
Conington	A 1538-1981	1538-1812	4,5,8	1538-1837	1538-1837	St Ives	1790-1812		7E
Coton	A 1538-1999		4,5,8	1538-1837	1540-1837	Chesterton			6D
Cottenham	A 1572-1937	1538-1876	4,5,8	1573-1837	1573-1837	Chesterton			5F
Coveney	A 1676-1970	1600-1866	4,5,8	1600-1837	1600-1837	Ely			5H
Croxton	A 1538-1957	1538-1877	4,5,8	1538-1892	1538-1837	Caxton			8D
Croydon with Clopton	A 1672-1990	1599-1876	4,5,8	1599-1845	1600-1837	Caxton	1790-1837		8C
Doddington	A 1681-1992	1681-1876	4,5,8	1600-1900	1600-1837	North Witchford			6I
Downham		1558-1876	4,5,8	1558-1837	1558-1837	Ely			5H
Dry Drayton	A 1565-1972	1564-1871	4,5,8	1564-1851	1565-1837	Chesterton	1790-1812		7E
Dullingham	A 1558-1945	1558-1875	4,5,8	1558-1873	1599-1837	Newmarket			3D
Duxford								1788-1836	5B
St John	A 1684-1934	1599-1877	4,5,8	1599-1851	1599-1837	Linton			5B
St Peter	A 1684-1996	1599-1877	4,5,8	1599-1851	1599-1837	Linton			5B
East Hatley	A 1585-1974	1585-1834	4,5,8	1585-1837	1590-1837	Caxton			8C
Elm	B 1539-1974	1539-1877	4,5,8	1539-1877	1539-1837	Wisbech			5J
Elsworth	A 1538-1867	1538-1848	4,5,8	1538-1867	1539-1837	Caxton	1790-1837		8E
Eltisley	A 1653-1957	1599-1877	4,5,8	1599-1900	1599-1837	Caxton	1790-1837		8D
Ely Cathedral	D 1690-1812		4,5,8	1690-1974	1691-1752	Ely			4G(C)
Ely Holy Trinity	A 1559-1881		4,5,8	1559-1837	1599-1837	Ely			4G(D)
Ely St Mary	A 1670-1888		4,5,8	1599-1837	1599-1754	Ely		1787-1837	4G
Ely Trinity & Mary Common Lands			4,5,8			Ely			4G(B)
Ely Trinity & St Mary (intermixed)			4,5,8			Ely			4G
Fen Ditton			4,5,8	1538-1902	1538-1837	Caxton			5D
Fen Drayton	A 1573-1912	1576-1812	4,5,8	1575-1916	1580-1837	St Ives	1790-1812		7F
Fordham	A 1567-1916		4,5,8	1567-1852	1568-1837	Newmarket		1819-1835	3F
Fowlmere	A 1561-1999	1561-1845	4,5,8	1561-1991	1562-1837	Royston		1812-1837	6B
Foxton	A 1678-1977	1599-1875	4,5,8	1599-1892	1599-1837	Royston			6C
Fulbourn All Saints	A 1558-1971	1558-1876	4,5,8	1558-1851	1560-1837	Chesterton		1816-1817	5D
Fulbourn St Vigor	A 1538-1971	1538-1877	4,5,8	1538-1851		Chesterton	1816-1817		5D
Gamlingay	A 1698-1976	1542-1876	4,5,8	1542-1851	1551-1837	Caxton		1820-1836	9C
Girton	A 1630-1973	1599-1811	4,5,8	1599-1908	1599-1837	Chesterton	1790-1818		6E
Grantchester	A 1539-1988	1539-1876	4,5,8	1539-1851	1539-1837	Chesterton			6D(N)
Graveley	A 1654-1939	1599-1876	4,5,8	1599-1939	1599-1837	St Neots	1790-1837		8E
Great Abington	A 1664-1983	1599-1877	4,5,8	1599-1844	1599-1837	Linton			5B
Great Eversden	A 1538-1991	1541-1877	4,5,8	1538-1992	1565-1837	Caxton		1797-1836	7C(O)
Great Shelford			4,5,8	1557-1844	1557-1844	Chesterton			5C
Great Wilbraham	A 1561-1987	1561-1854	4,5,8	1561-1851	1600-1837	Chesterton			4D
Grunty Fen (ex.par.)			4,5,8			Ely			5G
Guilden Morden	A 1653-1966	1598-1845	4,5,8	1599-1845	1599-1837	Royston			8B
Haddenham	A 1570-1970	1570-1876	4,5,8	1570-1851	1570-1837	Ely			6F
Hardwick	A 1564-1985	1564-1876	4,5,8	1578-1885	1578-1837	Caxton			7D
Harlton	A 1567-1906		4,5,8	1574-1837	1574-1837	Chesterton			6C

CAMBRIDGESHIRE

parish name	deposited original registers	I.G.I.	local census indexes	copies of registers at Soc. Gen.	Boyd's marriage index	1837-1851 Registration District	Pallot's marriage index	non-conform. records at P.R.O.	map ref.
Harston	A 1687-1995	1599-1877	4,5,8	1599-1840	1599-1837	Chesterton			6C
Haslingfield	A 1709-1996	1599-1853	4,5,8	1599-1929	1599-1837	Chesterton			6C
Hatley St George	A 1589-1980	1580-1837	4,5,8	1500-1837	1591-1837	Caxton			8C
Hauxton	A 1561-1993	1560-1877	4,5,8	1560-1842	1560-1837	Chesterton			6C(Q)
Hildersham	A 1559-1904	1559-1885	4,5,8	1541-1938	1599-1837	Linton			4B
Hinxton	A 1538-1938	1538-1876	4,5,8	1538-1938	1538-1837	Linton			5B
Histon	A 1653-1984	1599-1875	4,5,8	1599-1900	1590-1837	Chesterton	1790-1837		6E
Horningsea	A 1628-1979	1628-1876	4,5,8	1599-1878	1599-1837	Chesterton			5E
Horseheath	A 1558-1990	1558-1876	4,5,8	1558-1927	1558-1837	Linton			3B
Ickleton	A 1558-1995	1558-1875	4,5,8	1558-1880	1599-1837	Linton			5B
Impington	A 1562-1992	1562-1877	4,5,8	1562-1837	1562-1837	Chesterton	1790-1837		6E
Isleham	A 1566-1992	1566-1851	4,5,8	1566-1851	1566-1837	Newmarket		1821-1837	3F
Kennett	A 1754-1991		4,5,6,8	1558-1837	1558-1837	Newmarket			2E
Kingston	A 1654-1995	1655-1880	4,5,8	1589-1837	1589-1837	Caxton			7C
Kirtling	A 1585-1953	1585-1876	4,5,8	1576-1851	1592-1837	Newmarket			2D
Knapwell	A 1678-1996	1592-1837	4,5,8	1598-1996	1598-1837	Caxton	1790-1812		7D(J)
Landbeach	A 1538-1957		4,5,8	1538-1851	1539-1837	Chesterton			5E
Landwade			4,5,6,8	1693-1802	1695-1837	Newmarket			3E
Leverington		1558-1859	4,5,8	1558-1837	1568-1837	Wisbech			6L
Linton	A 1560-1966	1559-1876	4,5,8	1559-1844	1559-1837	Linton		1787-1837	4B
Litlington	A 1642-1955	1599-1845	4,5,8	1599-1845	1599-1837	Royston			7B
Little Abington	A 1687-1953	1599-1878	4,5,8	1599-1844	1602-1837	Linton			4C
Little Eversden	A 1704-2000	1703-1878	4,5,8	1599-1993	1599-1837	Caxton			7C(P)
Little Gransden	A 1730-1985	1600-1878	4,5,8	1600-1837	1604-1837	Caxton			8D
Littleport	A 1753-1994		4,5,8	1599-1837	1599-1837	Ely		1819-1840	4H
Little Shelford	A 1686-1994	1600-1876	4,5,8	1600-1842	1600-1837	Chesterton		1828-1836	5C(R)
Little Wilbraham	A 1538-1987	1538-1876	4,5,8	1538-1852	1599-1837	Chesterton			4D
Lolworth	A 1566-1898	1567-1810	4,5,8	1565-1920	1567-1837	St Ives	1790-1812		7E(G)
Long Stanton									6E
All Saints	A 1672-1974	1599-1877	4,5,8	1599-1974	1599-1837	Chesterton	1790-1812		6E(E)
St Michael	A 1559-1968	1559-1877	4,5,8	1559-1968	1563-1837	Chesterton	1790-1812		6E(F)
Long Stowe	A 1570-1923	1569-1876	4,5,8	1568-1861	1570-1837	Caxton			8D
Madingley	A 1539-1997	1539-1876	4,5,8	1539-1875	1539-1837	Chesterton	1790-1812		6D
Manea	A 1708-1966	1708-1876	4,5,8	1646-1900	1646-1837	North Witchford			5I
March	A 1548-1974		4,5,8	1548-1872	1548-1837	North Witchford		1798-1837	6I
Melbourn	A 1558-1977	1558-1877	4,5,8	1558-1851	1559-1837	Royston		1800-1837	7B
Meldreth	A 1678-1968	1599-1877	4,5,8	1599-1851	1599-1837	Royston			7B
Mepal		1659-1878	4,5,8	1600-1837	1600-1837	Ely			6G
Milton	A 1705-1967	1599-1837	4,5,8	1599-1871	1599-1837	Chesterton	1790-1837		5E
Newmarket All Saints	C 1622-1963		4,5,8			Newmarket			3E
Newton (nr Cambridge)	A 1557-1969	1557-1877	4,5,8	1557-1988	1557-1837	Chesterton			6C
Newton (in the Isle)	B 1653-1970		4,5,8	1600-1852	1600-1837	Wisbech			5L
Oakington	A 1561-1930	1561-1812	4,5,8	1561-1858	1561-1837	Chesterton			6E
Orwell	A 1560-1992	1560-1876	4,5,8	1560-1901	1560-1837	Caxton	1790-1837		7C
Outwell (Norfolk)						Wisbech			4J
Over	A 1577-1968	1577-1812	4,5,8	1577-1852	1559-1837	St Ives	1790-1818		6F
Pampisford	A 1560-1990	1560-1877	4,5,8	1560-1889	1599-1837	Linton			5C
Papworth Agnes	A 1558-1965	1558-1878	4,5,8	1558-1965	1558-1837	Caxton	1790-1837		8E
Papworth Everard	A 1695-1977	1565-1877	4,5,8	1565-1905	1565-1837	Caxton	1790-1837		8E
Parson Drove	B 1657-1971		4,5,8	1603-1754	1603-1837	Wisbech			6K
Rampton	A 1674-1996	1599-1876	4,5,8	1599-1837	1599-1837	Chesterton	1790-1812		6E
Royston (see Herts)						Royston			7B
Sawston	A 1640-1998		4,5,8	1599-1940	1599-1837	Linton		1813-1837	5C
Shepreth	A 1559-1968	1559-1837	4,5,8	1559-1837	1599-1837	Royston			6C
Shingay			4,5,8			Royston			8B
Shudy Camps	A 1558-1969	1558-1862	4,5,8	1558-1841	1599-1837	Linton			3B
Snailwell	A 1629-1992		4,5,6,8	1629-1903	1629-1832	Newmarket			3E
Soham	A 1558-1930	1558-1812	4,5,8	1558-1883	1599-1837	Newmarket		1801-1836	4F
Stanground (Hunts)						Peterborough			9J
Stapleford	A 1557-1967	1557-1885	4,5,8	1557-1837	1557-1837	Chesterton			5C
Steeple Morden	A 1675-1984	1599-1851	4,5,8	1599-1851	1599-1837	Royston			8B
Stetchworth	A 1666-1987	1599-1876	4,5,8	1596-1840	1596-1837	Newmarket			3D
Stow cum Quy	A 1649-1995	1541-1877	4,5,8	1539-1902	1599-1837	Chesterton			5D
Stretham	A 1558-1963		4,5,8	1558-1945	1558-1837	Ely			5F
Stuntney	A 1849-1902	1545-1850	4,5,8	1545-1837	1545-1837	Ely			4G
Sutton	A 1558-1996	1558-1876	4,5,8	1558-1837	1558-1837	Ely			6G
Swaffham Bulbeck	A 1558-1968		4,5,8	1558-1982	1558-1837	Newmarket			4E
Swaffham Prior							1559-1837		4E
St Cyriac & Julitta	A 1559-2000	1559-1876	4,5,6,8	1559-1662		Newmarket			4E
St Mary	A 1559-1662	1559-1876	4,5,6,8	1559-1851		Newmarket			4E
Swavesey		1576-1876	4,5,8	1599-1837	1599-1837	St Ives	1790-1812		7F
Tadlow	A 1653-1996	1599-1837	4,5,8	1599-1837	1599-1837	Caxton			8C
Teversham	A 1593-1989	1592-1840	4,5,8	1592-1840	1595-1837	Chesterton			5D
Thetford	A 1654-1970	1599-1784	4,5,8	1599-1963		Ely			4F
Thorney Abbey	A 1653-1963	1653-1876	4,5,8	1653-1837	1600-1754	Peterborough			8K
Thriplow	A 1538-1996	1538-1840	4,5,8	1538-1840	1603-1837	Royston			6B
Toft		1539-1878	4,5,8	1539-1918	1539-1837	Caxton			7D
Trumpington			4,5,8	1599-1876	1599-1837	Chesterton			6D
Tydd St Giles	B 1687-1992		4,5,8	1559-1837	1559-1837	Wisbech			6L
Upwell (Norfolk)						Wisbech			5J
Waterbeach			4,5,8	1599-1837	1599-1837	Chesterton			5E
Welches Dam (ex.par.)			4,5,8	1711-1727		North Witchford			5H
Welney (Norfolk)	A 1642-1969		4,5,8	1653-1753	1653-1753	Downham			4I
Wendy-with-Shingay	A 1550-1911	1550-1845	4,5,8	1550-1845	1550-1837	Royston			7B
Wentworth	A 1684-1991		4,5,8	1600-1837	1600-1837	Ely			5G(A)
Westley Waterless	A 1557-1965	1558-1877	4,5,8	1557-1901	1597-1812	Newmarket			3D
Weston Colville	A 1712-1979		4,5,8	1599-1851	1601-1837	Linton			3C
West Wickham	A 1682-1995	1599-1858	4,5,8	1565-1922	1565-1837	Linton			3C
West Wratting	A 1579-1980		4,5,8	1579-1889	1599-1837	Linton			4C

CAMBRIDGESHIRE

parish name	deposited original registers	I.G.I.	local census indexes	copies of registers at Soc. Gen.	Boyd's marriage index	1837-1851 Registration District	Pallot's marriage index	non-conform. records at P.R.O.	map ref.
Whaddon	A 1691-1995	1599-1878	4,5,8	1599-1851	1599-1837	Royston			7C
Whittlesey								1810-1837	8J
St Andrew	A 1653-1969		4,5,8	1602-1851	1602-1837	Whittlesey			8J
St Mary	A 1654-1976	1662-1694	4,5,8	1599-1851	1599-1837	Whittlesey			8J
Whittlesford	A 1559-1971	1559-1876	4,5,8	1559-1837	1559-1837	Linton			5C
Wicken	A 1564-1968		4,5,8	1564-1866	1599-1837	Newmarket			4F
Wilburton	A 1736-1964	1559-1851	4,5,8	1599-1851	1599-1837	Ely			5F
Willingham	A 1559-1989	1559-1876	4,5,8	1559-1851	1559-1837	Chesterton	1790-1812		6F
Wimpole	A 1560-1990	1560-1863	4,5,8	1560-1863	1560-1837	Caxton			7C
Wisbech								1700-1837	6K
St Mary	B 1557-1960	1557-1877	4,5,8	1560-1837	1560-1837	Wisbech			6K
St Peter	B 1558-1950	1558-1876	4,5,8	1558-1837	1558-1754	Wisbech			5K
Witcham		1663-1876	4,5,8	1559-1900	1599-1837	Ely			5G
Witchford	A 1754-1968		4,5,8	1599-1837	1599-1837	Ely			5G
Wood Ditton	A 1567-1971	1567-1876	4,5,8	1567-1837	1567-1837	Newmarket			3D

Original registers are deposited at:
A = Cambridge Record Office, Shire Hall, Castle Hill, Cambridge CB3 OAP
B = Wisbech & Fenland Museum, Museum Square, Wisbech, Cambs. PE13 1ES
C = Suffolk Record Office, Bury St Edmunds Branch, Raingate Street, Bury St Edmunds IP33 2AR
D= Cambridge University Library, Dept. of Manuscripts, West Road, Cambridge, CB3 9DR

Study adjacent parishes in counties of Northamptonshire, Lincolnshire, Norfolk, Huntingdonshire, Suffolk, Essex, Hertfordshire and Bedfordshire

Cambridgeshire Record Office – Shire Hall, Castle Hill, Cambridge, CB3 0AP
Cambridge University Library (Manuscript Room), West Road, Cambridge, CB3 9DR
Wisbech and Fenland Museum, Museum Square, Wisbech, Cambridgeshire, PE13 1ES

The following useful indexes have been compiled – see Introduction
Census Indexes 1841 & 1851 – Cambridgeshire FHS, Mr & Mrs Noble, 22 St Margarets Road, Girton, Cambridge, CB3 0LT
Census Index 1851 Cambridge Borough – Mrs B. Ward, 1 Ascham Lane, Whittlesford, Cambridge, CB2 4NT
Census Index 1871 Cambridge Town – County Archivist, Cambridge Record Office
Census Index 1851 Cambridge Prison and County Gaols – Society of Genealogists
Cambridgeshire Marriage Index – County Record Office, Shire Hall, Castle Hill, Cambridge, CB3 0AP
Cambridge Baptisms 1801-1837 & Burials 1801-1837 – Cambridgeshire FHS, Mr & Mrs Noble, 22 St Margarets Road, Girton, Cambridge, CB3 0LT
Cambridge Birth Registrations in Dr Williams' Library and Wesleyan Methodists Metropolitan Registry – Mrs V Uffindell, 21 Gaveston Drive, Berkhamsted, Herts, HP4 1JF
Monumental Inscriptions – Cambridge FHS, Ms Kennedy, 20 High Street, Oakington, Cambridge, CB4 5AG

Cambridgeshire's greatest length from north to south is nearly 50 miles and its breadth at the south and widest extremity over 25 miles. It is watered by two princpal rivers: the Ouse and the Granta or Cam. The population in 1841 was 164,459; in 1851, 191,894; in 1861, 175,950; in 1871, 186,906; in 1881, 185,594.

The soils are principally a mixture of clay and sand and, in the fens, a strong black mould and gravel. Oats were particularly abundant and saffron, hemp, flax, wheat and barley were also cultivated. A considerable number of sheep were raised. With the exception of a sort of white brick for cleaning irons, brass,etc., and the making of coarse pottery ware, there was little manufacturing industry.

The information in the Index is abbreviated, and may mislead the searcher if reference is not made to the details contained in the several publications listed in the Introduction. It is essential that users of this book check the appropriate works before making further enquiries.

CHESHIRE

parish name	deposited original registers	I.G.I.	local census indexes	copies of registers at Soc. Gen.	Boyd's marriage index	1837-1851 Registration District	Pallot's marriage index	non-conform. records at P.R.O.	map ref.
Acton	A 1653-1882	1653-1812	5,8	1653-1812		Nantwich			4G
Adlington		1757-1794	5,8	1704-1794		Macclesfield			7J
Alderley	A 1629-1941	1629-1837	5,8	1629-1837	1629-1837	Gt Boughton	1790-1837		6J
Aldford	A 1639-1983		5,8			Gt Boughton			4D
Alsager	A 1789-1908		5,8			Congleton			4I
Altrincham	A 1799-1962		5,8,9			Altrincham		1752-1837	8I
Alvanley	A 1791-1970		5,8			Runcorn			6E
Ashton-upon-Mersey	A 1636-1960		5,8,9			Altrincham		1799-1837	8I
Astbury	A 1572-1970	1754-1815	5,8	1750-1815		Congleton			4I
Aston by Sutton	A 1635-1997		5,8			Runcorn			6F
Audlem	A 1557-1947		5,8			Nantwich			2G
Backford	A 1562-1981		5,8			Gt Boughton			6D
Baddiley	A 1579-1991		5,8			Nantwich			3G
Barrow	A 1572-1921		5,8	1571-1880		Gt Boughton			5E
Barthomley	A 1562-1923		5,8	1562-1839		Nantwich			4H
Bebington	A 1558-1971	1558-1701	5,8	1558-1701		Wirral			7C
Bidston	A 1679-1986	1581-1699	5,8			Wirral			8B
Birkenhead	A 1719-1974	1721-1844	5,8	1719-1837		Wirral	1790-1812	1830-1837	8C
Bosley	A 1728-1847	1729-1847	5,8	1729-1750	1729-1750	Macclesfield			5J
Bowdon	A 1628-1973		5,8,9			Altrincham		1796-1837	8H
Brereton cum Smethwick	A 1538-1869		5,8	1754-1837		Congleton			5I
Bromborough	A 1580-1954	1600-1727	5,8	1600-1726		Wirral			7C
Bruera	A 1657-1983	1657-1812	5,8	1662-1812	1665-1837	Gt Boughton			4E
Bunbury	A 1559-1982		5,8			Nantwich			4F
Burley Dam	A 1770-1958		5,8			Nantwich			2G
Burton	A 1538-1993	1538-1770	5,8			Wirral			6C
Burwardsley	A 1818-1935		5,8			Nantwich			4F
Capesthorne	A 1722-1995	1722-1747	5,8	1722-1747	1722-1747	Macclesfield			6J
Carrington	A 1759-1894		5,8,9			Altrincham			8H
Chadkirk	A 1748-1971		5,8,9			Stockport			8K
Cheadle	A 1558-1913	1677-1713	5,8,9			Stockport		1794-1837	7J
Chelford	A 1674-1894	1674-1794	5,8	1674-1752	1674-1752	Macclesfield			6I
Chester								1713-1857	5D
Cathedral	A 1688-1981	1687-1812	5,8	1687-1812		Gt Boughton			5D
Holy Trinity	A 1654-1939	1598-1837	5,8	1532-1837		Gt Boughton	1790-1837		5D
St Bridget	A 1649-1972		5,8	1560-1832		Gt Boughton			5D
St John the Baptist	A 1559-1956	1559-1793	5,8	1735-1791		Gt Boughton			5D
St Martin	A 1671-1963		5,8			Gt Boughton			5D
St Mary on the Hill	A 1628-1975	1547-1812	5,8	1547-1831		Gt Boughton			5D
St Michael	A 1581-1972		5,8			Gt Boughton			5D
St Olave	A 1611-1861		5,8			Gt Boughton			5D
St Oswald	A 1581-1969		5,8	1581-1700		Gt Boughton	1790-1810		5D(A,B,F)
St Peter	A 1559-1970		5,8			Gt Boughton			5D
Christleton	A 1697-1970	1697-1812	5,8	1600-1812	1701-1812	Gt Boughton	1790-1812		5E
Church Hulme	A 1613-1903		5,8			Congleton			5H
Church Lawton	A 1559-1991		5,8	1596-1830		Congleton			4I
Church Minshull	A 1561-1874		5,8			Nantwich			4G
Coddington	A 1680-1998		5,8			Gt Boughton			4E
Congleton	A 1719-1931	1750-1769	5,8	1750-1769		Congleton		1785-1837	5J
Coppenhall	A 1653-1935		5,8			Nantwich			4H
Daresbury	A 1617-1975		5,8			Runcorn			7F
Davenham	A 1560-1988	1665-1819	4,5,8,9	1560-1888		Northwich			6G
Delamere	A 1817-1991		4,5,8,9			Northwich			5F
Disley	A 1591-1980	1591-1880	5,8,9	1591-1739	1651-1750	Hayfield			7K
Dodleston	A 1570-1903		5,8	1662-1724		Gt Boughton			4D
Eastham	A 1598-1884	1598-1700	5,8	1598-1700		Wirral			6D
Eccleston	A 1593-1892		5,8			Gt Boughton			4D
Farndon	A 1603-1961		5,8			Gt Boughton			4D
Frodsham	A 1558-1963	1558-1812	5,8	1558-1812		Runcorn	1790-1812		6F
Gawsworth	A 1557-1987	1557-1837	5,8	1557-1837	1557-1812	Macclesfield	1790-1812		6J
Goostrey	A 1561-1964		4,5,8,9			Northwich			6I
Grappenhall	A 1574-1942		5,8			Warrington			7G
Great Budworth	A 1558-1989		5,8			Runcorn		1792-1829	6G
Great Stanney (ex.par.)			5,8			Gt Boughton			6D
Guilden Sutton	A 1595-1967	1645-1781	5,8	1595-1880		Gt Boughton			5E(C)
Halton	A 1732-1979		5,8			Runcorn			7F
Handley	A 1570-1981		5,8			Gt Boughton			4E
Hargrave	A 1744-1883		5,8			Gt Boughton			5E
Harthill	A 1730-1830		5,8	1599-1837		Gt Boughton			4E
Haslington	A 1645-1926		5,8			Nantwich			4H
Heswall	A 1539-1963	1559-1729	5,8	1559-1729		Wirral			7B
High Legh	A 1815-1989		5,8,9			Altrincham			7H
Hyde St George	A 1832-1983		5,8,9			Stockport		1822-1837	8K
Ince	A 1687-1912		5,8	1600-1812	1687-1812	Gt Boughton			6E
Kings Marsh (ex.par.)			5,8			Gt Boughton			4E
Knutsford	A 1582-1972		5,8,9			Altrincham		1792-1837	6H
Latchford	A 1777-1961		5,8			Warrington			8G
Little Budworth	A 1561-1921		4,5,8,9			Northwich		1792-1839	5G
Little Leigh	A 1782-1997	1782-1804	4,5,8,9	1782-1804		Northwich			6G
Lower Peover	A 1570-1974	1628-1793	4,5,8,9	1576-1836		Northwich		1688-1823	6H
Lower Whitley	A 1777-1989		5,8			Runcorn			7G
Lymm	A 1568-1909	1568-1812	5,8,9	1568-1812	1651-1812	Altrincham	1790-1812	1811-1837	8H
Macclesfield								1713-1837	6K
St Michael	A 1572-1940	1572-1812	5,8	1572-1810		Macclesfield			6J
Christchurch	A 1775-1983	1793-1837	5,8	1793-1837		Macclesfield			6K
Forest	A 1675-1971		5,8			Macclesfield			6K
Malpas	A 1561-1987		5,8			Wrexham		1819-1837	3E
Marbury	A 1538-1955		4,5,8,9			Northwich			3F
Marple	A 1655-1972	1656-1754	5,8,9	1656-1754	1656-1750	Stockport		1804-1840	8K

CHESHIRE

parish name	deposited original registers	I.G.I.	local census indexes	copies of registers at Soc. Gen.	Boyd's marriage index	1837-1851 Registration District	Pallot's marriage index	non-conform. records at P.R.O.	map ref.
Marton	A 1563-1846	1563-1895	5,8	1563-1769	1563-1775	Macclesfield			5J
Middlewich	A 1613-1945	1751-1812	4,5,8,9	1751-1812		Northwich		1809-1837	5H
Mobberley	A 1578-1933	1578-1877	5,8,9			Altrincham		1806-1837	7I
Mottram in Longdendale	A 1558-1993	1559-1837	5,8	1770-1810		Ashton under Lyne		1747-1837	9K
Nantwich	A 1539-1949	1539-1812	5,8			Nantwich		1783-1837	4G
Neston	A 1559-1974	1565-1671	5,8			Wirral			6C
Northenden	B 1561-1914	1564-1852	5,8,9			Altrincham			8I
Odd Rode St Thomas	A 1809-1816		5,8			Congleton			4I
Over	A 1558-1917	1700-1837	4,5,8,9	1700-1812		Northwich			5G
Over Peover	A 1664-1956	1668-1877	5,8,9			Altrincham			6I
Plemstall	A 1558-1949		5,8			Gt Boughton			5E
Pott Shrigley	A 1630-1991	1685-1751	5,8	1685-1751	1685-1775	Macclesfield			7K
Poynton	A 1723-1994	1723-1753	5,8	1723-1753	1723-1753	Macclesfield			7J
Prestbury	A 1560-1990	1560-1803	5,8	1560-1812	1626-1812	Macclesfield		1808-1837	7J
Priors Heys (ex.par.)			5,8			Gt Boughton			5F(D)
Pulford	A 1559-1956		5,8	1582-1771		Gt Boughton			4D
Rainow	A 1765-1941		5,8			Macclesfield		1808-1836	6K
Ringway	A 1751-1967		5,8,9			Altrincham			7I
Rostherne	A 1594-1919		5,8,9	1594-1735		Altrincham		1835-1836	7H
Runcorn	A 1558-1984		5,8			Runcorn		1818-1837	7F
Saltersford	A 1770-1921		5,8			Macclesfield			6K
Sandbach	A 1563-1911	1799-1837	5,8	1736-1837		Congleton		1799-1838	4I
Shocklach	A 1538-1981		5,8			Wrexham			3E
Shotwick	A 1681-1992	1591-1723	5,8			Gt Boughton			6D
Shotwick Park (ex.par.)			5,8			Gt Boughton			6D
Siddington	A 1718-1895	1722-1754	5,8	1722-1783	1722-1800	Macclesfield			6I
Stalybridge (Lancs)						Ashton under Lyne			9K
Stanlow (ex.par.)			5,8			Gt Boughton			6D
Stockport	A 1584-1909	1584-1802	5,8,9	1584-1849		Stockport		1676-1840	8J
Stoke	A 1573-1993		5,8			Gt Boughton			6D
Stretton	A 1827-1960		5,8			Runcorn			7G
Swettenham	A 1570-1890		5,8	1561-1835		Congleton			5I
Tarporley	A 1558-1923		5,8	1559-1755		Nantwich		1801-1837	5F
Tarvin	A 1563-1993		5,8			Gt Boughton			5E
Tattenhall	A 1654-1947		5,8	1812-1835		Gt Boughton			4E
Taxal	A 1610-1894	1611-1837	5,8	1610-1837	1651-1837	Macclesfield		1827-1837	6K
Thelwall	A 1782-1981		5,8			Warrington			8G
Thornton-le-Moors	A 1574-1901		5,8			Gt Boughton			6E
Threapwood (ex.par.)	A 1817-1989		5,8			Wrexham			3E
Thurstaston	A 1706-1907	1581-1836	5,8	1706-1747		Wirral			7B
Tilston	A 1558-1837		5,8		1559-1837	Gt Boughton			3E
Upton in Overchurch	A 1755-1941	1600-1812	5,8	1600-1812		Wirral			8C
Wallasey	A 1574-1946	1574-1812	5,8	1574-1812		Wirral			8C
Warburton	A 1611-1935		5,8,9		1655-1837	Altrincham			8H
Warmingham	A 1538-1907		5,8			Nantwich			4H
Waverton	A 1582-1966	1562-1863	5,8			Gt Boughton			4E
Weaverham	A 1576-1925		4,5,8,9			Northwich			6G
West Kirby	A 1561-1964		5,8	1561-1619		Wirral			7B
Whitchurch (Salop)						Wem			2F
Whitegate	A 1565-1951	1702-1834	4,5,8,9	1702-1834		Northwich			5G
Willington (ex.par.)			5,8			Gt Boughton			5F(E)
Wilmslow	A 1558-1902	1558-1812	5,8,9	1558-1847		Altrincham		1807-1837	7I
Wincle	A 1803-1925		5,8			Macclesfield			5K
Wistaston	A 1572-1985		5,8			Nantwich			4H
Witton	A 1561-1973		4,5,8,9	1754-1851		Northwich			6G
Woodchurch	A 1571-1951		5,8	1571-1840		Wirral			7C
Woodhead	A 1780-1992		5,8			Ashton under Lyne			9L
Wrenbury	A 1593-1965		5,8	1593-1812		Nantwich			3F
Wybunbury	A 1558-1973	1653-1812	5,8			Nantwich			3H

CHESHIRE

Original registers deposited at:
A = Cheshire Record Office, Duke Street, Chester CH1 IRL
B = Manchester Central Library, St Peter's Square, Manchester, M2 5PD

Study adjacent parishes in counties of Lancashire, Yorkshire, Derbyshire, Staffordshire, Shropshire, Flintshire, Denbighshire

Cheshire Record Office – Duke Street, Chester, CH1 1RL
Chester City Record Office, Town Hall, Chester, CH1 2HJ
Stockport Archive Service, Central Library, Wellington Road South, Stockport, SK1 3RS
Wirral Archives Service, Central Reference Library, Borough Road, Birkenhead, L41 2XB

The following useful indexes have been compiled – see Introduction
Census Index, 1841, 1851, 1891 – Family History Society of Cheshire, D Johnson, 91 Stretford House, Chapel Lane, Stretford, Manchester, M32 9AY
Census Index 1891 (Stockport & Altrincham RD's) – North Cheshire FHS, Phil Spivey, 22 Davenport Road, Hazel Grove, Stockport, Cheshire, SK7 4EZ
1891 Database Wills and Monumental Inscriptions – Mr Peter Chadwick, 208 Bedford Street, Crewe, Cheshire, CW2 6JL
Cheshire Marriage Index 1650-1837 – Bertram Merrell, 3912 South 2520 West, West Valley City, Utah 84119, U.S.A.
North and East Cheshire Marriage Index – Mrs P.M. Litton, 2 Florence Road, Harrogate, North Yorks., HG2 0LD 1754-1837 complete, pre 1754 in progress
Mid-Cheshire Marriage Index (Northwich area) 1700-1900 – Mr & Mrs C. Thomson, 15 Mayfield Grove, Cuddington, Northwich, Cheshire, CW8 2LT
Marriage Index for Wirral Peninsula 1580-1850 – Cheshire & Chester Archives Service, Duke Street, Chester, CH1 1RL
The Hayes Computerised Marriage Index (Welsh Borders) – Mr D Hayes, Pen y Cae, Ffordd Hendy, Gwernymynydd, Flintshire, CH7 5JP
Memorial Inscriptions – North Cheshire FHS, D Wright, 51 Bakewell Road, Hazel Grove, Stockport, Cheshire, SK7 6JT

Cheshire's length from east to west is about 58 miles; its breadth from north to south about 30 miles. It is watered by eight principal rivers: the Dee, Mersey, Weaver, Bollin, Dane, Wheelock, Pover and Tame. The population in 1841 was 395,660; in 1851, 455,725; in 1861, 470,174; in 1871, 561,201; in 1881, 644,037.

The soils, generally, are clay and sand and there were large tracts of peat moss towards Yorkshire and Derbyshire. Salt and cheese were the principal staple commodities of Cheshire, both of them being exported in considerable amount beyond the county. Large numbers of cattle were raised and other productions were potatoes, corn, millstones and timber. The late 18th century saw the construction of important canals which afforded cheap communication, especially between such towns as Chester, Liverpool and Manchester and beyond into Staffordshire, Shropshire and the north of England.

The information in the Index is abbreviated, and may mislead the searcher if reference is not made to the details contained in the several publications listed in the Introduction. It is essential that users of this book check the appropriate works before making further enquiries.

CORNWALL

parish name	deposited original registers	I.G.I.	local census indexes	copies of registers at Soc. Gen.	Boyd's marriage index	1837-1851 Registration District	Pallot's marriage index	non-conform. records at P.R.O.	map ref.
Advent	1709-1979	1676-1805	4,5,6,7,8	1616-1801	1608-1801	Camelford	1790-1812		7H
Altarnun	1610-1980	1610-1875	4,5,6,7,8	1611-1673	1611-1673	Launceston			7I
Antony	1678-1925	1569-1807	5,6,7,8,9		1608-1664	St Germans		1815-1837	5K
Blisland	1539-1901	1539-1875	4,5,6,7,8,9	1539-1837	1539-1812	Bodmin	1790-1812		6H
Boconnoc	1709-1918	1709-1850	4,5,6,7,8	1608-1837	1608-1664	Liskeard			5I
Bodmin	1558-1983	1558-1876	5,6,7,8	1558-1812	1559-1812	Bodmin	1790-1812	1804-1837	6H
Botus Fleming	1548-1982	1547-1837	5,6,7,8	1550-1812	1550-1812	St Germans	1800-1812		5K
Boyton	1568-1970	1568-1876	5,6,7,8	1568-1837	1568-1812	Launceston	1790-1812		8J
Breage	1559-1982	1559-1875	4,5,6,7,8	1559-1812	1559-1812	Helston	1800-1812	1821-1837	3D
Bridgerule	1558-1956	1702-1812	4,5,7,8			Holsworthy			9J
Broadoak	1555-1980	1578-1850	4,5,6,7,8	1600-1837	1611-1633	Liskeard			6I
Bryher (Scillies)	1579-1979		4,5,6,7,8			Scilly Isles			1C
Budock	1653-1966	1649-1875	4,5,6,7,8	1610-1812	1610-1812	Falmouth	1800-1812		3F
Callington	1558-1900	1676-1773	5,6,7,8,9	1598-1673	1597-1673	Liskeard			6J
Calstock	1656-1987	1684-1772	4,5,6,7,8	1602-1673	1602-1673	Liskeard			6K
Camborne	1538-1946	1538-1837	4,5,7,8	1538-1837	1538-1812	Redruth	1800-1812	1828-1837	3E
Cardinham	1701-1890	1675-1875	5,7,8	1613-1812	1613-1812	Bodmin	1790-1812		6H
Colan	1747-1949	1597-1875	4,5,6,7,8	1600-1812	1600-1812	St Columb	1800-1812		5F
Constantine	1562-1974	1571-1875	5,6,7,8	1571-1875	1571-1812	Falmouth	1800-1812		3E
Cornelly	1561-1956	1561-1875	4,5,6,7,8,9	1612-1812	1612-1812	Truro	1800-1812		4G
Crantock	1559-1983	1608-1772	5,6,7,8	1559-1812	1559-1812	St Columb	1800-1812		5F
Creed with Grampound	1653-1950	1603-1837	4,5,6,7,8,9	1602-1837	1602-1668	St Austell	1790-1837		4G
Crowan	1691-1979	1674-1875	4,5,6,7,8	1614-1812	1614-1812	Helston	1790-1812		3E
Cubert	1733-1960	1608-1875	5,6,7,8,9	1608-1812	1608-1812	St Columb	1800-1812		5F
Cuby with Tregony	1661-1961	1611-1875	4,5,6,7,8	1611-1837	1611-1812	Truro	1800-1812		4G(F)
Cury	1690-1954	1676-1875	4,5,6,7,8	1608-1674	1608-1837	Helston			2E
Davidstow	1708-1980	1676-1811	5,6,7,8	1614-1812	1608-1811	Camelford	1790-1811		7I
Duloe	1668-1984	1607-1837	4,5,6,7,8	1607-1837	1607-1673	Liskeard			5I
East Looe	1709-1980		5,6,7,8	1709-1807		Liskeard		1815-1836	5J
East Newlyn	1559-1900	1559-1876	4,5,6,7,8	1559-1812	1559-1812	St Columb	1800-1812		5F
Egloshayle	1600-1989	1600-1875	5,7,8	1600-1812	1600-1812	Bodmin	1790-1812		6H
Egloskerry	1573-1909	1576-1875	5,6,7,8	1574-1812	1574-1812	Launceston	1790-1812		8J
Falmouth	1663-1900	1663-1839	5,6,7,8	1664-1812	1663-1812	Falmouth	1790-1812	1783-1837	3F
Feock	1671-1971	1597-1875	4,5,6,7,8	1671-1812	1597-1672	Truro			3F
Forrabury	1710-1987	1692-1812	4,5,6,7,8	1601-1812	1611-1812	Camelford	1790-1812		8H
Fowey	1543-1970	1543-1804	4,5,6,7,8	1568-1836	1568-1812	St Austell	1790-1812	1798-1836	5H
Germoe	1679-1991	1610-1895	5,6,7,8	1610-1837	1610-1812	Helston	1800-1812		3D
Gerrans	1538-1970	1538-1895	4,5,6,7,8	1538-1837	1617-1675	Truro	1790-1837	1826-1836	3F
Gorran	1661-1989	1661-1837	4,5,6,7,8	1607-1840	1607-1812	St Austell			4G
Grade	1700-1988	1597-1885	4,5,6,7,8,9	1597-1837	1597-1812	Helston	1790-1812		1E
Gulval (alias Lanisly)	1598-1925	1598-1895	4,5,6,7,8	1598-1837	1598-1812	Penzance	1800-1812		3C
Gunwalloe (alias Winnington)	1716-1837	1716-1994	4,5,6,7,8	1608-1665	1608-1665	Helston	1608-1794		2E
Gwennap	1658-1990	1674-1772	4,5,7,8	1610-1819	1610-1812	Redruth	1790-1812	1820-1857	3E
Gwinear	1560-1900	1560-1895	4,5,6,7,8	1560-1812	1560-1812	Redruth	1800-1812		3D
Gwithian	1560-1916	1560-1895	5,6,7,8	1560-1812	1560-1812	Redruth	1790-1812		3D
Helland	1722-1836	1677-1812	4,5,6,7,8	1608-1812	1608-1812	Bodmin	1790-1812		6H
Helston	1598-1974	1599-1853	5,6,7,8	1599-1812	1599-1812	Helston	1800-1812	1805-1837	2E(H)
Illogan	1539-1985	1600-1837	4,5,6,7,8	1613-1674	1613-1673	Redruth			4E
Isles of Scilly	1579-1979			1726-1940		Scilly Isles		1817-1837	1C
Jacobstow	1653-1869	1612-1895	4,5,6,7,8	1612-1837	1612-1812	Stratton	1790-1812		8I
Kea	1559-1915	1607-1837	4,5,7,8	1607-1812	1607-1812	Truro	1800-1812		4F
Kenwyn	1662-1988	1608-1875	4,5,6,7,8	1559-1812	1559-1812	Truro	1800-1812		4F
Kenwyn (det.)			4,5,6,7,8			Truro			4E
Kilkhampton	1537-1966	1539-1876	4,5,6,7,8,9	1539-1839	1539-1812	Stratton	1800-1812	1817-1837	10I
Ladock	1662-1970	1669-1875	4,5,6,7,8	1609-1837	1609-1812	Truro	1800-1812		4G
Lamorran	1572-1948	1572-1871	4,5,7,8,9	1572-1812	1621-1636	Truro			4G
Landewednack	1578-1971	1578-1837	4,5,7,8	1598-1812	1598-1812	Helston	1790-1812		1E
Landrake	1583-1987	1583-1812	4,5,6,7,8	1583-1812	1583-1812	St Germans	1800-1812		5J
Landulph	1540-1979	1540-1872	5,6,7,8	1540-1812	1541-1812	St Germans	1800-1812		6K
Laneast	1700-1979	1676-1875	5,6,7,8	1597-1812	1597-1812	Launceston	1790-1812		7I
Lanhydrock	1558-1913	1559-1812	4,5,6,7,8,9	1558-1812	1559-1812	Bodmin	1790-1812		6H
Lanivet	1656-1968	1608-1875	5,6,7,8	1608-1812	1608-1812	Bodmin	1790-1812		6H
Lanlivery	1600-1951	1583-1876	4,5,7,8	1585-1812	1600-1812	Bodmin	1800-1812		5H
Lanreath	1555-1992	1555-1875	5,6,7,8	1555-1837	1597-1673	Liskeard		1816-1827	5I
Lansallos	1600-1946	1682-1805	4,5,6,7,8	1600-1837	1607-1672	Liskeard			5I
Lanteglos-by-Camelford	1558-1975	1558-1812	5,6,7,8	1558-1812	1558-1812	Camelford	1790-1812	1800-1837	7H
Lanteglos-by-Fowey	1661-1967	1674-1773	4,5,6,7,8	1610-1674	1607-1673	Liskeard			5I
Launcells	1642-1989	1618-1836	4,5,6,7,8	1618-1812	1618-1812	Stratton			9I
Launceston (St Mary)	1559-1949	1681-1772	4,5,6,7,8	1559-1812	1559-1812	Launceston	1800-1812	1777-1837	7J(A)
Lawhitton	1640-1982		4,5,6,7,8,9	1608-1812	1608-1675	Launceston			7J
Lelant	1684-1928	1669-1875	5,6,7,8	1611-1812	1611-1812	Penzance	1800-1812		3D
Lesnewth	1563-1980	1569-1811	4,5,6,7,8	1559-1812	1569-1812	Camelford			8H
Lewannick	1660-1992	1660-1812	4,5,6,7,8	1597-1812	1597-1812	Launceston	1800-1812		7J
Lezant	1539-1981	1539-1812	4,5,6,7,8	1539-1812	1539-1812	Launceston	1790-1812		7J
Linkinhorne	1576-1966	1570-1876	5,6,7,8	1576-1812	1576-1812	Liskeard	1790-1812		6J
Liskeard	1539-1958	1691-1773	5,6,7,8	1597-1837	1597-1665	Liskeard		1806-1837	6I
Little Petherick	1706-1837	1706-1812	4,5,6,7,8	1636-1812	1608-1812	St Columb	1800-1812		6G(B)
Lostwithiel	1609-1980	1609-1837	4,5,6,7,8	1609-1812	1609-1812	Bodmin	1790-1812	1812-1837	5H(J)
Ludgvan	1563-1980	1563-1875	5,6,7,8	1563-1837	1563-1812	Penzance	1800-1812		3C
Luxulyan	1594-1902	1594-1875	4,5,6,7,8	1594-1812	1594-1812	Bodmin	1790-1812	1820-1837	5H
Mabe	1654-1975	1653-1875	4,5,6,7,8	1611-1812	1610-1675	Falmouth			3E
Madron	1577-1888	1577-1876	4,5,7,8	1577-1876	1577-1812	Penzance	1790-1812	1812-1837	3C
Maker	1630-1849	1630-1837	4,5,6,7,8,9	1607-1849	1607-1673	St Germans			5K
Manaccan	1624-1981	1597-1875	4,5,7,8	1597-1812	1597-1812	Helston	1800-1812		2F
Marazion	1813-1979		4,5,7,8	1754-1812		Penzance			3D
Marhamchurch	1558-1977	1559-1837	4,5,6,7,8	1558-1812	1558-1812	Stratton	1800-1812		9I
Mawgan in Menage	1559-1971	1559-1875	4,5,7,8	1563-1812	1563-1812	Helston	1800-1812		2E

CORNWALL

parish name	deposited original registers	I.G.I.	local census indexes	copies of registers at Soc. Gen.	Boyd's marriage index	1837-1851 Registration District	Pallot's marriage index	non-conform. records at P.R.O.	map ref.
Mawgan-in-Pydar	1674-1971	1608-1875	4,5,6,7,8	1608-1812	1608-1812	St Columb	1800-1812		6F
Mawnan	1553-1966	1581-1875	4,5,7,8	1553-1812	1553-1812	Falmouth	1800-1812		3F
Menheniot	1554-1981	1554-1837	5,6,7,8	1554-1812	1554-1812	Liskeard	1800-1812		6J
Merther	1675-1992	1658-1875	4,5,6,7,8	1608-1812	1608-1665	Truro			4F
Mevagissey	1590-1967	1590-1876	4,5,6,7,8	1590-1841	1598-1673	St Austell		1786-1837	4H
Michaelstow	1544-1974	1548-1812	4,5,6,7,8	1544-1812	1548-1812	Camelford	1790-1812	1822-1837	7H
Minster	1678-1979	1676-1812	4,5,6,7,8	1611-1812	1616-1812	Camelford	1790-1812		7H
Morvah	1617-1993	1650-1875	4,5,6,7,8	1617-1837	1614-1772	Penzance			3C
Morval	1538-1946	1538-1837	5,6,7,8,9	1610-1671	1597-1670	Liskeard			5J
Morwenstow	1558-1956	1558-1875	4,5,6,7,8,9	1558-1877	1558-1812	Stratton	1790-1812		10I
Mullion	1598-1981	1598-1875	4,5,7,8	1610-1837	1610-1673	Helston			2E
Mylor	1673-1955	1601-1875	4,5,6,7,8	1607-1812	1607-1812	Falmouth	1800-1812	1816-1837	3F
North Hill	1555-1990	1555-1875	4,5,6,7,8	1555-1865	1608-1673	Launceston			7J
North Petherwin	1653-1899		5,6,7,8	1611-1673	1611-1673	Launceston			8J
North Tamerton	1560-1962	1542-1837	5,7,8	1599-1674	1597-1673	Holsworthy			8J
Otterham	1667-1979	1681-1811	4,5,6,7,8	1614-1812	1612-1811	Camelford	1790-1812		8I
Padstow	1599-1951	1600-1812	4,5,6,7,8	1599-1812	1599-1812	St Columb	1790-1812	1820-1837	6G
Paul	1595-1981	1595-1875	4,5,7,8	1595-1812	1595-1812	Penzance	1800-1812		2C
Pelynt	1678-1993	1610-1837	5,6,7,8	1693-1837	1610-1673	Liskeard			5I
Penryn (see St Gluvias)						Falmouth		1806-1837	3F(G)
Penzance	1789-1967	1700-1812	5,7,8			Penzance		1791-1837	2C
Perranarworthal	1739-1984	1597-1875	4,5,6,7,8	1601-1812	1601-1812	Falmouth	1800-1812		3F
Perranuthnoe	1562-1971	1562-1875	4,5,6,7,8	1562-1812	1589-1812	Penzance	1800-1812		2D
Perranzabuloe	1558-1963	1558-1837	4,5,6,7,8	1619-1812	1619-1812	Truro	1800-1812		4F
Phillack	1560-1985	1561-1875	4,5,7,8	1572-1812	1572-1812	Redruth	1790-1812	1819-1837	3D
Philleigh	1733-1979	1612-1875	4,5,6,7,8	1613-1837	1597-1673	Truro	1790-1812		3F
Pillaton	1557-1979	1557-1812	5,6,7,8	1557-1812	1557-1812	St Germans	1790-1812		6K
Poughill	1537-1967	1537-1875	4,5,6,7,8	1537-1812	1537-1812	Stratton	1800-1812		9I
Poundstock	1614-1975	1597-1875	4,5,6,7,8	1597-1875	1597-1812	Stratton	1790-1814		9I
Probus	1641-1981	1597-1875	4,5,6,7,8,9	1597-1812	1597-1812	Truro	1800-1812	1815-1837	4G
Quethiock	1574-1984	1573-1852	4,5,6,7,8	1573-1776	1597-1673	St Germans			6J
Rame	1653-1837	1653-1812	5,6,7,8,9	1619-1840	1619-1673	St Germans		1810-1837	4K
Redruth	1560-1972	1560-1837	4,5,6,7,8	1560-1812	1560-1837	Redruth	1800-1813	1817-1837	4E
Roche	1571-1966	1571-1875	4,5,6,7,8	1578-1812	1578-1812	St Austell	1790-1812		5G
Ruan Lanihorne	1608-1992	1608-1875	4,5,6,7,8	1608-1837	1608-1670	Truro	1790-1837		4G
Ruan Major	1682-1986	1610-1837	4,5,6,7,8	1611-1812	1610-1812	Helston	1790-1812		2E
Ruan Minor	1653-1984	1608-1875	4,5,6,7,8	1625-1837	1608-1812	Helston	1790-1812		1E
St Agnes	1653-1969	1596-1837	4,5,6,7,8	1596-1837	1596-1812	Truro	1790-1812	1799-1837	4E
St Agnes (Scillies)	1579-1979		4,5,6,7,8			Scilly Isles			1C
St Allen	1680-1977	1611-1875	4,5,6,7,8	1611-1840	1611-1812	Truro	1790-1812		4F
St Anthony in Meneage	1602-1981	1597-1875	4,5,6,7,8	1597-1812	1597-1812	Helston	1800-1812		2F
St Anthony in Roseland	1660-1983	1623-1875	4,5,6,7,8	1623-1837	1623-1700	Truro			3F
St Austell	1564-1972	1696-1875	4,5,6,7,8	1564-1840	1600-1672	St Austell		1789-1837	5H
St Blazey	1710-1970	1608-1875	5,7,8	1608-1674	1608-1673	St Austell			5H
St Breock	1561-1962		5,6,7,8	1561-1812	1561-1812	St Columb	1790-1812		6G
St Breward	1558-1917	1558-1875	4,5,6,7,8	1558-1900	1558-1812	Camelford	1813-1837		7H
St Buryan	1653-1992	1653-1847	4,5,6,7,8	1653-1812	1654-1812	Penzance	1790-1812		2C
St Cleer	1675-1968	1597-1837	5,7,8	1597-1812	1597-1812	Liskeard	1790-1812		6I
St Clement	1538-1978	1543-1837	5,6,7,8	1538-1837	1608-1672	Truro	1790-1812		4F
St Clether	1640-1979	1640-1875	4,5,6,7,8	1610-1812	1610-1811	Camelford	1790-1812		7I
St Columb Major	1539-1970	1540-1780	4,5,7,8	1539-1812	1539-1812	St Columb	1800-1812	1795-1837	5G
St Columb Minor	1560-1960	1560-1875	5,6,7,8	1560-1812	1560-1812	St Columb	1781-1812	1795-1837	5F
St Day	1833-1962		5,7,8			Redruth			4E
St Dennis	1687-1985	1687-1875	4,5,6,7,8	1610-1815	1610-1812	St Austell	1800-1812		5G
St Dominic	1559-1978	1559-1875	5,6,7,8,9	1559-1812	1607-1672	Liskeard			6K
St Endellion	1732-1970	1684-1812	4,5,6,7,8	1684-1812	1614-1812	Bodmin			7G
St Enoder	1570-1974	1571-1875	4,5,6,7,8	1571-1812	1571-1812	St Columb	1800-1812		5G
St Erme	1671-1967	1671-1875	4,5,6,7,8	1614-1840	1614-1812	Truro	1800-1812		4F
St Erney	1555-1978	1555-1811	5,6,7,8	1555-1812	1555-1812	St Germans	1800-1812		5K
St Erth	1563-1980	1563-1875	5,6,7,8	1563-1812	1563-1812	Penzance	1800-1812		3D
St Ervan	1674-1917	1602-1875	4,5,6,7,8	1602-1812	1602-1812	St Columb	1800-1812	1820-1837	6G
St Eval	1695-1980	1612-1885	4,5,6,7,8	1631-1812	1612-1812	St Columb	1800-1812		6F
St Ewe	1559-1993	1560-1875	4,5,6,7,8	1560-1812	1560-1812	St Austell	1800-1812		4G
St Gennys	1702-1901	1687-1875	4,5,6,7,8	1612-1674	1612-1673	Stratton			8I
St Germans	1590-1906	1590-1837	4,5,6,7,8,9	1590-1837	1608-1675	St Germans			5J
St Giles on the Heath	1653-1982		5,6,7,8	1601-1673	1601-1673	Holsworthy			8J
St Gluvias	1598-1977	1599-1876	4,5,7,8	1599-1812	1599-1812	Falmouth	1800-1812	1813-1837	3F
St Hilary	1677-1975	1687-1875	5,7,8	1609-1812	1609-1812	Penzance	1800-1812		3D
St Issey	1596-1872	1596-1875	4,5,6,7,8	1596-1812	1596-1812	St Columb	1800-1812		6G
St Ive	1683-1972	1675-1713	5,7,8	1614-1837	1614-1672	Liskeard			6J
St Ives	1651-1977	1651-1812	5,6,7,8,9	1653-1812	1607-1812	Penzance	1800-1812	1800-1837	3C
St John	1582-1980	1675-1772	4,5,6,7,8,9	1611-1674	1611-1673	St Germans			5K
St Juliot	1656-1983	1656-1812	5,6,7,8	1623-1812	1623-1812	Camelford	1800-1812		8H
St Just in Penwith	1599-1980	1599-1877	4,5,6,7,8	1599-1812	1599-1812	Penzance	1800-1812		3B
St Just in Roseland	1538-1978	1540-1853	4,5,6,7,8	1538-1837	1597-1673	Truro	1790-1837	1807-1837	3F
St Keverne	1581-1906	1580-1875	4,5,6,7,8	1597-1812	1597-1812	Helston	1800-1812		2F
St Kew	1564-1910	1564-1875	5,6,7,8	1564-1812	1563-1812	Bodmin	1790-1812		7H
St Keyne	1721-1978	1539-1837	4,5,6,7,8	1533-1812	1608-1673	Liskeard			5I
St Levan	1700-1981	1694-1875	5,6,7,8	1694-1812	1694-1812	Penzance	1790-1812		2B
St Mabyn	1537-1983	1562-1812	4,5,6,7,8	1562-1812	1562-1812	Bodmin	1790-1812		6H
St Martin by Looe	1653-1974	1597-1837	5,6,7,8	1597-1673	1597-1673	Liskeard			5J
St Martin in Meneage	1571-1963	1571-1875	4,5,6,7,8	1571-1812	1571-1812	Helston	1800-1812		2E
St Martin (Scillies)	1579-1973		4,5,6,7,8			Scilly Isles			1C
St Mary's (Scillies)	1579-1973	1726-1875	4,5,6,7,8			Scilly Isles		1819-1837	1C
St Mellion	1558-1979	1558-1812	5,6,7,8	1558-1812	1558-1812	St Germans	1790-1812		6J
St Merryn	1688-1952	1616-1877	4,5,6,7,8	1616-1877	1616-1812	St Columb	1790-1812		6F
St Mewan	1693-1978	1607-1875	4,5,6,7,8,9	1607-1674	1607-1673	St Austell			5G
St Michael Caerhays	1588-1837	1677-1772	4,5,6,7,8	1608-1673	1608-1673	St Austell			4G
St Michael Penkevil	1546-1939	1546-1875	4,5,7,8	1577-1836	1597-1623	Truro	1790-1837		4F

CORNWALL

parish name	deposited original registers	I.G.I.	local census indexes	copies of registers at Soc. Gen.	Boyd's marriage index	1837-1851 Registration District	Pallot's marriage index	non-conform. records at P.R.O.	map ref.
St Michael's Mount (ex.par.)			4,5,6,7,8,9	1754-1812		Penzance			3C
St Minver	1559-1978	1558-1877	4,5,6,7,8	1558-1812	1559-1812	Bodmin	1790-1812		7G
St Neot	1549-1950	1549-1855	4,5,6,7,8	1610-1675	1610-1673	Liskeard		1820-1837	6I
St Pinnock	1539-1978	1682-1772	4,5,6,7,8	1539-1837	1597-1673	Liskeard			5I
St Sampson (alias Golant)	1568-1984	1568-1876	4,5,6,7,8	1568-1812	1568-1812	St Austell	1790-1812		5H(K)
St Stephen by Launceston	1566-1968	1568-1812	4,5,6,7,8	1566-1812	1566-1812	Launceston	1800-1812		7J
St Stephen in Brannel	1694-1951	1694-1876	4,5,6,7,8	1608-1850	1608-1812	St Austell	1800-1812		5G
St Stephen's by Saltash	1545-1978	1679-1772	5,6,7,8,9	1608-1673	1599-1673	St Germans		1820-1837	5K
St Teath	1558-1994	1558-1812	4,5,6,7,8	1558-1812	1558-1812	Camelford	1790-1812		7H
St Thomas-by-Launceston	1672-1971	1681-1804	4,5,6,7,8	1563-1812	1623-1672	Launceston			7J
St Tudy	1559-1963	1559-1875	4,5,6,7,8	1559-1812	1560-1812	Bodmin	1790-1812		7H
St Veep	1538-1992	1676-1772	4,5,6,7,8	1611-1673	1611-1673	Liskeard			5I
St Wenn	1706-1968	1608-1875	5,7,8	1609-1812	1609-1812	St Columb	1790-1812		6G
St Winnow	1622-1970	1612-1837	5,6,7,8	1612-1812	1612-1812	Bodmin	1800-1812		5H
Saltash	1697-1975		5,6,7,8,9	1599-1617		St Germans			5K
Sancreed	1559-1973	1566-1875	5,6,7,8	1559-1812	1559-1812	Penzance	1800-1812		3C
Sennen	1700-1966	1699-1847	4,5,6,7,8	1699-1812	1699-1812	Penzance	1790-1812		2B
Sheviock	1569-1890	1570-1871	4,5,6,7,8,9	1570-1812	1570-1812	St Germans	1790-1812		5K
Sithney	1664-1981	1666-1875	5,7,8	1608-1812	1608-1812	Helston	1800-1812		3E
South Hill	1549-1653	1676-1772	5,6,7,8	1598-1673		Liskeard			6J
South Petherwin	1656-1979		4,5,6,7,8	1608-1812	1608-1812	Launceston	1790-1812		7J
Stithians	1656-1983	1597-1875	5,6,7,8	1598-1812	1598-1812	Redruth	1800-1812		3E
Stoke Climsland	1538-1975	1675-1773	5,6,7,8	1597-1674	1597-1673	Launceston			6J
Stratton	1687-1989	1611-1860	4,5,6,7,8	1611-1860	1611-1812	Stratton	1800-1812		9I
Talland	1653-1988	1617-1837	4,5,6,7,8	1617-1674	1617-1673	Liskeard	1790-1812	1818-1837	5I
Temple	1884-1960		4,5,6,7,8,9			Bodmin			6I
Tintagel	1546-1980	1588-1812	5,6,7,8	1588-1812	1588-1812	Camelford	1790-1812		8H
Torpoint	1819-1975		5,7,8			St Germans			5K
Towednack	1676-1985	1676-1812	5,6,7,8	1671-1812	1597-1812	Penzance	1790-1812		3C
Tregavethan (ex.par.)			5,7,8			Truro			4F(D)
Tremaine	1726-1968	1674-1884	5,6,7,8	1612-1812	1612-1812	Launceston	1790-1812		8I
Treneglos	1675-1838	1676-1813	4,5,6,7,8	1614-1812	1597-1812	Launceston	1790-1812		8I
Tresco (Scillies)	1549-1979		4,5,6,7,8			Scilly Isles			1C
Tresmere	1574-1979	1625-1875	5,6,7,8	1613-1665	1597-1673	Launceston			8I
Trevalga	1538-1977	1539-1812	4,5,6,7,8	1539-1812	1539-1812	Camelford	1790-1812		8H
Trewen	1616-1979		4,5,6,7,8,9	1610-1837	1608-1675	Launceston			7J
Truro St Mary	1591-1968	1597-1875	5,6,7,8	1597-1837	1597-1839	Truro	1790-1812	1760-1837	4F(E)
Tywardreath	1642-1975	1608-1875	5,7,8	1608-1812	1608-1812	St Austell	1790-1812		5H
Veryan	1683-1974	1602-1875	4,5,6,7,8	1602-1812	1602-1812	Truro	1800-1812		4G
Warbstow	1695-1838	1681-1805	5,6,7,8	1612-1812	1612-1812	Launceston	1790-1812		8I
Warleggan	1548-1904	1547-1875	4,5,7,8	1547-1812	1547-1812	Bodmin	1790-1812		6I
Week St Mary	1602-1982	1602-1812	4,5,6,7,8	1602-1812	1602-1812	Stratton	1790-1812		8I
Wendron	1560-1979	1562-1837	4,5,7,8	1560-1812	1560-1812	Helston	1800-1812	1804-1837	3E
Werrington (Devon)									8J
West Looe	1709-1980		4,5,6,7,8			Liskeard		1788-1836	5J
Whitstone	1663-1981	1597-1875	4,5,6,7,8	1598-1674	1597-1673	Stratton			9J
Withiel	1567-1979	1567-1875	5,7,8	1567-1812	1568-1812	Bodmin	1790-1812		6G
Zennor	1600-1978	1599-1837	5,6,7,8	1599-1837	1611-1812	Penzance	1800-1812		3C

Original registers deposited at:
Cornwall Record Office, County Hall, Truro TR1 3AY

Study adjacent parishes in Devon

Cornwall Record Office – County Hall, Truro, TR1 3AY

The following useful indexes have been compiled – see Introduction
Census Indexes 1841, 1861, 1871, 1891 – Cornwall FHS, 5 Victoria Square, Truro, Cornwall, TR1 2RS
Census Index 1851 – Cornwall FHS, Ray Woodbine, 5 Priory Close, Tywardreath, Par, Cornwall, PL24 2PG
Census Index 1851 – Cornish Research Group of The New Zealand Society of Genealogists C/O Cornwall FHS, 5 Victoria Square, Truro, Cornwall, TR1 2RS
Cornwall Marriage Index – Cornwall FHS, 5 Victoria Square, Truro, Cornwall, TR1 2RS complete for 1813-1837, earlier period in progress
Monumental Inscriptions – Cornwall FHS, 5 Victoria Square, Truro, Cornwall, TR1 2RS
Cornwall Burial Index 1813-1837 – Cornwall FHS, 5 Victoria Square, Truro, Cornwall, TR1 2RS

Cornwall is the most westerly county of England, its extreme length being 90 miles and its medium breadth 25 miles until approaching Mount's Bay, between which place and St Ives it is not more than 5½ miles wide. It is watered by six principal rivers: the Tamar, Lynher, Fowey, Camel or Alan, Fal and Hayle. The population in 1841 was 341,279; in 1851, 353,637; in 1861, 369,390; in 1871, 362,343; in 1881, 329,484.

From earliest times Cornwall has been noted for its tin but other minerals are found there, including copper, lead, pyrites, bismuth, zinc, cobalt, arsenic, wolfram and menachenite. Barley was the most succesful grain, of which large crops were grown on the banks of the River Camel. Potatoes were grown extensively in some parts and cider made in the eastern portion of the county. Fishing was an important industry, pilchards being the most numerous catch.

The information in the Index is abbreviated, and may mislead the searcher if reference is not made to the details contained in the several publications listed in the Introduction. It is essential that users of this book check the appropriate works before making further enquiries.

CUMBERLAND

parish name	deposited original registers	I.G.I.	local census indexes	copies of registers at Soc. Gen.	Boyd's marriage index	1837-1851 Registration District	Pallot's marriage index	non-conform. records at P.R.O.	map ref.
Addingham	A 1601-1979	1660-1866	8	1814-1866		Skipton			3H
Aikton	A 1694-1993	1665-1895	8			Wigton			7I
Ainstable	A 1679-1990	1664-1883	8	1665-1875	1665-1775	Penrith			4H
Allhallows	A 1666-1973	1663-1875	5,8			Wigton			8H(J)
Allonby	A 1776-1948	1755-1880	8			Wigton			9H
Alston	D 1700-1993	1701-1895	5,8	1837-1900	1701-1815	Alston		1764-1837	2H
Arlecdon	C 1730-1982	1720-1877	5,8	1720-1877		Whitehaven			9E
Armathwaite	A 1749-1997	1775-1877	8			Penrith			4H
Arthuret	A 1610-1997	1666-1870	5,8	1792-1804		Longtown			5K
Aspatria	A 1660-1997	1663-1865	5,8	1754-1899		Wigton		1826-1837	8H
Bassenthwaite	A 1574-1978	1663-1877	8			Cockermouth			7G
Beaumont	A 1677-1991	1665-1877	8	1674-1877		Carlisle			6J(A)
Beckermet									9D
St Bridget	C 1687-1980	1702-1870	8	1687-1824		Whitehaven			9D
St John	C 1735-1984	1689-1877	8	1779-1826		Whitehaven			9D
Bewcastle	A 1737-1991	1665-1895	5,8	1665-1877		Longtown		1788-1838	4L
Bolton	A 1619-1992	1581-1872	5,8			Wigton			7H
Bootle		1690-1860	5,8			Bootle			8B
Borrowdale	A 1736-1994	1775-1870	8			Cockermouth			7E
Bowness	A 1663-1992	1663-1875	8			Wigton			7J
Brampton	A 1663-1995	1661-1895	5,8	1680-1839		Brampton		1817-1837	4J
Bridekirk	A 1585-1966	1584-1876	8	1584-1812	1584-1700	Cockermouth	1790-1812		9G
Brigham	C 1564-1970	1676-1874	8			Cockermouth			9F
Bromfield	A 1654-1998	1663-1877	8			Wigton			8H
Burgh by Sands	A 1653-1992	1653-1883	8			Carlisle			6J
Buttermere	C 1868-1976	1801-1877	8			Cockermouth			8E
Caldbeck	A 1657-1993	1663-1865	8			Wigton			6G
Calder Bridge			8						9D
Camerton	A 1599-1980	1663-1870	8	1813-1870		Cockermouth			10F
Carlatton (ex.par.)			8			Brampton			4I(H)
Carlisle								1785-1837	5I
Christ Church	A 1831-1951		4,5,8	1831-1839		Carlisle			5I
Holy Trinity	A 1831-1992		4,5,8			Carlisle			5I
St Cuthbert	A 1663-1997	1666-1875	4,5,8			Carlisle			5I
St Mary	A 1645-1978	1648-1877	4,5,8			Carlisle			5I
Castle Carrock	A 1688-1982	1689-1876	8			Brampton			4I
Castle Sowerby	A 1609-1991	1664-1875	8			Brampton			5G
Cleator	C 1572-1962	1813-1869	5,8	1690-1812		Penrith			9E
Clifton	C 1822-1977	1822-1877	5,8	1822-1877		Cockermouth			9F
Cockermouth All Saints	C 1632-1986	1689-1862	5,8	1632-1855		Cockermouth		1737-1835	8F
Copeland Forest (ex.par.)			5,8			Bootle			8D(R)
Corney		1676-1872	5,8			Bootle			8B
Croglin	A 1646-1991	1646-1875	8	1813-1839		Penrith			3I
Crosby on Eden	A 1649-1978	1665-1877	5,8	1665-1837	1665-1837	Carlisle	1790-1837		5J(E)
Crosscanonby	A 1663-1967	1669-1875	8			Cockermouth			9G
Crosthwaite	A 1562-1969	1562-1875	5,8	1562-1893	1562-1600	Cockermouth	1790-1812		7F
Culgaith	A 1749-1992	1758-1875	5,8			Penrith			3G
Cumrew	A 1679-1973	1665-1875	8	1651-1700	1651-1700	Brampton			4I
Cumwhitton	A 1695-1953	1665-1876	8	1665-1695	1651-1675	Brampton			4I
Dacre	A 1596-1992	1559-1871	5,8	1559-1716	1601-1700	Penrith			5F
Dalston	A 1570-1990	1570-1870	5,8	1601-1700	1601-1700	Carlisle	1790-1812		6I
Dean	C 1542-1979	1689-1880	8	1689-1704		Cockermouth			9F
Dearham	A 1662-1994	1737-1869	8			Cockermouth			9G
Distington	C 1653-1995	1755-1864	5,8	1672-1837	1653-1837	Whitehaven			9F
Drigg	A 1631-1960	1732-1870	5,8	1632-1653		Bootle			9C
Edenhall	A 1558-1995	1737-1874	5,8			Penrith			4G
Egremont	C 1630-1979	1780-1875	5,8	1726-1875		Whitehaven			10D
Embleton	C 1626-1915	1676-1871	8			Cockermouth			8F
Ennerdale	C 1638-1938	1676-1877	5,8	1643-1846		Whitehaven			9E
Eskdale	C 1625-1937	1778-1871	4,5,6,7,8	1676-1758		Bootle			8C
Farlam	A 1668-1995	1663-1876	8	1681-1839		Brampton			3J
Flimby	A 1686-1994	1713-1866	8			Cockermouth			9G
Garrigill	D 1699-1993	1699-1880	5,8	1699-1837	1699-1812	Alston		1811-1837	2H
Geltsdale (ex.par.)			8			Brampton			3I
Gilcrux	A 1589-1995	1740-1875	8			Cockermouth			8G(L)
Gosforth	C 1571-1988	1572-1875	5,8	1571-1837	1572-1837	Whitehaven	1790-1837		9D
Great Orton	A 1568-1994	1568-1875	8	1568-1812	1601-1700	Carlisle	1790-1812		6I
Great Salkeld	A 1571-1967	1813-1863	8			Penrith			4G
Greystoke	A 1559-1994	1559-1875	5,8	1559-1757	1601-1700	Penrith			5G
Grinsdale	A 1738-1993	1688-1875	8			Carlisle			6I(C)
Haile	C 1544-1990	1689-1878	5,8	1676-1845		Whitehaven			9D
Harrington	C 1653-1966	1652-1875	5,8	1535-1862	1652-1812	Whitehaven	1790-1837		10F
Hayton Carlisle	A 1619-1986	1665-1874	5,8	1775-1777		Brampton			4I
Hensingham	C 1811-1871	1811-1875	5,8	1823-1848		Whitehaven			10E
Hesket in the Forest	A 1662-1992	1667-1875	8			Penrith			5H
Holme Cultram	A 1544-1993	1580-1871	5,8	1580-1597		Wigton			8I
Hutton in the Forest	A 1649-1974	1662-1877	8	1662-1701	1662-1700	Penrith			5G(K)
Ireby	A 1705-1988	1666-1876	8	1666-1725	1666-1725	Wigton			7G
Irthington	A 1705-1983	1669-1871	5,8	1667-1812	1667-1812	Brampton			4J
Irton	C 1697-1959	1689-1875	5,8	1676-1841		Bootle			8C
Isell	A 1669-1977	1666-1876	8	1666-1921	1666-1670	Cockermouth			8G
Ivegill (or High Head)	A 1709-1994	1771-1867	8			Carlisle			5H
Kingmoor (ex.par.)			8			Carlisle			5J(D)
Kirkandrews on Eden	A 1677-1989	1686-1812	8			Carlisle			6I(B)
Kirkandrews on Esk	A 1665-1995	1682-1867	5,8	1813-1839		Longtown			6K
Kirkbampton	A 1695-1996	1669-1885	8	1669-1696	1669-1696	Wigton			7I
Kirkbride	A 1662-1992	1663-1875	8	1726-1875		Wigton			7I(G)

CUMBERLAND

parish name	deposited original registers	I.G.I.	local census indexes	copies of registers at Soc. Gen.	Boyd's marriage index	1837-1851 Registration District	Pallot's marriage index	non-conform. records at P.R.O.	map ref.
Kirkland	A 1620-1973	1663-1876	5,8			Penrith			2G
Kirklinton	A 1651-1977	1664-1878	8	1760-1766		Longtown			5J
Kirkoswald	A 1577-1999	1577-1863	5,8	1577-1812	1601-1700	Penrith	1790-1812	1700-1836	3H
Lamplugh	C 1581-1950	1581-1865	5,8	1581-1812		Whitehaven			9E
Lanercost	A 1684-1999	1666-1876	8	1731-1839		Brampton	1790-1837		3K
Langwathby	A 1576-1989	1587-1874	8			Penrith			3G(O)
Lazonby	A 1538-1997	1662-1875	8			Penrith			4H
Lorton	C 1538-1978	1689-1871	8			Cockermouth			8F
Loweswater	C 1625-1978	1676-1875	8			Cockermouth			8E
Maryport	A 1761-1990	1761-1866	8			Cockermouth		1765-1837	9G
Matterdale	A 1634-1995	1634-1877	8	1634-1720	1634-1700	Penrith			5F
Melmerby	A 1693-1997	1660-1867	8	1660-1702	1660-1700	Penrith			3G
Millom									8A
Holy Trinity	B 1590-1980	1591-1875	5,8	1591-1839	1601-1700	Bootle	1790-1812		8A
St George	B 1877-1957		5,8			Bootle			8A
Moresby	C 1717-1990	1690-1875	5,8	1676-1837	1676-1837	Whitehaven	1790-1837		10E
Mosser	C 1783-1990	1803-1868	8			Cockermouth			8F
Muncaster	C 1583-1930	1676-1874	5,8	1735-1842		Bootle			8C
Mungrisdale	A 1718-1993	1738-1875	8			Penrith			6G
Nether Denton	A 1703-1991	1667-1885	8			Brampton			3J
Nether Wasdale	C 1711-1991	1689-1854	5,8	1701-1854	1701-1812	Whitehaven			8D
Newlands	A 1868-1996	1782-1877	8			Cockermouth			7E
Newton Reigny	A 1571-1992	1571-1871	8	1571-1812	1572-1700	Penrith	1790-1812		4G(N)
Nichol Forest	A 1761-1992	1756-1873	5,8	1776-1812	1776-1812	Longtown			5L
Ousby	A 1663-1983	1663-1875	5,8			Penrith			3G
Over Denton (see Upper Denton)									3J
Penrith	A 1556-1990	1556-1847	5,8	1556-1812		Penrith		1799-1838	4G
Plumbland	A 1677-1996	1664-1874	8	1664-1674	1664-1674	Cockermouth			8G(M)
Plumpton Wall	A 1750-1985	1828-1875	5,8			Penrith			4G
Ponsonby	C 1723-1957	1702-1870	5,8	1723-1850		Whitehaven			9D
Raughton Head	A 1663-1984	1679-1869	8			Carlisle			6H
Renwick	A 1649-1979	1664-1867	8			Penrith			3H
Rockcliffe	A 1679-1978	1667-1875	8	1651-1680	1651-1837	Carlisle			6J
St Bees	C 1538-1995	1538-1883	5,8	1538-1837		Whitehaven		1789-1836	10E
St John's in the Vale	A 1718-1981	1776-1877	5,8	1776-1877					6F
Salter & Eskett (ex.par.)			8			Whitehaven			9E(P)
Scaleby	A 1724-1972	1816-1857	8			Longtown			5J
Sebergham	A 1694-1992	1813-1867	5,8	1667-1695	1667-1695	Wigton			6H
Setmurthy		1813-1875	8			Cockermouth			8G
Skelton	A 1580-1997	1580-1877	8	1580-1812	1601-1700	Penrith	1790-1812		5G
Skiddaw Forest (ex.par.)			8						7F
Stanwix	A 1662-1992	1662-1875	8	1662-1837	1662-1812	Carlisle	1790-1937		5J
Stapleton	A 1725-1991	1813-1874	5,8			Longtown			5K
Thornthwaite	A 1775-1999	1776-1871	8			Cockermouth			7F
Threlkeld	A 1573-1997	1646-1875	8	1761-1875		Penrith			6F
Thursby	A 1649-1995	1665-1875	8			Wigton			6I
Thwaites	B 1724-1978	1725-1873	5,8	1724-1837		Bootle			8B
Torpenhow	A 1651-1996	1813-1873	5,8			Wigton			8G
Uldale	A 1642-1991	1663-1870	8			Wigton			7G
Ulpha	B 1703-1991	1689-1857	5,8			Bootle			7C
Upper Denton	A 1813-1971	1813-1879	8			Brampton			3J
Waberthwaite	B 1656-1991	1813-1875	5,8	1657-1850	1657-1700	Bootle			8C
Walton	A 1684-1988	1813-1874	5,8			Brampton			4J
Warwick	A 1684-1992	1813-1875	5,8			Carlisle			5I(F)
Wasdale Head	C 1721-1992	1718-1871	4,5,6,7,8			Bootle			8D
Watermillock	A 1580-1996	1579-1855	8	1579-1812	1601-1700	Penrith	1790-1812		5F
Westward	A 1605-1993	1813-1877	5,8			Wigton			7H
Wetheral	A 1674-1998	1665-1880	5,8			Carlisle			5I
Whicham		1569-1862	5,8	1569-1862	1601-1700	Bootle	1790-1812		8B
Whitbeck		1689-1880	5,8	1813-1875		Bootle			8B
Whitehaven								1756-1858	10E
Holy Trinity	C 1715-1948	1717-1856	5,8	1718-1845		Whitehaven			10E
St James	C 1753-1962	1753-1875	5,8	1753-1837		Whitehaven			10E
St Nicholas	C 1694-1989	1696-1837	5,8	1694-1851		Whitehaven			10E
St Nicholas Old Chapel			5,8	1705-1709		Whitehaven			10E
Wigton	A 1604-1980	1604-1876	5,8	1604-1797		Wigton		1823-1837	7H
Workington								1745-1837	10F
St John	C 1824-1969	1824-1879	5,8			Cockermouth			10F
St Michael	C 1664-1994	1670-1855	5,8	1670-1837	1670-1812	Cockermouth	1790-1812		10F
Wreay	A 1749-1993	1750-1885	5,8			Carlisle			5H
Wythburn	A 1777-1980	1777-1874	8			Cockermouth			6E
Wythop	C 1792-1993	1813-1877	8			Cockermouth			7F

CUMBERLAND

Original registers deposited at:
A = Cumbria Record Office, The Castle, Carlisle, Cumbria CA3 8UR
B = Cumbria Record Office, 140 Duke Street, Barrow-in-Furness LA14 1XW
C = Cumbria Record Office, Scotch Street, Whitehaven, CA28 7BJ
D = Northumberland Record Office, Melton Park, North Gosforth, Newcastle-upon-Tyne NE3 5QX

Study adjacent parishes in counties of Lancashire, Westmorland, Durham, Northumberland and Scotland

Cumbria Record Office, The Castle, Carlisle, CA3 8UR
Cumbria Record Office, 140 Duke Street, Barrow-in-Furness, LA14 1XW
Cumbria Record Office, Scotch Street, Whitehaven, CA28 7BJ
Cumbria Record Office, County Offices, Kendal, LA9 4RQ

The following useful indexes have been compiled – see Introduction
Census Index 1841 Carlisle – Carlisle Library, 11 Globe Lane, Carlisle, CA3 8NX
Census Indexes 1841-1881 Eskdale and Wasdale – Cumbria FHS, Mrs MM Russell, Ulpha, 32 Granada Road, Denton, Manchester, M34 2LJ
Census Index 1851 – Cumbria FHS, Mrs MM Russell, Ulpha, 32 Granada Road, Denton, Manchester, M34 2LJ
Census Index 1851 South Cumberland at either Barrow or Carlisle Record Office
Cumberland Marriage Index pre 1813 – Cumbria Record Office, The Castle, Carlisle, CA3 8UR
Ramsden Marriage Index for South Cumberland 1650-1813 – Barrow Branch, Cumbria Record Office, 140 Duke Street, Barrow-in-Furness, LA14 1XW
Geldart Index of South Cumberland (A-M males only) – Barrow Branch, Cumbria Record Office, 140 Duke Street, Barrow-in-Furness, LA14 1XW

Cumberland's greatest extent is about 80 miles but its mean length is not more than 60 miles and its greatest breadth 35 miles. It is watered by seventeen principal rivers: the Eden, Eamont, Duddon, Ehen, Derwent, Greata, Cocker, Ellen, Waver, Wampool, Caldew, Peteril, Esk, Liddal, Line, Irthing and Gelt. The population in 1841 was 178,038; in 1851, 195,492; in 1861, 205,276; in 1871, 220,253; in 1881, 266,549.

The soils include various loams, light sandy soils and, in the mountainous districts, black forest peat earth. Near Carlisle was an immense bed of gypsum or plaster of Paris, which was worked to great profit. The mineral productions of the county were rich and varied and included lead, copper and iron ores, zinc, cobalt and black lead. The lead mines were chiefly in Alstone moor; the principal copper mines near Caldbeck, at Hesket Newmarket, in Borrowdale, and at Newlands near Keswick. At Crowgarth in the parish of Egremont was an important iron mine. The principal manufactures were the spinning and making of cotton into fabrics and calico printing. Coarse linens, checks, woollens, etc., are produced in several towns and Carlisle was long famous for ginghams. Earthenware was made near Dearham and there were ironworks near Workington.

The information in the Index is abbreviated, and may mislead the searcher if reference is not made to the details contained in the several publications listed in the Introduction. It is essential that users of this book check the appropriate works before making further enquiries.

parish name	deposited original registers	I.G.I.	local census indexes	copies of registers at Soc. Gen.	Boyd's marriage index	1837-1851 Registration District	Pallot's marriage index	non-conform. records at P.R.O.	map ref.
Alder Wasley	A 1861-1979		5,8,9			Belper			5G
Alfreton	A 1706-1963	1704-1894	5,8,9	1706-1837	1706-1837	Belper	1790-1837	1823-1837	3G
Allestree	A 1595-1986	1595-1895	5,8,9	1593-1812	1593-1812	Belper	1790-1812		4E(K)
Alvaston	A 1614-1944	1614-1895	5,8,9	1614-1812	1614-1812	Shardlow	1790-1812		4D
Appleby Magna (Leics.)	B 1573-1973		5,8,9			Ashby-de-la-Zouch			5A
Ashbourne	A 1538-1993	1538-1883	5,8,9	1538-1945		Ashbourne		1787-1837	6F
Ashford	A 1687-1959	1687-1880	5,8,9			Bakewell			7I
Ashover	A 1621-1998	1622-1894	5,8,9	1642-1888		Chesterfield			4H
Aston upon Trent	A 1667-1986	1667-1895	5,8,9	1667-1812	1667-1812	Shardlow	1790-1812		3D
Atlow	A 1685-1992	1685-1884	5,8,9			Ashbourne			6F
Ault Hucknall	A 1662-1996	1660-1875	5,8,9	1660-1812	1660-1812	Mansfield	1790-1812		3I
Bakewell	A 1614-1980	1813-1885	5,8,9			Bakewell		1799-1837	6I
Ballidon			5,8,9			Ashbourne			6G
Barleborough	A 1648-1990	1766-1852	5,8,9			Worksop			3J
Barlow	A 1573-1942	1573-1864	5,8,9			Chesterfield			5J
Barrow on Trent	A 1657-2000	1662-1869	5,8,9	1657-1812	1657-1812	Shardlow	1790-1812		4D
Barton Blount	A 1763-1973	1763-1853	5,8,9			Burton-upon-Trent			6D
Baslow	A 1569-1984	1569-1881	5,8,9			Bakewell			6J
Beauchief (ex.par.)	D 1670-1973	1696-1833	5,8,9	1696-1837	1696-1837	Ecclesall	1790-1837		5K(B)
Beeley	A 1538-1981	1542-1881	5,8,9	1542-1837	1542-1837	Bakewell			5I
Beighton	D 1653-1991	1654-1871	5,8,9	1653-1837	1653-1837	Rotherham	1790-1837		3K
Belper	A 1783-1990	1813-1832	5,8,9			Belper		1794-1837	4F
Birchover	A 1899-1967		5,8,9			Bakewell			6H(E)
Blackwell	A 1685-1991	1664-1864	5,8,9	1685-1912		Bakewell			3H
Bolsover	A 1603-1984	1603-1884	5,8,9	1813-1865		Chesterfield		1819-1836	3I
Bonsall	A 1634-1973	1813-1893	5,8,9			Ashbourne			5H
Boulton	A 1614-1975	1756-1875	5,8,9	1756-1812	1756-1812	Shardlow	1790-1812		4D
Boyleston	A 1734-1995	1660-1895	5,8,9			Uttoxeter			7D
Brackenfield	A 1845-1991	1855-1869	5,8,9			Chesterfield			4H
Bradbourne	A 1713-1992	1713-1882	5,8,9			Ashbourne			6G
Bradley	A 1579-1899	1591-1885	5,8,9			Ashbourne			6F
Brailsford	A 1647-1965	1647-1885	5,8,9	1653-1812	1653-1812	Ashbourne	1790-1812		6E
Brassington	A 1716-1984	1716-1881	5,8,9			Ashbourne			6G
Breadsall	A 1573-1984	1573-1895	5,8,9	1573-1837	1573-1837	Shardlow	1790-1837		4E
Breaston	A 1719-1983	1719-1895	5,8,9	1719-1936	1719-1810	Shardlow	1790-1812		3D
Bretby	A 1766-1959		5,8,9			Burton-upon-Trent			5C
Brimington	A 1813-1978	1813-1896	5,8,9	1813-1871		Chesterfield			4J(D)
Buxton	A 1718-1967	1813-1899	5,8,9	1718-1840	1718-1837	Chapel-en-le-Frith	1790-1837	1810-1837	8I
Caldwell	A 1898-1978		5,8,9			Burton-upon-Trent			5B
Calke	A 1699-1996	1699-1869	5,8,9	1813-1981		Ashby-de-la-Zouch			4C
Carsington	A 1592-1996	1592-1888	5,8,9			Ashbourne			6G(G)
Castleton	A 1647-1958	1791-1857	5,8,9	1646-1754	1662-1754	Chapel-en-le-Frith			7K
Chaddesden	A 1718-1981	1786-1871	5,8,9	1718-1812	1718-1812	Shardlow	1790-1812		4E
Chapel en le Frith	A 1620-1966	1620-1892	5,8,9	1620-1837	1621-1837	Chapel-en-le-Frith	1790-1837		9K
Chellaston	A 1570-1997	1570-1895	5,8,9	1570-1812	1570-1812	Shardlow	1790-1812		4D(T)
Chelmorton	A 1587-1991	1590-1879	5,8,9			Bakewell			8I
Chesterfield	A 1558-1981	1558-1875	5,8,9	1558-1635		Chesterfield		1705-1837	4I
Chilcote	C 1595-1812	1660-1860	5,8,9			Tamworth			5A
Chinley			5,8,9			Chapel-en-le-Frith		1702-1837	9K
Church Broughton	A 1538-1925	1538-1895	5,8,9	1538-1812	1538-1812	Burton-upon-Trent	1790-1812		6D
Church Gresley	A 1574-1967	1664-1895	5,8,9	1664-1812		Burton-upon-Trent		1807-1837	5B
Clifton Campville (Staffs)			5,8,9			Tamworth			5A
Clown	A 1558-1988	1558-1885	5,8,9			Worksop			2J
Codnor Park (ex.par.)			5,8,9			Basford			3G
Crich	A 1600-1991	1565-1885	5,8,9			Bakewell			4G
Cromford	A 1794-1990	1797-1911	5,8,9			Bakewell		1806-1837	5G
Croxall	A 1678-1993	1586-1895	5,8,9	1586-1812	1587-1812	Burton-uon-Trent			6B
Cubley	A 1566-1944	1813-1874	5,8,9			Uttoxeter			7E
Dalbury with Lees	A 1545-1990	1545-1895	5,8,9	1722-1732		Burton-upon-Trent			5E
Dale Abbey (ex.par.)	A 1667-1992	1667-1853	5,8,9	1667-1813	1667-1812	Shardlow	1790-1812		3E
Darley	A 1541-1969	1541-1879	5,8,9	1541-1837	1541-1837	Bakewell			5H
Denby	A 1577-1978	1573-1895	5,8,9	1557-1837	1557-1837	Belper	1790-1837		4F
Derby								1698-1840	4E
All Saints	A 1558-1947	1559-1895	5,8,9	1558-1837	1558-1837	Derby	1790-1812		4E(N)
St Alkmund	A 1538-1983	1538-1875	5,8,9	1538-1812	1538-1812	Derby	1790-1812		4E(L)
St Michael	A 1559-1958	1560-1895	5,8,9	1559-1812	1559-1812	Derby	1790-1812		4D(P)
St Peter	A 1558-1968	1795-1856	5,8,9	1558-1812	1558-1812	Derby	1790-1812		4D(O)
St Werburgh	A 1562-1984	1562-1844	5,8,9	1558-1837	1562-1837	Derby	1790-1837		4D(M)
Derby Hills (ex.par.)			5,8,9			Shardlow			4C(W)
Derwent Woodlands	A 1813-1943	1813-1875	5,8,9	1813-1843		Chapel-en-Frith			6L
Dore	A 1738-1814	1809-1868	5,8,9			Ecclesall Bierlow			5K
Doveridge	A 1574-1983	1574-1881	5,8,9			Uttoxeter			7D
Dronfield	A 1560-1988	1560-1875	5,8,9	1560-1837	1560-1837	Chesterfield	1790-1837	1812-1826	4J
Duffield	A 1598-1980	1598-1885	5,8,9	1598-1812	1598-1812	Belper	1790-1812	1750-1835	5F
Earl Sterndale	A 1765-1963	1765-1882	5,8,9			Bakewell			8I
Eaton and Alsop	A 1701-1992	1702-1882	5,8,9	1701-1837	1701-1837	Ashbourne	1790-1837		7G
Eckington	A 1559-1997	1800-1865	5,8,9			Chesterfield		1810-1837(?)	4K
Edale	A 1643-1927	1643-1882	5,8,9			Chapel-en-le-Frith			8K
Edensor	A 1539-1981	1539-1882	5,8,9	1539-1602		Bakewell			6I
Edlaston	A 1573-1997	1573-1895	5,8,9			Ashbourne			7F
Egginton	A 1561-1978	1561-1895	5,8,9			Burton-upon-Trent			5D
Elmton	A 1598-1997	1673-1868	5,8,9	1673-1868		Worksop			2J
Elton	A 1734-1982	1813-1837	5,8,9			Bakewell			6H
Elvaston	A 1651-1967	1662-1868	5,8,9	1651-1837	1651-1837	Shardlow	1790-1837		3D
Etwall	A 1557-1986	1558-1882	5,8,9	1557-1837	1557-1837	Burton-upon-Trent	1790-1837		5D
Eyam	A 1630-1964	1787-1868	5,8,9	1630-1700		Bakewell			6J
Fairfield	A 1738-1995	1738-1888	5,8,9	1738-1840	1756-1837	Chapel-en-le-Frith	1790-1837		8J
Fenny Bentley	A 1604-1991	1604-1885	5,8,9			Ashbourne			7F(F)

DERBYSHIRE

parish name	deposited original registers	I.G.I.	local census indexes	copies of registers at Soc. Gen.	Boyd's marriage index	1837-1851 Registration District	Pallot's marriage index	non-conform. records at P.R.O.	map ref.
Findern	A 1558-1998	1827-1869	5,8,9	1558-1600		Burton-upon-Trent		1785-1794	5D
Foremark	A 1662-1992	1662-1895	5,8,9	1663-1836	1663-1836	Burton-upon-Trent	1790-1837		4C
Foston and Scropton	A 1680-1996	1813-1864	5,8,9			Burton-upon-Trent			6D
Glapwell			5,8,9			Mansfield			2I
Glossop	A 1620-2000	1813-1845	5,8,9	1620-1733	1620-1730	Hayfield		1786-1857	9L
Hartington	A 1610-1984	1610-1884	5,8,9			Ashbourne			8I
Hartshorne	A 1594-1978	1673-1869	5,8,9	1813-1869		Ashby-de-la-Zouch			5C
Hathersage	A 1628-1980	1627-1881	5,8,9	1627-1980		Bakewell			6K
Hayfield	A 1622-1963	1813-1875	5,8,9			Hayfield		1795-1837	8L
Heage	A 1819-1969	1819-1897	5,8,9			Belper		1794-1836	4G
Heanor	A 1559-1997	1813-1868	5,8,9	1558-1899	1559-1837	Basford	1790-1837	1822-1837	3F
Heath	A 1682-1998	1682-1875	5,8,9	1682-1812	1682-1812	Chesterfield	1790-1812		3I
Hognaston	A 1661-1993	1675-1895	5,8,9			Ashbourne			6G(H)
Holbrook	A 1834-1987		5,8,9	1834-1838		Belper			4F
Holmesfield	A 1724-1990	1813-1876	5,8,9	1813-1876		Chesterfield			5J
Hope	A 1598-1987	1802-1857	5,8,9	1598-1858		Chapel-en-le-Frith		1789-1837	7K
Horsley	A 1558-1995	1767-1844	5,8,9	1558-1812	1558-1812	Belper	1790-1812		4F
Hulland	A 1838-1990	1838-1885	5,8,9			Ashbourne			5F
Ilkeston	A 1588-1988	1813-1835	5,8,9	1588-1812	1588-1812	Basford	1790-1812	1735-1837	3E
Kedleston	A 1600-1982	1597-1885	5,8,9	1600-1837	1600-1837	Belper	1790-1837		5E
Killamarsh	A 1638-1975	1820-1868	5,8,9			Chesterfield			3K
Kirk Hallam	A 1700-1966	1700-1888	5,8,9	1700-1837	1700-1837	Shardlow	1790-1837		3E
Kirk Ireton	A 1572-1980	1576-1869	5,8,9	1576-1812	1572-1812	Ashbourne	1790-1812		5F
Kirk Langley	A 1654-1993	1654-1885	5,8,9	1654-1837	1654-1812	Belper	1790-1812		5E
Kniveton	A 1591-1989	1591-1895	5,8,9			Ashbourne			6F
Langwith	A 1685-1997	1666-1868	5,8,9			Mansfield			2I
Little Eaton	A 1790-1990	1791-1875	5,8,9			Shardlow			4E(I)
Littleover	A 1680-1981	1662-1875	5,8,9	1680-1812	1680-1812	Shardlow	1790-1812		5D
Long Eaton	A 1813-1966	1813-1876	5,8,9			Shardlow	1831-1837		2D
Longford	A 1538-1954	1538-1895	5,8,9	1538-1837	1538-1837	Ashbourne	1790-1837		6E
Longstone	A 1637-1968	1637-1875	5,8,9			Bakewell			6J
Lullington	A 1560-1975	1811-1868	5,8,9			Burton-upon-Trent			6B
Mackworth	A 1611-1992	1603-1885	5,8,9	1603-1837	1603-1812	Belper	1790-1812		5E
Mapleton	A 1704-1992	1703-1883	5,8,9			Ashbourne			7F
Marston Montgomery	A 1661-1997	1813-1869	5,8,9	1662-1810		Uttoxeter			7E
Marston on Dove	A 1654-1965	1654-1898	5,8,9	1661-1810		Burton-upon-Trent			6D
Matlock	A 1637-1993	1756-1856	5,8,9	1637-1812	1637-1812	Bakewell	1790-1812	1785-1836	5H
Measham	B 1681-1993	1755-1875	5,8,9	1681-1993		Ashby-de-la-Zouch	1790-1837	1797-1837	4A
Melbourne	A 1653-1986	1758-1869	5,8,9	1653-1812	1653-1812	Shardlow	1790-1812	1753-1837	4C
Mellor	A 1624-1909	1678-1835	5,8,9	1678-1775	1678-1775	Blackborn	1790-1812	1761-1837	9L
Mickleover	A 1607-1981	1607-1885	5,8,9	1607-1812	1607-1812	Burton-upon-Trent	1790-1812		5D
Monyash	A 1754-1991	1754-1895	5,8,9			Bakewell			7I
Morley	A 1540-1999	1540-1885	5,8,9	1540-1837	1540-1837	Belper	1790-1837		4E
Morton	A 1575-1979	1576-1881	5,8,9	1575-1863	1575-1812	Chesterfield	1790-1812		3H
Muggington	A 1674-1993	1674-1895	5,8,9			Belper			5E
Newton Solney	A 1663-1998	1664-1895	5,8,9	1664-1841		Burton-upon-Trent			5C
Norbury	A 1686-1981	1673-1895	5,8,9	1673-1812		Uttoxeter			7E
Normanton	A 1769-1988	1810-1869	5,8,9	1769-1812	1760-1812	Mansfield	1790-1812		4D
North Wingfield	A 1567-1985	1569-1886	5,8,9			Chesterfield			4I
Norton	D 1559-1948	1559-1877	5,8,9	1559-1812	1559-1812	Ecclesall Bierlow	1790-1812	1777-1836	4K
Ockbrook	A 1630-1973	1631-1889	5,8,9	1630-1812	1631-1812	Shardlow	1790-1812	1746-1837	3E
Old Brampton	A 1658-1959	1658-1898	5,8,9	1658-1752		Chesterfield		1826-1837	5I
Osmaston by Ashbourne	A 1606-1999	1606-1895	5,8,9			Ashbourne	1790-1812		6F
Osmaston by Derby	A 1743-1972	1743-1885	5,8,9	1743-1812	1743-1812	Shardlow			4D(R)
Packington	B 1677-1993		5,8,9			Ashby-de-le-Zouch			4B
Parwich	A 1640-1992	1640-1882	5,8,9	1639-1837	1639-1837	Ashbourne	1790-1837		7G
Peak Forest (ex.par.)	A 1698-1938	1700-1875	5,8,9	1727-1815		Chapel-en-le-Frith	1790-1815		8J
Pentrich	A 1621-1980	1652-1868	5,8,9	1621-1837	1621-1837	Belper	1790-1837		4G
Pinxton	A 1561-1981	1561-1875	5,8,9	1561-1883		Mansfield			3G
Pleasley	A 1553-1988	1553-1895	5,8,9			Mansfield			2I
Quarndon	A 1712-1985	1772-1895	5,8,9	1755-1837	1755-1812	Belper	1790-1812		4E(J)
Radbourne	A 1571-1994	1571-1895	5,8,9			Burton-upon-trent			5E
Ravenstone	B 1705-1989	1673-1812	5,8,9			Ashby-de-la-Zouch			3A
Repton	A 1579-1974	1578-1881	5,8,9	1578-1670	1578-1837	Burton-upon-trent	1790-1837	1814-1837	5C
Risley	A 1719-1993	1696-1885	5,8,9	1720-1812	1720-1812	Shardlow	1790-1812		3E
Rosliston	A 1756-1996	1662-1895	5,8,9			Burton-upon-Trent			6B
Sandiacre	A 1711-1977	1581-1898	5,8,9	1570-1812	1570-1812	Shardlow	1790-1812		2E
Sawley	A 1654-1982	1654-1895	5,8,9	1656-1837	1656-1837	Shardlow	1790-1837		2D
Scarcliffe	A 1727-1993	1665-1875	5,8,9			Mansfield			2I
Seale	A 1566-1994	1813-1871	5,8,9			Ashby-de-la-Zouch			5B
Sheldon	A 1737-1990	1671-1882	5,8,9	1672-1812		Bakewell			7I
Shirland	A 1678-1982	1695-1798	5,8,9	1661-1837	1678-1837	Chesterfield	1790-1837		4H
Shirley	A 1663-1999	1663-1895	5,8,9			Ashourne			6E
Sinfrin Moor (ex.par.)			5,8,9			Shardlow			4D
Smalley	A 1623-1994	1623-1885	5,8,9	1623-1862	1624-1837	Belper	1790-1837		3F
Smisby	A 1720-2001	1679-1875	5,8,9	1720-1812	1720-1812	Ashby-de-la-Zouch	1790-1812		4B
Snelston	A 1575-1993	1575-1885	5,8,9			Ashbourne			7E
Somersall Herbert	A 1538-1993	1664-1867	5,8,9			Uttoxeter			7D(S)
South Normanton	A 1540-1979	1664-1868	5,8,9	1540-1868		Mansfield			3G
South Wingfield	A 1585-1974	1585-1881	5,8,9	1585-1838	1585-1837	Belper	1790-1837		4G
Spondon	A 1653-1986	1653-1862	5,8,9	1654-1812	1653-1812	Shardlow	1790-1812		3E
Stanley	A 1675-1992	1661-1852	5,8,9	1754-1837	1654-1837	Shardlow	1790-1837		3E
Stanton			5,8,9			Bakewell			6H
Stanton and Newhall	A 1833-1991		5,8,9			Burton-upon-Trent			5B
Stanton by Bridge	A 1664-1991	1660-1868	5,8,9	1662-1837	1664-1837	Shardlow	1790-1837		4C
Stanton by Dale	A 1604-1993	1605-1856	5,8,9	1605-1812	1605-1812	Shardlow	1790-1812		3E
Stapenhill	A 1679-1992	1666-1869	5,8,9			Burton-upon-Trent			5C
Staveley	A 1558-1988	1558-1887	5,8,9	1558-1618		Chesterfield			3J
Stoney Middleton	A 1715-1947	1663-1864	5,8,9			Bakewell			6J(A)

DERBYSHIRE

parish name	deposited original registers	I.G.I.	local census indexes	copies of registers at Soc. Gen.	Boyd's marriage index	1837-1851 Registration District	Pallot's marriage index	non-conform. records at P.R.O.	map ref.
Stretton en le Field	B 1638-1981	1662-1871	5,8,9			Ashby-de-la-Zouch			5A
Sudbury	A 1673-1993	1812-1875	5,8,9	1634-1810		Uttoxeter			7D
Sutton-cum-Duckmanton	A 1662-1974	1668-1868	5,8,9	1662-1837		Chesterfield			3I
Sutton Hill	A 1567-1980	1567-1895	5,8,9			Burton-upon-Trent			6D
Swarkeston	A 1604-1975	1663-1895	5,8,9	1604-1868	1604-1837	Shardlow	1790-1837		4D(U)
Taddington	A 1642-1986	1813-1882	5,8,9			Bakewell			7I
Tansley	A 1840-1952		5,8,9			Bakewell			5H
Thorpe	A 1538-1992	1538-1880	5,8,9			Ashbourne			7G
Tibshelf	A 1627-1990	1663-1871	5,8,9			Mansfield			3H
Ticknell	A 1626-1998	1626-1895	5,8,9	1628-1812	1628-1812	Ashby-de-la-Zouch	1790-1812	1817-1837	4C
Tideswell	A 1635-1989	1671-1885	5,8,9			Bakewell			7J
Tissington	A 1659-1992	1658-1883	5,8,9			Ashbourne			7G
Trusley	A 1538-1938	1538-1895	5,8,9			Burton-upon-Trent			6D
Turnditch	A 1813-1906	1783-1875	5,8,9			Belper			5F
Twyford and Stenson	A 1838-2001	1676-1895	5,8,9			Burton-upon-Trent	1790-1812		4D
Walton-on-Trent	A 1586-1996	1586-1885	5,8,9		1586-1751	Burton-upon-Trent			6B
West Hallam	A 1538-1993	1538-1895	5,8,9	1638-1812	1638-1812	Shardlow	1790-1812		3E
Weston-upon-Trent	A 1565-1949	1565-1895	5,8,9	1565-1837	1565-1812	Shardlow	1790-1812		4D
Whittington	A 1650-1977	1668-1859	5,8,9			Chesterfield			4J(C)
Whitwell	A 1672-1992	1672-1885	5,8,9			Worksop			2J
Willesley	B 1677-1985	1677-1868	5,8,9	1677-1868		Ashby-de-la-Zouch			4B
Willington	A 1698-1987	1810-1854	5,8,9	1698-1812	1698-1812	Burton-upon-Trent	1790-1812		5D(V)
Wilne	A 1540-1955	1540-1895	5,8,9	1540-1880	1540-1837	Shardlow	1790-1837		3D
Wingerworth	A 1540-1990	1539-1895	5,8,9			Chesterfield			4I
Winster	A 1674-1980	1814-1875	5,8,9			Bakewell		1825-1837	6H
Wirksworth	A 1608-1998	1608-1875	5,8,9			Belper		1813-1837	5G
Wormhill	A 1674-1987	1674-1882	5,8,9			Chapel-en-le-Frith			8J
Yeavely	A 1841-1989	1841-1867	5,8,9			Ashbourne		1816-1824	7E
Youlgreave	A 1558-1988	1805-1837	5,8,9	1598-1694	1598-1694	Bakewell			7H

Original registers deposited at:
A = Derbyshire Record Office, New Street, Matlock, Derbyshire
B = Leicestershire Record Office, Long Street, Wigston Magna, Leicestershire LE18 2AH
C = Staffordshire Record Office, Eastgate Street, Stafford ST16 2LZ
D = Sheffield Archives, 52 Shoreham Street, Sheffield, Yorkshire S1 4SP

Study adjacent parishes in counties of Yorkshire, Nottinghamshire, Leicestershire and Staffordshire

Derbyshire Record Office, New Street, Matlock, DE4 3AG
Derby Library, Local Studies Department, 25 Longate, Derby, DE1 3GL

The following useful indexes have been compiled – see Introduction
Census Index 1851 and 1891 – Derbyshire FHS, Bridge Chapel House, St Mary's Bridge, Sowter Road, Derby, DE1 3AT
Derbyshire Marriage Index – Miss S. Brown, 25 Homecroft Drive, Packington, Ashby-de-la-Zouch, Leics., LE65 1WG
Derbyshire Burial Index – Mrs H. Eaton, 24 Hopping Hill, Milford, Belper, Derbyshire, DE56 0RJ

Derbyshire is extremely irregular in shape; its greatest extent from north to south is nearly 55 miles, its breadth at the northern extremity is about 33 miles. It is watered by six principal rivers: the Trent, Dove, Derwent, Wye, Erewash and Rother. The population in 1841 was 272,202; in 1851, 296,084; in 1861, 339,327; in 1871, 379,394; in 1881, 461,914.

The most common soil is a reddish clay or marl but there is also sand, gravel, limestone and peat. Dairy-farming was important as was the cultivation of corn. Lead, copper and iron ores, coal, antimony, alabaster and millstones were also sources of wealth. The manufactures carried on in the county were various and extensive including cotton, stocking-weaving, silk, woollen cloths and iron.

The information in the Index is abbreviated, and may mislead the searcher if reference is not made to the details contained in the several publications listed in the Introduction. It is essential that users of this book check the appropriate works before making further enquiries.

DEVON

parish name	deposited original registers	I.G.I.	local census indexes	copies of registers at Soc. Gen.	Boyd's marriage index	1837-1851 Registration District	Pallot's marriage index	non-conform. records at P.R.O.	map ref.
Abbots Bickington	A 1717-1833	1615-1836	5,8	1609-1837	1615-1631	Holsworthy			7D
Abbotsham	E 1653-1939	1597-1875	5,8	1597-1637	1597-1636	Bideford			8D
Abbotskerswell	A 1607-1919	1607-1837	5,8			Newton Abbot			3H(AA)
Alfington	A 1884-1974	1603-1837	5,8		1603-1837	St Thomas			5H
Alverdiscott	E 1602-1989		5,8	1602-1896		Torrington			8E
Alwington	E 1550-1978	1550-1812	5,8	1551-1799	1555-1812	Kingsbridge			8D
Arlington	E 1598-1996	1640-1850	5,8	1596-1644	1597-1638	Barnstaple			10F
Ashburton	A 1603-1966	1603-1837	5,8		1603-1837	Newton Abbot		1801-1837	4G
Ashbury			5,8	1596-1644	1610-1613	Okehampton			6E
Ashcombe	A 1732-1992	1581-1836	5,8	1581-1837	1633-1636	St Thomas	1790-1837		4H
Ashford	E 1701-1966	1774-1875	5,8	1596-1966	1597-1640	Barnstaple			9E(A)
Ashprington	A 1607-1940		5,8	1596-1940	1597-1601	Totnes			3H
Ashreigney	E 1653-1867		5,8	1596-1982	1607-1636	Torrington		1820-1837	7F
Ashton	A 1547-1992		5,8			St Thomas			5H
Ashwater	A 1558-1875	1558-1837	5,8		1559-1837	Holsworthy		1828-1837	6D
Atherington	A 1538-1973	1541-1812	5,8	1596-1644	1548-1812	Barnstaple			8F
Aveton Gifford	A 1603-1986		5,8	1596-1644		Kingsbridge			2F
Awliscombe	A 1559-1979		5,8	1559-1855		Honiton			6J
Axminster	A 1559-1948	1559-1812	5,8	1596-1644	1606-1635	Axminster		1786-1837	6L
Axmouth	A 1603-1992	1603-1837	5,8		1603-1837	Axminster			5K
Aylesbeare	A 1580-1883	1580-1854	5,8	1580-1883		St Thomas			6I
Bampton	A 1653-1989		5,8	1609-1617	1609-1616	Tiverton			8I
Barnstaple (St Peter)	E 1538-1979	1538-1812	5,8	1538-1812	1538-1812	Barnstaple	1790-1812	1701-1837	9E
Beaford	E 1653-1972	1653-1729	5,8	1598-1615	1598-1729	Torrington			7E
Beaworthy	A 1758-1972		5,8	1602-1636	1602-1635	Okehampton			6D
Beer Ferris	A 1538-1979		5,8	1605-1606	1605-1606	Axminster		1813-1837	3D
Belstone	A 1552-1906	1553-1837	5,8	1553-1809	1601-1837	Okehampton			5F
Berrynarbor	E 1540-1974	1540-1812	5,8	1540-1783	1540-1812	Barnstaple			10E
Berry Pomeroy	A 1602-1957	1596-1837	5,8	1596-1602	1596-1837	Totnes			3H
Bickington	A 1603-1951		5,8	1620-1636	1631-1636	Newton Abbot			4G(Y)
Bickleigh (nr Plymouth)	B 1694-1985		5,8	1609-1642	1609-1641	Plympton St Mary			3E
Bickleigh (nr Tiverton)	A 1569-1979	1570-1837	5,8			Tiverton	1570-1837		7H
Bicton	A 1557-1926		5,8	1557-1974	1620-1638	St Thomas			5I
Bideford	E 1561-1972	1561-1812	5,8	1561-1968	1561-1812	Bideford		1753-1837	8D
Bigbury	A 1678-1959		5,8	1613-1627	1613-1626	Kingsbridge			2F
Bishop Nympton	E 1556-1987	1556-1837	5,8	1558-1633	1601-1660	St Molton			8G
Bishop Teignton	A 1558-1993		5,8	1558-1949		Newton Abbot			4H
Bishops Tawton	E 1558-1990	1558-1840	5,8			Barnstaple			9E
Bittadon			5,8			Barnstaple			10E
Blackawton	A 1538-1913		5,8	1538-1837		Kingsbridge			2G
Blackborough	A 1840-1973		5,8	1840-1973		Tiverton			7J
Black Torrington	A 1547-1978	1547-1837	5,8	1545-1879		Holsworthy			6D
Bondleigh	A 1754-1837		5,8	1607-1837	1607-1636	Okehampton			6F
Bovey Tracey	A 1538-1973	1538-1837	5,8	1538-1973	1598-1836	Newton Abbot		1778-1837	4G
Bow	A 1604-1978	1598-1836	5,8	1598-1639		Crediton		1825-1836	6G
Boyton (Cornwall)			5,8			Launceston			5C
Bradford	A 1558-1991	1559-1837	5,8	1558-1927	1558-1754	Holsworthy			6D
Bradninch	A 1559-1978		5,8	1557-1840		Exeter			7I
Bradstone	A 1654-1922		5,8	1611-1627	1611-1626	Tavistock			4D
Bradworthy	A 1548-1935	1548-1860	5,8	1548-1860		Bideford			7C
Brampford Speke	A 1739-1939	1608-1837	5,8	1608-1645	1608-1644	St. Thomas			6H(R)
Branscombe	A 1539-1989	1539-1812	5,8	1539-1812	1545-1812	Honiton	1790-1812		5K
Bratton Clovelly	A 1555-1972		5,8			Okehampton			6E
Bratton Fleming	E 1673-1913	1673-1850	5,8	1560-1656	1562-1644	Barnstaple			9F
Braunton	E 1538-1944	1538-1812	5,8	1538-1837	1538-1812	Barnstaple		1818-1837	9D
Brendon	E 1610-1992	1610-1850	5,8			Barnstaple			10G
Brentor	B 1720-1887		5,8			Tavistock			5E
Bridestowe	A 1696-1970		5,8			Okehampton			5E
Bridford	A 1538-1993	1538-1837	5,8			St Thomas			5G
Bridgerule, East	A 1702-1977	1702-1753	5,8	1692-1812	1702-1755	Holsworthy			6C
Brixham (St Mary)	A 1556-1984	1556-1837	5,8		1556-1837	Totnes		1811-1837	2H
Brixham (All Saints)	A 1826-1909		5,8			Totnes			2H
Brixton	B 1668-1979		5,8			Plympton St Mary			2E
Broadclyst	A 1653-1989	1653-1850	5,8			St Thomas			6I
Broadhembury	A 1538-1991		5,8			Honiton		1816-1832	7J
Broadhempston	A 1678-1920	1681-1822	5,8			Newton Abbot			3G
Broadwoodkelly	E 1609-1992		5,8			Okehampton			7F
Broadwoodwidger	A 1654-1874		5,8			Holsworthy			5D
Brushford	E 1694-1838		5,8			Crediton			7F
Buckerell	A 1650-1950	1650-1850	5,8			Honiton			6J
Buckfastleigh	A 1602-1966	1597-1812	5,8		1602-1812	Totnes		1787-1837	3G
Buckland Brewer	E 1603-1979	1604-1837	5,8		1603-1812	Bideford			8D
Buckland Filleigh	E 1619-1979	1603-1837	5,8	1603-1837		Torrington			7E
Buckland in the Moor	A 1692-1860		5,8			Newton Abbot			4G(AM)
Buckland Monachorum	B 1538-1977	1540-1778	5,8	1538-1892		Tavistock			3E
Buckland Tout Saints	A 1815-1988		5,8	1818-1822		Kingsbridge			2G
Bulkworthy	A 1709-1836	1605-1837	5,8	1605-1837		Bideford			7D
Burlescombe	A 1579-1989		5,8			Wellington			8J
Burrington	A 1592-1975	1601-1837	5,8		1601-1837	South Molton			8F
Butterleigh	A 1698-1976	1624-1837	5,8			Tiverton			7I(M)
Cadbury	A 1756-1971	1606-1837	5,8		1756-1837	Tiverton			7H
Cadeleigh	A 1665-1992	1606-1837	5,8			Tiverton			7H
Calverleigh	A 1679-1995		5,8			Tiverton			7H(K)
Chagford	A 1598-1996	1598-1850	5,8			Okehampton			5F
Challacombe	E 1673-1955		5,8	1673-1955	1597-1837	Barnstaple			10F
Charles	E 1531-1812	1538-1837	5,8	1531-1837	1539-1837	South Molton		1831-1837	9F
Charleton	A 1561-1983		5,8	1560-1861		Kingsbridge			1G(AL)
Chawleigh	A 1544-1894		5,8			Crediton			7G
Cheldon	A 1673-1835		5,8			South Moldon			7G

132

DEVON

parish name	deposited original registers	I.G.I.	local census indexes	copies of registers at Soc. Gen.	Boyd's marriage index	1837-1851 Registration District	Pallot's marriage index	non-conform. records at P.R.O.	map ref.
Cheriton Bishop	A 1538-1888		5,8			Crediton			6G
Cheriton Fitzpaine	A 1660-1954	1610-1837	5,8			Crediton			7H
Chittlehampton	E 1575-1986	1575-1812	5,8		1575-1812	South Molton			8F
Chivelstone	A 1630-1953	1684-1812	5,8	1630-1920	1684-1812	Kingsbridge		1772-1837	1G
Christow	A 1655-1963		5,8	1557-1855		St Thomas			5G
Chudleigh	A 1558-1917		5,8	1538-1858		Newton Abbot		1711-1837	4H
Chulmleigh	A 1653-1989	1610-1726	5,8	1610-1812	1653-1726	South Molton		1812-1837	7F
Churchstanton	D 1662-1960		5,8			Taunton			7K
Churchstow	A 1539-1993		5,8	1539-1876		Kingsbridge			2G
Churston Ferrers	A 1590-1936	1589-1837	5,8		1590-1836	Totnes			2H
Clannaborough	A 1696-1913	1696-1849	5,8			Crediton			6G(J)
Clawton	A 1693-1977	1612-1837	5,8		1604-1837	Holsworthy			6C
Clayhanger	A 1538-1961	1538-1837	5,8		1538-1770	Tiverton			8I
Clayhidon	A 1637-1948		5,8			Wellington			7J
Clovelly	E 1686-1989		5,8	1686-1946		Bideford			8C
Clyst Honiton	A 1683-1915	1683-1875	5,8		1683-1837	St Thomas			6I
Clyst Hydon	A 1548-1988	1548-1837	5,8			St Thomas			6I
Clyst St George	A 1754-1993	1567-1837	5,8	1565-1837	1565-1837	St Thomas	1790-1812		5I
Clyst St Lawrence	A 1539-1995		5,8			St Thomas			6I(T)
Clyst St Mary	A 1662-1971		5,8	1662-1958		St Thomas			5I(V)
Cockington	A 1628-1923		5,8			Newton Abbot			3H(AE)
Coffinswell	A 1560-1837	1560-1837	5,8	1601-1625	1601-1625	Newton Abbot			3H
Colaton Raleigh	A 1673-1982		5,8	1673-1871		St. Thomas			5I
Coldridge	A 1556-1978	1556-1837	5,8		1556-1750	Crediton			7F
Colebrooke	A 1558-1976		5,8	1558-1865		Crediton			6G
Colyton	A 1538-1940	1538-1837	5,8	1538-1837	1538-1837	Axminster	1790-1837	1773-1862	6K
Combeinteignhead	A 1653-1913		5,8	1653-1913		Newton Abbot			4H
Combe Martin	E 1671-1980		5,8			Barnstaple		1829-1836	10F
Combe Rawleigh	A 1653-1914		5,8	1653-1914		Honiton			6J
Combpyne	A 1685-1988	1685-1837	5,8			Axminster			6K
Compton Gifford	B 1870-1941		5,8			Plympton St Mary			2E(AF)
Cookbury	A 1746-1990	1609-1837	5,8	1609-1837		Holsworthy			7D
Cornwood	B 1669-1957	1665-1811	5,8	1685-1834		Plympton St Mary			3F
Cornworthy	A 1562-1889		5,8	1562-1889		Totnes			2H
Coryton	B 1654-1992		5,8			Tavistock			5D
Cotleigh	A 1653-1926	1608-1837	5,8			Honiton			6K
Countisbury	E 1676-1973	1676-1850	5,8	1676-1837	1676-1837	Barnstaple	1790-1836		10G
Cove	A 1680-1987		5,8			Tiverton			8I
Creacombe	E 1695-1990	1704-1837	5,8		1759-1835	South Molton			8G
Crediton	A 1557-1986	1558-1843	5,8			Crediton		1735-1837	6G
Cruwys Morchard	A 1572-1978	1572-1812	5,8			Tiverton			7H
Cullompton	A 1601-1906		5,8	1601-1844		Tiverton		1693-1837	7I
Culmstock	A 1645-1941	1608-1837	5,8		1646-1837	Wellington		1786-1836	7J
Dalwood	A 1568-1978		5,8	1568-1915		Axminster			6K
Dartington	A 1538-1890	1538-1852	5,8			Totnes			3G
Dartmouth								1726-1837	2H
St Petrox	A 1652-1901	1610-1837	5,8			Totnes			2H
St Saviour	A 1586-1883	1586-1837	5,8		1586-1756	Totnes			2H
Townstall	A 1653-1894	1597-1837	5,8			Totnes			2H
Dawlish St Gregory	A 1627-1975		5,8			Newton Abbot		1814-1837	4I
Dean Prior	A 1557-1812	1557-1837	5,8			Totnes			3G
Denbury	A 1559-1997		5,8	1559-1924	1601-1625	Newton Abbot			4G
Diptford	A 1653-1908		5,8			Totnes			2G
Dittisham	A 1650-1988	1603-1837	5,8	1650-1884		Totnes			2H
Dodbrooke	B 1725-1974		5,8	1725-1881		Kingsbridge		1819-1836	1G(AK)
Doddiscombsleigh	A 1678-1995		5,8			St Thomas			5H
Dolton	E 1608-1989	1602-1837	5,8	1610-1812	1608-1812	Torrington			7E
Dowland	E 1742-1984	1742-1840	5,8			Torrington			7E
Down St Mary	A 1696-1947	1696-1850	5,8			Crediton			6G
Drewsteignton	A 1557-1990		5,8	1599-1812	1599-1812	Okehampton			5G
Dunchideock	A 1538-1986	1538-1837	5,8	1538-1837	1539-1836	St Thomas			5H
Dunkeswell	A 1740-1993		5,8	1740-1876		Honiton			7J
Dunsford	A 1594-1986		5,8			St Thomas			5G
Dunterton	B 1580-1995		5,8			Tavistock			4D
East Allington	B 1554-1968		5,8			Kingsbridge			2G
East Anstey	A 1596-1990	1596-1812	5,8	1610	1610-1812	South Molton			8H
East Buckland	E 1684-1836		5,8	1684-1872		South Molton			9F
East Budleigh	A 1555-1954		5,8	1555-1863		St Thomas		1762-1837	5J
East Down	E 1538-1987	1538-1837	5,8	1539-1837		Barnstaple			10E
East Ogwell	A 1674-1996		5,8	1674-1909		Newton Abbot			4H(AB)
East Portlemouth	A 1562-1983		5,8	1562-1978		Kingsbridge			1G
East Putford	A 1799-1953	1605-1799	5,8			Bideford			7D
East Stonehouse	B 1697-1954		5,8	1697-1812		East Stonehouse		1794-1836	2E
East Teignmouth	A 1665-1979	1606-1837	5,8			Newton Abbot		1804-1837	4I
East Woolfardisworthy	E 1643-1973		5,8			Crediton			7G
East Worlington	E 1725-1990	1725-1851	5,8	1725-1884		South Molton			7G
Egg Buckland	B 1653-1984		5,8			Plympton St Mary			3E
Eggesford	A 1594-1948		5,8	1580-1702		Crediton			7F
Ermington	B 1603-1959	1603-1850	5,8			Plympton St Mary			2F
Exbourne	A 1755-1870		5,8			Okehampton			6F
Exeter									6H
All Hallows, Goldsmith St.	A 1809-1902	1561-1837	5,8	1561-1837	1561-1837	Exeter	1809-1837	1687-1837	6H
All Hallows on The Walls	A 1694-1938	1614-1837	5,8		1561-1837	Exeter			6H
Bedford Chapel	A 1833-1960		5,8			Exeter			6H
Bradninch			5,8	1559-1840		Exeter			6H
Exeter Castle			5,8			Exeter			6H
Exeter Cathedral	A 1593-1977	1594-1837	5,8	1594-1837	1594-1812	Exeter	1790-1812		6H

DEVON

parish name	deposited original registers	I.G.I.	local census indexes	copies of registers at Soc. Gen.	Boyd's marriage index	1837-1851 Registration District	Pallot's marriage index	non-conform. records at P.R.O.	map ref.
Exeter (cont'd)									
Holy Trinity	A 1564-1968	1563-1837	5,8			Exeter			6H
St David	A 1559-1983	1559-1837	5,8			Exeter	1780-1806		6H
St Edmund	A 1571-1956	1571-1837	5,8			Exeter			6H
St George the Martyr	A 1682-1925	1609-1837	5,8			Exeter			6H
St John	A 1682-1934	1609-1812	5,8			Exeter			6H
St Kerrian	A 1558-1933	1539-1837	5,8		1558-1837	Exeter			6H
St Lawrence	A 1754-1979	1604-1837	5,8		1604-1837	Exeter			6H
St Leonard	A 1704-1949	1704-1837	5,8		1708-1837	Exeter			6H
St Martin	A 1754-1973	1572-1836	5,8		1572-1837	Exeter			6H
St Mary Arches	A 1538-1964	1538-1837	5,8		1538-1837	Exeter			6H
St Mary Major	A 1561-1965	1561-1837	5,8			Exeter			6H
St Mary Steps	A 1655-1890	1558-1837	5,8			Exeter			6H
St Olave	A 1601-1981	1601-1838	5,8			Exeter			6H
St Pancras	A 1664-1933	1664-1837	5,8	1664-1837	1664-1796	Exeter	1790-1796		6H
St Paul	A 1754-1934	1562-1837	5,8	1562-1837	1562-1821	Exeter	1790-1837		6H
St Petrock	A 1538-1974	1538-1837	5,8		1538-1810	Exeter			6H
St Sidwell	A 1569-1968	1569-1837	5,8		1569-1837	Exeter			6H
St Stephen	A 1754-1928	1668-1837	5,8			Exeter			6H
St Thomas the Apostle	A 1541-1899	1541-1837	5,8	1541-1837		Exeter			6H
Exminster	A 1562-1957	1562-1836	5,8	1562-1837	1562-1836	St Thomas			5I
Farringdon	A 1678-1897	1610-1850	5,8	1620-1788	1620-1788	St Thomas			5I
Farway	A 1567-1994	1567-1875	5,8			Honiton			6J
Feniton	A 1549-1959	1549-1837	5,8		1550-1837	Honiton			6J
Filleigh	E 1685-1946	1597-1601	5,8			South Molton			8F
Fremington	E 1602-1948	1602-1837	5,8	1602-1948	1602-1837	Barnstaple			9E
Frithelstock	E 1556-1911	1556-1873	5,8			Torrington			8D
Georgeham	E 1538-1986	1538-1850	5,8			Barnstaple		1821-1835	9D
George Nympton	E 1599-1992		5,8			South Molton			8F
Germansweek	A 1652-1892		5,8			Okehampton			6D
Gidley	A 1599-1989	1599-1812	5,8			Okehampton			5F
Gittisham	A 1559-1990		5,8	1559-1952		Honiton			6J
Goodleigh	E 1538-1981		5,8			Barnstaple			9F
Great Torrington	E 1616-1978		5,8			Torrington			8E
Halberton	A 1605-1989	1813-1837	5,8	1605-1837		Tiverton	1790-1837		7I
Halwell	A 1560-1952	1695-1837	5,8			Totnes			2G
Halwill	A 1695-1965		5,8			Holsworthy			6D
Harberton	A 1624-1978		5,8			Totnes			3G
Harford	A 1724-1993		5,8			Plympton St. Mary			3F
Harpford	A 1638-1996	1638-1837	5,8			Honiton			5J
Hartland	E 1559-1949	1558-1837	5,8	1558-1837	1558-1837	Bideford	1790-1837	1821-1837	8C
Hatherleigh	A 1558-1975	1558-1837	5,8	1558-1872	1558-1823	Okehampton		1729-1789	6E
Heanton Punchardon	E 1559-1990	1560-1877	5,8		1559-1812	Barnstaple			9E
Heavitree	A 1556-1935	1555-1837	5,8			St Thomas			6I
Hemyock	A 1635-1923	1602-1837	5,8	1635-1837	1602-1837	Wellington	1790-1837		7J
Hennock	A 1541-1973	1541-1752	5,8	1552-1850	1544-1753	Newton Abbot			5H
High Bickington	E 1707-1992	1597-1837	5,8		1751-1837	Torrington			8E
Highampton	A 1653-1992	1609-1837	5,8	1653-1837		Okehampton			6E
High Bray	E 1605-1991		5,8	1605-1837		Barnstaple			9F
Highweek	A 1653-1984	1609-1837	5,8			Newton Abbot			4H
Hittisleigh	A 1676-1979	1676-1837	5,8		1678-1837	Crediton			6G
Hockworthy	A 1577-1978		5,8			Tiverton			8I
Holbeton	B 1619-1974	1620-1850	5,8			Plymptom St Mary			2F
Holcombe Burnell	A 1657-1976		5,8			St Thomas			5H
Holcombe Rogus	A 1540-1979		5,8			Wellington			8I
Hollacombe	A 1638-1979	1608-1871	5,8	1638-1837	1628-1739	Holsworthy			6D
Holne	A 1603-1877		5,8			Totnes			4F
Holsworthy	A 1563-1988	1563-1837	5,8	1563-1837		Holsworthy		1817-1837	7C
Honeychurch	A 1728-1837		5,8	1728-1837		Okehampton			6F
Honiton	A 1562-1967	1562-1837	5,8	1598-1850	1598-1837	Honiton		1697-1837	6J
Horwood	E 1653-1992		5,8	1653-1837		Barnstaple			8E
Huish	E 1595-1981	1595-1812	5,8	1595-1981		Torrington			7E
Huntsham	A 1558-1937	1559-1875	5,8	1559-1900	1597-1837	Tiverton			8I
Huntshaw	E 1746-1992	1607-1812	5,8		1755-1812	Torrington			8E
Huxham	A 1667-1976	1614-1837	5,8			St Thomas			6I(S)
Iddesleigh	E 1541-1903	1540-1840	5,8	1542-1801		Okehampton			7E
Ide	A 1591-1855	1590-1811	5,8		1653-1736	St Thomas			5H
Ideford	A 1598-1993	1598-1837	5,8			Newton Abbot			4H
Ilfracombe	E 1567-1907	1567-1837	5,8			Barnstaple		1729-1837	10E
Ilsington	A 1558-1868	1558-1837	5,8		1539-1837	Newton Abbot			4G
Instow	E 1717-1988		5,8			Barnstable			9E
Inwardleigh	A 1699-1978		5,8	1608-1842		Okehampton			6E
Ipplepen	A 1558-1973		5,8	1612-1837	1612-1837	Newton Abbot	1790-1837		3H
Ivybridge	B 1835-1990		5,8			Plympton St Mary			3F
Jacobstowe	A 1586-1837		5,8			Okehampton			6E
Kelly	A 1653-1837		5,8			Tavistock			5D
Kenn	A 1538-1979	1538-1837	5,8	1538-1837	1538-1669	St Thomas			5H
Kennerleigh	A 1645-1835		5,8			Crediton			7H(L)
Kentisbeare	A 1695-1925		5,8	1695-1865		Tiverton		1806-1837	7J
Kentisbury	E 1675-1990	1675-1841	5,8			Barnstaple			10F
Kenton	A 1694-1990	1694-1837	5,8	1694-1837		St Thomas			5I
Kilmington	A 1577-1994	1577-1837	5,8	1577-1891		Axminster			6K
Kingsbridge	A 1612-1980	1612-1837	5,8			Kingsbridge		1775-1857	1G(AJ)
Kingskerswell	A 1752-1914		5,8	1752-1837	1752-1837	Newton Abbot	1790-1837		3H
Kings Nympton	E 1538-1958		5,8	1538-1860		South Molton			8F
Kingsteignton	A 1670-1987	1606-1837	5,8			Newton Abbot		1808-1835	4H
Kingston	A 1630-1865	1631-1836	5,8			Kingsbridge			2F
Kingswear	A 1601-1960		5,8	1601-1925		Totnes			2H
Knowstone	E 1690-1991	1538-1837	5,8		1693-1712	South Molton			8G

DEVON

parish name	deposited original registers	I.G.I.	local census indexes	copies of registers at Soc. Gen.	Boyd's marriage index	1837-1851 Registration District	Pallot's marriage index	non-conform. records at P.R.O.	map ref.
Lamerton	B 1538-1994		5,8	1538-1854		Tavistock			4D
Landcross	E 1595-1989		5,8			Bideford			8D(D)
Landkey	E 1602-1988	1602-1850	5,8			Barnstaple		1816-1837	9E
Langtree	E 1659-1995	1603-1850	5,8		1659-1837	Torrington			7D
Lapford	A 1567-1986	1567-1850	5,8	1567-1850		Crediton			7G
Lew Trenchard	B 1706-1992		5,8			Tavistock			5E
Lifton	A 1653-1979		5,8			Tavistock			5D
Littleham (Bideford)	E 1539-1983	1538-1836	5,8		1538-1837	Bideford			8D
Littleham (Exmouth)	A 1603-1952		5,8			St Thomas			5I
Littlehempston	A 1539-1956	1539-1875	5,8			Totnes			3G(AD)
Little Torrington	E 1672-1968	1597-1812	5,8		1672-1812	Torrington			7E
Loddiswell	A 1559-1906		5,8			Kingsbridge			2G
Loxbeare	A 1560-1983		5,8			Tiverton			7H
Loxhore	E 1652-1988		5,8			Barnstaple			9F
Luffincott	A 1654-1961	1608-1812	5,8		1610-1753	Holsworthy			6C
Lundy			5,8			Bideford			10C
Luppitt	A 1711-1993		5,8	1711-1884		Honiton			7J
Lustleigh	A 1631-1971	1608-1837	5,8	1608-1837	1608-1837	Newton Abbot	1790-1837		5G
Lydford	B 1716-1995		5,8	1716-1869		Tavistock			5F
Lympstone	A 1654-1985	1654-1875	5,8		1654-1837	St Thomas			5I
Lynton	E 1568-1992	1569-1850	5,8	1568-1837	1591-1837	Barnstaple			10F
Malborough	A 1558-1946	1558-1837	5,8			Kingsbridge			lG
Mamhead	A 1556-1974	1549-1837	5,8	1556-1837		St Thomas			4H
Manaton	A 1653-1991		5,8	1653-1898		Newton Abbot			4G
Mariansleigh	A 1727-1987	1597-1837	5,8		1598-1837	South Molton			8G
Marldon	A 1598-1979	1650-1765	5,8			Totnes			3H
Martinhoe	E 1632-1980	1597-1729	5,8	1500-1812	1597-1812	Barnstaple	1790-1812		10F
Marwood	E 1602-1986	1602-1812	5,8		1602-1812	Barnstaple			9E
Marystowe	B 1651-1993		5,8			Tavistock			5D
Mary Tavy	A 1560-1966	1560-1837	5,8	1562-1809		Tavistock			4E
Meavy	B 1655-1992		5,8			Tavistock			3E
Meeth	A 1653-1986	1597-1812	5,8	1653-1981	1653-1812	Okehampton			7E
Membury	A 1637-1959	1620-1837	5,8	1637-1868	1637-1837	Axminster			6K
Merton	E 1687-1997	1597-1812	5,8	1687-1981	1687-1812	Torrington			7E
Meshaw	E 1580-1989	1580-1807	5,8			South Molton			8G
Milton Abbot	B 1653-1994	1653-1786	5,8		1654-1767	Tavistock			4D
Milton Damerel	A 1678-1958	1606-1837	5,8	1606-1837		Holsworthy			7D
Modbury	A 1553-1875	1553-1837	5,8		1553-1812	Kingsbridge			2F
Molland	E 1538-1987	1538-1837	5,8			South Molton			9G
Monkleigh	E 1548-1901	1548-1850	5,8			Bideford			8D
Monk Okehampton	E 1653-1838	1609-1811	5,8			Okehampton			6F(H)
Monkton	A 1737-1992		5,8			Honiton			6K
Morchard Bishop	A 1660-1940	1660-1850	5,8	1606-1850		Crediton			7G
Morebath	A 1558-1979		5,8			Tiverton			8I
Moreleigh	A 1695-1836		5,8			Totnes			2G(AH)
Moretonhampstead	A 1603-1906	1603-1850	5,8	1603-1864		Newton Abbot		1672-1836	5G
Mortehoe	E 1727-1944		5,8			Barnstaple			10D
Musbury	A 1622-1978	1614-1837	5,8		1614-1837	Haslington			6K
Nether Exe	A 1731-1924	1714-1837	5,8			St Thomas			6H(P)
Newton Ferrers	B 1600-1968	1600-1836	5,8			Plympton St Mary			2E
Newton Poppleford	A 1862-1970	1580-1678	5,8			St Thomas			5J(W)
Newton St Cyres	A 1554-1959	1554-1837	5,8	1555-1887	1554-1837	Crediton			6H
Newton St Petrock	E 1578-1989	1578-1837	5,8	1578-1837	1578-1812	Bideford			7D
Newton Tracey	E 1562-1993		5,8	1562-1837		Barnstaple			8E(B)
Northam	E 1538-1971	1538-1836	5,8		1601-1837	Bideford		1837	9D
Northam (detached)			5,8			Bideford			8D(C)
North Bovey	A 1572-1954	1572-1791	5,8	1572-1840		Newton Abbot			5G
North Huish	E 1656-1981		5,8			Totnes			2G
Northleigh	A 1697-1978	1700-1812	5,8			Honiton			6K(U)
North Lew	A 1690-1973		5,8			Okehampton			6E
North Molton	E 1539-1985	1539-1850	5,8			South Molton			9G
North Petherwin (Cornwall)						Launceston			5C
North Tawton	A 1538-1973		5,8	1538-1868		Okehampton		1812-1836	6F
Nymet Rowland	E 1719-1981	1719-1812	5,8	1719-1812		Crediton			7G(G)
Oakford	A 1568-1978	1568-1812	5,8	1568-1812		Tiverton			8H
Offwell	A 1551-1965	1551-1840	5,8	1943-1964		Honiton			6K
Okehampton	A 1634-1951	1608-1843	5,8			Okehampton		1799-1837	6E
Otterton	A 1559-1995	1558-1700	5,8	1558-1837	1559-1659	St Thomas			5J
Ottery St Mary	A 1601-1973	1601-1837	5,8	1601-1837	1601-1837	Honiton	1790-1837	1746-1837	6J
Paignton	A 1559-1992	1559-1837	5,8			Totnes		1818-1836	3H
Pancrasweek	A 1653-1977	1654-1837	5,8			Holsworthy			7C
Parkham	E 1537-1978	1537-1837	5,8	1537-1837	1538-1837	Bideford	1790-1812		8D
Parracombe	E 1687-1992	1597-1837	5,8	1597-1836	1597-1837	Barnstaple	1790-1837		10F
Payhembury	A 1559-1991		5,8			Honiton			6J
Pennycross	B 1634-1973	1634-1812	5,8	1634-1812		Plympton St Mary			3E
Peter Tavy	A 1674-1977		5,8			Tavistock			4E
Petermarland	E 1696-1997		5,8	1696-1980		Torrington			7E
Petrockstowe	E 1597-1979		5,8	1597-1979		Torrington			7E
Petton	A 1701-1926	1701-1837	5,8			Tiverton			8I
Pilton	E 1566-1965		5,8			Barnstaple			9E
Pinhoe	A 1561-1952		5,8	1687-1901	1687-1837	St Thomas			6I
Plymouth								1662-1837	2E
Charles the Martyr	B 1644-1962		5,8	1644-1841		Plymouth			2E
St Andrew	B 1581-1997	1581-1744	5,8	1581-1843	1581-1674	Plymouth			2E
Plympton St Mary	B 1603-1977	1603-1728	5,8	1627-1849		Plympton St Mary		1836-1837	2E
Plympton St Maurice	B 1616-1971	1616-1812	5,8			Plympton St Mary			2E(AG)
Plymstock	B 1591-1933		5,8	1591-1852	1591-1812	Plympton St Mary			2E
Plymtree	A 1538-1991	1538-1837	5,8	1538-1837		Honiton			6I
Poltimore	A 1718-1976	1614-1837	5,8			St Thomas			6I

parish name	deposited original registers	I.G.I.	local census indexes	copies of registers at Soc. Gen.	Boyd's marriage index	1837-1851 Registration District	Pallot's marriage index	non-conform. records at P.R.O.	map ref.
Poughill	A 1653-1908	1603-1837	5,8			Crediton			7H
Powderham	A 1558-1981	1559-1847	5,8	1558-1837		St Thomas			5I
Princetown	B 1807-1993		5,8			Tavistock			4F
Puddington	A 1555-1848		5,8	1555-1848		Crediton			7H
Pyworthy	A 1653-1992		5,8	1653-1891		Holsworthy			6C
Rackenford	A 1561-1992		5,8			South Molton			8H
Rattery	A 1653-1993	1609-1837	5,8			Totnes			3G
Revelstoke	B 1649-1977		5,8			Plympton St Mary			2E
Rewe	A 1675-1887	1609-1837	5,8	1686-1837	1611-1837	St Thomas			6I(Q)
Rewe (detached)			5,8			St Thomas			6I(O)
Ringmore	A 1719-1860	1719-1814	5,8			Kingsbridge			1F
Roborough	E 1549-1972	1549-1812	5,8		1549-1812	Torrington			8E
Rockbeare	A 1645-1953	1645-1837	5,8			St Thomas			6I
Romansleigh	E 1539-1995		5,8	1539-1836		South Molton			8G
Rose Ash	A 1591-1987	1591-1837	5,8		1591-1836	South Molton			8G
Rousdon	A 1872-1988		5,8			Axminster			5L
St Budeaux	B 1538-1988	1539-1875	5,8	1539-1837		Plympton St Mary			3D
St Giles in the Wood	A 1556-1985	1555-1743	5,8		1556-1747	Torrington			8E
St Giles on the Heath (Cornwall)			5,8			Holsworthy			5D
St Marychurch	A 1641-1972		5,8	1641-1812		Newton Abbot			3H
Salcombe	A 1802-1867		5,8			Honiton			1G
Salcombe Regis	A 1702-1995	1609-1875	5,8		1609-1837	Honiton			5J
Sampford Courtenay	A 1558-1955		5,8			Okehampton			6F
Sampford Peverell	A 1672-1972		5,8			Tiverton		1825-1833	7I
Sampford Spinney	B 1654-1989		5,8			Tavistock			4E
Sandford	A 1603-1991	1603-1837	5,8		1603-1812	Crediton			6G
Satterleigh	E 1574-1989		5,8	1574-1935		South Molton			8F(E)
Seaton and Beer	A 1584-1972	1584-1838	5,8		1584-1837	Axminster		1814-1835	5K
Shaldon with Ringmore	A 1616-1936		5,8			Kingsbridge		1824-1836	4I
Shaugh Prior	B 1565-1993		5,8	1897-1899		Plympton St Mary			3E
Shebbear	E 1576-1994	1576-1837	5,8	1576-1837	1576-1812	Torrington		1818-1837	7D
Sheepstor	B 1691-1979	1610-1837	5,8		1610-1837	Tavistock			3E
Sheepwash	E 1674-1989	1602-1838	5,8	1602-1838		Torrington			7E
Sheldon	A 1715-1991		5,8	1715-1836		Honiton			7J
Sherford	A 1713-1946		5,8	1713-1946		Kingsbridge			1G
Shillingford St George	A 1565-1991	1569-1837	5,8	1565-1837	1569-1835	St Thomas			5H(X)
Shirwell	E 1538-1971	1538-1772	5,8	1540-1599	1601-1754	Barnstaple			9E
Shobrooke	A 1539-1983	1538-1812	5,8		1538-1812	Crediton			6H
Shute	A 1561-1978		5,8	1561-1883		Axminster			6K
Sidbury	A 1813-1927	1609-1824	5,8			Honiton		1771-1836	6J
Sidmouth	A 1586-1979	1586-1801	5,8	1871-1872		Honiton		1753-1836	5J
Silverton	A 1626-1945	1620-1837	5,8			Tiverton			7I
Slapton	A 1634-1971	1606-1853	5,8		1616-1837	Kingsbridge			2G
Sourton	A 1722-1951		5,8			Okehampton			5E
South Brent	A 1677-1961		5,8	1677-1921		Totnes			3F
South Huish	A 1564-1986	1566-1837	5,8			Kingsbridge			1F
Southleigh	A 1754-1995		5,8			Honiton			6K
South Milton	A 1686-1963		5,8	1686-1963		Kingsbridge			1F
South Molton	E 1601-1982	1601-1812	5,8	1601-1704	1601-1786	South Molton		1758-1837	8F
South Molton(detached)			5,8			South Molton			8G(F)
South Pool	A 1664-1982		5,8	1664-1941		Kingsbridge			1G
South Tawton	A 1541-1964	1540-1738	5,8	1541-1866		Okehampton			5F
Sowton	A 1560-1919	1560-1837	5,8			St Thomas			5I
Spreyton	A 1563-1992	1563-1837	5,8		1563-1837	Okehampton			6F
Starcross	A 1828-1992	1828-1843	5,8	1828-1837	1828-1837	St Thomas			5I
Staverton	A 1614-1975	1614-1837	5,8		1614-1812	Totnes			3G
Stockland	A 1640-1976		5,8	1640-1976		Axminster			6K
Stockleigh English	A 1610-1975	1606-1837	5,8			Crediton			7H
Stockleigh Pomeroy	A 1558-1837	1560-1837	5,8			Crediton			6H
Stoke Canon	A 1654-1920	1608-1837	5,8		1616-1837	St Thomas			6H
Stoke Damerel	B 1595-1957	1595-1840	5,8	1596-1840	1595-1782	Stoke Damerel		1787-1837	2D
Stoke Fleming	A 1538-1968	1538-1837	5,8	1538-1863		Kingsbridge			2H
Stoke Gabriel	A 1539-1974	1539-1855	5,8		1539-1837	Totnes			3H
Stoke in Teignhead	A 1538-1964	1538-1837	5,8			Newton Abbot			4I
Stokenham	A 1570-1935	1574-1591	5,8	1574-1883	1578-1582	Kingsbridge		1772-1837	1G
Stoke Rivers	E 1553-1837	1553-1744	5,8	1553-1837	1556-1744	Barnstaple			9F
Stoodleigh	A 1597-1991		5,8			Tiverton			8H
Stowford	B 1707-1992		5,8			Tavistock			5D
Sutcombe	A 1653-1979	1597-1872	5,8			Holsworthy			7C
Swimbridge	E 1562-1957	1562-1850	5,8			Barnstaple			9F
Sydenham Damerel	B 1539-1994		5,8	1539-1870		Tavistock			4D
Talaton	A 1621-1979	1621-1837	5,8		1621-1837	Honiton			6J
Tamerton Foliott	B 1794-1948		5,8	1794-1897		Plympton St Mary			3E
Tavistock St Eustacius	A 1614-1980		5,8	1745-1856		Tavistock		1692-1837	4D
Tawstock	E 1538-1997		5,8	1754-1966		Barnstaple			8E
Tedburn St Mary	A 1558-1883	1557-1837	5,8		1558-1708	St Thomas			6G
Teigngrace	A 1684-1990	1683-1875	5,8			Newton Abbot			4H
Templeton	A 1556-1837		5,8			Tiverton			7H
Tetcott	A 1596-1836	1597-1837	5,8		1599-1836	Holsworthy			6C
Thelbridge	E 1632-1991	1633-1837	5,8			Crediton			7G
Thornbury	A 1652-1992	1600-1837	5,8	1652-1837		Holsworthy			7D
Thorncombe (Dorset)						Axminster			7L
Thorverton	A 1725-1968	1606-1837	5,8		1606-1750	Tiverton			6H
Throwleigh	A 1653-1989	1606-1837	5,8			Okehampton			5F
Thrushelton	B 1654-1992		5,8			Tavistock			5D
Thurlestone	A 1558-1994		5,8	1558-1878		Kingsbridge			1F
Tiverton St Peter	A 1560-1987	1605-1812	5,8			Tiverton		1766-1837	7H
Topsham	A 1600-1965	1600-1875	5,8	1600-1837	1600-1744	St Thomas	1790-1837	1744-1837	5I

DEVON

parish name	deposited original registers	I.G.I.	local census indexes	copies of registers at Soc. Gen.	Boyd's marriage index	1837-1851 Registration District	Pallot's marriage index	non-conform. records at P.R.O.	map ref.
Torbryan	A 1564-1982		5,8	1653-1838		Newton Abbot			3H
Tormoham	A 1637-1979	1637-1743	5,8	1637-1849		Newton Abbot		1813-1837	3H
Totnes	A 1556-1939	1556-1812	5,8	1556-1751	1601-1691	Totnes		1794-1837	3G
Trentishoe	E 1695-1987	1695-1875	5,8	1697-1812	1695-1812	Barnstaple	1790-1812		10F
Trusham	A 1559-1991		5,8			Newton Abbot			5H(AN)
Twitchen	E 1708-1991	1708-1850	5,8			South Molton			9G
Uffculme	A 1538-1990	1538-1837	5,8	1538-1837	1538-1837	Tiverton	1790-1837	1806-1836	7J
Ugborough	B 1538-1990	1538-1837	5,8		1538-1837	Totnes			3F
Uplowman	A 1662-1978	1607-1837	5,8			Axminster			7I
Uplyme	A 1684-1977		5,8	1710-1857		Axminster			6L
Upottery	A 1559-1971	1559-1837	5,8	1559-1862	1576-1837	Honiton			7K
Upton Hellions	A 1678-1928	1611-1837	5,8			Crediton			6H(N)
Upton Pyne	A 1673-1921	1612-1837	5,8			St Thomas			6H
Venn Ottery	A 1587-1946	1591-1837	5,8			Honiton			5J
Virginstow	C 1730-1982		5,8			Holsworthy			5D
Walkhampton	B 1674-1996		5,8			Tavistock			4E
Warkleigh	E 1538-1993		5,8	1538-1932		South Molton			8F
Washfield	A 1554-1979		5,8			Tiverton			8H
Washford Pyne	A 1586-1836		5,8			Crediton			7G
Weare Gifford	E 1583-1959	1583-1812	5,8		1583-1812	Torrington			8E
Welcombe (Chapelry of Hartland)	E 1757-1992		5,8	1757-1836		Bideford			8C
Wembury	B 1611-1989	1611-1837	5,8		1612-1750	Plympton St Mary			2E
Wembworthy	A 1674-1947		5,8	1674-1750		Crediton			7F
Werrington	C 1653-1980		5,8	1608-1812	1608-1812	Launceston	1790-1812		5C
West Alvington	A 1558-1990		5,8	1558-1947	1627-1628	Kingsbridge			1G
West Anstey	E 1653-1988	1608-1812	5,8	1608-1636	1608-1812	South Molton			8H
West Buckland	E 1625-1904		5,8			South Molton			9F
West Down	E 1582-1849	1583-1812	5,8		1583-1812	Barnstaple			10E
Westleigh	E 1560-1988	1560-1697	5,8	1812-1837	1561-1757	Barnstaple			8E
West Ogwell	A 1684-1988		5,8	1684-1843		Newton Abbot			4H(AC)
West Putford	A 1668-1968	1614-1812	5,8		1668-1812	Bideford			7D
West Teignmouth	A 1706-1877	1615-1837	5,8			Newton Abbot		1804-1837	4I
West Woolfardisworthy	E 1723-1993	1607-1812	5,8	1723-1885	1723-1812	Bideford			8C
West Worlington	E 1681-1846	1693-1850	5,8	1681-1850		South Molton			7G
Whimple	A 1653-1984	1653-1836	5,8			St Thomas			6I
Whitchurch	B 1559-1987		5,8	1559-1881		Tavistock			4E
Whitestone	A 1594-1981	1594-1837	5,8			St Thomas			6H
Widecombe in the Moor	A 1560-1992	1560-1837	5,8	1573-1837		Newtn Abbot			4F
Widworthy	A 1540-1993	1544-1840	5,8			Honiton			6K
Willand	A 1670-1989	1607-1837	5,8			Tiverton			7I
Winkleigh	E 1569-1944	1569-1837	5,8			Torrington			7F
Witheridge	E 1586-1965	1585-1837	5,8	1585-1837	1646-1837	South Molton			7G
Withycombe Raleigh	A 1562-1947	1562-1812	5,8	1562-1600	1601-1708	St Thomas		1779-1837	5I
Wolborough	A 1558-1977	1558-1805	5,8			Newton Abbot		1726-1836	4H(Z)
Woodbury	A 1557-1991	1557-1837	5,8			St Thomas		1773-1836	5I
Woodland	A 1560-1835		5,8			Newton Abbot			4G
Woodleigh	A 1635-1938		5,8			Kingsbridge			2G
Yarcombe	A 1539-1958	1539-1837	5,8			Chard			7K
Yarnscombe	E 1653-1983	1606-1812	5,8	1653-1888	1653-1812	Torrington			8E
Yealmpton	B 1600-1943	1600-1850	5,8	1600-1650		Plympton St Mary			2F
Zeal Monachorum	A 1594-1986	1594-1837	5,8			Crediton			6G

Original registers deposited at:
A = Devon Record Office, Castle Street, Exeter EX4 3PQ
B = West Devon Area Record Office, Unit 3, Clare Place, Coxside, Plymouth PL4 0JW
C = Cornwall Record Office, County Hall, Truro, Cornwall TR1 3AY
D = Somerset Record Office, Obridge Road, Taunton TA2 4BU
E = North Devon Record Office, Tuly Street, Barnstaple EX32 7EJ

Study adjacent parishes in counties of Cornwall, Somerset and Dorset

Devon Record Office, Castle Street, Exeter, EX4 3PU
West Devon Area Record Office, Unit 3, Clare Place, Coxside, Plymouth, PL4 0JW
North Devon Record Office, North Devon Library, Tuly Street, Barnstaple, EX32 7EJ

The following useful indexes have been compiled – see Introduction
Census Index 1851 – Devon FHS, PO Box 9, Exeter, EX2 6YP
Census Index 1851 (CD-Rom with Norfolk & Warwickshire) – The Church of the Latter Day Saints, 399 Garretts Green Lane, Sheldon, Birmingham, B33 0UH
Devon Marriage Index – Devon FHS, PO Box 9, Exeter, EX2 6YP complete 1754-1837
The Fursdon Index – Devon and Cornwall Record Society, c/o Westcountry Studies Library, Exeter, EX4 3PQ
Plymouth Post 1837 Marriage Index – Devon FHS, PO Box 9, Exeter, EX2 6YP
Devon Burial Index 1813-1837 – Devon FHS, PO Box 9, Exeter, EX2 6YP

Devon is exceeded in size only by Yorkshire, its greatest length from north to south being nearly 71 miles, and its breadth from east to west about the same. It is watered by ten principal rivers: The Exe, Torridge, Oke, Dart, Plym, Teign, Otter, Axe, Lyn and Tamar. The population in 1841 was 532,959; in 1851, 567,098; in 1861, 584,373; in 1871, 601,374; in 1881, 604,397.

The soils vary considerably and include red loam, shillet of foliated clay, iron-stone, sand and gravel. Wheat, barley, oats, beans, peas, turnips and potatoes were extensively grown and some flax. Sheep and cattle were bred and dairy products were important. Coarse woollen goods were manufactured but mainly for foreign markets, the items being shipped from Exeter, Plymouth and Dartmouth. Axminster was pre-eminent in the making of carpets.

The information in the Index is abbreviated, and may mislead the searcher if reference is not made to the details contained in the several publications listed in the Introduction. It is essential that users of this book check the appropriate works before making further enquiries.

DORSET

parish name	deposited original registers	I.G.I.	local census indexes	copies of registers at Soc. Gen.	Boyd's marriage index	1837-1851 Registration District	Pallot's marriage index	non-conform. records at P.R.O.	map ref.
Abbotsbury	A 1567-1976		5,8,9	1574-1704	1567-1812	Weymouth			3E
Affpuddle	A 1722-1900		5,8,9	1731-1837		Wareham			4I
Allington	A 1570-1998		5,8,9	1570-1812	1570-1812	Bridport	1790-1812		5D(d)
Almer	A 1538-1993	1538-1812	5,8,9	1538-1836		Blandford	1790-1811		5J
Alton Pancras	A 1674-1997		5,8,9	1674-1812	1673-1812	Dorchester	1790-1812		6G
Arne	A 1762-1994		5,8,9	1763-1840		Wareham			4K
Ashmore	A 1651-1994	1653-1820	5,8,9	1651-1900		Shaftesbury	1790-1820		8J
Askerswell	A 1560-1999		5,8,9	1559-1812	1560-1812	Bridport	1790-1812		4E
Athelhampton with Burleston	A 1755-1976		5,8,9	1755-1851		Dorchester			5H(Er)
Batcombe	A 1767-1991			1767-1808		Dorchester			6F(V)
Beaminster	A 1585-1993		5,8,9	1558-1837	1558-1812	Beaminster	1790-1812	1796-1836	6D
Beer Hackett	A 1549-1993	1549-1812	5,8,9			Sherborne	1790-1812		7F(R)
Belchalwell	A 1754-1998		5,8,9	1573-1807		Sturminster			7H(Bs)
Bere Regis	A 1788-1989		5,8,9	1585-1713	1585-1594	Wareham			5I
Bettiscombe	A 1746-1991		5,8,9	1746-1836	1824-1836	Beaminster			5C(C)
Bincombe	A 1658-1992		5,8,9	1658-1837		Weymouth			3G(x)
Bishops Caundle	A 1570-1993	1570-1814	5,8,9	1570-1837		Sherborne	1790-1812		7G(a)
Blandford Forum	A 1731-1993		5,8,9	1731-1883		Blandford		1760-1837	6J(Cx)
Blandford St Mary	A 1581-1953	1708-1718	5,8,9	1581-1812		Blandford			6J
Bloxworth	A 1579-1992		5,8,9	1579-1870		Wareham	1790-1837		5J
Bothenhampton	A 1725-1992		5,8,9	1636-1837	1636-1812	Bridport	1790-1812		4D
Bourton	A 1812-1990		5,8,9			Mere			10H
Bradford Abbas	A 1579-1992		5,8,9	1572-1836		Sherborne			8E
Bradford Peverell	A 1653-1992	1572-1796	5,8,9	1572-1838		Dorchester			4F
Bradpole	A 1695-1996		5,8,9	1695-1837	1695-1812	Bridport	1790-1812		5D(e)
Bridport	A 1600-1991		5,8,9	1600-1680		Bridport		1720-1837	4D
Broadmayne	A 1663-1981		5,8,9	1667-1837		Dorchester			3G(z)
Broadwey	A 1661-1977		5,8,9	1673-1837		Weymouth			3G(v)
Broadwinsor	A 1562-1999		5,8,9	1563-1812	1563-1775	Beaminster	1790-1812		6C
Bryanston	A 1598-1975		5,8,9	1598-1899		Blandford			6I
Buckhorn Weston	A 1677-1992		5,8,9			Wincanton			9H
Buckland Newton	A 1568-1995		5,8,9	1568-1839		Dorchester			6G
Buckland Ripers	A 1695-1982		5,8,9	1695-1840		Weymouth			3F(p)
Burstock	A 1560-1981		5,8,9	1563-1811	1563-1812	Beaminster	1790-1812		6C(A)
Burton Bradstock	A 1614-1990		5,8,9	1614-1837	1614-1812	Bridport	1790-1812		4D
Canford Magna	A 1656-1998		5,8,9			Poole			5L
Cann	A 1563-1969		5,8,9	1582-1827		Shaftesbury			9J
Castleton	A 1715-1992		5,8,9	1716-1836		Sherborne			8F(P)
Cattistock	A 1558-1977	1558-1876	5,8,9	1558-1838	1558-1812	Dorchester	1790-1812		6E
Caundle Marsh	A 1704-1992		5,8,9	1704-1831		Sherborne			7G(Z)
Cerne Abbas	A 1653-1985		5,8,9	1654-1841	1654-1775	Dorchester	1790-1812		6G
Chalbury	A 1629-1993	1629-1697	5,8,9	1629-1700		Wimborne			7L(Db)
Chaldon Herring	A 1621-1993		5,8,9			Wareham			3H
Chardstock	B 1597-1987	1597-1748	5,8,9	1597-1850	1597-1837	Axminster			6A
Charlton Marshall	A 1575-1978		5,8,9	1575-1900		Blandford			6J
Charminster	A 1561-2000		5,8,9	1561-1837	1561-1812	Dorchester	1790-1812		5G
Charmouth	A 1653-1932		5,8,9	1654-1837	1654-1812	Axminster	1790-1812	1780-1837	4B
Chedington	A 1756-1980		5,8,9	1756-1812	1556-1812	Beaminster	1790-1812		6D(D)
Cheselbourne	A 1644-1992		5,8,9	1633-1838	1664-1812	Dorchester			6H
Chetnole	A 1827-1992		5,8,9			Sherborne			7F(T)
Chettle	A 1538-1931		5,8,9	1538-1814		Wimborne			8K
Chickerell	A 1699-1990		5,8,9	1723-1837	1723-1812	Weymouth	1790-1812		3F
Chideock	A 1654-1995		5,8,9	1652-1837	1654-1812	Bridport	1790-1812		4C
Chilcombe	A 1748-1993		5,8,9	1748-1828		Bridport			4E(g)
Child Okeford	A 1653-1973	1731-1878	5,8,9			Sturminster			7I
Chilfrome	A 1678-2000		5,8,9	1678-1834	1709-1812	Dorchester	1790-1812		5E(L)
Church Knowle	A 1547-1961		5,8,9	1560-1837		Wareham			3K
Compton Abbas	A 1640-1985		5,8,9	1538-1837		Dorchester			8I
Compton Valence	A 1655-1992		5,8,9	1655-1812		Dorchester			4F(k)
Coombe Keynes	A 1813-1975		5,8,9			Wareham			3I
Corfe Castle	A 1653-1963		4,5,6,7,8,9	1653-1947		Wareham		1810-1835	3K
Corfe Mullen	A 1651-1994		5,8,9	1651-1840		Wimborne			5K
Corscombe	A 1595-1944		5,8,9	1595-1837	1595-1837	Beaminster	1790-1837		6D
Cranborne	A 1602-1985		5,8,9	1602-1837	1602-1717	Wimborne			7M
Dewlish	A 1616-1987		5,8,9	1610-1812		Dorchester			5H
Dorchester								1750-1837	4G
All Saints	A 1653-1970	1653-1836	5,8,9	1653-1845		Dorchester			4G(r)
Holy Trinity	A 1559-1975		5,8,9	1559-1837	1560-1812	Dorchester	1790-1812		4G(r)
St Peter	A 1653-1979		5,8,9	1653-1812	1653-1812	Dorchester			4G(r)
Durweston	A 1730-1974		5,8,9	1731-1899		Blandford			7I
East Chelborough	A 1682-1950		5,8,9	1690-1812	1690-1812	Beaminster	1790-1812		6E(F)
East Lulworth	A 1561-1991	1731-1875	5,8,9	1561-1846		Wareham			3I
East Orchard	A 1783-1836	1731-1880	5,8,9	1783-1836		Shaftesbury			8I(Bh)
East Stoke	A 1742-1984	1732-1880	5,8,9			Wareham			4J
East Stour (Stower)	A 1584-1998	1731-1879	5,8,9	1584-1812	1584-1812	Shaftesbury			9I
Edmondsham	A 1573-1996		5,8,9	1573-1645		Wimborne			7L
Evershot	A 1694-1973		5,8,9			Beaminster			6E
Farnham	A 1737-1992		5,8,9			Wimborne			8K
Fifehead Magdalen	A 1564-1994		5,8,9	1565-1839		Sturminster			9H(Ac)
Fifehead Neville	A 1573-1999		5,8,9	1573-1807		Sturminster			7H(Bm)
Fleet	A 1663-1995		5,8,9	1663-1835	1663-1753	Weymouth			3F
Folke	A 1538-1993		5,8,9	1538-1837		Sherborne			7G
Fontmell Magna	A 1653-1993		5,8,9	1654-1837		Shaftesbury			8I
Fordington	A 1705-1973		5,8,9	1564-1812	1577-1812	Dorchester	1790-1812		4G
Frampton	A 1627-1993		5,8,9	1627-1812		Dorchester			5F
Frome St Quintin	A 1653-1837		5,8,9			Dorchester			6F(U)
Frome Vauchurch	A 1642-1924		5,8,9	1643-1835	1667-1775	Dorchester	1790-1812		5F(N)
Gillingham	A 1559-1992		5,8,9			Shaftesbury		1796-1824	9H

DORSET

parish name	deposited original registers	I.G.I.	local census indexes	copies of registers at Soc. Gen.	Boyd's marriage index	1837-1851 Registration District	Pallot's marriage index	non-conform. records at P.R.O.	map ref.
Godmanstone	A 1654-1990		5,8,9	1654-1836	1654-1812	Dorchester	1790-1812		5F(c)
Gussage									7K
All Saints	A 1560-1993		5,8,9	1560-1840		Wimborne			7L
St Andrew	A 1785-1992		5,8,9			Wimborne			8K
St Michael	A 1653-1995		5,8,9	1654-1848		Wimborne			7K
Halstock	A 1698-1969		5,8,9	1698-1812	1701-1775	Beaminster	1790-1812		7D
Hammoon	A 1656-1963		5,8,9	1657-1765		Sturminster			7I(Bk)
Hampreston	A 1617-1972	1617-1659	5,8,9	1617-1662		Wimborne			6L
Hamworthy	A 1811-1989		5,8,9			Poole		1833-1837	4K
Hanford	A 1815-1954		5,8,9	1669-1864		Blandford			7I(Bn)
Hawkchurch	B 1664-1978		5,8,9	1663-1846	1669-1812	Axminster	1790-1812		5B
Haydon	A 1711-1976	1708-1812	5,8,9	1711-1812		Sherborne			8G(Y)
Hazelbury Bryan	A 1562-1999		5,8,9	1562-1837		Sturminster			7H
Hermitage	A 1712-1991	1712-1849	5,8,9	1712-1849		Dorchester			7F(W)
Hilton	A 1603-1994		5,8,9			Blandford			6H
Hinton Martel	A 1661-1992		5,8,9	1566-1837		Wimborne			6L
Hinton Parva	A 1621-1987		5,8,9			Wimborne			6L(Dc)
Hinton St Mary	A 1581-1983	1813-1880	5,8,9			Sturminster			8H(Af)
Holme East (ex.par.)			5,8,9			Wareham			3J
Holnest	A 1589-1996	1590-1877	5,8,9	1589-1835		Sherborne	1790-1812		7F
Holwell	A 1653-1992	1731-1880	5,8,9	1655-1837		Sherborne			7G
Hooke	A 1813-1999	1732-1880	5,8,9	1734-1837	1771-1812	Beaminster	1790-1812		5E
Horton with Woodlands	A 1563-1993	1734-1880	5,8,9	1563-1870		Wimborne			7L
Ibberton	A 1761-1988	1731-1880	5,8,9	1801-1837		Sturminster			7H
Iwerne Courtney	A 1562-1988	1731-1876	5,8,9	1562-1900	1563-1708	Blandford			7I
Iwerne Minster	A 1742-1994	1731-1880	5,8,9			Shaftesbury			8J
Iwerne Steepleton	A 1755-1987	1760-1880	5,8,9	1755-1945		Blandford			7J(Bp)
Kimmeridge	A 1684-1977	1802-1880	5,8,9	1702-1837		Wareham			2J
Kington Magna	A 1670-1985	1731-1877	5,8,9	1671-1837		Wincanton			9H
Kinson	A 1680-1992		5,8,9			Poole			5L
Langton Herring	A 1681-1916	1731-1880	5,8,9	1681-1835	1681-1812	Weymouth	1790-1812		3F
Langton Long Blandford	A 1591-1995	1739-1880	5,8,9	1591-1728		Blandford			6J(Cy)
Langton Matravers	A 1670-1985	1670-1880	5,8,9	1670-1837		Wareham		1833-1837	2L
Leweston (ex.par.)			5,8,9			Sherborne			8F(Q)
Lillington	A 1712-1975	1581-1880	5,8,9	1712-1843		Sherborne			7F
Little Bredy	A 1717-1976		5,8,9	1717-1836		Dorchester			4F
Litton Cheney	A 1614-1999	1726-1880	5,8,9	1614-1812	1614-1812	Bridport	1790-1812		4E
Loders	A 1636-1993	1752-1880	5,8,9	1636-1837	1636-1812	Bridport	1790-1812		5D
Longbredy	A 1628-1999		5,8,9	1680-1837		Dorchester			4E
Longburton	A 1589-1999	1580-1877	5,8,9	1580-1812		Sherborne	1790-1812		7F
Long Crichel	A 1663-1970		5,8,9	1663-1837		Wimborne			7K
Lydlinch	A 1559-1966	1560-1875	5,8,9	1559-1812		Sturminster	1790-1812		7H
Lyme Regis	A 1543-1996	1579-1880	5,8,9	1654-1812	1651-1775	Axminster	1790-1812	1775-1857	4B
Lytchett Matravers	A 1656-1991	1731-1880	5,8,9	1656-1808		Poole			5K
Lytchett Minster	A 1554-1994	1814-1880	5,8,9			Poole			4K
Maiden Newton	A 1553-1975	1731-1880	5,8,9	1553-1812	1555-1812	Dorchester	1790-1812	1833-1835	5F
Manston	A 1620-1992	1732-1880	5,8,9	1620-1837		Sturminster			8I
Mapperton	A 1669-1977	1585-1880	5,8,9	1669-1837	1669-1812	Beaminster	1790-1812		5D(J)
Mappowder	A 1650-1999	1731-1880	5,8,9			Dorchester			6H
Margaret Marsh	A 1682-1834	1731-1880	5,8,9	1694-1837		Shaftesbury			8I(Ae)
Marnhull	A 1559-1992	1731-1880	5,8,9	1560-1742		Sturminster			8H
Marshwood	A 1614-1992		5,8,9	1614-1728	1614-1675	Beaminster			5C
Melbury Abbas	A 1716-1968	1732-1880	5,8,9	1717-1837		Shaftesbury			8J
Melbury Bubb	A 1679-1836	1731-1880	5,8,9			Dorchester			7D
Melbury Osmond	A 1580-1970	1731-1880	5,8,9			Beaminster			7E(G)
Melbury Sampford	A 1606-1978		5,8,9			Beaminster			6E(H)
Melcombe Horsey	A 1690-1992	1731-1880	5,8,9	1690-1838		Dorchester			6H
Melcombe Regis	A 1560-1962	1731-1880	5,8,9			Weymouth			3G
Milborne St Andrew	A 1570-1993	1731-1880	5,8,9	1570-1838		Blandford			5I(Eh)
Milborne Stileham	A 1687-1742		5,8,9	1687-1742		Blandford			5I(Ek)
Milton Abbas	A 1651-1994	1731-1880	5,8,9	1569-1812	1559-1812	Blandford	1790-1812		6I
Minterne Magna	A 1635-1992	1731-1880	5,8,9	1636-1837		Dorchester			6F
Moor Crichel	A 1664-1958		5,8,9	1664-1836		Wimborne			7K
Morden	A 1575-1989	1731-1880	5,8,9	1575-1691		Wareham			5J
Moreton	A 1565-1994	1731-1880	5,8,9	1565-1838		Wareham			4I
Mosterton	A 1651-1977	1733-1880	5,8,9	1539-1837		Beaminster	1790-1812		6C
Motcombe	A 1675-1951	1749-1879	5,8,9	1676-1837		Shaftesbury			9I
Netherbury	A 1592-1989	1585-1880	5,8,9	1592-1851	1592-1837	Beaminster	1790-1839		5D
Nether Cerne	A 1693-1972		5,8,9	1716-1830	1716-1750	Dorchester			5G(b)
Nether Compton	A 1538-1994		5,8,9	1541-1837		Sherborne			8F
North Poorton	A 1694-1995	1749-1880	5,8,9	1698-1837	1608-1812	Beaminster	1790-1812		5D(K)
North Wootton	A 1538-1971	1539-1880	5,8,9	1539-1837		Sherborne			8F(X)
Oborne	A 1567-1993	1579-1876	5,8,9	1568-1840		Sherborne			8F
Okeford Fitzpaine	A 1592-1983	1731-1880	5,8,9			Sturminster			7H
Osmington	A 1678-1991	1731-1880	5,8,9			Weymouth			3H
Over Compton	A 1726-1995		5,8,9	1723-1837		Sherborne			8E
Owermoigne	A 1569-1993	1569-1880	5,8,9	1569-1837		Weymouth			3H
Pentridge	A 1713-1987	1731-1880	5,8,9	1713-1835		Wimborne			8L
Piddlehinton	A 1539-1993	1539-1880	5,8,9	1539-1837	1539-1768	Dorchester			5G
Piddletrenthide	A 1646-1997	1731-1880	5,8,9			Dorchester			5G
Pilsdon	A 1754-1994	1733-1880	5,8,9	1754-1809	1754-1809	Beaminster	1790-1809		5C(B)
Pimperne	A 1559-1976	1732-1880	5,8,9	1559-1900		Blandford			7J
Poole St James	A 1538-1997	1802-1880	5,8,9			Poole		1741-1840	4L(Fa)
Portesham	A 1568-1983	1731-1880	5,8,9	1568-1837	1568-1812	Weymouth			3F
Portland	A 1564-1991	1731-1880	5,8,9	1591-1803		Weymouth		1796-1837	1G
Powerstock	A 1568-1995	1568-1880	5,8,9	1568-1812	1568-1812	Beaminster			5D
Poxwell	A 1674-1968	1731-1880	5,8,9	1675-1837		Weymouth			3H(Fb)
Preston	A 1693-1994	1592-1880	5,8,9	1693-1837	1693-1812	Weymouth	1790-1837		3G
Puddletown (Piddletown)	A 1538-1979	1738-1880	5,8,9	1538-1837	1538-1812	Dorchester	1790-1812		5H

139

DORSET

parish name	deposited original registers	I.G.I.	local census indexes	copies of registers at Soc. Gen.	Boyd's marriage index	1837-1851 Registration District	Pallot's marriage index	non-conform. records at P.R.O.	map ref.
Pulham	A 1734-1993	1731-1880	5,8,9	1734-1902		Sherborne			7G
Puncknowle	A 1630-1981	1731-1880	5,8,9	1632-1836	1632-1753	Bridport			4E
Purse Caundle	A 1730-1992		5,8,9	1731-1841		Sherborne			8G
Radipole	A 1797-1994		5,8,9			Weymouth			3G
Rampisham	A 1574-1932	1731-1880	5,8,9	1574-1841	1574-1741	Beaminster			6E
Ryme Intrinseca	A 1630-1992	1631-1880	5,8,9	1631-1836	1631-1836	Sherborne			7E
Shaftesbury								1796-1839	9J
Holy Trinity	A 1695-1913	1731-1880	5,8,9	1560-1842		Shaftesbury			9J
St James	A 1559-1971	1731-1881	5,8,9			Shaftesbury			9I
St Peter	A 1623-1984	1731-1880	5,8,9			Shaftesbury			9J
Shapwick	A 1654-1948	1731-1880	5,8,9	1654-1732		Wimborne			6K
Sherborne	A 1538-1983	1585-1880	5,8,9	1538-1812		Sherborne		1785-1837	8F
Shillingstone	A 1653-1973	1653-1880	5,8,9	1654-1812		Sturminster			7I
Shipton Gorge	A 1813-1967	1745-1879	5,8,9	1614-1837		Bridport	1790-1812		4D
Silton	A 1653-1837	1731-1876	5,8,9	1653-1837		Mere			10H
Sixpenny Handley	A 1754-1976		5,8,9	1754-1837		Wimborne			8K
South Perrott	A 1538-1981	1731-1880	5,8,9	1539-1837	1538-1812	Beaminster	1790-1812		7C
Spetisbury	A 1705-1993	1731-1844	5,8,9	1705-1899		Blandford			6J
Stalbridge	A 1690-1996		5,8,9	1691-1837	1690-1812	Sturminster	1790-1812	1810-1837	8G
Steeple	A 1548-1836		5,8,9	1546-1836		Wareham			3J
Stinsford	A 1577-1988		5,8,9	1577-1812		Dorchester			4G
Stock Gaylard	A 1567-1838		5,8,9	1567-1838		Sturminster			7H
Stockwood	A 1813-1937	1618-1880	5,8,9	1586-1851		Sherborne			7E(S)
Stoke Abbot	A 1559-1983	1560-1880	5,8,9	1560-1837	1562-1812	Beaminster	1780-1837		5C
Stoke Wake	A 1546-1982	1732-1880	5,8,9	1546-1838		Sturminster			6H(Bq)
Stourpaine	A 1631-1978	1620-1880	5,8,9	1631-1799		Blandford			7J
Stour Provost	A 1701-1993	1731-1880	5,8,9			Shaftesbury			9I
Stourton Caundle	A 1670-1993		5,8,9	1670-1836	1670-1763	Sturminster			8G
Stratton	A 1561-1993	1561-1812	5,8,9	1561-1812	1562-1837	Dorchester			5F
Studland	A 1581-1971		5,8,9	1637-1837		Wareham			3L
Sturminster Marshall	A 1562-1972	1561-1812	5,8,9	1563-1812		Wimborne	1790-1812		6K
Sturminster Newton	A 1681-1958		5,8,9	1681-1837		Sturminster			7H
Sutton Waldron	A 1678-1994		5,8,9	1678-1837		Shaftesbury			8I(Bj)
Swanage	A 1563-1922	1563-1812	4,5,6,7,8,9	1563-1841		Wareham	1790-1812	1794-1836	2L
Swyre	A 1587-1998		5,8,9	1587-1837	1588-1837	Bridport	1790-1837		4D
Sydling St Nicholas	A 1565-2000		5,8,9	1565-1812		Dorchester		1816-1835	6F
Symondsbury	A 1558-1998		5,8,9	1558-1812	1558-1812	Bridport	1790-1812		5C
Tarrant Crawford	A 1597-1940		5,8,9	1597-1940		Blandford			6J(Dg)
Tarrant Gunville	A 1719-1996		5,8,9	1719-1919		Blandford			8J
Tarrant Hinton	A 1545-1992	1545-1812	5,8,9	1545-1812		Blandford	1790-1812		7K
Tarrant Keynston	A 1737-1994		5,8,9	1737-1939		Blandford			6J(Df)
Tarrant Monkton with Tarrant Launceston	A 1564-1992		5,8,9			Blandford			7K
Tarrant Rawston	A 1760-1957		5,8,9	1760-1931		Blandford			6J(Da)
Tarrant Rushton	A 1696-1993		5,8,9	1696-1919		Blandord			6K
Thorncombe	A 1551-1989		5,8,9	1551-1850	1552-1812	Axminster	1790-1812		6B
Thornford	A 1676-1998		5,8,9	1677-1837		Sherborne			7F
Tincleton	A 1576-1998		5,8,9	1576-1837		Dorchester			4H(Es)
Todber	A 1754-1994		5,8,9	1754-1836		Shaftesbury			8I(Ad)
Toller Fratrum	A 1558-1949		5,8,9	1616-1836	1616-1837	Dorchester			5E(M)
Toller Porcorum	A 1758-1972	1615-1639	5,8,9	1615-1680	1615-1775	Dorchester	1790-1812		5E
Tolpuddle	A 1718-1996		5,8,9	1719-1837		Dorchester			5I
Turners Puddle	A 1640-1969	1579-1880	5,8,9	1745-1837		Wareham			4I(Et)
Turnworth	A 1577-1972	1731-1880	5,8,9	1577-1684		Blandford			7I(Cs)
Tyneham	A 1694-1943	1731-1880	5,8,9	1694-1836		Wareham			3J
Upcerne	A 1650-1968		5,8,9	1682-1837	1676-1776	Dorchester	1790-1811		6F
Upwey	A 1654-1973	1731-1880	5,8,9	1654-1837		Weymouth			3G
Walditch	A 1738-1988	1733-1880	5,8,9	1738-1837	1726-1812	Bridport	1790-1812		4D(f)
Wambrook	C 1653-1970	1579-1880	5,8,9	1655-1837	1655-1837	Chard			7A
Wareham								1740-1857	4K
Holy Trinity	A 1754-1980	1731-1824	4,5,6,7,8,9	1754-1781		Wareham			3K(Fe)
Lady St Mary and			4,5,6,7,8,9			Wareham			4J(Fd)
St Martin		1731-1824	4,5,6,7,8,9			Wareham			4K
Warmwell	A 1641-1992	1731-1880	5,8,9	1641-1836		Dorchester			3H
Watercombe (ex.par.)			5,8,9			Weymouth			4H(Fc)
West Chelborough	A 1662-1996		5,8,9	1673-1835	1676-1812	Beaminster	1790-1812		6E(E)
West Compton	A 1538-1978		5,8,9	1538-1812	1539-1812	Dorchester			5E(j)
West Knighton	A 1693-1993		5,8,9	1693-1837		Dorchester			4H
West Lulworth	A 1745-1994	1731-1880	5,8,9			Wareham		1755-1840	3I
West Orchard	A 1754-1839		5,8,9	1754-1839		Shaftesbury			8I(Ag)
West Parley	A 1715-1984	1731-1877	5,8,9			Wimborne			6M
West Stafford	A 1558-1958		5,8,9	1558-1837		Dorchester			4H(Aa)
West Stour (Stower)	A 1678-1990	1732-1879	5,8,9			Shaftesbury			9H(Ab)
West Woodyates (ex.par.)			5,8,9			Wimborne			8L
Weymouth			5,8,9			Weymouth		1734-1837	2G
Whitcombe	A 1762-1968	1732-1880	5,8,9			Dorchester			4G(y)
Whitechurch Canonicorum	A 1558-1985	1730-1880	5,8,9	1558-1812	1538-1812	Bridport	1790-1812		5B
Wimborne All Saints	A 1687-1731*		5,8,9	1600-1727	1687-1837	Wimborne			7L
Wimborne Minster	A 1635-1998	1721-1862	5,8,9	1635-1812	1721-1813	Wimborne		1768-1837	6L
Wimborne St Giles	A 1594-1990		5,8,9	1594-1837		Wimborne			7L
Winfrith Newburgh	A 1585-1992		5,8,9	1585-1837		Wareham			3I
Winterbourne Abbas	A 1754-1992		5,8,9	1754-1837		Dorchester			4F(m)
Winterbourne Anderson	A 1757-1974		5,8,9	1757-1837		Dorchester			5J(En)
Winterbourne Came	A 1696-1995		5,8,9	1696-1837		Dorchester			4G(u)
Winterbourne Clenston	A 1684-1991		5,8,9	1684-1835		Dorchester			6I(Dd)
Winterbourne Houghton	A 1558-1996		5,8,9			Dorchester		6I(Cu)	
Winterbourne Kingston	A 1588-1975		5,8,9	1597-1837		Dorchester			5J
Winterbourne Monkton	A 1754-1998	1731-1880	5,8,9	1756-1836		Dorchester			4G(s)

DORSET

parish name	deposited original registers	I.G.I.	local census indexes	copies of registers at Soc. Gen.	Boyd's marriage index	1837-1851 Registration District	Pallot's marriage index	non-conform. records at P.R.O.	map ref.
Winterbourne St Martin	A 1653-1992	1732-1880	5,8,9	1655-1837		Dorchester			4F
Winterbourne Steepleton	A 1559-1992	1731-1846	5,8,9	1558-1837		Dorchester			4F(n)
Winterbourne Stickland	A 1615-1969	1731-1880	5,8,9	1615-1837	1616-1750	Dorchester			6I(Cw)
Winterbourne Tomson	A 1723-1970		5,8,9	1751-1893		Dorchester	1793-1802		5J(Ep)
Winterbourne Whitechurch	A 1599-1993		5,8,9	1599-1837		Dorchester			6I(De)
Winterbourne Zelstone	A 1548-1993	1731-1880	5,8,9	1548-1740		Dorchester			5J(Eu)
Witchampton	A 1656-1988	1733-1880	5,8,9	1838-1992		Wimborne			6K
Woodsford	A 1678-1993	1678-1880	5,8,9	1678-1837		Dorchester			4H
Wool	A 1583-1975	1733-1880	5,8,9	1583-1847		Wareham			4I
Woolland	A 1726-1996	1731-1880	5,8,9	1731-1837		Dorchester			6H(Cr)
Wootton Fitzpaine	A 1678-1983	1731-1880	5,8,9	1677-1812	1676-1812	Bridport	1790-1812		5B
Wootton Glanville	A 1546-1997	1731-1880	5,8,9	1546-1731		Dorchester			7G
Worth Matravers	A 1584-1978	1697-1880	5,8,9	1584-1696		Wareham			2K
Wraxall	A 1648-1840	1648-1880	5,8,9	1648-1840	1710-1775	Beaminster	1790-1812		5E
Wyke Regis	A 1676-1990	1731-1880	5,8,9	1676-1812	1676-1812	Weymouth	1790-1812		2G
Wynford Eagle	A 1754-1892		5,8,9	1560-1836	1560-1715	Dorchester			5E
Yetminster	A 1677-1992	1579-1880	5,8,9	1579-1621	1677-1837	Sherborne			7F

* joined with Wimborne St Giles in 1732

Original registers deposited at:
A = Dorset Record Office, Bridport Road, Dorchester, Dorset DT1 1RP
B = Devon Record Office, Castle Street, Exeter EX4 3PQ
C = Somerset Record Office, Obridge Road, Taunton TA2 4BU

Study adjacent parishes in counties of Somerset, Wiltshire, Hampshire and Devon

Dorset Record Office, Bridport Road, Dorchester, DT1 1RP

The following useful indexes have been compiled – see Introduction
Census Indexes 1841, 1851, 1861, 1871 & 1891 – Somerset and Dorset FHS, PO Box 4502, Sherborne, Dorset DT9 6YL
Census Index 1891- Dorset FHS, Mrs R Clipson, 7 Coppercourt Leaze, Wimborne, Dorset, BH2 1QX
Corfe Castle Census 1790-91 – Dorset FHS, Mrs S Smith, 3 Fernside Road, Bournemouth, Dorset, BH9 2LA
Dorset Marriage Index – Somerset and Dorset FHS, Mr & Mrs Andrew, 69 Sopwith Crescent, Merley, Wimborne, Dorset, BH21 1SW complete to 1837
Dorset Wills Database – Brian Churchill, 47 All Saints Road, Wyke Regis, Weymouth, Dorset DT4 9EZ
Dorset Burial Index – Somerset & Dorset FHS, 18 Bincleaves Road, Weymouth, Dorset, DT4 8RL
Monumental Inscriptions Index – Somerset & Dorset FHS, Mrs Olive Damon, 37 Beaucroft Lane, Colehill, Wimborne, Dorset BH21 2PD

Dorset is of irregular shape; its extent from north to south is about 35 miles and its breadth from east to west about 55 miles. It is watered by five principal rivers: the Frome, Stour, Piddle, Ivel and Hooke or Owke. The population in 1841 was 175,043; in 1851, 184,207; in 1861, 188,789; in 1871, 195,537; in 1881, 191,028.

The soils are rich loam, sandy loam intermixed with flint, stone-brack or brash and chalk. The principal sheep district was around Dorchester and other products were corn, cattle, wool, timber, flax and hemp. The quarries of Purbeck were well known for their stone. Chief manufactures were from flax and hemp, chiefly carried on in the neighbourhood of Bridport and Beaminster. At Shaftesbury were made shirt buttons and coarse woollen cloths; at Blandford, shirt buttons; and at Stalbridge and Sherborne silk was spun. Worsted stockings were knitted at Wimborne and sail-cloth, sacking, cables, ropes, large nets and cod-lines for the Newfoundland fisheries were made at Abbotsbury.

The information in the Index is abbreviated, and may mislead the searcher if reference is not made to the details contained in the several publications listed in the Introduction. It is essential that users of this book check the appropriate works before making further enquiries.

DURHAM

parish name	deposited original registers	I.G.I.	local census indexes	copies of registers at Soc. Gen.	Boyd's marriage index	1837-1851 Registration District	Pallot's marriage index	non-conform. records at P.R.O.	map ref.
Auckland St Andrew	A 1558-1999	1558-1877	5,8,9	1558-1907	1558-1653	Auckland			4H
Auckland St Helen	A 1593-1931	1653-1812	5,8	1593-1837	1653-1773	Auckland			4G
Aycliffe	A 1560-1991	1560-1901	5,8	1560-1885	1560-1812	Darlington			3I
Barnard Castle	A 1609-1954	1609-1812	5,8,9	1601-1839	1601-1812	Teesdale		1803-1837	2F
Billingham	A 1569-1990	1569-1877	5,8,9	1754-1946		Stockton			3L
Bishop Auckland (St Anne)			5,8,9			Auckland			4H
Bishop Middleham	A 1559-1995	1559-1812	5,8,9	1559-1837	1559-1812	Stockton	1790-1812		5J
Bishopton	A 1649-1970		5,8,9	1653-1965		Stockton			3J
Bishopwearmouth	A 1567-1971	1567-1877	5,8	1568-1837	1568-1812	Sunderland		1797-1854	8K
Boldon	A 1571-1970	1572-1812	5,8	1573-1914	1573-1812	South Shields			9J
Brancepeth	A 1599-1992	1599-1812	8,9	1599-1945	1599-1812	Durham			6H
Carlton			8			Stockton			3K
Castle Eden	A 1694-1991	1661-1871	5,8	1661-1871	1698-1800	Easington	1790-1794		6K
Chester-le-Street	A 1582-1988	1582-1827	5,8,9	1582-1886	1582-1826	Chester-le-Street		1813-1837	8I
Cockfield	A 1578-1966	1578-1812	5,8,9	1579-1840	1579-1812	Teesdale			3G
Coniscliffe	A 1590-1988	1590-1812	5,8,9	1590-1837	1590-1812	Darlington	1790-1812		2H
Croxdale	A 1696-1995		8	1696-1869		Durham			6I
Dalton-le-Dale	A 1653-1966	1652-1901	5,8	1651-1839	1651-1812	Easington	1790-1812		7K
Darlington	A 1590-1992		5,8,9	1590-1953		Darlington		1783-1840	2I
Denton	A 1576-1995	1579-1812	5,8,9	1579-1839	1579-1812	Darlington			3H
Dinsdale	A 1556-1996	1556-1812	5,8,9	1556-1837	1556-1812	Darlington	1790-1812		1J
Durham								1739-1840	6I
Cathedral	B 1609-1896	1609-1896	5,8	1609-1896	1609-1826	Durham			6I(A)
St Giles	A 1584-1991	1584-1814	5,8	1584-1926	1584-1814	Durham			7J
St Margaret	A 1558-1983	1558-1812	5,8	1558-1900	1558-1812	Durham	1790-1812		6I(A)
St Mary le Bow	A 1571-1979	1572-1814	5,8	1837-1968	1573-1814	Durham	1790-1812		6I(A)
St Mary the Less	A 1558-1993	1559-1812	5,8	1559-1964	1559-1812	Durham	1790-1812		6I(A)
St Nicholas	A 1540-1963	1540-1812	5,8	1550-1923	1550-1812	Durham	1790-1812		6I(A)
St Oswald	A 1538-1979	1538-1751	5,8	1538-1912	1538-1751	Durham			6I
Easington	A 1570-1988	1570-1831	5,8,9	1570-1839	1570-1812	Easington			6K
Ebchester	A 1619-1973	1610-1812	8	1619-1839	1619-1812	Durham	1790-1812		8G
Edmondbyers	A 1717-1987	1717-1901	5,8	1746-1840		Weardale			8E
Egglescliffe	A 1539-1969	1539-1812	5,8	1540-1837	1540-1812	Stockton			2K
Egglestone	A 1795-1920	1795-1901	5,8,9	1795-1840		Teesdale			4E
Elton	A 1573-2000	1573-1812	5,8,9	1534-1837	1574-1812	Auckland			2K
Elwick	A 1592-1987		5,8,9	1592-1900		Stockton			4L
Embleton	A 1651-1760	1650-1760	5,8,9	1650-1760	1653-1753	Stockton			4K
Escomb	A 1543-1993	1543-1877	5,8,9	1543-1837	1543-1812	Auckland			5H
Esh	A 1567-1995	1567-1877	8	1567-1877	1570-1812	Durham	1790-1812	1795-1839	7H
Gainford	A 1560-1980	1560-1812	5,8,9	1560-1839	1569-1812	Teesdale		1806-1837	2H
Garmondsway Moor (ex.par.)			5,8,9			Stockton			5J
Gateshead	A 1559-1979	1559-1877	5,8,9	1559-1837	1559-1662	Gateshead		1783-1837	9I
Gateshead Fell	A 1825-1986		5,8,9	1825-1917		Gateshead			9I
Greatham	A 1564-1982	1564-1812	5,8,9	1564-1837	1564-1812	Stockton			4L
Great Lumley	A 1858-1987		5,8	1882-1927		Chester-le-Street			7I
Grindon	A 1565-1938	1565-1812	5,8,9	1565-1837	1565-1758	Stockton			4K
Hamsterley	A 1580-1992	1580-1812	5,8,9	1580-1848	1580-1812	Auckland		1768-1837	4F
Hart	A 1577-1979		5,8,9	1577-1968		Stockton			5L
Hartlepool	A 1566-1887		5,8,9	1566-1839		Stockton		1834-1840	5M
Haughton-le-Skerne	A 1569-1993	1569-1877	5,8,9			Darlington			2J
Heatherycleugh	A 1824-1907		8	1828-1837		Chester-le-Street			7B
Heighington	A 1559-1994		5,8,9	1559-1894	1571-1812	Darlington			3I
Heworth	A 1696-1993	1696-1880	5,8	1696-1839	1696-1812	Gateshead			9I
Houghton-le-Spring	A 1563-1996	1563-1812	5,8,9	1563-1837	1563-1812	Houghton-le-Spring		1831-1840	7J
Hunstanworth	D 1659-1995	1672-1876	5,8	1659-1851		Weardale			7D
Hurworth	A 1559-1998	1559-1812	5,8,9	1559-1837	1559-1851	Darlington			1J
Jarrow	A 1571-1900	1572-1812	5,8	1568-1837	1572-1812	South Shields		1834-1837	10J
Kelloe	A 1693-1991	1754-1900	5,8,9	1693-1837	1693-1837	Easington			6J
Lamesley	A 1603-1987		5,8	1603-1837		Chester-le-Street			9I
Lanchester	A 1560-1987	1560-1848	8	1560-1839	1560-1837	Durham		1778-1839	7G
Long Newton	A 1564-1981	1564-1902	5,8,9	1564-1952	1564-1812	Stockton			2K
Medomsley	A 1608-1987	1612-1875	8	1608-1839	1608-1730	Durham			8G
Merrington	A 1579-1968	1579-1812	5,8,9	1787-1944	1579-1812	Auckland			5I
Middleton in Teesdale	A 1578-1952	1578-1752	5,8,9	1621-1840	1621-1752	Teesdale		1829-1836	4D
Middleton St George	A 1616-1972	1616-1901	5,8,9	1616-1972	1616-1812	Darlington	1790-1812		2J
Monk Hesledon	A 1578-1948	1578-1812	5,8	1578-1839	1578-1812	Easington		1808-1839	5L
Monkwearmouth	A 1683-1987	1683-1853	6,8	1790-1901		Sunderland		1778-1856	9K
Muggleswick	AC 1780-1975	1784-1902	8	1755-1991	1776-1812	Durham	1790-1812	1786-1836	7E
Norton	A 1574-1989	1574-1877	5,8			Stockton			3L
Penshaw	A 1754-1994		8	1754-1851		Houghton-le-Spring			8J
Pittington	A 1574-1977	1574-1827	8	1575-1837	1575-1812	Durham			6J
Redmarshall	A 1559-1988	1560-1812	5,8,9	1560-1837	1560-1812	Stockton			3K
Ryton	A 1581-1986	1581-1812	5,8	1581-1839	1581-1812	Gateshead	1790-1812	1775-1853	9G
Sadberge	A 1662-1992		5,8,9	1662-1967		Darlington			2J
Satley	A 1797-1960		8	1560-1839	1797-1812	Durham			7G
Seaham	A 1646-1999	1646-1812	8	1646-1839	1651-1812	Easington	1790-1812		7K
Sedgefield	A 1580-1991	1580-1877	5,8,9	1581-1837	1581-1812	Stockton			4K
Sherburn Hospital (ex.par.)	A 1678-1994	1692-1812	8	1678-1812	1695-1763	Durham			6J
Sockburn	A 1580-1993	1580-1812	5,8,9	1580-1837	1580-1812	Darlington			1J
South Shields	A 1653-1953	1653-1812	5,8,9	1653-1901	1653-1812	South Shields		1785-1857	10K
Staindrop	A 1635-1989	1635-1812	5,8,9	1635-1840	1635-1812	Teesdale		1806-1837	3G
Stainton le Street	A 1561-1975	1561-1812	5,8,9		1561-1812	Stockton			4J
Stanhope	A 1607-1974	1609-1812	5,8	1607-1974	1613-1812	Weardale	1790-1812	1813-1837	6E
Stillington	A 1872-1979		8,9			Stockton			3J
Stockton-on-Tees	A 1621-1992		5,8,9	1637-1958		Stockton		1688-1858	2L
Stranton	A 1580-1995		5,8,9	1580-1901		Stockton			4M
Sunderland	A 1719-1988	1719-1839	8	1719-1908	1719-1812	Sunderland		1717-1837	9K

DURHAM

parish name	deposited original registers	I.G.I.	local census indexes	copies of registers at Soc. Gen.	Boyd's marriage index	1837-1851 Registration District	Pallot's marriage index	non-conform. records at P.R.O.	map ref.
Tanfield	A 1719-1982	1719-1877	8	1719-1839	1720-1812	Durham			8H
Trimdon	A 1720-1987	1720-1812	5,8,9	1721-1837	1721-1812	Durham			5K
Washington	A 1604-1998	1601-1812	5,8	1603-1900	1603-1812	Chester-le-Street			9J
Weardale St John	A 1788-1994		8	1828-1837		Weardale		1813-1828	6C
West Rainton	A 1825-1987		8	1825-1839		Houghton-le-Spring			7J
Whickham	A 1576-1995	1576-1876	5,8	1576-1839	1579-1837	Gateshead	1790-1812	1733-1836	9H
Whitburn	A 1579-1936	1579-1812	5,8	1579-1904	1579-1812	South Shields	1790-1812		10K
Whitwell House (ex.par.)			8			Durham			6J
Whitworth	A 1569-1958		5,8,9	1569-1958		Auckland			5I
Whorlton	A 1626-1982	1626-1812	5,8,9	1626-1982	1713-1812	Teesdale	1790-1812		2G
Winston	A 1572-1988	1572-1875	5,8,9	1572-1840	1574-1812	Teesdale	1790-1812		2G
Witton Gilbert	A 1570-1984	1568-1812	5,8	1568-1837	1568-1812	Chester-le-Street			7I
Witton le Wear	A 1558-1980	1558-1757	5,8,9	1558-1837	1558-1757	Auckland			5G
Wolsingham	A 1631-1965	1631-1812	5,8	1655-1837	1655-1812	Weardale		1813-1828	6F
Wolsingham Park Moor (ex.par.)			5,8			Weardale			6F
Wolviston	A 1759-1996		5,8,9	1759-1965		Stockton			4L

Original registers deposited at:
A = Durham Record Office, County Hall, Durham DH1 5UL
B = Durham University Library Archives, 5 The College, Durham DH1 3EQ
C = Durham University Library Archives, Palace Green, Durham, DR1 3RN
D = Northumberland Record Office, Melton Park, North Gosforth, Newcastle upon Tyne NE3 5QX

Study adjacent parishes in counties of Cumberland, Northumberland and Yorkshire North Riding

Durham County Record Office, Durham, DH1 5UL

The following useful indexes have been compiled – see Introduction
Census Indexes 1851, 1861 & 1891 – Northumberland and Durham FHS, 2nd Floor, Bolbeck Hall, Westgate Road, Newcastle upon Tyne, NE1 1SE
Census Index 1851 Cleveland, North Yorkshire & South Durham FHS – D.W. Taylor, 106 The Avenue, Nunthorpe, Middlesbrough, Cleveland, TS7 0AH
Census Index Gateshead 1851 – Gateshead Library
Census Index 1891 (Consett) – K. Williams, 9 The Ridge Way, Kenton, Newcastle upon Tyne, NE3 4LP
Durham Marriage Index – Northumberland and Durham FHS, Mr. K. Dalkin, 12 St Aidan's Crescent, Crossgate Moor, Durham DH1 4AR complete 1813-1837, earlier period for 8 parishes in north and middle of the county
South Durham Marriage Index – Mr P. Joiner, Greystones, The Spital, Yarm, Cleveland, TS15 9EX

Durham Parish Registers Index – J. Lloyd, 1 Roysten Road, Manchester, M16 0EU
West Durham Database – Ron Nobley, 66 Alderside Crescent, Lanchester, Durham, DH7 0PZ baptisms, marriages and burials to 1851
Monumental Inscriptions – Northumberland and Durham FHS, 2nd Floor, Bolbeck Hall, Westgate Road, Newcastle upon Tyne, NE1 1SE
South Durham Burial Database – Mr D. Parkin, 28 Allendale Road, Billingham, Co Durham TS23 1PP

Durham's greatest extent from north to south is about 36 miles, its greatest length from east to west is about 45 miles. It is watered by three principal rivers: the Tees, Wear and Derwent. The population in 1841 was 307,963; in 1851, 390,997; in 1861, 508,666; in 1871, 685,045; in 1881, 867,258.

The soils are loam, clay and gravel. The principal crops were wheat, barley, oats and peas; cattle and sheep were raised. Manufactures were numerous and various: at Chester-le-Street, Washington, Salwell, Winlaton and Lumley, extensive iron-foundries and works; at Shortley Bridge, Derwentcoat and Blackhall mills, steel for sword blades; at Durham, worsted cloth, carpets and waistcoatings; at Darlington, worsteds, carpets, coarse linens, flax-spinning and grinding of optical glasses. There were extensive salt works at South Shields; sail cloth, glass and other articles were made at Stockton and Sunderland; and there was ship-building at Shields, Sunderland and Hartlepool.

The information in the Index is abbreviated, and may mislead the searcher if reference is not made to the details contained in the several publications listed in the Introduction. It is essential that users of this book check the appropriate works before making further enquiries.

ESSEX

parish name	deposited original registers	I.G.I.	local census indexes	copies of registers at Soc. Gen.	Boyd's marriage index	1837-1851 Registration District	Pallot's marriage index	non-conform. records at P.R.O.	map ref.
Abberton	B 1560-1971	1813-1851		1754-1851	1560-1752	Lexden			7I
Abbess Roding	A 1560-1837		5,6,8	1756-1837	1567-1753	Ongar		1707-1837	6D
Aldham	B 1558-1984	1813-1851	5,6,8	1755-1865	1558-1754	Lexden			7H
Alphamstone	A 1705-1939	1705-1814	5,6,8	1705-1837	1707-1836	Sudbury			9H
Alresford	B 1742-1975	1742-1813	5,8	1743-1865		Tendring			7J
Althorne	A 1800-1981	1800-1881	5,6,8	1800-1929	1800-1837	Maldon			4H
Ardleigh	B 1555-1985	1754-1851	5,8	1754-1865	1555-1754	Tendring			8J
Arkesden	A 1690-1985		5,6,8	1690-1865	1690-1837	Saffron Walden			9C
Ashdon	A 1553-1980	1557-1812	5,6,8	1553-1851	1557-1812	Saffron Walden	1790-1812		9D
Asheldham	A 1755-1966		5,6,8	1721-1937	1721-1837	Maldon			5I
Ashen	A 1558-1951		5,6,8	1754-1851	1558-1753	Risbridge			10F
Ashingdon	A 1564-1971	1566-1835	5,6,8	1804-1835	1568-1837	Rochford			4G
Aveley	A 1563-1970	1813-1845	5,8	1813-1865	1718-1812	Orsett			2D
Aythorpe Roding	A 1559-1970	1559-1812	5,6,8	1559-1851	1560-1837	Dunmow			6D
Ballingdon-cum-Brundon			5,6,8			Sudbury			9H
Bardfield Saling (Little Saling)	A 1561-1901		5,6,8	1561-1839	1561-1837	Dunmow			8F(D)
Barking	A 1558-1993		5,8	1754-1851	1558-1753	Romford		1804-1836	3C
Barling	A 1555-1950		5,6,8	1813-1865	1695-1754	Rochford			3H
Barnston	A 1539-1971		5,6,8	1539-1865	1539-1837	Dunmow			7E
Basildon	A 1777-1957		5,8	1813-1865		Billericay			3F
Beauchamp Roding	A 1688-1836		5,6,8	1754-1865	1688-1751	Ongar			6D(Q)
Beaumont cum Moze	B 1548-1918	1548-1678	5,8	1564-1837	1557-1753	Tendring			7K
Belchamp Otton	A 1578-1968		5,6,8	1578-1837	1578-1837	Sudbury			9G
Belchamps St Paul	A 1538-1992		5,6,8	1538-1865	1578-1837	Sudbury			9G
Belchamps Walter	A 1559-1989	1559-1812	5,6,8	1559-1865	1560-1837	Sudbury			9G
Berden	A 1715-1984		5,6,8	1754-1865	1715-1764	Bishop's Stortford			8C
Berechurch	B 1664-1985	1664-1837	5,8	1664-1865	1664-1740	Colchester			7I
Berners Roding	A 1590-1985		5,6,8	1589-1865	1538-1837	Ongar			6D
Birchanger	A 1688-1949		5,6,8		1688-1837	Bishop's Stortford			7C
Birdbrook	A 1633-1904		5,6,8	1633-1865	1633-1837	Risbridge			9F
Blackmore	A 1602-1992	1602-1852	5,6,8	1602-1865	1602-1750	Ongar			5D
Black Notley	A 1570-1996	1813-1851	5,6,8	1570-1865	1570-1754	Braintree			7F
Bobbingworth	A 1558-1967	1558-1812	5,6,8	1559-1865	1559-1753	Ongar			5D
Bocking	A 1558-1992	1561-1639	5,6,8	1655-1865	1593-1837	Braintree		1738-1857	8F
Boreham	A 1559-1994		5,6,8	1767-1837	1559-1767	Chelmsford			6F
Borley	A 1653-1988	1652-1823	5,6,8	1652-1836	1709-1837	Sudbury			10G
Bowers Gifford	A 1558-1987	1558-1812	5,8	1813-1865	1559-1812	Billericay			3F
Boxted	B 1559-1986		5,6,8	1559-1865	1559-1837	Lexden	1790-1837		8I
Bradfield	B 1564-1994		5,8	1813-1865	1564-1837	Tendring			8K
Bradwell-next-Coggeshall	A 1704-1923		5,6,8	1755-1865	1704-1754	Braintree			7G
Bradwell Juxta Mare	A 1558-1977	1558-1879		1558-1879	1558-1837	Braintree			5I
Braintree	A 1660-1996		5,6,8	1660-1865	1664-1837	Braintree		1813-1837	7F
Brentwood	A 1695-1911		5,8	1832-1865	1695-1753	Billericay		1707-1837	4D(g)
Brightlingsea	B 1697-1997		5,6,8	1754-1865	1701-1754	Lexden		1804-1859	7J
Broomfield	A 1546-1997		5,6,8	1754-1868	1547-1754	Chelmsford			6F
Broxted	A 1654-1995		5,6,8	1801-1865	1654-1837	Dunmow			8D
Bulmer	A 1559-1992	1556-1837	5,6,8	1558-1865	1558-1752	Sudbury			9G
Bulphan	A 1723-1989		5,8	1755-1811	1723-1753	Orsett			3E
Bures St Mary (Suffolk)						Sudbury			8H
Burnham	A 1559-1970		5,6,8	1559-1871	1559-1870	Maldon	1790-1837		4I
Buttsbury	A 1657-1837	1657-1803	5,6,8	1657-1837	1669-1727	Chelmsford			4E
Canewdon	A 1636-1981		5,6,8	1636-1899	1636-1740	Rochford			4H
Canvey Island	A 1813-1981		5,6,8			Orsett			3F
Castle Hedingham	A 1558-1960		5,8	1754-1851	1558-1754	Halstead		1775-1837	9G
Chadwell	A 1539-1947		5,8	1813-1865	1578-1812	Orsett			2E
Chappel	B 1538-1998	1538-1863	5,6,8	1754-1838	1539-1753	Lexden			8H
Chelmsford	A 1538-1970		5,6,8	1538-1851	1538-1837	Chelmsford	1790-1837	1759-1837	5F
Chickney	A 1554-1971	1554-1811	5,6,8	1554-1943	1556-1837	Dunmow			8D
Chignall Smealy	A 1600-1997		5,6,8	1600-1851	1650-1750	Chelmsford			6E(R)
Chignall St James	A 1724-1997	1539-1836	5,6,8	1723-1851	1725-1812	Chelmsford			6E(S)
Chigwell	A 1555-1971	1555-1853	5,6,8	1555-1865	1555-1753	Epping		1806-1837	4B
Childerditch	A 1537-1992	1538-1710	5,8	1538-1851	1540-1751	Billericay			3E
Chingford	C 1755-1970		5,6,8	1639-1865	1813-1851	Epping		1755-1812	4B
Chipping Ongar	A 1559-1975	1558-1750	5,6,8	1558-1865	1560-1749	Ongar		1764-1837	5D(Z)
Chrishall	A 1661-1912	1661-1812	5,6,8	1687-1865	1665-1837	Saffron Walden		1832-1837	9C
Clavering	A 1554-1971		5,6,8	1554-1865	1554-1837	Saffron Walden		1791-1837	8C
Coggeshall	A 1558-1991		5,8	1754-1865		Witham			7G
Colchester								1764-1837	7I(F)
All Saints	B 1609-1953		5,8	1754-1812	1609-1754	Colchester			7I(F)
Holy Trinity	B 1696-1955		5,8	1696-1865	1696-1753	Colchester			7I(F)
St Botolph	B 1560-1987	1680-1739	5,8	1813-1865	1560-1688	Colchester			7I(F)
St Giles	B 1693-1953		5,8	1749-1865	1692-1754	Colchester			7I(F)
St James	B 1561-1979	1561-1774	5,8	1754-1812	1653-1754	Colchester			7I(F)
St Leonard	B 1539-1983	1541-1853	5,8	1754-1865	1542-1751	Colchester			7I(F)
St Martin	B 1622-1950		5,8	1750-1865	1695-1753	Colchester			7I(F)
St Mary at the Walls	B 1559-1975	1561-1885	5,8	1754-1865	1661-1754	Colchester			7I(F)
St Mary Magdalene	B 1708-1986		5,8	1750-1865	1721-1753	Colchester			7I(F)
St Nicholas	B 1541-1953	1541-1812	5,8	1754-1812	1541-1754	Colchester			7I(F)
St Peter	B 1611-1915		5,8	1754-1851	1611-1754	Colchester			7I(F)
St Runwald	B 1598-1872		5,8	1762-1811	1599-1760	Colchester			7I(F)
Cold Norton	A 1539-1991	1539-1838	5,6,8	1539-1869	1541-1754	Maldon			4G
Colne Engaine	A 1629-1928		5,8	1754-1865	1629-1764	Halstead			8G
Copford	A 1558-1967	1558-1812	5,6,8	1754-1865	1558-1753	Lexden			7H
Corringham	A 1558-1955		5,8	1760-1865	1558-1753	Orsett			2F
Cranham	A 1558-1995		5,6,8	1559-1865	1559-1837	Romford			3D
Creeksea	A 1753-1982		5,6,8	1753-1899	1761-1837	Maldon			4H
Cressing	A 1733-1971	1754-1782	5,6,8	1754-1865	1732-1782	Braintree			7G

parish name	deposited original registers	I.G.I.	local census indexes	copies of registers at Soc. Gen.	Boyd's marriage index	1837-1851 Registration District	Pallot's marriage index	non-conform. records at P.R.O.	map ref.
Dagenham	A 1598-1968		5,8	1754-1865	1568-1753	Romford			3C
Danbury	A 1673-1972		5,6,8	1637-1865	1675-1753	Chelmsford			5F
Debden	A 1558-1997		5,6,8	1556-1851	1557-1837	Saffron Walden			8D
Dedham	B 1560-1998		5,6,8	1560-1905	1560-1812	Lexden		1755-1837	8J
Dengie	A 1550-1995		5,6,8	1550-1930	1550-1837	Maldon			5I
Doddinghurst	A 1560-1977	1560-1812	5,6,8	1560-1865	1560-1752	Ongar			4D
Dovercourt	B 1706-1981		5,8	1755-1865	1706-1753	Tendring			8L
Downham	A 1559-1992	1754-1837	5,8	1754-1865	1559-1750	Billericay			4F
Dunton	A 1538-1976		5,8	1813-1865	1538-1752	Billericay			3E
Earls Colne	A 1558-1942	1559-1693	5,8	1754-1865	1559-1753	Halstead			8G
East Donyland	B 1731-1965		5,6,8	1813-1851	1731-1754	Lexden			7I
East Ham	A 1696-1982	1803-1851	6,8	1803-1851	1695-1803	West Ham			2B
East Hanningfield	A 1538-1989	1538-1810	5,6,8	1539-1865	1538-1753	Chelmsford			4F
East Horndon	A 1557-1978	1557-1804	5,8	1557-1865	1557-1753	Billericay			3E
Easthorpe	B 1572-1956		5,6,8	1838-1851	1576-1834	Lexden			7H
East Mersea	B 1813-2000		5,6,8	1725-1755		Lexden			6J
East Tilbury	A 1626-1977		5,8	1754-1851	1627-1754	Orsett			2E
Eastwood	A 1685-1971		5,6,8	1755-1865	1686-1753	Rochford			3G
Elmdon	A 1618-1973	1618-1812	5,6,8	1618-1870	1618-1837	Saffron Walden			9C
Elmstead	A 1557-1997	1813-1851	5,8	1754-1871	1559-1754	Tendring			7J
Elsenham	A 1731-1900	1731-1876	5,6,8	1731-1865	1731-1837	Bishop's Stortford			8D
Epping	A 1539-1984	1538-1812	5,6,8	1538-1851	1539-1754	Epping		1768-1839	5C
Fairsted	A 1538-1976	1538-1840	5,8	1538-1840	1538-1753	Witham			7F
Farnham	A 1559-1909		5,6,8	1801-1865	1559-1837	Bishop's Stortford			8C
Faulkbourne	A 1574-1812	1574-1703	5,8	1574-1812	1576-1753	Witham			6G(K)
Feering	A 1563-1948		5,8	1754-1865	1563-1754	Witham			7H
Felstead	A 1558-1891		5,8	1754-1865	1558-1753	Dunmow		1807-1837	7F
Finchingfield	A 1617-1993		5,6,8	1617-1865	1617-1752	Braintree		1815-1837	9F
Fingringhoe	A 1653-1976		5,6,8	1813-1865	1681-1812	Lexden			7I
Fobbing	A 1539-1935		5,8	1813-1865	1539-1753	Orsett			3F
Fordham	B 1563-1974		5,6,8	1754-1865	1564-1753	Lexden		1784-1837	8H
Foulness	A 1695-1899	1813-1836	5,6,8	1695-1865	1695-1754	Rochford			4I
Foxearth	A 1551-1989		5,6,8	1754-1812	1707-1754	Sudbury			10G
Frating	B 1560-1986	1560-1812	5,8	1560-1851	1560-1753	Tendring			7J
Frinton	B 1738-1990		5,8	1762-1829		Tendring			7L
Fryerning	A 1595-1968		5,6,8	1754-1865	1619-1752	Chelmsford			5E
Fyfield	A 1538-1885	1538-1700	5,6,8	1538-1865	1538-1754	Ongar			5D
Gestingthorpe	A 1609-1892	1626-1812	5,6,8	1813-1865	1626-1837	Sudbury			9G
Goldhanger	A 1558-1879		5,6,8	1754-1865	1558-1744	Maldon			5H
Good Easter	A 1538-1941		5,6,8	1539-1865	1538-1837	Chelmsford			6E
Gosfield	A 1538-1961		5,8	1538-1865	1538-1837	Halstead			8F
Grays Thurrock	A 1674-1976		5,8	1755-1865	1674-1753	Orsett			2D
Great Baddow	A 1538-1946		5,6,8	1754-1865	1543-1752	Chelmsford			5F
Great Bardfield	A 1662-1980	1754-1876	5,8	1662-1876	1662-1753	Dunmow			8E
Great Bentley	B 1558-1968	1558-1677	5,8	1678-1865		Tendring			7J
Great Birch	B 1560-1990		5,6,8	1754-1866	1560-1753	Lexden			7H
Great Braxted	A 1558-1988		5,8	1754-1865	1559-1753	Witham			6G
Great Bromley	B 1559-1993	1559-1731	5,8	1559-1865	1559-1753	Tendring			8J
Great Burstead	A 1653-1857	1559-1654	5,8	1559-1837	1559-1761	Billericay		1778-1837	4E
Great Canfield	A 1538-1931	1538-1837	5,6,8	1538-1865	1538-1812	Dunmow			7D
Great Chesterford	A 1586-1992	1586-1812	5,6,8	1586-1837	1586-1837	Saffron Walden			10D
Great Chishall	A 1583-1997		5,6,8	1801-1837	1583-1837	Royston			9B
Great Clacton	B 1543-1984		5,6,8	1542-1865	1543-1754	Tendring			6K
Great Dunmow	A 1538-1890		5,6,8	1538-1851	1558-1837	Dunmow		1733-1856	7E
Great Easton	A 1562-1997	1813-1851	5,6,8	1561-1865	1561-1837	Dunmow			8E
Great Hallingbury	A 1538-1981		5,6,8	1801-1865	1538-1837	Bishop's Stortford			7C
Great Henny	A 1678-1976	1668-1881	5,6,8	1678-1945	1695-1837	Sudbury			9H
Great Holland	B 1539-1995		5,8	1754-1837	1547-1754	Tendring			7L
Great Horkesley	B 1558-1895		5,6,8	1558-1865	1558-1836	Lexden	1790-1836		8I
Great Leighs	A 1558-1897		5,6,8	1560-1837	1560-1837	Chelmsford	1790-1837		6F
Great Maplestead	A 1678-1976		5,8	1678-1865	1697-1754	Halstead			9G
Great Oakley	B 1559-1992	1673-1766	5,8	1754-1865	1559-1754	Tendring			8K
Great Parndon	A 1547-1981		5,6,7,8	1547-1865	1548-1753	Epping			5C
Great Saling	A 1715-1975		5,6,8	1715-1837	1732-1837	Braintree			7F
Great Sampford	A 1559-1879		5,6,8	1559-1865		Saffron Walden			9E
Great Stambridge	A 1559-1990		5,8	1754-1865	1559-1754	Rochford			3H
Great Tey	B 1559-1984		5,6,8	1754-1865	1559-1753	Lexden			8H
Great Totham	A 1557-1901		5,6,8	1754-1865	1559-1753	Maldon			6G
Great Wakering	A 1685-1915		5,6,8	1754-1865	1685-1753	Rochford			3I
Great Waltham	A 1566-1984	1566-1812	5,6,8	1756-1851	1704-1755	Chelmsford			6E
Great Warley	A 1539-1981		5,6,8	1539-1887	1539-1753	Romford			3D
Great Wigborough	B 1560-1997	1560-1812	5,6,8	1754-1837	1560-1750	Lexden	1790-1812	1743-1836	6I
Great Yeldham	A 1560-1958	1560-1812	5,8	1560-1851	1560-1753	Halsted			9F(B)
Greenstead (near Colchester)	B 1676-1983	1576-1812	5,8	1754-1851	1676-1753	Colchester			7I(G)
Greenstead (near Ongar)	A 1561-1966	1562-1812	5,6,8	1562-1865	1576-1812	Ongar	1790-1812		5D(Y)
Hadleigh	A 1568-1899		5,6,8	1568-1865	1568-1753	Rochford			3G
Hadstock	A 1558-1993	1558-1812	5,6,8	1558-1865	1559-1837	Linton			10D
Halstead					1564-1818			1796-1837	8G
Holy Trinity	A 1844-1978		5,8	1844-1865		Halstead	1844-1865		
St Andrew's	A 1564-1975		5,8	1564-1865		Halstead	1813-1865		
Harlow								1778-1837	6C
St Mary and St Hugh	A 1755-1973		5,6,7,8	1629-1865		Epping			
St John the Baptist	A 1841-1978		5,6,7,8	1841-1865		Epping			
Harwich	B 1559-1989		5,8	1754-1865	1559-1754	Tendring		1783-1837	8L
Hatfield Broad Oak		1662-1753	5,6,8	1662-1753	1662-1753	Dunmow		1731-1837	7D
Hatfield Peverel	A 1614-1988		5,8	1614-1851	1614-1851	Witham			6G
Havengore Island (ex.par.)			5,6,8			Rochford			3I

parish name	deposited original registers	I.G.I.	local census indexes	copies of registers at Soc. Gen.	Boyd's marriage index	1837-1851 Registration District	Pallot's marriage index	non-conform. records at P.R.O.	map ref.
Havering-atte-Bower	A 1657-1993		5,6,8	1837-1851	1691-1837	Romford			4C
Hawkwell	A 1693-1977		5,6,8	1752-1865	1696-1751	Rochford			3G
Hazeleigh	A 1589-1952	1573-1812	5,6,8	1575-1986	1589-1748	Maldon			5G
Helions Bumpstead	A 1558-1941		5,6,8	1558-1865	1559-1837	Risbridge			10E
Hempstead	A 1664-1979		5,6,8	1664-1812		Saffron Walden			9E
Henham	A 1539-1890		5,6,8	1539-1865	1539-1837	Bishop's Stortford		1806-1837	8D
Heybridge	A 1558-1922		5,6,8	1754-1865	1559-1773	Maldon			6G
Heydon	A 1538-1997		5,6,8	1538-1837	1538-1837	Royston			9C
High Easter	A 1654-1857		5,6,8	1654-1851	1654-1837	Dunmow			6E
High Laver	A 1593-1944		5,6,8	1754-1838	1616-1753	Ongar			6C
High Ongar	A 1538-1914		5,6,8	1743-1836	1539-1773	Ongar			5D
High Ongar (detached)			5,6,8			Ongar			5C(X)
High Roding	A 1538-1838		5,6,8	1538-1838	1538-1837	Dunmow			6D
Hockley	A 1728-1976	1729-1814	5,6,8	1732-1865	1732-1865	Rochford			4G
Hornchurch	A 1576-1948	1576-1812	5,6,8	1576-1851	1576-1753	Romford			3D
Horndon on the Hill	A 1622-1986		5,8	1754-1851	1628-1751	Orsett			3E
Hutton	A 1654-1876		5,8	1654-1876	1654-1727	Billericay			4E
Ingatestone	A 1558-1951	1558-1812	5,6,8	1558-1865	1559-1754	Chelmsford		1814-1837	5E
Ingrave	A 1678-1964		5,8	1679-1865		Billericay			4E
Inworth	B 1732-1996		5,8	1754-1837	1733-1753	Witham			6H
Kedington (Suffolk)						Risbridge			10F
Kelvedon	A 1558-1940	1558-1881	5,8	1558-1907	1559-1753	Witham		1811-1837	7G
Kelvedon Hatch	A 1559-1935		5,6,8	1561-1865	1561-1837	Ongar			5D
Kirby le Soken	A 1681-1982		5,8	1754-1865	1681-1754	Tendring			7L
Laindon	A 1653-1971		5,8	1755-1851	1654-1754	Billericay			3E
Lamarsh	A 1555-1993	1555-1812	5,6,8	1555-1837	1556-1837	Sudbury			9H
Lambourne	A 1582-1981	1582-1709	5,6,8	1582-1840	1584-1752	Ongar			4C
Langdon Hills	A 1686-1986	1686-1877	5,8	1754-1865	1690-1752	Orsett			3E
Langenhoe	B 1660-1960		5,6,8	1796-1865	1721-1796	Lexden			7I
Langford	A 1558-1993		5,6,8	1754-1836	1559-1754	Maldon			6G
Langham	B 1638-1979		5,6,8	1638-1979	1638-1754	Lexden		1782-1836	8I
Langley	A 1678-1984		5,6,8	1678-1851	1690-1837	Saffron Walden			9C
Latchingdon	A 1725-1943		5,6,8	1725-1865	1725-1754	Maldon			4H
Latton	A 1567-1988	1683-1837	5,6,7,8	1683-1851	1569-1726	Epping			6C
Lawford	B 1558-1998		5,8	1755-1865	1555-1753	Tendring			8J
Layer Breton	A 1749-1997		5,6,8	1755-1865		Lexden			7I(L)
Layer de la Haye	B 1755-1979	1813-1837	5,6,8	1755-1851		Lexden			7I
Layer Marney	B 1742-1985		5,6,8	1754-1851	1742-1754	Lexden			7H
Leaden Roding	A 1572-1833	1572-1812	5,6,8	1574-1865		Dunmow			6D(M)
Leigh	A 1684-1899		5,6,8	1684-1851	1691-1754	Rochford	1790-1812	1813-1837	3G
Lexden	B 1560-1972	1560-1657	5,8	1560-1865	1560-1754	Colchester			8I
Leyton	C 1575-1997		5,6,8	1574-1865	1575-1754	West Ham		1818-1837	3B
Lindsell	A 1568-1881		5,6,8	1568-1837	1568-1754	Dunmow			8E
Liston	A 1599-1968		5,6,8	1599-1837	1601-1837	Sudbury			10H
Little Baddow	A 1559-1983	1559-1789	5,6,8	1559-1865	1559-1753	Chelmsford		1764-1837	5F
Little Bardfield	A 1537-1958		5,6,8	1538-1958	1539-1753	Dunmow			8E
Little Bentley	B 1558-1942		5,8	1754-1865	1558-1752	Tendring			7J
Little Braxted	A 1730-1993	1730-1812	5,8	1730-1851	1730-1753	Witham			6G(O)
Little Bromley	B 1538-1990	1538-1592	5,8	1538-1865	1539-1753	Tendring			8J
Little Burstead	A 1678-1956	1679-1812	5,8	1678-1865	1679-1750	Billericay			3E
Littlebury	A 1545-1958		5,6,8	1545-1851	1545-1837	Saffron Walden			9C
Little Canfield	A 1561-1982		5,6,8	1561-1837	1561-1837	Dunmow			7D
Little Chesterford	A 1559-1992	1559-1812	5,6,8	1559-1866	1559-1837	Saffron Walden			10D
Little Chishall	A 1577-1997		5,6,8	1577-1837	1579-1806	Royston			9B
Little Clacton	B 1538-1963		5,8	1754-1865	1538-1754	Tendring			7K
Little Dunmow	A 1549-1992		5,6,8	1549-1943	1551-1837	Dunmow		1733-1837	7E
Little Easton	A 1559-1994		5,6,8	1559-1931	1559-1837	Dunmow			7D
Little Hallingbury	A 1690-1975	1710-1753	5,6,8	1710-1865	1710-1753	Bishop's Stortford			7C
Little Henny			5,6,8			Sudbury	1678-1945		9H
Little Holland			5,8	1542-1865		Tendring			6L
Little Horkesley	B 1568-1995	1568-1812	5,6,8	1568-1851	1568-1835	Lexden	1790-1835		8I
Little Ilford	A 1539-1903	1539-1875	6,8	1755-1875	1539-1753	West Ham	1790-1812		3B
Little Laver	A 1538-1999		5,6,8	1813-1838	1541-1812	Ongar			6D
Little Leighs	A 1679-1997		5,6,8	1680-1837	1680-1837	Chelmsford	1790-1837		7F(J)
Little Maplestead	A 1688-1982		5,8	1688-1813	1691-1755	Halstead			8G
Little Oakley	B 1558-1990		5,8	1558-1837	1558-1753	Tendring			8L
Little Parndon	A 1621-1997		5,6,7,8	1622-1851	1622-1745	Epping			6B
Little Sampford	A 1562-1977		5,6,8	1754-1851	1565-1754	Saffron Walden			9E
Little Stambridge	A 1654-1894		5,6,8	1752-1865	1659-1754	Rochford			4H(h)
Little Tey	B 1660-1992		5,6,8	1757-1853	1671-1753	Lexden			7H(E)
Little Thurrock	A 1654-1966		5,8	1813-1865	1654-1754	Orsett			2E
Little Totham	A 1558-1970		5,6,8	1754-1865	1559-1744	Maldon			6H
Little Wakering	A 1754-1961		5,6,8	1754-1865		Rochford			3H
Little Waltham	A 1538-1875		5,6,8	1539-1837	1539-1754	Chelmsford		1803-1837	6F
Little Warley	A 1539-1974		5,8	1539-1835	1538-1750	Billericay			3D
Little Wigborough	B 1586-1996	1586-1812	5,6,8		1592-1812	Lexden	1790-1812		6I
Little Yeldham	A 1564-1992	1564-1812	5,8	1756-1851		Halstead			9G
Loughton	A 1674-1913	1675-1812	5,6,8	1674-1840	1675-1837	Epping	1780-1837	1817-1837	4B
Magdalen Laver	A 1557-1945	1556-1812	5,6,8	1754-1836	1557-1753	Epping			5C(T)
Maldon								1776-1837	5G
All Saints	A 1558-1987	1754-1837	5,6,8	1695-1837	1558-1754	Maldon			5G
St Mary	A 1558-1971		5,6,8	1813-1865	1575-1754	Maldon			5G
St Peter	A 1556-1987		5,6,8	1695-1837	1556-1709	Maldon			5G
Manningtree	B 1695-1966		5,8	1754-1865	1696-1754	Tendring		1795-1837	8K
Manuden	A 1561-1986	1561-1812	5,6,8	1561-1865	1564-1837	Bishop's Stortford			8C
Maplestead									
Magna				1678-1812					
Parva				1690-1813					
Margaret Roding	A 1538-1954	1538-1812	5,6,8	1538-1851		Dunmow			6D

parish name	deposited original registers	I.G.I.	local census indexes	copies of registers at Soc. Gen.	Boyd's marriage index	1837-1851 Registration District	Pallot's marriage index	non-conform. records at P.R.O.	map ref.
Margaretting	A 1627-1969		5,6,8	1754-1865	1628-1754	Chelmsford			5E
Markshall	A 1582-1928		5,8	1755-1865	1585-1753	Witham			7G
Marks Tey	B 1560-1993	1560-1812	5,6,8	1560-1865	1562-1753	Lexden			7H
Mashbury	A 1539-1997	1539-1804	5,6,8	1539-1851	1540-1804	Chelmsford			6E(H)
Matching	A 1558-1969		5,6,7,8	1754-1865	1559-1753	Epping			6C
Mayland	A 1748-1997		5,6,8	1754-1837		Maldon			5H
Messing	A 1558-1965		5,8	1754-1865	1606-1754	Witham			7H
Middleton	A 1700-1991		5,6,8	1700-1851	1700-1837	Sudbury			9H
Mistley	B 1559-1933	1559-1812	5,8	1559-1851	1559-1754	Tendring			8K
Moreton	A 1558-1996	1558-1812	5,6,8	1558-1865	1559-1752	Ongar			5D
Mount Bures	B 1540-1958	1813-1837	5,6,8	1754-1837	1558-1753	Lexden			8H
Mountnessing	A 1653-1940	1653-1827	5,8	1653-1851	1654-1752	Billericay			4E
Mucking	A 1559-1991		5,8	1801-1851	1561-1812	Orsett			2E
Mundon	A 1741-1955	1741-1882	5,6,8	1741-1940	1741-1750	Maldon			5H
Navestock	A 1538-1871		5,6,8	1538-1837	1538-1812	Ongar	1790-1812		4D
Nazeing			5,6,8		1559-1739	Epping			5B
Netteswell	A 1558-1894	1558-1753	5,6,7,8	1558-1836	1558-1754	Epping			6C
Nevendon	A 1638-1979		5,8	1755-1851	1638-1753	Billericay			3F
Newport	A 1558-1981		5,6,8	1558-1865	1559-1837	Saffron Walden		1797-1837	9D
North Benfleet	A 1647-1993		5,8	1756-1865	1573-1752	Billericay			3F
North Fambridge	A 1556-1993		5,6,8	1556-1900	1556-1755	Maldon			4G
North Ockendon	A 1570-1948		5,8	1570-1850	1571-1837	Orsett			3D
North Shoebury	A 1680-1992		5,6,8	1687-1865		Rochford			3I
North Weald Bassett	A 1557-1951		5,6,8	1754-1865	1557-1754	Epping			5C
Northwood			5,8			Sudbury			9G(A)
Norton Mandeville	A 1779-1836	1779-1836	5,6,8	1779-1836		Ongar			5D(a)
Orsett	A 1669-1986	1758-1812	5,8	1670-1812	1670-1756	Orsett			2E
Orsett (det.)			5,8			Orsett			5F
Ovington	A 1559-1971		5,6,8	1755-1836	1559-1725	Risbridge			10F
Paglesham	A 1719-1986		5,6,8		1733-1739	Rochford			4H
Panfield	A 1570-1838		5,6,8	1570-1838	1570-1837	Braintree			8F
Pattiswick	A 1677-1980		5,6,8	1755-1837	1677-1753	Braintree			7G
Pebmarsh	A 1684-1971		5,8	1654-1837	1654-1837	Halstead			8G
Peldon	B 1725-1980		5,6,8	1724-1812	1724-1753	Lexden			6I
Pentlow	A 1539-1812		5,6,8	1539-1836	1539-1837	Sudbury			10G
Pitsea	A 1688-1953	1757-1840	5,8	1688-1865	1688-1754	Billericay			3F
Pleshey	A 1656-1993		5,6,8	1656-1865	1657-1737	Chelmsford			6E(N)
Prittlewell	A 1645-1898	1645-1812	5,6,8	1645-1851	1645-1812	Rochford	1790-1812	1830-1837	3H
Purleigh	A 1592-1959		5,6,8	1593-1919	1674-1754	Maldon			5G
Purleigh (det.)			5,6,8			Maldon			5F(c)
Quendon	A 1687-1992		5,6,8	1687-1860	1687-1735	Saffron Walden			8B
Radwinter	A 1638-1974		5,6,8	1638-1812	1638-1837	Saffon Walden			9E
Rainham	A 1570-1962		5,6,8	1570-1859	1668-1812	Romford			2D
Ramsden Bellhouse	A 1562-1956		5,8	1565-1865	1565-1753	Billericay			4F
Ramsden Greys	A 1558-1923		5,8	1754-1837	1572-1753	Billericay			4F(f)
Ramsey	B 1645-1998		5,8	1754-1865	1645-1753	Tendring			8K
Rawreth	A 1539-1965		5,6,8	1754-1812	1539-1751	Rochford			4F
Rayleigh	A 1548-1936	1754-1812	5,6,8	1548-1936	1548-1754	Rochford			3G
Rayne	A 1558-1979		5,6,8	1538-1865	1558-1837	Braintree			7F
Rettendon	A 1674-1973		5,6,8	1754-1865	1678-1744	Chelmsford			4F
Rickling	A 1662-1977		5,6,8	1660-1860	1663-1837	Saffron Walden			8C
Ridgewell	A 1562-1888		5,8	1745-1865	1562-1749	Halstead		1814-1836	9F
Rivenhall	A 1634-1973		5,8	1754-1865	1639-1769	Witham			7G
Rochford	A 1678-1905		5,6,8	1680-1865	1680-1865	Rochford		1770-1837	3G
Romford	A 1561-1946	1561-1812	4,5,6,8	1746-1837	1561-1753	Romford		1812-1837	3C
Roxwell	A 1559-1989	1558-1812	5,6,8	1558-1837	1559-1836	Chelmsford	1790-1837		6E
Roydon	A 1567-1982		5,6,7,8	1754-1865	1568-1752	Epping			6B
Runwell	A 1558-1960		5,6,8	1755-1865	1558-1743	Chelmsford			4F
St Lawrence	A 1704-2000		5,6,8	1704-1899	1705-1753	Maldon			5I
St Michael Mile End	B 1668-1982		5,8	1754-1865	1674-1754	Colchester			8I
St Osyth	B 1666-1920		5,8	1754-1865	1674-1754	Tendring			6J
Saffron Walden	A 1558-1982		5,8	1558-1865	1559-1837	Saffron Walden		1787-1837	9D
Salcott	B 1813-1991		5,8	1813-1865		Lexden			6I
Sandon	A 1554-1947		5,6,8	1813-1836	1554-1812	Chelmsford			5F
Shalford	A 1559-1997		5,6,8	1558-1837	1559-1754	Braintree			8F
Sheering	A 1558-1952		5,6,7,8	1754-1865	1559-1754	Epping			6C
Shelley	A 1687-1955		5,6,8	1813-1836	1709-1812	Ongar			5D
Shellow Bowells	A 1553-1926	1553-1783	5,6,8	1553-1865		Ongar			5E(V)
Shenfield	A 1538-1934		5,8	1538-1865	1539-1753	Billericay			4D
Shopland	A 1741-1952		5,6,8	1742-1865		Rochford			3H
Sible Hedingham	A 1560-1903		5,8	1560-1903	1599-1837	Halstead			9F
South Benfleet	A 1573-1993		5,6,8	1754-1865	1573-1752	Rochford			3G
Southchurch	A 1695-1946		5,6,8	1695-1899	1695-1754	Rochford			3H
South Fambridge	A 1754-1992		5,6,8	1754-1837		Rochford			4G
South Hanningfield	A 1654-1997		5,6,8	1654-1837	1661-1701	Chelmsford			4F(e)
Southminster	A 1700-1977		5,6,8	1700-1865	1701-1840	Maldon		1831-1836	4I
South Ockendon	A 1538-1977		5,8	1754-1865	1562-1700	Orsett		1815-1837	3D
South Shoebury	A 1704-1924		5,6,8	1754-1865	1705-1751	Rochford			3I
South Weald	A 1538-1939	1538-1573	5,8	1539-1865	1540-1753	Billericay			4D
Springfield	A 1653-1921		5,6,8	1797-1851	1651-1796	Chelmsford			6F
Stambourne	A 1559-1956	1559-1812	5,8	1559-1865	1678-1837	Halstead		1810-1837	9F
Stanford le Hope	A 1680-1985		5,8	1754-1865	1696-1754	Orsett			2E
Stanford Rivers	A 1538-1959	1538-1837	5,6,8	1538-1867	1538-1837	Ongar		1823-1837	5D
Stansted Montfichet	A 1558-1929		5,6,8	1558-1837	1558-1837	Bishop's Stortford		1812-1837	7D
Stanway	B 1704-1994		5,6,8	1754-1865	1703-1754	Lexden			7I
Stapleford Abbots	A 1653-1897		5,6,8	1766-1865	1654-1766	Ongar			4C
Stapleford Tawney	A 1558-1979	1558-1821	5,6,8	1558-1865	1558-1752	Ongar			4C
Stebbing	A 1712-1987	1813-1851	5,6,8	1754-1865	1712-1754	Dunmow		1793-1837	8E
Steeple	A 1660-1894		5,6,8	1660-1900	1660-1753	Maldon			5H

parish name	deposited original registers	I.G.I.	local census indexes	copies of registers at Soc. Gen.	Boyd's marriage index	1837-1851 Registration District	Pallot's marriage index	non-conform. records at P.R.O.	map ref.
Steeple Bumpstead	A 1676-1970		5,6,8	1676-1865	1689-1837	Risbridge			9E
Stifford	A 1568-1933	1561-1783	5,8	1568-1812	1572-1753	Orsett			2D
Stisted	A 1538-1997		5,6,8	1538-1851	1539-1837	Braintree			8G
Stock Harward	A 1563-1985	1563-1699	5,6,8	1563-1950	1563-1754	Chelmsford		1814-1837	4E
Stondon Massey	A 1708-1984		5,6,8	1754-1851	1708-1752	Ongar			5D(d)
Stow Maries	A 1559-1992	1754-1836	5,8	1559-1943	1561-1750	Maldon			4G
Strethall	A 1739-1992	1742-1836	5,6,8	1740-1865	1714-1811	Saffron Walden			10C
Sturmer	A 1733-1968		5,6,8	1733-1865	1733-1837	Risbridge			10F
Sutton	A 1740-1993		5,6,8	1740-1836		Rochford			3H
Takeley	A 1661-1989		5,6,8	1661-1851	1661-1837	Dunmow			7D
Tendring	B 1538-1882		5,8	1754-1865	1563-1753	Tendring			7K
Terling	A 1538-1977	1538-1840	5,8	1538-1865	1538-1754	Witham			6F
Thaxted	A 1538-1985	1783-1812	5,6,8	1538-1851	1538-1754	Dunmow		1789-1837	8E
Theydon Bois	A 1717-1933		5,6,8		1718-1837	Epping			4C
Theydon Garnon	A 1558-1872		5,6,8	1813-1865	1558-1837	Epping			5C
Theydon Mount	A 1564-1963	1564-1851	5,6,8	1564-1865	1564-1810	Ongar	1790-1810		5C
Thorpe le Soken	B 1682-1918		5,8	1754-1865	1682-1753	Tendring		1803-1837	7K
Thorrington	B 1558-1965		5,8	1558-1865	1558-1752	Tendring			7J
Thundersley	A 1569-1929		5,6,8	1569-1929	1569-1753	Rochford			3G
Tilbury Juxta Clare	A 1560-1996		5,8	1755-1837	1611-1725	Halstead			9F
Tillingham	A 1561-1969	1641-1836	5,6,8	1561-1910		Maldon			5I
Tilty	A 1673-1991	1672-1811	5,6,8	1673-1865	1727-1812	Dunmow			8D(C)
Tollesbury	A 1558-1976		5,6,8	1754-1913	1558-1754	Maldon		1817-1837	6I
Tolleshunt D'Arcy			5,6,8		1582-1753	Maldon			6H
Tolleshunt Knights	A 1695-1963	1630-1836	5,6,8	1696-1865	1696-1747	Maldon			6H
Tolleshunt Major	A 1559-1986		5,6,8	1813-1865	1561-1753	Maldon			6H
Toppesfield	A 1559-1974	1559-1851	5,8	1559-1865	1559-1753	Halstead			9F
Twinstead	A 1567-1993	1567-1721	5,6,8	1562-1865	1567-1837	Sudbury			9H
Ugley	A 1559-1993		5,6,8	1599-1865	1559-1837	Bishop's Stortford			8C
Ulting	A 1723-1836		5,8	1754-1836	1723-1752	Witham			6G
Upminster	A 1543-1978		5,6,8	1813-1865	1625-1837	Romford		1801-1837	3D
Vange	A 1558-1980		5,8	1756-1865	1560-1752	Billericay			3F
Virley	A 1628-1883		5,6,8	1761-1865	1732-1739	Lexden			6I(P)
Wakes Colne	B 1559-1957		5,6,8	1559-1865	1605-1836	Lexden			8H
Wallasea Island			5,6,8			Rochford			4I
Waltham Holy Cross	A 1563-1953	1564-1682	5,6,8	1563-1865	1563-1754	Edmonton		1770-1856	5B
Walthamstow	C 1645-1989	1650-1840	5,6,8	1650-1837	1650-1837	West Ham	1790-1837	1788-1837	3B
Walton le Soken	B 1688-1966		5,8	1754-1865	1688-1753	Edmonton			7L
Wanstead	A 1640-1837		5,6,8	1640-1865	1640-1749	West Ham			3B
Weeley	B 1562-1993		5,8	1754-1837	1562-1754	Tendring			7K
Wendens Ambo	A 1540-1995		5,6,8	1540-1865	1540-1837	Saffron Walden			9C
Wendon Lofts	A 1674-1932	1754-1812	5,6,8	1538-1878	1678-1837	Saffron Walden			9B
Wennington	A 1654-1997		5,6,8	1654-1850	1652-1814	Romford			2D
West Bergholt	B 1559-1975		5,6,8	1754-1865	1561-1753	Lexden			8I
West Ham	A 1653-1950		8	1653-1847	1653-1800	West Ham		1774-1854	3B
West Hanningfield	A 1558-1986	1558-1812	5,6,8	1558-1865	1558-1787	Chelmsford			5F
West Horndon	A 1560-1747		5,8	1742-1865	1560-1751	Billericay			3E
West Mersea	B 1625-1994		5,6,8		1625-1753	Lexden		1805-1837	6I
West Thurrock	A 1668-1977		5,8	1754-1836	1668-1751	Orsett			2D
West Tilbury	A 1540-1979		5,8	1540-1865	1567-1753	Orsett			2E
Wethersfield	A 1647-1997	1646-1724	5,6,8	1647-1865	1681-1752	Braintree		1797-1837	8F
White Colne	A 1558-1964	1709-1812	5,8	1560-1835	1561-1759	Halstead			8H
White Notley	A 1538-1969	1538-1882	5,6,8	1538-1932	1539-1837	Braintree			7F
White Roding	A 1547-1924		5,6,8	1547-1865	1547-1837	Dunmow			6D
Wicken Bonhunt	A 1588-1995		5,6,8	1590-1837	1590-1837	Saffron Walden			8B
Wickford	A 1538-1944		5,8	1755-1865	1561-1753	Billericay		1814-1837	4F
Wickham Bishops	A 1662-1985	1662-1856	5,8	1662-1865	1663-1754	Witham			6G
Wickham St Paul's	A 1609-1992		5,6,8	1609-1837	1609-1837	Witham			9G
Widdington	A 1666-1984		5,6,8	1666-1865	1666-1837	Saffron Walden			8D
Widford	A 1589-1948		5,6,8	1619-1837	1619-1836	Chelmsford	1790-1837		5F(b)
Willingale Doe	A 1570-1931	1570-1812	5,6,8	1705-1865	1705-1837	Ongar			6D(U)
Willingale Spain	A 1576-1928		5,6,8	1576-1851	1576-1837	Ongar			5E(W)
Wimbish	A 1572-1994	1729-1812	5,6,8	1572-1865	1582-1837	Saffron Walden			9D
Witham	A 1650-1969		5,8	1754-1851	1667-1754	Witham		1752-1837	6G
Wivenhoe	B 1560-2000		5,6,8	1754-1851	1560-1754	Lexden		1807-1836	7J
Wix	B 1560-1871		5,8	1696-1837	1560-1753	Tendring			8K
Woodford	A 1638-1978		5,6,8	1628-1851	1638-1837	West Ham	1780-1837		4B
Woodham Ferrers	A 1558-1987		5,6,8	1558-1919	1559-1753	Chelmsford			4G
Woodham Mortimer	A 1662-1968	1662-1812	5,6,8	1662-1981	1664-1754	Maldon			5G
Woodham Walter	A 1563-1958	1565-1812	5,6,8	1754-1865	1565-1753	Maldon			5G
Wormingford	B 1557-1943		5,6,8	1559-1837	1559-1837	Lexden	1790-1837		8H
Wrabness	B 1650-1992		5,8	1754-1851	1677-1753	Tendring			8K
Writtle	A 1634-1996		5,6,8	1634-1837	1634-1837	Chelmsford	1790-1837		5E

ESSEX

Original Registers deposited at:
A = Essex Record Office, Wharf Road, Chelmsford CM12 6YT
B = Essex Record Office, Colchester and North East Essex Branch, Stanwell House, Stanwell Street, Colchester CO2 7DL
C = Waltham Forest Archives and Local Studies Library, Vestry Road, Walthamstow, London E17 9NH

Study adjacent parishes in counties of Cambridgeshire, Suffolk, Hertfordshire and Middlesex

Essex Record Office, Wharf Road, Chelmsford, CM12 6YT
Essex Record Office, Colchester and North East Branch, Stanwell House, Stanwell Street, Colchester, Essex, CO2 7DL

The following useful indexes have been compiled – see Introduction
Census Index 1851, 1861 & 1871 – Essex FHS, c/o Mr.s B Poole, 14 Roche Avenue, Rochford, Essex, SS4 1NG
Census Index 1851 & 1861 – East of London FHS, c/o M.r D Filby, 19 Cavendish Gardens, Ilford, Essex, IG1 3EA
Essex Marriage Index – Jack H. Baxter, 16 Chandos Parade, Benfleet, Essex, SS7 2HT 1754-1851
Essex Marriages in London – A. Benton, 46 Waldegrave Gardens, Upminster, Essex, RM14 1UX cover the period 1675-1754
Catholic Marriage Index – Institute of Heraldic & Genealogical Studies, Northgate, Canterbury, CT1 1BA for some south Essex parishes 1837-1870
Essex Baptism Index 1780-1840 – Mrs J.D.E. Nutt, 15 Westfield Close, Wickford, Essex, SS11 8JR
Essex Burials 1813-1865 – Jack Baxter, 16 Chandos Parade, Benfleet, Essex, SS7 2HT
Essex Wills Beneficiaries Index – Mrs Thora Broughton, 43 Pertwee Drive, Chelmsford, CM2 8DY

Essex's extent from east to west is rather more than 60 miles and from north to south about 50 miles. It is watered by seven principal rivers: the Colne, Blackwater, Chelmer, Crouch, Ingerbourn, Rodering and Cam. The population in 1841 was 344,979; in 1851, 344,110; in 1861, 404,834; in 1871, 466,436; in 1881, 576,434.

The soils include gravel, clay, marl and every species of loam. Agriculture was the principal feature of the county, the produce consisting of livestock, wheat and other grains, hops, coriander, caraway, saffron, teazle, etc. Towards the west there were large dairy farms. Large manufactories of serges, baizes and other woollen goods were established in several towns and villages, especially Colchester.

The information in the Index is abbreviated, and may mislead the searcher if reference is not made to the details contained in the several publications listed in the Introduction. It is essential that users of this book check the appropriate works before making further enquiries.

GLOUCESTERSHIRE

parish name	deposited original registers	I.G.I.	local census indexes	copies of registers at Soc. Gen.	Boyd's marriage index	1837-1851 Registration District	Pallot's marriage index	non-conform. records at P.R.O.	map ref.
Abenhall	A 1596-1988	1596-1860	5,8	1596-1860		Westbury-on-Severn			6E
Acton Turville	A 1665-1972	1599-1836	5,8,9	1671-1837	1671-1837	Chipping Sodbury	1790-1812		2G
Adlestrop	A 1538-1992	1538-1812	5,8	1800-1837		Stow-on-the-Wold			7K
Alderley	A 1557-1996	1557-1812	5,8,9	1559-1837	1559-1837	Chipping Sodbury	1790-1812		3F
Alderton	A 1596-1948	1596-1882	5,8	1800-1837		Winchcombe			8I
Aldsworth	A 1683-1970	1571-1749	5,8	1683-1970		Northleach			5J
Almondsbury	B 1653-1975		5,8,9	1813-1837		Thornbury			3D
Alstone	C 1546-1978	1813-1874	5,8	1550-1805	1651-1675	Winchcombe	1550-1805		8I
Alveston	B 1742-1969		5,8,9	1813-1837		Thornbury			3E
Alvington	A 1688-1988	1629-1812	5,8	1688-1914	1698-1836	Chepstow	1790-1836		5E
Ampney Crucis	A 1559-1986	1561-1837	5,8	1561-1930	1561-1837	Cirencester	1790-1837		5I
Ampney Crucis (det.)			5,8			Cirencester			4J
Ampney St Mary	A 1602-1996	1608-1812	5,8	1800-1837		Cirencester			5J(U)
Ampney St Peter	A 1599-1995	1579-1812	5,8	1800-1837		Cirencester			4J
Arlingham	A 1539-1985	1539-1882	4,5,6,7,8,9	1661-1837	1661-1837	Wheatenhurst			6F
Ashchurch	A 1555-1986	1555-1875	5,8	1555-1837	1555-1837	Tewkesbury	1790-1837		8H
Ashleworth	A 1566-1998	1566-1885	5,8	1660-1812	1660-1812	Gloucester			7G
Ashton under Hill	C 1586-1982	1586-1895	5,8	1586-1837	1586-1778	Evesham			8I
Aston Blank	A 1727-1970	1599-1881	5,8	1580-1726		Northleach			6J
Aston Somerville	A 1660-1812		5,8	1661-1835	1661-1812	Evesham	1790-1812		8J
Aston Subedge	A 1539-1992	1539-1812	5,8	1539-1837	1559-1812	Evesham	1790-1812		9J
Aust	B 1538-1990		5,8,9	1538-1648		Thornbury			3D
Avening	A 1557-1970	1578-1812	5,8	1557-1837	1557-1837	Stroud	1790-1813	1776-1837	4G
Awre	A 1538-1995	1538-1875	5,8	1538-1837		Westbury-on-Severn			5F
Aylburton			5,8			Chepstow			5E
Badgeworth	A 1558-1981	1570-1812	5,8	1559-1947		Cheltenham			6H
Bagendon	A 1630-1976	1577-1884	5,8	1800-1837		Cirencester			5I
Barnsley	A 1574-1995		5,8	1800-1837		Cirencester			5I
Barnwood	A 1651-1959	1569-1885	5,8	1651-1913		Gloucester			6G
Batsford	A 1562-1998	1562-1878	5,8	1562-1812	1565-1812	Shipston-on-Stour	1790-1812		8K
Baunton	A 1625-1950	1625-1877	5,8	1625-1950		Cirencester			5I
Beckford	C 1538-1973	1600-1895	5,8	1600-1836	1607-1700	Winchcombe			8I
Bedminster (Somerset)						Bedminster			1D
Berkeley	A 1558-1978	1571-1877	5,8,9	1560-1877	1571-1837	Thornbury		1822-1836	4E
Beverstone	A 1563-1988	1570-1812	5,8	1563-1837	1563-1837	Tetbury	1790-1812		4G
Bibury	A 1551-1984		5,8	1551-1946		Northleach			5J
Bishops Cleeve		1599-1813	5,8	1563-1837	1563-1812	Winchcombe	1790-1812		7H
Bisley	A 1547-1942	1608-1812	5,8	1548-1942		Stroud		1782-1837	5H
Bitton	B 1571-1934	1571-1674	5,8,9	1571-1837	1571-1674	Keynsham		1822-1832	1E
Blaisdon	A 1635-1992	1584-1875	5,8	1800-1836		Westbury-on-Severn			6F
Blakeney	A 1813-1966	1813-1860	5,8			Westbury-on-Severn		1823-1837	5E
Bledington	A 1703-1994	1605-1882	5,8	1703-1930		Stow-on-the-Wold			7K
Boddington	A 1653-1979	1612-1813	5,8	1695-1979	1676-1813	Tewkesbury			7H
Bourton on the Hill	A 1568-1931	1568-1877	5,8	1800-1837		Shipston on Stour			8J
Bourton on the Water	A 1655-1980	1605-1813	5,8	1654-1837	1655-1837	Stow-on-the-Wold	1790-1837	1801-1836	6J
Boxwell with Leighterton	A 1582-1992	1605-1813	5,8	1572-1837	1572-1837	Tetbury	1790-1812		4G
Bream	A 1751-1986	1813-1876	5,8	1823-1857		Monmouth			5E
Brimpsfield	A 1587-1976	1616-1812	5,8	1800-1837		Cirencester			6H
Bristol								1679-1856	2D
All Saints (City)	B 1556-1983		4,5,6,7,8,9	1780-1837		Bristol			2D
Cathedral	B 1669-1837		4,5,6,7,8,9	1669-1837	1669-1837	Bristol			2D
Christchurch (City)	B 1538-1984		4,5,6,7,8,9	1780-1837		Bristol			2D
Holy Trinity (St Philip)	B 1832-1966		4,5,6,7,8,9	1800-1852		Bristol			2D
St Augustine the Less	B 1577-1940	1577-1700	4,5,6,7,8,9	1577-1837		Bristol	1813-1818		2D
St Ewen	B 1538-1793		4,5,6,7,8,9			Bristol			2D
St George	B 1756-1991	1756-1783	4,5,6,7,8,9	1800-1837		Clifton			2D
St James	B 1559-1984		4,5,6,7,8,9	1800-1885		Clifton			2D
St John Baptist (City)	B 1558-1983		4,5,6,7,8,9	1780-1837		Bristol			2D
St Leonard	B 1689-1768		4,5,6,7,8,9			Bristol			2D
St Mary le Port	B 1837-1867	1561-1654	4,5,6,7,8,9	1780-1837		Bristol			2D
St Mary Redcliffe	B 1559-1994		4,5,6,7,8,9	1800-1837		Bristol			2D
St Michael the Archangel	B 1653-1960		4,5,6,7,8,9	1800-1837		Bristol			2D
St Nicholas	B 1538-1958		4,5,6,7,8,9	1800-1837		Bristol			2D
St Paul (Portland Sq)	B 1794-1988		4,5,6,7,8,9	1800-1837		Clifton			2D
St Peter			4,5,6,7,8,9	1780-1837		Bristol			2D
St Philip & St Jacob	B 1576-1952		4,5,6,7,8,9	1800-1837		Clifton			2D
St Stephen (City)	B 1559-1997		4,5,6,7,8,9	1800-1837		Bristol			2D
St Thomas	B 1552-1979		4,5,6,7,8,9	1800-1900		Bristol			2D
St Werburgh	B 1558-1988		4,5,6,7,8,9	1677-1867		Bristol			2D
Temple or Holy Cross	B 1558-1940		4,5,6,7,8,9	1800-1837		Bristol			2D
Broadwell	A 1539-1939	1539-1812	5,8	1539-1939	1605-1812	Stow-on-the-Wold	1790-1812		7K
Brockworth	A 1559-1985	1580-1812	5,8	1800-1837		Gloucester			6H
Bromsberrow	A 1558-1990	1558-1877	5,8	1558-1837	1558-1837	Newent	1790-1837		8F
Brookthorpe	A 1730-1996	1569-1882	5,8	1612-1812	1612-1812	Wheatenhurst	1790-1812		6G(K)
Buckland	A 1539-1987	1539-1812	5,8	1539-1837	1539-1812	Winchcombe	1790-1812		8I
Bulley	A 1673-1836	1602-1857	5,8	1541-1837		Westbury-on-Severn			7F
Cam	A 1569-1977	1599-1812	5,8	1569-1837	1651-1725	Dursley	1790-1812		4F
Charfield	A 1587-1972	1607-1812	5,8,9	1585-1837	1664-1837	Thornbury			4F
Charlton Abbots	A 1723-1996	1738-1877	5,8	1802-1833		Winchcombe			7I
Charlton Kings	A 1538-1967	1538-1885	5,8	1538-1812	1538-1812	Cheltenham	1790-1812		7H
Chedworth	A 1653-1971	1580-1882	5,8	1653-1837	1653-1812	Northleach	1790-1812	1799-1837	6I
Cheltenham	A 1558-1812	1604-1812	5,8	1558-1837	1558-1812	Cheltenham	1790-1812	1810-1837	7H
Cherington	A 1567-1944	1580-1812	5,8	1569-1837	1569-1812	Tetbury	1790-1812		4H
Childs Wickham	C 1552-1950	1560-1885	5,8	1560-1837	1560-1812	Evesham	1790-1812		9I
Chipping Campden	A 1717-1973	1616-1854	5,8	1616-1973	1616-1837	Shipston-on-Stour		1729-1837	8J
Chipping Sodbury	A 1661-1989	1607-1812	5,8,9	1629-1837	1662-1812	Chipping Sodbury	1790-1812		3F(W)

parish name	deposited original registers	I.G.I.	local census indexes	copies of registers at Soc. Gen.	Boyd's marriage index	1837-1851 Registration District	Pallot's marriage index	non-conform. records at P.R.O.	map ref.
Christchurch	A 1814-1970		5,8	1820-1842		Monmouth			6D
Churcham	A 1541-1872	1541-1857	5,8	1541-1837		Westbury-on-Severn			6F
Churchdown	A 1563-1984	1596-1812	5,8	1800-1837		Gloucester			6G
Cirencester	A 1560-1925	1578-1812	5,8	1560-1908		Cirencester		1651-1839	5I
Clapton			5,8			Stow-on-the-Wold			6J
Clearwell	A 1830-1986		5,8	1830-1961		Monmouth			5D
Clifford Chambers	D 1538-1954	1538-1878	5,8	1538-1837	1538-1812	Stratford-on-Avon	1790-1812		10K
Clifton	B 1538-1951		4,5,6,7,8,9	1538-1837		Clifton		1833-1837	2D
Coaley	A 1569-1996	1580-1812	5,8	1625-1837	1625-1837	Dursley	1790-1812		5F
Coates	A 1566-1972	1608-1812	5,8	1801-1836		Cirencester			4H
Coberley	A 1539-1979	1578-1812	5,8	1539-1979	1780-1812	Cheltenham			6H
Cold Ashton	A 1734-1942	1599-1881	5,8,9	1728-1837	1728-1837	Chipping Sodbury	1790-1812		1F
Coleford	A 1767-1969	1768-1815	5,8			Monmouth		1838-1854	5D
Colesbourne	A 1632-1964	1578-1877	5,8	1801-1837		Cirencester			6I
Coln Rogers	A 1755-1997	1613-1882	5,8	1755-1837	1755-1812	Northleach	1790-1812		5I
Coln St Aldwyn	A 1650-1977	1580-1870	5,8	1650-1928		Northleach			5J
Coln St Dennis	A 1561-1996	1561-1882	5,8	1801-1835		Northleach			6J
Compton Abdale	A 1720-1992	1616-1812	5,8	1800-1837		Northleach			6I
Compton Greenfield	B 1583-1988		5,8,9			Clifton			3D
Condicote	A 1688-1996	1610-1812	5,8	1688-1836		Stow-on-the-Wold			7J
Corse	A 1661-1919	1609-1885	5,8	1661-1919	1662-1812	Newent			7G
Cowley	A 1676-1835	1596-1812	5,8	1596-1835		Cheltenham			6H
Cranham	A 1666-1966	1618-1877	5,8	1800-1837		Stroud			6H
Cromhall	A 1653-1991	1571-1812	5,8,9	1571-1837	1670-1837	Thornbury			3E
Daglingworth	A 1561-1994	1577-1812	5,8	1800-1837		Cirencester			5I
Deerhurst	A 1559-1969	1559-1885	5,8	1700-1837	1700-1812	Tewkesbury			7G
Didbrook	A 1558-1837	1616-1812	5,8	1588-1837	1558-1804	Winchcombe			7I
Didmarton	A 1674-1991	1599-1812	5,8	1675-1837	1675-1812	Tetbury	1790-1812		3G
Dodington	B 1574-1964		5,8,9	1661-1837	1661-1837	Chipping Sodbury			2F
Donnington	A 1754-1987		5,8	1754-1835		Stow-on-the-Wold			7K
Dorsington	D 1572-1836	1594-1812	5,8	1602-1836	1602-1812	Stratford-on-Avon	1790-1812		10J
Dowdeswell	A 1575-1970	1599-1812	5,8	1575-1970		Northleach			6I
Down Ampney	A 1603-1980	1578-1812	5,8	1603-1979		Cirencester			4J
Down Hatherley	A 1559-1944	1578-1812	5,8			Gloucester			7G(B)
Doynton	B 1567-1983		5,8,9	1813-1837		Chipping Sodbury			2F
Driffield	A 1561-1995	1613-1813	5,8	1561-1835		Cirencester			4I
Drybrook	A 1817-1972		5,8	1817-1926		Westbury-on-Severn			6E
Dumbleton	A 1738-1961	1599-1812	5,8	1738-1837	1738-1812	Winchcombe			8I
Duntisbourne Abbots	A 1683-1999	1606-1812	5,8	1607-1837	1607-1812	Cirencester	1790-1837		5H
Duntisbourne Rouse	A 1545-1998	1545-1812	5,8	1545-1941	1549-1837	Cirencester	1790-1837		5H
Dursley	A 1639-1982	1606-1812	5,8	1636-1896	1636-1812	Dursley	1790-1837	1754-1837	4F
Dymock	A 1538-1964	1538-1876	5,8	1538-1837		Newent			8F
Dyrham	B 1568-1969		5,8,9	1813-1837		Chipping Sodbury			2F
East Dean (ex.par.)			5,8			Westbury-on-Severn			6E
Eastington	A 1558-1987	1578-1812	5,8	1558-1954	1558-1812	Wheatenhurst	1790-1812	1802-1837	5F
Eastington			5,8			Northleach			6J
Eastleach Martin	A 1538-1979	1570-1812	5,8	1558-1913		Northleach			5K
Eastleach Turville	A 1654-1980	1578-1812	5,8	1654-1964		Northleach			5K
Ebrington	A 1568-1812	1568-1812	5,8	1570-1837	1653-1812	Shipston-on-Stour	1790-1812		9K
Edgeworth	A 1554-1979	1579-1813	5,8	1554-1837	1554-1812	Cirencester	1790-1812		5H
Elberton	B 1763-1981		5,8,9	1683-1869	1683-1837	Thornbury			3D
Elkstone	A 1592-1889	1578-1812	5,8	1592-1836	1592-1812	Cirencester	1790-1812		6H
Elmore	A 1556-1986	1560-1877	5,8	1560-1837	1660-1837	Gloucester			6F
Elmstone Hardwicke	A 1564-1929	1605-1813	5,8	1688-1835	1688-1812	Tewkesbury			7H
English Bicknor	A 1561-1923	1561-1877	5,8	1752-1837		Monmouth			6D
Eyford (ex.par.)			5,8			Stow-on-the-Wold			7J
Fairford	A 1607-1975	1607-1854	5,8	1619-1837	1619-1837	Cirencester	1790-1837	1787-1837	5J
Falfield	A 1813-1877		5,8,9			Thornbury			4E
Farmington	A 1613-1965	1617-1812	5,8	1800-1837		Northleach			6J
Filton	B 1654-1977		4,5,6,7,8,9	1653-1870	1653-1812	Clifton	1790-1812		2E
Flaxley	A 1562-1989	1562-1862	5,8	1565-1989		Westbury-on-Severn			6E
Forthampton	A 1678-1965	1578-1812	5,8	1687-1837	1687-1812	Tewkesbury	1790-1812		8G
Frampton Cotterell	B 1561-1995		5,8,9	1612-1837		Chipping Sodbury		1801-1837	3E
Frampton on Severn	A 1626-1987	1577-1882	5,8	1625-1837	1625-1813	Wheatenhurst	1790-1812	1777-1837	5F
Fretherne	A 1631-1950	1617-1875	5,8	1618-1837	1671-1837	Wheatenhurst			5F
Frocester	A 1559-1973	1559-1812	5,8	1559-1971	1559-1837	Wheatenhurst	1790-1837		5F
Gloucester								1740-1837	6G
Cathedral	A 1662-1914	1717-1862	5,8	1661-1872		Gloucester			6G
Christchurch	A 1823-1963		5,8	1825-1889		Gloucester			6G
Holy Trinty	A 1557-1667	1613-1640	5,8	1557-1730		Gloucester			6G
Littleworth (ex.par.)			5,8			Gloucester			6G
St Aldate	A 1572-1931	1619-1812	5,8	1573-1837		Gloucester			6G
St Catherine	A 1687-1968	1571-1812	5,8	1605-1888		Gloucester			6G
St John the Baptist	A 1559-1974	1570-1750	5,8	1558-1848		Gloucester			6G
St Mary de Crypt with St Owen	A 1653-1906	1570-1812	5,8	1653-1849		Gloucester			6G
St Mary de Lode	A 1675-1986	1606-1812	5,8	1656-1887		Gloucester			6G
St Mary Magdalene with St Margaret	A 1790-1901		5,8			Gloucester			6G
St Michael	A 1553-1940	1602-1812	5,8	1653-1837		Gloucester	1790-1812		6G
St Nicholas	A 1558-1966	1558-1882	5,8	1558-1854		Gloucester			6G
St Peter's Abbey			5,8	1717-1914			1717-1914		6G
Great Badminton	A 1538-1931	1596-1871	5,8,9	1538-1837	1538-1837	Chipping Sodbury	1790-1812		3G
Great Barrington	A 1547-1978	1548-1882	5,8	1800-1837		Stow-on-the-Wold			6K
Great Rissington	A 1538-1995	1538-1812	5,8	1538-1913	1538-1837	Stow-on-the-Wold	1790-1837		6K
Great Washbourne	A 1757-1966	1600-1813	5,8	1800-1837		Winchcombe			8I(C)
Great Witcome	A 1749-1982	1570-1877	5,8	1800-1837		Cheltenham			6H(M)
Guiting Power	A 1560-1993	1560-1885	5,8	1560-1837	1560-1812	Winchcombe	1790-1812		7J

parish name	deposited original registers	I.G.I.	local census indexes	copies of registers at Soc. Gen.	Boyd's marriage index	1837-1851 Registration District	Pallot's marriage index	non-conform. records at P.R.O.	map ref.
Hailes	A 1814-1975		5,8	1813-1837		Winchcombe			8I
Hampnett	A 1591-1969	1571-1877	5,8	1737-1754		Northleach			6J
Hanham Abbots	B 1584-1989	1584-1696	5,8,9	1584-1681	1584-1657	Keynsham			1E
Hardwicke	A 1566-1979	1578-1885	5,8	1566-1837	1556-1812	Wheatenhurst	1790-1812		6F
Harescombe	A 1741-1812	1569-1812	5,8	1742-1913	1744-1812	Wheatenhurst	1790-1812		5G
Haresfield	A 1558-1992	1559-1812	5,8	1558-1964		Wheatenhurst			6G
Harnhill	A 1730-1994	1613-1812	5,8	1730-1844		Cirencester			4I
Hartpury	A 1571-1977	1571-1884	5,8	1662-1837	1662-1812	Newent			7F
Hasfield	A 1559-1995	1559-1877	5,8	1662-1837	1662-1812	Tewkesbury			7G
Hatherop	A 1578-1990	1578-1876	5,8	1578-1913	1651-1837	Cirencester	1790-1837		5J
Hawkesbury	A 1603-1901	1578-1885	5,8,9	1603-1837	1603-1812	Chipping Sodbury	1790-1812	1767-1837	3F
Hawling	A 1677-1996	1605-1812	5,8	1800-1837		Winchcombe			7I
Hazleton	A 1590-1979	1609-1811	5,8	1597-1978		Northleach			6J
Hempstead	A 1558-1971	1618-1812	5,8	1558-1837		Gloucester			6G
Henbury	B 1582-1987		4,5,6,7,8,9	1544-1812	1544-1812	Clifton	1790-1812		2D
Hewelsfield	A 1664-1993	1587-1812	5,8	1727-1837		Chepstow			5D
Hill	A 1653-1837	1571-1812	5,8,9	1653-1837	1653-1812	Thornbury	1790-1812		4E
Hinton on the Green	C 1735-1981	1618-1812	5,8	1735-1837	1735-1812	Evesham	1790-1812		9I
Honeybourne (Worcs.)						Evesham			9J
Horfield	B 1543-1974		4,5,6,7,8,9			Clifton			2D
Horsley	A 1587-1994	1580-1881	5,8	1591-1909	1591-1812	Stroud	1790-1812	1749-1806	4G
Horton	A 1567-1811	1578-1812	5,8,9	1567-1837	1567-1812	Chipping Sodbury	1790-1812		3F
Huntley	A 1661-1940	1583-1812	5,8	1583-1957	1583-1837	Westbury-on-Severn	1790-1837		6F
Ilmington (Warwicks.)						Shipston-on-Stour			9K
Incomb	A 1545-1995	1613-1701	5,8	1563-1833	1563-1812	Stow-on-the-Wold	1790-1812		7K
Iron Acton	B 1570-1992		5,8,9	1570-1837	1660-1837	Chipping Sodbury			3E
Kemerton		1576-1882	5,8	1572-1948	1575-1812	Tewkesbury	1790-1812		8H
Kempley	A 1637-1979	1569-1858	5,8	1637-1903		Newent			8E
Kempsford	A 1573-1990	1573-1882	5,8	1653-1837	1653-1700	Cirencester			4J
Kingscote	A 1651-1995	1578-1812	5,8	1652-1837	1652-1725	Tetbury	1790-1812		4G
Kings Stanley	A 1573-1993	1573-1882	5,8	1573-1837	1573-1837	Stroud	1790-1812		5G
Kingswood	A 1598-1984	1578-1812	5,8	1598-1837	1598-1812	Dursley	1790-1812	1757-1840	3F
Lancaut			5,8			Chepstow			4D
Lasborough	A 1826-1987		5,8	1559-1844		Tetbury			4G
Lassington	A 1655-1966	1570-1860	5,8	1800-1837		Gloucester			7G(A)
Lechlade	A 1686-1988	1612-1812	5,8	1686-1847		Faringdon			4K
Leckhampton	A 1682-1978	1601-1812	5,8	1601-1978		Cheltenham			7H
Leigh (Lye)	A 1560-1976	1569-1812	5,8	1560-1837	1560-1837	Tewkesbury			7G
Leonard Stanley	A 1570-1985	1570-1877	5,8	1570-1837	1570-1812	Stroud	1790-1812		5G(R)
Little Barrington	A 1685-1996	1581-1885	5,8	1800-1837		Northleach			5K
Littledean	A 1684-1987	1617-1875	5,8	1684-1936		Westbury-on-Severn		1803-1837	6E
Little Rissington	A 1543-1995	1599-1812	5,8	1544-1837	1550-1837	Stow-on-the-Wold	1790-1837		6K
Little Sodbury	A 1754-1845	1599-1813	5,8,9	1660-1837	1660-1837	Chipping Sodbury			3F
Little Washbourne	C 1813-1981	1813-1877	5,8	1813-1981		Winchomb			8I(D)
Littleton On Severn	B 1701-1981		5,8,9	1684-1837	1688-1812	Thornbury			4D
Longborough	A 1676-1964	1612-1812	5,8	1676-1964		Stow-on-the-Wold			8K
Longhope	A 1702-1976	1583-1812	5,8	1702-1965		Westbury-on-Severn			6E
Long Marston	D 1603-1980	1603-1895	5,8	1680-1837	1680-1812	Stratford-on-Avon	1790-1812		10J
Longney	A 1661-1987	1600-1868	5,8	1660-1837	1660-1837	Wheatenhurst			6F
Lower Lemington	A 1685-1930	1571-1813	5,8	1813-1833	1576-1812	Shipston-on-Stour	1790-1812		8K
Lower Slaughter	A 1814-1995		5,8	1813-1837	1812-1837	Stow-on-the-Wold	1790-1837		7J
Lower Swell	A 1655-1978	1605-1875	5,8	1612-1837	1686-1812	Stow-on-the-Wold	1790-1812		7J
Lydney	A 1678-1988	1661-1876	5,8	1628-1837		Chepstow			5E
Maisemore	A 1538-1998	1557-1882	5,8	1538-1837	1557-1812	Gloucester	1790-1813		7G
Maiseyhampton	A 1570-1966	1578-1812	5,8	1570-1979		Cirencester			5J
Mangotsfield	B 1579-1992		5,8,9	1762-1837		Keynsham		1824-1837	2E
Marshfield	A 1558-1978	1558-1693	5,8,9	1558-1837	1558-1693	Chipping Sodbury		1806-1833	2F
Matson	A 1553-1986	1555-1812	5,8	1553-1837	1553-1812	Gloucester	1790-1812		6G(H)
Mickleton	A 1590-1978	1572-1812	5,8	1594-1837	1594-1812	Shipston-on-Stour	1790-1812		9J
Minchinhampton	A 1558-1975	1561-1878	5,8	1566-1837	1566-1812	Stroud	1790-1812	1814-1837	4G
Minsterworth	A 1633-1963	1575-1858	5,8	1633-1837	1633-1837	Westbury-on-Severn	1790-1812		6F
Miserden	A 1574-1953	1613-1812	5,8	1801-1837		Stroud			5H
Mitcheldean	A 1680-1991	1588-1853	5,8	1680-1954	1630-1812	Westbury-on-Severn	1790-1812	1759-1837	6E
Moreton-in-Marsh	A 1643-1997	1607-1885	5,8	1607-1975	1672-1812	Shipston-on-Stour	1790-1812	1801-1837	8K
Morton Valence	A 1681-1991	1569-1835	5,8	1605-1837	1664-1837	Wheatenhurst			5F(N)
Nailsworth	A 1794-1962		5,8			Stroud		1776-1837	4G
Naunton	A 1539-1982	1545-1812	5,8	1545-1837	1545-1812	Stow-on-the-Wold	1790-1812		7J
Newent	A 1672-1966	1597-1862	5,8	1754-1949		Newent		1818-1837	7F
Newington Bagpath	A 1754-1968	1578-1812	5,8	1599-1837	1601-1812	Tetbury	1790-1812		4G
Newland	A 1560-1989	1560-1877	5,8	1741-1837		Monmouth			5D
Newnham	A 1547-1998	1609-1812	5,8	1547-1837	1661-1837	Westbury-on-Severn		1823-1837	6E
North Cerney	A 1568-1990	1568-1885	5,8	1800-1837		Cirencester			5I
Northleach	A 1556-1967	1620-1812	5,8	1800-1837		Northleach		1801-1831	6J(T)
North Nibley	A 1567-1968	1567-1882	5,8	1567-1837	1617-1837	Dursley			4F
Norton	A 1686-1974	1569-1812	5,8	1686-1837		Gloucester			7G
Notgrove	A 1660-1981	1605-1877	5,8	1800-1837	1800-1837	Stow-on-the-Wold			7J
Nympsfield	A 1678-1993	1578-1877	5,8	1609-1837	1609-1812	Dursley	1790-1812		4G
Oddington	A 1549-1941	1580-1812	5,8	1549-1837		Stow-on-the-Wold			7K
Oldbury on the Hill	A 1567-1978	1596-1812	5,8	1568-1837	1568-1750	Tetbury	1790-1812		3G
Oldbury on Severn	A 1538-1741	1537-1747	5,8,9	1538-1733	1538-1733	Thornbury			4E
Oldland	B 1813-1991	1584-1696	5,8,9	1584-1681	1584-1657	Keynsham			2E
Old Sodbury	A 1684-1990	1605-1812	5,8,9	1600-1837	1684-1837	Chipping Sodbury	1790-1812		2F
Olveston	B 1560-1966		5,8,9	1560-1837	1560-1812	Thornbury	1790-1812		3D
Owlpen	A 1677-1993	1613-1877	5,8	1686-1897	1687-1837	Dursley	1790-1812		4G
Oxenhall	A 1665-1979	1583-1877	5,8	1800-1837		Newent			7F
Oxenton	A 1678-1979	1578-1812	5,8	1679-1906		Tewkesbury			8H
Ozleworth	A 1698-1836	1576-1812	5,8	1698-1837	1698-1812	Tetbury	1790-1812		4F
Painswick	A 1547-1975	1544-1877	5,8		1651-1725	Stroud	1790-1812	1780-1837	5G
Parkend	A 1822-1989		5,8			Monmouth			5E

GLOUCESTERSHIRE

parish name	deposited original registers	I.G.I.	local census indexes	copies of registers at Soc. Gen.	Boyd's marriage index	1837-1851 Registration District	Pallot's marriage index	non-conform. records at P.R.O.	map ref.
Pauntley	A 1538-1994	1538-1856	5,8	1538-1837		Newent			8F
Pebworth	C 1595-1970	1595-1812	5,8	1595-1837	1612-1726	Evesham			9J
Pitchcombe	A 1709-1955	1639-1885	5,8	1709-1837		Stroud		1828-1837	5G(Q)
Poulton	A 1635-1991		5,8	1695-1979		Cirencester			4J
Prescott (ex.par.)			5,8			Winchcombe			7I
Prestbury	A 1633-1982	1605-1837	5,8	1633-1837	1633-1837	Cheltenham	1790-1837		7H
Preston	A 1676-1997	1578-1812	5,8	1800-1837		Cirencester			5I
Preston	A 1665-1988	1586-1857	5,8	1801-1832		Newent			8E
Preston on Stour	D 1540-1970	1540-1895	5,8	1541-1913	1541-1812	Stratford-on-Avon	1790-1812		10K
Prinknash Park (ex.par.)			5,8			Gloucester			6G(L)
Pucklechurch	B 1590-1988		5,8,9	1813-1837		Chipping Sodbury			2E
Quedgeley	A 1559-1974	1559-1836	5,8	1559-1837	1559-1837	Gloucester	1790-1812		6G
Quenington	A 1653-1977	1578-1882	5,8	1800-1837		Cirencester			5J
Quinton	D 1547-1976	1547-1895	5,8	1548-1837	1548-1812	Shipston-on-Stour	1790-1812		9K
Randwick	A 1662-1877	1607-1812	5,8	1662-1837		Stroud		1797-1837	5G(P)
Rangeworthy	A 1704-1977	1575-1812	5,8,9	1663-1837	1663-1837	Thornbury			3E(V)
Redwick & Northwick	B 1645-1988		5,8,9			Thornbury			3D
Rendcomb	A 1566-1996	1566-1881	5,8	1566-1837	1566-1812	Cirencester	1790-1812		6I
Rockhampton	A 1563-1979	1580-1812	5,8,9	1563-1837	1661-1837	Thornbury			4E
Rodborough	A 1692-1939	1620-1837	5,8	1620-1837	1620-1837	Stroud		1762-1837	5G
Rodmarton	A 1605-1879	1578-1813	5,8	1800-1837		Cirencester			4H
Roel (ex.par.)			5,8			Winchcombe			7I
Ruardean	A 1538-1940	1538-1812	5,8	1540-1837		Ross		1795-1837	6E
Rudford	A 1729-1995	1583-1812	5,8	1800-1837		Newent			7F
St Briavels	A 1660-1996	1618-1812	5,8	1618-1839		Chepstow			5D
St George	B 1756-1991		4,5,6,7,8,9			Clifton		1820-1837	2E
Saintbury	A 1561-1976	1561-1884	5,8	1585-1837	1585-1812	Evesham	1790-1812		9J
Salperton	A 1617-1988	1609-1812	5,8	1800-1837		Northleach			7I
Sandhurst	A 1537-1971	1569-1812	5,8	1800-1837		Gloucester			7G
Sapperton	A 1661-1914	1578-1812	5,8	1662-1836	1662-1836	Cirencester			5H
Saul	A 1573-1996	1596-1812	5,8	1583-1837	1574-1837	Wheatenhurst			5F
Sevenhampton	A 1588-1985	1588-1837	5,8	1605-1837	1605-1837	Northleach	1790-1837		7I
Sezincote			5,8			Stow-on-the-Wold			8J
Sheepscombe	A 1821-1980		5,8			Stroud			6G
Sherborne	A 1570-1990	1572-1882	5,8	1800-1836		Northleach			6J
Shipton	A 1666-1988	1571-1877	5,8			Northleach			6I
Shipton Moyne	A 1570-1987	1570-1812	5,8	1587-1837	1587-1812	Tetbury	1790-1812		3G
Shirehampton	B 1727-1973		4,5,6,7,8,9			Clifton			2D
Shurdington	A 1556-1988	1578-1812	5,8	1800-1837		Cheltenham			6H(G)
Siddington St Mary	A 1606-1778	1578-1812	5,8			Cirencester			4I
Siddington St Peter	A 1687-1980	1578-1812	5,8	1801-1837		Cirencester			4I
Siston	B 1576-1980	1576-1641	5,8,9	1576-1641	1574-1641	Keynsham			2E
Slimbridge	A 1635-1989	1571-1812	5,8	1571-1837	1626-1812	Dursley	1790-1812		5F
Snowshill	A 1732-1985	1606-1812	5,8	1593-1837	1593-1603	Winchcombe			8J
South Cerney	A 1583-1998	1578-1861	5,8	1800-1837		Cirencester			4I
Southrop	A 1656-1983	1617-1812	5,8	1656-1837	1656-1837	Northleach	1790-1837		5K
Standish	A 1559-1979	1560-1812	5,8	1559-1978	1559-1812	Wheatenhurst	1790-1812		5G
Stanley Pontlarge			5,8			Winchcombe			8I(E)
Stanton	A 1572-1950	1612-1812	5,8	1572-1837	1572-1812	Winchcombe	1790-1812		8I
Stanway	A 1573-1902	1580-1812	5,8	1800-1837		Winchcombe			8I
Stapleton	B 1720-1994		4,5,6,7,8,9	1675-1812	1675-1738	Clifton			2E
Staunton	A 1653-1980	1583-1812	5,8	1754-1837		Monmouth			6D
Staverton	A 1538-1979	1539-1812	5,8	1538-1976		Cheltenham			7H
Stinchcombe	A 1582-1984	1606-1812	5,8	1582-1837	1583-1812	Dursley	1790-1812		4F
Stoke Gifford	B 1556-1987		4,5,6,7,8,9	1748-1837		Clifton			2E
Stone	A 1594-1979	1578-1812	5,8	1594-1812	1594-1812	Thornbury	1790-1812		4E
Stonehouse	A 1558-1958	1558-1867	5,8	1558-1837	1558-1812	Stroud	1790-1812	1824-1837	5G
Stow on the Wold	A 1558-1985	1610-1812	5,8	1800-1837		Stow-on-the-Wold		1821-1837	7K
Stratton	A 1600-1980	1578-1867	5,8	1800-1837		Cirencester			5I
Stroud	A 1624-1972	1578-1812	5,8	1580-1837		Stroud		1712-1837	5G
Sudeley Manor	A 1705-1972	1714-1817	5,8	1801		Winchcombe			7I
Sutton-under-Brailes (see Warwickshire)									
Swindon	A 1608-1987	1570-1813	5,8	1638-1837	1638-1837	Cheltenham	1790-1812		7H
Syde	A 1686-1990	1578-1812	5,8	1686-1837	1686-1812	Cirencester	1790-1812		6H
Taynton	A 1538-1909	1538-1858	5,8	1800-1837		Newent			7F
Temple Guiting	A 1570-1995	1580-1870	5,8	1580-1837	1676-1812	Winchcombe			7J
Tetbury	A 1631-1976	1578-1875	5,8	1626-1837	1631-1812	Tetbury	1790-1812	1822-1837	4G
Tewkesbury	A 1559-1974	1570-1850	5,8	1800-1837	1561-1808	Tewkesbury		1752-1837	8H
Thornbury	A 1550-1988	1550-1812	5,8,9	1550-1837	1550-1812	Thornbury	1790-1812	1796-1837	4E
Tibberton	A 1659-1953	1586-1858	5,8	1764-1858		Newent			7F
Tidenham	A 1708-1988	1585-1812	5,8	1750-1837		Chepstow			4D
Tirley (Trinley)	A 1653-1992	1601-1867	5,8	1655-1837	1655-1812	Tewkesbury	1790-1812		7G
Toddington	A 1655-1979	1599-1812	5,8	1710-1836	1710-1783	Winchcombe			8I
Todenham	A 1721-1951	1583-1811	5,8	1583-1951	1583-1812	Shipston-on-Stour	1781-1812		8K
Tormarton	B 1679-1931	1678-1882	5,8,9	1600-1995	1600-1812	Chipping Sodbury	1790-1812		2F
Tortworth	A 1592-1990	1599-1811	5,8,9	1620-1837	1620-1812	Thornbury	1790-1812		4F
Tredington	A 1550-1837	1599-1812	5,8	1675-1812	1675-1812	Tewkesbury			8H
Turkdean	A 1572-1962	1572-1885	5,8	1572-1837	1572-1837	Northleach	1790-1837		6J
Twyning	A 1648-1975	1618-1812	5,8	1674-1837	1674-1812	Tewkesbury	1790-1812		8H
Tytherington	A 1662-1990	1609-1812	5,8,9	1662-1837	1662-1837	Thornbury			3E
Uley	A 1668-1992	1599-1877	5,8	1599-1837	1668-1812	Dursley	1790-1812	1793-1837	4F
Upleadon	A 1538-1990	1538-1857	5,8	1800-1857		Newent			7F
Upper Slaughter	A 1538-1982	1580-1812	5,8	1538-1837	1538-1837	Stow-on-the-Wold	1790-1837		7J
Upper Swell	A 1543-1980	1605-1812	5,8	1800-1837		Stow-on-the-Wold			7J
Upton St Leonard	A 1539-1986	1569-1812	5,8	1736-1837		Gloucester			6G
Walton Cardiff	A 1677-1948	1732-1812	5,8	1677-1855		Tewkesbury			8H
Wapley & Codrington	B 1662-1974		5,8,9	1664-1837	1664-1837	Chipping Sodbury			2F
Welford	D 1561-1922	1561-1885	5,8	1561-1934	1561-1716	Stratford-on-Avon			10J
Westbury on Severn	A 1538-1993	1538-1857	5,8	1538-1941		Westbury-on-Severn			6F

153

GLOUCESTERSHIRE

parish name	deposited original registers	I.G.I.	local census indexes	copies of registers at Soc. Gen.	Boyd's marriage index	1837-1851 Registration District	Pallot's marriage index	non-conform. records at P.R.O.	map ref.
Westbury on Trym	B 1559-1979	1559-1713	4,5,6,7,8,9	1559-1763	1559-1763	Clifton		1793-1837	2D
Westcote	A 1630-1995		5,8	1630-1837	1630-1812	Stow-on-the-Wold			7K
West Dean (ex.par.)			5,8			Monmouth			5E
Westerleigh	B 1693-1973		5,8,9	1660-1837	1660-1837	Chipping Sodbury			2E
West Littleton		1838-1878	5,8,9	1600-1812	1600-1812	Chipping Sodbury	1790-1812		2F
Westonbirt	A 1654-1996	1610-1812	5,8	1596-1837	1596-1812	Tetbury	1790-1812		3G
Weston Subedge	A 1654-1985	1612-1812	5,8	1612-1837	1612-1812	Evesham	1790-1812		9J
Weston upon Avon	D 1685-1999	1686-1841	5,8	1685-1841	1690-1812	Stratford-on-Avon	1790-1812		10J
Whaddon	A 1674-1991	1617-1812	5,8	1620-1837	1620-1812	Gloucester	1790-1812		6G(J)
Whitminster (Wheatenhurst)	A 1538-1970	1571-1812	5,8	1538-1837	1660-1837	Wheatenhurst			5F(O)
Whittington	A 1539-1997	1529-1882	5,8	1774-1836		Northleach			7I
Wick & Abson	B 1687-1993		5,8,9	1813-1837		Chipping Sodbury			2F
Wickwar	A 1689-1983	1578-1812	5,8,9	1637-1837	1689-1812	Chipping Sodbury	1790-1812	1818-1836	3F
Willersey	A 1721-1933	1620-1812	5,8	1606-1837	1723-1812	Evesham	1790-1812		9J
Winchcombe	A 1539-1983	1607-1812	5,8	1539-1837	1539-1812	Winchcombe	1790-1812		7I
Windrush	A 1586-1961	1586-1882	5,8	1791-1837		Northleach			6K
Winson	A 1577-1985		5,8	1801-1836		Northleach			5J
Winstone	A 1540-1836	1607-1812	5,8	1540-1837	1540-1837	Cirencester	1790-1837		5H
Winterbourne	B 1600-1986		4,5,6,7,8,9	1600-1837	1600-1812	Clifton		1806-1837	2E
Withington	A 1609-1981	1600-1877	5,8	1800-1837		Northleach			6I
Woodchester	A 1563-1981	1563-1877	5,8	1563-1861	1563-1836	Stroud			5G(S)
Woolaston	A 1688-1969	1587-1765	5,8	1688-1864	1697-1837	Chepstow	1790-1837		4D
Woolstone	A 1814-1979	1570-1812	5,8	1800-1837		Tewkesbury			8H
Wormington	A 1719-1960	1620-1812	5,8	1719-1837	1719-1812	Winchcombe	1790-1812		8I(F)
Wotton under Edge	A 1571-1924	1578-1812	5,8	1571-1900	1660-1837	Dursley		1767-1837	4F
Wyck Rissington	A 1739-1995	1605-1812	5,8	1605-1837	1605-1837	Stow-on-the-Wold	1790-1838		7K
Yanworth	A 1695-1987	1605-1877	5,8	1800-1836		Northleach			6I
Yate	B 1660-1966	1609-1812	5,8,9	1660-1837	1660-1837	Chipping Sodbury			3F

Original registers deposited at:
A = Gloucestershire Record Office, Clarence Row, Alvin Street, Gloucester, GL1 3DW
B = Bristol Record Office, B Bond Warehouse, Smeaton Road, Bristol, BS1 6XN
C = Worcestershire Record Office, County Hall, Spetchley, Worcester WR5 2NP
D = Warwickshire County Record Office, Priory Park, Cape Road, Warwick CV34 4JS

Study adjacent parishes in counties of Oxfordshire, Wiltshire, Somerset, Monmouth, Hereford, Worcestershire and Warwickshire

Gloucestershire Record Office, Clarence Row, Alvin Street, Gloucester, GL1 3DW
Bristol Record Office, B Bond Warehouse, Smeaton Road, Bristol, BS1 6XN

The following useful indexes have been compiled – see Introduction
Bristol & Bedminster Census Indexes 1841, 1861, 1871 and 1891 – Miss J. Baker, Bristol Record Office, B Bond Warehouse, Smeaton Road, Bristol, BS1 6XN
Bath & District Census Indexes 1841 & 1851 – Bristol & Avon FHS, Mrs Pam Bishop, 8 Benville Avenue, Coombe Dingle, Bristol, BS9 2RX
Census Index 1851 – County Record Office (excluding Bristol)
Bristol and District Census Index 1851 – Bristol & Avon FHS, Mrs Pam Bishop, 8 Benville Avenue, Coombe Dingle, Bristol, BS9 2RX
Arlingham Census Index 1841-1891 – Gloucester Library, Quayside Wing, Gloucester, GL1 2HY
Gloucestershire Marriage Index 1800-1837 – Gloucestershire FHS, c/o Mrs Janet Selley, Penlea, Selsey West, Stroud, Gloucestershire, GL5 5LJ
Bristol and South Glos. 1754-1837 – Mr M.L. Browning, Elm Tree Farm, Harts Lane, Hallatrow, Bristol, BS39 6EA
Gloucestershire Marriage Allegations 1701-1823 – Gloucestershire Record Office, Clarence Row, Alvin Street, Gloucester, GL1 3DW
Bristol Marriages 1800-1837 – Mrs Pam Bishop, 8 Benville Avenue, Coombe Dingle, Bristol, BS9 2RX
Kingswood Index 1600-1900 – Mrs D.P. Lindegaard, 49 Clayfield Road, Brislington, Bristol, BS4 4NH
Avon Monumental Inscriptions – Bristol & Avon FHS, c/o R.A. Lewin, 7 South Croft, Henleaze, Bristol, BS9 4PS
Gloucestershire Monumental Inscriptions Index – Gloucestershire FHS, c/o Mr J. Rawes, 11 Trowscoed Avenue, Cheltenham, Gloucestershire, GL53 7BP

Gloucestershire's length from north-east to south-west is about 70 miles and its breadth from east to north-west about 40 miles. It is watered by five principal rivers: the Severn, Wye, Frome or Stroud and the two Avons. The population in 1841 was 431,495; in 1851, 458,805; in 1861, 485,770; in 1871 534,640; in 1881, 572,433.

The soils are various loams and gravel. Produce included wheat, barley and turnips. Cattle were raised and dairy-farming was important. Manufactures were various and included woollen cloths, hats, leather, wire, pins, brass, edge-tools and paper. Coal was found in great abundance in the forests of Dean and Kingswood, at Bitton, Bucklechurch, Siston, Iron Acton, Wick and Abson.

The information in the Index is abbreviated, and may mislead the searcher if reference is not made to the details contained in the several publications listed in the Introduction. It is essential that users of this book check the appropriate works before making further enquiries.

HAMPSHIRE

parish name	deposited original registers	I.G.I.	local census indexes	copies of registers at Soc. Gen.	Boyd's marriage index	1837-1851 Registration District	Pallot's marriage index	non-conform. records at P.R.O.	map ref.
Abbots Ann	A 1561-1989	1561-1877	5,8,9	1561-1883		Andover			8D
Aldershot	E 1571-1998	1572-1876	5,8	1590-1859	1590-1812	Aldershot	1790-1812		9J
Alton	A 1615-1975	1615-1876	5,8,9	1711-1759		Alton		1788-1837	7H
Alverstoke	C 1559-2000	1559-1875	5,8,9	1559-1975		Alverstoke	1780-1837		2G
Amport	A 1665-1994	1665-1876	5,8,9	1665-1812	1665-1812	Andover	1790-1812		8C
Andover	A 1587-1983	1587-1875	5,8,9	1587-1876		Andover		1739-1837	8D
Appleshaw	A 1695-1995		5,8,9			Andover			9C
Arreton	B 1653-1968		5,8	1654-1837	1654-1837	Isle of Wight		1799-1837	3L
Ashe	A 1617-1991	1607-1876	5,8,9	1606-1887		Whitchurch			8F
Ashley	A 1725-1980		5,8,9			Stockbridge			6E
Ashmansworth	A 1811-1993		5,8,9	1811-1965	1813-1836	Kingsclere			9E
Avington	A 1609-1991		5,8,9	1609-1920		Winchester			6F
Barton Stacey	A 1713-1986		5,8,9	1713-1896		Andover			7E
Basingstoke	A 1638-1985	1639-1875	5,8,9	1638-1919	1638-1812	Basingstoke	1790-1837	1739-1837	9G
Baughurst	A 1678-1992		5,8,9	1678-1837	1678-1812	Kingsclere	1790-1812		10G
Beaulieu	A 1653-1994		5,8,9	1653-1745		New Forest			2D
Bedhampton	C 1688-1989	1688-1876	5,8,9			Havant			3H
Bembridge	B 1827-1990		5,8,9			Isle of Wight			3M
Bentley	A 1538-1958	1539-1877	5,8,9	1538-1838	1541-1812	Alton	1790-1812		8I
Bentworth	A 1559-1989		5,8,9	1603-1837	1603-1837	Alton	1790-1837		7H
Bighton	A 1573-1992	1573-1876	5,8,9			Alresford			7G
Binstead	B 1708-1976		5,8,9	1708-1837		Isle of Wight			3L
Binstead	A 1653-1983	1653-1864	5,8,9	1653-1813		Alton			7I
Bishopstoke	A 1658-1985		5,8,9	1657-1837		Winchester		1817-1828	5F
Bishops Sutton	A 1711-1981	1711-1876	5,8,9	1711-1912		Alresford			6G
Bishops Waltham	A 1612-1992	1612-1876	5,8,9	1780-1812		Droxford			4F
Blendworth	C 1586-1965	1586-1876	5,8,9	1780-1871		Catherington			4I
Boarhunt	A 1654-1988	1683-1805	5,8	1654-1909		Fareham			4G
Boldre	A 1596-1992	1626-1840	5,8,9	1596-1813	1596-1812	Lymington	1790-1813		2D
Bonchurch	B 1734-1992	1754-1836	5,8	1754-1837	1754-1837	Isle of Wight	1780-1836		2M
Bossington	A 1763-1990	1764-1879	5,8,9	1763-1832		Stockbridge			6D
Botley	A 1679-1986	1679-1876	5,8,9	1679-1837		South Stoneham			4F
Brading	B 1547-1987		5,8,9	1547-1857	1547-1812	Isle of Wight	1790-1812		2M
Bradley	A 1725-1994		5,8,9	1725-1812		Basingstoke			7G
Bramdean	A 1573-1992	1573-1876	5,8,9	1573-1948		Alresford			6G
Bramley	A 1580-1984	1580-1875	5,8,9	1580-1812	1580-1812	Basingstoke	1580-1812		10H
Bramshaw	A 1597-1992	1597-1812	5,8,9			New Forest			4C
Bramshott	A 1560-1972	1560-1876	5,8,9			Farnborough			6J
Bransgore	A 1822-1993	1822-1876	5,8,9	1822-1840		Christchurch			2B
Breamore	A 1675-1958		5,8,9	1675-1840		Fordingbridge			5B
Brixton	B 1644-1987		5,8			Isle of Wight			2K
Brockenhurst	A 1594-1940		5,8,9	1594-1940	1629-1837	Lymington			3C
Brook	B 1653-1978		5,8,9	1654-1776		Isle of Wight			2J
Broughton	A 1639-1972	1639-1876	5,8,9	1639-1868		Stockbridge			7C
Broughton (detached)			5,8,9			Stockbridge			6C
Brown Candover	A 1611-1992	1612-1837	5,8,9	1612-1889	1612-1837	Alresford			7G
Buckholt (ex.par.)			5,8			Stockbridge			6C
Bullington	A 1715-1986		5,8,9	1754-1812	1755-1812	Andover	1755-1812		8E
Burghclere	A 1559-1981		5,8,9	1559-1812	1559-1812	Kingsclere	1790-1812		10E
Buriton	A 1678-1992	1695-1876	5,8,9			Petersfield			5I
Bursledon	A 1648-1980		5,8,9	1648-1836		South Stoneham			4F
Calbourne	B 1559-1980		5,8,9	1559-1837	1559-1837	Isle of Wight	1790-1812		3K
Carisbrooke	B 1572-1982	1572-1837	5,8	1572-1837	1572-1837	Isle of Wight	1780-1837	1853-1858	3K
Carisbrooke									
Castle (detached)			5,8			Isle of Wight			2J(a)
Castle (detached)			5,8			Isle of Wight			3K(b)
Castle (St Nicholas)	B 1723-1988		5,8	1723-1754	1723-1754	Isle of Wight			3K(c)
Catherington	C 1602-1999	1599-1876	5,8,9			Catherington			4H
Chale	B 1679-1989		5,8	1699-1837	1699-1837	Isle of Wight			2K
Chalton	C 1538-1973	1537-1883	5,8,9			Catherington		1799-1837	4I
Chawton	A 1596-1984		5,8,9			Alton			7H
Cheriton	A 1557-1990	1557-1877	5,8,9	1742-1885		Alresford			6G
Chilbolton	A 1699-1977		5,8,9	1774-1812		Andover			7E
Chilcomb	A 1556-1950		5,8			Winchester			6F
Chilton Candover	A 1672-1877	1612-1837	5,8,9	1672-1877		Alresford			7G
Chilworth	A 1721-1990	1721-1879	5,8,9	1721-1837		South Stoneham			5E
Christchurch			5,8,9	1576-1927	1682-1812	Christchurch		1780-1837	2A
Church Oakley	A 1559-1985		5,8,9	1559-1812	1559-1812	Basingstoke	1790-1812		9G
Clanfield	C 1548-1992	1563-1882	5,8,9	1678-1820		Catherington			5I
Cliddesden	A 1636-1993	1636-1876	5,8,9	1636-1812	1636-1812	Basingstoke	1636-1812		8H
Colemore	A 1563-1975	1563-1879	5,8,9	1563-1812		Petersfield	1790-1837		6H
Combe	F 1560-1985		5,8	1560-1835	1560-1812	Hungerford	1790-1812		10D
Compton	A 1678-1977		5,8,9	1695-1837	1695-1837	Winchester			6E
Corhampton	A 1665-1988		5,8,9			Droxford			5G
Crawley	A 1649-1984		5,8,9	1675-1812	1675-1812	Winchester	1790-1812		7E
Crondall	E 1569-1889		5,8,9	1569-1867	1546-1812	Hartley Wintney	1790-1812	1792-1836	8I
Crux Easton	A 1737-1994		5,8,9			Kingsclere			9E
Deane	A 1659-1992*	1659-1840	5,8,9	1659-1840	1679-1812	Basingstoke	1679-1812		9G
Dibden	A 1673-1986		5,8,9	1731-1854		New Forest			4E
Dogmersfield	A 1675-1994		5,8,9	1675-1835	1695-1812	Hartley Wintney	1790-1812		9I
Droxford	A 1633-1987	1633-1876	5,8,9			Droxford			4G
Dummer	A 1541-1987		5,8,9	1541-1812	1541-1812	Basingstoke	1541-1812		8G
Dunwood (ex.par.)			5,8,9			Romsey			5D
Durley	A 1560-1991		5,8,9	1561-1850		Droxford			5F
East Cowes	B 1834-1987		5,8	1836	1836-1837	Isle of Wight		1829-1837	4L
East Dean	A 1682-1993		5,8,9			Romsey			6C
East Meon	A 1560-1995	1560-1875	5,8,9	1560-1963		Petersfield			5H
Easton	A 1692-1999		5,8,9			Winchester			6F

155

HAMPSHIRE

parish name	deposited original registers	I.G.I.	local census indexes	copies of registers at Soc. Gen.	Boyd's marriage index	1837-1851 Registration District	Pallot's marriage index	non-conform. records at P.R.O.	map ref.
Eastrop	A 1759-1994	1750-1840	5,8,9	1750-1840	1759-1807	Basingstoke	1790-1807		9H(B)
East Stratton	A 1538-1989	1538-1809	5,8,9			Winchester			7F
East Tisted	A 1538-1992	1538-1877	5,8,9	1538-1987		Alton			6H
East Tytherley	A 1562-1993	1562-1875	5,8,9			Stockbridge			6C
East Wellow	A 1570-1988*	1570-1876	5,8,9	1570-1940		Romsey	1790-1837		5D
East Woodhay	A 1610-1950		5,8,9	1618-1812	1610-1812	Kingsclere	1790-1812		10E
East Worldham	A 1690-1986	1690-1876	5,8,9	1653-1854		Alton			7I
Ecchinswell	A 1610-1976		5,8,9			Kingsclere			10F
Eling	A 1537-1983		5,8,9	1538-1812	1539-1812	New Forest	1790-1812	1818-1837	4D
Ellingham	A 1596-1978		5,8,9			Ringwood			3B
Ellisfield	A 1540-1987		5,8,9	1606-1952		Basingstoke			8G
Elvetham	A 1638-1980		5,8,9	1639-1812	1639-1812	Hartley Wintney	1790-1812		9I
Empshott	A 1718-1993	1718-1875	5,8,9			Petersfield			6I
Eversley	A 1559-1992		5,8,9	1559-1812	1559-1812	Hartley Wintney	1790-1812		10I
Ewhurst	A 1682-1960		5,8,9	1682-1839	1682-1812	Kingsclere	1790-1823		9G(A)
Exbury	A 1756-1995	1787-1812	5,8,9	1756-1913		New Forest			3E
Exton	A 1579-1991		5,8,9		1580-1720	Droxford			5G
Faccombe	A 1580-1989	1580-1878	5,8,9	1580-1836	1546-1812	Andover	1790-1812		9D
Fareham	C 1558-1992	1558-1876	5,8	1558-1992		Fareham			3G
Farley Chamberlayne	A 1593-1992		5,8,9			Winchester			6E
Farlington	C 1538-1967	1538-1877	5,8,9			Havant			3H
Farnborough	E 1584-1981		5,8,9	1584-1837	1584-1812	Farnborough	1790-1812		9J
Farringdon	A 1559-1984		5,8,9			Alton			7H
Fawley	A 1673-1991	1678-1876	5,8,9	1673-1857		New Forest			3E
Fordingbridge	A 1642-1981	1642-1876	5,8,9	1642-1840		Fordingbridge		1795-1837	4A
Foxcott	A 1814-1903		5,8			Andover			8D
Freefolk	A 1820-1873		5,8,9			Whitchurch			8F
Frensham (Surrey)						Farnham			7J
Freshwater	B 1576-1987		5,8,9	1576-1837	1559-1837	Isle of Wight	1790-1812		3J
Froxfield	A 1544-1981	1544-1876	5,8,9			Petersfield			6H
Froyle	A 1653-1973	1653-1876	5,8,9	1653-1868		Alton			8I
Fyfield	A 1628-1996		5,8,9			Andover			8C
Gatcombe	B 1560-1979	1560-1835	5,8	1560-1835	1560-1835	Isle of Wight	1780-1835		2K
Godsfield (ex.par.)			5,8,9			Alresford			7G(H)
Godshill	B 1678-1986	1678-1837	5,8	1678-1837	1678-1837	Isle of Wight	1780-1837		2L
Goodworth Clatford	A 1538-1993	1538-1876	5,8,9	1538-1906		Andover			8D
Gosport	C 1696-1992	1696-1875	5,8	1696-1929		Alverstoke		1691-1837	3G
Grateley	A 1654-1999	1624-1877	5,8,9	1740-1957		Andover			7C
Greatham	A 1558-1994		5,8,9			Petersfield			6I
Great Salterns (ex.par.)			5,8,9			Portsea Island			3H
Greywell	A 1604-1992		5,8,9	1604-1979		Hartley Wintney			9H
Hale	A 1626-1985		5,8,9	1626-1950		Fordingbridge			5B
Hamble-le-Rice	A 1674-1978		5,8,9	1674-1920		South Stoneham			3F
Hambledon	A 1595-1960	1569-1876	5,8,9			Droxford		1820-1837	4H
Hannington	A 1768-1994		5,8,9	1768-1962	1768-1837	Kingsclere	1790-1837		9G
Harbridge	A 1572-1992		5,8,9	1571-1840		Ringwood			4A
Hartley Mauditt	A 1672-1993	1672-1876	5,8,9	1672-1812		Alton			7I
Hartley Wespall	A 1540-1992	1540-1877	5,8,9	1558-1837	1558-1812	Basingstoke	1790-1812		9H
Hartley Wintney	A 1658-1994		5,8,9	1658-1812	1658-1812	Hartley Wintney	1790-1812		9I
Havant	C 1653-1971	1653-1876	5,8,9	1653-1854		Havant		1779-1837	4H
Hawkley	A 1640-1981	1640-1876	5,8,9			Petersfield			6I
Headbourne Worthy	A 1615-1988		5,8,9			Winchester			7E
Headley	E 1539-1967	1539-1876	5,8,9	1539-1915		Farnborough			7J
Heckfield	A 1538-1968	1538-1812	5,8,9	1538-1968	1538-1812	Hartley Wintney	1790-1812		10I
Herriard	A 1666-1963	1666-1876	5,8,9	1701-1937	1701-1812	Basingstoke	1790-1812		8H
Highclere	A 1652-1985		5,8,9	1656-1813	1656-1812	Kingsclere	1790-1812		10E
Hinton Admiral	A 1810-1990		5,8			Christchurch			2A
Hinton Ampner	A 1561-1990	1561-1876	5,8,9			Alresford	1790-1812		6G
Holdenhurst	A 1679-1991	1845-1876	5,8,9	1680-1837		Christchurch			2A
Holybourne	A 1690-1977	1690-1876	5,8,9	1690-1878		Alton			8I
Hordle	A 1754-1993	1754-1812	5,8,9		1754-1812	Lymington			2C
Houghton	A 1669-1992	1669-1876	5,8,9	1669-1930		Stockbridge			7D
Hound	A 1660-1972		5,8,9	1660-1837		South Stoneham			4E
Hunton	A 1564-1995	1564-1885	5,8,9	1575-1810	1575-1812	Winchester			7F
Hursley	A 1600-1991	1599-1876	5,8,9	1599-1858	1600-1837	Winchester			5E
Hurstbourne Priors	A 1604-1985		5,8,9	1604-1838	1604-1812	Whitchurch	1604-1812		8E
Hurstbourne Tarrant	A 1546-1998	1546-1876	5,8,9	1546-1812	1546-1812	Andover	1546-1812		9D
Hythe	A 1823-1993		5,8,9	1823-1837		New Forest			3E
Ibsley	A 1654-1993		5,8,9	1654-1840		Ringwood			4B
Ipley Farm (ex.par.)			5,8			New Forest			3D
Itchin Abbas	A 1586-2000		5,8,9			Winchester			7F
Itchin Stoke	A 1719-1991		5,8,9	1719-1986		Alresford			7G
Kilmeston	A 1661-1992	1661-1877	5,8,9			Alresford			6G
Kimpton	A 1589-1996		5,8,9			Andover			8C
Kingsclere	A 1538-1967	1538-1876	5,8	1538-1920		Kingsclere			9F
Kingsley	A 1568-1989	1568-1877	5,8,9	1568-1977		Farnborough			7I
Kings Somborne	A 1567-1971		5,8,9	1672-1888		Stockbridge			6D
Kingston	B 1647-1984		5,8	1647-1832	1647-1832	Isle of Wight			2K
Kingsworthy	A 1538-1989		5,8,9	1538-1812	1538-1812	Winchester	1790-1812		7F
Knights Enham	A 1683-1992	1683-1836	5,8,9	1683-1805	1683-1812	Andover	1683-1812		8D
Lasham	A 1560-1978		5,8,9	1813-1837		Alton			8H
Laverstoke	A 1656-1990		5,8,9	1657-1838	1657-1837	Whitchurch	1790-1812		8F
Leckford	A 1757-1992		5,8,9			Stockbridge			7D
Linkenholt	A 1577-1989	1579-1812	5,8,9	1579-1810	1579-1812	Andover	1790-1816		10D
Liss	A 1599-1986		5,8,9			Petersfield			6I
Litchfield	A 1626-1992	1626-1883	5,8,9	1624-1838	1629-1837	Kingsclere	1790-1812		9E
Littleton	A 1736-1997		5,8,9			Winchester			6E
Lockerley	A 1538-1981	1583-1876	5,8,9			Romsey			5C

HAMPSHIRE

parish name	deposited original registers	I.G.I.	local census indexes	copies of registers at Soc. Gen.	Boyd's marriage index	1837-1851 Registration District	Pallot's marriage index	non-conform. records at P.R.O.	map ref.
Longparish	A 1654-1994		5,8,9	1654-1837		Andover			8E
Longstock	A 1718-1988		5,8,9			Stockbridge			7D
Long Sutton	A 1561-1995		5,8,9	1561-1836	1561-1812	Farnborough	1790-1812		8I
Lymington	A 1658-1970		5,8,9	1658-1886		Lymington		1753-1840	2D
Lyndhurst	A 1737-1992	1737-1876	5,8,9			New Forest		1786-1837	3C
Mapledurwell	A 1618-1988		5,8,9	1629-1837	1629-1812	Basingstoke	1790-1837		9H(C)
Martyr Worthy	A 1539-1998		5,8,9	1560-1630		Winchester			7F
Medstead	A 1560-1991	1560-1876	5,8,9	1560-1947		Alton			7H
Meonstoke	A 1599-1994		5,8,9			Droxford			5G
Micheldever	A 1538-1979	1538-1875	5,8,9			Winchester		1833-1837	7F
Michelmersh	A 1558-1996		5,8,9			Romsey			6D
Milford	A 1594-1972		5,8,9			Lymington			2C
Milland (ex.par.)			5,8			Winchester			6F(L)
Millbrook	D 1633-1981	1780-1812	5,8,9	1633-1837		South Stoneham			4D
Milton	A 1654-1990		5,8,9			Lymington			2C
Minstead	A 1682-1957	1688-1812	5,8,9	1688-1837	1688-1812	New Forest			4C
Monk Sherborne	A 1618-1986	1618-1811	5,8,9	1618-1826	1618-1812	Basingstoke			9G
Monxton	A 1716-1994	1716-1877	5,8,9	1716-1812	1716-1812	Andover	1716-1812		8D
Morestead	A 1549-1992		5,8	1549-1980		Winchester			6F
Mottisfont	A 1701-1983	1701-1877	5,8,9	1701-1950		Romsey			6D
Mottistone	B 1680-1977	1680-1813	5,8,9	1680-1835	1680-1835	Isle of Wight	1790-1812		2J
Nately Scures	A 1666-1988		5,8,9	1684-1836	1694-1812	Basingstoke	1790-1812		9H(D)
Nether Wallop	A 1629-1988		5,8,9	1628-1864		Stockbridge			7C
Newchurch	B 1690-1987		5,8,9	1692-1811		Isle of Wight			2L
New Alresford	A 1678-1991		5,8,9			Alresford		1832-1837	6G
New Forest (ex.par.)			5,8,9			New Forest			3B
New Forest (ex.par.)			5,8,9			New Forest			3D
Newnham	A 1752-1988		5,8,9	1753-1836	1754-1812	Basingstoke	1790-1812		9H
Newport	B 1541-1971		5,8	1541-1900	1651-1675	Isle of Wight	1790-1837	1739-1837	3L(d)
Newton Valence	A 1538-1992		5,8,9			Alton			7H
Newtown	A 1666-1978		5,8,9	1679-1811	1679-1812	Newbury	1790-1812		10E
Niton	B 1559-1987		5,8	1561-1837	1560-1837	Isle of Wight	1790-1812		1L
North Baddesley	A 1682-1990	1682-1876	5,8,9	1682-1967		Winchester			5E
North Hayling	C 1571-1984	1571-1879	5,8,9	1571-1812	1571-1812	Havant			3I
Northington	A 1579-1993	1579-1726	5,8,9	1579-1906		Alresford			7F
North Stoneham	A 1640-1988		5,8,9	1640-1837		South Stoneham			5E
North Waltham	A 1654-1996	1654-1876	5,8,9	1654-1812	1654-1812	Basingstoke	1790-1812		8G
Northwood	B 1538-1983	1538-1837	5,8	1538-1837	1538-1837	Isle of Wight	1780-1837	1832-1837	3K
Nursling	A 1617-1968	1736-1876	5,8,9	1617-1943		Romsey			4D
Nutley	A 1758-1950		5,8,9	1758-1813		Basingstoke			8G
Odiham	A 1538-1993		5,8,9	1538-1979	1538-1812	Hartley Wintney	1790-1812	1795-1836	9I
Old Alresford	A 1539-1979	1540-1866	5,8,9	1678-1909		Alresford			7G
Old Basing	A 1655-1965		5,8,9	1655-1812	1665-1812	Basingstoke	1790-1812		9H
Otterbourne	A 1647-1988		5,8,9			Winchester			5E
Overton	A 1617-1977		5,8,9	1640-1812	1640-1812	Whitchurch	1790-1812		8F
Over Wallop	A 1538-1988		5,8,9	1538-1988		Stockbridge			7C
Ovington	A 1591-1991		5,8,9			Alresford			6F
Owslebury	A 1678-1990		5,8,9			Winchester			5F
Pamber	A 1659-1980	1661-1812	5,8,9	1661-1812	1661-1812	Basingstoke			10G
Parkhurst Forest (ex.par.)			5,8			Isle of Wight			3K
Penton Mewsey	A 1647-1995		5,8,9	1649-1812	1649-1812	Andover	1649-1812		8D
Petersfield	A 1558-1995		5,8,9			Petersfield			5I
Popham	A 1628-1979		5,8,9	1628-1809	1628-1812	Basingstoke	1790-1812		8F
Portchester	C 1608-1994	1607-1877	5,8			Fareham			3G
Portsea (St Mary)	C 1654-1996	1666-1875	5,8,9	1654-1902		Portsea Island		1775-1837	3H
Portsea (All Saints)	C 1828-1999		5,8,9	1828-1838		Portsea Island			3H
Portsmouth								1676-1857	3H
St John	C 1789-1951	1789-1875	5,8,9	1789-1848		Portsea Island			3H
St Thomas	C 1654-1980	1653-1873	5,8,9	1653-1874	1653-1837	Portsea Island	1790-1812		3H
Preston Candover	A 1584-1992		5,8,9	1584-1812	1584-1812	Basingstoke	1790-1812		8G
Priors Dean	A 1538-1978	1538-1876	5,8,9	1538-1812		Petersfield	1790-1837		6I
Privett	A 1538-1980		5,8,9			Petersfield			6H
Quarley	A 1559-1993	1559-1851	5,8,9			Andover			8C
Ringwood	A 1561-1930	1561-1840	5,8,9	1561-1840		Ringwood		1748-1837	3B
Rockbourne	A 1561-1978	1561-1876	5,8,9			Fordingbridge			5A
Romsey	A 1569-1983	1569-1876	5,8,9	1569-1856		Romsey		1758-1837	5D
Ropley	A 1539-1989	1538-1876	5,8,9			Alresford			6H
Rotherwick	A 1560-1991	1560-1876	5,8,9	1560-1812	1560-1812	Hartley Wintney	1790-1812		9H
Rowner	C 1583-1995	1590-1878	5,8	1590-1922	1590-1812	Fareham	1790-1812		3G
Ryde St Thomas	B 1719-1957	1719-1837	5,8,9		1719-1837	Isle of Wight	1811-1837	1817-1837	3L
St Helens	B 1653-1998		5,8,9			Isle of Wight			3M
St Lawrence	B 1738-1986	1747-1836	5,8,9	1747-1836	1747-1836	Isle of Wight	1780-1837		1L
St Mary Bourne	A 1661-1960		5,8,9	1662-1812	1663-1837	Isle of Wight	1663-1812		9E
Selborne	A 1556-1975	1557-1672	5,8,9			Alton			6I
Shalden	A 1686-1979	1687-1836	5,8,9		1687-1837	Alton			8H
Shalfleet	B 1604-1987	1604-1812	5,8,9	1604-1837	1614-1837	Isle of Wight	1780-1812		3J
Shanklin	B 1724-1986	1766-1836	5,8,9	1724-1913	1754-1836	Isle of Wight	1780-1837		2M
Sherborne St John	A 1652-1980	1652-1852	5,8,9	1652-1837	1652-1812	Basingstoke	1790-1812		9G
Sherfield English	A 1640-1980	1640-1878	5,8,9			Romsey			5C
Sherfield on Loddon	A 1574-1994	1574-1876	5,8,9	1574-1812	1574-1812	Basingstoke	1790-1812		9H
Shipton Bellinger	A 1546-1978		5,8,9			Andover			8C
Shorwell	B 1674-1985	1676-1812	5,8	15851838	1676-1836	Isle of Wight	1780-1812		2K
Silchester	A 1653-1930		5,8,9	1653-1812	1653-1812	Basingstoke	1790-1812		10G
Soberton	A 1538-1987		5,8,9			Droxford			4G
Sopley	A 1678-1988		5,8,9	1682-1812	1676-1812	Christchurch	1790-1812	1829-1837	2B
Southampton								1783-1837	4E
All Saints	D 1653-1940	1653-1862	5,8,9	1723-1865		Southampton			4E
Holy Rood	D 1653-1812		5,8,9	1653-1858		Southampton			4E

HAMPSHIRE

parish name	deposited original registers	I.G.I.	local census indexes	copies of registers at Soc. Gen.	Boyd's marriage index	1837-1851 Registration District	Pallot's marriage index	non-conform. records at P.R.O.	map ref.
Southampton (cont'd)									
St Lawrence & John	D 1754-1813		5,8,9	1754-1836		Southampton			4E
St Mary	D 1675-1976		5,8,9	1675-1837		Southampton			4E
St Mary Extra	D 1671-1986		5,8,9			Southampton			4E
St Michael	D 1552-1985		5,8,9	1552-1943		Southampton			4E
Southampton Common (ex.par.)			5,8,9			Southampton			4E(M)
South Hayling	C 1672-1980	1676-1876	5,8,9	1672-1812	1676-1812	Havant			2H
South Stoneham	D 1663-1992	1663-1885	5,8,9	1663-1837		South Stoneham			4E
South Tidworth	A 1599-1992		5,8,9			Andover			8C
South Warnborough	A 1539-1989		5,8,9	1539-1811	1538-1812	Hartley Wintney	1790-1812		8I
Southwick	A 1584-1994	1628-1876	5,8			Fareham			4G
Sparsholt	A 1607-1995		5,8,9			Winchester			6E
Steep	A 1610-1974		5,8,9	1610-1840		Petersfield			6I
Steventon	A 1604-1989	1604-1840	5,8,9	1604-1891	1604-1812	Basingstoke	1604-1812		8F
Stockbridge	A 1663-1973	1663-1876	5,8,9			Stockbridge		1815-1836	7D
Stoke Charity	A 1540-1995	1541-1873	5,8,9	1542-1812	1542-1812	Winchester	1790-1812		7F
Stratfield Mortimer (Berks.)						Bradfield			10G
Stratfield Saye	A 1539-1966	1539-1876	5,8,9	1539-1837	1539-1812	Basingstoke	1790-1812		10H
Stratfield Turgis	A 1672-1974	1672-1876	5,8,9	1672-1837	1672-1812	Basingstoke	1790-1812		10H
Swarraton	A 1584-1885		5,8,9	1584-1694		Alresford			7G(G)
Sydmonton			5,8,9	1610-1673		Kingsclere			10F
Tadley	A 1683-1985	1683-1837	5,8,9	1683-1812	1683-1812	Kingsclere	1790-1812	1788-1835	10G
Tangley	A 1679-1995		5,8,9	1703-1812	1703-1812	Andover	1790-1812		9D
Thorley	B 1614-1976	1614-1853	5,8	1614-1837	1614-1837	Isle of Wight	1780-1853		3J
Thruxton	A 1600-1992		5,8,9	1702-1847		Andover			8C
Tichborne	A 1667-1992	1667-1883	5,8,9			Alresford			6F
Timsbury	A 1564-1997		5,8,9	1564-1812	1564-1812	Romsey			6D
Titchfield	A 1590-1984		5,8	1763-1812		Fareham		1803-1837	3F
Tufton	A 1714-1992	1716-1879	5,8,9	1716-1838	1754-1812	Whitchurch	1754-1812		8E
Tunworth	A 1749-1907	1749-1878	5,8,9			Basingstoke			8H
Twyford	A 1626-1987		5,8,9	1626-1837		Winchester			5F
Upham	A 1598-1993		5,8,9			Droxford			5F
Up Nately	A 1695-1988		5,8,9	1695-1837	1695-1750	Basingstoke			9H
Upper Clatford	A 1570-1990	1576-1876	5,8,9			Andover			8D
Upton Grey	A 1558-1990	1558-1875	5,8,9			Basingstoke			8H
Vernham Dean	A 1598-1991	1598-1875	5,8,9	1598-1812	1607-1812	Andover	1790-1812		9D
Warblington	C 1631-1993	1635-1877	5,8,9	1644-1930	1701-1837	Havant	1791-1837	1817-1837	3I
Warnford	A 1541-1997		5,8,9			Droxford			5G
Waterlooville	C 1831-1976		5,8,9			Catherington			4H
Weeke	A 1573-1991	1573-1876	5,8,9	1573-1837	1573-1837	Winchester			6E
West Cowes	B 1679-1977	1680-1703	5,8	1680-1703	1680-1703	Isle of Wight		1804-1837	4K
West Meon	A 1536-1973		5,8,9	1538-1800	1538-1800	Droxford	1790-1800		5H
Weston Corbett (ex.par.)			5,8,9			Basingstoke			8H(E)
Weston Patrick	A 1574-1996		5,8,9	1780-1820		Basingstoke			8H
West Tisted	A 1538-1981	1837-1878	5,8,9			Alresford			6H
West Tytherley	A 1654-1987	1654-1876	5,8,9			Stockbridge			6C
West Worldham	A 1653-1994	1649-1875	5,8,9	1649-1845		Alton			7I(J)
Weyhill	A 1564-1988		5,8,9	1564-1812	1564-1812	Andover	1790-1812		8D
Wherwell	A 1634-1986		5,8	1634-1986		Andover			7D
Whippingham	B 1727-1992	1728-1812	5,8	1728-1837	1728-1837	Isle of Wight	1760-1812		3L
Whitchurch	A 1605-1984	1605-1876	5,8,9	1605-1838	1605-1837	Whitchurch	1790-1812		8E
Whitwell	B 1678-1976		5,8	1699-1837	1699-1837	Isle of Wight	1790-1837		1L
Wickham	A 1556-1990		5,8	1780-1782		Fareham			4G
Widley	C 1654-1934	1653-1877	5,8			Fareham			3H
Wield	A 1539-1970	1538-1877	5,8,9	1539-1812		Alton			7G
Winchester								1716-1837	6F
Cathedral		1599-1811	5,8,9	1599-1812	1599-1812	Winchester			6F
St Bartholemew	A 1563-1981		5,8,9	1563-1837	1563-1837	Winchester	1790-1837		6F
St Faith	A 1670-1977		5,8,9	1674-1837	1674-1837	Winchester	1790-1837		6F
St John	A 1578-1967		5,8,9	1578-1837		Winchester			6F
St Lawrence	A 1754-1978	1754-1877	5,8,9	1754-1812	1754-1812	Winchester	1790-1837		6F
St Mary Kalender	A 1538-1955		5,8,9			Winchester			6F
St Maurice	A 1538-1955	1538-1876	5,8,9	1538-1837	1651-1775	Winchester	1790-1837		6F
St Michael	A 1632-1984		5,8,9	1632-1812	1632-1812	Winchester	1790-1812		6F
St Peter Chesil	A 1597-1948		5,8,9	1597-1837	1595-1837	Winchester	1790-1837		6F
St Peter Colebrook	A 1538-1955		5,8,9			Winchester			6F
St Swithin	A 1562-1976	1562-1878	5,8,9	1562-1812	1562-1812	Winchester	1790-1812		6F
SS Thomas & Clement	A 1671-1969	1678-1876	5,8,9	1685-1837	1685-1837	Winchester	1790-1837		6F
Winchester College			5,8,9	1409-1903	1678-1903	Winchester			6F
Winchfield	A 1659-1993		5,8,9	1660-1837	1660-1812	Hartley Wintney	1790-1812		9I
Winnall	A 1680-1965		5,8	1697-1837	1697-1837	Winchester			6F(K)
Winslade	A 1723-1977	1723-1877	5,8,9	1723-1812	1723-1812	Basingstoke	1790-1812		8H
Wolverton	A 1717-1996		5,8,9	1717-1840	1707-1812	Kingsclere	1790-1812		9F
Wonston		1570-1876	5,8,9	1570-1812	1570-1812	Winchester	1790-1812		7E
Woodcott			5,8,9			Kingsclere			9E
Woodmancote	A 1762-1988		5,8,9	1772-1812	1762-1812	Basingstoke	1790-1812		8G
Wootton St Edmund	B 1760-1994	1760-1833	5,8	1760-1833	1760-1833	Isle of Wight	1780-1837		3L,2K(e)
Wootton St Lawrence	A 1560-1989	1560-1876	5,8,9	1560-1812	1560-1812	Basingstoke	1560-1812		9G
Worting	A 1604-1913		5,8,9	1609-1812	1604-1812	Basingstoke	1790-1812		9G
Wymering	C 1654-1995	1653-1876	5,8			Fareham			3G
Yarmouth	B 1614-2000		5,8,9	1614-1812	1614-1812	Isle of Wight	1790-1812	1810-1837	3J
Yateley	A 1636-1979		5,8,9	1636-1812	1636-1812	Farnborough			9J
Yaverland	B 1632-1986		5,8,9	1632-1836	1682-1836	Isle of Wight	1790-1812		2M

HAMPSHIRE

Original registers deposited at:
A = Hampshire Record Office, Sussex Street, Winchester, SO23 8TH
B = Isle of Wight Record Office, 26 Hillside, Newport, Isle of Wight, PO30 2EB
C = Portsmouth City Record Office, 3 Museum Road, Portsmouth, PO1 2LJ
D = Southampton City Record Office, South Block, Civic Centre, Southampton, SO14 7LY
E = Surrey History Centre, 130 Goldsworth Road, Woking, Surrey, GU21 1ND
F = Berkshire Record Office, 9 Coley Avenue, Reading, Berkshire, RG1 6AF

Study adjacent parishes in counties of Berkshire, Surrey, Sussex, Dorset and Wiltshire

Hampshire Record Office, Sussex Street, Winchester, SO23 8TH
Southampton City Record Office, South Block, Civic Centre, Southampton, SO14 7LY
Portsmouth City Records Office, 3 Museum Road, Portsmouth, PO1 2LJ
Isle of Wight Record Office, 26 Hillside, Newport, Isle of Wight, PO30 2EB

The following useful indexes have been compiled – see Introduction
Census Indexes 1851 & 1891 – Hampshire Genealogical Society, PO Box 48, Cosham, Hampshire, PO6 3UN
Census Index West Wight 1891 – Mrs J. Few, 12 Ranelagh Road, Lake, Isle of Wight, PO36 8NX
Marriage Index 1538-1837 – Hampshire Genealogical Society, D. Knott, 2 Careys Cottages, Brockenhurst, Hampshire, SO42 7TF
Isle of Wight Marriage Index 1539-1837 – County Archivist, I.o.W. Record Office, 26 Hillside, Newport, I.o.W.
Isle of Wight Marriage Index 1837-1900 – Isle of Wight FHS, Barry Hall, 1A Hungerberry Close, Shanklin, I.o.W.
Wills Beneficiaries Index – Hampshire Genealogical Society, Mr.s M Proudfoot, Three Carpenters, Grange Road, Alresford, Hampshire, SO24 9HE

Hampshire extends in length from north to south about 55 miles, in breadth from east to west about 40 miles. It is watered by six principal rivers: the Itchen, Avon, Boldre water, Exe, Anton and Tese or Test. The population in 1841 was 354,682; in 1851, 245,370; in 1861, 481,815; in 1871, 524,836; in 1881, 575,409.

The soils are very numerous but the greater proportion tends to chalk. Heavy crops of wheat, barley and other grains were produced and great quantities of malt. Valuable salt marshes were found near Redbridge and hops were cultivated around Alton and along the Surrey border. Sheep and hogs were bred. Manufactures consisted of a few stuff-goods such as denims, serges and other coarse woollens as well as white brick from a variety of potter's clay.

The information in the Index is abbreviated, and may mislead the searcher if reference is not made to the details contained in the several publications listed in the Introduction. It is essential that users of this book check the appropriate works before making further enquiries.

HEREFORDSHIRE

parish name	deposited original registers	I.G.I.	local census indexes	copies of registers at Soc. Gen.	Boyd's marriage index	1837-1851 Registration District	Pallot's marriage index	non-conform. records at P.R.O.	map ref.
Abbey Dore	1634-1874	1635-1854	5,8,9	1634-1928		Hereford			7E
Aconbury	1736-1971	1665-1883	5,8,9	1665-1971		Hereford			5E
Allensmore	1698-1980	1660-1863	5,8,9	1660-1888		Hereford			6E
Almeley	1596-1997	1596-1860	5,8,9	1595-1860	1598-1754	Weobley			8H
Amberley			5,8,9	1770-1817		Hereford			5G
Ashperton	1538-1995	1538-1884	5,8,9	1538-1899		Ledbury			3F
Aston	1692-1991	1630-1845	5,8	1630-1846		Ludlow			6K
Aston Ingham	1633-1967	1662-1857	5,8	1662-1855		Newent			3C
Avenbury	1661-1940	1660-1886	5,8	1661-1940		Bromyard			3H
Aylton	1733-1837	1749-1991	5,8,9	1661-1865		Ledbury			3F
Aymestrey	1568-1894	1569-1875	5,8	1568-1953		Leominster			7J
Bacton	1724-1839	1663-1846	5,8	1660-1846		Hereford			7E
Ballingham	1595-1837	1595-1856	5,8	1595-1855		Ross			4E(a)
Birley	1757-1837	1663-1845	5,8,9			Weobley			6H
Bishops Frome	1564-1978	1564-1885	5,8	1564-1924		Bromyard			3G
Bishopstone	1727-1946	1660-1846	5,8,9	1727-1845		Weobley			7F(L)
Blakemere	1662-1988	1662-1850	5,8,9	1662-1847		Weobley			7F(Q)
Bockleton (Worcs.)						Tenbury			4I
Bodenham	1584-1961	1584-1885	5,8	1574-1961		Leominster			5H
Bolstone	1758-1977	1744-1854	5,8,9	1758-1855		Hereford			5E(Y)
Bosbury	1558-1945	1559-1861	5,8,9	1559-1819		Ledbury			2G
Brampton Abbotts	1561-1960	1561-1875	5,8	1561-1960		Ross			4D
Brampton Bryan	1823-1976	1663-1849	5,8	1638-1976		Knighton			8K
Bredenbury	1607-1975	1607-1846	5,8	1607-1857		Bromyard			4H(E)
Bredwardine	1723-1908	1660-1875	5,8	1660-1871	1660-1837	Hay	1790-1837		8G
Breinton	1662-1996	1662-1885	5,8,9	1662-1980	1662-1980	Hereford			6F
Bridge Sollers	1615-1836	1615-1853	5,8,9	1615-1853		Weobley			7F(R)
Bridstow	1560-1918	1580-1875	5,8	1560-1918		Ross			4D
Brilley	1580-1995	1580-1860	5,8	1580-1903		Presteigne			9G
Brimfield	1561-1883	1661-1865	5,8	1701-1833		Tenbury			5J
Brinsop	1695-1836	1660-1862	5,8,9	1660-1922		Weobley			6G
Brobury	1723-1922	1660-1882	5,8,9	1660-1933		Weobley	1790-1837		8G(J)
Brockhampton	1558-1992	1576-1852	5,8	1590-1852		Ross			4E
Brockhampton in Bromyard	1757-1812	1757-1841	5,8	1700-1841		Bromyard			3H
Bromyard	1538-1965	1538-1875	5,8	1538-1947		Bromyard		1696-1836	3H
Bucknell (Salop)						Knighton			7K
Bullingham	1682-1933	1683-1875	5,8,9	1682-1933		Hereford			5E
Burghill	1655-1929	1655-1885	5,8,9	1662-1929		Hereford			6G
Burrington	1541-1996	1541-1854	5,8	1541-1969		Ludlow			6K
Byford	1660-1991	1660-1853	5,8,9	1660-1852		Weobley			7F
Byton	1772-1837	1660-1866	5,8	1660-1866		Presteigne			7J
Callow	1576-1835	1576-1849	5,8,9	1576-1850		Hereford			5E(X)
Canon Frome	1680-1993	1664-1884	5,8,9	1660-1968		Ledbury	1790-1811		3G
Canon Pyon	1707-1957	1662-1849	5,8,9	1660-1837		Weobley			6G
Castle Frome	1678-1968	1660-1865	5,8,9	1714-1833		Ledbury			3G
Clehonger	1671-2000	1670-1875	5,8,9	1670-1940		Hereford			6F
Clifford	1690-1996	1660-1873	5,8	1662-1837		Hay			9G
Clodock	1714-1943	1825-1839	5,8,9	1714-1943		Hereford			8D
Coddington	1754-1994	1660-1872	5,8,9	1660-1849		Ledbury			2G
Collington	1566-1993	1566-1872	5,8	1566-1872		Bromyard			3I
Colwall	1588-1933	1553-1895	5,8,9	1553-1933		Ledbury			2F
Cradley	1560-1988	1560-1895	5,8	1560-1946		Bromyard		1818-1837	2G
Craswall		1662-1875	5,8,9			Hereford			9E
Credenhill	1671-1964	1662-1875	5,8,9	1662-1965		Hereford			6G
Croft	1565-1961	1565-1846	5,8	1565-1961		Leominster			6J
Cusop	1698-1971	1662-1862	5,8	1662-1899		Hay			9F
Dewsall	1582-1837	1582-1849	5,8,9	1582-1851		Hereford			6E(W)
Dilwyn	1559-1947	1558-1895	5,8,9	1558-1947		Weobley			7H
Dinedor	1750-1943	1660-1885	5,8,9	1671-1943		Hereford			5E
Dinmore (ex.par.)			5,8,9			Hereford			6H(F)
Docklow	1584-1985	1660-1856	5,8	1661-1856		Leominster			4I
Donnington		1666-1885	5,8,9	1746-1841		Ledbury			2E
Dormington	1690-1836	1660-1884	5,8,9	1661-1884		Hereford			4F
Dorstone	1733-1993	1662-1875	5,8	1660-1853		Hay			9F
Downton	1728-1991	1621-1876	5,8	1605-1837		Ludlow			7K
Dulas	1757-1828	1757-1850	5,8,9	1770-1850		Hereford			7D
Eardisland	1614-1968	1560-1858	5,8,9	1560-1968		Weobley			7I
Eardisley	1630-1964	1660-1885	5,8	1660-1964		Presteigne			8G
Eastnor	1561-1812	1660-1851	5,8,9	1754-1771		Ledbury			2F
Eaton Bishop	1558-1989	1588-1885	5,8,9	1588-1920		Hereford			6F
Edvin Loach	1576-1996	1576-1832	5,8	1576-1832		Bromyard			3I
Edvin Ralph	1651-1998	1652-1835	5,8	1651-1835		Bromyard			3I
Elton	1657-1992	1657-1845	5,8	1657-1824		Ludlow			6K
Evesbatch	1700-1991	1660-1865	5,8	1700-1921		Bromyard			2G
Ewyas Harold	1734-1987	1734-1885	5,8,9	1734-1975		Hereford			7D
Eye	1573-1983	1573-1875	5,8	1573-1906		Leominster			5J
Eyton	1682-1836	1682-1849	5,8			Leominster			6I
Felton	1637-1962	1637-1875	5,8	1639-1951		Bromyard			4G
Ford	1742-1985		5,8	1743-1812		Leominster			
Fownhope	1560-1979	1538-1885	5,8,9	1538-1969		Hereford			4E
Fawley Chapelry	1854-1898		5,8,9	1539-1898		Hereford			4E
Foy	1570-1948	1661-1849	5,8	1661-1861		Ross			4D
Fwddog (in Cwmyoy, Mon.)						Abergavenny			9D
Ganarew	1657-1997	1661-1876	5,8	1661-1876		Monmouth			5B
Garway	1664-1943	1660-1871	5,8	1661-1943		Monmouth			6C
Goodrich	1558-1884	1661-1874	5,8	1661-1874		Ross			4C
Grendon Bishop	1662-1946	1662-1884	5,8	1662-1946		Bromyard			4H
Grendon Warren			5,8			Bromyard			4H

160

HEREFORDSHIRE

parish name	deposited original registers	I.G.I.	local census indexes	copies of registers at Soc. Gen.	Boyd's marriage index	1837-1851 Registration District	Pallot's marriage index	non-conform. records at P.R.O.	map ref.
Hampton Bishop	1670-1999	1669-1862	5,8,9	1669-1862		Hereford			5F
Harewood	1781-1943	1671-1812	5,8	1768-1943		Ross			5D(c)
Hatfield	1615-1987	1615-1877	5,8	1615-1926		Leominster			4I
Haywood (ex.par.)			5,8,9			Hereford			6E
Hentland	1558-1894	1558-1860	5,8	1558-1894		Ross			5D
Hereford								1690-1854	5F
All Saints	1669-1995	1662-1858	5,8,9	1639-1820		Hereford			5F
Holy Trinity	1885-1988		5,8,9	1885-1938		Hereford			5F
St James	1870-1920	1870-1885	5,8,9	1870-1920		Hereford			5F
St John Baptist		1662-1860	5,8,9	1604-1969		Hereford			5F
St Martin	1559-1960	1559-1885	5,8,9	1559-1951		Hereford			5F
St Nicholas	1556-1996	1556-1885	5,8,9	1556-1926		Hereford			5F
St Owen	1626-1921	1626-1885	5,8,9	1626-1921		Hereford			5F
St Peter	1556-1936	1556-1885	5,8,9	1556-1921		Hereford			5F
Holme Lacy	1562-1921	1561-1885	5,8,9	1561-1921		Hereford			5E
Holmer	1712-1980	1660-1885	5,8,9	1712-1980		Hereford			5F
Hope Mansel	1556-1887	1555-1875	5,8	1560-1887		Ross			3C
Hope under Dinmore	1701-1981	1660-1875	5,8	1701-1980		Leominster			6H
How Caple	1677-1812	1661-1849	5,8	1701-1830		Ross			4E
Humber	1585-1984	1660-1867	5,8	1660-1867		Leominster			5H
Huntington	1930-1952	1720-1857	5,8,9	1718-1857		Hereford			6F(S)
Huntington (Kington)	1754-1837	1754-1846	5,8	1661-1846		Presteigne			9H
Kenchester	1757-1945	1663-1850	5,8,9	1663-1945		Hereford			6F(M)
Kenderchurch	1755-1834	1661-1856	5,8,9	1661-1856		Hereford			7D
Kentchurch	1686-1964	1661-1849	5,8,9	1661-1964		Hereford			7D
Kilpeck	1678-1981	1661-1875	5,8,9	1661-1916		Hereford			6D
Kimbolton	1565-1964	1661-1875	5,8	1565-1837		Leominster			5I
King's Caple	1631-1812	1661-1851	5,8	1661-1857		Ross			4D
Kingsland	1539-1974	1539-1895	5,8	1539-1974		Leominster			6I
King's Pyon	1538-1574	1538-1881	5,8	1538-1945		Weobley			6G
Kingstone	1659-1992	1661-1865	5,8,9			Hereford			6E
Kington	1667-1971	1661-1875	5,8	1660-1957		Presteigne	1791-1837		9H
Kinnersley	1626-1930	1626-1846	5,8	1626-1837		Weobley			8G
Kinsham	1593-1833	1599-1868	5,8	1599-1699		Presteigne			8J
Knill	1585-1836	1586-1857	5,8	1585-1836		Presteigne			9I
Laysters	1703-1947	1660-1877	5,8			Leominster			4I
Lea	1581-1924	1581-1875	5,8	1581-1924		Ross			3C
Ledbury	1556-1985	1556-1576	5,8,9	1556-1865		Ledbury	1785-1837		2F
Leinthall Earles	1766-1937	1766-1880	5,8	1830-1880		Leominster			6J
Leinthall Starkes	1740-1994	1660-1869	5,8	1660-1869		Ludlow			6J(A)
Leintwardine	1547-1969	1547-1885	5,8	1547-1925		Ludlow/Knighton			7K
Leominster	1550-1911	1660-1875	5,8			Leominster	1702-1837		6I
Letton	1762-1976	1660-1885	5,8,9	1754-1976		Weobley			8G
Lingen	1751-1958	1660-1875	5,8	1660-1958		Presteigne			8J
Linton	1570-1994	1662-1847	5,8	1662-1847		Newent	1831-1837		3D
Little Birch	1557-1963	1557-1885	5,8,9	1557-1963		Hereford			5E
Little Cowarne	1563-1998	1563-1885	5,8	1563-1957		Bromyard			4H(G)
Little Dewchurch	1730-1919	1660-1875	5,8,9	1660-1925		Hereford			5E
Little Hereford	1725-1938	1667-1877	5,8	1667-1938		Tenbury			5K
Little Marcle	1748-1995	1660-1875	5,8,9	1660-1969		Ledbury			3E
Llancillo	1727-1910	1727-1872	5,8,9	1707-1910		Hereford			7C
Llandinabo	1595-1994	1596-1863	5,8	1596-1863		Ross	1790-1812		5D(b)
Llangarren	1569-1999	1569-1881	5,8	1569-1951		Ross			5C
Llanrothal	1740-1937	1663-1748	5,8	1663-1937		Monmouth			6C
Llanveynor see Clodock			5,8,9			Hereford			9F
Llanwarne	1675-1993	1660-1875	5,8	1660-1909		Ross			5D
Longtown		1714-1885	5,8,9			Hereford			8D
Lucton	1711-1968	1662-1884	5,8	1711-1969		Leominster			6J
Ludford (Salop)						Ludlow			5K
Lugwardine	1538-1981	1538-1885	5,8,9	1538-1930	1538-1758	Hereford			5F
Lyonshall	1682-1973	1660-1874	5,8	1660-1882		Presteigne			8H
Madley	1559-1995	1661-1850	5,8,9			Hereford			7F
Mansell Gamage	1664-1967	1660-1855	5,8,9	1664-1967		Weobley			7G
Mansell Lacy	1714-1956	1660-1875	5,8,9	1714-1956		Weobley			7G
Marden	1616-1983	1660-1866	5,8,9	1660-1886		Hereford			5G
Marstow	1707-1836	1662-1853	5,8	1662-1853		Ross			4C
Michaelchurch	1741-1964		5,8	1662-1852		Ross			5D(db)
Michaelchurch Escley	1719-1894		5,8,9	1750-1761		Hereford			8E
Middleton on the Hill	1650-1911	1650-1911	5,8	1650-1871		Leominster			5J
Moccas	1673-1993	1660-1886	5,8,9	1660-1977		Weobley			8F
Monkland	1592-1961	1660-1856	5,8	1660-1856		Leominster			6I
Monnington on Wye		1660-1846	5,8,9	1660-1846		Weobley			7G(K)
Mordiford	1621-1995	1661-1853	5,8,9	1621-1874		Hereford			4F
Moreton Jefferys	1711-1855	1670-1873	5,8	1670-1872		Bromyard			4G(H)
Moreton on Lugg	1754-1990	1681-1836	5,8,9	1681-1835		Hereford			5G(N)
Much Birch	1599-1966	1599-1875	5,8,9	1599-1966		Hereford			5D
Much Cowarne	1599-1954	1559-1885	5,8	1559-1954		Bromyard			3G
Much Dewchurch	1558-1893	1558-1869	5,8,9	1558-1915		Hereford			6D
Much Marcle	1556-1886	1556-1875	5,8,9	1556-1886		Ledbury			3E
Munsley	1708-1837	1662-1869	5,8,9	1662-1812		Ledbury	1790-1812		3F
Norton Canon	1716-1836	1661-1861	5,8,9	1661-1861		Weobley			7G
Ocle Pychard	1780-1956	1660-1875	5,8	1660-1956		Bromyard			4G
Old Radnor (Radnor)	1736-1946		5,8			Presteigne			9I
Orcop	1672-1895	1661-1863	5,8,9	1672-1889		Hereford			6D
Orleton	1565-1989	1660-1851	5,8	1660-1851		Leominster			6J
Pembridge	1564-1960	1564-1885	5,8	1564-1960		Presteigne	1822-1836		7I
Pencombe	1538-1994	1538-1871	5,8	1538-1913		Bromyard			4H
Pencoyd	1563-1837	1564-1851	5,8	1563-1851		Ross	1790-1812		5D
Peterchurch	1711-1867	1660-1846	5,8	1660-1846		Hereford			8F

161

HEREFORDSHIRE

parish name	deposited original registers	I.G.I.	local census indexes	copies of registers at Soc. Gen.	Boyd's marriage index	1837-1851 Registration District	Pallot's marriage index	non-conform. records at P.R.O.	map ref.
Peterstow	1538-1945	1538-1875	5,8	1538-1945		Ross			4D
Pipe	1558-1966	1559-1885	5,8,9	1558-1966	1558-1780	Hereford			5G
Pixley	1751-1834	1660-1869	5,8,9	1660-1869		Ledbury			3F
Presteigne (Radnor)	1561-1948		5,8			Presteigne			8J
Preston Wye	1813-1989	1664-1849	5,8,9			Weobley			7F
Preston Wynne	1730-1991	1730-1875	5,8,9	1730-1980		Hereford			4G
Pudleston	1562-1984	1660-1876	5,8			Leominster			4I
Putley	1561-1930	1662-1863	5,8,9	1765-1772		Ledbury			3F
Richard's Castle (Salop)						Ludlow			6K
Ross	1671-1889	1671-1887	5,8	1671-1889		Ross		1732-1837	4C
Rowlestone	1727-1954	1702-1886	5,8,9	1727-1954		Hereford			7D
St Devereux	1669-1994	1669-1885	5,8,9	1669-1975		Hereford	1790-1812		6E
St Margaret	1702-1915	1813-1851	5,8,9	1750-1780		Hereford			8E
St Weonard	1624-1876	1624-1864	5,8	1624-1876		Ross			6D
Sarnesfield	1764-1851	1660-1875	5,8,9	1660-1897		Weobley	1790-1895		7H(C)
Sellack	1566-1992	1566-1678	5,8	1566-1769		Ross			4D
Shobdon	1556-1903	1556-1869	5,8	1566-1903		Leominster			7I
Sollers Hope	1696-1999		5,8	1701-1817		Ross			3E
Stanford Bishop	1699-1988	1669-1812	5,8	1699-1837		Bromyard			3H
Staunton on Arrow	1558-1936	1558-1875	5,8	1558-1936		Presteigne			8I
Staunton on Wye	1677-1944	1677-1875	5,8,9	1677-1944		Weobley			8G
Stoke Bliss		1571-1885	5,8	1712-1820		Tenbury			3J
Stoke Edith	1538-1838	1538-1840	5,8,9	1538-1840		Hereford			4F
Stoke Lacy	1567-1969	1567-1885	5,8	1567-1969		Bromyard			3H
Stoke Prior	1678-1982	1648-1875	5,8	1678-1912		Leominster			5H
Stretford	1720-1970	1720-1889	5,8,9	1712-1970		Weobley			6H(D)
Stretton Grandison	1558-1976	1559-1875	5,8,9	1558-1976		Ledbury			3G(P)
Stretton Sugwas	1733-1946	1733-1875	5,8,9	1733-1946		Hereford			6F
Sutton									5G
St Michael	1593-2001	1678-1837	5,8,9	1539-1837		Hereford			5G(Oa)
St Nicholas	1593-1995	1589-1837	5,8,9	1539-1837		Hereford			5G(Ob)
Tarrington	1561-1937	1561-1875	5,8,9	1561-1937	1562-1812	Ledbury			4F
Tedstone De La Mere	1690-1998		5,8	1691-1990		Bromyard			2I
Tedstone Wafer	1729-1836	1729-1836	5,8	1729-1836		Bromyard			3I
Thornbury	1538-1993	1538-1875	5,8	1538-1953		Bromyard	1790-1812		4I
Thruxton	1582-1985	1582-1875	5,8,9	1582-1835		Hereford			6E(V)
Titley	1570-1983	1570-1885	5,8	1570-1899		Presteigne			8I
Tretire	1586-1942	1586-1884	5,8	1586-1942		Ross			5D(da)
Treville (ex.par.)			5,8,9			Hereford			6E
Turnastone	1678-1993		5,8,9	1754-1813		Hereford			8E(U)
Tyberton	1672-1988		5,8,9	1700-1814		Hereford			8F
Ullingswick	1561-1919	1561-1875	5,8	1561-1919		Bromyard			4H
Upper Sapey	1674-1997		5,8	1679-1986		Bromyard			3J
Upton Bishop	1571-1999	1571-1875	5,8	1571-1910		Ross	1790-1882		3D
Vowchurch	1754-1992		5,8,9	1755-1823		Hereford			7E
Wacton	1660-1877	1660-1877	5,8	1660-1877		Bromyard			4I
Walford	1663-1972		5,8	1661-1792		Ross			4C
Walterstone	1761-1835	1712-1835	5,8,9	1780-1835		Hereford			7C
Wellington	1559-1915	1559-1875	5,8,9	1559-1973		Hereford			5G
Welsh Bicknor	1699-1988		5,8	1704-1833		Monmouth			4C
Welsh Newton	1758-1984	1758-1875	5,8	1758-1917		Monmouth			5C
Weobley	1635-1885	1635-1885	5,8,9	1635-1885		Weobley			7H
Westhide	1575-1999	1575-1835	5,8,9	1575-1971		Hereford			4G
Weston Beggard	1587-1992	1587-1875	5,8,9	1581-1932		Hereford			4F(T)
Weston under Penyard	1568-1999	1568-1885	5,8	1568-1956		Ross		1785-1837	3C
Whitbourne	1740-1998		5,8	1588-1867		Bromyard			2H
Whitchurch	1813-1950	1761-1875	5,8	1660-1951		Monmouth		1820-1833	5C
Whitney	1740-1994	1740-1875	5,8	1660-1967		Hay			10G
Wigmore	1572-1905	1572-1869	5,8	1572-1965		Ludlow			7J
Willersley	1815-1962	1815-1875	5,8	1754-1962		Presteigne			8G(B)
Winforton	1691-1992	1690-1835	5,8	1690-1959		Presteigne			10G
Withington	1671-1995	1573-1840	5,8,9	1573-1950		Hereford			4G
Wolferlow	1629-1994		5,8	1824-1933		Bromyard			3J
Woolhope	1558-1992		5,8,9	1558-1812		Ledbury			4E
Wormbridge	1611-1833	1612-1833	5,8,9	1611-1812	1612-1812	Hereford	1790-1812		7E(Z)
Wormsley	1749-1969	1749-1884	5,8,9	1749-1969		Weobley			7G
Yarkhill	1559-1973	1563-1876	5,8,9	1562-1918		Ledbury			4F
Yarpole	1561-1981	1561-1857	5,8	1561-1877		Leominster			6J
Yatton			5,8			Ross			3E
Yazor	1621-1839	1620-1839	5,8,9	1621-1839		Weobley			7G

HEREFORDSHIRE

Original registers are deposited at:
A = Herefordshire Record Office, The Old Barracks, Harold Street, Hereford HR1 2QX

Study adjacent parishes in Radnorshire, Shropshire, Worcestershire, Gloucestershire, Monmouthshire and Breconshire

Hereford and Worcester Record Office (Hereford branch), The Old Barracks, Harold Street, Hereford, HR1 2QX

The following useful indexes have been compiled - see Introduction
Census Indexes 1851 & 1891 - Herefordshire FHS, c/o Mr A Charles, 79 College Road, Hereford, HR1 1ED
Herefordshire FHS Marriage Index. For parishes 1538-1753: Mr. J. Harnden, 11 Longworth Road, Tupsley, Hereford HR1 1SP; For parishes 1754-1837: Mrs V. Hadley, 255 Whitecross Road, Hereford HR4 0LT
Herefordshire Burial Index 1813-1839 - Herefordshire FHS, c/o Mr. A. Whitfield, 1 Castle Barn, Dilwyn, Herefordshire, HR4 8HZ
Herefordshire Monumental Inscription Index - c/o Mr A. Charles, 79 College Road, Hereford, HR1 1ED

Herefordshire's greatest extent from north to south is 38 miles, its greatest width from east to west 35 miles. It is watered by seven principal rivers; the Wye, Lugg, Munnow, Arrow, Frome, Team or Teme and Leddon. The population in 1841 was 113,272; in 1851, 115,489; in 1861, 123,650; in 1871, 125,370; in 1881, 121,062.

The soils are generally a mixture of marl and clay, containing a large proportion of calcareous earth. There are also beds of gravel, fuller's earth, red and yellow ochres and pipe clay. Cattle, sheep and pigs are bred and corn, apples and hops cultivated.

The information in the Index is abbreviated, and may mislead the searcher if reference is not made to the details contained in the several publications listed in the Introduction. It is essential that users of this book check the appropriate works before making further enquiries.

parish name	deposited original registers	I.G.I.	local census indexes	copies of registers at Soc. Gen.	Boyd's marriage index	1837-1851 Registration District	Pallot's marriage index	non-conform. records at P.R.O.	map ref.
Abbots Langley	A 1538-1994	1538-1882	5,8	1538-1904		Watford			3F
Albury	A 1558-1998	1558-1875	5,8	1558-1912	1693-1812	Bishop's Stortford			7K
Aldbury	A 1694-1968	1693-1875	5,8	1604-1896		Berkhamsted	1790-1812		5D
Aldenham	A 1559-1968	1559-1827	5,8	1559-1895		Watford	1790-1812		3G
Anstey	A 1540-1923	1541-1857	5,8	1540-1923		Royston			8K
Ardeley	A 1546-1880	1700-1850	5,8	1546-1880	1546-1812	Royston	1790-1812		7I
Ashwell	A 1678-1975	1604-1891	5,8	1604-1968	1610-1717	Royston		1797-1837	9H
Aspenden	A 1559-2000	1559-1875	5,8	1559-1948		Royston			7J(E)
Aston	A 1558-1986	1558-1875	5,8	1558-1922	1676-1812	Hertford			6I
Ayot									5H
St Lawrence	A 1566-1999	1566-1850	5,8	1562-1836		Hatfield			5G(L)
St Peter	A 1686-1986	1609-1896	5,8	1601-1895	1601-1700	Hatfield			5H(M)
Baldock	A 1558-1967	1558-1837	5,8	1558-1883		Hitchin			8H(A)
Barkway	A 1539-1984	1538-1875	5,8	1538-1967		Royston		1812-1837	8J
Barley	A 1559-1988	1559-1847	5,8	1559-1874	1566-1812	Royston	1790-1812		9J
Bayford	A 1538-1878	1538-1871	5,8	1538-1871		Hertford			4I
Bengeo	A 1539-1992	1539-1875	5,8	1539-1895	1539-1837	Hertford			5I
Benington	A 1538-1980	1538-1885	5,8	1538-1885	1538-1812	Hertford	1790-1813		6I
Berkhamsted									4D
St Mary			5,8			Berkhamsted			4D
St Peter	A 1538-1981	1604-1851	5,8	1538-1905	1538-1812	Berkhamsted	1790-1812	1787-1837	4D
								1748-1855	
Bishops Stortford									6L
Holy Trinity	A 1859-1985		5,8	1859-1972		Bishop's Stortford			6L
St Michael	A 1561-1995	1561-1903	5,8	1561-1979		Bishop's Stortford			6L
Bovingdon	A 1674-1992	1674-1875	5,8	1604-1905	1609-1837	Hemel Hempstead			3E
Boxmoor	A 1830-1969		5,8						4E
Bramfield	A 1559-1989	1559-1840	5,8	1559-1958		Hertford			5I
Braughing	A 1563-1971	1563-1875	5,8	1563-1925		Bishop's Stortford		1812-1836	7J
Brent Pelham	A 1539-1932		5,8	1538-1932		Bishop's Stortford			7K
Broxbourne	A 1688-1949	1688-1857	5,8	1688-1906		Ware			4J
Buckland	A 1658-1976	1658-1875	5,8	1659-1922		Royston			8J
Bushey	A 1684-1970	1581-1875	5,8	1560-1891	1581-1837	Watford	1609-1725	1816-1837	2F
Bygrave	A 1765-1980	1765-1834	5,8	1614-1834		Hitchin			8H
Caddington (Beds)						Luton			6E
Caldecote	A 1726-1974	1609-1834	5,8	1609-1970	1609-1802	Hitchin			9H
Cheshunt	A 1559-1995	1559-1837	5,8	1559-1910		Edmonton		1729-1837	3I
Chipping Barnet	A 1560-1984	1560-1885	5,8	1560-1894	1569-1700	Barnet			2H
Clothall	A 1717-1990	1604-1852	5,8	1605-1837	1610-1725	Hitchin			8I
Codicote	A 1559-1970	1559-1885	5,8	1558-1867		Hitchin			6H
Cottered	A 1558-1974	1558-1875	5,8	1558-1971		Royston			7I
Datchworth	A 1570-1990	1570-1892	5,8	1570-1895	1570-1812	Hertford	1790-1812		6H
Digswell	A 1538-1993	1538-1911	5,8	1538-1971		Hatfield	1790-1812		5H
East Barnet		1560-1682	5,8	1553-1935		Barnet			2I
Eastwick	A 1555-1977	1555-1879	5,8	1556-1930	1556-1812	Ware	1790-1812		5K
Elstree	A 1656-1991	1755-1800	5,8	1575-1851	1585-1803	Barnet	1800-1837		2G
Essendon	A 1653-1970	1653-1849	5,8	1604-1948		Hatfield			4H
Flamstead	A 1548-1929	1838-1874	5,8	1548-1869		Hemel Hempstead			5E
Flaunden	B 1729-1971	1729-1875	5,8	1613-1949	1731-1837	Hemel Hempstead			3E
Furneux Pelham	A 1561-1992	1560-1853	5,8	1560-1837		Bishop's Stortford			7K
Gilston	A 1558-1993	1558-1896	5,8	1558-1896	1559-1812	Ware	1800-1812		5K
Graveley	A 1555-1974	1555-1880	5,8	1555-1946	1556-1812	Hitchin	1790-1812		7H
Great Amwell	A 1528-1993	1559-1856	5,8	1558-1942		Ware			4K
Great Gaddesden	A 1558-1959	1559-1871	5,8	1558-1894		Hemel Hempstead			5E
Great Hormead	A 1538-1988	1538-1876	5,8	1538-1956	1576-1812	Royston	1790-1812		7J
Great Munden	A 1558-1988	1558-1876	5,8	1558-1939		Ware			7J
Great Wymondley	A 1561-1993	1561-1897	5,8	1561-1897		Hitchin	1790-1812		7H(B)
Harpenden	A 1562-1961	1562-1875	5,8	1562-1879		St Albans	1819-1821		5F
Hatfield		1604-1875	5,8	1604-1954	1609-1703	Hatfield			4H
Hemel Hempstead	A 1558-1975	1558-1881	5,8	1558-1949	1558-1837	Hemel Hempstead		1785-1837	4E
Hertford									5I
All Saints	A 1559-1975	1559-1875	5,8	1560-1881		Hertford			4I
St Andrew	A 1560-1988	1560-1875	5,8	1561-1927		Hertford			5I(P)
St John			5,8	1621-1835		Hertford			
Hertingfordbury	A 1679-1967	1545-1883	5,8	1541-1951		Hertford			5I
Hexton	A 1538-1990	1538-1875	5,8	1538-1927		Hitchin	1790-1812		7F
Hinxworth	A 1558-1994	1558-1871	5,8	1558-1963		Royston			9H
Hitchin	A 1562-1998	1562-1875	5,8	1562-1943	1601-1812	Hitchin	1790-1812	1717-1837	7G
Hoddesdon	A 1841-1949	1841-1875	5,8	1844-1895		Ware		1818-1837	4J
Hunsdon	A 1546-1986	1546-1863	5,8	1546-1931		Ware	1790-1837		5K
Ickleford	A 1749-1988	1604-1875	5,8	1604-1895		Hitchin	1790-1812		8G
Ippollitts	A 1625-1993	1625-1875	5,8	1604-1943	1625-1812	Hitchin			7G
Kelshall	A 1538-1987	1538-1875	5,8	1538-1916		Royston			8I
Kensworth	C 1615-2000	1615-1885	5,8	1605-1914	1615-1812	Luton	1790-1812		6E
Kimpton	A 1559-1993	1559-1890	5,8	1568-1890		Hitchin			6G
Kings Langley	A 1558-1995	1755-1850	5,8	1558-1922		Hemel Hempstead		1834-1837	3E
Kings Walden	A 1558-1985	1557-1885	5,8	1558-1917		Hitchin		1837	6G
Knebworth	A 1596-1951	1596-1875	5,8	1596-1837	1606-1812	Hitchin	1790-1812		6H
Layston	A 1563-1996	1563-1875	5,8	1563-1930		Royston		1810-1836	7J(F)
Letchworth	A 1695-1985	1695-1850	5,8	1610-1937	1614-1812	Hitchin	1790-1812		8H
Letchworth (detached)			5,8			Hitchin			6H(J)
Lilley	A 1711-1985	1604-1875	5,8	1609-1897		Hitchin	1609-1712		7F
Little Berkhampstead	A 1647-1915	1604-1875	5,8	1604-1915	1609-1812	Hertford	1800-1812		4I(Q)
Little Gaddesden		1743-1850	5,8	1604-1984		Berkhamsted			5D
Little Hadham	A 1559-1994	1559-1871	5,8	1559-1871		Bishop's Stortford	1790-1812	1804-1836	6K
Little Hormead	A 1588-1994	1588-1886	5,8	1588-1916	1598-1836	Royston			7J(G)
Little Munden	A 1680-1989	1604-1852	5,8	1604-1895		Ware			6I
Little Wymondley	A 1577-1987	1577-1885	5,8	1575-1964		Hitchin	1790-1812		7H(C)
London Colney	A 1826-1992		5,8	1826-1940		St Albans			3E
Long Marston (Bucks)	A 1820-1993	1805-1871	5,8	1609-1871	1614-1637	Berkhamsted			5C

HERTFORDSHIRE

parish name	deposited original registers	I.G.I.	local census indexes	copies of registers at Soc. Gen.	Boyd's marriage index	1837-1851 Registration District	Pallot's marriage index	non-conform. records at P.R.O.	map ref.
Meesden	A 1737-1837	1737-1837	5,8	1737-1837		Royston			8K
Much Hadham	A 1559-1986	1559-1858	5,8	1559-1882		Bishop's Stortford			6K
Newnham	A 1676-1983	1581-1837	5,8	1581-1898		Hitchin			8H
Northaw	A 1571-1964	1564-1881	5,8	1564-1881	1564-1750	Hatfield	1581-1747		3I
Northchurch	A 1564-1903	1564-1875	5,8	1604-1886		Berkhamsted			4D
North Mimms	A 1565-1998	1565-1875	5,8	1565-1901		Hatfield			4H
Norton	A 1579-1989	1571-1900	5,8	1579-1950		Hitchin	1790-1812		8H
Offley	A 1653-1987	1653-1876	5,8	1604-1943	1653-1812	Hitchin	1609-1812		7G
Pirton	A 1558-1995	1813-1850	5,8	1558-1914		Hitchin			8G
Puttenham	A 1678-1993	1614-1837	5,8	1605-1837	1614-1837	Berkhamsted			5C
Radwell	A 1590-1989	1590-1835	5,8	1590-1896	1610-1812	Hitchin			8H
Redbourn	A 1617-1917	1581-1839	5,8	1560-1876	1703-1798	St Albans		1813-1836	5F
Reed	A 1539-1988	1539-1875	5,8	1538-1966		Royston			8J
Rickmansworth	A 1653-1966	1569-1812	5,8	1562-1895	1569-1812	Watford	1800-1812	1795-1836	2E
Ridge	A 1558-1932	1558-1875	5,8	1558-1932		Barnet			4G
Royston	A 1662-1990	1662-1875	5,8	1662-1901		Royston		1759-1850	9J
Rushden	A 1607-1992	1607-1899	5,8	1604-1910		Royston			8I
St Albans								1751-1837	4G
Abbey	A 1558-1940	1558-1875	5,8	1558-1895		St Albans		1751-1837	4G(O)
St Michael	A 1643-1901	1572-1875	5,8	1570-1899	1572-1625	St Albans			4F
St Peter	A 1558-1997	1558-1875	5,8	1558-1895		St Albans			4G
St Stephen	A 1558-1995	1561-1875	5,8	1558-1962	1561-1600	St Albans			3F
St Margarets (Stanstead)	A 1697-1995	1772-1840	5,8	1697-1840		Ware			4K
St Pauls Walden	A 1558-1985	1559-1875	5,8	1558-1926		Hitchin			6G
Sacombe	A 1726-1979	1726-1903	5,8	1604-1979	1609-1704	Hertford			6I
Sandon	A 1678-1993	1678-1885	5,8	1538-1976	1609-1700	Royston		1814-1836	8I
Sandridge	A 1558-1977		5,8	1558-1934		St Albans			5G
Sarratt	A 1560-1986	1560-1885	5,8	1560-1970		Watford			3E
Sawbridgeworth	A 1558-1982	1558-1875	5,8	1558-1929		Bishop's Stortford		1817-1836	5K
Shenley	A 1653-1972	1811-1849	5,8	1604-1920		Barnet			3G
Shephall	A 1560-1992		5,8	1560-1958	1561-1812	Hitchin	1790-1811		6H(K)
Standon	A 1672-1985	1671-1875	5,8	1671-1926		Ware			6J
Stanstead Abbots	A 1679-1995	1695-1885	5,8	1678-1923		Ware			5J
Stapleford	A 1578-1985	1578-1885	5,8	1578-1972		Hertford			5I(N)
Stevenage	A 1538-1983	1538-1875	5,8	1538-1875		Hitchin			7H
Stocking Pelham	A 1695-1992	1695-1875	5,8	1695-1961		Bishop's Stortford			7K
Studham (Beds)						Luton			5E
Tewin	A 1559-1975	1559-1875	5,8	1559-1926		Hertford			5H
Therfield	A 1538-1988	1538-1850	5,8	1538-1961		Royston			8J
Thorley	A 1539-1986	1539-1875	5,8	1539-1961		Bishop's Stortford			6L
Throcking	A 1612-1836	1608-1875	5,8	1608-1976	1626-1812	Royston			7J(D)
Thundridge	A 1556-1994	1556-1875	5,8	1556-1915		Ware			5J
Totteridge	A 1546-1945	1570-1875	5,8	1556-1886	1570-1837	Barnet	1813-1837	1788-1837	2H
Tring	A 1566-1969	1566-1875	5,8	1566-1947		Berkhamsted			5C
Wakeley (ex.par.)			5,8			Royston			7J(H)
Walkern	A 1559-1985	1559-1877	5,8	1559-1963	1680-1812	Hertford	1790-1812	1814-1837	7I
Wallington	A 1661-1991	1634-1835	5,8	1538-1837		Royston			8I
Ware	A 1558-1985	1558-1882	5,8	1558-1893	1558-1754	Ware		1783-1840	5J
Watford	A 1539-1994	1539-1812	5,8	1539-1880		Watford		1785-1837	3F
Watton-at-Stone	A 1560-1967	1539-1875	5,8	1560-1967	1560-1812	Hertford	1790-1812		6I
Welwyn	A 1558-1988	1558-1876	5,8	1559-1939		Hatfield		1793-1837	5H
Westmill	A 1562-1930	1562-1868	5,8	1562-1930		Royston			7J
Weston	A 1539-1937	1539-1875	5,8	1539-1932		Hitchin			7H
Wheathampstead	A 1690-1973	1604-1850	5,8	1604-1893	1622-1812	St Albans			5G
Whipsnade (Beds) (detached)						Luton			6D
Widford	A 1558-1996	1558-1838	5,8	1558-1894		Ware			5L
Wigginton	A 1610-1838	1601-1838	5,8	1601-1837	1601-1675	Berkhamsted			4D
Willian	A 1557-1990	1557-1899	5,8	1557-1939		Hitchin	1790-1812		8H
Wormley	A 1674-1985	1674-1859	5,8	1674-1891		Ware			4I
Wyddial	A 1665-1995	1665-1837	5,8	1666-1837		Royston			8J

Original registers deposited at:
A = Hertfordshire Archives and Local Studies, County Hall, Hertford SG13 8DE
B = Buckinghamshire Record Office, County Hall, Aylesbury, Bucks. HP20 1UU
C = Bedfordshire Record Office, County Hall, Bedford MK42 9AP

Study adjacent parishes in counties of Bedfordshire, Cambridgeshire, Essex, Middlesex and Buckinghamshire

Hertfordshire Archives and Local Studies, County Hall, Hertford, SG13 8DE

The following useful indexes have been compiled – see Introduction
Census Index 1851 – Hertfordshire Archives and Local Studies
The Allen Index (marriages up to 1837) – Hertfordshire Archives and Local Studies
Parish Settlement, Removal, Examination, Bastardy and Apprenticeship papers – Hertford Archives and Local Studies
Monumental Inscriptions – Hertfordshire FHS, Mrs D. Thomas, 56 Dalkeith Road, Harpenden, Hertfordshire, AL5 5PW

Hertfordshire is almost elliptical in shape; its medium length is 34 miles and its breadth 26 miles. It is watered by two principal rivers: the Leigh and Colne. The population in 1841 was 157,207; in 1851, 167,856; in 1861, 173,294; in 1871, 192,226; in 1881, 203,069.

The soils are clay, loams, gravel and chalk. Produce includes the best white wheat and other grains, turnips and other vegetables, apples, cherries, currants and strawberries. Hay was produced for the London market and many cattle, sheep, pigs and poultry raised. Straw plait, silk and paper were manufactured and there was a malt trade, brewing, tanning, brick, tile and pipe making, weaving, coach and lace making.

The information in the Index is abbreviated, and may mislead the searcher if reference is not made to the details contained in the several publications listed in the Introduction. It is essential that users of this book check the appropriate works before making further enquiries.

HUNTINGDONSHIRE

parish name	deposited original registers	I.G.I.	local census indexes	copies of registers at Soc. Gen.	Boyd's marriage index	1837-1851 Registration District	Pallot's marriage index	non-conform. records at P.R.O.	map ref.
Abbotsley	A 1754-1963		4,5,8,9	1704-1848		St Neots			5D
Abbots Ripton	A 1559-1885		4,5,8,9			Huntingdon			5H
Alconbury			4,5,8,9			Huntingdon			6G
Alconbury Weston	A 1559-1944		4,5,8,9			Huntingdon			6H
Alwalton	A 1572-1969		4,5,8,9			Peterborough			7K
Barham	A 1688-1987		4,5,8,9	1604-1851		Huntingdon			7G(C)
Bluntisham cum Earith	A 1538-1996		4,5,8,9	1539-1837	1579-1837	St Ives		1771-1837	3G
Botolph Bridge	A 1556-1837		4,5,8,9			Peterborough			6L
Brampton	A 1653-1993		4,5,8,9	1618-1851		Huntingdon			6F
Brington	A 1685-1994	1604-1858	4,5,8,9			Thrapston			8H
Broughton	A 1572-1988	1785-1818	4,5,8,9	1785-1788		St Ives			4H
Buckden	A 1559-1992		4,5,8,9			St Neots			6F
Buckworth	A 1665-1838	1604-1858	4,5,8,9	1604-1851		Huntingdon			7H
Bury cum Hepmangrove	A 1561-1973		4,5,8,9	1561-1837	1561-1837	St Ives	1790-1837		4I
Bythorn	A 1560-1960	1604-1858	4,5,8,9	1560-1900		Thrapston			9H
Caldecote	A 1739-1972		4,5,8,9	1605-1972		Peterborough			7J
Chesterton	A 1561-1956	1604-1858	4,5,8,9			Peterborough			7K
Colne	A 1663-1958		4,5,8,9	1663-1837		St Ives			2G
Conington	A 1583-1992	1604-1824	4,5,8,9	1583-1699		Huntingdon			6I
Coppingford			4,5,8,9			Huntingdon			7H(A)
Covington	A 1649-1985		4,5,8,9	1604-1851		Thrapston			9F
Denton	A 1546-1960		4,5,8,9	1546-1900		Peterborough			7J
Diddington	A 1689-1965		4,5,8,9			St Neots			6E
Earith	A 1538-1997		4,5,8,9			St Ives			2G
Easton	A 1708-1948		4,5,8,9	1604-1851		Huntingdon			7F
Ellington	A 1608-1967		4,5,8,9	1608-1967		Huntingdon			7F
Elton	A 1560-1957		4,5,8,9			Oundle			8K
Eynesbury	A 1538-1969		4,5,8,9			St Neots			6D
Farcett	A 1641-1976		4,5,8,9			Peterborough			5K
Fen Stanton	A 1611-1982		4,5,8,9	1612-1837	1613-1837	St Ives			4F
Fletton	A 1604-1941		4,5,8,9			Peterborough			6K
Folksworth	A 1564-1972		4,5,8,9			Peterborough			7J
Glatton	A 1578-1962		4,5,8,9			Peterborough			7I
Godmanchester	A 1604-1974		4,5,8,9	1604-1837	1604-1837	Huntingdon			5F
Grafham	A 1581-1993		4,5,8,9	1580-1851		St Neots			7F
Great Catworth	A 1679-1896		4,5,8,9	1679-1852		St Neots			8G
Great Gidding	A 1574-1975		4,5,8,9	1675-1812		Oundle			7I
Great Gransden	A 1538-1995		4,5,8,9			Caxton			5D
Great Paxton	A 1583-1972		4,5,8,9			St Neots			6E
Great Raveley	A 1558-1957		4,5,8,9	1558-1812		Huntingdon			5H
Great Staughton	A 1541-1896		4,5,8,9	1540-1837		St Neots			7E
Great Stukeley	A 1569-1995		4,5,8,9			Huntingdon			5G
Haddon	A 1538-1955		4,5,8,9			Peterborough			7K
Hail Weston	A 1644-1963		4,5,8,9			St Neots			7E
Hamerton			4,5,8,9	1604-1845		Huntingdon			7H
Hartford	A 1538-1958		4,5,8,9	1538-1890		Huntingdon			5G
Hemingford Abbots	A 1692-1991		4,5,8,9	1604-1851	1643-1775	St Ives			4F
Hemingford Grey	A 1673-1992		4,5,8,9	1674-1837	1674-1837	St Ives			4F
Hilton	A 1558-1973		4,5,8,9	1558-1966	1558-1837	St Ives			4E
Holme	A 1684-1956		4,5,8,9			Peterborough			5J
Holywell cum Needingworth	A 1667-1986		4,5,8,9	1667-1812	1667-1812	St Ives		1824-1837	3G
Houghton	A 1633-1988		4,5,8,9	1605-1838		St Ives			4G
Huntingdon								1797-1837	5G(E)
All Saints	A 1558-1912		4,5,8,9	1559-1838	1559-1837	Huntingdon	1780-1837		5G(E)
All Saints & St John			4,5,8,9	1678-1838		Huntingdon			5G(E)
St Benedict	A 1574-1667		4,5,8,9	1575-1837	1575-1700	Huntingdon	1780-1837		5G(E)
St Benedict & St Mary			4,5,8,9	1701-1837	1692-1837	Huntingdon			5G(E)
St John	A 1585-1668		4,5,8,9	1585-1838	1586-1651	Huntingdon	1780-1837		5G(E)
St Mary	A 1593-1979		4,5,8,9	1593-1837	1593-1837	Huntingdon	1780-1837		5G(E)
Keyston	A 1637-1994		4,5,8,9	1604-1851		Thrapston			9G
Kimbolton	A 1647-1993		4,5,8,9			St Neots		1818-1837	8F
Kings Ripton	A 1597-1957		4,5,8,9			Huntingdon			5G
Leighton Bromswold	A 1653-1986		4,5,8,9			Huntingdon			7G
Little Catworth			4,5,8,9		1701-1837	St Neots			8G
Little Gidding	A 1637-1993		4,5,8,9			Oundle			7I
Little Paxton	A 1559-1972		4,5,8,9	1559-1966		St Neots			6E
Little Raveley	A 1576-1970		4,5,8,9	1577-1839	1577-1837	Huntingdon	1790-1839		5H(B)
Little Stukeley	A 1566-1969		4,5,8,9	1567-1812		Huntingdon			6G
Luddington (Northants)						Oundle			8I
Lutton (Northants)						Oundle			7J
Midloe (ex.par.)			4,5,8,9			St Neots			7E
Molesworth	A 1564-1992		4,5,8,9			Thrapston			8G
Morborne	A 1724-1952		4,5,8,9			Peterborough			7J
Offord Cluny	A 1573-1995		4,5,8,9			St Neots			5F
Offord Darcy	A 1563-1976		4,5,8,9			St Neots			5E
Old Hurst	A 1654-1964		4,5,8,9	1654-1836		St Ives			4G
Old Weston	A 1754-1994		4,5,8,9	1604-1851		Thrapston			8H
Orton Longueville	A 1556-1837		4,5,8,9	1696-1955		Peterborough			6K
Orton Waterville	A 1538-1887		4,5,8,9			Peterborough			7K
Papworth Agnes (Cambs.)						Caxton			4E
Pidley cum Fenton	A 1558-1876		4,5,8,9	1558-1837		St Ives			3H
Ramsey	A 1559-1959		4,5,8,9	1559-1837	1559-1837	Huntingdon	1790-1837		4I
St Ives	A 1561-1975		4,5,8,9	1561-1837	1561-1837	St Ives	1779-1837	1742-1807	4G
St Neots	A 1691-1974		4,5,8,9			St Neots		1797-1837	6D
Sapley (ex.par.)			4,5,8,9			Huntingdon			5G(D)
Sawtry									7I
All Saints	A 1591-1971		4,5,8,9			Huntingdon			7I
St Andrew	A 1662-1886		4,5,8,9			Huntingdon			6I

parish name	deposited original registers	I.G.I.	local census indexes	copies of registers at Soc. Gen.	Boyd's marriage index	1837-1851 Registration District	Pallot's marriage index	non-conform. records at P.R.O.	map ref.
Sawtry (cont'd)									7I
St Judith (ex.par.)			4,5,8,9			Huntingdon			6H
Sibson-cum-Stibbington	A 1595-1963		4,5,8,9			Stamford			8L
Somersham	A 1558-1972		4,5,8,9	1558-1838		St Ives			3H
Southoe	A 1558-1963		4,5,8,9			St Neots			6E
Spaldwick	A 1683-1981		4,5,8,9	1604-1851		Huntingdon		1793-1837	7G
Stanground	A 1538-1979		4,5,8,9			Peterborough			5K
Steeple Gidding	A 1571-1974		4,5,8,9			Huntingdon			7H
Stilton	A 1616-1978		4,5,8,9			Peterborough			6J
Stow Longa	A 1698-1955		4,5,8,9	1698-1837		St Neots			9F
with Little Catworth									
Swineshead	B 1549-1981	1548-1836	4,5,8,9	1549-1892		St Neots	1790-1812		9F
Tetworth	A 1650-1958		4,5,8,9			St Neots			6C
Thurning (Northants.)			4,5,8,9			Oundle			8I
Tilbrook (Beds.)						St Neots			8F
Toseland	A 1559-1900		4,5,8,9	1567-1837		St Neots			5E
Upton			4,5,8,9	1604-1851		Huntingdon			6H
Upwood	A 1558-1990		4,5,8,9	1558-1812	1558-1812	Huntingdon			5I
with Great Raveley									
Warboys	A 1551-1997		4,5,8,9	1551-1845		St Ives			3I
Waresley	A 1647-1973		4,5,8,9			St Neots			5C
Washingley			4,5,8,9			Peterborough			7J
Water Newton	A 1688-1839		4,5,8,9			Peterborough			7L
Winwick	A 1539-1944		4,5,8,9			Oundle			8H
Wistow	A 1628-1988		4,5,8,9	1604-1837	1604-1837	St Ives	1790-1837		4H
Woodhurst	A 1681-1981		4,5,8,9			St Ives			4G
Woodston	A 1551-1919		4,5,8,9			Peterborough			6K
Woodwalton	A 1754-1967		4,5,8,9	1605-1812		Huntingdon			5I
Woolley	A 1576-1987		4,5,8,9	1576-1850		Huntingdon			7G
Wyton	A 1635-1974		4,5,8,9	1605-1838		St Ives			4G
Yaxley	A 1653-1960		4,5,8,9			Peterborough		1820-1837	6J
Yelling	A 1583-1997	1583-1877	4,5,8,9			Caxton			5E

Original registers are deposited at:
A = Huntingdonshire Record Office, Grammar School Walk, Huntingdon PE29 6LF
B = Bedfordshire Record Office, County Hall, Bedford MK42 9AP

Study adjacent parishes in counties of Northamptonshire, Cambridgeshire and Bedfordshire

County Record Office, Grammar School Walk, Huntingdon, PE29 6LF

The following useful indexes have been compiled – see Introduction
Census Indexes 1841, 1851 & 1891 – Huntingdonshire FHS, 16 Kidmans Close, Hilton, Huntingdon, PE28 6UQ
Huntingdonshire Marriage Index 1601-1837 – Record Office, Grammar School Walk, Huntingdon, PE29 6LF or for purchase from Huntingdonshire FHS (as above)
Huntingdonshire Marriage Allegations and Bonds Index – Record Office, Grammar School Walk, Huntingdon, PE29 6LF
Monumental Inscriptions – Huntingdonshire FHS, 16 Kidmans Close, Hilton, Huntingdon, PE28 6UQ

Huntingdonshire is in the general form of an irregular square; its extent from north to south is about 30 miles, from east to west 23 miles. It is watered by two principal rivers: the Ouse and Nene or Nen. The population in 1841 was 58,594; in 1851, 64,183; 1n 1861, 64,250; in 1871, 63,708; in 1881, 59,491.

The soils vary considerably and include shallow staple, limestone, clays, loams and iron-stone. Corn was grown and cattle raised. There was also wool-stapling and the spinning of yarn.

The information in the Index is abbreviated, and may mislead the searcher if reference is not made to the details contained in the several publications listed in the Introduction. It is essential that users of this book check the appropriate works before making further enquiries.

KENT

parish name	deposited original registers	I.G.I.	local census indexes	copies of registers at Soc. Gen.	Boyd's marriage index	1837-1851 Registration District	Pallot's marriage index	non-conform. records at P.R.O.	map ref.
Acol			5,8			Thanet			7L
Acrise	B 1541-2000		4,5,8	1541-1926		Elham			4K
Addington	A 1562-1922	1562-1875	5,8	1562-1812	1651-1725	Malling			6D
Adisham	B 1538-1990		4,5,6,7,8			Bridge			5K
Aldington	A 1558-1990		5,6,8	1563-1772		East Ashford			3I
Alkham	B 1558-1992		4,5,8			Dover			4K
Allington	A 1630-1995	1630-1877	5,8	1630-1812	1651-1725	Malling			6E(J)
Appledore	A 1700-2001		5,8	1563-1886	1700-1800	Tenterden			3H
Ash		d1813-1837	8			Eastry			6L
Ash	F 1553-1997	1560-1872	5,8	1553-1812		Dartford			7D
Ashford	A 1696-1904		5,6,8	1570-1856		West Ashford		1785-1837	4H
Ashurst	A 1813-1998	1716-1885	5,8,9	1692-1812		Tonbridge			4B
Aylesford	A 1653-1955	1653-1861	5,8	1653-1812		Malling			6E
Badlesmere	B 1557-1999		5,6,8	1563-1984		Faversham			6I
Bapchild	A 1561-1919		4,5,6,7,8,9			Milton			7H
Barfreyston	B 1572-1996		4,5,6,7,8	1572-1936	1651-1725	Eastry			5L
Barham	B 1558-1994		4,5,8	1754-1812		Bridge			5K
Bearsted	A 1563-1977	1563-1847	5,6,8,9	1563-1641	1659-1837	Maidstone			6F
Beckenham		1718-1875	5,8	1538-1851		Bromley			8A
Bekesbourne	B 1558-1999	1558-1812	5,8	1558-1812	1651-1725	Bridge	1790-1812		6K
Benenden	A 1558-1980		5,8	1558-1940	1560-1754	Cranbrook			3F
Bethersden			5,6,8	1558-1600		West Ashford			4G
Betteshanger	B 1562-1992		4,5,6,7,8			Eastry			5L(AE)A
Bexley		1565-1876	5,6,7,8,9	1565-1812	1651-1725	Dartford		1827-1837	8B
Bicknor	A 1572-1811		5,6,8			Hollingbourne			6G
Bidborough	A 1593-1984	1716-1885	5,8,9	1593-1837	1701-1725	Tonbridge			5C
Biddenden	A 1538-1975		5,8	1538-1877		Tenterden			4F
Bilsington	A 1562-1992		5,6,8			East Ashford			3I
Birchington	B 1538-1909	1538-1675	5,8	1676-1837		Thanet		1819-1837	7L
Birling	F 1558-1950	1558-1877	5,8	1558-1840	1711-1725	Malling			7E
Bishopsbourne	B 1561-1992		5,8			Bridge			5J
Blackmanstone			5,8			Romney Marsh			3I(AF)
Blean	B 1558-1966		5,8	1558-1812		Blean			6J
Bobbing	A 1738-1983		4,6,7,8,9			Milton			7G
Bonnington	A 1679-1986		5,6,8	1564-1680	1651-1675	East Ashford			3I
Borden	A 1555-1883	1555-1839	4,5,6,7,8,9			Milton			7G
Boughton Aluph	A 1558-1971		5,6,8			East Ashford			5I
Boughton Malherbe	A 1671-1962		5,8	1665-1839	1653-1671	Hollingbourne			5G
Boughton Monchelsea	A 1560-1988		5,6,8,9			Maidstone			5F
Boughton under Blean	B 1558-1980	1558-1626	5,6,8	1558-1812		Faversham			6I
Boxley	A 1558-1997	1558-1808	5,6,8			Hollingbourne			6F
Brabourne	A 1558-1893		5,6,8	1558-1693		East Ashford		1817-1837	4I
Brasted	B 1557-1994	1813-1841	5,8	1557-1867		Sevenoaks			6B
Bredgar	A 1546-1972		4,6,7,8,9		1563-1799	Milton			6G
Bredhurst	F 1546-1998	1564-1812	5,6,8	1547-1837		Hollingbourne			7F(L)
Brenchley	A 1560-1916	1560-1876	5,8,9	1560-1837		Tonbridge			4D
Brenzett	A 1538-1987		5,8			Romney Marsh			2H
Bridge	B 1579-1960		5,8			Bridge			5J
Bromley		1558-1881	5,8	1558-1941		Bromley		1788-1832	8A
Brook	B 1695-1988		5,6,8			East Ashford			4I
Brookland	A 1558-1990		5,8		1560-1795	Romney Marsh			2H
Broomfield	A 1579-1980		5,8			Hollingbourne			5F
Broomhill			5,8			Rye			1H
Buckland			5,6,8		1577-1733	Faversham			6H(N)
Buckland, St Andrew	B 1577-1993		5,8			Dartford			4L
Burham	F 1627-1981	1625-1879	5,8	1626-1812		Malling			7E
Burmarsh	A 1572-1983		5,8	1572-1836	1651-1725	Romney Marsh			3I
Canterbury									6J
All Saints	B 1559-1959		8	1559-1891		Canterbury		1646-1855	6J(S)
Cathedral (Christ-Church)	B 1564-1991	1564-1878	5,8	1564-1878	1651-1725	Blean	1790-1837		6J(S)
Holy Cross	B 1563-1969		8	1563-1880		Canterbury			6J(S)
St Alphege	B 1558-1980	1558-1800	5,8	1558-1864	1651-1705	Blean	1790-1800		6J(S)
St Andrew	B 1564-1880		8	1538-1880		Canterbury			6J(S)
St Dunstan	B 1576-1995	1560-1800	5,8	1559-1969	1651-1725	Blean	1790-1800		6J(T)
St George	B 1538-1958	1538-1800	8	1538-1800		Canterbury	1790-1800		6J(S)
St Margaret	B 1653-1942		8	1654-1942		Canterbury			6J(S)
St Martin	B 1662-1988		8	1662-1897	1573-1671	Canterbury			6J(W)
St Mary Bredin	B 1633-1983	1563-1812	8	1563-1840	1564-1636	Canterbury			6J(Y)
St Mary Bredman	B 1558-1887		8	1558-1868		Canterbury			6J(S)
St Mary Magdalen	B 1634-1868	1559-1800	8	1559-1800	1651-1725	Canterbury	1790-1800		6J(S)
St Mary Northgate	B 1640-1887		8	1640-1846		Canterbury			6J(U)
St Mildred	B 1559-1992		8	1559-1950		Canterbury			6J(S)
St Paul	B 1562-1973	1562-1800	8	1562-1930		Canterbury			6J(X)
St Peter	B 1560-1993	1560-1800	8	1560-1863	1651-1725	Canterbury	1790-1800		6J(S)
Capel	A 1663-1939	1663-1870	5,8,9	1663-1812		Tonbridge			5D
Capel-le-Ferne	B 1593-1983		4,5,6,8,9			Dover		1831-1837	4K
Chalk	F 1661-1954	1661-1876	5,8	1661-1812	1651-1725	North Aylesford			8E
Challock	B 1558-1994		5,6,8	1754-1812		East Ashford			5H
Charing	A 1590-1965	1590-1812	5,6,8	1590-1686		West Ashford			5H
Charlton	D 1653-1933	1653-1872	4,5,8	1653-1850		Lewisham			9B
Charlton	B 1564-1990		5,8,9	1565-1837	1564-1837	Dover	1790-1837		4L(AK)
Chartham	B 1558-1991		5,8	1558-1813	1558-1740	Bridge			6J
Chart Sutton	A 1558-1937		5,8			Hollingbourne			5F
Chatham	F 1568-1974	1735-1838	4,5,6,7,8	1676-1837		Medway		1700-1837	7F
Chelsfield		1538-1887	5,8	1558-1986	1651-1725	Bromley			7B
Cheriton	B 1563-1971		4,5,6,7,8	1563-1837	1651-1725	Elham			3K
Chevening	A 1561-1957	1561-1887	5,8	1561-1812	1651-1725	Sevenoaks			6B

KENT

parish name	deposited original registers	I.G.I.	local census indexes	copies of registers at Soc. Gen.	Boyd's marriage index	1837-1851 Registration District	Pallot's marriage index	non-conform. records at P.R.O.	map ref.
Chiddingstone	A 1631-1944	1813-1863	5,8	1558-1911	1651-1725	Sevenoaks			5B
Chilham	B 1558-1987	1558-1836	5,6,8	1558-1836		East Ashford			5I
Chillenden	B 1559-1984		8			Eastry			5L(AB)
Chislehurst		1558-1887	8	1558-1930		Bromley			8B
Chislet	B 1538-1990	1538-1707	5,8	1538-1707	1651-1707	Blean			7K
Cliffe	F 1558-1990	1813-1849	5,6,7,8,9			North Aylesford			9E
Cobham	F 1655-1992	1718-1879	5,8	1655-1812	1701-1725	North Aylesford			8E
Coldred	B 1560-1999		4,5,6,7,8	1560-1836		Dover			4L
Cooling	F 1707-1977	1719-1875	5,6,7,8,9	1707-1812		Hoo			8F
Cowden	A 1566-1805	1566-1846	5,8	1566-1842		Sevenoaks			4B
Cranbrook	A 1559-1881		5,8	1559-1840		Cranbrook		1682-1837	4F
Crayford		1813-1887	5,8,9	1558-1812	1651-1725	Dartford			9C
Crundale	B 1554-1994		5,6,8			East Ashford			5I
Cudham		1801-1825	5,8	1653-1851	1653-1725	Bromley			7A
Cuxton	F 1560-1994	1560-1876	5,6,7,8,9	1560-1877	1651-1725	North Aylesford			7E
Darenth	F 1678-1996	1813-1877	5,8	1678-1988	1701-1725	Dartford			8C
Dartford	F 1561-1984	1561-1843	5,8	1561-1812		Dartford		1797-1837	8C
Davington	B 1549-1991	1549-1812	5,6,8	1549-1837	1549-1831	Faversham			6H(O)
Deal									5M
St George	B 1717-1967		5,8	1717-1956		Eastry			5M
St Leonard	B 1559-1961		5,8	1559-1837		Eastry		1681-1837	5M
Denton	B 1560-1986		4,5,6,7,8,9			Dover			4K
Deptford					1570-1653			1755-1837	9A(A)
St Nicholas	E 1563-1933	1564-1872	4,5,8,9			Greenwich			9A(A)
St Paul	E 1730-1966	1730-1882	5,8,9	1730-1763		Greenwich	1780-1837		9A(A)
Detling	A 1558-1987		5,8			Hollingbourne			6F
Ditton	A 1663-1891	1663-1885	5,8	1663-1812	1665-1725	Malling			6E
Doddington	B 1589-1992		5,6,8	1695-1722		Faversham			6H
Dover								1646-1837	4L
St James the Apostle	B 1614-1940	1595-1842	5,8	1591-1923		Dover			4L
St Mary	B 1558-1993	1557-1849	5,8	1557-1849		Dover			4L
St Mary in the Castle			5,8			Dover			4L
Downe		1813-1875	5,8	1538-1851	1538-1732	Bromley			7B
Dunkirk (ex.par.)			5,6,8			Faversham			6I
Dymchurch	A 1624-1980		5,8	1624-1837	1651-1725	Romney Marsh			3I
East Barming	A 1541-1989	1541-1885	5,6,8,9	1541-1813		Maidstone			6E
Eastbridge			5,8			Romney Marsh			3I
Eastchurch	A 1677-1867		5,8,9			Sheppey			8H
East Farleigh	A 1580-1907	1580-1842	5,6,8,9	1580-1840		Maidstone			6E
East Langdon			4,5,6,7,8,9			Dover			4L
Eastling	B 1558-1990		5,6,8			Faversham			6H
East Malling	A 1570-1929	1570-1895	5,8	1570-1839		Malling			6E
East Peckham		1813-1879			1651-1725				5D
Holy Trinity	A 1558-1977		5,8	1558-1812		Malling			5D
St Michael			5,8	1813-1850		Malling			5D
Eastry	B 1559-1985		8	1559-1905		Eastry			5L
East Sutton	A 1648-1938		5,8			Hollingbourne			5F
Eastwell	A 1538-1965		5,8			East Ashford			5H
East Wickham		1718-1876	4,5,8,9	1715-1812		Dartford			9B(C)
Ebony	A 1708-1837		5,8	1578-1837		Tenterden			3G
Edenbridge	A 1545-1944	1546-1863	5,8	1545-1899		Sevenoaks		1806-1837	5B
Egerton			4,5,6,7,8	1569-1850		West Ashford		1816-1837	5G
Elham	B 1556-1974		5,8	1566-1918		Elham			4J
Elmley	A 1827-1942		5,8,9			Sheppey			7H
Elmstead	B 1538-1999		5,8			Elham			4J
Elmstone	B 1551-1995	1552-1812	8	1552-1812	1651-1725	Eastry	1790-1812		6L(AA)
Eltham		1718-1875	4,5,8	1583-1803		Lewisham			8B
Erith		1625-1875	4,5,8,9			Dartford		1807-1832	9B
Ewell, Temple	B 1581-1994		4,5,6,7,8			Dover			4L
Eynsford	A 1538-1862	1538-1846	5,8	1538-1837	1538-1812	Dartford	1790-1812	1799-1837	7C
Eythorne	B 1559-1965		4,8	1754-1812		Eastry		1723-1837	5L
Fairfield	A 1558-1932		5,8			Romney Marsh			2H
Farnborough		1558-1875	5,8	1558-1851		Bromley	1790-1812		7B
Farningham	A 1589-1964	1589-1865	5,8	1589-1812	1651-1725	Dartford			7C
Faversham	B 1620-1983		5,6,8		1560-1621	Faversham		1790-1837	6I
Fawkham	F 1568-1986	1718-1871	5,8	1568-1812	1651-1725	Dartford			7D
Folkestone	B 1635-1962	1635-1840	4,5,6,7,8	1635-1840	1651-1725	Elham		1779-1837	3K
Foots Cray		1799-1855	5,8	1559-1812	1651-1725	Bromley			8B
Fordwich	B 1683-1997		5,8	1683-1927		Bridge			6K
Frant (Sussex)									4D
Frindsbury	F 1669-1977	1718-1832	5,6,7,8,9	1669-1812		North Aylesford		1816-1837	8E
Frinsted	A 1560-1843		5,6,7,8,9			Hollingbourne			6G
Frittenden	A 1678-1879		5,8	1558-1601	1563-1798	Cranbrook			4F
Gillingham	F 1558-1976	1558-1882	4,5,6,7,8,9	1558-1752		Medway		1796-1837	7F
Godmersham	B 1600-1993		5,6,8	1564-1812	1651-1725	East Ashford			5I
Goodnestone	B 1558-1984	1558-1877	8	1558-1880	1651-1725(?)	Eastry	1790-1837		5L
Goodnestone (Faversham)	B 1759-1835		5,6,8	1813-1837	1651-1725(?)	Faversham			6I(P)
Goudhurst	A 1558-1970		5,8	1558-1714	1651-1714	Cranbrook		1815-1836	4E
Grain, Isle of	F 1653-1992	1813-1856	5,6,7,8,9			Hoo			8G
Graveney	B 1653-1913		5,6,8	1813-1837		Faversham			7I
Gravesend	F 1547-1951	1553-1876	5,8	1547-1812		Gravesend		1761-1855	8D
Great Chart	A 1558-1946		5,6,8			West Ashford			4H
Great Mongeham	B 1685-1991		4,5,6,7,8	1754-1812		Eastry			5M
Greenwich	E 1615-1989	1615-1866	4,5,8,9	1615-1637		Greenwich		1705-1864	9A
Groombridge	A 1845-1975		8	1588-1836		Tonbridge			4C
Guston	B 1667-1968		4,6,7,8			Dover			4L
Hackington	B 1567-1993		5,8	1567-1886		Blean			6J
Hadlow	A 1558-1887	1558-1870	5,8,9	1557-1836	1559-1753	Tonbridge			5D

KENT

parish name	deposited original registers	I.G.I.	local census indexes	copies of registers at Soc. Gen.	Boyd's marriage index	1837-1851 Registration District	Pallot's marriage index	non-conform. records at P.R.O.	map ref.
Halling	F 1705-1995	1705-1883	5,6,7,8,9	1705-1840		North Aylesford			7E
Halsted	A 1561-2000	1561-1895	5,8	1561-1837	1561-1837	Sevenoaks	1790-1836		7B
Ham	B 1552-1978		4,5,6,7,8			Eastry			5L(AD)
Harbledown	B 1557-1992	1557-1800	5,8	1557-1800	1651-1725	Bridge	1790-1800		6J
Harrietsham	A 1538-1997	1538-1569	5,8	1538-1837		Hollingbourne			5G
Hartley	F 1712-1984	1718-1883	5,8	1712-1814	1713-1725	Dartford			7D
Hartlip	A 1538-1945		4,6,7,8,9			Milton			7F
Harty	A 1679-1835		5,8,9			Sheppey			7I
Hastingleigh	B 1730-1993		5,6,8			East Ashford			4I
Hawkhurst	A 1550-1988		5,8	1558-1601		Cranbrook			3E
Hawkinge	B 1691-1977		5,8	1691-1812	1701-1725	Elham			4K(AJ)
Hayes		1539-1876	5,8	1539-1812	1651-1725	Bromley			8A
Headcorn	A 1560-1962		5,8	1558-1601		Hollingbourne		1731-1837	5F
Herne	B 1558-1992		5,8	1728-1740		Blean		1826-1836	7J
Hernehill	B 1557-1995		5,6,8	1653-1837		Faversham			6I
Hever	A 1632-1937	1813-1877	5,8	1632-1937		Sevenoaks			5B
Higham	F 1653-1982	1653-1877	5,6,7,8,9	1653-1812	1654-1725	North Aylesford			8E
High Halden	A 1558-1937		5,8	1558-1601		Tenterden			4G
High Halstow	F 1653-1991	1653-1874	5,6,7,8,9	1654-1812		Hoo			9F
Hinxhill	A 1577-1995		5,8			East Ashford			4I
Hoath	B 1554-1990		5,8			Blean			7K
Hollingbournee	A 1556-1979		5,6,8			Hollingbourne			6F
Hoo									8F
All Hallows	F 1629-1976	1629-1873	5,6,7,8,9			Hoo			9G
St Mary	F 1695-1978	1695-1874	5,6,7,8,9	1695-1812		Hoo			8F
St Werbergh	F 1587-1987	1587-1879	5,6,7,8,9			Hoo			8F
Hope	A 1589-1707		5,8			Romney Marsh			2I
Horsmonden	A 1558-1893	1558-1895	5,8,9			Tonbridge			4E
Horton Kirkby	F 1671-1998	1684-1876	5,8	1678-1812	1701-1725	Dartford	1790-1812		8C
Hothfield	A 1570-1978		5,6,8			West Ashford			4H
Hougham	B 1659-1989		5,8	1661-1838		Dover			4L
Hucking	A 1556-1836		5,6,8			Hollingbourne			6F
Hunton	A 1585-1978	1585-1870	5,6,8,9	1585-1812		Maidstone			5E
Hurst			5,6,8			East Ashford			3I
Hythe	B 1566-1937		5,8	1586-1837	1651-1725	Elham		1810-1837	3J
Ickham	B 1557-1886		5,8			Bridge			6K
Ifield	F 1751-1976	1813-1871	5,8	1751-1812		North Aylesford			8D(D)
Ightham	A 1559-1995	1559-1895	5,8	1559-1812	1651-1725	Malling			6D
Ivychurch	A 1715-1950		5,8			Romney Marsh			2H
Iwade	A 1560-1953		4,6,7,8,9			Milton			7G
Kemsing	A 1561-1874	1719-1853	5,8	1561-1812	1651-1725	Sevenoaks			6C
Kenardington	A 1546-1990		5,8			Tenterden			3H
Kennington	A 1671-1987		5,6,8			East Ashford			4I
Keston		1540-1876	5,8	1540-1851		Bromley			7A
Kidbrook (ex.par.)			4,5,8			Lewisham			9B(B)
Kingsdown	B 1560-1984	1719-1851	4,5,6,7,8,9	1725-1812		Dartford			6H
Kingsnorth	A 1538-1982		5,6,8			West Ashford			4H
Kingston	B 1558-1990	1558-1837	5,8	1558-1837	1651-1725	Bridge	1790-1837		5K
Knockholt	A 1548-1987	1813-1895	5,8	1548-1851	1651-1725	Bromley			7B
Knowlton	B 1711-1981		4,5,6,7,8	1640-1976		Eastry			5L(AC)
Lamberhurst	A 1564-1898	1563-1895	4,5,8	1564-1837	1563-1837	Ticehurst	1790-1837		4D
Langley	A 1665-1980		5,8			Hollingbourne			5F
Leaveland	B 1553-2001		5,6,8	1553-1812		Faversham			6H(R)
Lee	C 1579-1979	1579-1862	5,8	1579-1850	1579-1775	Lewisham			8A
Leeds	A 1557-1972		5,8			Hollingbourne			6F
Leigh	A 1592-1918	1592-1885	5,8	1560-1837	1651-1725	Sevenoaks			5C
Lenham			5,8			Hollingbourne		1779-1837	5G
Lewisham	C 1703-1975	1559-1875	5,8	1558-1750	1559-1775	Lewisham			8A
Leybourne	A 1560-1987	1560-1891	5,8	1560-1841	1651-1725	Malling			6E(G),6D9
Leysdown	A 1701-1921		5,8	1884-1913		Sheppey			7I
Linton	A 1561-1987	1681-1878	5,6,8,9			Maidstone			5E
Littlebourne	B 1559-1955		5,8			Bridge			6K
Little Chart	A 1538-1836	1537-1813	5,6,8	1538-1813	1651-1725	West Ashford	1790-1813		5H
Little Mongeham			4,5,6,7,8			Eastry			5L
Longfield	F 1757-1973	1718-1878	5,8	1558-1812	1651-1725	Dartford			8D(E)
Loose	A 1556-1991		5,6,8,9	1556-1966		Maidstone			5E
Lower Halstow	A 1691-1876		4,6,7,8,9	1756-1840		Milton			7G
Lower Hardres	B 1563-1917		5,8			Bridge			5J
Luddenham	B 1547-1971		5,6,8			Faversham			7H
Luddesdown	F 1682-1997	1587-1890	5,8	1681-1812	1701-1725	North Aylesford			7D
Lullingstone	A 1578-1840	1578-1853	5,8	1578-1812	1701-1725	Dartford	1790-1812		7C
Lydd	A 1542-1981		5,8	1539-1848		Romney Marsh		1814-1837	2I
Lydden	B 1540-1990		4,5,6,7,8,9	1540-1837	1651-1725	Dover			4K
Lyminge	B 1679-1993	1795-1837	5,8	1538-1837	1679-1837	Elham			4J
Lympne	A 1617-1984		5,8	1617-1836	1651-1725	Elham			3J
Lynsted	B 1653-1992		5,6,8			Faversham			6H
Maidstone			5,8,9	1542-1754		Maidstone		1732-1839	6E
Marden	A 1559-1950		5,6,8,9	1558-1601		Maidstone		1812-1836	5E
Margate (see St John the Baptist)									
Meopham	F 1561-1991	1561-1871	5,8	1561-1812	1651-1725	North Aylesford			7D
Mereworth	A 1559-1960	1560-1886	5,8	1559-1837	1651-1725	Malling			6D
Mersham	A 1558-1959		5,6,8			East Ashford			4I
Midley			5,8			Romney Marsh			2H
Milstead	A 1542-1999		4,6,7,8,9	1754-1842		Milton			6G
Milton	B 1688-1980		5,8			Bridge			6J(Z)
Milton (Gravesend)	F 1558-1889		5,8	1559-1812		Gravesend		1807-1836	7G
Milton (Sittingbourne)	A 1559-1889	1559-1883	4,6,7,8,9	1538-1669		Milton		1813-1854	8D
Minster in Sheppey	A 1568-1952		5,8,9	1883-1918		Sheppey		1833-1837	8H

KENT

parish name	deposited original registers	I.G.I.	local census indexes	copies of registers at Soc. Gen.	Boyd's marriage index	1837-1851 Registration District	Pallot's marriage index	non-conform. records at P.R.O.	map ref.
Minster in Thanet	B 1557-1972		5,8	1557-1880	1557-1837	Thanet			7L
Molash	B 1557-1992		5,6,8	1755-1812		East Ashford			5I
Monks Horton	A 1558-1836		5,8	1558-1766		Elham			4J
Monkton	B 1700-1991		5,8	1700-1952		Thanet			7L
Murston	A 1561-1933		4,6,7,8,9		1702-1725	Milton			7H
Nackington	B 1563-1995		5,8			Bridge			5J
Nettlested	A 1640-1975	1640-1885	5,6,8,9	1640-1812	1651-1725	Maidstone			5D
Newchurch	A 1604-1982		5,8			Romney Marsh			3I
Newenden	A 1559-1990	1559-1813	5,8	1559-1813	1651-1725	Tenterden	1790-1813		3F
Newington (Hythe)	B 1559-2000		5,8	1559-1837	1559-1837	Elham			3J
Newington (Sittingbourne)	A 1558-1969		4,6,7,8,9		1558-1836	Milton	1790-1837		7G
Newnham	B 1722-1994		5,6,8			Faversham		1825-1837	6H
New Romney	A 1662-1977		5,8			Romney Marsh			2I
Nonington	B 1538-1939	1538-1727	8			Eastry			5K
Northbourne	B 1586-1958		4,5,6,7,8			Eastry			5L
North Cray		1538-1881	5,8	1538-1812	1651-1725	Bromley			8B
Northfleet	F 1539-1955	1813-1837	5,8	1539-1812	1701-1725	North Aylesford			8D
Norton	B 1559-1983		5,6,8			Faversham			6H
Nursted	F 1561-1997	1720-1883	5,8	1561-1812	1651-1725	North Aylesford			8D
Oare	B 1714-1996		4,5,6,7,8,9			Faversham			7I
Offham	A 1538-1937	1538-1875	5,8	1538-1852	1651-1725	Malling			6D
Old Romney	A 1538-1813		5,8			Romney Marsh			2H
Orgarswick			5,8			Romney Marsh			3I(AG)
Orlestone			5,6,8			East Ashford		1805-1837	3H
Orpington	A 1554-1985	1560-1876	5,8	1560-1935	1651-1725	Bromley		1650-1837	7B
Ospringe	B 1561-1985		5,6,8	1754-1812		Faversham			6H
Otford	A 1562-1972	1813-1844	5,8	1630-1812	1651-1725	Sevenoaks			6C
Otham	A 1538-1972		5,6,8,9			Maidstone			6F
Otterden	B 1660-1993		5,8	1754-1812		Hollingbourne			5H
Oxney			4,5,6,7,8,9			Dover			4M(AL)
Paddlesworth	B 1813-1991		5,8			Elham			4K(AH)
Patrixbourne	B 1556-1969		5,8			Bridge			5K
Pembury	A 1560-1994	1716-1842	5,8,9	1560-1837		Tonbridge			4D
Penshurst	A 1558-1812	1813-1842	5,8	1558-1836	1626-1812	Sevenoaks	1790-1812		5C
Petham	B 1559-1997		5,8	1634-1661		Bridge			5J
Plaxtol	A 1648-1902	1813-1904	8	1648-1812	1651-1725	Malling			6D
Pluckley	A 1660-1945		5,6,8			West Ashford			4G
Plumstead	E 1654-1898	1744-1855	4,5,7,8,9	1783-1787		Lewisham			9B
Postling	B 1687-1991		5,8			Elham			4J
Poulton			4,5,6,7,8			Dover			4L
Preston (Faversham)	B 1599-1942		5,6,8			Faversham			6I
Preston	B 1558-1984		8			Eastry			6K
Queenborough	A 1719-1960		5,8,9	1719-1918		Sheppey		1797-1836	8G
Rainham	F 1592-1985	1560-1812	4,6,7,8,9			Milton			7F
Ramsgate St George	B 1827-1976		4,5,8			Thanet		1695-1837	6M
Reculver	B 1602-1991		5,8			Blean			7K
Ridley	F 1625-1962	1626-1875	5,8	1626-1812	1631-1837	Dartford			7D
Ringwould	B 1569-1983		4,5,6,7,8,9			Dover			4M
Ripple	B 1560-1893		4,5,6,7,8			Eastry			5M
River	B 1620-1997		4,5,6,7,8	1566-1840		Dover			4L
Rochester								1700-1837	7E(F)
Cathedral	F 1633-1994	1660-1837	4,5,6,7,8	1657-1837	1669-1725	Medway			7E(F)
St Margaret	F 1653-1980	1718-1866	4,5,6,7,8	1639-1885		Medway			7E(F)
St Nicholas	F 1624-1950	1624-1876	4,5,6,7,8	1624-1840		Medway			7E(F)
Rodmersham	A 1538-1950		4,6,7,8,9			Milton			6G
Rolvenden	A 1558-1991		5,8	1557-1812		Tenterden			3F
Ruckinge	A 1538-1976		5,6,8			East Ashford			3H
Ryarsh	A 1560-1960	1559-1901	5,8	1560-1837	1651-1725	Malling			6D
St John the Baptist (Margate)	B 1559-1990		5,8	1559-1847		Margate		1802-1837	7M
St Lawrence in Thanet	B 1559-1984	1559-1653	4,5,8	1560-1653		Thanet			7M
St Margaret at Cliffe	B 1558-1946		4,5,6,7,8,9			Dover			4M
St Mary Cray		1579-1874	5,8	1579-1851	1651-1725	Bromley			8B
St Mary in the Marsh	A 1831-1891		5,8			Romney Marsh			2I
St Nicholas at Wade	B 1653-1993		5,8			Thanet		1824-1835	7L
St Pauls Cray		1584-1875	5,8	1579-1837	1651-1725	Bromley			8B
St Peter in Thanet	B 1582-1991	1582-1777	5,8	1582-1837		Thanet		1789-1836	7M
Saltwood	B 1560-1995		5,8	1562-1837	1651-1725	Elham			3J
Sandhurst	A 1563-1990		5,8	1560-1840		Cranbrook		1785-1837	3F
Sandwich								1690-1837	6L
St Clement	B 1563-1967		8			Eastry			6L
St Mary	B 1538-1966		8			Eastry			6L
St Peter	B 1538-1967		8	1538-1812		Eastry			6L
Sarre			5,8			Thanet			7L
Seal	A 1561-1812	1561-1904	5,8	1561-1845	1651-1655	Sevenoaks			6C
Seasalter	B 1558-1998		5,8	1555-1845		Blean			7J
Sellindge	A 1559-1957		5,8			Elham			4I
Selling	B 1558-1950		5,6,8	1557-1979		Faversham			6I
Sevenoaks	A 1559-1980	1816-1904	5,8	1559-1837	1651-1725	Sevenoaks		1796-1837	6C
Sevington	A 1554-1962		5,6,8	1554-1962		East Ashford			4I
Shadoxhurst	A 1538-1931		5,6,8			West Ashford			4H
Sheerness						Sheppey		1791-1837	8H
Holy Trinity	A 1836-1969		5,8,9	1883-1918		Sheppey	1883-1918		8H
St Paul			5,8,9	1911-1918		Sheppey	1911-1918		8H
Sheldwich	B 1558-1969		5,6,8	1560-1984		Faversham			6I
Shipbourne	A 1560-1940	1560-1904	4,5,6,7,8	1560-1812	1659-1812	Malling			6C
Sholden	B 1591-1965		4,5,6,7,8			Eastry			5M
Shoreham	A 1558-1982	1558-1904	5,8	1558-1812	1651-1725	Sevenoaks			7C

171

KENT

parish name	deposited original registers	I.G.I.	local census indexes	copies of registers at Soc. Gen.	Boyd's marriage index	1837-1851 Registration District	Pallot's marriage index	non-conform. records at P.R.O.	map ref.
Shorne	F 1538-1992	1538-1875	5,8	1538-1812	1651-1725	North Aylesford			8E
Sibertswold	B 1563-1980		8	1560-1953		Dover			5K
Sittingbourne	A 1561-1922		4,6,7,8,9	1538-1668		Milton		1798-1837	7G(M)
Smarden	A 1632-1966		5,6,8	1558-1601		West Ashford			4G
Smeeth	A 1662-1916		5,6,8	1569-1838		East Ashford			4I
Snargate	A 1552-1990		5,8			Romney Marsh			2H
Snave	A 1619-1838		5,8			Romney Marsh			3H
Snodland	F 1559-1971	1559-1860	5,8	1559-1860		Malling			7E
Southborough		1831-1909	5,8,9			Tonbridge			5C
Southfleet	F 1558-1932	1718-1851	5,8	1558-1812	1651-1725	Dartford			8D
Speldhurst	A 1538-1936	1716-1889	5,8,9	1558-1836	1651-1725	Tonbridge			4C
Stalisfield	B 1699-1992		5,6,8			Faversham			5H
Stanford, All Saints	B 1556-1991		5,8			Elham			3J
Stansted	A 1564-1991	1813-1901	5,8	1564-1812	1651-1725	Malling			7D
Staple	B 1544-1961		4,8			Eastry			6L
Staplehurst	A 1538-1902		5,6,8,9	1538-1812	1538-1812	Maidstone	1790-1812	1797-1836	4F
Stelling Minnis	B 1557-1989		5,8			Elham			5J
Stockbury	A 1653-1983		5,8	1653-1983		Hollingbourne			7F
Stodmarsh	B 1558-1936		5,8			Bridge			6K
Stoke	F 1666-1906	1573-1829	5,6,7,8,9	1755-1812		Hoo			8F
Stonar			8			Thanet			6L
Stone in Oxney	A 1538-1929	1567-1812	5,8	1569-1929		Tenterden			2G
Stone			5,6,8			Faversham			6H
Stone (Dartford)	F 1718-1995		5,8	1718-1812	1722-1725	Dartford			8C
Stourmouth	B 1538-1986		8	1538-1812	1651-1725	Eastry			6L
Stowting	A 1539-1932		5,8			Elham			4J
Strood	F 1565-1978	1565-1875	4,5,6,7,8,9			North Aylesford		1791-1836	8E
Sturry	B 1538-1993		5,8	1538-1890		Blean			6K
Sundridge	A 1562-1955	1813-1904	5,8	1562-1812	1651-1725	Sevenoaks			6B
Sutton	B 1538-1896		4,5,6,7,8	1538-1812	1651-1725	Eastry			5L
Sutton at Hone	F 1607-1979	1607-1868	5,8	1607-1851	1651-1725	Dartford			8C
Sutton Valence	A 1576-1951		5,8			Hollingbourne		1795-1836	5F
Swalecliffe	B 1538-1980		5,8			Blean			7J
Swanscombe	F 1559-1987	1718-1871	5,8	1559-1812	1651-1725	Dartford			8D
Swingfield	B 1698-2000		5,8			Elham			4K
Tenterden	A 1544-1980		5,8	1558-1601		Tenterden		1736-1837	3G
Teston	A 1538-1975	1538-1882	5,6,8,9	1538-1840		Maidstone			6E
Teynham	B 1538-1989		5,6,8			Faversham			7H
Thanington	B 1558-1973		5,8			Bridge			6J
Throwley	B 1557-1889		5,6,8	1557-1980		Faversham			6H
Thurnham	A 1625-1971		5,8	1838-1971		Hollingbourne			6F
Tilmanstone	B 1558-1993		8	1558-1900		Eastry			5L
Tonbridge	A 1547-1890	1553-1837	4,5,6,8,9	1547-1837	1651-1725	Tonbridge	1790-1837	1752-1837	5C
Tonge			4,6,7,8,9			Milton			7H
Trottescliffe	A 1540-1884	1540-1885	5,8	1540-1812	1651-1725	Malling			7D
Tudley	A 1663-2000	1663-1870	5,8,9	1663-1812	1663-1725	Tonbridge			5D
Tonbridge Wells								1769-1837	4C(K)
King Charles	A 1745-1996	1729-1904	5,8,9	1729-1812		Tonbridge			4C(K)
Holy Trinity	A 1830-1946		5,8,9			Tonbridge			4C(K)
Tunstall	A 1538-1951		4,6,7,8,9			Milton			6G
Ulcombe	A 1560-1987		5,8	1561-1968		Hollingbourne			5G
Upchurch	A 1633-1968		4,6,7,8,9			Milton			7G
Upper Hardres	B 1754-1989		5,8			Bridge			5J
Waldershare	B 1561-1999		4,5,6,7,8			Eastry			5L
Walmer	B 1560-1976		8	1560-1988		Eastry			5M
Waltham	B 1538-1966		5,8			Bridge			5J
Warden	A 1759-1884		5,8,9			Sheppey			8I
Warehorne	A 1727-1973		5,6,8			East Ashford			3H
Wateringbury	A 1705-1915	1705-1875	5,8	1705-1812	1705-1725	Malling			6E
Westbere	B 1577-1993		5,8	1577-1947		Blean			6K
Westcliffe	B 1576-1811		4,5,6,7,8,9			Dover			4L
Westerham	A 1559-1968	1716-1870	5,8	1559-1916	1559-1837	Sevenoaks	1790-1837		6B
West Farleigh	A 1539-1905	1539-1875	5,6,8,9	1558-1812	1539-1812	Maidstone	1790-1812		6E
West Hythe	A 1617-1962		5,8	1743-1809		Romney Marsh			3J
West Kingsdown	A 1725-1970		8	1725-1812	1725-1812	Dover			7C
West Langdon	B 1640-1811		4,5,6,7,8,9		1622-1775	Dover			4L
West Malling	A 1698-1961	1698-1864	5,8	1698-1840		Malling			6E
West Peckham	A 1561-1923	1561-1879	5,8	1561-1812	1651-1725	Malling			6D
Westwell	A 1558-1984		5,6,8			West Ashford			5H
West Wickham		1720-1849	5,8	1558-1900		Bromley			7A
Whitfield	B 1586-1984		4,5,6,7,8,9			Dover			4L
Whitstable	B 1549-1992		5,8			Blean			7J
Wichling			5,8	1577-1837	1577-1837	Hollingbournee	1813-1837		6G
Wickhambreux	B 1558-1956		5,8	1558-1651		Bridge			6K
Willesborough	A 1538-1975	1538-1838	5,6,8	1538-1837	1538-1837	East Ashford	1814-1837		4I
Wilmington	F 1683-1977	1683-1813	5,8	1684-1860	1701-1725	Dartford			8C
Wingham	B 1568-1972		8			Eastry			6K
Wittersham	A 1550-1906		5,8	1550-1860		Tenterden`		1819-1837	2G
Womenswold	B 1574-1989	1574-1837	4,5,8	1754-1812	1651-1725	Bridge	1790-1837		5K
Woodchurch	A 1538-1990		5,8	1558-1601	1578-1584	Tenterden		1797-1836	3H
Woodnesborough	B 1561-1967		8			Eastry			6L
Woolwich	E 1670-1941	1813-1875	4,5,8,9	1719-1803		Greenwich		1786-1854	9B
Wooton	B 1546-1995		8			Dover			4K
Wormshill			4,5,6,7,8,9			Hollingbourne			6G
Worth	B 1726-1988		4,8			Eastry			5L
Wouldham	F 1538-1990	1538-1877	5,8	1538-1852		Malling			7E
Wrotham	A 1558-1971	1813-1885	5,8	1558-1870		Malling		1818-1837	6D
Wye	B 1538-1996		5,6,8	1538-1812		East Ashford			5I
Yalding	A 1559-1923	1716-1880	5,6,8,9	1559-1812		Maidstone			5E

KENT

Original registers deposited:
A = Centre for Kentish Studies, Sessions House, County Hall, Maidstone ME14 1XQ
B = Canterbury Cathedral Archives, The Precincts, Canterbury, Kent, CT1 2EH
C = Lewisham Local Studies and Archives, Lewisham Library, 199-201 Lewisham High Street, Lewisham, London SE13 6LG
D = Greenwich Local History Library, Woodlands, 90 Mycenae Road, Blackheath, London, SE3 7SE
E = London Metropolitan Archives, 40 Northampton Road, London, EC1 0AB
F = Medway Area Archives Office, Civic Centre, Strood, Rochester, Kent ME2 4AU

Study adjacent parishes in counties of Essex, Middlesex, Surrey and Sussex

Canterbury City and Cathedral Archives, The Precincts, Canterbury, CT1 2EH
Centre for Kentish Studies, Sessions House, County Hall, Maidstone, ME14 1XQ
Medway Area Archives Office, Civic Centre, Strood, Rochester, Kent, ME2 4AU
East Kent Archives Office, Enterprize Road, Honeywood Road, Whitfield, Dover, CT16 3EH

The following useful indexes have been compiled – see Introduction
There are many index holders of census material for one or two parishes or single registration districts. A guide to these is produced by Gillian Rickards.
Kent Census Surnames Index – G. Rickards, 99 Strangers Lane, Canterbury, Kent, CT1 3XN
Major indexes are held or published by -
Census Indexes 1841, 1851, 1861, 1871 & 1891 – Kent FHS, c/o Mrs R.J. Bailey, 41 The Street, Kennington, Ashford, Kent, TN24 9HD
Census Index 1851 – North West Kent FHS, c/o Mrs B Attwaters, 141 Princes Road, Dartford, Kent, DA1 3HJ
West Kent Census Index 1851 – Matthew Copus, 58 Thorold Road, Chatham, Kent, ME5 7EB
Isle of Sheppey Census Index 1851 – T.J. Wood, 4 Georgian Houses, Ludborough Road, North Thoresby, Grimsby, Lincolnshire, DN36 5RF
Census Index 1871 & 1891 – Woolwich and District FHS, c/o F Reynolds, Parkhill Road, Bexley, Kent, DA5 1HY
Isle of Sheppey and Milton Registration Districts Census Index 1891 – TJ Wood (as above)
Kent Marriage Index 1813-1837 – M.J. Gandy, 140 Hampden Way, Southgate, London, N14 5AX
East Kent Marriage Index 1754-1813 – M.J. Gandy (as above)
East Kent Marriage Index 1538-1753 – Mrs J. Jones, Weir Bank Lodge, Monkey Island Lane, Bray, Maidenhead, Berks SL6 2ED
West Kent Marriage Index 1538-1812 – S.G. Smith, 59 Friar Road, Orpington, Kent BR5 2BW
Thames Riverside Parish Index – R.J. Cottrell, 19 Bellevue Rd., Bexleyheath, Kent, DA6 8ND
The SELON Index – Peter R. Shilham, 6 Beckford Close, Wokingham, Berks. RG41 1HN
West Kent Baptismal Index 1813-40 – Mathew Copus (as above)
Nonconformist Index – Mathew Copus (as above)
East Kent Settlement and Removal Index 1598-1865 – Miss G. Rickards (as above)
West Kent Settlement and Removal Index 1602-1872 – Miss G. Rickards (as above)
Vagrants, Gypsies & Travellers in Kent 1538-1837 – Miss G. Rickards (as above)
East Kent Burial Index 1813-41 – Dr David Wright, 71 Island Wall, Whitstable, Kent, CT5 1EL

Kent is about 63 miles in length on its northern side and nearly 40 miles on its eastern side. It is watered by four principal rivers: The Thames, Medway, Stour and Rother. The population in 1841 was 549,353; in 1851, 617,766; in 1861, 733,887; in 1871, 848,294; in 1881, 977,585.

The soils are chalk, flint, iron and rag-stone, clay, gravel and marl. Produce included wheat, barley, oats, beans, peas, asparagus, potatoes, turnips, hops and fruits of many kinds. Horses, cattle, sheep, pigs, poultry and game are reared. Manufactures were unimportant.

The information in the Index is abbreviated, and may mislead the searcher if reference is not made to the details contained in the several publications listed in the Introduction. It is essential that users of this book check the appropriate works before making further enquiries.

LANCASHIRE

parish name	deposited original registers	I.G.I.	local census indexes	copies of registers at Soc. Gen.	Boyd's marriage index	1837-1851 Registration District	Pallot's marriage index	non-conform. records at P.R.O.	map ref.
Admarsh	A 1779-1982		8			Lancaster			7I
Ainsworth	B 1727-1894	1727-1861	8			Bury		1769-1837	5D
Aldingham	E 1539-1978	1539-1756	6,7,8	1542-1837	1542-1837	Ulverstone			9J
Altcar	A 1664-1938		5,8,9	1663-1812		Ormskirk			9D
Altham	A 1596-1946	1596-1848	8	1596-1695	1596-1695	Burnley			5F
Ancoats (see Manchester)						Manchester			4C
Ardwick	B 1740-1976	1740-1873	5,8			Chorlton			4C
Arkholme	A 1828-1864		5,8,9			Lancaster			6J
Ashton	D 1698-1955			1698-1755		Wigan		1786-1837	6C
in Makerfield			5,8,9						3C
Ashton-under-Lyne				1594-1837	1594-1720			1794-1837	3C
St Michael	B 1594-1840	1594-1843	5,6,7,8			Ashton-under-Lyne			3C
St Peter	B 1824-1973		5,6,7,8			Ashton-under-Lyne			3C
Ashworth	B 1813-1958	1813-1843	8			Bury			4E
Astley	B 1724-1969	1724-1844	8			Bolton		1825-1837	5C
Atherton	B 1724-1982	1724-1849	8	1724-1849		Leigh			6D
Aughton	A 1541-1951	1541-1882	5,7,8,9	1541-1764		Ormskirk			8D
Bacup	B 1788-1950	1788-1849	8			Haslingden		1759-1837	4E
Balderstone	A 1751-1976		8			Blackburn			6F
Billinge	D 1696-1995	1696-1856	8,9	1696-1812		Wigan			7D
Birch in Rusholme	B 1837-1979	1752-1877	8			Chorlton			4C
Birch in Hopwood	B 1829-1988		8			Bury			4D
Bispham	A 1599-1935	1599-1858	4,5,6,8	1599-1754	1631-1837	Fylde			9G
Blackburn				1660-1680				1751-1840	5F
St John	A 1789-1975		5,8			Blackburn			5F
St Mary	A 1569-1951	1568-1705	5,8		1600-1705	Blackburn			5F
St Paul	A 1792-1955		5,8			Blackburn			5F
St Peter	A 1821-1981		5,8			Blackburn			5F
Blackley	B 1655-1907	1655-1880	5,7,8	1655-1783	1668-1753	Manchester		1752-1837	4D
Blackpool (St John)	A 1821-1988		6,8			Fylde			9G
Blackrod	A 1607-1955	1606-1860	8,9	1606-1860	1606-1700	Wigan			6D
Blawith	E 1728-1956	1728-1837	8	1715-1837	1730-1837	Ulverstone			9L
Bolton-le-Moors				1573-1660				1753-1837	5D
All Saints	B 1796-1966	1797-1872	5,8			Bolton			5D
Holy Trinity, see Horwich			5,8			Bolton			5D
St George	B 1796-1975	1796-1856	5,8			Bolton			5D
St Peter	B 1573-1945	1573-1837	5,8		1573-1660	Bolton			5D
Bolton le Sands	A 1642-1964	1653-1885	6,7,8	1655-1736	1653-1837	Lancaster			7J
Bootle	C 1827-1962		4,8			West Derby			9C
Bradshaw	B 1814-1874		8			Bolton			5E
Brindle	A 1558-1972	1558-1895	5,8,9	1558-1714	1558-1837	Chorley			6F
Broughton	A 1653-1938	1653-1804	5,6,7,8	1653-1804	1654-1837	Preston			7G
Broughton in Furness	E 1634-1996	1634-1812	6,8	1634-1837	1662-1837	Ulverstone		1634-1810	9K
Burnley	A 1562-1956	1562-1847	5,8	1562-1653	1562-1653	Burnley		1807-1837	4F
Burscough Bridge	A 1832-1931		5,8,9			Ormskirk			8E
Burton			8			Kendal			7K
Burtonwood	F 1668-1942	1668-1876	8	1668-1837		Warrington			6C
Bury				1590-1837				1699-1837	4E
St John	B 1813-1906	1770-1859	5,7,8			Bury			4E
St Mary	B 1590-1947	1590-1876	5,7,8		1591-1698	Bury			4E
Cartmel	H 1559-1883	1559-1723	7,8,9	1559-1723	1559-1837	Ulverstone			8K
Cartmel Fell	H 1754-1996		6,7,8,9	1754-1790		Ulverstone			8L
Caton	A 1585-1954	1585-1718	5,7,8,9	1585-1718	1585-1837	Lancaster			7I
Cheetham	B 1794-1981	1794-1849	8			Manchester			4D
Childwall		1557-1850	8	1557-1753		West Derby/Prescot			8B
All Saints									
Chipping	A 1559-1959	1559-1694	5,8	1559-1694	1559-1837	Clitheroe			6G
Chorley	A 1548-1961	1548-1880	5,8,9	1548-1708	1548-1837	Chorley		1788-1837	6E
Chorlton-cum-Hardy	B 1737-1979		8	1737-1837		Chorlton			4C
Chorlton on Medlock								1789-1857	4C
All Saints	B 1819-1943		5,8			Chorlton			4C
St Luke	B 1805-1962		5,8			Chorlton			4C
Church Coniston	H 1599-1971	1599-1700	8	1599-1700	1604-1837	Ulverstone			9L
Church Kirk	A 1633-1968	1600-1880	8	1600-1747	1635-1747	Blackburn			5F
Claughton (in Lonsdale)	A 1701-1996	1701-1812	6,7,8,9	1701-1862	1701-1837	Blackburn	1790-1812		6I
Clitheroe	A 1570-1935	1570-1841	5,6,8			Clitheroe		1796-1837	5G
Cockerham	A 1595-1981	1595-1885	6,7,8,9	1595-1657	1595-1837	Lancaster		1785-1837	7H
Cockersand Abbey (ex.par.)			6,8			Lancaster			8H
Colne (St Bartholomew)	A 1599-1948	1599-1833	5,8,9	1599-1812	1599-1644	Burnley		1753-1837	3G
Colton	E 1623-1911	1623-1812	6,7,8,9	1623-1842	1623-1837	Ulverstone	1790-1812	1755-1837	9K
Coniston	H 1599-1968		8	1599-1700		Ulverstone			9L
Coppul	A 1757-1966	1812-1865	8,9			Chorley			7E
Croft	F 1833-1989		8	1833-1920		Warrington			6C
Croston	A 1538-1944	1538-1876	8,9	1538-1900	1538-1837	Chorley		1819-1837	7E
Croxteth Park (ex.par.)			4,8			West Derby			8C
Dalton-in-Furness	E 1565-1971	1565-1691	5,6,7,8,9	1565-1837	1565-1837	Ulverstone			9J
Deane	B 1636-1890	1604-1829	8	1613-1750	1604-1750	Bolton		1803-1838	5D
Dendron	E 1788-1962		8	1803-1812		Ulverstone			9J
Denton	B 1695-1939	1695-1837	5,8	1695-1837	1698-1754	Ashton-under-Lyne			3C
Didsbury	B 1561-1911	1561-1881	8	1561-1751	1561-1757	Chorlton			4C
Douglas	A 1719-1990		8		1721-1748	Chorley			7D
Downham	A 1653-1887	1653-1800	8	1606-1837	1655-1754	Clitheroe			4G
Eccles	B 1563-1970	1564-1632	8	1563-1841	1565-1632	Barton		1786-1837	5C
Eccleston	A 1603-1938	1603-1875	8,9	1603-1900	1603-1837	Chorley			7E
Edenfield	B 1728-1966	1728-1812	5,8	1813-1934		Haslingden			4E
Egton with Newland	E 1792-1966		6,7,8	1792-1841		Ulverstone			9K

LANCASHIRE

parish name	deposited original registers	I.G.I.	local census indexes	copies of registers at Soc. Gen.	Boyd's marriage index	1837-1851 Registration District	Pallot's marriage index	non-conform. records at P.R.O.	map ref.
Ellel	A 1828-1955	1727-1829	5,6,7,8,9			Lancaster			7I
Ellenbrook	B 1744-1902		8			Bolton			5D
Euxton	A 1711-1978	1734-1780	8,9	1734-1781		Chorley			7E
Everton								1825-1837	8C
St Augustine	C 1830-1941		4,5,8			West Derby			8C
St George	C 1814-1982	1814-1860	4,5,8			West Derby			8C
Failsworth	B 11845-1965		8			Manchester			5C
Farnworth	F 1538-1957	1538-1873	5,8	1538-1920		Prescot			7B
Farnworth	B 1826-1903	1826-1849	8			Bolton		1809-1837	5D
Feniscowles	A 1836-1985		8			Blackburn			6F
Finsthwaite	H 1725-1970	1726-1812	6,8		1727-1837	Ulverstone			8L
Flixton	B 1570-1886	1570-1812	8	1570-1812	1570-1754	Barton		1799-1837	5C
Formby	A 1710-1974	1620-1839	5,8,9	1620-1837	1710-1812	Ormskirk			9D
Garstang		1567-1885		1567-1982				1784-1837	7H
St Helen	A 1567-1978	1567-1734	4,5,6,7,8		1567-1837	Garstang			7H
St Thomas	A 1824-1982		4,5,6,7,8			Garstang			7G
Garston	C 1777-1988		4,8			West Derby		1711-1836	8B
Goldshaw Booth	B 1732-1907		8			Burnley			4F
Goosnargh	A 1639-1967	1639-1880	4,7,8	1639-1876	1639-1837	Preston	1790-1812	1828-1837	6G
Gorton	B 1600-1981	1599-1880	8	1599-1901	1601-1741	Chorlton			4C
Great Crosby	A 1749-1861	1749-1869	4,8	1749-1893		West Derby			9D
Great Harwood	A 1547-1979	1547-1880	8	1547-1812	1560-1683	Blackburn			5F
Great Sankey	F 1728-1993	1728-1885	8	1728-1839		Warrington			6B
Gressingham	A 1710-1993	1676-1828	6,7,8	1676-1828	1676-1835	Lancaster	1790-1828		6J
Hale	F 1620-1969	1572-1885	4,8	1572-1754		Prescot			7B
Halsall	A 1653-1956	1606-1885	5,8,9	1606-1754		Ormskirk			8D
Halton	A 1592-1972	1592-1791	6,7,8	1592-1837	1593-1837	Lancaster			7J
Hambleton	A 1695-1959	1695-1812	4,8	1695-1812		Garstang			8G
Haslingden	A 1603-1959	1721-1844	7,8			Haslingden		1785-1837	5F
Hawkshead	H 1568-1964	1568-1837	5,6,7,8,9	1568-1837	1568-1837	Ulverstone			8M
Heapey	A 1711-1962	1734-1780	8			Chorley			6E
Heaton Norris	B 1846-1983	1769-1845	8,9	1767-1851		Stockport		1793-1837	4C
Hesketh with Becconsall	A 1745-1975		5,8,9		1824-1837	Ormskirk			8F
Hey	B 1743-1915	1788-1812	8			Rochdale			3D
Heysham	A 1658-1982	1658-1854	6,7,8	1658-1813	1659-1837	Lancaster	1790-1812		8I
Heywood	B 1733-1906	1745-1800	5,8,9	1745-1846		Bury		1808-1837	4D
Hindley	D 1698-1971	1698-1879	5,8,9		1698-1837	Wigan		1642-1837	6D
Hoghton	A 1781-1966	1786-1850	8			Chorley			6F
Holcombe Emmanuel	B 1726-1974		5,8,9	1726-1858		Bury		1802-1817	4E
Hollinfare	F 1654-1987		8	1654-1837		Warrington			6C
Hollingwood	B 1769-1999		8	1769-1855		Oldham			3D
Holme	A 1742-1953	1792-1895	8	1742-1841		Burnley			4F
Hoole	A 1673-1970	1673-1775	8		1673-1836	Preston			7E
Hornby	A 1742-1998	1742-1789	6,8	1742-1790	1743-1798	Lancaster			6J
Horwich	B 1660-1881	1660-1841	8	1695-1841		Bolton		1751-1836	6D
Hulme	B 1828-1983		8			Chorlton		1810-1869	4C
Huyton (by Roby)		1578-1868	4,8	1578-1837		Prescot			8C
Ireleth	E 1865-1980		6,7,8	1745-1784		Ulverstone			9K
Kirkby	C 1678-1959	1678-1893	4,7,8	1610-1839		West Derby			8C
Kirkby Ireleth	E 1681-1998	1701-1812	8	1634-1837	1728-1837	Ulverstone			9K
Kirkham	A 1539-1989	1539-1653	4,5,6,7,8,9	1539-1653	1539-1837	Fylde		1810-1837	8G
Lancaster				1599-1786				1760-1857	7I
St Anne	A 1796-1958	1796-1812	5,6,7,8,9			Lancaster			7I
St John	A 1755-1958	1755-1813	5,6,7,8,9			Lancaster			7I
St Mary	A 1599-1908	1599-1818	5,6,7,8,9		1599-1837	Lancaster			7I
Langho	A 1733-1962		8	1725-1837		Blackburn			5G
Lathom	A 1855-1995		5,8,9	1758-1836		Ormskirk			7D
Leck	A 1800-1976		6,7,8,9			Lancaster			5K
Leigh	B 1558-1913	1558-1839	5,8	1558-1885	1560-1624	Leigh		1758-1837	6C
Leyland	A 1651-1963	1622-1880	5,8,9	1651-1838	1622-1837	Chorley			7E
Lindale	H 1734-1965		8	1754-1790		Ulverstone			8J
Littleborough	B 1716-1986		8			Rochdale		1805-1837	3E
Little Lever	B 1791-1969	1791-1866	8	1791-1840		Bolton			5D
Little Marsden	A 1811-1992		8			Burnley			4G
Liverpool								1709-1855	
All Saints			4,5,8			Liverpool			8C
Blessed Virgin Mary			4,5,8			Liverpool			8C
Christchurch	C 1799-1968	1799-1851	4,5,8			Liverpool			8C
Holy Trinity	C 1792-1966	1802-1843	4,5,8			Liverpool			8C
St Andrew	C 1815-1904		4,5,8			Liverpool			8C
St Anne	C 1773-1968	1773-1856	4,5,8			Liverpool			8C
St Bride	C 1831-1984		4,5,8			Liverpool			8C
St Catherine	C 1831-1952		4,5,8			Liverpool			8C
St David	C 1827-1974		4,5,8			Liverpool			8C
St George	C 1734-1897	1734-1875	4,5,8		1734-1837	Liverpool			8C
St John	C 1767-1898	1785-1875	4,5,8			Liverpool			8C
St Luke	C 1831-1959		4,5,8			Liverpool			8C
St Mark	C 1815-1973	1815-1843	4,5,8			Liverpool			8C
St Martin's Cemetery	C 1829-1861		4,5,8			Liverpool			8C
St Martin in the Fields	C 1829-1946	1829-1856	4,5,8			Liverpool			8C
St Mary's Cemetery	C 1806-1847		4,5,8			Liverpool			8C
St Mary (Blind)	C 1829-1926		4,5,8			Liverpool			8C
St Matthew	C 1798-1929	1798-1851	4,5,8			Liverpool			8C
St Michael (City)	C 1826-1902	1815-1893	4,5,8			Liverpool			8C
St Nicholas	C 1659-1961	1604-1879	4,5,8	1660-1725	1604-1704	Liverpool			8C
St Paul	C 1773-1901	1769-1881	8			Liverpool			8C

parish name	deposited original registers	I.G.I.	local census indexes	copies of registers at Soc. Gen.	Boyd's marriage index	1837-1851 Registration District	Pallot's marriage index	non-conform. records at P.R.O.	map ref.
Liverpool (con'd)									
St Peter	C 1704-1919	1704-1875	4,5,8	1704-1715		Liverpool			8C
St Philip	C 1816-1976	1816-1881	4,5,8			Liverpool			8C
St Simon	C 1831-1930	?-1837	4,5,8			Liverpool			8C
St Stephen	C 1792-1937	1801-1869	4,5,8			Liverpool			8C
St Thomas	C 1750-1905	1750-1875	4,5,8			Liverpool			8C
Longridge	A 1760-1975	1762-1812	6,8			Preston			6G
Longton	A 1754-1979	1753-1820	5,8,9	1895-1990		Preston			7F
Lower Darwen	A 1829-1952		8	1751-1794		Blackburn			5F
Lowick	E 1718-1947	1718-1837	6,8	1715-1837	1727-1837	Ulverstone			9K
Lowton	D 1733-1991		8			Leigh			6C
Lytham	A 1679-1989	1679-1797	4,5,6,7,8	1679-1761	1679-1837	Fylde			9F
Maghull	A 1729-1955	1729-1876	8,9	1660-1875		Ormskirk			8D
Manchester								1712-1857	4C
Ancoats, Christchurch			5,8			Manchester		1825-1837	4C
St Andrew (Ancoats)	B 1831-1958	1831-1877	8			Manchester			4C
St Ann	B 1736-1854	1736-1808	8			Manchester			4C
St Clement	B 1793-1878	1793-1871	8			Manchester			4C
St George	B 1798-1976	1798-1839	5,8			Manchester			4C
St James	B 1787-1928	1781-1875	8	1788-1837		Manchester			4C
St John	B 1769-1928	1686-1855	8	1769-1878		Manchester			4C
St Mary	B 1754-1888	1756-1875	8	1754-1888		Manchester			4C
St Mary, Dennis & George (Cathedral)		1573-1885	8	1573-1666	1573-1803	Manchester			4C
St Matthew	B 1826-1942		8			Manchester			4C
St Michael	B 1789-1930	1791-1812	8			Manchester			4C
St Paul	B 1838-1976	1765-1844	8			Manchester			4C
St Peter	B 1795-1906		8			Manchester			4C
Marton	A 1828-1985		6,7,8	1826-1900		Fylde			9G
Melling	A 1603-1960	1603-1837	5,6,7,8,9	1603-1837		Ormskirk			8D
Melling	A 1625-1982	1625-1752	5,6,7,8,9	1625-1853	1636-1837	Lancaster			6J
Mellor	A 1829-1958		5,8			Blackburn		1803-1837	6F
Middleton	B 1541-1903	1541-1752	5,6,7,8,9	1541-1838	1541-1752	Oldham		1769-1838	4D
Milnrow	B 1721-1990	1722-1851	8			Rochdale			3D
Mitton	A 1610-1917		8			Clitheroe		1807-1837	5G
Mossley		1756-1821	8			Ashton-under-Lyne			3D
Newchurch (in Culcheth)	F 1599-1994	1599-1893	5,8	1559-1842	1607-1751	Leigh			6C
Newchurch in Pendle	A 1721-1935	1720-1798	5,8		1574-1813	Clitheroe			4G
Newchurch in Rossendale	B 1653-1871	1653-1853	5,8	1653-1723	1654-1723	Haslingden		1759-1838	4F
Newton Heath	B 1655-1963	1654-1856	5,8	1655-1792		Manchester			4C
Newton in Makerfield	D 1735-1966		5,7,8	1756-1788		Warrington			6C
North Meols		1594-1812	5,8	1594-1838	1600-1837	Ormskirk	1790-1812	1806-1837	8E
Old Accrington	A 1766-1944		8			Haslingden		1785-1837	5F
Oldham								1763-1840	3D
St James			5,8			Ashton-under-Lyne			3D
St Mary	B 1558-1932	1558-1825	5,8	1558-1844	1598-1812	Ashton-under-Lyne			3D
St Peter	B 1768-1961		5,8			Ashton-under-Lyne			3D
Ormskirk	A 1557-1977	1537-1841	5,8,9	1557-1836	1557-1625	Ormskirk		1743-1837	8D
Over Darwen								1751-1837	5E
St John	A 1864-1974		8			Blackburn			5E
St Peter	A 1829-1981		8			Blackburn			5E
Over Kellet	A 1653-1920	1653-1812	6,8	1648-1812	1653-1837	Lancaster	1790-1812		7J
Overton	A 1722-1902	1718-1730	6,7,8,9	1718-1730		Lancaster			8I
Over Wyresdale	A 1715-1867	1714-1813	6,8	1714-1735		Lancaster			6H
Padiham	A 1573-1955	1573-1873	5,8	1573-1653	1573-1653	Burnley		1785-1837	4F
Peel	B 1772-1807	1760-1846	8			Bolton			5D
Pendleton	B 1776-1991		8	1776-1860		Salford		1813-1837	4C
Pennington	E 1612-1984	1613-1812	6,7,8	1612-1837	1616-1837	Ulverstone			9K
Penwortham	A 1857-1968	1608-1820	8	1608-1753	1608-1753	Preston			7F
Pilling	A 1630-1977	1630-1721	4,8	1630-1721	1630-1837	Garstang			8H
Poulton-le-Fylde	A 1591-1976	1591-1677	5,6,7,8	1591-1677	1591-1837	Fylde			8G
Poulton-le-Sands	A 1747-1950		8			Lancaster			7I
Prescot	A 1573-1974	1576-1632	5,8	1538-1694		Prescot/Warrington		1776-1837	7C
Preston								1762-1837	7F
Holy Trinity	A 1815-1951		5,6,8,9			Preston			7F
St. John	A 1603-1974	1611-1885	5,6,8,9	1611-1851	1611-1837	Preston			7F
Prestwich	B 1603-1972	1603-1712	5,8	1603-1843	1603-1712	Manchester		1765-1837	4D
Radcliffe					1557-1783			1803-1837	4D
St Mary	B 1557-1992	1560-1851	5,8,9		1560-1761	Bury			4D
St Thomas	B 1826-1987	1819-1859	5,8,9			Bury			4D
Rainford	A 1718-1973	1702-1874	8	1702-1837		Prescot		1746-1837	7C
Ribchester	A 1598-1966	1595-1885	6,8,9	1598-1801	1598-1837	Preston			6G
Ringley	B 1680-1960	1709-1825	8	1770-1841	1719-1753	Prestwich		1808-1831	5D
Rivington	B 1703-1877		8,9	1703-1873	1726-1837	Chorley		1786-1819	6E
Rochdale	B 1582-1898	1582-1802	5,8	1582-1906	1583-1801	Rochdale	1790-1801	1752-1837	3D
Royton	B 1755-1985	1755-1837	5,8			Ashton-under-Lyne			3D
Rufford	A 1673-1977	1632-1727	5,8,9	1632-1812	1670-1837	Ormskirk			8E
St Helen's	A 1713-1925	1713-1892	8	1713-1837		Prescot		1734-1837	7C
St Michael-on-Wyre	A 1660-1950	1659-1880	8	1662-1875	1622-1837	Garstang		1717-1837	7G
Salesbury	A 1809-1981	1807-1812	8			Blackburn			5F
Salford								1794-1840	4C
Christchurch	B 1831-1963		5,8	1831-1838		Salford			4C
St Phillip	B 1813-1935	1826-1848	5,8	1834-1888		Salford			4C
St Stephen	B 1794-1956	1794-1865	5,8	1794-1877		Salford			4C
Sacred Trinity	B 1709-1887	1636-1864	5,8			Salford			4C
Samlesbury	A 1678-1972	1635-1845	8		1685-1837	Preston			6F
Satterthwaite	E 1766-1893	1776-1812	6,8			Ulverstone			8L

parish name	deposited original registers	I.G.I.	local census indexes	copies of registers at Soc. Gen.	Boyd's marriage index	1837-1851 Registration District	Pallot's marriage index	non-conform. records at P.R.O.	map ref.
Seathwaite	E 1684-1990	1684-1812	6,8	1684-1837	1737-1836	Ulverstone			9L
Sefton	A 1597-1899	1597-1855	4,8	1597-1783	1600-1812	West Derby			8C
Shaw	B 1653-1889	1704-1837	8	1704-1837		Oldham		1816-1837	3D
Shireshead	A 1817-1946	1742-1829	8			Garstang			7H
Skelmersdale	A 1817-1992		8,9	1782-1836		Ormskirk			8D
Smallbridge			8			Rochdale			4E
Southport								1824-1837	9E
Christchurch	A 1821-1973		8	1820-1839		Ormskirk			9E
Holy Trinity	A 1837-1896		8	1874-1875		Ormskirk			9E
Spotland			5,6,7,8			Rochdale		1752-1837	4E
Stalmine	A 1583-1950	1583-1724	6,7,8,9	1583-1724	1583-1837	Garstang			8H
Stalybridge	B 1776-1930	1782-1823	5,8	1779-1852		Ashton-Under-Lyne		1789-1837	3C
Stand	B 1827-1923		8			Prestwich			4D
Standish	A 1560-1911	1558-1861	5,8,9	1558-1812	1560-1837	Wigan			7D
Stretford	B 1599-1960	1598-1836	5,8	1598-1883		Barton			4C
Swinton	B 1791-1981	1791-1852	8	1791-1837		Worsley		1814-1837	4C
Tarleton	A 1719-1945	1722-1727	5,8,9		1822-1837	Ormskirk			8E
Tatham	A 1558-1947	1558-1872	7,8	1558-1837	1558-1837	Lancaster	1790-1812		6J
Tatham Fell	A 1745-1951	1745-1865	8	1745-1837		Lancaster			5I
Thornton-in-Lonsdale	G 1576-1993	1576-1848	4,6,7,8	1567-1812	1576-1812	Settle	1790-1812		5J
Tockholes	A 1777-1951		8			Blackburn			6E
Todmorden	I 1666-1979		8	1666-1780	1669-1811	Todmorden		1816-1836	3E
Torver	H 1599-1977	1599-1792	6,8	1599-1837	1599-1837	Ulverstone			9L
Tottington	B 1799-1861	1799-1821	5,8,9	1799-1837		Bury		1699-1837	5E
Tottington Higher End	B 1728-1856		8			Haslingden			5E
Toxteth Park (ex.par.)								1778-1855	8B
St James	C 1775-1965		4,5,8			West Derby			8B
St Michael			4,5,8			West Derby			8B
Tunstall	A 1625-1952	1625-1874	5,7,8,9	1626-1812	1625-1825	Lancaster	1790-1812		6J
Turton	B 1719-1927	1720-1812	8	1720-1812		Bolton		1763-1837	5E
Tyldesley			8			Leigh		1789-1837	5D
Ulverston								1545-1812	9K
Holy Trinity	E 1832-1975		6,8,9	1832-1837		Ulverstone	1832-1837		9K
St Mary	E 1545-1975	1545-1813	6,8,9	1545-1837	1545-1837	Ulverstone	1790-1813	1819-1837	9K
Unsworth	B 1730-1891	1730-1827	8	1730-1840		Bury		1765-1837	4D
Upholland	A 1600-1957	1600-1879	5,8,9	1600-1840	1600-1735	Wigan			7D
Urswick	E 1608-1978	1608-1812	8	1608-1837	1608-1837	Ulverstone			9J
Walmesley	B 1794-1868		5,8			Bury		1803-1837	5E
Walney	E 1744-1990		5,8,9	1744-1900		Ulverstone			10J
Walton-le-Dale	A 1653-1978	1609-1812	5,7,8	1609-1900	1609-1837	Preston	1790-1812		6F
Walton-on-the-Hill		1586-1880							8C
St Mary	C 1586-1982	1586-1746	4,8	1586-1746	1586-1650	West Derby			8C
St Mary, Edge Hill	C 1813-1961		4,8			West Derby			8C
Wardleworth									3E
St James	B 1821-1873		5,8			Rochdale			3E
St Mary	B 1769-1936		5,8			Rochdale			3E
Warrington		1591-1869		1591-1841				1771-1870	6B
Holy Trinity	F 1816-1944		8			Warrington			6B
St Elphin	F 1591-1985	1591-1796	8	1591-1826		Warrington			6B
St Paul	F 1831-1985		8			Warrington			6B
Warton	A 1568-1988	1568-1885	4,5,7,8,9	1568-1813	1569-1837	Lancaster	1790-1812		7J
Wavertree	C 1794-1971	1806-1880	4,8	1704-1840	1794-1840	West Derby			8B
West Derby (St Mary)	C 1586-1947	1688-1880	5,8	1688-1837		West Derby			8C
Westhoughton	B 1732-1905	1732-1840	8	1732-1852		Bolton		1826-1837	6D
Whalley	A 1538-1958	1538-1875	5,8	1538-1653	1538-1601	Bolton		1787-1839	5G
Whitechapel	A 1818-1903		8	1818-1903		Clitheroe			7G
Whitewell	A 1713-1994	1756-1847	8			Fylde			6H
Whittington	A 1538-1914	1538-1764	4,6,7,8	1538-1764	1538-1837	Lancaster			6J
Whittle-le-Woods	A 1830-1989	1843-1845	8	1843-1845		Chorley			6E
Whitworth	B 1747-1969		5,8			Rochdale			3E
Wigan		1580-1869		1580-1625				1777-1837	6D
All Saints	D 1580-1958	1580-1852	5,8,9		1594-1814	Wigan			6D
St George	D 1814-1968		5,8,9			Wigan			6D
Winwick	F 1563-1970	1563-1890	8	1563-1841		Warrington		1786-1837	6C
Woodland	E 1735-1956		8	1735-1837		Ulverstone			9L
Woodplumpton	A 1604-1992	1604-1784	6,7,8	1604-1784	1604-1837	Preston			7G
Woolton	C 1826-1919	1826-1874	8			Prescot		1711-1836	8B

LANCASHIRE

Original records deposited at:
A = Lancashire Record Office, Bow Lane, Preston PR1 2RE
B = Manchester Archives and Local Studies, Central Library, St Peter's Square, Manchester M2 5PD
C = Liverpool Record Office, William Brown Street, Liverpool L3 8EW
D = Wigan Record Office, Town Hall, Leigh, Lancashire WN7 2DY
E = Cumbria Record Office, 140 Duke Street, Barrow-in-Furness LA14 1XW
F = Cheshire Record Office, Duke Street, Chester CH1 1RL
G = North Yorkshire County Record Office, Malpas Road, Northallerton, N.Yorks DL7 0TB
H = Cumbria Record Office, County Offices, Kendal LA9 4RQ
I = West Yorkshire Archive Service, Calderdale District Archives, Central Library, Northgate House, Northgate, Halifax, HX1 1UN

Study adjacent parishes in counties of Cumberland, Westmorland, Yorkshire and Cheshire

Lancashire Record Office, Bow Lane, Preston, PR1 2RE
Manchester Archives and Local Studies, Central Library, St. Peter's Square, Manchester, M2 5PD
Greater Manchester County Record Office, 56 Marshall Street, New Cross, Manchester, M4 5FU
John Rylands University Library of Manchester, Oxford Road, Manchester, M13 9PP
National Museum of Labour History, 103 Princess Street, Manchester, M11 6ED
Bolton Archive Service, Central Library, Le Mans Crescent, Bolton, BL1 1SE
Bury Archive Service, Edwin Street, Bury, BL9 0AS
Oldham Archives Service, Local Studies Library, Union Street, Oldham, OL1 1DN
Rochdale Libraries, Central Library, The Esplanade, Rochdale, OL16 1AQ
Wigan Record Office, Town Hall, Leigh, Lancashire, WN7 2DY
Salford Archives Centre, Liverpool Road, Irlam, Manchester, M44 5AD
Merseyside Record Office, Cunard Building, Pier Head, Liverpool, L3 1EG
National Museums and Galleries on Merseyside, Maritime Records Centre, Albert Dock, Liverpool, L3 4AA

The following useful indexes have been compiled – see Introduction
Census Indexes 1841 – These are held, for the appropriate areas, in Furness Library, Bury Central Library, Rewtenstall Library, Burnley Library, Nelson Library, Barnoldswick Library and Salford Library. Indexes have also been compiled by the major societies listed under 1851.
Census Indexes 1851 – Lancashire FH & HS, c/o Mrs D. Haworth, 12 Blakemere Avenue, Sale Moor, Greater Manchester, M33 2PL, Manchester and Lancashire FHS, Clayton House, 59 Piccadilly, Manchester, M1 2AQ, Liverpool & SW Lancashire FHS, c/o J.D. Griffiths, 9 Manor Road, Lymm, Cheshire, WA13 0AY, Ormskirk & Dstrict FHS, c/o Ormskirk College, Hants Lane, Ormskirk, L39 1PX and the libraries mentioned above.
Census Indexes 1861 – Lancashire FH & HS, c/o Mrs D. Haworth, 12 Blakemere Avenue, Sale Moor, Greater Manchester, M33 2PL, Manchester and Lancashire FHS, Clayton House, 59 Piccadilly, Manchester, M1 2AQ and the libraries mentioned above.
Census Indexes 1871 – Lancashire FH & HS, c/o Mrs D. Haworth, 12 Blakemere Avenue, Sale Moor, Greater Manchester, M33 2PL, Manchester and Lancashire FHS, Clayton House, 59 Piccadilly, Manchester, M1 2AQ and the libraries mentioned above.
Census Indexes 1891 – Lancashire FH & HS, c/o Mrs D. Haworth, 12 Blakemere Avenue, Sale Moor, Greater Manchester, M33 2PL, Ormskirk & Dstrict FHS, c/o Ormskirk College, Hants Lane, Ormskirk, L39 1PX and the libraries mentioned above.
Marriage Index 1813-1837 – Lancashire FH & HS, c/o Mrs D. Haworth, 12 Blakemere Avenue, Sale Moor, Greater Manchester, M33 2PL
Marriage Index of North Lancashire and Westmorland 1700-1837 – S.G. Smith, 59 Friar Road, Orpington, Kent, BR5 2BW
Marriage Index of NE Lancashire and Yorkshire Borders 1700-1837 – Mrs B.H. Smith, The Shieling, Old Back Lane, Wiswell, Clitheroe, Lancashire, BB7 9BS
Marriage Index of Liverpool – Liverpool & SW Lancashire FHS, c/o J.D. Griffiths, 9 Manor Road, Lymm, Cheshire, WA13 0AY
Marriage Index of Warrington pre 1837 – Liverpool & SW Lancashire FHS, c/o D. Forrest, 83 Wash Lane, Warrington, WA4 1JD
Marriage Index of Bolton – Manchester and Lancashire FHS, Clayton House, 59 Piccadilly, Manchester, M1 2AQ
Pendle Forest People 1750-1900 – A. Wilkins, 14 Carr Road, Nelson, Lancashire, BB9 7JS
Burial Index for Manchester and Salford pre 1837 – J. Lloyd, 1 Royston Road, Manchester, M16 0EU

Lancashire's extreme length from north to south is 74 miles and its greatest breadth, at the southern end, about 45 miles. It is watered by ten principal rivers: the Mersey, Ribble, Lune, Irwell, Douglas, Wyre, Ken, Leven, Dudden and Crake. The population in 1841 was 1,667,054; in 1851, 2,031,236; in 1861, 2,429,440; in 1871, 2,818,904; in 1881, 3,454,441.

The soils include loam, clay, gravel, sand and peat. The area known as the Fylde was a rich grain land. Cattle, sheep, goats, pigs and horses were bred. In some parts dairy-farming was important. The first potatoes raised in England were grown in the county. Woollens, flannels, linens, cotton fabrics and hats and silks ranked among the manufactures. There was also calico printing, bleaching, dyeing, machine-making and iron-founding. Paper, glass and earthenware were manufactured.

The information in the Index is abbreviated, and may mislead the searcher if reference is not made to the details contained in the several publications listed in the Introduction. It is essential that users of this book check the appropriate works before making further enquiries.

LEICESTERSHIRE

parish name	deposited original registers	I.G.I.	local census indexes	copies of registers at Soc. Gen.	Boyd's marriage index	1837-1851 Registration District	Pallot's marriage index	non-conform. records at P.R.O.	map ref.
Ab Kettleby	1580-1916	1734-1872	5,8	1580-1910	1651-1725	Melton Mowbray	1790-1812		7H
Allexton	1636-1951	1604-1857	5,8	1570-1836		Billesdon			4J
Anstey	1556-1992	1813-1862	5,8	1556-1892	1556-1837	Barrow-upon-Soar		1810-1837	5G(J)
Anstey Pastures (ex.par.)			5,8			Barrow-upon-Soar			5G(K)
Appleby	1573-1973	1570-1876	5,8	1572-1906		Ashby-de-la-Zouch			5D
Arnesby	1602-1992	1566-1851	5,8	1566-1640		Lutterworth		1752-1836	3H
Asfordby	1564-1961	1587-1852	5,8	1564-1837	1564-1837	Melton Mowbray	1790-1837		6I
Ashby de la Zouch	1561-1993	1561-1872	5,8	1561-1754	1651-1725	Ashby-de-la-Zouch		1756-1837	6E
Ashby Folville	1653-1968	1579-1876	5,8	1579-1812	1651-1725	Melton Mowbray	1790-1837		5I
Ashby Magna	1586-1992	1586-1892	5,8	1576-1836		Lutterworth			3G
Ashby Parva	1585-1992	1566-1848	5,8	1589-1836	1651-1725	Lutterworth	1790-1837		3G
Aston Flamville	1558-1996	1558-1836	5,8,9	1763-1812		Hinckley			3F
Aylestone	1560-1938	1726-1871	5,8	1561-1669	1651-1837	Blaby	1790-1837		4G
Bagworth	1781-1977	1723-1861	5,8	1559-1776		Market Bosworth			5F
Bardon (ex.par.)			5,8			Loughborough			6F
Barkby	1586-1963	1742-1830	5,8	1586-1963	1651-1725	Barrow-upon-Soar	1790-1812		5H
Barkestone	1569-1996	1750-1853	5,8	1569-1837	1651-1725	Bingham	1790-1837		8J
Barlestone	1652-1996	1754-1885	5,8	1652-1943		Market Bosworth			5F
Barrow upon Soar	1563-1982	1563-1564	5,8	1563-1966	1651-1725	Barrow-upon-Soar	1790-1837		6G
Barwell	1653-1993	1563-1856	5,8,9	1563-1640		Hinckley			4F
Bassett House (ex.par.)			5,8			Blaby			4F(Q)
Beaumont Leys (ex.par.)			5,8			Barrow-upon-Soar			5G(M)
Beeby	1538-1992	1728-1875	5,8	1538-1912	1651-1725	Barrow-upon-Soar	1790-1837		5H
Belgrave	1653-1996	1565-1875	5,8	1565-1851	1651-1750	Barrow-upon-Soar	1790-1837		5G
Belton	1538-1907	1578-1875	5,8			Loughborough			6F
Belvoir (ex.par.)			5,8			Grantham			8J
Bescaby (ex.par.)			5,8			Melton Mowbray			7J
Billesdon	1599-1979	1738-1857	5,8			Billesdon			4I
Birstall	1574-1984	1574-1870	5,8	1574-1857	1651-1750	Barrow-upon-Soar	1790-1837		5G
Bitteswell	1558-1936	1728-1866	5,8	1558-1936	1651-1725	Lutterworth	1790-1837		2G
Blaby	1560-1995	1728-1858	5,8	1568-1837	1568-1837	Blaby	1790-1837		4G
Blackfordby	1653-1980	1766-1875	5,8	1561-1854		Ashby-de-la-Zouch			6D
Blaston	1676-1902	1723-1849	5,8	1676-1845		Uppingham			3J
Bottesford	1563-1995	1563-1853	5,8	1563-1812	1651-1725	Grantham	1790-1812		8J
Branston	1591-1997	1578-1885	5,8	1591-1839	1651-1725	Melton Mowbray	1790-1839		7J
Braunstone	1561-1988	1561-1872	5,8	1561-1837	1561-1837	Blaby	1790-1837		4G
Breedon on the Hill	1562-1988	1562-1859	5,8	1562-1945		Shardlow		1795-1837	7E
Bringhurst	1640-1907		5,8	1604-1812		Uppingham			3J
Brooksby	1767-1822		5,8	1767-1811		Melton Mowbray	1790-1812		6H(D)
Broughton Astley	1581-1987	1582-1836	5,8			Lutterworth			3G
Bruntingthorpe	1574-1991	1736-1858	5,8	1574-1969		Lutterworth			3H
Buckminster	1585-1881	1705-1849	5,8		1538-1837	Melton Mowbray			6K
Burbage	1562-1994	1562-1865	5,8,9		1651-1675	Hinckley			3F
Burrow on the Hill	1612-1995	1750-1858	5,8	1612-1837	1651-1725	Melton Mowbray	1790-1837		5I
Burton Lazars	1762-1987	1742-1845	5,8	1762-1778		Melton Mowbray			6J
Burton Overy	1575-1990	1571-1851	5,8			Billesdon			4H
Cadeby	1574-1976	1564-1861	5,8			Market Bosworth			4E
Carlton	1714-1988	1573-1856	5,8	1714-1812	1651-1675	Market Bosworth			5E
Carlton Curlieu	1749-1835	1570-1870	5,8	1571-1678		Billesdon			4I
Castle Donington		1564-1865	5,8	1672-1692	1651-1675	Shardlow		1786-1837	7F
Catthorpe	1573-1937	1582-1859	5,8	1573-1836	1651-1725	Lutterworth	1790-1837		1G
Charley (ex.par.)			5,8			Loughborough			6F
Church Langton	1646-1990		5,8			Market Harborough			3I
Claybrooke	1564-1968	1563-1885	5,8	1563-1836	1705-1837	Lutterworth		1805-1837	3F
Cold Newton	1653-2000		5,8	1653-1837		Billesdon	1790-1837		5I
Cold Overton	1556-1996	1577-1847	5,8		1556-1837	Oakham			5J
Coleorton	1611-1993	1815-1874	5,8	1611-1962		Ashby-de-la-Zouch			6E
Congerstone	1756-1954	1604-1866	5,8	1608-1812		Market Bosworth	1790-1812		5E(W)
Cosby		1813-1860	5,8			Blaby			3G
Cossington	1544-1995	1813-1831	5,8	1649-1837		Barrow-upon-Soar	1790-1837		6H
Coston	1561-1997	1813-1877	5,8	1561-1812	1651-1675	Melton Mowbray	1790-1812		7J
Cotesbach	1558-1844	1813-1875	5,8	1558-1812		Lutterworth			2F
Countesthorpe	1577-1973	1561-1858	5,8			Blaby			4G
Cranoe	1653-1996		5,8	1653-1837		Market Harborough			3I
Croft	1583-1971	1565-1837	5,8	1548-1837	1651-1675	Blaby			3F
Cropston			5,8	1562-1836	1801-1837	Barrow-upon-Soar			5G(G)
Croxton Kerrial	1558-1998	1558-1885	5,8	1558-1837	1651-1725	Grantham	1790-1837		7J
Dadlington	1734-1993	1571-1850	5,8			Market Bosworth			4E
Desford	1559-1996	1559-1876	5,8	1559-1837	1651-1675	Market Bosworth			4F
Diseworth	1656-1989	1813-1849	5,8	1564-1907		Shardlow		1785-1837	7F
Dishley with Thorpe Acre	1681-1990		5,8	1700-1739		Loughborough			7G
Dunton Bassett	1653-1949	1562-1876	5,8			Lutterworth			3G
Earl Shilton	1552-1990	1570-1850	5,8,9	1552-1923		Hinckley		1810-1836	4F
East Norton	1690-1840	1562-1857	5,8		1651-1675	Billesdon			4J
Eastwell	1585-1990	1771-1846	5,8	1588-1832	1651-1725	Melton Mowbray	1790-1837		7I
Eaton	1724-1989	1813-1874	5,8	1724-1837	1651-1750	Melton Mowbray	1790-1837		7J
Edmondthorpe	1560-1997	1813-1844	5,8	1560-1812		Melton Mowbray			6J
Enderby	1559-1990	1559-1849	5,8	1559-1837		Blaby			4G
Evington	1601-1990	1813-1872	5,8	1601-1950	1651-1725	Billesdon	1790-1837		4H
Fenny Drayton	1709-1999	1570-1850	5,8	1570-1850		Atherstone			4D
Fleckney	1638-1994	1575-1850	5,8			Market Harborough		1799-1836	3H
Foston	1690-1994		5,8	1690-1836		Blaby			4G
Foxton	1653-1994	1564-1842	5,8	1715-1722	1651-1675	Market Harborough			3I
Freeby	1599-1822	1604-1866	5,8	1601-1775	1651-1725	Melton Mowbray			6J
Frisby			5,8			Billesdon			4I
Frisby on the Wreake	1659-1916	1561-1877	5,8	1561-1840	1659-1725	Melton Mowbray	1790-1837		6I

parish name	deposited original registers	I.G.I.	local census indexes	copies of registers at Soc. Gen.	Boyd's marriage index	1837-1851 Registration District	Pallot's marriage index	non-conform. records at P.R.O.	map ref.
Frowlesworth	1538-1934	1565-1870	5,8	1538-1836	1651-1725	Lutterworth	1790-1837		3F
Gaddesby	1568-1995	1606-1837	5,8	1568-1812	1651-1675	Melton Mowbray	1790-1812		6H
Galby	1583-1836	1813-1867	5,8			Billesdon			4I
Garthorpe	1568-1987	1568-1844	5,8		1651-1675	Melton Mowbray			6J
Gilmorton	1610-1999	1561-1851	5,8	1561-1837	1651-1725	Lutterworth	1790-1837		3G
Gilroes (ex.par.)			5,8			Barrow-upon-Soar			5G(N)
Glenfield	1604-1974	1566-1837	5,8	1566-1837	1601-1837	Blaby	1790-1837		5G
Glen Parva			5,8	1561-1837		Blaby	1790-1837		4G
Glooston	1564-1998	1575-1871	5,8			Market Harborough			4I
Goadby	1745-1837	1572-1865	5,8	1604-1695		Billesdon			4I
Goadby Marwood	1656-1989	1604-1857	5,8	1657-1837	1656-1837	Melton Mowbray	1790-1837		7J
Gopsall (ex.par.)			5,8			Market Bosworth			5D
Great Bowden	1559-1985	1813-1867	5,8	1559-1880		Market Harborough			3I
Great Dalby	1591-1988	1564-1860	5,8	1591-1812	1651-1725	Melton Mowbray	1790-1812		6I
Great Easton	1656-1891	1572-1863	5,8	1572-1812		Uppingham			3J
Great Glen	1687-1984	1813-1856	5,8	1687-1962	1571-1837	Billesdon		1826-1837	4H
Great Stretton	1585-1954	1602-1832	5,8	1585-1837	1602-1822	Billesdon			4H(U)
Grimston	1635-1812	1633-1863	5,8	1637-1837	1651-1725	Melton Mowbray	1790-1837		6I
Groby	1840-1996	1840-1876	5,8			Market Bosworth			5G
Gumley	1594-1983	1565-1854	5,8	1566-1687	1651-1675	Market Harborough			3H
Hallaton	1563-1877	1813-1875	5,8	1563-1877		Uppingham			4J
Harby	1700-1988	1813-1851	5,8	1700-1963	1651-1725	Melton Mowbray	1790-1837		8I
Harston	1707-1995	1582-1885	5,8	1707-1837	1651-1725	Grantham	1790-1837		8J
Hathern	1563-1984	1563-1836	5,8	1563-1757		Loughborough			7F
Heather	1619-1976	1563-1842	5,8			Ashby-de-la-Zouch			5E
Higham on the Hill	1754-1947	1563-1856	5,8,9			Nuneaton			4E
Hinckley	1554-1991	1554-1848	5,8,9		1651-1669	Hinckley		1706-1837	3E
Hoby	1562-1896	1562-1875	5,8	1562-1896	1651-1725	Melton Mowbray	1790-1812		6H
Holwell		1734-1872	5,8	1580-1812		Melton Mowbray	1790-1812		7I
Horninghold	1661-1839	1571-1858	5,8	1582-1638		Uppingham			4J
Hose	1688-1974	1761-1850	5,8	1688-1957	1701-1725	Melton Mowbray	1790-1837	1807-1834	7I
Hoton	1653-1987	1633-1836	5,8	1654-1826	1653-1725	Loughborough	1790-1837		7G
Houghton on the Hill	1651-1981		5,8	1582-1836	1651-1750	Billesdon	1790-1837		4H
Hugglescote	1581-1990	1563-1857	5,8	1563-1807	1651-1680	Ashby-de-la-Zouch			5F
Humberstone	1557-1975	1557-1875	5,8	1559-1837	1651-1750	Billesdon	1790-1837		5H
Huncote			5,8			Blaby			4G
Hungerton	1614-1985	1578-1854	5,8	1614-1836	1651-1725	Billesdon	1790-1837		5I
Husbands Bosworth	1558-1894	1563-1877	5,8			Market Harborough			2H
Ibstock	1568-1976	1561-1849	5,8	1568-1931	1651-1675	Market Bosworth			5E
Ilston on the Hill	1652-1835	1582-1876	5,8	1607-1691	1651-1675	Billesdon			4I
Isley Walton (ex.par.)	1710-1981	1710-1848	5,8			Shardlow			7E
Kegworth	1556-1984	1577-1859	5,8			Shardlow		1785-1837	7F
Keyham	1563-1836	1633-1859	5,8	1563-1836	1651-1725	Billesdon	1790-1837		5H
Kibworth Beauchamp	1726-1953	1595-1843	5,8			Market Harborough		1806-1837	3H
Kilby	1570-1998	1770-1864	5,8	1570-1886		Blaby		1752-1836	3H
Kimcote & Walton	1653-1999	1565-1876	5,8	1565-1710	1651-1675	Lutterworth			2G
Kings Norton	1589-1837	1563-1836	5,8			Billesdon			4H
Kirby Bellars	1713-1836	1575-1852	5,8	1563-1836	1651-1725	Melton Mowbray	1790-1837		6I
Kirby Muxloe	1597-1987	1561-1853	5,8	1561-1856	1619-1837	Blaby	1790-1837		4F
Kirkby Mallory	1598-1992	1813-1851	5,8	1571-1953		Market Bosworth			4F
Knaptoft			5,8			Lutterworth			3H
Knighton	1653-1971		5,8	1672-1837	1651-1837	Blaby	1790-1837		4G
Knipton	1561-1997	1813-1885	5,8	1561-1973	1651-1725	Grantham	1790-1837		8J
Knossington	1558-1995	1571-1874	5,8		1558-1837	Oakham			5J
Langley Priory(ex.par.)			5,8			Shardlow			7E
Laughton	1754-1997	1813-1836	5,8	1754-1837		Market Harborough			2H
Leicester								1711-1853	4G
All Saints	1571-1982	1575-1815	5,8			Leicester			4G
St George	1827-1966	1827-1875	5,8	1827-1830		Leicester			4G
St Leonard	1682-1981	1682-1837	5,8			Leicester			4G
St Margaret	1615-1936	1604-1837	5,8	1754-1855	1651-1675	Leicester			4G
St Martin	1558-1947	1558-1783	5,8	1679-1687		Leicester			4G
St Mary	1600-1954	1600-1837	5,8	1600-1837		Leicester			4G
St Nicholas	1559-1971	1560-1875	5,8			Leicester			4G
Leicester Abbey (ex.par.)			5,8			Barrow-upon-Soar			5G(O)
Leicester Forest East (ex.par.)			5,8			Blaby			4G(S)
Leicester Forest West (ex.par.)			5,8			Blaby			4F(R)
Leicester Frith (ex.par.)			5,8			Barrow-upon-Soar			5G(L)
Leire	1559-1992	1559-1932	5,8	1559-1932	1651-1725	Lutterworth	1790-1837		3G
Little Dalby	1559-1988	1580-1850	5,8	1559-1811	1651-1725	Melton Mowbray	1790-1812		6I
Little Stretton	1592-1837	1604-1836	5,8			Billesden			4H(V)
Lockington	1557-1968	1813-1868	5,8			Shardlow			7F
Loddington	1554-1998	1565-1870	5,8		1565-1837	Billesdon			4J
Long Clawson	1558-1993	1580-1845	5,8	1558-1837	1558-1837	Melton Mowbray	1790-1837		7I
Long Whatton	1549-1980	1754-1876	5,8	1549-1852		Loughborough		1794-1819	7F
Loughborough	1538-1978	1577-1875	5,8			Loughborough		1760-1837	6G
Lowesby	1653-2000	1813-1863	5,8	1561-1837	1651-1750	Billesdon	1790-1837		5I
Lubenham	1559-1971	1559-1860	5,8		1559-1837	Market Harborough			3I
Lutterworth	1653-1986	1563-1855	5,8	1564-1640		Lutterworth		1733-1837	2G
Market Bosworth	1567-1938	1567-1803	5,8	1567-1699	1651-1675	Market Bosworth		1812-1836	4E
Market Harborough	1584-1967	1754-1876	5,8	1584-1951		Market Harborough		1753-1837	3I
Markfield	1571-1998	1563-1853	5,8	1563-1812	1563-1812	Market Bosworth			5F
Medbourne	1588-1871	1588-1866	5,8			Uppingham		1804-1830	3J
Melton Mowbray	1546-1932	1561-1885	5,8	1546-1932	1651-1725	Melton Mowbray	1790-1812	1813-1837	6I
Misterton	1558-1993	1558-1866	5,8	1558-1838	1558-1753	Lutterworth			2G
Mountsorrel	1677-1982	1563-1845	5,8	1600-1837	1701-1725	Barrow-upon-Soar	1790-1837	1791-1838	6G
Mowsley	1660-1986	1583-1852	5,8			Market Harborough			3H
Muston	1561-1995	1561-1836	5,8	1561-1812	1651-1725	Grantham	1790-1812		8J

LEICESTERSHIRE

parish name	deposited original registers	I.G.I.	local census indexes	copies of registers at Soc. Gen.	Boyd's marriage index	1837-1851 Registration District	Pallot's marriage index	non-conform. records at P.R.O.	map ref.
Nailstone	1680-1989	1563-1836	5,8			Market Bosworth			5E
Narborough	1599-1984	1566-1852	5,8			Blaby		1755-1837	4G
Nether and Over Seal			5,8	1563-1724	1801-1837	Ashby-de-la-Zouch			6D
Nether Broughton	1570-1997	1563-1835	5,8	1577-1837	1577-1837	Melton Mowbray	1790-1837		7H
Newbold Verdon	1542-1986	1561-1872	5,8			Market Bosworth			5F
New Parks (ex.par.)			5,8			Leicester			5G(P)
Newton Harcourt	1588-1951	1676-1765	5,8	1588-1940		Billesdon			4H
Newton Linford	1654-1993	1608-1864	5,8	1633-1812	1651-1812	Barrow-upon-Soar			5G
Normanton le Heath	1695-1994	1585-1836	5,8			Ashby-de-la-Zouch			6E
North Kilworth	1553-1993	1565-1875	5,8			Lutterworth			2H
Norton Juxta Twycross	1686-1992	1564-1872	5,8	1605-1673	1687-1837	Market Bosworth			5D
Nosely			5,8			Billesdon			4I
Oadby	1653-1970	1568-1837	5,8	1569-1837	1655-1837	Blaby			4H
Oaks in Charnwood	1816-1955	1816-1855	5,8			Ashby-de-la-Zouch			6F
Old Dalby	1725-1997	1632-1877	5,8	1633-1837	1725-1837	Melton Mowbray	1790-1837		7H
Orton on the Hill	1594-1994	1594-1875	5,8			Market Bosworth			5D
Osgathorpe	1683-1979	1813-1863	5,8	1683-1865		Ashby-de-la-Zouch			6F(A)
Owston and Newbold	1701-1983	1572-1870	5,8	1701-1983	1651-1725	Billesdon	1790-1837		5I
Packington	1677-1993	1574-1862	5,8	1612-1765		Ashby-de-la-Zouch			6E
Peatling Magna	1565-1992	1565-1854	5,8	1565-1836		Lutterworth			3G
Peatling Parva	1538-1998		5,8			Lutterworth			3G(Y)
Peckleton	1567-1975	1567-1875	5,8	1567-1837		Market Bosworth			4F
Pickwell	1570-1991	1583-1875	5,8	1570-1841	1651-1725	Melton Mowbray	1790-1841		5J
Plungar	1695-1995	1578-1853	5,8	1695-1837	1651-1725	Bingham	1790-1837		8I
Potters Marston			5,8			Blaby			4F(T)
Prestwold	1561-1987	1578-1836	5,8	1560-1837	1651-1725	Loughborough	1790-1837		6G
Queniborough	1562-1973	1562-1845	5,8	1562-1836	1701-1725	Barrow-upon-Soar	1790-1837		5H
Quorndon	1577-1992	1576-1837	5,8	1576-1837	1651-1750	Barrow-upon-Soar	1790-1837	1760-1837	6G
Ragdale	1668-1836		5,8	1668-1836	1668-1725	Melton Mowbray	1790-1837		6H
Ratby	1754-1991	1624-1876	5,8	1624-1812	1701-1725	Market Bosworth	1790-1812		5F
Ratcliffe Culey	1585-1994	1562-1871	5,8			Atherstone			4D
Ratcliffe on the Wreak	1698-1994	1565-1852	5,8	1578-1837	1651-1725	Barrow-upon-Soar	1790-1837		6H(C)
Ravenstone with Snibston	1705-1989		5,8			Ashby-de-la-Zouch			6E
Rearsby	1648-1976	1637-1836	5,8	1654-1837	1651-1725	Barrow-upon-Soar	1790-1837		6H
Redmile	1654-1996	1578-1850	5,8	1653-1837	1653-1725	Grantham	1790-1837		8J
Rolleston	1754-1972		5,8			Billesdon			4I
Rotherby	1561-1835	1561-1849	5,8	1561-1812	1651-1725	Melton Mowbray	1790-1812		6H(E)
Rothley	1562-1937	1563-1811	5,8	1562-1837	1651-1725	Barrow-upon-Soar	1790-1837	1791-1836	5G
Saddington	1538-1983	1564-1836	5,8	1538-1685		Market Harborough			3H
Saltby	1565-1997	1790-1845	5,8	1565-1878	1651-1675	Melton Mowbray			7J
Sapcote	1564-2000	1754-1852	5,8,9	1564-1971		Hinckley			3F
Saxby	1678-1981	1771-1851	5,8	1593-1836	1651-1837	Melton Mowbray	1790-1837		6J
Saxelby	1538-1837	1716-1859	5,8	1555-1837	1555-1837	Melton Mowbray	1790-1837		7I
Scalford	1558-1990	1578-1845	5,8	1559-1811	1651-1725	Melton Mowbray	1790-1812		7I
Scraptoft	1539-1987	1572-1859	5,8	1539-1812	1651-1725	Billesdon	1790-1812		5H
Seagrave	1682-1995	1769-1875	5,8	1682-1836	1651-1725	Barrow-upon-Soar	1790-1837		6H
Sewstern			5,8		1801-1837	Melton Mowbray			6K
Shackerstone	1630-1988	1558-1685	5,8	1558-1667	1651-1675	Market Bosworth			5E
Shangton	1580-1994		5,8	1580-1829		Market Harborough			4I
Sharnford	1595-2000	1565-1837	5,8,9	1598-1837	1651-1725	Hinckley	1790-1837		3F
Shawell	1760-1836	1561-1849	5,8			Lutterworth			2G
Shearsby	1658-1992	1658-1851	5,8			Lutterworth			3H
Sheepy Magna	1607-1994	1561-1872	5,8	1561-1837		Atherstone		1832-1836	4D
Shenton	1625-1838	1584-1860	5,8			Market Bosworth			4E
Shepshed	1538-1990	1577-1875	5,8	1538-1896	1651-1675	Loughborough		1754-1837	6F
Shoby			5,8	1555-1837		Melton Mowbray			6H
Sibson	1561-1994	1561-1860	5,8	1561-1812	1651-1725	Market Bosworth	1790-1812		4E
Sileby	1568-1986	1563-1835	5,8	1563-1837	1651-1725	Barrow-upon-Soar	1790-1937	1791-1836	6H
Skeffington	1590-1975	1566-1864	5,8			Billesdon			4I
Slawston	1559-1835	1563-1875	5,8			Uppingham			3I
Snarestone	1665-1992	1574-1855	5,8	1561-1891		Ashby-de-la-Zouch			5D
Somerby	1601-1996	1601-1853	5,8	1590-1812	1651-1725	Melton Mowbray	1790-1812		5J
South Croxton	1662-1903	1562-1867	5,8	1561-1837	1662-1725	Barrow-upon-Soar	1790-1837		5H
South Kilworth	1559-1995	1558-1871	5,8	1559-1830	1651-1725	Lutterworth			2H
Sproxton	1640-1997	1580-1845	5,8	1581-1639	1651-1675	Melton Mowbray			7J
Stanton under Bardon			5,8	1559-1776		Market Bosworth			5F
Stapleford	1648-1990	1577-1851	5,8	1577-1837	1655-1837	Melton Mowbray	1790-1837		6J
Stapleton			5,8			Market Bosworth			4F
Stathern	1567-1987	1604-1847	5,8	1567-1837	1651-1725	Melton Mowbray	1790-1837		8I
Stockerston	1574-1837		5,8	1574-1837		Uppingham			4J
Stoke Golding	1656-1998	1561-1850	5,8,9	1561-1850	1651-1675	Nuneaton			4E
Stonesby	1625-1952	1578-1855	5,8			Melton Mowbray			7J
Stoney Stanton	1558-1987	1558-1860	5,8,9			Hinckley			3F
Stonton Wyville	1539-1992		5,8			Market Harborough			3I
Stoughton	1537-1953	1564-1875	5,8	1537-1835	1651-1750	Billesdon	1790-1837		4H
Sutton Cheney	1674-1997	1573-1875	5,8			Market Bosworth			4E
Swepstone	1561-1976	1782-1857	5,8	1561-1891		Ashby-de-la-Zouch		1803-1835	5D
Swinford	1559-1923		5,8	1559-1925		Lutterworth			2G
Swithland	1700-1926	1616-1861	5,8	1616-1837	1651-1750	Barrow-upon-Soar	1790-1837		6G
Sysonby			5,8			Melton Mowbray			6I
Syston	1644-1991	1809-1867	5,8	1562-1952	1663-1725	Barrow-upon-Soar	1790-1837	1823-1837	5H
Theddingworth	1635-1837	1604-1872	5,8			Market Harborough			2H
Thornton	1559-1995	1559-1861	5,8	1559-1776	1651-1725	Market Bosworth			5F
Thorpe Arnold	1558-1987	1578-1863	5,8	1558-1840	1558-1837	Melton Mowbray	1790-1840		6I
Thorpe Langton	1606-1991		5,8	1606-1837		Market Harborough			3I
Thorpe Satchville			5,8	1532-1812		Melton Mowbray			5I
Thrussington	1660-1942	1565-1865	5,8	1565-1812	1660-1725	Barrow-upon-Soar	1790-1812		6H
Thurcaston	1561-1981	1799-1866	5,8	1562-1836	1651-1750	Barrow-upon-Soar	1790-1837		5G(F)

parish name	deposited original registers	I.G.I.	local census indexes	copies of registers at Soc. Gen.	Boyd's marriage index	1837-1851 Registration District	Pallot's marriage index	non-conform. records at P.R.O.	map ref.
Thurlaston	1587-1976	1565-1855	5,8	1588-1837		Blaby		1815-1837	4F
Thurmaston (South)	1719-1974	1561-1832	5,8	1561-1837	1651-1750	Barrow-upon-Soar	1790-1937		5H(H)
Thurnby	1538-1966	1735-1879	5,8	1564-1836	1651-1750	Billesdon	1790-1837		4H
Tilton on the Hill	1610-1949	1562-1861	5,8	1561-1836	1651-1750	Billesdon	1790-1837		5I
Tugby	1568-1989		5,8	1568-1895		Billesdon			4I
Tur Langton	1693-1967	1571-1875	5,8	1693-1915		Market Harborough			3I
Twycross	1585-1994	1585-1867	5,8	1585-1872		Market Bosworth			5E
Twyford	1558-1958	1562-1853	5,8	1562-1812	1651-1725	Melton Mowbray	1790-1812		5I
Ulverscroft (ex.par.)			5,8			Barrow-upon-Soar			5F
Waltham on the Wolds	1564-1971	1577-1855	5,8		1651-1675	Melton Mowbray			7J
Walton on the Wolds	1566-1920	1700-1875	5,8	1568-1836	1651-1750	Barrow-upon-Soar	1790-1837		6G
Wanlip	1561-1995	1561-1857	5,8	1561-1838	1651-1838	Barrow-upon-Soar	1790-1837		5G
Wartnaby	1633-1961	1813-1863	5,8	1633-1838	1651-1725	Melton Mowbray	1790-1838		7I
Welby			5,8			Melton Mowbray			6I
Welham		1813-1858	5,8	1575-1697	1651-1675	Market Harborough			3I
West Langton	1646-1990		5,8			Market Harborough			3I
Westrill (ex.par.)			5,8			Rugby			2G
Whetstone	1538-1993	1717-1877	5,8	1571-1837		Blaby			4G
Whitwick	1601-1977	1815-1854	5,8	1608-1735	1651-1675	Ashby-de-la-Zouch		1822-1837	6F
Wigston Magna	1567-1909		5,8	1567-1909	1567-1837	Blaby	1790-1837	1772-1837	4H
Wigston Parva			5,8			Lutterworth			3F
Willoughby Waterless	1559-1992	1559-1875	5,8	1559-1837		Lutterworth			3G(X)
Wistow	1588-1940		5,8	1588-1940		Billesdon			3H
Withcote	1679-1977		5,8	1679-1836	1701-1725	Billesdon	1790-1837		5J
Witherley	1564-1998	1564-1769	5,8			Atherstone			4D
Woodhouse	1710-1971		5,8	1625-1837	1651-1750	Barrow-upon-Soar	1790-1837	1799-1837	6F
Worthington	1759-1990		5,8			Ashby-de-la-Zouch			6E
Wycombe & Chadwell	1700-1987	1607-1835	5,8	1633-1836	1701-1725	Melton Mowbray	1790-1837		7J(B)
Wyfordby with Brentingby	1557-1836		5,8	1557-1837	1558-1837	Melton Mowbray	1790-1837		6J
Wymeswold	1560-1970		5,8	1560-1970	1651-1725	Loughborough			7H
Wymondham	1538-1984		5,8	1538-1962	1538-1837	Melton Mowbray			6J

Original registers deposited at:
Leicestershire Record Office and Local Studies Centre, Long Street, Wigston Magna, Leicester LE18 2AH

Study adjacent parishes in counties of Derbyshire, Nottinghamshire, Lincolnshire, Rutland, Northamptonshire, Warwickshire and Staffordshire

Leicestershire Record Office and Local Studies Centre, Long Street, Wigston Magna, Leicester, LE18 2AH

The following useful indexes have been compiled – see Introduction
Census Index 1851 Leicester City – Leicestershire & Rutland FHS, Mr P. Cousins, 13 Langton Road, Wigston, Leicester, LE18 2HT
Census Index 1851 County – Leicestershire & Rutland FHS, Mr R. Hinton, 29 Mortimer Way, Leicester, LE3 1GR
Leicestershire Marriage Index 1754-1837 – R.E. Makins, 45 Westcotes Drive, Leicester, LE3 0QT
Leicestershire Marriage Index 1538-1837 – Mrs H. Schultka, 18 Edgeley Road, Countesthorpe, Leicestershire, LE8
Archdeaconry of Leicester Marriage Bonds 1570-1891 – Leicestershire Record Office and Local Studies Centre, Long Street, Wigston Magna, Leicester LE18 2AH
Leicester Borough Burials 1813-1885 – P Cragg, 17 Westdown Drive, Thurmaston, Leicester, LE4 8HU

Leicestershire is very irregular in shape and extends in length from north to south about 30 miles and from east to west about 25 miles. It is watered by four principal rivers: the Soar, Wreake, Trent and Anker. The population in 1841 was 215,867; in 1851, 230,318; in 1861, 237,412; in 1871, 269,311; in 1881, 321,258.

The soils for the most part are clay and marl. Produce included corn, grass, beans and cheese (particularly Stilton). Sheep were bred as well as cattle and large dray horses and in the north-west of the county were valuable coalmines. The rivers supplied many sorts of fish, especially the best kind of salmon. The principal manufacture was hosiery and many articles made from wool.

The information in the Index is abbreviated, and may mislead the searcher if reference is not made to the details contained in the several publications listed in the Introduction. It is essential that users of this book check the appropriate works before making further enquiries.

LINCOLNSHIRE

parish name	deposited original registers	I.G.I.	local census indexes	copies of registers at Soc. Gen.	Boyd's marriage index	1837-1851 Registration District	Pallot's marriage index	non-conform. records at P.R.O.	map ref.
Aby	1643-1729	1562-1728	4,5,6,7,8,9	1643-1725		Louth			4J(A)
Addlethorpe	1565-1981	1563-1839	4,5,6,7,8,9	1561-1969	1651-1750	Spilsby	1790-1837		3K(A)
Aisthorpe	1593-1992	1593-1838	4,5,6,7,8,9	1593-1966		Lincoln			5D(A)
Alford	1538-1987	1538-1836	4,5,6,7,8,9	1538-1972	1651-1750	Spilsby	1790-1837	1814-1837	4J(A)
Algarkirk	1678-1955	1561-1800	4,5,6,7,8,9	1700-1812		Boston			5I(B)
Alkborough	1538-1985	1599-1853	4,5,6,7,8,9	1538-1985		Glanford Brigg			10D(A)
Althorpe	1672-1975	1599-1836	4,5,6,7,8,9	1672-1975		Thorne			9C(A)
Alvingham	1583-1978	1561-1844	4,5,6,7,8,9	1583-1978	1584-1837	Louth			6I(A)
Ancaster	1722-1977	1562-1885	4,5,6,7,8,9	1661-1753		Grantham			6E(B)
Anderby	1563-1993	1562-1836	4,5,6,7,8,9	1561-1916	1651-1750	Spilsby	1790-1837		4K(A)
Anwick	1573-1906	1561-1838	4,5,6,7,8,9			Sleaford			7G(B)
Apley	1561-1817	1561-1834	4,5,6,7,8,9	1561-1817		Lincoln			4F(A)
Appleby	1570-1984	1599-1837	4,5,6,7,8,9	1626-1984		Glanford Brigg			9E(A)
Asgarby (Sleaford)	1676-1837	1561-1805	4,5,6,7,8,9			Sleaford			6G(B)
Asgarby (Spilsby)	1595-1963	1602-1845	4,5,6,7,8,9	1595-1834		Horncastle			3I(A)
Ashby by Partney	1770-1993	1562-1875	4,5,6,7,8,9	1754-1837		Spilsby			3J(A)
Ashby cum Fenby	1723-1989	1561-1824	4,5,6,7,8,9	1723-1989		Caistor			7H(A)
Ashby de la Launde	1695-1943	1561-1831	4,5,6,7,8,9			Sleaford			8F(B)
Ashby Puerorum	1653-1998	1562-1837	4,5,6,7,8,9	1653-1838		Horncastle			4I(A)
Aslackby	1558-1929	1558-1839	4,5,6,7,8,9	1558-1929		Bourne			5F(B)
Asterby	1686-1976	1561-1843	4,5,6,7,8,9	1668-1909		Horncastle			5H(A)
Aswarby	1755-1962	1561-1826	4,5,6,7,8,9	1753-1962		Sleaford			6F(B)
Aswardby	1754-1836	1561-1831	4,5,6,7,8,9			Spilsby			3I(A)
Aubourn	1749-2000	1562-1840	4,5,6,7,8,9	1562-1978	1651-1837	Lincoln	1790-1837		8D(B)
Aunsby	1681-1971	1561-1835	4,5,6,7,8,9			Sleaford			6F(B)
Authorpe	1561-1993	1561-1834	4,5,6,7,8,9	1561-1833		Louth			5J(A)
Aylesby	1561-2000	1561-1823	4,5,6,7,8,9	1813-1835		Caistor			8H(A)
Bag Enderby	1562-1997	1561-1811	4,5,6,7,8,9	1562-1837		Horncastle			4I(A)
Bardney	1653-1976	1561-1828	4,5,6,7,8,9	1653-1976		Lincoln			4F(A)
Barholm	1726-2001	1562-1835	4,5,6,7,8,9	1726-1836		Stamford			2F(B)
Barkston	1561-1944	1562-1837	4,5,6,7,8,9	1700-1753	1561-1837	Newark			6D(B)
Barlings	1626-1938	1599-1801	4,5,6,7,8,9	1626-1938		Lincoln			4F(A)
Barnetby le Wold	1753-1974	1561-1838	4,5,6,7,8,9	1753-1974		Glanford Brigg			8F(A)
Barnoldby le Beck	1571-1999	1561-1833	4,5,6,7,8,9	1571-1837		Caistor			8H(A)
Barrow on Humber	1560-1943	1561-1849	4,5,6,7,8,9	1560-1943		Glanford Brigg		1808-1834	10F(A)
Barrowby	1538-1983	1562-1842	4,5,6,7,8,9	1538-1837	1538-1937	Grantham	1790-1837		6D(B)
Barton on Humber								1789-1837	10F(A)
St Mary	1570-1980	1561-1866	4,5,6,7,8,9	1570-1980		Glanford Brigg			10F(A)
St Peter	1566-1968	1561-1875	4,5,6,7,8,9	1566-1968		Glanford Brigg			10F(A)
Bassingham	1572-1979	1562-1836	4,5,6,7,8,9	1572-1968	1651-1812	Newark	1790-1812		8D(B)
Bassingthorpe	1541-1991	1561-1836	4,5,6,7,8,9	1541-1837		Grantham			4E(B)
Baston	1558-1966	1562-1833	4,5,6,7,8,9	1558-1937		Bourne			3G(B)
Baumber	1691-1977	1561-1835	4,5,6,7,8,9	1691-1977		Horncastle			4G(A)
Beckingham	1558-1932	1561-1834	4,5,6,7,8,9	1700-1753		Newark			7D(B)
Beelsby	1559-1985	1559-1856	4,5,6,7,8,9	1559-1985		Caistor			7H(A)
Beesby	1743-1998	1562-1836	4,5,6,7,8,9	1565-1837	1651-1750	Louth	1790-1837		4K(A)
Belchford	1698-1985	1561-1834	4,5,6,7,8,9	1698-1985		Horncastle			4H(A)
Belleau (nr. Aby)	1697-1956	1562-1833	4,5,6,7,8,9	1697-1932		Louth			4J(A)
Belton (Axholme)	1542-1994	1562-1855	4,5,6,7,8,9	1542-1884		Thorne			6D(B)
Belton (Grantham)	1538-1836	1599-1830	4,5,6,7,8,9			Grantham			9B(A)
Benington	1539-1970	1561-1853	4,5,6,7,8,9	1559-1970		Boston			6J(B)
Benniworth	1691-1977	1561-1843	4,5,6,7,8,9	1691-1865		Horncastle			5G(A)
Bicker	1561-1979	1561-1837	4,5,6,7,8,9	1561-1979		Boston			5H(B)
Bigby	1697-1997	1561-1836	4,5,6,7,8,9	1697-1953		Caistor		1815-1837	8F(A)
Billingborough	1561-1963	1561-1827	4,5,6,7,8,9	1561-1963		Bourne			5G(B)
Billinghay	1565-1962	1562-1830	4,5,6,7,8,9			Sleaford			8G(B)
Bilsby	1669-1981	1561-1832	4,5,6,7,8,9	1561-1981	1651-1750	Spilsby	1790-1837		4K(A)
Binbrook									6H(A)
St Gabriel	1688-1847	1561-1842	4,5,6,7,8,9	1749-1847		Louth			6H(A)
St Mary	1694-1911	1561-1842	4,5,6,7,8,9	1694-1911		Louth			6H(A)
Biscathorpe	1688-1837	1561-1835	4,5,6,7,8,9	1688-1837		Louth			5H(A)
Bishop Norton	1587-1964	1578-1831	4,5,6,7,8,9			Caistor			6E(A)
Bitchfield	1675-1992	1561-1836	4,5,6,7,8,9	1674-1838		Grantham			4E(B)
Blankney	1558-1978	1562-1854	4,5,6,7,8,9			Sleaford			8F(B)
Bloxholm	1708-1993	1561-1837	4,5,6,7,8,9			Sleaford			7F(B)
Blyborough	1785-1996	1599-1830	4,5,6,7,8,9	1754-1867		Gainsborough			7D(A)
Blyton	1571-1985	1571-1837	4,5,6,7,8,9	1571-1933		Gainsborough			7C(A)
Bonby	1649-1989	1561-1837	4,5,6,7,8,9	1649-1989		Glanford Brigg			9E(A)
Boothby Graffoe	1720-2000	1562-1851	4,5,6,7,8,9	1562-1977	1651-1750	Lincoln	1790-1837		8E(B)
Boothby Pagnell	1559-1991	1562-1818	4,5,6,7,8,9	1559-1953		Grantham			5E(B)
Boston									6I(B)
St Aidan	1822-1850		4,5,6,7,8,9	1822-1850		Boston		1785-1858	6I(B)
St Botolph	1564-1983	1557-1834	4,5,6,7,8,9	1557-1983		Boston			6I(B)
St James	1893-1967		4,5,6,7,8,9	1893-1967		Boston			6I(B)
Bottesford	1603-1965	1599-1838	4,5,6,7,8,9	1599-1928		Glanford Brigg			8D(A)
Boultham	1561-1933	1561-1885	4,5,6,7,8,9	1561-1837	1651-1750	Lincoln	1790-1837		9E(B)
Bourne	1562-1938	1562-1833	4,5,6,7,8,9	1562-1938		Bourne		1814-1837	3F(B)
Braceborough	1593-1912	1562-1829	4,5,6,7,8,9	1593-1912		Stamford	1790-1837		3F(B)
Bracebridge	1663-1996	1562-1838	4,5,6,7,8,9	1562-1910	1651-1750	Lincoln			9E(B)
Braceby	1759-1837	1562-1830	4,5,6,7,8,9	1700-1837		Grantham			5E(B)
Bradley	1813-1998	1561-1825	4,5,6,7,8,9	1813-1987		Caistor			8H(A)
Branston	1625-1943	1562-1836	4,5,6,7,8,9	1625-1784		Lincoln			9F(B)
Brant Broughton	1710-1981	1562-1849	4,5,6,7,8,9	1700-1753	1561-1837	Newark			8D(B)
Bratoft	1685-1991	1695-1838	4,5,6,7,8,9	1685-1839		Spilsby			2K(A)
Brattleby	1686-1988	1599-1855	4,5,6,7,8,9	1685-1966		Lincoln			5D(A)
Brauncewell	1626-1973	1561-1838	4,5,6,7,8,9	1562-1855		Sleaford			7F(B)
Brigsley	1722-1971	1561-1837	4,5,6,7,8,9	1722-1961		Caistor			7H(A)
Brinkhill	1561-1998	1561-1836	4,5,6,7,8,9	1561-1944		Spilsby			4I(A)

parish name	deposited original registers	I.G.I.	local census indexes	copies of registers at Soc. Gen.	Boyd's marriage index	1837-1851 Registration District	Pallot's marriage index	non-conform. records at P.R.O.	map ref.
Brocklesby	1538-1998	1538-1859	4,5,6,7,8,9	1538-1837		Caistor	1790-1837		9G(A)
Brothertoft	1682-1990	1612-1837	4,5,6,7,8,9	1700-1753		Boston			7H(B)
Broughton (Brigg)	1538-1857	1538-1837	4,5,6,7,8,9	1538-1857		Glanford Brigg			8E(A)
Brox-Holme	1642-1989	1599-1866	4,5,6,7,8,9	1642-1987		Lincoln			5D(A)
Bucknall	1708-1992	1561-1835	4,5,6,7,8,9	1708-1956		Horncastle			3G(A)
Burgh on Bain	1578-2001	1561-1834	4,5,6,7,8,9	1578-1835		Louth			6H(A)
Burgh le Marsh	1538-1973	1562-1837	4,5,6,7,8,9	1538-1864		Spilsby			3K(A)
Burton Coggles	1565-1992	1561-1834	4,5,6,7,8,9	1754-1929		Grantham			4E(B)
Burton (Lincoln)	1558-1992	1599-1842	4,5,6,7,8,9	1558-1839		Lincoln			4D(A)
Burton Pedwardine	1754-1978	1561-1855	4,5,6,7,8,9	1561-1970		Sleaford			6G(B)
Burton upon Stather	1567-1929	1599-1855	4,5,6,7,8,9	1567-1929		Glanford Brigg			10D(A)
Burwell	1586-1976	1561-1826	4,5,6,7,8,9	1586-1976		Louth			5I(A)
Buslingthorpe	1760-1981	1599-1875	4,5,6,7,8,9	1754-1981		Caistor			6F(A)
Butterwick (nr. Boston)	1697-1876	1561-1838	4,5,6,7,8,9	1697-1876		Boston			6J(B)
Cabourne	1559-1981	1561-1842	4,5,6,7,8,9			Caistor			8G(A)
Cadney	1563-1951	1563-1819	4,5,6,7,8,9	1563-1951		Glanford Brigg			8E(A)
Caenby	1712-1954	1599-1827	4,5,6,7,8,9	1712-1954		Lincoln			6E(A)
Caistor (inc. Clixby)	1583-1959	1561-1787	4,5,6,7,8,9	1632-1923		Caistor			8F(A)
Calceby	1621-1723	1562-1746	4,5,6,7,8,9	1621-1723		Spilsby			4J(A)
Calcethorpe		1569-1642	4,5,6,7,8,9			Louth			6H(A)
Cammeringham	1662-1997	1599-1833	4,5,6,7,8,9	1662-1978		Lincoln			5D(A)
Candlesby	1753-1947	1562-1838	4,5,6,7,8,9	1753-1947		Spilsby			3J(A)
Canwick	1681-1994	1561-1885	4,5,6,7,8,9	1681-1837		Lincoln			9E(A)
Careby	1562-1837	1561-1844	4,5,6,7,8,9	1562-1837		Bourne			3E(B)
Carlby	1668-1989	1562-1831	4,5,6,7,8,9	1668-1836		Bourne			3F(B)
Carlton le Moorland	1561-1977	1561-1836	4,5,6,7,8,9	1561-1977	1651-1812	Newark	1790-1813	1793-1837	8D(B)
Carlton Scroop	1557-1913	1562-1833	4,5,6,7,8,9	1700-1753		Grantham			6D(B)
Carrington	1837-1960	1818-1859	4,5,6,7,8,9			Boston			2H(A)
Castle Bytham	1567-1909	1561-1838	4,5,6,7,8,9	1567-1909	1567-1751	Bourne			3E(B)
Castle Carlton	1571-1913	1565-1820	4,5,6,7,8,9	1571-1913		Louth			5J(A)
Cawkwell	1683-1900	1561-1839	4,5,6,7,8,9	1683-1900		Horncastle			5H(A)
Caythorpe	1663-1984	1562-1846	4,5,6,7,8,9	1700-1753		Newark			7E(B)
Chapel Hill	1816-1982		4,5,6,7,8,9			Boston			7H(B)
Chapel St Leonards	1665-1999	1568-1836	4,5,6,7,8,9	1665-1978	1666-1675	Spilsby			3L(A)
Cherry Willingham	1662-1990	1599-1837	4,5,6,7,8,9	1662-1985		Lincoln			4E(A)
Claxby (Alford)	1699-1978	1566-1885	4,5,6,7,8,9	1561-1978		Spilsby	1790-1837		7F(A)
Claxby (Normanby)	1566-1998	1561-1811	4,5,6,7,8,9	1566-1962	1651-1750	Caistor	1790-1837		3J(A)
Claxby Pluckacre	1561-1873	1561-1834	4,5,6,7,8,9	1561-1873		Horncastle			3H(A)
Claypole	1538-1895	1562-1844	4,5,6,7,8,9	1538-1837	1651-1837	Newark	1790-1837		7C(B)
Claythorpe			4,5,6,7,8,9	1700-1753		Louth			5J(A)
Clee	1900-1973	1561-1876	4,5,6,7,8,9	1562-1876		Caistor			8I(A)
Coates (Stow)	1664-1997	1601-1812	4,5,6,7,8,9	1664-1956		Gainsborough			6D(A)
Cold Hanworth	1725-1974	1599-1832	4,5,6,7,8,9	1725-1974		Lincoln			5E(A)
Coleby	1561-1994	1561-1880	4,5,6,7,8,9	1561-1966		Lincoln	1790-1812		8E(B)
Colsterworth	1571-1930	1561-1839	4,5,6,7,8,9	1571-1930	1573-1837	Grantham			4D(B)
Coningsby	1561-1963	1561-1837	4,5,6,7,8,9	1561-1963		Horncastle			2G(A)
Conisholme	1559-1998	1559-1836	4,5,6,7,8,9	1559-1951		Louth			6J(A)
Corby	1564-1896	1561-1836	4,5,6,7,8,9	1564-1896		Bourne			4E(B)
Corringham	1647-1981	1602-1842	4,5,6,7,8,9	1647-1859		Gainsborough			6C(A)
Covenham									6I(A)
St Bartholomew	1566-1992	1561-1836	4,5,6,7,8,9	1566-1974		Louth			6I(A)
St Mary	1596-1992	1561-1836	4,5,6,7,8,9	1596-1921		Louth			6I(A)
Cowbit	1595-1947	1561-1846	4,5,6,7,8,9	1561-1932	1651-1837	Spalding	1790-1850		3H(B)
Cranwell	1560-1985	1561-1834	4,5,6,7,8,9	1560-1837		Sleaford			7E(B)
Creeton	1692-1833	1561-1843	4,5,6,7,8,9	1692-1833		Bourne			4E(B)
Croft	1548-1981	1562-1857	4,5,6,7,8,9	1548-1981		Spilsby			2K(A)
Crowland	1639-1973	1561-1839	4,5,6,7,8,9	1629-1973		Peterborough			2H(B)
Crowle	1561-1973	1598-1841	4,5,6,7,8,9	1561-1973		Thorne			9B(A)
Croxby	1762-1994	1561-1856	4,5,6,7,8,9	1775-1969		Caistor			7G(A)
Croxton	1562-1812	1561-1833	4,5,6,7,8,9	1562-1812		Glanford Brigg			9F(A)
Culverthorpe			4,5,6,7,8,9			Sleaford			6E(B)
Cumberworth	1557-1989	1561-1836	4,5,6,7,8,9	1561-1989	1651-1750	Spilsby	1790-1837		4K(A)
Cuxwold	1683-1997	1561-1834	4,5,6,7,8,9	1683-1978		Caistor			7G(A)
Dalby	1721-1832	1589-1848	4,5,6,7,8,9	1721-1832		Spilsby			3J(A)
Dalderby	1690-1742	1561-1734	4,5,6,7,8,9	1690-1742		Horncastle			3H(A)
Deeping St James	1674-1993	1562-1860	4,5,6,7,8,9	1674-1919		Bourne			2G(B)
Deeping (St Nicholas)	1846-1981		4,5,6,7,8,9	1846-1981		Bourne			3G(B)
Dembleby	1763-1991	1562-1850	4,5,6,7,8,9	1813-1991		Sleaford			6F(B)
Denton	1538-1955	1562-1833	4,5,6,7,8,9	1558-1837	1651-1750	Grantham			5C(B)
Digby	1679-1959	1561-1837	4,5,6,7,8,9			Sleaford			8F(B)
Doddington	1643-1914	1562-1836	4,5,6,7,8,9		1651-1837	Lincoln	1790-1837		9D(B)
Donington (Pigot)	1690-1992	1561-1848	4,5,6,7,8,9	1562-1978		Spalding			5H(B)
Donington on Bain	1655-1961	1561-1842	4,5,6,7,8,9	1655-1887		Louth			5H(A)
Dorrington	1653-1993	1561-1835	4,5,6,7,8,9			Sleaford			7F(B)
Dowsby	1731-1994	1561-1838	4,5,6,7,8,9	1731-1930		Bourne			4G(B)
Driby	1622-1965	1562-1826	4,5,6,7,8,9	1622-1965		Spilsby			4J(A)
Dry Doddington (see Westborough)			4,5,6,7,8,9			Newark			7C(B)
Dunholme	1581-1881	1602-1835	4,5,6,7,8,9	1581-1881		Lincoln			5E(A)
Dunsby	1538-1837	1538-1835	4,5,6,7,8,9	1538-1837		Bourne			4G(B)
Dunston	1564-1977	1562-1855	4,5,6,7,8,9	1564-1977		Lincoln			8F(B)
Eagle	1588-1955	1561-1840	4,5,6,7,8,9	1588-1955	1651-1837	Lincoln	1790-1837		9D(B)
East Allington	1559-1940	1591-1836	4,5,6,7,8,9	1559-1812	1651-1812	Newark	1790-1812		6C(B)
East Barkwith	1695-1983	1561-1830	4,5,6,7,8,9	1695-1983		Horncastle			5G(A)
East Fen			4,5,6,7,8,9						2I(A)
East Firsby	1813-1840		4,5,6,7,8,9	1813-1840		Lincoln			6E(A)
East Halton	1574-1890	1561-1845	4,5,6,7,8,9	1574-1892		Glanford Brigg			10G(A)
East Keal	1707-1941	1562-1839	4,5,6,7,8,9	1707-1941		Spilsby			3I(A)
East Kirkby	1583-1865	1562-1835	4,5,6,7,8,9	1583-1865		Spilsby			3I(A)

LINCOLNSHIRE

parish name	deposited original registers	I.G.I.	local census indexes	copies of registers at Soc. Gen.	Boyd's marriage index	1837-1851 Registration District	Pallot's marriage index	non-conform. records at P.R.O.	map ref.
East Torrington	1594-1991	1561-1835	4,5,6,7,8,9	1593-1955		Caistor			5G(A)
Eastville	1840-1890		4,5,6,7,8,9	1840-1890		Spilsby			2J(A)
Edenham	1654-1964	1561-1840	4,5,6,7,8,9	1654-1964		Bourne			4F(B)
Edlington	1561-1837	1561-1841	4,5,6,7,8,9	1561-1837		Horncastle			4H(A)
Elsham	1566-1989	1561-1812	4,5,6,7,8,9	1566-1989		Glanford Brigg			9E(A)
Epworth	1538-1945	1538-1829	4,5,6,7,8,9	1538-1945		Thorne		1812-1835	8B(A)
Evedon	1561-1968	1562-1833	4,5,6,7,8,9	1560-1861	1560-1861	Sleaford			7F(B)
Ewerby	1755-1979	1561-1818	4,5,6,7,8,9	1661-1838		Sleaford			7G(B)
Faldingworth	1559-1993	1599-1832	4,5,6,7,8,9	1560-1978		Lincoln			6F(A)
Farforth	1784-1995	1561-1835	4,5,6,7,8,9	1784-1837		Louth			5I(A)
Farlesthorpe	1608-1998	1561-1836	4,5,6,7,8,9	1562-1837	1651-1750	Spilsby	1790-1837		4K(A)
Fenton	1538-1836	1536-1833	4,5,6,7,8,9	1700-1753		Newark			7D(B)
Fillingham	1661-1996	1599-1875	4,5,6,7,8,9	1661-1948		Gainsborough			6D(A)
Firsby (Spilsby)	1717-1837	1562-1837	4,5,6,7,8,9	1717-1812		Spilsby			2J(A)
Fishtoft	1696-1963	1561-1835	4,5,6,7,8,9	1696-1963		Boston			6J(B)
Fiskerton	1539-1992	1539-1874	4,5,6,7,8,9	1529-1906		Lincoln			4F(A)
Fleet	1652-1928	1561-1846	4,5,6,7,8,9	1561-1928	1651-1812	Holbeach	1790-1812	1709-1837	4J(B)
Flixborough	1660-1947	1599-1855	4,5,6,7,8,9	1660-1947		Glanford Brigg			9D(A)
Folkingham	1583-1989	1561-1827	4,5,6,7,8,9	1562-1812		Bourne			5F(B)
Fosdyke	1559-1978	1562-1885	4,5,6,7,8,9	1952-1992		Boston			5I(B)
Foston	1776-1981	1626-1839	4,5,6,7,8,9	1646-1837	1651-1837	Newark	1790-1837		6C(B)
Fotherby	1568-1992	1561-1812	4,5,6,7,8,9	1568-1973		Louth			6I(A)
Frampton	1556-1996	1558-1875	4,5,6,7,8,9	1700-1946		Boston			6I(B)
Friesthorpe	1620-1974	1603-1831	4,5,6,7,8,9	1620-1971		Lincoln			5F(A)
Frieston	1653-1891	1561-1838	4,5,6,7,8,9	1653-1895		Boston			6J(B)
Friskney	1559-1936	1562-1857	4,5,6,7,8,9	1559-1936		Spilsby			2J(A)
Frithville	1822-1886	1823-1859	4,5,6,7,8,9	1822-1886		Boston			1H(A)
Frodingham	1636-1812	1599-1852	4,5,6,7,8,9	1636-1836		Glanford Brigg			9D(A)
Fulbeck	1562-1954	1562-1840	4,5,6,7,8,9	1700-1753		Newark			7D(B)
Fulletby	1750-1947	1561-1846	4,5,6,7,8,9	1750-1947		Horncastle			4H(A)
Fulstow	1586-1992	1561-1846	4,5,6,7,8,9	1586-1890		Louth			7I(A)
Gainsborough	1564-1948	1564-1835	4,5,6,7,8,9	1564-1640		Gainsborough		1707-1837	6C(A)
Gate Burton	1735-1997	1599-1836	4,5,6,7,8,9	1735-1837		Gainsborough			6C(A)
Gautby	1570-1837	1813-1834	4,5,6,7,8,9	1570-1980		Horncastle			4G(A)
Gayton le Marsh	1687-1998	1561-1836	4,5,6,7,8,9	1687-1926		Louth			5J(A)
Gayton le Wold	1773-1837	1561-1837	4,5,6,7,8,9	1773-1837		Louth			5H(A)
Gedney	1558-1923	1558-1834	4,5,6,7,8,9	1558-1923		Holbeach			4K(B)
Gedney Hill	1693-1851	1562-1858	4,5,6,7,8,9	1693-1858		Holbeach			2I(B)
Glentham	1690-1984	1602-1840	4,5,6,7,8,9	1690-1859		Caistor			6E(A)
Glentworth	1586-1997	1599-1852	4,5,6,7,8,9	1586-1947		Gainsborough			6D(A)
Goltho	1672-1952	1638-1834	4,5,6,7,8,9	1672-1952		Lincoln			4F(A)
Gosberton	1656-1983	1561-1862	4,5,6,7,8,9	1656-1983		Spalding		1703-1836	5H(B)
Goulceby	1690-1989	1561-1835	4,5,6,7,8,9	1690-1922		Horncastle			4H(A)
Goxhill	1572-1987	1561-1837	4,5,6,7,8,9	1572-1987		Glanford Brigg			10G(A)
Grainsby	1561-1835	1561-1843	4,5,6,7,8,9	1561-1844		Louth			7H(A)
Grainthorpe	1653-1942	1562-1847	4,5,6,7,8,9	1653-1880		Louth			7J(A)
Grantham St Wulfram	1562-1990	1562-1835	4,5,6,7,8,9	1562-1884		Grantham		1813-1837	5D(A)
Grasby	1653-1966	1561-1811	4,5,6,7,8,9	1653-1837		Caistor			8F(A)
Grayingham	1576-1998	1599-1836	4,5,6,7,8,9	1576-1837		Gainsborough			7D(A)
Great Carlton	1561-1998	1561-1835	4,5,6,7,8,9	1561-1971		Louth			5J(A)
Great Coates	1653-1961	1561-1846	4,5,6,7,8,9	1653-1961		Caistor			8H(A)
Greatford	1755-1837	1562-1840	4,5,6,7,8,9	1754-1837		Stamford			2F(B)
Great Gonerby	1560-1885	1562-1836	4,5,6,7,8,9	1560-1837	1651-1750	Grantham	1790-1837		6D(B)
Great Grimsby	1538-1983	1538-1832	4,5,6,7,8,9	1538-1983		Caistor	1790-1812	1818-1837	8H(A)
Great Hale	1538-1988	1561-1847	4,5,6,7,8,9			Sleaford			6G(B)
Great Ponton	1622-1951	1562-1834	4,5,6,7,8,9	1622-1951		Grantham			5D(B)
Great Steeping	1712-1945	1563-1837	4,5,6,7,8,9	1711-1945		Spilsby		1786-1793	3J(A)
Great Sturton	1679-1948	1561-1844	4,5,6,7,8,9	1679-1837		Horncastle			4G(A)
Greetham	1653-1997	1561-1836	4,5,6,7,8,9	1653-1812		Horncastle			4H(A)
Greetwell	1755-1999	1599-1842	4,5,6,7,8,9	1755-1985	1723-1837	Lincoln			4E(A)
Grimoldby	1558-1974	1558-1836	4,5,6,7,8,9	1558-1974		Louth			6J(A)
Gunby (Grantham)	1560-1837	1561-1812	4,5,6,7,8,9	1560-1837	1561-1810	Grantham			4D(B)
Gunby (Spilsby)	1724-2000	1561-1851	4,5,6,7,8,9	1724-1832		Spilsby			3J(A)
Habrough	1538-1936	1539-1833	4,5,6,7,8,9	1538-1844		Caistor			9G(A)
Hacconby	1703-1941	1561-1846	4,5,6,7,8,9	1703-1941		Bourne			4F(B)
Haceby	1560-1981	1561-1850	4,5,6,7,8,9			Grantham			5E(B)
Hackthorn	1653-1997	1599-1833	4,5,6,7,8,9	1653-1944		Lincoln			5E(A)
Hagnaby	1683-1836	1562-1836	4,5,6,7,8,9	1683-1836		Spilsby			2I(A)
Hagworthingham	1562-1907	1561-1830	4,5,6,7,8,9	1562-1907		Horncastle			3I(A)
Hainton	1632-1961	1602-1830	4,5,6,7,8,9	1623-1961		Louth			5G(A)
Hallington		1561-1751	4,5,6,7,8,9	1654-1742		Louth			5I(A)
Haltham on Bain	1561-1974	1561-1844	4,5,6,7,8,9	1561-1837		Horncastle			3H(A)
Halton Holegate	1566-1912	1561-1826	4,5,6,7,8,9	1701-1912		Spilsby			3J(A)
Hameringham	1744-1998	1561-1845	4,5,6,7,8,9	1744-1837		Horncastle			3H(A)
Hannah cum Hagnaby	1559-1995	1561-1824	4,5,6,7,8,9	1559-1961	1651-1750	Louth	1790-1837		4K(A)
Hareby	1587-1836	1561-1824	4,5,6,7,8,9	1587-1836		Spilsby			3I(A)
Harlaxton	1558-1901	1812-1843	4,5,6,7,8,9	1558-1901	1651-1750	Grantham	1790-1837		5D(B)
Harmston	1563-1979	1562-1855	4,5,6,7,8,9	1563-1979	1651-1750	Lincoln	1790-1837		8E(B)
Harpswell	1559-1994	1595-1837	4,5,6,7,8,9	1559-1836		Gainsborough			6D(A)
Harrington	1697-1996	1561-1836	4,5,6,7,8,9	1697-1837		Spilsby			4I(A)
Hatcliffe	1695-1987	1561-1837	4,5,6,7,8,9	1695-1987		Caistor			7H(A)
Hatton	1552-1837	1561-1835	4,5,6,7,8,9	1552-1837		Horncastle			4G(A)
Haugh	1762-1836	1562-1639	4,5,6,7,8,9	1754-1836		Louth			4J(A)
Haugham	1756-1947	1561-1832	4,5,6,7,8,9	1700-1947		Louth			5I(A)
Hawerby cum Beesby	1596-1960	1562-1831	4,5,6,7,8,9	1596-1960		Caistor			7H(A)
Haxey	1559-1922	1599-1856	4,5,6,7,8,9	1556-1922		Gainsborough			8B(A)
Healing	1571-1963	1561-1830	4,5,6,7,8,9	1571-1963		Caistor			8H(A)
Heapham	1558-1997	1563-1842	4,5,6,7,8,9	1558-1837		Gainsborough			6C(A)

LINCOLNSHIRE

parish name	deposited original registers	I.G.I.	local census indexes	copies of registers at Soc. Gen.	Boyd's marriage index	1837-1851 Registration District	Pallot's marriage index	non-conform. records at P.R.O.	map ref.
Heckington	1559-1968	1561-1837	4,5,6,7,8,9	1561-1837	1651-1837	Sleaford	1790-1837		6G(B)
Helpringham	1558-1955	1561-1843	4,5,6,7,8,9	1559-1640		Sleaford			6G(B)
Hemingby	1578-1896	1561-1841	4,5,6,7,8,9	1578-1896		Horncastle			4H(A)
Hemswell	1683-1963	1599-1833	4,5,6,7,8,9	1683-1963		Gainsborough			6D(A)
Heydour	1559-1917	1559-1835	4,5,6,7,8,9	1650-1837		Grantham			6E(B)
Hibaldstow	1631-1985	1599-1846	4,5,6,7,8,9	1631-1945		Glanford Brigg			8E(A)
High Toynton	1715-1934	1561-1855	4,5,6,7,8,9	1715-1934		Horncastle			3H(A)
Hogsthorpe	1559-1999	1561-1840	4,5,6,7,8,9	1559-1940	1651-1750	Spilsby	1790-1837		3K(A)
Holbeach (All Saints)	1560-1996	1561-1847	4,5,6,7,8,9	1613-1964	1560-1837	Holbeach			4J(B)
Holland Fen	1813-1986	1813-1833	4,5,6,7,8,9			Boston			6H(B)
Holton cum Beckering	1560-1975	1561-1853	4,5,6,7,8,9	1560-1975		Lincoln			5F(A)
Holton le Clay	1753-1966	1561-1835	4,5,6,7,8,9	1753-1966		Louth			7I(A)
Holton le Moor	1813-1971	1593-1740	4,5,6,7,8,9	1813-1971		Caistor			7F(A)
Holywell	1558-1981	1558-1845	4,5,6,7,8,9	1558-1981		Bourne			3E(B)
Honington	1561-1837	1562-1828	4,5,6,7,8,9	1700-1753		Grantham			6D(A)
Horbling	1653-1961	1561-1837	4,5,6,7,8,9	1653-1961		Bourne	1790-1837		5G(B)
Horkstow	1562-1992	1561-1839	4,5,6,7,8,9			Glanford Brigg			10E(A)
Horncastle	1559-1959	1559-1852	4,5,6,7,8,9	1559-1965		Horncastle		1806-1849	3H(A)
Horsington	1558-1998	1561-1836	4,5,6,7,8,9	1558-1875		Horncastle			3G(A)
Hougham	1562-1890	1562-1875	4,5,6,7,8,9	1700-1838	1560-1837	Newark			6D(B)
Hough on the Hill	1646-1895	1562-1841	4,5,6,7,8,9	1562-1836	1566-1837	Grantham			7D(B)
Howell	1564-1832	1561-1864	4,5,6,7,8,9			Sleaford			6G(B)
Humberston	1748-1965	1561-1840	4,5,6,7,8,9	1813-1965		Caistor			8I(A)
Hundleby	1707-1953	1562-1827	4,5,6,7,8,9	1707-1953		Spilsby			3I(A)
Huttoft	1562-1919	1561-1833	4,5,6,7,8,9	1562-1919	1651-1750	Spilsby	1790-1837		4K(A)
Immingham	1564-1963	1561-1830	4,5,6,7,8,9	1724-1963		Caistor			9G(A)
Ingham	1567-1987	1599-1875	4,5,6,7,8,9	1567-1978		Lincoln			6D(A)
Ingoldmells	1728-1995	1562-1839	4,5,6,7,8,9	1561-1944	1651-1750	Spilsby	1790-1837		3L(A)
Ingoldsby	1566-1989	1561-1814	4,5,6,7,8,9	1566-1878		Grantham			5E(B)
Irby in the Marsh	1540-2000	1540-1843	4,5,6,7,8,9	1540-1836		Spilsby			2J(A)
Irby on Humber	1560-1998	1558-1841	4,5,6,7,8,9	1558-1812		Caistor			8H(A)
Irnham	1559-1968	1561-1836	4,5,6,7,8,9	1559-1968		Bourne			4F(B)
Keddington	1563-1997	1561-1847	4,5,6,7,8,9	1563-1977		Louth			6I(A)
Keelby	1565-1952	1544-1835	4,5,6,7,8,9	1565-1952		Caistor			8G(A)
Kelstern	1651-1876	1561-1882	4,5,6,7,8,9	1651-1879		Louth			6H(A)
Kettlethorpe	1653-1993	1599-1825	4,5,6,7,8,9	1653-1948		Gainsborough			5C(A)
Killingholme	1564-1897	1562-1833	4,5,6,7,8,9	1564-1897		Glanford Brigg			9G(A)
Kingerby	1765-1962	1562-1838	4,5,6,7,8,9	1562-1962		Caistor			6F(A)
Kirkby cum Osgodby	1555-1998	1563-1845	4,5,6,7,8,9	1558-1979		Caistor			6F(A)
Kirkby Green	1722-1973	1562-1831	4,5,6,7,8,9	1722-1973		Sleaford			8F(B)
Kirkby Laythorpe	1660-1979	1561-1836	4,5,6,7,8,9	1556-1837	1556-1837	Sleaford			6F(B)
Kirkby on Bain	1562-1897	1561-1830	4,5,6,7,8,9	1562-1922		Horncastle			3G(A)
Kirkby Underwood	1558-1940	1558-1852	4,5,6,7,8,9	1558-1838		Bourne			4F(B)
Kirkstead	1678-1994	1814-1845	4,5,6,7,8,9	1663-1970	1676-1837	Horncastle			3G(A)
Kirmington	1697-1978	1561-1811	4,5,6,7,8,9	1697-1965		Glanford Brigg			8F(A)
Kirmond le Mire	1751-1993	1561-1836	4,5,6,7,8,9	1751-1968		Caistor			6G(A)
Kirton (Holland)	1561-1935	1561-1875	4,5,6,7,8,9	1700-1753		Boston		1832-1836	6I(B)
Kirton in Lindsey	1708-1997	1582-1832	4,5,6,7,8,9	1708-1947		Glanford Brigg		1780-1837	7D(A)
Knaith	1732-1998	1609-1836	4,5,6,7,8,9	1732-1837		Gainsborough			6C(A)
Laceby	1538-1977	1538-1835	4,5,6,7,8,9	1538-1977		Caistor			8H(A)
Langrick	1831-1967		4,5,6,7,8,9			Boston			1H(A)
Langtoft	1649-1980	1561-1836	4,5,6,7,8,9	1649-1980		Bourne			3G(B)
Langton	1753-1997	1561-1875	4,5,6,7,8,9	1753-1944		Horncastle			3H(A)
Langton by Partney	1558-1837	1561-1834	4,5,6,7,8,9	1558-1837		Spilsby			3J(A)
Langton by Wragby	1653-1987	1561-1853	4,5,6,7,8,9	1653-1987		Horncastle			4G(A)
Laughton	1566-1997	1566-1881	4,5,6,7,8,9	1566-1881		Gainsborough			7C(A)
Lea	1660-1991	1599-1847	4,5,6,7,8,9	1600-1837		Gainsborough			6C(A)
Leadenham	1558-1972	1561-1830	4,5,6,7,8,9	1558-1753		Sleaford			7D(B)
Leake		1561-1831	4,5,6,7,8,9	1700-1753		Boston			7J(B)
Leasingham	1575-1949	1561-1840	4,5,6,7,8,9	1575-1837		Sleaford			7F(B)
Legbourne	1711-1919	1562-1838	4,5,6,7,8,9	1711-1919		Louth			5I(A)
Legsby	1563-1973	1561-1841	4,5,6,7,8,9	1563-1973		Caistor			5G(A)
Lenton	1576-1989	1561-1827	4,5,6,7,8,9	1576-1921		Grantham		1799-1840	5F(B)
Leverton	1562-1980	1561-1836	4,5,6,7,8,9	1562-1980		Boston			7J(B)
Limber Magna	1561-1978	1561-1842	4,5,6,7,8,9	1561-1814		Caistor			8G(A)
Lincoln								1756-1837	10E(B)
St Benedict	1645-1948	1562-1840	4,5,6,7,8,9	1562-1948		Lincoln			10E(B)
St Botolph	1561-1925	1561-1869	4,5,6,7,8,9	1561-1925		Lincoln			10E(B)
St John in Newport	1708-1861	1708-1861	4,5,6,7,8,9	1708-1861		Lincoln			10E(B)
St Margaret in the Close	1538-1930	1538-1837	4,5,6,7,8,9	1538-1930		Lincoln			10E(B)
St Mark	1660-1969	1561-1840	4,5,6,7,8,9	1561-1969		Lincoln			10E(B)
St Martin	1548-1968	1548-1841	4,5,6,7,8,9	1546-1968		Lincoln			10E(B)
St Mary le Wigford	1622-1992	1562-1842	4,5,6,7,8,9	1562-1971		Lincoln			10E(B)
St Mary Magdalen	1665-1964	1602-1840	4,5,6,7,8,9	1602-1964		Lincoln			10E(B)
St Michael	1562-1963	1562-1843	4,5,6,7,8,9	1562-1963		Lincoln			10E(B)
St Nicholas in Newport	1740-1933	1602-1879	4,5,6,7,8,9	1602-1933		Lincoln			10E(B)
St Paul in the Bail	1695-1968	1565-1836	4,5,6,7,8,9	1565-1968		Lincoln			10E(B)
St Peter at Arches	1561-1930	1561-1842	4,5,6,7,8,9	1561-1930		Lincoln	1826-1837(?)		10E(B)
St Peter at Gowts	1538-1984	1538-1861	4,5,6,7,8,9	1538-1911		Lincoln			10E(B)
St Peter in Eastgate	1662-1969	1562-1835	4,5,6,7,8,9	1562-1958		Lincoln	1826-1837(?)		10E(B)
St Swithin	1686-1961	1562-1866	4,5,6,7,8,9	1562-1961		Lincoln			10E(B)
The Monks Liberty			4,5,6,7,8,9			Lincoln			10E(B)
Linwood	1705-1935	1561-1827	4,5,6,7,8,9	1705-1935		Caistor			6F(A)
Lissington	1562-1978	1562-1875	4,5,6,7,8,9	1563-1978		Caistor			5F(A)
Little Bytham	1681-1930	1561-1838	4,5,6,7,8,9	1681-1930		Bourne			3E(B)
Little Carlton	1726-1978	1561-1812	4,5,6,7,8,9	1700-1978		Louth			5J(A)

186

LINCOLNSHIRE

parish name	deposited original registers	I.G.I.	local census indexes	copies of registers at Soc. Gen.	Boyd's marriage index	1837-1851 Registration District	Pallot's marriage index	non-conform. records at P.R.O.	map ref.
Little Cawthorpe	1677-1994	1565-1836	4,5,6,7,8,9	1700-1836		Louth			5I(A)
Little Coates St Michael	1726-1935	1561-1832	4,5,6,7,8,9	1726-1946		Caistor			8H(A)
Little Grimsby	1593-1989	1562-1851	4,5,6,7,8,9	1593-1835		Louth			6I(A)
Little Ponton	1729-1837	1562-1835	4,5,6,7,8,9	1700-1837		Grantham			5D(B)
Little Steeping	1559-1881	1559-1837	4,5,6,7,8,9	1559-1881		Spilsby			2J(A)
Londonthorpe	1539-1949	1562-1837	4,5,6,7,8,9	1539-1949		Grantham			6D(B)
Long Bennington	1560-1933	1562-1838	4,5,6,7,8,9	1560-1933	1651-1837	Newark	1790-1837		7C(B)
Long Sutton (Sutton St Mary)	1669-1936	1561-1859	4,5,6,7,8,9	1669-1873	1671-1837	Holbeach		1820-1837	3J(B)
Louth	1538-1943	1604-1858	4,5,6,7,8,9	1538-1943		Louth		1801-1837	6I(A)
Low Toynton	1585-1959	1561-1846	4,5,6,7,8,9	1585-1959		Horncastle			4H(A)
Ludborough	1598-1991	1561-1850	4,5,6,7,8,9	1598-1938		Louth			7I(A)
Luddington	1700-1976	1599-1843	4,5,6,7,8,9	1700-1976		Goole			9C(A)
Ludford	1696-1962	1561-1838	4,5,6,7,8,9	1696-1962		Louth			6G(A)
Lusby	1690-1836	1562-1820	4,5,6,7,8,9	1690-1836		Horncastle			3I(A)
Mablethorpe	1648-1971	1561-1841	4,5,6,7,8,9	1561-1971	1651-1750	Louth	1790-1837		5K(A)
Maltby le Marsh	1680-1998	1561-1835	4,5,6,7,8,9	1561-1837	1651-1750	Louth	1680-1837		5K(A)
Manby	1679-1989	1562-1841	4,5,6,7,8,9	1679-1973	1680-1837	Louth			5J(A)
Manton	1754-1997	1599-1873	4,5,6,7,8,9	1754-1905		Glanford Brigg			8D(A)
Mareham le Fen	1561-1988	1561-1840	4,5,6,7,8,9	1561-1988		Horncastle			2H(A)
Mareham on the Hill	1572-1999	1561-1855	4,5,6,7,8,9	1572-1837		Horncastle			3H(A)
Markby	1557-1998	1561-1836	4,5,6,7,8,9	1558-1967	1651-1750	Spilsby	1790-1837		4K(A)
Market Deeping	1709-1983	1562-1836	4,5,6,7,8,9	1709-1983		Bourne			2G(B)
Market Rasen	1559-1950	1561-1837	4,5,6,7,8,9	1560-1950		Caistor		1797-1857	6F(A)
Market Stainton	1689-1837	1561-1837	4,5,6,7,8,9	1689-1837		Horncastle			5H(A)
Marshchapel	1589-1938	1561-1835	4,5,6,7,8,9	1589-1916		Louth			7J(A)
Marston	1707-1934	1562-1883	4,5,6,7,8,9	1700-1753	1562-1837	Newark			6D(B)
Martin	1561-1835	1561-1834	4,5,6,7,8,9	1561-1836		Horncastle			3H(A)
Marton	1651-1981	1599-1863	4,5,6,7,8,9	1651-1964		Gainsborough			5C(A)
Mavis Enderby	1579-1837	1561-1836	4,5,6,7,8,9	1579-1837		Spilsby			3I(A)
Melton Ross	1568-1998	1562-1836	4,5,6,7,8,9	1568-1950		Glanford Brigg			9F(A)
Messingham	1558-1967	1599-1839	4,5,6,7,8,9	1558-1885		Glanford Brigg			8D(A)
Metheringham	1538-1977	1562-1858	4,5,6,7,8,9	1538-1977		Lincoln			8F(B)
Middle Rasen (Drax)	1755-1845	1561-1831	4,5,6,7,8,9	1755-1843		Caistor		1806-1857	6F(A)
Middle Rasen (Tupholme)	1708-1845	1562-1831	4,5,6,7,8,9	1708-1843		Caistor		1806-1857	6F(A)
Midville	1821-1923	1821-1837	4,5,6,7,8,9	1821-1923		Spilsby			2I(A)
Miningsby	1695-1971	1561-1845	4,5,6,7,8,9	1695-1971		Horncastle			3I(A)
Minting	1562-1876	1561-1876	4,5,6,7,8,9	1562-1876		Horncastle			4G(A)
Moorby	1561-1975	1562-1836	4,5,6,7,8,9	1561-1975		Horncastle			3H(A)
Morton	1549-1972	1541-1843	4,5,6,7,8,9	1549-1972		Bourne			4F(B)
Moulton	1558-1967	1561-1849	4,5,6,7,8,9	1558-1967	1651-1837	Spalding	1790-1837		3I(B)
Muckton	1695-1965	1561-1826	4,5,6,7,8,9	1695-1965		Louth			5I(A)
Mumby	1573-1929	1561-1836	4,5,6,7,8,9	1562-1929	1651-1750	Spilsby	1790-1837		4K(A)
Navenby	1681-1999	1562-1849	4,5,6,7,8,9	1562-1979	1651-1750	Lincoln	1790-1837		8E(B)
Nettleham	1583-1982	1598-1849	4,5,6,7,8,9	1582-1968		Lincoln			4E(A)
Nettleton	1679-1978	1561-1815	4,5,6,7,8,9	1684-1978		Caistor			7F(A)
New Sleaford	1653-1967	1561-1883	4,5,6,7,8,9	1561-1754		Sleaford		1789-1837	7F(B)
Newton	1580-1993	1561-1835	4,5,6,7,8,9			Sleaford			5F(B)
Newton by Toft	1592-1998	1561-1810	4,5,6,7,8,9	1630-1974		Caistor			6F(A)
Newton on Trent	1656-1992	1599-1836	4,5,6,7,8,9	1656-1909		Gainsborough			4C(A)
Nocton	1582-1969	1562-1845	4,5,6,7,8,9	1582-1969		Lincoln			9F(B)
Normanby by Spital	1653-1974	1599-1840	4,5,6,7,8,9	1654-1865		Lincoln			6E(A)
Normanby le Wold	1561-1998	1562-1813	4,5,6,7,8,9	1561-1975		Caistor			7G(A)
Normanton	1670-1968	1562-1834	4,5,6,7,8,9	1700-1753		Grantham			7E(B)
North Carlton	1653-1997	1596-1832	4,5,6,7,8,9	1653-1971		Lincoln			5D(A)
North Coates	1659-1979	1561-1854	4,5,6,7,8,9	1659-1979	1715-1753	Louth			7I(A)
North Cockerington	1645-1964	1561-1844	4,5,6,7,8,9	1645-1964	1647-1837	Louth			6J(A)
North Elkington	1701-1974	1561-1838	4,5,6,7,8,9	1700-1974		Louth			6I(A)
North Kelsey	1612-1992	1561-1853	4,5,6,7,8,9	1612-1944		Caistor			7E(A)
North Ormsby	1813-1974	1561-1839	4,5,6,7,8,9	1700-1974		Louth			6H(A)
Northorpe	1593-1985	1598-1839	4,5,6,7,8,9	1593-1985		Gainsborough			7D(A)
North Reston	1563-1996	1563-1836	4,5,6,7,8,9	1563-1829		Louth			5J(A)
North Scarle	1571-1901	1562-1835	4,5,6,7,8,9	1564-1901	1651-1812	Newark	1790-1812		9D(B)
North Somercotes	1558-1957	1561-1836	4,5,6,7,8,9	1563-1957		Louth			7J(A)
North Thoresby	1552-1999	1561-1844	4,5,6,7,8,9	1552-1982		Louth			7I(A)
North Willingham	1658-1997	1561-1835	4,5,6,7,8,9	1568-1972		Caistor			6G(A)
North Witham	1591-1837	1561-1840	4,5,6,7,8,9	1591-1837	1562-1837	Grantham			4D(B)
Norton Disney	1578-1983	1562-1836	4,5,6,7,8,9	1578-1983	1651-1812	Newark	1790-1812		8D(B)
Old Bolingbroke	1538-1894	1563-1831	4,5,6,7,8,9	1538-1894		Spilsby			3I(A)
Old Sleaford (see Quarrington)									6F(B)
Orby	1725-1990	1561-1843	4,5,6,7,8,9	1725-1989		Spilsby			3K(A)
Osbournby	1682-1968	1561-1840	4,5,6,7,8,9	1561-1812		Sleaford			6F(B)
Owersby	1559-1998	1562-1875	4,5,6,7,8,9	1559-1976		Caistor			7F(A)
Owmby by Spital	1700-1998	1599-1834	4,5,6,7,8,9	1700-1837		Lincoln			6E(A)
Owston	1638-1988	1599-1833	4,5,6,7,8,9	1638-1926		Gainsborough			8C(A)
Oxcombe	1813-1978	1561-1834	4,5,6,7,8,9	1787-1840		Louth			4I(A)
Panton	1736-1956	1561-1827	4,5,6,7,8,9	1736-1956		Horncastle			5G(A)
Partney	1699-1965	1562-1837	4,5,6,7,8,9	1699-1965		Spilsby			3J(A)
Pickworth	1538-1992	1538-1840	4,5,6,7,8,9			Grantham			5F(B)
Pilham	1677-1996	1559-1840	4,5,6,7,8,9	1677-1837		Gainsborough			7C(A)
Pinchbeck	1560-1994	1561-1855	4,5,6,7,8,9	1560-1940	1651-1812	Spalding	1790-1812	1785-1836	4H(B)
Potterhanworth	1683-1977	1562-1836	4,5,6,7,8,9	1663-1977		Lincoln			9F(B)
Quadring	1583-1979	1561-1836	4,5,6,7,8,9	1583-1979		Spalding			5H(B)
Quarrington	1558-1964	1561-1838	4,5,6,7,8,9	1561-1890		Sleaford		1789-1840	6F(B)
Raithby (Louth)	1654-1975	1561-1836	4,5,6,7,8,9	1664-1975		Louth			5I(A)
Raithby (Spilsby)	1558-1837	1561-1836	4,5,6,7,8,9	1558-1837		Spilsby			3I(A)
Ranby	1569-1813	1561-1828	4,5,6,7,8,9	1569-1813		Horncastle			5H(A)
Rand	1661-1966	1562-1836	4,5,6,7,8,9	1661-1966		Lincoln			5F(A)

187

LINCOLNSHIRE

parish name	deposited original registers	I.G.I.	local census indexes	copies of registers at Soc. Gen.	Boyd's marriage index	1837-1851 Registration District	Pallot's marriage index	non-conform. records at P.R.O.	map ref.
Rauceby	1688-1964	1561-1837	4,5,6,7,8,9	1700-1935		Sleaford			7E(B)
Ravendale	1723-1988	1561-1828	4,5,6,7,8,9	1723-1987		Caistor			7H(A)
Redbourne	1558-1976	1599-1836	4,5,6,7,8,9	1558-1976		Glanford Brigg			7E(A)
Reepham	1633-1995	1599-1855	4,5,6,7,8,9	1653-1890		Lincoln			4E(A)
Revesby	1594-1999	1594-1836	4,5,6,7,8,9	1594-1937		Horncastle			2H(A)
Riby	1560-1956	1561-1845	4,5,6,7,8,9	1560-1956		Caistor			8G(A)
Rigsby	1602-1998	1561-1850	4,5,6,7,8,9	1561-1837	1701-1750	Spilsby	1790-1837		4J(A)
Rippingale	1633-1943	1562-1836	4,5,6,7,8,9	1633-1943		Bourne			4F(B)
Ropsley	1558-1961	1561-1825	4,5,6,7,8,9	1558-1961		Grantham			5E(B)
Rothwell	1561-1942	1561-1784	4,5,6,7,8,9	1561-1962		Caistor			7G(A)
Roughton	1564-1835	1561-1842	4,5,6,7,8,9	1564-1835		Horncastle			3H(A)
Rowston	1561-1992	1561-1847	4,5,6,7,8,9			Sleaford			8F(B)
Roxby	1689-1953	1599-1836	4,5,6,7,8,9	1689-1953		Glanford Brigg			9D(A)
Ruckland	1757-1997	1561-1834	4,5,6,7,8,9	1757-1836		Louth			4I(A)
Ruskington	1558-1989	1561-1836	4,5,6,7,8,9	1558-1660		Sleaford			7F(B)
Saleby	1554-1998	1561-1876	4,5,6,7,8,9	1554-1837	1651-1750	Louth	1790-1837		4J(A)
Salmonby	1558-1975	1561-1834	4,5,6,7,8,9	1558-1965		Horncastle			4I(A)
Saltfleetby									6K(A)
All Saints	1558-1836	1558-1842	4,5,6,7,8,9	1558-1836	1558-1837	Louth			6K(A)
St Clements	1756-1835	1561-1837	4,5,6,7,8,9	1756-1835	1718-1837	Louth			6K(A)
St Peter	1653-1939	1561-1842	4,5,6,7,8,9	1653-1939	1608-1837	Louth			6J(A)
Sapperton	1818-1998	1562-1837	4,5,6,7,8,9	1700-1833		Grantham			5E(B)
Sausthorpe	1565-1995	1560-1834	4,5,6,7,8,9	1565-1837		Spilsby			3I(A)
Saxby (Owmby)	1666-1989	1599-1848	4,5,6,7,8,9	1666-1812		Lincoln			6E(A)
Saxby All Saints	1719-1992	1561-1812	4,5,6,7,8,9	1719-1988		Glanford Brigg			9E(A)
Saxilby	1563-1996	1599-1836	4,5,6,7,8,9	1563-1921		Lincoln			5C(A)
Scamblesby	1569-1900	1561-1843	4,5,6,7,8,9	1569-1900		Horncastle			4H(A)
Scampton	1548-1995	1599-1837	4,5,6,7,8,9	1548-1970		Lincoln			5D(A)
Scartho	1565-1960	1563-1841	4,5,6,7,8,9	1562-1953		Caistor	1790-1837		8H(A)
Scawby	1559-1954	1599-1815	4,5,6,7,8,9	1558-1954		Glanford Brigg			8E(A)
Scopwick	1695-1978	1562-1833	4,5,6,7,8,9	1695-1978		Sleaford			8F(B)
Scothorn	1630-1930	1599-1833	4,5,6,7,8,9	1630-1930		Lincoln			5E(A)
Scotter	1561-1985	1562-1837	4,5,6,7,8,9	1561-1985		Gainsborough		1825-1837	8C(A)
Scotton	1560-1988	1560-1828	4,5,6,7,8,9	1560-1952		Gainsborough			7D(A)
Scot Willoughby	1573-1964	1577-1753	4,5,6,7,8,9			Sleaford			6F(B)
Scrafield (see Hameringham)		1561-1748	4,5,6,7,8,9			Horncastle			3H(A)
Scredington	1738-2000	1561-1843	4,5,6,7,8,9	1561-1970		Sleaford			6F(B)
Scremby	1716-1836	1561-1841	4,5,6,7,8,9	1716-1836		Spilsby			3J(A)
Scrivelsby	1565-1836	1813-1839	4,5,6,7,8,9	1752-1836		Horncastle			3H(A)
Searby	1558-1992	1562-1821	4,5,6,7,8,9	1558-1836		Caistor			8F(A)
Sedgebrook	1559-1962	1561-1836	4,5,6,7,8,9	1559-1962	1651-1812	Newark	1790-1812		6C(B)
Sempringham	1558-1974	1558-1873	4,5,6,7,8,9	1558-1974		Bourne			5G(B)
Sibsey	1565-1994	1561-1834	4,5,6,7,8,9	1565-1923		Boston			1I(A)
Silk Willoughby	1561-1919	1561-1845	4,5,6,7,8,9	1625-1812		Sleaford			6F(B)
Sixhills	1672-1994	1561-1838	4,5,6,7,8,9	1672-1974		Caistor			6G(A)
Skegness									2L(A)
St Clement	1653-1972	1562-1857	4,5,6,7,8,9	1653-1959		Spilsby			2L(A)
St Matthew	1880-1959		4,5,6,7,8,9	1880-1959		Spilsby			2L(A)
Skellingthorpe	1563-1992	1563-1835	4,5,6,7,8,9	1563-1978	1651-1812	Lincoln	1790-1812		10E(B)
Skendleby	1723-1997	1562-1845	4,5,6,7,8,9	1723-1904		Spilsby			3J(A)
Skidbrooke	1563-1964	1561-1837	4,5,6,7,8,9	1563-1964		Louth			6K(A)
Skillington	1542-1967	1542-1866	4,5,6,7,8,9	1541-1867		Grantham			4D(B)
Skinnand	1813-1955	1562-1742	4,5,6,7,8,9	1589-1955	1651-1725	Lincoln			8E(B)
Skirbeck St Nicholas	1661-1940	1561-1833	4,5,6,7,8,9	1661-1940		Boston			6I(B)
Snarford	1718-1985	1599-1875	4,5,6,7,8,9	1718-1973		Lincoln			5F(A)
Snelland	1653-1977	1561-1875	4,5,6,7,8,9	1653-1977		Lincoln			5F(A)
Snitterby	1858-1990		4,5,6,7,8,9	1858-1990		Caistor			7E(A)
Somerby (Brigg)	1661-1994	1561-1840	4,5,6,7,8,9	1661-1965		Caistor			8F(A)
Somerby (Grantham)	1730-1988	1562-1812	4,5,6,7,8,9	1562-1837	1651-1750	Grantham			5E(B)
Somersby	1561-1998	1563-1811	4,5,6,7,8,9	1573-1836		Horncastle			4I(A)
Sotby	1658-1980	1562-1834	4,5,6,7,8,9	1658-1980		Horncastle			5G(A)
South Carlton	1653-1997	1602-1844	4,5,6,7,8,9	1655-1863		Lincoln			5D(A)
South Cockerington	1670-1998	1561-1845	4,5,6,7,8,9	1670-1837	1671-1837	Louth			6I(A)
South Elkington	1701-1975	1562-1846	4,5,6,7,8,9	1701-1975		Louth			6I(A)
South Ferriby	1538-1993	1595-1841	4,5,6,7,8,9	1538-1971		Glanford Brigg			10E(A)
South Hykeham	1694-1991	1562-1867	4,5,6,7,8,9	1562-1936	1651-1837	Lincoln	1790-1837		9E(B)
South Kelsey	1559-1978	1559-1849	4,5,6,7,8,9	1559-1978	1651-1812	Caistor	1790-1812		7E(A)
South Kyme	1654-1964	1561-1838	4,5,6,7,8,9			Sleaford			7G(B)
South Ormsby	1561-1998	1561-1828	4,5,6,7,8,9	1561-1920		Spilsby			4I(A)
South Reston	1757-1994	1561-1835	4,5,6,7,8,9	1757-1837		Louth			5J(A)
South Somercotes	1558-1986	1558-1846	4,5,6,7,8,9	1558-1963		Louth			6J(A)
South Stoke	1663-1958	1562-1841	4,5,6,7,8,9	1660-1958	1665-1837	Grantham			4D(B)
South Thoresby	1660-1998	1561-1833	4,5,6,7,8,9	1660-1836		Louth			4J(A)
South Willingham	1711-1920	1562-1843	4,5,6,7,8,9	1711-1920		Louth			5G(A)
South Witham	1687-1887	1561-1851	4,5,6,7,8,9	1687-1837	1688-1837	Grantham			3D(B)
Spalding	1538-1985	1561-1858	4,5,6,7,8,9	1538-1987	1651-1812	Spalding	1790-1812	1819-1837	3H(B)
SS Mary & Nicholas									
Spanby	1681-1965	1670-1835	4,5,6,7,8,9			Sleaford			5F(B)
Spilsby	1562-1938	1562-1845	4,5,6,7,8,9	1562-1938		Spilsby		1811-1837	3J(A)
Spridlington	1560-1990	1560-1831	4,5,6,7,8,9	1560-1922		Lincoln			5E(A)
Springthorpe	1558-1998	1559-1834	4,5,6,7,8,9	1558-1837		Gainsborough			6C(A)
Stainby	1653-1836	1561-1851	4,5,6,7,8,9	1653-1836	1651-1837	Grantham			4D(B)
Stainfield	1680-1967	1561-1826	4,5,6,7,8,9	1680-1967		Lincoln			4F(A)
Stainton (Langworth)	1720-1998	1561-1835	4,5,6,7,8,9	1720-1863		Lincoln			5F(A)
Stainton le Vale	1703-1998	1561-1880	4,5,6,7,8,9	1703-1813		Caistor			7G(A)
Stallingborough	1588-1908	1561-1833	4,5,6,7,8,9	1558-1908		Caistor			9H(A)
Stamford						Stamford		1797-1837	2E(B)
All Saints	1560-1972	1560-1872	4,5,6,7,8,9	1560-1883		Stamford			2E(B)

LINCOLNSHIRE

parish name	deposited original registers	I.G.I.	local census indexes	copies of registers at Soc. Gen.	Boyd's marriage index	1837-1851 Registration District	Pallot's marriage index	non-conform. records at P.R.O.	map ref.
Stamford (cont'd)									
St George	1560-1980	1562-1855	4,5,6,7,8,9	1559-1980		Stamford			2E(B)
St John Baptist	1561-1969	1562-1846	4,5,6,7,8,9	1561-1874		Stamford			2E(B)
St Mary	1569-1904	1573-1836	4,5,6,7,8,9	1569-1837		Stamford			2E(B)
St Michael	1560-1958	1562-1842	4,5,6,7,8,9	1560-1958		Stamford			2E(B)
Stapleford	1695-1984	1562-1835	4,5,6,7,8,9	1563-1984	1651-1809	Newark	1790-1809		8D(B)
Stenigot	1562-1836	1562-1834	4,5,6,7,8,9	1562-1836		Louth			5H(A)
Stewton	1700-1978	1562-1836	4,5,6,7,8,9	1700-1978		Louth			5I(A)
Stickford	1662-1944	1562-1860	4,5,6,7,8,9	1662-1836		Spilsby			2I(A)
Stickney	1648-1978	1562-1836	4,5,6,7,8,9	1648-1978		Spilsby			2I(A)
Stixwould	1547-1998	1561-1836	4,5,6,7,8,9	1547-1955		Horncastle			3G(A)
Stow (Lindsey)	1561-1977	1561-1833	4,5,6,7,8,9	1561-1977		Gainsborough			5C(A)
Stragglethorpe	1701-1971	1565-1828	4,5,6,7,8,9	1700-1753		Newark			7D(B)
Stroxton	1735-1812	1562-1839	4,5,6,7,8,9	1700-1754		Grantham			5D(B)
Strubby	1558-1996	1590-1841	4,5,6,7,8,9	1558-1947	1651-1750	Louth	1790-1837		5J(A)
Stubton	1577-1966	1562-1830	4,5,6,7,8,9	1562-1837	1651-1837	Newark	1790-1837		7D(B)
Sudbrooke	1579-1843	1579-1835	4,5,6,7,8,9	1579-1843		Lincoln			4E(A)
Surfleet	1662-1979	1561-1848	4,5,6,7,8,9	1562-1978	1651-1812	Spalding	1790-1812		4H(B)
Sutterby	1560-1959	1562-1848	4,5,6,7,8,9	1560-1959		Spilsby			4I(A)
Sutterton	1538-1988	1538-1875	4,5,6,7,8,9	1700-1753		Boston		1823-1836	5I(B)
Sutton le Marsh	1813-1983	1561-1836	4,5,6,7,8,9	1561-1983	1651-1750	Spilsby	1790-1837		4K(A)
Sutton St Edmund	1706-1977	1561-1835	4,5,6,7,8,9	1706-1977		Holbeach			2I(B)
Sutton St James	1570-1974	1561-1834	4,5,6,7,8,9	1706-1974		Holbeach			3J(B)
Sutton St Nicholas	1538-1941	1562-1836	4,5,6,7,8,9			Holbeach			4K(B)
Swaby	1660-1989	1561-1835	4,5,6,7,8,9	1660-1967		Louth			4J(A)
Swallow	1672-1992	1561-1840	4,5,6,7,8,9	1672-1988		Caistor			8G(A)
Swarby	1754-1992	1561-1840	4,5,6,7,8,9	1561-1811		Sleaford			6F(B)
Swaton	1681-1966	1561-1836	4,5,6,7,8,9	1686-1812		Sleaford			5G(B)
Swayfield	1724-1912	1561-1840	4,5,6,7,8,9	1700-1912		Bourne			4E(B)
Swinderby	1568-1978	1562-1840	4,5,6,7,8,9	1562-1978	1651-1812	Newark	1790-1812		9D(B)
Swineshead	1639-1985	1561-1850	4,5,6,7,8,9	1561-1812		Boston			6H(B)
Swinhope	1697-1835	1561-1836	4,5,6,7,8,9	1697-1835		Caistor			7H(A)
Swinstead	1733-1934	1565-1834	4,5,6,7,8,9	1700-1934		Bourne			4E(B)
Syston	1730-1837	1562-1873	4,5,6,7,8,9	1700-1873	1562-1837	Newark			6D(B)
Tallington	1754-2000	1562-1836	4,5,6,7,8,9	1690-1837		Stamford			2F(B)
Tathwell	1662-1890	1561-1836	4,5,6,7,8,9	1700-1812		Louth			5I(A)
Tattershall	1568-1969	1561-1846	4,5,6,7,8,9	1568-1969		Horncastle			2G(A)
Tealby	1714-1986	1562-1827	4,5,6,7,8,9	1714-1986		Caistor			6G(A)
Tetford	1579-1997	1561-1831	4,5,6,7,8,9	1579-1872		Horncastle			4I(A)
Tetney	1730-1866	1561-1837	4,5,6,7,8,9	1730-1866		Louth			7I(A)
Theddlethorpe									5K(A)
All Saints	1560-1971	1561-1812	4,5,6,7,8,9	1560-1971	1560-1837	Louth			5K(A)
St Helen	1566-1932	1561-1812	4,5,6,7,8,9	1566-1932		Louth			5K(A)
Thimbleby	1695-2000	1561-1800	4,5,6,7,8,9			Horncastle			4H(A)
Thoresway	1726-1991	1561-1836	4,5,6,7,8,9	1726-1978		Caistor			7G(A)
Thorganby	1561-1837	1561-1836	4,5,6,7,8,9	1561-1837		Caistor			7H(A)
Thornton (Horncastle)	1561-1839	1561-1841	4,5,6,7,8,9	1561-1839		Horncastle			3H(A)
Thornton Curtis	1567-1975	1561-1861	4,5,6,7,8,9	1567-1975		Glanford Brigg			9F(A)
Thornton le Moor	1711-1994	1561-1845	4,5,6,7,8,9	1711-1974		Caistor			7F(A)
Thorpe on the Hill	1694-1897	1562-1847	4,5,6,7,8,9	1563-1897	1651-1835	Lincoln	1790-1835		9D(B)
Thorpe St Peter	1653-1978	1561-1838	4,5,6,7,8,9	1653-1978		Spilsby			2J(A)
Threckingham	1572-1960	1561-1830	4,5,6,7,8,9	1754-1837		Sleaford			5F(B)
Thurlby (Bourne)	1560-1993	1562-1840	4,5,6,7,8,9	1560-1941	1651-1812	Bourne	1790-1812		3F(B)
Thurlby (Lincoln)	1575-1984	1602-1836	4,5,6,7,8,9	1575-1984		Newark			8D(B)
Timberland	1660-1964	1561-1841	4,5,6,7,8,9	1660-1964		Sleaford			8G(B)
Toft by Newton	1653-1993	1561-1834	4,5,6,7,8,9	1653-1976		Caistor			6F(A)
Torksey	1575-1981	1577-1836	4,5,6,7,8,9	1575-1968		Gainsborough			5C(A)
Tothill	1608-1963	1565-1838	4,5,6,7,8,9	1608-1963		Louth			5J(A)
Toynton All Saints	1689-1955	1561-1843	4,5,6,7,8,9	1689-1955		Spilsby			2I(A)
Toynton St Peter	1742-1970	1562-1837	4,5,6,7,8,9	1562-1970		Spilsby			2J(A)
Trusthorpe	1665-1952	1561-1836	4,5,6,7,8,9	1562-1952	1651-1750	Louth	1790-1837		5K(A)
Tupholme (ex.par.)			4,5,6,7,8,9			Horncastle			4G(A)
Tydd St Mary	1540-1986	1561-1851	4,5,6,7,8,9	1540-1986	1541-1837	Holbeach			3J(B)
Uffington	1799-1863	1562-1858	4,5,6,7,8,9	1562-1863		Stamford			2F(B)
Ulceby (Grimsby)	1567-1920	1562-1836	4,5,6,7,8,9	1567-1920		Glanford Brigg			9G(A)
Ulceby with Fordington	1749-1983	1561-1846	4,5,6,7,8,9	1733-1846		Spilsby			4J(A)
Upton cum Kexby	1563-1860	1563-1869	4,5,6,7,8,9	1563-1860		Gainsborough			6C(A)
Usselby	1564-1998	1561-1831	4,5,6,7,8,9	1564-1933		Caistor			7F(A)
Utterby	1695-1992	1562-1857	4,5,6,7,8,9	1695-1980		Louth			6I(A)
Waddingham	1653-1990	1599-1848	4,5,6,7,8,9	1653-1990		Caistor			7E(A)
Waddington	1675-1970	1562-1870	4,5,6,7,8,9	1563-1970	1651-1750	Lincoln	1790-1837		9E(B)
Waddingworth	1593-1959	1562-1884	4,5,6,7,8,9	1593-1959		Horncastle			4G(A)
Wainfleet								1816-1837	2J(A)
All Saints	1677-1967	1561-1841	4,5,6,7,8,9	1679-1967		Spilsby			2J(A)
St Mary	1611-2000	1562-1836	4,5,6,7,8,9	1611-1882		Spilsby			2K(A)
Waithe	1693-1979	1561-1834	4,5,6,7,8,9	1693-1981		Louth			7I(A)
Walcot	1546-1971	1539-1832	4,5,6,7,8,9			Sleaford			5F(B)
Walesby	1561-1978	1561-1827	4,5,6,7,8,9	1562-1978		Caistor			6G(A)
Walmesgate		1561-1826	4,5,6,7,8,9			Louth			4I(A)
Waltham	1561-1889	1561-1840	4,5,6,7,8,9	1561-1889		Caistor			8H(A)
Washingborough	1564-1960	1562-1836	4,5,6,7,8,9	1564-1960	1564-1837	Lincoln			9F(B)
Welbourn	1561-1918	1561-1859	4,5,6,7,8,9	1700-1753	1562-1837	Sleaford			8E(B)
Welby	1568-1949	1562-1834	4,5,6,7,8,9	1700-1834		Grantham			6E(B)
Well	1649-1997	1562-1811	4,5,6,7,8,9	1561-1955	1651-1750	Spilsby			4J(A)
Wellingore	1653-1999	1602-1868	4,5,6,7,8,9	1602-1868	1651-1750	Sleaford	1790-1837		8E(B)
Welton (Lincoln)	1568-1974	1813-1871	4,5,6,7,8,9	1568-1973		Lincoln			5E(A)
Welton le Marsh	1558-2000	1562-1841	4,5,6,7,8,9	1558-1944		Spilsby			3J(A)
Welton le Wold	1558-1969	1561-1843	4,5,6,7,8,9	1554-1969		Louth			6H(A)

LINCOLNSHIRE

parish name	deposited original registers	I.G.I.	local census indexes	copies of registers at Soc. Gen.	Boyd's marriage index	1837-1851 Registration District	Pallot's marriage index	non-conform. records at P.R.O.	map ref.
West Allington	1559-1949	1562-1839	4,5,6,7,8,9	1559-1812	1651-1812	Newark	1790-1812		6C(B)
West Ashby	1561-1959	1561-1840	4,5,6,7,8,9	1561-1959		Horncastle			4H(A)
West Barkwith	1681-1965	1561-1828	4,5,6,7,8,9	1681-1965		Horncastle			5G(A)
Westborough (nr. Dry Doddington)	1564-1957	1562-1866	4,5,6,7,8,9	1562-1837	1651-1837	Newark			7C(B)
West Deeping	1657-1991	1562-1838	4,5,6,7,8,9	1657-1894		Stamford			2F(B)
West Fen (ex.par.)			4,5,6,7,8,9			Spilsby			2I(A)
West Halton	1538-1950	1599-1847	4,5,6,7,8,9	1598-1950		Glanford Brigg			10D(A)
West Keal	1624-1901	1561-1830	4,5,6,7,8,9	1642-1901		Spilsby			3I(A)
Weston	1678-1948	1561-1837	4,5,6,7,8,9	1678-1957	1651-1837	Spalding	1790-1837		4I(B)
West Rasen	1683-1997	1561-1848	4,5,6,7,8,9	1561-1978		Caistor			6F(A)
West Torrington	1638-1836	1561-1831	4,5,6,7,8,9	1638-1836		Horncastle			5G(A)
Whaplode	1559-1953	1559-1875	4,5,6,7,8,9	1559-1953	1560-1837	Holbeach			3I(B)
Whaplode Drove	1713-1901	1562-1837	4,5,6,7,8,9	1713-1901		Holbeach			2I(B)
Whitton	1545-1998	1599-1852	4,5,6,7,8,9	1545-1852		Glanford Brigg			10D(A)
Wickenby	1558-1976	1561-1835	4,5,6,7,8,9	1558-1976		Lincoln			5F(A)
Wigtoft	1634-1984	1561-1836	4,5,6,7,8,9	1700-1753		Boston			5H(B)
Wildmore	1816-1973	1818-1854	4,5,6,7,8,9			Horncastle			2H(A)
Wilksby	1562-1994	1561-1851	4,5,6,7,8,9	1562-1979		Horncastle			3H(A)
Willingham by Stow	1562-1980	1562-1812	4,5,6,7,8,9	1562-1980		Gainsborough			6C(A)
Willoughby with Sloothby	1538-1980	1561-1837	4,5,6,7,8,9	1538-1980	1651-1750	Spilsby	1790-1837		3K(A)
Willoughton	1599-1961	1599-1832	4,5,6,7,8,9	1599-1898		Gainsborough			7D(A)
Wilsford	1668-1938	1562-1830	4,5,6,7,8,9	1562-1774		Sleaford			6E(B)
Wilsthorp (see Greatford)		1813-1841	4,5,6,7,8,9	1754-1836		Stamford			3F(B)
Winceby	1579-1962	1561-1839	4,5,6,7,8,9	1579-1962		Horncastle			3I(A)
Winteringham	1563-1976	1599-1846	4,5,6,7,8,9	1562-1981		Glanford Brigg			10E(A)
Winterton	1558-1950	1558-1855	4,5,6,7,8,9	1558-1950		Glanford Brigg			10E(A)
Winthorpe	1551-1977	1561-1837	4,5,6,7,8,9	1551-1960		Spilsby			3L(A)
Wispington	1662-1968	1561-1824	4,5,6,7,8,9	1662-1963		Horncastle			4G(A)
Witham on the Hill	1670-1942	1561-1833	4,5,6,7,8,9	1670-1942		Bourne			3F(B)
Withcall	1597-1940	1561-1836	4,5,6,7,8,9	1579-1940		Louth			5H(A)
Withern	1558-1994	1561-1835	4,5,6,7,8,9	1558-1929	1651-1750	Louth	1790-1837		5J(A)
Wold Newton	1578-1836	1561-1820	4,5,6,7,8,9	1578-1836		Caistor			7H(A)
Wood Enderby	1561-1979	1561-1855	4,5,6,7,8,9	1561-1979		Horncastle			3H(A)
Woodhall	1562-1970	1562-1877	4,5,6,7,8,9	1562-1970		Horncastle		1822-1836	3G(A)
Woolsthorpe by Belvoir	1661-1971	1561-1837	4,5,6,7,8,9	1562-1837	1651-1750	Grantham			5C(B)
Wootton	1563-1919	1561-1845	4,5,6,7,8,9	1563-1919		Glanford Brigg			9F(A)
Worlaby	1559-1989	1561-1837	4,5,6,7,8,9	1559-1989		Glanford Brigg			9E(A)
Wragby	1567-1989	1561-1827	4,5,6,7,8,9	1567-1977		Horncastle			5F(A)
Wrangle	1652-1914	1561-1866	4,5,6,7,8,9	1561-1914		Boston			7K(B)
Wrawby	1675-1989	1561-1836	4,5,6,7,8,9	1561-1918		Glanford Brigg		1815-1838	8E(A)
Wroot	1573-1968	1599-1851	4,5,6,7,8,9	1573-1968		Thorne			8B(A)
Wyberton	1538-1889	1561-1856	4,5,6,7,8,9	1561-1753		Boston			6I(B)
Wyham cum Cadeby	1695-1978	1562-1839	4,5,6,7,8,9	1695-1978		Louth			6H(A)
Wyville	1817-1842		4,5,6,7,8,9			Grantham			5D(B)
Yarburgh	1561-1978	1562-1837	4,5,6,7,8,9	1561-1978		Louth			6I(A)

Original registers are deposited at:
Lincolnshire Archives Office, St Rumbold Street, Lincoln, LN2 5AB

Study adjacent parishes in counties of Yorkshire, Nottinghamshire, Leicestershire, Rutland, Northamptonshire and Cambridgeshire

The following useful indexes have been compiled – see Introduction
Census Indexes 1841, 1851, 1861, 1871 & 1891 – Lincolnshire FHS, Postal Sales Officer, Unit 6, 33 Monks Way, Monks Road, Lincoln, Lincolnshire, LN2 5LN
Lincolnshire Marriage Index – Lincolnshire FHS, Postal Sales Officer, Unit 6, 33 Monks Way, Monks Road, Lincoln, Lincolnshire, LN2 5LN arranged by deanery, whole county covered 1700-1837, some deaneries also 1600-1699.
Lincolnshire Poor Law Index – Lincolnshire FHS, Postal Sales Officer, Unit 6, 33 Monks Way, Monks Road, Lincoln, Lincolnshire, LN2 5LN

Lincolnshire forms an irregular oblong; its length from north to south is 77 miles, its breadth from east to west 48 miles. It has five principal rivers: the Trent, Ancholme, Welland, Witham and Bain. The population in 1841 was 362,602; in 1851, 407,222; in 1871, 436,599; in 1881, 469,919.

Soils of every description are to be found in the county from the sharpest sand to the strongest clay. Grain was cultivated together with flax, hemp and turnips. Sheep, cattle, horses and geese were reared. Canvas and sail cloth were manufactured.

The information in the Index is abbreviated, and may mislead the searcher if reference is not made to the details contained in the several publications listed in the Introduction. It is essential that users of this book check the appropriate works before making further enquiries.

LONDON

parish name	deposited original registers	I.G.I.	local census indexes	copies of registers at Soc. Gen.	Boyd's marriage index	1837-1851 Registration District	Pallot's marriage index	non-conform. records at P.R.O.	map ref.
All Hallows Barking			5,8			City	1800-1812	(see note	3K
All Hallows Bread Street	1538-1992	1538-1875	5,8	1538-1892	1538-1990	City	1780-1837	at end of	5F
All Hallows Honeylane	1538-1992	1538-1875	5,8	1538-1851	1546-1836	City	1780-1837	section)	5F
All Hallows Lombard Street	1550-1982	1813-1846	5,8	1553-1853	1553-1837	City	1812-1837		4I
All Hallows London Wall	1559-1945	1559-1880	5,8	1559-1849	1559-1837	City	1801-1837		7I
All Hallows Staining	1642-1978	1642-1870	5,8	1642-1870	1653-1750	City	1800-1837		4K
All Hallows The Great	1667-1975	1668-1812	5,8	1667-1853	1671-1837	City	1800-1837		3G
All Hallows The Less	1558-1975	1558-1885	5,8	1558-1853	1558-1666	City	1800-1837		3H
Barnard's Inn (ex.par.)			5,8			West London			7A
Christchurch	1547-1940	1538-1880	5,8	1538-1812	1538-1754	City	1780-1837		6D
Furnival's Inn (ex.par.)			5,8			Holborn			8A
Holy Trinity the Less	1547-1971	1547-1836	5,8	1755-1852	1542-1730	City	1800-1837		4F
Holy Trinity Minories	1563-1945	1563-1875	5,8	1676-1868	1579-1663	Whitechapel			5M
Lamb Chapel	1619-1753		5,8	1618-1753		East London			8F
Precinct of Bridewell (ex.par.)	1667-1969		5,8	1665-1837	1671-1725	West London	1813-1837		4C
Precinct of St Katherine (ex.par.)			5,8			Whitechapel			2M
Precinct of Whitefriars (ex.par.)			5,8			City			4B
St Alban	1663-1934	1662-1852	5,8	1629-1852		City	1800-1837		7F
St Alphage	1613-1940	1754-1885	5,8	1813-1875		City	1800-1837		7F
St Andrew by the Wardrobe	1558-1940	1558-1885	5,8	1558-1838		City	1800-1837		4D
St Andrew Holborn	1558-1952	1558-1875	5,8	1754-1764		Holborn	1780-1837		7A
St Andrew Hubbard	1538-1988	1538-1837	5,8	1538-1846	1538-1622	City	1800-1837		4I
St Andrew Undershaft	1558-1970	1558-1875	5,8	1813-1849	1726-1837	City	1780-1837		5J
St Ann Blackfriars	1560-1940	1560-1861	5,8	1726-1812		City	1801-1837		5C
St Anne and St Agnes	1640-1938	1640-1875	5,8	1813-1853		City	1800-1837		7E
St Antholin	1539-1952	1538-1872	5,8	1538-1853	1538-1754	City	1800-1837		4G
St Augustine	1559-1940	1559-1875	5,8	1813-1853	1559-1836	City	1780-1837		5E
St Bartholomew by the Exchange	1558-1996	1558-1840	5,8	1558-1838	1558-1754	City	1800-1837		5H
St Bartholomew the Great	1616-1934	1616-1885	5,8	1843-1853		West London	1807-1837		8E
St Bartholomew the Less			5,8	1547-1941		West London	1807-1837		7D
St Benet Fink	1538-1986	1538-1880	5,8	1538-1845	1538-1836	City	1780-1837		5I
St Benet Gracechurch	1558-1982	1730-1866	5,8	1558-1852	1558-1837	City	1800-1837		4I
St Benet Paul's Wharf	1619-1975	1619-1879	5,8	1619-1853	1619-1837	City	1780-1837		4D
St Benet Sherehog	1670-1954	1557-1880	5,8	1516-1754	1557-1837	City	1780-1860		5G
St Botolph Billingsgate	1685-1988	1686-1875	5,8	1629-1845	1754-1835	City	1801-1836		3I
St Botolph without Aldersgate	1638-1984	1640-1872	5,8	1640-1755	1640-1755	East London	1807-1837		8E
St Botolph without Aldgate	1558-1945	1558-1875	5,8			East London	1779-1837		5L
St Botolph without Bishopsgate	1558-1958	1558-1862	5,8	1558-1753	1558-1754	East London	1800-1837		8K
St Bride	1587-1969	1587-1880	5,8	1587-1653		West London	1801-1837		5B
St Christopher Le Stock	1557-1996	1557-1781	5,8	1558-1837	1557-1780	City	1800-1837		5H
St Clement	1539-1964	1539-1877	5,8	1539-1853	1539-1839	City	1780-1837		4I
St Dionis Backchurch	1538-1982	1538-1877	5,8	1538-1849	1538-1837	City	1780-1837		4J
St Dunstan in the East	1558-1948	1558-1880	5,8	1558-1853	1605-1625	City	1799-1837		3J
St Dunstan in the West	1558-1990	1800-1840	5,8	1601-1777	1701-1812	West London	1800-1837		5A
St Edmund the King & Martyr	1670-1980	1670-1875	5,8	1670-1850	1670-1812	City	1780-1837		4I
St Ethelburga	1671-1986	1671-1873	5,8	1671-1915	1679-1837	City	1800-1837		6J
St Faith under St Paul's	1645-1940	1645-1875	5,8	1677-1853	1813-1837	City	1780-1837		6D
St Gabriel	1571-1952	1571-1872	5,8	1572-1851		City	1754-1837		4J
St George	1546-1988	1754-1885	5,8	1653-1875	1537-1837	City	1800-1837		3I
St Giles without Cripplegate	1561-1987	1561-1885	5,8	1627-1640	1561-1625	East London	1813-1837		8F
St Gregory by St Paul's	1559-1958	1559-1821	5,8	1559-1821	1559-1754	City	1800-1837		5D
St Helen	1575-1993	1575-1874	5,8	1575-1853	1575-1837	City	1780-1837		6J
St James Duke's Place	1664-1950	1664-1872	5,8	1664-1853	1664-1837	City	1780-1837		5K
St James Garlickhithe	1535-1971	1535-1868	5,8	1754-1853	1708-1754	City	1780-1837		3F
St John the Baptist	1682-1952	1682-1812	5,8	1629-1812		City	1800-1837		4G
St John the Evangelist	1653-1992	1653-1821	5,8	1653-1822	1653-1666	City	1780-1837		5F
St John Zachary	1693-1938	1640-1875	5,8	1665-1849		City	1800-1837		6F
St Katherine Coleman	1559-1978	1710-1876	5,8	1563-1853	1563-1754	City			4K
St Katherine Creechurch	1663-1950	1663-1885	5,8	1639-1837		City	1780-1837		5K
St Lawrence Jewry	1538-1983	1538-1880	5,8	1538-1853	1538-1764	City	1764-1837		6G
St Lawrence Pountney	1538-1978	1538-1812	5,8	1538-1853	1538-1837	City	1737-1837		3H
St Leonard Eastcheap	1538-1982	1538-1866	5,8	1538-1705	1538-1705	City	1800-1806		4I
St Leonard Foster Lane	1724-1940		5,8			City	1780-1837		6E
St Magnus the Martyr	1558-1991	1669-1850	5,8	1557-1853	1557-1837	City			3I
St Margaret Fish Street Hill	1670-1991	1669-1768	5,8	1629-1640		City	1800-1837		3I
St Margaret Lothbury	1558-1996	1558-1875	5,8	1558-1853	1558-1754	City	1800-1837		6H
St Margaret Moses	1558-1850	1558-1842	5,8	1559-1850	1558-1666	City	1813-1837		5F
St Margaret Pattens	1558-1952	1559-1875	5,8	1650-1853	1559-1660	City	1754-1837		4J
St Martin Ludgate	1538-1958	1539-1875	5,8	1754-1837	1626-1700	City	1800-1837		5D
St Martin Orgar	1624-1964	1539-1877	5,8	1625-1812	1625-1726	City	1780-1837		3H
St Martin Outwich	1670-1993	1670-1873	5,8	1664-1873	1670-1837	City	1780-1873		5I
St Martin Pomeroy	1539-1996	1539-1874	5,8	1539-1848	1539-1647	City	1800-1837		5G
St Mary Abchurch	1558-1978	1558-1837	5,8	1558-1853	1558-1837	City	1737-1837		4H
St Mary Aldermanbury	1538-1940	1538-1880	5,8	1538-1859	1701-1837	City	1780-1935		7G
St Mary Aldermary	1558-1952	1538-1875	5,8	1558-1851	1558-1754	City	1800-1837		5F
St Mary at Hill	1558-1988	1558-1837	5,8	1558-1850	1701-1754	City	1800-1837		3J
St Mary Bothaw	1536-1944	1536-1653	5,8	1536-1812	1754-1812	City	1804-1811		4G
St Mary Colechurch	1558-1996	1558-1870	5,8	1558-1654	1558-1684	City	1800-1837		5G
St Mary Le Bow	1538-1992	1538-1837	5,8	1538-1852	1538-1837	City	1780-1837		5F
St Mary Magdalen Milk Street	1558-1983	1538-1880	5,8	1558-1677	1559-1666	City	1764-1837		5F
St Mary Magdalen Old Fish Street	1539-1958	1538-1877	5,8	1539-1853	1664-1754	City	1800-1837		4E
St Mary Mountshaw	1568-1975	1568-1875	5,8	1568-1849	1568-1835	City	1780-1837		4E
St Mary Somerset	1558-1975	1558-1878	5,8	1557-1853	1558-1837	City	1780-1837		4E
St Mary Staining	1673-1934	1673-1812	5,8	1629-1820		City	1800-1837		7F
St Mary Woolchurch Haw	1558-1985	1558-1885	5,8	1558-1848	1559-1666	City	1800-1837		5H
St Mary Woolnoth	1538-1985	1538-1885	5,8	1538-1852	1538-1754	City	1800-1837		5H
St Matthew Friday Street	1813-1882	1538-1875	5,8	1538-1846	1538-1836	City	1780-1837		5F
St Michael Bassishaw	1538-1983	1538-1880	5,8	1538-1892	1538-1764	City	1800-1837		6G

191

LONDON

parish name	deposited original registers	I.G.I.	local census indexes	copies of registers at Soc. Gen.	Boyd's marriage index	1837-1851 Registration District	Pallot's marriage index	non-conform. records at P.R.O.	map ref.
St Michael Cornhill	1546-1986	1545-1836	5,8	1546-1853	1546-1836	City	1800-1837		5I
St Michael Crooked Lane	1538-1991	1749-1875	5,8	1539-1852	1539-1835	City	1780-1835		3H
St Michael Le Querne	1754-1884	1837-1877	5,8	1629-1849	1686-1836	City	1780-1837		6E
St Michael Paternoster Royal	1558-1975	1558-1885	5,8	1558-1850	1558-1837	City	1780-1837		4G
St Michael Queenhithe	1653-1971	1651-1875	5,8	1639-1852	1701-1753	City	1780-1837		4F
St Michael Wood Street	1559-1934	1559-1811	5,8	1754-1820	1674-1837	City	1800-1837		6F
St Mildred Bread Street	1754-1853	1658-1837	5,8	1629-1853	1670-1837	City	1780-1837		4F
St Mildred Poultry	1538-1996	1538-1870	5,8	1538-1852	1538-1754	City	1800-1837		5G
St Nicholas Acon	1539-1982	1539-1875	5,8	1539-1850	1539-1664	City	1780-1837		4H
St Nicholas Cole Abbey	1538-1975	1538-1885	5,8	1538-1873	1584-1812	City	1800-1837		4E
St Nicholas Olave	1670-1975	1704-1875	5,8	1704-1852		City	1800-1837		4F
St Olave Hart Street	1563-1978	1563-1878	5,8	1563-1893	1563-1754	City	1780-1837		4K
St Olave Old Jewry	1538-1996	1538-1875	5,8	1538-1837	1538-1754	City	1800-1837		5G
St Olave Silver Street	1561-1934	1616-1736	5,8	1562-1852		City	1800-1837		7F
St Pancras	1538-1992	1538-1875	5,8	1538-1849	1538-1836	City	1780-1837		5G
St Paul's Cathedral	1697-1812		5,8	1697-1899	1697-1758	City	1804-1837		5E
St Peter Cornhill	1538-1985	1538-1875	5,8	1538-1853	1538-1754	City	1780-1837		5I
St Peter Le Poer	1561-1986	1561-1875	5,8	1561-1837	1561-1837	City	1780-1837		6I
St Peter Paul's Wharf	1607-1975	1607-1837	5,8	1607-1849	1607-1834	City	1780-1837		4E
St Peter Westcheap	1538-1876	1538-1868	5,8	1813-1846	1538-1836	City	1800-1837		5F
St Sepulchre	1662-1987	1662-1875	5,8	1662-1904	1662-1754	West London	1800-1837		8D
St Stephen Coleman Street	1538-1952	1538-1875	5,8	1538-1754	1701-1754	City	1780-1837		7H
St Stephen Walbrook	1557-1954	1557-1880	5,8	1559-1860	1557-1837	City	1780-1860		4G
St Swithin	1614-1944	1615-1875	5,8	1614-1935	1726-1837	City	1780-1837		4H
St Thomas the Apostle	1558-1952	1558-1873	5,8	1558-1849	1558-1754	City	1800-1837		4G
St Vedast	1754-1981	1558-1875	5,8	1558-1853	1559-1837	City	1780-1837		6F
Sergeant's Inn (ex.par.)			5,8			West London			5A
Staple Inn (ex.par.)			5,8			Holborn			7A
Thavia's Inn (ex.par.)			5,8			West London			7B
The Temple (ex.par.)			5,8	1628-1853	1701-1760	West London			5A

Original registers deposited at:
Guildhall Library, Aldermanbury EC2P 2EJ

There were a large number of non-conformist chapels in the City of London and to assign them to a particular Church of England parish would be difficult and misleading, A listing is available at the Public Record Office. There were also a number of non-parochial establishments that recorded baptisms, marriages and burials such as Fleet Prison, The Guildhall Chapel, The Mitre Chapel and The Mercers Hall Chapel. These have not been included in this publication.

The following useful indexes have been compiled – see Introduction
Census Index 1851 – The Publications Officer, London and North Middlesex FHS, 1d Upland Park Road, Enfield , Middlesex,EN2 7PS
London Probate Index (London & Middlesex) – David Wright, 71 Island Wall, Whitstable, Kent, CT5 1EL

The City of London stands on the north bank of the river Thames, is roughly a parallelogram in shape and covers an area of 677 acres. The population in 1841 was 135,008; in 1851, 127,869; in 1861, 112,063; in 1871, 74,732; in 1881, 50,652.

The soils are London clay, sand and gravel. The City was not only the market of London but also the commercial and financial centre of Britain and the Empire. It contained the great money markets such as the Bank of England, joint-stock companies, merchant banks, discount houses and the Stock Exchange. Other exchanges included the Baltic (cereals) and those dealing in wool, iron, steel and coal. Billingsgate was the great fish market.

The information in the Index is abbreviated, and may mislead the searcher if reference is not made to the details contained in the several publications listed in the Introduction. It is essential that users of this book check the appropriate works before making further enquiries.

MIDDLESEX

parish name	deposited original registers	I.G.I.	local census indexes	copies of registers at Soc. Gen.	Boyd's marriage index	1837-1851 Registration District	Pallot's marriage index	non-conform. records at P.R.O.	map ref.
Acton	A 1539-1963		5,8	1566-1812	1566-1812	Brentford	1790-1812	(see note	5E
Ashford	A 1696-1904		5,8	1629-1837	1696-1812	Staines	1790-1812	at end of	3B
Bethnal Green, St Matthew	A 1746-1993	1746-1879	5,7,8,9	1746-1854		Bethnal Green	1783-1837	section)	6H
Bloomsbury, St George	A 1730-1927		5,8			St. Giles	1800-1837		3J
Bromley, St Leonard	A 1622-1960		5,8	1639-1640		Poplar	1780-1837		6I
Charter House		1671-1876	5,8	1671-1890	1671-1754	Holborn			3K
Chelsea, St Luke	A 1559-1987	1558-1876	5,8	1639-1800	1701-1754	Kensington	1803-1837		5G
Chiswick			5,8	1678-1872	1678-1800	Brentford	1790-1837		5E
Clerkenwell									4J
Pentonville Chapel	A 1790-1977	1810-1885	5,8	1790-1876		Clerkenwell			4J
St James	A 1551-1945	1551-1754	5,8	1551-1754	1551-1754	Clerkenwell	1806-1837		4J
St John the Baptist	A 1723-1930		5,8			Clerkenwell	1807-1837		4J
St Mark, Myddleton Square	A 1828-1931		5,8	1828-1856		Clerkenwell			4J
Covent Garden, St Paul	D 1653-1972	1653-1837	5,8	1653-1853	1653-1837	Strand	1800-1837		2J
Cowley	A 1562-1949		5,8	1563-1812	1563-1812	Uxbridge	1790-1837		5B
Cranford	A 1564-1908		5,8	1564-1834		Staines	1770-1837		4C
Ealing	A 1582-1979	1852-1875	4,5,6,8	1582-1837	1582-1837	Brentford	1790-1837		5D
East Bedfont	A 1678-1973		5,8	1659-1860		Staines			3B
Edgware	A 1717-1976		5,8	1630-1840		Hendon	1770-1837	1834-1836	8E
Edmonton									8G
All Saints	A 1558-1925	1834-1876	5,8	1557-1837	1557-1837	Edmonton	1790-1837	1819-1837	8G
Christ Church	A 1813-1953		5,8			Edmonton			8G
Weld Chapel	A 1695-1842		5,8			Edmonton			8G
Enfield	A 1550-1981	1550-1875	5,7,8	1550-1837	1550-1837	Edmonton	1790-1837	1727-1838	10G
Feltham	A 1634-1964	1813-1875	5,8	1634-1837	1634-1812	Staines	1790-1837		3C
Finchley	A 1558-1958		5,8	1560-1837	1560-1837	Barnet	1790-1837		8F
Friern Barnet	A 1674-1974	1813-1875	5,8	1675-1837		Barnet	1770-1837		9F
Fulham	A 1674-1946		5,8	1614		Kensington			5F
Gray's Inn			5,6,8	1695-1850	1695-1754	Holborn			3K
Great Stanmore	A 1599-1934	1754-1876	5,8	1599-1837	1599-1837	Hendon	1790-1837		8D
Greenford			5,8	1539-1812	1539-1812	Brentford	1790-1812		6D
Hackney									7H
St Barnabas with St Paul	A 1847-1948		5,8			Hackney	1825-1838		7H
St John	A 1556-1968	1545-1812	5,8	1540-1754	1540-1754	Hackney	1800-1837		7H
St John of Jerusalem	A 1826-1986		5,8			Hackney	1832-1837		7H
St Thomas	A 1827-1939		5,8			Hackney			7H
Hammersmith	C 1664-1990		5,8			Kensington	1800-1837	1758-1854	5F
Hampstead, St John			5,6,8			Edmonton	1769-1837		7F
Hampton, St Mary	A 1554-1973		5,8,9	1554-1837	1657-1812	Kingston	1790-1837		3D
Hampton Wick	A 1831-1967		5,8,9			Kingston			2D
Hanwell	A 1570-1966		5,8	1570-1812	1570-1812	Brentford	1790-1837		5D
Hanworth	A 1731-1968		5,8	1629-1837	1732-1837	Staines	1790-1837		3C
Harefield	A 1538-1898		5,8	1546-1837	1546-1837	Uxbridge	1790-1837		7A
Harlington			5,8	1540-1853	1540-1812	Staines	1790-1812		5B
Harmondsworth	A 1670-1979	1670-1876	5,8	1629-1840		Staines	1770-1837		4B
Harrow on the Hill	A 1558-1918	1558-1653	5,8	1558-1840	1558-1653	Hendon		1831-1836	8D
Hayes	A 1557-1943		5,8	1557-1840	1557-1813	Uxbridge	1790-1813		5C
Hendon	A 1653-1992		5,8	1653-1837	1726-1837	Hendon	1810-1837	1784-1837	8E
Heston	A 1560-1965		5,8	1559-1819	1559-1812	Brentford	1790-1837		4C
Highgate	A 1633-1952		5,8	1633-1903		Pancras/Edmonton		1785-1836	7G
Hillingdon	A 1559-1910		4,5,6,7,8	1559-1866	1559-1813	Uxbridge	1790-1812		6B
Holborn, St Andrew	B 1558-1952	1558-1875	5,8	1754-1764		Holborn	1780-1837		3J
Hornsey	A 1653-1966		5,8	1654-1812	1654-1700	Edmonton	1780-1837	1785-1836	7G
Hounslow	A 1708-1968	1836-1875	5,8	1708-1812	1708-1753	Brentford	1780-1812	1827-1836	4C
Ickenham	A 1536-1948	1754-1874	5,8	1558-1837	1558-1812	Uxbridge	1790-1837		6B
Isleworth	E 1566-1895	1813-1875	5,8	1566-1812		Brentford			4C
Islington									7G
Holy Trinity, Cloudsley Sq	A 1829-1978		5,7,8	1830-1837		Islington			7G
St John, Upper Holloway	A 1829-1954		5,7,8	1829-1854		Islington			7G
St Mary	A 1557-1921		5,7,8			Islington	1800-1814		7G
St Paul, Canonbury	A 1830-1980		5,7,8			Islington	1831-1837		7G
Kensington								1825-1837	5F
Holy Trinity, Brompton Rd	A 1829-1987		5,8			Kensington			5F
Holy Trinity, Knightsbridge	D 1658-1903		5,8	1658-1739	1658-1681	Kensington			5F
St Mary Abbots		1539-1675	5,8	1539-1853	1539-1675	Kensington	1800-1819		5F
Kingsbury	A 1732-1970		5,8	1639		Hendon			7E
Laleham	A 1538-1937		5,8	1538-1842		Staines			2B
Liberty of Glasshouse Yard			5,8			East London			3K
Liberty of Saffron Hill			5,8			Holborn			3K
Liberty of the Rolls			5,8		1736-1749	Strand			3K
Liberty of the Tower			5,8			Whitechapel			2K
Limehouse, St Anne	A 1730-1968		5,8			Stepney	1800-1837		6I
Lincoln's Inn		1695-1806	5,8		1695-1754	Holborn			3K
Little Stanmore	A 1558-1963		5,8	1829-1837		Hendon		1834-1836	8D
Littleton	A 1562-1984	1564-1812	5,8	1562-1852		Staines			2B
Mayfair, St George's Chapel	D 1735-1754	1728-1754	5,8	1735-1754	1729-1754	Holborn			2I
Monken Hadley	A 1619-1956	1732-1885	5,8	1619-1837	1619-1837	Barnet	1790-1837		9F
New Brentford	A 1570-1961		5,8	1618-1836	1618-1812	Brentford	1790-1812	1831-1837	5D
Northolt	A 1560-1995		4,5,6,7,8	1575-1812	1575-1812	Uxbridge	1790-1812		6C
Norwood	A 1654-1970		5,8	1654-1837		Uxbridge			5C
Old Artillery Ground			5,8			Whitechapel			3L
Old Brentford	A 1828-1959		5,8			Brentford		1831-1837	5E
Paddington									6F
St James	A 1655-1958	1655-1875	5,7,8	1784-1792		Kensington			6F
St Mary	A 1790-1955		5,7,8			Kensington	1802-1837		6F
Perivale	A 1707-1988	1707-1875	5,8	1707-1952		Brentford			6D
Pinner	A 1654-1942		4,5,6,7,8	1654-1837	1654-1837	Hendon	1790-1837		7C
Poplar	A 1711-1989	1711-1754	5,7,8	1670-1754		Poplar	1823-1837		5I

MIDDLESEX

parish name	deposited original registers	I.G.I.	local census indexes	copies of registers at Soc. Gen.	Boyd's marriage index	1837-1851 Registration District	Pallot's marriage index	non-conform. records at P.R.O.	map ref.
Precinct of Old Tower			5,8			Whitechapel			2K
Ruislip	A 1689-1957		5,8	1629-1875		Uxbridge			7B
St Botolph without Aldgate	B 1538-1945	1558-1875	5,8			East London	1799-1837		2L
St Clement Danes	D 1558-1986	1558-1885	5,8			Strand	1807-1837		3J
St George Hanover Square	D 1725-1914		5,8	1725-1845	1725-1837	St George Hanover			5G
St George in the East	A 1729-1901	1729-1840	5,8	1760-1837		St George in East	1796-1837		2M
St George the Martyr	A 1706-1955		5,8	1706-1800	1706-1801	Holborn	1800-1837		3J
St Giles in the Fields			5,7,8	1561-1650	1561-1650	St. Giles	1800-1837		3J
St James Westminster	D 1685-1963	1685-1882	5,7,8	1754-1762	1701-1754	Westminster	1786-1837		2I
St John the Baptist Savoy			5,8			Strand	1799-1837		2J
St John the Evangelist, Westminster	D 1728-1947	1728-1755	5,7,8			Westminster	1813-1837		1I
St Katherine by the Tower		1584-1875	5,8	1584-1726	1584-1625	Whitechapel			2L
St Luke Old Street	A 1733-1965	1733-1875	5,8	1742-1765	1742-1750	St Luke	1802-1837		4K
St Margaret Westminster	F 1538-1987	1539-1699	5,7,8	1539-1699	1539-1775	Westminster	1813-1822		2I
St Martin in the Fields	D 1525-1968	1550-1897	5,8	1550-1856	1550-1619	St Martin in Fields	1800-1837		2I
St Marylebone									6G
All Souls, Langham Place	A 1825-1992	1825-1876	5,7,8			Marylebone	1825-1837		6G
Christ Church, Cosway St	A 1825-1957		5,7,8	1825-1828		Marylebone	1825-1834		6G
Holy Trinity, Marylebone Rd	A 1828-1942		5,7,8			Marylebone	1828-1837		6G
Oxford Chapel	A 1736-1754	1736-1754	5,7,8	1736-1754	1736-1754	Marylebone			6G
St Marylebone	A 1668-1925	1668-1876	5,7,8	1668-1812	1668-1812	Marylebone	1812-1833		6G
St Mary, Bryanston Square	A 1825-1962		5,7,8			Marylebone	1825-1837		6G
St Mary Le Strand	D 1558-1990	1754-1885		1605-1754	1606-1754	Strand	1800-1837		2J
St Pancras									6G
All Saints, Camden Town Chapel	A 1824-1947		5,6,7,8			Pancras			6G
Fitzroy Chapel	A 1786-1913		5,7,8			Marylebone			6G
Percy Chapel	A 1776-1808		5,6,7,8			Pancras			6G
St John the Baptist, Kentish Town Chapel	A 1804-1990		5,6,7,8			Pancras			6G
St Mary the Virgin, Somers Town Chapel	A 1826-1986		5,6,7,8			Pancras			6G
St Pancras	A 1660-1950	1660-1876	5,6,7,8	1660-1752	1701-1754	Pancras	1780-1837		6G
St Peter, Regent Sq Chapel	A 1829-1943	1829-1885	5,6,7,8			Pancras			6G
St Peter on the Tower			5,8			Whitechapel			2K
St Sepulchre	B 1662-1987	1662-1875	5,8	1662-1761	1662-1754	Holborn/W London	1800-1837		3K
Shadwell, St Paul	A 1670-1934		5,8	1671-1700	1671-1754	Stepney	1779-1837		2M
Shepperton	A 1574-1911		5,8	1574-1866		Staines			2B
Shoreditch									4L
Aske's Hospital Chapel	B 1696-1854	1696-1753	5,7,8	1696-1852		Shoreditch			4L
Geffrey's Almshouses Chapel	B 1794-1850		5,7,8			Shoreditch			4L
St John the Baptist, Hoxton	A 1826-1947	1830-1875	5,7,8			Shoreditch			4L
St Leonard	B 1558-1930	1745-1875	5,7,8	1694-1709		Shoreditch	1806-1836		4L
St Leonard's Workhouse	B 1820-1871	1834-1873	5,7,8			Shoreditch			4L
St Mary, Haggerston	A 1829-1949		5,7,8	1830-1837		Shoreditch			4L
Soho, St Anne	D 1686-1940	1686-1897	5,8	1789-1808	1684-1754	Strand	1800-1837		3J
Somerset House Chapel		1714-1776	5,8	1714-1775	1714-1776	Strand			3K
Southgate	A 1813-1953	1805-1885	5,8	1812-1836		Edmonton		1812-1836	9G
South Mimms	A 1558-1906		5,8	1558-1983	1558-1837	Barnet	1790-1837		10E
Spitalfields									3L
Christchurch	A 1729-1964	1721-1876	5,8		1720-1752	Whitechapel	1800-1837		3L
St Mary, N. Folgate	A 1720-1911		5,8			Whitechapel			3L
Staines	A 1538-1962	1644-1694	5,8	1644-1694	1653-1660	Staines		1785-1837	3A
Stanwell	A 1632-1972		5,8	1632-1837	1632-1812	Staines	1790-1812	1820-1837	4A
Stepney, St Dunstan	A 1568-1962	1568-1875	5,8	1568-1754	1568-1754	Stepney	1800-1837		6I
Stoke Newington, St Mary	A 1559-1977	1559-1812	4,5,8	1560-1812	1560-1812	Hackney	1780-1812		7H
Stratford Le Bow, St Mary	A 1538-1968		5,8	1629		Poplar	1800-1837		6I
Sunbury	A 1565-1950	1565-1876	5,8	1566-1875	1566-1812	Staines	1790-1837		2C
Teddington	A 1558-1960		8,9	1560-1837	1560-1837	Kingston	1800-1837		3D
Tottenham	A 1557-1901		5,8	1558-1837	1558-1837	Edmonton	1780-1837	1819-1837	8G
Twickenham	A 1538-1837		5,8	1538-1838	1538-1812	Brentford	1800-1837		3D
Twyford	A 1722-1994		5,8			Hendon	1810-1835		6E
Uxbridge	A 1538-1973		5,8	1538-1694	1538-1694	Uxbridge		1789-1855	6B
Wapping	A 1618-1940		5,8	1617-1665		Stepney	1802-1837		2L
West Drayton	A 1568-1979	1813-1847	5,8	1568-1837	1568-1813	Uxbridge	1790-1837		5B
Westminster Abbey	F 1608-2001	1607-1875	5,7,8	1607-1875	1655-1775	Westminster			1J
Whitechapel	A 1558-1940	1558-1875	5,8	1558-1823	1616-1625	Whitechapel	1800-1837		3L
Whitehall, Chapel Royal			5,8		1701-1754	St Martin in Fields			2J
Willesden	A 1569-1979		5,6,8	1569-1838	1573-1838	Hendon			7E

MIDDLESEX

Original registers deposited at:
A = London Metropolitan Archives, 40 Northampton Road, EC1R 0HB
B = Guildhall Library, Aldermanbury, EC2P 2EJ
C = London Borough of Hammersmith and Fulham Archives & Local History Centre, The Lilla Huset, 191 Talgarth Road, London, W6 8BJ
D = Westminster City Archives, 10 St Ann's Street, London SW1P 2DE
E = Hounslow Library & Local Studies, 24 Treaty Centre, High Street, Hounslow, Middlesex, TW3 1ES
F = Westminster Abbey Muniment Room, Westminster Abbey, London, SW1P 3PA

LONDON/ MIDDLESEX

Study adjacent parishes in counties of Buckinghamshire, Hertfordshire, Essex, Berkshire, Surrey and Kent

College of Arms, Queen Victoria Street, EC4V 4BT
Corporation of London Records Office, PO Box 270, Guildhall, EC2P 2EJ (in Room 221, 2nd Floor, North Office Block, immediately behind Guildhall, reached from Basinghall Street)
Dr Williams's Library, 14 Gordon Square, London, WC1H 0AG
Family Records Centre, 1 Myddleton Street, London, EC1R 1UW
Guildhall Library, Aldermanbury, London, EC2P 2EJ
London Metropolitan Archives, 40 Northampton Road, London, EC1R 0HB
Public Record Office, Ruskin Avenue, Kew, Richmond, Surrey, TW9 4DU
Society of Friends' Library, Friends' House, Euston Road, London, NW1 2BJ
Society of Genealogists, 14 Charterhouse Buildings, Goswell Road, London, EC1M 7BA
The Principal Registry of the Family Division, First Avenue House, 42-49 High Holborn, London, WC1V 6NP
United Reformed Church History Society, 86 Tavistock Place, London, WC1H 9RT
Westminster City Archives, 10 St Ann's Street, London SW1P 2DE
Westminster (Roman Catholic) Diocesan Archives, 16a Abingdon Road, Kensington, Middlesex, W8 6AF

The following useful indexes have been compiled – see Introduction

Census Indexes 1841, 1851 & 1891 – East of London FHS, Mr D. Filby, 19 Cavendish Gardens, Ilford, Essex, IG1 3EA
Census Index 1841, 1851, 1861 & 1871 – Hillingdon FHS, Mrs G. May, 20 Moreland Drive, Gerrards Cross, Buckinghamshire, SL9 8BB
Census Index 1851 – London and North Middlesex FHS, C.A. Gibbens, 1d Uplands Park Road, Enfield, Middlesex, EN2 7PS
Census Indexes 1851 & 1891 – West Middlesex FHS, Mrs M.M. Harris, Westerwood, Gough's Lane, Warfield, Berkshire, RG12 2JR
Census Index of London and Other Prisons 1851 – Susan Bourne, 26 Brookside Road, Istead Rise, Northfleet, Kent, DA13 9JJ
Census Index 1871 – Clive Ayton, PO Box 19, West P.D.D., Nottingham, NG8 5JE
Boyd's Marriage Index – Guildhall Library
Pallot Marriage Index 1800-1837 – Institute of Heraldic & Genealogical Studies, Northgate, Canterbury, Kent, CT1 1BA
Catholic Marriage Index 1837-1870 – Institute of Heraldic & Genealogical Studies (as above)
Marriage Licences Index – Institute of Heraldic & Genealogical Studies (as above)
Selon Index – Peter R. Shilham, 6 Beckford Close, Wokingham, Berkshire, RG41 1HN
Marriage Index 1813-1837 – Mr C.R. Webb, Coldharbour Road, Pyrford, Woking, Surrey GU22 8SJ
Marriage Index West Middlesex FHS, Mr R. Chapman, 15 Willerton Lodge, Bridgewater Road, Weybridge, Surrey, KT13 0ED
London Probate Index (London & Middlesex) – David Wright, 71 Island Wall, Whitstable, Kent, CT5 1EL
Nonconformist registers of Middlesex – C.A. Gibbens (as above)
Boyd's London Burial Index 1538-1853 (Males only) – Society of Genealogists (as above)
Monumental Inscriptions – West Middlesex FHS, Mrs W. Mott, 24 Addison Avenue, Hounslow, Middlesex, TW3 4AP

There were a large number of non-conformist chapels in London and to assign these to a particular Church of England parish would be difficult and misleading. A listing is available at the Public Record Office. Where possible the available information has been entered.

Middlesex's greatest length does not exceed 24 miles and the breadth is about 18 miles. It is watered by five principal rivers: the Thames, Lea, Coln, Brent and the New River. The population in 1841 was 1,647,018; in 1851, 1,886,576, in 1861, 2,206,485, in 1871, 2,539,765, in 1881, 2,920,485.

The soil is chiefly London clay with occasional patches of plastic clay and gravel. Produce included wheat and barley with some oats and rye and large quantities of fruit and vegetables. Livestock was raised on only a small scale. Manufactures (the main ones being situated in the capital) included silk goods, pins, needles, and fancy articles in worsted, silk, gold and silver. Breweries and distilleries were numerous. In some towns there were bleaching and calico-printing works, iron-foundries, soap works and tanneries.

The information in the Index is abbreviated, and may mislead the searcher if reference is not made to the details contained in the several publications listed in the Introduction. It is essential that users of this book check the appropriate works before making further enquiries.

MONMOUTHSHIRE

parish name	deposited original registers	I.G.I.	local census indexes	copies of registers at Soc. Gen.	Boyd's marriage index	1837-1851 Registration District	Pallot's marriage index	non-conform. records at P.R.O.	map ref.
Abergavenny	B 1653-1990		5,6,8			Abergavenny		1711-1837	6J
Aberystruth	AB 1736-1974		5,6,8			Abergavenny		1802-1837	8H
Bassaleg	B 1742-1922		5,6,7,8			Newport		1812-1837	7D
Bedwas	B 1635-1971	1653-1875	5,6,7,8	1635-1739		Newport			9E
Bedwellty	B 1624-1979	1696-1875	5,6,8	1815-1817		Abergavenny		1806-1837	9H
Bettws	B 1696-1977	1813-1873	5,6,7,8			Newport			6D
Bettwsnewydd	A 1734-1974	1813-1876	5,6,8	1796-1974		Abergavenny			5H
Bishton	B 1793-1991	1696-1875	5,6,7,8	1793-1900		Newport			4D
Blaenavon	B 1804-1971		5,6,8,9			Abergavenny		1813-1837	7I
Bryngwyn	B 1660-1995	1696-1875	5,6,8			Abergavenny			4H
Caerwent	B 1568-1970	1659-1875	6,7,8	1568-1900		Chepstow		1817-1835	3E
Caldicote	B 1716-1976	1813-1874	6,7,8	1754-1900		Chepstow			3E
Chapel Hill	B 1695-1970	1726-1869	6,7,8	1813-1900		Chepstow			1G
Chepstow	B 1595-1925		6,7,8	1558-1924		Chepstow		1828-1837	1E
Christchurch	A 1695-1974	1725-1875	5,6,7,8			Newport		1826-1836	5D
Clytha (see Llanarth)			5,6,8			Abergavenny			5H
Coedcernew	A 1654-1987	1725-1873	5,6,7,8			Newport			7C
Cwmcarvan	A 1660-1976	1696-1875	6,7,8	1660-1900		Monmouth			3H
Cwmyoy	B 1708-1976	1686-1875	5,6,8	1754-1900		Abergavenny			6L
Dingestow	A 1742-1983	1725-1875	5,6,7,8	1742-1900		Monmouth			3I
Dinham (see Llanvairdiscoed)			6,7,8			Chepstow			2E
Dixton Newton	C 1661-1870	1843-1875	6,7,8	1661-1870		Monmouth			2I
Glascoed (see Usk)			5,6,8,9			Pontypool			6G
Goldcliff	B 1728-1981	1725-1875	5,6,7,8	1813-1981		Newport			5C
Goytre	B 1695-1971	1725-1865	5,6,8,9	1695-1869		Pontypool		1815-1833	6H
Grace-Dieu Park (ex.par.)			6,7,8			Monmouth			3I(D)
Grosmont	A 1589-1954	1589-1873	5,6,8	1589-1900		Hereford			5K
Gwernesney	A 1783-1990		5,6,8,9			Pontypool			4G(K)
Henllys	B 1813-1976	1726-1875	5,6,7,8			Newport			7E
Howick (ex.par.)			6,7,8			Chepstow			2E
Ifton			6,7,8			Chepstow			3D
Itton	B 1773-1991	1725-1868	6,7,8	1725-1900		Chepstow			2F
Kemeys Commander	A 1813-1984	1726-1875	5,6,8,9	1813-1973		Pontypool			5G(J)
Kemeys Inferior	A 1701-1959	1725-1875	5,6,7,8	1701-1840		Newport			5E(O)
Kilgwrwg	B 1774-1991	1814-1860	6,7,8	1813-1900		Chepstow			3F
Llanarth	B 1598-1896	1725-1875	5,6,8			Abergavenny			5I
Llanbadock	DA 1582-1969	1582-1870	5,6,8,9	1582-1709		Pontypool			5G
Llanddewi Fach	B 1741-1987	1725-1875	5,6,8	1741-1861		Pontypool			6F
Llanddewi Rhydderch (Llanthewyrytherch)	B 1670-1978	1670-1875	5,6,8	1670-1783		Abergavenny			5I
Llandegveth	B 1746-1986	1725-1832	5,6,8,9	1746-1859		Pontypool			5F(N)
Llandenny	B 1710-1992	1725-1872	6,7,8			Monmouth			4G
Llandogo	B 1694-1971	1725-1872	6,7,8	1755-1900		Monmouth			2H
Llanelen	A 1754-1971	1725-1870	5,6,8			Abergavenny			6I
Llanfihangel Gobion	B 1751-1977		5,6,8			Abergavenny			5H
Llanfoist	A 1736-1975	1725-1874	5,6,8,9			Abergavenny			7I
Llan-frechfa	B 1727-1971	1816-1874	5,6,8			Pontypool			6F
Llangatock	AB 1695-1971	1725-1875	5,6,7,8			Newport			5E
Llangattock Lingoed	A 1696-1982	1696-1875	5,6,8	1696-1900		Abergavenny		1696-1900	5J
Llangattock Nigh Usk	B 1598-1978		5,6,8			Abergavenny			5I(E)
Llangattock-Vibon-Avel	A 1683-1991	1813-1869	5,6,7,8			Monmouth			3J
Llangeview	A 1709-1992	1758-1865	5,6,8,9			Pontypool			4G
Llangibby	A 1679-1839	1679-1868	5,6,8,9	1678-1840		Pontypool			5F
Llangovan	A 1689-1982		6,7,8	1680-1900		Monmouth			3H
Llangstone	B 1755-1979	1725-1875	5,6,7,8			Newport			4E
Llangua	C 1714-1843		5,6,8			Hereford			4L
Llangwm	A 1663-1986	1663-1849	6,7,8			Chepstow			4F
Llanhennock	AB 1685-1991	1813-1874	5,6,7,8			Newport			5E
Llanhilleth	B 1813-1971	1725-1861	5,6,8,9			Pontypool			8G
Llanishen	B 1596-1992	1725-1875	6,7,8			Monmouth			3G
Llanllowel	A 1664-1991	1676-1867	5,6,8,9			Pontypool			4F(M)
Llanmartin	B 1813-1979	1815-1875	5,6,7,8			Newport		1813-1835	4D(P)
Llanover	A 1708-1973		5,6,8,9	1661-1896		Abergavenny			6H
Llansantffraed	B 1753-1990	1772-1866	5,6,8			Abergavenny			5I(G)
Llansoy	A 1592-1984	1592-1875	6,7,8			Chepstow			3G
Llanthewy Skirrid	A 1549-1982	1813-1875	5,6,8	1549-1900		Abergavenny			5J(A)
Llanthony	B 1769-1976	1843-1876	5,6,8	1769-1900		Abergavenny			6L
Llantiliocrossenny	B 1719-1971	1629-1871	5,6,7,8	1577-1644		Monmouth			4J
Llantilio-Pertholey	B 1591-1981		5,6,8	1591-1900		Abergavenny			6J
Llantrissent	A 1743-1992	1725-1868	5,6,8,9	1813-1843		Pontypool			4F
Llanvaches	B 1796-1992		5,6,7,8			Newport		1799-1837	4E
Llanvairdiscoed	B 1680-1991	1680-1812	6,7,8	1568-1900		Chepstow			3E
Llanvairkilgidin	B 1733-1984		5,6,8	1733-1844		Abergavenny			5H
Llanvapley	B 1699-1977	1699-1724	5,6,8			Abergavenny		1823-1833	5I(B)
Llanvetherine	A 1745-1984		5,6,8			Abergavenny			5J
Llanvihangel-juxta-Roggiett	B 1754-1991	1815-1869	6,7,8	1757-1899		Chepstow			3D
Llanvihangelcrucorney	B 1629-1971		5,6,8	1629-1900		Abergavenny			5K
Llanvihangellantarnam	B 1727-1971	1725-1740	5,6,7,8			Newport		1817-1836	6E
Llanvihangel Nigh Usk	B 1751-1977		5,6,8			Abergavenny			5H(F)
Llanvihangelpontymoil	B 1739-1976		5,6,8	1739-1869		Pontypool			6G
Llanvihangel-Tor-y-mynydd	A 1594-1990	1813-1862	6,7,8			Chepstow			3G(L)
Llanvihangel-ystern-Llewern	B 1695-1991	1685-1875	5,6,7,8	1685-1812		Monmouth			4J(C)
Llanwenarth	B 1725-1996	1813-1875	5,6,8,9			Abergavenny			7I
Llanwern	B 1750-1991	1763-1812	5,6,7,8	1750-1900		Newport			4D(Q)
Machen	B 1670-1996		5,6,7,8			Newport			8D
Magor	B 1754-1984	1725-1875	5,6,7,8	1793-1900		Newport			4D
Malpas	B 1759-1986	1725-1854	5,6,7,8	1759-1932		Newport			6E
Mamhilad	B 1686-1989	1725-1861	5,6,8,9	1682-1837		Pontypool			6G

MONMOUTHSHIRE

parish name	deposited original registers	I.G.I.	local census indexes	copies of registers at Soc. Gen.	Boyd's marriage index	1837-1851 Registration District	Pallot's marriage index	non-conform. records at P.R.O.	map ref.
Marshfield	A 1653-1973		5,6,7,8			Newport		1819-1837	7C
Mathern	A 1565-1942		6,7,8	1565-1900		Chepstow			2E
Michaelston-Fedwy	B 1658-1983	1781-1875	4,5,6,7,8			Newport			7C
Mitchel Troy	B 1590-1994	1592-1865	6,7,8	1720-1900		Monmouth			2I
Monks Wood (ex.par.)	B 1783-1962	1742-1875	5,6,8,9			Pontypool			5G
Monmouth	AB 1598-1918	1843-1869	6,7,8	1598-1900		Monmouth		1808-1850	2I
Mounton	A 1790-1991	1813-1875	6,7,8	1790-1900		Chepstow			2E
Mynyddislwyn	B 1656-1933	1717-1842	5,6,7,8			Newport		1787-1837	8F
Nash	B 1733-1984	1725-1870	5,6,7,8	1758-1970		Newport			5C
Newchurch	B 1710-1970	1725-1868	6,7,8	1710-1970		Chepstow		1819-1837	2F
Newport	B 1702-1931	1725-1875	5,6,7,8	1692-1905		Newport		1812-1837	6D
Oldcastle	B 1773-1976	1714-1875	5,6,8	1714-1900		Abergavenny			6K
Panteg	B 1598-1999	1598-1854	5,6,8,9	1598-1838		Pontypool		1766-1837	7F
Penallt	B 1765-1970	1725-1870	6,7,8	1765-1900		Monmouth			2H
Penhow	B 1725-1992	1813-1875	5,6,7,8			Newport			4E
Penrhos	AB 1718-1990	1560-1875	5,6,7,8	1577-1644		Monmouth			4I
Penterry	B 1721-1992		6,7,8	1813-1899		Chepstow			2F
Pen-y-Clawdd	A 1727-1982	1813-1875	6,7,8	1727-1900		Monmouth			3H(H)
Peterstone	A 1754-1985	1725-1864	5,6,7,8			Newport			7B
Portskewet	B 1593-1953	1725-1875	6,7,8	1593-1900		Chepstow			2D
Raglan	B 1722-1989	1725-1873	6,8			Monmouth		1820-1836	4H
Redwick	B 1699-1969	1813-1875	5,6,7,8	1754-1900		Newport			4C
Risca	B 1754-1958		5,6,7,8			Newport		1813-1837	7E
Rockfield	A 1696-1992	1725-1875	5,6,7,8			Monmouth			3J
Roggiett	B 1752-1993	1815-1867	6,7,8	1750-1900		Chepstow			3D
Rumney	A 1744-1837	1733-1865	6,8	1696-1840		Cardiff		1813-1836	7B
St Arvans	B 1683-1917	1829-1870	6,7,8	1792-1900		Chepstow			2F
St Brides Netherwent	B 1754-1992	1725-1875	5,6,7,8	1813-1900		Chepstow		1828-1837	3E(S)
St Brides Wentlloog	A 1695-1989	1725-1873	5,6,7,8			Newport			6C
St Maughans	A 1733-1992	1825-1872	5,6,7,8			Monmouth			3J
St Mellons	AB 1722-1993	1725-1869	6,8			Cardiff		1812-1837	7C
St Peirre	A 1813-1992		6,7,8	1813-1900		Chepstow			2E
Shire Newton	B 1730-1971		6,7,8			Chepstow			3F
Skenforth	A 1639-1928		5,6,7,8	1639-1900		Monmouth			4K
Tintern Parva	B 1756-1970		6,7,8	1756-1900		Chepstow			1G
Tredunnock	A 1695-1992		5,6,7,8			Newport			4E
Tregare	A 1751-1984		5,6,7,8	1751-1900		Monmouth			4I
Trelleck	A 1763-1976	1725-1875	6,7,8	1763-1900		Monmouth			2G
Trelleck Grange	B 1770-1991	1813-1873	6,7,8			Chepstow			2G
Trevethin	B 1655-1939	1653-1844	5,6,8,9	1652-1837		Pontypool		1801-1837	7G
Trostrey	A 1723-1975	1725-1875	5,6,8,9	1723-1975		Pontypool			5H
Undy	B 1754-1971	1697-1875	6,7,8	1754-1900		Chepstow			3D
Usk	B 1742-1963	1815-1875	5,6,8,9			Pontypool			5G
Whitson	B 1728-1991	1725-1875	5,6,7,8	1728-1986		Newport			4D
Wilcrick	B 1814-1974	1725-1876	5,6,7,8			Newport			4D(R)
Wolvesnewton	B 1716-1990	1725-1862	6,7,8			Chepstow		1819-1837	3G
Wonastow	A 1674-1992	1725-1861	6,7,8	1674-1900		Monmouth			3I

Original registers deposited at:
A = Department of Manuscripts and Records, National Library of Wales, Aberystwyth, Ceredigion, SY23 3BU
B = Gwent County Record Office, County Hall, Cwmbran, NP44 2XH
C = Herefordshire Record Office, The Old Barracks, Harold Street, Hereford, HR1 2QX
D = University College Cardiff, PO BOX 430, Cardiff, CF1 3XT

Study adjacent parishes in counties of Glamorgan, Breconshire, Herefordshire and Gloucestershire

Census Indexes 1851, 1861, 1871 & 1891 – Gwent FHS, 50 Queens Hill, Newport, Gwent, NP20 5HJ
Marriage Index 1813-1837 – Gwent FHS, 35 Trinity Street, Abergavenny, Gwent, NP7 5EA
Monmouthshire Marriage Index 1754-1812 –   Surnames A-L – A.A. Powell, 1 St Davids Close, Forest Park, Penedairhoel, Hengoed, Mid Glam. CF8 8BL;
                                                                    Surnames L-Z – B. Hemming, 1 Marianwen Street, Cefn Fforest, Blackwood, Gwent
Monmouthshire Marriage Index, Reference Librarian, Newport Central Library, John Frost Square, Newport, Gwent, NP9 1PA
Monumental Inscriptions Index- Gwent FHS, 51 Newport Road, Lower New Inn, Panteg, Pontypool, Gwent, NP4 0NU

The soils include marl, shale and sand. Corn was grown and great numbers of cattle and sheep and some goats raised. Coal and iron were abundant, the latter constituting the chief article of manufacture, coal giving rise to a considerable coasting trade. Newport and Chepstow had a trade in timber and ship-building and Abergavenny, in flannels.

The information in the Index is abbreviated, and may mislead the searcher if reference is not made to the details contained in the several publications listed in the Introduction. It is essential that users of this book check the appropriate works before making further enquiries.

NORFOLK

parish name	deposited original registers	I.G.I.	local census indexes	copies of registers at Soc. Gen.	Boyd's marriage index	1837-1851 Registration District	Pallot's marriage index	non-conform. records at P.R.O.	map ref.
Acle	A 1664-1883	1664-1847	5,8,9	1664-1815	1664-1812	Blofield	1664-1812		9L
Alburgh	A 1540-1978		5,8,9		1541-1753	Depwade			2I
Alby	A 1558-1983		5,8,9	1558-1983		Aylsham			7I
Aldborough	A 1538-1975	1538-1715	5,8,9	1725-1812	1538-1715	Erpingham			7H(Ek)
Aldeby	A 1558-1991		5,8,9			Loddon			3K
Alderford	A 1723-1836		5,8,9	1723-1836		StFaith's			5H(Ay)
Alpington (see Yelverton)			5,8,9			Loddon			8J
Anmer	A 1678-1987		5,8,9	1600-1837	1709-1835	Docking	1790-1837		7D
Antigham	A 1755-1987		5,8,9	1679-1812	1680-1754	Erpingham			7I
Arminghall	A 1570-1966		5,8,9	1560-1759	1570-1754	Henstead			9I
Ashby St Mary	A 1620-1992		4,5,6,8,9	1620-1874		Loddon			8K
Ashby with Oby (see Thurne)									10L
Ashill	A 1538-1979		5,8,9			Swaffham			4E
Ashmanhough	A 1562-1970	1562-1836	5,8,9	1562-1836	1563-1837	Tunstead			6J(Ob)
Ashwellthorpe	A 1558-1996		5,8,9			Depwade			3H(Oo)
Ashwicken with Leziate			5,8,9	1717-1815	1716-1837	Freebridge Lynn	1814-1835		6C
Aslacton	A 1556-1983		5,8,9			Depwade			2H(Ou)
Attleborough	A 1552-1913		5,8,9	1552-1840		Wayland			3G
Attlebridge	A 1712-1835		5,8,9	1712-1835		StFaith's			5H
Aylmerton	A 1696-1976		5,8,9	1696-1924		Erpingham			8H
Aylsham	A 1653-1960		5,8,9			Aylsham		1791-1837	6H
Babingley	A 1662-1981		5,8,9	1694-1805	1662-1812	Freebridge Lynn			6C
Baconsthorpe	A 1676-1993		5,8,9	1682-1812		Erpingham			7H
Bacton	A 1558-1919	1558-1812	5,8,9	1558-1812	1559-1812	Tunstead		1822-1837	7J
Bagthorp	A 1561-1997		5,8,9	1562-1837	1562-1837	Docking	1790-1837		7D(C)
Bale	A 1538-1998		5,8,9			Walsingham			7G
Banham	A 1558-1886		5,8,9			Guiltcross			2G
Banningham	A 1709-1984		5,8,9			Aylsham			6I(Eq)
Barford	A 1700-1837		5,8,9			Forehoe			4G
Barmer	A 1887-1975		5,8,9			Docking			7D
Barney	A 1538-1993		5,8,9	1538-1786		Walsingham			7F
Barnham Broom	A 1630-1921		5,8,9			Forehoe			4G
Barton Bendish									4C
St Andrew	A 1695-1902		5,8,9	1562-1837		Downham			4C
St Mary and All Saints	A 1726-1837		5,8,9	1691-1837		Downham			4C
Barton Turf	A 1558-1976		5,8,9	1558-1837	1558-1836	Tunstead	1790-1836		6J
Barwick (see Stanhoe)									7D
Bawburgh	A 1555-1948		5,8,9	1555-1871		Forehoe			4H
Bawdeswell	A 1557-1890		5,8,9			Mitford			6G
Bawsey	A 1539-1773	1539-1771	5,8,9	1539-1773	1539-1771	Freebridge Lynn	1539-1771		6C
Bedingham	A 1555-1992		5,8,9	1561-1871	1561-1812	Loddon	1790-1812		3I
Beechamwell	A 1558-1901		5,8,9	1558-1901		Swaffham	1790-1836		4D
Beeston next Mileham alias Bittering	A 1538-1954		5,8,9	1538-1753	1538-1753	Mitford			5E
Beeston Regis	A 1743-1993	1738-1812	5,8,9	1743-1853		Erpingham			8H
Beeston St Andrew (see Sprowston)									10J
Beeston St Lawrence	A 1558-1976	1558-1838	5,8,9	1558-1838	1558-1838	Tunstead			6J(Oc)
Beetley	A 1539-1986		4,5,6,7,8,9			Mitford			5F
Beighton	A 1589-1898		5,8,9		1589-1745	Blofield			9K
Belaugh	A 1538-2000		5,8,9			Aylsham			5J(Oa)
Bergh Apton	A 1556-1918		5,8,9	1556-1871	1556-1753	Loddon			8J
Bessingham	A 1695-1975		5,8,9	1695-1838		Erpingham			7H(Ef)
Besthorpe	A 1558-1918		5,8,9	1539-1871		Wayland			3G
Bexwell	A 1558-1837		5,8,9	1558-1871		Downham			4C
Billingford (nr Diss)	A 1640-1837		5,8,9		1640-1753	Depwade			1H
Billingford (nr Dereham)	A 1744-1975	1739-1740	5,8,9	1739-1740		Mitford			6G
Billockby	A 1561-1897		4,5,6,7,8,9	1561-1811	1561-1748	Flegg	1561-1748		10L
Binham	A 1559-1999			1559-1903		Walsingham			8F
Bintree	A 1558-1995		5,8,9	1558-1903		Mitford			6F
Bircham Newton	A 1744-1975	1562-1736	5,8,9	1562-1871	1562-1837	Docking	1790-1837		7D(B)
Bircham Tofts	A 1715-1956		5,8,9	1698-1837	1715-1837	Docking	1790-1837		7D
Bittering Parva (see Beeston with Bittering)									5F
Bixley	A 1561-1992		5,8,9	1563-1809	1561-1738	Henstead			9J
Blakeney alias Snitterly	A 1538-1986		5,8,9	1696-1789		Walsingham			8G
Blickling	A 1560-1994		5,8,9			Aylsham			6H
Blofield	A 1545-1961	1546-1812	5,8,9	1545-1901	1547-1786	Blofield			4J
Blo Norton	A 1562-1956		5,8,9	1562-1871		Guiltcross			1F
Bodham	A 1708-1992		5,8,9	1729-1812		Erpingham			8H
Bodney	A 1563-1998	1735-1740	5,8,9	1563-1837		Swaffham			3E
Booton	A 1558-1973		5,8,9	1560-1812	1560-1812	StFaith's	1790-1812		6H
Boughton	A 1729-1837		5,8,9	1691-1871		Downham			4C
Bowthorpe			5,8,9			Forehoe			4H
Bracon Ash	A 1563-1918		5,8,9	1814-1871		Henstead			3H(Og)
Bradfield	A 1725-1976	1725-1812	5,8,9	1725-1852	1725-1812	Tunstead		1692-1836	7I(Eo)
Bramerton	A 1561-1988		5,8,9	1551-1871	1566-1749	Henstead			9J
Brampton	A 1732-1991	1601-1812	5,8,9	1732-1812	1654-1812	Aylsham	1790-1812		6I(Et)
Brancaster	A 1538-2000		5,8,9	1814-1857	1538-1864	Docking			8D
Brandiston	A 1562-1979		5,8,9	1562-1902		StFaith's			6H(Ea)
Brandon Parva	A 1694-1839		5,8,9	1813-1871	1706-1808	Forehoe			4G(Aw)
Braydeston	A 1731-1837		5,8,9	1623-1812	1623-1812	Blofield	1623-1812		9K(g)
Breckles	A 1540-1837		5,8,9			Wayland			3F
Bressingham	A 1559-1972		5,8,9	1813-1857	1559-1753	Guiltcross			2G
Brettenham	A 1777-1993		5,8,9	1725-1871		Thetford			2E
Bridgham	A 1558-1993		5,8,9	1558-1930		Guiltcross			2F
Briningham	A 1709-1956		5,8,9	1719-1812		Walsingham			7G
Brinton	A 1547-1843		5,8,9	1706-1812		Erpingham			7G
Brisley	A 1698-2000		5,8,9			Mitford			6F

NORFOLK

parish name	deposited original registers	I.G.I.	local census indexes	copies of registers at Soc. Gen.	Boyd's marriage index	1837-1851 Registration District	Pallot's marriage index	non-conform. records at P.R.O.	map ref.
Briston	A 1689-1951		5,8,9	1813-1843	1559-1754	Erpingham		1786-1840	7G
Brockdish	A 1558-1984		5,8,9	1813-1856	1558-1812	Depwade			1H
Brooke	A 1558-1914		5,8,9	1761-1857	1538-1760	Loddon			3I
Broome	A 1538-1957		5,8,9	1563-1812	1566-1812	Loddon	1563-1812		3J
Brundall	A 1563-1971		5,8,9	1561-1949	1562-1837	Blofield			9K
Brunstead	A 1561-1949	1561-1845	5,8,9	1560-1857		Tunstead			6J(Od)
Buckenham St Nicholas alias Ferry	A 1714-1973		5,8,9			Blofield			9K
Buckenham Tofts or Parva (see West Tofts)									3E(O)
Bunwell			5,8,9	1813-1857		Depwade			3H
Burgh next Aylsham	A 1563-1997	1563-1662	5,8,9			Aylsham			6I(Es)
Burgh Parva	A 1594-1943		5,8,9			Erpingham			7G
Burgh St Margaret	A 1739-1973	1769-1770	4,5,6,7,8,9	1746-1863	1813-1837	Flegg	1813-1837		5K+10M
Burgh St Peter	A 1538-1992		5,8,9	1821-1857	1560-1812	Loddon			3K
Burlingham									9K
St Andrew	A 1538-1992		5,8,9	1538-1884	1540-1812	Blofield	1540-1812		10K(c)
St Andrew			5,8,9			Blofield			9M(D1)
St Edmund	A 1538-1836		5,8,9			Blofield			9K(e)
St Peter	A 1560-1932	1560-1875	5,8,9	1560-1884	1560-1812	Blofield	1560-1812		10K(d)
Burnham Deepdale	A 1539-1975	1538-1753	5,8,9	1538-1857	1539-1753	Docking			8E
Burnham Norton	A 1559-1987		5,8,9	1821-1848		Docking			8E
Burnham Overy	A 1653-1986		5,8,9	1838+1848		Docking			8E
Burnham Ulph and Sutton	A 1653-1987		5,8,9	1653-1848	1653-1837	Docking	1790-1837		8E
Burnham Thorpe	A 1559-1977		5,8,9	1819-1857		Docking			8E
Burnham Westgate	A 1538-1986		5,8,9	1848+1857		Docking		1810-1835	8E
Burston	A 1657-1983		5,8,9	1654-1814	1645-1753	Depwade			2H
Buxton	A 1665-1973		5,8,9	1600-1812		Aylsham		1804-1835	6I(Ev)
Bylaugh	A 1557-1836		5,8,9			Mitford			6G
Caister next Yarmouth	A 1563-1981		4,5,6,7,8,9	1550-1837	1563-1837	Flegg	1790-1837		5L
Caister St Edmund	A 1557-1846	1557-1879	5,8,9	1557-1719	1557-1810	Henstead			9I
Caldecote			5,8,9			Swaffham			4D(M)
Calthorpe	A 1539-1983		5,8,9	1558-1812	1558-1812	Aylsham	1558-1812		7H(E1)
Cantley	A 1558-1978	1569-1847	5,8,9	1813-1837		Blofield			9K
Carbrooke	A 1539-1996		5,8,9			Wayland			4F
Carleton Forehoe	A 1699-1969		5,8,9	1857		Forehoe			4G(Au)
Carleton Rode	A 1560-1962		5,8,9	1560-1812	1560-1812	Depwade	1790-1812		3G
Carleton St Peter	A 1540-1996		5,8,9			Loddon			8K
Castle Acre	A 1695-1960		5,8,9	1600-1813	1601-1813	Freebridge Lynn	1710-1812		5D
Castle Rising	A 1573-1976		5,8,9	1573-1840	1573-1837	Freebridge Lynn	1790-1837		6C
Caston	A 1538-1945	1538-1718	5,8,9	1539-1720	1539-1700	Wayland			3F
Catfield	A 1558-1984	1548-1837	5,8,9	1559-1837	1559-1837	Tunstead			6K
Catton (Old)	A 1668-1970		5,8,9	1688-1851		St Faith's			10I
Cawston	A 1538-1968		5,8,9			Aylsham			6H
Central Wingland (Lincs) (ex. par.)									6B
Chedgrave	A 1551-1991	1550-1812	5,8,9	1550-1842	1550-1812	Loddon	1550-1812		8K
Choseley (ex. par.)			5,8,9			Docking			8D(A)
Claxton	A 1747-1988	1691-1718	5,8,9	1691-1718		Loddon			9K
Clenchwarton	C 1720-1978		5,8,9			Wisbech			6B
Cley next the Sea	A 1538-1959		5,8,9	1539-1743		Erpingham			8G
Clippesby	A 1737-1977		4,5,6,7,8,9			Flegg			10L
Cockley Cley	A 1731-1996		5,8,9	1691-1861		Swaffham			4D
Cockthorpe	A 1560-1996		5,8,9	1560-1902		Walsingham			8F
Colby	A 1552-1984		5,8,9	1553-1812		Aylsham			7I
Colkirk	A 1539-1992		5,8,9			Mitford			6F
Colney	A 1741-1959		5,8,9	1705-1837		Henstead			9H
Coltishall	A 1558-1977		5,8,9	1558-1812	1558-1744	Aylsham			6I
Colton	A 1542-1993		5,8,9			Forehoe			4H
Colveston			5,8,9	1691-1837		Swaffham			3D(N)
Congham			5,8,9	1552-1837	1581-1837	Freebridge Lynn	1790-1837		6D
Corpusty	A 1718-1931		5,8,9	1730-1812		Aylsham			7H(Af)
Costessey	A 1538-1989		5,8,9	1538-1812		Forehoe			5H
Coston	A 1705-1968		5,8,9			Forehoe			4G(At)
Cranwich	A 1732-1836		5,8,9	1691-1837	1734-1753	Thetford			3D
Cranworth	A 1653-1980		5,8,9			Mitford			4F
Crimplesham	A 1561-1894	1561-1805	5,8,9			Downham			4C
Cringleford	A 1561-1968	1561-1854	5,8,9	1561-1854	1561-1837	Henstead	1790-1837		9H
Cromer	A 1689-1977		5,8,9			Erpingham			8I
Crostwick	A 1561-1834		5,8,9	1561-1753	1561-1753	St Faith's			10J
Crostwight	A 1698-1836	1698-1836	5,8,9	1698-1836	1712-1837	Tunstead			6J
Crownthorpe	A 1700-1966		5,8,9	1700-1920		Forehoe			4G(As)
Croxton	A 1558-1944		5,8,9	1727-1812	1564-1751	Thetford			2E
Denton	A 1559-1975		5,8,9		1559-1753	Depwade		1806-1837	2I
Denver	A 1670-1939		5,8,9		1540-1754	Downham			4B
Deopham with Hackford	A 1560-1983		5,8,9			Forehoe			4G
Dersingham	A 1653-1983		5,8,9	1653-1837	1653-1836	Docking	1790-1837		7C
Dickleburgh			5,8,9	1540-1754	1540-1754	Depwade			2H
Didlington	A 1717-1998		5,8,9	1691-1837	1730-1752	Swaffham			3D
Dilham	A 1563-1977	1563-1839	5,8,9	1563-1882	1563-1837	Tunstead			6J
Diss	A 1551-1915		5,8,9	1551-1837	1572-1754	Depwade		1761-1837	2H
Ditchingham	A 1559-1978		5,8,9	1559-1812	1559-1812	Loddon	1790-1812		3J
Docking	A 1813-1928		5,8,9	1558-1837	1558-1837	Docking	1790-1837		8D
Downham Market	A 1533-1956		5,8,9	1541-1726		Downham		1814-1837	4B
Drayton	A 1559-1874		5,8,9			St Faith's			5H
Dunston	A 1557-1985	1557-1885	5,8,9	1557-1837	1552-1811	Henstead			8I
Dunton cum Doughton	A 1784-1976		5,8,9	1784-1837	1784-1837	Walsingham	1790-1837		7E
Earlham St Mary	A 1622-1995		5,8,9	1621-1837	1559-1754	Norwich			4H

parish name	deposited original registers	I.G.I.	local census indexes	copies of registers at Soc. Gen.	Boyd's marriage index	1837-1851 Registration District	Pallot's marriage index	non-conform. records at P.R.O.	map ref.
Earsham	A 1559-1960		5,8,9			Depwade			2J
East Barsham	A 1657-1980		5,8,9	1658-1871	1658-1837	Walsingham	1790-1837		7F
East Beckham			5,8,9			Erpingham			8H
East Bilney	A 1713-1994		5,8,9			Mitford			6F(V)
East Bradenham	A 1695-1989		5,8,9	1691-1857		Swaffham			5F
East Carleton	A 1559-1998		5,8,9	1857		Henstead			4H
East Dereham	A 1549-1964		5,8,9			Mitford		1772-1837	5F
East Harling	A 1544-1993		5,8,9	1544-1730		Guiltcross			2F
East Lexham	A 1538-1974		5,8,9	1541-1812	1541-1812	Mitford	1541-1812		5E
Easton	A 1678-1926		5,8,9	1678-1903		Forehoe			5H
East Raynham	A 1627-1987		5,8,9	1627-1716	1601-1837	Walsingham	1790-1837		6E
East Rudham	A 1562-1980		5,8,9	1562-1837	1562-1837	Docking			7E
East Ruston	A 1558-1977		5,8,9	1558-1915	1558-1837	Tunstead			6J
East Somerton (see Winterton)									5L
East Tuddenham	A 1561-1968		5,8,9	1561-1752	1561-1747	Mitford			5G
East Walton	A 1560-1954	1560-1782	5,8,9	1560-1836	1562-1837	Freebridge Lynn	1790-1836		5D
East Winch	A 1678-1982		5,8,9	1690-1894	1690-1838	Freebridge Lynn	1790-1828		5C
East Wretham	A 1748-1985		5,8,9	1748-1891		Thetford			3E
Eaton St Andrew	A 1568-1989		5,8,9	1558-1812		Norwich			9I
Eccles	A 1538-1993		5,8,9	1538-1837		Guiltcross			2F
Edgefield	A 1653-1880		5,8,9	1730-1812		Erpingham			7G
Edingthorpe	A 1560-1845		5,8,9			Tunstead			7J
Edgmere			5,8,9			Walsingham			7E
Ellingham nr Bungay	A 1539-1993		5,8,9	1557-1810		Loddon			3J
Elsing	A 1558-1985		5,8,9			Mitford			5G
Emneth	C 1681-1968		5,8,9	1681-1968		Wisbech			4A
Erpingham	A 1559-1984		5,8,9			Aylsham			7I(Em)
Fakenham	A 1719-1988		5,8,9	1719-1910	1719-1837	Walsingham	1790-1837	1800-1837	7F
Felbrigg	A 1539-1997		5,8,9	1556-1812		Erpingham			8I
Felmingham	A 1754-1980		5,8,9	1725-1812		Tunstead			6I
Felthorpe	A 1712-1989		5,8,9	1723-1812		St Faith's			5H
Feltwell				1903					3C
Anchor (ex. par.)			5,8,9			Thetford			3B
St Mary	A 1562-1970		5,8,9			Thetford			3C
St Nicholas	A 1664-1970		5,8,9			Thetford			3C
Fersfield	A 1565-1970		5,8,9	1565-1735	1565-1754	Guiltcross			2G
Field Dalling	A 1538-1954	1538-1769	5,8,9			Walsingham			8G
Filby	A 1561-1987		4,5,6,7,8,9	1561-1837	1561-1837	Flegg	1790-1837		10M
Fincham, St Martin	A 1541-1931	1543-1812	5,8,9	1543-1812		Downham	1790-1812		4C
Fincham, St Michael	A 1585-1931		5,8,9	1587-1745		Downham			4C
Flitcham Cum Appleton	A 1755-1981		5,8,9	1755-1837	1755-1837	Freebridge Lynn	1790-1837		6D
Flordon	A 1559-1967		5,8,9	1558-1724		Henstead			3H
Fordham	A 1577-1836		5,8,9	1563-1837		Downham			4B
Forncett									3H
St Mary	A 1688-1976		5,8,9	1688-1812		Depwade			3H
St Peter	A 1561-1976		5,8,9	1561-1837		Depwade			3H
Foulden	A 1538-1997		5,8,9		1539-1753	Swaffham			4D
Foulsham	A 1558-1948		5,8,9	1559-1770		Aylsham		1815-1835	6G
Foxley	A 1700-1976		5,8,9			Mitford			6G
Framlington Earl	A 1721-1993	1707-1718	5,8,9	1707-1718	1721-1753	Henstead			8J(b)
Framlington Pigot	A 1553-1991		5,8,9		1553-1728	Henstead		1808-1836	9J(a)
Freethorpe	A 1755-1957		5,8,9			Blofield			9L
Frenze	A 1651-1978		5,8,9	1654-1877		Depwade			2H
Frettenham	A 1558-1906		5,8,9	1785-1881		St Faith's			5I
Fring	A 1671-1837		5,8,9	1700-1812	1700-1812	Docking	1790-1812		7D
Fritton	A 1558-1992		4,5,6,7,8,9	1558-1728		Depwade			3I
Fulmodeston cum Croxton	A 1556-1954		5,8,9	1727-1812		Walsingham			7F
Fundenhall	A 1559-1905		5,8,9			Depwade			3H
Garboldisham	A 1609-1986		5,8,9	1609-1881		Guiltcross			2F
Garveston	A 1538-1959		5,8,9	1813-1900		Mitford			4G(An)
Gasthorpe (see Riddlesworth with Gasthorpe)					1729-1742				2F
Gateley	A 1682-1996		5,8,9	1682-1812		Mitford			6F
Gayton	A 1701-1972		5,8,9	1702-1837	1702-1837	Freebridge Lynn	1790-1837		6D
Gayton Thorpe	A 1813-1817		5,8,9	1575-1837	1575-1837	Freebridge Lynn	1790-1837		6D
Gaywood	A 1654-1978		5,8,9	1653-1837	1653-1837	Freebridge Lynn	1790-1837		6C
Geldeston	A 1657-1993		5,8,9			Loddon			3J
Gillingham	A 1540-1993		5,8,9			Loddon			3K
Gimingham	A 1558-1962	1558-1845	5,8,9	1558-1845	1558-1837	Erpingham			7J
Gissing	A 1539-1992	1691-1796	5,8,9	1540-1968	1562-1753	Depwade			2H
Glandford with Bayfield	A 1654-1996		5,8,9	1687-1812		Erpingham			8G
Gooderstone	A 1702-1996		5,8,9	1563-1837		Swaffham			4D
Gorleston (Suffolk)			4,5,6,7,8,9						9M
Great Bircham	A 1669-1979		5,8,9	1669-1871	1669-1837	Docking			7D
Great Cressingham	A 1557-1995		5,8,9	1557-1812	1557-1812	Swaffham	1790-1812		4E
Great Dunham	A 1538-1992		5,8,9	1538-1812	1538-1812	Mitford	1538-1812		5E
Great Ellingham	A 1630-1980	1657-1853	5,8,9	1817-1837		Wayland		1817-1837	3G
Great Fransham	A 1559-1962		5,8,9			Mitford			5E
Great Hautbois	A 1563-1946		5,8,9			Aylsham			6I(Ex)
Great Massingham	A 1564-1981		5,8,9	1564-1837	1564-1837	Freebridge Lynn	1790-1836		6D
Great Melton	A 1538-1991		5,8,9			Henstead			4H
Great Plumstead	A 1558-1891		5,8,9	1558-1807		Blofield			5I
Great Ryburgh	A 1547-1965		5,8,9	1547-1965	1547-1837	Walsingham			6F
Great Snarehill			5,8,9			Thetford			2E
Great Snoring	A 1560-1996		5,8,9	1563-1837	1560-1837	Walsingham	1790-1837		7F
Great Walsingham	A 1558-1997		5,8,9	1558-1901		Walsingham			7F
Great Witchingham	A 1539-1858		5,8,9	1836+1885	1539-1752	St Faith's			5G
Great Yarmouth	A 1558-1962	1559-1689	4,5,6,7,8,9	1558-1901	1558-1758	Yarmouth		1706-1837	4L
Gresham	A 1559-1962	1559-1783	5,8,9	1559-1812	1690-1812	Erpingham	1790-1812		7H

NORFOLK

parish name	deposited original registers	I.G.I.	local census indexes	copies of registers at Soc. Gen.	Boyd's marriage index	1837-1851 Registration District	Pallot's marriage index	non-conform. records at P.R.O.	map ref.
Gressenhall			5,8,9			Mitford			5F
Grimstone			5,8,9	1552-1837	1552-1837	Freebridge Lynn	1790-1837		6C
Griston	A 1654-1964		5,8,9			Wayland			3F
Guestwick	A 1558-1965		5,8,9			Aylsham		1786-1840	6G
Guist	A 1557-1958		5,8,9	1557-1877		Mitford			6F
Gunthorpe	A 1558-1998		5,8,9	1540-1910		Walsingham			7G(Ab)
Gunton	A 1723-1973		4,5,6,8,9	1723-1963		Erpingham			7I
Hackford nr Wymondham	A 1689-1982		5,8,9			Forehoe			4G(Ar)
Hackford with Whitwell	A 1559-1935		5,8,9	1559-1901		Aylsham		1805-1837	6G(Aj)
Haddiscoe	A 1558-1950		5,8,9	1655-1753		Loddon			3K
Hainford	A 1556-1980		5,8,9			StFaith's			5I
Hales	A 1674-1967		5,8,9	1674-1907		Loddon			3J
Halvergate	A 1550-1908		5,8,9	1550-1784		Blofield			9L
Hanworth	A 1721-1990		5,8,9	1727-1812		Erpingham			7I
Happisburgh	A 1558-1924	1558-1837	5,8,9	1558-1837	1558-1837	Tunstead			7K
Hapton	A 1653-1973		5,8,9			Depwade		1803-1834	3H(Op)
Hardingham	A 1558-1939		5,8,9			Mitford			4G
Hardley	A 1715-1995	1707-1875	5,8,9	1708-1714		Loddon			8K
Hardwick	A 1561-1992		5,8,9	1516-1812		Depwade			2I(Ow)
Hargham	A 1561-1953		5,8,9	1561-1741		Wayland			3G
Harpley	A 1722-1867		5,8,9			Freebridge Lynn			6D
Hassingham	A 1563-1949		5,8,9			Blofield			9K
Haveringland	A 1694-1993		5,8,9	1600-1837		St Faith's			6H
Heacham	A 1558-1861		5,8,9	1558-1812	1558-1812	Docking	1558-1812		7C
Heckingham	A 1559-1993		5,8,9	1560-1875	1559-1812	Loddon			8L
Hedenham	A 1559-1993		5,8,9	1559-1812	1559-1812	Loddon	1790-1812		3J
Heigham	A 1563-1812		5,8,9	1538-1840		Norwich			9I
Helhoughton	A 1539-1985		5,8,9	1539-1921	1539-1837	Walsingham	1790-1837		6E
Hellesdon	A 1562-1994		5,8,9			Norwich/St Faith's			5I
Hellington	A 1563-1980		5,8,9	1562-1812		Loddon			8J
Hemblington	A 1562-1963		5,8,9	1563-1833	1564-1812	Blofield	1564-1812		10K
Hempnall	A 1560-1954		5,8,9	1560-1908		Depwade			3I
Hempstead by Holt	A 1558-1992		5,8,9	1558-1839		Erpingham			7H
Hempstead with Eccles	A 1707-2000		5,8,9	1707-1837	1707-1837	Tunstead			6K
Hempton	A 1856-1981		5,8,9			Walsingham			7E(X)
Hemsby	A 1556-1971	1556-1812	4,5,6,7,8,9	1556-1837	1556-1837	Flegg	1790-1837		5L
Hethel	A 1710-1835		5,8,9	1812-1814		Henstead			4H
Hethersett	A 1615-1984		5,8,9	1617-1838		Henstead			4H
Hevingham	A 1648-1975		5,8,9	1600-1839		Aylsham			6H
Heydon	A 1538-1994		5,8,9			Aylsham			6H
Hickling	A 1653-1976		5,8,9	1653-1871	1657-1812	Tunstead	1790-1812		6K
Hilborough	A 1561-1954		5,8,9	1813-1873		Swaffham			4D
Hilgay	A 1583-1877		5,8,9	1583-1760	1583-1760	Downham			3B
Hillington			5,8,9	1695-1837	1695-1837	Freebridge Lynn	1790-1837		6D
Hindolveston	A 1693-1932		5,8,9	1693-1784		Aylsham			7G
Hindringham	A 1660-1992		5,8,9			Walsingham			7F
Hingham	A 1600-1969		5,8,9	1600-1912	1600-1645	Forehoe			4G
Hockering	A 1561-1987		5,8,9	1561-1781	1561-1754	Mitford			5G
Hockham Gr. & Lt.	A 1563-1986		5,8,9	1721-1870		Wayland			3F
Hockwold cum Wilton	A 1640-1968		5,8,9	1640-1873	1662-1837	Thetford			2C
Hoe	A 1547-1994		5,8,9			Mitford			5F
Holkham	A 1542-1986		5,8,9	1542-1812	1542-1812	Walsingham	1542-1812		8E
Holme Hale	A 1538-1999		5,8,9	1539-1873	1539-1837	Swaffham	1790-1837		4E
Holme Next Sea	A 1704-1991	1698-1867	5,8,9	1705-1812	1704-1811	Docking	1790-1812		8C
Holt	A 1557-1969	1557-1695	5,8,9			Erpingham		1815-1837	7G
Holverston			5,8,9			Henstead			8J
Honing	A 1630-1981	1630-1836	5,8,9	1630-1908	1630-1836	Tunstead			6J
Honingham	A 1561-1995		5,8,9	1563-1727		St Faith's			5H
Horning	A 1558-1967		5,8,9	1559-1877	1558-1754	Tunstead			5J
Horningtoft	A 1539-1998		5,8,9	1539-1837	1539-1837	Mitford	1790-1837		6F
Horsey	A 1559-1964	1559-1824	5,8,9	1559-1964		Tunstead			6K
Horsford	A 1597-1999		5,8,9	1597-1972		St Faith's			5H
Horsham St Faith cum Newton			5,8,9			St Faith's			5I
Horstead with Staininghall	A 1558-1911		5,8,9	1558-1811	1558-1812	St Faith's	1790-1812		5I
Houghton next Harpley	A 1654-1988		5,8,9	1654-1905		Docking			7D
Houghton St Giles next Walsingham	A 1559-1997		5,8,9	1559-1902		Walsingham			7F
Houghton on the Hill	A 1695-1935		5,8,9	1813-1851		Swaffham			4E(Q)
Hoveton									5J
St John	A 1673-1971		5,8,9	1673-1914		Tunstead			5J
St Peter	A 1562-1994		5,8,9	1624-1905		Tunstead			5J
Howe	A 1602-1993	1708-1718	5,8,9	1708-1718	1607-1812	Loddon			3I(Om)
Hunstanton (old)	A 1538-1906		5,8,9	1538-1810		Docking			8C
Hunworth	A 1538-1835		5,8,9	1729-1812		Erpingham			7G(Ad)
Ickburgh	A 1755-1962		5,8,9	1693-1836		Swaffham			3D
Illington	A 1673-1972		5,8,9	1672-1871		Wayland			3F
Ingham	A 1800-1990	1713-1838	5,8,9	1713-1856	1801-1838	Tunstead		1770-1837	6K
Ingoldesthorpe	A 1754-1994		5,8,9	1739-1838	1754-1837	Docking	1790-1837		7C
Ingworth	A 1559-1983		5,8,9	1559-1812	1558-1812	Aylsham	1559-1812		7I(En)
Intwood with Keswick	A 1538-1991		5,8,9	1538-1726		Henstead			9H
Irmingland (see Heydon)									7H(Ag)
Irstead	A 1538-1976		5,8,9	1538-1627		Tunstead			5J
Islington	C 1559-1955		5,8,9			Wisbech			5B
Itteringham	A 1558-1946		5,8,9	1717-1812		Aylsham			7H(Eb)
Kelling	A 1558-1991		5,8,9			Erpingham			8G
Kempostone	A 1721-1946		5,8,9			Mitford			5E(R)
Kenninghall	A 1558-1973		5,8,9	1558-1727		Guiltcross			2G
Keswick (see Intwood)									9I

parish name	deposited original registers	I.G.I.	local census indexes	copies of registers at Soc. Gen.	Boyd's marriage index	1837-1851 Registration District	Pallot's marriage index	non-conform. records at P.R.O.	map ref.
Ketteringham	A 1695-1952		5,8,9	1695-1733		Henstead			4H
Kettlestone	A 1540-1989		5,8,9	1725-1812		Walsingham			7F
Kilverstone	A 1558-1982		5,8,9			Thetford			2E
Kimberley	A 1753-1837		5,8,9	1739-1740		Forehoe			4G
King's Lynn								1754-1857	6B
St Margaret	A 1559-1990		5,8,9	1559-1838		King's Lynn			6B(F)
St Nicholas	A 1562-1990		5,8,9	1562-1931		King's Lynn			6B(E)
Kirby Bedon	A 1558-1982		5,8,9	1856	1568-1753	Henstead			9J
Kirby Cane	A 1539-1996		5,8,9	1856		Loddon			3J
Kirstead	A 1663-1976		5,8,9			Loddon			3I(On)
Knapton	A 1687-1956	1687-1836	5,8,9	1687-1836	1687-1837	Erpingham			7J
Lakenham (Old) St John	A 1568-1990		5,8,9	1568-1902		Norwich		1826-1837	9I
Lamas with Little Hautbois	A 1539-1975	1539-1835	5,8,9	1539-1723	1539-1723	Aylsham			6I(Ew)
Langford	A 1755-1963			1692-1705		Swaffham			3D
Langham	A 1695-1999		5,8,9	1695-1880	1710-1812	Walsingham	1790-1812		8G
Langley	A 1695-2000		5,8,9	1695-1812	1701-1812	Loddon	1695-1812		8K
Larling	A 1678-1986		5,8,9	1678-1839		Wayland			3F
Lessingham	A 1557-1996	1557-1837	5,8,9	1557-1837	1557-1837	Tunstead	1557-1812		6K
Letheringsett	A 1653-1996	1601-1759	5,8,9	1601-1812	1662-1752	Erpingham			8G
Letton (see Cranworth)									4F
Leziate (see Ashwicken)									6C
Limpenhoe	A 1662-1978		5,8,9	1662-1793		Blofield			8L
Lingwood	A 1560-1996		5,8,9	1561-1838		Blofield			9K
Litcham	A 1554-1974		5,8,9	1555-1812	1555-1812	Mitford	1555-1812		6E
Little Barningham	A 1558-1929		5,8,9	1717-1812		Aylsham			7H
Little Cressingham	A 1692-1996		5,8,9	1691-1837		Swaffham			4E
Little Dunham	A 1562-1940		5,8,9			Mitford			5E
Little Ellingham	A 1649-1980	1649-1860	5,8,9			Wayland			3F
Little Fransham	A 1538-1984		5,8,9			Mitford			5E
Little Massingham	A 1558-1834		5,8,9	1559-1837	1539-1837	Freebridge Lynn	1790-1837		6D
Little Melton	A 1734-1991		5,8,9	1724-1837		Henstead			4H(Of)
Little Plumstead	A 1559-1892		5,8,9	1559-1724		Blofield			5J
Little Ryburgh	A 1689-1946		5,8,9	1688-1946	1695-1749	Walsingham			6F(Aa)
Little Snarehill			5,8,9			Thetford			2E
Little Snoring	A 1559-1999		5,8,9		1559-1837	Walsingham	1790-1837		7F
Little Walsingham	A 1558-1971		5,8,9	1558-1901		Walsingham		1812-1837	7F(Y)
Little Witchingham	A 1565-1834		5,8,9	1836	1565-1753	St Faith's			6H(Az)
Loddon	A 1556-1986		5,8,9			Loddon			3J
Longham	A 1560-1837	1560-1877	5,8,9	1560-1900		Mitford			5F
Ludham	A 1583-1990		5,8,9	1903-1904		Tunstead			5J
Lynford			5,8,9			Thetford			3D
Lyng	A 1538-1933		5,8,9			Mitford			5G
Mannington			5,8,9			Aylsham			7H(Ae)
Marham	A 1562-1969		5,8,9	1562-1730		Downham			5C
Markshall (see Caistor St Edmund)									9I
Marlingford	A 1558-1969		5,8,9			Forehoe			4H(Oe)
Marsham	A 1538-1976	1538-1837	5,8,9	1538-1836	1538-1837	Aylsham	1790-1837		6H
Martham		1559-1834	4,5,6,7,8,9		1559-1838	Flegg			5K
Matlaske	A 1558-1990		5,8,9	1558-1812		Erpingham			7H(Ee)
Mattishall			5,8,9		1653-1753	Mitford		1772-1837	5G
Mattishall Burgh	A 1653-1776		5,8,9	1812-1868		Mitford			5G(Al)
Mautby	A 1663-1993	1600-1834	4,5,7,8,9	1600-1834	1663-1834	Flegg	1790-1834		10M
Melton Constable	A 1561-1945		5,8,9			Walsingham			7G
Merton	A 1564-1835		5,8,9			Wayland			3E
Methwold	A 1683-1968		5,8,9	1683-1726		Thetford			3C
Metton	A 1738-1994		5,8,9	1731-1812		Erpingham			7I(Eg)
Middleton	A 1560-1947		5,8,9	1560-1839	1560-1837	Freebridge Lynn	1790-1839		5C
Mileham	A 1538-1991		5,8,9		1540-1753	Mitford			6F
Mintlyn (see Gaywood)									6C
Moreton-on-Hill	A 1559-1837		5,8,9	1559-1837		St Faith's			5H
Moreley St Botolph	A 1539-1980		5,8,9			Forehoe			4G(Aq)
Moreley St Peter	A 1562-1982		5,8,9			Forehoe			3G
Morningthorpe	A 1557-1991		5,8,9	1557-1727		Depwade			3I
Morston	A 1538-2000		5,8,9	1689-1915		Walsingham			8G
Moulton St Mary	A 1539-1975		4,5,8,9	1539-1906	1531-1752	Blofield			9L
Moulton St Michael	A 1557-1878		4,5,8,9			Depwade			2H
Mulbarton	A 1547-1862		5,8,9		1547-1732	Henstead			4H
Mundford	A 1699-1948		5,8,9	1699-1739	1700-1754	Thetford			3D
Mundham	A 1559-1965		5,8,9		1559-1812	Loddon			3J
Mundesley	A 1724-1979	1702-1812	5,8,9	1724-1812	1726-1812	Erpingham	1790-1812		7J
Narburgh	A 1558-1984	1558-1811	5,8,9	1538-1812	1558-1812	Swaffham	1558-1812		5D
Narford	A 1596-1912		5,8,9	1559-1811	1599-1811	Swaffham	1559-1812		5D
Neatishead	A 1676-1976		5,8,9	1676-1727		Tunstead		1801-1837	5J
Necton	A 1558-1995		5,8,9	1558-1812		Swaffham			5E
Needham	A 1643-1975		5,8,9	1644-1750	1644-1750	Depwade			2I
New Buckenham	A 1538-1579		5,8,9	1813-1857		Guiltcross		1812-1837	3G(Ot)
Newton by Castle Acre	A 1559-1989		5,8,9	1559-1822		Swaffham			5E
Newton Flotman	A 1759-1992		5,8,9		1561-1724	Henstead			3I(Oh)
North Barningham	A 1538-1956		5,8,9	1538-1956	1558-1753	Erpringham			7H
North Barsham	A 1557-1977		5,8,9	1726-1871	1557-1837	Walsingham	1790-1837		7E
North Creake	A 1538-1962		5,8,9	1538-1841		Aylsham			8E
North Elmham	A 1538-1982	1538-1858	5,8,9	1538-1934	1538-1631	Mitford			6F
North Lopham	A 1558-1972		5,8,9		1561-1753	Guiltcross			2G
North Lynn	A 1826-1845		5,8,9			King's Lynn			6B(D)
North Pickenham	A 1678-1995		5,8,9			Swaffham			4E
North Repps			5,8,9	1725-1811		Erpingham			8I
North Runcton	A 1563-1988		5,8,9	1563-1903	1563-1837	Freebridge Lynn	1790-1836		5C
North Tuddenham	A 1560-1959		5,8,9	1560-1753		Mitford			5G

NORFOLK

parish name	deposited original registers	I.G.I.	local census indexes	copies of registers at Soc. Gen.	Boyd's marriage index	1837-1851 Registration District	Pallot's marriage index	non-conform. records at P.R.O.	map ref.
North Walsham		1541-1837	5,7,8,9	1541-1837	1541-1837	Erpingham		1822-1837	7I
Northwold	A 1656-1967		5,8,9	1656-1827		Thetford			3C
North Wotton	A 1654-1947		5,8,9	1655-1837	1655-1837	Freebridge Lynn	1790-1837		6B
Norton Subcourse	A 1560-1991		5,8,9	1560-1873		Loddon			8L
Norwich								1691-1856	9I
All Saints	A 1573-1965	1573-1880	5,8,9			Norwich			9I
Cathedral		1697-1811	5,8,9	1697-1812	1697-1812	Norwich	1607-1754		9I
St Andrew	A 1558-1959	1558-1812	5,8,9			Norwich	1780-1837		9I
St Augustine	A 1559-1992	1558-1875	5,8,9	1558-1859		Norwich			9I
St Benedict	A 1562-1942	1562-1812	5,8,9	1562-1840		Norwich			9I
St Clement	A 1538-1973	1538-1875	5,8,9			Norwich			9I
St Edmund	A 1550-1932	1561-1875	5,8,9			Norwich			9I
St Etheldreda	A 1665-1961	1668-1885	5,8,9			Norwich			9I
St George at Colegate	A 1538-1932	1538-1875	5,8,9	1538-1838	1538-1707(?)	Norwich	1813-1819		9I
St George at Tombland	A 1538-1960	1538-1856	5,8,9	1538-1854	1538-1707(?)	Norwich			9I
St Giles	A 1538-1968	1538-1850	5,8,9	1538-1841		Norwich			9I
St Gregory	A 1571-1974	1571-1813	5,8,9			Norwich			9I
St Helen	A 1708-1856	1708-1841	5,8,9	1678-1856		Norwich			9I
St James with Pockthorpe	A 1556-1969	1556-1841	5,8,9	1556-1856		Norwich			9I
St John de Sepulchre	A 1632-1982	1632-1875	5,8,9			Norwich			9I
St John Maddermarket	A 1557-1973		5,8,9			Norwich			9I
St John of Timberhill	A 1559-1911	1559-1875	5,8,9			Norwich			9I
St Julian	A 1589-1941	1589-1812	5,8,9			Norwich			9I
St Lawrence	A 1558-1956		5,8,9			Norwich			9I
St Margaret	A 1559-1972		5,8,9	1559-1840		Norwich			9I
St Martin at Oak	A 1560-1954	1560-1875	5,8,9	1560-1873		Norwich			9I
St Martin at Palace	A 1538-1964	1538-1855	5,8,9	1538-1838		Norwich			9I
St Mary at Coslany	A 1557-1942	1557-1812	5,8,9	1557-1837	1557-1812	Norwich	1790-1812		9I
St Mary in the Marsh	A 1591-1973	1591-1812	5,8,9		1558-1812	St Faiths			9I
St Michael at Coslany	A 1558-1972	1558-1875	5,8,9	1558-1696		Norwich			9I
St Michael at Plea	A 1538-1961	1538-1812	5,8,9	1538-1837	1539-1700	Norwich			9I
St Michael at Thorn		1608-1812	5,8,9			Norwich			9I
St Paul	A 1785-1943	1614-1812	5,8,9			Norwich			9I
St Peter Hungate	A 1597-1901		5,8,9	1602-1812		Norwich			9I
St Peter of Mancroft	A 1538-1997	1538-1880	5,8,9	1538-1738		Norwich			9I
St Peter per Mountage	A 1538-1979	1538-1900	5,8,9	1538-1904		Norwich			9I
St Peter Southgate	A 1558-1882	1558-1882	5,8,9			Norwich			9I
St Saviour	A 1555-1967	1555-1812	5,8,9	1555-1856		Norwich			9I
St Simon and St Jude	A 1539-1894	1539-1864	5,8,9	1539-1864		Norwich			9I
St Stephen	A 1538-1914	1538-1812	5,8,9	1538-1904	1538-1722	Norwich			9I
St Swithin	A 1700-1951		5,8,9			Norwich			9I
Old Buckenham	A 1560-1986	1560-1649	5,8,9	1537-1857	1560-1649	Guiltcross			3G
Ormsby St Margaret with Scratby	A 1675-1971		4,5,6,7,8,9	1601-1837	1601-1837	Flegg	1790-1837		5L
Ormsby St Michael	A 1568-1948		4,5,6,7,8,9	1591-1837	1591-1837	Flegg	1790-1837		10M
Oulton	A 1706-1887		5,6,8,9			Aylsham		1725-1837	6H
Outwell	C 1559-1903		5,8,9			Wisbech			4A
Overstrand	A 1558-1966		5,8,9	1725-1812		Erpingham			8I
Ovington	A 1654-1941		5,8,9			Wayland			4F
Oxborough	A 1538-1998	1538-1743	5,8,9	1538-1743	1538-1743	Swaffham			4D
Oxnead	A 1574-1998		5,8,9	1573-1783		Aylsham			6I(Eu)
Oxwick & Pattesley	A 1538-1939		5,8,9			Mitford			6E(W)
Palling	A 1616-1994	1616-1812	5,8,9	1616-1994	1616-1676	Tunstead			6K
Paston	A 1538-1988	1538-1812	5,8,9	1538-1812		Tunstead			7J
Pensthorpe			5,8,9			Walsingham			7F(Z)
Pentney	A 1731-1986		5,8,9	1731-1837	1731-1837	Freebridge Lynn	1790-1837		5C
Plumstead by Holt	A 1551-1993		5,8,9	1559-1811		Erpingham			7H
Pockthorpe			5,8,9			Norwich			9I
Poringland	A 1560-1992		5,8,9			Henstead			4I
Postwick	A 1570-1807		5,8,9			Blofield			9J
Potter Heigham	A 1538-1976		5,8,9			Tunstead			5K
Pudding Norton			5,8,9			Walsingham			6F
Pulham				1813-1868					2H
St Mary Magdalene	A 1538-1965		5,8,9		1539-1753	Depwade			2H
St Mary The Virgin	A 1539-1890		5,8,9	1539-1754		Depwade			2I
Quarles (ex. par.)			5,8,9			Walsingham			8E
Quidenham	A 1538-1992		5,8,9	1538-1725		Guiltcross			2G
Rackheath	A 1646-1992		5,8,9	1645-1837		StFaith's			5I
Ranworth with Panxworth	A 1559-1915		5,8,9	1558-1915	1559-1812	Blofield	1790-1813		5J
Raveningham	A 1678-1992		5,8,9			Loddon			3K
Redenhall with Harleston & Wortwell	A 1558-1906		5,8,9			Depwade			2I
Redmere (ex. par.)			5,8,9			Thetford			2B
Reedham	A 1754-1976	1691-1837	5,8,9	1691-1709	1558-1753	Blofield			8L
Reepham with Kerdiston	A 1538-1992		5,8,9	1538-1903		Aylsham		1805-1827	6G
Repps with Bastwick	A 1563-1835	1563-1733	5,8,9	1563-1811		Flegg			5K
Reymerston	A 1559-1913		5,8,9			Mitford			4G
Riddlesworth with Gasthorpe	A 1686-1995		5,8,9		1688-1739	Guiltcross			2F
Ridlington	A 1559-1838	1559-1838	5,8,9	1559-1838	1559-1837	Tunstead			7J
Ringland	A 1559-1990		5,8,9			St Faith's			5H
Ringstead St Andrew	A 1575-1988		5,8,9	1813-1905		Docking			8C
Ringstead St Peter	A 1547-1812		5,8,9			Docking			8C
Rockland All Saints & St Andrew	A 1697-1984		5,8,9			Wayland			3F
Rockland St Mary	A 1558-1989		5,8,9	1539-1744		Henstead			9J
Rockland St Peter	A 1538-1984		5,8,9			Wayland		1835-1837	3F(Ap)
Rollesby	A 1558-1983		4,5,6,7,8,9			Flegg			5K

parish name	deposited original registers	I.G.I.	local census indexes	copies of registers at Soc. Gen.	Boyd's marriage index	1837-1851 Registration District	Pallot's marriage index	non-conform. records at P.R.O.	map ref.
Roudham	A 1663-1922		5,8,9	1663-1922		Wayland			2F
Rougham	A 1538-1967	1769-1770	5,8,9	1769-1770		Mitford			6E
Roughton	A 1562-1995		5,8,9	1562-1837	1563-1837	Erpingham			7I
Roxham (see Ryston)						Downham			4C(L)
Roydon nr Lynn			5,8,9		1721-1837	Freebridge Lynn	1790-1827(?)		6C
Roydon nr Diss	A 1559-1992		5,8,9	1559-1837	1559-1753	Guiltcross	1790-1827(?)		2G
Runcton Holme	A 1562-1957		5,8,9	1901-1903		Downham			5B
Runhall	A 1558-1997		5,8,9			Forehoe			4G
Runham	A 1539-1970	1539-1812	4,5,6,7,8,9	1538-1902	1539-1812	Flegg	1790-1812		10M
Runton	A 1743-1972		5,8,9	1743-1924		Erpingham			8I
Rushall	A 1561-1975		5,8,9	1562-1732	1562-1754	Depwade			2H
Rushford	A 1586-1837		5,8,9			Thetford			2E
Ryston	A 1687-1925		5,8,9	1687-1837		Downham			4B(K)
Saham Toney	A 1547-1981		5,8,9			Swaffham			4E
Salhouse	A 1561-1918		5,8,9			St Faith's		1802-1837	5J
Salle	A 1558-1992		5,8,9	1558-1812		Aylsham			6H
Salthouse	A 1538-1996		5,8,9			Erpingham			8G
Sandringham	A 1557-1993		5,8,9	1561-1812	1561-1812	Freebridge Lynn	1561-1812		7C
Santon	D 1770-1976		5,8,9	1707-1837	1780-1790	Thetford			2D
Saxlingham by Holt	A 1558-1995		5,8,9	1558-1905		Walsingham			8G
Saxlingham Thorpe and Nethergate	A 1557-1979	1556-1812	5,8,9	1556-1790	1558-1812	Henstead		1813-1836	3I
Saxthorpe	A 1559-1974		5,8,9	1695-1805		Aylsham			7H
Scarning	A 1538-1991		5,8,9			Mitford			5F
Scole	A 1561-1993		5,8,9		1563-1752	Depwade			1H
Sco Ruston	A 1707-1968	1707-1835	5,8,9	1707-1908	1726-1835	Tunstead			6J(Ey)
Scottow	A 1549-1971		5,8,9			Aylsham			6I
Scoulton	A 1550-1987		5,8,9			Wayland			4F
Sculthorpe	A 1561-1972		5,8,9	1561-1836	1563-1837	Walsingham	1790-1837		7E
Sedgford	A 1560-1975		5,8,9	1560-1837	1560-1837	Docking	1790-1837		7D
Seething	A 1561-1986		5,8,9		1561-1812	Loddon			3J
Sharrington	A 1672-1998	1672-1812	5,8,9	1672-1812		Walsingham			7G(Ac)
Shelfanger	A 1686-1971		5,8,9	1686-1837	1686-1837	Guiltcross		1814-1837	2G
Shelton	A 1557-1991	1597-1830	5,8,9	1557-1812		Depwade			3I
Shereford	A 1721-1988		5,8,9	1711-1837	1722-1837	Walsingham	1790-1837		7E
Shernborne	A 1749-1987		5,8,9	1755-1838	1755-1837	Docking	1790-1837		7D
Shimpling	A 1538-1955		5,8,9		1538-1753	Depwade			2H(Oz)
Shingham	A 1762-1836		5,8,9	1691-1837		Swaffham	1790-1837		4D
Shipdham	A 1558-1991		4,5,8,9	1558-1804		Mitford		1833-1837	4F
Shotesham									3I
All Saints	A 1538-1978		5,8,9	1561-1753		Henstead			3I(Ol)
St Mary	A 1687-1835		5,8,9	1687-1781	1687-1775	Henstead			3I(Ok)
Shouldham	A 1653-1994		5,8,9	1653-1725	1561-1751	Downham			5C
Shouldham Thorpe	A 1558-1994		5,8,9			Downham			5C
Shropham	A 1721-1985		5,8,9	1721-1918		Wayland			3F
Sidestrand		1558-1858	5,8,9	1735-1858		Erpingham			8I
Sisland	A 1584-2000		5,8,9		1584-1812	Loddon	1790-1837		8K
Skeyton	A 1706-1969		5,8,9			Aylsham			6I
Sloley	A 1560-1992		5,8,9	1560-1812		Tunstead			6J(Ez)
Smallburgh	A 1561-1970	1561-1812	5,8,9	1561-1837		Tunstead			6J
Snetterton	A 1669-1976		5,8,9	1669-1932		Wayland			3F
Snettisham	A 1682-1972		5,8,9	1682-1812	1682-1812	Docking	1582-1812		7C
South Acre	A 1572-1890		5,8,9	1576-1812	1576-1812	Swaffham	1576-1812		5D
Southburgh	A 1558-1958		5,8,9			Mitford			4F(Ao)
South Creake	A 1539-1991	1538-1840	5,8,9	1538-1841	1550-1837	Docking	1790-1837	1786-1853	7E
Southery	A 1706-1974		5,8,9		1706-1751	Downham			3B
South Lopham	A 1557-1998		5,8,9		1561-1753	Guiltcross			2G
South Lynn All Saints	A 1558-1965		5,8,9			King's Lynn			5B
South Pickenham	A 1694-1836		5,8,9			Swaffham			4E
South Raynham	A 1740-1987		5,8,9	1601-1837	1601-1837	Walsingham	1790-1837		6E
Southrepps	A 1558-1937		5,8,9	1725-1812		Erpingham			7I
South Runcton (see Runcton Holme)									5C(J)
South Walsham									10K
St Lawrence	A 1550-1959	1550-1756	5,8,9	1550-1756	1550-1756	Blofield			10K
St Lawrence			5,8,9			Blofield			9M(D5)
St Mary	A 1550-1936	1550-1743	5,8,9	1551-1743	1550-1750	Blofield			10K
Southwood	A 1630-1885		5,8,9			Blofield			9L(f)
South Wootton	A 1556-1973		5,8,9	1556-1837	1557-1837	Freebridge Lynn	1790-1837		6C
Sparham	A 1573-1969		5,8,9			Mitford			6G
Spixworth	A 1551-1973		5,8,9		1554-1753	St Faith's			10I
Sporle with Palgrave			5,8,9			Swaffham			5E
Sprowston with Beeston	A 1721-1973		5,8,9	1690-1838		St Faith's			10I
Stalham	A 1560-1995		5,8,9	1562-1742		Tunstead			6J
Stanfield	A 1560-1999		5,8,9			Mitford			6F
Stanford with Sturston	A 1755-1942		5,8,9	1699-1911		Swaffham			3E
Stanhoe with Barwick	A 1558-1982		5,8,9	1567-1837	1567-1837	Docking	1790-1859		7D
Starston	A 1558-1971		5,8,9	1561-1753	1561-1753	Depwade			2I
Stibbard	A 1733-1989		5,8,9	1691-1978		Walsingham			6F
Stiffkey with Morston	A 1548-1972		5,8,9	1548-1919		Walsingham			8F
Stockton	A 1561-1990	1722-1794	5,8,9			Loddon			3J
Stody	A 1661-1997		5,8,9	1713-1812	1662-1754	Erpingham			7G
Stoke Ferry	C 1736-1949		5,8,9	1904	1736-1754	Downham			4C
Stoke Holy Cross	A 1538-1988	1538-1885	5,8,9	1538-1812	1538-1812	Henstead			4I
Stokesby with Herringsby	A 1560-1993	1733-1812	4,5,6,7,8,9	1560-1927	1561-1812	Flegg	1790-1812		10L
Stow Bardolph	A 1559-1753	1559-1758	5,8,9			Downham			4B
Stow Bedon	A 1722-1922		5,8,9			Wayland			3F
Stradsett	A 1559-1836		5,8,9	1559-1633		Downham			4C
Stratton St Mary	A 1547-1979		5,8,9	1547-1742		Depwade			3H(Ov)

NORFOLK

parish name	deposited original registers	I.G.I.	local census indexes	copies of registers at Soc. Gen.	Boyd's marriage index	1837-1851 Registration District	Pallot's marriage index	non-conform. records at P.R.O.	map ref.
Stratton St Michael	A 1558-1991		5,8,9			Depwade		1825-1837	3H(Os)
Stratton Strawless	A 1562-1974		5,8,9			Aylsham			6I
Strumpshaw	A 1562-1999		5,8,9	1562-1812	1562-1812	Blofield	1562-1812		9K
Sturston			5,8,9			Thetford			3E
Suffield	A 1558-1977		5,8,9	1726-1812		Erpingham			7I(Ep)
Surlingham	A 1561-1982	1561-1875	5,8,9	1561-1890	1561-1811	Henstead			9J
Sustead	A 1558-1980		5,8,9	1725-1812		Erpingham			7H(Eh)
Sutton	A 1559-1969	1559-1836	5,8,9	1559-1836		Tunstead		1559-1812	6J
Swaffham	A 1559-1993		5,8,9	1559-1901	1599-1837	Swaffham	1790-1837	1815-1837	5D
Swafield	A 1660-1997	1660-1812	5,8,9	1660-1812	1660-1812	Tunstead			7J
Swainsthorpe	A 1558-1992		5,8,9	1559-1734	1559-1767	Henstead			4I(Oj)
Swanington	A 1538-1882	1539-1812	5,8,9	1538-1882		St Faith's			5H
Swanton Abbot	A 1538-1969	1539-1703	5,8,9	1538-1838	1540-1837	Aylsham		1824-1837	6I
Swanton Morley	A 1538-1986	1538-1785	4,5,6,7,8,9	1755-1891		Mitford			5G
Swanton Novers	A 1667-1989		5,8,9			Walsingham			7G
Swardeston	A 1538-1945		5,8,9	1538-1754		Henstead			9I
Syderstone	A 1585-1974	1585-1684	5,8,9	1558-1840	1586-1837	Aylsham	1790-1837		7E
Talconeston	A 1539-1947		5,8,9			Depwade			3H
Tasburgh	A 1558-1906		5,8,9	1558-1724		Depwade			3I(Oq)
Tatterford	A 1561-1954	1561-1765	5,8,9	1560-1954	1561-1837	Walsingham	1790-1837		7E
Tatterset alias Gatesend	A 1755-1985		5,8,9	1755-1908	1710-1837	Walsingham	1790-1837		7E
Taverham	A 1713-1995		5,8,9	1601-1837	1720-1753	St Faith's			5H
Terrington St Clement	C 1598-1964		5,8,9			Wisbech			6B
Terrington St John	C 1538-1976		5,8,9	1884		Wisbech			5B
Testerton			5,8,9			Walsingham			6F
Tharston			5,8,9			Depwade			3H
Thelveton			5,8,9		1539-1753	Depwade			2H
Themelthorpe	A 1715-1997		5,8,9			Aylsham			6G(Ah)
Thetford								1796-1837	2E
St Cuthbert	A 1653-1980		5,8,9	1653-1837		Thetford			2E
St Mary	A 1653-1974		5,8,9	1653-1913	1653-1751	Thetford			2E
St Peter	A 1653-1975		5,8,9	1653-1838		Thetford			2E
Thompson	A 1538-1926		5,8,9	1538-1812		Wayland			3E
Thornage	A 1561-1996		5,8,9	1696-1812		Erpingham			7G
Thornham	A 1716-2000		5,8,9	1873		Aylsham			8D
Thorpe Abbotts	A 1560-1836		5,8,9	1560-1727	1564-1758	Depwade			1H
Thorpe Market	A 1538-1959	1537-1739	5,8,9	1538-1812	1539-1739	Erpingham			7I
Thorpe Next Haddiscoe	A 1654-1990		5,8,9			Loddon			3K
Thorpe Next Norwich	A 1642-1946	1642-1812	5,8,9	1642-1812		Norwich/Blofield		1821-1837	9J
Threxton	A 1730-1998		5,8,9	1602-1629		Swaffham			4E(P)
Thrigby	A 1539-1992	1539-1812	4,5,7,8,9	1539-1836	1540-1812	Flegg	1790-1812		10M
Thurgarton	A 1538-1977		5,8,9	1725-1812		Erpingham			7H(Ej)
Thurlton	A 1558-1990	1558-1840	5,8,9	1538-1840		Loddon			3K
Thurne	A 1559-1979		4,5,6,7,8,9	1559-1837	1559-1837	Flegg			10L
Thurning			5,8,9	1891		Aylsham			7G
Thursford	A 1692-1989		5,8,9	1692-1837	1692-1837	Walsingham	1790-1837		7F
Thurton	A 1559-1992		5,8,9	1904		Loddon			8K
Thuxton	A 1538-1842		5,8,9			Mitford			4G
Thwaite Alby	A 1562-1984		5,8,9			Aylsham			7I
Thwaite St Mary			5,8,9	1539-1837	1545-1837	Loddon	1790-1837		3J(Or)
Tibenham	A 1560-1973		5,8,9	1560-1928		Depwade			2H
Tilney All Saints	C 1558-1985		5,8,9			Wisbech			6B
Tilney St Lawrence	C 1653-1976		5,8,9			Wisbech			5B
Titchwell	A 1558-2000		5,8,9			Aylsham			8D
Tittleshall with Godwick	A 1538-1987	1750-1812	5,8,9	1539-1904		Mitford		1826-1837	6E
Tivetshall St Margaret	A 1673-1983		5,8,9	1673-1837	1680-1754	Depwade			2H(Ox)
Tivetshall St Mary	A 1672-1968		5,8,9	1672-1837	1674-1754	Depwade			2H(Oy)
Toft Monks	A 1538-1992		5,8,9	1904		Loddon			3K
Toftrees	A 1753-1989		5,8,9	1739-1837	1757-1834	Walsingham	1790-1834		6E
Topcroft	A 1556-1990		5,8,9	1557-1813	1557-1812	Loddon	1790-1813		3I
Tottenhill	A 1678-1964		5,8,9			Downham			5C
Tottington	A 1711-1951		5,8,9			Wayland			3E
Town Barningham	A 1703-1994		5,8,9	1725-1812		Erpingham			7H
Trimingham	A 1557-1992	1557-1840	5,8,9	1557-1840		Erpingham			7I
Trowse	A 1695-1965		5,8,9	1696-1725	1695-1749	Henstead			9I
Trunch	A 1558-1976	1558-1837	5,8,9	1558-1837		Erpingham	1538-1837		7I
Tunstall	A 1557-1974		5,8,9	1557-1812		Blofield			9L
Tunstead	A 1678-1977		5,8,9	1677-1908		Tunstead			6J
Tuttington	A 1544-1984		5,8,9			Aylsham			6I(Er)
Twyford	A 1558-1997		5,8,9			Mitford			6G
Upper Sheringham	A 1670-1986		5,8,9	1670-1858		Erpingham			8H
Upton with Fishley	A 1558-1952	1557-1870	5,8,9	1558-1812	1558-1812	Blofield	1558-1812		10L
Upwell	C 1704-1902	1654-1668	5,8,9	1904		Wisbech			4A
Wacton	A 1553-1992		5,8,9	1560-1902		Depwade			3H
Walcott	A 1558-1972	1558-1836	5,8,9	1558-1836	1558-1837	Tunstead			7J
Wallington cum Thorpland (see Runcton Holme)			5,8,9			Downham			5B
Walpole St Andrew	C 1633-1969		5,8,9			Wisbech			6A
Walpole St Peter			5,8,9	1884+1887		Wisbech			5A
Walsoken	C 1528-1875		5,8,9	1572-1875		Wisbech			5A
Warham All Saints	A 1558-1982		5,8,9			Walsingham			8F
Warham St Mary	A 1565-1983		5,8,9			Walsingham			8F
Waterden	A 1730-1985		5,8,9	1730-1850	1743-1812	Docking	1790-1812		7E
Watlington	A 1570-1945		5,8,9			Downham			5B
Watton	A 1539-1979		5,8,9			Wayland		1822-1837	4F
Waxham	A 1755-1998	1786-1812	5,8,9	1780-1991		Tunstead			6K
Weasenham All Saints	A 1568-1987	1569-1812	5,8,9	1568-1812		Mitford			6E(T)
Weasenham St Peter	A 1581-1986		5,8,9	1581-1812		Mitford			6E
Weeting with Bromehill	A 1558-1891		5,8,9	1558-1746	1558-1812	Thetford	1790-1812		3D

NORFOLK

parish name	deposited original registers	I.G.I.	local census indexes	copies of registers at Soc. Gen.	Boyd's marriage index	1837-1851 Registration District	Pallot's marriage index	non-conform. records at P.R.O.	map ref.
Welborne	A 1695-1992		5,8,9			Forehoe			5G(Ax)
Wellingham	A 1765-1986		5,8,9	1756-1921		Mitford			6E(U)
Wells Next The Sea	A 1548-1996		5,8,9	1659-1900		Walsingham		1818-1837	8F
Welney	B 1642-1968	1642-1876	5,8,9	1653-1895	1653-1753	Downham			3B
Wendling			5,8,9	1890-1894		Mitford			5F
Wereham	A 1558-1977		5,8,9	1553-1753	1558-1753	Downham			4C
West Acre	A 1665-1995	1665-1812	5,8,9	1665-1837	1668-1837	Freebridge Lynn	1790-1837		5D
West Barsham			5,8,9	1856-1871	1813-1837	Walsingham	1813-1837		7E
West Beckham	A 1689-1996	1689-1812	5,8,9	1689-1836	1689-1836	Erpingham			8H
West Bilney	A 1562-1990		5,8,9	1562-1837	1562-1837	Freebridge Lynn	1790-1838		5C
West Bradenham	A 1538-1988		5,8,9	1538-1902		Swaffham			5F
West Dereham	A 1558-1972	1558-1753	5,8,9	1558-1753	1558-1753	Downham			4C
Westfield	A 1706-1968		4,5,6,7,8,9	1834		Mitford			5F(Am)
West Harling	A 1538-1988		5,8,9	1538-1906		Guiltcross			2F
West Lexham	A 1689-1985		5,8,9			Mitford			5E(S)
West Lynn	A 1695-1971		5,8,9	1695-1838		King's Lynn			6B
West Newton	A 1560-1993		5,8,9	1561-1837	1561-1837	Freebridge Lynn	1790-1837		6C
Weston Longville	A 1660-1928		5,8,9	1660-1928		St Faith's			5H
West Raynham	A 1538-1798		5,8,9	1538-1663	1538-1751	Walsingham	1790-1837		6E
West Rudham	A 1565-1973		5,8,9	1565-1837	1565-1837	Docking			6E
West Somerton	A 1736-1943	1736-1812	5,8,9	1737-1837	1736-1837	Flegg	1790-1837		5K
West Tofts	A 1733-1942		5,8,9	1705-1907		Thetford			3E
West Walton	C 1662-1979		5,8,9			Wisbech			5A
Westwick	A 1642-1836	1642-1836	5,8,9	1642-1836	1642-1836	Tunstead			6I
West Winch	A 1559-1976		5,8,9	1559-1812		Freebridge Lynn			5C
West Wretham	A 1783-1793		5,8,9	1745-1903		Thetford			3E
Weybourne	A 1727-1972		5,8,9	1729-1812		Erpingham			8H
Wheatacre	A 1558-1992		5,8,9	1834		Loddon			3K
Whinburgh	A 1703-1967		5,8,9	1834		Mitford			4F
Whissonsett	A 1577-1999		5,8,9	1700-1837	1700-1837	Mitford	1790-1837		6F
Whitlingham	A 1653-1709		5,8,9			Henstead			9J
Whitwell	A 1559-1968		5,8,9	1559-1908		Aylsham			6G
Wickhampton	A 1561-1940		5,8,9			Blofield			9L
Wicklewood	A 1561-1982		5,8,9	1834		Forehoe			4G
Wickmere	A 1559-1837		5,8,9	1665-1812		Aylsham			7H(Ed)
Wiggenhall				1893					5B
St German	C 1653-1977		5,8,9			Downham			5B
St Mary Magdalen	C 1562-1981		5,8,9	1558-1771		Downham			5B
St Mary The Virgin	C 1558-1980		5,8,9	1538-1654		Downham			5B
St Peter	C 1695-1929		5,8,9			Downham			5B(G)
Wighton	A 1558-1992		5,8,9			Walsingham			8F
Wilby	A 1541-1984		5,8,9	1541-1733		Guiltcross			2G
Wilton	A 1634-1957		5,8,9			Wilton			5G
Wimbotsham			5,8,9	1834		Downham			4B
Winfarthing	A 1614-1993		5,8,9	1834	1614-1754	Guiltcross			2G
Winterton with East Somerton	A 1717-1993		5,8,9	1717-1837	1626-1837	Flegg	1790-1837		5L
Witton nr Blofield	A 1571-1835		5,8,9	1582-1812	1558-1837	Blofield	1562-1812		9J
Witton nr North Walsham	A 1558-1958	1559-1875	5,8,9	1558-1903	1582-1812	Tunstead			7J
Wiveton	A 1558-1992		5,8,9	1832+1836		Walsingham			8G
Wolferton	A 1653-1993		5,8,9	1653-1812	1655-1812	Freebridge Lynn	1653-1812		7C
Wolterton	A 1560-1780		5,8,9	1719-1764		Aylsham			7H(Ec)
Woodbastwick with Panxiworth	A 1560-1987		5,8,9	1558-1920	1561-1812	Blofield	1790-1812		5J
Wood Dalling	A 1653-1990	1653-1812	5,8,9	1653-1836		Aylsham			6G
Wood Norton	A 1722-2000		5,8,9	1828-1836		Aylsham			6G
Wood Rising	A 1561-1836		5,8,9	1561-1836		Mitford			4F
Woodton	A 1538-1993		5,8,9	1538-1812	1538-1811	Loddon	1790-1812		3I
Wormegay	A 1561-1876		5,8,9	1565-1648		Downham			5C
Worstead	A 1558-1984	1561-1768	5,8,9	1558-1901	1558-1837	Tunstead			6J
Worthing	A 1654-1834		5,8,9	1826-1828		Mitford			5F(Ak)
Wortwell (see Redenhall)								1787-1836	2I
Wramplingham	A 1566-1839	1566-1747	5,8,9	1566-1725	1567-1747	Forehoe			4H(Av)
Wreningham	A 1656-1915		5,8,9	1834		Henstead			3H
Wretton	A 1693-1919		5,8,9	1697-1770	1697-1770	Downham			4C
Wroxham	A 1558-1959		5,8,9	1826-1836		St Faith's			5I
Wymondham	A 1615-1972		5,8,9			Forehoe		1820-1837	4H
Yaxham	A 1686-1893		5,8,9	1686-1734		Mitford			5G
Yelverton with Alpington	A 1558-1992	1559-1767	5,8,9		1559-1767	Loddon			8J

NORFOLK

Original registers deposited at:
A = Norfolk Record Office, Gildengate House, Anglia Square, Upper Green Lane, Norwich, Norfolk, NR3 1AX
B = Cambridgeshire Record Office, Shire Hall, Castle Hill, Cambridge CB3 OAP
C = Wisbech and Fenland Museum, Museum Square, Wisbech, Cambridge PE13 1ES
D = Suffolk Record Office, Bury St Edmunds Branch, Raingate Street, Bury St Edmunds IP33 2AR

Study adjacent parishes in counties of Lincolnshire, Cambridgeshire and Suffolk

Norfolk Record Office, Central Library, Norwich NR2 1NJ

The following useful indexes have been compiled – see Introduction

Census Indexes 1841-1891 – Great Yarmouth Central Library, Tolhouse Street, Great Yarmouth, Norfolk, NR30 2SH
Census Index 1851 (CD-Rom with Devon & Warwickshire) – The Church of the Latter Day Saints, 399 Garretts Green Lane, Sheldon, Birmingham, B33 0UH
Census Index 1891 – Trevor Read, 1 Chester Close, Greenham, Newbury, Berkshire RG14 7RR
Norwich Marriage Index 1813-1837 – Norfolk Genealogy, Vol.XIV (available from Norfolk and Norwich Genealogical Society)
Norfolk Marriage Licence Bonds 1624-1860 – Norfolk FHS, Kirkby Hall, 70 St Giles Street, Norwich, Norfolk, NR2 1LS
Marriage (and Obituary) Notices 1851, 1881, 1882, 1900 – Lynn Advertiser, Wisbech Constitutional Gazette & Norfolk & Cambridgeshire Herald – Janice Simons, 36
    Old Hospital Mews, Hospital Walk, London Road, King's Lynn PE30 5RU

Norfolk is almost entirely insulated by the sea and by the rivers which form its internal boundary. The shape is almost an oval, of which the diameter from north to south is 45 miles and that from east to west about 70 miles. It is watered by eight principal rivers: the Great Ouse, Little Ouse, Nene, Waveney, Wensum, Yare, Bure and Nar. The population in 1841 was 412,664; in 1851, 442,714; in 1861, 434,798; in 1871, 438,656, in 1881, 444,749.

The principal soils are sandy loam, sand, clay and gravel. All sorts of grain were cultivated together with peas, beans, vetches, cole-seed, clover, chicory, cabbages, turnips, carrots, potatoes, flax and hemp. Sheep, cattle, turkeys and game were reared. Manufactures included crepes, bombazines and other stuffs, Norwich being the centre of these industries. Yarmouth was of consequence both as a port and fishing town, herring fishing being particularly important.

The information in the Index is abbreviated, and may mislead the searcher if reference is not made to the details contained in the several publications listed in the Introduction. It is essential that users of this book check the appropriate works before making further enquiries.

NORTHAMPTONSHIRE

parish name	deposited original registers	I.G.I.	local census indexes	copies of registers at Soc. Gen.	Boyd's marriage index	1837-1851 Registration District	Pallot's marriage index	non-conform. records at P.R.O.	map ref.
Abington	A 1637-1972		5,8			Northampton			4G
Abthorpe	A 1813-1989		5,8			Towcester			2E
Adstone	A 1678-1972		5,8			Towcester			3E
Alderton	A 1597-1836		5,8			Potterspury			2G
Aldwinkle									6I
All Saints	A 1653-1837		5,8			Thrapston			6I
St Peter	A 1563-1837		5,8			Thrapston			6I
Apethorpe	A 1676-1840	1605-1831	5,8			Oundle			8I
Arthingworth	A 1650-1836		5,8			Mkt Harborough			6F
Ashby St Ledgers	A 1554-1973		5,8			Daventry			5D
Ashley	A 1588-1836		5,8			Mkt Harborough		1790-1836	7G
Ashton	A 1682-1996		5,8	1682-1944		Potterspury			3F
Ashwell	B 1595-1992	1701-1812	5,8	1595-1812		Oakham			10H
Aston Le Walls	A 1538-1980		5,8			Banbury			3C
Aynho	A 1562-1882		8			Brackley			1D
Ayston	B 1656-1853	1656-1834	5,8	1656-1812	1656-1837	Uppingham	1788-1834		9H
Badby	A 1559-1970		5,8			Daventry			4D
Bainton	A 1713-1834		8			Stamford			9J
Barby	A 1538-1993		5,8			Rugby			5D
Barford (ex.par.)			5,8			Kettering			6G(Q)
Barleythorpe (see Oakham)									9G
Barnack	A 1695-1974	1696-1836	8	1711-1812	1696-1837	Stamford			9J
Barnwell									7J
All Saints	A 1695-1831		5,8			Oundle			7J
St Andrew	A 1558-1876		5,8			Oundle			7J
Barrow	B 1655-1963		8	1655-1877		Oakham			10H
Barrowden	B 1603-1988	1603-1837	5,8	1603-1892	1603-1700	Uppingham		1798-1837	8H
Barton Seagrave	A 1609-1984		5,8			Kettering			6H
Beanfield Lawas (ex.par.)			8			Kettering			7G(R)
Beaumont Chase (ex.par.)			8			Uppingham			8G
Belton	B 1577-1885	1707-1812	5,8	1577-1884		Uppingham			9G
Benefield	A 1570-1904		5,8			Oundle			7I
Bisbrooke	B 1665-1996	1666-1812	5,8		1666-1775	Uppingham			8H(h)
Blakesley	A 1538-1978		5,8	1538-1978		Towcester			3E
Blatherwycke	A 1621-1968		5,8			Oundle			8I
Blisworth	A 1548-1947		5,8			Towcester		1804-1836	3F
Boddington	A 1558-1878		5,8			Banbury			3C
Borough Fen (ex.par.)			8			Peterborough			9K
Boughton	A 1549-1947		5,8	1600-1657		Brixworth			5F
Bozeat	A 1729-1988		5,8			Wellingborough	1780-1837		4H
Brackley	A 1560-1987		8		1637-1702	Brackley		1804-1837	2D
Bradden	A 1559-1919		5,8			Towcester			3E(D)
Brafield	A 1653-1971		5,8			Hardingstone			4G(N)
Brampton Ash	A 1580-1837		5,8			Mkt Harborough			7G
Braunston	A 1538-1978		5,8			Daventry		1805-1837	5D
Braunston	B 1558-1907	1701-1812	5,8	1558-1907		Oakham			9G
Braybrooke	A 1653-1972		5,8			Mkt Harborough			7F
Brigstock	A 1641-1924		5,8			Thrapston		1782-1837	7H
Brington	A 1558-1994		8	1558-1981		Brixworth			5E
Brixworth	A 1546-1956		5,8	1546-1956		Brixworth			5F
Brockhall	A 1561-1836		5,8			Daventry			4E(F)
Brooke	B 1574-1996	1707-1812	5,8	1574-1812		Oakham			9G
Broughton	A 1560-1896	1570-1746	5,8		1570-1746	Kettering			6G
Bugbrooke	A 1557-1874		5,8	1556-1791		Northampton			4E
Bulwick	A 1563-1950		5,8			Oundle			8I
Burley	B 1577-1996	1707-1812	5,8	1577-1983		Oakham			10H
Burton Latimer	A 1538-1979	1538-1713	5,8	1538-1812		Kettering		1809-1837	6H
Byfield	A 1636-1989		5,8	1688-1772		Daventry		1827-1836	3C
Caldecote	B 1605-1988	1616-1840	5,8			Uppingham			8H
Canons Ashby	A 1696-1951		5,8			Daventry			3D
Castle Ashby	A 1564-1842		5,8			Hardingstone			4G
Castor	A 1538-1928	1538-1837	8	1538-1812	1651-1837	Peterborough	1790-1812		8K
Catesby	A 1705-1812		5,8			Daventry			4D
Chacombe	A 1566-1922		8	1566-1812		Banbury			2C
Charwelton	A 1697-1836		5,8			Daventry			4D
Chelveston	A 1573-1995		5,8			Thrapston			5I
Chipping Warden	A 1579-1981		5,8			Banbury			3C
Church Brampton	A 1561-1994		8	1561-1970		Brixworth			5F
Clapton or Clopton	A 1558-1836		5,8			Thrapston			6J
Clay Coton	A 1541-1963	1541-1614	5,8	1541-1615		Rugby			6D
Clipsham	B 1717-1987		5,8			Stamford			10I
Clipston	A 1667-1966		5,8			Mkt Harborough			6F
Cogenhoe	A 1554-1986		5,8			Hardingstone			4G
Cold Ashby	A 1560-1963		5,8	1559-1733		Brixworth			6E
Cold Higham	A 1556-1980		5,8			Towcester			3E
Collingtree	A 1771-1935	1754-1837	5,8	1754-1837	1754-1837	Hardingstone			3F(K)
Collyweston	A 1541-1981		5,8			Stamford			9I
Corby	A 1684-1951		5,8			Kettering			7H
Cosgrove	A 1691-1877		5,8			Potterspury			2G
Cotterstock	A 1631-1921		5,8			Oundle			8J
Cottesbrooke	A 1630-1966		5,8			Brixworth			6F
Cottesmore	B 1655-1963	1701-1812	5,8	1655-1877		Oakham			10H
Cottingham	A 1574-1905		5,8	1577-1905		Kettering			7G
Courteenhall	A 1538-1890		5,8	1538-1812		Hardingstone			3F(L)
Cranford									6H
St Andrew	A 1695-1836	1754-1841	5,8		1695-1837	Kettering			6H(T)
St John	A 1627-1955	1623-1841	5,8		1629-1837	Kettering			6H(U)
Cransley	A 1561-1962		5,8			Kettering			6G
Creaton	A 1688-1981		5,8			Brixworth		1782-1837	5F

NORTHAMPTONSHIRE

parish name	deposited original registers	I.G.I.	local census indexes	copies of registers at Soc. Gen.	Boyd's marriage index	1837-1851 Registration District	Pallot's marriage index	non-conform. records at P.R.O.	map ref.
Crick	A 1559-1975		5,8			Rugby		1825-1836	5D
Croughton			8	1696-1812	1663-1812	Brackley	1790-1812		1D
Culworth	A 1563-1872		8	1562-1841		Brackley			3D
Dallington	A 1577-1961		8			Northampton			4F
Daventry	A 1560-1973		5,8			Daventry		1746-1837	4D
Deene	A 1558-1923		5,8	1558-1923		Oundle			8H
Denford	A 1596-1950		5,8			Thrapston			6I
Denton	A 1538-1960		5,8			Hardingstone			4G
Desborough	A 1571-1984		5,8			Kettering		1803-1837	7G
Dingley	A 1583-1837	1580-1812	5,8	1583-1811	1580-1812	Mkt Harborough	1790-1811		7F
Dodford	A 1581-1995		5,8	1581-1812	1651-1812	Daventry	1790-1812		4E
Draughton	A 1559-1980		5,8	1755-1836		Brixworth			6F
Duddington	A 1733-1966	1605-1842	5,8			Stamford			8I
Duston	A 1692-1993		8			Northampton			4F
Earls Barton	A 1558-1904		5,8	1724-1793		Wellingborough		1818-1836	4G
East Carlton	A 1625-1842		5,8			Kettering			7G
East Farndon	A 1562-1981		5,8	1562-1656		Mkt Harborough			7F
East Haddon	A 1552-1994		8			Brixworth			5E
Easton Maudit	A 1539-1989		5,8			Wellingborough			4H
Easton Neston	A 1559-1995		5,8	1707-1861		Towcester			3F
Easton on the Hill	A 1580-1989		5,8	1578-1859		Stamford			9I
Ecton	A 1559-1986		5,8			Wellingborough			4G
Edgcote	A 1716-1980		5,8			Banbury			3C
Edith Weston	B 1585-1992	1701-1812	5,8	1585-1882		Oakham			9H
Egleton	B 1538-1996		5,8	1538-1909		Oakham			9H
Elkington			5,8			Rugby			6E
Empingham	B 1563-1990	1563-1837	5,8		1563-1837	Oakham	1780-1837		9I
Essendine	B 1600-1835	1624-1835	5,8	1600-1835	1624-1837	Stamford	1780-1835		10J
Etton	A 1587-1991		8	1711-1804		Peterborough			9K
Evenley	A 1695-1889		8		1699-1837	Brackley			1D
Everdon	A 1558-1971		5,8	1558-1812	1684-1812	Daventry	1790-1812		4D
Exton	B 1579-1964	1701-1812	5,8	1597-1964		Oakham			10H
Eydon	A 1538-1975		5,8	1538-1907	1538-1837	Brackley			3D
Eye	A 1543-1945		8			Peterborough			9L
Farthinghoe	A 1560-1995		8			Brackley			2D
Farthingstone	A 1538-1980		5,8	1544-1812	1651-1812	Daventry	1790-1812		3E
Fawsley	A 1583-1998		5,8		1587-1812	Daventry			4D
Faxton	A 1569-1934		5,8	1568-1980	1776-1836	Brixworth	1790-1837		6G
Finedon			5,8			Wellingborough		1817-1837	5H
Fineshade (ex.par.)			5,8			Uppingham			8I
Flore	A 1653-1964		5,8			Daventry		1787-1837	4E
Fotheringhay	A 1557-1836		5,8			Oundle			8J
Furtho	A 1696-1977		5,8			Potterspury			2G
Gayton	A 1558-1943		5,8	1558-1744		Towcester			3F
Geddington	A 1680-1976		5,8			Kettering			6H
Glapthorne	A 1568-1957		5,8			Oundle			7I
Glaston	B 1556-1954	1701-1812	5,8			Uppingham			8H(j)
Glendon	A 1793-1812		5,8			Kettering			6G
Glinton	A 1567-1975	1567-1836	8	1568-1814	1651-1837	Peterborough	1790-1812		9K
Grafton Regis	A 1585-1837		5,8			Potterspury			2G
Grafton Underwood	A 1678-1881		5,8			Kettering			6H
Great Addington	A 1693-1901		5,8			Thrapston			6I
Great Billing	A 1662-1987		5,8			Northampton			4G
Great Casterton	B 1655-1982	1665-1837	5,8	1665-1891	1665-1812	Stamford	1780-1837		10I
Great Doddington	A 1560-1886		5,8			Wellingborough			4H
Great Harrowden	A 1672-1965		5,8			Wellingborough			5H
Great Houghton	A 1558-1900		5,8			Hardingstone			4G
Great Oakley	A 1562-1973		5,8	1562-1718		Kettering			7H
Great Oxendon	A 1564-1965		5,8			Mkt Harborough			7F
Great Weldon	A 1594-1941		5,8			Oundle			7H
Greatworth	A 1757-1979	1757-1813	5,8	1757-1813	1757-1813	Brackley			2D(A)
Greens Norton	A 1565-1978		5,8			Towcester			3E
Greetham	B 1576-1977	1644-1812	5,8	1576-1881		Oakham			10H
Grendon	A 1559-1969		5,8			Wellingborough			4H
Gretton	A 1557-1973	1731-1843	5,8			Uppingham		1812-1835	8H
Guilsborough	A 1560-1968		5,8			Brixworth			5E
Gunthorpe (see Belton)									9H(b)
Hackleton (see Piddington)								1797-1836	3G
Hambleton	B 1558-1978	1707-1812	5,8	1558-1978		Oakham			9H
Hannington	A 1539-1836		5,8			Brixworth			5G
Hanslope (Bucks)			8						3G
Hardingstone	A 1563-1991		5,8			Hardingstone			4F
Hardwick	A 1559-1847		5,8	1559-1839		Wellingborough			5G
Hargrave	A 1572-1978		5,8	1572-1978		Thrapston			5I
Harlestone	A 1570-1960		8			Brixworth			4F
Harpole	A 1538-1942		5,8	1538-1812	1651-1812	Northampton	1790-1812		4F
Harrington	A 1673-1974		5,8			Kettering			6F
Harringworth	A 1695-1997		5,8			Uppingham			8H
Hartwell	A 1684-1987		5,8	1684-1964		Potterspury			3G
Haselbech	A 1653-1919		5,8	1654-1911		Brixworth			6F
Hellidon	A 1571-1913		5,8			Daventry			4C
Helmdon	A 1572-1989		8			Brackley			2D
Helpston	A 1685-1984		8	1711-1807		Peterborough			9J
Hemington	A 1574-1961		5,8			Oundle			7J
Higham Ferrers	A 1579-1991		5,8			Wellingborough		1813-1837	5I
Higham Park (ex.par.)			8			Wellingborough			4I
Hinton in the Hedges	A 1558-1838	1558-1754	5,8	1558-1754	1559-1754	Brackley			1D
Holcot	A 1559-1964		5,8			Brixworth			5G
Holdenby	A 1754-1965		8			Brixworth			5F

parish name	deposited original registers	I.G.I.	local census indexes	copies of registers at Soc. Gen.	Boyd's marriage index	1837-1851 Registration District	Pallot's marriage index	non-conform. records at P.R.O.	map ref.
Horn (see Exton)									10I
Horton	A 1605-1989		5,8			Hardingstone			3G
Hulcote (see Easton Neston)									3F
Irchester	A 1622-1993		5,8			Wellingborough			5H
Irthlingborough	A 1562-1985		5,8			Wellingborough			5H
Isham	A 1701-1973		5,8	1701-1810		Wellingborough			5H
Islip	A 1695-1958		5,8			Thrapston			6I
Kelmarsh	A 1599-1920		5,8	1559-1837		Mkt Harborough			6F
Kettering	A 1637-1710		5,8			Kettering		1714-1837	6H
Ketton	B 1561-1917	1561-1842	5,8	1564-1961	1561-1837	Stamford	1780-1837	1823-1836	9I
Kilsby	A 1754-1944		5,8			Rugby		1795-1837	5D
Kingscliffe	A 1590-1996	1590-1877	5,8			Oundle			8I
Kings Sutton	A 1570-1844	1812-1813	8	1570-1811		Brackley		1823-1830	1C
Kingsthorpe	A 1539-1928		5,8			Northampton			4F
Kislingbury	A 1538-1972		5,8	1538-1972		Northampton			4F
Lamport	A 1587-1980		5,8	1587-1980	1651-1836	Brixworth	1790-1836		6F
Langham	B 1559-1978	1707-1812	5,8	1559-1974		Oakham			10G
Laxton	A 1689-1836		5,8			Uppingham			8I
Leighfield (ex.par.)			8			Oakham			9G
Liddington	B 1563-1996	1604-1840	8	1561-1948	1604-1837	Uppingham	1780-1837		8H
Lilbourne	A 1573-1943		5,8			Rugby			6D
Lilford	A 1560-1985	1564-1835	5,8		1564-1837	Oundle			6J
Litchborough	A 1728-1994	1732-1812	5,8	1732-1812	1732-1812	Towcester			3E
Little Addington	A 1588-1887		5,8			Thrapston			5H
Little Billing	A 1632-1987		5,8			Northampton			4G
Little Bowden	B 1653-1975	1661-1876	5,8		1661-1812	Mkt Harborough			7F
Little Casterton	B 1559-1847	1560-1837	5,8	1559-1812	1560-1837	Stamford	1780-1837		9J
Little Harrowden	A 1653-1944		5,8			Wellingborough			5G
Little Houghton	A 1541-1977		5,8			Hardingstone			4G
Little Oakley	A 1679-1972		5,8			Kettering			7H(S)
Loddington	A 1622-1958		5,8			Kettering			6G
Long Buckby	A 1558-1969	1558-1689	5,8	1558-1689		Daventry		1795-1836	5E
Lowick	A 1542-1962		5,8			Thrapston			6I
Luddington	A 1635-1837		5,8			Oundle			6J
Lutton			5,8	1653-1812		Oundle			7J
Lyndon	B 1580-1996	1707-1812	5,8	1580-1837		Oakham			9H(e)
Maidford	A 1711-1982		5,8	1711-1982		Towcester			3E(E)
Maidwell	A 1708-1980		5,8			Brixworth			6F
Manton	B 1573-1913		5,8	1573-1913		Oakham			9H
Marholm	A 1566-1836	1566-1836	8		1567-1837	Peterborough			9K
Market Overton	B 1573-1992	1701-1812	5,8			Oakham			10H
Marston St Lawrence	A 1813-1948		8	1664-1840		Brackley			2C
Marston Trussell	A 1561-1962		5,8			Mkt Harborough			7F
Martinsthorpe			8			Oakham			9H(a)
Mawsley (ex.par.)			5,8			Brixworth			6G
Maxey	A 1538-1958	1538-1812	5,8	1538-1812	1538-1803	Peterborough			9K
Mears Ashby	A 1670-1960		5,8			Wellingborough			5G
Middleton Cheney	A 1558-1987		5,8			Banbury		1785-1837	2C
Milton	A 1558-1982		5,8	1558-1889		Hardingstone			3F
Morcott	B 1539-1960	1701-1812	5,8	1539-1960		Uppingham		1798-1837	8H(k)
Moreton Pinkney	A 1641-1962		5,8	1641-1723		Brackley			3D
Moulton	A 1565-1950	1565-1812	5,8	1565-1812		Brixworth		1795-1836	5G
Moulton Park (ex.par.)			5,8			Northampton			5G
Naseby	A 1563-1980	1779-1812	5,8	1563-1844		Brixworth			6E
Nassington	A 1560-1893	1712-1847	5,8	1560-1883		Oundle			8J
Nether Heyford	A 1558-1961		5,8	1558-1837	1651-1837	Northampton	1790-1837		4E(G)
Newborough	A 1830-1973		8			Peterborough			9K
Newbottle	A 1538-1898		8			Brackley			1D
Newnham	A 1552-1944		5,8			Daventry			4D
Newton in the Willows	A 1662-1963		5,8			Kettering			7H
Newton Bromswold	A 1560-1994		5,8			Wellingborough			5I
Normanton	B 1755-1966	1707-1837	5,8	1755-1966	1720-1837	Oakham	....-1836	1770-1837	9H(d)
Northampton									4F
All Saints	A 1559-1992		5,8	1559-1904		Northampton			4F(M)
St Giles	A 1559-1987		5,8	1559-1890		Northampton			4F(M)
St Peter	A 1578-1969		5,8	1578-1884	1655-1812	Northampton	1790-1812		4F(M)
St Sepulchre	A 1566-1982		5,8	1566-1880		Northampton	1780-1837		4F(M)
Northborough	A 1671-1961	1814-1839		1538-1812	1651-1837	Peterborough	1790-1812		9K
North Luffenham	B 1572-1923	1565-1832	5,8	1565-1923	1565-1837	Uppingham	1790-1832		9H
Norton	A 1678-1987		5,8	1678-1752		Daventry			4E
Oakham	B 1564-1978	1565-1837	8	1564-1978	1564-1754	Oakham		1768-1855	9G
Old	A 1559-1937		5,8	1559-1937		Brixworth		1809-1837	5G
Orlingbury	A 1564-1920		5,8			Wellingborough			5G
Orton	A 1836-1961		5,8			Kettering			6G
Oundle	A 1625-1988		5,8	1625-1915		Oundle			7I
Overstone	A 1680-1964		5,8			Wellingborough			5G
Passenham	A 1695-1959		5,8			Potterspury			2F
Paston	A 1644-1983	1645-1837	8		1645-1837	Peterborough			9K
Pattishall	A 1556-1953		5,8			Towcester			3E
Paulerspury	A 1557-1965		5,8			Pottesbury			2F
Peakirk	A 1560-1980	1814-1837	8	1617-1812	1651-1837	Peterborough	1790-1812		9K
Peterborough								1810-1837	8K
Cathedral			5,8			Peterborough			8K
St John Baptist	A 1559-1959	1561-1726	5,8	1559-1891		Peterborough			8K
Pickworth	B 1660-1957	1661-1837	5,8	1660-1837	1661-1812	Stamford	1814-1837		10I
Piddington	A 1573-1988		5,8			Hardingstone			3G
Pilton	B 1548-1995	1701-1812	5,8	1553-1837		Uppingham			9H(g)
Pilton	A 1569-1837		5,8			Oundle			7I
Pitsford	A 1560-1990		5,8	1560-1943		Brixworth			5F

parish name	deposited original registers	I.G.I.	local census indexes	copies of registers at Soc. Gen.	Boyd's marriage index	1837-1851 Registration District	Pallot's marriage index	non-conform. records at P.R.O.	map ref.
Plumpton	A 1682-1949		5,8			Towcester			3E(B)
Polebrook	A 1653-1909		5,8			Oundle			7J
Potterspury	A 1674-1894		5,8			Potterspury		1739-1837	2F
Preston	B 1560-1991	1560-1836	5,8		1560-1837	Uppingham	1780-1836		9H(f)
Preston Capes	A 1614-1897		5,8			Daventry			3D
Preston Deanery	A 1670-1968		5,8			Hardingstone			3G
Pytchley	A 1695-1926	1697-1812	5,8	1697-1812	1613-1812	Kettering			6G
Quinton	A 1648-1978		5,8			Hardingstone			3G
Radstone	A 1565-1988		8	1573-1684		Brackley			2E
Raunds	A 1581-1966		5,8	1581-1837		Thrapston			5I
Ravensthorpe	A 1539-1984		8			Brixworth			5E
Ridlington	B 1559-1995	1707-1812	5,8			Uppingham			9G
Ringstead	A 1569-1950		5,8	1569-1886		Thrapston		1811-1836	6I
Roade	A 1587-1980		5,8			Hardingstone		1804-1837	3F
Rockingham	A 1562-1992	1722-1812	5,8	1562-1721		Uppingham			8G
Rothersthorpe	A 1562-1968	1614-1708	5,8			Hardingstone			4F(J)
Rothwell	A 1614-1915		5,8		1614-1708	Kettering		1629-1836	6G
Rushden	A 1559-1910		5,8	1726-1860		Wellingborough			5I
Rushton	A 1538-1983	1538-1837	5,8	1538-1837	1538-1837	Kettering	1790-1837		7G
Ryhall	B 1653-1946	1674-1838	5,8	1653-1878	1676-1837	Stamford	1838		10I
Scaldwell	A 1561-1981		5,8			Brixworth			5F
Seaton	B 1538-1981	1538-1837	5,8	1561-1974	1538-1837	Uppingham			8H
Shutlanger (see Stoke Bruerne)									3F
Sibbertoft	A 1680-1927		5,8	1680-1749		Mkt Harborough			6E
Silverstone	A 1831-1989		5,8			Towcester			2E
Slapton	A 1573-1835		5,8			Towcester			3E(C)
Slipton	A 1670-1812		5,8			Thrapston			6H
South Luffenham	B 1678-1994		5,8	1678-1971		Uppingham			9H
Southwick	A 1732-1837		5,8			Oundle			8I
Spratton	A 1538-1979		5,8	1538-1653		Brixworth			5F
Stamford Baron	A 1572-1957		8			Stamford			9J
Stanford	B 1607-1975		5,8			Rugby			6E
Stanion	A 1653-1977		5,8			Kettering			7H
Stanwick	A 1558-1965		5,8			Thrapston			5I
Staverton	A 1563-1970		5,8			Daventry			4D
Steane	A 1697-1752		5,8			Brackley			2D
Stoke Albany	A 1575-1960		5,8			Mkt Harborough			7G
Stoke Bruerne	A 1560-1976		5,8	1561-1812	1651-1812	Towcester	1790-1812		3F
Stoke Doyle	A 1560-1991		5,8			Oundle			7I
Stoke Dry	B 1559-1837	1707-1812	5,8	1559-1837		Uppingham			8G
Stowe Nine Churches	A 1558-1930		5,8	1560-1837	1665-1837	Daventry	1790-1837		4E
Stretton	B 1631-1997	1631-1837	5,8			Oakham			10H
Strixton	A 1730-1926		5,8			Wellingborough			4H
Stuchbury (see Helmdon)									2D
Sudborough	A 1661-1961		5,8			Thrapston			6I
Sulby (ex.par.)			5,8			Mkt Harborough			6E
Sulgrave	A 1668-1972		5,8			Brackley			2D
Sutton (by Castor)	A 1758-1930		8			Peterborough			8J
Sutton Bassett (see Weston by Welland)									7F
Syresham	A 1668-1939		8			Brackley			2E
Sywell	A 1572-1951		5,8			Wellingborough			5G
Tansor	A 1639-1926	1639-1837	5,8	1639-1926	1639-1837	Oundle			7J
Teigh	B 1572-1985		5,8		1572-1837	Oakham	1789-1837		10H
Theddingworth (Leics)									7E
Thenford	A 1562-1836		8	1567-1578		Brackley			2C
Thistleton	B 1574-1995	1574-1812	5,8			Oakham			10H
Thornby	A 1649-1984		5,8	1649-1781		Brixworth			6E
Thornhaugh	A 1562-1974	1654-1835	8		1654-1837	Stamford			8J
Thorpe Achurch	A 1591-1837	1592-1837	5,8		1591-1837	Oundle			6I
Thorpe Lubenham (see Marston Trussell)									7F
Thorpe Malsor	A 1538-1986		5,8			Kettering			6G(P)
Thorpe Mandeville	A 1559-1970	1559-1837	8		1560-1837	Brackley			3C
Thrapston	A 1560-1984		5,8	1685-1709		Thrapston		1794-1837	6J
Thurning (also Hunts)	A 1560-1955		5,8			Oundle			6J
Tickencote	B 1574-1995	1576-1837	5,8	1574-1836	1576-1837	Oakham	1781-1836		9I(c)
Tiffield	A 1559-1944		5,8	1559-1840		Towcester			3F
Tinwell	B 1561-1939	1561-1837	5,8	1561-1939	1562-1837	Stamford	1780-1837		9I
Titchmarsh	A 1543-1967	1754-1812	5,8	1754-1986		Thrapston			6I
Tixover	B 1754-1979	1561-1842	8		1754-1837	Stamford	1782-1837		9I(l)
Towcester	A 1678-1986		5,8			Towcester		1755-1837	3E
Twywell	A 1577-1964		5,8			Thrapston			6H
Ufford	A 1570-1977		8	1712-1812		Stamford			9J
Upper Heyford (see Nether)									4E(H)
Uppingham	B 1571-1984	1571-1812	5,8	1571-1862	1571-1753	Uppingham		1785-1836	8H
Upton (Northampton)	A 1594-1981		5,8			Northampton			4F
Upton (Peterborough)	A 1770-1930		8			Peterborough			8J
Wadenhoe	A 1559-1961		5,8			Oundle			7I
Wakerley	A 1540-1966		5,8			Uppingham			8I
Walgrave	A 1571-1984		5,8	1571-1905		Brixworth			5G
Wansford	A 1807-1962		8			Stamford			8J
Wappenham	A 1678-1965		8	1686-1965		Towcester			2E
Wardley	B 1574-1825	1701-1812	5,8	1574-1812		Uppingham			8G
Warkton	A 1558-1812		5,8			Kettering			6H
Warkworth	A 1814-1836		5,7,8,9	1664-1840		Banbury			2C
Warmington	A 1558-1958		8			Oundle			7J
Watford	A 1565-1969		5,8			Daventry			5E
Weedon Bec	A 1588-1997		5,8			Daventry		1787-1837	4E
Weedon Lois	A 1558-1930		5,8	1705-1812		Towcester		1780-1837	3D
Weekley	A 1550-1953		5,8			Kettering			6H

NORTHAMPTONSHIRE

parish name	deposited original registers	I.G.I.	local census indexes	copies of registers at Soc. Gen.	Boyd's marriage index	1837-1851 Registration District	Pallot's marriage index	non-conform. records at P.R.O.	map ref.
Welford	A 1561-1954		5,8	1561-1954		Lutterworth		1744-1837	6E
Welland (see Weston by Welland)									8F
Wellingborough	A 1586-1938		5,8	1586-1878		Wellingborough		1784-1837	5H
Welton	A 1578-1966		5,8			Daventry		1824-1837	5D
Werrington (see Paston)									9K
West Haddon	A 1653-1975		5,8	1653-1975		Daventry		1815-1837	5E
Weston by Welland	A 1576-1913		5,8	1576-1913	1662-1812	Mkt Harborough	1790-1812		8F
Weston Favell	A 1540-1987		5,8			Northampton			4G
Whilton	A 1570-1984		5,8			Daventry			5E
Whissendine	B 1563-1962	1707-1812	5,8	1577-1867	1563-1837	Oakham	1780-1837		10G
Whiston	A 1700-1835		5,8			Hardingstone			4G(O)
Whitfield	A 1689-1991	1696-1813	8	1696-1813	1696-1812	Brackley			2E
Whittlebury	A 1653-1958		5,8	1653-1958		Towcester			2F
Whitwell	B 1716-1995	1707-1812	5,8			Oakham			9H
Wicken	A 1559-1994		5,8			Potterspury			2F
Wilbarston	A 1746-1875		5,8			Mkt Harborough		1790-1836	7G
Wilby	A 1562-1983		5,8			Wellingborough			5G
Wing	B 1625-1996	1625-1836	5,8	1625-1891	1625-1837	Uppingham	1780-1836		9H
Winwick	A 1567-1837		5,8			Daventry			6E
Winwick (Hunts)									6J
Wittering	A 1763-1973	1742-1835	8		1742-1837	Stamford			9J
Wollaston	A 1663-1965		5,8			Wellingborough		1788-1836	4H
Woodford Halse	A 1602-1961		5,8	1602-1961		Daventry		1796-1840	3D
Woodford (Thrapston)	A 1680-1961		5,8			Thrapston			6I
Wood Newton	A 1588-1948	1604-1831	5,8			Oundle			8J
Wootton	A 1707-1978		5,8			Hardingstone			4F
Yardley Hastings	A 1550-1944		5,8			Hardingstone		1804-1836	3G
Yarwell	A 1572-1881	1605-1847	5,8	1813-1847		Oundle			8J
Yelvertoft	A 1575-1894		5,8			Rugby		1791-1837	6D

Original registers deposited at:
A =Northamptonshire Record Office, Wootton Hall Park, Northampton NN4 8BQ
B =Leicestershire Record Office and Local Studies Centre, Wigston Magna, Leicester LE18 2AH

Study adjacent parishes in counties of Oxfordshire, Warwickshire, Leicestershire, Lincolnshire, Huntingdonshire, Bedfordshire and Buckinghamshire

Northamptonshire Record Office, Wootton Hall Park, Northampton NN4 8BQ

The following useful indexes have been compiled – see Introduction
Census Index 1851 (Northamptonshire) – Northamptonshire FHS, Miss E Warwick, The Nurseries, Yardley Hastings, Northamptonshire, NN7 1HJ
Census Index 1851 (Rutland) – Leicestershire Record Office and Local Studies Centre, Wigston Magna, Leicester LE18 2AH
Northamptonshire Marriage Index – Northamptonshire Record Office, Wootton Hall Park, Northampton, NN4 8BQ complete for 1813-1837, 1707-1812 almost complete.
Rutland Marriage Index 1754-1837 – Leicestershire & Rutland FHS available on the internet at http://www.lrfhs.freeserve.co.uk/lrfhsdownloads.htm

Northamptonshire lies obliquely across the middle of England and borders on more surrounding counties than any other in the country. Its greatest length is 60 miles and its breadth only about 25 miles. It is watered by six principal rivers: the Nene, Welland, Ouse, Avon, Leam and Charwell. The population in 1841 was 199,208; in 1851, 213,844; in 1861, 227,704; in 1871, 243,891; in 1881, 272,555.

The soils are principally loams. Cattle, horses and sheep were reared; woad for dyeing was cultivated and there were some orchards. Butter and cheese were made. Manufactures were of little importance but silk stockings were woven and there was lace-making and wool-spinning. Shoes were made at Northampton and Wellingborough.

Rutland is the smallest county in England being only 18 miles in length and 16 miles at its greatest breadth. It is watered by two principal rivers: the Eye and Welland. The population in 1841 was 21,302; in 1851, 22,983; in 1861, 21,861; in 1871, 22,073; in 1881, 21,434.

The soils include clay, gravel, sand and marl. Corn and turnips were grown and sheep raised. Manufactures and minerals were negligible and the only quarries were those of limestone at Ketton.

The information in the Index is abbreviated, and may mislead the searcher if reference is not made to the details contained in the several publications listed in the Introduction. It is essential that users of this book check the appropriate works before making further enquiries.

NORTHUMBERLAND

parish name	deposited original registers	I.G.I.	local census indexes	copies of registers at Soc. Gen.	Boyd's marriage index	1837-1851 Registration District	Pallot's marriage index	non-conform. records at P.R.O.	map ref.
Allendale	1662-1972	1662-1877	5,8	1662-1851		Hexham			7C
Allenheads (see Allendale)		1785-1876				Hexham			7B
Alnham	1688-1993	1688-1896	8	1688-1812	1705-1812	Rothbury	1790-1812		6H
Alnwick	1645-1992	1645-1812	5,8	1645-1669	1646-1812	Alnwick		1762-1840	4I
Alwinton	1691-1992	1694-1812	8	1719-1815	1719-1812	Rothbury		1767-1840	6H
Ancroft	1742-1995	1742-1876	5,8	1813-1840	1742-1812	Berwick		1790-1840	5L
Bamburgh	1648-1960	1654-1757	5,8	1652-1809	1653-1758	Belford		1797-1838	4K
Beadnell	1766-1935	1766-1812	8	1766-1812	1767-1800	Belford			3J
Bedlington	1653-1989	1643-1812	5,8		1653-1812	Morpeth			3E
Belford	1688-1977	1701-1812	5,8	1688-1812	1702-1812	Belford		1820-1858	4K
Bellingham	1684-1992	1684-1880	5,8,9	1684-1851		Bellingham		1775-1837	7E
Berwick-upon-Tweed	1572-1992	1572-1812	5,8	1572-1841	1572-1812	Berwick		1764-1858	5M
Birtley	1728-1993	1728-1877	5,8			Bellingham			6E
Blanchland	1753-1977	1753-1877	5,8	1753-1851		Hexham			6B
Bolam	1662-1991	1661-1896	8		1662-1812	Castle Ward			4E
Bothal	1678-1986	1678-1812	5,8	1678-1812	1678-1812	Morpeth	1790-1812		3F
Branxton	1736-1997	1736-1812	8	1736-1812	1754-1811	Glendale			6K(A)
Brinkburn (ex.par.)	1865-1997	1865-1897	8			Rothbury			4G(E)
Byrness	1797-1978		8	1797-1813		Rothbury			7G
Bywell									5C
St Andrew	1668-1991	1668-1896	5,8		1685-1812	Hexham			5C(K)
St Peter	1663-1975	1663-1812	5,8		1663-1812	Hexham		1795-1840	5C
Carham	1684-1998	1684-1838	8	1815-1836	1690-1812	Glendale			7K
Carr Shield	1823-1982	1823-1875	8			Hexham			7B
Chatton	1712-1992	1712-1876	8	1712-1837	1712-1812	Glendale	1790-1812		5J
Chillingham	1692-1991	1692-1812	8		1692-1812	Glendale			5J(C)
Chollerton	1647-1995	1643-1877	5,8	1643-1851	1648-1814	Hexham			6D
Corbridge	1657-1991	1654-1812	5,8	1654-1851	1657-1812	Hexham	1790-1812		5C
Cornhill	1695-1995		8			Berwick			7K
Corsenside	1715-1993	1713-1876	5,8	1715-1843		Bellingham			6F
Cramlington	1665-1997	1665-1812	5,8		1666-1812	Tynemouth			2E(J)
Doddington	1688-1991	1688-1812	8	1688-1837	1701-1812	Glendale			5J
Earsdon	1589-1991	1589-1813	5,7,8		1589-1812	Tynemouth			2D
Edlingham	1658-1992	1658-1896	8	1658-1812	1658-1812	Alnwick	1790-1812		4H
Eglingham	1662-1951	1662-1896	5,8		1663-1812	Alnwick	1790-1812		4I
Ellingham	1695-1997	1695-1818	5,8	1695-1819	1695-1814	Belford		1775-1840	4J
Elsdon	1672-1984	1672-1885	5,8	1672-1812	1672-1780	Rothbury			6F
Embleton	1682-1983	1660-1897	5,8		1682-1812	Alnwick			3I
Falstone	1742-1984	1743-1877	5,8			Bellingham			9F
Felton	1653-1985	1653-1895	4,5,6,7,8,9		1656-1812	Alnwick		1792-1840	4G
Ford	1684-1984	1684-1877	5,8	1683-1812	1684-1812	Glendale		1785-1843	6K
Gosforth	1697-1985	1687-1885	8		1725-1812	Castle Ward			3D
Greystead	1818-1996		5,8			Bellingham			9E
Guizance (ex.par.)			4,5,6,7,8,9			Alnwick			3G(D)
Halton	1654-1983	1654-1886	8	1654-1812	1654-1769	Hexham			5D
Haltwistle	1656-1959	1656-1882	5,8,9	1656-1851		Haltwhistle		1752-1857	8D
Hartburn	1678-1986	1678-1895	5,8		1679-1812	Morpeth			5F
Haydon Bridge	1654-1953	1644-1895	5,8	1654-1991	1655-1812	Hexham			7C
Hebburn	1680-1984	1680-1896	5,8	1678-1812	1680-1812	Morpeth	1790-1812		3F
Heddon on the Wall	1656-1974	1664-1875	8	1671-1710		Castle Ward			4D
Hexham	1579-1972	1579-1894	5,8	1579-1851	1579-1812	Hexham		1787-1837	6C
Holy Island	1578-1960	1578-1885	5,8	1578-1960	1578-1812	Berwick			4L
Horton	1648-1987	1648-1812	5,8		1660-1809	Tynemouth			2E
Howick	1678-1995	1678-1895	8		1686-1812	Alnwick			3I
Ilderton	1724-1930	1724-1895	8	1724-1812	1727-1812	Glendale	1790-1812		5I
Ingram	1682-1992	1684-1895	8	1682-1837	1684-1812	Glendale	1790-1812		5I
Kidland (ex.par.)			8			Rothbury			6H
Kirkharle	1692-1980	1692-1877	5,8	1692-1875		Bellingham			5E(F)
Kirkhaugh	1761-1958	1760-1876	5,8		1760-1812	Haltwhistle			8B
Kirkheaton (ex.par.)	1814-1984		8	1705-1747		Castle Ward			5E(G)
Kirknewton	1670-1992	1659-1885	8	1762-1788		Glendale			6J
Kirkwhelpington	1679-1983	1679-1812	5,8		1684-1812	Bellingham			5F
Knaresdale	1695-1955	1695-1895	5,8		1701-1812	Haltwhistle			9B
Kyloe	1675-1982	1675-1897	5,8			Berwick			5K
Lambley	1742-1951	1742-1896	8	1697-1851	1743-1812	Haltwhistle			9C
Lesbury	1689-1972	1689-1877	5,8	1690-1812	1689-1812	Alnwick	1790-1812		3H
Longbenton	1653-1963	1653-1812	5,7,8	1653-1837	1653-1812	Tynemouth			2D
Longframlington	1653-1990	1653-1897	8		1685-1717	Rothbury			4G
Longhorsley	1667-1991	1668-1876	5,8		1694-1706	Morpeth			4G
Long Houghton	1646-1991	1646-1895	5,8	1646-1812	1646-1812	Alnwick	1790-1812		3I
Lowick	1718-1983	1716-1896	8	1716-1812	1729-1812	Glendale			5K
Lucker	1769-1994	1769-1875	8	1769-1875		Belford			4J
Meldon	1706-1939	1706-1896	5,8	1706-1812	1727-1812	Morpeth	1790-1812		4E(H)
Mitford	1651-1988	1659-1812	5,8		1659-1812	Morpeth			4F
Morpeth	1583-1956	1583-1812	5,8	1719-1812	1583-1812	Morpeth		1829-1837	3E
Netherwitton	1696-1951	1696-1896	5,8	1696-1812	1706-1812	Morpeth			4F
Newbiggin	1662-1995	1662-1812	8	1662-1812	1665-1780	Morpeth			2F
Newbrough	1695-1980	1725-1896	5,8	1695-1980		Hexham			7D
Newburn	1659-1977	1659-1812	8	1654-1739	1659-1812	Castle Ward			3D
Newcastle								1746-1837	2C
All Saints	1600-1963	1600-1895	5,7,8,9	1600-1902	1600-1812	Newcastle			2C
St Andrew	1597-1967	1597-1877	5,7,8		1597-1812	Newcastle			2C
St John	1587-1958	1587-1812	5,7,8		1587-1812	Newcastle			3C
St Nicholas	1558-1965	1558-1897	5,7,8	1574-1812	1574-1812	Newcastle	1790-1812		2C
Norham	1653-1969	1653-1877	5,8		1653-1812	Berwick			6L
Ovingham	1661-1979	1679-1896	5,8	1679-1812	1679-1812	Hexham		1785-1836	4C
Ponteland	1602-1958	1602-1812	5,8		1602-1812	Castle Ward			4D
Ramshope (ex.par.)			5,8			Bellingham			8H

parish name	deposited original registers	I.G.I.	local census indexes	copies of registers at Soc. Gen.	Boyd's marriage index	1837-1851 Registration District	Pallot's marriage index	non-conform. records at P.R.O.	map ref.
Rennington	1765-1992	1768-1895	8	1768-1814	1769-1779	Alnwick			3I
Rock	1768-1981	1769-1896	8	1768-1812	1771-1780	Alnwick			3I
Rothbury	1653-1970	1653-1812	5,8	1653-1812	1653-1812	Rothbury		1769-1840	5G
St John Lee	1664-1983	1664-1896	5,8	1664-1851	1664-1812	Hexham			6D
Shilbottle	1723-1996	1691-1815	5,8		1695-1851	Alnwick			3H
Shotley	1670-1995	1670-1837	5,8	1670-1812	1670-1818	Hexham			5B
Simonburn	1681-1959	1681-1877	5,8	1681-1851		Hexham			7D
Slaley	1703-1991	1703-1895	5,8	1703-1851	1725-1812	Hexham			6C
Stamfordham	1662-1978	1662-1812	5,8	1662-1851	1662-1812	Castle Ward			5D
Stannington	1658-1959	1658-1877	8			Castle Ward			3E
Thockrington	1715-1936	1715-1886	5,8	1715-1851		Bellingham			6E
Thorneyburn	1819-1994		5,8	1818-1838		Bellingham			8F
Tweedmouth	1711-1952	1711-1812	5,8	1711-1812		Berwick		1751-1785	5L
Tynemouth	1607-1981	1607-1884	5,7,8		1607-1733	Tynemouth		1756-1840	2D
Ulgham	1602-1962	1602-1875	5,8			Morpeth			3F
Wallsend	1669-1981	1669-1812	5,7,8		1669-1812	Tynemouth		1813-1837	2D
Warden	1695-1992	1695-1896	5,8	1695-1987	1695-1723	Hexham			6D
Wark	1818-1995	1818-1877	5,7,8			Bellingham			7E
Warkworth	1676-1974	1677-1812	5,8	1677-1812	1677-1812	Alnwick	1790-1812		3G
West Allen or Ninebanks	1767-1998	1767-1877	8			Hexham			7B
Whalton	1661-1987	1661-1896	8	1661-1812	1661-1812	Castle Ward	1790-1812		4E
Whitfield	1605-1980	1606-1877	5,8	1605-1812	1606-1812	Haltwhistle			8B
Whitley	1764-1995	1764-1896	5,8	1764-1851		Tynemouth			6B
Whittingham	1658-1991	1659-1876	5,8			Rothbury			5H
Whittonstall	1754-1960	1750-1877	5,8	1750-1851		Hexham			5C
Widdrington	1698-1975	1698-1876	5,8		1698-1781	Morpeth			2G
Woodhorn	1605-1986	1605-1812	5,8		1606-1812	Morpeth			2F
Wooler	1692-1968	1692-1895	5,8		1693-1812	Glendale			5J(B)

Original registers deposited at:
Northumberland Record Office, Melton Park, North Gosforth, Newcastle upon Tyne NE3 5QX

Study adjacent parishes in counties of Scotland, Cumberland and Durham

Northumberland Record Office, Mellton Park, North Gosforth, Newcastle-upon-Tyne NE3 5QX
Berwick-upon-Tweed Record Office, Council Offices, Wallace Green, Berwick-upon-Tweed TD15 1ED
Morpeth Records Centre, The Kylins, Loansdean, Morpeth, NE61 2EQ
Tyne and Wear Archive Service, Blandford House, Blandford Square, Newcastle-upon-Tyne NE1 4JA

The following indexes have been compiled – see Introduction
Census Indexes 1851, 1871 & 1891 – Northumberland & Durham FHS, c/o Ms Sheila Senior, 2nd Floor, Bolbec Hall, Westgate Road, Newcastle upon Tyne NE1 1SE
Census Indexes 1841 – 1891 for Felton & Guizance – Mr P. Cook, 23 Benlaw Grove, Felton, Morpeth, Northumberland, NE65 9NG
Northumberland Marriage Index 1813 -1837 – Northumberland and Durham FHS, 2nd Floor, Bolbec Hall, Westgate Road, Newcastle upon Tyne NE1 1SE
Northumberland Marriage Index – Mr P.R. Joiner, Greystones, The Spital, Yarm, North Yorkshire, TS15 9EX
Pre 1837 Non-Anglican Marriage Index – Original Indexes, 113 East View, Wideopen, Tyne & Wear, NE13 6EF
Northumberland Burials – Original Indexes, 113 East View, Wideopen, Tyne & Wear, NE13 6EF

Northumberland is triangular in shape; its greatest length from north to south is almost 70 miles and its breadth at the southern extremity from east to west almost 48 miles. It is watered by five principal rivers: the Trent, North Tyne, South Tyne, Coquet and Read. The population in 1841 was 266,020; in 1851, 303,568; in 1861, 343,025; in 1871, 386,959; in 1881, 434,086.

The soils include clay, loam, sand and gravel. The produce was corn, cattle, sheep, lead and coal, the latter being of particular importance. The principal manufactures were glass, pottery and iron and the rivers were the source of considerable numbers of fish, especially trout and salmon.

The information in the Index is abbreviated, and may mislead the searcher if reference is not made to the details contained in the several publications listed in the Introduction. It is essential that users of this book check the appropriate works before making further enquiries.

NOTTINGHAMSHIRE

parish name	deposited original registers	I.G.I.	local census indexes	copies of registers at Soc. Gen.	Boyd's marriage index	1837-1851 Registration District	Pallot's marriage index	non-conform. records at P.R.O.	map ref.
Annesley	1599-1990	1755-1867	4,5,6,7,8,9	1599-1901	1651-1675	Basford	1790-1812		9F
Arnold	1544-1989	1813-1845	4,5,6,7,8,9	1546-1901	1651-1675	Basford	1790-1812		7E
Askham	1538-1932	1781-1844	4,5,6,7,8,9	1538-1904	1651-1675	East Retford	1790-1837		5I
Aslockton	1538-1965		4,5,6,7,8,9			Bingham			5D
Attenborough	1559-1907	1601-1852	4,5,6,7,8,9	1559-1900		Shardlow	1560-1812		8D
Averham	1538-1964	1736-1856	4,5,6,7,8,9	1538-1907	1651-1675	Southwell	1790-1812		5F
Awsworth	1756-1942	1813-1836	4,5,6,7,8,9	1813-1900		Basford			9E
Babworth	1623-1958	1758-1848	4,5,6,7,8,9	1625-1901		East Retford			6J
Balderton	1538-1993	1750-1848	4,5,6,7,8,9	1538-1901	1651-1725	Newark	1538-1812	1796-1856	4F
Barnby in the Willows	1593-1967	1745-1841	4,5,6,7,8,9	1593-1904	1651-1725	Newark	1593-1812		4F
Barnstone (see Langar)						Bingham			5D
Barton in Fabis	1558-1978	1615-1871	4,5,6,7,8,9	1558-1997	1651-1675	Basford	1558-1812		8C
Basford	1561-1964	1772-1831	4,5,6,7,8,9	1561-1925	1651-1675	Basford	1568-1812	1801-1837	8E
Beckingham	1615-1991	1634-1865	4,5,6,7,8,9	1615-1902	1651-1675	Gainsborough	1790-1837		5K
Beeston	1558-1964	1813-1844	4,5,6,7,8,9	1558-1901	1651-1675	Basford	1790-1812	1829-1837	8D
Bestwood (see Lenton)									8E
Bevercotes (see Markham Clinton)									6I
Bilborough	1569-1973	1734-1847	4,5,6,7,8,9	1560-1901	1651-1675	Basford			8E(Q)
Bilsthorpe	1654-1983	1753-1853	4,5,6,7,8,9	1654-1904	1655-1754	Southwell	1790-1837		6G
Bingham	1598-1979	1821-1845	4,5,6,7,8,9	1598-1900	1651-1725	Bingham	1598-1812	1807-1837	6D
Bleasby	1573-1992	1744-1846	4,5,6,7,8,9	1573-1903	1651-1675	Southwell	1790-1812		6F
Blidworth	1566-1934	1741-1835	4,5,6,7,8,9	1566-1901	1651-1675	Mansfield	1790-1837	1833-1836	7F
Blyth	1556-1968	1813-1865	4,5,6,7,8,9	1556-1901		Worksop		1819-1837	7K
Bole	1755-1992	1754-1858	4,5,6,7,8,9	1755-1901		Gainsborough			4K
Bothamsall	1540-1900	1775-1844	4,5,6,7,8,9	1538-1812		East Retford			6I
Boughton	1685-1957	1760-1861	4,5,6,7,8,9	1685-1901		Southwell	1790-1837		6H
Bradmore (see Bunny)									7C
Bramcote	1562-1966	1813-1857	4,5,6,7,8,9	1562-1902	1561-1675	Shardlow	1562-1812	1829-1837	9D
Broughton Sulney	1571-1993	1813-1852	4,5,6,7,8,9	1570-1901	1651-1725	Melton Mowbray	1571-1812	1807-1834	6B
Bulwell	1621-1900	1813-1838	4,5,6,7,8,9	1620-1948	1651-1675	Basford	1790-1812	1804-1817	8E
Bunny	1556-1968	1600-1862	4,5,6,7,8,9	1556-1902	1651-1675	Basford	1790-1818		7C
Burton Joyce	1559-1900	1813-1866	4,5,6,7,8,9	1559-1901	1651-1675	Basford	1790-1812		7E
Calverton	1569-1975	1617-1853	4,5,6,7,8,9	1569-1901	1651-1675	Basford	1790-1812	1831-1836	7F
Carburton	1528-1983	1528-1841	4,5,6,7,8,9	1528-1812		Worksop			7I
Car Colston	1570-1994	1780-1843	4,5,6,7,8,9	1570-1902	1651-1725	Bingham	1570-1812		5E
Carlton in Lindrick	1559-1968	1813-1843	4,5,6,7,8,9	1559-1900		Worksop			7J
Carlton on Trent	1782-1960		4,5,6,7,8,9	1782-1901		Southwell			5H
Caunton	1709-1977	1614-1826	4,5,6,7,8,9	1709-1902		Southwell	1790-1837		5G
Clarborough	1567-1983	1813-1841	4,5,6,7,8,9	1567-1901	1567-1837	East Retford			5J
Clayworth	1540-1959	1813-1855	4,5,6,7,8,9	1540-1901		East Retford			5K
Clifton (with Glapton)	1573-1981	1789-1859	4,5,6,7,8,9	1573-1901	1661-1675	Basford	1573-1812		8C
Coddington	1676-1973	1793-1844	4,5,6,7,8,9	1676-1901	1701-1725	Newark			4F
Colston Basset	1591-1900	1770-1843	4,5,6,7,8,9	1591-1850	1651-1725	Bingham	1591-1837		6C
Colwick	1569-1989	1813-1840	4,5,6,7,8,9	1569-1901	1651-1675	Basford	1755-1812		7D
Cossall	1654-1944	1744-1854	4,5,6,7,8,9	1654-1853	1663-1675	Basford	1790-1812		9E
Costock	1558-1953	1750-1862	4,5,6,7,8,9	1558-1992	1651-1725	Loughborough	1558-1812		7B
Cotgrave	1569-1981	1758-1835	4,5,6,7,8,9	1569-1901	1651-1725	Bingham	1569-1812		7D
Cotham	1587-1979	1815-1841	4,5,6,7,8,9	1587-1902	1651-1725	Newark	1587-1812		4E
Cottam	1695-1900	1774-1864	4,5,6,7,8,9	1696-1905	1699-1837	East Retford			4J
Cromwell	1650-1900	1750-1849	4,5,6,7,8,9	1650-1903	1654-1675	Southwell	1790-1837		4G
Cropwell Bishop	1539-1972	1638-1830	4,5,6,7,8,9	1539-1850	1651-1725	Bingham	1539-1837		6D
Darlton	1568-1979	1633-1836	4,5,6,7,8,9	1568-1904	1569-1837	East Retford			5I
Dunham	1654-1980	1773-1836	4,5,6,7,8,9	1654-1902	1654-1836	East Retford			4I
Eakring	1563-1992	1758-1831	4,5,6,7,8,9	1563-1902	1654-1675	Southwell	1790-1837		6G
East Bridgford	1557-1975	1741-1861	4,5,6,7,8,9	1557-1901	1651-1725	Bingham	1614-1812		6E
East Drayton	1755-1900	1774-1838	4,5,6,7,8,9	1753-1904	1755-1837	East Retford			5I
East Leake	1600-1980	1626-1836	4,5,6,7,8,9	1600-1991	1651-1725	Loughborough	1600-1812	1763-1837	8B
East Markham	1561-1949	1703-1846	4,5,6,7,8,9	1561-1901		East Retford			5I
East Retford	1573-1900	1803-1837	4,5,6,7,8,9	1573-1901		East Retford		1800-1837	6J
East Stoke	1538-1966		4,5,6,7,8,9	1538-1902	1651-1725	Southwell	1538-1812		5E
Eastwood	1711-1970	1750-1859	4,5,6,7,8,9	1621-1862		Basford	1790-1812		9E
Eaton	1660-1978	1757-1843	4,5,6,7,8,9	1660-1902		East Retford			6I
Edingley	1580-1900	1766-1858	4,5,6,7,8,9	1580-1902	1651-1675	Southwell	1790-1837		6F
Edwalton	1545-1968	1813-1842	4,5,6,7,8,9	1538-1902	1651-1675	Bingham	1538-1812		7D(T)
Edwinstowe	1634-1990	1634-1877	4,5,6,7,8,9	1634-1901		Southwell			7H
Egmanton	1653-1979	1813-1838	4,5,6,7,8,9	1653-1902	1653-1675	Southwell	1790-1837		5H
Elkesley	1628-1966	1754-1843	4,5,6,7,8,9	1628-1901		East Retford			6I
Elston	1572-1940	1813-1843	4,5,6,7,8,9	1572-1901	1651-1725	Southwell	1573-1812		5E(G)
Elston Chapel	1584-1878		4,5,6,7,8,9	1584-1873	1651-1725	Southwell	1584-1814		5E(F)
Elton	1592-1933	1750-1840	4,5,6,7,8,9	1592-1904	1651-1725	Bingham	1593-1837		5D
Epperstone	1582-1907	1751-1848	4,5,6,7,8,9	1584-1901	1651-1675	Southwell	1790-1812		7F
Everton	1560-1962	1567-1851	4,5,6,7,8,9	1560-1901	1651-1675	East Retford	1790-1837		6L
Farndon	1695-1959	1695-1845	4,5,6,7,8,9	1558-1901	1651-1725	Newark	1559-1812		5F
Farnsfield	1572-1977	1790-1836	4,5,6,7,8,9	1572-1901	1651-1675	Southwell	1790-1837		7G
Finningley	1557-1992	1813-1852	4,5,6,7,8,9	1557-1901		Doncaster			6M
Flawborough	1680-1900	1770-1842	4,5,6,7,8,9	1674-1908	1701-1725	Bingham	1680-1812		4D
Fledborough cum Woodcoates	1562-1979	1626-1842	4,5,6,7,8,9	1562-1903	1651-1675	East Retford			5I
Flintham	1576-1992	1600-1841	4,5,6,7,8,9	1576-1904	1651-1725	Bingham	1629-1812		5E
Gamston (Retford)	1544-1978	1747-1843	4,5,6,7,8,9	1544-1902		East Retford			6I
Gedling	1558-1948	1813-1860	4,5,6,7,8,9	1558-1900	1651-1675	Basford	1790-1812		7E
Girton	1680-1900	1770-1842	4,5,6,7,8,9	1680-1901		Newark	1790-1807		4H
Gonalston	1538-1900	1753-1843	4,5,6,7,8,9	1538-1905	1651-1675	Southwell	1790-1812		6E(E)
Gotham	1560-1937	1813-1859	4,5,6,7,8,9	1560-1901	1651-1725	Basford	1558-1812		8C
Granby	1567-1972	1814-1864	4,5,6,7,8,9	1567-1901	1651-1725	Bingham	1567-1837		5D
Greasley	1600-1958	1814-1830	4,5,6,7,8,9	1600-1901	1651-1675	Basford	1790-1812	1831-1837	9E
Gringley on the Hill	1678-1900	1682-1885	4,5,6,7,8,9	1632-1902		East Retford			5L
Grove	1726-1900	1601-1836	4,5,6,7,8,9	1726-1906	1726-1812	East Retford			5J
Halam	1559-1932	1769-1849	4,5,6,7,8,9	1559-1901	1651-1675	Southwell	1790-1837		6F

NOTTINGHAMSHIRE

parish name	deposited original registers	I.G.I.	local census indexes	copies of registers at Soc. Gen.	Boyd's marriage index	1837-1851 Registration District	Pallot's marriage index	non-conform. records at P.R.O.	map ref.
Halloughton	1621-1992	1622-1848	4,5,6,7,8,9	1621-1909	1651-1675	Southwell	1790-1837		6F(D)
Harworth and Bircotes	1538-1942	1763-1852	4,5,6,7,8,9	1538-1901	1538-1837	Worksop			6L
Hawksworth	1569-1900	1626-1852	4,5,6,7,8,9	1569-1903	1651-1725	Bingham	1569-1812		5E(N)
Hawton	1564-1984	1608-1862	4,5,6,7,8,9	1564-1901	1651-1725	Newark	1564-1812		4F
Hayton	1655-1983	1769-1863	4,5,6,7,8,9	1655-1901	1655-1675	East Retford	1790-1837		5J
Headon	1566-1947	1567-1837	4,5,6,7,8,9	1566-1812		East Retford	1790-1812		5I
Hickling	1646-1992	1813-1841	4,5,6,7,8,9	1646-1902	1651-1725	Bingham	1646-1837		6C
Hockerton	1582-1900	1813-1851	4,5,6,7,8,9	1582-1837	1651-1675	Southwell	1790-1837		6G
Holme	1711-1989	1623-1843	4,5,6,7,8,9	1711-1905	1711-1837	Southwell	1790-1837		4G
Holme Pierrepont	1564-1971	1788-1847	4,5,6,7,8,9	1564-1901	1651-1725	Bingham	1564-1812		7D
Hoveringham	1553-1900	1813-1852	4,5,6,7,8,9	1553-1812	1651-1675	Southwell	1790-1837		6E
Hucknall Torkard	1560-1965	1600-1837	4,5,6,7,8,9	1560-1901	1651-1675	Basford	1790-1812		8E
Kelham	1663-1964	1813-1856	4,5,6,7,8,9	1663-1901	1663-1675	Southwell	1790-1837		5F
Keyworth	1653-1972	1813-1847	4,5,6,7,8,9	1653-1901	1657-1675	Bingham	1657-1812	1784-1837	7C
Kilvington	1538-1900	1611-1826	4,5,6,7,8,9	1538-1906	1651-1675	Newark	1538-1812		4D
Kingston on Soar	1688-1900	1626-1843	4,5,6,7,8,9	1630-1996	1755-1811	Shardlow	1755-1811		9C
Kinoulton	1606-1991	1662-1865	4,5,6,7,8,9	1569-1837	1651-1837	Bingham	1654-1837		6C
Kirkby in Ashfield	1620-1971	1600-1864	4,5,6,7,8,9	1621-1900	1651-1675	Basford	1790-1812	1748-1836	9F
Kirklington	1575-1956	1622-1848	4,5,6,7,8,9	1575-1902	1651-1675	Southwell	1790-1837		6G
Kirton	1538-1963	1771-1838	4,5,6,7,8,9	1538-1837	1651-1675	Southwell	1790-1837		6H
Kneesall	1682-1948	1777-1861	4,5,6,7,8,9	1682-1901	1682-1837	Southwell	1790-1837		6H
Kneeton	1591-1900	1813-1866	4,5,6,7,8,9	1591-1903	1651-1725	Bingham	1592-1812		5E(K)
Lambley	1652-1948	1813-1826	4,5,6,7,8,9	1569-1902	1651-1675	Basford	1790-1812		7E
Laneham	1538-1900	1760-1859	4,5,6,7,8,9	1538-1901	1651-1675	East Retford	1790-1837		4I
Langar	1595-1963	1761-1873	4,5,6,7,8,9	1595-1837	1651-1837	Bingham	1790-1837		5C
Langford	1669-1992	1761-1843	4,5,6,7,8,9	1669-1907	1703-1837	Newark	1790-1837		4G
Laxton	1563-1994	1564-1848	4,5,6,7,8,9	1563-1901	1651-1675	Southwell	1790-1837		5H
Lenton	1540-1973	1600-1836	4,5,6,7,8,9	1540-1901	1651-1837	Radford	1540-1812		8D
Linby	1692-1946	1627-1835	4,5,6,7,8,9	1692-1904	1692-1837	Basford	1790-1837		8F
Lindhurst (ex.par.)			4,5,6,7,8,9			Mansfield			8G
Littleborough	1539-1985	1609-1841	4,5,6,7,8,9	1539-1902		East Retford			4J
Lowdham	1559-1996	1749-1885	4,5,6,7,8,9	1559-1901	1651-1675	Southwell	1790-1812		6E
Mansfield	1559-1961	1813-1837	4,5,6,7,8,9	1559-1901	1651-1675	Mansfield	1790-1837	1738-1837	8G
Mansfield Woodhouse	1653-1995	1662-1846	4,5,6,7,8,9	1653-1901	1657-1675	Mansfield	1790-1837		8G
Maplebeck	1562-1993	1600-1838	4,5,6,7,8,9	1562-1901	1651-1675	Southwell	1790-1837		6G
Markham Clinton (West Markham)	1651-1950	1626-1838	4,5,6,7,8,9	1651-1902		East Retford			5I(A)
Marnham	1601-1967	1601-1843	4,5,6,7,8,9	1601-1904	1651-1675	East Retford	1790-1837		4H
Mattersey	1539-1954	1608-1843	4,5,6,7,8,9	1545-1902		East Retford			6K
Mering (ex.par.)			4,5,6,7,8,9			Southwell			4H
Misson	1653-1992	1600-1843	4,5,6,7,8,9	1636-1901		Doncaster			6L
Misterton	1540-1977	1635-1865	4,5,6,7,8,9	1540-1900		Gainsborough			5L
Morton	1640-1900	1622-1846	4,5,6,7,8,9	1640-1904	1651-1675	Southwell	1790-1837		5F
Newark on Trent	1599-1900	1599-1839	4,5,6,7,8,9	1599-1900	1651-1725	Newark	1599-1837	1796-1856	4F
Normanton on Soar	1559-1991		4,5,6,7,8,9	1559-1902	1651-1725	Loughborough	1559-1812		8B
Normanton on Trent	1673-1972		4,5,6,7,8,9	1673-1901	1673-1675	East Retford	1790-1837		4H
North and South Clifton	1539-1900	1813-1846	4,5,6,7,8,9	1539-1902	1654-1675	Newark	1790-1812		4H
North Collingham	1558-1986	1773-1843	4,5,6,7,8,9	1558-1901	1651-1675	Newark	1790-1837		4G
North Leverton with Hablesthorpe	1669-1938	1669-1840	4,5,6,7,8,9	1669-1901	1669-1837	East Retford			5J
North Muskham	1705-1943	1623-1843	4,5,6,7,8,9	1705-1901	1706-1837	Southwell	1790-1837		5G
North Wheatley	1649-1983	1601-1854	4,5,6,7,8,9	1649-1901		East Retford			5K
Norton Cuckney	1632-1918	1813-1841	4,5,6,7,8,9	1632-1901		Worksop			8I
Norwell	1681-1960	1635-1843	4,5,6,7,8,9	1638-1901	1651-1675	Southwell	1790-1837		5G
Nottingham								1690-1839	7D
St Mary	1566-1998	1756-1827	4,5,6,7,8,9	1566-1901	1651-1812	Nottingham	1790-1812		7D
St Nicholas	1562-1955	1601-1831	4,5,6,7,8,9	1562-1893	1683-1812	Nottingham			7D
St Peter	1570-1977	1572-1885	4,5,6,7,8,9	1572-1899	1651-1812	Nottingham	1790-1825		7D
Nuthall	1657-1971	1602-1873	4,5,6,7,8,9	1657-1902	1663-1675	Basford	1790-1812		8E
Ollerton	1592-1964	1592-1854	4,5,6,7,8,9	1592-1901		Southwell	1790-1812		6H
Ordsall	1538-1968	1628-1841	4,5,6,7,8,9	1538-1901		East Retford			6J
Orston	1590-1981	1606-1854	4,5,6,7,8,9	1590-1901	1651-1725	Bingham	1590-1812		5D
Ossington	1594-1979		4,5,6,7,8,9	1594-1903	1651-1675	Southwell	1790-1837		5H
Owthorpe	1731-1977	1605-1851	4,5,6,7,8,9	1731-1902	1813-1837	Bingham	1733-1837		6C
Oxton	1564-1999	1618-1844	4,5,6,7,8,9	1564-1901	1651-1675	Southwell	1790-1812	1834-1836	7F
Papplewick	1661-1983	1627-1835	4,5,6,7,8,9	1661-1901	1661-1675	Basford	1790-1837		8F
Park Leys (ex.par.)			4,5,6,7,8,9			Southwell			5G(B)
Perlethorpe	1528-1981	1530-1866	4,5,6,7,8,9	1528-1901		Southwell	1790-1812		6I
Pinxton (Derbys)									9G
Plumtree	1558-1969	1602-1862	4,5,6,7,8,9	1558-1812	1651-1675	Bingham	1790-1812		7C
Radcliffe on Trent	1632-1989	1626-1831	4,5,6,7,8,9	1632-1901	1651-1725	Bingham	1633-1812		6D
Radford	1563-1982	1813-1836	4,5,6,7,8,9	1563-1901	1651-1675	Radford	1790-1812	1824-1837	8D(R)
Ragnall	1700-1991	1623-1836	4,5,6,7,8,9	1700-1905	1701-1837	East Retford			4I
Rampton	1565-1931	1639-1843	4,5,6,7,8,9	1565-1901	1566-1837	East Retford			5I
Ratcliffe on Soar	1597-1900	1627-1854	4,5,6,7,8,9	1597-1901	1651-1675	Shardlow	1624-1812		9C
Rempstone	1570-1974	1600-1854	4,5,6,7,8,9	1570-1990	1651-1725	Loughborough	1570-1812		7B
Rolleston	1588-1900	1600-1846	4,5,6,7,8,9	1559-1901	1651-1675	Southwell	1790-1837		5F
Ruddington	1633-1981	1628-1862	4,5,6,7,8,9	1636-1852	1655-1675	Basford	1655-1813	1824-1837	8C
Rufford (ex.par.)			4,5,6,7,8,9			Southwell			7G
Saundby	1562-1977	1600-1844	4,5,6,7,8,9	1562-1908		Gainsborough			4K
Scarrington	1570-1900	1609-1854	4,5,6,7,8,9	1570-1902	1651-1725	Bingham	1571-1812		5D(M)
Screveton	1639-1980	1630-1843	4,5,6,7,8,9	1652-1902	1651-1725	Bingham	1640-1812		5E(L)
Scrooby	1695-1992	1628-1837	4,5,6,7,8,9	1695-1902	1695-1837	East Retford	1790-1837		6K
Selston	1557-1931	1557-1875	4,5,6,7,8,9	1557-1900	1651-1675	Basford	1790-1812	1794-1837	9F
Shelford	1563-1993	1627-1865	4,5,6,7,8,9	1563-1901	1651-1725	Bingham	1563-1812		6E
Shelton	1595-1966	1595-1853	4,5,6,7,8,9	1595-1905	1651-1725	Bingham	1596-1812		4E
Sibthorpe	1720-1900	1613-1853	4,5,6,7,8,9	1720-1904	1720-1725	Bingham	1720-1812		5E(J)
Skegby	1569-1986	1813-1885	4,5,6,7,8,9	1569-1901	1651-1675	Mansfield	1790-1812		9G
Sneinton	1654-1900	1601-1824	4,5,6,7,8,9	1651-1901	1655-1675	Radford	1790-1812		7D(S)

NOTTINGHAMSHIRE

parish name	deposited original registers	I.G.I.	local census indexes	copies of registers at Soc. Gen.	Boyd's marriage index	1837-1851 Registration District	Pallot's marriage index	non-conform. records at P.R.O.	map ref.
South Collingham	1558-1988	1790-1845	4,5,6,7,8,9	1558-1900	1651-1675	Newark	1790-1837		4G
South Leverton	1658-1924	1600-1840	4,5,6,7,8,9	1658-1901	1659-1837	East Retford			5J
South Muskham	1589-1936	1623-1861	4,5,6,7,8,9	1589-1901	1651-1675	Southwell	1790-1837		5G
South Scarle	1680-1939	1598-1843	4,5,6,7,8,9	1684-1902	1684-1837	Newark	1790-1837		4G
Southwell	1559-1900	1633-1838	4,5,6,7,8,9	1559-1901	1651-1675	Southwell	1790-1837		6F
South Wheatley	1546-1900	1686-1842	4,5,6,7,8,9	1546-1872		East Retford			4K
Stanford on Soar	1633-1900	1602-1841	4,5,6,7,8,9	1633-1991	1651-1725	Loughborough	1633-1812		8B
Stanton on the Wolds	1735-1980	1627-1846	4,5,6,7,8,9	1736-1904	1736-1753	Bingham	1824-1837		7C(V)
Stapleford	1656-1983	1603-1844	4,5,6,7,8,9	1656-1902	1656-1675	Shardlow	1790-1812		9D
Staunton	1654-1900	1608-1842	4,5,6,7,8,9	1654-1905	1654-1725	Newark	1654-1812		4E
Staunton Chapel	1663-1900		4,5,6,7,8,9	1663-1814	1663-1725	Newark	1663-1812		4E
Stokeham	1618-1900	1635-1838	4,5,6,7,8,9	1618-1916	1683-1837	East Retford			4I
Strelley	1654-1903	1626-1848	4,5,6,7,8,9	1654-1900	1665-1675	Basford	1790-1812		9E
Sturton le Steeple	1638-1983	1627-1845	4,5,6,7,8,9	1638-1901		East Retford			4J
Sutton Bonnington								1807-1837	8B
St Anne	1560-1989	1600-1829	4,5,6,7,8,9	1560-1900	1651-1675	Loughborough	1560-1812		8B
St Michael	1558-1978	1600-1852	4,5,6,7,8,9	1558-1901	1651-1725	Loughborough	1559-1812		8B
Sutton-cum-Lound	1538-1938	1627-1837	4,5,6,7,8,9	1538-1901	1651-1675	East Retford	1790-1837		6K
Sutton in Ashfield	1577-1995	1813-1823	4,5,6,7,8,9	1572-1901	1651-1675	Mansfield	1813-1837	1760-1837	9G
Sutton on Trent	1584-1975	1813-1868	4,5,6,7,8,9	1584-1901	1651-1675	Southwell	1790-1837		4H
Syerston	1567-1900	1799-1843	4,5,6,7,8,9	1568-1904	1651-1725	Southwell	1567-1812		5E(H)
Teversall	1571-1957	1793-1857	4,5,6,7,8,9	1571-1901	1651-1675	Mansfield	1790-1812		9G
Thorney	1562-1900	1813-1843	4,5,6,7,8,9	1561-1901	1651-1675	Newark	1790-1837		3I
Thoroton	1583-1953	1777-1854	4,5,6,7,8,9	1583-1903	1651-1725	Bingham	1583-1812		5E(O)
Thorpe in the Glebe			4,5,6,7,8,9			Loughborough			7B
Thorpe next to Newark	1542-1900	1813-1843	4,5,6,7,8,9	1542-1901	1651-1725	Southwell	1559-1800		5F
Thrumpton	1679-1975	1813-1857	4,5,6,7,8,9	1679-1902	1679-1812	Basford	1679-1812		9C
Thurgarton	1721-2000	1793-1847	4,5,6,7,8,9	1654-1903	1651-1675	Southwell	1790-1837		6F
Tithby	1559-1900	1813-1843	4,5,6,7,8,9	1559-1905	1651-1837	Bingham	1790-1837		6D
Tollerton	1558-1972	1793-1852	4,5,6,7,8,9	1558-1902	1651-1725	Bingham	1559-1812		7D(U)
Treswell	1557-1900	1760-1841	4,5,6,7,8,9	1557-1902		East Retford			4J
Trowell	1567-1945	1783-1843	4,5,6,7,8,9	1568-1901	1651-1675	Basford	1790-1812		9D
Tuxford	1624-1975	1813-1843	4,5,6,7,8,9	1624-1901		East Retford			5H
Upton	1585-1902	1633-1843	4,5,6,7,8,9	1585-1902	1651-1675	Southwell	1790-1837		5F
Walesby	1580-1988	1580-1865	4,5,6,7,8,9	1580-1901		Southwell			6I
Walkeringham	1605-1955	1755-1852	4,5,6,7,8,9	1605-1901		Gainsborough			5L
Wallingwells (ex.par.)			4,5,6,7,8,9			Worksop			8J
Warsop	1538-1971	1813-1858	4,5,6,7,8,9	1538-1901		Mansfield			8H
Welbeck (ex.par.)			4,5,6,7,8,9			Worksop			7I
Wellow	1703-1983	1622-1839	4,5,6,7,8,9	1703-1812		Southwell	1723-1812		6H
West Bridgford	1559-1948	1752-1842	4,5,6,7,8,9	1559-1901	1651-1675	Basford	1559-1812		7D
West Burton	1602-1955	1745-1837	4,5,6,7,8,9	1602-1878		Gainsborough			4K
West Drayton	1632-1900	1760-1846	4,5,6,7,8,9	1632-1902		East Retford			6I
West Leake	1616-1900	1813-1835	4,5,6,7,8,9	1614-1989	1651-1725	Loughborough	1617-1812		8B
Weston	1559-1960	1813-1842	4,5,6,7,8,9	1559-1901	1651-1675	Southwell	1790-1837		5H
West Retford	1722-1972	1622-1841	4,5,6,7,8,9	1754-1901		East Retford		1800-1837	6J
Whatton	1538-1965	1813-1851	4,5,6,7,8,9	1538-1904	1651-1725	Bingham	1538-1812		5D
Widmerpool	1539-1900	1813-1864	4,5,6,7,8,9	1539-1904	1651-1725	Bingham		1807-1834	7C
Wilford	1657-1970		4,5,6,7,8,9	1657-1901	1657-1675	Basford	1657-1812		8D
Willoughby on the Wolds	1680-1970	1813-1844	4,5,6,7,8,9	1680-1900	1682-1812	Loughborough	1682-1812		7B
Winkburn	1541-1992		4,5,6,7,8,9	1541-1929	1651-1675	Southwell	1773		6G
Winthorpe	1687-1992	1813-1842	4,5,6,7,8,9	1687-1901	1701-1725	Newark	1695-1812		4F(C)
Wiverton Hall (ex.par.)			4,5,6,7,8,9			Bingham			6D(P)
Wollaton	1576-1960	1813-1860	4,5,6,7,8,9	1576-1901	1651-1675	Basford	1790-1812		8D
Woodborough	1547-1952	1623-1835	4,5,6,7,8,9	1547-1901	1651-1675	Basford	1790-1812		7E
Woodhouse Hall (ex.par.)			4,5,6,7,8,9			Worksop			8I
Worksop	1558-1939	1558-1857	4,5,6,7,8,9	1558-1901	1654-1675	Worksop	1654-1812	1814-1837	7I
Wysall	1654-1997	1813-1853	4,5,6,7,8,9	1654-1900		Loughborough			7C

Original registers deposited at:
Nottinghamshire Archives, County House, Castle Meadow Road, Nottingham NG2 1AG

Study adjacent parishes in counties of Derbyshire, Yorkshire, Lincolnshire and Leicestershire

Nottinghamshire Archives Office, County House, Castle Meadow Road, Nottingham NG2 1AG
Nottingham University Manuscripts Department, Hallward Library, University Park, Nottingham NG7 2RD

The following indexes have been compiled – see Introduction
Census Indexes 1841-1891 – Nottinghamshire FHS, c/o Mrs S. Greenall, 10 Sherwin Walk, Nottingham, NG3 1AH
Marriage Index – Nottinghamshire FHS, c/o Mrs S. Greenall, 10 Sherwin Walk, Nottingham, NG3 1AH from start of registers up to 1837, some parishes to 1900
Nottingham Marriage Index 1562-1812 – Nottinghamshire Archives, County House, Castle Meadow Road, Nottingham NG2 1AG
Monumental Inscriptions – Nottinghamshire FHS, c/o Mrs S. Greenall, 10 Sherwin Walk, Nottingham, NG3 1AH

Nottinghamshire's length from north to south is about 50 miles, its greatest breadth 25 miles. It is watered by three principal rivers: the Trent, Idle and Erwash. The population in 1841 was 249,910; in 1851, 270,427; in 1861, 293,867; in 1871, 319,758; in 1881, 391,815.

The soils are sand, gravel, clay and loam and along the Derbyshire border there is lime and coal. Barley and other grains were grown as well as hops and there were extensive pastures. Great numbers of pigeons were kept.

The information in the Index is abbreviated, and may mislead the searcher if reference is not made to the details contained in the several publications listed in the Introduction. It is essential that users of this book check the appropriate works before making further enquiries.

OXFORDSHIRE

parish name	deposited original registers	I.G.I.	local census indexes	copies of registers at Soc. Gen.	Boyd's marriage index	1837-1851 Registration District	Pallot's marriage index	non-conform. records at P.R.O.	map ref.
Adderbury	A 1598-1898	1598-1856	5,6,7,8,9	1589-1994	1598-1840	Banbury			6K
Adwell	A 1539-1992	1539-1866	4,5,6,7,8,9	1539-1974	1540-1809	Thame			3F(Z)
Albury	A 1639-1995	1680-1851	4,5,6,7,8,9	1639-1980		Thame			3G
Alkerton	A 1544-1975	1546-1851	5,6,7,8,9	1544-1986	1546-1836	Banbury			7L
Alvescot	A 1662-1996	1721-1851	5,6,7,8,9	1645-1950		Witney			9G
Ambrosden	A 1611-1997	1611-1852	4,5,6,7,8,9	1611-1878	1611-1878	Bicester			4I
Ardley	A 1758-1835	1680-1851	4,5,6,7,8,9	1680-1851	1713-1835	Bicester			5J
Arncott (see Ambrosden)									4H
Ascott under Wychwood	A 1569-1980	1721-1851	4,5,6,7,8,9	1569-1977		Chipping Norton			8I
Asthall	A 1684-1984	1667-1851	5,6,7,8,9	1667-1975		Witney			8H
Aston Rowant	A 1554-1978	1554-1871	4,5,6,7,8,9	1554-1871	1555-1812	Thame			2F
Attington (ex.par.)			4,5,6,7,8,9			Thame			3F
Balscote	A 1821-1977	1813-1853	5,6,7,8,9	1821-1988		Banbury			7L
Bampton	A 1538-1972	1538-1868	4,5,6,7,8,9	1538-1909		Witney		1647-1837	8F
Banbury	A 1558-1964	1558-1851	5,6,7,8,9	1558-1935	1558-1837	Banbury		1789-1837	6K
Barford St John	A 1629-1928	1669-1852	5,6,7,8,9	1629-1983	1669-1737	Banbury			6K
Barford St Michael	A 1755-1961	1721-1852	4,5,6,7,8,9	1643-1988	1755-1849	Banbury			7J(B)
Beckley	A 1703-1979	1678-1851	4,5,6,7,8,9	1703-1979		Headington			4H
Begbroke	A 1664-1991	1721-1852	4,5,6,7,8,9	1664-1852		Woodstock			6H(P)
Benson (Bensington)	A 1565-1975	1565-1858	4,5,6,7,8,9	1565-1964	1569-1812	Wallingford		1835-1836	4E
Benson (detached)			4,5,6,7,8,9			Wallingford			4E(d)
Berrick-Salome	A 1609-1985	1815-1853	4,5,6,7,8,9	1609-1979		Wallingford			4E
Berrick-Salome (det.)			4,5,6,7,8,9			Wallingford			4E(d)
Bicester	A 1539-1963	1539-1840	4,5,6,7,8,9	1539-1960	1539-1840	Bicester		1786-1837	4I
Binsey	A 1754-1979	1754-1885	5,6,7,8,9	1754-1987		Abingdon			6G
Bix Brand	A 1577-1952	1639-1852	4,5,6,7,8,9	1577-1952		Henley			2D
Black Bourton		1678-1853	5,6,7,8,9	1542-1864		Witney			9G
Blackthorn (see Ambrosden)									4I
Bladon	A 1545-1978	1684-1856	4,5,6,7,8,9	1545-1978		Woodstock			6H(L)
Blenheim Park (ex.par.)			5,6,7,8,9			Woodstock			7H
Bletchingdon	A 1559-1993	1713-1865	4,5,6,7,8,9	1559-1865	1713-1835	Bicester			6H
Bloxham	A 1630-1970	1630-1871	5,6,7,8,9	1630-1970	1630-1837	Banbury		1789-1837	7K
Bodicote	A 1563-1933	1564-1852	5,6,7,8,9	1563-1988	1564-1840	Banbury			6K
Bourton	A 1863-1978		5,6,7,8,9	1863-1995		Banbury			6L
Brightwell Baldwin	A 1546-1979	1547-1812	4,5,6,7,8,9	1546-1981	1547-1812	Henley			3E(e)
Britwell Salome	A 1574-1987	1696-1852	5,6,7,8,9	1574-1982	1575-1812	Henley			3E(g)
Brize Norton	A 1548-1997	1548-1875	5,6,7,8,9	1538-1877	1569-1837	Witney			8G
Broadwell		1721-1852	5,6,7,8,9	1615-1917		Witney			9G
Broughton	A 1683-1893	1680-1850	5,6,7,8,9	1680-1893	1680-1840	Banbury			7L
Broughton Poggs	A 1556-1710	1721-1852	5,6,7,8,9	1556-1852		Witney			10G
Bruern (ex.par.)			4,5,6,7,8,9			Chipping Norton			9H
Bucknell	A 1653-1979	1653-1852	4,5,6,7,8,9	1653-1979	1654-1840	Bicester			5I
Burford	A 1612-1944	1613-1860	5,6,7,8,9	1612-1937	1612-1840	Witney		1809-1837	9H
Cassington	A 1652-1947	1673-1852	4,5,6,7,8,9	1603-1939	1673-1837	Woodstock	1800-1837		6H
Caversfield	A 1641-1976	1755-1865	5,6,7,8,9	1606-1976	1754-1840	Bicester			4I
Caversham	B 1597-1958	1639-1869	5,6,7,8,9	1597-1869		Henley			3C
Chadlington	A 1565-1977	1669-1851	4,5,6,7,8,9	1567-1967		Chipping Norton			8I
Chalgrove	A 1531-1999	1639-1853	4,5,6,7,8,9	1531-1853		Thame			4F
Charlbury	A 1559-1932	1559-1851	4,5,6,7,8,9	1559-1900	1559-1764	Chipping Norton			8I
Charlton on Otmoor	A 1562-1907	1700-1854	4,5,6,7,8,9	1562-1875		Bicester			4H
Chastleton	A 1572-1985	1682-1852	4,5,6,7,8,9	1572-1985		Chipping Norton			9J
Checkendon	A 1719-1977	1639-1860	4,5,6,7,8,9	1639-1979		Henley			3D
Chesterton	A 1538-1929	1538-1855	4,5,6,7,8,9	1538-1855	1538-1837	Bicester			5I
Chilson (see Charlbury)									8I
Chinnor	A 1581-1923	1622-1855	4,5,6,7,8,9	1581-1978	1622-1754	Wycombe		1804-1837	2F
Chipping Norton	A 1560-1990	1560-1856	4,5,6,7,8,9	1560-1990	1626-1675	Chipping Norton	1800-1837	1767-1837	8J
Chislehampton	A 1567-1976	1569-1833	4,5,6,7,8,9	1569-1840	1569-1762	Abingdon			4F(U)
Churchill	A 1630-1978	1630-1875	4,5,6,7,8,9	1630-1993	1631-1837	Chipping Norton			9I
Clanfield	A 1633-1995	1721-1852	5,6,7,8,9	1633-1880		Witney			9F
Clattercott (ex.par.)			5,6,7,8,9			Banbury			6M
Claydon	A 1569-1990	1569-1851	5,6,7,8,9	1569-1999	1569-1837	Banbury			6M
Clifton Hampden	A 1578-1992	1787-1866	4,5,6,7,8,9	1576-1866		Abingdon			5E
Cogges	A 1653-1995	1655-1852	4,5,6,7,8,9	1653-1973	1655-1755	Witney			7G
Combe	A 1646-1932	1646-1851	4,5,6,7,8,9	1646-1992	1654-1692	Woodstock			7H
Cornbury Park (ex.par.)			5,6,7,8,9			Chipping Norton			8I(G)
Cornwell	A 1662-1979	1669-1853	4,5,6,7,8,9	1662-1982		Chipping Norton			9J
Cottisford	A 1610-1978	1678-1852	4,5,6,7,8,9	1610-1997	1678-1836	Bicester			4J
Cowley	A 1678-1972	1721-1854	4,5,6,7,8,9	1678-1904		Headington			5G
Cropredy	A 1538-1990	1538-1837	5,6,7,8,9	1538-1995	1538-1837	Banbury		1823-1837	6M
Crowell	A 1594-1979	1602-1852	4,5,6,7,8,9	1594-1979	1602-1837	Thame	1800-1836		2F
Crowmarsh Gifford	B 1575-1992	1575-1875	4,5,6,7,8,9	1576-1900	1576-1836	Wallingford			4D
Cuddesdon	A 1541-1979	1542-1829	4,5,6,7,8,9	1541-1979	1542-1754	Headington			4F(S)
Culham	A 1747-1882	1666-1875	4,5,6,7,8,9	1648-1987		Abingdon			5E
Cuxham	A 1578-1840	1639-1864	4,5,6,7,8,9	1578-1982	1648-1840	Henley			3E(f)
Deddington	A 1631-1969	1669-1851	4,5,6,7,8,9	1631-1902	1669-1837	Woodstock			6J
Denton (see Cuddesdon)									4F
Dorchester	A 1638-1919	1661-1816	4,5,6,7,8,9	1638-1961		Wallingford			5E
Drayton (near Banbury)	A 1577-1965	1577-1859	5,6,7,8,9	1577-1987	1577-1837	Banbury			6L
Drayton (St Leonard)	A 1568-1977	1813-1857	4,5,6,7,8,9	1568-1857		Abingdon			4E
Ducklington	A 1550-1992		5,6,7,8,9	1550-1917		Witney	1790-1837		8G
Dunstew	A 1654-1995	1669-1837	4,5,6,7,8,9	1593-1996	1670-1837	Woodstock			6J
Easington	A 1754-1834	1669-1865	4,5,6,7,8,9	1630-1979		Thame			3E(c)
Elsfield	A 1686-1993	1670-1852	4,5,6,7,8,9	1670-1979		Headington			5G
Emmington	A 1539-1854	1539-1852	4,5,6,7,8,9	1538-1983	1539-1836	Thame			2G
Enstone	A 1558-1985	1558-1841	4,5,6,7,8,9	1558-1976	1558-1837	Chipping Norton			7I
Epwell	A 1577-1952	1577-1875	5,6,7,8,9	1577-1993	1580-1777	Banbury			8L
Ewelme	A 1599-1986	1802-1852	4,5,6,7,8,9	1559-1982		Wallingford			3E
Ewelme (detached)			4,5,6,7,8,9			Wallingford			4E(d)
Eynsham	A 1653-1994	1665-1844	5,6,7,8,9	1653-1900	1665-1675	Witney	1800-1837		7G
Fifield	A 1700-1994	1794-1851	4,5,6,7,8,9	1659-1984		Chipping Norton			9I

OXFORDSHIRE

parish name	deposited original registers	I.G.I.	local census indexes	copies of registers at Soc. Gen.	Boyd's marriage index	1837-1851 Registration District	Pallot's marriage index	non-conform. records at P.R.O.	map ref.
Finmere	A 1560-1962	1700-1853	4,5,6,7,8,9	1560-1996	1700-1837	Brackley			4K
Forest Hill	A 1564-1836	1566-1952	4,5,6,7,8,9	1564-1852		Headington			5G
Fringford	A 1586-1980	1721-1856	4,5,6,7,8,9	1586-1997	1721-1837	Bicester			4J
Fritwell	A 1558-1892	1558-1837	4,5,6,7,8,9	1558-1952	1558-1837	Bicester			5J
Fulbrook	A 1616-1996	1615-1885	4,5,6,7,8,9	1615-1996	1615-1837	Witney			9H
Garsington	A 1562-1960		4,5,6,7,8,9	1562-1855		Headington			5F
Glympton	EA 1567-1995	1568-1812	4,5,6,7,8,9	1567-1863	1567-1754	Woodstock			7I
Godington	A 1678-1953	1678-1834	4,5,6,7,8,9	1678-1997	1678-1837	Bicester			3J
Goring	A 1673-1888		4,5,6,7,8,9	1673-1982		Bradfield		1790-1834	4C
Goring Heath	A 1742-1958		4,5,6,7,8,9			Bradfield			4C
Great Haseley	A 1538-1992	1538-1837	4,5,6,7,8,9	1538-1958	1538-1837	Thame			3F
Great Milton	A 1550-1991	1550-1840	4,5,6,7,8,9	1550-1967	1550-1840	Thame			4F
Great Rollright	A 1560-1935	1668-1837	4,5,6,7,8,9	1560-1935	1668-1837	Chipping Norton			8J
Great Tew	A 1606-1975	1606-1836	4,5,6,7,8,9	1606-1993	1606-1836	Chipping Norton			7J
Hailey (with Crawley)	A 1797-1983		5,6,7,8,9	1797-1932		Witney			8H
Hampton Gay	A 1622-1836		4,5,6,7,8,9	1622-1852		Woodstock			6H(N)
Hampton Poyle	A 1540-1982	1545-1754	4,5,6,7,8,9	1540-1978	1545-1754	Woodstock			5H(O)
Hanborough	A 1560-1992	1560-1837	4,5,6,7,8,9	1560-1860	1651-1675	Witney	1800-1837		7H
Hanwell	A 1586-1930	1586-1837	5,6,7,8,9	1586-1991	1586-1837	Banbury			6L
Hardwick	A 1758-1977	1755-1837	4,5,6,7,8,9	1739-1997	1753-1837	Bicester			4J(J)
Harpsden	A 1558-1994	1563-1754	4,5,6,7,8,9	1560-1928	1563-1754	Henley	1790-1836		2C
Headington	A 1681-1993	1681-1848	4,5,6,7,8,9	1598-1900	1678-1837	Headington			5G
Henley	A 1558-1979	1558-1653	4,5,6,7,8,9	1558-1979	1558-1653	Henley		1685-1837	2D
Hethe	A 1678-1994	1700-1837	4,5,6,7,8,9	1678-1997	1700-1837	Bicester			4J
Heythrop	A 1600-1994	1668-1833	4,5,6,7,8,9	1600-1981	1668-1833	Chipping Norton			8J
Holton	A 1633-1995		4,5,6,7,8,9	1633-1982		Headington			4G
Holwell			5,6,7,8,9	1844-1996		Witney			9G
Hook Norton	A 1550-1982	1669-1837	4,5,6,7,8,9	1550-1979	1669-1837	Banbury			8K
Horley	A 1538-1968	1538-1837	5,6,7,8,9	1538-1992	1538-1837	Banbury			7L
Hornton	A 1703-1880	1723-1837	5,6,7,8,9	1703-1992	1703-1837	Banbury			7L
Horspath	A 1561-1978	1561-1836	4,5,6,7,8,9	1561-1900	1561-1837	Headington			5G
Ibstone (Bucks.)	C 1665-1973	1665-1812	4,5,6,7,8,9	1639-1973	1665-1812	Wycombe	1790-1812		2E
Ickford (Bucks.)									3G
Idbury	A 1754-1991		4,5,6,7,8,9	1669-1985		Chipping Norton			9I
Iffley	A 1572-1986		4,5,6,7,8,9	1572-1986	1574-1812	Headington			5F
Ipsden	A 1560-1983	1509-1840	4,5,6,7,8,9	1560-1983	1569-1840	Henley		1818-1833	4D
Islip	A 1590-1978	1590-1885	4,5,6,7,8,9	1590-1871		Bicester			5H
Kelmscott	A 1740-1992		5,6,7,8,9	1538-1850		Witney			9F
Kencot	A 1544-1849		5,6,7,8,9	1538-1994		Witney			9G
Kiddington	A 1573-1977	1576-1837	4,5,6,7,8,9	1573-1977	1576-1837	Woodstock			7I
Kidlington	A 1574-1960	1574-1837	4,5,6,7,8,9	1574-1960	1574-1754	Woodstock			6H
Kingham	A 1663-1969		4,5,6,7,8,9	1663-1963		Chipping Norton			9I
Kingsey (Bucks.)									2G
Kirtlington	A 1558-1966	1558-1837	4,5,6,7,8,9	1558-1840	1558-1837	Bicester			6I
Langford	A 1538-1880		5,6,7,8,9	1538-1880	1589-1837	Faringdon			9F
Launton	A 1648-1978	1672-1837	4,5,6,7,8,9	1648-1979	1671-1837	Bicester			4I
Leafield	A 1784-1983		4,5,6,7,8,9	1784-1983		Chipping Norton			8H
Lewknor	A 1666-1999	1666-1753	4,5,6,7,8,9	1666-1884	1666-1812	Thame/Wycombe			2E
Little Milton	A 1844-1992		4,5,6,7,8,9			Thame		1789-1837	9I
Littlemore	A 1836-1959		4,5,6,7,8,9	1814-1936		Abingdon			5F
Little Rollright	A 1754-1972	1721-1829	4,5,6,7,8,9	1721-1985	1721-1985	Chipping Norton			9J
Little Tew			4,5,6,7,8,9	1854-1994		Chipping Norton			7J
Lower Heyford	A 1539-1888	1539-1840	4,5,6,7,8,9	1539-1840	1539-1840	Bicester			6I
Lyneham (see Shipton)						Chipping Norton			9I
Mapledurham	A 1627-1960	1627-1867	4,5,6,7,8,9	1627-1960		Bradfield			3C
Marsh Baldon	A 1559-1976	1662-1851	4,5,6,7,8,9	1559-1851		Abingdon			5F(T)
Marston	A 1653-1944		4,5,6,7,8,9	1653-1944		Headington			5G
Merton	A 1635-1990	1729-1837	4,5,6,7,8,9	1635-1972	1721-1837	Bicester	1790-1837		4I
Middleton Stoney	A 1598-1916	1679-1830	4,5,6,7,8,9	1598-1978	1679-1830	Bicester			5I
Milcombe	A 1562-1993	1562-1791	5,6,7,8,9	1562-1990	1562-1711	Banbury			7K
Minster Lovell	A 1754-1978	1813-1865	4,5,6,7,8,9	1656-1973		Witney			8G
Mixbury	A 1645-1977	1645-1882	4,5,6,7,8,9	1645-1996	1657-1837	Brackley			4K
Mollington	A 1561-1988	1565-1840	5,6,7,8,9	1565-1999	1565-1840	Banbury			7M
Mongewell	A 1660-1931	1682-1812	4,5,6,7,8,9	1660-1931	1682-1812	Wallingford			4D
Nether Worton	A 1560-1929	1813-1830	4,5,6,7,8,9	1560-1881	1813-1830	Woodstock			7J(C)
Nettlebed	A 1641-1970		4,5,6,7,8,9	1641-1883		Henley			2D
Newington	A 1572-1977		4,5,6,7,8,9	1572-1869		Wallingford			4E
Newnham Murren	B 1678-1992	1685-1840	4,5,6,7,8,9	1678-1992	1685-1840	Wallingford			4D
Newton Purcell	A 1538-1933	1700-1837	4,5,6,7,8,9	1538-1996	1700-1837	Bicester			4J
Noke	A 1574-1955	1574-1883	4,5,6,7,8,9	1574-1976		Bicester			5H
North Aston	A 1565-1958	1722-1853	4,5,6,7,8,9	1565-1853	1725-1836	Woodstock			6J
Northleigh	A 1572-1966		4,5,6,7,8,9	1572-1966		Witney			7H
Northmoor	A 1653-1964	1654-1837	4,5,6,7,8,9	1653-1899	1654-1837	Witney	1800-1837		7F
North Stoke	A 1740-1835	1744-1837	4,5,6,7,8,9	1721-1982	1639-1837	Wallingford			4D
Nuffield			4,5,6,7,8,9	1570-1853		Henley			3D
Nuneham Courtenay	A 1715-1971		4,5,6,7,8,9	1715-1840		Abingdon			5F
Oddington	A 1571-1969		4,5,6,7,8,9	1571-1977		Bicester			5H
Over Worton	A 1628-1995	1721-1835	4,5,6,7,8,9	1628-1995	1721-1835	Woodstock			6J(D)
Oxford								1784-1837	5G
All Saints	A 1559-1984		4,5,6,7,8,9	1559-1895		Oxford			5G
Christ Church	F 1633+	1642-1754	4,5,6,7,8,9	1633-1884	1642-1754	Oxford			5G
Magdalen College	G 1728-1867		4,5,6,7,8,9	1728-1867		Oxford			5G
Merton College (see St John Baptist)			4,5,6,7,8,9	1616-1892		Oxford			5G
New College	G 1703-1903		4,5,6,7,8,9	1703-1803		Oxford			5G
Radcliffe Infirmary			4,5,6,7,8,9			Oxford			5G
St Aldate	A 1678-1952		4,5,6,7,8,9	1538-1900		Oxford			5G
St Clement	A 1665-1964		4,5,6,7,8,9	1626-1938		Headington			5G
St Cross	A 1653-1965		4,5,6,7,8,9	1653-1900		Oxford			5G
St Ebbe	A 1557-1947		4,5,6,7,8,9	1557-1952		Oxford			5G
St Giles	A 1576-1980	1576-1885	4,5,6,7,8,9	1576-1963	1599-1754	Headington			5G

SHROPSHIRE

parish name	deposited original registers	I.G.I.	local census indexes	copies of registers at Soc. Gen.	Boyd's marriage index	1837-1851 Registration District	Pallot's marriage index	non-conform. records at P.R.O.	map ref.
Abdon	A 1554-1850	1561-1857	5,8	1561-1857		Ludlow			3H
Acton Burnell	A 1568-1981	1568-1855	5,8	1568-1840		Atcham	1790-1837		5G
Acton Round	A 1585-1812	1585-1848	5,8	1638-1844		Bridgnorth			4H
Acton Scott	A 1690-1875	1638-1879	5,8	1660-1713		Church Stretton			3F
Adderley	A 1692-1930	1692-1875	5,8	1692-1812	1692-1812	Market Drayton			9I
Alberbury	A 1564-1991	1564-1864	5,8	1564-1812	1564-1812	Atcham	1790-1812		6E
Albrighton	A 1555-1953	1555-1866	5,8	1555-1812	1555-1812	Shifnal	1790-1812		5J
Albrighton	A 1649-1812	1649-1812	5,8	1649-1812	1684-1757	Atcham			7G(B)
Alveley	A 1561-1970	1561-1837	5,8	1662-1735	1662-1750	Bridgnorth			3J
Ashford Bowdler	A 1603-1837	1601-1865	5,8	1602-1837		Ludlow			1G
Ashford Carbonell	A 1653-1980	1670-1846	5,8			Ludlow			7G
Astley	A 1695-1957	1695-1875	5,8	1692-1812	1726-1812	Atcham	1790-1812		7G
Astley Abbots	A 1561-1923	1561-1852	5,8			Bridgnorth			4I
Aston Botterell	A 1559-1837	1559-1867	5,8	1661-1867		Cleobury Mortimer			3H
Aston Eyre (see Morvill)									4I
Atcham	A 1619-1932	1621-1871	5,8	1813-1840	1621-1837	Atcham	1790-1837		6G
Badger	A 1662-1837	1602-1870	5,8	1660-1870	1662-1836	Shifnal	1790-1862		5J
Barrow	A 1611-1930	1660-1859	5,8	1660-1859		Madeley			5I
Baschurch	A 1600-1977	1600-1868	5,8			Ellesmere			7F
Battlefield	A 1663-1979	1663-1848	5,8	1663-1812	1665-1775	Atcham	1774		7G
Beckbury	A 1661-1854	1610-1878	5,8	1660-1878		Shifnal			5J
Bedstone	A 1719-1992	1660-1854	5,8	1660-1854	1720-1812	Knighton	1790-1812		2E
Benthall	A 1558-1882	1558-1854	5,8			Madeley			5I
Berrington	A 1559-1979	1559-1875	5,8	1559-1837	1561-1837	Atcham	1790-1837		6G
Bettwys-y-Crwyn	A 1695-1838	1661-1854	8			Knighton			3C
Bicton	A 1853-1946		8			Atcham			6F
Billingsley	A 1626-1848	1625-1854	8	1625-1812	1628-1812	Bridgnorth			3I
Bishops Castle	A 1559-1997	1559-1876	4,5,6,8			Clun		1814-1837	3E
Bitterley	A 1658-1978	1658-1876	5,8	1658-1852	1658-1812	Ludlow	1790-1812		2G
Bobbington (see Staffs.)									4K
Bolas Magna	A 1582-1872	1582-1868	8	1582-1812	1584-1812	Wellington	1790-1812		7I
Boningale	A 1698-1941	1654-1875	5,8	1698-1812	1698-1812	Shifnal	1790-1812		5J
Boscobel (ex.par.)			5,8			Shifnal			6K
Bridgnorth								1769-1840	4I
St Leonard	A 1556-1976	1556-1873	8	1636-1812	1636-1812	Bridgnorth			4I(O)
St Mary Magdalene	A 1610-1980	1610-1877	8	1665-1725	1665-1725	Bridgnorth	1795-1812		4I(P)
Bromfield	A 1598-1996	1559-1875	5,8	1559-1812	1559-1812	Ludlow	1790-1812		2G
Broseley	A 1570-1916	1570-1840	8	1570-1750	1571-1750	Madeley		1794-1837	5I
Broughton	A 1705-1812	1630-1856	5,8	1586-1812	1586-1812	Wem	1790-1812		8G
Bucknell	A 1598-1974	1598-1879	5,8	1598-1675		Knighton			2E
Buildwas	A 1665-1972	1659-1868	5,8	1659-1837	1665-1837	Madeley	1790-1837		5H
Burford	A 1558-1928	1558-1876	8	1558-1812	1559-1812	Tenbury	1790-1812		1H
Burwarton	A 1575-1845	1575-1812	8			Bridgnorth		1796-1829	3H
Calverhall	A 1771-1992	1791-1869	8			Wem			9H
Cardeston	A 1706-1975	1663-1846	8	1678-1703	1664-1812	Atcham	1790-1812		6E
Cardington	A 1598-1910	1598-1876	5,8			Church Stretton			4G
Caynham	A 1558-1886	1660-1874	5,8			Ludlow			2G
Chelmarsh	A 1557-1923	1556-1879	8	1557-1812	1558-1812	Bridgnorth	1790-1812		3I
Cheswardine	A 1558-1982	1558-1868	5,8		1556-1662	Market Drayton			8I
Chetton	A 1538-1886	1538-1879	8			Bridgnorth			4I
Chetwynd	A 1585-1927	1585-1865	8			Newport			8I
Childs Ercall	A 1569-1979	1569-1869	5,8			Market Drayton			8I
Chirbury	A 1629-1900	1629-1860	5,8	1629-1812	1629-1812	Montgomery	1790-1812	1827-1836	5D
Church Aston	A 1620-1979	1620-1856	8	1810-1855		Newport			7J
Church Preen	A 1813-1977	1680-1879	5,8	1680-1813	1680-1812	Atcham	1790-1812		5G
Church Stoke (Montgomery)	A 1558-1853		8			Montgomery			4D
Church Stretton	A 1661-1959	1653-1865	5,8	1661-1865	1663-1812	Church Stretton	1790-1812		4F
Claverley	A 1568-1982	1568-1837	8	1568-1837	1568-1837	Bridgnorth	1790-1837		4J
Clee St Margaret	A 1634-1875	1660-1877	5,8	1663-1855		Ludlow			3H
Cleobury Mortimer	A 1601-1931	1601-1861	5,8	1601-1812	1601-1812	Cleobury Mortimer	1790-1812		2I
Cleobury North	A 1680-1836	1860-1865	5,8			Bridgnorth			3H
Clive	A 1671-1999	1667-1867	5,8	1667-1866	1667-1750	Wem	1790-1812	1800-1837	8G
Clun	A 1653-1967	1653-1812	5,8			Clun			2D
Clunbury	A 1574-1968	1574-1858	5,8	1574-1858	1574-1812	Clun	1790-1812		2E
Clungunford	A 1559-1992	1559-1850	5,8	1660-1850		Clun			2F
Cockshut	A 1772-1979	1772-1875	8			Ellesmere			8F
Cold Weston	A 1689-1977	1784-1885	8	1660-1860		Ludlow			3G(R)
Condover	A 1570-1968	1570-1870	5,8	1570-1812	1570-1812	Atcham	1790-1812	1808-1837	5G
Coreley	A 1543-1882	1543-1857	5,8			Cleobury Mortimer			2H
Cound	A 1608-1981	1562-1812	5,8	1562-1812	1562-1812	Atcham	1790-1812		5G
Cressage	A 1722-1999	1660-1879	5,8	1722-1741	1701-1775	Atcham			5H
Culmington	A 1579-1996	1575-1850	5,8	1660-1850		Ludlow			3F
Dawley Magna	A 1666-1992	1666-1871	5,8	1666-1837	1666-1837	Madeley	1790-1837	1829-1835	6I
Deuxhill	A 1598-1849	1656-1864	8	1654-1812	1659-1812	Bridgnorth	1790-1812		3I(T)
Diddlebury	A 1583-1971	1583-1871	5,8	1583-1812	1583-1812	Ludlow	1790-1812		3G
Ditton Priors	A 1673-1877	1660-1859	5,8	1813-1837		Bridgnorth		1801-1834	4H
Donington	A 1556-1952	1556-1880	5,8	1556-1812	1556-1812	Shifnal	1790-1812		6J
Dowles	B 1572-1972	1630-1855	8	1660-1845		Kidderminster			2J
Dudleston	A 1693-1910	1665-1856	8			Ellesmere			9E
Easthope	A 1624-1978	1623-1895	5,8	1623-1830		Church Stretton			4H
Eaton Constantine	A 1684-1926	1684-1812	5,8	1684-1812	1684-1812	Atcham	1790-1812		6H(L)
Eaton under Haywood	A 1688-1953	1581-1894	5,8	1660-1837		Church Stretton			4G
Edgmond	A 1660-1881	1559-1878	8	1669-1812	1676-1812	Newport	1790-1812		7I
Edgton	A 1722-1939	1660-1812	5,8	1722-1812	1722-1811	Clun	1790-1812		3E
Edstaston	A 1712-1885	1646-1875	8	1712-1885	1712-1775	Wem			9G
Ellesmere	A 1654-1940	1630-1875	8	1653-1909		Ellesmere		1788-1837	9E
Ercall Magna	A 1585-1958	1585-1861	8	1585-1837		Wellington	1790-1837		7H
Eyton upon the Weald Moors	A 1698-1997	1698-1885	8			Wellington			7H(J)

222

parish name	deposited original registers	I.G.I.	local census indexes	copies of registers at Soc. Gen.	Boyd's marriage index	1837-1851 Registration District	Pallot's marriage index	non-conform. records at P.R.O.	map ref.
Farlow	A 1813-1996		5,8			Cleobury Mortimer			2H
Fitz	A 1559-1980	1560-1868	5,8	1559-1812	1564-1812	Atcham	1790-1812		7F
Ford	A 1569-1990	1569-1850	5,8	1589-1812	1569-1812	Atcham	1790-1812		6F
Frodesley	A 1547-1973	1547-1862	5,8	1547-1812	1547-1812	Atcham	1790-1812		5G
Glazeley	A 1598-1849	1656-1864	8	1654-1812	1659-1812	Bridgnorth	1790-1812		3I(U)
Great Hanwood	A 1559-1993	1560-1880	5,8	1560-1880	1561-1754	Atcham			6F(G)
Great Ness	A 1589-1960	1589-1876	5,8	1589-1837		Ellesmere	1790-1837		7E
Greet	A 1663-1834	1663-1847	5,8	1663-1812	1666-1812	Tenbury	1790-1812		1H
Grinshill	A 1592-1992	1592-1856	5,8	1592-1812	1595-1812	Wem	1790-1812		8G
Habberley	A 1598-1894	1598-1849	5,8	1670-1812	1600-1812	Atcham	1790-1812		5F
Hadnall	A 1732-1998	1730-1856	8			Ellesmere		1800-1837	7G
Halford	A 1597-1759	1594-1875	8			Ludlow			3F
Halston	A 1686-1897	1686-1849	8	1668-1891	1699-1826	Oswestry	1790-1812		9E
Harley	A 1745-1989	1745-1877	5,8	1590-1812	1601-1812	Atcham	1790-1812		5H
Heath (see Stoke St Milborough)									3H
Highley	A 1551-1914	1551-1877	5,8			Cleobury Mortimer			3J
Hinstock	A 1695-1936	1673-1868	5,8			Market Drayton			8I
Hodnet	A 1539-1864	1540-1849	5,8	1539-1812	1540-1812	Market Drayton	1790-1812	1814-1837	8H
Holdgate	A 1660-1837	1661-1851	5,8	1651-1701		Ludlow			4H
Hope Bagot	A 1715-1937	1661-1867	5,8	1714-1837		Ludlow			2H(W)
Hope Bowdler	A 1567-1994	1563-1877	5,8			Church Stretton			4F
Hopesay	A 1678-1953	1660-1847	5,8	1660-1837	1662-1837	Clun	1790-1837		3F
Hopton Cangeford	A 1788-1875	1790-1878	5,8			Ludlow			3G
Hopton Castle	A 1538-1991	1538-1850	5,8	1538-1812	1549-1812	Clun	1790-1812		2E
Hopton Wafers	A 1660-1904	1627-1872	5,6,7,8	1638-1837	1638-1812	Cleobury Mortimer	1790-1812		2H
Hordley	A 1686-1952	1634-1869	5,8	1656-1812	1656-1812	Ellesmere	1790-1811		8E
Hughley	A 1576-1977	1576-1891	5,8	1576-1812	1582-1812	Atcham	1790-1812		4H
Ightfield	A 1557-1953	1681-1830	8			Wem			9H
Kemberton	A 1659-1837	1659-1859	5,8			Shifnal			5I
Kenley	A 1631-1968	1631-1877	5,8	1682-1812	1690-1812	Atcham	1790-1812		5H
Kinlet	A 1657-1978	1657-1847	5,8	1657-1840	1651-1837	Cleobury Mortimer	1790-1837		2I
Kinnerley	A 1677-1993	1677-1840	8	1677-1813	1677-1812	Oswestry	1790-1812		7D
Knockin	A 1661-1948	1661-1846	5,8	1661-1812	1679-1812	Oswestry	1790-1812		7E
Kynnersley	A 1691-1920	1676-1869	8			Wellington			7I
Langley (see Acton Burnell)									5G
Leebotwood	A 1548-1998	1548-1856	5,8	1547-1812	1547-1812	Church Stretton	1790-1812		5F
Lee Brockhurst	A 1566-1837	1567-1854	5,8	1567-1838		Wem	1790-1837		8G(A)
Leighton	A 1660-1996	1661-1868	5,8	1661-1812	1661-1837	Atcham	1790-1837		6H
Leinthwardine North (see Herefordshire)									2F
Lilleshall	A 1656-1997	1656-1877	8			Newport			7I
Little Ness	A 1605-1737	1605-1742	8	1605-1737		Ellesmere			7F
Little Wenlock	A 1689-1971	1689-1837	5,8			Madeley			6H
Llanvair Waterdine	A 1593-1895	1676-1853	5,8	1660-1853		Knighton			2D
Llansilin (Denbigh)									8C
Llanyblodwel	A 1695-1990	1599-1850	8	1597-1812	1599-1812	Oswestry	1790-1812		8C
Llanymynech (Denbigh)	A 1666-1898	1666-1857	5,8	1666-1812	1683-1812	Oswestry		1825-1836	7D
Longdon upon Tern	A 1692-1969	1692-1875	8	1692-1812	1701-1812	Wellington	1790-1812		7H(H)
Longford	A 1558-1979	1674-1868	8			Newport			7I
Longnor	A 1586-1997	1586-1852	5,8	1586-1812	1584-1812	Church Stretton			5G(M)
Long Stanton	A 1568-1978	1546-1878	5,8			Bridgnorth			4H
Loppington	A 1654-1970	1558-1864	5,8	1607-1859		Wem			8F
Loughton	A 1821-1991		5,8			Cleobury Mortimer			3H
Ludford	A 1643-1969	1647-1855	5,8			Ludlow			2G
Ludlow	A 1558-1976	1558-1876	5,8,9	1558-1853	1558-1812	Ludlow	1790-1812	1802-1837	2G
Lydbury North	A 1563-1958	1563-1846	5,8	1660-1846		Clun			3E
Lydham	A 1596-1981	1596-1880	5,8	1596-1850	1596-1812	Clun	1790-1812		4E
Madeley	A 1645-1989	1645-1885	5,8	1638-1754		Madeley		1818-1837	5I
Mainstone	A 1590-1956	1590-1876	5,8			Clun			3D
Market Drayton	A 1558-1941	1681-1872	5,8			Market Drayton		1776-1836	9I
Melverley	A 1723-1992	1723-1860	5,8	1723-1812	1724-1812	Atcham	1790-1812		7E
Meole Brace	A 1681-1987	1660-1849	8	1660-1849		Shrewsbury	1790-1837		6F
Middle	A 1541-1942	1541-1852	4,5,6,7,8	1541-1837	1541-1837	Ellesmere	1790-1837		8F
Middleton Scriven	A 1604-1837	1601-1855	8	1631-1855	1734-1812	Bridgnorth	1790-1812		3I(S)
Milson	A 1656-1848	1660-1846	5,8	1660-1846	1708-1812	Cleobury Mortimer	1790-1812		2H
Mindtown	A 1813-1829	1660-1852	5,8			Clun			4F
Minsterley		1815-1859	5,8	1777-1858		Atcham		1807-1837	5E
Monkhopton	A 1699-1835	1698-1848	5,8	1660-1848	1700-1812	Bridgnorth	1790-1812		4H
Montford	A 1661-1972	1573-1860	5,8	1577-1812	1573-1812	Atcham	1790-1812		7F
More	A 1687-1950	1570-1877	5,8	1570-1862	1574-1812	Clun	1790-1812		4E
Moreton Corbet	A 1580-1973	1580-1878	5,8	1580-1812	1580-1812	Wem	1790-1812		8G
Moreton Say	A 1691-1891	1690-1875	5,8	1690-1812	1690-1812	Market Drayton	1790-1812		9H
Morton	A 1823-1957		5,8			Oswestry			8D
Morville	A 1562-1832	1562-1876	5,8	1660-1876		Bridgnorth			4I
Much Wenlock	A 1558-1960	1558-1880	5,8	1558-1935		Madeley			4H
Munslow	A 1538-1899	1538-1859	5,8	1538-1812	1538-1812	Ludlow	1790-1812		3G
Neen Savage	A 1575-1979	1575-1858	5,8	1575-1812	1575-1812	Cleobury Mortimer	1790-1812		2I
Neen Sollars	A 1656-1851	1660-1851	5,8	1678-1851	1710-1851	Cleobury Mortimer	1790-1851		1I
Neenton	A 1558-1838	1558-1846	5,8	1558-1812	1558-1812	Bridgnorth	1794-1805		3H
Newport	A 1569-1951	1572-1877	4,5,8			Newport		1814-1837	7J
Newtown	A 1779-1963	1763-1874	8	1779-1963		Wem			9F
Norbury	A 1560-1992	1560-1867	5,8	1560-1867		Clun			4E
Norton in Hales	A 1573-1978	1572-1875	5,8	1573-1880	1573-1836	Market Drayton	1790-1837		10I
Oldbury	A 1582-1992	1582-1872	8	1582-1812	1583-1812	Bridgnorth	1790-1812	1715-1837	4I
Onibury	A 1578-1998	1577-1849	5,8	1577-1849	1577-1836	Ludlow	1790-1837		2F
Oswestry	A 1558-1961	1558-1860	5,8	1558-1812	1551-1812	Oswestry	1790-1812	1779-1837	8D
Petton	A 1694-1935	1677-1862	5,8			Ellesmere			8F
Pitchford	A 1558-1980	1543-1875	5,8	1558-1812	1558-1812	Atcham	1790-1812		5G
Pontesbury	A 1886-1997	1538-1882	5,8	1538-1812	1538-1812	Atcham	1790-1812	1828-1837	6F
Prees	A 1597-1952	1597-1868	8			Wem		1805-1837	9G

parish name	deposited original registers	I.G.I.	local census indexes	copies of registers at Soc. Gen.	Boyd's marriage index	1837-1851 Registration District	Pallot's marriage index	non-conform. records at P.R.O.	map ref.
Preston Gubbals	A 1601-1967	1560-1868	5,8	1560-1837		Atcham		1827-1836	7F
Preston upon the Weald Moors	A 1679-1944	1679-1944	8			Wellington			7I(K)
Priors Lee	A 1813-1964	1808-1875	8	1678-1837		Shifnal			6I
Pulverbatch	A 1542-1988	1542-1812	5,8	1542-1812		Atcham			5F
Quatford	A 1577-1971	1577-1835	8	1687-1688	1665-1700	Bridgnorth			4I
Quatt	A 1672-1949	1662-1872	8			Bridgnorth			4J
Ratlinghope	A 1702-1963	1755-1813	5,8	1755-1813	1755-1813	Clun	1790-1812		5E
Richards Castle	A 1559-1890	1558-1812	5,8	1559-1902		Ludlow			1G
Rodington	A 1678-1972	1631-1868	8	1678-1837		Wellington			7H
Romsley (ex.par.)			8			Bridgnorth			3J
Rudge (see Pattingham)						Wolverhampton			5J
Rushbury	A 1538-1924	1538-1877	5,8			Church Stretton			4G
Ruyton of the Eleven Towns	A 1719-1974	1630-1858	5,8	1719-1812	1719-1812	Oswestry	1790-1812		8E
Ryton	A 1659-1992	1657-1864	5,8			Shifnal			5J
St Martin	A 1603-1971	1663-1841	5,8	1579-1837	1579-1837	Oswestry	1790-1837		9D
Selattyn	A 1557-1852	1577-1860	4,5,8	1557-1812	1559-1812	Oswestry	1790-1812		9D
Shawbury	A 1561-1966	1561-1876	5,8	1561-1711		Wem			7G
Sheinton	A 1711-1989	1658-1878	5,8	1658-1812	1658-1812	Atcham	1790-1812		5H
Shelve	A 1584-1977	1584-1835	5,8			Clun			4E
Sheriff Hales (Staffs)									6J
Shifnal	A 1676-1979	1679-1865	5,8	1678-1837		Shifnal		1811-1836	6J
Shipton	A 1538-1978	1538-1880	5,8	1538-1812	1538-1812	Church Stretton	1790-1804		4G
Shrawardine	A 1637-1992	1638-1812	5,8	1637-1812		Atcham	1790-1812		7E
Shrewsbury								1692-1857	6G
Holycross	A 1541-1904	1540-1875	5,6,8	1542-1854		Shrewsbury			6G
St Alkmond	A 1559-1958	1559-1871	5,6,8			Shrewsbury			7G
St Chad	A 1616-1990	1616-1868	5,6,8	1616-1812	1616-1812	Shrewsbury	1790-1812		6G(E)
St Julian	A 1559-1976	1559-1872	5,6,8	1559-1881		Shrewsbury			6G(F)
St Mary	A 1584-1987	1584-1838	5,6,8	1584-1812	1584-1812	Shrewsbury	1790-1812		6G(D)
Sibdon Carwood	A 1582-1835	1582-1812	5,8	1583-1814	1583-1812	Church Stretton	1790-1812		3F(Q)
Sidbury	A 1560-1997	1560-1812	8	1560-1812	1560-1812	Bridgnorth	1790-1812		3I
Silvington	A 1663-1997		5,8	1663-1837		Cleobury Mortimer			2H(V)
Smethcott	A 1609-1997	1609-1856	5,8	1609-1812	1613-1812	Church Stretton	1790-1811		5F
Stanton Lacy	A 1561-1992	1561-1812	5,8	1561-1812	1561-1812	Ludlow	1790-1812		2G
Stanton upon Hine Heath	A 1665-1957	1739-1875	5,8	1655-1682		Wem			8H
Stapleton	A 1635-1997	1546-1853	5,8	1635-1812	1546-1812	Atcham	1790-1812		5F
Stirchley	A 1658-1973	1658-1876	5,8	1658-1812	1658-1812	Madeley	1790-1812		6I
Stockton	A 1558-1918	1664-1878	5,8			Shifnal			5I
Stokesay	A 1558-1987	1559-1877	8	1559-1837	1561-1837	Ludlow	1790-1837		2F
Stoke St Milborough	A 1654-1941	1587-1876	5,8	1654-1839		Ludlow			3H
Stoke upon Tern	A 1654-1968	1668-1875	5,8	1654-1700	1662-1699	Market Drayton			8H
Stottesden	A 1565-1998	1565-1812	5,8			Cleobury Mortimer			3I
Stow	A 1576-1835	1576-1811	5,8			Knighton			1D
Sutton	A 1769-1870	1709-1868	5,8	1709-1870		Atcham	1790-1837		6G
Sutton Maddock	A 1559-1917	1559-1878	5,8			Shifnal			5I
Tasley	A 1563-1982	1563-1813	8	1563-1813	1564-1812	Bridgnorth	1790-1812		4I
Tibberton	A 1719-1883	1681-1856	8	1719-1812	1719-1753	Newport			7I
Tong	A 1620-1963	1629-1876	5,8	1588-1812	1630-1812	Shifnal	1790-1812		6J
Tugford	A 1637-1837	1754-1841	5,8			Ludlow			3G
Uffington	A 1578-1944	1581-1868	5,8	1578-1812	1581-1812	Atcham	1790-1812		7G
Uppington	A 1650-1993	1650-1874	5,8	1650-1812	1676-1812	Atcham	1790-1812		6H
Upton Cressett	A 1637-1957	1766-1812	5,8	1637-1840		Bridgnorth			4I
Upton Magna	A 1563-1875	1577-1877	5,8			Atcham			6G
Waters Upton	A 1547-1870	1547-1868	8	1547-1816	1547-1815	Wellington	1790-1811		7H(C)
Wellington	A 1626-1980	1628-1875	4,5,8	1628-1701		Wellington		1827-1837	6H
Welshampton	A 1772-1939	1636-1856	5,8			Ellesmere			9F
Wem	A 1583-1951	1582-1875	5,8	1582-1880	1576-1812	Wem	1790-1812	1755-1836	8G
Wentnor	A 1662-1915	1660-1812	5,8			Clun			4E
Westbury	A 1637-1990	1637-1812	5,8	1637-1812	1637-1812	Atcham	1790-1812	1807-1837	6E
West Felton	A 1628-1970	1628-1865	8			Oswestry			8E
Weston and Wixhill	A 1565-1993	1565-1875	8	1565-1812	1574-1754	Wem			8G
Wheathill	A 1573-1993	1573-1812	5,8			Cleobury Mortimer			3H
Whitchurch	A 1627-1898	1627-1858	8	1627-1797		Wem		1708-1837	10G
Whittington	A 1591-1979	1591-1840	5,8	1591-1812	1591-1800	Oswestry	1790-1812	1832-1837	9D
Whixall	A 1758-1900	1757-1876	8			Wem		1805-1837	9G
Willey	A 1644-1975	1644-1812	5,8	1644-1812	1665-1812	Madeley	1790-1812		5I
Wistanstow	A 1687-1949	1661-1876	5,8	1688-1837	1638-1837	Church Stretton	1790-1837		3F
Withington	A 1591-1948	1591-1868	5,8	1591-1812	1592-1812	Atcham			6H
Wollaston	A 1601-1997	1814-1837	8			Atcham			6D
Wombridge	A 1721-1947	1721-1836	8			Wellington		1817-1837	6I
Woodcote	A 1862-1991		8			Newport			7J
Woodhouse (ex.par.)						Cleobury Mortimer			2I(X)
Woolstaston	A 1601-1955	1601-1812	5,8	1601-1812	1607-1812	Church Stretton	1790-1812		5F
Woore	A 1769-1984	1769-1804	5,8	1773-1808		Market Drayton			10I
Worfield	A 1560-1940	1562-1871	8	1562-1812		Bridgnorth			4J
Worthen	A 1558-1982	1558-1812	5,8	1558-1812	1558-1812	Montgomery	1790-1812		5E
Wrockwardine	A 1591-1970	1591-1877	8	1591-1812	1592-1812	Wellington	1790-1812	1818-1837	6H
Wroxeter	A 1618-1989	1613-1868	5,8	1613-1812	1613-1812	Atcham			6H

SHROPSHIRE

Original registers deposited at:
A = Shropshire Records and Research Centre, Castle Gates, Shrewsbury SY2 6ND
B = Worcestershire Library and History Centre, Trinity Street, Worcester WR1 2PW

Study adjacent parishes in counties of Denbighshire, Flintshire, Cheshire, Staffordshire, Worcestershire, Herefordshire, Radnor and Montgomery

Shropshire Records and Research Centre, Castle Gates, Shrewsbury SY2 6ND

The following useful indexes have been compiled – see Introduction
Census Indexes 1841-1891 – Shropshire FHS, c/o Mrs R Wilford, 68 Oakley Street, Belle Vue, Shrewsbury, SY3 7JZ
Marriage Index 1813-1837 – R.W. Gwynne, 26 Derwent Close, Dane Bank, Denton, Manchester M34 2FW
Marriage Index 1750-1812 – Mr D. Lewis, The Berringtons, Woodseaves, Market Drayton, Shropshire, TF9 2AU
The Hayes Computerised Marriage Index – V. Masters, 34 Bryn Awalon, Buckley, Clwyd, CH7 2QB
Shropshire Monumental Inscriptions – M.J. Hulme, 19 Brook Road, Bomere Heath, Shrewsbury, SY4 3PU
Shropshire Burials 1813-1837 – Shropshire FHS, c/o Mr J. Ravenscroft, 19 Upper Bar, Newport, Shropshire, TF10 7EH

Shropshire's average extent from north to south is nearly 50 miles, its extreme breadth from east to west being about 40 miles. It is watered by seven principal rivers: the Severn, Teme, Clun, Warren, Rea, Tern and Rodan. The population in 1841 was 225,820; in 1851, 229,341; in 1861, 240,959; in 1871, 248,111; in 1881, 248,014.

Few counties possess a greater variety of soils. The principal crops were grain, hops and fruit and cattle and sheep were bred. Large quantities of milk and cheese were produced. Lead, iron, lime-stone, free-stone, pipe-clay and coal were found in abundance and the main manufactures were porcelain and flannel.

The information in the Index is abbreviated, and may mislead the searcher if reference is not made to the details contained in the several publications listed in the Introduction. It is essential that users of this book check the appropriate works before making further enquiries.

parish name	deposited original registers	I.G.I.	local census indexes	copies of registers at Soc. Gen.	Boyd's marriage index	1837-1851 Registration District	Pallot's marriage index	non-conform. records at P.R.O.	map ref.
Abbas and Templecombe	A 1563-1981	1597-1812	4,5,6,7,8,9	1597-1812		Wincanton	1802-1812	1816-1836	4K
Abbots Leigh	C 1656-1991		4,5,6,7,8,9			Bedminster			9I
Aisholt	A 1652-1994	1598-1812	4,5,6,7,8,9	1598-1812	1654-1812	Bridgwater	1790-1812		5F
Alford	A 1758-1994	1575-1812	4,5,6,7,8,9	1594-1811		Wincanton	1700-1811		5J(Eu)
Aller	A 1560-1966	1560-1812	4,5,6,7,8,9	1560-1812	1560-1812	Langport	1560-1812		4H
Angersleigh	A 1678-1991	1594-1812	4,5,6,7,8,9	1595-1811	1693-1812	Taunton	1790-1812		3F
Ansford	A 1554-1978	1554-1837	4,5,6,7,8,9	1554-1837		Wincanton	1802-1812		5J(Ev)
Ashbrittle	A 1563-1981	1599-1812	4,5,6,7,8,9	1563-1812	1563-1812	Wellington	1790-1812		4D
Ashcott	A 1743-1996	1559-1812	4,5,6,7,8,9	1599-1812		Bridgwater	1801-1812		5H
Ashill	A 1558-1985	1598-1757	4,5,6,7,8,9	1558-1815	1558-1815	Chard	1790-1815		3G
Ashington	A 1567-1836	1572-1812	4,5,6,7,8,9	1572-1812		Yeovil	1803-1812		4J(Em)
Ash Prior	A 1700-1970	1594-1812	4,5,6,7,8,9	1595-1812	1676-1812	Taunton	1790-1812		4E
Ashwick	A 1701-1982	1595-1812	4,5,6,7,8,9	1598-1812		Shepton Mallet	1805-1812	1761-1837	6J
Axbridge	A 1561-1971	1597-1812	4,5,6,7,8,9	1597-1812		Axbridge			7H(L)
Babcary	A 1754-1975	1598-1812	4,5,6,7,8,9	1598-1812		Langport	1801-1812		4J
Babington	A 1725-1992	1606-1812	4,5,6,7,8,9	1607-1812		Frome	1805-1813		7K(T)
Backwell	A 1558-1968	1598-1812	4,5,6,7,8,9	1598-1813		Bedminster		1833-1837	8I
Badgworth	A 1671-1985	1559-1813	4,5,6,7,8,9	1598-1813		Axbridge	1790-1812		7H
Baltonsborough	A 1538-1987	1599-1813	4,5,6,7,8,9	1599-1668		Wells	1800-1812		5I
Banwell	A 1569-1977		4,5,6,7,8,9	1569-1901		Axbridge		1796-1837	8H
Barrington	A 1653-1983	1597-1813	4,5,6,7,8,9	1654-1837	1654-1812	Langport	1790-1812		3H(Ao)
Barrow Gurney	A 1591-1984	1593-1813	4,5,6,7,8,9	1590-1900	1593-1812	Bedminster	1593-1812		8I
Barton St David	A 1714-1993	1607-1679	4,5,6,7,8,9	1607-1679		Langport			5I(Eo)
Barwick	A 1560-1977		4,5,6,7,8,9	1560-1887		Yeovil			3J
Batcombe	A 1642-1997	1597-1669	4,5,6,7,8,9	1597-1669		Shepton Mallet			5K
Bath								1719-1840	8L
St James	A 1569-1942	1603-1802	4,5,6,7,8,9	1813-1840		Bath	1790-1812		8L(G)
St Michael	A 1569-1929	1598-1802	4,5,6,7,8,9	1559-1840		Bath	1790-1812		8L(G)
St Peter & Paul	A 1569-1965	1569-1839	4,5,6,7,8,9	1569-1840	1569-1800	Bath	1790-1802		8L(G)
Bathampton	A 1754-1972		4,5,6,7,8,9	1599-1980		Bath			8L
Bathealton	A 1712-1981		4,5,6,7,8,9	1712-1979		Wellington			4D
Batheaston	A 1634-1967	1604-1623	4,5,6,7,8,9	1609-1812		Bath	1790-1812		8L
Bathford	A 1727-1990	1608-1662	4,5,6,7,8,9	1608-1810		Bath	1790-1812		8L
Bathwick	A 1668-1915		4,5,6,7,8,9	1668-1840		Bath	1790-1812		8L
Bawdrip	A 1748-1970	1602-1636	4,5,6,7,8,9	1602-1636		Bridgwater			5G
Beckington	A 1559-1973		4,5,6,7,8,9	1559-1900		Frome			7L
Bedminster				1599-1624				1813-1837	9J
St John the Baptist	C 1643-1965		4,5,6,7,8,9			Bedminster			9J
St Paul	C 1852-1979		4,5,6,7,8,9			Bedminster			9J
Beercrocombe	A 1542-1980	1542-1812	4,5,6,7,8,9	1542-1812	1542-1812	Langport	1790-1812		3G(Ak)
Berkley	A 1546-1942		4,5,6,7,8,9	1546-1903		Frome			7L
Berrow	A 1700-1967		4,5,6,7,8,9	1700-1901		Axbridge			7G
Bickenhall	A 1682-1991		4,5,6,7,8,9	1682-1812	1682-1812	Taunton	1790-1812		3G
Bicknoller	A 1557-1973		4,5,6,7,8,9	1557-1903		Williton			5E
Biddisham	A 1621-1985		4,5,6,7,8,9	1621-1985		Axbridge			7H(K)
Binegar	A 1769-1922		4,5,6,7,8,9	1769-1903		Shepton Mallet			7J
Bishops Hull	A 1562-1988	1733-1837	4,5,6,7,8,9	1562-1837	1562-1812	Taunton	1790-1812	1734-1837	4F
Bishops Lydeard	A 1674-1978		4,5,6,7,8,9	1595-1638		Taunton			4F
Blackford	A 1684-1991		4,5,6,7,8,9	1684-1899		Wincanton			4K(Od)
Blagdon	A 1555-1965		4,5,6,7,8,9	1555-1886		Axbridge			8I
Bleadon	A 1706-1969	1608-1623	4,5,6,7,8,9	1608-1939		Axbridge			7G
Bradford	A 1558-1990	1594-1622	4,5,6,7,8,9	1558-1812	1558-1812	Wellington	1790-1812		4F
Bratton Seymour	A 1754-1996		4,5,6,7,8,9	1813-1851		Wincanton			4K
Brean	A 1730-1977		4,5,6,7,8,9	1730-1906		Axbridge			7G
Brent Knoll	A 1678-1982	1622-1846	4,5,6,7,8,9	1622-1811		Axbridge			7G
Brewham	A 1659-1958		4,5,6,7,8,9	1607-1985		Wincanton			5K
Bridgwater	A 1558-1976	1597-1669	4,5,6,7,8,9	1597-1669		Bridgwater		1755-1837	5G
Brislington	C 1566-1983		4,5,6,7,8,9	1566-1812		Keynsham	1790-1810		9J
Broadway	A 1678-1958	1598-1811	4,5,6,7,8,9	1598-1837		Chard	1789-1811	1777-1840	3G
Brockley	A 1696-1980	1599-1640	4,5,6,7,8,9	1598-1640		Bedminster			8I(B)
Brompton Ralph	A 1558-1978		4,5,6,7,8,9	1603-1642		Williton			5E
Brompton Regis	A 1690-1954		4,5,6,7,8,9	1690-1900		Tiverton		1823-1837	4C
Broomfield	A 1630-1870		4,5,6,7,8,9	1630-1870	1630-1812	Bridgwater	1790-1812		5F
Brushford	A 1558-1976		4,5,6,7,8,9	1558-1905		Tiverton			4C
Bruton	A 1554-1928	1554-1680	4,5,6,7,8,9	1554-1812	1554-1812	Wincanton	1790-1812	1802-1837	5K
Brympton	A 1699-1836	1638-1678	4,5,6,7,8,9	1602-1695		Yeovil			3I(Ef)
Buckland Dinham	A 1540-1973	1603-1630	4,5,6,7,8,9	1603-1630		Frome			7L
Buckland St Mary	A 1538-1990	1538-1812	4,5,6,7,8,9	1538-1886	1538-1812	Chard	1790-1812		3F
Burnett	A 1749-1846		4,5,6,7,8,9	1599-1639		Keynsham			8K
Burnham on Sea	A 1630-1986		4,5,6,7,8,9	1630-1840		Axbridge			6G
Burrington	A 1687-1945		4,5,6,7,8,9	1598-1841		Axbridge			7I
Butcombe	A 1692-1999		4,5,6,7,8,9	1605-1835	1693-1835	Axbridge	1790-1835		8I
Butleigh	A 1578-1987	1598-1637	4,5,6,7,8,9	1598-1637		Wells			5I
Cameley	A 1561-1979		4,5,6,7,8,9	1605-1679		Clutton			7J
Camerton	A 1654-1941	1607-1608	4,5,6,7,8,9	1654-1812		Clutton			7K
Cannington	A 1559-1988		4,5,6,7,8,9	1559-1812	1559-1812	Bridgwater	1790-1812		5F
Carhampton	A 1634-1888		4,5,6,7,8,9	1634-1888		Williton			6D
Castle Cary	A 1564-1891	1615-1639	4,5,6,7,8,9	1564-1775		Wincanton			5J
Catcott	A 1691-1928	1597-1640	4,5,6,7,8,9	1597-1902		Bridgwater			6H
Chaffcombe	A 1680-1992		4,5,6,7,8,9	1700-1837		Chard			2G
Chapel Allerton	A 1690-1988	1598-1812	4,5,6,7,8,9	1598-1810		Axbridge	1803-1812		7H
Chard	A 1649-1981		4,5,6,7,8,9	1540-1729		Chard		1786-1837	2G
Charlcombe	A 1710-1980		4,5,6,7,8,9	1712-1837		Bath			9L
Charlinch	A 1744-1982	1607-1621	4,5,6,7,8,9	1607-1779	1754-1779	Bridgwater	1779		5F
Charlton Adam	A 1704-1927	1607-1812	4,5,6,7,8,9	1607-1812	1707-1812	Langport	1707-1812		4I
Charlton Horethorne	A 1695-1988		4,5,6,7,8,9	1695-1889		Wincanton			4K
Charlton Mackrell	A 1575-1874	1575-1812	4,5,6,7,8,9	1575-1812	1575-1812	Langport	1575-1812		4I
Charlton Musgrove	A 1538-1985		4,5,6,7,8,9	1615-1679		Wincanton			5K
Charterhouse on Mendip (see Blagdon)									7I

SOMERSET

parish name	deposited original registers	I.G.I.	local census indexes	copies of registers at Soc. Gen.	Boyd's marriage index	1837-1851 Registration District	Pallot's marriage index	non-conform. records at P.R.O.	map ref.
Cheddar	A 1601-1920	1608-1675	4,5,6,7,8,9	1608-1675		Axbridge			7H
Cheddon Fitzpaine	A 1558-1998		4,5,6,7,8,9	1559-1812	1559-1812	Taunton	1790-1812		4F(Ab)
Chedzoy	A 1558-1970		4,5,6,7,8,9	1558-1812	1558-1812	Bridgwater	1790-1812		5G
Chelvey	A 1574-1980	1599-1639	4,5,6,7,8,9	1599-1663		Bedminster			8I(A)
Chelwood	A 1720-1984	1721-1837	4,5,6,7,8,9	1720-1903		Clutton	1721-1837		8J
Chew Magna	A 1560-1989	1605-1621	4,5,6,7,8,9	1605-1623		Clutton			8J
Chew Stoke	A 1663-1975	1605-1623	4,5,6,7,8,9	1666-1888		Clutton	1822-1836		8J
Chewton Mendip	A 1554-1992		4,5,6,7,8,9	1623-1639		Wells			7J
Chilcompton	A 1649-1981	1607-1636	4,5,6,7,8,9	1607-1631		Clutton			7J
Chillington	A 1750-1984		4,5,6,7,8,9	1750-1913		Chard			2H(Ay)
Chilthorne Domer	A 1678-1980		4,5,6,7,8,9	1615-1636		Yeovil			3I(Ej)
Chilton Cantelo	A 1714-1836	1607-1623	4,5,6,7,8,9	1607-1666		Yeovil			4J(En)
Chilton Polden	A 1710-1953	1621-1623	4,5,6,7,8,9	1710-1921		Bridgwater			6H
Chilton Trinity	A 1732-1993		4,5,6,7,8,9	1661-1685		Bridgwater			6G(Y)
Chipstable	A 1694-1992	1603-1837	4,5,6,7,8,9	1607-1837		Wellington			4D
Chiselborough	A 1558-1979		4,5,6,7,8,9	1558-1979		Yeovil			3I(Eb)
Christon	A 1548-1985	1549-1711	4,5,6,7,8,9	1549-1722		Axbridge			7H(J)
Churchill	A 1653-1976	1609-1667	4,5,6,7,8,9	1609-1667		Axbridge			8H
Clapton in Gordano	A 1558-1956	1615-1617	4,5,6,7,8,9	1599-1663		Bedminster			9H
Clatworthy	A 1561-1937		4,5,6,7,8,9	1561-1922		Williton			5D
Claverton	A 1582-1991		4,5,6,7,8,9	1582-1812		Bath			8L
Clevedon	A 1727-1976	1607-1666	4,5,6,7,8,9	1607-1666		Bedminster			9H
Cloford	A 1561-1979		4,5,6,7,8,9	1561-1903		Frome			6K
Closworth	A 1685-1982	1598-1603	4,5,6,7,8,9	1598-1603		Yeovil			3J
Clutton	A 1691-1890	1615-1623	4,5,6,7,8,9	1609-1638		Clutton			8J
Combe Florey	A 1566-1906	1566-1837	4,5,6,7,8,9	1566-1837		Taunton			5E
Combe Hay	A 1539-1938		4,5,6,7,8,9			Bath			8K
Combe St Nicholas	A 1678-1984	1653-1812	4,5,6,7,8,9	1636-1812	1678-1812	Chard	1790-1812		3G
Compton Bishop	A 1641-1943	1606-1621	4,5,6,7,8,9	1606-1621		Axbridge			7H
Compton Dando	A 1653-1973		4,5,6,7,8,9	1616-1679		Keynsham			8J
Compton Dundon	A 1682-1995		4,5,6,7,8,9	1682-1962		Langport			5I
Compton Martin	A 1559-1982		4,5,6,7,8,9	1559-1812		Clutton			7I
Compton Pauncefoot	A 1559-1993	1606-1638	4,5,6,7,8,9	1590-1638		Wincanton			4J(Oc)
Congresbury	A 1543-1957	1605-1807	4,5,6,7,8,9	1543-1837		Axbridge			8H
Corfe	A 1566-1989	1609-1663	4,5,6,7,8,9	1566-1840	1687-1812	Taunton	1790-1812		3F
Corston	A 1568-1950		4,5,6,7,8,9	1567-1812		Keynsham			8K
Corton Denham	A 1538-1992		4,5,6,7,8,9	1538-1937		Wincanton			4J
Cossington	A 1675-1984	1639-1640	4,5,6,7,8,9	1606-1640		Bridgwater			6H
Cothelstone	A 1658-1993	1678+	4,5,6,7,8,9	1607-1715	1664-1715	Taunton	1715-		5F
Creech St Michael	A 1665-1992	1623-1639	4,5,6,7,8,9	1607-1814	1665-1814	Taunton	1790-1814		4G
Crewkerne	A 1558-1972	1599-1812	4,5,6,7,8,9	1559-1812	1559-1812	Chard	1790-1812	1785-1837	2H
Cricket Malherbie	A 1723-1992	1615-1621	4,5,6,7,8,9	1754-1837		Chard			3H(Ax)
Cricket St Thomas	A 1564-1992	1621-1639	4,5,6,7,8,9	1599-1678		Chard			2H
Croscombe	A 1558-1992	1607-1672	4,5,6,7,8,9	1607-1672		Shepton Mallet			6J
Crowcombe	A 1641-1948	1594-1670	4,5,6,7,8,9	1594-1812	1641-1812	Williton	1790-1812		5E
Cucklington	A 1558-1992		4,5,6,7,8,9	1558-1904	1559-1837	Wincanton			4L
Cudworth	A 1699-1992		4,5,6,7,8,9	1754-1836		Chard			2H
Culbone	A 1683-1836		4,5,6,7,8,9	1699-1951		Williton			6B
Curland	A 1634-1970		4,5,6,7,8,9	1634-1901		Taunton			3G(Aj)
Curry Mallet	A 1682-1995	1597-1615	4,5,6,7,8,9	1597-1750		Langport			4G
Curry Rivel	A 1606-1983	1629-1638	4,5,6,7,8,9	1607-1812	1642-1812	Langport	1642-1812		4H
Cutcombe	A 1636-1971		4,5,6,7,8,9	1636-1886		Williton			5C
Dinder	A 1578-1992	1598-1640	4,5,6,7,8,9	1598-1640		Wells			6J
Dinnington	A 1592-1837		4,5,6,7,8,9	1599-1674		Chard			3H(Az)
Ditcheat	A 1562-1999	1605-1624	4,5,6,7,8,9	1605-1623		Shepton Mallet			5J
Dodington	A 1538-1835	1597-1679	4,5,6,7,8,9	1538-1805	1538-1805	Williton	1790-1805		5E
Donyatt	A 1712-1882	1623-1629	4,5,6,7,8,9	1712-1837		Chard			3G
Doulting	A 1634-1994	1615-1629	4,5,6,7,8,9	1615-1629		Shepton Mallet			6J
Dowlish Wake	A 1644-1984	1599-1619	4,5,6,7,8,9	1599-1619		Chard			3H(Aw)
Downhead	A 1695-1978	1615-1630	4,5,6,7,8,9	1615-1630		Shepton Mallet			6K
Drayton	A 1558-1979		4,5,6,7,8,9	1577-1812	1577-1812	Langport	1577-1812		4H
Dulverton	A 1558-1967	1830-1836	4,5,6,7,8,9	1558-1886		Tiverton		1831-1836	4C
Dundry	A 1560-1979		4,5,6,7,8,9			Bedminster			8J
Dunkerton	A 1748-1888	1608-1615	4,5,6,7,8,9	1748-1888		Bath			8K(H)
Dunster	A 1559-1979	1803-1837	4,5,6,7,8,9	1559-1903		Williton		1803-1837	6D
Durleigh	A 1683-1992	1609-1666	4,5,6,7,8,9	1599-1807	1683-1807	Bridgwater	1790-1807		5G(X)
Durston	A 1712-1946	1606-1812	4,5,6,7,8,9	1606-1812	1712-1812	Taunton	1606-1812		4G
Earnshill & Hambridge	A 1844-1982		4,5,6,7,8,9	1844-1982		Langport			4H(Al)
East Brent	A 1558-1975	1588-1611	4,5,6,7,8,9	1558-1622		Axbridge			7G
East Chinnock	A 1647-1872		4,5,6,7,8,9	1647-1872		Yeovil			3I(Ee)
East Coker	A 1560-1980		4,5,6,7,8,9	1560-1888	1560-1714	Yeovil			3I
East Cranmore	A 1783-1955		4,5,6,7,8,9	1597-1663		Shepton Mallet			6K
East Harptree	A 1663-1980	1606-1635	4,5,6,7,8,9	1597-1635		Clutton		1816-1834	7J
East Lambrook	A 1771-1946		4,5,6,7,8,9	1770-1860		Langport			3H
East Lydford	A 1730-1990		4,5,6,7,8,9	1730-1902		Shepton Mallet			5J(Eq)
Easton in Gordano	A 1559-1962		4,5,6,7,8,9	1559-1919		Bedminster			9I
East Pennard	A 1608-1988	1608-1639	4,5,6,7,8,9	1599-1812	1608-1812	Shepton Mallet	1790-1812		5J
East Quantoxhead	A 1559-1836	1608-1681	4,5,6,7,8,9	1608-1812	1654-1812	Williton	1790-1812		6E
Edington	A 1552-1909		4,5,6,7,8,9	1552-1900		Bridgwater			6H
Elm	A 1697-1958		4,5,6,7,8,9			Frome			7L(V)
Elworthy	A 1685-1978		4,5,6,7,8,9	1685-1888		Williton			5E
Emborough	A 1569-1977	1598-1640	4,5,6,7,8,9	1569-1769		Shepton Mallet			7J
Englishcombe	A 1728-1987		4,5,6,7,8,9	1609-1812		Bath	1790-1812		8K
Enmore	A 1653-1979	1607-1679	4,5,6,7,8,9	1607-1812	1655-1812	Bridgwater	1790-1812		5F
Evercreech	A 1540-1969		4,5,6,7,8,9	1540-1969		Shepton Mallet			5J
Exford	A 1618-1986		4,5,6,7,8,9	1618-1902		Tiverton			5B
Exmoor (ex.par.)			4,5,6,7,8,9	1856-1899		Tiverton			5A
Exton	A 1559-1975		4,5,6,7,8,9	1559-1901		Tiverton			5C
Farleigh Hungerford	A 1673-1996		4,5,6,7,8,9	1616		Frome			7L

SOMERSET

parish name	deposited original registers	I.G.I.	local census indexes	copies of registers at Soc. Gen.	Boyd's marriage index	1837-1851 Registration District	Pallot's marriage index	non-conform. records at P.R.O.	map ref.
Farmborough	A 1559-1987		4,5,6,7,8,9	1559-1812		Clutton	1790-1812		8K
Farrington Gurney	A 1681-1976		4,5,6,7,8,9			Clutton			7J(O)
Fiddington	A 1706-1998		4,5,6,7,8,9	1706-1922	1706-1812	Bridgwater	1790-1812		5F
Fitzhead	A 1558-2000		4,5,6,7,8,9	1609-1663		Wellington			4E
Fivehead	A 1654-1983	1656-1812	4,5,6,7,8,9	1598-1837	1656-1812	Langport	1790-1812		4G
Flax Bourton	A 1701-1984		4,5,6,7,8,9			Bedminster			9I(C)
Foxcote	A 1691-1836		4,5,6,7,8,9	1598-1639		Frome			7K
Freshford	A 1653-1958	1601-1688	4,5,6,7,8,9	1601-1812		Bradford-on-Avon	1790-1812		8L
Frome			4,5,6,7,8,9	1558-1837		Frome		1764-1837 1814-1837	6L
Glastonbury									5I
St Benedict	A 1663-1955	1607-1629	4,5,6,7,8,9	1607-1663		Wells			5I
St John	A 1603-1980	1597-1598	4,5,6,7,8,9	1597-1598		Wells			5I
Goathill	B 1699-1837	1702-1743	4,5,6,7,8,9			Sherborne			3K
Goathurst	A 1539-1979	1598-1670	4,5,6,7,8,9	1539-1812	1539-1812	Bridgwater	1790-1812		5F
Godney	A 1741-1869		4,5,6,7,8,9			Wells			6I
Greinton	A 1655-1989		4,5,6,7,8,9			Bridgwater			5H
Halse	A 1558-1970		4,5,6,7,8,9	1559-1812	1559-1812	Taunton	1790-l812		4E
Hardington (see Hemington)				1598-1649		Frome			7K(U)
Hardington Mandeville	A 1688-1893		4,5,6,7,8,9	1813-1893		Yeovil			2I
Haslebury Plucknett	A 1672-1956		4,5,6,7,8,9	1754-1836		Yeovil			2I
Hatch Beauchamp	A 1760-1995		4,5,6,7,8,9	1609-1638		Taunton			3G
Hawkridge	A 1653-1911		4,5,6,7,8,9	1598-1623		Tiverton			5B
Heathfield	A 1698-1992		4,5,6,7,8,9	1700-1756	1700-1756	Taunton			4E(Ac)
Hemington	A 1539-1950		4,5,6,7,8,9			Frome			7K
Henstridge	A 1653-1910		4,5,6,7,8,9			Wincanton			3K
High Ham	A 1569-1968	1569-1812	4,5,6,7,8,9	1569-1812	1569-1812	Langport	1569-1812		5H
High Littleton	A 1657-1961		4,5,6,7,8,9			Clutton			7J
Hillfarrance	A 1701-1992	1615-1623	4,5,6,7,8,9	1701-1812	1701-1812	Wellington	1790-1812		4F(Ae)
Hinton Blewett	A 1563-1979		4,5,6,7,8,9	1623-1629		Clutton			7J(N)
Hinton Charterhouse	A 1546-1996		4,5,6,7,8,9	1546-1733		Bath			7L
Hinton St George	A 1632-1955	1597-1669	4,5,6,7,8,9	1597-1837	1632-1837	Chard	1790-1837		3H
Holcombe	A 1698-1982		4,5,6,7,8,9	1604-1639		Shepton Mallet			7K(R)
Holford	A 1558-1977		4,5,6,7,8,9	1558-1812	1558-1812	Williton	1790-1812		6E
Holton	A 1558-1993	1629-1636	4,5,6,7,8,9	1813-1837		Wincanton			4K
Hornblotton	A 1763-1993		4,5,6,7,8,9	1768-1849		Shepton Mallet			5J(Et)
Horsington	A 1559-1978	1558-1837	4,5,6,7,8,9	1558-1836	1558-1836	Wincanton			4K
Huish Champflower	A 1559-1982	1616-1638	4,5,6,7,8,9	1597-1638		Tiverton			5D
Huish Episcopi	A 1692-1989	1615-1812	4,5,6,7,8,9	1698-1812	1698-1812	Langport	1698-1812		4H(Am)
Huntspill	A 1654-1994		4,5,6,7,8,9	1623		Bridgwater			6G
Hutton	A 1715-1916	1621-1629	4,5,6,7,8,9	1621-1668		Axbridge			7G
Ilchester	A 1690-1979	1594-1812	4,5,6,7,8,9	1594-1666		Yeovil	1802-1812	1806-1837	4I(Ek)
Ilminster			4,5,6,7,8,9	1660-1837	1662-1811	Chard	1790-1812	1726-1837	3G
Ilton	A 1642-1982	1616-1812	4,5,6,7,8,9	1616-1837	1645-1811	Chard	1790-1811		3G
Isle Abbots	A 1561-1992	1562-1837	4,5,6,7,8,9	1562-1837	1562-1837	Langport	1790-1837		3G
Isle Brewer	A 1705-1994	1598-1635	4,5,6,7,8,9	1598-1837	1705-1812	Langport	1790-1812		3H
Keinton Mandeville	A 1728-1993		4,5,6,7,8,9	1736-1851		Langport			5J(Ep)
Kelston	A 1538-1993		4,5,6,7,8,9	1538-1812		Keynsham	1790-1812		9K
Kenn	A 1540-1950	1607-1640	4,5,6,7,8,9	1607-1621		Bedminster			9H
Kewstoke	A 1667-1958		4,5,6,7,8,9			Axbridge			8G
Keynsham	A 1628-1912		4,5,6,7,8,9	1628-1812		Keynsham			8K
Kilmersdon	A 1653-1987	1603-1635	4,5,6,7,8,9	1603-1635		Frome			7K
Kilmington	A 1582-1954	1582-1885	4,5,6,7,8,9	1582-1837	1582-1837	Mere	1790-1837		5L
Kilton	A 1683-1835	1621-1623	4,5,6,7,8,9	1621-1812	1683-1812	Williton	1790-1812		6E
Kilve	A 1539-1837	1621-1636	4,5,6,7,8,9	1618-1812	1638-1812	Williton	1790-1812		5E
Kingsbury Episcopi	A 1557-1992	1557-1812	4,5,6,7,8,9	1557-1869	1557-1812	Langport	1790-1812	1681-1837	3H
Kingsdon	A 1538-1955	1540-1812	4,5,6,7,8,9	1540-1812	1540-1812	Langport	1540-1812	1809-1834	4I
Kingston St Mary	A 1677-2000		4,5,6,7,8,9	1677-1840		Taunton		1823-1837	4F
Kingston Seymour	A 1727-1983	1622-1837	4,5,6,7,8,9	1622-1639		Bedminster			8H
Kingstone	A 1715-1992		4,5,6,7,8,9	1714-1837		Chard			3H(Au)
Kingweston	A 1653-1993		4,5,6,7,8,9			Langport			5I
Kittisford	A 1694-1981	1621-1837	4,5,6,7,8,9	1621-1837	1695-1812	Wellington	1790-1837		4D
Knowle St Giles	A 1695-1981		4,5,6,7,8,9			Chard			2G
Lamyatt	A 1613-1993		4,5,6,7,8,9			Shepton Mallet			5K
Langford Budville	A 1537-1973		4,5,6,7,8,9	1607-1812	1607-1812	Wellington	1790-1812		4E
Langport	A 1728-1992	1728-1812	4,5,6,7,8,9	1728-1812	1728-1812	Langport	1728-1812	1832-1837	4H
Langridge	A 1756-1970		4,5,6,7,8,9	1763-1840		Bath			9K
Laverton	A 1678-1836		4,5,6,7,8,9	1609-1639		Frome			7L
Leighland	A 1755-1976		4,5,6,7,8,9			Williton			5D
Leigh on Mendip	A 1566-1987	1607-1608	4,5,6,7,8,9	1607-1622		Frome			6K
Lilstock	A 1654-1974	1678-1679	4,5,6,7,8,9	1607-1812	1661-1812	Williton	1790-1812		6F
Limington	A 1684-1979	1695-1812	4,5,6,7,8,9	1695-1812	1695-1812	Yeovil	1695-1812		4I
Litton	A 1587-1992		4,5,6,7,8,9			Clutton			7J
Locking	A 1750-1960		4,5,6,7,8,9			Axbridge			8G
Long Ashton	A 1558-1911	1623-1679	4,5,6,7,8,9	1558-1901		Bedminster		1826-1837	9I
Long Load	A 1749-1981		4,5,6,7,8,9	1749-1888	1749-1808	Yeovil	1749-1808		4I
Long Sutton	A 1559-1989	1559-1812	4,5,6,7,8,9	1559-1840	1559-1812	Langport	1559-1812		4I
Lopen	A 1693-1925		4,5,6,7,8,9	1609-1812	1723-1812	Chard	1790-1812		3H(At)
Lovington	A 1677-1992		4,5,6,7,8,9			Wincanton			5J(Es)
Loxton	A 1558-1982		4,5,6,7,8,9			Axbridge			7H
Luccombe	A 1653-1966		4,5,6,7,8,9			Williton			6C
Lufton	A 1748-1823		4,5,6,7,8,9	1598		Yeovil			3I(Eg)
Lullington	A 1712-1837		4,5,6,7,8,9	1598-1840		Frome			7L
Luxborough	A 1590-1968		4,5,6,7,8,9			Williton			5C
Lydeard St Lawrence	A 1573-1915		4,5,6,7,8,9			Taunton			5E
Lympsham	A 1737-1973		4,5,6,7,8,9	1737-1841		Axbridge			7G
Lyncombe and Widcombe	A 1574-1977	1739-1802	4,5,6,7,8,9	1784-1840		Bath		1834-1837	8L
Lyng	A 1691-1992		4,5,6,7,8,9	1813-1837		Bridgwater			4G
Maiden Bradley (Wilts.)									5L
Maperton	A 1558-1992	1613-1678	4,5,6,7,8,9	1613-1679	1566-1837	Wincanton			4K(Oe)

SOMERSET

parish name	deposited original registers	I.G.I.	local census indexes	copies of registers at Soc. Gen.	Boyd's marriage index	1837-1851 Registration District	Pallot's marriage index	non-conform. records at P.R.O.	map ref.
Mark	A 1568-1998		4,5,6,7,8,9	1568-1756		Axbridge			6H
Marksbury	A 1563-1981		4,5,6,7,8,9	1563-1812		Keynsham	1790-1812		8K
Marston Bigot	A 1654-1993	1607-1639	4,5,6,7,8,9	1607-1639		Frome			6L
Marston Magna	A 1562-1946	1621-1625	4,5,6,7,8,9			Sherborne			4J
Martock	A 1558-1986		4,5,6,7,8,9	1558-1901	1559-1812	Yeovil	1559-1812	1681-1837	3I
Meare	A 1559-1975	1605-1668	4,5,6,7,8,9	1559-1902		Wells			6H
Mells	A 1565-1970		4,5,6,7,8,9	1565-1901		Frome			7K
Merriot	A 1646-1952	1646-1812	4,5,6,7,8,9	1646-1812	1653-1813	Chard			3H
Middle Chinnock	A 1695-1837		4,5,6,7,8,9			Yeovil			3I(Ed)
Middlezoy	A 1653-1904		4,5,6,7,8,9			Bridgwater			5H
Midsomer Norton	A 1697-1974	1637-1663	4,5,6,7,8,9	1701-1837	1701-1837	Clutton	1790-1812	1801-1857	7K
Milborne Port	A 1538-1924		4,5,6,7,8,9	1538-1813		Wincanton		1780-1837	3K
Milton Clevedon	A 1596-1996	1607-1668	4,5,6,7,8,9	1607-1668		Shepton Mallet			5K(Ew)
Milverton	A 1538-1947		4,5,6,7,8,9	1538-1812	1538-1837	Wellington	1790-1812	1784-1837	4E
Minehead	A 1548-1924		4,5,6,7,8,9	1548-1840		Williton			6C
Misterton	A 1558-1977		4,5,6,7,8,9	1613-1886		Beaminster			2I
Monksilver	A 1653-1979		4,5,6,7,8,9			Williton			5D
Monkton Combe	A 1561-1853		4,5,6,7,8,9	1559-1812		Bath	1790-1797		8L
Montacute	A 1558-1949	1598-1695	4,5,6,7,8,9			Yeovil			3I
Moorlinch	A 1653-1935		4,5,6,7,8,9	1598-1623		Bridgwater			5H
Muchelney	A 1702-1977	1620-1812	4,5,6,7,8,9	1620-1812	1703-1812	Langport	1703-1812		4H
Mudford	A 1563-1941		4,5,6,7,8,9		1563-1837	Yeovil			3J
Nailsea	A 1554-1911		4,5,6,7,8,9			Bedminster			9H
Nempnett Thrubwell	A 1556-1836		4,5,6,7,8,9			Clutton			8I
Nether Stowey	A 1640-1973	1631-1639	4,5,6,7,8,9	1631-1812	1645-1812	Bridgwater	1790-1812		6F(W)
Nettlecombe	A 1540-1979	1598-1763	4,5,6,7,8,9	1598-1673		Williton			5D
Newton St Loe	A 1538-1890		4,5,6,7,8,9	1538-1812		Keynsham	1790-1812		8K
North Barrow	A 1568-1991		4,5,6,7,8,9	1598		Wincanton			4J(Ey)
North Cadbury	A 1558-1957	1558-1734	4,5,6,7,8,9	1558-1734		Wincanton			4J
North Cheriton	A 1558-1996		4,5,6,7,8,9			Wincanton			4K
North Curry	A 1539-1986	1539-1812	4,5,6,7,8,9	1539-1812	1538-1812	Taunton	1539-1812		4G
North Newton	A 1778-1943		4,5,6,7,8,9			Bridgwater			5G
Northover	A 1531-1982		4,5,6,7,8,9	1531-1850	1531-1812	Yeovil	1531-1812		4I(El)
North Perrot	A 1648-1937		4,5,6,7,8,9	1599-1637		Yeovil			2I
North Petherton	A 1558-1980	1558-1837	4,5,6,7,8,9	1558-1837	1558-1837	Bridgwater	1790-1837		5G
North Stoke	A 1649-1975		4,5,6,7,8,9	1559-1840		Keynsham	1790-1810		9K
North Wootton	A 1565-1987	1613-1636	4,5,6,7,8,9	1608-1639		Wells			6I
Norton Fitzwarren	A 1556-1998	1556-1725	4,5,6,7,8,9	1556-1812	1565-1812	Taunton	1790-1812	1826-1837	4F
Norton Malreward	A 1554-1835		4,5,6,7,8,9			Clutton			8J
Norton St Philip	A 1585-1973	1609-1639	4,5,6,7,8,9			Frome			7L
Norton sub Hamdon	A 1558-1948		4,5,6,7,8,9	1558-1850		Yeovil			3I(Ea)
Nunney	A 1547-1993	1636-1639	4,5,6,7,8,9	1636-1639		Frome			6K
Nyland			4,5,6,7,8,9			Axbridge			7I
Nynehead	A 1670-1984	1605-1669	4,5,6,7,8,9	1605-1812	1670-1812	Wellington	1790-1812		4E
Oake	A 1630-1991		4,5,6,7,8,9	1594-1625		Wellington			4E(Ad)
Oare	A 1674-1989		4,5,6,7,8,9	1599-1851		Williton			6B
Odcombe	A 1669-1966		4,5,6,7,8,9			Yeovil			3I
Old Cleeve	A 1661-1965		4,5,6,7,8,9			Williton			6D
Orchardleigh	A 1623-1820		4,5,6,7,8,9	1623-1839		Frome			7L
Orchard Portman	A 1538-1991	1606-1676	4,5,6,7,8,9	1538-1842	1538-1812	Taunton	1790-1812		3F(Ag)
Othery	A 1560-1994		4,5,6,7,8,9	1608		Bridgwater			5H
Otterford	A 1558-1986		4,5,6,7,8,9	1588-1837	1588-1812	Taunton	1790-1812		3F
Otterhampton	A 1650-1981		4,5,6,7,8,9	1656-1749	1646-1749	Bridgwater	1749		6F
Over Stowey	A 1558-1992		4,5,6,7,8,9	1558-1812	1558-1812	Bridgwater	1790-1812		5F
Paulton	A 1728-1990	1785-1836	4,5,6,7,8,9			Clutton		1785-1836	7K
Pawlett	A 1667-1943	1622-1623	4,5,6,7,8,9	1597-1623		Bridgwater			6G
Pendomer	A 1730-1839		4,5,6,7,8,9	1609-1754		Yeovil			2I
Penselwood	A 1721-1924		4,5,6,7,8,9	1597-1623		Wincanton			5L
Pensford	A 1651-1967		4,5,6,7,8,9			Clutton		1794-1837	8J(E)
Pilton	A 1558-1992	1616-1669	4,5,6,7,8,9	1616-1669		Shepton Mallet			6J
Pitcombe	A 1538-1958	1538-1837	4,5,6,7,8,9	1567-1836		Wincanton	1790-1837		5K
Pitminster	A 1544-1994		4,5,6,7,8,9	1544-1836	1542-1812	Taunton	1790-1812	1709-1836	3F
Pitney	A 1623-1976		4,5,6,7,8,9	1623-1812	1623-1812	Langport	1623-1812		4H
Podimore Milton	A 1635-1979		4,5,6,7,8,9	1744-1851	1744-1812	Yeovil	1744-1811		4I
Porlock	A 1618-1982		4,5,6,7,8,9	1837-1957		Williton			6B
Portbury	A 1559-1913		4,5,6,7,8,9	1637		Bedminster			9I
Portishead	A 1554-1980		4,5,6,7,8,9			Bedminster			9I
Poyntington	B 1618-1897		4,5,6,7,8,9			Sherborne			3J
Preston Plucknett			4,5,6,7,8,9			Yeovil			3I
Priddy	A 1759-1987		4,5,6,7,8,9	1813-1836		Wells			7I
Priston	A 1723-1992		4,5,6,7,8,9	1723-1812		Keynsham	1790-1847		8K
Publow	A 1569-1972		4,5,6,7,8,9			Clutton		1794-1837	8J(D)
Puckington	A 1692-1834	1695-1812	4,5,6,7,8,9	1695-1812	1695-1812	Langport	1790-1812		3H(An)
Puriton	A 1558-1912		4,5,6,7,8,9			Bridgwater			6G
Puxton	A 1543-1981		4,5,6,7,8,9			Axbridge			8H
Pylle	A 1591-1998		4,5,6,7,8,9	1622-1627		Shepton Mallet			5J
Queen Camel	A 1639-1993		4,5,6,7,8,9	1607		Wincanton			4J
Queen Charlton	A 1562-1889		4,5,6,7,8,9	1562-1752		Keynsham			8J
Raddington	A 1814-1961	1602-1836	4,5,6,7,8,9	1814-1836		Wellington	1789-1812		4D
Radstock	A 1652-1986		4,5,6,7,8,9			Clutton			7K
Rimpton	A 1537-1931		4,5,6,7,8,9			Sherborne			4J
Road	A 1587-1995		4,5,6,7,8,9	1714-1840		Frome			7L
Rodden	A 1659-1964		4,5,6,7,8,9			Frome			6L
Rode Hill	A 1824-1995		4,5,6,7,8,9			Frome			7L
Rodney Stoke	A 1654-1984	1602-1745	4,5,6,7,8,9	1602-1906		Wells			7I
Rowberrow	A 1723-1989		4,5,6,7,8,9			Axbridge		1816-1837	7I(M)
Ruishton	A 1678-1985		4,5,6,7,8,9	1679-1812	1679-1812	Taunton	1790-1812		4G
Runnington	A 1585-1836		4,5,6,7,8,9	1586-1851	1586-1812	Wellington	1790-1812		4E
St Catherine	A 1752-1837	1623-1629	4,5,6,7,8,9	1598-1630		Bath			9L

SOMERSET

parish name	deposited original registers	I.G.I.	local census indexes	copies of registers at Soc. Gen.	Boyd's marriage index	1837-1851 Registration District	Pallot's marriage index	non-conform. records at P.R.O.	map ref.
St Decumans	A 1600-1984		4,5,6,7,8,9			Williton			6D
St Michaelchurch	A 1695-1960	1695-1884	4,5,6,7,8,9	1605-1812	1695-1812	Bridgwater	1695-1837		5G(Z)
Saltford	A 1709-1971		4,5,6,7,8,9	1709-1837		Keynsham	1790-1812		8K
Sampford Arundel	A 1695-1994		4,5,6,7,8,9	1698-1812	1698-1812	Wellington	1790-1812		3E
Sampford Brett	A 1629-1965	1609-1679	4,5,6,7,8,9	1609-1679		Williton			6E
Sandford Orcas	B 1538-1993		4,5,6,7,8,9			Sherborne			3J
Seaborough	B 1562-1978	1596-1598	4,5,6,7,8,9	1594-1623		Beaminster			2H
Seavington St Mary	A 1716-1985	1621-1623	4,5,6,7,8,9	1621-1903		Chard			3H(Ar)
Seavington St Michael	A 1558-1986		4,5,6,7,8,9	1558-1905		Chard			3H(As)
Selworthy	A 1653-1994		4,5,6,7,8,9			Williton			6C
Shapwick	A 1590-1996	1605-1640	4,5,6,7,8,9	1605-1640		Bridgwater			5H
Shepton Beauchamp	A 1558-1984	1588-1812	4,5,6,7,8,9	1558-1812	1558-1812	Chard	1790-1812		3H(Aq)
Shepton Mallet	A 1635-1988	1566-1679	4,5,6,7,8,9	1566-1679		Shepton Mallet		1757-1837	6J
Shepton Montague	A 1779-1964	1623-1630	4,5,6,7,8,9	1617-1630		Wincanton			5K
Shipham	A 1560-1961		4,5,6,7,8,9	1560-1794		Axbridge			8H
Skilgate	A 1674-1960		4,5,6,7,8,9			Tiverton			4D
Somerton	A 1697-1970	1599-1812	4,5,6,7,8,9	1599-1812	1697-1812	Langport	1696-1818	1805-1837	4I
South Barrow	A 1678-1992	1605-1786	4,5,6,7,8,9			Wincanton			4J(Ez)
South Cadbury	A 1559-1993	1617-1623	4,5,6,7,8,9	1607-1679		Wincanton			4J(Ob)
South Petherton	A 1574-1985		4,5,6,7,8,9	1574-1901		Yeovil		1694-1857	3H
South Stoke	A 1704-1935		4,5,6,7,8,9	1704-1812		Bath	1790-1810		8L
Sparkford	A 1729-1994		4,5,6,7,8,9			Wincanton			4J
Spaxton	A 1558-1979		4,5,6,7,8,9	1558-1812	1558-1812	Bridgwater	1790-1812		5F
Stanton Drew	A 1652-1983	1607-1615	4,5,6,7,8,9	1599-1668		Clutton			8J
Stanton Prior	A 1572-1991		4,5,6,7,8,9	1571-1812		Keynsham	1791-1810		8K(F)
Staple Fitzpaine	A 1684-1991		4,5,6,7,8,9	1682-1812	1682-1812	Taunton	1790-1812		3F
Staplegrove	A 1558-1982		4,5,6,7,8,9			Taunton			4F
Stawell	A 1675-1812		4,5,6,7,8,9	1598-1623		Bridgwater			5H
Stawley	A 1653-1980		4,5,6,7,8,9			Wellington			4D
Stockland Bristol	A 1538-1996		4,5,6,7,8,9	1813-1990	1538-1812	Bridgwater			6F
Stocklinch Magdalen	A 1712-1993	1712-1776	4,5,6,7,8,9	1712-1927	1712-1755	Chard	1776		3H(Ap)
Stocklinch Ottersey	A 1558-1976	1558-1812	4,5,6,7,8,9	1558-1907	1558-1812	Chard	1790-1812		3H(Ba)
Stogumber	A 1559-1984		4,5,6,7,8,9	1559-1712		Williton			5E
Stogursey	A 1598-1999		4,5,6,7,8,9	1595-1812	1595-1812	Williton	1790-1812		6F
Stoke Pero	A 1712-1838		4,5,6,7,8,9	1613-1630		Williton			6B
Stoke St Gregory	A 1561-1986		4,5,6,7,8,9			Taunton			4G
Stoke St Mary	A 1676-1988		4,5,6,7,8,9	1679-1812	1679-1812	Taunton	1790-1812		4F
Stoke sub Hamdon	A 1558-1996	1621-1623	4,5,6,7,8,9	1621-1623		Yeovil			3I
Stoke St Michael	A 1644-1995		4,5,6,7,8,9	1622		Shepton Mallet			6K
Stoke Trister	A 1751-1985		4,5,6,7,8,9		1751-1837	Wincanton			4K
Stone Easton	A 1813-1968	1594-1669	4,5,6,7,8,9	1594-1669		Clutton			7J(P)
Stourton (Wilts)									5L
Stowell	A 1574-1836		4,5,6,7,8,9	1613-1636		Wincanton			4K
Stowey	A 1570-1992		4,5,6,7,8,9	1570-1983		Clutton			8J
Stratton on the Fosse	A 1641-1965	1607-1666	4,5,6,7,8,9	1599-1666		Shepton Mallet			7K(Q)
Street	A 1636-1989	1598-1755	4,5,6,7,8,9	1599-1762		Wells		1814-1837	5I
Stringston	A 1557-1836		4,5,6,7,8,9	1609-1812	1633-1812	Williton	1790-1812		6F
Sutton Bingham	A 1742-1983		4,5,6,7,8,9	1605-1621		Yeovil			2I
Sutton Mallet	A 1781-1989		4,5,6,7,8,9	1598-1623		Bridgwater			5H
Sutton Montis	A 1701-1994		4,5,6,7,8,9			Wincanton			4J(Of)
Swainswick	A 1557-1948		4,5,6,7,8,9	1557-1840		Bath	1790-1811		9L
Swell	A 1559-1983	1599-1812	4,5,6,7,8,9	1559-1812	1559-1812	Langport	1790-1812		4H
Taunton			4,5,6,7,8,9					1699-1837	4F
St James	A 1610-1998		4,5,6,7,8,9	1610-1837	1610-1837	Taunton	1790-1837		4F
St Mary Magdalen	A 1558-1991		4,5,6,7,8,9	1558-1812	1558-1812	Taunton	1790-1812		4F
Tellisford	A 1538-1995		4,5,6,7,8,9			Frome			7L
Thorne Coffin	A 1695-1978		4,5,6,7,8,9	1609-1623		Yeovil			3I(Eh)
Thorne St Margaret	A 1761-1992		4,5,6,7,8,9	1721-1812	1721-1812	Wellington	1790-1812		3E
Thornfalcon	A 1725-1991		4,5,6,7,8,9	1726-1812	1726-1812	Taunton	1790-1812		4G(Ah)
Thurlbear	A 1700-1991		4,5,6,7,8,9	1613-1812	1700-1812	Taunton	1790-1812		4F
Thurloxton	A 1559-1961		4,5,6,7,8,9	1558-1812	1558-1812	Bridgwater	1790-1812		4G(Aa)
Tickenham	A 1538-1993		4,5,6,7,8,9			Bedminster			9H
Timberscombe	A 1656-1994		4,5,6,7,8,9	1598-1678		Williton			6C
Timsbury	A 1561-1918	1621-1627	4,5,6,7,8,9	1561-1812		Clutton	1790-1812	1803-1837	7K
Tintinhull	A 1561-1986	1609-1623	4,5,6,7,8,9	1598-1623		Yeovil			3I
Tolland	A 1706-1971		4,5,6,7,8,9			Taunton			5E
Treborough	A 1693-1977		4,5,6,7,8,9			Williton			5D
Trent	B 1558-1976		4,5,6,7,8,9	1598-1675		Sherborne			3J
Trull	A 1538-1972		4,5,6,7,8,9	1598-1812	1671-1812	Taunton	1790-1812		4F
Twerton	A 1538-1985		4,5,6,7,8,9	1538-1840		Bath	1790-1812		8K
Ubley	A 1671-1975	1609-1616	4,5,6,7,8,9	1609-1623		Clutton			7I
Uphill	A 1701-1959		4,5,6,7,8,9	1598-1623		Axbridge			8G
Upton	A 1708-1940		4,5,6,7,8,9	1623		Tiverton			4D
Upton Noble	A 1677-1982		4,5,6,7,8,9			Shepton Mallet			5K(Ex)
Walcot	A 1691-1971		4,5,6,7,8,9	1699		Bath		1813-1837	8L
Walton	A 1671-1992		4,5,6,7,8,9	1617-1663		Wells			5I
Walton In Gordano	A 1667-1837		4,5,6,7,8,9	1599-1662		Bedminster			9H
Wanstrow	A 1570-1987		4,5,6,7,8,9	1605-1678		Frome			6K
Wayford	A 1704-1981		4,5,6,7,8,9	1613-1896		Chard			2H
Weare	A 1637-1985	1621-1623	4,5,6,7,8,9	1598-1639		Axbridge			7H
Wedmore	A 1561-1941	1561-1839	4,5,6,7,8,9	1561-1860	1561-1837	Axbridge	1800-1839		6H
Wellington	A 1683-1976	1616-1682	4,5,6,7,8,9	1616-1812	1683-1812	Wellington	1790-1812	1784-1837	3E
Wellow	A 1561-1967		4,5,6,7,8,9	1599-1623		Bath			7K
Wells			4,5,6,7,8,9					1790-1836	6I
St Andrew			4,5,6,7,8,9	1660-1982		Wells			6J
St Cuthbert	A 1609-1956		4,5,6,7,8,9			Wells			6I
Wembdon	A 1665-1993		4,5,6,7,8,9			Bridgwater			5G
West Bagborough	A 1558-1933	1565-1812	4,5,6,7,8,9	1565-1812	1565-1812	Taunton	1790-1812		5E
West Bradley	A 1633-1997	1607-1667	4,5,6,7,8,9	1605-1673		Wells			5J

SOMERSET

parish name	deposited original registers	I.G.I.	local census indexes	copies of registers at Soc. Gen.	Boyd's marriage index	1837-1851 Registration District	Pallot's marriage index	non-conform. records at P.R.O.	map ref.
West Buckland	A 1538-1975	1621-1629	4,5,6,7,8,9	1538-1812	1538-1812	Wellington	1790-1812		3F
Westbury	A 1654-1911	1636-1639	4,5,6,7,8,9	1623-1639		Wells			6I
West Camel	A 1678-1930		4,5,6,7,8,9	1597-1629		Yeovil			4J
West Chinnock	A 1678-1966		4,5,6,7,8,9			Yeovil			3I(Ec)
West Coker	A 1697-1973	1608-1639	4,5,6,7,8,9	1608-1639		Yeovil			3I
West Cranmore	A 1562-1937	1629-1663	4,5,6,7,8,9	1597-1663		Shepton Mallet			6K
West Dowlish	A 1816-1905		4,5,6,7,8,9			Chard			3H(Av)
West Harptree	A 1656-1971	1598-1680	4,5,6,7,8,9	1598-1680		Clutton			7I
West Hatch	A 1604-1992	1604-1812	4,5,6,7,8,9	1604-1812	1604-1812	Taunton	1604-1812		3G
West Lydford	A 1733-1993		4,5,6,7,8,9	1623		Shepton Mallet			5J
West Monkton	A 1710-1975	1618-1639	4,5,6,7,8,9	1710-1812	1710-1837	Taunton	1790-1812		4F
Weston	A 1538-1969		4,5,6,7,8,9	1538-1840		Bath	1812		8K
Weston Bampfylde	A 1728-1993	1623-1672	4,5,6,7,8,9	1623-1683		Wincanton			4J(Oa)
Weston in Gordano	A 1684-1920		4,5,6,7,8,9	1593-1639		Bedminster			9H
Weston-Super-Mare	A 1668-1933	1682-1837	4,5,6,7,8,9	1668-1837	1682-1837	Axbridge	1790-1837	1829-1836	8G
Weston Zoyland	A 1558-1970		4,5,6,7,8,9			Bridgwater			5G
West Pennard	A 1538-1980		4,5,6,7,8,9	1607-1639		Wells			5J
West Quantoxhead	A 1558-1992		4,5,6,7,8,9	1613		Williton			6E
Whatley	A 1673-1949		4,5,6,7,8,9			Frome			6K
Wheathill	A 1813-1939		4,5,6,7,8,9	1623		Wincanton			5J(Er)
Whitchurch	C 1565-1969		4,5,6,7,8,9			Keynsham			8J
Whitelackington	A 1678-1992	1621-1623	4,5,6,7,8,9	1609-1900	1695-1837	Chard	1790-1837		3H
Whitestaunton	A 1659-1985	1606-1636	4,5,6,7,8,9	1606-1812	1606-1811	Chard	1790-1811		2G
Wick	A 1615-1910		4,5,6,7,8,9			Axbridge			8H
Williton	A 1792-1973		4,5,6,7,8,9			Williton			6E
Wilton	A 1558-1995	1558-1837	4,5,6,7,8,9	1558-1837	1558-1837	Taunton	1800-1837		4F(Af)
Wincanton	A 1636-1978	1629-1672	4,5,6,7,8,9	1629-1889		Wincanton		1798-1837	4K
Winford	A 1655-1983	1630-1639	4,5,6,7,8,9	1609-1639		Bedminster			8I
Winscombe	A 1658-1944		4,5,6,7,8,9	1598-1623		Axbridge			7H
Winsford	A 1660-1978	1621-1639	4,5,6,7,8,9	1621-1639		Tiverton			5C
Winsham	A 1559-1982		4,5,6,7,8,9			Chard		1810-1837	2H
Witham Friary	A 1684-1974		4,5,6,7,8,9	1684-1837		Frome			6K
Withel Florey	A 1697-1970	1609-1623	4,5,6,7,8,9	1609-1629		Williton			5D
Withycombe	A 1669-1897		4,5,6,7,8,9			Williton			5D
Withypool	A 1771-1970		4,5,6,7,8,9			Tiverton			5B
Wiveliscombe	A 1558-1893	1622-1637	4,5,6,7,8,9	1598-1637		Wellington		1710-1837	4E
Wookey	A 1565-1964		4,5,6,7,8,9			Wells			6I
Woolavington	A 1694-1985		4,5,6,7,8,9			Bridgwater			6G
Woolley	A 1560-1935		4,5,6,7,8,9	1560-1840		Bath	1790-1835		9L
Woolverton	A 1813-1995		4,5,6,7,8,9			Frome			7L
Wootton Courtney	A 1558-1994		4,5,6,7,8,9			Williton			6C
Worle	A 1598-1990		4,5,6,7,8,9			Axbridge			8G
Wraxall	A 1562-1999	1562-1812	4,5,6,7,8,9	1562-1812	1562-1812	Bedminster	1790-1812		9I
Wrington	A 1538-1986	1806-1807	4,5,6,7,8,9	1806-1807		Axbridge	1806		8I
Writhlington	A 1675-1978		4,5,6,7,8,9			Frome			7K(S)
Wyke Champflower	A 1625-1993		4,5,6,7,8,9			Wincanton			5K
Yarlington	A 1655-1993		4,5,6,7,8,9	1599-1851		Wincanton			4K
Yatton	A 1675-1979	1662-1679	4,5,6,7,8,9	1623-1679		Bedminster			8H
Yeovil	A 1563-1960		4,5,6,7,8,9			Yeovil		1793-1836	3J
Yeovilton	A 1710-1979	1621-1623	4,5,6,7,8,9	1599-1812	1655-1812	Yeovil	1655-1812		4I

Original registers deposited at;
A = Somerset Record Office, Obridge Road, Taunton TA2 7PU
B = Dorset Record Office, Bridport Road, Dorchester DT1 1RP
C = Bristol Record Office, B Bond Warehouse, Smeaton Road, Bristol BS1 6XN

Study adjacent parishes in counties of Devon, Dorset, Wiltshire and Gloucestershire

Bath and North East Somerset Record Office, Guildhall, Bath BA1 5AW
Somerset Record Office, Obridge Road, Taunton TA2 7PU

The following useful indexes have been compiled – see Introduction
Census Indexes 1841-1891 – Robert Studley, 3559 Burningelm Crescent, Mississauga, Ontario, L4Y 3L2, Canada
Census Index 1851 and 1891 – Somerset and Dorset FHS c/o Mrs M. Monk, 65 Wyke Road, Weymouth, DT4 9QN
Census Index 1851 – Bristol & Avon FHS c/o Mr. P. Portch, 60 Redcatsh Road, Knowle, Bristol BS4 2EY for Bath and Mrs. J. Hiscocks, Beanacre, Easter Compton, Bristol BS12 3RJ for Bristol
Somerset Marriage Index 1754-1837 – Mr B. Welchman, The Cottage, Manor Terrace, Paignton, Devon, TQ3 3RQ
Somerset Marriage Index pre 1754 – J. Hodges, Flat 21, Thornton Lodge, 24-26 Thornton Hill, London, SW19 4HS
North Somerset Marriage Index – Somerset Record Office, Obridge Road, Taunton, TA2 7PU
North Somerset Marriage Index 1754 – 1837 – M.L. Browning, Elm Tree Farm, Hart's Lane, Hallatrow, Bristol, BS39 6EA
Bath and Wells Diocese Marriage Index – G.S.W. Smith, Middle Whites Farm, Burtle, Bridgwater, Somerset TA7 8NH
Monumental Inscriptions in Somerset – Somerset and Dorset FHS, c/o Mr P. Abbott, 1 Eymore Close, Selly Oak, Birmingham, B29 4LB
Somerset Genealogical Index – Bernard Welchman (as above)

Somerset's form is oblong, being in length from north-east to south-west some 80 miles and in breadth from east to west about 36 miles. It is watered by four principal rivers: the Avon, Parret, Axe and Brue. The population in 1841 was 435,599; in 1851, 443,916; in 1861, 463,368; in 1871, 482,652; in 1881, 469,010.

There is a great variety of soils. Hemp, flax and woad were cultivated in great quantities and fine cheese was produced. Cattle and sheep were raised and copper, lead and coal mined. The principal manufactures were fine woollen cloths, coarse woollen goods and coarse linen. Bricks and tiles were made and there were brass and iron foundries.

The information in the Index is abbreviated, and may mislead the searcher if reference is not made to the details contained in the several publications listed in the Introduction. It is essential that users of this book check the appropriate works before making further enquiries.

STAFFORDSHIRE

parish name	deposited original registers	I.G.I.	local census indexes	copies of registers at Soc. Gen.	Boyd's marriage index	1837-1851 Registration District	Pallot's marriage index	non-conform. records at P.R.O.	map ref.
Abbots Bromley	A 1558-1992	1668-1859	5,8			Uttoxeter			5G
Acton Trussell	A 1571-1997	1659-1872	5,8			Penkridge			7F
Adbaston	A 1600-1967	1600-1856	8	1600-1839		Newport		1819-1837	9G
Aldridge	A 1660-1988	1660-1856	8	1660-1771	1654-1750	Walsall			5D
Alrewas	A 1547-1978	1664-1852	5,8	1547-1795		Lichfield			4E
Alstonefield	A 1538-1992	1538-1868	8	1538-1812		Leek	1790-1812		5K
Alton	A 1681-1952	1676-1852	5,8	1676-1758		Cheadle		1811-1835	5I
Armitage	A 1673-1992	1623-1862	5,8	1623-1837		Lichfield		1821-1837	5E
Ashley	A 1551-1982	1551-1857	5,8	1551-1743		Market Drayton			9H
Audley	A 1538-1875	1674-1857	5,8	1538-1713		Newcastle-u-Lyme			8J
Barlaston	A 1551-1933	1573-1868	8	1551-1812		Stone	1790-1812		7H
Barton-under-Needwood		1571-1868	5,8	1571-1813		Burton-upon-Trent	1790-1812		4F
Baswich	A 1601-1974	1601-1812	5,8	1601-1812		Stafford/Penkridge	1790-1812		6F
Bednall	A 1678-1997		5,8			Penkridge			6F
Betley (Berkswich)	A 1538-1950	1538-1887	5,8	1653-1812		Newcastle-u-Lyme	1790-1812		9I
Biddulph	A 1558-1906	1559-1867	8	1559-1856		Congleton			7K
Bilston St Leonard	A 1684-1988	1684-1835	5,8	1684-1760		Wolverhampton		1785-1837	7C
Blithfield	A 1538-1992	1693-1877	5,8			Uttoxeter			5G
Blore-Ray	A 1558-1994	1668-1872	8			Ashbourne			5J
Bloxwich	A 1733-1954	1736-1869	5,8,9	1669-1791		Walsall			6D(S)
Blurton	A 1754-1990	1814-1838	8	1558-1812		Stone			7I(D)
Blymhill	A 1561-1989	1561-1898	5,8	1561-1837		Shiffnall	1790-1812		8E
Bobbington (Salop)	A 1571-1947	1813-1831	5,8	1669-1791	1651-1812	Wolverhampton			8B
Bradley	A 1538-1944	1636-1864	5,8	1538-1779		Penkridge	1790-1812		7F
Bradley-in-the-Moors	A 1674-1993	1674-1868	5,8	1674-1812		Cheadle			5I(F)
Bramshall	A 1587-1996	1673-1877	5,8			Uttoxeter			5H
Brewood	A 1562-1989	1561-1875	5,8	1561-1650		Penkridge		1810-1837	8D
Brierley Hill	B 1766-1899	1776-1864	5,8	1766-1899		Stourbridge			7B
Bucknall-cum-Bagnall	A 1758-1947	1762-1897	5,8	1762-1812		Stoke-upon-Trent	1790-1812		7J(C)
Burntwood	A 1820-1968	1820-1897	4,5,6,7,8			Lichfield			5E
Burslem St John	A 1637-1947	1578-1837	5,8	1578-1812		Wolstanton	1790-1812	1801-1837	7J
Burslem St Paul	A 1831-1958		5,8			Wolstanton			7J
Burton-upon-Trent	A 1538-1980	1663-1877	5,8			Burton-upon-Trent		1793-1837	3F
Bushbury	A 1662-1908	1561-1868	5,8	1560-1813		Penkridge			7D
Butterton	A 1660-1982	1660-1864	8	1660-1751		Leek			5K
Calton	A 1760-1992	1809-1844	8			Ashbourne			5J
Cannock	A 1659-1949	1659-1867	5,8	1659-1802		Penkridge		1789-1837	6E
Cauldon	A 1580-1992	1668-1856	5,8	1580-1869		Cheadle			5J
Caverswall	A 1552-1920	1663-1864	5,8	1552-1813		Cheadle			7I
Chapel Chorlton	A 1564-1996	1681-1876	5,8			Newcastle-u-Lyme			8H
Chartley Holme (ex.par.)			8			Stafford			6G
Cheadle	A 1575-1937	1660-1856	5,8	1573-1682		Cheadle		1800-1837	6I
Chebsey	A 1713-1869	1660-1845	8	1660-1812		Stone			8G
Checkley	A 1625-1975	1661-1897	5,8			Cheadle		1803-1837	6H
Cheddleton	A 1696-1958	1676-1840	5,8			Cheadle			6J
Church Eaton	A 1538-1945	1660-1888	5,8	1538-1812		Penkridge			8F
Clifton Campville	A 1662-1989	1664-1866	5,8			Tamworth			3E
Codsall	A 1587-1973	1587-1857	5,8	1587-1843		Wolverhampton			8D
Colton	A 1647-1987	1647-1898	5,8			Lichfield			5F
Colwich	A 1590-1978	1659-1871	8			Stafford			6F
Coppenhall	A 1678-1996	1762-1859	8	1678-1837		Penkridge			7F(P)
Cotton	A 1795-1809		5,8			Cheadle			5I
Creswell (ex.par.)			8			Stafford			7G(L)
Croxall (Derbys)									3E
Croxden	A 1673-1837	1674-1856	5,8	1671-1873		Uttoxeter	1790-1812		5I
Darlaston	A 1539-1987	1660-1844	8	1544-1692		Walsall		1832-1837	6C(Y)
Dilhorne	A 1599-1960	1662-1862	5,8			Cheadle			6I
Draycott-in-the-Moors	A 1669-1978	1676-1868	5,8	1671-1868		Cheadle			6H
Drayton-Bassett	A 1559-1943	1664-1881	5,8	1559-1943		Tamworth			4C
Eccleshall	A 1573-1944	1573-1875	8	1573-1667		Stone/Newcastle		1822-1836	8G
Edingale	A 1575-1967	1669-1870	5,8			Tamworth			3E
Elford	A 1558-1966	1663-1871	5,8			Lichfield			4E
Elkstone	A 1785-1991		8			Leek			5K
Ellastone	A 1538-1922	1538-1869	8	1538-1812		Ashbourne	1790-1812	1826-1837	5I
Ellen Hall	A 1539-1964	1563-1875	8	1539-1812		Stafford			8G
Endon with Stanley	A 1731-1984	1805-1873	8			Leek			7J
Enville	A 1627-1986	1660-1874	5,8			Wolverhampton			8B
Farewell	A 1693-1971	1663-1867	5,8			Lichfield			5E(R)
Fazeley	A 1816-1907	1842-1867	8			Tamworth			4D
Forton	A 1558-1916	1660-1868	8			Newport			9F
Fradswell	A 1578-1978	1666-1857	8			Stafford			6G(J)
Fulford	A 1800-1983	1813-1863	8			Stone			6H(G)
Gayton	A 1593-1926	1661-1836	8			Stafford			6G
Gnosall	A 1572-1950	1572-1836	8	1572-1785		Newport			8F
Gratwich	A 1680-1991	1680-1864	5,8			Uttoxeter			5G(K)
Great Barr		1660-1870	8	1654-1749		Walsall			5C
Grindon	A 1697-1992	1679-1852	5,8			Leek			5J
Hammerwich	A 1724-1970	1727-1865	5,8			Lichfield			5D
Hamstall Ridware	A 1598-1988	1598-1856	5,8	1598-1812		Lichfield			5F
Hanbury	A 1574-1881	1661-1856	5,8	1574-1812		Uttoxeter/Burton	1790-1812		4G
Handsworth	F 1558-1980	1805-1865	5,8	1558-1837		West Bromwich		1788-1837	5B
Hanley	A 1789-1976	1789-1835	5,8	1743-1803		Stoke-upon-Trent		1786-1837	7I(B)
Harborne	F 1538-1954	1660-1869	8			Kings Norton			6B
Harlaston	A 1693-1967	1665-1870	8			Tamworth			3E
Haughton	A 1570-1907	1570-1876	8	1570-1812		Stafford	1790-1812		8F
High Offley	A 1689-1876	1659-1875	8	1659-1812		Newport			9G
Hilderstone	A 1830-2000	1833-1868	8			Stone			6H(H)
Himley	B 1668-1882	1665-1875	5,8	1665-1837		Wolvehampton			7B
Hints	A 1559-1948	1558-1828	5,8	1558-1812		Tamworth	1790-1812		4D

STAFFORDSHIRE

parish name	deposited original registers	I.G.I.	local census indexes	copies of registers at Soc. Gen.	Boyd's marriage index	1837-1851 Registration District	Pallot's marriage index	non-conform. records at P.R.O.	map ref.
Hopwas Hays (ex.par.)			5,8			Tamworth			4D(V)
Horton	A 1653-1992	1673-1870	5,8			Leek			7K
Ilam	A 1651-1990	1661-1868	8	1651-1995		Ashbourne			4J
Ingestre	A 1691-1948	1676-1839	8			Stafford			6G(O)
Ipstones	A 1561-1948	1560-1847	5,8	1560-1716		Cheadle			6J
Keele	A 1540-1980	1540-1870	5,8	1540-1812		Newcastle-u-Lyme			8I
Kings Bromley	A 1673-1984	1632-1869	5,8			Lichfield			5E
Kingsley	A 1561-1945	1561-1857	5,8	1561-1795		Cheadle			6I
Kingstone	A 1755-1938	1679-1868	5,8			Uttoxeter			5G
Kingswinford	B 1603-1958	1718-1837	5,6,8	1603-1761		Stourbridge	1793-1836		7B
Kinver	A 1560-1915	1560-1876	8	1560-1804		Wolverhampton			8B
Lapley	A 1538-1993	1664-1877	5,8	1538-1756		Penkridge			8E
Leek	A 1634-1973	1562-1853	5,8	1634-1812		Leek		1787-1837	6K
Leigh	A 1541-1988	1541-1872	5,8			Uttoxeter			6H
Lichfield								1801-1837	4E
Cathedral	D 1660-1984	1660-1885	5,8	1660-1754		Lichfield			4E
St Chad	D 1635-1953	1659-1877	5,8			Lichfield			5E
St Mary	D 1566-1947	1659-1868	5,8			Lichfield			4D
St Michael	D 1574-1945	1663-1895	5,8			Lichfield			5D
Longdon	A 1687-1980	1663-1872	5,8			Lichfield			5E
Longnor	A 1691-1985		8			Leek			5L
Longton								1811-1837	7I(E)
St James	A 1834-1948	1834-1839	8			Stoke-upon-Trent			7I(E)
St John	A 1764-1978	1764-1868	8			Stoke-upon-Trent			7I(E)
Lower Gornal	B 1823-1911	1823-1847	8	1823-1837		Dudley			7B
Madeley	A 1678-1938	1567-1876	5,8	1567-1812		Newcastle-u-Lyme			9I
Maer	A 1558-1996	1674-1878	5,8			Newcastle-u-Lyme			9H
Marchington	A 1612-1985	1665-1865	8	1609-1812	1617-1632	Uttoxeter			4G
Marston	A 1565-1983	1566-1877	8			Stafford			7G
Mavesyn Ridware	A 1538-1990	1663-1868	5,8	1538-1812		Lichfield			5F
Mayfield	A 1576-1968	1676-1868	8			Ashbourne/Leek			4I
Meerbrook	A 1738-1925	1791-1863	8			Leek			6K
Milwich	A 1573-1991	1573-1875	8	1573-1812		Stone			6H
Mucklestone	A 1555-1998	1555-1869	5,8	1555-1812		Market Drayton			9H
Needwood, Christchurch	A 1809-1996					Burton-upon-Trent			4G
Newborough	A 1601-1899	1660-1844	8			Uttoxeter			4G
Newcastle-under-Lyme	A 1563-1982	1563-1874	5,8	1563-1812		Newcastle-u-Lyme		1777-1837	8I(A)
Newchapel	A 1723-1910	1726-1856	8			Wolstanton			7J
Norbury	A 1538-1894	1673-1868	8	1538-1837		Newport			9F
Norton-le-Moors	A 1576-1970	1574-1875	5,8	1574-1837		Leek			7J
Norton Canes	A 1567-1907	1659-1859	5,8			Penkridge			6D
Ogley Hay (ex.par.)		1849-1876	5,8			Lichfield			5D(U)
Okeover	A 1759-1955		8			Ashbourne			4I
Onecote	A 1755-1995	1782-1834	8			Leek			5J
Patshull	A 1559-1990	1656-1874	8			Shifnall			8D
Pattingham	A 1559-1936	1559-1874	5,8	1559-1874		Wolverhampton	1790-1812		8C
Pelsall	A 1746-1997	1799-1839	8	1763-1812		Walsall			6D(T)
Penkridge	A 1572-1951	1572-1876	5,8	1572-1837		Penkridge			7E
Penn	A 1569-1876	1569-1852	8	1569-1837		Wolverhampton			7C
Pipe Ridware	A 1561-1998	1565-1869	5,8	1561-1812		Lichfield	1790-1812		5F(Q)
Quarnford	A 1744-1996	1795-1856	8			Leek			6L
Ranton	A 1655-1993	1655-1868	8	1655-1812		Stafford			8F
Rocester	A 1564-1812	1565-1868	5,8	1565-1812		Uttoxeter	1790-1812		5H
Rolleston	A 1569-1982	1662-1866	5,8			Burton-upon-Trent			3G
Rowley Regis	C 1539-1983	1539-1812	5,8	1539-1874	1685-1714	Dudley	1790-1812		6B
Rugeley	A 1569-1996	1569-1875	5,8	1569-1812		Lichfield		1821-1837	6E
Rushall	A 1686-1982	1660-1868	8	1660-1812		Walsall			6C(X)
Rushton Spencer	A 1700-1992	1693-1856	8			Leek			7K
Sandon	A 1636-1873	1660-1868	8			Stone			6G
Sedgley	A 1558-1971	1558-1876	5,8	1558-1876		Dudley		1778-1837	7C
Seighford	A 1560-1945	1561-1850	8	1561-1812		Stafford			7G
Shareshill	A 1565-1982	1687-1868	5,8			Penkridge			7D
Sheen	A 1595-1996	1660-1852	5,8			Leek			5K
Shenstone	A 1579-1975	1653-1875	5,8			Lichfield	1579-1812		5D
Sheriffhales	E 1557-1972	1557-1812	8		1551-1812	Shifnall	1790-1812		9E
Smethwick	C 1732-1989	1774-1857	8	1732-1924		Kings Norton			6B
Stafford									7G
Castle Church	A 1567-1887	1837-1868	8	1547-1812		Stafford	1790-1812		7F
St Chad	A 1636-1956	1636-1864	8	1636-1812		Stafford	1790-1811		7G
St Mary	A 1559-1980	1559-1876	8	1599-1671		Stafford		1795-1837	7G
Standon	A 1558-1896	1558-1856	8	1558-1812		Stone	1790-1812		8H
Statfold			5,8			Tamworth			3D
Stoke-upon-Trent	A 1629-1978	1629-1838	5,8	1629-1812		Stoke-upon-Trent	1790-1812	1786-1837	7I
Stone	A 1568-1960	1568-1885	8			Stone		1787-1837	7H
Stonnall	A 1823-1984	1823-1836	8			Lichfield			5D(W)
Stowe by Chartley	A 1575-1943	1574-1867	8	1574-1689		Stafford			6G
Stretton	A 1659-1973	1678-1877	5,8			Penkridge			7E
Swynnerton	A 1558-1986	1676-1868	8	1558-1837		Stone			8H
Tamworth	A 1558-1949	1556-1868	5,8	1556-1635		Tamworth		1695-1837	4D
Tatenhill	A 1563-1994	1563-1868	5,8	1563-1812		Burton-upon-Trent	1790-1812		4F
Teddesley Hay (ex.par.)			5,8			Penkridge			6E
Tettenhall-Regis	A 1602-1968	1602-1876	5,8	1602-1839		Wolverhampton			8D
Thorpe Constantine	A 1539-1812	1667-1866	5,8			Tamworth			3D
Tipton St Martin	A 1573-1901	1574-1868	5,8	1513-1969		Dudley		1809-1837	6C
Tixall	A 1707-1836	1663-1865	8			Stafford			6F
Trentham	A 1558-1956	1558-1852	8	1558-1812		Stone	1790-1812		7I
Trysull	A 1572-1980	1655-1856	5,8	1558-1812		Wolverhampton			8C
Tutbury	A 1668-1916	1673-1838	5,8	1673-1809		Burton-upon-Trent		1801-1837	3G
Upper Arley	G 1564-1964	1564-1812	8	1564-1812		Kidderminster	1790-1812		9A

233

STAFFORDSHIRE

parish name	deposited original registers	I.G.I.	local census indexes	copies of registers at Soc. Gen.	Boyd's marriage index	1837-1851 Registration District	Pallot's marriage index	non-conform. records at P.R.O.	map ref.
Uttoxeter	A 1596-1987	1668-1856	5,8			Uttoxeter		1793-1837	5G
Walsall	A 1646-1985	1570-1858	4,5,6,7,8	1570-1842		Walsall		1786-1837	6C
Warslow	A 1785-1980	1805-1857	8			Leek			5K
Waterfall	A 1602-1992	1661-1856	8	1602-1931		Ashbourne			5J
Wednesbury	A 1561-1934	1673-1844	8	1562-1926		West Bromwich		1800-1837	6C
Wednesfield	A 1751-1986	1751-1837	5,8	1751-1837		Wolverhampton			7D
Weeford	A 1562-1975	1562-1835	5,8	1562-1812		Lichfield			4D
West Bromwich								1787-1837	6C
All Saints	C 1608-1984	1608-1868	5,8	1608-1837		West Bromwich			6C
Christchurch	A 1829-1970	1829-1835	5,8	1829-1962		West Bromwich			6C
Weston under Lizard	A 1701-1998	1653-1877	8	1652-1837		Shiffnall	1790-1812		8E
Weston-upon-Trent	A 1583-1985	1666-1864	8			Stafford			6G(M)
Wetton	A 1657-1992	1660-1877	8			Leek			5K
Whitmore	A 1558-1964	1674-1837	8			Newcastle-u-Lyme			8I
Whittington	A 1574-1954	1663-1870	5,8			Lichfield			4D
Wichnor	A 1731-1989	1660-1835	5,8			Burton-u-Trent			4E
Willenhall	A 1642-1965	1799-1825	5,8	1642-1812		Wolverhampton			6C
Wolstanton	A 1628-1966	1624-1875	5,8	1624-1812		Wolstanton	1790-1812	1795-1837	8J
Wolverhampton								1726-1838	7C
St George	A 1832-1977		5,8			Wolverhampton			7C
St Peter	A 1603-1949	1538-1844	5,8	1603-1776		Wolverhampton			7C
Wombourne	A 1570-1983	1655-1856	5,8			Wolverhampton			8B
Woodford Grange (ex. par.)			8			Wolverhampton			8C
Yoxall	A 1645-1915	1666-1856	5,8	1644-1754		Lichfield			4F

Original registers are deposited at:
A = Staffordshire Record Office, Eastgate Street, Stafford, ST16 2LZ
B = Dudley Libraries, Archives and Local History Service, Mount Pleasant Street, Coseley, Dudley, WR14 9JR
C = Smethwick District Library, High Street, Smethwick, Warley, West Midlands, B66 1AB
D = Lichfield Joint Record Office, The Friary, Lichfield, WS13 9QG
E = Shropshire Records and Research Centre, Castle Gates, Shrewsbury SY2 6ND
F = Birmingham Reference Library, Chamberlain Square, Birmingham, B3 3HQ
G = Worcestershire Library and History Centre, Trinity Street, Worcester, WR1 2PW

Study adjacent parishes in counties of Worcestershire, Warwickshire, Derbyshire, Cheshire and Shropshire

Walsall Local History Centre, Essex Street, Walsall, WS2 7AS
Wolverhampton Borough Archives, Central Library, Snow Hill, Wolverhampton, WV1 3AX
Staffordshire Record Office, Eastgate Street, Stafford, ST16 2LZ
Lichfield Joint Record Office, The Friary, Lichfield, WS13 9QG
Stoke on Trent City Archives, Hanley Library, Bethesda Street, Stoke on Trent, ST1 3RS
Burton upon Trent Archives, Burton Library, Riverside, High Street, Burton upon Trent, DE14 1AH
William Salt Library, 19 Eastgate Street, Stafford, ST16 2LZ

The following useful indexes have been compiled – see Introduction
Census Index 1851 – Birmingham and Midland SGH, c/o Mr Garner, 29a Windmill Close, Kenilworth, Warwickshire, CV8 2GQ
Census Indexes 1841-1871 Burntwood – Burntwood FHG, 10 Squirrels Hollow, Burntwood, Staffordshire, WS7 8YS
Census Index 1891 Bloxwich – Walsall Local History Centre, Essex Street, Walsall, WS2 7AS
Census Indexes 1841-1871 Walsall – Walsall Local History Centre, Essex Street, Walsall, WS2 7AS
Staffordshire Marriage Index – Mrs. Sue Smith, 5 Woodhayes Road, Wednesfield, Wolverhampton, West Midlands WV11 1AD
Marriage Index for Greater Birmingham 1776-1837 – (see under Warwickshire for details)
Staffordshire Burial Index – T. Bowers, 272 Walsall Road, Perry Barr, Birmingham, B42 1UB

Staffordshire is 55 miles in length at its extreme points from north-west to south-east, its greatest breadth from north-east to south-west being 35 miles. It is watered by eight principal rivers:the Trent, Dove, Blyth, Sow, Penk, Churnet, Tame and Stour. The population in 1841 was 510,504; in 1851, 630,545; in 1861, 769,541; in 1871, 857,333; in 1881, 981,013.

The soils include gravel, clay, shale, marl and loam. Agriculture and stock-raising were inportant and dairy-farming produced much good butter and cheese. Coal was abundant and lead, copper and iron were also mined. Fuller's earth, pipe-clay, marble and ochre were also found in the county. Pottery was the main manufacture.

The information in the Index is abbreviated, and may mislead the searcher if reference is not made to the details contained in the several publications listed in the Introduction. It is essential that users of this book check the appropriate works before making further enquiries.

SUFFOLK

parish name	deposited original registers	I.G.I.	local census indexes	copies of registers at Soc. Gen.	Boyd's marriage index	1837-1851 Registration District	Pallot's marriage index	non-conform. records at P.R.O.	map ref.
Acton	B 1605-1989		5,8		1564-1754	Sudbury			3D
Akenham	A 1538-1973		5,8	1538-1905	1540-1750	Bosmere			4G
Aldeburgh	A 1558-1965		5,8	1558-1907	1558-1754	Plomesgate			4J
Alderton	A 1674-1986		5,8	1674-1901	1674-1753	Woodbridge			3I
Aldham	B 1666-1947		5,8	1564-1812	1668-1757	Cosford			3F
Aldringham-with-Thorpe	A 1538-1970	1545-1876	5,8	1538-1900	1545-1758	Blything		1812-1837	5J
Alnesbourn Priory (ex.par.)			8			Ipswich			3G(Uo)
Alpheton	B 1571-1901		5,8	1574-1836	1574-1837	Sudbury			4D
Ampton	B 1559-1834		5,8	1564-1812	1562-1752	Thingoe			6D(B)
Ashbocking	A 1555-1952		5,8	1555-1900	1555-1754	Bosmere			4G(Ey)
Ashby	C 1553-1835		5,8	1553-1835	1553-1835	Mutford	1790-1837		9J
Ashfield	A 1693-1978	1691-1836	5,8	1691-1901	1695-1754	Bosmere			5G
Aspall	A 1558-1996		5,8	1564-1812	1559-1753	Hartismere			5G(Aw)
Assington	B 1598-1897	1598-1836	5,8		1599-1823	Sudbury			2D
Athelington	A 1694-1845		5,8	1694-1904	1695-1753	Hoxne			6G(Al)
Bacton	A 1559-1879		5,8	1539-1879	1539-1754	Hartismere			5F
Badingham			5,8		1596-1754	Hoxne			5H
Badley	A 1589-1834		5,8		1556-1753	Bosmere			4F
Badwell Ash	B 1559-1964	1560-1811	5,8	1559-1811	1559-1751	Stow			6E
Bardwell	B 1538-1989	1538-1844	5,8	1538-1837	1538-1837	Thingoe		1821-1837	6E
Barham	A 1562-1969		5,8	1538-1900	1563-1753	Bosmere			4G
Barking	A 1563-1985		5,8		1562-1754	Bosmere		1833-1837	4F
Barnardiston	B 1540-1983		5,8	1540-1904	1545-1837	Risbridge			4B(Y)
Barnby	D 1555-1987	1558-1875	5,8	1555-1901	1554-1754	Mutford			8J
Barnham	B 1730-1980	1730-1872	5,8	1563-1812	1730-1754	Thetford			7D
Barningham	B 1538-1939		5,8	1561-1812	1538-1724	Erpingham		1812-1837	7E
Barrow	B 1542-1988	1542-1876	5,8	1542-1837	1544-1837	Thingoe			5C
Barsham	D 1558-1988		5,8	1558-1901	1561-1757	Wangford			8I
Barton Mills	B 1663-1915		5,8	1663-1835	1663-1837	Mildenhall	1790-1837		6B
Battisford	A 1711-1986		5,8	1707-1709	1713-1750	Bosmere			4F
Bawdsey	A 1744-1986	1739-1740	5,8	1698-1902	1744-1752	Woodbridge			2I
Baylham	A 1661-1962		5,8	1661-1761	1661-1753	Bosmere			4F
Beccles	D 1586-1949	1813-1837	5,8		1586-1749	Wangford		1773-1837	8J
Bedfield	A 1584-1978		5,8	1584-1907	1584-1756	Hoxne			5H
Bedingfield	A 1538-1900		5,8	1538-1935	1542-1749	Hoxne	1790-1837		6G
Belstead	A 1539-1986		5,8	1539-1986	1539-1753	Samford			3G
Belton	C 1560-1980	1813-1834	5,8		1560-1755	Mutford			9J
Benacre	D 1727-1980	1727-1875	5,8		1728-1754	Blything			7K
Benhall	A 1560-1987		5,8	1560-1900	1561-1754	Plomesgate			5I
Bentley	A 1538-1993		5,8	1539-1761	1539-1761	Samford			2F
Beyton	B 1539-1995		5,8	1552-1837	1539-1837	Stow			5E(L)
Bildeston	B 1558-1977	1558-1876	5,8	1558-1900	1559-1754	Cosford			4E(Od)
Blaxhall	A 1673-1965		5,8		1673-1754	Plomesgate			4I
Blundeston	C 1558-1972		5,8		1560-1753	Mutford			8K
Blyford	D 1695-1996		5,8	1695-1901	1695-1727	Blything			6J
Blythburgh	A 1563-1970		5,8	1690-1900	1690-1753	Blything			6J
Botesdale (see Redgrave with Botesdale)									6F(Ac)
Boulge	A 1621-1901		5,8	1621-1986	1628-1812	Woodbridge			4H(Uu)
Boxford	B 1557-1978		5,8		1575-1805	Cosford		1824-1837	3E
Boxted	B 1539-1965		5,8	1539-1850	1539-1837	Sudbury			4C
Boyton with Capel	A 1538-1970		5,8		1538-1754	Woodbridge			3I
Bradfield Combust	B 1538-1835	1538-1835	5,8	1538-1835	1538-1837	Thingoe			5D(R)
Bradfield St Clare	B 1539-1992	1538-1836	5,8	1538-1811	1541-1837	Thingoe			5D(S)
Bradfield St George	B 1555-1990	1555-1875	5,8	1555-1901	1555-1837	Thingoe			5D(T)
Bradwell	C 1556-1985		5,8		1565-1753	Mutford			9K
Braiseworth	A 1709-1972		5,8	1565-1812	1701-1753	Hartismere			6G(Af)
Bramfield	A 1539-1985	1539-1875	5,8	1539-1889	1540-1837	Blything	1790-1837		6I
Bramford	A 1553-1988		5,8	1553-1900	1553-1754	Bosmere			3F
Brampton	D 1760-1998	1739-1875	5,8	1755-1900		Blything			7J
Brandeston	A 1559-1993		5,8	1559-1901	1559-1812	Plomesgate		1836-1837	5H
Brandon	B 1653-1978		5,8	1565-1812	1728-1754	Thetford		1811-1836	7C
Brantham	A 1634-1983	1634-1876	5,8	1634-1900	1634-1759	Samford			2F
Bredfield	A 1711-1933		5,8	1708-1709	1711-1751	Woodbridge			4H
Brent Eleigh	B 1589-1948		5,8	1589-1836	1590-1837	Cosford			4D
Brettenham	B 1584-1886	1739-1770	5,8	1584-1752	1584-1752	Cosford			4E(Oa)
Brightwell	A 1653-1966	1629-1793	5,8,9	1538-1902	1654-1812	Woodbridge			3H(Uj)
Brockley	B 1560-1909		5,8	1560-1900	1560-1836	Thingoe			4C
Brome	A 1559-1978		5,8	1559-1900	1563-1752	Hartismere			7G
Bromeswell	A 1634-1993		5,8		1634-1761	Woodbridge			4H
Bruisyard	A 1566-1994		5,8		1566-1753	Plomesgate			5I(En)
Brundish	A 1562-1995	1562-1785	5,8	1562-1904	1563-1749	Hoxne			6H
Bucklesham	A 1678-1986		5,8,9	1678-1901	1678-1751	Woodbridge			3H
Bungay		1813-1837						1783-1850	8I
Holy Trinity	D 1557-1986	1813-1837	5,8	1557-1900	1557-1752	Wangford			8I
St Mary	D 1557-1977	1813-1837	5,8	1558-1901	1558-1752	Wangford			8I
Bures St Mary	B 1538-1975		5,8	1538-1900	1538-1750	Sudbury			2D
Burgate	A 1560-1959		5,8	1560-1903	1560-1753	Hartismere			6F
Burgh	A 1547-1954	1547-1877	5,8	1547-1812	1559-1812	Woodbridge	1790-1812		4H
Burgh Castle	C 1694-1984		5,8		1694-1752	Mutford			9J
Burstall	A 1540-1966	1540-1877	5,8	1540-1887	1542-1837	Samford			3F(Ou)
Bury St Edmunds								1689-1837	5D
St James	B 1558-1985	1558-1800	5,8	1558-1837	1562-1837	Bury St Edmunds	1790-1800		5D
St Mary	B 1538-1984	1558-1837	5,8	1558-1837	1538-1837	Bury St Edmunds			5D
Butley	A 1785-1967		5,8	1693-1901		Plomesgate			4I
Buxhall	A 1558-1970	1558-1875	5,8	1558-1900	1559-1799	Stow			4E
Campsea Ash	A 1559-1958	1559-1875	5,8		1559-1812	Plomesgate			4I
Capel St Andrew (see Boyton with Capel)									3I
Capel St Mary	A 1538-1992		5,8	1538-1837	1539-1837	Samford	1790-1837		2F
Carlton	A 1538-1958	1538-1885	5,8	1538-1886	1538-1837	Blything	1790-1837		5I(Uw)

SUFFOLK

parish name	deposited original registers	I.G.I.	local census indexes	copies of registers at Soc. Gen.	Boyd's marriage index	1837-1851 Registration District	Pallot's marriage index	non-conform. records at P.R.O.	map ref.
Carlton Colville	C 1710-1970		5,8	1710-1912	1710-1753	Mutford			8K
Cavendish	B 1594-1963	1594-1837	5,8	1594-1837	1595-1837	Sudbury			3C
Cavenham	B 1539-1980	1539-1837	5,8	1539-1836	1540-1836	Mildenhall			6C
Charsfield	A 1727-1978		5,8	1698-1901	1730-1823	Woodbridge			4H
Chattisham	A 1559-1934		5,8		1559-1812	Samford			3F(Ox)
Chedburgh	B 1538-1993		5,8	1538-1905	1542-1837	Thingoe			5C(O)
Chediston	A 1653-1981	1654-1895	5,8	1653-1924	1654-1837	Blything	1790-1837		7I
Chelmondiston	A 1727-1992		5,8	1698-1900	1728-1753	Samford		1831-1834	2G(Ut)
Chelsworth	B 1559-1996	1559-1875	5,8		1559-1812	Cosford			3E(Oc)
Chevington	B 1559-1895	1559-1812	8	1559-1896	1559-1837	Thingoe	1790-1812		5C
Chillesford	A 1740-1836	1740-1812	5,8	1715-1900	1742-1743	Plomesgate			4I
Chilton	B 1623-1980	1813-1875	5,8		1624-1753	Sudbury			3D
Clare	B 1558-1983		5,8	1558-1900	1574-1837	Risbridge		1779-1837	3C
Claydon	A 1559-1975		5,8	1559-1901	1560-1764	Bosmere			4G(Or)
Clopton	A 1735-1836		5,8	1698-1812	1726-1812	Woodbridge			4H
Cockfield	B 1561-1992		5,8	1561-1812	1561-1760	Cosford			4D
Coddenham	A 1538-1967		5,8	1538-1900	1543-1752	Bosmere			4F
Combs	A 1568-1972		5,8	1568-1837	1568-1837	Stow	1790-1837		4F
Coney Weston	B 1562-1836		5,8	1563-1812	1562-1751	Thetford			7E
Cookley	A 1538-1996		5,8	1538-1900	1538-1756	Blything			6I
Copdock	A 1701-1994	1701-1876	5,8	1701-1752	1701-1752	Samford			3F(Oz)
Corton	C 1579-1912		5,8	1579-1930	1595-1754	Mutford			8K
Cotton	A 1538-1871		5,8	1538-1899	1539-1754	Hartismere			5F
Covehithe	D 1559-1995	1574-1876	5,8		1600-1754	Blything			7K
Cowlinge	B 1558-1992		5,8	1558-1901	1558-1837	Risbridge			4B
Cransford	A 1653-1996		5,8		1665-1837	Plomesgate			5I(Em)
Cratfield	A 1539-1965	1539-1877	5,8	1539-1900	1539-1812	Blything		1813-1837	6H
Creeting									4F
All Saints	A 1754-1812		8	1563-1812		Bosmere			4F
St Mary	A 1681-1989		5,8		1681-1753	Bosmere			4F
St Peter	A 1558-1990		5,8	1562-1812	1558-1751	Stow			4F(Eg)
Cretingham	A 1557-1992		5,8	1557-1901	1561-1812	Plomesgate			5H(Ek)
Crowfield	A 1756-1969		5,8	1538-1900		Bosmere			4G
Culford	B 1560-1910	1560-1778	5,8	1560-1910	1560-1773	Thingoe			6D
Culpho	A 1700-1978	1700-1875	5,8	1720-1886	1727-1821	Woodbridge	1790-1837		4G(Ud)
Dalham	B 1558-1974		8	1558-1837	1558-1837	Newmarket			5B
Dallinghoo	A 1560-1996	1559-1875	5,8	1559-1752	1560-1752	Woodbridge			4H
Darsham	A 1536-1984		5,8	1536-1901	1536-1754	Blything			6J
Debach	A 1539-1980		5,8	1539-1904	1543-1812	Woodbridge			4H(Ez)
Debenham	A 1559-1980		5,8	1559-1805	1559-1754	Bosmere		1706-1837	5G
Denham (near Bury St Edmunds)	B 1538-1990	1539-1877		1538-1850	1566-1837	Thingoe	1790-1850		5C
Denham (near Eye)	A 1708-1949		5,8	1708-1812	1711-1753	Hartismere	1790-1850		6G
Dennington	A 1571-1997		5,8	1570-1900	1571-1830	Hoxne			5H
Denston	B 1561-1989		5,8	1564-1812	1561-1771	Risbridge			4C
Depden	B 1538-1992		5,8	1564-1837	1586-1837	Thingoe			4C
Drinkstone	B 1666-1924	1579-1679	5,8	1579-1812	1582-1754	Stow			5E
Dunwich									5J
All Saints	A 1672-1821		5,8	1672-1900	1677-1752	Blything			5J
St James (formerly All Saints)	A 1822-1984		5,8			Blything			5J
St Peter	E 1539-1657		5,8	1549-1658	1549-1658	Blything			5J
Earl Soham	A 1558-1972		5,8	1558-1900	1558-1812	Plomesgate			5H
Earl Stonham	A 1654-1994		5,8	1654-1902	1654-1753	Bosmere			5F
East Bergholt	A 1653-1966		5,8	1653-1906	1661-1754	Samford		1689-1836	2F
Easton	A 1561-1979		5,8	1561-1950	1561-1812	Plomesgate			5H
Easton Bevents (see Benacre)									6K
Edwardstone	B 1645-1995	1645-1876	5,8	1645-1901	1645-1812	Cosford		1824-1837	3E
Ellough	D 1540-1966	1540-1812	5,8	1540-1812	1545-1754	Wangford			7J
Elmsett	B 1684-1961	1684-1877	5,8	1564-1812	1685-1754	Cosford			3F
Elmswell	B 1655-1992		5,8	1561-1899	1661-1756	Stow			5E
Elveden	B 1652-1984		5,8	1570-1812	1653-1753	Mildenhall			7C
Eriswell	B 1669-1955	1678-1875	5,8	1567-1812	1678-1753	Mildenhall			7C
Erwarton	A 1558-1993		5,8	1558-1901	1560-1751	Samford			2G
Euston	B 1566-1980	1566-1839	5,8	1561-1812	1572-1753	Thetford			7D
Exning	B 1558-1947	1558-1880		1558-1812	1558-1812	Newmarket	1790-1812		5A
Eye	A 1538-1990		5,8	1538-1812	1538-1753	Hartismere		1812-1834	6G
Eyke	A 1538-1950		5,8		1539-1812	Plomesgate			4I
Fakenham Magna	B 1559-1980	1559-1837	5,8	1563-1812	1561-1749	Thetford			6D
Falkenham	A 1538-1961		5,8,9	1538-1900	1538-1754	Woodbridge			2H
Farnham	A 1707-1996		5,8	1559-1804	1718-1753	Plomesgate			5I(Ew)
Felixstowe	A 1653-1965	1652-1876	5,8,9	1652-1900	1654-1753	Woodbridge			2H
Felsham	B 1656-1992	1656-1876	5,8	1568-1812	1656-1752	Stow			4E
Finningham	A 1560-1970		5,8	1560-1812	1560-1754	Hartismere			6F
Flempton	B 1561-1955		5,8	1561-1874	1561-1837	Thingoe			6C(A)
Flixton	D 1547-1995	1547-1879	5,8		1560-1753	Wangford			7I
Flixton			5,8			Mutford			8K
Flowton	A 1572-1994		5,8			Bosmere			3F(Ot)
Fornham									6D
All Saints	B 1558-1991		5,8	1558-1837	1578-1753	Thingoe			6D
St Genevieve	B 1753-1876		5,8	1564-1805	1753-1774	Thingoe			6D
St Martin	B 1538-1995		5,8	1541-1836	1541-1836	Thingoe			6D
Foxhall			5,8	1538-1902		Woodbridge			3H
Framlingham	A 1560-1989		5,8	1560-1900	1560-1754	Plomesgate		1752-1853	5H
Framsden	A 1558-1971		5,8	1558-1900	1560-1756	Bosmere		1831-1837	5G
Freckenham	B 1550-1996		5,8	1550-1837	1550-1837	Mildenhall			6B
Fressingfield	A 1554-1986	1554-1875	8	1554-1838	1554-1837	Hoxne	1790-1837		6H
Freston	A 1538-1968	1539-1877	5,8		1538-1753	Samford	1790-1837		2G
Friston	A 1541-1968		5,8	1541-1900	1543-1753	Plomesgate			4J

SUFFOLK

parish name	deposited original registers	I.G.I.	local census indexes	copies of registers at Soc. Gen.	Boyd's marriage index	1837-1851 Registration District	Pallot's marriage index	non-conform. records at P.R.O.	map ref.
Fritton	C 1706-1994		5,8	1706-1904	1708-1751	Mutford			9J
Frostenden	D 1538-1949	1538-1813	5,8	1538-1791	1538-1754	Blything			7J
Gazeley	B 1538-1974		8	1539-1837	1540-1837	Newmarket			5B
Gedding	B 1543-1997	1543-1879	5,8	1543-1812	1566-1753	Stow			5E(U)A
Gedgrave (ex par)			8			Plomesgate			3I
Gipping (see Stowmarket and Old Newton)			5,8						5F(Ef)
Gisleham	C 1559-1992		5,8	1559-1905	1559-1750	Mutford			8K
Gislingham	A 1558-1945		5,8	1558-1790	1558-1754	Hartismere			6F
Glemsford	B 1550-1994	1550-1880	5,8	1550-1837	1550-1837	Sudbury			4C
Gorleston	C 1668-1852	1813-1837	5,8	1679-1808	1675-1751	Mutford		1828-1837	9K
Gosbeck	A 1561-1977		5,8	1561-1900	1564-1751	Bosmere			4G
Great Ashfield	B 1765-1985		5,8	1563-1812		Stow			6E
Great Barton	B 1561-1997		5,8	1574-1812	1562-1753	Thingoe			5D
Great Bealings	A 1538-1976	1539-1809	5,8	1541-1840	1542-1812	Woodbridge	1790-1812		4H(Ue)
Great Blakenham	A 1545-1967		5,8	1665-1794	1549-1752	Bosmere			4F(Oo)
Great Bradley	B 1703-1987		5,8	1786-1901	1703-1837	Risbridge			4B
Great Bricett	A 1525-1976		5,8		1592-1750	Bosmere			4F(Oj)
Great Cornard	B 1540-1972		5,8	1540-1837	1597-1754	Sudbury			3D
Great Finborough	A 1558-1929		5,8	1558-1900	1558-1812	Stow			4E(Ee)
Great Glemham	A 1559-1974		5,8		1559-1753	Plomesgate			5I
Great Livermere	B 1538-1907		5,8	1564-1812	1538-1753	Thingoe			6D(D)
Great Saxham	B 1555-1992	1555-1812	5,8	1555-1836	1561-1837	Thingoe			5C
Great Thurlow	B 1636-1983		5,8	1636-1900	1636-1837	Risbridge			4B
Great Waldingfield	B 1539-1997	1539-1876	5,8	1563-1812	1539-1812	Sudbury			3D
Great Wenham	A 1642-1975	1643-1812	5,8	1670-1837	1670-1837	Samford	1790-1837		2F(Ov)
Great Whelnetham	B 1561-1991	1561-1850	5,8	1561-1954	1562-1837	Thingoe	1790-1850		5D(P)
Great Wratting	B 1593-1986		5,8	1598-1900	1598-1837	Risbridge			3B
Great Yarmouth (Norfolk)									9K
Groton	B 1562-1987	1704-1875	5,8	1562-1901	1563-1812	Cosford			3E
Grundisburgh	A 1538-1983	1538-1876	5,8	1538-1851	1539-1837	Woodbridge	1790-1837		4G
Gunton	C 1739-1992		5,8	1691-1759	1740-1754	Mutford			8K
Hacheston	A 1538-1991	1538-1869	5,8	1538-1985	1538-1812	Plomesgate			4H
Hadleigh	A 1558-1991	1558-1876	5,8	1631-1918	1559-1754	Cosford		1690-1837	3E
Halesworth	D 1653-1978	1813-1837	5,8	1653-1900	1653-1837	Blything		1796-1836	6I(Au)
Hargrave	B 1710-1975		5,8	1574-1836	1710-1837	Thingoe			5C
Harkstead	A 1653-1985		5,8	1653-1901	1654-1754	Samford			2G
Harleston	A 1560-1827		5,8	1596-1812	1579-1812	Stow			5E(Eb)
Hartest	B 1556-1959		5,8	1559-1850	1559-1837	Sudbury			4C
Hasketon	A 1538-1985	1540-1813	5,8	1538-1813	1545-1812	Woodbridge	1790-1812		4H
Haslewood			8			Plomesgate			5J
Haughley	A 1557-1978		5,8	1561-1812	1559-1757	Stow			5F
Haverhill	B 1600-1976		5,8	1562-1837	1670-1837	Risbridge		1709-1839	3B
Hawkedon	B 1709-1996		5,8	1564-1839	1710-1837	Sudbury			4C
Hawstead	B 1558-1926		5,8	1558-1857	1559-1837	Thingoe			5D
Helmingham	A 1559-1921		5,8	1559-1901	1559-1753	Bosmere			4G
Hemingstone	A 1553-1986		5,8	1553-1901	1556-1753	Bosmere			4G(Op)
Hemley	A 1698-1980		5,8,9	1698-1837	1698-1741	Bosmere			3H(Um)
Hengrave	B 1561-1955	1813-1837	5,8	1561-1874		Thingoe			6C
Henham (see Wangford)									6J
Henley	A 1559-1986		5,8	1559-1901	1559-1850	Bosmere			4G(Oq)
Henstead	D 1539-1986		5,8	1539-1709	1539-1753	Blything			7J
Hepworth	B 1688-1948		5,8	1562-1812	1563-1764	Thetford			6E
Herringfleet	C 1706-1994	1691-1692	5,8	1706-1912	1709-1752	Mutford			9J
Herringswell	B 1748-1933		5,8	1563-1837	1749-1837	Mildenhall			6B
Hessett	B 1538-1969		5,8	1539-1837	1538-1837	Stow			5F
Heveningham	A 1539-1886	1539-1875	5,8	1539-1886	1539-1753	Blything			6I(Ay)
Higham	A 1538-1836	1538-1812	5,8	1744-1902	1538-1774	Samford			2F
Hinderclay	B 1567-1957		5,8	1563-1812	1570-1812	Stow			7F
Hintlesham	A 1652-1965		5,8		1655-1757	Samford			3F
Hitcham	B 1575-1966		5,8	1564-1868	1600-1754	Cosford			4E
Holbrook	A 1559-1985		5,8	1559-1900	1559-1754	Samford			2G
Hollesley	A 1623-1969	1623-1812	5,8	1623-1812	1623-1812	Woodbridge	1790-1812		3I
Holton St Mary	A 1568-1835	1754-1835	5,8	1568-1902	1568-1753	Samford	1790-1837(?)		2F
Holton St Peter	D 1538-1979	1538-1875	5,8	1538-1924	1568-1753	Blything	1790-1837(?)		7I
Homersfield	D 1558-1995	1558-1875	5,8		1559-1740	Wangford			7H
Honington	B 1559-1970		5,8	1563-1812	1559-1753	Thetford			6D(E)
Hoo	A 1653-1992		5,8	1653-1903	1653-1812	Plomesgate			5H
Hopton (by Thetford)	B 1691-1952		5,8	1566-1812	1691-1754	Thetford			7E
Hopton (by Lowestoft)	C 1673-1965		5,8	1673-1902	1677-1751	Mutford			9K
Horham	A 1593-1997		5,8	1593-1753	1599-1753	Hoxne			6G
Horringer	B 1558-1984	1558-1850	5,8	1558-1850	1559-1850	Thingoe	1790-1837		5C
Hoxne	A 1548-1968		5,8	1548-1837	1581-1837	Hoxne	1790-1837		6G
Hundon	B 1538-1985	1813-1837	5,8	1562-1812		Risbridge			4B
Hunston	B 1557-1962		5,8	1561-1812	1561-1753	Stow			6E(H)
Huntingfield	A 1539-1966		5,8	1539-1900	1539-1758	Blything			6I
Icklingham All Saints	B 1559-1949	1560-1884	5,8	1559-1812	1559-1753	Mildenhall			6C
Icklingham St James	B 1775-1907	1775-1875	5,8	1563-1812		Mildenhall			6C
Ickworth	B 1566-1983	1566-1875	5,8	1564-1890	1566-1887	Thingoe	1790-1837		5C
Iken	A 1669-1951		5,8	1669-1902	1669-1754	Plomesgate			4I
Ilketshall									7I
St Andrew	D 1541-1988		5,8	1541-1677	1559-1753	Wangford			7I
St John	D 1538-1984		5,8		1538-1642	Wangford			7I
St Lawrence	D 1539-1982		5,8		1559-1754	Wangford			7I
St Margaret	D 1538-1982		5,8		1538-1754	Wangford			7I
Ingham	B 1538-1838	1538-1804	5,8	1538-1812	1540-1787	Thingoe	1780-1787		6D
Ipswich								1708-1858	3G
St Clement	A 1563-1978		5,8	1710-1812	1564-1753	Ipswich			3G
St Helen	A 1677-1945		5,8		1677-1753	Ipswich			3G
St Lawrence	A 1539-1973		5,8	1539-1812	1539-1755	Ipswich			3G

SUFFOLK

parish name	deposited original registers	I.G.I.	local census indexes	copies of registers at Soc. Gen.	Boyd's marriage index	1837-1851 Registration District	Pallot's marriage index	non-conform. records at P.R.O.	map ref.
Ipswich (cont'd)									
St Margaret	A 1537-1980		5,8	1754-1781	1538-1754	Ipswich			3G
St Mary at the Elms	A 1554-1936		5,8		1554-1753	Ipswich			3G
St Mary at the Quay	A 1559-1941	1562-1737	5,8	1559-1737	1601-1735	Ipswich			3G
St Mary at the Tower	A 1538-1945		5,8		1616-1754	Ipswich			3G
St Mary Stoke	A 1563-1986	1565-1876	5,8		1563-1754	Ipswich			3G
St Matthew	A 1559-1956	1559-1876	5,8		1559-1753	Ipswich			3G
St Nicholas	A 1539-1983	1539-1709	5,8	1539-1710	1539-1753	Ipswich			3G
St Peter	A 1657-1969	1662-1796	5,8	1657-1790	1662-1790	Ipswich			3G
St Stephen	A 1585-1973		5,8		1586-1753	Ipswich			3G
Ixworth	B 1557-1996	1559-1829	5,8	1557-1837	1559-1837	Thingoe			6D
Ixworth Thorpe	B 1718-1965		5,8	1561-1812	1719-1753	Thingoe			6D(F)
Kedington	B 1654-1970		5,8	1563-1900	1654-1837	Risbridge			3B
Kelsale-cum-Charlton	A 1538-1968	1538-1886	5,8	1538-1886	1538-1837	Blything	1790-1837		5I
Kentford	B 1709-1959		5,8	1608-1837	1718-1837	Mildenhall			6B
Kenton	A 1538-1993	1813-1876	5,8	1538-1812	1539-1754	Plomesgate			5G
Kersey	B 1561-1907	1561-1876	5,8	1563-1837	1541-1754	Cosford			3E
Kesgrave	A 1654-1971		5,8	1660-1840	1653-1812	Woodbridge			3H(Uh)
Kessingland	C 1561-1984		5,8	1531-1912	1561-1755	Mutford			7K
Kettle Baston	B 1578-1963		5,8	1572-1812	1578-1753	Cosford			4E(Ob)
Kettle-Burgh	A 1561-1881		5,8	1561-1901	1561-1753	Plomesgate			5H(El)
Kirkley	C 1701-1980	1686-1740	5,8	1686-1755	1543-1812	Mutford			8K
Kirton	A 1623-1994		5,8,9	1623-1899	1623-1754	Woodbridge			3H
Knettishall	C 1773-1949		5,8	1561-1812		Thetford			7E
Knodishall	A 1566-1971	1556-1703	5,8	1566-1901	1567-1754	Blything			5J
Lackford	B 1587-1993		5,8	1587-1900	1587-1837	Thingoe			6C
Lakenheath	B 1712-1968		5,8	1563-1812	1712-1754	Mildenhall			7B
Langham	B 1561-1966		5,8	1561-1812	1561-1753	Stow			6E
Lavenham	B 1558-1983	1558-1708	5,8	1564-1812	1558-1837	Cosford		1739-1835	4D
Lawshall	B 1558-1982		5,8	1559-1837	1559-1837	Sudbury			4D
Laxfield	A 1579-1941		5,8	1579-1900	1579-1753	Hoxne			6H
Layham	B 1538-1899	1538-1867	5,8	1538-1902	1544-1812	Cosford			3E
Leiston	A 1538-1989		5,8	1538-1900	1538-1753	Blything			5J
Letheringham	A 1588-1979	1588-1812	5,8	1588-1812	1591-1758	Plomesgate			4H(Es)
Levington	A 1562-1986	1563-1876	5,8,9	1562-1812	1564-1751	Woodbridge			3H(Uq)
Lidgate	B 1547-1992		8	1548-1902	1548-1837	Newmarket			5B
Lindsey	B 1559-1984	1559-1875	5,8	1563-1904	1550-1812	Cosford			3E
Linstead Magna	A 1558-1920	1653-1783	5,8		1653-1763	Blything			6I(An)
Linstead Parva	A 1538-1964	1539-1850	5,8		1541-1750	Blything			6I(Ao)
Little Bealings	A 1558-1986	1558-1875	5,8	1544-1886	1559-1883	Woodbridge			3H(Ug)
Little Blakenham	A 1728-1991		5,8	1698-1727	1728-1746	Bosmere			4F(On)
Little Bradley	B 1561-1991		5,8	1561-1902	1760-1835	Risbridge			4B
Little Cornard	B 1565-1938		5,8	1563-1812	1569-1758	Sudbury			3D
Little Finborough	A 1560-1936		8	1598-1812	1561-1812	Stow			4E(Ex)
Little Glemham	A 1550-1974		5,8		1550-1753	Plomesgate			5I(Eu)
Little Livermere	B 1559-1917		5,8	1563-1811	1560-1753	Thingoe			6D(C)
Little Saxham	B 1559-1993	1559-1850	5,8	1559-1850	1560-1836	Thingoe	1790-1837		5C(J)
Little Stonham	A 1542-1988		5,8	1542-1839	1542-1754	Bosmere			5F(Eh)
Little Thurlow	B 1561-1982		5,8	1561-1902	1561-1837	Risbridge			4B
Little Waldingfield	B 1568-1983		5,8	1564-1900	1572-1761	Sudbury			3D(Os)
Little Wenham	A 1558-1979		5,8	1564-1810	1567-1812	Samford	1790-1812		3F(Ow)
Little Whelnetham	B 1557-1992	1557-1850	5,8	1557-1850	1557-1837	Thingoe	1790-1850		5D(Q)
Little Wratting	B 1656-1965		5,8	1564-1900	1676-1837	Risbridge			3B
Long Melford (Sudbury)	B 1559-1978		5,8	1563-1897	1570-1837	Sudbury		1733-1837	3D
Lound	C 1696-1972		5,8		1698-1768	Mutford			9K
Lowestoft	C 1561-1937	1561-1875	5,8	1561-1840	1561-1812	Mutford	1790-1812	1812-1837	8K
Market Weston	B 1563-1946		5,8	1563-1812	1566-1753	Thetford			7E
Marlesford	A 1661-1978	1661-1876	5,8	1661-1978	1661-1812	Plomesgate			5I(Et)
Martlesham	A 1653-1967	1655-1812	5,8,9	1653-1900	1653-1837	Woodbridge	1790-1837		3H
Mellis	A 1559-1987		5,8	1559-1812	1560-1751	Blything			6F
Melton	A 1558-1970	1558-1876	5,8		1559-1753	Woodbridge			4H
Mendham	A 1678-1877		5,8	1678-1837	1678-1837	Hoxne	1790-1837	1807-1837	7H
Mendlesham	A 1558-1960		5,8	1560-1812	1558-1754	Hartismere			5F
Metfield	A 1559-1985		5,8	1559-1920	1560-1837	Hoxne	1790-1837		7H
Mettingham	D 1653-1983		5,8	1647-1900	1653-1754	Wangford			8I
Mickfield	A 1558-1973		5,8	1558-1837	1558-1837	Bosmere	1790-1837		5G
Middleton	A 1652-1966		5,8	1653-1899	1653-1750	Blything			5J
Milden	B 1559-1992		5,8	1558-1837	1560-1837	Cosford			3E
Mildenhall	B 1559-1976		5,8	1559-1837	1559-1837	Mildenhall		1796-1837	7B
Monewden	A 1705-1992		5,8	1698-1900	1705-1813	Plomesgate			4H(Er)
Monk Soham	A 1712-1997	1565-1875	5,8	1691-1919	1713-1837	Hoxne	1790-1837		5G
Monks Eleigh	B 1557-1946	1754-1846	5,8		1557-1837	Cosford			3E
Moulton	B 1560-1961		8	1561-1836	1561-1836	Newmarket			5B
Mutford	C 1681-1969	1558-1679	5,8	1681-1901	1681-1749	Mutford			8J
Nacton	A 1562-1980	1562-1878	5,8,9	1705-1756	1562-1754	Woodbridge			3G
Naughton	B 1561-1954	1561-1877	5,8	1563-1837	1561-1837	Cosford			4E(Oh)
Nayland	B 1557-1947		5,8	1558-1901	1558-1753	Sudbury		1785-1836	2E
Nedging	B 1559-1982	1559-1874	5,8	1559-1837	1560-1837	Cosford			4E(Of)
Nettlestead	A 1618-1939		5,8		1625-1755	Bosmere			4F(Om)
Newbourn	A 1561-1980		5,8,9		1561-1750	Woodbridge			3H(Ul)
Newmarket All Saints	B 1622-1963		8	1594-1837	1813-1837	Newmarket			5A
Newmarket St Mary's	B 1638-1966	1638-1880	8	1567-1837	1633-1837	Newmarket		1787-1828	5A
Newton	B 1558-1909		5,8	1559-1812	1559-1812	Sudbury			3D
North Cove with Willingham	D 1696-1995	1685-1875	5,8	1696-1901	1699-1753	Wangford			8J
Norton	B 1539-1948	1539-1879	5,8	1539-1837	1539-1837	Stow			5E
Nowton	B 1562-1844		5,8	1558-1900	1565-1837	Thingoe			5D
Oakley	A 1538-1976		5,8	1538-1900	1539-1754	Hartismere			7G
Occold	A 1681-1972		5,8	1564-1812	1680-1753	Hartismere			6G

238

SUFFOLK

parish name	deposited original registers	I.G.I.	local census indexes	copies of registers at Soc. Gen.	Boyd's marriage index	1837-1851 Registration District	Pallot's marriage index	non-conform. records at P.R.O.	map ref.
Offton	A 1558-1994		5,8		1563-1755	Bosmere			4F
Old Newton	A 1653-1969		8	1566-1885	1654-1754	Stow			5F
Onehouse	A 1552-1961		5,8	1564-1812	1552-1812	Stow			5F(Ec)
Orford	A 1538-1992		5,8	1538-1900	1551-1836	Plomesgate			4J
Otley	A 1734-1956		5,8	1692-1889	1734-1812	Woodbridge		1800-1836	4G
Oulton	C 1564-1978	1564-1659	5,8	1564-1915	1659-1757	Mutford			8K
Ousden	B 1675-1993		8	1567-1900	1675-1837	Newmarket			5B
Pakefield	C 1678-1965		5,8			Mutford			8K
Pakenham	B 1563-1939	1564-1876	5,8	1568-1812	1681-1811	Thingoe			6D
Palgrave	A 1559-1954		5,8	1564-1900	1563-1753	Hartismere		1761-1836	7F
Parham	A 1538-1977	1538-1876	5,8	1538-1977	1538-1812	Plomesgate			5H
Peasenhall	A 1558-1947		5,8	1558-1899	1558-1753	Blything		1800-1853	6I
Pettaugh	A 1653-1996		5,8	1653-1900	1659-1733	Bosmere			5G(Ej)
Pettistree	A 1539-1932	1539-1836	5,8	1539-1985	1539-1751	Woodbridge	1539-1803		4H
Playford	A 1660-1976		5,8	1660-1900	1661-1769	Woodbridge			3G
Polstead	B 1538-1983	1538-1876	5,8	1538-1902	1539-1753	Cosford			3E
Poslingford	B 1559-1981		5,8	1559-1922	1559-1837	Risbridge			4C
Preston	B 1628-1994		5,8	1628-1843	1628-1835	Cosford			4E
Purdis Farm (ex.par.)			8			Woodbridge			3G(Up)
Ramsholt	A 1706-1952		5,8	1698-1906	1709-1752	Woodbridge			3H
Rattlesden	B 1558-1929	1559-1758	5,8	1558-1812	1559-1758	Stow			5E
Raydon	A 1558-1975	1813-1875	5,8	1682-1900	1563-1753	Samford			3F
Rede	B 1538-1961		5,8	1538-1835	1538-1837	Thingoe			4C
Redgrave	A 1538-1970		5,8	1538-1900	1562-1812	Hartismere			7F
Redisham	D 1537-1986		5,8	1537-1904	1537-1751	Wangford			7I(Ap)
Redlingfield	A 1739-1951		5,8	1582-1812	1740-1836	Hartismere			6G(Ak)
Rendham	A 1554-1921	1554-1823	5,8		1554-1754	Plomesgate		1723-1837	5I
Rendlesham	A 1722-1992		5,8		1724-1812	Plomesgate			4I
Reydon	D 1712-1989	1712-1876	5,8		1725-1754	Blything			6J
Rickinghall Inferior	A 1653-1979		5,8	1653-1900	1654-1812	Stow			6F(Aa)
Rickinghall Superior	A 1558-1974		5,8	1558-1900	1558-1812	Hartismere			6F(Ab)
Ringsfield	D 1751-1987	1751-1876	5,8			Wangford			7I
Ringshall	A 1539-1986		5,8		1539-1753	Bosmere			4F
Risby	B 1674-1989		5,8	1561-1837	1564-1837	Thingoe	1790-1837		6C
Rishangles	A 1593-1967		5,8	1593-1786	1593-1767	Hartismere			6G(Aj)
Rougham	B 1565-1982		5,8	1565-1838		Thingoe			5D
Rumburgh	D 1559-1984		5,8	1559-1901	1566-1837	Blything			7I
Rushbrooke	B 1567-1965	1568-1877	5,8	1567-1850	1572-1837	Thingoe	1790-1837		5D(K)
Rushford (Norfolk)									7E
Rushmere (All Saints)	C 1718-1836		5,8	1691-1842		Mutford			7K(As)
Rushmere (St Andrew's)	A 1582-1976		5,8	1582-1889	1582-1755	Woodbridge			3G
Santon Downham	B 1579-1976		5,8	1754-1800	1580-1755	Thetford			8C
Sapiston	B 1680-1970		5,8	1560-1812	1680-1759	Thetford			6E
Saxmundham	A 1538-1997		5,8	1538-1900	1538-1754	Plomesgate			5I(Ep)
Saxtead	A 1528-1983		5,8	1546-1983	1546-1753	Hoxne			5H
Semer	B 1558-1835	1538-1876	5,8	1538-1904	1539-1755	Cosford			3E
Shadingfield	D 1539-1985		5,8		1542-1753	Wangford			7J(Aq)
Shelland	A 1722-1923	1725-1876	5,8	1592-1812	1758-1812	Stow			5E(Ea)
Shelley	A 1747-1994	1714-1876	5,8	1715-1744	1711-1800	Samford	1780-1790		2E
Shimpling	B 1539-1924		5,8	1539-1837	1539-1837	Sudbury			4D
Shipmeadow	D 1561-1980		5,8	1561-1902	1561-1753	Wangford			8I
Shotley	A 1571-1993	1571-1850	5,8	1571-1850	1587-1850	Samford	1790-1837		2H
Shottisham	A 1618-1981		5,8	1618-1900	1618-1753	Woodbridge			3I(Un)
Sibton	A 1557-1969		5,8	1557-1900	1557-1753	Blything			6I
Snape	A 1560-1958		5,8	1560-1900	1562-1751	Plomesgate			5I
Somerleyton	C 1558-1905	1571-1873	5,8	1558-1905	1558-1837	Mutford	1790-1837		8J
Somersham	A 1675-1977		5,8	1789-1801	1675-1753	Bosmere			3F(Ol)
Somerton	B 1538-1837		5,8	1538-1837	1538-1837	Sudbury			4C(X)
Sotherton	D 1558-1962		5,8		1561-1752	Blything			7J
Sotterley	D 1547-1989		5,8		1558-1756	Wangford			7J
South Cove	D 1538-1988	1538-1812	5,8		1539-1750	Blything			7K
South Elmham									7H
All Saints	D 1708-1979	1539-1812	5,8	1539-1812	1580-1753	Wangford			7H
St Cross	D 1558-1996	1858-1875	5,8		1562-1751	Wangford			7H
St James	D 1558-1983		5,8		1668-1754	Wangford			7H
St Margaret	D 1679-1973	1679-1875	5,8		1582-1754	Wangford			7H
St Michael	D 1559-1983		5,8	1761-1813	1560-1753	Wangford			7H
St Peter	A 1678-1996	1695-1875	5,8		1695-1753	Wangford			7H
Southolt	A 1538-1971		5,8	1538-1904	1540-1688	Hoxne			6G(Am)
Southwell Park (see Hargrave)									5C(N)
Southwold	D 1602-1944		5,8	1602-1900	1602-1802	Blything		1730-1837	6K
Spexhall	D 1537-1984	1538-1777	5,8	1777-1924	1538-1777	Blything			7I
Sproughton	A 1538-1985	1540-1711	5,8		1540-1754	Samford			3F
Stanningfield	B 1561-1928	1561-1837	5,8	1561-1837	1561-1837	Thingoe			4D(V)
Stansfield	B 1538-1979		5,8	1538-1902	1539-1837	Risbridge		1834-1837	4C
Stanstead	B 1570-1948		5,8	1563-1837	1570-1837	Sudbury			4D(Z)
Stanton All Saints	B 1584-1986		5,8	1562-1900	1584-1837	Thingoe			6E
Stanton St John the Baptist	B 1579-1896		5,8	1579-1836	1580-1837	Thingoe			6E
Sternfield	A 1558-1961		5,8	1558-1900	1558-1754	Plomesgate			5I(Eq)
Stoke Ash	A 1538-1892		5,8	1564-1812	1539-1753	Hartismere			6F(Ag)
Stoke by Clare	B 1538-1956		5,8	1538-1837	1588-1837	Risbridge			3B
Stoke Nayland	B 1558-1964	1558-1876	5,8	1559-1812	1588-1837	Sudbury			2E
Stonham Aspall	A 1541-1972		5,8		1588-1837	Bosmere			5G
Stoven	D 1781-1987		5,8			Blything			7J(At)
Stowlangtoft	B 1559-1966		5,8	1561-1812	1559-1750	Stow			6E(G)
Stowmarket	A 1559-1975		5,8	1559-1812	1559-1754	Stow		1780-1838	5F(Ed)
Stowupland	A 1559-1975		5,8	1592-1900	1693-1763	Stow			5F
Stradbroke	A 1538-1923		5,8	1761-1812	1538-1754	Hoxne		1814-1836	6H

SUFFOLK

parish name	deposited original registers	I.G.I.	local census indexes	copies of registers at Soc. Gen.	Boyd's marriage index	1837-1851 Registration District	Pallot's marriage index	non-conform. records at P.R.O.	map ref.
Stradishall	B 1548-1964		5,8	1561-1835	1576-1835	Risbridge			4B(W)
Stratford St Andrew	A 1692-1994		5,8	1698-1752	1724-1752	Plomesgate			5I(Ev)
Stratford St Mary	A 1562-1966	1562-1812	5,8	1588-1956	1588-1754	Samford			2F
Stratton Hall (ex par)			8			Woodbridge			2H(Ur)
Stuston	A 1631-1977		5,8	1563-1901	1631-1750	Hartismere			7G
Stutton	A 1645-1969		5,8	1645-1880	1646-1753	Samford			2G
Sudbourne	A 1661-1983		5,8	1661-1900	1651-1754	Plomesgate			4J
Sudbury								1707-1837	3D
All Saints	B 1564-1982	1564-1876	5,8	1564-1812	1564-1754	Sudbury			3D
St Gregory	B 1653-1951	1653-1872	5,8	1653-1872	1653-1754	Sudbury			3D
St Peter	B 1590-1971	1653-1872	5,8	1593-1861	1590-1754	Sudbury			3D
Sutton	A 1555-1903		5,8	1625-1901	1555-1750	Woodbridge			3H
Sweffling	A 1695-1963	1570-1850	5,8	1572-1752	1573-1752	Plomesgate			5I(Eo)
Swilland	A 1678-1836		5,8	1678-1856	1680-1754	Bosmere			4G
Syleham	A 1538-1923		5,8	1538-1837	1538-1837	Hoxne	1790-1837		7G
Tannington	A 1539-1837	1539-1660	5,8	1539-1902	1539-1754	Hoxne			5H
Tattingstone	A 1654-1968		5,8		1654-1751	Samford			2G
Theberton	A 1548-1970		5,8	1548-1900	1558-1752	Blything			5J
Thelnetham	B 1538-1932		5,8	1538-1812	1538-1753	Thetford			7E
Thetford St Mary	C 1653-1974		5,8		1653-1751	Thetford		1796-1837	7D
Thorington	A 1561-1984	1561-1875	5,8	1561-1905	1591-1837	Blything	1790-1881		6J(Az)
Thorndon	A 1538-1915	1538-1710	5,8	1538-1812	1538-1753	Hartismere			6G
Thornham Magna	A 1555-1914		8	1555-1814	1582-1753	Hartismere			6F(Ae)
Thornham Parva	A 1711-1995	1746-1747	8	1711-1818	1711-1753	Hartismere			6F(Ad)
Thorpe Morieux	B 1538-1949		5,8	1538-1837	1538-1837	Cosford			4E
Thrandeston	A 1558-1978		5,8	1559-1901	1559-1837	Hartismere	1790-1837		7G
Thurston	B 1707-1974		5,8	1661-1836	1707-1837	Stow			5D
Thwaite St George	A 1709-1994		5,8	1563-1812	1711-1779	Hartismere			6F(Ah)
Timworth	B 1558-1995	1565-1715	5,8	1558-1812	1558-1753	Thingoe			6D
Tostock	B 1675-1897	1675-1879	5,8	1564-1836	1675-1837	Stow			5E(M)
Trimley St Martin	A 1538-1968		5,8,9	1715-1756	1539-1754	Woodbridge			2H
Trimley St Mary	A 1654-1986		5,8,9	1655-1785	1654-1754	Woodbridge			2H
Troston	B 1558-1884		5,8	1560-1812	1559-1754	Thingoe			6D
Tuddenham St Martin	A 1664-1977		5,8	1813-1900	1696-1812	Woodbridge			3G(Uc)
Tuddenham St Mary	B 1558-1956	1558-1874	5,8	1563-1836	1601-1836	Mildenhall			6C
Tunstall	A 1539-1941		5,8		1539-1754	Plomesgate			4I
Ubbeston	A 1555-1968	1555-1812	5,8	1555-1902	1557-1754	Blything			6I(Ax)
Ufford	A 1558-1911	1555-1614	5,8	1555-1900	1558-1753	Woodbridge	1538-1789		4H
Uggeshall	D 1558-1970		5,8		1564-1754	Blything			7J
Walberswick	A 1656-1976		5,8	1656-1900	1651-1812	Blything			6J
Waldringfield	A 1695-1980		5,8,9	1695-1837	1700-1812	Woodbridge			3H(Uk)
Walpole	A 1753-1984		5,8	1691-1901		Blything	1706-1837	1706-1837	6I
Walsham le Willows	B 1539-1949	1538-1839	5,8	1538-1837	1539-1837	Stow		1811-1837	6E
Walton	A 1559-1975		5,8,9	1559-1900	1654-1753	Woodbridge		1807-1836	2H
Wangford (Nr Brandon)	B 1754-1980		5,8	1754-1831		Mildenhall			7C
Wangford (Nr Southwold)	D 1678-1994		5,8	1567-1812	1690-1751	Blything		1832-1837	7J(Av)
Wantisden	A 1708-1836		5,8	1711-1754	1711-1754	Plomesgate			4I
Washbrook	A 1559-1994		5,8	1559-1985	1561-1752	Samford			3F(Oy)
Wattisfield	B 1540-1892	1540-1551	5,8	1540-1812	1540-1754	Stow		1735-1837	6E
Wattisham	B 1680-1971	1582-1842	5,8	1563-1900	1572-1743	Cosford			4E(Oe)
Wenhaston	A 1687-1984		5,8	1687-1730	1687-1752	Blything			6J
Westerfield	A 1539-1969		5,8	1538-1901	1539-1753	Ipswich			3G(Ub)
Westhall	D 1559-1994	1559-1868	5,8	1559-1899	1559-1753	Blything			7J
Westhorpe	A 1538-1996		5,8	1538-1813	1539-1753	Hartismere			6F
Westleton	A 1545-1983		5,8	1545-1899	1545-1750	Blything			6J
Westley	B 1565-1993		5,8	1565-1835	1569-1834	Thingoe			5C
Weston	D 1538-1997		5,8		1545-1753	Wangford			7J
West Stow	B 1558-1991	1558-1850	5,8	1558-1882	1560-1837	Thingoe	1790-1837		6C
Wetherden	A 1538-1972		5,8	1563-1812	1539-1753	Stow			5E
Wetheringsett with Brockford	A 1556-1973		5,8	1564-1811	1556-1754	Hartismere			5G
Weybread	A 1687-1990		5,8	1687-1901	1687-1837	Hoxne	1790-1837		7H
Whatfield	B 1558-1836	1558-1875	5,8	1564-1812	1558-1753	Cosford			3E
Whepstead	B 1538-1975		5,8	1564-1812	1538-1773	Thingoe			5C
Wherstead	A 1590-1977	1590-1683	5,8	1590-1718	1590-1753	Samford			3G
Whitton-cum-Thurlston	A 1559-1978		5,8	1599-1823	1600-1751	Ipswich			3G(Ua)
Wickhambrook	B 1559-1967		5,8	1567-1812	1559-1765	Risbridge		1726-1837	4C
Wickham Market	A 1557-1951		5,8	1557-1900	1557-1751	Plomesgate		1820-1837	4H
Wickham Skeith	A 1558-1984		5,8	1558-1812	1558-1753	Hartismere			6F
Wilby	A 1538-1959		5,8	1813-1838	1541-1755	Hoxne			6H
Willingham (see North Cove)									7J(Ar)
Willisham	A 1838-1974		5,8		1562-1753	Bosmere			4F(Ok)
Wingfield	A 1538-1904	1538-1838	5,8	1538-1838	1539-1838	Hoxne	1790-1837		6H
Winston	A 1558-1934		5,8	1558-1901	1559-1756	Bosmere			5G
Wissett	D 1559-1977	1599-1875	5,8	1559-1924	1559-1837	Blything			7I
Wissington	B 1538-1983		5,8	1563-1812	1538-1754	Sudbury		1785-1836	2E
Withersdale	A 1653-1837		5,8	1653-1936	1653-1837	Hoxne	1790-1837		7H
Withersfield	B 1558-1962	1558-1853	5,8	1558-1901	1588-1837	Risbridge			4B
Witnesham	A 1538-1982		5,8	1538-1899	1539-1752	Woodbridge			4G
Wixoe	B 1674-1836		5,8	1563-1836	1676-1836	Risbridge			3B
Woodbridge	A 1545-1969	1545-1876	5,8	1545-1837	1545-1855	Woodbridge	1780-1837	1710-1837	3H(Uf)
Woolpit	B 1558-1979		5,8	1558-1837	1559-1837	Stow			5E
Woolverstone	A 1939-1984	1539-1875	5,8		1539-1757	Samford			2G(Us)
Wordwell	B 1579-1979	1581-1850	5,8	1561-1850	1580-1837	Thingoe	1800-1849		6C
Worlingham	D 1538-1993	1538-1876	5,8	1538-1900	1540-1753	Wangford			8J
Worlington	B 1719-1974		5,8	1563-1836	1719-1837	Mildenhall			6B
Worlingworth	A 1558-1964		5,8	1558-1899	1558-1754	Hoxne			6H
Wortham	A 1538-1958		5,8	1564-1900	1538-1837	Hartismere			7F
Wrentham	D 1602-1986	1602-1875	5,8		1603-1754	Blything		1650-1837	7J

SUFFOLK

parish name	deposited original registers	I.G.I.	local census indexes	copies of registers at Soc. Gen.	Boyd's marriage index	1837-1851 Registration District	Pallot's marriage index	non-conform. records at P.R.O.	map ref.
Wyverstone	A 1558-1837		5,8	1558-1813	1561-1753	Hartismere			6F
Yaxley	A 1684-1939		5,8	1564-1812	1560-1753	Hartismere			6G
Yoxford	A 1559-1972		5,8	1559-1900	1559-1753	Blything			6I

Original registers deposited at:
A = Suffolk Record Office, Ipswich Branch, Gatacre Road, Ipswich IP1 2LQ
B = Suffolk Record Office, Bury St Edmunds Branch, Raingate Street, Bury St Edmunds IP33 2AR
C = Norfolk Record Office, Gildengate House, Anglia Square, Upper Green Lane, Norwich NR3 1AX
D = Suffolk Record Office, Lowestoft Central Library, Clapham Road, Lowestoft NR32 1DR
E = British Library, 96 Euston Road, London NW1 2DB

Study adjacent parishes in counties of Cambridgeshire, Norfolk and Essex

Suffolk Record Office, Gatacre Road, Ipswich IP1 2LQ
Suffolk Record Office, Bury St Edmunds Branch, Raingate Street, Bury St Edmunds IP33 2AR
Suffolk Record Office, Central Library, Clapham Road, Lowestoft NR32 1DR

The following useful indexes have been compiled – see Introduction
Census Index 1851 – Suffolk FHS c/o Mrs. P. Turner, 48 Princethorpe Road, Ipswich, Suffolk IP3 8NX
Census Index 1891 – Felixstowe FHS, c/o Mr J. Woollan, The Pines, Manor Road, Trimley St Mary, Felixstowe, Suffolk IP11 0TU
Marriage Index 1813-1837 – Suffolk FHS, c/o Mrs. Pamela Palgrave, Crossfields, Dale Road, Stanton, Bury St Edmunds, Suffolk IP31 2DY
Suffolk Wills Beneficiaries – Suffolk FHS, c/o Mrs. S. Piper, The Old School, Bridge Street, Long Melford, Suffolk LO10 9BQ
Monumental Inscriptions Index – Suffolk FHS, c/o Mr J. Roffey, 52 Park Drive, Worlingham, Beccles, Suffolk NR34 7DL
Suffolk Burial Index – Suffolk FHS, c/o Mrs A. Youngs, 6 Gresham Close, Oulton Broad, Lowestoft, Suffolk NR32 3DH

N.B. At both branches of the Suffolk Record Office there are many microfilm copies of parish registers, the originals of which are deposited in the branch covering the other part of the county.

Suffolk is oblong in shape being about 47 miles in length and 27 miles in breadth. It is watered by ten principal rivers: the Stour, Lesser Ouse, Waveney, Deben, Ald, Blyth, Gipping, Ore, Orwell and Larke. The population in 1841 was 315,073; in 1851, 337,215; in 1861, 337,070; in 1871, 348,869; in 1881, 356,893.

The soils are clay, sand, loam and fen. Produce included wheat, beans, cabbages and other vegetables as well as hemp. Stock-raising was important and horses were bred. Light stuffs, buntings, crepes and yarns were the principal manufactures and there were mackerel and herring fisheries.

The information in the Index is abbreviated, and may mislead the searcher if reference is not made to the details contained in the several publications listed in the Introduction. It is essential that users of this book check the appropriate works before making further enquiries.

SURREY

parish name	deposited original registers	I.G.I.	local census indexes	copies of registers at Soc. Gen.	Boyd's marriage index	1837-1851 Registration District	Pallot's marriage index	non-conform. records at P.R.O.	map ref.
Abinger	A 1559-1959	1559-1876	5,8	1559-1840	1559-1812	Dorking	1780-1812		4G
Addington	A 1559-1990	1560-1812	5,8	1560-1890	1560-1812	Croydon	1780-1812		7K
Albury	A 1559-1973	1559-1875	5,8	1734-1841	1559-1665	Guildford		1833-1840	4G
Albury (detached)			5,8			Guildford			2G
Alfold	A 1658-1901	1658-1876	5,8	1658-1840		Hambledon			2F
Ash	A 1549-1981	1548-1876	5,8	1548-1849		Farnborough			5D
Ashtead	A 1662-1990	1699-1876	5,8	1662-1841		Epsom			6H
Banstead	A 1547-1973	1547-1876	5,8	1547-1837	1754-1837	Epsom	1780-1876		6I
Barnes	A 1538-1973	1813-1839	8	1538-1699		Richmond			9I
Battersea (St Mary)	C 1559-1878	1684-1875	5,8	1802-1837		Wandsworth			8J
Battersea (detached)		1561-1880	5,8			Wandsworth			8K
Beddington	B 1538-1985	1538-1876	5,8	1538-1812	1561-1812	Croydon			7J
Bermondsey								1781-1872	9K
St James	C 1829-1952	1830-1855	5,7,8	1830-1837		Bermondsey			9K
St Mary Magdalen	C 1548-1968	1548-1856	5,8	1548-1763	1548-1700	Bermondsey	1777-1837	1781-1835	9K
Betchworth	A 1558-1893	1801-1875	5,8	1558-1837	1562-1837	Reigate			5I
Bisley	A 1561-1965	1561-1882	4,5,6,8	1561-1851		Chertsey			6E
Bletchingley	A 1538-1986	1538-1857	5,8	1538-1923	1654-1812	Godstone			5K
Bramley	A 1563-1988	1566-1881	5,8	1563-1840		Hambledon			4F
Buckland	A 1560-1967	1560-1878	5,8	1560-1840		Reigate			5I
Burstow	A 1546-2000	1813-1848	5,8	1547-1942		Reigate			4J
Byfleet	A 1698-1977	1800-1844	5,8	1698-1840		Chertsey			6G
Camberwell								1801-1841	8K
St George	C 1826-1968	1826-1830	5,8			Camberwell			8K
St Giles	C 1557-1960	1763-1845	5,8	1568-1802	1558-1725	Camberwell			8K
Capel	A 1653-1975	1653-1876	5,8	1653-1840		Dorking			3H
Carshalton	B 1538-1900	1538-1875	5,8	1538-1837	1538-1837	Epsom	1790-1837		7J
Caterham	A 1543-1989	1543-1876	5,8	1543-1851	1543-1837	Godstone	1790-1837		5K
Chaldon	A 1564-1981	1564-1855	5,8	1564-1851	1570-1836	Reigate			5J
Charlwood	A 1595-1912	1837-1886	5,8	1595-1840		Reigate		1818-1837	3I
Cheam	B 1538-1954		5,8	1538-1837	1538-1837	Epsom	1790-1837		7I
Chelsham	A 1680-1981	1669-1878	5,8	1680-1840	1681-1812	Godstone	1780-1812		6K
Chertsey	A 1606-1951	1616-1880	5,8	1610-1753		Chertsey		1758-1837	7F
Chessington	A 1656-1990	1656-1876	5,8	1656-1837	1656-1837	Epsom			6H
Chiddingfold	A 1563-2000	1563-1881	5,8			Hambledon			2E
Chilworth	A 1785-1835	1779-1875	8	1779-1900		Hambledon			4F(H)
Chipstead	A 1656-1941	1656-1876	5,8	1656-1840	1663-1812	Reigate	1780-1812		5J
Chobham	A 1654-1952	1654-1876	5,6,8	1587-1837		Chertsey		1810-1836	6E
Clapham								1781-1837	9J
Holy Trinity	C 1551-1967	1792-1873	5,8	1551-1854	1551-1754	Wandsworth			9J
St James, Clapham Park	C 1829-1976		5,8			Wandsworth			9J
Cobham	A 1562-1928	1562-1880	5,8	1562-1812	1562-1812	Epsom			6G
Compton	A 1639-1951	1638-1876	5,8	1639-1840		Guildford			4E
Coulsdon	A 1653-1957	1653-1876	5,8	1653-1880	1655-1837	Croydon	1780-1812		6J
Cranleigh	A 1566-1959	1566-1877	4,5,8		1609-1837	Hambledon			3G
Crowhurst	A 1567-1890	1567-1885	5,8		1573-1812	Godstone			4K
Croydon	A 1538-1929	1538-1895	5,8			Croydon		1797-1837	7K
Cuddington			5,8			Epsom			7I
Deptford (Kent)									9K
Dorking	A 1538-1952	1538-1876	5,8,9	1538-1812		Dorking		1718-1855	4H
Dunsfold	A 1628-1973	1628-1876	5,8	1628-1840		Hambledon			2F
East Clandon	A 1558-1909	1559-1876	5,8	1558-1840		Guildford			5G
East Horsley	A 1666-1959	1666-1878	5,8	1666-1840	1667-1750	Guildford			5G
East Molesey	A 1668-1966	1668-1876	5,8	1668-1840		Kingston			7H
Effingham	A 1565-1932	1565-1844	5,8	1565-1851	1565-1837	Dorking			5G
Egham	A 1560-1899	1560-1895	5,8	1771-1812		Windsor			8F
Elstead	A 1538-1992	1538-1876	5,8	1538-1841		Hambledon		1834-1837	4D
Epsom	A 1695-1965	1686-1874	5,8	1695-1913	1695-1812	Epsom		1779-1837	6I
Esher	A 1678-1977	1682-1876	5,8			Kingston			7H
Ewell	A 1604-1969	1597-1875	5,8	1723-1812	1608-1837	Epsom			7I
Ewhurst	A 1614-1955	1614-1877	5,6,8	1614-1838		Hambledon		1823-1836	3G
Farleigh	A 1679-1972	1678-1879	5,8	1678-1840	1678-1812	Godstone	1780-1810		6K
Farnham	A 1539-1895	1539-1876	4,5,8	1539-1840		Farnham		1794-1837	4C
Fetcham	A 1559-1953	1559-1876	5,8	1559-1840	1565-1753	Epsom			6H
Frensham	A 1649-1971	1649-1876	5,6,8			Farnham			3D
Frimley	A 1590-1991	1681-1876	5,8	1590-1840		Farnham			6D
Gatton	A 1599-1992	1599-1882	5,8	1601-1831	1599-1812	Reigate	1780-1812		5J
Godalming	A 1582-1970	1582-1877	5,8	1582-1840	1583-1688	Guildford		1786-1837	4E
Godstone	A 1662-1907	1662-1876	5,8		1662-1663	Godstone			5K
Great Bookham	A 1632-1869	1632-1876	5,8	1680-1840		Epsom			5H
Guildford					1701-1739			1707-1840	5E
Holy Trinity	A 1558-1967	1558-1875	5,6,8	1813-1840		Guildford			5F(C)
St Mary	A 1540-1971	1540-1877	5,6,8	1540-1840		Guildford			5F(B)
St Nicholas	A 1561-1925	1561-1876	5,6,8	1561-1840		Guildford			5E
Hambledon	A 1617-1966	1714-1876	5,8	1586-1915		Hambledon			3E
Hascombe	A 1646-1869	1646-1869	5,8	1658-1754		Hambledon			3F(G)
Haslemere	A 1573-1972	1573-1876	5,8	1573-1842	1573-1812	Hambledon	1790-1812	1789-1834	2D
Headley	A 1663-1895	1663-1875	5,8	1663-1836	1663-1837	Reigate	1790-1836		5I
Horley	A 1577-1931	1578-1876	5,7,8	1578-1840		Reigate			4J
Horne	A 1614-1888	1614-1854	5,8	1614-1840	1709-1710	Godstone			4K
Horsell	A 1653-1973	1653-1876	5,6,8	1653-1840		Chertsey			6E
Kew	A 1714-1982		5,8	1714-1840		Richmond			9I
Kingston	A 1541-1954	1541-1876	4,5,6,7,8,9	1542-1882	1543-1740	Kingston		1698-1856	8I
Lambeth								1787-1837	9J
Renfrew Road Workhouse		1803-1875	5,8,9			Lambeth			9J
St John, Waterloo	C 1824-1973	1825-1875	5,8,9			Lambeth			9J
St Luke, W. Norwood	C 1825-1963	1825-1844	5,8,9	1825-1837		Lambeth		1821-1837	9J
St Mark, Kennington	C 1825-1951	1825-1875	5,8,9			Lambeth		1817-1837	9J

SURREY

parish name	deposited original registers	I.G.I.	local census indexes	copies of registers at Soc. Gen.	Boyd's marriage index	1837-1851 Registration District	Pallot's marriage index	non-conform. records at P.R.O.	map ref.
Lambeth (cont'd)									
St Mary	C 1539-1971	1800-1837	5,8,9	1695-1710		Lambeth			9J
St Matthew, Brixton	C 1825-1964	1825-1845	5,8,9			Lambeth		1824-1837	9J
Leatherhead	A 1656-1954	1656-1876	5,7,8	1647-1840		Epsom		1832-1835	6H
Leigh	A 1579-1976	1579-1876	5,8	1579-1838		Reigate			4I
Limpsfield	A 1539-1941	1539-1876	5,8	1543-1916	1540-1837	Godstone		1812-1836	5L
Lingfield	A 1559-1994	1559-1882	5,6,8	1663-1780	1561-1586	East Grinstead			4L
Little Bookham	A 1642-1949	1631-1835	5,8	1642-1840	1632-1812	Epsom	1780-1812		5H(E)
Long Ditton	A 1564-1982	1564-1869	5,8	1564-1858	1564-1652	Kingston			7H
Malden	A 1676-1983	1676-1881	5,8,9	1676-1754	1676-1837	Kingston			7I
Merrow	A 1538-1979	1538-1876	5,8	1536-1836		Guildford			5F
Merstham	A 1538-1970	1538-1876	5,8	1538-1840	1540-1812	Reigate	1790-1812		5J
Merton	A 1559-1998	1559-1876	5,8			Croydon			7I
Mickleham	A 1549-1955	1549-1881	5,8			Dorking			5H
Mitcham	A 1563-1970	1563-1876	5,8	1563-1884	1563-1753	Croydon			7J
Morden	A 1634-1962	1634-1865	5,8	1634-1840	1634-1812	Croydon	1790-1812		7I
Mortlake	A 1599-1970	1599-1881	5,8	1599-1678		Richmond		1719-1752	8I
Newdigate	A 1559-1945	1706-1862	5,8	1559-1840		Dorking			3I
Newington									9K
Holy Trinity	C 1825-1959	1825-1875	5,8,9			Newington			9K
St Mary	C 1561-1975	1813-1837	5,8,9			Newington			9K
St Peter, Walworth	C 1825-1980	1825-1861	5,8,9			Newington		1791-1852	9K
Nutfield	A 1558-1924	1558-1876	5,8	1558-1913	1558-1807	Reigate			5J
Ockham	A 1568-1995	1568-1875	5,6,8	1568-1840		Guildford			6G
Ockley	A 1539-1976	1538-1876	5,8	1539-1840		Dorking			3H
Okewood	A 1696-1981	1697-1876	8	1696-1840	1697-1751	Dorking			3H
Oxted	A 1603-1958	1613-1876	5,8	1655-1837	1655-1813	Godstone		1812-1836	5K
Peperharow	A 1697-1926	1697-1885	5,8	1587-1986		Hambledon			4E
Petersham	A 1574-1978		8			Richmond			8H
Pirbright	A 1574-1947	1754-1876	5,6,8	1574-1842		Guildford			6E
Putney (St Mary)	C 1620-1973	1620-1870	5,8	1620-1870	1620-1837	Wandsworth	1780-1837	1817-1834	8I
Puttenham	A 1562-1917	1562-1882	5,8	1562-1885		Farnborough			4E
Pyrford	A 1665-1991	1665-1876	4,5,8	1665-1840		Chertsey			6F
Reigate	A 1556-1996	1558-1869	5,8		1559-1698	Reigate		1835-1837	5I
Richmond	A 1584-1989	1583-1876	5,8	1583-1812	1583-1780	Richmond		1831-1836	8H
Ripley	A 1794-1992	1653-1876	6,8	1773-1840		Guildford			6F
Rotherhithe (St Mary)	C 1555-1943	1783-1868	5,8	1556-1804		Rotherhithe	1785-1804	1812-1836	9K
St Martha on the Hill (see Chilworth)									4F(H)
Sanderstead	A 1564-1971	1564-1876	5,8	1564-1840	1564-1812	Croydon	1780-1812		6K
Seale	A 1539-1908	1539-1876	5,8	1653-1837		Farnborough			4D
Send	A 1653-1977	1653-1876	5,6,8	1653-1877		Guildford			5F
Shalford	A 1564-1985	1564-1875	5,8	1558-1841		Hambledon			4F
Shere	A 1547-1998	1547-1884	5,8	1547-1691	1547-1691	Guildford			4G
Southwark								1723-1853	9K
Christchurch	C 1671-1941	1670-1880	4,5,6,7,8,9	1807-1833		St Sav Southwark	1781-1837		9K
St George the Martyr	C 1602-1953	1800-1836	5,7,8,9		1602-1754	St Geo Southwark	1780-1837		9K
St John Horsleydown	C 1733-1960	1803-1853	5,6,7,8,9	1803-1853	1733-1791	St Olave Southwark	1792-1837	1656-1837	9K
St Olave	C 1582-1918	1639-1885	5,6,7,8,9		1583-1754	St Olave Southwark			9K
St Saviour	C 1538-1923	1759-1835	5,6,7,8,9		1605-1625	St Sav Southwark	1782-1837		9K
St Thomas	C 1614-1898	1801-1866	5,6,7,8,9		1614-1753	St Olave Southwark	1792-1837		9K
Stoke	A 1662-1971	1662-1883	5,8			Guildford			5F
Stoke D'Abernon	A 1619-1944	1619-1877	5,8	1619-1837	1620-1835	Epsom	1780-1812		6H
Streatham	C 1538-1963	1801-1872	5,8	1538-1753	1538-1663	Wandsworth			8J
Sutton	B 1636-1960	1636-1882	5,8	1636-1852		Epsom	1780-1837		7I
Tandridge	A 1672-1928	1669-1877	5,8	1695-1840		Godstone			5K
Tatsfield	A 1674-1976	1689-1875	5,8	1689-1865	1689-1812	Godstone	1780-1812		5L
Thames Ditton	A 1663-1888	1663-1881	5,8	1693-1694		Kingston		1816-1836	7H
Thorpe	A 1653-1996	1802-1846	4,5,8			Windsor			7F
Thursley	A 1613-1964	1613-1876	5,8			Hambledon			3D
Titsey	A 1579-1972	1579-1844	5,8	1579-1844	1579-1812	Godstone	1780-1812		5L
Tooting Graveney	C 1555-1970	1800-1844	5,8	1555-1841		Wandsworth		1786-1837	8J(A)
Walton-on-Thames	A 1639-1918	1639-1883	5,8			Chertsey			7G
Walton-on-the-Hill	A 1581-1906	1581-1878	5,8	1581-1840	1631-1837	Reigate	1790-1837		5I
Wanborough	A 1561-1786	1561-1774	5,8	1561-1786	1561-1658	Guildford			5E
Wandsworth	C 1603-1937	1603-1854	5,8,9	1603-1837	1603-1788	Wandsworth	1780-1820	1811-1836	8I
Warlingham	A 1653-1985	1653-1876	5,8	1653-1841	1667-1812	Godstone	1780-1812		6K
Waverley (ex.par.)			8			Farnham			4D
West Clandon	A 1536-1935	1536-1877	5,8	1536-1837		Guildford			5F(D)
West Horsley	A 1600-1996	1754-1875	5,8	1600-1840		Guildford			5G
West Molesey	A 1729-1931	1729-1876	5,8	1729-1840		Kingston			7H
Weybridge	A 1625-1991	1625-1876	5,8	1625-1836	1625-1812	Chertsey			7G
Wimbledon	A 1539-1977	1538-1876	5,8	1538-1812	1594-1812	Kingston	1780-1812		8I
Windlesham	A 1677-1881	1677-1876	5,8	1677-1899		Chertsey			7D
Wisley	A 1666-1996	1666-1878	5,6,8	1666-1901		Guildford			6G
Witley	A 1653-1964	1736-1875	5,8	1653-1900		Hambledon			3E
Woking	A 1653-1932	1800-1846	5,6,8	1654-1840		Guildford		1778-1836	6E
Woldingham	A 1813-1992	1766-1877	5,8	1765-1865	1769-1810	Godstone	1804-1812		5K
Wonersh	A 1539-1995	1539-1881	5,8	1539-1812		Hambledon			4F
Woodmansterne	A 1566-1942	1568-1876	5,8	1566-1838	1568-1843	Croydon	1790-1843		6J(F)
Worplesdon	A 1539-1976	1540-1876	5,6,8,9	1538-1840		Guildford		1823-1837	5E
Wotton	A 1596-1911	1596-1876	5,8	1596-1840	1603-1812	Dorking	1780-1812		4H

SURREY

Original registers deposited at:
A = Surrey History Centre, 130 Goldsworthy Road, Woking, GU21 1ND
B = Sutton Heritage Centre Library, St Nicholas Way, Sutton, Surrey, SM1 1EA
C = London Metropolitan Archives, 40 Northampton Road, London, EC1R 0HB

Study adjacent parishes in counties of Hampshire, Berkshire, Middlesex, London, Kent and Sussex

Surrey History Centre, 130 Goldsworthy Road, Woking, GU21 1ND
Sutton Heritage Centre Library, St Nicholas Way, Sutton, Surrey, SM1 1EA
London Metropolitan Archives, 40 Northampton Road, London, EC1R 0HB

The following useful indexes have been compiled – see Introduction
Census Indexes 1851 – East Surrey FHS, c/o Mrs G. Hallett, 9 Spa Drive, The Wells, Epsom, Surrey, KT18 7LR for the east of the county and metropolitan Surrey.
West Surrey FHS c/o Mrs. R. Cleaver, 17 Lane End Drive, Knaphill, Woking, Surrey GU21 2QQ for remainder of the county but also some metropolian areas.
Census Indexes 1861 – West Surrey FHS c/o Mrs. R. Cleaver, 17 Lane End Drive, Knaphill, Woking, Surrey GU21 2QQ Mainly west of the county but also some metropolian areas.
Census Index 1871 Bermondsey – East Surrey FHS, c/o Mrs G. Hallett, 9 Spa Drive, The Wells, Epsom, Surrey, KT18 7LR
Census Indexes 1891 – Census Indexes 1851 – East Surrey FHS, c/o Mrs G. Hallett, 9 Spa Drive, The Wells, Epsom, Surrey, KT18 7LR for the east of the county and metropolitan Surrey. West Surrey FHS c/o Mrs. R. Cleaver, 17 Lane End Drive, Knaphill, Woking, Surrey GU21 2QQ for remainder of the county but also some metropolian areas.
Census Indexes 1841- 1891 for metropolitan areas – The SELON Index, Mr P. Shilham, 6 Beckford Close, Wokingham, Berkshire, RG41 1HN
Census Indexes 1841- 1891 Kingston – Kingston Museum and Heritage Service, Wheatfield Way, Kingston upon Thames, Surrey, KT1 2PS
Surrey Marriage Index pre 1813 – Mr C.R. Webb, Cold Arbor, Coldharbour Road, Pyrford, Woking, Surrey GU22 8SJ
Surrey Marriage Index 1813 – 1837 – Mr C.R. Webb, Cold Arbor, Coldharbour Road, Pyrford, Woking, Surrey GU22 8SJ
The SELON INDEX, Mr P Shilham, 6 Beckford Close, Wokingham, Berkshire RG41 1HN
Surrey Monumental Inscriptions Index pre-1866 – Cliff Webb, Cold Arbor, Coldharbour Road, Pyrford, Woking, Surrey, GU22 8SJ

Surrey is 39 miles in length from east to west and 25 miles in breadth from north to south. It is watered by three principal rivers: The Mole, Wandle and Wey. The population in 1841 was 584,036; in 1851, 683,082; in 1861, 831,093; in 1871, 1,091,635; in 1881, 1,435,842.

The soils are chiefly clay, loam and chalk. Fine hops were grown but otherwise agriculture was not of the first order but because of the county's vicinity to the capital farmers and gardeners found ready markets. House-lamb suckling was an important aspect of farming. Manufactures consisted of starch, tobacco, snuff, gunpowder, paper, vinegar, pottery and hats (of the latter great numbers were made in Southwark). There were also extensive distilleries, breweries, bleaching and printing works.

The information in the Index is abbreviated, and may mislead the searcher if reference is not made to the details contained in the several publications listed in the Introduction. It is essential that users of this book check the appropriate works before making further enquiries.

SUSSEX

parish name	deposited original registers	I.G.I.	local census indexes	copies of registers at Soc. Gen.	Boyd's marriage index	1837-1851 Registration District	Pallot's marriage index	non-conform. records at P.R.O.	map ref.
Albourne	A 1550-1975	1550-1900	5,8	1813-1893		Cuckfield			5F
Alciston	B 1575-1994	1575-1892	5,8	1755-1892		Lewes			4H
Aldingbourne	A 1558-1989	1558-1876	8	1558-1870		Westhampnett			4C
Alfold (Surrey)									7D
Alfriston	B 1538-1973	1538-1893	4,5,8	1754-1836		Eastbourne		1804-1837	4H
Amberley	A 1559-1993	1559-1878	4,5,6,7,8,9	1560-1875		Worthing			5D
Angmering	A 1563-1965	1562-1877	8	1562-1812		Worthing			4D
Appledram	A 1661-1939	1594-1879	4,5,6,7,8,9	1594-1894	1599-1812	Westhampnett	1790-1816		4B(X)
Ardingly	A 1558-1953	1558-1876	5,8	1558-1880		Cuckfield	1790-1812		6G
Arlington	B 1607-1994	1607-1698	4,5,8	1755-1898		Hailsham			4I
Arundel	A 1560-1964	1560-1876	8	1560-1840	1560-1680	Worthing		1796-1837	5D
Ashburnham	B 1538-1993		4,5,8	1607-1837		Battle			5J
Ashington	A 1736-1989		5,8	1538-1878	1611-1810	Thakeham	1790-1811		5E(P)
Ashurst	A 1560-1998		4,5,6,7,8,9			Steyning			5E
Balcombe	A 1539-1969	1539-1877	5,8	1539-1837		Cuckfield			7G
Barcombe	B 1580-1990	1580-1888	4,5,8	1580-1837		Lewes			5H
Barlavington	A 1656-1994	1572-1811	5,8			Chichester			5C
Barnham	A 1675-1986	1584-1877	8	1675-1896		Westhampnett			4C(c)
Battle	B 1610-1967		4,5,8	1653-1837		Battle		1769-1836	5K
Beckley	B 1597-1991		5,8			Rye			5L
Beddingham	B 1686-1993		5,8	1593-1840		Lewes			4H
Bepton	A 1723-2000	1584-1876	4,5,6,7,8,9	1613-1845	1613-1723	Midhurst			6B
Berwick	B 1611-1994	1611-1893	5,8	1800-1897		Lewes			4I
Bexhill	B 1558-1996		4,5,8	1558-1837		Battle			4K
Bignor	A 1563-1998	1556-1836	5,8		1683-1836	Chichester	1809-1836		5C
Bignor (detached)			5,8			Chichester			6C(B)
Billingshurst	A 1558-1889	1575-1899	8			Petworth		1821-1836	6E
Binderton (see West Dean)		1579-1641		1584-1641		Westhampnett			5B
Binsted	A 1638-1999	1572-1878	8	1638-1851		Westhampnett			4C
Birdham	A 1538-1988	1538-1877	4,5,6,7,8,9	1777-1837		Westhampnett			4B
Bishopstone	B 1561-1995		5,8	1633-1893		Lewes			3H
Bodiam	B 1557-1938	1557-1885	5,8	1557-1837		Ticehurst			6K
Bolney	A 1541-1986	1541-1894	4,5,6,7,8,9	1541-1812		Cuckfield	1790-1812		6F
Bosham	A 1557-1969	1557-1875	8	1557-1988		Westbourne		1823-1836	4B
Botolphs	A 1601-1834		4,5,6,7,8,9			Steyning			4E
Boxgrove	A 1561-1973	1560-1885	8	1561-1812		Westhampnett			5C
Bramber	A 1601-1966		4,5,6,7,8,9	1584-1812		Steyning			5E
Bramshott (Hants)									7B
Brede	B 1559-1995		5,8	1559-1812		Rye		1833-1837	5L
Brightling	B 1560-1989	1560-1885	4,5,8	1606-1837		Battle			5J
Brighton (St Nicholas)	B 1558-1972	1558-1881	4,5,8	1558-1837		Brighton		1700-1854	4G
Brighton Chapel Royal	B 1823-1953	1823-1885	4,5,8			Brighton			4G
Broadwater	A 1558-1974	1558-1894	8	1558-1842		Worthing			4E
Broomhill (Kent)									5M
Burpham	A 1653-1922		8	1854-1912		Worthing			5D
Burton	A 1559-1999	1863-1886	4,5,6,7,8,9	1789-1812		Chichester			6D(J)
Burton (detached)			4,5,6,7,8,9			Chichester			5C(R)
Burwash	B 1558-1976	1558-1885	4,5,8	1558-1827		Ticehurst		1767-1835	6J
Bury	A 1558-1996		4,5,6,7,8,9			Chichester			5D
Buxted	B 1567-1994	1568-1881	5,8		1567-1750	Uckfield			6I
Catsfield	B 1612-1992	1606-1892	4,5,8	1606-1852		Battle			5K
Chailey	B 1538-1999		4,5,8	1538-1842		Lewes			5G
Chalvington	B 1538-1994	1538-1895	5,8	1539-1893		Lewes			4I(g)
Chichester								1730-1837	4B(W)
All Saints	A 1563-1951	1563-1875	8	1563-1870	1699-1754	Chichester			4B(W)
Cathedral	A 1664-1904	1664-1885	8	1664-1751		Chichester			4B(W)
Palace Chapel	A 1699-1754	1699-1754	8	1699-1754		Chichester			4B(W)
St Andrew	A 1563-1945	1568-1871	8	1563-1871	1568-1812	Chichester			4B(W)
St Bartholomew	A 1571-1994	1571-1876	5,8	1571-1840		Chichester			4B(W)
St James (ex.par.)			8			Chichester			4B(W)
St John New Town (ex.par.)			8			Chichester			4B(W)
St Martin	A 1560-1903	1560-1878	8	1561-1878	1569-1812	Chichester			4B(W)
St Olave	A 1569-1949	1569-1882	5,8	1569-1879	1569-1812	Chichester			4B(W)
St Pancras	A 1558-1950	1558-1812	8	1558-1874		Chichester			4B(W)
St Peter the Great	A 1558-1980	1558-1894	8	1558-1840		Chichester	1780-1799		4B(W)
St Peter the Less	A 1680-1949	1591-1843	8	1587-1838	1674-1812	Chichester			4B(W)
Chiddingly	B 1621-1992	1621-1846	5,8	1605-1837		Hailsham			5I
Chidham	A 1652-1975	1625-1812	8		1625-1812	Westbourne			4B
Chithurst	A 1628-1988	1615-1875	5,8			Midhurst	1790-1837		6B
Clapham	A 1685-1998	1571-1887	8	1571-1837		Petworth			4E
Clayton	A 1601-1958	1601-1895	5,8	1601-1840		Cuckfield			5G
Climping	A 1678-1981	1572-1878	4,5,6,7,8,9			Worthing	1790-1837		4D
Coates	A 1559-1999	1559-1881	4,5,6,7,8,9	1789-1837		Chichester			5D(K)
Cocking	A 1558-1999	1558-1875	4,5,6,7,8,9	1558-1837	1558-1837	Midhurst	1792-1837		6B
Coldwaltham	A 1561-1992	1561-1877	4,5,6,7,8,9			Thakeham			5D(L)
Compton	A 1558-1992	1558-1876	8	1813-1839		Westbourne			5A
Coombes	A 1538-1998	1538-1879	4,5,6,7,8,9	1542-1837		Steyning			4E
Cowfold	A 1558-1964	1558-1880	4,5,6,7,8,9	1558-1840		Cuckfield	1790-1812		6F
Crawley	A 1653-1977	1611-1877	4,5,6,7,8,9	1611-1839		East Grinstead			7G
Crowhurst	B 1558-1984	1558-1895	4,5,8	1558-1837		Battle			4K
Cuckfield	A 1598-1964	1598-1699	5,8	1598-1837		Cuckfield			6G
Dallington	B 1643-1995	1598-1885	4,5,8	1813-1842		Battle		1821-1837	5J
Denton	B 1567-1989		5,8	1754-1894		Lewes			4H
Didling	A 1717-1782	1573-1877	4,5,6,7,8,9	1663-1745	1681-1694	Midhurst			6B
Ditchling	B 1557-1907	1557-1750	4,5,8	1556-1837		Lewes		1798-1837	5G
Donnington	A 1559-1999	1559-1878	4,5,6,7,8,9	1813-1911		Westhampnett			4B(Y)
Duncton	A 1548-1996	1548-1877	5,8			Chichester			5C
Durrington	A 1627-1914	1610-1880	8	1753-1812		Worthing			4E(m)

SUSSEX

parish name	deposited original registers	I.G.I.	local census indexes	copies of registers at Soc. Gen.	Boyd's marriage index	1837-1851 Registration District	Pallot's marriage index	non-conform. records at P.R.O.	map ref.
Earnley	A 1562-1979	1590-1885	4,5,6,7,8,9	1562-1781		Westhampnett	1562-1781		4B
Eartham	A 1754-2001	1591-1880	8	1754-1840		Westhampnett			5C
Easebourne	A 1538-1953	1538-1876	5,8	1770-1780		Midhurst			6C
East Blatchington	B 1563-1997	1563-1894	5,8	1563-1894		Lewes			3H
Eastbourne, St Mary	B 1558-1996	1558-1744	4,5,6,8	1558-1837		Eastbourne		1808-1825	3I
East Chiltington	B 1587-1987		4,5,8	1601-1812		Lewes			3I
East Dean (Eastbourne)	B 1559-1997		4,5,8	1559-1891		Eastbourne			3I
East Dean (Chichester)	A 1653-1999	1571-1876	8	1571-1840		Westhampnett			5C
Eastergate	A 1564-1964	1563-1881	8			Westhampnett			4C(b)
East Grinstead	A 1558-1961	1558-1876	5,8	1558-1840		East Grinstead		1812-1836	7H
East Guldeford	B 1705-1994	1605-1885	5,8	1606-1837		Rye			5M
East Hoathly	B 1559-1969		4,5,6,7,8,9	1753-1882		Uckfield			5I
East Lavant	A 1653-1987	1609-1876	8	1653-1812	1653-1753	Westhampnett			5B
East Marden	A 1691-1992	1571-1881	8	1571-1839		Westbourne			5B(F)
East Preston	A 1708-1981	1573-1878	8	1573-1840		Worthing			4D
East Wittering	A 1653-1976	1571-1895	4,5,6,7,8,9	1590-1908	1625-1639	Westhampnett			4B
Edburton	A 1558-1999	1558-1812	4,5,6,7,8,9	1558-1812		Steyning	1790-1812		5F
Egdean	A 1646-1990	1630-1880	4,5,6,7,8,9			Chichester			6D
Elsted	A 1571-1993	1571-1886	5,8		1734-1810	Midhurst	1790-1810		6B
Etchingham	B 1561-1959	1561-1887	4,5,8	1561-1837	1561-1812	Ticehurst			6K
Ewhurst	B 1558-1988	1558-1885	4,5,8	1632-1837		Battle		1832-1837	5K
Fairlight	B 1651-1983		4,5,8	1651-1830		Hastings			4L
Falmer	B 1649-1994	1606-1889	5,8	1606-1840		Lewes			4G
Felpham	A 1557-1963	1554-1876	8	1554-1875		Westhampnett	1780-1837		4C
Fernhurst	A 1547-1990	1547-1876	5,8	1932-1964	1547-1752	Midhurst			7C
Ferring	A 1558-1971	1558-1877	8	1558-1840		Worthing			4D
Findon	A 1557-1987	1557-1876	5,8			Thakeham			5E
Fittleworth	A 1559-1991	1559-1876	5,8			Chichester			6D
Fletching	B 1554-1989	1554-1898	5,8	1551-1812	1552-1653	Uckfield			6H
Folkington	B 1560-1979	1664-1791	4,5,8	1754-1882	1560-1754	Eastbourne			4I(k)
Ford	A 1630-1997	1572-1881	4,5,6,7,8,9	1572-1900	1646-1809	Worthing			4D
Framfield	B 1538-1996		5,8	1687-1812		Uckfield			5I
Frant	B 1543-1984	1543-1887	4,5,8	1543-1812	1543-1812	Ticehurst			7I
Friston	B 1545-1994	1546-1845	4,5,8	1547-1891		Eastbourne			3I
Funtington	A 1560-1965	1564-1876	8		1705-1754	Westbourne			5B
Glynde	B 1558-1994	1558-1812	5,8	1558-1840		Lewes			4H
Goring	A 1560-1993	1560-1876	8	1560-1840		Worthing			4E
Graffham	A 1655-1999	1589-1877	8		1754-1813	Westhampnett	1790-1812		6C
Greatham (see Wiggonholt)						Chichester			5D(M)
Guestling	B 1686-1998		4,5,8	1686-1837		Hastings			4L
Hailsham	B 1558-1999		4,5,8	1558-1838		Hailsham		1795-1837	4I
Hamsey	B 1583-1974	1583-1885	4,5,8	1583-1894		Lewes			5H
Hangleton	B 1727-1978	1697-1888	5,8	1727-1851		Steyning			4F
Hardham	A 1643-1996	1584-1880	4,5,6,7,8,9	1642-1812	1688-1752	Thakeham			5D
Hartfield	B 1648-1978	1648-1899	5,8	1696-1837		East Grinstead			7H
Harting	A 1567-1970	1567-1876	5,8	1567-1812		Midhurst		1827-1837 1817-1855	6B
Hastings									4K
All Saints	B 1559-1986	1599-1895	4,5,8	1559-1749	1559-1749	Hastings			4K
St Clement	B 1558-1964	1558-1895	5,8	1677-1772	1610-1724	Hastings			4K
St Mary in the Castle	B 1828-1970		5,8	1828-1837		Hastings			4K
Hawkhurst (Kent)									6K
Heathfield	B 1581-1991		5,8	1581-1837		Hailsham		1775-1836	5J
Heene	A 1594-1965	1594-1876	8			Worthing			4E
Hellingly	B 1618-1999	1607-1887	5,8	1753-1812		Hailsham		1830-1837	4I
Henfield	A 1595-1900	1810-1876	4,5,6,7,8,9	1800-1810		Steyning		1832-1837	5F
Herstmonceux	B 1538-1973	1606-1893	4,5,8	1813-1893		Hailsham		1812-1836	4J
Heyshott	A 1690-1837	1587-1880	4,5,6,7,8,9			Chichester			6C
Hollington	B 1636-1992		4,5,8	1606-1813	1636-1837	Battle			4K
Hooe	B 1609-1989	1606-1887	4,5,8			Hailsham			4J
Horsham	A 1540-1965	1540-1876	4,5,6,7,8	1541-1635		Horsham		1669-1837	7E
Horsted Keynes	A 1638-1986	1605-1876	5,8	1638-1837		Cuckfield			6G
Houghton	A 1560-1999		4,5,6,7,8,9	1560-1839		Worthing			5D
Hove, St Andrew	B 1538-1973	1538-1882	5,8	1538-1812		Steyning			4F
Hove (Waterloo Street)	B 1830-1988		5,8			Steyning			4F
Hunston	A 1678-1999		4,5,6,7,8,9	1583-1902		Westhampnett			4B
Hurstpierpoint	A 1558-1992	1558-1877	5,8		1559-1812	Cuckfield			5F
Icklesham	B 1669-1990	1666-1892	5,8	1670-1812		Rye			5L
Iden	B 1560-1993	1558-1886	5,8	1606-1837		Rye			5M
Ifield	A 1568-1985		8	1568-1754		Horsham			7F
Iford	B 1654-1984	1606-1895	5,8	1557-1883	1608-1812	Lewes	1790-1836		4G
Iping	A 1653-1999	1584-1876	5,8			Midhurst			6B
Isfield	B 1570-1993		5,8	1570-1837		Uckfield			5H0
Itchingfield	A 1700-1990	1591-1887	4,5,6,7,8,9	1584-1837		Horsham			6E
Jevington	B 1661-1988		4,5,8			Eastbourne			3I
Keymer	A 1601-1943	1601-1888	5,8	1601-1812		Cuckfield			5G
Kingston (Ferring)	A 1570-1660	1570-1671	8	1570-1672		Worthing	1790-1836(?)		4D
Kingston (Lewes)	B 1557-1948	1557-1765	5,8	1557-1883	1557-1837	Lewes	1790-1836(?)		4G
Kingston by Sea	A 1591-1970	1607-1885	5,8	1592-1893		Steyning	1790-1836(?)		4F
Kirdford	A 1558-1996	1558-1876	8			Petworth			6D
Lamberhurst (Kent)									7J
Lancing	A 1560-1989	1559-1882	4,5,6,7,8,9			Worthing			4E
Laughton	B 1561-1996	1557-1885	5,8	1557-1891		Hailsham			5H
Lewes								1783-1837	4G
All Saints	B 1561-1972	1561-1881	5,8	1573-1837		Lewes			4G
St Anne	B 1679-1993	1608-1863	5,8	1679-1812		Lewes			4G
St John sub Castro	B 1602-1965		5,8	1602-1812		Lewes			4G
St Michael	B 1579-1988	1579-1886	5,8	1575-1812		Lewes			4G
St Thomas à Becket at Cliffe	B 1606-1996		5,8	1606-1837		Lewes			4G

parish name	deposited original registers	I.G.I.	local census indexes	copies of registers at Soc. Gen.	Boyd's marriage index	1837-1851 Registration District	Pallot's marriage index	non-conform. records at P.R.O.	map ref.
Lewes (cont'd)									
Southover St John Baptist	B 1558-1991	1558-1886	5,8	1559-1812		Lewes			4G
Linch	A 1701-1999	1701-1876	5,8	1693-1840	1706-1834	Midhurst	1785-1837		7B(A)
Linch (detached)			5,8			Midhurst			6B(D)
Linchmere	A 1558-1980		5,8	1558-1812	1566-1812	Midhurst	1790-1812		7C
Lindfield	A 1558-1974	1590-1885	5,8	1558-1812		Cuckfield		1815-1836	6G
Litlington	B 1695-1994	1695-1894	4,5,8	1728-1894		Eastbourne			3I
Littlehampton	A 1611-1953	1584-1876	8	1591-1753		Worthing			4D
Little Horsted	B 1540-1994		5,8			Uckfield			5H
Lodsworth	A 1557-1975	1557-1876	5,8	1557-1902	1630-1735	Midhurst			6C
Lower Beeding	A 1840-1990	1840-1876	8	1561-1891		Horsham			6F
Lullington	B 1721-1981	1606-1895	4,5,8	1754-1836		Eastbourne			4I(h)
Lurgashall	A 1559-1950	1559-1877	5,8	1559-1840	1559-1837	Midhurst			7C
Lyminster	A 1566-1985	1566-1876	8			Worthing			4D
Madehurst	A 1639-2000		8	1572-1837		Westhampnett			5C
Maresfield	B 1538-1909		5,8	1538-1758		Uckfield			6H
Mayfield	B 1570-1992	1570-1885	5,8	1570-1837		Uckfield			6I
Merston	A 1685-1993		8	1587-1892		Westhampnett			4C
Middleton	A 1553-1998	1560-1877	8			Westhampnett	1551-1819		4C
Midhurst	A 1565-1975	1565-1876	5,8	1565-1812	1565-1812	Midhurst	1790-1812		6B(C)
Mid Lavant	A 1567-1964	1567-1876	8		1567-1745	Westhampnett			5B(U)
Milland	A 1581-1990	1581-1878	8			Midhurst			7B
Mountfield	B 1558-1983		4,5,8	1649-1837		Battle			5K
New Fishbourne	A 1589-1971	1589-1877	8	1589-1837		Westhampnett			4B(V)
Newhaven, St Michael	B 1553-1994	1553-1885	5,8	1553-1837		Lewes		1798-1832	3H
Newick	B 1558-1937		4,5,8			Lewes			5H
New Shoreham	A 1565-1955		5,8	1564-1837		Steyning		1802-1836	4F
Newtimber	A 1558-1998	1558-1877	5,8	1558-1840		Cuckfield			5F
Ninfield	B 1663-1993	1559-1885	4,5,8			Hailsham			4J
North Chapel	A 1716-1998		5,8	1716-1837		Midhurst			7C
Northiam	B 1558-1993		5,8	1738-1837		Rye			5L
North Marden	A 1813-1991	1584-1897	8	1590-1840		Westbourne			5B(E)
North Mundham	A 1558-1988		4,5,6,7,8,9	1558-1919		Westhampnett			4B
North Stoke	A 1566-1993	1565-1883	4,5,6,7,8,9	1565-1812		Worthing			5D(e)
Nuthurst	A 1559-1972	1562-1869	4,5,6,7,8,9	1559-1840		Horsham			6F
Old Shoreham	A 1565-1964		5,8	1565-1837		Steyning			4F
Ore	B 1558-2000		4,5,8	1659-1837		Hastings			4L
Oving	A 1561-1988	1561-1877	8	1561-1837		Westhampnett			4C
Ovingdean	B 1719-1992	1606-1887	5,8	1704-1841		Lewes			4G
Pagham	A 1707-1978	1610-1876	8	1662-1841	1662-1811	Westhampnett	1790-1812		4B
Parham	A 1538-1993		5,8	1538-1840		Thakeham			5D
Patcham	B 1558-1990	1558-1885	5,8	1558-1840		Steyning			4G
Patching	A 1560-1998	1560-1886	8			Petworth			4D
Peasmarsh	B 1568-1986		5,8	1608-1837		Rye			5L
Penhurst	B 1558-1994		5,8	1577-1834		Battle			5J
Pett	B 1675-1961		4,5,8	1607-1837		Hastings			4L
Petworth	A 1559-1971	1559-1876	4,5,6,7,8,9	1559-1700		Petworth		1827-1837	6D
Pevensey	B 1569-1995	1569-1885	4,5,8	1569-1891		Eastbourne			4J
Piddinghoe	B 1540-1994	1540-1884	5,8	1540-1884		Lewes			4H
Playden	B 1638-1988	1606-1885	5,8	1606-1837		Rye	1790-1798		5M
Plumpton	B 1558-1987		4,5,8	1558-1906		Lewes			5G
Poling	A 1653-1985	1584-1877	8	1665-1742	1630-1641	Worthing			4D(f)
Portslade, St Nicholas	B 1666-1974	1608-1875	5,8		1666-1812	Steyning			4F
Poynings	A 1558-1998		4,5,6,7,8,9	1559-1894		Steyning			5F
Preston, St Peter	B 1754-1889	1551-1785	5,8	1754-1840		Steyning			4G
Pulborough	A 1595-1989	1583-1876	5,8	1595-1617		Thakeham			6D
Pyecombe	A 1561-1999	1561-1895	5,8			Cuckfield			5F
Racton	A 1680-1992	1599-1877	8			Westbourne			5A
Ringmer	B 1605-1995	1605-1885	4,5,8	1605-1837		Lewes			5H
Ripe	B 1538-1994	1538-1893	5,8	1813-1893		Lewes			4I
Rodmell	B 1701-1995	1610-1895	5,8	1610-1893		Lewes			4H
Rogate	A 1558-1940	1558-1876	5,8			Midhurst			6B
Rotherfield	B 1539-1997	1539-1886	5,8	1539-1850		Uckfield		1748-1836	6I
Rottingdean	B 1558-1922	1558-1887	5,8	1558-1841		Lewes			4G
Rudgwick	A 1538-1994	1538-1877	8	1538-1812		Petworth			7E
Rumboldswyke	A 1670-1978	1613-1877	8	1630-1812	1613-1776	Westhampnett	1780-1837		4B(Z)
Rusper	A 1560-1935	1560-1877	7,8	1560-1812		Horsham			7F
Rustington	A 1569-1951	1569-1877	8	1568-1840		Worthing			4D
Rye	B 1538-1993	1538-1893	5,8	1538-1635		Rye		1765-1837	5M
St Leonards, Hastings	B 1833-1984		5,8			Hastings			4K
Salehurst	B 1575-1991	1575-1885	5,8	1575-1837		Ticehurst		1832-1837	6K
Seaford	B 1559-1992	1559-1890	4,5,8	1559-1892		Eastbourne			3H
Sedlescombe	B 1559-1992		4,5,8	1607-1838		Battle			5K
Selham	A 1566-1999	1565-1891	5,8	1565-1840		Midhurst			6C(H)
Selmeston	B 1667-1994	1608-1893	5,8	1756-1893		Lewes			4I
Selsey	A 1663-1992	1584-1876	4,5,6,7,8,9	1584-1862	1581-1792	Westhampnett			3B
Shermanbury	A 1653-1995	1606-1876	4,5,6,7,8,9			Steyning			5F(Q)
Shipley	A 1609-1966	1584-1877	4,5,6,7,8,9	1754-1812		Horsham			6E
Sidlesham	A 1566-1969	1566-1876	4,5,6,7,8,9	1566-1812	1567-1812	Westhampnett			4B
Singleton	A 1558-1999	1558-1877	8	1558-1840		Westhampnett			5C
Slaugham	A 1654-1897	1606-1876	5,8	1654-1880		Cuckfield			6F
Slindon	A 1558-2001	1558-1877	5,8	1765-1812		Westhampnett			5C
Slinfold	A 1556-1943	1556-1876	8	1556-1714		Horsham		1813-1837	7E
Sompting	A 1547-1974	1590-1908	4,5,6,7,8,9			Steyning			4E
South Bersted	A 1564-1989	1564-1876	8			Chichester		1827-1836	4C
Southease	B 1556-1995	1556-1894	5,8	1813-1893		Lewes			4G
South Heighton	B 1542-1895		5,8	1557-1749		Lewes			4H
South Malling	B 1629-1991		5,8	1629-1812		Lewes			4H

247

SUSSEX

parish name	deposited original registers	I.G.I.	local census indexes	copies of registers at Soc. Gen.	Boyd's marriage index	1837-1851 Registration District	Pallot's marriage index	non-conform. records at P.R.O.	map ref.
South Stoke	A 1553-1995	1553-1875	4,5,6,7,8,9	1553-1839		Worthing			5D
Southwick	A 1654-1983	1606-1876	5,8	1725-1741		Steyning			4F
Stanmer	B 1550-1966	1550-1888	5,8	1663-1900		Lewes			4G
Stedham	A 1538-1994	1538-1882	5,8		1712-1718	Midhurst			6B
Steep (see Hampshire)									6C
Steyning	A 1565-1991	1565-1895	4,5,6,7,8,9	1565-1925		Steyning			5E
Stopham	A 1545-1999	1544-1879	4,5,6,7,8,9	1544-1803		Thakeham			6D
Storrington	A 1547-1976		5,8	1549-1837		Thakeham			5D
Stoughton	A 1671-1992	1571-1876	8		1630-1666	Westbourne			5A
Streat	B 1561-1995	1561-1888	4,5,8	1813-1908		Lewes			5G
Sullington	A 1555-1993		5,8	1555-1700	1555-1700	Thakeham			5E
Sutton	A 1656-1999	1587-1806	4,5,6,7,8,9	1813-1871	1633-1783	Chichester			5C
Tangmere	A 1538-1981	1538-1877	8	1538-1837	1539-1812	Westhampnett			4C(a)
Tarring Neville	B 1569-1996		5,8	1571-1894		Lewes			4H
Telscombe	B 1684-1993		5,8	1684-1840		Lewes			4G
Terwick	A 1571-1999	1571-1876	5,8	1813-1883		Midhurst			6B
Thakeham	A 1558-1990	1559-1876	5,8			Thakeham			5E
The Gumber (ex.par.)						Chichester			5C(S)
Ticehurst	B 1559-1971	1559-1870	4,5,8	1558-1843	1559-1812	Ticehurst			6J
Tillington	A 1572-1938	1571-1899	5,8	1640-1837		Midhurst			6C
Tortington	A 1560-1987	1560-1877	4,5,6,7,8,9	1813-1878		Worthing			4D(d)
Treyford	A 1728-1992	1573-1877	5,8	1632-1745	1633-1745	Midhurst			6B
Trotton	A 1660-1993	1571-1881	5,8			Midhurst			7B
Tuxlith (see Milland and Trotton)									
Twineham	A 1716-1999	1606-1890	5,8	1606-1840		Cuckfield			5F
Uckfield	B 1538-1991		5,8			Uckfield		1783-1836	5H
Udimore	B 1560-1994		5,8	1559-1893		Rye			5L
Up Marden	A 1714-1992	1559-1878	8		1630-1714	Westbourne			5B
Up Waltham	A 1762-1999	1554-1887	8	1601-1836	1571-1776	Westhampnett			5C
Upper Beeding	A 1544-1952		4,5,6,7,8,9			Steyning			5F
Wadhurst	B 1604-1975		5,8			Ticehurst		1818-1837	6J
Walberton	A 1556-1972	1556-1876	8	1556-1850		Westhampnett			4C
Waldron	B 1564-1996		5,8	1564-1857	1564-1812	Uckfield			5I
Warbleton	B 1559-1994	1559-1896	5,8	1644-1930		Hailsham			5J
Warminghurst	A 1714-1978	1560-1878	5,8	1716-1754		Thakeham			5E(O)
Warnham	A 1559-1960	1558-1897	8	1558-1870		Horsham			7E
Warningcamp	A 1572-1717	1571-1717	8	1633-1640		Petworth			4D(n)
Wartling	B 1538-1977	1538-1885	4,5,8	1813-1894		Hailsham			4J
Washington	A 1559-1993		5,8			Thakeham			5E
West Blatchington			5,8	1636-1640		Steyning			4F
Westbourne	A 1550-1998	1550-1880	8		1550-1753	Westbourne			5A
West Chiltington	A 1711-1957	1571-1879	5,8			Thakeham			6E
West Dean (Chichester)	A 1554-1991	1559-1876	8	1571-1840		Westbourne			5B
West Dean (Lewes)	B 1631-1993		4,5,8	1813-1894		Eastbourne			3I
Westfield	B 1552-1993		4,5,8	1552-1837		Battle			5K
West Firle	B 1668-1988		5,8	1606-1894		Lewes			4H
West Grinstead	A 1558-1953	1591-1895	4,5,6,7,8,9			Horsham			6E
Westham	B 1571-1984	1571-1812	4,5,8	1571-1879	1571-1812	Eastbourne	1790-1812		4J
West Hampnett	A 1734-1996		8			Westhampnett			5C
West Hoathly	A 1645-1991	1606-1876	5,8	1606-1812		East Grinstead		1828-1837	7G
West Itchenor	A 1561-1987	1561-1878	4,5,6,7,8,9			Westhampnett			4B
Westmeston	B 1587-1995	1587-1894	4,5,8	1813-1894		Lewes			5G
West Stoke	A 1555-1999	1560-1880	8	1554-1841		Westhampnett			5B(T)
West Tarring	A 1540-1963		8	1540-1753		Worthing			4E
West Thorney	A 1570-1999	1570-1890	8			Westbourne			4A
West Wittering	A 1621-1986	1538-1879	4,5,6,7,8,9	1621-1909		Westhampnett			4A
Whatlington	B 1558-1994		4,5,8	1640-1837		Battle			5K(l)
Wiggonholt	A 1597-1993		4,5,6,7,8,9	1583-1883		Worthing			5D(N)
Willingdon	B 1560-1992	1560-1894	4,5,8	1560-1894		Eastbourne			3I
Wilmington	B 1538-1998	1560-1676	4,5,8	1616-1890		Eastbourne			4I(j)
Winchelsea	B 1651-1987	1606-1893	5,8	1606-1837		Rye			5L
Wisborough Green	A 1560-1972	1560-1876	8			Petworth		1821-1836	6D
Wiston	A 1638-2000	1570-1876	4,5,6,7,8,9			Thakeham			5E
Withyham	B 1661-1990	1606-1891	5,8	1606-1754		East Grinstead			7I
Wivelsfield	B 1559-1997	1559-1881	4,5,8	1559-1666		Lewes		1784-1837	6G
Woodmancote	A 1582-1997	1582-1885	4,5,6,7,8,9	1582-1812		Steyning	1790-1812		5F
Woolavington	A 1668-1972	1571-1937	5,8			Midhurst			6C(G)
Woolbeding	A 1548-1999	1556-1876	5,8	1667-1811	1556-1753	Midhurst			6B
Worth	A 1558-1938	1558-1876	5,8	1558-1840		East Grinstead		1828-1837	7G
Worthing St Paul	A 1813-1979	1868-1876	8			Worthing		1808-1837	4E
Yapton	A 1538-1982	1538-1876	8			Westhampnett			4C

SUSSEX

Original registers deposited at:
A = West Sussex Record Office, County Hall, Chichester, West Sussex PO19 1RN
B = East Sussex Record Office, The Maltings, Castle Precincts, Lewes, East Sussex BN7 1YT

Study adjacent parishes in counties of Hampshire, Surrey and Kent

West Sussex Record Office, County Hall, Chichester, West Sussex PO19 1RN
East Sussex Record Office, The Maltings, Castle Precincts, Lewes, East Sussex BN7 1YT

The following useful indexes have been compiled - see Introduction
Census Indexes 1841 for East Sussex parishes - PBN Publications, 22 Abbey Road, Eastbourne, East Sussex BN20 8TE
Census Indexes 1851 for East Sussex parishes - C. June Barnes, 50 St Helen's Park Road, Hastings, East Sussex TN34 2DN
Census Indexes 1851 for West Sussex parishes - Sussex FHG, Mr J. Bysh, 40 Tanbridge Park, Horsham, West Sussex RH12 1SZ
Census Indexes 1841 - 1891 for West Sussex parishes - Sussex FHG, Mr J. Bysh, 40 Tanbridge Park, Horsham, West Sussex RH12 1SZ
Census Indexes 1841 - 1891 for East Hoathly - Jane Seabrook, 9 High Street, East Hoathly, East Sussex BN8 6DR
Sussex Parish Register Transcript Collection - Institute of Heraldic and Genealogical Studies, Northgate, Canterbury, Kent CT1 1BA
Marriage Index - Mr. F.L. Leeson, 108 Sea Lane, Ferring, West Sussex BN12 5NB up to 1837
Sussex Burials Index 1813-1841 - Lord & Lady Teviot, 28 Hazel Grove, Burgess Hill, West Sussex RH15 0BY

Sussex is long and narrow in shape measuring 76 miles from east to west and varying from 20 to 27 miles from north to south. It is watered by five principal rivers: the Ouse, Adur, Arun, Rother and Cuckmere. The population in 1841 was 300,075; in 1851, 336,844; in 1861, 363,735; in 1871, 417,456; in 1881, 496,316.

The soils are chalk, clay, loam, sand and gravel. Produce includes wheat, oats, barley, beans, cabbages, turnips and fruit. Cattle and sheep are bred. Manufactures were not extensive (paper was made in some towns and gunpowder at Battle) but shipping and ship-building were important.

The information in the Index is abbreviated, and may mislead the searcher if reference is not made to the details contained in the several publications listed in the Introduction. It is essential that users of this book check the appropriate works before making further enquiries.

WARWICKSHIRE

parish name	deposited original registers	I.G.I.	local census indexes	copies of registers at Soc. Gen.	Boyd's marriage index	1837-1851 Registration District	Pallot's marriage index	non-conform. records at P.R.O.	map ref.
Alcester	A 1560-1991	1560-1876	5,8			Alcester		1774-1836	8E
Allesley	A 1562-1966	1567-1876	5,8,9	1561-1863		Meriden			6H
Alveston	A 1539-1948	1538-1876	5,8	1539-1814		Stratford on Avon	1529-1769		7E
Ansley	A 1637-1981	1637-1876	5,8	1637-1877		Atherstone		1799-1837	6I
Ansty	A 1589-1983	1662-1875	5,8,9	1589-1880		Foleshill		1790-1812	5H
Arley	A 1557-1939	1557-1875	5,8			Nuneaton			6I
Arrow	A 1588-1992	1591-1895	5,8	1837-1974		Alcester			8E
Ashow	A 1733-1995	1663-1895	5,8,9	1733-1979		Warwick			6F
Ashted	B 1810-1970	1810-1877	5,8			Aston			8I
Astley	A 1670-1985	1670-1878	5,8	1670-1953		Nuneaton			6I
Aston	B 1544-1969	1544-1870	5,8,9	1544-1744		Aston			8I
Aston Cantlow	A 1560-1996	1612-1895	5,8			Alcester		1822-1856	8E
Atherstone	A 1825-1982	1825-1876	5,8			Atherstone		1708-1837	5J
Atherstone on Stour	A 1654-1979	1654-1895	5,8	1611-1865	1651-1675	Stratford on Avon	1780-1837		7D
Austrey	A 1558-1983	1558-1895	5,8	1558-1809		Tamworth			6K
Avon Dassett	A 1559-1979	1559-1895	5,7,8,9	1559-1799		Banbury			4D
Baddesley Clinton	A 1632-1986	1632-1875	5,8	1813-1865		Solihull			7G(D)
Baddesley Ensor	A 1688-1965	1676-1875	5,8			Atherstone		1801-1836	6J
Bagington	A 1628-1993	1635-1877	5,8,9	1813-1837		Warwick			5G
Balsall	A 1736-1982	1809-1831	5,8	1828-1833		Solihull			7G
Barcheston	A 1559-1979	1559-1877	5,8		1561-1754	Shipston on Stour			6C
Barford	A 1538-1980	1539-1876	5,8	1538-1812	1539-1812	Warwick			6E
Barston	A 1598-1964	1598-1876	5,8	1598-1876		Solihull			7G
Barton on the Heath	A 1575-1979	1575-1879	5,8,9	1575-1876	1651-1675	Chipping Norton	1790-1812		6B
Baxterley	A 1673-1899	1654-1875	5,8	1662-1674		Atherstone			6J
Bearley	A 1550-1972	1549-1880	5,8	1550-1883		Stratford on Avon			7E(O)
Beaudesert	A 1661-1994	1607-1876	5,8			Stratford on Avon	1790-1837		8F
Beausale (ex.par.)			5,8			Warwick			6F
Bedworth	A 1644-1964	1653-1876	5,8,9	1875-1907		Foleshill		1688-1837	5I
Bentley	A 1837-1987		5,8	1837-1967		Atherstone			6I
Berkswell	A 1653-1984	1665-1836	5,8,9	1653-1933		Meriden			6G
Bickenhill	A 1558-1976	1558-1875	5,8			Meriden			7H
Bidford-on-Avon	A 1664-1979	1711-1876	5,8	1612-1876		Alcester			8D
Billesley	A 1816-1974	1816-1888	5,8	1817-1865		Stratford on Avon			8E(N)
Bilton	A 1643-1966	1662-1852	5,8			Rugby			3G
Binley	A 1660-1987	1600-1876	5,8,9	1800-1946		Foleshill			5G
Binton	A 1539-1979	1539-1895	5,8	1540-1978		Stratford on Avon			8E
Birdingbury	A 1559-1979	1559-1865	5,8	1559-1977		Rugby	1780-1837		4F(L)
Birmingham								1719-1858	9H
All Saints	B 1833-1972	1833-1876	5,8,9			Birmingham			9H
St George	B 1823-1973	1823-1875	5,8,9			Birmingham			9H
St Martin	B 1554-1981	1554-1879	5,8,9	1554-1839		Birmingham			9H
St Mary	B 1774-1925	1813-1847	5,8,9	1774-1779		Birmingham			9H
St Paul	B 1779-1982	1779-1812	5,8,9			Birmingham			9H
St Peter	B 1842-1898	1842-1875	5,8,9	1657-1824		Birmingham			9H
St Philip	B 1715-1965	1715-1875	5,8,9	1715-1940		Birmingham			9H
St Thomas	B 1829-1948	1829-1875	5,8,9			Birmingham			9H
Bishop's Itchington	A 1559-1995	1559-1876	5,8	1698-1837		Southam			5E
Bishop's Tachbrook	A 1538-1970	1538-1885	5,8	1538-1877	1651-1675	Warwick	1790-1812		6E
Bishopston	AC 1590-1966	1590-1895	5,8	1598-1966		Stratford on Avon			7E
Bordesley	B 1823-1965	1823-1876	5,8			Aston			8H
Bourton on Dunsmore	A 1560-1995	1560-1875	5,8	1560-1813	1651-1675	Rugby	1790-1812		4G
Brailes	A 1570-1997	1570-1876	5,8			Shipston on Stour			6C
Brinklow	A 1558-1995	1558-1876	5,8	1750-1799		Rugby			4G
Brownsover	A 1593-1979	1593-1895	5,8	1593-1865		Rugby			3G
Bubbenhall	A 1698-1995	1558-1852	5,8,9	1738-1914		Warwick			5G
Budbrooke	A 1539-1985	1539-1876	5,8	1702-1812		Warwick			6F
Bulkington	A 1606-1984	1660-1877	5,8	1660-1876		Nuneaton		1812-1836	5H
Burmington	A 1582-1979	1583-1878	5,8	1583-1865	1583-1834	Shipston on Stour			6B
Burton Dassett	A 1564-1976	1642-1876	5,8	1642-1876		Southam			5D
Burton Hastings	A 1574-1992	1574-1885	5,8	1574-1938		Hinckley			4I
Butlers Marston	A 1539-1946	1538-1895	5,8	1538-1812	1651-1675	Shipston on Stour	1790-1812		6D
Caldecote	A 1725-1975	1674-1877	5,8	1813-1961		Nuneaton			5J
Camberfields (ex.par.)			5,8						4H
Castle Bromwich	A 1619-1940	1619-1875	5,8			Aston			8I
Chadshunt	A 1701-1930	1660-1835	5,8			Southam			5D
Chapel Ascote (see Ladbroke)						Southam			4E(T)
Charlecote	A 1539-1980	1543-1877	5,8	1543-1978	1651-1675	Stratford on Avon	1790-1812		6E
Cherington	A 1538-1978	1538-1880	5,8	1538-1978	1540-1812	Shipston on Stour			6B(X)
Chesterton	A 1538-1982	1746-1846	5,8	1538-1842		Southam			5E
Chilvers Coton	A 1654-1992	1754-1876	5,8	1654-1878		Nuneaton		1818-1837	5I
Church Lawford	A 1575-1984	1575-1877	5,8	1575-1948		Rugby			4G
Churchover	A 1658-1984	1658-1876	5,8		1658-1812	Rugby		1822-1836	3H
Claverdon	A 1593-1978	1593-1877	5,8	1596-1990		Stratford on Avon			7F
Clifton upon Dunsmore	A 1594-1979	1734-1876	5,8	1594-1883		Rugby			3G
Coleshill	A 1538-1982	1538-1875	5,8	1538-1704		Meriden		1835-1836	7I
Combroke	A 1701-1995	1608-1895	5,8	1803-1881	1608-1786	Stratford on Avon			6D
Compton Verney (ex.par.)			5,8	1880-1923		Stratford on Avon			5D
Compton Wynyates	A 1683-1935		5,8	1683-1935	1713-1774	Shipston on Stour			5C
Copston Magna (see Monks Kirby)		1575-1875							4I
Corley	A 1540-1973	1540-1877	5,8,9	1662-1686		Meriden			6H
Coughton	A 1673-1964	1616-1876	5,8,9	1673-1768		Alcester			8E
Coventry								1766-1837	5H
Holy Trinity	A 1561-1971	1561-1895	4,5,8,9	1561-1904		Coventry			5H
St John Baptist	A 1734-1967	1734-1876	4,5,8,9			Coventry			5H
St Michael	A 1662-1934	1662-1876	4,5,8,9	1640-1837		Coventry			5H
Cubbington	A 1559-1987	1590-1876	5,8	1559-1840		Warwick			5F
Curdworth	A 1653-1956	1653-1844	5,8	1875-1936		Aston			7I
Deritend	B 1699-1940	1699-1869	5,8,9			Aston			8I

WARWICKSHIRE

parish name	deposited original registers	I.G.I.	local census indexes	copies of registers at Soc. Gen.	Boyd's marriage index	1837-1851 Registration District	Pallot's marriage index	non-conform. records at P.R.O.	map ref.
Dunchurch	A 1538-1974	1748-1876	5,8	1538-1876		Rugby			4F
Edgbaston	B 1635-1983	1635-1838	5,8	1635-1868		King's Norton	1790-1812		9H
Elmdon	A 1538-1979	1538-1878	5,8	1693-1968		Solihull			7H
Erdington	B 1824-1985		5,8,9			Aston		1822-1856	8I
Ettington	A 1661-1945	1612-1857	5,8	1623-1812	1651-1675	Stratford on Avon	1790-1812		6D
Exhall	A 1540-1978	1540-1895	5,8,9	1803-1837		Foleshill			5H
Exhall (nr. Alcester)	A 1605-1978	1540-1895	5,8	1540-1812		Alcester			8E(M)
Farnborough	A 1558-1999	1725-1875	5,7,8,9	1558-1896		Banbury			4D
Fenny Compton	A 1627-1973	1745-1876	5,8	1627-1882	1651-1675	Southam	1790-1812		4D
Fillongley	A 1538-1981	1538-1876	5,8,9	1538-1947		Meriden			6I
Foleshill	A 1564-1974	1564-1877	5,8,9	1564-1877		Foleshill		1788-1837	5H
Frankton	A 1559-1992	1559-1877	5,8	1813-1949		Rugby			4F
Fullbrook *see* Sherbourn		1587-1880				Stratford on Avon			6E(S)
Gaydon	A 1701-1930	1660-1835	5,8	1754-1930		Southam			5E
Grandborough	A 1581-1895	1744-1885	5,8	1581-1982		Rugby			4F
Great Alne	A 1612-1981	1604-1895	5,8	1616-1753		Alcester			8E
Great Packington	A 1538-1993	1754-1895	5,8	1538-1948		Meriden			7H
Great Wolford	A 1654-1979	1612-1895	5,8	1654-1878	1626-1812	Shipston on Stour			6B
Grendon	A 1567-1956	1766-1876	5,8	1567-1940		Atherstone			6J
Halford	A 1545-1987	1545-1812	5,8	1552-1912	1651-1675	Shipston on Stour	1790-1812		6C
Hampton in Arden	A 1599-1908	1599-1877	5,8,9	1590-1848		Meriden			7H
Hampton Lucy	A 1556-1998	1602-1700	5,8	1556-1977	1553-1812	Stratford on Avon			6E
Harborough Magna	A 1540-1974	1540-1878	5,8	1540-1968		Rugby			4H
Harbury	A 1564-1976	1564-1876	5,8	1822-1931		Southam			5E
Haseley	A 1588-1993	1588-1876	5,8	1588-1879		Warwick			7F
Haselor	A 1589-1978	1589-1875	5,8			Alcester			8E
Hatton	A 1539-1985	1615-1876	5,8	1538-1812	1651-1675	Warwick	1790-1812		7F(G)
Henley in Arden	A 1679-1994		5,8	1546-1700		Stratford on Avon		1791-1830	8F
Hillmorton	A 1564-1959	1564-1876	5,8	1564-1917		Rugby			3G
Hinckley (Leics.)									4I
Hodnell (ex.par.)						Southam			4E(U)
Honiley	A 1745-1987	1813-1875	5,8	1745-1865		Warwick			6G(E)
Honington	A 1571-1927	1571-1877	5,8	1571-1812	1651-1675	Shipston on Stour	1790-1812		6C
Hunningham	A 1718-1983	1662-1878	5,8	1717-1865		Warwick			5F(K)
Idlicote	A 1556-1901	1556-1885	5,8	1557-1865	1651-1675	Shipston on Stour	1790-1812		6C
Ilmington	A 1588-1979	1685-1875	5,8	1588-1881		Shipston on Stour			7C
Ipsley	D 1608-1976	1601-1885	5,8			Alcester			9F
Kenilworth	A 1630-1979	1740-1876	5,8,9	1630-1880		Warwick		1819-1836	6G
Kineton	A 1539-1971	1611-1877	5,8	1546-1886		Stratford on Avon			5D
Kingsbury	A 1539-1975	1539-1874	5,8			Tamworth			7J
Kings Newnham (see Church Lawford)									4G
Kinwarton	A 1566-1994	1566-1895	5,8	1566-1725		Alcester			8E
Knowle	A 1682-1992	1682-1877	5,8	1682-1915		Solihull	1790-1812		7G
Ladbroke	A 1558-1992	1745-1875	5,8	1559-1919		Southam			4E
Lapworth	A 1561-1985	1561-1885	5,8	1835-1961		Solihull			7F
Lea Marston	A 1570-1989	1570-1895	5,8	1662-1674		Meriden			7I(A)
Leamington Hastings	A 1559-1993	1705-1895	5,8	1559-1886		Rugby		1831-1837	4F
Leamington Priors	A 1618-1965	1618-1895	5,8	1618-1901	1704-1812	Warwick	1790-1812	1822-1840	6F
Leek Wootton	A 1581-1973	1709-1885	5,8,9	1581-1865		Warwick			6F
Lighthorne	A 1538-1985	1735-1895	5,8	1538-1885		Southam			5E
Lillington	A 1539-1985	1728-1895	5,8	1539-1885		Warwick			5F
Little Compton	E 1588-1985	1605-1812	5,7,8,9	1588-1985		Chipping Norton			6B
Little Packington	A 1629-1967	1739-1895	5,8	1629-1967		Meriden			7H(C)
Long Compton	A 1670-1987	1608-1876	5,7,8,9	1608-1812	1651-1675	Chipping Norton	1790-1812	1820-1836	6B
Long Itchington	A 1653-1972	1653-1876	5,8	1813-1865		Southam			5F
Lower Radbourn (ex.par.)						Southam			4E
Lower Shuckburgh	A 1678-1994	1800-1885	5,8	1800-1984		Southam	1780-1827		3E
Loxley	A 1540-1991	1754-1895	5,8	1540-1981	1539-1812	Stratford on Avon			6D
Mancetter	A 1576-1990	1576-1895	5,8	1576-1935		Atherstone			5I
Marton	A 1660-1983	1660-1885	5,8	1660-1865		Rugby			4F
Maxstoke	A 1653-1983	1653-1895	5,8	1653-1914		Meriden			7I
Merevale	A 1727-1984	1727-1875	5,8	1813-1837		Atherstone			6J
Meriden	A 1646-1980	1754-1895	5,8,9	1687-1876		Meriden			6H
Middleton	A 1676-1943	1755-1895	5,7,8,9	1675-1900		Tamworth			7J
Milverton	A 1742-1939	1665-1872	5,8	1742-1851		Warwick			6F(H)
Mollington (Oxford)									4D
Monks Kirby	A 1653-1998	1754-1876	5,8	1649-1973		Lutterworth			4H
Moreton Morrell	A 1678-1978	1608-1895	5,8	1678-1878		Stratford on Avon			6E
Morton Bagot	A 1644-1979	1614-1895	5,8	1664-1857		Alcester			8F
Napton on the Hill	A 1604-1997	1813-1895	5,8	1813-1847		Southam			4E
Nether Whitacre	A 1539-1991	1539-1885	5,8	1813-1845		Meriden			6I
Newbold on Avon	A 1559-1983	1710-1895	5,8	1559-1882		Rugby			4G
Newbold Pacey	A 1554-1973	1731-1895	5,8	1554-1883		Stratford on Avon			6E
Newton Regis	A 1591-1995	1602-1895	5,8	1591-1875		Tamworth			6K
Norton Lindsey	A 1742-1992	1742-1895	5,8	1742-1865		Warwick			7F(Q)
Nuneaton	A 1577-1980	1577-1895	5,8			Nuneaton		1818-1836	5I
Nuthurst (see Hampton in Arden)									8G
Offchurch	A 1694-1918	1694-1895	5,8			Warwick			5F
Old Stratford	C 1558-1970	1558-1895	5,8	1558-1902		Stratford on Avon	1790-1812	1786-1836	7E
Over Whitacre	A 1561-1983	1561-1875	5,8	1568-1953		Meriden			6I(B)
Oxhill	A 1568-1996	1748-1885	5,8	1568-1881		Shipston on Stour			6D
Packwood	A 1668-1927	1668-1875	5,8			Solihull			7G
Pillerton Hersey	A 1539-1992	1539-1895	5,8	1611-1700		Shipston on Stour			6D
Pillerton Priors	A 1594-1992	1604-1854	5,8	1613-1667		Shipston on Stour			6D
Polesworth	A 1631-1992	1631-1885	5,8	1631-1947		Atherstone		1832-1836	6J
Preston Bagot	A 1677-1973	1612-1895	5,8	1612-1973		Stratford on Avon			7F(F)
Priors Marston	A 1689-1987	1689-1854	5,8	1727-1865		Southam			4E
Priors Hardwick	A 1661-1991	1754-1875	5,8	1662-1865	1662-1675	Southam	1790-1812		4E
Radford Semele	A 1565-1974	1565-1895	5,8	1565-1967		Warwick			5F

parish name	deposited original registers	I.G.I.	local census indexes	copies of registers at Soc. Gen.	Boyd's marriage index	1837-1851 Registration District	Pallot's marriage index	non-conform. records at P.R.O.	map ref.
Radway	A 1605-1978	1755-1895	5,7,8,9	1605-1879		Banbury			5D
Ratley	A 1701-1979	1754-1895	5,8	1662-1837		Banbury			5D
Rowington	A 1638-1998	1612-1895	5,8	1612-1812		Warwick	1790-1812		7F
Rugby	A 1621-1976	1739-1895	5,8	1621-1876		Rugby		1815-1837	3G
Ryton on Dunsmore	A 1539-1969	1755-1885	5,8	1539-1879		Rugby			5G
Salford Priors	A 1568-1970	1854-1895	5,8	1614-1701		Alcester			9D
Seckington	A 1644-1973	1612-1895	5,8	1813-1865		Tamworth			6K
Sheldon	B 1558-1967	1558-1895	5,8	1558-1858		Meriden			8H
Sherbourn	A 1587-1995	1737-1895	5,8	1587-1879		Warwick			6E(R)
Shilton	A 1695-1986	1750-1871	5,8,9	1695-1879		Foleshill			5H
Shirley (see Solihull)									8G
Shotteswell	A 1564-1979	1755-1895	5,8	1564-1979		Banbury			4C
Shrewley (see Hatton)									7F
Shustoke	A 1538-1989	1538-1875	5,8	1539-1841	1538-1812	Meriden			7I
Shuttington	A 1557-1995	1715-1895	5,8	1557-1933		Tamworth			6K
Snitterfield	A 1561-1969	1561-1895	5,8	1561-1953	1651-1675	Stratford on Avon	1790-1812		7E
Solihull	A 1538-1945	1538-1880	4,5,8	1538-1668		Solihull		1836-1837	8G
Southam	A 1539-1967	1539-1895	5,8	1539-1812		Southam			4E
Spernall	A 1562-1970	1701-1895	5,8	1562-1836		Alcester			8F
Stivichall	A 1648-1987	1824-1895	5,8,9	1813-1844		Warwick			5I
Stockingford	A 1824-1960	1824-1895	5,8	1824-1844		Nuneaton			5I
Stockton	A 1566-1998	1566-1895	5,8	1704-1876		Southam			4F
Stoke	A 1573-1942	1573-1895	5,8,9	1755-1918		Foleshill			5H
Stoneleigh	A 1634-1992	1754-1895	5,8,9	1634-1980		Warwick			6G
Stretton Baskerville (see Burton Bassett)									4I
Stretton on Dunsmore	A 1682-1958	1742-1895	5,8	1695-1935		Rugby			5G
Stretton on the Foss	A 1538-1978	1538-1862	5,8	1839-1978		Shipston on Stour		1787-1836	7C
Studley	A 1663-1970	1663-1895	5,8	1874-1908		Alcester			8F
Sutton Coldfield	A 1565-1924	1603-1895	5,8,9	1565-1710		Aston			8J
Sutton under Brailes	A 1605-1992	1605-1878	5,8	1578-1865	1578-1837	Shipston on Stour	1790-1812		5B
Tanworth-in-Arden	A 1558-1961	1558-1875	5,8	1558-1924		Solihull	1790-1837		8G
Temple Grafton	A 1612-1979	1754-1875	5,8	1612-1812	1651-1675	Stratford on Avon	1790-1812		8D
Tysoe	A 1575-1999	1768-1895	5,8	1575-1837		Shipston on Stour			5C
Ufton	A 1660-1981	1750-1885	5,8	1660-1840		Southam			5E
Ullenhall (see Wootton Warwen)		1855-1885	5,8	1546-1700		Stratford on Avon			8F
Upper Radbourn (ex.par.)						Southam			4E(V)
Upper Shuckburgh	A 1781-1993	1813-1846	5,8	1781-1865		Southam			3E
Walsgrave-on-Sowe	A 1538-1993	1748-1895	5,8	1558-1877		Foleshill			5H
Wappenbury	A 1753-1984	1753-1895	5,8	1753-1865		Warwick			5F
Warmington	A 1636-1979	1728-1895	5,7,8,9			Banbury			5D
Warwick								1784-1837	6F
St Mary	A 1611-1996	1754-1895	5,8	1611-1639		Warwick			6F
St Nicholas	A 1539-1991	1813-1895	5,8	1652-1861		Warwick			6F
Wasperton	A 1538-1980	1737-1895	5,8	1539-1841		Warwick			6E
Watergall (ex.par.)						Southam			4E(W)
Water Orton	A 1785-1992	1785-1885	5,8			Aston			7I
Weddington	A 1662-1989	1663-1895	5,8	1663-1886		Nuneaton	1790-1812		5I
Weethley	A 1572-1979	1813-1895	5,8	1813-1979		Alcester			9E
Welford (Glos.)									8D
Wellesbourne	A 1560-1970	1754-1897	5,8	1560-1942		Stratford on Avon			6E
Weston under Wetherley	A 1661-1984	1754-1895	5,8	1813-1984		Warwick			5F(J)
Whatcote	A 1571-1996	1571-1885	5,8	1572-1980		Shipston on Stour			6C
Whichford	A 1540-1995		5,8	1610-1700		Shipston on Stour			6B
Whitchurch	A 1561-1995	1813-1885	5,8	1562-1865	1651-1675	Stratford on Avon	1780-1837		7D
Whitnash	A 1679-1976	1679-1895	5,8	1758-1840		Warwick			5E
Wibtoft (see Claybrooke, Leics)									4H
Willey	A 1661-1992	1744-1895	5,8	1661-1865		Lutterworth			3H
Willoughby	A 1625-1991	1754-1885	5,8	1625-1878		Rugby			3F
Wills Pastures (ex.par.)						Southam			4E
Wilnecote (see Tamworth)									7J
Wishaw	A 1688-1925	1815-1832	5,8	1815-1832		Aston			7I
Withybrook	A 1653-1995	1809-1885	5,8	1653-1879		Foleshill			4H
Wixford	A 1539-1994		5,8	1540-1812		Alcester			9D
Wolfhamcote	A 1558-1982	1558-1895	5,8	1558-1768		Rugby			3F
Wolston	A 1558-1983	1735-1895	5,8	1665-1876		Rugby		1811-1837	4G
Wolverton	A 1680-1991	1614-1895	5,8	1813-1865		Stratford on Avon			7E(P)
Wolvey	A 1653-1992	1653-1895	5,8	1653-1979		Nuneaton			4H
Wootton Wawen	A 1546-1994	1546-1895	5,8	1546-1700		Stratford on Avon			8F
Wormleighton	A 1586-1990	1662-1895	5,8	1586-1972		Southam			4D
Wroxhall	A 1586-1993	1587-1885	5,8	1587-1963		Warwick			7G
Wyken	A 1600-1987	1600-1895	5,8,9	1662-1942		Foleshill			5H

WARWICKSHIRE

Original registers deposited at:
A = Warwick County Record Office, Priory Park, Cape Road, Warwick CV34 4JS
B = Birmingham City Archives, Central Library, Chamberlain Square, Birmingham B3 3HQ
C = Shakespeare Birthplace Trust Record Office, Henley Street, Stratford upon Avon CV37 6QW
D = Worcestershire Library and History Centre, Trinity Street, Worcester WR1 2PW
E = Oxfordshire Record Office, St. Luke's Church, Cowley, Oxford OX4 2EX

Study adjacent parishes in counties of Gloucestershire, Worcestershire, Staffordshire, Derbyshire, Leicestershire, Northamptonshire and Oxfordshire

Birmingham City Archives, Central Library, Chamberlain Square, Birmingham, B3 3HQ
Coventry Archives, Mandela House, Bayley Lane, Coventry, CV1 5RG
Warwickshire County Record Office, Priory Park, Cape Road, Warwick, CV34 4JS
The Shakespeare Birthplace Trust Record Office, Henley Street, Stratford-upon-Avon, CV37 6QW

The following useful indexes have been compiled – see Introduction
Census Indexes 1841 & 1851 – Birmingham & Midland SGH, c/o Mr M. Harrison, 121 Rowood Drive, Solihull, West Midlands B92 9LJ
Census Index 1851 (CD-Rom with Norfolk & Devon) – The Church of the Latter Day Saints, 399 Garretts Green Lane, Sheldon, Birmingham, B33 0UH
Census Index 1871 – Oxfordshire FHS, c/o Dr H. Kearsey, Windmill Place, Windmill Road, Minchinhampton, Stroud GL6 9EE
Census Index 1891 – Mr J. Wilson, 71 Heath Croft Road, Four Oaks, Sutton Coldfield, B75 6NQ
Census Index pre 1841 – Birmingham & Midland SGH, c/o Mrs H. Workman, 16 Bickenhill Road, Marston Green, Birmingham B37 7EL
Warwickshire (Rural) Marriage Index – Mrs D. Durrant, 21 Thornby Road, Kenilworth, Warwickshire CV8 2DT
Greater Birmingham Marriage Index 1801-1837 – Mrs P. Archer, 56 St Andrew's Road, Lillington, Leamington Spa, CV32 7EX
Greater Birmingham Burial Index 1538-1837 and 1838 onwards – Mr D. Pullar, 1 Kemble Close, Trent Park, Willenhall, West Midlands WV12 4DQ
Warwickshire Rural Burial Index 1813-1837 – Birmingham & Midland SGH, c/o Mrs D. Inett, 139 Cotwall End Road, Sedgley, Dudley, DY3 3YQ
Warwickshire Poor Law Index – Birmingham & Midland SGH, c/o Mrs H. Workman, 16 Bickenhill Road, Marston Green, Birmingham B37 7EL

Warwickshire's length from north to south is about 50 miles:its breadth from east to west nearly 35 miles. It is watered by three principal rivers:the Avon, Leam and Tame. The population in 1841 was 401,715;in 1851, 479,157; in 1861, 561,334; in 1871, 633,902; in 1881, 737,339.

The soils include gravel and clay. Flax is grown, dairy-farming is of great importance and sheep are raised. There was a great diversity of manufactures – ribbons, gauzes, other silk fabrics and thread, especially at Coventry; hardware, cutlery, steam-engines and firearms, especially at Birmingham; toys and glass.

The information in the Index is abbreviated, and may mislead the searcher if reference is not made to the details contained in the several publications listed in the Introduction. It is essential that users of this book check the appropriate works before making further enquiries.

WESTMORLAND

parish name	deposited original registers	I.G.I.	local census indexes	copies of registers at Soc. Gen.	Boyd's marriage index	1837-1851 Registration District	Pallot's marriage index	non-conform. records at P.R.O.	map ref.
Ambleside	1642-1977	1795-1876	5,8			Kendal			5D
Appleby								1816-1837	8I
St Lawrence	1694-1992	1661-1869	5,8			East Ward			8H
St Michael Bongate	1582-1975	1665-1870	8	1695-1690	1583-1677	East Ward			8I
Asby	1657-1971	1726-1874	5,8		1651-1700	East Ward			7H
Askham	1566-1991	1566-1877	5,8	1566-1812	1601-1700	West Ward	1790-1812		8F
Bampton	1637-1972	1637-1877	5,8	1641-1812	1626-1700	West Ward	1790-1812		7F
Barbon	1790-1991	1813-1870	5,8			Kendal			2H
Barton	1676-1961	1666-1877	5,8	1666-1830	1651-1700	West Ward	1790-1812		8E
Beetham	1604-1971	1813-1870	5,8			Kendal			2F
Birkbeck Fell (ex.par.)						West Ward			6G
Bolton	1647-1980	1647-1879	5,8	1647-1812		West Ward			8H
Brough	1559-1994	1556-1874	5,8	1556-1812	1601-1675	East Ward	1790-1812		7J
Brougham	1681-1992	1645-1877	5,8	1645-1812		West Ward			9G
Burnside	1717-1991	1813-1875	8	1764-1812		Kendal			4F
Burton in Kendal	1653-1951	1806-1875	5,8	1653-1726	1651-1719	Kendal			1F
Casterton	1833-1993	1833-1875	5,8			Kendal			2H
Cliburn	1565-1991	1565-1878	5,8	1565-1812		West Ward	1790-1812		8G
Clifton	1675-1991	1644-1875	5,8			West Ward			9F
Crook	1813-1993	1813-1870	5,8	1764-1812		Kendal			4E
Crosby Garrett	1559-1973	1559-1871	5,8	1559-1812		East Ward			6I
Crosby Ravensworth	1568-1982	1568-1874	5,8	1568-1812	1569-1651	West Ward			7G
Crosby Ravensworth Fell (ex.par.)						West Ward			6G
Crosscrake	1755-1979	1825-1869	8			Kendal			3F
Crosthwaite cum Lyth	1570-1980	1569-1871	8	1568-1812		Kendal	1790-1812		3E
Dufton	1571-1992	1665-1870	5,8	1571-1837		East Ward			8I
Firbank	1746-1969	1813-1867	5,8			Kendal			4H
Grasmere	1570-1971	1676-1875	5,8	1813-1818		Kendal			6C
Grayrigg	1730-1978	1813-1871	8	1764-1812		Kendal			4G
Great Musgrave	1558-1974	1665-1868	8			East Ward			7J
Helsington	1813-1993	1813-1875	5,8	1764-1812		Kendal			3F
Heversham	1605-1958	1694-1885	8			Kendal		1797-1835	2F
Holme	1842-1990	1856-1875	5,8			Kendal			2F
Hugill (Ings)	1732-1978	1813-1862	5,8	1764-1812		Kendal			4E
Hutton Roof	1799-1975	1813-1871	5,8			Kendal			1G
Kendal	1558-1953	1558-1845	5,8	1555-1823		Kendal		1687-1855	3F
Kentmere	1701-1993	1813-1875	5,8	1764-1812		Kendal			5E
Killington	1619-1969	1689-1873	5,8			Kendal			3H
Kirkby Lonsdale	1538-1973	1813-1858	5,8			Kendal		1816-1836	1G
Kirkby Stephen	1647-1990	1746-1861	5,8	1647-1812		East Ward			6J
Kirkby Thore	1593-1993	1674-1875	5,8			East Ward			9H
Langdale	1827-1985	1799-1871	5,8			Kendal			5C
Levens	1836-1979	1856-1875	8			Kendal			2F
Long Marton	1586-1997	1809-1872	5,8	1586-1837		East Ward			8H
Long Sleddale	1670-1993	1813-1861	8	1764-1812		Kendal			5F
Lowther	1540-1982	1539-1872	5,8	1539-1812		West Ward	1790-1812		8F
Mallerstang	1714-1996	1774-1875	5,8	1714-1839		East Ward			5J
Mansergh	1813-1992	1813-1870	5,8			Kendal			2G
Mardale	1684-1935	1793-1878	5,8			West Ward			6E
Martindale	1633-1982	1749-1875	5,8	1633-1904		West Ward	1790-1871		7E
Middleton	1671-1992	1670-1877	5,8	1670-1812	1676-1700	Kendal	1790-1812		3H
Milburn	1678-1992	1679-1877	5,8	1678-1812	1676-1700	East Ward	1790-1812		9H
Morland	1538-1993	1538-1879	5,8	1538-1743		West Ward			8G
Natland	1777-1898	1813-1870	5,8	1764-1812		Kendal			3F
New Hutton	1741-1979	1813-1875	5,8			Kendal			3G
Newbiggin	1571-1990	1571-1875	5,8	1571-1812		East Ward	1790-1812		9H
Old Hutton	1685-1982	1813-1862	5,8	1764-1812		Kendal			3G
Ormside	1560-1992	1762-1863	5,8			East Ward			7I
Orton	1596-1977	1746-1875	5,8	1877-1879		East Ward			6H
Over Staveley	1651-1971	1813-1857	5,8	1764-1812		Kendal			5E
Patterdale	1612-1986	1746-1872	5,8			West Ward			7D
Preston Patrick	1703-1976	1704-1870	8	1704-1800		Kendal			2G
Ravenstone Dale	1571-1988	1571-1875	5,8	1571-1813	1601-1800	East Ward	1790-1812	1775-1837	5I
Rydal	1826-1979	1831-1855	5,8			Kendal			5D
Selside	1753-1947	1813-1871	5,8	1753-1812		Kendal			5F
Shap	1559-1951	1559-1876	5,8	1559-1848	1601-1700	West Ward	1790-1837		7G
Soulby	1813-1990	1813-1875	5,8			East Ward			6J
Stainmore	1708-1985	1795-1856	5,8			East Ward			7K
Temple Sowerby	1669-1992	1774-1875	5,8	1700-1855		East Ward			9H
Thrimby	1813-1986		5,8			West Ward			8G
Troutbeck	1578-1932	1698-1874	5,8			Kendal	1579-1837		5D
Underbarrow	1735-1996	1813-1865	5,8	1764-1812		Kendal			4E
Warcop	1597-1991	1597-1870	5,8	1597-1744	1601-1700	East Ward		1757-1836	7I
Windermere	1613-1981	1694-1863	8			Kendal			4D
Winster	1720-1837	1813-1871	8	1720-1882		Kendal			4E
Witherslack	1671-1969	1694-1875	5,8			Kendal			2E

WESTMORLAND

Original registers deposited at:
Cumbria Record Office (Kendal), County Offices, Kendal LA9 4RQ

Study adjacent parishes in counties of Cumberland, Durham, Yorkshire and Lancashire

Cumbria Rcord Office, County Offices, Kendal, LA9 4RQ

The following useful indexes have been compiled – see Introduction
Census Index 1851 – Mr D. Lowis, 6 Doomgate, Appleby-in-Westmorland, Cumbria, CA16 6RB for North Westmorland.
Census Index 1851 – Cumbria FHS, c/o Mrs M. Russell, Ulpha, 32 Granada Road, Denton, Manchester, M34 2LJ
Westmorland and North Lancashire Marriage Index 1700-1837 – Mr S.G. Smith, 59 Friar Road, Orpington, Kent, BR5 2BW
Westmorland Marriage Database – Mr P.R. Joiner, The Spital, Yarm-on-Tees, Yorkshire, TS15 9EX

Westmorland is about 40 miles in length from north-east to south-west and varies in breadth from 16 to nearly 40 miles. It is watered by five principal rivers: the Eden, Eimot, Loder, Ken and Lune. The population in 1841 was 56,454; in 1851, 58,287; in 1861, 60,809; in 1871, 65,010; in 1881, 64,191.

The soil is mainly dry gravelly mould but clay and a heavy moist soil also occur. Produce included oats and smaller quantities of wheat and barley. Cattle and sheep were raised and there was dairy-farming. Copper was mined and there were slate, limestone and marble quarries. Manufactures were principally woollen goods, particularly the coarser kinds.

The information in the Index is abbreviated, and may mislead the searcher if reference is not made to the details contained in the several publications listed in the Introduction. It is essential that users of this book check the appropriate works before making further enquiries.

WILTSHIRE

parish name	deposited original registers	I.G.I.	local census indexes	copies of registers at Soc. Gen.	Boyd's marriage index	1837-1851 Registration District	Pallot's marriage index	non-conform. records at P.R.O.	map ref.
Aldbourne	A 1637-1992		5,7,8	1637-1881		Hungerford			3J
Alderbury	A 1606-1985		5,7,8,9	1800-1837	1606-1671	Alderbury			3D
Alderton	A 1606-1991		5,7,8	1605-1812	1651-1675	Malmesbury	1790-1812		7K
All Cannings	A 1578-1992	1577-1885	5,7,8	1578-1813		Devizes	1790-1813	1829-1837	4I
Allington	A 1655-1992	1655-1895	5,7,8,9	1623-1837	1651-1765	Amesbury	1790-1812		3F
Alton Barnes	A 1592-1987		5,7,8	1592-1838	1651-1675	Devizes	1790-1812		4H(Ae)
Alton Priors	A 1664-1984		5,7,8	1605-1838		Pewsey			4I(Ad)
Alvediston	A 1592-1992	1592-1837	5,7,8,9	1592-1908		Tisbury			6D
Amesbury	A 1579-1987	1579-1895	5,7,8,9	1599-1878	1599-1665	Amesbury			4F
Ansty	A 1654-1992	1752-1856	5,7,8	1655-1838		Tisbury			6D
Ashley	B 1664-1991		5,7,8	1607-1837	1658-1675	Tetbury	1790-1812		6M
Ashton Keynes	A 1582-1967		5,7,8	1582-1840		Cricklade			5M
Atworth	A 1645-1993		5,7,8,9	1585-1837		Bradford-on-Avon		1790-1836	7I
Avebury	A 1679-1999		5,7,8	1621-1837		Marlborough		1807-1837	4I
Barford	A 1653-1979		5,7,8,9	1623-1755		Wilton			5E
Baverstock	A 1559-1996		5,7,8	1559-1837	1651-1675	Wilton	1790-1812		5E(Ss)
Baydon	A 1673-1999	1673-1885	5,7,8	1578-1837		Hungerford			2J
Beechingstoke	A 1566-1987		5,7,8	1566-1837	1651-1675	Devizes	1790-1812		4H(Em)
Bemerton	A 1657-1950		5,7,8	1631-1837	1651-1675	Wilton	1790-1812		4E(Th)
Berwick Bassett	A 1674-1970	1674-1875	5,7,8	1580-1875		Marlborough			4J(r)
Berwick St James	A 1731-1994	1731-1837	5,7,8	1609-1837		Wilton			5F
Berwick St John	A 1559-1965	1712-1895	5,7,8,9	1559-1965	1559-1642	Tisbury			6C
Berwick St Leonard	A 1723-1992	1723-1895	5,7,8,9	1723-1961		Tisbury			6E(Sp)
Biddestone	A 1688-1993	1688-1885	5,7,8	1605-1837		Chippenham			7J
Bishops Canning	A 1591-1973	1591-1895	5,7,8	1591-1837		Devizes	1790-1812		5I
Bishopstone (Salisbury)	A 1601-1987	1636-1880	5,7,8	1606-1842		Wilton			5D
Bishopstone (Swindon)	A 1573-1952		5,7,8,9	1573-1899		Highworth			2K
Bishopstrow	A 1685-1992		5,7,8	1611-1890		Warminster			6G(Ew)
Blackland	A 1757-1992	1757-1835	5,7,8	1594-1835		Calne			5I
Blunsdon St Andrew	A 1654-1992		5,7,8,9	1650-1839		Highworth			4L
Boscombe	A 1696-1992		5,7,8	1624-1840	1651-1675	Amesbury	1790-1812		3E
Bowerchalke	A 1694-1998	1701-1895	5,7,8,9	1701-1837		Wilton			5C
Box	A 1538-1965	1538-1895	5,7,8	1538-1951		Chippenham			8I
Boyton	A 1560-1991		5,7,8	1560-1841	1651-1675	Warminster	1790-1837		6E
Bradford on Avon	A 1579-1977	1566-1880	5,7,8	1566-1837		Bradford-on-Avon		1772-1857	8H
Bramshaw	C 1597-1993	1597-1812	5,7,8	1597-1835		New Forest			2C
Bratton	A 1542-1999	1542-1877	5,7,8,9	1542-1837	1651-1675	Westbury	1790-1837		7G
Bremhill	A 1590-1990	1590-1882	5,7,8	1590-1837		Calne		1748-1840	6J
Bremilham	A 1813-1992	1813-1840	5,7,8	1677-1904		Malmesbury			7K(Uy)
Brinkworth	A 1653-1963	1653-1895	5,7,8	1572-1925	1653-1675	Malmesbury	1790-1812	1829-1837	5K
Britford	A 1572-1991		5,7,8,9	1573-1880	1651-1675	Alderbury	1790-1812		4D
Brixton Deverill	A 1653-1980		5,7,8,9	1655-1838		Warminster			7E
Broad Blunsdon	A 1679-1996		5,7,8,9	1585-1840		Highworth			3L
Broad Chalke	A 1538-1972	1538-1895	5,7,8,9	1538-1780		Wilton		1808-1836	5D
Broad Hinton	A 1612-1999	1603-1885	5,7,8	1603-1837		Marlborough			4J
Brokenborough	A 1697-1992		5,7,8	1609-1859		Malmesbury			6L
Bromham	A 1560-1989	1567-1880	5,7,8	1560-1837		Devizes	1790-1800		6I
Broughton Gifford	A 1665-1991	1665-1885	5,7,8,9	1622-1978		Bradford-on-Avon			7I(X)
Bulford	A 1654-1986	1654-1880	5,7,8	1608-1837	1651-1675	Amesbury	1790-1812	1806-1837	3F
Burbage	A 1561-1974		5,7,8,9	1561-1837		Pewsey			3H
Burcombe	A 1682-1998		5,7,8,9	1611-1837	1683-1812	Wilton			5E
Buttermere	A 1720-1967	1720-1842	5,7,8	1786-1842		Hungerford			1H
Calne	A 1537-1994	1760-1855	5,7,8	1538-1812		Calne			6J
Calstone Wellington	A 1760-1980	1760-1863	5,7,8	1760-1836		Calne		1835-1837	5I(k)
Castle Combe	A 1653-1996	1653-1857	5,7,8	1602-1892		Chippenham		1810-1836	7J(S)
Castle Eaton	A 1549-1994		5,7,8,9	1549-1840	1651-1675	Highworth	1790-1812		3M
Chalfield Magna	A 1545-1993		5,7,8	1605-1848		Bradford-on-Avon			7I
Charlton (Malmesbury)	A 1661-1991		5,7,8,9	1607-1859		Malmesbury			6L
Charlton (Pewsey)	A 1695-1986	1695-1838	5,7,8	1611-1986		Pewsey	1790-1812		4H(Es)
Cherhill	A 1690-1990	1690-1868	5,7,8	1588-1837		Calne			5I
Chicklade	A 1721-1989	1721-1812	5,7,8	1721-1837		Tisbury			7E(Sn)
Chilmark	A 1653-1996		5,7,8,9	1611-1837		Tisbury			6E
Chilton Foliat	A 1569-1994	1568-1895	5,7,8	1568-1837		Hungerford			1J
Chippenham	A 1578-1983	1570-1884	5,7,8	1578-1912		Chippenham		1789-1837	7J
Chirton	A 1579-1987	1579-1873	5,7,8	1579-1987	1651-1675	Devizes	1790-1812		5H
Chisledon	A 1641-1987		5,7,8,9	1605-1842	1651-1675	Highworth	1790-1812		3K
Chitterne All Saints	A 1653-1993		5,7,8,9	1653-1921		Warminster			5F
Chitterne St Mary	A 1653-1993		5,7,8,9	1653-1862		Warminster			6F(Re)
Chittoe	A 1846-1978	1846-1880	5,7,8			Devizes			6I
(see also Bishops Canning)									
Cholderton	A 1652-1992		5,7,8	1652-1974	1664-1675	Amesbury	1790-1812		3F
Christian Malford	A 1653-1988	1605-1837	5,7,8	1653-1837	1653-1675	Chippenham	1790-1812	1809-1836	6K
Chute	A 1580-1996		5,7,8	1580-1996		Andover			2G
Chute Forest (ex.par.)	A 1871-1971		5,7,8,9			Andover			1G
Clarendon Park (ex.par.)			5,7,8,9			Alderbury			3E
Cliffe Pypard	A 1576-1999		5,7,8	1576-1874	1651-1675	Cricklade	1790-1837		5J
Codford St Mary	A 1653-1991	1623-1880	5,7,8	1800-1837		Warminster		1813-1836	6F
Codford St Peter	A 1597-1991	1597-1879	5,7,8,9	1597-1900	1682-1837	Warminster			6F
Colerne	A 1560-1986	1560-1895	5,7,8	1560-1837	1661-1675	Chippenham	1790-1812	1801-1837	8J
Collingbourne Ducis	A 1653-1994		5,7,8,9	1654-1835	1654-1675	Pewsey	1790-1837		2G
Collingbourne Kingston	A 1653-1986	1799-1877	5,7,8,9	1606-1837		Pewsey			3H
Compton Basset	A 1558-1982		5,7,8	1559-1982		Calne			5J
Compton Chamberlain	A 1538-1990		5,7,8,9	1800-1837		Wilton			5D(Ta)
Coombe Bisset	A 1637-1988	1558-1882	5,7,8,9	1636-1840		Alderbury			4D(Us)
Corsham	A 1563-1995	1563-1895	5,7,8	1563-1837		Chippenham		1787-1836	7I
Corsley	A 1686-1978		5,7,8,9	1608-1838		Warminster		1765-1837	8F
Cricklade St Mary	A 1683-1954	1683-1895	5,7,8	1605-1840		Cricklade			4L(h)
Cricklade St Sampson	A 1672-1969	1672-1895	5,7,8	1599-1840		Cricklade			4L
Crudwell	A 1659-1995		5,7,8	1662-1812	1662-1675	Malmesbury	1790-1812		6L

parish name	deposited original registers	I.G.I.	local census indexes	copies of registers at Soc. Gen.	Boyd's marriage index	1837-1851 Registration District	Pallot's marriage index	non-conform. records at P.R.O.	map ref.
Dauntsey	A 1653-1973	1653-1895	5,7,8	1605-1950		Malmesbury			6K
Devizes					1651-1675			1772-1837	5H
St John the Baptist	A 1559-1959	1888-1895	5,7,8	1559-1837		Devizes	1790-1837		6H(Z)
St Mary the Virgin	A 1569-1971		5,7,8	1559-1837		Devizes			5H(Y)
Dilton	A 1585-1921	1556-1895	5,7,8,9	1585-1869		Westbury			7G
Dinton	A 1558-1997		5,7,8,9	1754-1799		Wilton			5E
Ditteridge	A 1584-1993		5,7,8	1584-1840		Chippenham			8I
Donhead St Andrew	A 1655-1922		5,7,8	1622-1837		Tisbury			6D
Donhead St Mary	A 1678-1981		5,7,8	1621-1840		Tisbury		1800-1837	7D
Downton	A 1601-1980	1601-1895	5,7,8	1601-1927		Alderbury		1767-1837	3D
Draycot Cerne	A 1691-1994	1691-1875	5,7,8	1604-1837		Chippenham			6K(P)
Draycot Foliat	A 1817-1830		5,7,8			Highworth			3J
Durnford	A 1574-1966	1574-1864	5,7,8,9	1574-1837	1574-1719	Amesbury			4E
Durrington	A 1591-1965		5,7,8	1591-1837	1651-1675	Amesbury	1790-1812		4F
East Coulston	A 1714-1992		5,7,8,9	1622-1838		Westbury			6H(Eu)
East Kennett	A 1655-1991		5,7,8	1607-1836		Marlborough			4I(Ab)
East Knoyle	A 1538-1990	1538-1874	5,7,8	1538-1907	1651-1675	Mere	1790-1812	1821-1837	7E
Easton Royal	A 1580-1992	1580-1741	5,7,8,9	1580-1837		Pewsey			3H
Ebbesbourne Wake	A 1653-1991	1653-1841	5,7,8,9	1622-1841		Wilton		1783-1837	6C
Edington	A 1678-1990	1695-1885	5,7,8,9	1597-1929		Westbury			6G
Eisey	A 1574-1947		5,7,8	1574-1864	1651-1675	Cricklade	1790-1837		4M
Enford	A 1631-1946		5,7,8	1800-1812		Pewsey			4G
Erlestoke	A 1689-1996	1578-1880	5,7,8	1578-1850		Devizes			6G
Etchilhampton	A 1630-1992	1606-1895	5,7,8	1630-1982		Devizes	1790-1812		5H(f)
Everleigh	A 1598-1984		5,7,8,9	1605-1984		Pewsey			3H
Fifield Bavant	A 1696-1991	1622-1895	5,7,8	1696-1922		Wilton			5D(Tb)
Figheldean	A 1653-1993	1660-1880	5,7,8,9	1654-1837		Amesbury			3G
Fisherton Anger	A 1653-1999	1627-1895	5,7,8	1608-1975		Alderbury			4D(Um)
Fisherton Delamere	A 1561-1992		5,7,8	1561-1837		Wilton			6E
Fittleton	A 1624-1992		5,7,8	1778-1837		Pewsey			3G
Fonthill Bishop	A 1754-1998	1754-1885	5,7,8	1624-1949		Tisbury			6E(Sr)
Fonthill Gifford	A 1661-1891	1661-1865	5,7,8	1622-1891	1667-1718	Tisbury			6E(Su)
Fovant	A 1541-1991		5,7,8,9	1541-1837		Wilton		1816-1836	5D
Foxley	A 1713-1992	1713-1835	5,7,8	1605-1860		Malmesbury			7K(D)
Froxfield	A 1561-1990		5,7,8	1561-1889		Hungerford			2I
Fugglestone St Peter	A 1568-1991	1568-1895	5,7,8,9	1568-1879	1651-1675	Wilton	1790-1837		4E(Th)
Fyfield	A 1732-1995	1813-1878	5,7,8	1605-1969		Marlborough			4I(Aa)
Garsdon	A 1682-1991		5,7,8	1603-1865		Malmesbury			6L(F)
Great Bedwin	A 1538-1992	1754-1895	5,7,8	1539-1956		Hungerford			2H
Great Cheverell	A 1653-1987	1653-1895	5,7,8	1622-1987		Devizes			6G
Great Somerford	A 1707-1992	1605-1875	5,7,8	1605-1837	1651-1675	Malmesbury	1790-1812		6K(K)
Great Wishford	A 1558-1983	1558-1895	5,7,8,9	1558-1838		Wilton			5E(Rj)
Grey Easton	A 1725-1991		5,7,8	1837-1880		Malmesbury			7L(C)
Grittleton	A 1573-1993		5,7,8	1570-1859	1651-1675	Chippenham	1790-1812		7K
Groveley wood (ex.par.)						Wilton			5E(St)
Ham	A 1720-1993	1720-1885	5,7,8	1604-1880		Hungerford			1H
Hankerton	A 1699-1994		5,7,8	1607-1859		Malmesbury	1790-1837		6L
Hannington	A 1571-1990		5,7,8,9	1571-1855		Highworth			3L
Hardenhuish	A 1730-1991	1607-1895	5,7,8	1730-1958		Chippenham			7J(V)
Heddington	A 1538-1993	1538-1885	5,7,8	1539-1836		Calne			5I
Heytesbury	A 1653-1999	1582-1895	5,7,8,9	1582-1837	1582-1675	Warminster	1790-1837	1811-1837	6F
Highway	A 1742-1990	1606-1895	5,7,8	1609-1833		Calne			5J
Highworth	A 1539-1975	1743-1895	5,7,8	1538-1840		Highworth		1821-1836	3L
Hill Deverill	A 1661-1981		5,7,8	1587-1837		Warminster			7F(Rf)
Hilmarton	A 1645-1980	1645-1878	5,7,8	1648-1837		Calne			5J
Hilperton	A 1694-1992	1622-1880	5,7,8	1622-1861		Melksham			7H(d)
Hindon	A 1599-1945	1599-1886	5,7,8	1599-1945		Tisbury			7E(Sm)
Hippenscombe (ex.par.)						Hungerford			2H(Et)
Holt	A 1568-1988	1845-1880	5,7,8,9	1568-1965		Bradford-on-Avon			7H
Homington	A 1675-1991	1621-1880	5,7,8	1675-1840		Alderbury			4D(Ut)
Horningsham	A 1561-1991	1561-1895	5,7,8,9	1561-1857		Warminster		1784-1837	8F
Huish	A 1603-1987		5,7,8,9	1684-1836		Pewsey	1790-1812		4I(Af)
Hullavington	A 1654-1928		5,7,8	1605-1836		Malmesbury		1825-1836	7K
Hungerford (see Berks)									1I
Idmiston	A 1577-1990	1577-1895	5,7,8,9	1577-1975	1651-1675	Amesbury	1790-1812		3E
Imber	A 1709-1967		5,7,8,9	1623-1976		Warminster			6G
Inglesham	A 1589-1972		5,7,8,9	1589-1972		Highworth			3M
Keevil	A 1559-1993		5,7,8,9	1559-1954		Westbury			6H
Kemble	B 1679-1950		5,7,8	1605-1837	1679-1812	Cirencester	1790-1812		6M
Kingston Deverill	A 1706-1982		5,7,8,9	1608-1836		Mere	1790-1812		8E
Kingswood (see Gloucs)									
Kington St Michael	A 1563-1966		5,7,8	1563-1837	1651-1675	Chippenham	1790-1837		7J
Knook	A 1687-1983	1687-1895	5,7,8	1591-1837		Warminster	1790-1837		6F
Lacock	A 1559-1989		5,7,8	1559-1879		Chippenham			7I
Landford	A 1671-1986	1757-1876	5,7,8,9	1608-1837		Alderbury			2C
Langley Burrell	A 1607-1990	1607-1874	5,7,8	1609-1978		Chippenham			6J
Latton	A 1576-1992		5,7,8	1576-1925	1651-1675	Cricklade	1790-1837		4M
Laverstock & Ford	A 1726-1982		5,7,8,9	1726-1977		Alderbury	1790-1812		4E(Tf)
Lea & Cleverton	A 1751-1991		5,7,8	1605-1865		Malmesbury			6K(G)
Leigh	A 1683-1972		5,7,8	1605-1865		Cricklade			5L
Leigh Delamere	A 1712-1991		5,7,8	1605-1875		Chippenham	1790-1812		7K(M)
Liddington	A 1692-1992	1692-1872	5,7,8,9	1604-1842		Highworth			3K
Limpley Stoke	A 1707-1986		5,7,8,9	1611-1837		Bradford-on-Avon			8H
Little Bedwin	A 1722-1959		5,7,8	1591-1933		Hungerford			2I
Little Cheverell	A 1653-1997	1755-1895	5,7,8	1622-1987		Devizes			6G(Ev)
Little Hinton	A 1654-1946	1605-1837	5,7,8	1605-1840		Highworth			3K
Little Langford	A 1699-1991		5,7,8	1699-1835		Wilton			5E(Rh)
Little Somerford	A 1708-1991	1708-1875	5,7,8	1605-1837	1651-1675	Malmesbury	1790-1812		6K(J)
Littleton Drew	A 1706-1992		5,7,8	1605-1900		Chippenham		1825-1837	7K(L)

WILTSHIRE

parish name	deposited original registers	I.G.I.	local census indexes	copies of registers at Soc. Gen.	Boyd's marriage index	1837-1851 Registration District	Pallot's marriage index	non-conform. records at P.R.O.	map ref.
Longbridge Deverill	A 1682-1975	1607-1880	5,7,8	1682-1837		Warminster			7F
Long Newnton	B 1648-1907		5,7,8	1609-1836	1653-1675	Tetbury	1790-1812		7L
Luckington	A 1572-1991		5,7,8	1574-1860	1651-1675	Malmesbury	1790-1837		8K
Ludgershall		1609-1895	5,7,8,9	1600-1837		Andover		1817-1837	2G
Lydiard Millicent	A 1579-1992		5,7,8	1579-1860	1651-1675	Cricklade	1790-1837		4K(m)
Lydiard Tregoze	A 1666-1992		5,7,8	1666-1967		Cricklade			5K
Lyneham	A 1653-1990		5,7,8	1605-1837		Cricklade		1810-1836	5K
Maddington	A 1652-1975	1652-1895	5,7,8,9	1610-1836		Amesbury			5F
Maiden Bradley	A 1662-1968	1662-1885	5,7,8	1666-1837		Mere		1825-1837	8F
Malmesbury	A 1590-1992		5,7,8	1590-1837		Malmesbury		1794-1840	6K
Manningford Abbas	A 1538-1982		5,7,8,9	1538-1863		Pewsey			4H(Ep)
Manningford Bruce	A 1657-1986		5,7,8	1605-1837		Pewsey			4H(En)
Marden	A 1684-1986	1685-1841	5,7,8	1622-1971		Devizes			4H
Market Lavington	A 1673-1988	1673-1876	5,7,8	1622-1839	1673-1675	Devizes	1790-1812	1797-1836	5H
Marlborough								1807-1837	3I
St Mary the Virgin	A 1602-1995	1602-1874		1581-1837	1651-1675	Marlborough	1790-1812		3I(u)
St Peter & St Paul	A 1611-1975	1611-1855		1607-1846	1651-1675	Marlborough	1790-1812		3I(y)
Marston Meysey	B 1742-1974		5,7,8	1742-1974		Cirencester			4M
Martin	C 1589-1978		5,7,8	1813-1837		Fordingbridge			5C
Melchet Park (ex.par.)						Romsey			2C
Melksham	A 1568-1992	1568-1895	5,7,8,9	1568-1903		Melksham		1776-1837	7I
Mere	A 1561-1996	1561-1895	5,7,8,9	1561-1837	1651-1675	Mere	1790-1812	1796-1837	8E
Mildenhall	A 1560-1996		5,7,8	1560-1880		Marlborough			3I
Milford (see Laverstock)									4E(Tj)
Milston	A 1540-1997		5,7,8	1539-1838	1651-1675	Amesbury	1790-1812		3G
Milton Lilborne	A 1686-1999	1686-1812	5,7,8,9	1602-1837		Pewsey			3H
Minety	A 1663-1978		5,7,8	1605-1881	1663-1675	Malmesbury	1790-1812		5L
Monkton Deverill	A 1695-1980		5,7,8	1608-1833		Mere	1790-1812		7E(Rk)
Monkton Farleigh	A 1570-1982	1623-1880	5,7,8,9	1570-1837		Bradford-on-Avon			8I
Netheravon	A 1582-1992		5,7,8	1579-1837		Pewsey		1814-1837	4G
Netherhampton	A 1755-1992	1755-1895	5,7,8,9	1622-1837		Wilton			4D(Tk)
Nettleton	A 1557-1981	1551-1895	5,7,8	1556-1837		Chippenham		1827-1836	8K
Newton Tony	A 1568-1991	1568-1895	5,7,8	1568-1977	1651-1675	Amesbury	1790-1812		3F
North Bradley	A 1646-1994	1661-1887	5,7,8,9	1603-1922		Westbury		1779-1837	7H
North Newnton	A 1755-1987		5,7,8,9	1767-1839		Pewsey			4H(Er)
North Tidworth	A 1700-1983		5,7,8			Andover			3G
North Wraxall	A 1677-1992	1677-1885	5,7,8	1677-1837		Chippenham			8J
Norton Bavant	A 1653-1993	1653-1895	5,7,8	1622-1842		Warminster	1790-1812(?)		6F(Ey)
Norton Coleparle	A 1663-1992		5,7,8	1606-1837	1663-1675	Malmesbury	1790-1812(?)		7K(H)
Nunton & Bodenham	A 1672-1974		5,7,8	1624-1837		Alderbury			3D(Uu)
Oaksey	A 1670-1981		5,7,8		1670-1782	Malmesbury			6L
Odstock	A 1541-1991		5,7,8	1541-1839		Alderbury			4D
Ogbourne St Andrew	A 1538-1978		5,7,8	1603-1696		Marlborough			3J
Ogbourne St George	A 1663-1997	1663-1875	5,7,8			Marlborough			3J
Orcheston St George	A 1647-1989	1756-1875	5,7,8,9	1609-1836		Amesbury			5F(Rb)
Orcheston St Mary	A 1688-1993	1608-1875	5,7,8	1608-1835		Amesbury			5G(Ra)
Overton	A 1682-1995	1682-1879	5,7,8	1605-1907		Marlborough			4I
Patney	A 1592-1990	1592-1840	5,7,8	1592-1986	1651-1675	Devizes	1790-1812		5H(Aj)
Pertwood	A 1813-1923	1840-1895	5,7,8	1813-1923		Mere			7E(So)
Pewsey	A 1568-1985		5,7,8	1568-1840		Pewsey			3H
Pewsham (ex.par.)						Chippenham			6J
Pitton & Farley	A 1661-1990		5,7,8,9	1669-1837		Alderbury			3E
Plaitford	C 1710-1992		5,7,8	1622-1762		Romsey			2C(Uv)
Poole Keynes	B 1632-1985		5,7,8	1605-1837		Cirencester			5M(A)
Porton	A 1754-1990	1754-1895	5,7,8	1754-1920		Amesbury	1790-1812		3E
Potterne	A 1556-1999	1653-1895	5,7,8	1558-1907		Devizes			6H
Poulshot	A 1627-1996	1627-1885	5,7,8	1596-1945		Devizes			6H
Preshute	A 1606-1952	1607-1875	5,7,8	1606-1839	1651-1675	Marlborough	1790-1812		3I
Purton	A 1558-1986		5,7,8	1558-1876	1651-1675	Cricklade	1790-1812		5L
Ramsbury	A 1678-1985	1678-1875	5,7,8	1597-1945		Hungerford			2J
Rodbourne Cheney	A 1653-1947		5,7,8	1605-1837		Highworth			4L
Rollstone	A 1654-1992	1654-1829	5,7,8,9	1608-1829	1654-1675	Amesbury	1790-1812		4F(Rc)
Rowde	A 1606-1990	1606-1895	5,7,8	1606-1924		Devizes			6H
Rushall	A 1652-1991	1652-1837	5,7,8,9	1652-1837		Pewsey			4G
Salisbury								1723-1857	4D (Um)
Cathedral			5,7,8,9	1570-1837	1651-1675	Salisbury	1790-1812		4D(Um)
St Edmund	A 1559-1973	1813-1895	5,7,8,9	1559-1837	1651-1675	Salisbury	1790-1837		4D(Um)
St Martin	A 1559-1943	1559-1885	5,7,8,9	1559-1812	1651-1675	Salisbury	1790-1812		4D(Um)
St Thomas	A 1570-1943		5,7,8,9	1570-1812	1651-1675	Salisbury	1790-1812		4D(Um)
Savernake (ex.par.)	A 1854-1970	1861-1885				Marlborough			3I
Seagry	A 1610-1991		5,7,8	1611-1837		Chippenham			6K
Sedgehill	A 1755-1992	1755-1837	5,7,8,9	1607-1837		Mere			7D
Seend	A 1612-1996	1612-1874	5,7,8,9	1612-1969		Melksham			6H
Semington	A 1586-1981		5,7,8,9	1586-1973		Melksham			7H(e)
Semley	A 1708-1995	1709-1885	5,7,8,9	1708-1851		Tisbury		1821-1837	7D
Sevenhampton (see Highworth)				1649-1663		Highworth			3L
Shalbourne	A 1677-1996	1665-1840	5,7,8	1587-1837		Hungerford			2H
Sherrington	A 1677-1991		5,7,8	1608-1841		Warminster			6E(Rg)
Sherston Magna	A 1653-1969		5,7,8	1601-1837	1653-1675	Malmesbury	1790-1837		7L
Shorncote	B 1708-1837	1705-1837	5,7,8	1622-1837		Cirencester	1790-1812		5M
Shrewton	A 1557-1986	1557-1873	5,7,8,9			Amesbury			4F
Slaughterford	A 1813-1992	1814-1835	5,7,8	1605-1837		Chippenham			7J(U)
Somerford Keynes	B 1560-1927	1560-1812	5,7,8	1561-1836		Cirencester			5M(B)
Sopworth	A 1698-1992		5,7,8	1697-1837		Malmesbury	1790-1812		8L
Southbroom	A 1572-1979	1572-1883	5,7,8	1572-1837	1651-1675	Devizes	1790-1817		5I
South Damerham	C 1678-1968		5,7,8	1622-1799		Fordingbridge			4C
South Marston			5,7,8	1539-1840		Highworth			3L
South Newton	A 1695-1994	1695-1885	5,7,8,9	1604-1984		Wilton			4E
South Wraxall	A 1672-1995		5,7,8,9	1622-1835		Bradford-on-Avon			8I

WILTSHIRE

parish name	deposited original registers	I.G.I.	local census indexes	copies of registers at Soc. Gen.	Boyd's marriage index	1837-1851 Registration District	Pallot's marriage index	non-conform. records at P.R.O.	map ref.
Stanton Fitzwarren	A 1542-1992		5,7,8,9	1542-1840		Highworth			3L(j)
Stanton St Bernard	A 1568-1986		5,7,8	1568-1836		Devizes			4I(Ac)
Stanton St Quintin	A 1679-1993		5,7,8	1679-1843		Chippenham			7K(N)
Stapleford	A 1633-1992	1637-1837	5,7,8,9	1637-1837		Wilton			5E
Staverton	A 1673-1992		5,7,8	1641-1837		Melksham			7H(a)
Steeple Ashton	A 1538-1987		5,7,8,9	1538-1900		Westbury			7H
Steeple Langford	A 1674-1980		5,7,8			Wilton			5E
Stert	A 1579-1986	1579-1838	5,7,8	1579-1986	1651-1675	Devizes	1790-1812		5H(Ah)
Stockton	A 1589-1992		5,7,8,9	1590-1837	1651-1675	Warminster	1790-1812		6E
Stourton	A 1570-1998	1570-1895	5,7,8,9	1570-1836		Mere	1790-1800		8E
Stratford Subcastle	A 1654-1967		5,7,8,9	1654-1837		Alderbury	1790-1812		4E(Tg)
Stratford Tony	A 1562-1988		5,7,8	1562-1837	1562-1776	Alderbury			4D(Ur)
Stratton St Margaret	A 1608-1982		5,7,8	1608-1840		Highworth			3L
Sutton Benger	A 1653-2000		5,7,8	1654-1838		Chippenham			6J(Q)
Sutton Mandeville	A 1654-1995		5,7,8,9	1622-1837		Tisbury			6D(Sy)
Sutton Veny	A 1564-1998	1564-1884	5,7,8,9	1653-1837	1599-1637	Warminster		1801-1837	7F
Swallowcliffe	A 1737-1998	1813-1877	5,7,8	1585-1837		Tisbury			6D(Sw)
Swindon	A 1623-1992		5,7,8	1589-1840		Highworth		1804-1856	4K
Teffont Evias	A 1683-1994		5,7,8,9	1623-1835		Tisbury			6E(Sv)
Teffont Magna (see Dinton)				1800-1837		Tisbury			6E
Tidcombe	A 1731-1992	1731-1885	5,7,8	1639-1992					1H
Tilshead	A 1664-1927	1603-1870	5,7,8,9	1603-1837		Amesbury			5G
Tisbury	A 1563-1991	1599-1880	5,7,8	1563-1660		Tisbury		1723-1837	6D
Tockenham	A 1653-1999	1620-1871	5,7,8	1620-1836		Cricklade			5K(R)
Tollard Royal	A 1688-1951	1609-1880	5,7,8,9	1609-1840		Tisbury			6C
Trowbridge	A 1539-1987	1538-1875	5,7,8,9	1538-1971		Melksham		1757-1837	7H
Tytherton Kellaways	A 1815-1994		5,7,8			Chippenham			6J(W)
Tytherton Lucas	A 1813-2000	1813-1837	5,7,8	1578-1912		Warminster			6J
Upavon	A 1687-1986	1687-1875	5,7,8,9	1625-1837		Pewsey			4H
Upton Lovell	A 1653-1992		5,7,8,9	1611-1837		Warminster			6F(Rd)
Upton Scudamore	A 1654-1992	1654-1837	5,7,8,9	1605-1992		Warminster			7G
Urchfont	A 1538-1989	1632-1895	5,7,8	1538-1926	1651-1675	Devizes	1790-1812		5H
Wanborough	A 1582-1990		5,7,8,9	1582-1837		Highworth			3K
Wardour (see Tisbury)									6D
Warminster	A 1556-1999		5,7,8,9	1587-1837				1762-1837	7F
Christchurch	A 1831-1992	1831-1880				Warminster			7F
Westbury	A 1556-1998		5,7,8	1556-1837		Westbury		1769-1837	7G
West Dean	A 1754-1990	1754-1875	5,7,8,9	1754-1947		Stockbridge			2D
West Grimstead	A 1717-1983		5,7,8	1622-1983		Alderbury			3D(Up)
West Harnham	A 1567-1987	1567-1880	5,7,8,9			Alderbury			4D(Un)
West Kington	A 1754-1990	1754-1885	5,7,8			Chippenham			8J
West Knoyle	A 1718-1991	1718-1895	5,7,8,9	1607-1837		Mere	1790-1837		7E
West Lavington	A 1598-1988	1598-1876	5,7,8	1597-1907		Devizes			5G
Westport St Mary	A 1678-1944		5,7,8	1605-1837		Malmesbury			6K(E)
West Wellow	C 1570-1940		5,7,8	1570-1940		Romsey	1790-1837		2C
Westwood	A 1666-1978	1666-1876	5,7,8	1671-1832		Bradford-on-Avon			8H
Whaddon	A 1653-1996		5,7,8,9	1582-1838		Melksham			7H(b)
Whiteparish	A 1560-1977		5,7,8	1560-1837	1651-1675	Alderbury	1790-1837		3D
Whitsbury	D 1714-1992		5,7,8			Fordingbridge			4C
Wilcot	A 1564-1987		5,7,8,9	1754-1837		Pewsey			4H
Wilsford	A 1588-1987	1588-1885	5,7,8	1588-1901		Pewsey			4H
Wilsford Withlake	A 1655-1992	1681-1812	5,7,8,9	1671-1812		Amesbury			4F
Wilton	A 1615-1977	1622-1895	5,7,8,9	1615-1837	1615-1704	Wilton		1753-1836	4D
Wingfield	A 1654-1993		5,7,8			Bradford-on-Avon			8H
Winsley	A 1724-1985	1724-1825	5,7,8,9	1623-1861		Bradford-on-Avon			8II
Winterbourne Bassett	A 1681-1982		5,7,8	1607-1838		Marlborough			4J(n)
Winterbourne Dauntsey	A 1561-1888		5,7,8,9	1560-1837		Amesbury			3E(Tc)
Winterbourne Earls	A 1557-1982		5,7,8	1557-1837		Amesbury			3E(Te)
Winterbourne Gunner	A 1560-1992		5,7,8	1560-1837		Amesbury			3E(Td)
Winterbourne Monkton	A 1656-1991		5,7,8	1605-1837		Marlborough			4J(t)
Winterbourne Stoke	A 1726-1991	1726-1895	5,7,8	1608-1840		Amesbury			4F
Winterslow			5,7,8,9	1598-1812	1651-1675	Alderbury	1790-1812		3E
Woodborough	A 1567-1994		5,7,8,9	1567-1837	1651-1675	Pewsey	1790-1837		4H(Ak)
Woodford	A 1538-1986	1538-1885	5,7,8,9	1538-1837		Amesbury			4E
Wootton Bassett	A 1584-1989	1584-1895	5,7,8	1584-1938		Cricklade		1826-1836	5K
Wootton Rivers	A 1728-1992		5,7,8,9	1607-1837		Pewsey			3I(Ag)
Worton & Marston	A 1841-1994	1841-1885	5,7,8	1841-1954		Devizes			6H(g)
Wroughton	A 1653-1973		5,7,8	1606-1838		Highworth			4K
Wylye	A 1581-1991	1581-1837	5,7,8,9	1581-1837		Wilton	1790-1837	1813-1836	5E
Yatesbury	A 1706-1992	1706-1885	5,7,8	1606-1892		Calne			5J
Yatton Keynell	A 1653-1988	1653-1885	5,7,8	1653-1837	1653-1675	Chippenham	1790-1812		7J(T)

WILTSHIRE

Original registers deposited at:
A = Wiltshire Record Office, County Hall, Trowbridge BA14 8BS
B = Gloucestershire Record Office, Clarence Row, Alvin Street, Gloucester GL1 3DW
C = Hampshire Record Office, Sussex Street, Winchester SO23 8TH

Study adjacent parishes in counties of Somerset, Gloucestershire, Berkshire, Hampshire and Dorset

Wiltshire Record Office, County Hall, Trowbridge, BA14 8BS

The following useful indexes have been compiled – see Introduction
Census Index 1851 – Wiltshire FHS, c/o The Research Co-ordinator, 10 Castle Lane, Devizes, Wiltshire, SN10 1HU
Census Index 1851 & 1871 – Wiltshire Index Service, Mrs P Wilson, 11 Ardmore Close, Tuffley, Gloucester, GL4 0BJ
Census Indexes 1851 & 1891 – The Nimrod Index, B. &. J. Carter, 1 Lansdown Road, Swindon, Wiltshire, SN1 3NE
Census Index 1891 – Moonraker Genealogical Services, Sodum Hall, Mulberry Grove, Swindon, SN2 1HU
Marriage Index – The Nimrod Index, as above, 1538-1837
Marriage Index – Wiltshire Index Service, as above, pre 1837
Wiltshire Personal Names Index and Wills Index 1242-1887 – B. and J. Carter (as above)
Wiltshire Varied Index – B. and J. Carter (as above)
White Horse Baptism Index – Rev. Robert Marsh, 56 The Boulevard, Worthing, Sussex BN13 1LA
Nonconformist Registers of Wiltshire – Wiltshire FHS (as above)
Monumental Inscriptions Index – Wiltshire FHS (as above)

Wiltshire's length is nearly 54 miles and its breadth 34 miles. It is watered by seven principal rivers: the Thames, Upper and Lower Avon, Nadder, Wiley, Bourne and Kennet. The population in 1841 was 256,280; in 1851, 254,221; in 1861, 249,311; in 1871, 257,177; in 1881, 258,965.

The soils include clay, sand, fuller's earth and chalk. Wheat and barley were cultivated and cattle and pigs bred, the county being particularly celebrated for its bacon (and cheese). Wiltshire was conspicuous for its manufactures – various woollen cloths and serges and coarse linens. Wilton was noted for its carpets and Bradford was the centre of the greatest fabric of superfine cloths in England.

The information in the Index is abbreviated, and may mislead the searcher if reference is not made to the details contained in the several publications listed in the Introduction. It is essential that users of this book check the appropriate works before making further enquiries.

WORCESTERSHIRE

parish name	deposited original registers	I.G.I.	local census indexes	copies of registers at Soc. Gen.	Boyd's marriage index	1837-1851 Registration District	Pallot's marriage index	non-conform. records at P.R.O.	map ref.
Abberley	A 1559-1990	1558-1885	5,8	1662-1856		Martley			7E
Abberton	A 1661-1993	1608-1875	5,8			Pershore			5I
Abbots Morton	A 1728-1956	1611-1700	5,8			Alcester			5I
Acton Beauchamp	C 1577-1994	1571-1885	5,8	1577-1980		Bromyard			5E
Alderminster	F 1651-1981	1611-1877	5,8	1613-1812	1651-1675	Stratford-on-Avon	1641-1837		5L
Alfrick	A 1656-1967	1622-1876	5,8			Martley			5E
Alvechurch	A 1545-1967	1545-1876	5,8			Bromsgrove			8I
Areley Kings	A 1539-1893	1539-1895	5,8	1564-1812		Martley			7F
Astley	A 1539-1987	1539-1885	5,8	1950-1976	1539-1630	Martley			7F
Badsey	A 1538-1906	1538-1877	5,8	1538-1708	1539-1733	Evesham			4J
Bayton	A 1564-1995	1564-1885	5,8	1638-1858		Cleobury Mortimer			8E
Belbroughton	A 1540-1980	1540-1877	5,8	1615-1700		Bromsgrove			8H
Bengeworth	A 1538-1910	1611-1867	5,8	1538-1966		Evesham			4I
Beoley	A 1538-1996	1622-1875	5,8	1538-1964		King's Norton			7J
Berrow	A 1698-1973	1611-1700	5,8	1611-1700		Upton-on-Severn			3F
Besford	A 1539-1959	1539-1875	5,8			Pershore			4G
Bewdley (see Ribbesford)						Kidderminster		1722-1836	8F
Birlingham	A 1566-1959	1566-1895	5,8			Pershore			4H
Birtsmorton	A 1539-1983	1539-1837	5,8	1539-1804	1651-1675	Upton-on-Severn	1790-1812		3F
Bishampton	A 1599-1932	1616-1880	5,8	1599-1949		Pershore			5H
Blockley	E 1538-1980	1613-1700	5,8		1543-1651	Shipston-on-Stour			3K
Bockleton	C 1574-1850	1574-1877	5,8	1574-1871		Tenbury			6C
Bordesley	A 1704-1770		5,8			Bromsgrove			7I
Bradley	A 1562-1993	1612-1875	5,8	1562-1812	1645-1754	Droitwich	1630-1812		6H
Bransford	A 1767-1944	1538-1882	5,8			Martley			5F
Bredicot	A 1702-1991	1702-1877	5,8			Pershore			5G(N)
Bredon	A 1559-1968	1559-1875	5,8			Tewkesbury			3H
Bredons Norton	A 1754-1891	1612-1877	5,8			Tewkesbury			3H
Bretforton	A 1538-1950	1538-1876	5,8	1538-1837		Evesham	1790-1837		4J
Bricklehampton	A 1718-1837	1611-1884	5,8	1718-1784		Pershore			4H(X)
Broadwas	A 1676-1992	1612-1700	5,8			Martley			5F
Broadway	A 1539-1992	1539-1880	5,8	1539-1966		Evesham	1790-1812	1801-1837	3J
Bromsgrove	A 1590-1879	1590-1875	5,8	1589-1712		Bromsgrove		1739-1837	8H
Broom		1616-1877	5,8	1666-1972		Kidderminster			8G
Broughton Hackett	A 1759-1836	1611-1881	5,8			Pershore			5H(O)
Bushley	A 1538-1959	1538-1875	5,8	1538-1837	1651-1675	Upton-on-Severn	1790-1837		3G
Castle Morton	A 1558-1953	1558-1878	5,8	1609-1641	1609-1641	Upton-on-Severn			3F
Chaceley	E 1538-1978	1540-1833	5,8		1540-1837	Tewkesbury			2G
Chaddesley Corbett		1538-1877	5,8	1601-1626		Kidderminster			8G
Church Honeybourne	A 1673-1948	1581-1832	5,8			Evesham			4J
Churchill (nr. Worcester)	A 1564-1924	1564-1880	5,8	1564-1839	1601-1675	Pershore	1790-1839		5H(P)
Churchill	A 1540-1905	1612-1700	5,8			Kidderminster	1790-1812		9G
Church Lench	A 1696-1951	1615-1700	5,8	1702-1812		Evesham	1702-1812		5I
Claines	A 1538-1948	1538-1875	5,8			Droitwich			6G
Cleeve Prior	A 1598-1964	1598-1875	5,8	1599-1837	1651-1675	Evesham	1790-1837		4J
Clent	A 1562-1997	1562-1885	5,8	1562-1812		Bromsgrove		1807-1836	8H
Clifton on Teme	A 1598-1993	1598-1877	5,8	1598-1840		Martley			6E
Cofton Hackett	A 1549-1979	1550-1700	5,8			Bromsgrove			8I
Cotheridge	A 1653-1947	1611-1882	5,8			Martley			5F
Cradley	B 1798-1987	1785-1877	5,8	1785-1844		Stourbridge		1761-1837	9H
Croome D'Abitot	A 1560-1973	1608-1875	5,8			Upton-on-Severn			4G
Cropthorne	A 1557-1992	1577-1885	5,8	1557-1717	1557-1751	Pershore			4I
Crowle	A 1539-1998	1539-1875	5,8	1539-1890		Droitwich			6H
Crutch (ex.par.)						Droitwich			7G(F)
Cutsdean	E 1695-1993	1634-1675	5,8			Winchcombe			2J
Daylesford	H 1679-1837	1661-1700	5,8	1660-1971		Stow-on-theWold			1L
Defford	A 1540-1932	1540-1812	5,8			Pershore			4G
Doddenham	A 1538-1960	1538-1875	5,8	1538-1809		Martley	1790-1812		5E
Dodderhill	A 1651-1893	1613-1875	5,8			Droitwich			7H
Dormston	A 1716-1836	1613-1862	5,8	1612-1739	1612-1736	Pershore			5I
Doverdale	A 1704-1837	1615-1875	5,8			Droitwich			7G(E)
Droitwich									6G
St Andrew	A 1571-1971	1571-1875	5,8			Droitwich			6G(Hb)
St Peter	A 1544-1978	1544-1882	5,8	1544-1840		Droitwich			6G(Hc)
Dudley								1743-1837	10H
St Edmund	B 1540-1646	1540-1611	5,6,8	1540-1649		Dudley			10H
St Thomas	B 1541-1954	1541-1877	5,6,8	1541-1954		Dudley			10H
Earls Croome	A 1644-1993	1612-1875	5,8	1660-1836		Upton-on-Severn			4G(U)
Eastham	A 1571-1962	1571-1880	5,8	1571-1837	1651-1675	Tenbury	1790-1837		7D
Eckington	A 1678-1968	1612-1880	5,8			Pershore			3H
Edvin Loach	C 1576-1996		5,8	1813-1837		Bromyard			6D
Eldersfield	A 1718-1969	1611-1700	5,8			Upton-on-Severn			2F
Elmbridge	A 1570-1892	1613-1875	5,8	1570-1812	1651-1675	Droitwich	1590-1812		7G
Elmley Castle	A 1657-1998	1612-1879	5,8	1813-1937		Pershore			3H
Elmley Lovett		1608-1700	5,8			Droitwich			7G
Evenlode	E 1562-1992	1562-1885	5,8	1561-1909		Stow-on-theWold			2L
Evesham								1778-1837	4I
All Saints		1613-1700	5,8		1538-1812	Evesham			4I(Yb)
St Lawrence			5,8		1556-1725	Evesham			4I(Ya)
Feckenham	A 1538-1900	1538-1875	5,8			Alcester		1788-1837	6I
Fladbury	A 1560-1957	1560-1885	5,8			Pershore			4I
Flyford Flavell	A 1676-1997	1813-1875	5,8	1676-1966		Pershore			5H(S)
Frankley (see Romsley)			5,8	1598-1900	1651-1675	Bromsgrove	1790-1812		9H
Grafton Flyford	A 1676-1996	1676-1875	5,8			Pershore			5H
Grafton Manor (ex.par.)						Droitwich			7H
Great Comberton	A 1540-1963	1755-1885	5,8	1540-1964	1540-1964	Pershore			4H
Great Malvern	A 1556-1940	1709-1875	5,8	1556-1868		Upton-on-Severn		1828-1837	4F

WORCESTERSHIRE

parish name	deposited original registers	I.G.I.	local census indexes	copies of registers at Soc. Gen.	Boyd's marriage index	1837-1851 Registration District	Pallot's marriage index	non-conform. records at P.R.O.	map ref.
Great Witley	A 1538-1975	1739-1875	5,8	1538-1908		Martley			7E
Grimley	A 1573-1990	1731-1875	5,8			Martley			6F
Hadzor	A 1554-1968	1554-1877	5,8			Droitwich			6H
Hagley			5,8	1538-1969		Bromsgrove			9H
Halesowen	B 1559-1929	1559-1881	5,6,8	1559-1971		Stourbridge		1715-1837	9H
Hallow	A 1584-1982	1583-1876	5,8	1962-1970		Martley			6F
Hampton Lovett	A 1666-1954	1615-1700	5,8	1577-1837		Droitwich			7G
Hanbury	A 1577-1990	1577-1875	5,8	1577-1837		Droitwich			6H
Hanley Castle	A 1538-1989	1538-1885	5,8			Upton-on-Severn			4F
Hanley Child	A 1813-1992	1813-1885	5,8	1571-1836	1790-1836	Tenbury			7D
Hanley William	A 1586-1992	1586-1847	5,8	1586-1847	1651-1675	Tenbury	1790-1837		7D
Hartlebury	A 1540-1950	1540-1886	5,8	1540-1812		Droitwich			7F
Harvington	A 1570-1961	1734-1875	5,8	1570-1972		Evesham			5I
Hill Croome	A 1721-1835	1611-1700	5,8			Upton-on-Severn			3G
Himbleton	A 1713-1995	1611-1875	5,8	1711-1812	1713-1812	Droitwich	1790-1812		6H
Hindlip	A 1736-1997	1612-1875	5,8			Droitwich			6G
Holt	A 1538-1975	1538-1875	5,8	1538-1837		Martley			6F
Huddington	A 1695-1992	1695-1872	5,8	1695-1835	1790-1837	Droitwich			6H
Inkberrow	A 1675-1976	1598-1875	5,8	1615-1778		Alcester			6I
Kempsey	A 1688-1986	1608-1885	5,8	1690-1812	1690-1812	Upton-on-Severn			4G
Kenswick (see Knightwick)									6F(D)
Kidderminster	A 1539-1950	1539-1875	5,8	1539-1636		Kidderminster		1727-1837	8F
Kings Norton	G 1546-1990	1612-1877	5,8	1546-1998	1546-1754	King's Norton			8I
Kington	A 1587-1836	1587-1863	5,8	1587-1836	1651-1675	Pershore			5H
Knighton-on-Teme	A 1559-1960	1560-1875	5,8			Tenbury			7D
Knightwick	A 1539-1927	1539-1880	5,8	1742-1875		Tenbury			6D
Kyre Parva (Hereford.)									6D
Leigh	A 1538-1981	1538-1882	5,8	1538-1906		Martley		1818-1837	5F
Lenchwick (see Norton)									
Lindridge	A 1574-1961	1574-1885	5,8		1574-1727	Tenbury			7D
Little Comberton	A 1540-1947	1754-1885	5,8	1540-1964	1651-1675	Pershore	1790-1812		4H(W)
Little Malvern	A 1691-1886	1691-1836	5,8	1691-1838		Upton-on-Severn			3F
Little Washbourne	A 1813-1959			1813-1981		Winchcombe			3H
Little Witley	A 1680-1973	1680-1875	5,8	1680-1846		Martley			6F
Longdon	A 1538-1929	1612-1875	5,8	1737-1929	1538-1837	Upton-on-Severn			3F
Lower Mitton (Stourport)	A 1693-1923	1603-1700	5,8	1693-1840		Kidderminster		1788-1837	7F
Lower Sapey	A 1674-1993	1661-1844	5,8	1636-1849		Bromyard			6E
Lulsley	A 1656-1969	1622-1875	5,8			Martley			5E
Lye	B 1839-1980		5,8	1839-1911		Stourbridge			9H
Madresfield	A 1742-1836	1611-1836	5,8	1742-1836		Upton-on-Severn			4F
Mamble	A 1692-1955	1662-1871	5,8			Cleobury Mortimer			7E
Martin Hussingtree	A 1538-1996	1539-1708	5,8			Droitwich			6G(J)
Martley	A 1625-1971		5,8	1625-1953		Martley			6E
Mathon	C 1631-1943	1613-1875	5,8	1631-1943		Ledbury			4E
Moseley	G 1758-1979	1796-1885	5,8	1761-1850		King's Norton			9J
Naunton Beauchamp	A 1559-1992	1559-1812	5,8			Pershore			5H(T)
Netherton (see Cropthorne)									3I
Newland	A 1562-1973	1612-1700	5,8			Upton-on-Severn			4F
North and Middle Littleton	A 1661-1978	1661-1875	5,8	1662-1809	1662-1675	Evesham	1790-1812		4J
Northfield	G 1560-1990	1612-1700	5,8	1560-1875		King's Norton			9I
North Piddle	A 1565-1997	1612-1875	5,8	1565-1812	1571-1810	Pershore	1790-1810		5H(R)
Norton (and Lenchwick)	A 1538-1950	1538-1875	5,8	1538-1923		Evesham			4I
Norton	A 1538-1986	1613-1875	5,8			Pershore			5G
Oddingley	A 1661-1970	1611-1875	5,8			Droitwich			6H
Offenham		1539-1621	5,8	1543-1812	1651-1675	Evesham	1543-1812		4I
Oldberrow	F 1659-1979	1756-1895	5,8			Alcester			7J
Oldbury	D 1714-1970		5,8	1813-1970		West Bromwich		1823-1837	10I
Oldswinford	A 1602-1889	1602-1877	5,8	1719-1819		Stourbridge		1792-1837	9G
Ombersley	A 1574-1918	1574-1882	5,8			Droitwich			6G
Orleton	A 1815-1947		5,8	1571-1947		Tenbury	1790-1837		7E
Overbury	A 1563-1985	1748-1882	5,8			Tewkesbury			3H
Pedmore	B 1539-1960	1539-1875	5,8	1539-1963		Bromsgrove			9G
Pendock	A 1558-1937	1755-1875	5,8	1584-1948		Tewkesbury			2F
Pensax	A 1563-1895	1620-1885	5,8	1563-1963		Martley			7E
Peopleton	A 1632-1992	1612-1885	5,8			Pershore			5H
Pershore									4H
Holy Cross	A 1539-1908	1540-1812	5,8			Pershore			4H
St Andrew	A 1641-1958	1609-1812	5,8			Pershore			4H
Pinvin	A 1559-1984	1559-1885	5,8	1559-1968		Pershore			4H
Pirton	A 1764-1990	1538-1882	5,8	1612-1700		Pershore			4G
Powick	A 1662-1983	1611-1875	5,8	1611-1731		Upton-on-Severn			5F
Queenhill	A 1580-1837	1580-1837	5,8	1581-1837		Upton-on-Severn			3G
Redditch	A 1770-1983	1770-1882	5,8	1808-1811		Bromsgrove	1790-1812	1810-1837	7I
Redmarley D'Abitot	E 1539-1993	1539-1885	5,8	1539-1969		Newent			2F
Ribbesford	A 1574-1996		5,8	1574-1765		Kidderminster			8F
Ripple	A 1568-1926	1568-1885	5,8			Upton-on-Severn			3G
Rochford	A 1561-1993	1561-1875	5,8			Tenbury			7D
Rock	A 1548-1994	1548-1875	5,8			Cleobury Mortimer			7E
Romsley	A 1736-1985	1736-1882	5,8	1736-1841		Bromsgrove			9H
Rous Lench	A 1538-1988	1813-1875	5,8	1539-1811	1651-1675	Evesham	1539-1812		5I
Rushock	A 1666-1979		5,8	1608-1837	1667-1675	Kidderminster	1790-1837		7G
Salwarpe	A 1666-1993	1608-1875	5,8	1613-1968		Droitwich			6G
Sedgeberrow	A 1566-1986	1566-1885	5,8	1566-1972		Evesham			3I
Severn Stoke	A 1538-1982	1538-1851	5,8	1538-1621		Upton-on-Severn			4G
Shelsley Beauchamp	A 1538-1994	1538-1885	5,8			Martley			7E
Shelsley Walsh	A 1729-1968	1729-1882	5,8	1729-1968		Martley			6E(C)
Shipston on Stour	F 1572-1976	1727-1895	5,8	1572-1812	1651-1675	Shipston-on-Stour	1571-1812	1783-1836	3L

262

WORCESTERSHIRE

parish name	deposited original registers	I.G.I.	local census indexes	copies of registers at Soc. Gen.	Boyd's marriage index	1837-1851 Registration District	Pallot's marriage index	non-conform. records at P.R.O.	map ref.
Shrawley	A 1537-1940	1755-1882	5,8	1719-1967		Martley			7F
South Littleton	A 1538-1978	1538-1885	5,8	1538-1811	1651-1675	Evesham	1790-1812		4J
Spetchley	A 1539-1986	1764-1874	5,8	1539-1966		Pershore			5G(M)
Stanford on Teme	A 1594-1963	1594-1885	5,8	1594-1964		Martley			7E
Staunton	E 1559-1916		5,8			Newent			2F
Stockton on Teme	A 1539-1993	1539-1875	5,8			Martley			7E(B)
Stoke Prior	A 1557-1976	1564-1882	5,8			Bromsgrove			7H
Stone	A 1601-1892	1754-1882	5,8	1601-1966		Kidderminster			8G
Stoulton	A 1542-1987	1721-1875	5,8			Pershore			5G
Strensham	A 1569-1908	1569-1906	5,8	1569-1908		Pershore			3G
Suckley	A 1695-1976	1613-1877	5,8			Martley		1818-1837	5E
Tardebigge	A 1566-1968	1730-1882	5,8	1566-1908		Bromsgrove			7I
Teddington	A 1560-1977	1550-1885	5,8			Tewkesbury			2H
Tenbury	A 1653-1983		5,8			Tenbury		1820-1836	7C
Throckmorton	A 1546-1995	1545-1812	5,8	1717-1812		Pershore			5H
Tibberton	A 1756-1999	1612-1877	5,8			Droitwich			5G
Tidmington	F 1691-1833	1691-1833	5,8	1611-1851		Shipston-on-Stour	1693-1812		3L
Tredington	F 1541-1994	1541-1895	5,8	1541-1907		Shipston-on-Stour			4L
Upton on Severn	A 1546-1988	1546-1882	5,8	1577-1837	1651-1675	Pershore	1790-1837		5H
Upton Warren	A 1604-1957	1604-1882	5,8			Droitwich			7H
Warndon	A 1561-1985	1759-1882	5,8	1561-1962		Droitwich			5G(K)
Welland	A 1670-1973	1608-1885	5,8	1608-1812	1605-1812	Upton-on-Severn	1780-1812		3F
Westwood Park (ex. par.)						Droitwich			6G(G)
Whiteladies Aston	A 1558-1975	1558-1882	5,8	1558-1840		Pershore	1816-1844		5H(Q)
Whittington	A 1653-1979	1755-1877	5,8	1653-1895		Pershore			5G(L)
Wichenford	A 1690-1976	1599-1875	5,8	1599-1700	1690-1812	Martley			6F
Wick	A 1695-1978	1608-1882	5,8	1608-1971		Pershore			4H
Wickhamford	A 1538-1992	1613-1882	5,8	1538-1967		Evesham			3J
Wolverley	A 1539-1909	1616-1837	5,8	1539-1860		Kidderminster			9F
Worcester								1699-1837	5G
Cathedral		1693-1811	5,8	1693-1811		Worcester			5G
All Saints	A 1560-1970	1560-1875	5,8			Worcester			5G
St Alban	A 1630-1934	1630-1880	5,8	1630-1812		Worcester	1790-1812		5G
St Andrew	A 1656-1936	1770-1875	5,8	1770-1936	1656-1755	Worcester			5G
St Clement	A 1694-1985	1608-1875	5,8		1694-1753	Worcester			5G
St Helen	A 1538-1939	1538-1875	5,8	1538-1812		Worcester	1790-1812		5G
St John Bedwardine	A 1558-1994	1558-1875	5,8	1558-1870	1559-1812	Worcester	1790-1812		5F
St Martin	A 1538-1978	1762-1878	5,8	1762-1841		Worcester			5G
St Michael	A 1546-1908	1546-1880	5,8	1546-1908	1548-1755	Worcester			5G
St Nicholas	A 1563-1984		5,8	1563-1966		Worcester			5G
St Oswald's Hospital	A 1695-1964		5,8		1700-1754	Worcester			5G
St Peter the Great	A 1686-1974	1752-1875	5,8	1686-1856		Worcester			5G
St Swithin	A 1538-1973	1538-1875	5,8	1538-1953	1538-1754	Worcester			5G
Wyre Piddle	A 1670-1971	1716-1871	5,8	1716-1971		Pershore			4H(V)
Wythall	A 1760-1983	1760-1885	5,8	1760-1967		King's Norton			8J
Yardley	G 1539-1969	1608-1701	5,8	1704-1840		Solihull			9J

Original registers deposited at:
A = Worcestershire Library and History Centre, Trinity Street, Worcester, WR1 2PW
B = Dudley Archives and Local History Service, Mount Pleasant Street, Coseley, Dudley, WV14 9JR
C = Herefordshire Record Office, The Old Barracks, Harold Street, Hereford HR1 2QX
D = Smethwick District Library, High Street, Smethwick, Warley, West Midlands, B66 1AB
E = Gloucestershire Record Office, Clarence Row, Alvin Street, Gloucester, GL1 3DW
F = Warwickshire County Record Office, Priory Park, Cape Road, Warwick CV34 4JS
G = Birmingham City Archives, Central Library, Chamberlain Square, Birmingham B3 3HQ
H = Oxfordshire Record Office, St. Luke's Church, Cowley, Oxford OX4 3EX

Study adjacent parishes in counties of Shropshire, Staffordshire, Warwickshire, Gloucestershire and Herefordshire

Worcestershire Library and History Centre, Trinity Street, Worcester, WR1 2PW
Dudley Archives and Local History Service, Mount Pleasant Street, Coseley, Dudley, WV14 9JR

The following useful indexes have been compiled – see Introduction
Census Index 1851 – Birmingham & Midland SHG, c/o Mr M. Harrison, 121 Rowood Drive, Solihull, West Midlands B92 9JL
Census Index 1851 – S & N Genealogy Supplies, West Wing, Manor Farm, Salisbury Road, Chilmark, Wiltshire SP3 5AF
Census Index 1861 – Mr R. Griffiths, http://griffs.treehouse.tripod.com/census/intro.html
Marriage Index 1701-1837 – Worcestershire Library and History Centre (as above)
Marriage Index 1701-1837 – Birmingham & Midland SGH, c/o Mrs A. Purcell, 8 Ironside Close, Bewdley, Worcestershire DY12 2HX
Greater Birmingham Marriage Index 1801-1837 – Birmingham & Midland SGH, c/o Mrs P. Archer, 56 St. Andrew's Road, Lillington, Leamington Spa CV32 7EX
Worcestershire Burials – Mr D. Pullar, 1 Kemble Close, Trent Park, Willenhall, West Midlands WV12 4DQ
Evesham Index – Mrs S. Minney, 20 Walpole Court, Hampton Road, Twickenham, Middlesex TW2 5QH

Worcestershire is extremely irregular in shape; its extent from the south-west to the north-east is about 44 miles; from north to south about 24 miles. It is watered by four principal rivers: the Severn, Avon, Tame and Stour. The population in 1841 was 248,460; in 1851, 276,926; in 1861, 307,397; in 1871, 338,848; in 1881, 380,283.

The soils are marl, loam, clay and gravel. Produce includes grain and fruit, whilst the principal manufactures were found in Worcester city; glove-making, porcelain and cabinet ware. In other towns were considerable tanneries, glass and iron works. Wool-spinning, linen-weaving and the making of needles and nails were also practised widely. Kidderminster was a centre for carpets.

The information in the Index is abbreviated, and may mislead the searcher if reference is not made to the details contained in the several publications listed in the Introduction. It is essential that users of this book check the appropriate works before making further enquiries.

parish name	deposited original registers	I.G.I.	local census indexes	copies of registers at Soc. Gen.	Boyd's marriage index	1837-1851 Registration District	Pallot's marriage index	non-conform. records at P.R.O.	map ref.
Acaster Malbis	B 1693-1979	1720-1871	5,8			York			5C
Acklam	B 1716-1988	1737-1875	5,6,8,9	1626-1861		Malton			7F
Acomb	B 1634-1990	1634-1886	5,8,9	1634-1875		York			6B
Aldbrough	A 1570-1985	1813-1856	5,6,8,9		1538-1703	Skirlaugh		1802-1837	4K
Allerthorpe	B 1616-1989	1626-1871	5,6,8,9	1600-1848		Pocklington			6F
Askham Bryan	B 1695-1992	1604-1886	5,8	1604-1837		York			6B
Askham Richard	B 1579-1992	1578-1885	5,8	1579-1837	1579-1812	York	1790-1812		6B(f)
Atwick	A 1538-1998	1538-1841	6,8	1538-1812		Skirlaugh			6K
Aughton	B 1610-1988	1602-1888	5,6,8,9	1600-1865	1602-1812	Howden	1790-1812		5E
Bainton	A 1561-1995	1721-1867	6,8	1600-1882		Driffield			6H
Barlby	B 1780-1993	1781-1860	5,8,9	1781-1860		Selby			4D
Barmby on the Marsh	A 1777-1976	1763-1860	5,6,8,9			Howden			3E
Barmby on the Moor	B 1720-1990	1706-1880	5,8	1600-1852		Pocklington			6F
Barmston	A 1571-1993	1721-1844	6,8			Bridlington			7J
Beeford	A 1563-1984	1715-1838	6,8	1609-1838		Driffield			6J
Bempton	A 1597-1989	1715-1867	6,8	1600-1889		Bridlington			8K
Bessingby	A 1698-1989	1734-1836	6,8	1600-1836		Bridlington			8J
Beswick	A 1657-1990	1731-1869	6,8	1600-1869		Beverley			6I
Beverley								1701-1837	5I
St John	A 1558-1989	1813-1864	5,8			Beverley			4I
St Mary	A 1561-1977	1718-1875	5,8			Beverley			5I
Bilbrough	B 1695-1991	1695-1888	5,6,8			Tadcaster			6B(g)
Bilton	B 1571-1868	1571-1842	5,6,8	1571-1864		Tadcaster			6A
Bilton	A 1692-1993	1726-1871	5,6,8			Skirlaugh			4J
Birdsall	B 1558-1981	1568-1887	5,8,9	1583-1848		Malton			8F
Bishop Burton	A 1562-1978	1730-1835	6,8			Beverley		1755-1836	5H
Bishopthorpe	B 1692-1973	1692-1886	5,8	1631-1837		York			6C(j)
Bishop Wilton	B 1613-1973	1613-1887	5,6,8,9	1601-1856		Pocklington			7F
Blacktoft	A 1700-1985	1700-1878	6,8	1700-1812	1700-1812	Howden	1790-1812		3G
Bolton Percy	B 1571-1992	1571-1886	5,8	1604-1854		Pocklington			5B
Boynton	A 1563-1992	1573-1867	8	1563-1840		Bridlington			8J
Brandesburton	A 1558-2000	1558-1845	6,8	1558-1845		Skirlaugh			6J
Brantingham	A 1653-1994	1653-1866	6,8	1653-1841	1653-1812	Beverley	1790-1812		3H
Bridlington	A 1564-1977	1722-1873	5,6,8	1600-1873		Bridlington		1698-1837	8K
Bubwith	B 1623-1986	1600-1886	5,6,8,9	1600-1865	1601-1837	Howden			4E
Bugthorpe	B 1661-1993	1661-1888	5,6,8,9	1631-1856		Pocklington			7F
Burnby	B 1584-1992	1726-1842	5,6,8,9	1601-1842		Pocklington			6G
Burstwick	A 1747-1993	1813-1842	6,8			Patrington			3K
Burton Agnes	A 1700-1990	1730-1842	6,8	1718-1842		Bridlington			7J
Burton Fleming	A 1538-1988	1538-1826	6,8	1538-1840	1538-1812	Bridlington	1790-1812		8I
Burton Pidsea	A 1714-1992	1718-1864	6,8			Patrington			3K
Burythorpe	B 1720-1992	1715-1889	5,6,8,9	1661-1857		Malton			8F
Butterwick	A 1796-1993	1728-1858	5,6,8,9	1601-1859		Driffield			8H
Carnaby	A 1634-1988	1745-1868	5,6,8,9	1600-1867		Pocklington			6E
Catton	B 1592-1978	1737-1886	5,8,9	1600-1867		Pocklington			6E
Catwick	A 1586-1992	1730-1843	6,8	1601-1843		Skirlaugh			5J
Cherry Burton	A 1561-1989	1562-1860	6,8	1561-1841	1561-1740	Beverley			5H
Copmanthorpe	B 1759-1981	1759-1883	5,8	1759-1874		York			6B
Cottingham	A 1563-1986	1730-1836	5,6,8			Sculcoates		1690-1837	4I
Cowlam	A 1799-1978	....-1855	6,8,9			Driffield			8H
Drypool	A 1712-1979	1572-1866	5,6,8	1572-1812	1572-1812	Sculcoates			3J
Dunnington	B 1573-1953	1573-1866	5,6,8	1628-1847		Skirlaugh			6D
Easington	A 1654-1998	1720-1855	5,6,8,9			Patrington			2M
Eastrington	A 1563-1969	1724-1863	6,8,9			Howden		1820-1837	4F
Ellerton Priory	B 1675-1987	1675-1889	5,8,9		1602-1724	Howden			5E
Elloughton	A 1600-1984	1715-1865	6,8	1601-1865		Beverley		1809-1829	3H
Elvington	B 1600-1978	1600-1873	5,6,8	1600-1873		York			6E
Escrick	B 1617-1992	1617-1886	5,6,8	1608-1886		York			5D
Etton	A 1557-1984	1730-1867	5,6,8,9	1600-1887		Beverley			5H
Everingham	B 1653-1992	1653-1889	5,6,8,9	1600-1883	1751-1816	Pocklington		1771-1840	5F
Fangfoss	B 1655-1991	1655-1889	5,6,8	1813-1837		Pocklington			6F
Filey	A 1571-1986	1571-1867	5,6,8	1571-1840		Scarborough			10J
Flamborough	A 1564-1992	1724-1856	5,6,8			Bridlington			8K
Folkton	A 1665-1978	1720-1875	5,6,8			Scarborough			9I
Foston on the Wolds	A 1653-1988	1720-1872	5,6,8	1599-1872		Driffield		1815-1836	7J
Foxholes	A 1654-1992	1725-1860	6,8,9	1600-1860		Driffield			9H
Fraisthorpe	A 1595-1717	1736-1771	6,8	1600-1775		Bridlington			7J
Fridaythorpe	A 1685-1991	1706-1849	5,8,9	1626-1849		Pocklington			7G(A)
Fulford	B 1653-1962	1716-1868	8	1603-1865		York			6D
Full Sutton	B 1713-1978	1713-1887	5,6,8,9	1597-1864		Pocklington			7E(C)
Ganton	A 1553-1982	1720-1867	6,8,9	1790-1867		Scarborough			9H
Garton	A 1582-1993	1752-1856	6,8	1600-1856		Skirlaugh			4L
Garton on the Wolds	A 1653-1985	1722-1875	6,8	1722-1887		Driffield			7H
Goodmanham	B 1678-1991	1678-1887	5,8,9	1600-1874		Pocklington			5G
Goxhill	A 1561-1991	1705-1871	6,8			Skirlaugh			5K(F)
Great Driffield	A 1556-1993	1710-1875	6,8			Driffield		1796-1837	7I
Great Givendale	B 1657-1991	1657-1860	5,6,8,9	1606-1860		Pocklington			6F(D)
Grindale	A 1591-1983	1703-1873	6,8	1703-1768		Bridlington			8J
Halsham	A 1563-1992	1736-1852	6,8		1563-1837	Patrington			3L
Harpham	A 1720-1990	1730-1842	6,8	1700-1842		Driffield			7J
Harswell	B 1653-1993	1653-1897	5,6,8,9	1600-1852		Pocklington			5F(G)
Hayton	B 1610-1976	1610-1886	5,6,8	1601-1867		Pocklington			5F
Healaugh	B 1698-1991	1698-1890	5,8,9	1633-1869		Tadcaster			5B
Hedon	A 1549-1989	1721-1841	5,6,8	1552-1893		Sculcoates			3K(K)
Helperthorpe	B 1733-1977	1715-1892	6,8,9	1631-1870		Driffield			8H
Hemingbrough	B 1605-1977	1605-1886	5,6,8,9	1661-1867		Howden			4D
Heslington	B 1653-1994	1653-1887	5,6,8	1683-1870		York			6D
Hessle	A 1560-1993	1720-1836	5,6,8	1600-1836		Sculcoates			3I
Hilston	A 1654-1988	1731-1840	6,8			Patrington			4L(J)

YORKSHIRE (EAST RIDING)

parish name	deposited original registers	I.G.I.	local census indexes	copies of registers at Soc. Gen.	Boyd's marriage index	1837-1851 Registration District	Pallot's marriage index	non-conform. records at P.R.O.	map ref.
Hollym	A 1564-1984	1722-1855	6,8			Patrington			3L
Holme on the Wolds	A 1539-1861	1726-1853	6,8			Beverley			5H(H)
Holme upon Spalding Moor	B 1559-1989	1558-1849	8 5,6,8	1559-1650	1726-1800	Howden		1743-1840	4F
Holmpton	A 1739-1992	1813-1857	6,8	1739-1837		Patrington			3M
Hornsea	A 1654-1982	1721-1856	6,8			Skirlaugh		1820-1837	6K
Hotham	A 1706-1989	1720-1848	6,8			Howden			4G
Howden	A 1541-1972	1542-1861	6,8,9	1543-1837	1571-1770	Howden		1781-1836	3F
Huggate	B 1539-1981	1539-1885	5,6,8,9	1539-1812	1564-1812	Pocklington	1790-1812		7G
Hull				1554-1892				1705-1837	3I
Holy Trinity	A 1554-1971	1723-1875	5,8	1538-1600	1636-1837	Hull			3I
St James	A 1831-1956	1831-1836	5,8			Hull			3I
St Mary	A 1564-1938	1716-1833	5,8	1569-1785	1633-1837	Hull			3I
Humbleton	A 1577-2000	1731-1856	6,8	1681-1685		Skirlaugh			4K
Hunmanby	A 1583-1981	1730-1875	6,8			Bridlington		1786-1836	9J
Hutton Cranswick	A 1653-1988	1705-1869	6,8	1601-1869		Driffield			6I
Keyingham	A 1604-1986	1717-1865	6,8			Patrington			3K
Kilham	A 1653-1994	1716-1875	8,9	1693-1876		Driffield		1821-1836	8I
Kilnsea	A 1711-1995	1731-1853	6,7,8			Patrington			2M
Kilnwick Juxta Watton	A 1558-2001	1558-1852	8	1558-1852	1607-1837(?)	Beverley			6I
Kilnwick Percy	B 1688-1993	1718-1891	5,6,8,9	1661-1877	1607-1837(?)	Pocklington			6F
Kirby Grindalythe	B 1722-1978	1605-1886	5,6,8	1605-1866	1836-1837	Malton			8G
Kirby Underdale	B 1557-1993	1557-1891	5,6,8,9	1636-1840		Pocklington			7F
Kirkburn	A 1686-1992	1710-1875	6,8	1691-1875		Driffield			7H
Kirk Ella	A 1558-1901	1558-1875	6,8	1558-1877	1558-1842	Sculcoates	1790-1842	1739-1836	3I
Kirk Hammerton	C 1714-1933	1714-1847	5,8,9	1714-1812	1755-1812	Knaresborough			6A
Knapton (see Acomb)						York			6B(c)
Knapton	B 1760-1970	1805-1875	5,6,8,9	1805-1878		York			9G
Langtoft	A 1587-1994	1724-1854	8,9	1601-1854		Driffield			8H
Langton	B 1653-1981	1653-1887	5,6,8,9	1653-1871		Malton			8F
Laxton	A 1779-1989	1763-1848	6,8			Howden			3F
Leconfield	A 1551-1990	1551-1861	6,8	1551-1861		Beverley			5I
Leven	A 1653-1991	1727-1864	6,8	1600-1880		Beverley			5J
Lissett	A 1653-1988	1719-1838	6,8	1600-1838		Bridlington			7J
Little Driffield	A 1579-1982	1714-1875	6,8			Driffield			7I
Lockington	A 1547-1996	1730-1875	6,8	1599-1874	1649-1680	Beverley			5H
Londesborough	B 1580-1992	1580-1889	5,6,8,9	1600-1865		Pocklington			5G
Long Marston	B 1645-1994	1634-1888	5,8	1645-1885		Tadcaster/York			6B
Long Riston	A 1653-1985	1710-1845	6,8			Skirlaugh			5J
Lowthorpe	A 1546-1992	1725-1875	6,8	1706-1889		Driffield		1813-1837	7I
Lund	A 1587-1984	1587-1867	5,6,8,9	1586-1687	1612-1837	Beverley			6H
Mappleton	A 1682-1991	1711-1869	6,8			Skirlaugh			5K
Marfleet	A 1713-1990	1731-1846	8			Sculcoates			3J
Market Weighton	B 1653-1960	1653-1886	6,8	1600-1881		Pocklington		1819-1836	5G
Middlethorpe (see St Mary Bishophill senior)						York			6C(h)
Middleton on the Wolds	A 1678-2000	1715-1867	6,8			Driffield			6H
Millington	B 1609-1994	1716-1859	5,6,8,9			Pocklington			6F
Moor Monkton	B 1697-1995	1697-1890	5,8,9	1628-1870		York			7B
Muston	A 1541-1983	1729-1878	6,8			Scarborough			9J
Naburn	B 1653-1987	1653-1887	6,8	1662-1849		York			5D
Nafferton	A 1653-1992	1720-1875	6,8	1689-1898		Driffield			7I
Nether Poppleton	B 1640-1996	1736-1873	8,9	1661-1878		York			7B(a)
New Village (ex.par.)			8			Howden			4G
North Cave	A 1678-1966	1726-1836	6,8	1629-1736		Howden			4G
North Dalton	A 1653-1992	1719-1862	6,8	1600-1862		Driffield			6H
North Ferriby	A 1561-1991	1715-1851	5,6,8	1600-1852		Sculcoates		1739-1836	3H
North Frodingham	A 1559-1992	1725-1849	6,8	1600-1849		Driffield		1815-1836	6J
North Grimston	B 1689-1977	1686-1889	5,6,8,9	1606-1862		Malton			8G
North Newbald	A 1600-1994	1721-1864	6,8			Beverley			4G
Norton	B 1558-1945	1558-1886	5,6,8,9	1605-1879		Malton			8F
Nunburnholme	B 1586-1992	1586-1887	5,8,9	1605-1855		Pocklington			6G(E)
Nunkeeling	A 1559-1993	1598-1873	6,8	1559-1812		Skirlaugh			6J
Ottringham	A 1566-1992	1727-1852	6,8			Patrington			3L
Owthorne	A 1574-1945	1729-1865	6,8			Patrington			3L
Patrington	A 1570-1996	1570-1866	5,6,8	1570-1731	1570-1731	Patrington		1805-1838	2L
Paull	A 1657-1989	1730-1840	6,8			Patrington			3K
Pocklington	B 1599-1923	1559-1886	5,6,8,9	1601-1856		Pocklington		1771-1840	6F
Preston	A 1559-1988	1720-1827	5,6,8,9			Sculcoates			4K
Reighton	A 1559-1993	1715-1836	6,8			Bridlington			9J
Riccall	B 1669-1995	1669-1861	5,6,8	1669-1813		Selby			4D
Rillington	B 1638-1993	1638-1889	5,6,8,9	1638-1845	1640-1837	Malton		1819-1837	9G
Rise	A 1559-1993	1725-1846	6,8			Skirlaugh			5J
Roos	A 1571-1998	1571-1842	6,8	1571-1679	1572-1837	Patrington			4L
Routh	A 1631-1993	1731-1860	6,8	1750-1837		Beverley			5I
Rowley	A 1653-1998	1731-1861	8	1605-1861		Beverley			4H
Rudston	A 1550-1995	1550-1856	6,8	1694-1842		Bridlington			8J
Rufforth	B 1655-1992	1655-1889	8	1582-1852		York			6B
Ruston Parva	A 1572-1992	1730-1875	6,8,9	1710-1879		Driffield			7I(B)
Sancton	B 1538-1915	1728-1864	5,6,8,9	1599-1864		Pocklington		1787-1840	5G
Scampston	B 1783-1992	1866-1867	5,6,8	1638-1845		Malton			9G
Scarborough	A 1653-1993	1653-1861	5,6,8,9	1653-1791	1653-1812	Beverley			5I(I)
Scrayingham	B 1648-1977	1648-1889	5,6,8,9	1626-1865		Pocklington			7E
Sculcoates								1797-1840	3I
All Saints	A 1538-1973	1538-1870	6,8	1538-1837		Sculcoates			3I
Christchurch	A 1822-1962	1822-1841	6,8	1822-1841		Sculcoates			3I
Seaton Ross	B 1653-1980	1653-1887	5,6,8,9	1600-1920		Pocklington			5F
Settrington	B 1559-1979	1559-1887	5,6,8,9	1559-1856	1560-1812	Malton	1790-1812		8G
Sherburn	B 1653-1991	1653-1886	6,8	1604-1889		Scarborough			9H
Shipton	B 1675-1981	1675-1886	5,6,8,9	1600-1870		Pocklington			5G

YORKSHIRE (EAST RIDING)

parish name	deposited original registers	I.G.I.	local census indexes	copies of registers at Soc. Gen.	Boyd's marriage index	1837-1851 Registration District	Pallot's marriage index	non-conform. records at P.R.O.	map ref.
Sigglesthorne	A 1562-1990	1732-1850	6,8	1600-1850		Skirlaugh			5J
Skeffling	A 1585-1992	1734-1853	6,8			Patrington			2M
Skerne	A 1561-1992	1723-1870	6,8	1600-1872		Driffield			6I
Skidby	A 1653-1990	1726-1835	6,8	1600-1835		Beverley		1824-1836	4H
Skipsea	A 1720-1978	1728-1865	6,8	1750-1837		Bridlington		1807-1836	6J
Skipwith	B 1670-1999	1670-1886	5,6,8,9	1670-1754		Selby			5D
Skirlaugh	A 1711-1986	1722-1866	5,6,8			Skirlaugh		1774-1816	5J
Skirpenbeck	B 1660-1993	1660-1875	5,6,8,9	1631-1876		Pocklington			7E
Sledmere	A 1696-1986	1720-1866	6,8,9	1626-1866		Driffield			8H
South Cave	A 1558-1992	1558-1875	6,8	1558-1783		Beverley	1790-1837	1791-1831	3G
South Dalton	A 1649-1861	1706-1849	6,8	1600-1849		Beverley			5H
Speeton	A 1636-1992	1722-1768	6,8			Bridlington			9J
Sproatley	A 1657-1995	1720-1846	6,8			Skirlaugh			4K
Stillingfleet	B 1598-1993	1598-1886	5,6,8	1599-1883		York			5C
Sunk Island	A 1820-1983	1820-1852	6,8			Patrington			2L
Sutton on Hull	A 1558-2000	1721-1834	5,6,8			Sculcoates			4J
Sutton upon Derwent	B 1593-1993	1593-1875	6,8,9	1628-1883		Pocklington			6E
Swine	A 1706-1993	1725-1867	6,8			Skirlaugh			4J
Tadcaster	B 1570-1989	1570-1859	5,6,8	1598-1859		Tadcaster		1763-1840	5B
Thorganby	B 1653-1973	1653-1886	5,6,8	1610-1874		York			5E
Thornton	B 1615-1987	1615-1887	5,6,8	1602-1848		Pocklington			5E
Thorp Arch	B 1595-1970	1705-1860	5,6,8	1603-1860		Tadcaster			5A(e)
Thorpe Bassett	B 1656-1979	1656-1892	5,6,8,9	1604-1874	1672-1837	Malton			9G
Thwing	A 1692-1992	1732-1836	6,8	1599-1641		Bridlington			8I
Tunstall	A 1567-1991	1724-1856	6,8,9			Patrington			4L
Ulrome	A 1813-1992	1720-1870	6,8			Bridlington			7J
Upper Poppleton	B 1829-1980	1829-1873	8,9	1846-1873		York			6B(b)
Walkington	A 1754-1992	1813-1847	6,8			Beverley			4H
Walton	B 1619-1993	1600-1875	5,8	1619-1837		Tadcaster			6A(d)
Warter	B 1653-1981	1653-1886	5,6,8,9	1598-1887		Pocklington			6G
Watton	A 1558-1993	1712-1848	6,8	1626-1865		Driffield			6I
Wawne	A 1653-1999	1707-1870	6,8			Beverley			4J
Weaverthorpe	B 1682-1978	1682-1886	6,8,9	1631-1852		Driffield			8H
Welton	A 1713-2000	1723-1852	6,8			Sculcoates			3H
Welwick	A 1653-1971	1725-1857	6,8	1754-1840		Patrington			2L
West Heslerton	B 1561-1931	1561-1867	5,6,8,9	1561-1840	1585-1837	Malton			9H
Westow	B 1549-1993	1549-1874	5,6,8,9	1626-1873		Malton			8F
Wetwang	A 1653-1988	1747-1868	6,8	1632-1868		Driffield			7H
Wharram le Street	B 1538-1978	1538-1888	5,6,8,9	1631-1836	1538-1645	Malton			8G
Wharram Percy	B 1554-1933	1538-1858	5,6,8,9	1628-1848		Malton			7G
Wheldrake	B 1603-1975	1603-1886	5,6,8	1631-1781		York			5D
Wighill	B 1717-1992	1715-1891	5,8	1600-1861		Tadcaster			6A
Wilberfoss	B 1618-1989	1618-1886	5,6,8	1600-1875		Pocklington			6E
Willerby	A 1653-1978	1705-1865	6,8,9	1601-1865		Scarborough			9I
Winestead	A 1578-1995	1578-1848	6,8	1578-1812	1578-1812	Patrington	1790-1812		3L
Wintringham	B 1558-1993	1558-1885	5,6,8	1558-1914	1558-1812	Malton	1790-1812		9G
Withernwick	A 1652-1988	1712-1874	6,8			Skirlaugh			5K
Wold Newton	A 1708-1993	1722-1859	6,8	1708-1840	1725-1785	Bridlington			9I
Wressell	A 1724-1992	1720-1866	5,8,9	1600-1866		Howden		1795-1840	4E
Yapham	B 1654-1988	1654-1856	6,8	1696-1856		Pocklington			6F
Yedingham	B 1707-1993	1813-1892	6,8	1626-1878		Malton			9H
York								1721-1838	6C
All Saints, North St	B 1578-1981	1578-1886	5,8,9	1626-1865		York			6C
All Saints, Pavement	B 1554-1987	1554-1886	5,8,9	1554-1738		York			6C
Holy Trinity, Goodramgate	B 1573-1957	1573-1899	5,8,9	1573-1865	1582-1837	York	1790-1812		6C
Holy Trinity, Kings Court	B 1616-1885	1616-1885	5,8,9	1716-1837	1631-1837	York	1790-1812		6C
Holy Trinity, Micklegate	B 1586-1947	1586-1888	5,8,9	1586-1837	1586-1837	York			6C
Minster			5,8,9	1634-1836	1681-1762	York			6C
Minster (Bedern Chapel)		1821-1856	5,8,9			York			6C
St Crux	B 1539-1896	1540-1887	5,8,9	1539-1872	1541-1677	York			6C
St Cuthbert	B 1581-1975	1718-1875	5,8,9	1581-1975		York			6C
St Denis	B 1558-1964	1558-1886	5,8,9	1558-1812		York			6C
St Helen, Stonegate	B 1568-1967	1568-1885	5,8,9	1601-1892		York			6C
St John, Micklegate	B 1570-1933	1570-1874	5,8,9	1570-1874		York			6C
St Lawrence	B 1606-1975	1606-1886	5,8,9	1606-1812	1620-1837	York	1790-1812		6C
St Margaret	B 1558-1973	1574-1886	5,8,9	1600-1866		York			6C
St Martin, Coney St.	B 1557-1942	1557-1887	5,8,9	1557-1837	1557-1812	York	1790-1812		6C
St Martin cum Gregory, Micklegate	B 1539-1939	1537-1887	5,8,9	1539-1869	1538-1734	York			6C
St Mary Bishophill Jr	B 1602-1951	1602-1892	5,8,9	1602-1857	1603-1837	York	1790-1812		6C
St Mary Bishophill Sr	B 1598-1897	1598-1892	5,8,9	1600-1871		York			6C
St Mary Castlegate	B 1604-1974	1604-1887	5,8,9	1604-1837	1641-1837	York			6C
St Maurice	B 1650-1966	1647-1886	5,8,9	1648-1812	1648-1837	York	1780-1812		6C
St Michael le Belfrey	B 1565-1983	1565-1875	5,8,9	1565-1875	1563-1837	York			6C
St Michael Spurriergate	B 1598-1964	1598-1887	5,8,9	1598-1691	1598-1691	York			6C
St Olave	B 1538-1962	1538-1891	5,8,9	1538-1785	1538-1644	York	1780-1834		6C
St Sampson	B 1640-1965	1640-1880	5,8,9	1626-1851		York			6C
St Saviour	B 1567-1939	1567-1888	5,8,9	1626-1869		York			6C

YORKSHIRE (EAST RIDING)

Original registers deposited at:
A = East Riding of Yorkshire Archive Office, County Hall, Beverley HU17 9BA
B = The Borthwick Institute of Historical Research, St Anthony's Hall, Peasholme Green, York YO1 7PW
C = North Yorkshire County Record Office, County Hall, Northallerton, North Yorkshire DL7 8AF

Study adjacent parishes in counties of North Riding, West Riding and Lincolnshire

East Riding of Yorkshire Archive Office, County Hall, Beverley HU17 9BA
Borthwick Institute of Historical Research, University of York, St Anthony's Hall, Peaseholme Green, York, YO1 7PW
Hull City Archives, 79 Lowgate, Hull HU1 1HN
York City Archives Department, Art Gallery Building, Exhibition Square, York, YO1 2EW

The following useful indexes have been compiled – see Introduction
Census Indexes 1851, 1861 & 1891 – East Yorkshire FHS, c/o Mrs J. Bangs, 5 Curlew Close, Molescroft, Beverley, East Yorkshire HU17 7QN
Census Indexes 1851 & 1891 – City of York and District FHS, c/o Mrs C. Mennell, 4 Orchard Close, Dringhouses, York YO24 2XN
Census Index 1891 – Mr T. Lamyman, 6 Godber Drive, Bracebridge Heath, Lincoln LN4 2LN for Hull and Sculcoates RD's.
Marriage Index 1754-1837 – Mrs P.M. Pattinson, 250 Longridge Road, Grimsargh, Preston, Lancashire PR2 5AQ
Marriage Index – East Riding of Yorkshire Archives Service, Beverley (as above)
Marriage Index – Mr P.R. Joiner, Greystones, The Spital, Yarm-on-Tees, Yorkshire TS15 9EX
Settlement and Removal Index – H. Woledge, 23 Woodlands, Beverley, East Yorkshire HU17 8BT
Monumental Inscriptions – East Yorkshire FHS, c/o Mrs J.P. Morris, 1 Eppleworth Road, Cottingham, East Yorkshire HU16 5YE
Archbishop of York's Marriage Bonds and Allegations – The Borthwick Institute of Historical Research (as above)

The East Riding's length from east to west is 45 miles and from north to south about 35 miles but on the coast from Filey to Spurn Head is 50 miles. It is watered by four principal rivers: the Humber, Hull, Ouse and Derwent. The population in 1841 was 194,936; in 1851, 220,983; in 1861, 240,227; in 1871, 290,505; in 1881, 315,460.

The soils are mainly sand, gravel, loam and clay. Produce included wheat, barley, oats, flax, potatoes, cabbages, beans and turnips. Cattle, sheep and horses were bred and there was a fishing industry. Manufactures were circumscribed – there were some paint and colour works, oil mills, soap and white lead works; comb-making and coarse hosiery.

The information in the Index is abbreviated, and may mislead the searcher if reference is not made to the details contained in the several publications listed in the Introduction. It is essential that users of this book check the appropriate works before making further enquiries.

YORKSHIRE (NORTH RIDING)

parish name	deposited original registers	I.G.I.	local census indexes	copies of registers at Soc. Gen.	Boyd's marriage index	1837-1851 Registration District	Pallot's marriage index	non-conform. records at P.R.O.	map ref.
Ainderby Steeple	A 1667-1992	1813-1854	5,8,9			Northallerton			6F
Aldborough	A 1538-1965	1538-1829	5,6,8,9			Richmond		1802-1837	3G
Allerston	A 1680-1980	1680-1879	5,6,8	1604-1868		Pickering			5K
Alne	B 1560-1980	1560-1885	5,6,8,9	1600-1838		Easingwold			3H
Ampleforth	A 1644-1997	1725-1891	5,6,8,9			Helmsley		1802-1818	4I
Appleton le Street	B 1715-1989	1723-1853	5,8,9	1600-1853		Malton			4J
Appleton Wiske	A 1596-1991	1730-1848	5,8,9			Northallerton			7G
Arkengarthdale	A 1726-1938	1754-1879	5,8,9	1727-1812		Reeth			7B
Askrigg	A 1701-1961	1674-1848	4,5,6,7,8,9	1674-1701		Askrigg			6B
Aysgarth	A 1709-1946	1691-1848	4,5,6,7,8,9	1709-1840		Askrigg			5C
Bagby	A 1556-1995	1556-1875	5,8,9	1556-1894		Thirsk			5G
Barningham	E 1581-1995	1674-1844	5,8	1732-1844		Teesdale			7C
Barton									7E
St Cuthberts	A 1582-1978	1755-1879	5,8			Darlington			7E
St Mary	A 1619-1842	1619-1879	5,6,8			Darlington			7E
Barton le Street	B 1701-1978	1720-1840	5,8,9	1600-1840		Malton			4J
Bedale	A 1560-1989	1732-1847	5,8,9	1732-1734	1560-1653	Bedale		1785-1840	6E
Bilsdale	A 1590-1958	1588-1864	5,6,8,9			Helmsley			7H
Birdforth	B 1616-1991	1739-1872	5,8,9	1632-1872		Thirsk			4H(A)
Birkby	A 1721-1993	1813-1832	5,8,9			Northallerton			7F
Bolton upon Swale	A 1656-1981	1663-1846	5,8,9			Richmond			7E
Bossall	B 1611-1972	1611-1889	5,6,8	1601-1863		York			3J
Bowes	E 1670-1996	1615-1847	5,6,8	1615-1837		Teesdale			8B
Brafferton	B 1798-1970	1720-1867	8,9			Easingwold			4G
Brandsby	B 1575-1982	1720-1875	6,8,9	1631-1888		Easingwold		1820-1840	4I
Brignall	A 1588-1836	1779-1847	8			Teesdale			8C
Brompton	A 1584-1980	1584-1875	6,8,9	1788-1951		Scarborough			5L
Brompton	A 1593-1984	1594-1878	6,8,9			Northallerton			6F
Brotton	C 1641-1962	1641-1878	5,6,8,9			Guisborough			9I
Bulmer	B 1571-1975	1572-1889	5,8,9	1596-1865		Malton			4J
Burneston	A 1566-1993	1786-1847	5,6,8			Bedale			5F
Buttercrambe	B 1635-1772	1640-1763	5,6,8	1631-1681		York			2J
Carlton	A 1700-1979	1730-1858	5,7,8,9			Stokesley		1815-1837	7H
Carlton Miniott	A 1707-1967	1835-1866	5,8,9			Thirsk			5G
Castle Bolton	A 1684-1978	1678-1848	4,5,6,7,8,9	1753-1848		Leyburn			6C
Catterick	A 1653-1988	1615-1885	5,8,9			Richmond		1758-1837	6E
Cayton	D 1684-1986	1684-1860	6,8,9	1684-1840	1676-1837	Scarborough	1790-1800		5M
Cleasby	A 1712-1993	1790-1847	5,8			Darlington			8E
Clifton (see York St Michael Le Belfrey, St Olave and St Mary Castlegate)									2I
Cloughton	D 1685-1986	1730-1874	6,8,9			Scarborough			6M
Cold Kirby	A 1738-1979	1763-1870	5,8,9			Helmsley			5H
Coverham	A 1707-1985	1805-1848	8	1805-1845		Leyburn			5C
Cowesby	A 1697-1990	1813-1861	5,8,9			Thirsk			6G
Coxwold	B 1583-1962	1583-1848	5,8,9	1583-1848		Easingwold			4H
Crambe	B 1711-1939	1718-1886	5,6,8,9	1601-1835		Malton			3J
Crathorne	A 1723-1984	1731-1875	5,8,9			Stokesley		1777-1839	7G
Crayke	B 1558-1982	1558-1837	5,8	1558-1812	1558-1812	Easingwold			4H
Croft	A 1615-1994		5,8			Darlington			7E
Cropton	A 1754-1991	1710-1868	5,6,8			Pickering			6J
Cundall	A 1582-1997	1582-1847	8	1582-1780	1582-1780	Ripon			4G
Dalby	B 1656-1975	1656-1889	5,8,9	1656-1881	1656-1837	Easingwold			4I
Danby	A 1585-1991	1585-1875	5,8,9	1585-1812	1585-l812	Guisborough	1790-1812	1663-1837	7J
Danby Wiske	A 1621-1992	1690-1847	5,8,9			Northallerton			6F
Deighton	A 1686-1993	1758-1876	5,8,9			Northallerton			7F
Downholme	A 1736-1995	1813-1848	5,8,9	1813-1848		Richmond			6D
Easby	A 1670-1968	1801-1848	5,8,9	1801-1848		Richmond			7E
Easington	C 1606-1956	1720-1876	5,8,9			Guisborough			8J
Easingwold	B 1599-1967	1599-1886	5,8	1599-1837	1599-1812	Easingwold	1790-1812	1815-1840	4H
East Cowton	A 1754-1985	1752-1848	5,8			Northallerton			7F
East Harsley	A 1693-1991	1693-1868	5,8			Northallerton			7G
East Rounton	A 1595-1982	1595-1845	5,8,9	1595-1837	1596-1837	Stokesley	1790-1837		7G
East Witton	A 1670-1955	1663-1847	5,8,9	1751-1836		Leyburn			5D
Ebberston	A 1678-2000	1680-1868	5,6,8	1723		Pickering			5L
Egton	A 1622-1996	1617-1869	5,6,8,9	1723-1812		Whitby		1835-1840	7K
Ellerburn	A 1691-1967	1702-1875	8	1718-1738		Pickering			5K
Eryholme	A 1568-1978	1674-1847	8	1575-1789	1568-1754	Darlington			7F
Eskdaleside	A 1723-1973	1813-1865	6,8,9			Whitby			7K
Eston	C 1590-1992	1590-1878	5,6,8,9	1590-1878	1590-1812	Guisborough	1790-1812		9H
Faceby	A 1768-1983	1731-1858	5,8,9	1731-1859		Stokesley			7H
Farlington	B 1614-1989	1718-1837	5,8,9	1632-1837		Easingwold			3I
Felixkirk	A 1598-1993	1718-1866	5,8,9	1598-1866		Thirsk		1808-1831	5H
Finghall	A 1592-1990		5,8,9			Leyburn			6D
Forcett	A 1596-1993	1664-1847	5,8,9			Richmond			8D
Foston	B 1588-1966	1718-1888	5,6,8,9	1622-1835		Malton			3J
Fylingdales	A 1653-1964	1740-1875	6,8	1600-1841		Whitby			7L
Gate Helmsley	B 1689-1993	1689-1887	5,6,8	1689-1837	1691-1753	York			2J(E)
Gilling	A 1571-1997	1572-1877	5,8,9	1573-1812		Helmsley			4I
Gilling	A 1639-1996	1678-1834	5,8,9			Richmond			7E
Glaisdale	A 1758-1974	1672-1875	5,6,8,9			Whitby			7J
Goathland	A 1669-1924	1723-1867	5,6,8,9	1669-1736	1670-1731	Whitby			7K
Great Ayton	A 1666-1995	1601-1875	5,8,9	1600-1812	1729-1837	Stokesley	1790-1812	1763-1836	8H
Great Edstone	A 1557-1944	1557-1876	6,8			Helmsley			5J
Great Langton	A 1695-1996		5,8			Northallerton			6F
Great Smeaton	A 1573-1989	1679-1847	5,8,9			Northallerton			7F
Grinton	A 1640-1950	1640-1876	5,6,8	1640-1847	1640-1802	Reeth	1790-1802	1787-1837	6C
Guisborough	C 1661-1979	1775-1870	5,6,8,9	1600-1615		Guisborough		1799-1836	8I
Hackness	D 1566-1984	1566-1875	6,8,9	1557-1840	1566-1785	Scarborough			6L
Hardraw	A 1750-1978	1750-1847	8,9			Askrigg			6A
Harum	A 1600-1690	1863-1873	5,8,9			Helmsley			5I

YORKSHIRE (NORTH RIDING)

parish name	deposited original registers	I.G.I.	local census indexes	copies of registers at Soc. Gen.	Boyd's marriage index	1837-1851 Registration District	Pallot's marriage index	non-conform. records at P.R.O.	map ref.
Harwood Dale	D 1757-1992	1720-1875	6,8,9	1757-1840		Scarborough			6L
Haukswell	A 1593-1989	1637-1848	5,8,9			Leyburn			6D
Hawes	A 1695-1864	1687-1848	4,5,6,7,8,9			Askrigg			6A
Hawnby	A 1653-1996	1653-1852	5,8,9	1653-1722	1653-1722	Helmsley			6H
Haxby	B 1667-1993	1700-1867	5,8	1605-1867		York			2I
Helmsley	A 1575-1971	1716-1868	5,6,8,9		1691-1753	Helmsley			5I
Helperby (see Brafferton)			5,8,9						4G
Henderskelfe (see Bulmer)			5,8,9						4J(F)
Heworth (see York St Cuthbert and St Giles)									2I
High Worsall	A 1720-1997	1813-1860	5,8			Stockton			7G
Hilton	A 1698-1993	1749-1865	5,8,9			Stokesley			8G
Hinderwell	A 1601-1978	1601-1876	5,8	1601-1872		Whitby			8J
Hipswell	A 1664-1988	1664-1875	5,8,9	1770-1875		Richmond			6E
Holtby	B 1679-1992	1679-1843	5,6,8	1679-1812	1679-1754	York			2I
Hornby	A 1582-1978	1714-1824	5,8,9	1558-1824	1679-1753	Leyburn			6E
Horsehouse	A 1770-1975	1808-1848	8,9	1616-1817		Leyburn			5C
Hovingham	B 1642-1989	1642-1870	5,6,8,9	1598-1856		Malton			4I
Hudswell	A 1602-1992	1674-1847	5,8	1736-1840		Richmond			7D
Huntington	B 1590-1991	1590-1718	5,8	1598-1853	1590-1836	York			2I
Husthwaite	AB 1674-1983	1703-1877	5,8,9	1660-1877		Easingwold			4H
Hutton Bonville	A 1727-1990	1813-1876	5,8,9			Northallerton			7F
Hutton Buscel	A 1572-1992	1572-1864	6,8,9	1572-1864		Scarborough			5L
Hutton Conyers (ex.par.)			8			Ripon			4F
Hutton Magna	A 1670-1962	1679-1847	5,8			Teesdale			8D
Huttons Ambo	B 1714-1990	1714-1867	5,6,8,9	1632-1839		Malton			4J
Ingleby Arncliffe	A 1654-1991	1654-1878	5,8,9			Stokesley			7G
Ingleby Greenhow	A 1539-1997	1539-1861	5,8,9	1539-1800	1560-1798	Stokesley	1790-1800		7I
Kilburn	A 1575-1994	1575-1867	5,8,9	1600-1812	1600-1812	Thirsk	1790-1812		5H
Kildale	A 1719-1998	1730-1870	8,9			Stokesley			7I
Kirby Hill	A 1576-1995	1576-1848	5,8,9	1576-1812	1606-1812	Ripon	1790-1812		4G
Kirby in Cleveland	A 1627-1987	1627-1875	8,9			Stokesley			7H
Kirby Knowle	A 1642-1994	1731-1875	5,8,9			Thirsk			5G
Kirby Misperton	A 1788-1976	1721-1876	5,6,8,9	1600-1837		Pickering			4J
Kirby Sigston	A 1574-1985	1574-1867	5,8,9			Northallerton			6G
Kirby Wiske	A 1616-1941	1674-1847	5,8,9			Thirsk			5F
Kirkby Fleetham	A 1591-1998	1591-1848	5,8,9	1591-1848		Bedale			6F
Kirkby Moorside	A 1622-1992	1813-1851	5,8,9	1600-1854		Helmsley		1814-1837	5J
Kirkby Ravensworth	A 1599-1990	1662-1884	8	1737-1884		Richmond			7D
Kirkdale	A 1579-1962	1728-1869	8	1603-1869		Helmsley			5I
Kirkleatham	C 1559-1986	1559-1879	5,6,8,9	1559-1975	1559-1812	Guisborough	1790-1812		9H
Kirkleavington	C 1734-1997	1730-1867	5,8,9			Stockton			8G
Kirklington	A 1568-1993	1568-1847	8,9	1568-1812	1569-1812	Bedale	1790-1812		5F
Lastingham	A 1559-1895	1721-1876	5,6,8,9			Pickering			6J
Leake	A 1570-1980	1570-1878	5,8,9	1810-1875		Northallerton			6G
Leeming	A 1823-1979		5,8			Bedale			5F
Levisham	A 1700-1979	1720-1864	5,8			Pickering			6K
Liverton	C 1665-1982	1720-1875	6,8,9			Guisborough			8J
Lockton	A 1713-1971	1718-1868	5,8			Pickering			6K
Lofthouse	C 1697-1981	1813-1872	6,8			Guisborough			8J
Lunds	A 1749-1971		5,6,8,9			Askrigg			6A
Lythe	A 1634-1985	1619-1857	5,6,8,9	1619-1837		Whitby		1814-1836	8K
Manfield	A 1593-1993	1595-1848	5,8	1594-1812	1595-1812	Darlington	1790-1812	1785-1840	8E
Marrick	A 1687-1951	1680-1846	5,8,9			Reeth			7C
Marske	A 1594-1996	1678-1848	5,6,8,9	1570-1984		Richmond		1786-1830	7D
Marske in Cleveland	C 1569-1972	1570-1865	5,8,9	1569-1984	1570-1812	Guisborough	1790-1812		9I
Marton	C 1572-1983	1730-1860	5,6,8,9	1572-1866		Pickering			8H
Marton le Forest	B 1539-1992	1720-1837	5,8	1601-1837		Easingwold			4I
Masham	A 1599-1965		8	1754-1847		Bedale	1780-1837		5D
Melsonby	A 1574-1999	1573-1863	5,8,9			Richmond			7E
Middleham	A 1604-1986		5,8,9			Leyburn		1815-1837	5D
Middleton	A 1671-1978	1710-1868	5,6,7,8,9			Pickering			5J
Middleton-on-Leven	A 1614-1996	1763-1840	5,8,9			Stokesley			8G
Middleton Tyas	A 1539-1979	1754-1875	5,8,9			Richmond			7E
Muker	A 1638-1954	1638-1848	5,8,9	1638-1842		Reeth		1766-1837	6B
Myton on Swale	B 1654-1993	1654-1854	5,8,9	1654-1856	1654-1750	Easingwold			3G
New Malton								1770-1837	4J
St Leonard	B 1600-1956	1600-1886	5,8	1601-1843		Malton			4J
St Michael	B 1570-1974	1570-1886	5,8	1600-1876		Malton			4J
Newton	C 1725-1984	1720-1860	5,6,8,9	1725-1812		Pickering		1791-1837	8H
Newton on Ouse	B 1653-1996	1718-1875	5,8,9	1631-1878	1776-1837	Easingwold			3H
Normanby	A 1699-1990	1711-1853	5,6,8,9	1699-1812		Helmsley			5J
Northallerton	A 1592-1991	1592-1875	5,8,9			Northallerton	1780-1837	1806-1837	6F
North Otterington	A 1589-1986	1813-1856	5,8,9			Northallerton			6F
Nunnington	A 1539-1985	1566-1878	5,6,8,9			Helmsley			5I
Old Byland	A 1654-1974	1755-1875	5,6,8,9	1777-1875		Helmsley			5H
Old Malton	B 1606-1959	1606-1850	5,8	1606-1863		Malton		1814-1837	4K
Ormesby	C 1599-1994	1701-1838	5,6,8	1599-1899		Guisborough			8H
Osbaldwick	B 1581-1983	1581-1886	5,6,8	1632-1875		York			2I
Osmotherley	A 1696-1979	1696-1876	5,8,9			Northallerton		1771-1839	6G
Oswaldkirk	A 1538-1996	1538-1867	5,8,9	1538-1837	1538-1659	Helmsley			5I
Over Silton	A 1678-1997	1678-1877	5,8	1601-1877		Northallerton			6G
Overton	B 1593-1962	1732-1848	5,8	1601-1848		York			2H
Patrick Brompton	A 1558-1991	1663-1848	8,9	1727-1848		Leyburn			6E
Pickering	A 1559-1967	1709-1873	5,6,8,9	1600-1873		Pickering		1789-1837	5K
Pickhill	A 1571-1988	1567-1848	5,8,9	1567-1812	1567-1812	Thirsk	1790-1812		5F
Raskelf	B 1747-1909	1747-1875	5,8	1600-1837		Easingwold			4H
Richmond	A 1556-1978	1636-1847	5,8,9	1556-1632		Richmond		1748-1840	7D
Rokeby	E 1589-1993	1598-1847	5,8	1598-1837		Teesdale			8D
Romaldkirk	E 1578-1993	1578-1773	5,8	1655-1812	1578-1753	Teesdale		1748-1837	9B

parish name	deposited original registers	I.G.I.	local census indexes	copies of registers at Soc. Gen.	Boyd's marriage index	1837-1851 Registration District	Pallot's marriage index	non-conform. records at P.R.O.	map ref.
Rosedale	A 1616-1917	1616-1876	5,6,8,9	1783-1876		Pickering			6J
Roxby	A 1758-1841	1757-1831	5,6,8,9	1758-1835		Whitby	1790-1812		8J
Rudby	A 1584-1972	1736-1856	8			Stokesley			7G
Salton	A 1573-1978	1707-1838	5,6,8,9	1573-1905		Helmsley			5J
Sandhutton	A 1707-1988	1748-1874	5,6,8	1634-1681		Thirsk			5G
Scalby	D 1556-1972	1730-1873	8,9			Scarborough			6M
Scarborough	D 1687-1987	1602-1847	5,6,9	1601-1647		Scarborough	1790-1800	1703-1837	5M
Scawton	A 1720-1980	1720-1880	5,8,9			Helmsley			5H
Scruton	A 1572-1992	1572-1778	5,8,9	1572-1837		Bedale			6F
Seamer	D 1559-1990	1710-1860	5,8,9	1559-1838	1560-1837	Scarborough			5M
Seamer in Cleveland	A 1638-1992	1737-1871	8			Stokesley			8H
Sessay	A 1612-1999	1600-1837	5,8,9	1600-1837		Thirsk	1790-1812		4G
Sheriff Hutton	B 1628-1992	1718-1856	5,6,8,9	1628-1856		Malton			3I
Sinnington	A 1577-1976	1725-1870	5,6,8,9			Pickering			5J
Skelton by York	B 1538-1996	1732-1874	5,6,8	1600-1872		York			2H
Skelton in Cleveland	C 1567-1981	1727-1874	5,6,8			Guisborough			8I
Slingsby	B 1687-1971	1813-1854	5,8,9	1600-1854		Malton			4J
Snainton	A 1713-1984		6,8,9			Scarborough			5L
Sneaton	A 1581-1992	1719-1875	5,6,8,9			Whitby			7K
Sockburn (Durham)									7F
South Cowton	A 1568-1986	1615-1848	8			Northallerton			7F
South Kilvington	A 1572-1963	1744-1860	5,8,9			Thirsk			5G
South Otherington	A 1715-1996	1731-1855	5,8	1601-1855		Thirsk			5G
Sowerby	A 1569-1985	1733-1864	5,8,9			Thirsk		1740-1837	5G
Spennithorne	A 1573-1978	1637-1847	5,8,9			Leyburn			6D
Stainton	C 1551-1992	1551-1838	5,8,9	1754-1837	1556-1837	Stockton			8G
Stalling Busk	A 1743-1968	1792-1875	8,9						5B
Stanwick St John	A 1652-1993	1615-1847	5,8,9			Richmond			8E
Startforth	E 1668-1988	1656-1848	5,8	1665-1700	1665-1701	Teesdale			8C
Stillington	B 1666-1971	1710-1864	5,8,9			Easingwold			3H
Stockton on the Forest	B 1653-1996	1653-1886	5,6,8	1600-1864		York			2I
Stokesley	A 1571-1948	1571-1860	5,8,9	1571-1750	1571-1750	Stokesley		1799-1837	7H
Stonegrave	A 1584-1990	1585-1856	5,6,8,9			Helmsley			4I
Strensall	B 1566-1968	1566-1886	5,6,8	1600-1882		York			3I
Sutton on the Forest	B 1557-1996	1719-1856	5,6,8	1603-1856		Easingwold		1808-1831	3H
Terrington	B 1599-1993	1599-1863	5,6,8,9	1598-1863	1599-1812	Malton	1790-1812		4I
Thirkleby	A 1611-1994	1718-1861	5,6,8,9	1611-1836		Thirsk			4G
Thirsk	A 1556-1986	1556-1864	5,8,9	1556-1721	1556-1710	Thirsk		1775-1840	5G
Thormanby	B 1658-1993	1730-1835	5,8,9	1605-1835		Easingwold			4H(B)
Thornton Dale	A 1538-1973	1716-1858	5,6,8			Pickering			5K
Thornton le Moor (see North Otterington)									5G
Thornton le Street	A 1598-1995	1813-1875	5,6,8,9			Thirsk		1775-1840	5G
Thornton Steward	A 1563-1837	1637-1841	5,8,9		1750-1800	Leyburn		1663-1837	5D
Thornton Watlass	A 1574-1979	1674-1848	8	1746-1848		Northallerton			5E
Topcliffe	A 1570-1985	1714-1856	5,8,9			Thirsk			4G
Ugglebarnby	A 1732-1899	1813-1865	5,6,8			Whitby			7K
Upleatham	C 1654-1947	1724-1873	5,6,8,9	1654-1812		Guisborough			8I
Upper Helmsley	B 1642-1993	1642-1889	5,6,8	1631-1857	1665-1752	York			2J(D)
Warthill	B 1689-1992	1689-1889	5,6,8		1691-1752	York			2I(C)
Wath	A 1571-1969	1782-1848	5,6,7,8			Ripon			4F
Welbury	A 1697-1993	1633-1861	5,8,9			Northallerton			7G
Well	A 1558-1990	1656-1846	5,8,9	1558-1850		Bedale			5E
Wensley	A 1538-1962	1538-1877	5,8,9	1538-1847	1538-1754	Leyburn		1812-1836	6D
West Acklam	C 1735-1979	1737-1875	5,8			Stockton			8G
Westerdale	A 1562-1979	1730-1865	5,8,9			Guisborough			7I
West Rounton	A 1725-1982	1725-1885	5,8	1725-1917	1725-1837	Northallerton			7G
West Tanfield	A 1653-1991	1637-1839	8			Ripon			5E
West Witton	A 1576-1898	1725-1869	4,5,6,7,8,9			Leyburn		1663-1837	5C
Whenby	B 1556-1981	1556-1892	6,8,9	1600-1982		Easingwold			4I
Whitby	A 1608-1945	1600-1862	5,6,8,9	1600-1812	1676-1739	Whitby		1695-1840	8K
Whorlton	A 1721-1994	1721-1875	5,8,9			Stokesley			7G
Wigginton	B 1691-1992	1691-1887	5,8	1598-1876		York			3I
Wilton	C 1719-1972	1719-1880	5,8,9	1601-1983		Guisborough			9H
Wycliffe	A 1681-1837	1692-1847	5,8			Teesdale		1743-1838	8D
Wykeham	A 1653-1992	1653-1851	5,6,8,9	1601-1851		Scarborough			5L
Yafforth	A 1675-1985	1761-1812	5,8,9			Northallerton			6F
Yarm	C 1649-1990	1751-1875	5,8,9	1649-1837		Stockton		1795-1840	8G

YORKSHIRE (NORTH RIDING)

Original registers deposited at:
A = North Yorkshire County Record Office, County Hall, Northallerton, North Yorkshire DL7 8AF
B = The Borthwick Institute of Historical Research, St Anthony's Hall, Peasholme Green, York YO1 7PW
C = Teeside Archives, Exchange House, 6 Marton Road, Middlesbrough TS1 1DB
D = East Riding County Record Office, County Hall, Beverley HU17 9BA
E = Durham County Record Office, County Hall, Durham DH1 5UL

Study adjacent parishes in counties of Durham, Westmorland, West Riding and East Riding

North Yorkshire County Record Office, County Hall, Northallerton, North Yorkshire, DL7 8AF
Teeside Archives, Exchange House, 6 Marton Road, Middlesbrough TS1 1DB

The following useful indexes have been compiled – see Introduction
Census Indexes 1841-1891 Bishopdale area – Bishopdale Archives, West Lane House, Bishopdale, Leyburn, North Yorkshire DL8 3TG
Census Index 1851 – Yorkshire Archaeological Society, c/o Mrs A.M. Hill, 23 Claremont, 23 Clarendon Road, Leeds, Yorkshire LS2 9NZ
Census Indexes 1851 & 1891 – City of York and District FHS, c/o Mrs C. Mennell, 4 Orchard Close, Dringhouses, York YO24 2XN
Census Index 1851 & 1891 – Cleveland, North Yorkshire & South Durham FHS, c/o Mr D.W. Taylor, 106 The Avenue, Nunthorpe, Middlesbrough, Cleveland TS7 0AH
Census Index 1861 – East Yorkshire FHS, c/o Mrs J. Bangs, 5 Curlew Close, Molescroft, Beverley, East Yorkshire HU17 7QN
Marriage Index – Mr P.R. Joiner, Greystones, The Spital, Yarm, Cleveland, TS15 9EX
Marriage Index 1813-1837 – Durham Record Office, County Hall, Durham DH1 5UL
Archbishop of York's Marriage Bonds and Allegations – Borthwick Institute (as above)

The North Riding's greatest length from north to south is about 45 miles, which diminishes in one part to about 20; and from west to east it is about 80 miles long. It is watered by eight principal rivers: The Tees, Derwent, Ouse, Rye, Swale, Fosse, Esk and Ure. The population in 1841 was 204,701; in 1851, 215,214; in 1861, 245,154; in 1871, 291,589; in 1881, 346,260;

Among the soils are shale, marl and clay. Oats were grown and, to a lesser extent, barley and rye, as well as turnips and clover. Timber was important and cattle, sheep and horses bred. Manufactures were not highly developed but there were oil mills, comb-making, coarse hosiery, soap and paint-works.

The information in the Index is abbreviated, and may mislead the searcher if reference is not made to the details contained in the several publications listed in the Introduction. It is essential that users of this book check the appropriate works before making further enquiries.

YORKSHIRE (WEST RIDING)

parish name	deposited original registers	I.G.I.	local census indexes	copies of registers at Soc. Gen.	Boyd's marriage index	1837-1851 Registration District	Pallot's marriage index	non-conform. records at P.R.O.	map ref.
Aberford	B 1540-1946	1540-1886	5,6,8	1540-1812		Tadcaster	1790-1813	1806-1838	3L(A)
Ackworth	A 1558-1957	1558-1875	5,8	1558-1840		Hemsworth			6H(B)
Addingham	E 1612-1949	1612-1846	5,7,8,9	1612-1812	1612-1812	Skipton	1790-1812	1829-1836	4G(A)
Adel	C 1606-1876	1606-1847	5,7,8,9	1606-1812	1606-1807	Otley	1790-1812		3J(A)
Adlingfleet	F 1694-1972	1720-1844	5,8	1694-1820		Goole			5L(B)
Adwick le Street	F 1547-1956	1547-1867	5,8	1547-1867	1547-1907	Doncaster			5H(B)
Adwick upon Dearne	F 1690-1985	1718-1841	5,8			Doncaster			4H(B)
Airmyn	F 1726-1999	1726-1874	5,8			Goole			6K(B)
Aldborough	D 1538-1965	1538-1829	5,8,9	1538-1611		Knaresborough		1802-1837	6K(A)
Aldfield	D 1809-1994		8,9			Ripon			6J(A)
Allerton Mauleverer	D 1557-1971	1557-1846	5,8	1557-1812		Knaresborough	1790-1812		5K(A)
Almondbury	A 1557-1987	1557-1835	4,5,8	1557-1806		Huddersfield		1807-1837	5D(B)
Alverthorpe	A 1825-1974	1825-1840	5,8			Wakefield			6F(B)
Anston	G 1544-1977	1707-1848	8	1598-1890		Worksop			1H(B)
Arkendale	D 1793-2000	1813-1848	5,8	1813-1848		Knaresborough			5K(A)
Arksey	F 1558-1974	1718-1875	8		1562-1837	Doncaster		1829-1837	4I(B)
Armley	C 1664-1964	1664-1845	5,8	1664-1812	1725-1753	Hunslet		1809-1837	8F(B)
Armthorpe	F 1653-1946	1718-1870	5,8		1653-1837	Doncaster			4J(B)
Arncliffe	D 1669-1941	1669-1844	5,7,8,9	1663-1812	1669-1812	Settle	1790-1812		7E(A)
Aston	G 1560-1969	1718-1837	8			Rotherham			2H(B)
Attercliffe	G 1719-1969	1748-1829	6,8			Sheffield		1798-1837	2F(B)
Austerfield	H 1559-1976	1559-1660	5,8	1559-1812	1560-1812	Doncaster	1790-1812		3J(B)
Badsworth	A 1583-1976	1584-1848	5,8	1583-1879		Hemsworth			5H(B)
Baildon	E 1621-1994	1621-1846	4,5,8,9	1621-1812		Otley		1807-1837	3H(A)
Bardsey	C 1538-1937	1538-1848	5,7,8,9	1538-1812	1539-1754	Tadcaster			3J(A)
Barnburgh	F 1557-1983	1557-1837	5,8			Doncaster			4H(B)
Barnby upon Don	F 1599-1975	1720-1854	5,8		1599-1837	Doncaster			5J(B)
Barnoldswick		1588-1835	8	1587-1837		Skipton		1753-1837	3E(A)
Barnsley	A 1568-1974	1568-1831	5,8	1568-1808	1569-1724	Barnsley		1785-1837	4F(B)
Barwick in Elmet	C 1653-1976	1600-1845	5,8	1600-1812	1631-1812	Tadcaster	1790-1812		3K(A)
Batley	A 1559-1976	1724-1841	5,6,8,9			Dewsbury		1796-1837	7E(B)
Bawtry	H 1653-1960	1813-1860	5,8	1653-1900		Doncaster		1819-1837	3J(B)
Beeston	C 1720-1964	1717-1837	5,8	1720-1812	1720-1753	Hunslet			7F(B)
Bentham	D 1666-1987	1673-1812	8	1666-1812	1668-1837	Settle	1790-1812		6B(A)
Bierley	E 1824-1992	1824-1846	8,9			Bradford			7E(B)
Bingley	E 1577-1936	1577-1841	4,5,6,7,8,9	1577-1686	1577-1686	Keighley		1754-1837	3H(A)
Birkenshaw	A 1831-1980	1831-1846	8			Dewsbury			7E(B)
Birkin	B 1649-1873	1649-1873	5,8,9	1631-1862		Pontefract			7I(B)
Birstall	A 1558-1919	1724-1847	8	1558-1687		Dewsbury		1724-1837	7E(B)
Bishop Thornton	D 1816-1998	1816-1835	8,9			Ripon		1806-1840	6J(A)
Blubberhouses (see Fewston)									5H(A)
Blyth	H 1556-1968	1813-1865	8			Worksop/E Retford		1819-1837	3J(B)
Bolsterstone	G 1736-1972	1778-1872	8			Wortley			3E(B)
Bolton Abbey	D 1689-1981	1634-1847	5,7,8	1689-1812	1689-1812	Skipton	1790-1812		5G(A)
Bolton by Bowland	I 1558-1880	1558-1841	8	1558-1812	1560-1812	Clitheroe	1790-1812		4D(A)
Bolton upon Dearne	G 1561-1986	1561-1853	5,8	1561-1673		Doncaster			4H(B)
Boroughbridge	D 1823-1973		5,8,9			Knaresborough		1802-1837	6K(A)
Bracewell	I 1587-1986	1731-1855	8	1600-1639		Skipton			4E(A)
Bradfield	G 1559-1989	1559-1860	6,8	1559-1914	1559-1722	Wortley		1833-1840	3E(B)
Bradford	E 1599-1983	1718-1845	4,6,7,8,9	1596-1735	1596-1708	Bradford		1730-1857	8D(B)
Braithwell	F 1559-1994	1559-1867	5,8	1559-1837	1559-1837	Doncaster			3H(B)
Bramham	B 1586-1995	1586-1886	5,8	1586-1737	1679-1737	Tadcaster			9G(B)
Bramley	C 1717-1987	1717-1842	5,8	1717-1812	1724-1753	Rotherham		1783-1837	8E(B)
Brayton	B 1614-1982	1759-1836	5,8,9	1617-1836		Selby			7I(B)
Brighouse	A 1831-1985	1842-1846	8			Halifax		1782-1837	6D(B)
Brodsworth	F 1538-1987	1539-1871	5,8	1538-1813	1539-1837	Doncaster	1790-1812		4H(B)
Brotherton	A 1562-1985	1709-1871	8,9			Pontefract		1833-1837	7H(B)
Broughton in Craven	D 1671-1939	1741-1843	8			Skipton		1757-1837	4F(A)
Browsholme (ex.par.)			8			Clitheroe			3C(A)
Burghwallis	F 1596-1980	1593-1875	5,8	1596-1814		Doncaster		1761-1836	5I(B)
Burley in Wharfedale	E 1774-1980	1786-1846	5,7,8,9			Otley			4H(A)
Burnsall	D 1559-1871	1559-1900	5,7,8,9	1559-1812	1559-1700	Skipton	1790-1837		5F(A)
Burton in Lonsdale	D 1821-1998		8			Settle			7C(A)
Burton Leonard	D 1672-1905	1672-1846	8,9	1672-1812	1675-1755	Ripon			6J(A)
Calverley	C 1574-1988	1574-1834	4,5,6,7,8,9	1574-1720	1596-1720	Bradford		1742-1837	8E(B)
Campsall	F 1563-1990	1720-1875	5,8		1564-1837	Doncaster			5I(B)
Cantley	F 1539-1990	1539-1844	5,8	1539-1812	1540-1837	Doncaster			4J(B)
Carleton	A 1537-1896	1713-1846	5,8			Pontefract			4F(A)
Carleton Juxta Snaith	B 1617-1982	1598-1867	8	1598-1812	1618-1812	Selby	1790-1812		6J(B)
Castleford	A 1653-1978	1731-1870	5,8			Pontefract			6G(B)
Cawood	B 1591-1971	1591-1886	5,8,9	1636-1839		Selby			8I(B)
Cawthorne	A 1653-1966	1716-1845	5,8,9			Wortley		1815-1837	4E(B)
Chapel Allerton	C 1762-1981	1724-1837	5,8	1723-1812	1725-1753	Hunslet		1835-1837	8F(B)
Chapel le Dale	D 1754-1975	1775-1843	8		1762-1837	Settle	1790-1812		7C(A)
Chapel Thorpe	A 1829-1980		8			Wakefield			5G(B)
Church Fenton	B 1627-1996	1716-1866	8	1630-1693		Tadcaster			8I(B)
Clapham	D 1595-1959	1595-1845	8	1595-1812	1683-1812	Settle		1745-1840	6C(A)
Claton with Frickley	F 1577-1985	1577-1870	8,9	1577-1812	1580-1837	Doncaster	1790-1812	1748-1837	4H(B)
Cleckheaton	A 1761-1962	1743-1847	4,5,6,7,8,9			Bradford		1724-1837	7E(B)
Coley	A 1734-1970	1720-1846	8	1644-1752		Halifax			7D(B)
Collingham	C 1579-1941	1579-1837	5,8	1579-1837		Tadcaster			4K(A)
Conisbrough	F 1555-1992	1702-1844	5,8		1559-1836	Doncaster			3H(B)
Conistone	D 1567-1940	1567-1845	5,7,8,9	1559-1812	1568-1812	Skipton	1790-1812		6F(A)
Copgrove	D 1584-1997	1584-1847	5,8	1584-1790	1586-1790	Knaresborough	1781-1790		6K(A)
Cowthorpe	C 1568-1973	1568-1841	5,8	1568-1797	1568-1812	Knaresborough	1790-1812		5L(B)
Crofton	A 1615-1980	1615-1867	5,8	1615-1812	1615-1811	Wakefield	1790-1811		6G(B)
Cross Stone		1813-1838	8			Todmorden			7B(B)
Cumberworth	A 1708-1994	1731-1840	4,5,8	1708-1779		Huddersfield		1795-1837	4E(B)
Darfield	F 1628-1983	1628-1871	5,8	1598-1854		Barnsley			4G(B)

YORKSHIRE (WEST RIDING)

parish name	deposited original registers	I.G.I.	local census indexes	copies of registers at Soc. Gen.	Boyd's marriage index	1837-1851 Registration District	Pallot's marriage index	non-conform. records at P.R.O.	map ref.
Darrington	A 1567-1928	1567-1871	5,8	1567-1849	1567-1812	Pontefract	1790-1812		6H(B)
Darton	A 1539-1994	1700-1842	8	1609-1842		Barnsley			5F(B)
Dent	K 1611-1992	1611-1848	8	1611-1812	1611-1669	Sedbergh		1806-1837	9C(A)
Denton	C 1766-1989	1786-1847	5,7,8,9			Otley			4H(A)
Dewsbury	A 1538-1999	1538-1847	4,5,8	1538-1653	1538-1650	Dewsbury		1741-1837	6E(B)
Dinnington	G 1730-1966	1701-1834	8			Worksop			2I(B)
Dob Cross	J 1787-1999	1787-1790	8			Saddleworth			4B(B)
Doncaster	F 1557-1925	1735-1838	5,7,8	1557-1837	1701-1843	Doncaster	1790-1837	1797-1840	4I(B)
Drax	B 1597-1980	1720-1875	5,8,9	1632-1892		Selby			7J(B)
Drighlington	A 1816-1966	1816-1847	5,8,9			Bradford			7E(B)
Earls Heaton	A 1827-1960	1827-1847	8			Dewsbury			6F(B)
East Ardsley	A 1654-1994	1598-1847	5,8	1598-1812		Wakefield			7F(B)
Ecclesall	G 1784-1989	1748-1828	6,8,9			Ecclesall Bierlow			2F(B)
Ecclesfield	G 1558-1986	1558-1835	6,8	1558-1912	1550-1621	Wortley		1823-1836	3F(B)
Edlington	F 1731-1962	1718-1842	5,8			Doncaster			3I(B)
Elland	A 1559-1967	1559-1841	4,5,8	1559-1714	1671-1714	Halifax		1741-1837	6C(B)
Emley	A 1600-1983	1600-1846	4,5,8	1600-1836	1601-1812	Wakefield	1790-1837	1815-1837	5E(B)
Farnham	D 1570-1956	1569-1830	5,8,9	1569-1812	1570-1812	Knaresborough	1790-1812		6K(A)
Farnley	C 1791-1991	1724-1833	5,7,8,9	1724-1812	1729-1730	Hunslet		1816-1837	7E(B)
Featherstone	A 1558-1984	1558-1871	5,8	1558-1812	1558-1812	Pontefract			6G(B)
Felkirk with Bierley	A 1701-1978	1701-1834	5,8	1701-1812	1706-1812	Hemsworth	1790-1812		5G(B)
Ferry Fryston	A 1674-1966	1720-1856	5,8			Pontefract			7H(B)
Fewston	D 1594-1992	1593-1845	5,7,8,9	1593-1812	1593-1812	Otley	1790-1812		5I(A)
Finningley	H 1557-1992	1813-1852	5,8			Doncaster			3J(B)
Firbeck	G 1721-1954	1719-1836	8			Worksop			2I(B)
Fishlake	F 1561-1995	1718-1875	5,8		1561-1853	Thorne			5J(B)
Flockton	A 1813-1972	1713-1847	5,8,9	1713-1812		Wakefield		1795-1836	5E(B)
Friarmere	J 1769-1992	1767-1771	8			Saddleworth			5B(B)
Garforth	C 1663-1985	1631-1841	8	1631-1812	1631-1812	Pontefract	1790-1812	1833-1837	2L(A)
Gargrave	D 1558-1976	1558-1846	8	1558-1812	1538-1837	Skipton	1790-1812	1811-1836	5F(A)
Garsdale	K 1693-1919	1694-1843	8	1805-1843		Sedbergh			9C(A)
Giggleswick	D 1558-1976	1558-1847	8	1558-1769		Settle		1816-1837	6D(A)
Gildersome	A 1813-1981	1796-1840	5,8			Hunslet		1799-1819	7E(B)
Gisburn	I 1558-1967	1561-1847	8	1558-1838		Clitheroe		1773-1837	4E(A)
Golcar	A 1829-1989	1836-1846	4,5,8			Huddersfield		1835-1838	6C(B)
Goldsborough	D 1707-1979	1674-1829	5,8,9	1707-1812	1708-1812	Knaresborough			5K(A)
Greasborough	G 1747-1973	1768-1848	8			Rotherham			3G(B)
Great Ouseburn	D 1659-1997	1658-1848	5,8,9	1658-1822	1658-1812	Knaresborough			6L(A)
Grindleton	I 1744-1875	1744-1847	8	1813-1924		Clitheroe			3D(A)
Guiseley	C 1585-1956	1584-1836	5,7,8,9	1584-1837	1585-1720	Otley		1808-1837	3I(A)
Halifax								1742-1837	7C(B)
St James	A 1832-1952	1832-1844	5,8			Halifax			7C(B)
St John the Baptist	A 1538-1981	1538-1847	5,8	1538-1827	1538-1593	Halifax			7C(B)
Trinity	A 1798-1978	1832-1845	5,8			Halifax			7C(B)
Halton Gill	D 1813-1973	1790-1841	5,7,8,9	1663-1812		Settle	1790-1812		7E(A)
Hampsthwaite	D 1603-1992	1603-1846	5,8	1603-1807	1603-1807	Knaresborough	1790-1807	1823-1837	5I(A)
Handsworth	G 1558-1994	1708-1874	6,8			Sheffield			2G(B)
Hanging Heaton	A 1825-1982	1825-1847	8			Dewsbury			6E(B)
Harewood	C 1614-1977	1600-1842	4,5,7,8,9	1614-1812	1621-1812	Otley	1790-1812		4J(A)
Harrogate	C 1748-1959	1748-1847	5,8	1748-1812	1748-1812	Knaresborough		1817-1835	5J(A)
Harthill	G 1587-1970	1813-1864	8			Worksop			1H(B)
Hartshead	A 1612-1973	1612-1845	4,8	1600-1812	1612-1812	Halifax	1790-1812		6D(B)
Hartwith	D 1751-1972	1751-1812	8,9	1751-1812		Pateley Bridge			6I(A)
Hatfield	F 1566-1943	1720-1875	5,8	1556-1838	1566-1838	Thorne		1818-1837	5J(B)
Haverah Park (ex.par.)			8			Otley			5I(A)
Haworth	E 1645-1981	1645-1847	8	1645-1911	1645-1725	Keighley		1806-1837	8B(B)
Headingley	C 1722-1979	1717-1840	5,8	1634-1837	1627-1758	Hunslet	1733-1754		8F(B)
Heckmondwike	A 1831-1988	1831-1847	4,5,8			Dewsbury			6E(B)
Hemsworth	A 1654-1984	1538-1876	5,8	1654-1812	1599-1812	Hemsworth	1790-1812		5G(B)
Heptonstall	A 1593-1986	1599-1885	8	1593-1660	1593-1837	Todmorden		1745-1837	7B(B)
Hickleton	F 1694-1979	1626-1863	5,8	1626-1812		Doncaster			4H(B)
High Hoyland	A 1720-1982	1731-1855	4,5,8	1752-1861		Wortley		1797-1837	5F(B)
High Melton	F 1538-1987	1722-1881	5,8		1538-1836	Doncaster			4H(B)
Holbeck	C 1717-1976	1717-1835	5,8	1764-1812	1726-1752	Hunslet		1785-1854	7F(B)
Holmfirth	A 1736-1998	1813-1846	8			Huddersfield		1779-1840	5D(B)
Honley	A 1812-1964	1813-1847	4,8	1828-1855		Huddersfield		1795-1837	5C(B)
Hook	F 1678-1999	1688-1841	5,8	1678-1878		Goole		1829-1837	6K(B)
Hooton Pagnell	F 1538-1985	1538-1858	5,8	1538-1812	1569-1837	Doncaster	1790-1811		4H(B)
Hooton Roberts	G 1702-1977	1720-1846	8			Rotherham			3H(B)
Horbury	A 1598-1984	1598-1853	5,8	1598-1812	1598-1812	Wakefield	1790-1812		6F(B)
Horsforth	C 1693-1991	1620-1835	5,6,7,8,9			Hunslet		1800-1837	3I(A)
Horton (see Bradford)		1809-1833				Bradford			8C(B)
Horton in Ribblesdale	D 1556-1973	1556-1847	8	1556-1812	1557-1812	Settle			7D(A)
Howgill (see Sedbergh)						Sedbergh			10B(A)
Hubberholme	D 1663-1903	1663-1835	7,8,9	1663-1812	1667-1812	Settle	1790-1812		8E(A)
Huddersfield				1562-1819				1772-1840	6D(B)
St Paul	A 1831-1955		5,8	1831-1880		Huddersfield			6D(B)
St Peter	A 1562-1995	1566-1824	5,8	1562-1884		Huddersfield			6D(B)
Trinity Church	A 1819-1968	1819-1837	5,8	1819-1894		Huddersfield			6D(B)
Hunsingore	D 1626-1893	1626-1801	5,8,9	1626-1812	1626-1812	Knaresborough			5L(A)
Hunslet	C 1686-1967	1687-1837	8	1686-1812	1724-1753	Hunslet		1815-1854	7F(B)
Idle	E 1788-1972	1760-1844	4,6,7,8,9			Bradford		1790-1837	8D(B)
Ilkley	E 1597-1955	1597-1846	4,5,7,8,9	1597-1812	1597-1812	Otley	1790-1812		4H(A)
Illingworth	A 1695-1984	1720-1835	8			Halifax		1798-1837	7C(B)
Ingleton	D 1607-1970	1607-1848	5,8	1607-1837	1617-1837	Settle	1790-1812		7C(A)
Keighley	E 1562-1945	1562-1859	8	1562-1736	1562-1688	Keighley		1749-1840	3G(A)
Kellington	A 1705-1951	1720-1851	5,8			Pontefract			6I(B)
Kettlewell	D 1698-1940	1713-1835	5,7,8,9			Skipton			7F(A)
Kildwick	D 1572-1980	1575-1843		1575-1789	1576-1750	Skipton		1753-1837	3G(A)

parish name	deposited original registers	I.G.I.	local census indexes	copies of registers at Soc. Gen.	Boyd's marriage index	1837-1851 Registration District	Pallot's marriage index	non-conform. records at P.R.O.	map ref.
Kippax	C 1539-1969	1539-1840	5,8	1539-1812	1540-1812	Pontefract	1790-1812		2L(A)
Kirk Bramwith	F 1700-1979	1718-1849	5,8		1700-1837	Doncaster			5I(B)
Kirkburton	C 1540-1990	1540-1837	4,5,8	1541-1837	1541-1710	Huddersfield		1700-1840	5D(B)
Kirkby Malham	D 1597-1961	1597-1846	8	1597-1846	1607-1837	Settle			6E(A)
Kirkby Malzeard	D 1653-1995	1653-1764	8,9			Ripon		1832-1837(?)	7I(A)
Kirkby Overblow	C 1647-1993	1647-1837	5,8	1647-1812	1647-1812	Knaresborough			4J(A)
Kirkby Wharfe	B 1583-1968		5,8	1666-1868		Tadcaster			8H(B)
Kirk Deighton	C 1600-1979	1600-1844	5,8	1600-1786		Knaresborough			4K(A)
Kirk Hammerton	D 1714-1933	1714-1847	5,8,9	1714-1812	1755-1812	Knaresborough			5L(A)
Kirkheaton	A 1653-1970	1600-1836	4,5,8	1600-1822	1600-1616	Huddersfield			6D(B)
Kirk Sandall	F 1679-1988	1728-1848	5,8		1679-1837	Doncaster			4J(B)
Kirk Smeaton	A 1604-1965	1724-1863	5,8			Hemsworth			5H(B)
Kirkstall	C 1829-1950	1829-1837	5,8			Hunslet		1835-1837	8E(B)
Knaresborough		1670-1839	5,8	1560-1753	1801-1840	Knaresborough		1765-1840	5K(A)
Knottingley	A 1724-1975	1813-1870	5,8			Pontefract		1813-1837	6H(B)
Laughton en le Morthen	G 1561-1981	1708-1836	8			Rotherham			2H(B)
Leathley	D 1673-1993	1718-1836	5,7,8,9			Otley			4J(A)
Ledsham	B 1539-1967	1539-1875	8	1539-1812	1540-1812	Pontefract	1790-1812		7H(B)
Leeds			8	1571-1832				1654-1855	8F(B)
Christ Church	C 1827-1971	1827-1837	5,8			Leeds			7G(B)
Holy Trinity	C 1730-1923	1731-1752	5,8		1750-1751	Leeds			8G(B)
St John	C 1773-1953	1723-1845	5,8		1725-1754	Leeds			8G(B)
St Mark		1826-1846	5,8			Leeds			8G(B)
St Mary	C 1826-1977	1826-1840	5,8			Leeds			8G(B)
St Paul	C 1851-1905		5,8			Leeds			8G(B)
St Peter	C 1572-1916	1572-1837	5,8	1571-1769	1572-1776	Leeds			8G(B)
Letwell (see Laughton)						Worksop			2I(B)
Lightcliffe	A 1703-1989	1720-1846	8			Halifax			7D(B)
Linthwaite	A 1828-1993		4,5,8	1828-1860		Huddersfield		1807-1837	5C(B)
Linton	D 1562-1878	1562-1847	5,7,8,9	1562-1812	1565-1812	Skipton	1790-1812	1771-1840	6G(A)
Little Ouseburn	D 1565-1989	1565-1846	5,8,9	1565-1846	1558-1812	Knaresborough			6L(A)
Liversedge	A 1816-1975	1816-1847	4,5,8			Dewsbury		1787-1837	7E(B)
Lockwood	A 1830-1989		4,5,8			Huddersfield		1793-1837	5D(B)
Long Preston	D 1563-1968	1717-1847	8			Settle		1814-1836	5D(A)
Longwood	A 1797-1990	1813-1846	4,5,8			Huddersfield			6C(B)
Loversall	F 1814-1980	1718-1835	5,8			Doncaster			3I(B)
Luddenden	A 1653-1996	1720-1832	5,8			Halifax		1803-1837	7B(B)
Lydgate	J 1788-1952	1788-1791	8			Saddleworth			4B(B)
Maltby	G 1597-1948	1597-1836	8,9	1597-1812	1606-1837	Rotherham	1790-1812		2I(B)
Marr	F 1729-1980	1718-1840	5,8			Doncaster			4H(B)
Marsden	A 1734-1968	1813-1835	4,5,8			Huddersfield		1796-1837	5C(B)
Marton cum Grafton	D 1648-1979	1650-1844	5,8,9			Knaresborough			6K(A)
Marton in Craven	D 1548-1890	1724-1838	8			Skipton			4E(A)
Meltham	A 1669-1984	1813-1835	4,5,8			Huddersfield			5C(B)
Methley	C 1559-1950	1560-1845	5,8	1560-1812	1559-1812	Pontefract	1790-1812		7G(B)
Mexborough	F 1562-1980	1724-1877	5,8			Doncaster			3H(B)
Middlesmoor	D 1700-1977		8			Ripon			7G(A)
Midhope	A 1813-1973	1789-1855	8			Wortley			3E(B)
Mirfield	A 1559-1990	1559-1846	4,5,8	1559-1826	1559-1754	Dewsbury		1733-1837	6E(B)
Mitton	I 1610-1917	1813-1841	8			Clitheroe		1807-1837	3C(A)
Monk Bretton	A 1839-1979	....-1842	5,8			Barnsley			5G(B)
Monk Fryston	B 1538-1943	1538-1885	8,9	1538-1812	1679-1812	Pontefract			7H(B)
Nether Hoyland	G 1740-1977	1748-1864	8			Barnsley			4G(B)
Netherthong	A 1830-1984	1830-1838	4,5,8			Huddersfield			5D(B)
Newton Kyme	B 1632-1991	1632-1889	5,8			Tadcaster			9H(B)
Nidd	D 1666-1995	1637-1848	5,8			Knaresborough			5J(A)
Normanton	A 1537-1991	1538-1868	5,8	1538-1812	1539-1600	Wakefield			6G(B)
Northowram			5,8	1644-1752	1646-1837	Halifax		1744-1837	7C(B)
Nun Monkton	D 1708-1883	1637-1848	5,8,9			Knaresborough			5L(A)
Ossett	A 1792-1978	1813-1848	5,8			Dewsbury		1741-1837	6F(B)
Otley	C 1562-1943	1563-1847	4,5,7,8,9	1562-1797	1562-1750	Otley		1807-1837	4I(A)
Oulton-cum-Woodlesford	C 1830-1954	1830-1838	5,8			Wakefield			7G(B)
Owston	F 1683-1955	1718-1878	5,8	1600-1837		Doncaster			5I(B)
Paddock	A 1830-1967		4,5,8			Huddersfield			6D(B)
Pannal	C 1585-1974	1585-1835	5,8	1558-1775		Knaresborough			5J(A)
Pateley Bridge	D 1551-1962	1551-1844	8	1551-1715		Pateley Bridge		1772-1837	6H(A)
Penistone	A 1644-1966	1643-1846	5,8	1643-1844		Wortley		1788-1837	4E(B)
Pontefract	A 1585-1972	1585-1875	4,5,8	1585-1672		Pontefract		1787-1840	6H(B)
Pool (see Brotherton)		1787-1846	8			Otley			4I(A)
Pudsey	C 1775-1986	1760-1845	5,8,9			Bradford		1787-1837	8E(B)
Rastrick	A 1719-1985	1774-1836	5,8			Halifax			6D(B)
Ravenfield	G 1563-1974	1724-1872	8			Rotherham			3H(B)
Rawcliffe	F 1689-1987	1773-1878	5,8			Goole			6K(B)
Rawdon	C 1753-1984	1684-1847	7,8,9			Otley		1756-1837	3I(A)
Rawmarsh	G 1558-1977	1718-1849	8	1558-1812		Rotherham			3G(B)
Ripley	D 1560-1929	1560-1846	5,8	1560-1812		Knaresborough		1817-1829	5J(A)
Ripon			8					1817-1840	7J(A)
St Peter and	D 1574-1900	1573-1616	8,9	1574-1628	1572-1628	Ripon			7J(A)
St Wilfred			8,9			Ripon			7J(A)
Holy Trinity	D 1827-1993	1827-1834	8,9			Ripon			7J(A)
Ripponden	A 1684-1985	1684-1875	8	1684-1817		Halifax		1804-1837	6B(B)
Rochdale (see Lancs.)									5B(B)
Rossington	F 1538-1988	1538-1875	5,8		1538-1837	Doncaster			3J(B)
Rotherham	G 1540-1907	1540-1837	6,8,9	1540-1837	1540-1837	Rotherham	1800-1837	1748-1837	3G(B)
Rothwell	C 1538-1995	1538-1839	5,8	1538-1812	1538-1837	Hunslet	1790-1812	1832-1837(?)	7F(B)
Roundhay	C 1826-1964	1827-1832	5,8			Hunslet			2J(A)
Royston	A 1557-1987	1558-1842	5,6,8	1558-1633		Barnsley			5F(B)
Rylstone	D 1559-1900	1559-1835	5,7,8,9	1559-1812	1560-1812	Skipton	1797-1812		5F(A)
Ryther	B 1558-1993	1570-1887	5,8	1550-1812		Selby			8I(B)

YORKSHIRE (WEST RIDING)

parish name	deposited original registers	I.G.I.	local census indexes	copies of registers at Soc. Gen.	Boyd's marriage index	1837-1851 Registration District	Pallot's marriage index	non-conform. records at P.R.O.	map ref.
Saddleworth	J 1632-1935	1613-1800	8	1613-1837	1613-1800	Saddleworth	1790-1800	1786-1837	4B(B)
Sandal Magna	A 1651-1991	1598-1843	5,8	1598-1832	1598-1631	Wakefield		1822-1837	5F(B)
Sawley (ex.par.)	D 1812-1917		8			Clitheroe			4D(A)
Saxton in Elmet	B 1538-1992	1539-1887	5,8	1539-1812	1560-1837	Tadcaster	1790-1812		8H(B)
Scammonden	A 1746-1986	1813-1845	4,5,8	1746-1812		Huddersfield			5C(B)
Sedbergh	K 1594-1998	1594-1847	8	1594-1886	1594-1800	Sedbergh	1790-1800	1806-1837	9B(A)
Selby	B 1579-1993	1780-1886	5,8	1579-1886		Selby		1797-1840	7J(B)
Sharow	D 1825-1988	1825-1837	8			Ripon			7K(A)
Sheffield				1560-1752				1681-1840	2F(B)
St George	G 1825-1977		6,8,9			Sheffield			1F(B)
St James	G 1813-1940		6,8,9			Sheffield			1F(B)
St Mary	G 1830-1990		6,8,9			Sheffield			1F(B)
St Paul	G 1768-1937	1793-1829	6,8,9		1703-1719	Sheffield			1F(B)
St Peter and Paul	G 1560-1985	1560-1828	6,8,9	1560-1752	1560-1703	Sheffield			1F(B)
St Philip	G 1828-1977	1828-1883	6,8,9			Sheffield			1F(B)
Sherburn in Elmet	B 1640-1981	1653-1886	5,8,9	1603-1866		Tadcaster			7H(B)
Shipley	E 1826-1955	1826-1844	4,6,7,8,9	1826-1955		Bradford		1831-1837	8D(B)
Silkstone	A 1558-1970	1558-1846	5,8	1558-1830	1558-1837	Wortley		1795-1837	4F(B)
Silsden	E 1768-1978	1644-1843	5,8	1740-1843		Keighley		1823-1837	4G(A)
Skelbrooke	F 1587-1995	1745-1880	5,8			Hemsworth			5H(B)
Skelton-cum-Newby	D 1811-1876		8			Ripon			6J(A)
Skipton	D 1592-1908	1592-1845	5,8,9	1592-1837	1592-1812	Skipton	1790-1812	1783-1857	4F(A)
Slaidburn	I 1662-1968	1631-1843	8	1600-1812		Clitheroe			4C(A)
Slaithwaite	A 1679-1967	1813-1842	4,5,8			Huddersfield			6C(B)
Snaith	F 1587-1950	1537-1858	5,8	1537-1727	1537-1838	Goole		1826-1837	6J(B)
South Crosland	A 1829-1993		4,5,8			Huddersfield			5D(B)
South Kirkby	A 1620-1978	1718-1853	5,8			Hemsworth			5H(B)
Southowram	A 1813-1991	1723-1846	5,8			Halifax			6D(B)
South Stainley	D 1658-1998	1658-1840	8,9	1658-1812		Ripon		1807-1840	6J(A)
Sowerby	A 1643-1992	1813-1837	5,8,9			Halifax		1740-1837	6C(B)
Sowerby Bridge	A 1709-1994	1720-1846	8			Halifax			7C(B)
Spofforth	C 1599-1974	1600-1847	5,8	1598-1732	1599-1837	Knaresborough		1785-1840	4K(A)
Sprotbrough	F 1559-1996	1718-1846	5,8		1559-1837	Doncaster			4I(B)
Stainburn		1780-1843	5,7,8,9			Otley			4J(A)
Stainland	A 1782-1962	1841-1843	5,8			Halifax		1779-1836	6C(B)
Stainton	F 1556-1959	1721-1842	5,8,9			Doncaster			3I(B)
Stanley	A 1824-1984	1824-1844	5,8			Wakefield			6F(B)
Stannington	G 1830-1986	1830-1876	8			Wortley		1718-1837	2E(B)
Staveley	D 1583-1997	1582-1847	5,8			Knaresborough			6K(A)
Swillington	C 1539-1966	1540-1849	5,8	1539-1812	1540-1837	Hunslet			2K(A)
Swinefleet	F 1813-1967	1810-1841	5,8			Goole		1832-1837	6L(B)
Swinton	F 1800-1982	1815-1849	5,8,9			Rotherham			3G(B)
Sykehouse	F 1860-1974		5,8			Thorne			5J(B)
Tadcaster	B 1570-1989	1570-1859	5,8	1598-1859		Tadcaster		1763-1840	9H(B)
Tankersley	G 1598-1965	1729-1861	5,8	1588-1840		Wortley			4F(B)
Thorne		1724-1861	5,8	1565-1697	1565-1837	Thorne		1805-1837	5K(B)
Thorner	C 1622-1971	1728-1842	5,8	1606-1842		Tadcaster		1796-1806	3K(A)
Thornes	A 1831-1976	1831-1840	8			Wakefield			6F(B)
Thornhill	A 1580-1986	1580-1845	4,5,8	1580-1895	1580-1812	Dewsbury	1790-1812		6E(B)
Thornthwaite (see Hampsthwaite)		1687-1812	8			Pateley Bridge			6H(A)
Thornton	E 1678-1955	1730-1837	7,8,9	1682-1837		Bradford		1756-1857	7D(B)
Thornton in Craven	D 1566-1942	1735-1841	8			Skipton		1802-1837	4F(A)
Thornton in Lonsdale	D 1576-1993	1576-1848	8		1576-1812	Settle	1790-1812		7C(A)
Thorpe Salvin	G 1592-1993	1592-1835	8	1592-1726	1593-1726	Worksop			1H(B)
Throapham	G 1547-1977	1709-1836	8			Worksop			2I(B)
Thrybergh	G 1599-1981		8			Rotherham			3H(B)
Thurnscoe	F 1619-1993	1720-1857	5,8		1619-1709	Doncaster			4H(B)
Tickhill	F 1542-1910	1718-1866	5,8	1542-1812	1538-1838	Doncaster			3I(B)
Tinsley	G 1711-1968	1712-1856	8	1711-1854	1713-1837	Rotherham			2G(B)
Todmorden	A 1666-1979	1624-1780	4,5,8			Todmorden		1807-1837	6B(B)
Todwick	G 1577-1997	1718-1862	8		1577-1835	Worksop			2H(B)
Tong	E 1550-1990	1725-1835	4,7,8,9			Bradford			7E(B)
Tosside	I 1749-1987	1749-1776	8			Settle			5D(A)
Treeton	G 1677-1919	1721-1876	8			Rotherham			2H(B)
Waddington		1599-1854	8	1599-1812	1599-1812	Clitheroe	1790-1812		3C(A)
Wadworth	F 1574-1963	1715-1839	5,8	1574-1920	1575-1837	Doncaster			3I(B)
Wakefield								1761-1840	6F(B)
Cathedral	A 1613-1988	1600-1846	5,8	1600-1812	1613-1812	Wakefield			6F(B)
St John	A 1795-1983	1795-1832	5,8	1795-1812	1795-1812	Wakefield			6F(B)
Wales	G 1578-1920	1720-1870	8			Worksop			1H(B)
Warmfield	A 1595-1967	1727-1875	5,8	1590-1609		Wakefield			6G(B)
Warmsworth	F 1594-1969	1718-1848	5,8			Doncaster			3I(B)
Wath upon Dearne	F 1598-1984	1598-1858	5,8,9	1598-1779	1598-1779	Rotherham			4G(B)
Wentworth	F 1654-1958	1718-1856	5,8			Rotherham			3G(B)
West Ardsley or Wood Kirk	A 1652-1978	1652-1847	5,8	1652-1832		Wakefield			7F(B)
West Bretton	A 1750-1991	1753-1813	5,8	1753-1784		Wakefield			5F(B)
West Clayton	A 1720-1982		8	1752-1861		Wortley		1818-1837	5E(B)
Weston	C 1672-1993	1604-1847	5,8	1639-1812	1639-1812	Otley	1790-1812		4I(A)
Wetherby	C 1783-1909	1786-1847	5,8			Knaresborough		1805-1816	4K(A)
Whalley (detached) (see Lancs.)									3B(A)
Whiston	G 1587-1979	1720-1855	8			Rotherham			2H(B)
Whitewell	I 1713-1994		5,8			Clitheroe			3B(A)
Whitgift	F 1562-1962	1562-1838	4,8	1562-1812		Goole			6L(B)
Whitkirk	C 1603-1979	1600-1847	5,8	1603-1837	1603-1700	Hunslet			2K(A)
Whixley	D 1568-1973	1568-1846	5,8,9	1568-1812	1569-1753	Knaresborough		1798-1836	5L(A)
Wibsey	E 1674-1955	1618-1835	4,6,7,8,9			Bradford			7D(B)
Wickersley		1718-1843	8			Rotherham			2H(B)
Wilsden	E 1826-1965	1826-1838	4,6,7,8,9			Bradford		1793-1837	8C(B)

YORKSHIRE (WEST RIDING)

parish name	deposited original registers	I.G.I.	local census indexes	copies of registers at Soc. Gen.	Boyd's marriage index	1837-1851 Registration District	Pallot's marriage index	non-conform. records at P.R.O.	map ref.
Winksley	D 1747-1954		8,9			Ripon			6I(A)
Wistow	B 1590-1990	1710-1839	5,8,9	1635-1839		Selby			8I(B)
Womersley	A 1564-1953	1730-1865	5,8			Pontefract			6I(B)
Woodhouse	A 1824-1996	1824-1843	4,5,8			Wakefield		1817-1837	6D(B)
Woolley	C 1651-1955	1600-1885	5,8	1600-1936		Barnsley			5F(B)
Worsborough	G 1559-1950	1720-1862	8		1565-1675	Barnsley			4G(B)
Wortley	G 1678-1989	1727-1863	5,8			Wortley			3F(B)
Wortley	C 1813-1990	1813-1837	5,8			Hunslet		1819-1837	8F(B)
Wragby	A 1538-1965	1538-1846	5,8	1538-1812	1538-1812	Hemsworth			5G(B)

Original registers deposited at:
A = West Yorkshire Record Office, Newstead Road, Wakefield WF1 2DE
B = The Borthwick Institute of Historical Research, St Anthony's Hall, Peasholme Green, York YO1 7PW
C = Leeds District Archives, Chapeltown Road, Sheepscar, Leeds LS7 3AP
D = North Yorkshire County Record Office, County Hall, Northallerton, North Yorks DL7 8AF
E = Bradford Central Library, Archives Department, Prince's Way, Bradford BD1 1NN
F = Doncaster Archives Department, King Edward Road, Balby, Doncaster DN4 ONA
G = Sheffield Archives, 52 Shoreham Street, Sheffield S1 4SP
H = Nottinghamshire Record Office, County House, Castle Meadow Road, Nottingham NG2 1AG
I = Lancashire Record Office, Bow Lane, Preston PR1 2RE
J = Manchester City Archives, Central Library, St Peter's Square, Manchester M2 5PD
K = Cumbria Record Office (Kendal), County Offices, Kendal, Cumbria LA9 4RQ

Study adjacent parishes in counties of Westmorland, North Riding, Lancashire, Cheshire, Derbyshire, Nottinghamshire, Lincolnshire and the East Riding

West Yorkshire Archive Service, Newstead Road, Wakefield, WF1 2DE
Leeds District Archives, Chapeltown Road, Sheepscar, Leeds, LS7 3AP
Bradford District Archives, 15 Canal Road, Bradford, BD1 4AT
Calderdale District Archives, Calderdale Central Library, Northgate House, Northgate, Halifax, HX1 1UN
Kirklees District Archives, Huddersfield Central Library, Princess Alexandra Walk, Huddersfield, HD1 2SU
Barnsley Archive Service, Central Library, Shambles Street, Barnsley, South Yorkshire, S70 2JF
Rotherham Archives and Local Studies Department, Central Library, Walker Place, Rotherham, S65 1JH
Doncaster Archives Department, King Edward Road, Balby, Doncaster, DN4 0NA
Sheffield Archives, 52 Shoreham Street, Sheffield, S1 4SP
Wakefield Local Studies and Archives, District Library HQ, Balne Lane, Wakefield, WF2 0DQ
Yorkshire Archaeological Society, Claremont, 23 Clarendon Road, Leeds, LS2 9NZ

The following useful indexes have been compiled – see Introduction
Census Indexes 1841-1891 – Yorkshire Archaeological Society, c/o Mrs A.M. Hill, 23 Claremont, 23 Clarendon Road, Leeds, Yorkshire LS2 9NZ
Census Indexes 1841- 1891 – Bradford FHS, c/o Mrs W. Evans, 6 Bempton Place, Great Horton, Bradford, West Yorkshire BD7 3DB
Census Indexes 1841 & 1851 – Calderdale FHS, c/o Mr J. Sutcliffe, 12 Ewood Drive, Mytholmroyd, Hebden Bridge, West Yorkshire HX7 5PQ
Census Indexes 1841 & 1851 – Huddersfield FHS, c/o The Librarian, 28 Bishops Way, Meltham, Huddersfield, West Yorkshire HD9 4BW
Census Indexes 1841 & 1851 – Pontefract FHS, c/o B. Graham, 10 Saddlers Grove, Badsworth, Pontefract, West Yorkshire WF9 1PE
Census Indexes 1841- 1891 – Wharfedale FHS, c/o Mr S. Merridew, 206 Moseley Wood Gardens, Leeds LS16 7JE
Census Index 1851 – Barnsley FHS, c/o Mrs D. Poulter, 10 Scarr Lane, Ardsley, Barnsley, South Yorkshire S71 5BB
Census Index 1851 – Doncaster FHS, c/o Mrs J. Wade, 6 Melford Drive, Balby, Doncaster DN4 9AT
Census Index 1851 – Wakefield FHS, c/o J. Welch, 101 Thornes Road, Wakefield WF2 8QD
Census Indexes 1851, 1861 & 1891 – Morley FHS, c/o Mr R. Taylor, 32 Romford Avenue, Morley, West Yorkshire LS27 0RN
Census Indexes 1851 & 1891 – Ripon FHS, c/o Mr J. Hebden, Aldergarth, Galphay, Ripon, North Yorkshire HG4 3NJ
Census Indexes 1861 & 1891 – Sheffield FHS, c/o A. Gillar, 17 Firshill Road, Sheffield, South Yorkshire S4 7BB
Census Index 1871 – Rotherham FHS, c/o Mrs E. Lewis, 184 Margate Drive, Grimesthorpe, Sheffield, South Yorkshire S4 8FH
Marriage Index – Mr P.R. Joiner, Greystones, The Spital, Yarm-on-Tees, Yorkshire TS15 9EX
Marriage Index Archdeaconry of Doncaster – Mrs. L. Peabody, 22 Horsehills Lane, Armthorpe, Doncaster, South Yorkshire DN3 3ET
Marriage Index Wharfedale 1813-1837 – Mr B. Clayton, 26 St Philip's Way, Burley in Wharfedale, Ilkley, West Yorkshire LS29 7EW
Marriage Index Huddersfield – Huddersfield FHS (as above)
N.E. Lancashire & Yorkshire Borders Marriage Index – Mrs B.H. Smith, The Shieling, Old Back Lane, Wiswell, Clitheroe, Lancashire BB7 9BS
Archbishop of York's Marriage Bonds and Allegations – Borthwick Institute (as above)
Registry of Deeds – West Yorkshire Record Office, Wakefield (as above)

The West Riding is irregular in shape but the greatest length across the county in a straight line is from Spurn Head on the south-east to the junction of counties Westmorland and Durham on the north-east, a distance of about 124 miles. In the opposite direction, from the junction of Lancashire and Cheshire on the south-west to Whitby on the north-east, the breadth is about 90 miles. It is watered by nine principal rivers: the Ouse, Aire, Worth, Colne, Don, Wharfe, Nidd, Ure and Ribble. The population in 1841 was 1,325,495; in 1851, 1,325,495; in 1861, 1,507,796; in 1871, 1,874,611; in 1881, 2,175,314.

The soils include clay, sand and shale. Produce included all types of grain, flax, teasels, dyer's woad, potatoes, clover, turnips and mustard. Cattle, sheep and horses were raised. The principal manufactures were woollen cloth and worsted fabrics, cotton and linen goods, carpets and blankets. There were iron and steel works and cutlery and tools made. The coal-mining industry was important.

The information in the Index is abbreviated, and may mislead the searcher if reference is not made to the details contained in the several publications listed in the Introduction. It is essential that users of this book check the appropriate works before making further enquiries.

CENTRAL WALES

parish name	deposited original registers	I.G.I.	local census indexes	copies of registers at Soc. Gen.	Boyd's marriage index	1837-1851 Registration District	Pallot's marriage index	non-conform. records at P.R.O.	map ref.
Abbey-Cwmhir	A 1831-1981	1831-1867	4,6,8			Rhayader			3E
Aberedw	A 1740-1992	1813-1843	4,6,8			Builth			3C
Aberhafesp	A 1578-1993	1787-1835	4,5,6,8			Newtown			3G
Aberporth	A 1662-1971		8	1813-1837		Cardigan		1808-1837	10C
Aberystwyth	A 1788-1971	1811-1874	4,5,6,7,8,9			Aberystwyth		1805-1837	7F
Alberbury (Salop)	E 1564-1991		4,5,8						7I
Bangor	A 1802-1991	1813-1875	8	1813-1837		Newcastle-in-Emlyn			9C
Beddgelert (Caernavon)	A 1734-1857								7L
Beguildy	A 1703-1986	1813-1844	4,6,8			Knighton			2F
Berriew	A 1596-1985	1795-1854	4,5,8			Montgomery		1825-1837	2H
Bettws-Bledrws	A 1813-1984	1801-1880	4,5,6,7,8,9	1813-1837		Lampeter			7D
Bettws-Cadewain	A 1661-1984	1773-1853	4,5,8			Newtown		1826-1836	2G
Bettws-Disserth	A 1731-1980		4,6,8			Builth			3D
Bettws-Evan	A 1726-1941	1806-1861	6,8	1813-1837		Newcastle-in-Emlyn			9C
Bettws-Gwerfil-Goch	D 1685-1981		8			Corwen			4L
Bettws-Lleuch	A 1813-1986	1813-1872	4,5,6,7,8,9	1813-1837		Tregaron			7D
Blaenpenal	A 1813-1986	1813-1875	8	1813-1837		Tregaron			7E
Blaenporth	A 1716-1992	1802-1866	8	1716-1837		Cardigan			10C
Bleddfa	A 1603-1986	1813-1867	4,6,8			Knighton			2E
Boughrood	A 1689-1979	1813-1847	4,6,8			Hay			2C
Brampton Bryan (see Herefordshire)									1E
Brongwyn	A 1726-1992	1803-1852	8			Newcastle-in-Emlyn		1785-1837	9C
Bryngwyn	A 1614-1982	1813-1852	4,6,8			Hay			2D
Buttington	A 1736-1971		4,5,8	1813-1848		Montgomery			1H
Capel Cynon	A 1822-1978	1824-1872	8	1813-1837		Aberayron			9D
Cardigan	A 1653-1971		5,6,8	1813-1837		Cardigan		1803-1837	10C
Cardigan Island (e.p.)			5,8			Cardigan			10D
Carno	A 1638-1916		4,5,6,8			Newtown		1812-1836	4G
Caron-uwch-Clawdd (or Strata Florida)	A 1750-1971	1811-1874		1813-1837		Tregaron		1810-1837	6E
Cascob	A 1678-1986	1813-1853	4,5,6,8			Presteigne			2E
Castle Caereinion	A 1689-1992	1770-1844	4,5,8			Montgomery			2H
Cefnllys	A 1671-1971	1813-1870	4,5,6,8			Rhayader			3D
Cellan	A 1779-1993	1779-1875	4,5,6,7,8,9	1813-1837		Lampeter			7C
Cemmaes	A 1711-1970	1739-1851	4,5,8			Machynlleth		1828-1837	5H
Church Stoke	E 1558-1853		4,5,8			Montgomery			1G
Cilcennin	A 1734-1993		8	1813-1837		Aberayron			7D
Ciliau-Aeron	A 1775-1991	1775-1875	8	1813-1837		Aberayron			8D
Clyro	A 1688-1989	1813-1871	4,6,8			Hay			2C
Colva	A 1663-1991		4,5,6,8			Presteigne			2D
Corwen	D 1719-1968	1813-1834	8			Corwen		1807-1837	3K
Cregrina	A 1685-1991	1813-1848	4,6,8			Builth			3D
Darowen	A 1633-1876	1773-1854	4,5,8			Machynlleth		1812-1837	5H
Dihewid	A 1807-1993	1800-1878	8	1813-1837		Aberayron			8D
Discoed	C 1680-1933		4,5,6,8	1680-1933		Presteigne			1E
Disserth	A 1734-1991	1813-1867	4,6,8	1734-1812		Builth			3D
Dolgelley	A 1640-1812	1814-1870	8			Dolgelly		1795-1837	6I
Ffestiniog	D 1695-1990		5,8			Ffestiniog		1826-1837	6K
Forden	A 1598-1980	1660-1843	4,5,8			Montgomery		1827-1836	2H
Garthbeibie	A 1710-1941	1748-1855	4,5,8			Llanfyllin			4I
Gartheli	A 1813-1986	1813-1875	4,5,6,7,8,9	1813-1837		Tregaron			7D
Gladestry	A 1683-1971	1813-1852	4,5,6,8			Presteigne			2D
Glasbury	A 1660-1976	1813-1874	4,6,8	1660-1836		Hay	1790-1837	1801-1837	2C
Glascwm	A 1679-1992	1813-1845	4,5,6,8			Presteigne			2D
Guilsfield	A 1572-1994	1780-1858	4,5,8			Montgomery			2I
Gwyddelwern	A 1691-1980	1807-1837	8			Corwen		1807-1837	3L
Henfynyw	A 1772-1993	1799-1868	8	1813-1837		Aberayron		1791-1837	8D
Henllan	A 1798-1991	1813-1875	8	1813-1837		Newcastle-in-Emlyn			9C
Heyop	A 1679-1986	1813-1853	4,6,8			Knighton			2F
Hirnant	A 1600-1992	1758-1854	4,5,8			Llanfyllin			3J
Hyssington			4,5,8	1660-1870		Clun			1G
Kerry	A 1602-1993	1602-1847	4,5,6,8	1602-1812		Newtown	1790-1812		2G
Knighton	A 1599-1971		4,5,6,8			Knighton			1E
Lampeter (or Llanbedr Pont Steffan)	A 1695-1970	1695-1875	8	1813-1837		Lampeter		1818-1837	7C
Llanaber	D 1750-1978					Dolgelly		1811-1837	7I
Llanafan	A 1767-1993	1811-1875	4,5,6,7,8	1813-1837		Aberystwyth		1822-1837	6E
Llananno	A 1721-1987		4,6,8			Knighton			3F
Llanarth	A 1688-1969	1799-1875	8	1813-1837		Aberayron			8D
Llanbadarn-fawr	A 1696-1971	1813-1865	4,6,8			Rhayader			3E
Llanbadarn-fynydd	A 1678-1997	1813-1847	4,6,8			Knighton			3F
Llanbadarn-Odwyn	A 1808-1956	1811-1877	8	1813-1837		Tregaron			6D
Llanbadarn-Trefeglwys	A 1724-1993	1724-1873	4,5,6,7,8,9	1813-1837		Aberayron		1821-1837	7E
Llanbadarn-y-garreg	A 1750-1992	1813-1847	4,6,8			Builth			3D
Llanbadarn Vawr	A 1678-1969	1815-1875	4,5,6,7,8			Aberystwyth		1811-1837	6F
Llanbedr	AD 1627-1838	1810-1837	8			Ffestiniog		1810-1837	6J
Llanbedr-Painscastle	A 1726-1981	1813-1850	4,5,6,8	1687-1850		Hay			2C
Llanbister	A 1705-1994	1813-1840	4,6,8	1702-1840		Knighton			2F
Llanbrynmair	A 1663-1965		4,5,8			Machynlleth		1762-1837	4H
Llancynfelyn	A 1754-1970	1803-1875	4,5,6,7,8			Aberystwyth		1821-1836	8G
Llandanwg	D 1725-1902		5,8			Ffestiniog		1812-1835	7K
Llanddeiniol	A 1754-1978	1811-1875	8	1813-1837		Aberystwyth		1835-1837	7E
Llandderfel	D 1598-1994	1814-1837	8	1602-1757		Bala		1814-1837	4K
Llanddewi-Aberarth	A 1737-1993	1812-1872	8	1813-1837		Aberayron		1818-1836	8E
Llanddewi-Brefi	A 1775-1992	1776-1875	4,5,6,7,8,9	1813-1837		Tregaron		1814-1837	6D
Llanddewi-Fach	A 1754-1981		4,6,8	1741-1837		Hay			2C
Llanddewi-Ystradenny	A 1732-1981	1813-1859	4,6,8			Knighton			3E
Llanddwywe	A 1674-1837		8						7J

277

parish name	deposited original registers	I.G.I.	local census indexes	copies of registers at Soc. Gen.	Boyd's marriage index	1837-1851 Registration District	Pallot's marriage index	non-conform. records at P.R.O.	map ref.
Llandecwyn	D 1668-1992		8			Ffestiniog			7K
Llandegley	A 1727-1990		4,5,6,8			Presteigne			2E
Llandeilo-graban	A 1813-1992		4,6,8			Hay			3C
Llandinam	A 1587-1970	1775-1864	4,5,6,8			Newtown		1811-1837	3G
Llandrillo	D 1686-1994	1820-1837	8			Corwen		1816-1837	3K
Llandrindod	A 1734-1971		4,6,8			Builth			3D
Llandrinio	A 1662-1993	1735-1833	4,5,8			Llanfyllin		1832-1836	1I
Llandyfriog	A 1725-1971	1799-1874	8	1725-1837		Newcastle-in-Emlyn		1810-1837	9C
Llandygwydd	A 1677-1988	1799-1875	8	1677-1837		Cardigan			10C
Llandysilio	A 1662-1986	1751-1848	4,5,8			Llanfyllin		1819-1837	1I
Llandyssil	A 1755-1925	1799-1873	8			Newcastle-in-Emlyn		1797-1837	8C
Llandyssil	A 1689-1971	1733-1857	4,5,6,8			Montgomery			2G
Llandyssiliogogo	A 1727-1993	1799-1875	8			Aberayron		1815-1837	9D
Llanegryn	D 1723-1970		8			Dolgelly		1819-1837	7H
Llanelltyd	D 1681-1990		8			Dolgelly		1822-1837	6J
Llanelwedd	A 1773-1982		4,6,8			Builth			3D
Llanenddwyn	AD 1694-1971		8			Dolgelly		1813-1837	7J
Llanerch-Aeron	A 1754-1993	1799-1878	8	1813-1837		Aberayron			8D
Llanerfyl	A 1626-1991	1736-1836	4,5,8			Llanfyllin			4H
Llanfachairn	A 1603-1993	1813-1850	4,5,8			Llanfyllin			2J
Llanfachreth	D 1635-1982	1814-1836	8			Dolgelly		1818-1837	6J
Llanfair	AD 1746-1993	1813-1838	5,8			Ffestiniog		1809-1837	7J
Llanfair-Caereinion	A 1608-1992	1749-1852	4,5,8			Llanfyllin		1812-1837	3H
Llanfair-Clydogau	A 1813-1970	1806-1875	4,5,6,7,8,9	1813-1837		Lampeter			7D
Llanfair-Orllwyn	A 1813-1991	1799-1879	8	1813-1837		Newcastle-in-Emlyn			9C
Llanfair-Treflygen (see Llandyfriog)									9C
Llanfaredd	A 1698-1984		4,6,8			Builth			3D
Llanfawr	D 1722-1992		8			Bala		1814-1837	4K
Llanfihangel Geneur-y-Glyn	A 1736-1982	1811-1874	4,5,6,7,8	1835-1837		Aberystwyth		1805-1837	7G
Llanfigangel-Helygen	A 1732-1991		4,6,8			Rhayader			3E
Llanfihangel-Lledrod	A 1766-1992	1811-1875	8			Tregaron		1819-1837	6E
Llanfihangel-nant-Melan	A 1700-1991		4,5,6,8			Presteigne			2D
Llanfihangel-Rhydithon	A 1725-1990		4,6,8	1732-1944		Knighton			2E
Llanfihangel-yn-Ngwynfa	A 1663-1968	1814-1857	4,5,8			Llanfyllin		1826-1837	3I
Llanfihangel-y-Pennant	D 1754-1995	1814-1865	8			Dolgelly			6I
Llanfihangel-y-Strad	A 1712-1993	1799-1875	8	1813-1837		Aberayron		1821-1837	7D
Llanfihangel-y-Traethau	D 1690-1992	1813-1872	8			Ffestiniog		1808-1837	7K
Llanfrothen	D 1722-1992	1813-1845	5,8			Ffestiniog		1810-1837	7K
Llanfyllin	A 1654-1956	1745-1846	4,5,8			Llanfyllin		1764-1837	3I
Llangadfan	A 1673-1970	1813-1836	4,5,8			Llanfyllin			3I
Llangar	D 1614-1970		8	1614-1811		Corwen			3K
Llangeitho	A 1761-1986	1769-1875	8	1813-1837		Tregaron			7D
Llangelynin	A 1618-1919	1813-1847	8	1754-1837		Dolgelly		1809-1837	7H
Llangoedmor	A 1754-1985	1799-1875	8	1813-1837		Cardigan			10C
Llangower	AD 1603-1993	1813-1852	8			Bala		1813-1837	4J
Llangranog	A 1762-1993	1799-1875	8	1813-1837		Newcastle-in-Emlyn			9D
Llangurig	A 1683-1969	1775-1867	4,5,8			Newtown			4F
Llangwyryfon	A 1729-1992	1812-1875	8	1813-1837		Aberystwyth		1816-1837	7E
Llangybi	A 1813-1993	1799-1875	4,5,6,7,8,9	1813-1837		Lampeter		1821-1837	7D
Llangyniew	A 1584-1991	1730-1839	4,5,8			Llanfyllin			3I
Llangynllo	A 1755-1970	1799-1875	8	1813-1837		Newcastle-in-Emlyn			9C
Llangynllo	A 1744-1986		4,6,8			Knighton			2E
Llangynog	A 1720-1971	1743-1859	4,5,8			Llanfyllin			3J
Llanidloes	A 1614-1990	1813-1840	4,5,8	1711-1718		Newtown		1804-1837	4G
Llanilar	A 1685-1992	1811-1876	8	1813-1837		Aberystwyth		1814-1837	7F
Llanina	A 1688-1992	1810-1874	8	1813-1837		Aberayron			8D
Llanllugan	A 1603-1991	1793-1850	4,5,6,8			Newtown			3H
Llanllwchaiarn	A 1658-1993	1743-1850	4,5,6,8	1813-1837		Newtown			3G
Llanllwchaiarn	A 1720-1998	1799-1874				Aberayron		1815-1837	9D
Llanmerewig	A 1661-1993	1750-1837	4,5,6,8			Montgomery			2G
Llanrhaiadr-yn-Mochnant (see North Wales)									3J
Llanrhystyd	A 1738-1978	1810-1878	8	1813-1837		Aberystwyth			7E
Llansantffraid	A 1754-1993	1811-1875	8	1813-1837		Aberayron		1815-1837	7E
Llansantffraid-Cwmdeuddwr	A 1737-1978		4,6,8			Rhayader			5E
Llansantffraid-Glyn-Dyfrdwy	D 1767-1905		8	1813-1837		Corwen		1807-1837	3L
Llansantffraid-in-Elvel	A 1767-1980		4,6,8	1813-1837		Builth			3D
Llansantffraid-yn-Mechan	A 1582-1993	1755-1844	4,5,8	1759-1911		Llanfyllin		1793-1837	2I
Llanstephan	A 1754-1981		4,6,8			Hay			2C
Llanuwchllyn	AD 1697-1972		8			Bala		1807-1837	5J
Llanwddyn	A 1623-1968	1740-1851	4,5,8			Llanfyllin			4J
Llanwenog	A 1722-1993	1799-1866	4,5,6,7,8,9	1813-1837		Lampeter			8C
Llanwnen	A 1765-1993	1799-1875	8	1813-1837		Lampeter			7C
Llanwnnog	A 1668-1911	1799-1852	4,5,6,8			Newtown		1820-1837	3G
Llanwnws (or Gwnnws)	A 1760-1991	1811-1875	8	1813-1837		Tregaron			6E
Llanwrin	A 1671-1917	1730-1857	4,5,8			Machynlleth		1811-1837	5H
Llanwyddelan	A 1783-1993	1755-1846	5,6,8			Newtown		1812-1837	3C
Llanychaiarn	A 1754-1993	1811-1875	4,5,6,7,8	1813-1837		Aberystwyth		1808-1837	7F
Llanycil	D 1615-1969		8			Bala		1810-1837	5K
Llanymawddwy	A 1627-1993		8			Dolgelly			5I
Llanymynech	E 1666-1898		4,5,8	1666-1812		Oswestry			1J
Llanyre	A 1759-1971		4,6,8			Rhayader			3E
Llechryd	A 1805-1996	1799-1863	8	1813-1837		Cardigan			10C
Llowes	A 1701-1971		4,6,8			Hay			2C
Lower-Llanfihangel-y-Creuddyn	A 1781-1993	1811-1876	4,5,6,7,8			Aberystwyth			6F

parish name	deposited original registers	I.G.I.	local census indexes	copies of registers at Soc. Gen.	Boyd's marriage index	1837-1851 Registration District	Pallot's marriage index	non-conform. records at P.R.O.	map ref.
Machynlleth	A 1684-1993	1731-1857	4,5,6,8			Machynlleth		1791-1857	5H
Maentwrog	D 1695-1970	1814-1851	8			Ffestiniog		1811-1837	6K
Mainstone (Salop)									1G
Mallwyd	A 1568-1967		8			Dolgelly		1795-1837	5I
Manafon	A 1596-1971	1735-1850	4,5,6,8			Newtown		1810-1837	3H
Meifod	A 1597-1970	1735-1836	4,5,8			Llanfyllin		1807-1837	2I
Michaelchurch-on-Arrow	C 1741-1993		4,5,6,8	1662-1837		Presteigne			2D
Mochdre	A 1682-1993	1813-1841	4,5,6,8			Newtown			3F
Montgomery	A 1574-1981		4,5,6,8			Montgomery			2G
Mount	A 1813-1993	1799-1852	4,5,6,7,8,9	1813-1837		Cardigan			10D
Nantcwnlle	A 1813-1987	1769-1875	8	1813-1837		Tregaron			7D
Nantmel	A 1742-1992		4,6,8			Rhayader		1831-1837	3E
New Church	A 1708-1981		4,5,6,7,8			Presteigne			2D
New Radnor	A 1644-1971	1660-1846	4,5,6,8	1644-1708		Presteigne			2E
Newtown	A 1660-1993	1813-1841	4,5,8			Newtown		1813-1837	3G
Norton	A 1704-1992		4,5,6,8,9			Presteigne			1E
Old Radnor	C 1682-1961		4,5,6,8	1736-1870		Presteigne		1805-1836	2D
Penbryn	A 1726-1993	1799-1877	8	1726-1838		Newcastle-in-Emlyn		1785-1837	9C
Penegoes	A 1679-1993		4,5,6,8			Machynlleth			5G
Pennal	D 1721-1991	1813-1840	5,8			Machynlleth		1802-1836	6H
Pennant	A 1680-1991	1744-1853	4,5,8			Llanfyllin		1828-1837	3J
Penstrowed	A 1628-1994	1777-1869	4,5,6,8			Newtown			3G
Pilleth	A 1771-1980		4,5,6,8			Presteigne			1E
Presteigne	C 1561-1922		4,5,6,8	1561-1922		Presteigne			1E
Rhayader	A 1751-1992		4,5,6,8			Rhayader		1817-1836	4E
Rhostie	A 1815-1925	1816-1865	8	1813-1837		Aberystwyth			6E
Silian	A 1776-1984	1811-1875	8	1813-1837		Lampeter			7D
Snead	E 1665-1988		4,5,8			Clun			1G
St Harmon	A 1751-1971		4,6,8			Rhayader		1826-1837	4F
Talyllyn	D 1683-1978	1813-1875	8			Dolgelly		1812-1837	6I
Towyn	D 1663-1918	1813-1839	5,8			Machynlleth		1808-1837	7H
Trawsfynydd	D 1730-1934	1813-1839	5,8			Ffestiniog		1790-1837	6K
Trefeglwys	A 1625-1988	1794-1836	4,5,8			Newtown		1810-1837	4G
Trefilan	A 1705-1993	1811-1875	8	1813-1837		Lampeter			7D
Tregaron	A 1653-1979	1811-1875	4,5,6,7,8,9	1813-1837		Tregaron			6D
Tregynon	A 1677-1993	1738-1839	4,5,6,8			Newtown		1812-1837	3H
Tremain	A 1763-1990	1799-1866	4,5,6,7,8,9	1813-1837		Cardigan			10C
Troedyraur	A 1655-1990	1799-1875	8	1655-1837		Newcastle-in-Emlyn		1785-1837	9C
Upper Llanfihangel-y-Creuddyn (or Eglwys Newydd)	A 1773-1992	1823-1875	4,5,6,7,8	1811-1888		Aberystwyth			5F
Verwick	A 1769-1992	1814-1866	4,5,6,7,8,9	1813-1837		Cardigan		1811-1837	10C
Welshpool	A 1634-1992	1730-1853	4,5,8			Montgomery		1796-1837	2H
Whitton	A 1600-1986		4,5,6,8			Presteigne			1E
Worthen (Salop)									1H
Ysgubor-y-coed (or Eglwys-Fach)	A 1754-1993	1813-1869	6,8	1754-1837		Aberystwyth			6G
Yspytty Cynfyn	A 1762-1991	1813-1874	8	1762-1837		Aberystwyth			5F
Yspytty-Ystwyth	A 1781-1992	1811-1875	8	1813-1837		Tregaron			5E
Ystraid-Meurig	A 1798-1976	1813-1875	8	1813-1837		Tregaron			6E

CENTRAL WALES

A = National Library of Wales, Aberystwyth, Ceredigion SY23 3BU
B = Ceredigion Archives, County Offices, Marine Terrace, Aberystwyth, Ceredigion SW23 2DE
C = Herefordshire Record Office, The Old Barracks, Harold Street, Hereford HR1 2QX
D = Gwynedd Archives, Archifdy Merion, Cae Penariag, Dolgellau, Gwynedd LL40 2YB
E = Shropshire Records and Research Centre, Castle Gates, Shrewsbury SY1 2AQ

Study adjacent parishes in counties of Denbighshire, Shropshire, Herefordshire

National Library of Wales, Aberystwyth, Ceredigion SY23 3BU
Ceredigion Archives, County Offices, Marine Terrace, Aberystwyth, Ceredigion, SY23 2DE
Powys County Archives Office, County Hall, Llandrindod Wells, Powys, LD1 5LG
Gwynedd Archives, Archifdy Merion, Cae Penariag, Dolgellau, Gwynedd LL40 2YB

The following useful indexes have been compiled – see Introduction
Census Indexes 1841-1891 – National Library of Wales (as above)
Census Indexes 1841-1871 – Powys FHS, c/o Mr M. MacSorley, 20 Hospital Road, Penpedairheol, Caerphilly, Mid-Glamorgan CF82 8DG
Census Index 1841 – Montgomeryshire Genealogical Society, c/o Mrs S.I. Pryce, 4 Erw Wen, Welshpool, Montgomeryshire, Powys SY21 7HJ
Census Index 1851 – Dyfed FHS, c/o Mrs E.A.Davies, Rhydybont, Bronwydd, Carmarthen, Carmarthenshire SA33 6HX
Census Index 1851 – Gywnedd FHS, C/ O Y. Edwards, 36 Y Wern, Y Felinheli, Gwynedd, LL56 4TX
Cardiganshire Marriage Index – Cardiganshire FHS, c/o Dr E.L. James, PO Box 37, Aberystwyth SY23 2WL
Dyfed Marriage Index 1813-1837 – Dyfed FHS (as above)
Cardiganshire 1813-1875 – R. James, PO Box 41, Llanelli, Carmarthenshire SA15 2YF
The Hayes Computerised Marriage Index, Dafydd Hayes, Pen Y Cae, Ffordd Hendy, Gwernymyndd, Clwyd, CH7 5JP
Merioneth Marriage Index 1754-1837 – Gywnedd FHS (as above)
Montgomeryshire Marriage Index – T.E. Gwynne, 5 Newtonmere Drive, Wellington, Telford, Shropshire TF1 3HG
Radnorshire Marriage Index pre 1754 – D. Foster, Mansion View, Gwystre, Llandrindod Wells, Powys LD1 6RN
Radnorshire Marriage Index 1754-1812
    Surnames A-L A.A. Powell, 1 St. David's Close, Forest Park, Penpedairheol, Hengoed, Mid-Glamorgan CF8 8BL
    Surnames M-Z B. Hemmings, 1 Marianwen Street, Cefn Fforest, Blackwood, Gwent

CARDIGANSHIRE
Cardiganshire is roughly triangular in shape, its greatest length, from north-east to south-west being about 50 miles and from west to east, about 40 miles. It is watered by three principal rivers: the Teivy, Ystwyth and Rheidol. The population in 1841 was 68,766; in 1851, 97,614; in 1861, 97,401; in 1871, 73,488; in 1881, 70,270.

The soils include light mould, sand, clay, shale, loam and peat. Wheat, barley, oats, rye, peas, beans, turnips, potatoes and hops were grown and cattle, sheep and pigs raised. There was silver and lead mining. Manufactures were mainly coarse stockings, flannel and hats. There were also fisheries.

MERIONETH
Merioneth is roughly triangular in shape, its greatest length, from east to west being some 40 miles and from north to south, about 35 miles. It is watered by three principal rivers: the Dee, Maw and Dovey. The population in 1841 was 39,332; in 1851, 51,307; in 1861, 53,230; in 1871, 47,369; in 1881, 52,028.

Clay, gravel, shale, loam, peat and light mould are among the soils. Produce included oats, barley, potatoes, clover, fruit, butter and cheese. Cattle, sheep and small ponies were bred and there was lead and copper mining. Woollen stockings were made and skins dressed.

MONTGOMERYSHIRE
Montgomeryshire's greatest length, from south-west to north-east is about 40 miles and from north-west to south-east, it is approximately the same. It is watered by five principal rivers: the Severn, Vyrnwy, Tanat, Dovey and Wye. The population in 1841 was 69,219; om 1851, 77,142; in 1861, 76,923; in 1871, 67,789; in 1881, 65,718.

The soils include clay, sand, loam, shale, peat and light mould. Among the produce were wheat, oats, barley, peas, turnips, potatoes, clover and fruit. Cattle and sheep were raised. Flannel was an important manufacture and other woollens were made. There was lead and copper mining and timber was produced.

RADNORSHIRE
Radnorshire is in shape a trapezium, its greatest length from east to west being about 35 miles and from north to south, about 30 miles. It is watered by five principal rivers: the Wye, Lugg, Somergill, Arrowe and Teme. The population in 1841 was 25,356; in 1851, 31,425; in 1861, 32,866; in 1871, 25,428; in 1881, 23,528.

Wheat, barley and oats were grown but only for personal consumption and turnips, clover, potatoes, peas, flax and hops were raised in varying quantities. The main interest was in the breeding of cattle, sheep and ponies. Manufactures were only poorly developed—chiefly flannel—but considerable quantities of hides were tanned and dressed.

The information in the Index is abbreviated, and may mislead the searcher if reference is not made to the details contained in the several publications listed in the Introduction. It is essential that users of this book check the appropriate works before making further enquiries.

NORTH WALES

parish name	deposited original registers	I.G.I.	local census indexes	copies of registers at Soc. Gen.	Boyd's marriage index	1837-1851 Registration District	Pallot's marriage index	non-conform. records at P.R.O.	map ref.
Aber	AD 1682-1971	1745-1854	5,8			Bangor			7F
Aberdaron	AD 1753-1969	1751-1864	8			Pwllheli		1811-1837	3A
Abererch	D 1600-1868	1813-1875	5,8			Pwllheli		1813-1837	4C
Aberffraw	C 1719-1970	1813-1871	5,8			Anglesey		1807-1837	7C
Abergele	A 1647-1928		4,5,8	1810-1837		St Asaph		1810-1837	8H
Amlwch	AC 1630-1971	1813-1858	5,8			Anglesey		1790-1837	9C
Bangor Cathedral	AD 1727-1932	1813-1829	8	1754-1932		Bangor		1790-1837	7D
Bangor	B 1675-1939		4,5,8	1675-1812		Wrexham			5L
Bardsey Island (ex. par.)			8			Pwllheli			2A
Beaumaris	A 1649-1971	1813-1848	5,8	1723-1781		Bangor		1791-1837	7E
Beddgelert	A 1734-1857	1813-1866	8			Ffestiniog		1809-1837	5E
Bethesda	D 1813-1917		8			Bangor			7E
Bettws Garmon	D 1778-1962	1809-1867	5,8			Caernarvon			6E
Bettws Gwerfil Goch	E 1685-1981		4,5,8			Corwen			5I
Bettws-y-Coed	D 1731-1942	1745-1858	5,8			Llanrwst		1806-1837	6G
Bettws-yn-Rhos	F 1705-1992		4,5,8			St Asaph			7G
Bodedern	AC 1695-1985	1813-1871	5,8			Anglesey		1811-1837	8B
Bodewryd	C 1755-1991	1817-1874	5,8			Anglesey			9C
Bodfari	B 1571-1986	1823-1836	4,5,8	1571-1812		St Asaph			7I
Bodfean	D 1678-1992	1755-1875	8			Pwllheli		1833-1837	4B
Bodferin			8			Pwllheli			3A
Bodwrog	C 1754-1993	1813-1875	5,8			Anglesey			8C
Bottwnog	AD 1741-1991	1745-1874	8			Pwllheli		1814-1837	3B(E)
Broughton	B 1824-1990		4,5,8			Wrexham			7L
Buckley	B 1822-1992		4,5,8			Great Boughton			7K
Bryncroes	D 1731-1970	1777-1868	8			Pwllheli		1815-1836	3B
Bryn Eglwys	F 1687-1970		4,5,8	1820-1837		Corwen		1820-1837	5J
Caerhun	D 1662-1970	1799-1875	5,8			Conway			7F
Caerwys	B 1673-1983		4,5,8	1673-1728		Holywell		1810-1836	8J
Capel Curig	D 1754-1969	1780-1846	5,8			Llanrwst			6F
Capel Garmon	F 1702-1969	1818-1853	5,8			Llanrwst		1813-1837	6G
Carnguwch	D 1754-1861	1780-1868	8			Pwllheli			4C
Ceirchiog	C 1813-1997	1813-1843	5,8			Anglesey			7C
Ceidio	D 1754-1810	1842-1870	8			Pwllheli			4B
Ceidio (or Rhodogeidio)	C 1754-1964		5,8			Anglesey			8C
Cerrigceinwen	C 1721-1992	1813-1867	5,8			Anglesey			7C
Cerrigydrudion	F 1590-1970		4,5,8	1799-1837		Corwen		1799-1837	5H
Chirk	A 1611-1975		4,5,8	1705-1812	1612-1812	Oswestry			4K
Cilcain	B 1576-1971	1813-1875	4,5,8	1576-1843		Holywell		1812-1836	7J
Clocaenog	F 1672-1965	1813-1863	4,5,8			Ruthin			6I
Clynnog	D 1624-1891	1813-1875	8			Caernarvon		1807-1837	5D
Coedana	C 1813-1995	1813-1873	5,8			Anglesey			8C
Conway	A 1541-1973	1541-1868	5,8	1541-1793		Conway		1811-1837	8F
Criccieth	A 1675-1991	1810-1875	5,8			Pwllheli		1813-1837	4D
Cwm	B 1727-1971		4,5,8			St Asaph			8I
Denbigh	F 1683-1984	1815-1842	4,5,8	1684-1837		St Asaph		1763-1837	7I
Deneio	A 1686-1812	1770-1862	5,8			Pwllheli		1785-1837	4C
Derwen	F 1632-1968	1813-1851	4,5,8			Ruthin		1818-1837	5I
Dodleston (Cheshire)									6L
Dolbenmaen	A 1672-1974	1778-1875	8			Ffestiniog		1812-1837	5D
Dolgarrog (see Llanbedr-y-cennin)									6F
Dolwyddelan	D 1701-1971	1782-1875	5,8			Llanrwst		1817-1836	5F
Dwygyfylchi	D 1813-1991	1761-1871	5,8			Conway		1804-1837	8F
Dyserth	B 1602-1974	1813-1830	4,5,8	1602-1812		St Asaph		1823-1837	8I
Edern	D 1700-1931	1745-1868	5,8			Pwllheli		1811-1837	4B
Efenechtid	F 1693-1995	1813-1864	4,5,8	1693-1812	1693-1811	Ruthin		1826-1837	6J
Eglwysbach	F 1601-1929		4,5,8			Llanrwst		1813-1837	7G
Eglwys-Rhos (or Llanrhos)	D 1754-1993	1753-1847	4,5,8			Conway			8G
Ellesmere (Salop.)									5L
Erbistock	F 1679-1991		4,5,8	1679-1812		Wrexham			5L
Flint	B 1598-1955	1820-1837	4,5,8	1707-1786		Holywell		1820-1837	7K
Gresford	F 1661-1988		4,5,8		1660-1812	Wrexham			6L
Gwaenysgor	B 1538-1995	1813-1850	4,5,8	1538-1812		Holywell			8I
Gwytherin	AF 1718-1994		4,5,8	1814-1837		Llanrwst		1814-1837	6G
Gyffin	A 1707-1970	1753-1864	5,8			Conway			8F
Gyffylliog	F 1617-1967	1796-1861	4,5,8	1812-1837		Ruthin			6I
Halkyn	B 1594-1993	1815-1850	4,5,8	1594-1803		Holywell		1808-1837	7J
Hanmer	B 1563-1960		4,5,8	1563-1850		Ellesmere			5M
Hawarden	B 1586-1994	1771-1875	4,5,8			Great Boughton			7L
Heneglwys	C 1693-1993	1813-1875	5,8			Anglesey			7C
Henllan	F 1684-1983	1818-1849	4,5,8	1684-1746		St Asaph		1810-1837	7I
Holt	F 1661-1997	1850-1869	4,5,8	1740-1812	1661-1837	Wrexham			6L
Holyhead	AC 1737-1991	1682-1859	5,8	1682-1840		Anglesey		1806-1837	8B
Holywell	B 1677-1995	1823-1848	4,5,8	1714-1812		Holywell		1800-1837	8J
Hope	B 1668-1943		4,5,8	1668-1812		Wrexham			6K
Isycoed	F 1749-1970		4,5,8	1749-1837	1750-1837	Ellesmere			6L
Llanaelhaearn	AD 1725-1971	1756-1869	8			Pwllheli			5C
Llanallgo	C 1725-1992	1813-1871	5,8			Anglesey		1805-1837	8D
Llanarmon	F 1676-1969	1730-1836	4,5,8	1812-1861		Ruthin			6J
Llanarmon	A 1705-1993	1813-1875	8			Pwllheli		1821-1836	4C
LLanarmon Dyffryn Ceiriog	F 1624-1991	1758-1835	4,5,8		1690-1868	Corwen			4J
Llanarmon Mynydd Mawr	F 1695-1989		4,5,8			Llanfyllin			3J
LLanasa	B 1629-1890	1814-1837	4,5,8	1619-1812		Holywell		1818-1837	8I
Llanbabo	C 1740-1986	1813-1870	5,8			Anglesey			8C
Llanbadrig	C 1731-1992	1813-1875	5,8			Anglesey		1807-1837	9C
Llanbeblig	D 1699-1975	1813-1875	5,8			Caernarvon		1785-1837	6D
Llanbedr Dyffrin Clwyd	F 1650-1968	1813-1860	4,5,8	1652-1891		Ruthin			6J
Llanbedr Goch	C 1754-1987	1813-1866	5,8			Anglesey			8D

parish name	deposited original registers	I.G.I.	local census indexes	copies of registers at Soc. Gen.	Boyd's marriage index	1837-1851 Registration District	Pallot's marriage index	non-conform. records at P.R.O.	map ref.
Llanbedrog	D 1691-1988	1795-1875	8			Pwllheli			4C
Llanbedr-y-cennin	D 1663-1837	1799-1875	5,8			Conway			7F
Llanberis	D 1726-1995	1802-1867	5,8			Caernarvon		1809-1837	6E
Llanbeulan	A 1754-1959	1813-1874	5,8			Anglesey			7C
Llanddanielfab	C 1746-1992	1813-1860	5,8			Bangor		1819-1837	7D
Llanddeiniolen	D 1575-1999	1813-1875	8			Caernarvon		1809-1837	6E
Llanddeusant	AC 1754-1991	1813-1870	5,8			Anglesey		1824-1837	8C
Llanddoged	F 1600-1990	1768-1850	4,5,8			Llanwrst			6G
Llanddona	C 1762-1992	1813-1864	5,8			Bangor		1815-1837	8E
Llanddulas	F 1755-1971		4,5,8			St Asaph			8H
Llanddyfnan	C 1661-1993	1813-1875	5,8			Anglesey		1803-1837	8D
Llandegai	A 1674-1908	1813-1875	5,8			Bangor			6E
Llandegfan	A 1547-1976	1547-1860	5,8			Bangor		1817-1837	7E
Llandegla	F 1710-1970		4,5,8	1741-1812		Ruthin			5J
Llandegwning	AD 1761-1969	1792-1865	8	1779-1812		Pwllheli			3B
Llandrillo-yn-Rhos	F 1693-1921		4,5,8			Conway			8G
Llandrygarn	C 1739-1993	1813-1875	5,8			Anglesey		1807-1837	8C
Llandudno	D 1750-1920	1805-1875	5,6,8			Conway		1821-1837	8F
Llandudwen	D 1754-1980					Pwllheli			4B
Llandwrog	D 1593-1887	1813-1874	5,8			Caernarvon		1812-1837	6D
Llandyfrydog	A 1690-1943	1813-1875	5,8			Anglesey		1814-1837	8C
Llandyrnog	F 1664-1986	1813-1856	4,5,8			Ruthin		1811-1837	7I
Llandysilio	C 1755-1959		5,8			Bangor			7D(D)
Llanedwen	C 1747-1994	1797-1862	5,8			Bangor			7D
Llaneilian	A 1733-1888	1796-1875	5,8	1825-1837		Anglesey		1826-1837	9D
Llanelian-yn-Rhos	F 1589-1992		4,5,8			Conway		1825-1837	7G
Llanelidan	F 1686-1995	1813-1869	4,5,8	1686-1870	1696-1812	Ruthin		1810-1837	5J
Llanengan	A 1679-1967	1791-1875	8			Pwllheli		1811-1837	3B
Llanerchymedd	C 1754-1998		5,8			Anglesey		1802-1837	8C
Llaneugrad	C 1725-1991	1813-1870	5,8			Anglesey			8D
Llanfachreth	C 1682-1993		5,8			Anglesey			8B
Llanfaelog	A 1754-1971	1806-1875	5,8			Anglesey		1807-1837	7C
Llanfaelrhys	D 1811-1992	1796-1874	8			Pwllheli			3B
Llanfaes	C 1727-1975		5,8			Bangor			8E
Llanfaethlu	C 1743-1974	1794-1874	5,8	1678-1840		Anglesey			8B
Llanfaglan	AD 1602-1992	1813-1875	5,8			Caernarvon			6D
Llanfair Dyffryn Clwyd	F 1680-1979		4,5,8	1680-1812		Ruthin			6J
Llanfair-Fechan	D 1634-1992	1812-1875	5,8	1635-1812		Bangor		1804-1837	7F
Llanfair-is-gaer	A 1675-1907	1813-1875	5,8			Caernarvon		1832-1836	7D
Llanfair-mathafarn-eithaf	C 1753-1996	1790-1875	5,8			Anglesey			8D
Llanfair Talhaearn	F 1669-1999		4,5,8	1822-1837		St Asaph			7H
Llanfair-yn-neubwll	AC 1774-1990	1744-1862	5,8	1677-1841		Anglesey			7B
Llanfairynghornwy	C 1732-1974	1758-1870	5,8			Anglesey			9B
Llanfairynycwmwd			5,8			Caernarvon			7D(B)
Llanfair-Pwllgwyngyll	A 1754-1882	1800-1865	5,8			Bangor			7D(C)
Llanfechell	C 1691-1992	1799-1866	5,8			Anglesey			9C
Llanferres	F 1586-1998	1814-1837	4,5,8	1611-1897	1588-1837	Ruthin		1821-1837	6J
Llanffinan	C 1690-1992	1791-1862	5,8			Bangor			7D
Llanfflewin	C 1784-1990	1794-1872	5,8			Anglesey			8C
Llanfigael	C 1682-1991	1754-1873	5,8			Anglesey		1808-1836	8B(A)
Llanfihangel Bachellaeth	D 1692-1995	1798-1875	8			Pwllheli			4B
Llanfihangel Dinsylwy	C 1762-1943	1764-1858	5,8			Bangor			8E
Llanfihangel Glyn Myfyr	F 1662-1991	1813-1843	4,5,8			Corwen		1819-1837	5H
Llanfihangel Tre'r-Beirdd	C 1695-1992	1734-1875	5,8			Anglesey			9D
Llanfihangel-yn-Nhywyn	C 1813-1996		5,8	1679-1838		Anglesey			7B
Llanfihangel-y-Pennant	A 1698-1971	1813-1875	8			Ffestiniog		1819-1837	4E
Llanfihangel Ysgeifiog	C 1703-1996		5,8			Bangor			7D
Llanfwrog	F 1638-1945		4,5,8	1638-1840	1638-1840	Ruthin		1792-1837	6I
Llanfwrog	C 1754-1992		5,8	1672-1840	1638-1840	Anglesey		1814-1837	8B
Llangadwaladr	C 1610-1999		5,8			Anglesey			7C
Llangadwaladr	F 1736-1995	1813-1854	4,5,8			Oswestry			4J
Llangaffo	C 1659-1992		5,8			Caernarvon			7C
Llangedwyn	A 1672-1952		4,5,8			Llanfyllin			3J
Llangefni	C 1709-1999		5,8			Anglesey		1798-1837	7D
Llangeinwen	C 1688-1993		8			Llanwrst		1812-1837	6D
Llangelynnin	D 1733-1992	1811-1866	5,8			Conway		1819-1836	7F
Llangernyw	AF 1570-1998		4,5,8			Llanwrst		1810-1837	7G
Llangian	A 1679-1970	1810-1875	8			Pwllheli		1810-1837	3B
Llangoed	C 1754-1970		5,8			Bangor		1811-1837	8E
Llangollen	F 1587-1986	1813-1852	4,5,8	1670-1812	1670-1786	Corwen		1805-1837	5K
Llangristiolus	C 1754-1967		5,8			Anglesey		1785-1837	7C
Llangwyfan	F 1723-1992		4,5,8	1834-1837		Ruthin			7J(F)
Llangwyfan	C 1754-1991		5,8			Anglesey			7C
Llangwyllog	C 1777-1996		5,8			Anglesey			8C
Llangwm	F 1738-1977		4,5,8		1738-1812	Corwen		1799-1837	5H
Llangwnnadl	D 1755-1992	1808-1874	8			Pwllheli		1812-1837	4A
Llangwstenin	A 1608-1970	1805-1850	4,5,8			Conway		1820-1836	8G
Llangybi	A 1695-1992	1810-1875	8			Pwllheli		1810-1837	4C
Llangynhafal	F 1704-1940		4,5,8	1706-1837	1706-1747	Ruthin		1814-1837	7J
Llanidan	AC 1666-1993		5,8			Caernarvon		1808-1837	7D
Llaniestyn	C 1813-1992		5,8			Bangor			8E
Llaniestyn	AD 1765-1970	1813-1870	8			Pwllheli		1811-1836	4B
Llanllechid	A 1690-1907	1813-1865	5,8			Bangor		1790-1837	7E
Llanllibio			5,8			Anglesey			8B
Llanllyfni	A 1744-1924	1813-1864	8			Caernarvon		1811-1837	5D
Llannefydd	F 1754-1989		4,5,8	1754-1812		St Asaph			7H
Llannore	AD 1724-1990	1810-1862	5,8	1757-1811		Pwllheli		1808-1837	4C
Llanrhaeadr yng Nghinmeirch	F 1683-1971		4,5,8			Ruthin		1812-1837(?)	6I

parish name	deposited original registers	I.G.I.	local census indexes	copies of registers at Soc. Gen.	Boyd's marriage index	1837-1851 Registration District	Pallot's marriage index	non-conform. records at P.R.O.	map ref.
Llanrhaeadr yn Mochnant	F 1678-1930		4,5,8			Llanfyllin		1806-1837	3J
Llanrhychwyn	D 1594-1987	1813-1858	5,8			Llanrwst		1814-1836	6F
Llanrhuddlad	C 1813-1994		5,8			Anglesey		1789-1837	9B
Llanrhwydrus	C 1747-1974		5,8			Anglesey			9B
Llanrhydd	F 1608-1991		4,5,8			Ruthin			6J
Llanrug	D 1674-1923	1813-1874	5,8			Caernarvon		1809-1837	6D
Llanrwst	F 1613-1973		4,5,8			Llanrwst		1806-1837	6G
Llansadwrn	C 1584-1991		5,8			Bangor			7D
Llansanffraid Glan Conway	F 1660-1993		4,5,8			Conway			7G
Llansanffraid Glyn Ceiriog	F 1754-1970		4,5,8		1754-1814	Corwen			4J
Llansannan	F 1730-1998	1666-1832	4,5,8	1667-1812		St Asaph	1790-1812	1811-1837	6H
Llansilin	A 1668-1932	1813-1855	4,5,8			Oswestry		1818-1836	3J
Llantrisant	C 1745-1969		5,8			Anglesey			8C
LLantysilio	F 1677-1992		4,5,8	1671-1812	1671-1812	Corwen		1821-1836	5J
Llanwenllwyfo	A 1762-1969		5,8			Anglesey		1808-1837	9D
Llanwnda	AD 1600-1902	1813-1875	5,8			Caernarvon		1825-1837	6D
Llanychan	F 1696-1991		4,5,8	1676-1874	1677-1833	Ruthin			6J(G)
Llanynghenedl	C 1713-1983		5,8			Anglesey			8B
Llanynys	F 1626-1971	1813-1867	4,5,8	1626-1880	1626-1837	Ruthin			6I
Llanystumdwy	A 1596-1993	1813-1875	5,8			Pwllheli		1811-1837	4D
Llechgynfarwy	C 1743-1986		5,8			Anglesey			8C
Llechylched	AC 1803-1997		5,8			Anglesey		1801-1837	7B
Llysfaen	F 1661-1938	1822-1844	4,5,8			Conway		1834-1836	8G
Maenan Abbey (ex.par.)			8			Llanrwst			6F
Malpas (Cheshire)									5M
Marchwiel	F 1653-1970		4,5,8		1665-1812	Wrexham			5L
Meliden	B 1602-1996	1813-1851	4,5,82	1602-1812		St Asaph		1825-1837	8I
Meyllteyrn	AD 1741-1987	1795-1875	8			Pwllheli			3B
Minera	F 1786-1971		4,5,8			Wrexham			6K
Mold	B 1604-1988	1817-1834	4,5,8	1604-1812		Holywell		1807-1837	7J
Nannerch	A 1664-1970	1813-1851	4,5,8	1664-1812		Holywell		1820-1837	7J
Nantglyn	F 1719-1993		4,5,8	1720-1779	1720-1745	Ruthin		1811-1837	6H
Nercwys	B 1665-1970	1813-1851	4,5,8	1665-1812		Holywell			6K
Nevin	AD 1692-1913	1814-1867	8			Pwllheli		1823-1837	4B
Newborough	C 1721-1971		5,8			Caernarvon		1809-1837	6C
Newmarket (or Trelawnyd)	B 1696-1970	1820-1858	4,5,8			Holywell		1796-1837	8I
Northop	B 1590-1993	1813-1847	4,5,8	1656-1812		Holywell		1806-1837	7K
Overton	B 1602-1957		4,5,8	1602-1837		Ellesmere			5L
Penley	B 1752-1970	1813-1877	4,5,8			Ellesmere			4L
Penllech	D 1785-1949	1813-1875	5,8			Pwllheli			4B
Pennant (Montgom.)									3I
Penmachno	D 1710-1970	1813-1875	5,8			Llanrwst		1812-1837	5F
Penmon	C 1693-1995		5,8			Bangor			8E
Penmorfa	D 1672-1986	1814-1875	8			Ffestiniog		1823-1837	4D
Penmynydd	C 1754-1994		5,8			Bangor		1824-1837	7D
Penrhos	A 1813-1944		5,8			Pwllheli			4C
Penrhosllggwy	C 1578-1997		5,8			Anglesey			8D
Pentir	DG 1616-1992	1813-1829	5,8			Bangor			7D
Pentraeth	C 1740-1992		5,8			Anglesey		1808-1837	8D
Pentrefoelas	F 1772-1966	1782-1854	4,5,8			Llanrwst			6G
Pistyll	D 1773-1990	1789-1869	8			Pwllheli		1812-1837	4C
Puffin Island (Priestholme)			5,8			Bangor			8E
Rhiw	D 1782-1990	1813-1875	8			Pwllheli			3B
Rhosbeirio	C 1813-1962		5,8			Anglesey			9C
Rhoscolyn	AC 1732-1990		5,8			Anglesey		1815-1837	7B
Rhuddlan	B 1681-1940	1815-1834	4,5,8	1681-1742		St Asaph		1815-1837	8I
Ruabon	A 1559-1964		4,5,8	1559-1812	1559-1812	Wrexham		1810-1837	5K
Ruthin	F 1592-1991	1813-1860	4,5,8	1608-1720	1608-1720	Ruthin		1813-1837	6J(H)
St Asaph	B 1593-1983	1813-1836	4,5,8	1671-1812		St Asaph		1810-1837	7I
St George	F 1694-1971	1681-1846	4,5,8		1695-1812	St Asaph		1832-1837	8H
Threapwood (Cheshire)									5M
Trefdraeth	C 1551-1999		5,8			Anglesey		1806-1837	7C
Treflys	A 1813-1937	1813-1875	8			Ffestiniog		1809-1837	4D
Trefriw	D 1594-1969	1800-1858	5,8			Llanrwst		1815-1837	6G
Tregaean	C 1708-1992		5,8			Anglesey			8D
Tremeirchion	B 1599-1992	1813-1835	4,5,8	1604-1812		St Asaph			7I
Treuddyn	B 1611-1923		4,5,8	1611-1812		Wrexham		1826-1837	6K
Trewalchmai	C 1727-1999		5,8			Anglesey		1806-1837	7C
Tudweiliog	D 1759-1932	1813-1874	8			Pwllheli		1811-1835	4B
Whitford	B 1643-1938	1814-1837	4,5,8	1643-1812		Holywell		1814-1837	8L
Worthenbury	B 1597-1970	1850-1876	4,5,8			Wrexham			5L
Wrexham	F 1618-1994		5,8	1618-1775	1632-1754	Wrexham		1713-1837	5K
Ynyscynhaiarn	A 1754-1907	1813-1870	8			Ffestiniog		1812-1837	4E
Ysbyty Ifan	F 1732-1968		5,8			Llanrwst		1806-1837	5G
Ysceifiog	B 1662-1996		4,5,8			Holywell		1819-1836	7J

NORTH WALES

Original Registers deposited at:
A = National Library of Wales, Aberystwyth, Ceredigion SY23 3BU
B = Flintshire Record Office, The Old Rectory, Hawarden, Flintshire CH5 3NR
C = Anglesey County Record Office, Shire Hall, Glanhwfa Road, Llangefni, Anglesey LL77 7TW
D = Gwynedd Archives Service, Caernarfon Area Record Office, County Offices, Shirehall Street, Caernarfon, Gwynedd LL55 1SH
E = Gwynedd Archives, Archifdy Meirion, Cae Penarlag, Dolgellau, Gwynedd LL40 2YB
F = Denbighshire Record Office, 46 Clwyd Street, Ruthin, Denbighshire LL15 1HP
G = British Libary, Euston Road, London, NW1 2DB

Study adjacent parishes in counties of Cheshire and Shropshire

National Library of Wales, Aberystwyth, Ceredigion SY23 3BU
Flintshire Record Office, The Old Rectory, Hawarden, Flintshire, CH5 3NR
Anglesey County Record Office, Shire Hall, Llangefni, Anglesey LL77 7TW
Denbighshire Record Office, 46 Clwyd Street, Ruthin, Denbighshire LL15 1HP
Gwynedd Archives Service, Caernarfon Area Record Office, County Offices, Shirehall Street, Caernarfon, Gwynedd LL55 1SH
Gwynedd Archives, Archifdy Meirion, Cae Penarlag, Dolgellau, Gwynedd LL40 2YB
Dept. of Manuscripts, Main Library, University College of North Wales, Bangor, Gwynedd, LL57 2DG

The following useful indexes have been compiled - see Introduction
Census Indexes 1841 & 1851 Denbighshire & Flintshire - D. Hayes, Pen Y Cae, Ffordd Hendy, Gwernymyndd, Clwyd, CH7 5JP
Census Index 1851 - Gywnedd FHS, C/ O Y. Edwards, 36 Y Wern, Y Felinheli, Gwynedd, LL56 4TX
The Hayes Computerised Marriage Index - D. Hayes (as above)
Marriage Index Gwynedd - Gwynedd FHS (as above)

ANGLESEY
Anglesey is an island, its greatest length, from north-west to south-east, being some 20 miles. Its length from south-west to north-east is almost uniformly about 15 miles except around Beaumaris, where it reaches 20 miles. It is watered by four principal rivers: The Cefni, Alaw, Fraw and Dulas. The population in 1841 was 50,891; in 1851, 39,732; in 1861, 38,157; in 1871, 50,919; in 1881, 51,416.

Sand, marl, loam, shale, peat and mould are among the soils. Produce included oats, barley, wheat, peas, potatoes, turnips and some hemp. Cattle and sheep were bred, and there was coal and copper mining. Manufactures were negligible, being confined almost entirely to coarse woollens.

CAERNARVONSHIRE
Caernarvonshire stongly resembles Cornwall in shape. Its greatest length, from south-west to north-east is almost 60 miles and north-west to south-east about 25 miles. It is watered by five principal rivers: The Conway, Seiont, Gorfai, Ogwen and Gwynedd. The population in 1841 was 81,093; in 1851, 98,185; in 1861, 103,538; in 1871, 106,122; in 1881, 119,349.

The soils are extremely various and include loams, sand, gravel, peat, shingle and mould. Wheat, barley, oats and rye were grown together with potatoes, turnips and clover. Cattle, sheep, pigs and horses were bred. Manufactures were of minor importance. Cloths and coarse linen yarns were made and woollen stockings knitted. Slate was quarried.

DENBIGHSHIRE
Denbighshire's shape is very irregular, its greatest length, from north-west to south-east, being about 40 miles and from south-west to north-east, some 20 miles. It is watered by three principal rivers: The Dee, Clwyd and Conway. The population in 1841 was 88,866; in 1851, 94,698; in 1861, 104,346; in 1871, 104,266; in 1881, 111,740.

Soils include loams, sand, peat, gravel and mould. Wheat, barley, oats and rye were cultivated and other produce were peas, turnips, apples and clover. Cattle and sheep were bred and considerable quantities of butter and cheese were made. Coal was mined. Manufactures were mainly coarse woollen cloth and knitted woollen stockings. Skins were dressed and many made into gloves and shoes.

FLINTSHIRE
Flintshire exists in two separated parts, Denbighshire intervening. The greatest length of the larger portion, from north-west to south-east, being about 30 miles and from south-west to north-east, some 15 miles. It is watered by three principal rivers: The Dee, Clwydd and Allen. The population in 1841 was 66,919; in 1851, 41,047; in 1861, 39,941; in 1871, 76,245; in 1881, 80,587.

Clay, gravel, loams and marl are among the soils. Produce included wheat, barley, oats, turnips, peas and clover. Cattle, sheep and horses were bred and butter and cheese were made. Coal was a major industry and lead and limestone were also mined extensively. Manufactures were mainly copper and brass articles; pottery, ropes and cotton items.

The information in the Index is abbreviated, and may mislead the searcher if reference is not made to the details contained in the several publications listed in the Introduction. It is essential that users of this book check the appropriate works before making further enquiries.

parish name	deposited original registers	I.G.I.	local census indexes	copies of registers at Soc. Gen.	Boyd's marriage index	1837-1851 Registration District	Pallot's marriage index	non-conform. records at P.R.O.	map ref.
Aberavon	G 1747-1955	1696-1869	4,5,8,9			Neath		1815-1837	4I
Aberdare	G 1734-1937		4,5,6,8,9			Merthyr Tydfil		1790-1837	5K
Abergorlech	D 1813-1993		8	1813-1988		Lampeter			8H
Abergwili	A 1661-1934	1813-1875	8	1661-1934	1661-1934	Carmarthen		1810-1837	7G
Aberllynfi			5,8			Hay			8L
Abernant	AD 1754-1993		8	1754-1875	1754-1875	Carmarthen		1805-1857	7F
Aberyscir	A 1755-1991	1813-1871	5,8			Brecknock			8K
Alltmawr	A 1912-1971	1814-1844	5,8			Builth			9L
Ambleston	A 1765-1974	1799-1864	4,5,8,9	1813-1837		Haverfordwest		1811-1837	7C
Amroth	E 1754-1970	1799-1875	4,5,8	1813-1837		Narberth			6D
Angle	A 1755-1993	1799-1875	4,5,8	1813-1837		Pembroke			5B
Baglan	G 1769-1923		4,5,8			Neath			4I
Barry	G 1724-1958		4,5,8,9			Cardiff			2L
Battle	A 1720-1992	1813-1841	5,8	1813-1837		Brecknock			8K
Bayvil	A 1813-1908		4,5,8			Cardigan			8D
Bedwas (Mon.)									4L
Begelly	A 1759-1934		4,5,8,9	1757-1837		Narberth		1820-1837	6D
Bettws	AG 1722-1950	1813-1876	4,5,8,9	1813-1837	1813-1837	Bridgend			4J
Bettws	D 1706-1973		8	1813-1837	1813-1837	Llandilofawr		1812-1837	6H
Bishopston	A 1716-1979		4,5,8,9			Swansea			4H
Blaen-Gwrach (see Glyncorrwg)									5J
Bletherston	A 1653-1980	1806-1875	4,5,8	1813-1837		Narberth			7D
Bonvilston	G 1758-1983	1696-1875	4,5,8,9			Cardiff			3L
Bosherston	A 1670-1991	1799-1875	4,5,8	1813-1837		Pembroke			5C
Boulston	E 1754-1939	1813-1839	4,5,8,9	1754-1939		Haverfordwest			6C
Brawdy	E 1813-1966	1799-1875	4,5,8,9	1813-1837		Haverfordwest		1809-1837	7B
Brechfa	D 1780-1970		8	1806-1970	1813-1837	Llandilofawr			7G
Brecon								1810-1837	7K
St David	A 1730-1971	1813-1844	5,6,8			Brecknock			7K
St John	A 1727-1982	1813-1865	5,6,8			Brecknock			7K
St Mary	A 1684-1976		5,6,8			Brecknock			7K(F)
Bridell	A 1810-1993		4,5,8	1813-1837		Cardigan			8E
Briton-Ferry	G 1668-1969	1813-1867	4,5,8			Neath			5I
Bronllys	A 1755-1992	1813-1872	5,8			Hay			8L
Builth	A 1681-1987	1813-1841	5,6,8			Builth		1805-1837	9K
Burton	A 1689-1922	1799-1873	4,5,8	1754-1837		Pembroke			6C
Cadoxton	G 1752-1982	1818-1869	4,5,8,9			Cardiff			2L
Cadoxton	G 1738-1965	1813-1872	4,5,8			Neath		1820-1837	5I
Caerau	G 1741-1974	1724-1870	4,5,8,9			Cardiff			3L
Caerphilly	G 1813-1925	1834-1875	4,5,6,8,9			Cardiff			4L
Caldy Island (ex par)			5,8			Pembroke			5D
Camrose	A 1754-1992	1799-1875	4,5,8,9	1813-1837		Haverfordwest		1827-1840	7B
Cantref	A 1754-1992	1813-1834	5,8			Brecknock			7K
Capel Colman	A 1770-1991	1806-1875	5,8	1813-1837		Newcastle-in-Emlyn			8E
Cardiff								1798-1837	3M
St John	G 1669-1921	1813-1875	4,5,6,8,9	1813-1868		Cardiff			3M
St Mary	G 1843-1932	1813-1877	4,5,6,8,9	1813-1868		Cardiff			3M
Carew	E 1718-1971	1813-1875	4,5,8	1778-1837		Pembroke			5C
Carmarthen (St Peter)	D 1671-1923	1671-1875	5,8	1671-1837	1813-1837	Carmarthen		1785-1858	7F
Castellan (see Penrith)									8E
Castelldwyran	A 1754-1926		4,5,8			Narberth			7D
Castlebythe	A 1752-1980	1799-1875	4,5,8,9	1813-1837		Haverfordwest			7C
Castlemartin	A 1783-1993	1799-1875	4,5,8	1813-1837		Pembroke			5B
Cathedine	A 1732-1991	1813-1867	5,8			Brecknock			7L
Cenarth	A 1701-1975		4,5,8		1701-1837	Newcastle-in-Emlyn		1810-1837	8E
Cheriton	A 1757-1992		4,5,8,9			Swansea			4G
Cilgerran	A 1708-1992	1799-1875	4,5,8	1813-1837		Cardigan		1820-1836	8E
Cilrhedyn	A 1754-1978	1799-1874	5,8	1813-1837		Newcastle-in-Emlyn			8F
Cil-y-bebyll	G 1768-1931	1776-1868	4,5,8			Neath		1760-1837	5I
Cilycwm	D 1701-1970		8	1813-1837	1813-1837	Llandovery		1812-1837	8I
Cilymaenllwyd	AD 1742-1977		8	1813-1837	1813-1837	Narberth			7D
Clarbeston	E 1718-1993	1799-1867	5,8	1813-1837		Narberth			7C
Clydey	A 1701-1991	1799-1873	5,8						8E
Coedcanlass (see Martletwy and Lawrenny)									6C(D)
Cogan	AG 1784-1979	1813-1830	4,5,8,9			Cardiff			3M
Coity	G 1717-1950	1820-1875	4,5,8,9			Bridgend		1785-1837	3J
Colwynston	A 1766-1992	1813-1862	4,5,8,9			Bridgend			3K
Conwil-Elvet	A 1743-1982	1764-1864	8		1743-1837	Carmarthen		1806-1837	7F
Conwil-Gaio	A 1698-1979	1749-1856	8		1697-1970	Llandovery		1812-1837	8H
Cosherton	E 1723-1970	1799-1875	4,5,8	1723-1840		Pembroke			5C
Cowbridge	G 1718-1983	1819-1875	4,5,8,9			Bridgend			3K(R)
Coychurch	G 1736-1959	1820-1861	4,5,8,9	1760-1850		Bridgend			4K
Crickadarn	A 1734-1992	1813-1873	5,8	1734-1983		Builth			8L
Crickhowell	A 1633-1944		5,8			Crickhowell		1813-1837	7M
Crinow	A 1757-1970	1829-1872	4,5,8	1813-1837		Narberth			6D
Crunwear	E 1754-1979	1799-1875	4,5,8	1813-1837		Narberth			6D
Cyffic	D 1813-1979		5,8	1813-1837	1813-1837	Narberth			6E
Dale	A 1723-1958	1799-1875	4,5,8,9	1813-1837		Haverfordwest			6A
Defynnog	A 1695-1997		5,6,8			Brecknock		1775-1837	7J
Dinas	A 1676-1993	1799-1875	4,5,8	1675-1879		Cardigan		1812-1835	8C
Eglwsfair-a-churig	D 1813-1941		4,5,8		1813-1875	Narberth			7E
Eglwys-Brewis	G 1750-1970		4,5,8,9		1813-1837	Bridgend			2K
Eglwys-Cymmyn	D 1731-1984	1750-1869	5,8	1690-1837	1813-1837	Narberth			6E
Eglwysilan	G 1679-1930	1813-1875	4,5,8,9			Cardiff			4L
Eglwyswrw	A 1740-1993	1799-1874	4,5,8	1813-1837		Cardigan			8D
Egremont	D 1813-1968	1794-1876	5,8	1813-1837		Narberth			7D
Ewenny	G 1714-1992	1813-1875	4,5,8,9			Bridgend			3J
Fishguard	A 1785-1964	1799-1864	4,5,8,9	1813-1837		Haverfordwest		1775-1837	8C
Flemingston	AG 1576-1992	1813-1870	4,5,8,9	1576-1725		Bridgend			3K(Q)

parish name	deposited original registers	I.G.I.	local census indexes	copies of registers at Soc. Gen.	Boyd's marriage index	1837-1851 Registration District	Pallot's marriage index	non-conform. records at P.R.O.	map ref.
Ford	AE 1801-1963		4,5,8			Haverfordwest			7C
Freystrop	E 1729-1969	1799-1870	4,5,8,9	1813-1837		Haverfordwest		1831-1837	6C
Garthbrengy	A 1733-1982	1775-1854	5,8			Brecknock			8K
Gelligaer	G 1755-1933	1813-1870	4,5,6,8,9			Merthyr Tydfil		1832-1837	5L
Gileston	G 1701-1812	1814-1875	4,5,8,9			Bridgend			2K
Glasbury	A 1660-1976	1813-1874	5,8	1660-1836		Hay	1790-1837	1801-1837	8M
Glyn-corwg	AG 1702-1914	1821-1860	4,5,8			Neath			5J
Glyntawe (or Callwen)	C 1685-1971	1813-1840	5,8			Brecknock			6J
Granston	E 1778-1991		4,5,8,9	1813-1837		Haverfordwest			8B
Gumfreston	E 1647-1970	1799-1873	4,5,8	1813-1837		Pembroke			5D
Gwenddwr	A 1752-1992	1778-1873	5,8			Builth		1824-1837	9K
Haroldston West	E 1748-1992	1798-1870	4,5,8,9	1813-1837		Haverfordwest			6B
Hasguard	E 1813-1969	1800-1870	4,5,8,9	1813-1837		Haverfordwest			6B
Haverfordwest				1745-1772				1705-1837	6C
St Martin	E 1721-1974	1800-1871	4,5,8	1722-1884		Haverfordwest			6C(Ba)
St Mary	E 1590-1966	1799-1875	4,5,8	1594-1850		Haverfordwest			6C(Bc)
St Thomas	E 1710-1962	1813-1875	4,5,8	1713-1907		Haverfordwest			6C(Bb)
Hay	A 1688-1991	1776-1867	5,8			Hay			8M
Haycastle	E 1813-1992	1799-1875	4,5,8,9	1813-1837		Haverfordwest			7B
Henllan Amgoed	D 1826-1989		5,8	1813-1837		Narberth		1748-1837	7E
Henry's Moat	A 1755-1993	1799-1874	4,5,8,9	1813-1837		Haverfordwest			7C
Herbrandston	E 1717-1992	1799-1870	4,5,8,9	1813-1837		Haverfordwest			6B
Highlight (ex.par.)			4,5,8,9			Cardiff			3L(T)
Hodgeston	E 1755-1961	1799-1875	4,5,8	1813-1837		Pembroke			5C
Hubberston	A 1702-1986	1800-1867	4,5,8,9	1813-1837		Haverfordwest			6B
Ilston	A 1653-1992	1813-1875	4,5,8,9			Swansea			4G
Jeffreston	A 1695-1977	1799-1875	4,5,8,9	1730-1837		Narberth			6D
Johnston	E 1637-1987	1799-1866	4,5,8	1813-1837		Haverfordwest			6C
Jordanston	A 1802-1851	1799-1866	4,5,8,9	1813-1837		Haverfordwest			8B
Kenfig	G 1695-1925	1813-1872	4,5,8,9			Bridgend			4I
Kidwelly (St Mary)	D 1626-1971	1627-1875	5,8	1627-1837	1627-1809	Llanelly			6F
Knelston (see Llanddewi)									4G(Y)
Laleston	AG 1742-1971	1813-1875	4,5,8,9			Bridgend		1809-1837	4J
Lambston	E 1737-1991	1799-1868	4,5,8,9	1813-1837		Haverfordwest			6B
Lampeter Velfrey	E 1755-1992	1763-1875	4,5,8	1813-1837		Narberth			6D
Lamphey	E 1755-1975	1799-1875	4,5,8	1813-1837		Pembroke			5C
Laugharne	D 1639-1974		8	1639-1837	1639-1837	Carmarthen		1825-1837	6F
Lavernock	G 1769-1964	1724-1875	4,5,8,9			Cardiff			2M
Lawrenny	E 1708-1970	1800-1875	4,5,8	1716-1836		Pembroke			6C
Leckwith	A 1781-1986	1724-1875	4,5,8,9			Cardiff			3M
Letterston	E 1801-1982		4,5,8,9	1813-1837		Haverfordwest			7C
Lisvane	G 1755-1992	1724-1875	4,5,8,9			Cardiff			4M
Lis-y-Fran	A 1728-1993	1799-1869	4,5,8	1813-1837		Haverfordwest			7C
Little Newcastle	A 1783-1977	1799-1875	4,5,8,9	1813-1837		Haverfordwest			7C
Llanafan-fawr	A 1720-1992	1771-1844	5,8			Builth		1804-1837	9J
Llanafanfechan	A 1755-1998		5,8			Builth			9K
Llanarthney	D 1720-1953	1740-1875	5,8	1720-1875	1720-1875	Carmarthen		1816-1837	7G
Llanbedr	A 1675-1971	1765-1836	5,8	1704-1849		Crickhowell			7M
Llanblethian	G 1661-1992	1661-1875	4,5,8,9			Bridgend		1803-1837	3K
Llanboidy	D 1748-1992		4,5,8	1796-1875	1813-1837	Narberth		1748-1837	7E
Llancarfan	G 1618-1976	1813-1871	4,5,8,9			Cardiff			3K
Llandaff	G 1724-1968	1813-1875	4,5,6,8,9			Cardiff			3L
Llandarog	D 1736-1944	1746-1872	5,8	1736-1875		Carmarthen		1811-1837	6G
Llandawke	D 1771-1963		8	1813-1837	1813-1837	Carmarthen			6E
Llandetty	A 1740-1975		5,8			Brecknock			6L
Llanddew	A 1813-1991		5,8			Brecknock			8L
Llanddewi	C 1718-1978	1814-1875	4,5,8,9			Swansea			4G
Llanddewi Abergewsyn	A 1813-1986		5,8		1813-1837	Builth			10J
Llanddewi Cwm	A 1754-1992		5,8			Builth			9K
Llanddewi Velfrey	A 1727-1992	1733-1873	4,5,8	1813-1837		Narberth			6D
Llandefaelogfach	A 1715-1981	1713-1873	5,8	1712-1837		Brecknock		1818-1836	8K
Llandefaelog-tre'r-graig	A 1755-1971		5,8	1710-1839		Brecknock			7L(G)
Llandefalle	A 1813-1981	1771-1847	5,8	1813-1981		Brecknock			8L
Llandeilo'r-Fan	A 1809-1971	1809-1844	5,8		1813-1837	Brecknock		1822-1834	8J
Llandeilo-Talybont	A 1662-1990	1814-1873	4,5,8,9	1813-1857		Swansea			5H
Llandeloy	AE 1754-1991	1799-1873	4,5,8,9	1813-1837		Haverfordwest			7B
Llandeusant	D 1813-1980		8		1813-1837	Llandovery		1816-1837	7I
Llandilo	A 1813-1860		4,5,8	1679-1779		Narberth			7D
Llandilo-Abercowin	AD 1707-1947	1736-1866	8	1813-1837		Carmarthen			6F
Llandilo-Fawr	D 1732-1966	1733-1876	8	1679-1779		Llandilofawr		1779-1837	7H
Llandingat	A 1733-1965	1745-1865	8		1733-1965	Llandovery		1804-1837	8I
Llandissilio	D 1720-1969	1749-1876	4,5,8	1813-1837		Narberth		1828-1837	7D
Llandough juxta Cardiff	A 1755-1991	1813-1875	4,5,8,9			Cardiff			3M
Llandough juxta Cowbridge	G 1583-1986	1583-1812	4,5,8,9			Bridgend			3K(N)
Llandow	AG 1688-1992	1813-1865	4,5,8,9			Bridgend			3K
Llandowror	D 1726-1979	1736-1856	8		1720-1875	Carmarthen		1807-1837	6E
Llandulas	A 1813-1986		5,8			Llandovery			8J
Llandybie	D 1695-1948		8	1813-1837	1813-1837	Llandilofawr		1812-1837	6H
Llandyfaelog	A 1695-1970	1735-1862	5,8	1813-1837	1813-1837	Camarthen			6F
Llandyfeisant	D 1784-1970	1813-1871	8	1813-1837	1813-1837	Llandilofawr			7H
Llandyfodwg	A 1755-1905	1813-1864	4,5,8,9			Bridgend			4K
Llanedeyrn	G 1701-1982	1795-1869	4,5,8,9	1700-1837		Cardiff			4M
Llanedy	D 1708-1977	1738-1862	5,8	1813-1837		Llanelly		1745-1837	6H
Llanegwad	A 1701-1953	1750-1875	8	1701-1905	1813-1837	Llandilofawr		1820-1837	7G
Llanelieu	A 1754-1971		5,8	1687-1886		Hay			8M
Llanelly	D 1684-1971	1813-1875	5,8			Llanelly	1790-1837(?)	1783-1838	5G
Llanelly	B 1701-1933	1814-1837	5,8	1688-1886		Crickhowell	1790-1837(?)	1829-1837	6M
Llanfabon	A 1754-1922	1752-1870	4,5,6,7,8,9			Merthyr Tydfil			5L
Llan-fair-ar-y-bryn	A 1735-1865	1735-1865	8	1813-1837	1813-1837	Llandovery		1769-1837	8I

SOUTH WALES

parish name	deposited original registers	I.G.I.	local census indexes	copies of registers at Soc. Gen.	Boyd's marriage index	1837-1851 Registration District	Pallot's marriage index	non-conform. records at P.R.O.	map ref.
Llanfair-Nant-Gwyn	A 1776-1992	1803-1875	4,5,8,9	1813-1837		Cardigan			8D
Llanfair-Nant-y-Gof	E 1801-1975	1809-1864	4,5,8			Haverfordwest			8C
Llanfallteg	E 1711-1978		5,8	1813-1837	1813-1837	Narberth			7D
Llanfeigan	A 1747-1988	1762-1868	5,8			Brecknock		1792-1837	7L
Llanfihangel Aberbythych	D 1674-1970	1674-1866	4,8	1675-1922	1698-1875	Llandilofawr			7H
Llanfihangel Aberonwin	D 1754-1993		8	1813-1875		Carmarthen		1811-1837	6E
Llanfihangel Abergwesyn	A 1730-1987		5,8			Builth			10J
Llanfihangel-ar-arth	D 1756-1977		4,5,8	1756-1875	1756-1875	Newcastle-in-Emlyn		1817-1837	8G
Llanfihangel-Bryn-Pabuan	A 1755-1991	1762-1844	5,8			Builth			10K
Llanfihangel-Cilfargan	D 1746-1985	1761-1872		1755-1934	1755-1838	Llandilofawr			7H
Llanfihangel-Cwm-du	A 1734-1992	1688-1840	5,8	1688-1799		Crickhowell			7L
Llanfihangel-fechan	A 1819-1981	1819-1854	5,8			Brecknock			8K
Llanfihangel-Nant-Bran	A 1813-1991	1765-1844	5,8			Brecknock		1812-1837	8K
Llanfihangel-Penbedw	A 1680-1970	1799-1878	4,5,8	1813-1837		Cardigan			8E
Llanfihangel-Rhos-y-carn	D 1754-1967	1741-1872	8	1754-1989	1754-1966	Lampeter			8G
Llanfihangel-Tal-y-llyn	A 1767-1992	1713-1873	5,8			Brecknock			7L(H)
Llanfilo	A 1680-1990		5,8			Brecknock			8L
Llanfrynach	A 1754-1971	1799-1877	5,8			Brecknock			7K
Llanfynydd	D 1692-1967	1745-1856	8	1698-1989	1698-1875	Llandilofawr			7H
Llanfyrnach	E 1754-1993		5,8	1813-1837		Newcstle-in-Emlyn		1785-1837	7E
Llangadock	D 1708-1970		8	1813-1837	1813-1837	Llandovery		1822-1837	7I
Llangain	D 1772-1993	1740-1864	8	1772-1875	1813-1837	Carmarthen			6F
Llangammarch	A 1763-1971	1775-1868	5,8			Builth		1811-1837	9J
Llan-gan	G 1688-1984	1813-1860	4,5,8,9			Bridgend			3K
Llangan	E 1768-1992	1740-1840	4,5,8	1813-1837	1813-1837	Narberth			7E
Llanganten	A 1754-1998	1826-1853	5,8		1747-1970	Builth			9K
Llangasty-Tal-y-llyn	A 1718-1991		5,8			Brecknock			7L(I)
Llangathen	D 1747-1972	1754-1865	8	1747-1972		Llandilofawr			7H
Llangattwg	A 1703-1992	1815-1837	5,8			Crickhowell		1826-1837	6L
Llangeinwyr	A 1755-1898	1801-1865	4,5,8,9			Bridgend			4J
Llangeler	A 1704-2000	1799-1874	4,5,8	1704-1921	1704-1921	Newcastle-in-Emlyn			8F
Llangennech	D 1742-1970	1678-1853	5,8	1813-1837	1813-1837	Llanelly			5H
Llangenny	A 1695-1971	1770-1839	5,8			Crickhowell			7M
Llangenydd	G 1726-1993		4,5,8,9			Swansea			4G
Llangiwg	C 1703-1979	1813-1866	4,5,8			Neath		1760-1837	6I
Llanglydwen	AD 1755-1989	1763-1877	4,5,8	1813-1837	1813-1837	Narberth		1818-1837	7D
Llangolman	A 1755-1991		4,5,8	1813-1837		Narberth			7D
Llangorse	A 1693-1971		5,8			Brecknock		1810-1836	7L
Llangunnor	D 1678-1975		5,8	1675-1875	1675-1837	Carmarthen			7G
Llangwm	E 1716-1966		4,5,8,9	1813-1837		Haverfordwest		1820-1836	6C
Llangyfelach	C 1693-1975		4,5,8,9	1676-1794		Swansea		1767-1837	5H
Llangyndeyrn	D 1735-1972	1733-1866	5,8	1665-1811	1813-1837	Carmarthen		1815-1837	6G
Llangynidr	A 1754-1992	1813-1841	5,8			Crickhowell			6L
Llangynin	D 1736-1977	1747-1855	8		1813-1837	Carmarthen		1820-1837	7E
Llangynog	A 1768-1992		8	1813-1875	1813-1837	Carmarthen		1801-1837	6F
Llangynog	A 1745-1934		5,8			Builth			9K
Llangynwyd	AG 1662-1909	1813-1875	4,5,8,9			Bridgend/Neath		1809-1837	4J
Llanhamlach	A 1717-1991	1716-1834	5,8			Brecknock			7L
Llanharan	G 1615-1984	1813-1876	4,5,8,9			Bridgend			4K
Llanharry	G 1813-1983	1823-1875	4,5,8,9			Bridgend			3K
Llanhowel	A 1796-1993		4,5,8,9	1813-1837		Haverfordwest			7B
Llanigon	A 1712-1971	1720-1852	5,8			Hay			8M
Llanilid	AG 1706-1987	1696-1875	4,5,8,9			Bridgend			4K
Llanilltern	A 1756-1767	1800-1867	4,5,8,9			Cardiff			3L(U)
Llanishen	G 1752-1939	1813-1875	4,5,8,9			Cardiff			4L
Llanllawddog	D 1698-1969		8	1695-1875	1695-1875	Carmarthen		1812-1837	7G
Llanllawer	A 1770-1968		4,5,8,9	1813-1837		Haverfordwest			8C
Llanlleonfel	A 1794-1998		5,8			Builth			9J
Llanllwch	D 1754-1999	1802-1858	8	1754-1875	1754-1875	Carmarthen			7F
Llanllwni	A 1739-1983	1740-1872	8	1739-1971	1739-1971	Lampeter			8G
Llanmadog	A 1724-1992	1814-1875	4,5,8,9			Swansea			5G
Llanmaes	A 1583-1988	1796-1871	4,5,8,9			Bridgend			3K(O)
Llanmihangel	A 1755-1969	1813-1874	4,5,8,9			Bridgend			3K(M)
Llannon	A 1679-1978	1730-1852	5,8		1813-1837	Llanelly			6G
Llanpumsaint	D 1755-1971		8	1695-1875	1695-1875	Carmarthen		1810-1837	7F
Llanreithan	E 1799-1977	1799-1877	4,5,8,9	1813-1837		Haverfordwest			7B(A)
Llanrhidian	A 1730-1969	1813-1875	4,5,8,9			Swansea			4G
Llanrian	A 1729-1993	1798-1875	4,5,8,9	1813-1837		Haverfordwest		1811-1837	8B
Llansaduren	D 1663-1993		8	1813-1837	1667-1812	Carmarthen			6E
Llansadwrn	A 1739-1971		8	1663-1837	1813-1837	Llandovery			8I
Llansamlet	C 1704-1992	1815-1872	4,5,8,9	1807-1812		Neath		1794-1837	5I
Llansannor	A 1727-1992	1724-1868	4,5,8			Bridgend			3K
Llansantffraid	A 1718-1988		5,8			Brecknock			7L
Llansawell	A 1751-1980		8	1813-1837	1813-1837	Llandilofawr		1818-1836	8H
Llanspyddyd	A 1699-1983	1759-1869	5,8			Brecknock			7K
Llanstadwell	A 1714-1948	1800-1867	4,5,8	1813-1837		Pembroke			6C
Llanstephan	AD 1697-1982		8	1677-1837	1697-1739	Carmarthen		1814-1837	6F
Llanstinan	A 1797-1979	1799-1871	4,5,8,9	1813-1837		Haverfordwest			8C
Llantood	A 1768-1993	1799-1875	4,5,8			Cardigan			8D
Llantrisant	AG 1728-1962	1717-1875	4,5,6,8,9	1813-1844		Cardiff			4K
Llantrithyd	G 1571-1979	1597-1874	4,5,8,9	1571-1810		Cardiff			3K
Llantwit Major	A 1721-1991	1813-1870	4,5,6,7,8,9			Bridgend		1798-1837	3K
Llantwit-Fardre	G 1626-1972	1813-1874	4,5,8,9			Cardiff			4L
Llantwit-Lower	G 1695-1919	1813-1861	4,5,8			Neath			5I
Llanwinio	D 1767-1877		8		1754-1875	Carmarthen		1799-1837	7E
Llanwnda	E 1799-1993	1799-1871	4,5,8,9	1813-1837		Haverfordwest			8B
Llanwonno	A 1717-1910	1826-1860	4,5,8,9			Merthyr Tydfil			5K
Llanwrda	A 1689-1970		8		1813-1837	Llandovery		1800-1837	8I
Llanwrthwl	A 1813-1971		5,8			Rhayader		1831-1837	10J

parish name	deposited original registers	I.G.I.	local census indexes	copies of registers at Soc. Gen.	Boyd's marriage index	1837-1851 Registration District	Pallot's marriage index	non-conform. records at P.R.O.	map ref.
Llanwrtyd	A 1748-1991	1749-1868	5,8			Llandovery		1800-1837	9J
Llanybyther	D 1754-1994		8		1813-1837	Lampeter		1775-1837	8G
Llancefn	A 1816-1980	1799-1879	4,5,8	1813-1837		Narberth			7D
Llanychaer	A 1787-1993	1799-1865	4,5,8,9	1813-1837		Haverfordwest			8C
Llanychlwydog	AE 1770-1965		4,5,8	1783-1837		Cardigan			8C
Llancrwys	A 1813-1992	1725-1876	8	1813-1837	1813-1837	Lampeter		1765-1837	9H
Llanynis	A 1731-1988	1749-1848	5,8			Builth			9K
Llan-y-wern	A 1653-1990	1713-1850	5,8			Brecknock			7L
Llewhaden	A 1653-1980		4,5,8	1754-1837		Narbeth			6D
Llyswen	A 1718-1981	1716-1853	5,8			Hay			8L
Llysworney	AG 1588-1992	1721-1867	4,5,8,9			Bridgend			3K(K)
Llywel	A 1694-1971	1791-1858	5,8			Brecknock		1813-1837	7J
Loughor	C 1717-1994	1813-1875		1754-1837		Llanelly			5H
Loveston	E 1783-1977		4,5,8,9	1799-1839		Narberth			6D
Ludchurch	A 1732-1993	1799-1877	4,5,8	1779-1839		Narberth			6D
Maenclochog	A 1770-1993		4,5,8	1813-1837		Narberth			7D
Maesmynis	A 1684-1992	1744-1848	5,8			Builth			9K
Manorbier	E 1755-1993	1800-1875	4,5,8	1813-1837		Pembroke			5D
Manordeilo	D 1813-1970		8			Llandovery			7H
Manordeifi	A 1724-1992	1799-1875	4,5,8	1724-1837		Cardigan		1810-1837	8E
Manorowen	E 1779-1993		4,5,8,9			Haverfordwest			8C
Marcross	G 1756-1997	1813-1870	4,5,8,9			Bridgend			3K
Margam	G 1672-1953	1814-1875	4,5,8,9	1763-1843		Neath		1815-1837	4I
Marloes	E 1749-1969	1799-1877	4,5,8,9	1813-1837		Haverfordwest			6A
Marros	D 1738-1984		5,8	1813-1837	1813-1837	Narberth			6E
Martletwy	E 1728-1971	1799-1875	4,5,8	1757-1837		Narberth			6C
Mathry	E 1729-1992	1799-1876	4,5,8,9	1813-1837		Haverfordwest			8B
Mechan (Mon.)									4M
Meline	A 1702-1993	1799-1879	4,5,8	1813-1837		Cardigan			8D
Merthyr	D 1681-1980	1735-1842	8	1686-1875	1686-1875	Carmarthen			7F
Merthyr Cynog	A 1756-1981	1783-1871	5,6,8			Brecknock		1802-1837	8K
Merthyr Dovan	AG 1754-1990	1814-1875	4,5,8,9			Cardiff			3L
Merthyr-Mawr	G 1749-1988	1813-1871	4,5,8,9			Bridgend			3J
Merthyr-Tydfil	A 1704-1968	1820-1858	4,5,6,8,9			Merthyr Tydfil		1786-1837	5L
Michaelston-Fedwy (Mon.)									4M
Michaelston le Pit	G 1783-1980	1813-1875	4,5,8,9			Cardiff			3M
Michaelston super Avon	G 1785-1930		4,5,8			Neath			5J
Michaelston super Ely	A 1754-1993	1813-1870	4,5,8,9			Cardiff			3L(X)
Milford Haven	E 1808-1975		4,5,8			Haverfordwest		1796-1837	6B
Minwear	E 1753-1991		4,5,8	1753-1837		Narberth			6C
Monington	A 1773-1993		4,5,8	1813-1837		Cardigan			9D
Monk-Nash	G 1754-1987	1812-1873	4,5,8,9			Bridgend			3J
Monkton	AE 1711-1970	1799-1875	4,5,8	1813-1837		Pembroke			5C
Morvil	E 1813-1965	1804-1840	4,5,8	1813-1837		Haverfordwest			8C
Mounton (see Narberth)									6D
Moylgrove	A 1769-1988	1799-1875	4,5,8	1813-1837		Cardigan			9D
Myddfai	A 1653-1992	1732-1868	8	1813-1837	1813-1837	Llandovery		1822-1837	7I
Mydrim	D 1653-1994	1761-1857	8			Carmarthen			7E
Mynachlog-ddu	E 1813-1993	1799-1871	4,5,8	1813-1837		Narberth			8D
Nant Ddu	A 1779-1971	1813-1871	5,8			Brecknock			6K
Narberth	E 1676-1964	1681-1873	4,5,8	1813-1837		Narberth		1787-1837	6D
Nash	E 1742-1976	1800-1875	4,5,8			Pembroke			5C
Neath	G 1692-1900	1813-1861	4,5,8			Neath		1773-1837	5I
Nevern	A 1663-1993	1799-1870	4,5,8	1663-1837		Cardigan			8D
Newcastle	A 1739-1943	1813-1876	4,5,8,9			Bridgend		1803-1837	4J
Newchurch	D 1742-1980	1807-1848	8	1742-1875	1742-1875	Carmarthen			7F
New Moat	E 1754-1993	1799-1871	4,5,8	1813-1837		Narberth			7D
Newport	E 1765-1940	1765-1875	4,5,8	1813-1837		Cardigan		1783-1837	8C
Newton	E 1814-1890		4,5,8	1813-1837		Narberth			6D
Newton-Nottage	A 1715-1957	1820-1861	4,5,7,8,9			Bridgend			3J
Nicholaston	C 1787-1985	1815-1875	4,5,8,9			Swansea			4G
Nolton	E 1704-1991	1844-1875	4,5,8,9	1813-1837		Haverfordwest			6B
Oxwich	H 1772-1984	1813-1875	4,5,8,9			Swansea			4G
Oystermouth	A 1719-1984	1813-1871	4,5,8,9	1714-1840		Swansea		1820-1836	4H
Partrishoe	A 1728-1992		5,8			Crickhowell			7M
Pembroke								1814-1858	5C
St Mary	A 1711-1961	1799-1875	4,5,8	1813-1837		Pembroke			5C
St Michael	A 1711-1930	1799-1875	4,5,8	1813-1837		Pembroke			5C
Penally	E 1738-1993	1799-1875	4,5,8	1813-1837		Pembroke			5D
Penard	A 1743-1992	1813-1875	4,5,8,9			Swansea			4H
Penarth	G 1813-1940	1819-1875	4,5,6,8,9	1831-1886		Cardiff			3M
Penboyr	A 1752-1994	1799-1875	4,5,8	1752-1970	1752-1970	Newcastle-in-Emlyn			8F
Pen-Bre	D 1700-1965	1766-1867	8	1813-1837		Llanelly		1814-1837	5G
Pencarreg	A 1754-1992	1739-1875	8	1813-1837	1813-1837	Lampeter		1765-1837	9H
Penderyn	A 1754-1990	1813-1836	4,5,8,9		1813-1837	Merthyr Tydfil			6K
Pendine	D 1783-1978	1743-1875	5,8	1813-1837	1813-1837	Narberth			6E
Pendoylan	AG 1569-1975	1813-1868	4,5,8,9			Cardiff		1821-1837	3K
Pen-llin	A 1813-1992		4,5,8,9			Bridgend			3K
Penmaen	C 1765-1985	1813-1875	4,5,8,9			Swansea			4G
Penmark	AG 1751-1985	1791-1875	4,5,8,9			Cardiff		1818-1837	2K
Penrice	C 1631-1993	1813-1875	4,5,8,9			Swansea			4G
Penrydd	A 1813-1973	1799-1882	5,8	1813-1837		Newcastle-in-Emlyn			8E
Pentyrch	G 1678-1946	1823-1874	4,5,8,9			Cardiff			4L
Peterston super Ely	G 1749-1989	1772-1857	4,5,8,9	1749-1812		Cardiff	1700-1812		3L
Peterston super Montem	G 1745-1992	1820-1860	4,5,8,9			Bridgend		1777-1837	4K
Pontfaen	E 1813-1993	1800-1855	4,5,8	1813-1837		Haverfordwest			8C
Port Eynon	C 1740-1970		4,5,8,9			Swansea			4G
Porthkerry	G 1754-1985		4,5,8,9			Cardiff			2L
Prendergast	A 1696-1985	1801-1873	4,5,8,9	1702-1837		Haverfordwest			7C

SOUTH WALES

parish name	deposited original registers	I.G.I.	local census indexes	copies of registers at Soc. Gen.	Boyd's marriage index	1837-1851 Registration District	Pallot's marriage index	non-conform. records at P.R.O.	map ref.
Puncheston	A 1789-1985	1799-1859	4,5,8,9	1813-1837		Haverfordwest			7C
Pwllcrochan	A 1695-1982	1799-1875	4,5,8	1813-1837		Pembroke			5B
Pyle	G 1695-1925	1813-1872	4,5,8,9			Bridgend			4J
Radyr	G 1725-1994		4,5,8,9			Cardiff			3L
Ramsey Island			4,5,8			Haverfordwest			7A
Redberth	E 1794-1993	1802-1875	4,5,8	1802-1837		Pembroke			5D
Reynalton	A 1786-1977	1799-1875	4,5,8	1813-1837		Narberth			6D
Reynoldston	C 1713-1993		4,5,8,9	1786-1802		Swansea			4G(Z)
Rhoscrowther	A 1731-1993	1799-1875	4,5,8	1813-1837		Pembroke			5B
Rhossili	C 1641-1978		4,5,8,9			Swansea			4G
Roath	G 1731-1926		4,5,6,7,8,9			Cardiff			3M
Robeston Wathen	E 1790-1970	1737-1867	4,5,8	1813-1837		Narberth			6D
Robeston West	A 1731-1992	1799-1869	4,5,8,9	1813-1837		Haverfordwest			6B
Roch	E 1677-1963	1799-1875	4,5,8,9	1813-1837		Haverfordwest			7B
Rosemarket	E 1772-1969	1799-1858	4,5,8	1813-1837		Pembroke			6C
Rudbaxton	E 1735-1992	1799-1875	4,5,8,9	1799-1886		Haverfordwest			7C
Rudry	G 1626-1970		4,5,8,9			Cardiff			4M
St Andrew's Major	G 1744-1940	1791-1873	4,5,8,9			Cardiff			3L
St Andrew's Minor			4,5,8,9			Bridgend			3J(J)
St Athan	G 1663-1964	1813-1876	4,5,6,7,8,9	1721-1780		Bridgend			2K
St Bride's	E 1725-1992	1800-1877	4,5,8,9	1799-1877		Haverfordwest			6A
St Bride's Major	G 1723-1992	1813-1864	4,5,8,9			Bridgend			3J
St Bride's Minor	G 1723-1947	1813-1873	4,5,8,9			Bridgend			4J
St Bride's super Ely	G 1747-1991	1717-1870	4,5,8,9			Cardiff			3L(V)
St Clear's	D 1681-1970		8	1672-1875	1682-1875	Carmarthen		1770-1837	6E
St David's	A 1724-1984	1813-1874	4,5,8,9	1813-1837		Haverfordwest		1812-1837	7A
St Dogmael's	A 1699-1970	1799-1876	4,5,8	1813-1837		Cardigan			9D
St Dogwell's	A 1718-1973	1799-1875	4,5,8,9	1813-1837		Haverfordwest			7C
St Donat's	A 1570-1999	1696-1875	4,5,8,9			Bridgend			2K
St Edren's	E 1788-1959	1799-1845	4,5,8,9	1813-1837		Haverfordwest			7B
St Elvis	E 1784-1839	1813-1836	4,5,8,9	1813-1837		Haverfordwest			7B
St Fagan's	A 1689-1966		4,5,8,9			Cardiff			3L
St Florence	E 1755-1994	1799-1875	4,5,8	1799-1837		Pembroke		1803-1837	5D
St George's	G 1693-1984		4,5,8,9	1694-1742		Cardiff			3L(W)
St Hilary	G 1690-1994		4,5,8,9			Bridgend			3K
St Illtyd	A 1776-1963		5,8			Brecknock			7J
St Ishmael	D 1560-1969	1561-1753	5,8	1561-1837	1561-1837	Carmarthen		1815-1829	6F
St Ishmael's	E 1755-1970	1799-1875	4,5,8,9	1813-1837		Haverfordwest			6B
St Issels	A 1766-1938	1799-1875	4,5,8,9	1656-1837		Narberth			6D
St Issels Haroldston	E 1813-1990		4,5,8,9	1813-1837		Haverfordwest			6C(C)
St Lawrence	E 1766-1992	1799-1874	4,5,8,9			Haverfordwest			7B
St Lythans	G 1748-1985		4,5,8,9	1724-1800		Cardiff			3L
St Mary Church	G 1577-1985	1600-1863	4,5,6,7,8,9			Bridgend			3K(P)
St Mary Hill	AG 1755-1970	1696-1860	4,5,8,9			Bridgend			3K
St Nicholas	G 1755-1966	1724-1871	4,5,6,8,9	1813-1837		Cardiff		1823-1836	3L
St Nicholas	E 1779-1993		4,5,8,9			Haverfordwest			8B
St Petrox	A 1640-1989	1799-1875	4,5,8	1813-1837		Pembroke			5C
St Twynnell	A 1729-1991		4,5,8	1813-1837		Pembroke			5C
Sker (ex.par.)			4,5,8,9			Bridgend			3I
Skokholm Island (ex.par.)			4,5,8			Haverfordwest			5A
Skomer Island (in parish of St Martin Haverfordwest)			4,5,8			Haverfordwest			6A
Slebech	A 1762-1972		4,5,8	1799-1837		Narberth			6C
Spittal	E 1754-1992	1803-1866	4,5,8,9	1813-1837		Haverfordwest		1796-1837	7C
Stackpole Elidor	A 1724-1992	1800-1874	4,5,8	1813-1837		Pembroke			5C
Steynton	E 1637-1987		4,5,8	1813-1837		Haverfordwest			6B
Sully	G 1754-1964		4,5,8,9			Cardiff			2L
Swansea								1766-1837	4H
St John	C 1797-1971	1813-1873	4,5,8,9			Swansea			5H
St Mary	C 1631-1989	1631-1978	4,5,8,9			Swansea			4H
Talachddu	A 1601-1992		5,8	1600-1679		Brecknock		1822-1837	8L
Talbenny	E 1764-1990		4,5,8,9	1813-1837		Haverfordwest		1822-1837	6B
Talgarth	A 1695-1971	1768-1840	5,8			Hay		1700-1837	7L
Talley	D 1685-1979		8	1813-1837	1813-1837	Llandilofawr			8H
Tenby	E 1711-1971	1799-1875	4,5,8	1813-1837		Pembroke		1803-1837	5D
Trallong	A 1752-1992	1772-1870	5,8			Brecknock			8K
Trefgarn	A 1727-1990	1799-1859	4,5,8,9	1813-1837		Haverfordwest			7C
Tr-elech-a'r-Bettws	D 1663-1970		8		1663-1875	Carmarthen		1735-1837	7E
Tythegoston	AG 1757-1987	1818-1875	4,5,8,9			Bridgend			4J
Upton and Nash	E 1742-1976		4,5,8	1800-1826		Pembroke			5C(E)
Uzmaston	E 1720-1993	1799-1870	4,5,8,9	1813-1837		Haverfordwest			6C
Vaynor	A 1755-1975	1757-1841	5,8,9	1755-1950		Merthyr Tydfil		1829-1837	6K
Walton East	A 1721-1974	1799-1871	4,5,8,9	1813-1837		Haverfordwest			7C
Walton West	E 1763-1992	1800-1874	4,5,8,9	1813-1837		Haverfordwest			6B
Walwyn's Castle	A 1755-1993	1801-1874	4,5,8,9	1813-1837		Haverfordwest			6B
Warren	A 1755-1990		4,5,8	1813-1837		Pembroke			5C
Welsh St Donats	G 1726-1982	1813-1873	4,5,8,9			Cardiff			3K
Wenvoe	G 1585-1983		4,5,8,9			Cardiff			3L
Whitchurch	G 1732-1938		4,5,8,9	1813-1837		Cardiff			4L
Whitchurch	E 1752-1989	1799-1875	4,5,8,9			Haverfordwest		1798-1837	7B
Whitechurch	A 1704-1992	1799-1875	4,5,8	1813-1837		Cardigan			8D
Wick	G 1754-1993	1723-1864	4,5,8,9			Bridgend			3J
Wiston	A 1653-1993	1799-1875	4,5,8,9	1813-1837		Haverfordwest		1820-1837	7C
Yerbeston	E 1813-1976	1799-1875	4,5,8,9	1801-1837		Narberth			6D
Ystraddyfodwg	G 1719-1973		4,5,8,9			Merthyr Tydfil			5K
Ystradfellte	C 1754-1971		5,8			Neath			6J
Ystradgynlais	C 1721-1990	1796-1836	5,8			Neath		1813-1837	6J
Ystradowain	A 1754-1974		4,5,8,9			Bridgend			3K(S)

SOUTH WALES

Original registers deposited at:
A = National Library of Wales, Aberystwyth, Ceredigion SY23 3BU
B = Gwent Record Office, County Hall, Cwbran NP44 2XH
C = West Glamorgan Archive Service, County Hall, Oystermouth Road, Swansea SA1 3SN
D = Carmarthenshire Archives Service, County Hall, Carmarthen, Carmarthenshire SA31 1JP
E = Pembrokeshire Record Office, The Castle, Haverfordwest, Pembrokeshire SA61 2EF
F = Denbighshire Record Office, 46 Clwyd Street, Ruthin, Denbighshire LL15 1HP
G = Glamorgan Record Office, Glamorgan Building, King Edward VII Avenue, Cathays Park, Cardiff CF10 3NE

Study adjacent parishes in counties of Herefordshire and Monmouth

National Library of Wales, Aberystwyth, Ceredigion SY23 3BU
Gwent Record Office, County Hall, Cwbran NP44 2XH
West Glamorgan Archive Service, County Hall, Oystermouth Road, Swansea SA1 3SN
Carmarthenshire Archives Service, County Hall, Carmarthen, Carmarthenshire SA31 1JP
Pembrokeshire Record Office, The Castle, Haverfordwest, Pembrokeshire SA61 2EF
Denbighshire Record Office, 46 Clwyd Street, Ruthin, Denbighshire LL15 1HP
Glamorgan Record Office, Glamorgan Building, King Edward VII Avenue, Cathays Park, Cardiff CF10 3NE
Powys County Archives Office, County Hall, Llandrindod Wells, Powys LD1 5LG

The following useful indexes have been compiled – see Introduction
Census Indexes 1841-1861 – Powys FHS, c/o Mr M. MacSorley, 20 Hospital Road, Penpedairheol, Caerphilly, Mid-Glamorgan CF82 8DG
Census Indexes 1841-1891 – Glamorgan FHS, c/o 1 Dyfed House, Glenside Court, Ty-Gwyn Road, Penylan, Cardiff CF23 5JS
Census Index 1851 – Carmarthenshire FHS, c/o R. James, PO Box 41, Llanelli, Carmarthenshire SA15 2YF
Census Index 1851 – Dyfed FHS, c/o Mrs E.A.Davies, Rhydybont, Bronwydd, Carmarthen, Carmarthenshire SA33 6HX
Breconshire Marriage Index 1754-1812
 Surnames A-L A.A. Powell, 1 St. David's Close, Forest Park, Penpedairheol, Hengoed, Mid-Glamorgan CF8 8BL
 Surnames M-Z B. Hemmings, 1 Marianwen Street, Cefn Fforest, Blackwood, Gwent
Carmarthenshire Marriage Index 1754-1837 – c/o Carmarthernshire FHS (as above)
Glamorgan Marriage Index – Glamorgan FHS (as above)
Williams Marriage Index for Glamorganshire – Newport Borough Libraries, Central Library, John Frost Square, Kingsway, Newport, Gwent, NP20 1PA
Dyfed Marriage Index 1813-1837 – Dyfed FHS (as above)
Pembrokeshire Marriage Index 1813-1837 – Carmarthenshire FHS (as above)
Breconshire Monumental Inscriptions – Powys FHS (as above)
Glamorgan Monumental Inscriptions – Glamorgan FHS (as above)
Glamorgan Baptism & Burial Indexes pre 1900 – Glamorgan FHS (as above)

BRECON
Brecon is roughly triangular in shape, its greatest length, from the north-west to the south-east, being some 40 miles and from the south-west to north-east about 35 miles. In the north it narrows to about 10 miles.It is watered by six principal rivers: the Wye, Usk, Taff, Neath, Tawe and Yrfon. The population in 1841 was 55,603; in 1851, 59,178; in 1861, 58,860; in 1871, 59,904; in 1881, 57,746.

The soils include shale, loam, clay, sand and peat. Wheat, barley and oats were grown as well as peas, vetches, turnips, potatoes, hops and fruit. Cattle, sheep, and horses were bred. The iron-works were the chief industry but woollens and linen and flannel were made and large quantities of hides and skins tanned.

CARMARTHENSHIRE
Carmarthenshire's greatest length, from south-west to north-east is about 60 miles, and from north to south, about 35 miles. It is watered by six principal rivers: the Towy, Taff, Loughor, Teivy and Greater and Lesser Gwendraeth. The population in 1841 was 106,326; in 1851, 98,185; in 1861, 103,538; in 1871, 116,944; in 1881, 124,864.

The soils include clay, sand and peat. The main produce was wheat, barley, oats, potatoes, peas, turnips, flax and hemp. Cattle, sheep and pigs were reared. The most important minerals were coal and iron but there were also tin and copper works and woollens were manufactured and hides and skinned tanned.

GLAMORGAN
Glamorgan's greatest length, from east to west, is some 55 miles and from north to south, about 30 miles. It is watered by five principal rivers: the Taff, Tawe, Neath, Loughor and Rhymney. The population in 1841 was 171,188; in 1851, 240,095; in 1861, 326,254; in 1871, 396,010; in 1881, 511,433.

The soils are clay, sand, loam, gravel and peat. Produce included wheat, barley, oats, turnips, beans, peas, clover and potatoes. Butter and cheese were made and sheep and cattle bred. The main minerals were iron, coal and lead, the former providing material for the principal manufactures. There were tin and copper works and woollens and earthenware were made. There was also a fishing industry.

PEMBROKESHIRE
Pembrokeshire's greatest length, from north-east to south-west, is approximately 40 miles and from north-west to south-east, about 30 miles. It is watered by five principal rivers: the Western and Eastern Cleddy, Gwayne, Nevern and Teivy. The population in 1841 was 88,044; in 1851, 84,472; in 1861, 87,690; in 1871, 91,939; in 1818, 91,824.

The soils include loam, shale, clay, marl and peat. Wheat, barley, oats, beans, potatoes, turnips and clover were grown and cattle, sheep, horses and pigs bred. There were no important manufactures but coarse woollen articles were made and there was tanning and fishing.

The information in the Index is abbreviated, and may mislead the searcher if reference is not made to the details contained in the several publications listed in the Introduction. It is essential that users of this book check the appropriate works before making further enquiries.

SCOTLAND

S.W. SCOTLAND	deposited original registers	map ref.		deposited original registers	map ref.		deposited original registers	map ref.
Anwoth	1727	B5	Fenwick	1691	I5	Muirkirk	1718	H4
Ardrossan	1734	I7	Galston	1670	H5	New Abbey	1691	C2
Auchinleck	1693	H4	Girthon	1699	C5	New Cumnock	1706	F5
Avondale	1698	I4	Girvan	1733	E7	New Luce	1694	C8
Ayr	1664	G6	Glasgow Royalty	1609	K5	New Monkland	1693	K3
Ballantrae	1731	D8	Glasserton	1700	B6	Newton-upon-Ayr	1780	H6
Balmaclellan	1747	D4	Glassford	1692	J4	Ochiltree	1642	G5
Balmaghie	1768	C4	Gorbals	1771	K5	Old Cumnock	1704	H4
Barony	1672	K4	Govan	1690	K5	Old Luce	1731	C7
Barr	1689	E6	Hamilton	1645	J4	Old Monkland	1695	K3
Beith	1659	J6	Inch	1729	C8	Parton	1714	C4
Biggar	1730	I1	Irongrey	1757	D2	Penninghame	1695	C6
Blantyre	1677	J4	Irvine	1687	I6	Pettinain	1689	I2
Borgue	1741	B4	Kells	1698	D5	Port Patrick	1720	C9
Bothwell	1671	J3	Kelton	1717	B3	Prestwick see Monkton		
Buittle	1736	B3	Kilbirnie	1688	J7	Rerrick	1736	B3
Cadder	1662	K4	Kilbride	1723	H8	Riccarton	1695	H6
Cambuslang	1657	K5	Kilmarnock	1640	I6	Roberton see Wiston		
Cambusnethan	1634	J2	Kilmaurs	1688	I6	Rothesay	1691	K9
Carluke	1690	J2	Kilmory (includes	1701	H8	Rutherglen	1698	K5
Carmichael	1694	I2	Lochranza 1732)			Shotts	1707	K3
Carmunnock	1653	K5	Kilwinning	1678	I6	Sorbie	1700	B6
Carnwath	1705	J1	Kingarth	1727	J8	Sorn	1692	H5
Carsphairn	1758	E5	Kircudbright	1743	B4	Southwick see Colvend		
Carstairs	1672	J2	Kirkbean	1714	B2	St Quivox	1735	H6
Colmonell	1759	D7	Kirkcolm	1779	C9	Stair	1736	H5
Colvend & Southwick	1781	B2	Kirkcowan	1788	C7	Stevenston	1700	I7
Covington & Thankerton	1772	I2	Kirkgunzeon	1702	C2	Stewarton	1693	I6
Coylton	1723	G6	Kirkinner	1694	B6	Stonehouse	1696	I3
Craigie	1679	H6	Kirkmabreck	1703	C5	Stoneykirk	1744	B9
Crawford see Leadhills			Kirkmaiden	1699	A8	Straiton	1644	F6
Crawfordjohn	1693	H3	Kirkmichael	1638	F6	Stranraer	1695	C9
Crossmichael	1751	C3	Kirkoswald	1694	F7	Symington	1692	I1
Culter	1700	I2	Kirkpatrick Durham	1693	D3	Symington	1642	H6
Cumbraes	1730	J8	Lanark	1647	I2	Tarbolton	1730	H4
Dailly	1691	F7	Largs	1723	K7	Terregles	1724	D2
Dalmellington	1641	F5	Leadhills (includes	1698	G1	Thankerton see Covington		
Dalry	1691	E4	Crawford 1741)			Tongland	1693	B4
Dalry	1679	J7	Lesmahagow	1692	I3	Troqueer	1690	D2
Dalrymple	1699	G6	Leswalt	1729	C9	Twynholm	1694	B4
Dalserf	1738	J3	Libberton	1717	I1	Urr	1760	C3
Dalziel	1648	J3	Lochranza see Kilmory			Walston	1679	I1
Dolphinton	1717	J1	Lochrutton	1697	D2	Wandell & Lamington	1645	H2
Douglas	1691	H3	Loudon	1673	I5	West Kilbride	1691	J7
Dreghorn	1749	I6	Mauchline	1670	H5	Whithorn	1763	B6
Dundonald	1673	H6	Maybole	1712	G7	Wigtown	1731	C6
Dunlop	1700	J6	Minnigaff	1694	D6	Wiston & Roberton	1689	H2
Dunsyre	1687	J1	Mochrum	1720	B7			
East Kilbride	1688	J5	Monkton & Prestwick	1702	H6			

SCOTLAND

LOTHIAN AND S.E.. LOWLANDS	deposited original registers	map ref.
Abbey St. Bathans	1715	J3
Abbotrule see Southdean		
		I8
Aberlady	1632	J6
Ancrum	1703	G3
Annan	1703	B3
Applegarth & Sibbaldie	1749	C5
Ashkirk	1630	F4
Athelstaneford	1664	J5
Ayton	1743	K2
Bara see Garvald		
Bathgate	1672	H8
Bedrule	1690	G2
Berwick (Liberties of)	nd	J1
Bolton	1685	J5
Borrowstounness	1648	H8
Borthwick	1700	I6
Bowden	1697	G3
Broughton	1697	F7
Bunkle & Preston	1704	J3
Canonbie	1693	C2
Canongate	1564	I7
Carlaverock	1749	A5
Carriden	1687	I8
Carrington or Primrose	1653	H6
Castleton	1749	E2
Cavers	1694	E3
Channelkirk	1651	I5
Chirnside	1660	J2
Closeburn	1765	C6
Cockburnspath	1642	K3
Cockpen	1690	I6
Coldingham	1690	K3
Coldstream	1690	I2
Colinton or Hailes	1654	I7
Corrie see Hutton		
Corstorphine	1634	I7
Crailing	1708	G2
Cramond	1651	I7
Cranshaws	1731	I4
Cranston	1682	I6
Crichton	1679	I5
Cummertrees	1733	B4
Currie	1638	H7
Dalkeith	1609	I6
Dalmeny	1628	I7
Dalton	1723	B4
Dirleton	1664	K5
Dornock	1773	B3
Drumelzier	1649	F6
Dryfesdale	1732	C4
Duddingston	1631	J6
Dumfries	1605	B6
Dunbar	1651	K4
Dunscore	1777	A7
Dunse	1615	J3
Durrisdeer	1758	C7
Earlston	1694	H3
East Calder see Kirknewton		
Eccles	1697	I2
Ecclesmachan	1717	H8
Eckford	1694	H2
Eddlestone	1713	G6
Edinburgh	1595	J7
Ednam	1666	H2
Edrom	1721	J2
Eskdalemuir	1724	D4
Ettrick	1693	E5
Ewes	1700	D3
Eyemouth	1710	K2
Fala & Soutra	1673	I5
Fogo	1660	I3
Foulden	1682	J2
Galashiels	1714	G4
Garvald & Bara	1694	J4
Gifford see Yester		
Gladsmuir	1688	J6
Glencairn	1693	B7
Glencorse (Woodhouselee)	1672	I7
Glenholm	1747	F6
Gordon	1652	H3
Graitney see Gretna		
Greenlaw	1648	I3
Gretna (or Graitney)	1730	B3
Haddington	1619	J5
Hailes see Colinton		
Halfmorton	1787	C3
Hawick	1634	E3
Heriot	1685	H5
Hilton see Whitsome		
Hobkirk	1726	F2
Hoddam	1746	B4
Holywood	1687	A6
Hownam	1689	G2
Humbie	1643	I5
Hume see Stitchel		
Hume	1640	H3
Hutton	1700	J2
Hutton & Corrie	1745	D4
Innerleithen	1642	G5
Innerwick	1614	J4
Inveresk	1606	J6
Jedburgh	1639	G2
Johnstone	1734	C5
Keir	1721	B7
Kelso	1598	H2
Kilbucho	1749	F7
Kirkconnel	1742	C8
Kirkliston	1675	H8
Kirkmahoe	1720	B6
Kirkmichael	1727	C5
Kirknewton & East Calder	1642	H8
Kirkpatrick Fleming	1748	B3
Kirkpatrick Juxta	1694	D6
Kirktown	1707	F3
Kirkurd	1705	F7
Ladykirk	1697	J2
Langholm (Staplegortoun)	1688	C3
Langton	1728	I3
Lasswade	1617	I6
Lauder	1677	I4
Legerwood	1689	H4
Liberton	1624	I6
Lilliesleaf	1737	G3
Linlithgow	1613	H8
Linton	1732	H2
Livingstone	1639	H8
Lochmaben	1741	C5
Longformacus	1654	J4
Lyne & Megget	1649	F6
Makerston	1692	H3
Manor	1663	F6
Maxton	1689	G3
Megget see Lyne		
Melrose	1642	H4
Merton	1729	H3
Mid Calder	1604	H8
Middlebie	1744	C3
Minto	1703	F3
Moffat	1709	D6
Mordington	1721	J2
Morebattle	1726	H1
Morham	1712	J5
Morton	1692	C7
Mousewald	1751	B4
Nenthorn	1702	H3
Newbattle	1618	I6
Newlands	1677	G6
Newton	1629	I6
North Leith	1605	J7
North Berwick	1653	K5
Oldhamstocks	1664	K4
Ormiston	1637	I5
Oxnam	1700	G2
Peebles	1622	G6
Pencaitland	1598	J5
Penicuik	1654	H7
Penpont	1728	B7
Polwarth	1652	I3
Preston see Bunkle		
Prestonkirk	1658	J5
Prestonpans	1687	J6
Primrose see Carrington		
Queensferry	1635	I8
Ratho & Stobhill	1682	I8
Roberton	1679	F4
Roberton	1679	F4
Roxborough	1642	H3
Ruthwell	1723	A5
Salton	1635	J5
Sanquhar	1757	C8
Selkirk	1697	G4
Sibbaldie see Applegarth		
Skirling	1665	F7
Smailholm	1648	H3
South Leith	1588	J7
Southdean & Abbotrule	1696	F2
Soutra see Fala		
Spott	1683	K4
Sprouston	1633	H2
St Boswells	1692	G3
St Cuthberts	1573	I7
St Mungo	1700	B4
Staplegortoun see Langholm		
Stenton	1668	K4
Stitchel & Hume	1640	H3
Stobhill see Ratho		
Stobo	1783	F6
Stow	1626	H5
Swinton	1697	I2
Temple	1688	H6
Teviothead	1824	E3
Tinwald	1789	B5
Torpichen	1693	H8
Torthorwald	1696	B5
Tranent	1611	J5
Traquair	1694	G5
Tundergarth	1791	C4
Tweedsmuir	1656	E6
Tynninghame see Whitekirk		
Tynron	1742	B7
Uphall	1598	H8
Wamphray	1709	D5
West Calder	1645	G8
West Linton	1656	G7
Westerkirk	1693	D3
Westruther	1657	I4
Whitburn	1719	G8
Whitekirk & Tynninghame	1695	K5
Whitsome & Hilton	1724	J2
Whittinghame	1627	J4
Wilton	1694	F3
Woodhouselee see Glencorse		
Yarrow	1691	F5
Yester (or Gifford)	1654	J5
Yetholm	1689	H1

SCOTLAND

SCOTLAND

PERTHSHIRE AND ADJOINING COUNTIES	deposited original registers	map ref.
Abbotshall	1650	I1
Abdie	1620	H3
Abercrombie see St Monace		
Aberdalgie	1612	G3
Aberdour	1658	H1
Aberfoyle	1692	B1
Aberlemno	1706	J6
Abernethy	1690	H3
Abernyte	1667	H4
Airlie	1682	I6
Alloa	1609	F1
Alva	1655	F1
Alyth	1623	G6
Anstruther Easter	1641	K3
Anstruther Wester	1577	K3
Arbirlot	1632	J5
Arbroath	1653	J5
Ardoch see Muthill		
Arngask	1686	H3
Auchterarder	1661	G3
Auchterderran	1664	H2
Auchtergaven	1741	G4
Auchterhouse	1645	I5
Auchtermuchty	1649	H3
Auchtertool	1708	H1
Ballingry	1670	H2
Balmerino	1632	I3
Balquhidder	1696	B2
Barry	1704	J5
Beath	1643	H1
Bendochy	1642	H5
Benvie see Liff		
Blackford	1738	F2
Blairathol & Strowan	1718	D7
Blairgowrie	1647	G6
Brechin	1612	J7
Burntisland	1672	I1
Callander	1710	D2
Cameron	1695	J3
Caputh	1670	G5
Careston	1714	J6
Cargill	1652	H4
Carmyllie	1684	J5
Carnbee	1646	J3
Carnock	1652	G1
Ceres	1620	J3
Clackmannan	1593	F1
Cleish	1700	H2
Clova see Cortachy		
Clunie	1702	G5
Collace	1713	H4
Collessie	1696	I3
Comrie	1693	D3
Cortachy & Clova	1662	H7
Coupar Angus	1682	H5
Craig	1657	K6
Crail	1655	K3
Creich	1694	I3
Crieff	1692	E4
Culross	1640	G1
Cults	1693	I3
Cupar	1654	I3
Dairsie	1645	I3
Dalgetty	1644	H1
Dollar	1700	F1
Dowally	1705	F5
Dron	1682	H3
Dull	1703	E5
Dun	1642	K7
Dunbarney	1594	H3
Dunbog	1695	I3
Dundee	1645	I4
Dunfermline	1561	H1
Dunino	1643	K3
Dunkeld	1672	F5
Dunnichen	1683	J5
Dunning	1691	G3
Dysart	1582	I2
Eassie & Nevay	1728	I5
Edzell	1641	J8
Elie	1639	J2
Errol	1533	H4
Falkland	1661	H2
Farnell	1699	J6
Fearn	1762	I7
Ferryport-on-Craig	1634	J4
Findo-Gask	1669	G3
Flisk	1697	I3
Forfar	1633	I6
Forgan	1695	I4
Forgandenny	1695	G3
Forteviot	1710	G3
Fortingall	1748	B5
Fossoway & Tulliebole	1609	G2
Fowlis Easter see Lundie		
Powlis Wester	1674	F3
Glammis	1685	I5
Glendevon	1710	F2
Glenisla	1719	G7
Guthrie	1663	J6
Inchture	1619	H4
Inverarity	1710	I5
Invergowrie see Liff		
Inverkeillor	1717	K6
Inverkeithing	1676	H1
Kemback	1648	I3
Kenmore	1636	D4
Kennoway	1638	I2
Kettins	1650	H5
Kettle	1632	I3
Kilconquhar	1637	J3
Kilmadock	1623	D1
Kilmany	1706	I3
Kilrenny	1647	K3
Kilspindie	1656	H4
Kincardine	1691	E1
Kinclaven	1726	G5
Kinfauns	1624	G3
Kinghorn	1576	I1
Kingoldrum	1700	H6
Kinglassie	1627	H2
Kingsbarns	1642	K3
Kinloch see Lethendy		
Kinnaird	1632	H4
Kinnell	1657	J6
Kinnettles	1696	I5
Kinnoull	1618	G3
Kinross	1676	H2
Kippen	1700	D1
Kirkcaldy	1614	I2
Kirkden	1650	J6
Kirkmichael	1650	G7
Kirriemuir	1716	H7
Largo	1636	J3
Lecropt	1720	E1
Leslie	1673	H2
Lethendy & Kinloch	1698	G6
Lethnott & Navar	1728	I8
Leuchars	1665	J4
Liff, Benvie & Invergowrie	1650	I4
Lintrathen	1717	H6
Little Dunkeld	1759	F5
Lochlee	1731	I8
Logie	1660	J3
Logie	1688	E1
Logiepert	1717	K7
Logierait	1673	F5
Longforgan	1633	H4
Lunan	1654	K6
Lundie & Fowlis Easter	1667	H5
Madderty	1701	F3
Mains	1635	I4
Markinch	1634	I2
Maryton	1727	K7
Meigle	1727	H5
Menmuir	1701	J7
Menteith (Port of) see Port of Menteith		
Methven	1662	G4
Moneydie	1655	G4
Monifieth	1562	J4
Monikie	1613	J5
Monimail	1656	I3
Montrose	1615	K7
Monzie	1700	F4
Monzievaird & Strowan	1697	E3
Moonzie	1713	I3
Moulin	1740	F6
Muckart	1698	G2
Murroes	1698	I5
Muthill including Ardoch	1676	E3
Navar see Lethnott		
Nevay see Eassie		
Newburgh	1654	H3
Newburn	1628	J3
Newtyle	1713	H5
Oathlaw	1717	I6
Orwell	1688	G2
Panbride	1693	J5
Perth	1561	G3
Pittenween	1611	K3
Port of Menteith	1697	C1
Portmoak	1701	H2
Rattray	1665	G5
Redgorton	1706	G4
Rescobie	1688	I6
Rhynd	1698	H3
Ruthven	1744	H5
Saline	1746	G1
Scone	1620	H4
Scoonie	1667	I3
St Andrews and St Leonards	1627	J3
St Leonards see St Andrews		
St Maddoes	1591	H3
St Martins	1686	G4
St Monace or Abercrombie	1628	J3
St Vigeans	1669	K5
Stracathro	1709	J7
Strathmartine	1744	I5
Strathmiglo	1702	H3
Strowan see Blairathol and also Monzievaird		
Tannadice	1694	I6
Tealing	1599	I5
Tibbermore	1694	G3
Tillycoultry	1639	F2
Torryburn	1629	G1
Trinity Gask	1641	G3
Tulliallan	1673	F1
Tulliebole see Fossoway		
Weem	1692	B4
Wemyss	1660	I2

SCOTLAND

	deposited original registers	map ref.
Aberdour	1698	I8
Aberlour	1708	E6
Abernethy	1737	C5
Aboyne	1752	G3
Advie see Cromdale		
Alford	1717	G4
Alvah	1718	H8
Alves	1648	D8
Arbuthnott	1631	I2
Ardclach	1642	B6
Auchindoir & Kearn	1694	F5
Auchterless	1680	H6
Auldearn	1687	B7
Banchory Devenick	1713	J3
Banchory Ternan	1670	H3
Banff	1620	G8
Belhelvie	1624	J5
Bellie	1709	E8
Benholm	1684	I1
Bervie	1698	I1
Birnie	1712	D8
Birse	1758	G3
Boharm	1634	E8
Botriphnie	1683	E7
Bourtie	1709	I5
Boyndie	1700	G8
Braemar see Crathie		
Cabrach	1711	F5
Cairney	1738	F6
Catterline see Kinneff		
Cawdor	1719	B6
Chapel of Garioch	1763	H5
Clatt	1680	G5
Cluny	1751	H4
Coull	1752	G3
Crathie & Braemar	1717	D2
Crimond	1743	J8
Cromdale, Inverallan & Advie	1729	C6
Croy	1719	A7
Cruden	1707	J6
Cullen	1668	G8
Culsamond	1735	H6
Cushnie see Leochel		
Dalcross	1747	C6
Dallas	1742	D7
Daviot	1723	H5
Deskford	1660	F8
Drainie	1631	D9
Drumblade	1702	G6
Drumoak	1692	I3
Duffus	1629	D8
Dundurcas see Rothes		
Dunnottar	1672	I2
Durris	1716	H3
Duthil	1766	B5
Dyce	1646	I4
Dyke	1635	C8
Echt	1648	H3
Edinkillie	1702	C7
Edzell	1641	G1
Elgin	1609	D8
Ellon	1640	J6
Essie see Rhynie		
Fettercairn	1669	H1
Fetteresso	1620	I3
Fintray	1728	I5
Forbes see Tullynessle		
Fordoun	1693	H2
Fordyce	1665	G8
Forglen	1647	H7
Forgue	1684	G6
Forres	1675	C8
Foveran	1658	J5
Fraserburgh	1733	J8
Fyvie	1685	H6
Gamrie	1704	H8
Gartly	1709	F6
Garvock	1703	H1
Glass	1736	F6
Glenbervie	1721	H2
Glenbucket	1719	E5
Glengairn see Glenmuick		
Glenmuick, Tullich & Glengairn	1744	F3
Grange	1684	F7
Huntly	1680	F6
Insch	1683	G6
Inverallan see Cromdale		
Inveravon	1630	D5
Inverkeithny	1721	G7
Inverurie	1609	H5
Kearn see Auchindoir		
Keig	1750	G5
Keith	1686	F7
Keithhall & Kinkell	1678	I5
Kemnay	1660	H4
Kildrummy	1678	F5
Kincardine O'Neil	1706	H3
King Edward	1701	H8
Kinkell see Keithhall		
Kinloss	1699	C8
Kinneff & Catterline	1616	I2
Kinnellar	1697	I4
Kinnethmont	1728	G5
Kintore	1717	H4
Kirkmichael	1725	D4
Knockando	1757	D6
Laurencekirk	1702	H1
Leochel-Cushnie	1657	G4
Leslie	1699	G5
Lhanbryde	1723	D8
Logie Buchan	1698	J6
Logie Coldstone	1716	F3
Longside	1621	J7
Lonmay	1687	J8
Lumphannan	1740	G3
Marnoch	1672	G7
Maryculter	1696	I3
Marykirk	1695	H1
Methlic	1663	I6
Midmar	1717	H4
Migvy see Tarland		
Monquhitter	1670	H7
Monymusk	1678	H4
Mortlach	1741	E6
Nairn	1705	B7
New Deer	1684	I7
New Machar	1676	I5
New Spynie	1709	D8
Newhills	1700	I4
Nigg	1675	J3
Old Deer	1735	J7
Old Machar	1621	J4
Old Meldrum	1713	I6
Ordiquhill	1704	G8
Oyne	1703	H5
Peterculter	1645	I3
Peterhead	1664	K7
Pitsligo	1720	J8
Premnay	1718	G5
Rafford	1682	C7
Rathen	1704	J8
Rathven	1716	F8
Rayne	1672	H6
Rhynie & Essie	1740	F5
Rothes (inc. Dundurcas)	1698	D7
Rothiemay	1658	F7
Skene	1726	I4
Slains	1707	J6
Speymouth	1651	E8
St Andrews	1701	D8
St Cyrus	1696	H1
St Fergus	1688	K7
Strachan	1704	G2
Strathdon	1667	E4
Strichen	1672	J7
Tarland & Migvy	1764	F4
Tarves	1695	I6
Tough	1706	G4
Towie	1751	F4
Tullich see Glenmuick		
Tullynessle & Forbes (with Kearn area until 1811)	1718	G5
Turriff	1696	H7
Tyrie	1710	I8
Udny	1744	I5
Urquhart	1647	E8

SCOTLAND

INVERNESS	deposited original registers	map ref.
Abernethy & Kincardine	1737	J3
Abertarff	1737	F4
Advie see Cromdale		
Alvie	1713	I3
Ardersier	1719	I6
Boleskine	1777	F4
Cromdale, Inverallan & Advie	1729	K5
Croy & Dalcross	1719	I6
Dalarossie see Moy		
Dalcross see Croy		
Daviot & Dunlichtly	1774	H5
Dores	1734	G5
Dunlichtly see Daviot		
Glenelg	1792	A5
Glenmoriston see Urquhart		
Harris	1823	B9
Insh	1783	H2
Inverallan see Cromdale		
Inverness	1602	H6
Kilmalie	1773	B2
Kilmonivaig	1730	D2
Kilmorack	1674	E6
Kiltarlity	1714	G6
Kincardine see Abernethy		
Kingussie	1724	H2
Kirkhill	1726	H6
Laggan	1775	F2
Moy & Dalarossie	1788	H4
Petty	1633	I6
Rothiemurchus	1774	I2
St Kilda	1830	B9
Urquhart & Glenmoriston	1739	E5

W. INVERNESS AND N.ARGYLL	deposited original registers	map ref.
Ardnamurchan	1777	C5
Barra	1836	E8
Bracadale	1802	H4
Coll	1776	E5
Duirinish	1817	J5
Glenelg	1792	E2
Kilfinchen & Kilviceuen	1804	A8
Kilmalie	1773	C3
Kilmonivaig	1730	D2
Kilmore see Kilninian		
Kilmuir	1823	J3
Kilninian & Kilmore	1776	C7
Kilviceuen see Kilfinchen		
Morvern	1803	C5
North Uist	1821	J7
Portree	1800	H4
Sleat	1813	F4
Snizort	1823	I4
South Uist	1839	G7
Strath	1820	G3
Tiree	1775	E7
Torosay	1772	A6

ROSS AND CROMARTY	deposited original registers	map ref.
Alness	1783	I7
Applecross	1797	F2
Avoch	1727	K7
Barvas	1810	A4
Contin	1778	H5
Cromarty	1675	K8
Cullicudden see Resolis		
Dingwall	1662	J7
Edderton	1799	I8
Fearn	1749	K1
Fodderty	1735	I6
Gairloch	1781	F4
Glenshiel	1785	I1
Killearnan	1744	K6
Kilmuir Easter	1738	J8
Kilmuir Wester see Knockbain		
Kiltearn	1702	H7
Kincardine	1804	H8
Kintail	1776	H2
Kirkmichael see Resolis		
Knockbain or Kilmuir Wester & Suddy	1749	K6
Lochalsh	1775	H3
Lochbroom	1810	G6
Lochcarron	1819	G3
Lochs	1831	C2
Logie Easter	1775	J8
Logie Wester see Urquhart		
Nigg	1730	K9
Resolis or Kirkmichael & Cullicudden	1731	J7
Rosemarkie	1739	K7
Rosskeen	1781	I7
Stornoway	1762	B4
Suddy see Knockbain		
Tain	1719	J1/J9
Tarbat	1801	K1
Uig	1824	B2
Urquhart or Logie Wester	1715	J7

SCOTLAND

<table>
<tr><td>SUTHERLAND
AND CAITHNESS</td><td>deposited
original
registers</td><td>map
ref.</td></tr>
<tr><td>Assynt</td><td>1798</td><td>B4</td></tr>
<tr><td>Bower</td><td>1770</td><td>J7</td></tr>
<tr><td>Canisbay</td><td>1706</td><td>J8</td></tr>
<tr><td>Clyne</td><td>1782</td><td>F4</td></tr>
<tr><td>Creich</td><td>1785</td><td>C3</td></tr>
<tr><td>Dornoch</td><td>1730</td><td>F2</td></tr>
<tr><td>Dunnet</td><td>1751</td><td>J8</td></tr>
<tr><td>Durness</td><td>1764</td><td>C7</td></tr>
<tr><td>Eddrachillis</td><td>1808</td><td>B5</td></tr>
<tr><td>Farr</td><td>1790</td><td>E5</td></tr>
<tr><td>Golspie</td><td>1739</td><td>F3</td></tr>
<tr><td>Halkirk</td><td>1772</td><td>H6</td></tr>
<tr><td>Kildonan</td><td>1790</td><td>F5</td></tr>
<tr><td>Lairg</td><td>1768</td><td>D4</td></tr>
<tr><td>Latheron</td><td>1740</td><td>H5</td></tr>
<tr><td>Loth</td><td>1795</td><td>G4</td></tr>
<tr><td>Olrig</td><td>1699</td><td>I7</td></tr>
<tr><td>Reay</td><td>1732</td><td>G6</td></tr>
<tr><td>Rogart</td><td>1795</td><td>E3</td></tr>
<tr><td>Thurso</td><td>1647</td><td>H7</td></tr>
<tr><td>Tongue</td><td>1789</td><td>D6</td></tr>
<tr><td>Watten</td><td>1714</td><td>I6</td></tr>
<tr><td>Wick</td><td>1701</td><td>J6</td></tr>
</table>

<table>
<tr><td>ORKNEYS AND
SHETLANDS</td><td>deposited
original
registers</td><td>map
ref.</td></tr>
<tr><td>Birsay</td><td>1645</td><td>D5</td></tr>
<tr><td>Bressay, including Burra
  & Quarff</td><td>1737</td><td>D6</td></tr>
<tr><td>Burness see Cross and also Sanday</td><td></td><td></td></tr>
<tr><td>Burra see Bressay</td><td></td><td></td></tr>
<tr><td>Burray see South Ronaldshay</td><td></td><td></td></tr>
<tr><td>Cross & Burness</td><td>1758</td><td>F2</td></tr>
<tr><td>Cross see also Sanday</td><td></td><td></td></tr>
<tr><td>Deerness</td><td>1703</td><td>C2</td></tr>
<tr><td>Delting</td><td>1751</td><td>H7</td></tr>
<tr><td>Dunrossness</td><td>1746</td><td>C7</td></tr>
<tr><td>East Gilsay see Rousay</td><td></td><td></td></tr>
<tr><td>Eday and Pharay</td><td>1789</td><td>E3</td></tr>
<tr><td>Evie & Rendall</td><td>1725</td><td>D4</td></tr>
<tr><td>Fetlar & North Yell</td><td>1754/1787</td><td>J6</td></tr>
<tr><td>Firth & Stennes</td><td>1732</td><td>C4</td></tr>
<tr><td>Flotta see Walls</td><td></td><td></td></tr>
<tr><td>Foula see Walls</td><td></td><td></td></tr>
<tr><td>Graemsay see Hoy</td><td></td><td></td></tr>
<tr><td>Harray</td><td>1784</td><td>C4</td></tr>
<tr><td>Holm & Paplay</td><td>1654</td><td>B3</td></tr>
<tr><td>Hoy & Graemsay</td><td>1776</td><td>B5</td></tr>
<tr><td>Kirkwall & St Ola</td><td>1657</td><td>C3</td></tr>
<tr><td>Lady see Sanday</td><td></td><td></td></tr>
<tr><td>Lerwick</td><td>1706</td><td>E6</td></tr>
<tr><td>Lunnasting see Nesting</td><td></td><td></td></tr>
<tr><td>Mid and South Yell</td><td>1723</td><td>I6</td></tr>
<tr><td>Nesting including
  Lunnasting, Whalsay & Skerries</td><td>1781</td><td>G6</td></tr>
<tr><td>North Mavine</td><td>1758</td><td>I7</td></tr>
<tr><td>North Yell see Fetlar</td><td></td><td></td></tr>
</table>

<table>
<tr><td>ORKNEYS AND
SHETLANDS</td><td>deposited
original
registers</td><td>map
ref.</td></tr>
<tr><td>Orphir</td><td>1708</td><td>C4</td></tr>
<tr><td>Papa Stour see Walls</td><td></td><td></td></tr>
<tr><td>Papa Westray see Westray</td><td></td><td></td></tr>
<tr><td>Paplay see Holm</td><td></td><td></td></tr>
<tr><td>Pharay see Eday</td><td></td><td></td></tr>
<tr><td>Quarff see Bressay</td><td></td><td></td></tr>
<tr><td>Rendall see Evie</td><td></td><td></td></tr>
<tr><td>Rousay & Egilsay</td><td>1733</td><td>E4</td></tr>
<tr><td>St Andrews</td><td></td><td></td></tr>
<tr><td>St Ola see Kirkwall</td><td></td><td></td></tr>
<tr><td>Sanday</td><td>1735</td><td>F2</td></tr>
<tr><td>Sandness see Walls</td><td></td><td></td></tr>
<tr><td>Sandwick</td><td>1727</td><td>D5</td></tr>
<tr><td>Shapinshay</td><td>1632</td><td>D3</td></tr>
<tr><td>Skerries see Nesting</td><td></td><td></td></tr>
<tr><td>South Ronaldshay &
  Burray</td><td>1749/1765</td><td>B3</td></tr>
<tr><td>South Yell see Mid Yell</td><td></td><td></td></tr>
<tr><td>Stennes see Firth</td><td></td><td></td></tr>
<tr><td>Stromness</td><td>1695</td><td>C5</td></tr>
<tr><td>Stronsay</td><td>1743</td><td>E2</td></tr>
<tr><td>Tingwall including
  Whiteness & Weisdale</td><td>1695</td><td></td></tr>
<tr><td>Unst</td><td>1776</td><td>L6</td></tr>
<tr><td>Walls including
  Sandness, Papa Stour & Foula</td><td>1771</td><td>G9</td></tr>
<tr><td>Walls & Flotta</td><td>1753</td><td>B5</td></tr>
<tr><td>Westray & Papa Westray</td><td>1733/1784</td><td>G3</td></tr>
<tr><td>Weisdale see Tingwall</td><td></td><td></td></tr>
<tr><td>Whalsay see Nesting</td><td></td><td></td></tr>
<tr><td>Whiteness see Tingwall</td><td></td><td></td></tr>
</table>